Call to FREEDOM

Beginnings to 1914

Sterling Stuckey ■ **Linda Kerrigan Salvucci**

WELLS, FARGO & COMPANY.

U.S. MAIL

HOLT, RINEHART AND WINSTON

Harcourt Brace & Company

Austin • • Orlando • Atlanta • San Francisco • Boston • Dallas • Toronto • London

About the Authors

Sterling Stuckey is Professor of History and holds the President's Chair at the University of California, Riverside. Dr. Stuckey is the author of *Slave Culture: Nationalist Theory and the Foundations of Black America* and *Going Through the Storm: The Influence of African American Art in History.*

Linda Kerrigan Salvucci is Associate Professor of History at Trinity University, San Antonio, Texas. Dr. Salvucci is currently working on a book entitled *Ironies of Empire: The United States–Cuba Trade Under Spanish Rule.*

Editorial
Sue Miller, *Executive Editor*
Jim Eckel, *Managing Editor*
Steven L. Hayes, *Senior Editor*

Pupil's Edition
Hadley Lewis Watson,
    Project Editor
Doug Sims, *Associate Editor*
Melissa Langley Biegert, *Editor*
W. H. Bass III, *Editor*
Ed Connolly, *Associate Editor*
Dwonna N. Goldstone,
    Associate Editor
Kevin N. Christensen, *Associate Editor*
Carmen J. Saegert,
    Administrative Assistant

Teacher's Edition
Holly Hammett Norman,
    Project Editor
Anthony Pozeck,
    Associate Editor
Catherine Turner,
    Associate Editor

Ancillaries
Katharine Graydon,
    Project Editor
Amy Barden, *Associate Editor*

Fact Checking
Bob Fullilove, *Editor*
Vaishali Jhaveri,
    Assistant Editor

Copy Editing
Nancy Katapodis Hicks,
    Senior Copy Editor
Joseph S. Schofield IV,
    Copy Editor

Editorial Permissions
Ann B. Farrar

Art, Design and Photo

Book Design
Diane Motz, *Art Director*
Candace Moore,
    Senior Designer
Robin Bouvette, *Designer II*
Tonia Klingensmith, *Designer*
Rhonda Holcomb, *Ancillaries Designer*
Jane Dixon, *Design Assistant*
Anne Wright, *Design Assistant*
Teresa Carrera-Paprota, *Design Assistant*
Ben Plimpton, *Design Assistant*
Sally Bess, *Design Assistant*
Julie Ray, *Design Assistant*
Holly Trapp, *Teacher's Edition Design Assistant*

Photo Research
Peggy Cooper,
    Photo Research Manager
Bob McClellan, *Photo Researcher*
Terry Janecek, *Photo Researcher*
Andy Christiansen, *Photo Coordinator*
Seana Piatt, *Photo Coordinator*

Image Services
Debra Schorn, *Director*
Elaine Tate,
    Art Buyer Supervisor
Linda Richey, *Art Buyer*
Sherry France, *Art Buyer*
Kristy Sprott,
    Technical Specialist
Michelle Shukers,
    Image Librarian

New Media Design
Susan Michael, *Art Director*
Carey Smith,
    Design Manager

Book and Media Design
Joe Melomo, *Design Manager*

Cover Design
Decode, Inc.

New Media
Kate Bennet,
    Associate Director
Debra Doran,
    Senior Project Manager
Stacy Dooe,
    Project Manager
Lydia Dot, *Project Manager*
Armin Guer
    Managing and Technical Support
Cathy Ku
    Technical Assistant
Nina Dedo, *Intern*
Henry C, *Project Associate*

Production
Gene R,
    Production Manager
Leanna
    Production Assistant

Media Production
Kim An-Scott,
    Media Production Manager
Susan,
    Production Coordinator
Nanc,
    Production Supervisor

Manufacturing
Jenit,
    Manufacturing Coordinator

COVER: *The Concord Stageco*ant but rugged. *Built for Wells, Fargo & Co. b*owning Co. of *Concord, New Hampshire. B*Wells Fargo had *the largest staging operatio*world.

ii

Content Reviewers

Dr. Richard Abbott
Eastern Michigan University
Reconstruction

Dr. Larry Conyers
University of Denver
Anthropology

Dr. R. Douglas Cope
Brown University
Colonial Latin America

Dr. Paul A. Gilje
University of Oklahoma
U.S., 1492–1865

Dr. Christopher Hendricks
Armstrong Atlantic State University
Early U.S.

Dr. Melvin Holli
University of Illinois at Chicago
U.S. urban and ethnic

Dr. Raymond Hyser
James Madison University
Gilded Age and Progressive Era

Dr. Elizabeth Jameson
University of New Mexico
American West and U.S. social

Dr. Beverly Jones
North Carolina Central University
Reconstruction

Dr. Yasuhide Kawashima
University of Texas at El Paso
*Colonial and revolutionary America,
American legal*

Dr. F. Daniel Larkin
State University of New York-Oneonta
19th-century U.S.

Dr. Helen Nader
University of Arizona
Renaissance, Spain

Dr. Edward Peters
University of Pennsylvania
Medieval European

Dr. Jack Rakove
Stanford University
*American Revolution, early
American political*

Dr. Leonard Richards
University of Massachusetts
Jacksonian America

Dr. Joel Silbey
Cornell University
19th-century U.S.

Dr. David Switzer
Plymouth State College
Civil War and Reconstruction

Dr. Patricia Tracy
Williams College
Colonial America

Dr. Clarence E. Walker
University of California at Davis
African American 1450–present

Dr. John R. Wunder
University of Nebraska
American West

Educational Reviewers

Anistacio Asuncion
Piedmont Middle School
San Jose, California

Michelle Bohanek
Orozco Academy
Chicago, Illinois

Jeri Goodspeed-Gross
Minnetonka Middle School West
Chaska, Minnesota

Cynthia Gore
Castillero Middle School
San Jose, California

Tom Harris
Oak Park Middle School
Leesburg, Florida

Valerie Hill
Gaston Middle School
Dallas, Texas

Robert Jones
Perry Junior High School
New Hartford, New York

Marilyn Kretzer
Johnston Middle School
Houston, Texas

Steve Munzel
Jane Lathrop Stanford Middle School
Palo Alto, California

Milt Perlman
Junior High School 185
Flushing, New York

Pat Tobbe
Newburg Middle School
Louisville, Kentucky

Helen Webb
Wynn Seale Middle School
Corpus Christi, Texas

George Wood
Gregory-Portland Junior High School
Portland, Texas

Field Test Teachers

Sandra Poe Borowiecki
New Hartford Perry Junior High
School
New Hartford, New York

Mary Beth Breshears
Wood Middle School
Fort Leonard Wood, Missouri

Richard J. Giannicchi
West Seneca Junior High School
West Seneca, New York

Kim Gravell
Dripping Springs Middle School
Dripping Springs, Texas

Deborah K. Lofton
Charles F. Blackstock Junior High
School
Port Hueneme, California

Stan Mendenhall
Broadmoor Junior High School
Pekin, Illinois

Daniel Murray
Hackett Middle School
Albany, New York

Martha Potter
John Jay Middle School
Katonah, New York

Linda B. Rothrock
Harlandale Middle School
San Antonio, Texas

Amy Thompson
Union Middle School
San Jose, California

Call to *FREEDOM*

Beginnings to 1914

CONTENTS

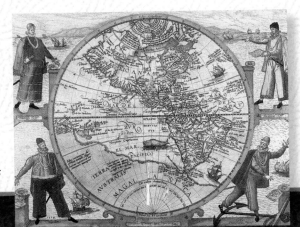

A map of the Americas from the 1500s

Detail, Courtesy of the Pilgrim Society, Plymouth Massachusetts

Henry Bacon's Landing of the Pilgrims

Washington crossing the Delaware River

The Granger Collection, New York

Conestoga wagon

The Granger Collection, New York

The U.S. Constitution

Sacagawea guiding Lewis and Clark

Harriet Tubman (far left) and escaped slaves

*A wealthy
southerner's fan*

Colonial Williamsburg Foundation

Sutter's Fort in California

The Granger Collection, New York

A military drum

Workers on the Northern Pacific Railroad

Theodore Roosevelt campaigning in 1912

A Granger poster

FEATURES

American Arts

American Literature

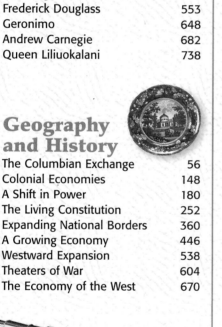
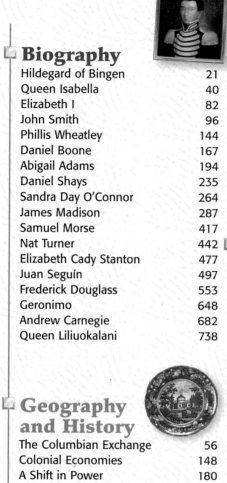

Themes in American History

Call to Freedom begins every chapter with a set of theme questions. These questions are drawn from seven broad themes central to American history: Global Relations, Constitutional Heritage, Citizenship and Democracy, Technology and Society, Cultural Diversity, Geographic Diversity, and Economic Development. These themes provide a framework for the historical events in each chapter. This framework will help you understand the connections between historical events and see how past events relate to the social, political, and economic challenges our nation faces today.

As you begin each chapter, examine the theme questions and answer them based on your own experiences or prior knowledge. As you read the chapter, explore how the theme questions relate to its history. By tracing the themes through the book, you will be able to see how each theme has developed over time.

Global Relations

Since the first Asian nomads crossed a land bridge to the continent thousands of years ago, America has been

Native American pottery

involved in global events. The Global Relations theme invites you to trace ways in which our nation's political, social, and economic development has affected–and been affected by–other countries and their people.

Constitutional Heritage

No study of American history would be complete without examining the U.S. Constitution, the document that provides the legal framework for our democratic government. The Constitutional Heritage theme will help you understand the Constitution's origins and how it has evolved through constitutional amendments, Supreme Court rulings, and congressional actions. This theme also explores how individuals and different groups in the nation's history have influenced the Constitution and have been affected by it. Finally, this theme asks you to consider how the relationship between Americans and their government has changed over time.

Citizenship and Democracy

Throughout our history, Americans have struggled to define, possess, and protect individual rights and personal freedoms, such as the freedom of speech and religion, the right to vote, and the right to privacy. Americans have also worked to uphold the responsibilities of citizenship that accompany membership in our democracy. The Citizenship and

Colonial pottery

Democracy theme explores how changing social, economic, and political conditions have influenced the theory and practices of these rights, freedoms, and responsibilities. This theme also examines the many conflicts that have arisen over these democratic values, and Americans' attempts to resolve these conflicts.

Technology and Society

From the adobe bricks that Hopi and Zuni Indians used in building cliff villages hundreds of years ago to the computers that help you with your school assignments and personal projects today, technology has influ-

A telegraph key

enced every aspect of our culture and society. The Technology and Society theme explores technological developments and their influence on the U.S. economy and life.

Cultural Diversity

Our nation's rich and unique culture comes from its many ethnic, racial, and religious groups. The Cultural Diversity theme examines America's experience in dealing with diverse culture groups from the time of the Spanish explorers to recent immigration from around the world.

Geographic Diversity

The Geographic Diversity theme explores ways in which the nation's vast and diverse geography has played an important role in American history. The theme examines how the development of the nation's resources has helped shape its economy, society, and politics. In addition, the Geographic Diversity theme traces how public and government attitudes about resources and the environment have changed over time.

Economic Development

President Calvin Coolidge said in 1925 that "the business of America is business." The Economic Development theme asks you to explore the

The Granger Collection, New York

Advertisement for barbed wire

relationship between history and economics in the United States. The theme traces the relationship between government, business, and labor in America. It examines how the growth of a strong national economy has influenced the country's domestic and global politics, as well as individual lives and American society.

★ Geography Themes ★

History and geography share many elements. History describes important events that have taken place from ancient times until the present day. Geography describes how physical environments affect human events and how people influence the environment around them. To describe a series of events without placing them in their physical settings is to tell only part of the story. Geography themes include:

Location describes a site's position. It is the spot on the earth where something is found, often expressed in terms of its position in relation to other places.

Place refers to the physical features and the human influences that define a site and make it different from other sites. Physical features include landscape, climate, and vegetation. Human influences include land use, architecture, and population size.

Region is the common cultural or physical features of an area that distinguish it from other areas. One region may be different from another area because of physical characteristics, such as landforms or climate, or because of cultural features, such as dominant languages or religions.

Movement describes the way people interact as they travel, communicate, and trade goods and services. Movement includes human migration as well as the exchange of goods and ideas.

Human-Environment Interaction deals with the ways in which people interact with their natural environments, such as clearing forests, irrigating the land, and building cities. This theme is particularly important to the study of history in that it shows how people shape and are shaped by their surroundings.

Critical Thinking and the Study of History

Throughout *Call to Freedom*, you are asked to think critically about the events and issues that have shaped U.S. history. Critical thinking is the reasoned judgment of information and ideas. People who think critically study information to determine its accuracy. They evaluate arguments and analyze conclusions before accepting them. Critical thinkers are able to recognize and define problems and develop strategies for resolving them.

The development of critical thinking skills is essential to effective citizenship. Such skills empower you to exercise your civic rights and responsibilities. For example, critical thinking skills equip you to judge the messages of candidates for office and to evaluate news reports.

Helping you develop critical thinking skills is an important goal of *Call to Freedom*. The following eight critical thinking skills appear in the section reviews and chapter reviews.

Identifying Cause and Effect is part of interpreting the relationships between historical events. A cause is any action that leads to an event; the outcome of that action is an effect. To explain historical events, historians often point out multiple causes and effects. For example, economic and political differences between the North and the South, as well as conflict over the issue of slavery, brought about the Civil War—which in turn had many far-reaching effects.

Newspaper announcing the end of the Civil War

The Museum of the Confederacy, Richmond, Virginia

Evaluating is assessing the significance or overall importance of something, such as the success of a reform movement, the actions of a president, or the results of a major conflict. You should base your judgment on standards that others will understand and are likely to share. For example, you might consider the outcome of the Mexican War and evaluate its importance to American politics and expansion. You could also evaluate the impact of this war on the peoples already living in the West.

Synthesizing Information involves combining information and ideas from several sources or points in time to gain a new under-

Corliss engine

standing of a topic or event. Much of the narrative writing in *Call to Freedom* is a synthesis. It pulls together historical data from many sources and perspectives from many people into a chronological story of our nation. Synthesizing information is important to understanding how many individual stories add up to create the big picture of events. Synthesizing the history of the Second Industrial Revolution, for example, might involve studying descriptions or images of factories and cities from the late 1800s, together with population and economic statistics. You could also examine the writings of industrial workers, business owners, immigrants, inventors, and others who lived during the period.

◻ Drawing Conclusions

Drawing Conclusions is forming a possible explanation for an event, a situation, or a problem. This explanation should be an educated guess based on available evidence. Often you must be prepared to test your conclusions against new evidence or arguments. For example, a historian might conclude that women's leadership roles in the abolition movement led to the development of the early women's movement. The historian would then organize the evidence needed to support this conclusion and challenge other explanations of the origins.

◻ Determining the Strength of an Argument

Determining the Strength of an Argument involves understanding the main points of an argument and determining if the argument is logical, well organized, and based on factual information. You should look for flaws in reasoning as well as possible errors in the conclusions of an argument. In addition, you need to consider whether the statements that the argument uses to support its points are accurate. For example, a historian might examine the Roosevelt Corollary to the Monroe Doctrine and ask whether President Roosevelt had a strong justification for telling the nations of Europe that they should not interfere in the Americas.

◻ Making Comparisons

Making Comparisons is examining events, situations, or points of view for their similarities and differences. *Comparing* focuses on both the similarities and the differences. *Contrasting* focuses only on the differences. For example, a comparison of early Irish and Chinese immigrants to the United States would point out that both groups were recruited to help build railroads and that both groups faced discrimination

and had difficulties in finding well-paying jobs. In contrast, language and racial barriers generally proved more of a problem for Chinese immigrants. Other factors to compare and contrast could include the reasons that each group had for immigrating to the United States.

◻ Identifying Generalizations and Stereotypes

Identifying Generalizations and Stereotypes means viewing historical events and situations in ways that are fair to all cultural groups affected. Determining whether statements about a given group are consistent with each other and with the available facts helps you identify bias and unfair generalizations. Understanding how individuals and groups are sometimes inaccurately stereotyped by factors such as age, gender, religion, race, political views and economic status broadens your knowledge of American history. For example, learning about American Indian cultures in the West before the arrival of American settlers helps you understand that settlers did not move into an empty western landscape. They encountered a land already settled by people with rich cultures.

◻ Supporting a Point of View

Supporting a Point of View involves choosing a viewpoint on a particular event or issue and persuasively arguing for that position. Your argument should be well organized and based on specific evidence that supports the point of view you have chosen. Supporting a point of view often involves working with controversial or emotional issues. For example, you might consider the points of view involving the struggles of labor unions against businesses in the late 1800s. Whether you choose a position in favor of unions or in favor of businesses, you would state your opinion clearly and give reasons to defend it.

Labor union banner

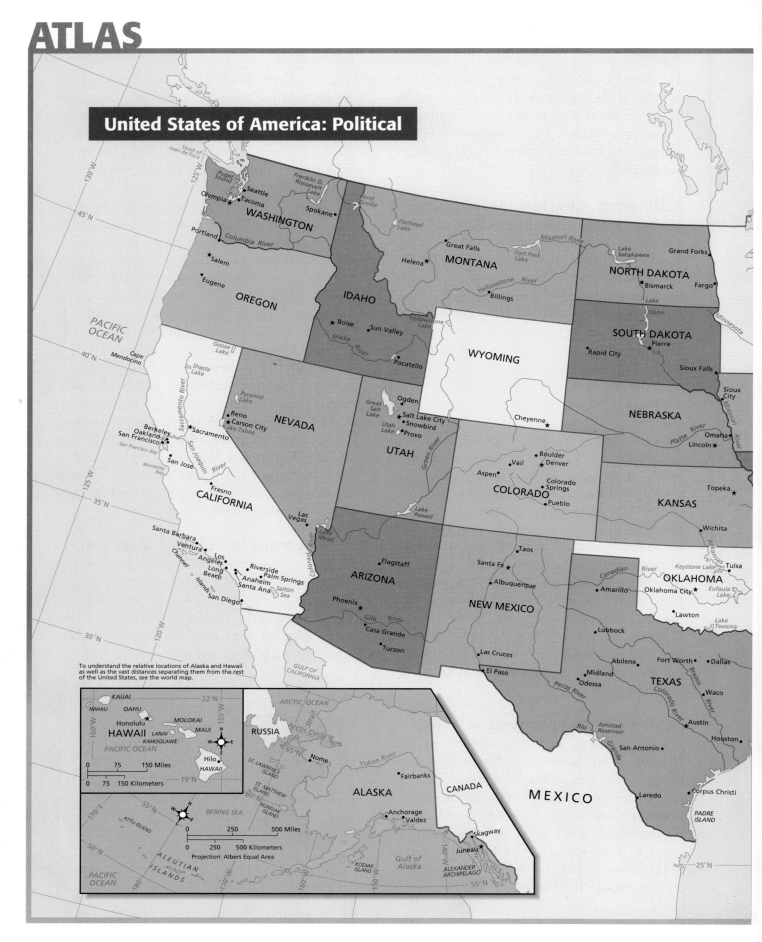

United States of America: Political

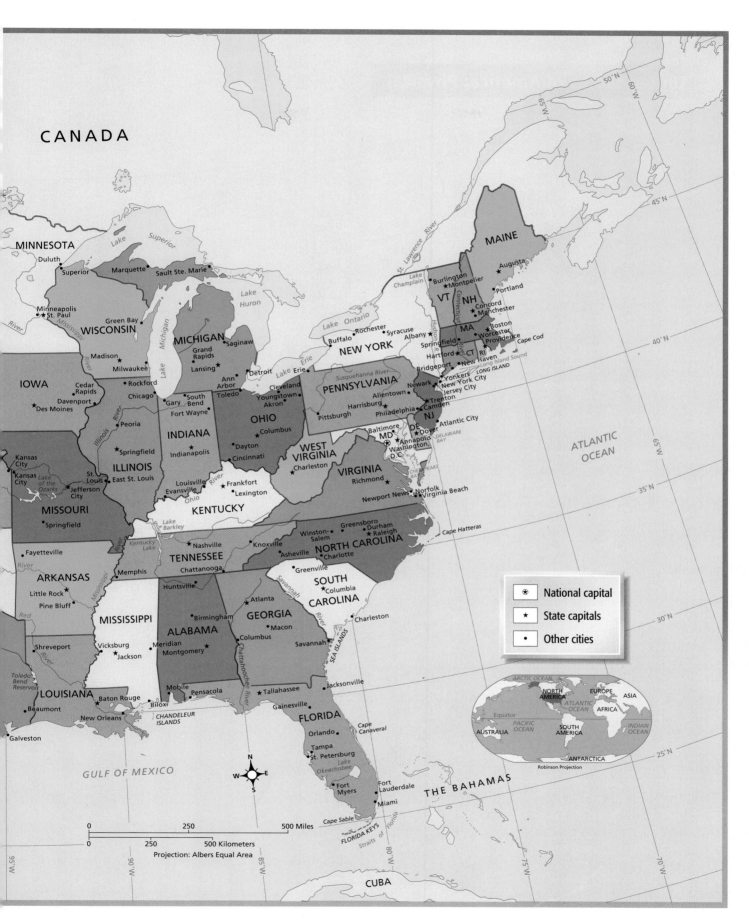

CANADA

MINNESOTA
Duluth
Superior
Marquette
Sault Ste. Marie
Lake Superior

Minneapolis
St. Paul
Green Bay
WISCONSIN
Madison
Milwaukee

Lake Michigan
MICHIGAN
Saginaw
Grand Rapids
Lansing
Detroit

IOWA
Cedar Rapids
Rockford
Chicago
Davenport
Des Moines

Lake Huron

Ann Arbor
Toledo
Lake Erie
Cleveland
Youngstown
Akron

South Bend
Gary
Fort Wayne
OHIO
Columbus
Dayton
Cincinnati

INDIANA
Peoria
Springfield
Indianapolis

ILLINOIS
East St. Louis
St. Louis
Kansas City
Kansas City
Lake of the Ozarks
Jefferson City
MISSOURI
Springfield

Louisville
Evansville
Frankfort
Lexington
KENTUCKY

Lake Barkley

WEST VIRGINIA
Charleston

VIRGINIA
Richmond

PENNSYLVANIA
Pittsburgh
Harrisburg
Philadelphia
Baltimore
Allentown
Camden
Trenton
NJ
Atlantic City

NEW YORK
Buffalo
Rochester
Syracuse
Albany
Lake Ontario
Lake Erie
Susquehanna River

MAINE
Augusta
Burlington
Montpelier
VT
NH
Concord
Manchester
Portland
Lake Champlain

MA
Boston
Worcester
Providence
Springfield
Hartford
CT
RI
New Haven
Bridgeport
Cape Cod
Long Island Sound
Yonkers
Newark
New York City
LONG ISLAND
Jersey City

St. Lawrence River
Hudson River
Connecticut River

MD
DE
Dover
Annapolis
Washington, D.C.
DELAWARE BAY
CHESAPEAKE BAY

Norfolk
Newport News
Virginia Beach
Cape Hatteras

Fayetteville
ARKANSAS
Little Rock
Pine Bluff

Nashville
Memphis
TENNESSEE
Chattanooga
Kentucky Lake
Knoxville
Asheville

Winston-Salem
Greensboro
Durham
Raleigh
NORTH CAROLINA
Charlotte

Greenville
SOUTH CAROLINA
Columbia

Huntsville

Shreveport
Vicksburg
MISSISSIPPI
Jackson
Meridian

Birmingham
ALABAMA
Montgomery
Columbus
Macon
GEORGIA
Atlanta

Savannah River
Charleston

ATLANTIC OCEAN

Red River

LOUISIANA
Beaumont
Baton Rouge
New Orleans
Galveston

Toledo Bend Reservoir

Mobile
Pensacola
Biloxi
CHANDELEUR ISLANDS

Tallahassee
Savannah
SEA ISLANDS
Jacksonville
Gainesville

Chattahoochee River

FLORIDA
Orlando
Tampa
St. Petersburg
Lake Okeechobee
Fort Myers
Cape Canaveral

Fort Lauderdale
Miami
Cape Sable
FLORIDA KEYS
Straits of Florida

THE BAHAMAS

GULF OF MEXICO

CUBA

National capital
State capitals
Other cities

ARCTIC OCEAN
NORTH AMERICA
EUROPE
ASIA
ATLANTIC OCEAN
AFRICA
PACIFIC OCEAN
Equator
SOUTH AMERICA
INDIAN OCEAN
AUSTRALIA
ANTARCTICA
Robinson Projection

0   250   500 Miles
0   250   500 Kilometers
Projection: Albers Equal Area

N E S W

50°N
45°N
40°N
35°N
30°N
25°N

60°W
65°W
70°W
75°W
80°W
85°W
90°W
95°W

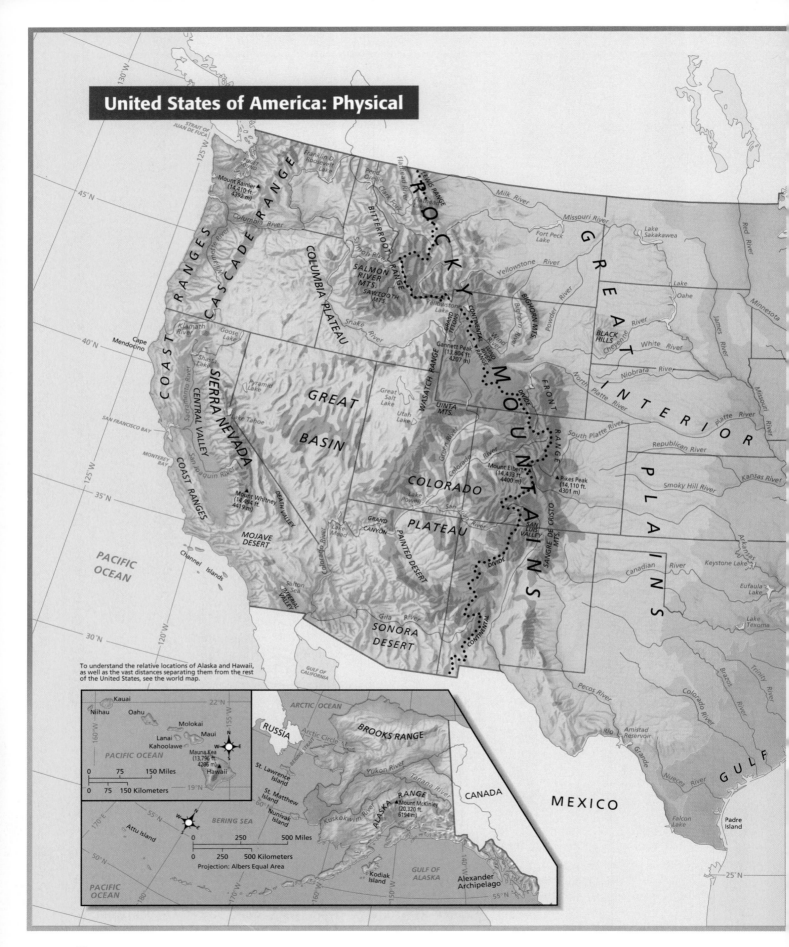

United States of America: Physical

STRAIT OF JUAN DE FUCA

PUGET SOUND

Mount Rainier ▲
(14,410 ft.
4392 m)

Columbia River

Willamette River

Franklin D. Roosevelt Lake

Pend Oreille

Flathead Lake

Clark Fork

Milk River

Missouri River

Fort Peck Lake

Lake Sakakawea

Red River

COAST RANGES

CASCADE RANGE

COLUMBIA PLATEAU

BITTERROOT RANGE

SALMON RIVER MTS.

Salmon River

SAWTOOTH MTS.

ROCKY

LEWIS RANGE

Yellowstone Lake

GRAND TETONS

CONTINENTAL

Wind River

WIND RIVER RANGE

Gannett Peak
(13,804 ft.
4207 m) ▲

Yellowstone River

BIGHORN MTS.

Bighorn River

Powder River

GREAT

Lake Oahe

Minnesota

Cape Mendocino

Klamath River

Goose Lake

Snake River

Shasta Lake

SIERRA NEVADA

Pyramid Lake

CENTRAL VALLEY

Lake Tahoe

GREAT BASIN

Great Salt Lake

Utah Lake

WASATCH RANGE

UINTA MTS.

Green River

DIVIDE

FRONT RANGE

Mount Elbert
(14,433 ft.
4400 m) ▲

MOUNTAINS

▲ Pikes Peak
(14,110 ft.
4301 m)

North Platte River

South Platte River

BLACK HILLS

Cheyenne

White River

Niobrara River

Republican River

INTERIOR

James River

Missouri River

Platte River

Kansas River

Smoky Hill River

PLAINS

Sacramento River

SAN FRANCISCO BAY

MONTEREY BAY

San Joaquin River

COAST RANGES

Mount Whitney
(14,494 ft.
4419 m) ▲

DEATH VALLEY

Colorado River

Lake Mead

MOJAVE DESERT

GRAND CANYON

Lake Powell

PAINTED DESERT

COLORADO PLATEAU

San Juan River

San Luis River

SAN LUIS VALLEY

SANGRE DE CRISTO MTS.

DIVIDE

CONTINENTAL

PACIFIC OCEAN

Channel Islands

Salton Sea

IMPERIAL VALLEY

SONORA DESERT

Gila River

GULF OF CALIFORNIA

Canadian River

Keystone Lake

Eufaula Lake

Arkansas River

Lake Texoma

Pecos River

Colorado River

Brazos River

Trinity River

Rio Grande

Amistad Reservoir

Nueces River

Falcon Lake

Padre Island

GULF

MEXICO

CANADA

To understand the relative locations of Alaska and Hawaii, as well as the vast distances separating them from the rest of the United States, see the world map.

Kauai

Niihau

Oahu

Molokai

Lanai

Maui

Kahoolawe

Mauna Kea
(13,796 ft.
4206 m)

Hawaii

PACIFIC OCEAN

0   75   150 Miles

0   75   150 Kilometers

RUSSIA

ARCTIC OCEAN

Arctic Circle

BROOKS RANGE

BERING STRAIT

St. Lawrence Island

St. Matthew Island

Nunivak Island

Yukon River

Tanana River

ALASKA RANGE

▲ Mount McKinley
(20,320 ft.
6194 m)

CANADA

Kuskokwim River

Kodiak Island

GULF OF ALASKA

Alexander Archipelago

Attu Island

BERING SEA

0   250   500 Miles

0   250   500 Kilometers

Projection: Albers Equal Area

PACIFIC OCEAN

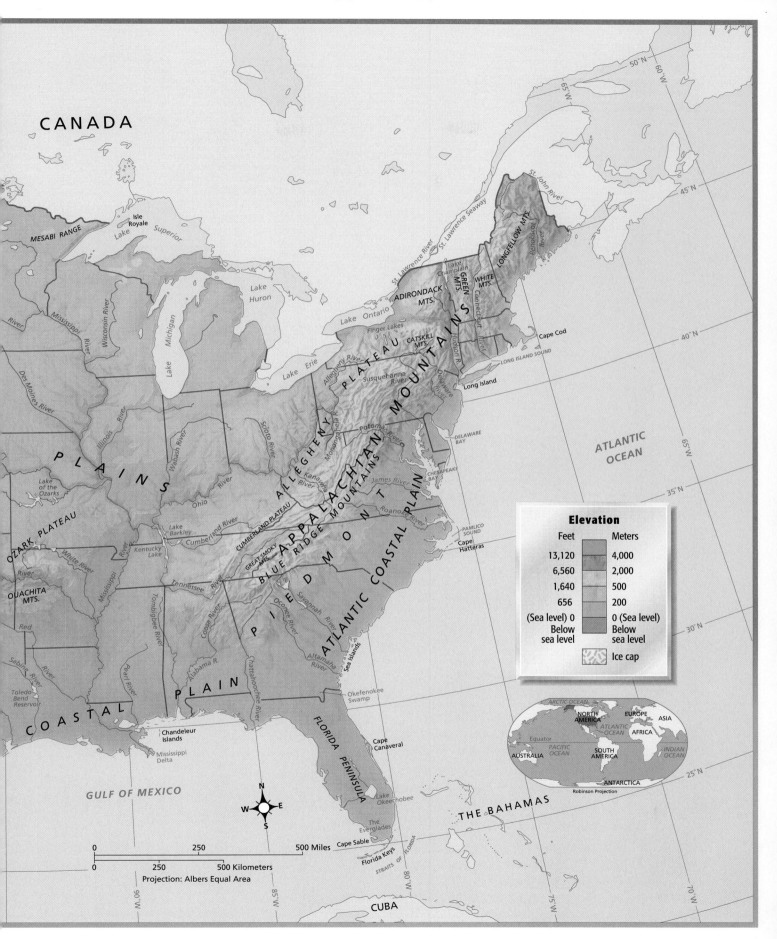

CANADA

MESABI RANGE

Isle
Royale

Lake Superior

Lake Huron

Lake Michigan

Lake Ontario

Lake Erie

Finger Lakes

St. Lawrence River

St. Lawrence Seaway

Lake Champlain

ADIRONDACK MTS.

GREEN MTS.

WHITE MTS.

LONGFELLOW MTS.

Penobscot River

St. John River

Cape Cod

Long Island

LONG ISLAND SOUND

Connecticut River

Hudson R.

Delaware River

CATSKILL MTS.

ALLEGHENY PLATEAU

Susquehanna River

Monongahela River

Potomac River

Kanawha River

DELAWARE BAY

CHESAPEAKE BAY

APPALACHIAN MOUNTAINS

BLUE RIDGE MOUNTAINS

PIEDMONT

ATLANTIC COASTAL PLAIN

ATLANTIC OCEAN

P L A I N S

Mississippi River

Wisconsin River

Des Moines River

Illinois River

Wabash River

Scioto River

Ohio River

Lake of the Ozarks

OZARK PLATEAU

White River

River

OUACHITA MTS.

Red River

Kentucky Lake

Lake Barkley

Cumberland River

CUMBERLAND PLATEAU

GREAT SMOKY MTS.

Tennessee River

James River

Roanoke River

PAMLICO SOUND

Cape Hatteras

Sabine River

Toledo Bend Reservoir

Tombigbee River

Pearl River

Alabama R.

Coosa River

Ococee River

Savannah River

Chattahoochee River

Altamaha River

Sea Islands

C O A S T A L   P L A I N

Chandeleur Islands

Mississippi Delta

GULF OF MEXICO

Okefenokee Swamp

FLORIDA PENINSULA

Cape Canaveral

Lake Okeechobee

The Everglades

Cape Sable

Florida Keys

STRAITS OF FLORIDA

THE BAHAMAS

CUBA

Elevation

Feet		Meters
13,120		4,000
6,560		2,000
1,640		500
656		200
(Sea level) 0		0 (Sea level)
Below sea level		Below sea level

Ice cap

ARCTIC OCEAN

NORTH AMERICA

EUROPE

ASIA

ATLANTIC OCEAN

AFRICA

Equator

PACIFIC OCEAN

SOUTH AMERICA

INDIAN OCEAN

AUSTRALIA

ANTARCTICA

Robinson Projection

N
W E
S

0   250   500 Miles

0   250   500 Kilometers

Projection: Albers Equal Area

50° N
45° N
40° N
35° N
30° N
25° N

60° W
65° W
70° W
75° W
80° W
85° W
90° W

Atlas **xxiii**

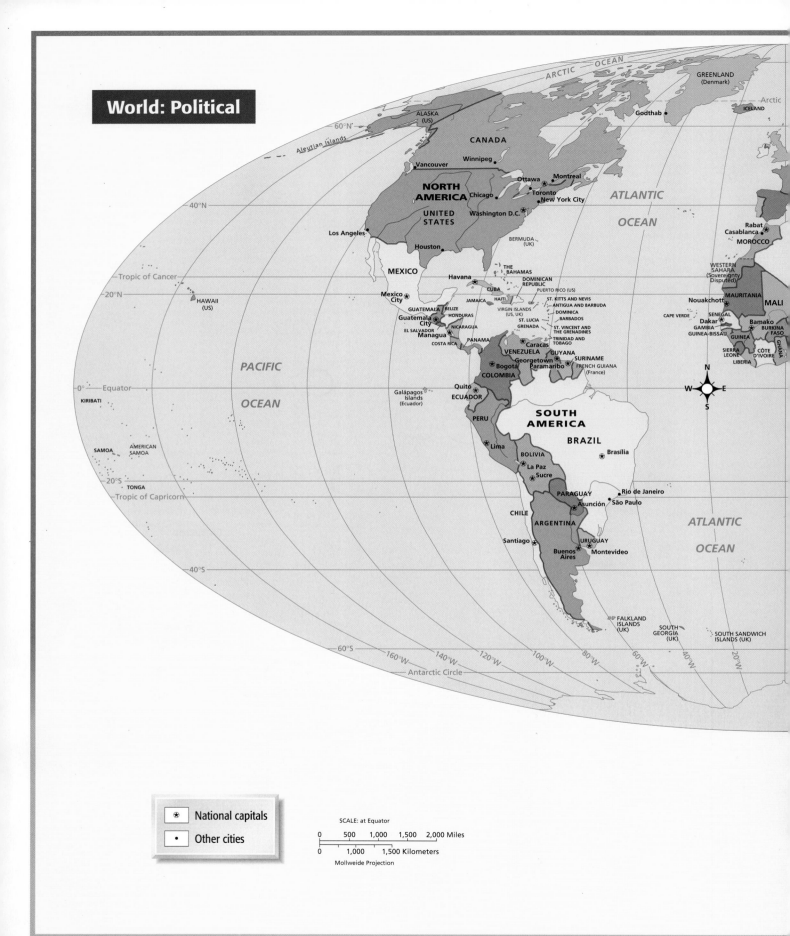

World: Political

ARCTIC OCEAN

GREENLAND
(Denmark)

Arctic

ICELAND

ALASKA
(US)

60°N

Aleutian Islands

CANADA

NORTH
AMERICA

Vancouver
Winnipeg

Ottawa
Montreal

Chicago
Toronto
New York City

UNITED
STATES
Washington D.C.

40°N

ATLANTIC

OCEAN

Los Angeles

Rabat
Casablanca
MOROCCO

Houston

BERMUDA
(UK)

WESTERN
SAHARA
(Sovereignty
Disputed)

MEXICO

Tropic of Cancer

Havana

THE
BAHAMAS

DOMINICAN
REPUBLIC

20°N

HAWAII
(US)

CUBA

PUERTO RICO (US)

Nouakchott

MAURITANIA

MALI

Mexico
City

HAITI

ST. KITTS AND NEVIS
ANTIGUA AND BARBUDA

CAPE VERDE

JAMAICA

GUATEMALA BELIZE

VIRGIN ISLANDS
(US, UK)

DOMINICA

Dakar
SENEGAL

Bamako

BURKINA
FASO

Guatemala
City

HONDURAS

ST. LUCIA

BARBADOS

GAMBIA
GUINEA-BISSAU

GHANA

EL SALVADOR

NICARAGUA

ST. VINCENT AND
THE GRENADINES

GUINEA

Managua

GRENADA

CÔTE
D'IVOIRE

COSTA RICA

PANAMA

Caracas

TRINIDAD AND
TOBAGO

SIERRA
LEONE

VENEZUELA

GUYANA

LIBERIA

Bogotá

Georgetown
Paramaribo

SURINAME

FRENCH GUIANA
(France)

N

COLOMBIA

PACIFIC

Galápagos
Islands
(Ecuador)

Quito

ECUADOR

W   E

0° Equator

KIRIBATI

OCEAN

SOUTH
AMERICA

S

PERU

BRAZIL

SAMOA

AMERICAN
SAMOA

Lima

Brasília

BOLIVIA

La Paz

20°S

TONGA

Sucre

Rio de Janeiro

Tropic of Capricorn

PARAGUAY

São Paulo

Asunción

CHILE

ATLANTIC

ARGENTINA

URUGUAY

OCEAN

Santiago

Buenos
Aires

Montevideo

40°S

60°S

FALKLAND
ISLANDS
(UK)

SOUTH
GEORGIA
(UK)

SOUTH SANDWICH
ISLANDS (UK)

160°W   140°W   120°W   100°W   80°W   60°W   40°W   20°W

Antarctic Circle

| ⊛ | National capitals |
| • | Other cities |

SCALE: at Equator

0   500   1,000   1,500   2,000 Miles

0   1,000   1,500 Kilometers

Mollweide Projection

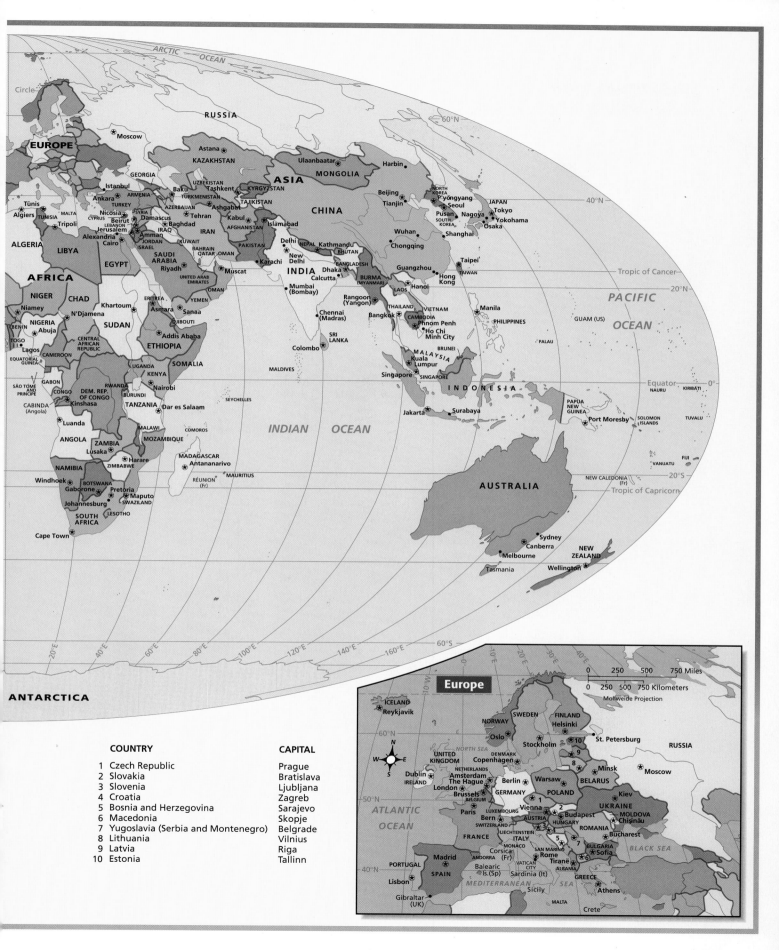

ARCTIC OCEAN

Circle

EUROPE

RUSSIA

Moscow

KAZAKHSTAN

Astana

Ulaanbaatar

MONGOLIA

Harbin

60°N

GEORGIA

Istanbul

UZBEKISTAN

Tashkent

KYRGYZSTAN

ASIA

Beijing

NORTH KOREA

P'yŏngyang

JAPAN

40°N

Ankara

ARMENIA

Baku

TURKMENISTAN

TAJIKISTAN

CHINA

Tianjin

Seoul

Pusan

SOUTH KOREA

Nagoya

Tokyo

Yokohama

TURKEY

AZERBAIJAN

Ashgabat

Tūnis

MALTA

Nicosia

CYPRUS

SYRIA

Tehran

Kabul

Islamabad

Wuhan

Osaka

Algiers

TUNISIA

Tripoli

LEBANON

Beirut

Damascus

Baghdad

IRAN

AFGHANISTAN

Shanghai

Jerusalem

ISRAEL

Amman

JORDAN

IRAQ

KUWAIT

PAKISTAN

Delhi

NEPAL

Kathmandu

Chongqing

Alexandria

Cairo

BAHRAIN

QATAR

New Delhi

BHUTAN

Taipei

ALGERIA

LIBYA

EGYPT

SAUDI ARABIA

Riyadh

UNITED ARAB EMIRATES

OMAN

Muscat

Karachi

INDIA

BANGLADESH

Dhaka

Guangzhou

TAIWAN

Hong Kong

Tropic of Cancer

AFRICA

NIGER

CHAD

Khartoum

ERITREA

Asmara

YEMEN

Sanaa

Mumbai (Bombay)

Calcutta

BURMA (MYANMAR)

Hanoi

LAOS

PACIFIC OCEAN

20°N

Niamey

N'Djamena

SUDAN

DJIBOUTI

Rangoon (Yangon)

Chennai (Madras)

THAILAND

VIETNAM

Manila

GUAM (US)

NIGERIA

Abuja

BENIN

TOGO

Lagos

CENTRAL AFRICAN REPUBLIC

Addis Ababa

ETHIOPIA

SOMALIA

Bangkok

CAMBODIA

Phnom Penh

Ho Chi Minh City

PHILIPPINES

PALAU

EQUATORIAL GUINEA

SÃO TOMÉ AND PRINCIPE

GABON

CONGO

UGANDA

KENYA

SRI LANKA

Colombo

MALDIVES

BRUNEI

MALAYSIA

Kuala Lumpur

Equator

NAURU

KIRIBATI

0°

CABINDA (Angola)

Kinshasa

DEM. REP. OF CONGO

RWANDA

BURUNDI

Nairobi

SEYCHELLES

Singapore

SINGAPORE

INDONESIA

Luanda

TANZANIA

Dar es Salaam

INDIAN OCEAN

Jakarta

Surabaya

PAPUA NEW GUINEA

Port Moresby

SOLOMON ISLANDS

TUVALU

ANGOLA

ZAMBIA

Lusaka

MALAWI

MOZAMBIQUE

COMOROS

Windhoek

NAMIBIA

ZIMBABWE

Harare

MADAGASCAR

Antananarivo

RÉUNION (Fr)

MAURITIUS

FIJI

VANUATU

20°S

Gaborone

BOTSWANA

Pretoria

Maputo

SWAZILAND

Johannesburg

LESOTHO

SOUTH AFRICA

AUSTRALIA

NEW CALEDONIA (Fr)

Tropic of Capricorn

Cape Town

Sydney

Canberra

NEW ZEALAND

Melbourne

Tasmania

Wellington

ANTARCTICA

20°E 40°E 60°E 80°E 100°E 120°E 140°E 160°E 60°S

COUNTRY	CAPITAL
1 Czech Republic	Prague
2 Slovakia	Bratislava
3 Slovenia	Ljubljana
4 Croatia	Zagreb
5 Bosnia and Herzegovina	Sarajevo
6 Macedonia	Skopje
7 Yugoslavia (Serbia and Montenegro)	Belgrade
8 Lithuania	Vilnius
9 Latvia	Riga
10 Estonia	Tallinn

Europe

ICELAND

Reykjavik

NORWAY

SWEDEN

FINLAND

Helsinki

60°N

St. Petersburg

RUSSIA

NORTH SEA

Oslo

Stockholm

10

9

Moscow

N W E S

UNITED KINGDOM

DENMARK

Copenhagen

8

Minsk

Dublin

IRELAND

NETHERLANDS

Amsterdam

The Hague

Berlin

Warsaw

BELARUS

London

Brussels

BELGIUM

GERMANY

POLAND

Kiev

50°N

Paris

LUXEMBOURG

1

Vienna

2

Budapest

UKRAINE

MOLDOVA

Chişinău

ATLANTIC OCEAN

FRANCE

SWITZERLAND

LIECHTENSTEIN

AUSTRIA

HUNGARY

ROMANIA

3

4

5

7

Bucharest

MONACO

ITALY

SAN MARINO

BULGARIA

Sofia

6

BLACK SEA

Madrid

ANDORRA

Corsica (Fr)

Rome

VATICAN CITY

Tiranë

ALBANIA

PORTUGAL

SPAIN

Balearic Is. (Sp)

Sardinia (It)

GREECE

40°N

Lisbon

Gibraltar (UK)

MEDITERRANEAN SEA

Sicily

MALTA

Athens

Crete

0 250 500 750 Miles

0 250 500 750 Kilometers

Mollweide Projection

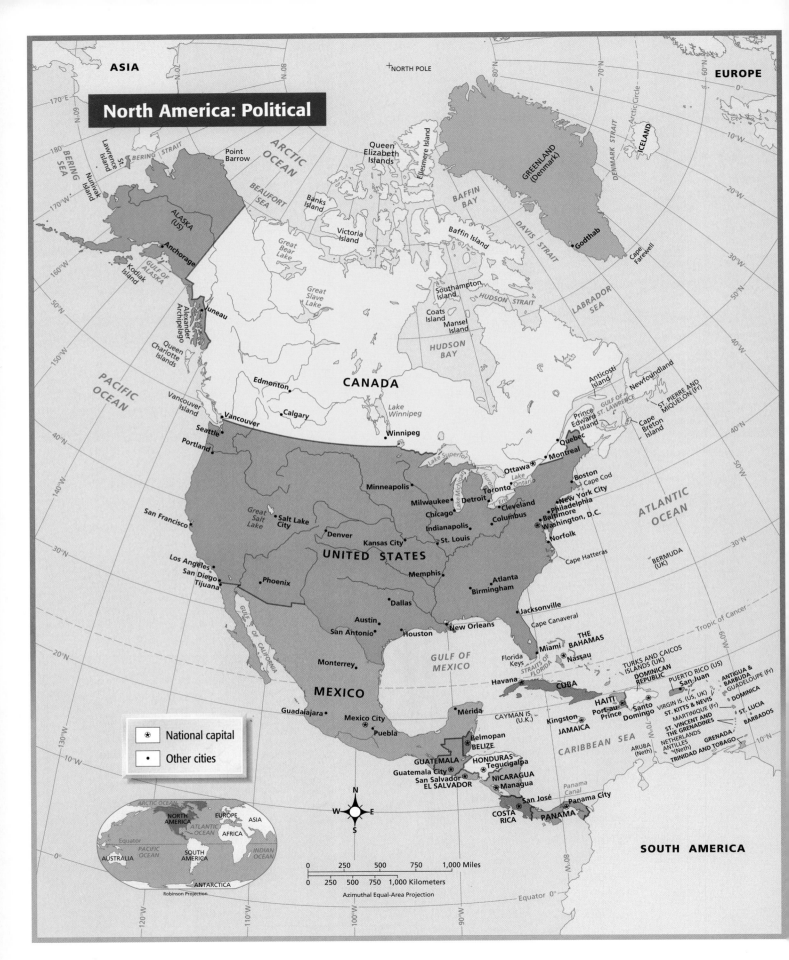

North America: Political

ASIA

EUROPE

NORTH POLE

ARCTIC OCEAN

BERING SEA
St. Lawrence Island
Nunivak Island
BERING STRAIT
Point Barrow

Queen Elizabeth Islands
Ellesmere Island

GREENLAND (Denmark)

ICELAND
DENMARK STRAIT
Arctic Circle

ALASKA (US)
Anchorage

GULF OF ALASKA
Kodiak Island

Banks Island
Victoria Island
Great Bear Lake

Baffin Island

BAFFIN BAY

Godthab

Cape Farewell

DAVIS STRAIT

LABRADOR SEA

Alexander Archipelago
Juneau

Queen Charlotte Islands

Great Slave Lake

Southampton Island
Coats Island
Mansel Island

HUDSON STRAIT

PACIFIC OCEAN

CANADA

HUDSON BAY

Anticosti Island
Newfoundland

Edmonton

Vancouver Island
Vancouver
Calgary

Lake Winnipeg

GULF OF ST. LAWRENCE
ST. PIERRE AND MIQUELON (Fr)

Prince Edward Island
Cape Breton Island

Seattle
Portland

Winnipeg

Lake Superior

Quebec
Montreal
Ottawa ⊛

ATLANTIC OCEAN

Minneapolis

Milwaukee
Chicago

Lake Michigan
Lake Huron

Detroit
Toronto
Lake Ontario
Lake Erie

Boston
Cape Cod

Cleveland
Columbus
Baltimore
Philadelphia
New York City

San Francisco

Great Salt Lake
Salt Lake City

Denver

Indianapolis
Washington, D.C. ⊛
Norfolk

UNITED STATES

Kansas City

St. Louis

Cape Hatteras

Los Angeles
San Diego
Tijuana

Phoenix

Memphis

Atlanta
Birmingham

BERMUDA (UK)

Dallas

Austin
San Antonio

Houston

New Orleans

Jacksonville
Cape Canaveral

Monterrey

Tropic of Cancer

GULF OF CALIFORNIA

GULF OF MEXICO

Florida Keys
Miami

THE BAHAMAS
Nassau ⊛

TURKS AND CAICOS ISLANDS (UK)

PUERTO RICO (US)
San Juan

ANTIGUA & BARBUDA
GUADELOUPE (Fr)

MEXICO

Guadalajara

Mexico City ⊛
Puebla

Mérida

STRAITS OF FLORIDA
Havana ⊛

CUBA

DOMINICAN REPUBLIC

CAYMAN IS. (U.K.)

HAITI
Port-au-Prince ⊛

Kingston
JAMAICA

Santo Domingo ⊛

VIRGIN IS. (US, UK)
ST. KITTS & NEVIS
MARTINIQUE (Fr)
ST. VINCENT AND THE GRENADINES

DOMINICA

ST. LUCIA
BARBADOS

Belmopan ⊛
BELIZE

GUATEMALA
Guatemala City ⊛
San Salvador ⊛
EL SALVADOR

HONDURAS
Tegucigalpa ⊛

NICARAGUA
Managua ⊛

NETHERLANDS ANTILLES (Neth)
ARUBA (Neth)

CARIBBEAN SEA

GRENADA
TRINIDAD AND TOBAGO

San José ⊛

Panama Canal

COSTA RICA

PANAMA

Panama City ⊛

SOUTH AMERICA

Equator 0°

Legend

⊛	National capital
•	Other cities

N W E S

| 0 | 250 | 500 | 750 | 1,000 Miles |

| 0 | 250 | 500 | 750 | 1,000 Kilometers |

Azimuthal Equal-Area Projection

ARCTIC OCEAN
NORTH AMERICA
EUROPE
ASIA
ATLANTIC OCEAN
AFRICA
Equator
PACIFIC OCEAN
SOUTH AMERICA
INDIAN OCEAN
AUSTRALIA
ANTARCTICA
Robinson Projection

South America: Political

CENTRAL
AMERICA

CARIBBEAN SEA

Barranquilla
Cartagena
Caracas

Lake
Maracaibo

VENEZUELA

Medellín

Bogotá

COLOMBIA

Cali

GUYANA

Georgetown
Paramaribo

SURINAME

Cayenne

FRENCH
GUIANA
(Fr)

Malpelo
Island
(Colombia)

Quito

ECUADOR

Guayaquil

Galápagos
Islands
(Ecuador)

Equator

Rio Negro

Amazon River

Belém

ATLANTIC
OCEAN

PERU

Marañón River

Trujillo

Ucayali River

Amazon River

BRAZIL

Recife

Callao
Lima

Lake
Titicaca

Arequipa

BOLIVIA

La Paz

Lake
Poopó

Sucre

River

PACIFIC
OCEAN

Brasília

São Francisco River

Salvador

Belo Horizonte

PARAGUAY

Paraguay River

Asunción

Campinas
São Paulo

Curitiba

Rio de Janeiro

Tropic of Capricorn

San Ambrosio
Island
(Chile)

San Félix Island
(Chile)

Paraná River

Uruguay River

Pôrto Alegre

ATLANTIC
OCEAN

CHILE

Córdoba

Juan Fernández
Islands
(Chile)

Valparaíso
Santiago

Rosario

Buenos Aires
Morón
San Justo
Lomas de Zamora

URUGUAY

Montevideo

RIO DE LA PLATA

ARGENTINA

N
W   E
S

| | National capital |
| | Other cities |

0   250   500   750   1,000 Miles
0   250   500   750   1,000 Kilometers
Azimuthal Equal-Area Projection

STRAIT OF
MAGELLAN

FALKLAND
ISLANDS (UK)

Tierra del
Fuego

SOUTH GEORGIA
ISLAND
(UK)

ARCTIC OCEAN

NORTH
AMERICA

EUROPE

ASIA

ATLANTIC
OCEAN

AFRICA

Equator

PACIFIC
OCEAN

SOUTH
AMERICA

INDIAN
OCEAN

AUSTRALIA

ANTARCTICA

Robinson Projection

Atlas **xxvii**

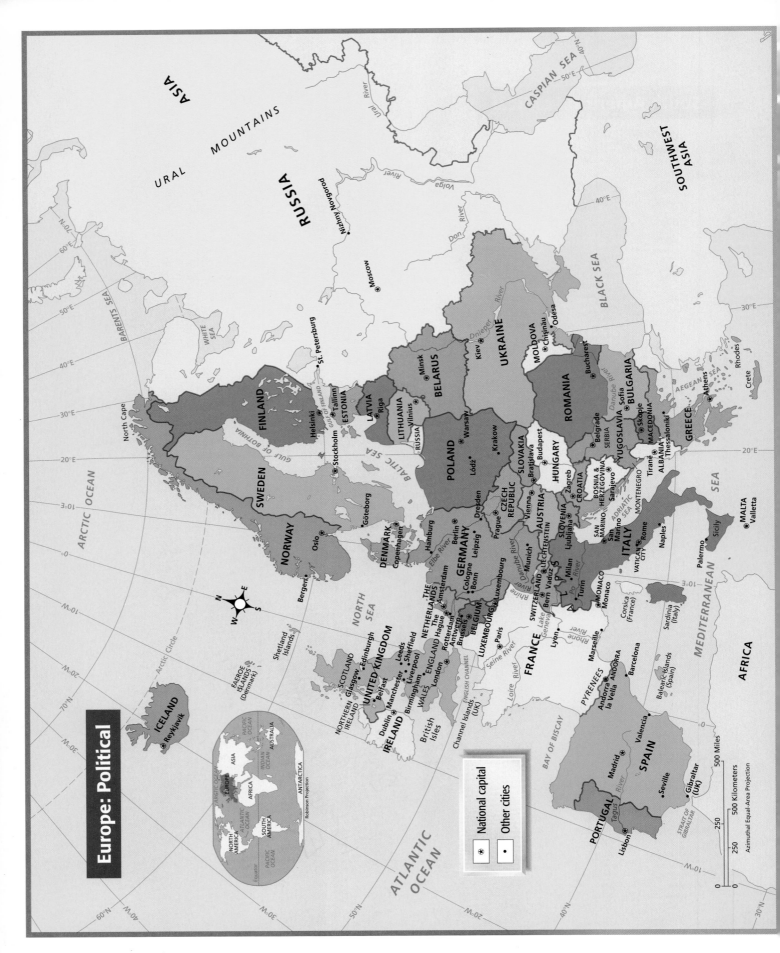

Europe: Political

ASIA

URAL MOUNTAINS

RUSSIA

Nizhny Novgorod

Moscow

St. Petersburg

WHITE SEA

BARENTS SEA

CASPIAN SEA

SOUTHWEST ASIA

BLACK SEA

Ural River

Volga River

Don River

Dnieper River

FINLAND
Helsinki

ESTONIA
Tallinn

LATVIA
Riga

LITHUANIA
Vilnius

RUSSIA

BELARUS
Minsk

Kiev

UKRAINE

MOLDOVA
Chişinău

Odesa

ROMANIA
Bucharest

BULGARIA
Sofia

Danube River

SWEDEN
Stockholm

Göteborg

GULF OF FINLAND

GULF OF BOTHNIA

BALTIC SEA

POLAND
Warsaw

Łódź

Kraków

SLOVAKIA
Bratislava

HUNGARY
Budapest

Vienna

AUSTRIA

SERBIA
Belgrade

Zagreb

CROATIA

BOSNIA & HERZEGOVINA
Sarajevo

YUGOSLAVIA

MONTENEGRO

MACEDONIA
Skopje

Thessaloniki

ALBANIA
Tiranë

GREECE
Athens

AEGEAN SEA

Rhodes

Crete

NORWAY
Oslo

Bergen

DENMARK
Copenhagen

Hamburg

Berlin

Leipzig

Dresden

GERMANY

CZECH REPUBLIC
Prague

Elbe River

Munich

LIECHTENSTEIN
Vaduz

SLOVENIA
Ljubljana

SAN MARINO
San Marino

VATICAN CITY
Rome

ITALY

Naples

ADRIATIC SEA

Corsica (France)

Sardinia (Italy)

Palermo

Sicily

MALTA
Valletta

MEDITERRANEAN SEA

ARCTIC OCEAN

NORTH CAPE

Arctic Circle

N E W S

NORTH SEA

Shetland Islands

FAEROE ISLANDS (Denmark)

SCOTLAND
Edinburgh
Glasgow

NORTHERN IRELAND
Belfast

IRELAND
Dublin

UNITED KINGDOM

Leeds
Sheffield
Manchester
Liverpool
Birmingham

WALES

ENGLAND
London

British Isles

Channel Islands (UK)

ENGLISH CHANNEL

NETHERLANDS
The Hague
Amsterdam
Rotterdam
Antwerp

BELGIUM
Brussels

LUXEMBOURG
Luxembourg

Cologne
Bonn

Rhine River

Seine River

Paris

FRANCE

Loire River

Lyon

SWITZERLAND
Bern

Lake Geneva

Rhône River

Milan

Turin

Po River

Genoa

MONACO
Monaco

Marseille

PYRENEES

ANDORRA
Andorra la Vella

Barcelona

Balearic Islands (Spain)

BAY OF BISCAY

SPAIN
Madrid

Valencia

Seville

Gibraltar (UK)

STRAIT OF GIBRALTAR

PORTUGAL
Lisbon

Tagus River

AFRICA

ICELAND
Reykjavík

ATLANTIC OCEAN

Legend

⊛ National capital

• Other cities

0   250   500 Miles

0   250   500 Kilometers

Azimuthal Equal-Area Projection

ARCTIC OCEAN

PACIFIC OCEAN

ASIA

EUROPE

AFRICA

INDIAN OCEAN

AUSTRALIA

NORTH AMERICA

SOUTH AMERICA

ANTARCTICA

ATLANTIC OCEAN

PACIFIC OCEAN

Equator

Robinson Projection

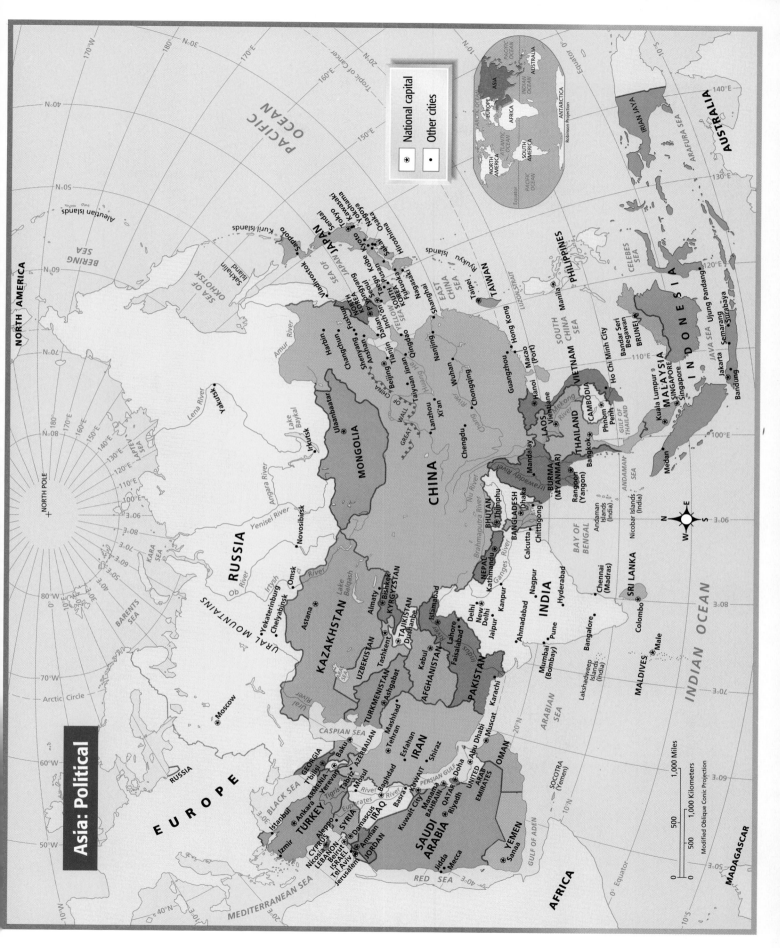

Asia: Political

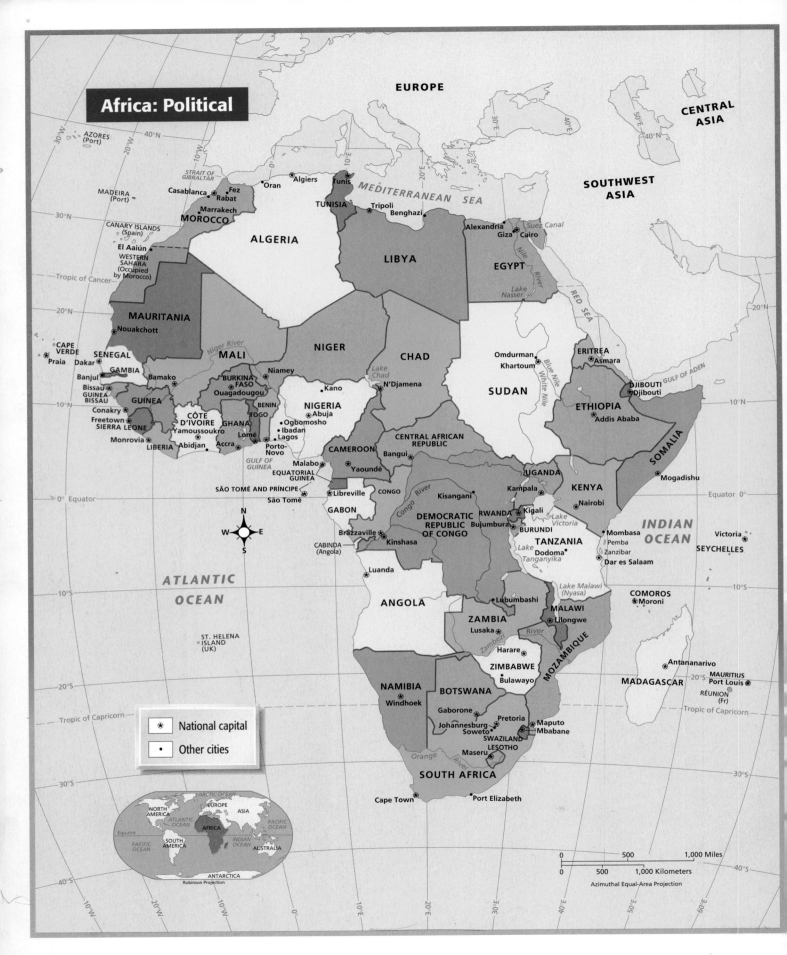

Africa: Political

EUROPE

CENTRAL ASIA

SOUTHWEST ASIA

MEDITERRANEAN SEA

AZORES (Port)

MADEIRA (Port)

STRAIT OF GIBRALTAR

Casablanca • Fez
Oran • Algiers
Rabat
Marrakech
MOROCCO

Tunis
TUNISIA
Tripoli
Benghazi

Alexandria
Giza • Cairo
Suez Canal

CANARY ISLANDS (Spain)

El Aaiún

WESTERN SAHARA (Occupied by Morocco)

Tropic of Cancer

ALGERIA

LIBYA

EGYPT

Nile River
Lake Nasser

RED SEA

MAURITANIA
• Nouakchott

CAPE VERDE
Praia

SENEGAL
Dakar
GAMBIA
Banjul
Bissau
GUINEA-BISSAU
GUINEA
Conakry
Freetown
SIERRA LEONE
Monrovia
LIBERIA

Niger River

MALI
Bamako

NIGER
Niamey
• Kano

BURKINA FASO
Ouagadougou

BENIN
TOGO
NIGERIA
Abuja
• Ogbomosho
• Ibadan
• Lagos

CÔTE D'IVOIRE
GHANA
Yamoussoukro
Lomé
Accra
Abidjan
Porto-Novo

CHAD
Lake Chad
N'Djamena

Omdurman
Khartoum

SUDAN

Blue Nile
White Nile

ERITREA
Asmara

DJIBOUTI
Djibouti

GULF OF ADEN

ETHIOPIA
• Addis Ababa

SOMALIA
• Mogadishu

GULF OF GUINEA

CAMEROON
Malabo
EQUATORIAL GUINEA
Yaoundé
Bangui

SÃO TOMÉ AND PRÍNCIPE
São Tomé

Libreville

CONGO
GABON

CENTRAL AFRICAN REPUBLIC

Congo River
• Kisangani

UGANDA
Kampala

RWANDA
Kigali
Bujumbura
BURUNDI

KENYA
• Nairobi

Equator 0°

Equator

Brazzaville
CABINDA (Angola)
Kinshasa

DEMOCRATIC REPUBLIC OF CONGO

Lake Victoria

TANZANIA
Dodoma
Dar es Salaam

Lake Tanganyika

Mombasa
Pemba
Zanzibar

INDIAN OCEAN

Victoria
SEYCHELLES

ATLANTIC OCEAN

Luanda

ST. HELENA ISLAND (UK)

ANGOLA

• Lubumbashi

ZAMBIA
Lusaka

Lake Malawi (Nyasa)

MALAWI
Lilongwe

COMOROS
Moroni

Zambezi River

Harare

ZIMBABWE
• Bulawayo

MOZAMBIQUE

• Antananarivo

MADAGASCAR

MAURITIUS
Port Louis

RÉUNION (Fr)

Tropic of Capricorn

NAMIBIA
Windhoek

BOTSWANA
Gaborone

Johannesburg
Soweto
Pretoria
Maputo
Mbabane
SWAZILAND
Maseru
LESOTHO

SOUTH AFRICA

Orange River

Cape Town
Port Elizabeth

N
W E
S

Legend	
✷	National capital
•	Other cities

ARCTIC OCEAN
NORTH AMERICA
EUROPE
ASIA
ATLANTIC OCEAN
PACIFIC OCEAN
Equator
AFRICA
SOUTH AMERICA
PACIFIC OCEAN
INDIAN OCEAN
AUSTRALIA
ANTARCTICA
Robinson Projection

0   500   1,000 Miles
0   500   1,000 Kilometers
Azimuthal Equal-Area Projection

XXX Atlas

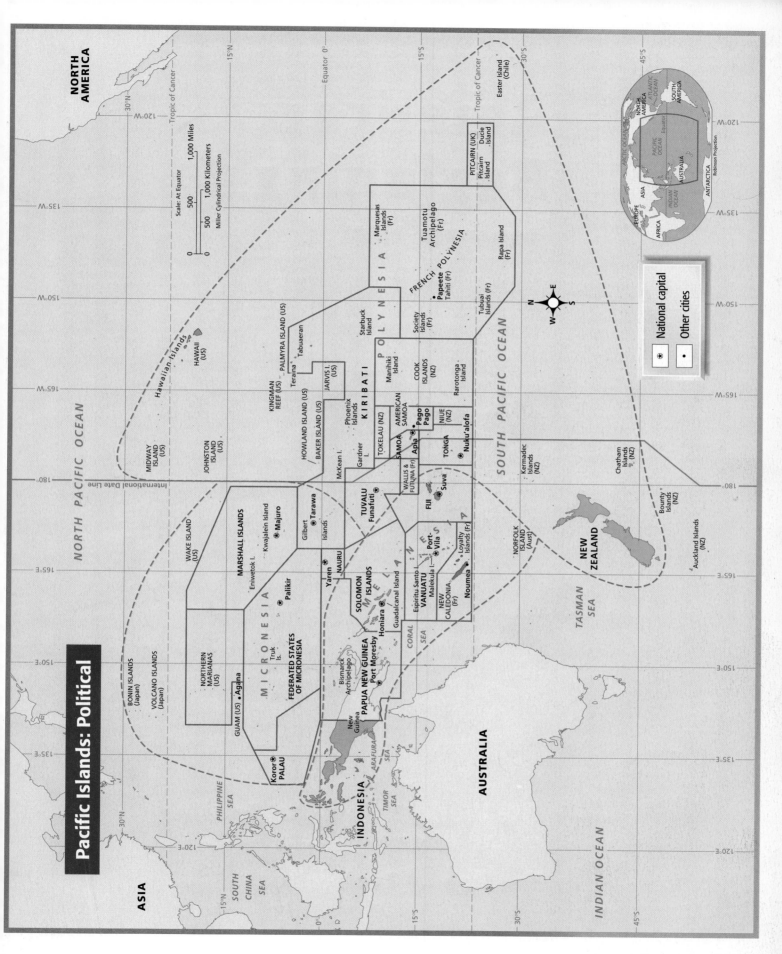

Pacific Islands: Political

ASIA

NORTH AMERICA

SOUTH CHINA SEA

PHILIPPINE SEA

NORTH PACIFIC OCEAN

International Date Line

Tropic of Cancer

BONIN ISLANDS (Japan)
VOLCANO ISLANDS (Japan)

NORTHERN MARIANAS (US)

GUAM (US) Agaña

PALAU Koror

FEDERATED STATES OF MICRONESIA
Truk Is.
Palikir

M I C R O N E S I A

MARSHALL ISLANDS
Eniwetok I.
Kwajalein Island
Majuro

WAKE ISLAND (US)

MIDWAY ISLAND (US)

JOHNSTON ISLAND (US)

Hawaiian Islands
HAWAII (US)

Tropic of Cancer

KINGMAN REEF (US)
PALMYRA ISLAND (US)
Teraina
Tabuaeran

Starbuck Island

MARQUESAS Islands (Fr)

Tuamotu Archipelago (Fr)

FRENCH POLYNESIA

P O L Y N E S I A

PITCAIRN (UK)
Pitcairn Island
Ducie Island

Easter Island (Chile)

Rapa Island (Fr)

Society Islands (Fr)
Papeete Tahiti (Fr)

Tubuai Islands (Fr)

INDONESIA

New Guinea
PAPUA NEW GUINEA
Port Moresby
Bismarck Archipelago

SOLOMON ISLANDS
Honiara
Guadalcanal Island

NAURU Yaren

Tarawa
Gilbert Islands

K I R I B A T I

HOWLAND ISLAND (US)
BAKER ISLAND (US)
JARVIS I. (US)

McKean I.
Gardner I.
Phoenix Islands

Manihiki Island

COOK ISLANDS (NZ)

Rarotonga Island

TUVALU Funafuti

TOKELAU (NZ)

SAMOA Apia
AMERICAN SAMOA
Pago Pago

NIUE (NZ)

TONGA Nuku'alofa

M E L A N E S I A

VANUATU
Espíritu Santo
Malekula
Port-Vila

NEW CALEDONIA (Fr)
Loyalty Islands (Fr)
Noumea

WALLIS & FUTUNA (Fr)

FIJI
Suva

CORAL SEA

ARAFURA SEA
TIMOR SEA

AUSTRALIA

SOUTH PACIFIC OCEAN

NORFOLK ISLAND (Aust)

Kermadec Islands (NZ)

Chatham Islands (NZ)

Bounty Islands (NZ)

NEW ZEALAND

TASMAN SEA

Auckland Islands (NZ)

INDIAN OCEAN

N
W E
S

National capital
Other cities

Scale: At Equator
1,000 Miles
500
0
1,000 Kilometers
500
0
Miller Cylindrical Projection

NORTH AMERICA
EUROPE
ASIA
AFRICA
ATLANTIC OCEAN
ARCTIC OCEAN
PACIFIC OCEAN
INDIAN OCEAN
SOUTH AMERICA
AUSTRALIA
ANTARCTICA
Equator
Robinson Projection

UNIT 1

American Beginnings

(Beginnings–1550)

CHAPTER 1 **The World Before the Opening of the Atlantic** (BEGINNINGS–1500)

CHAPTER 2 **The Age of Exploration** (1350–1550)

Young People

IN HISTORY

Young Sailors

During the early days of European exploration, sailors kept track of time by turning over sand-filled hourglasses every half hour. On Spanish ships while some crew members stood watch, or lookout, a young boy would announce that watch's eighth turning of the glass:

> *Good is that which passeth,*
> *better that which cometh,*
> *seven is past and eight floweth,*
> *more shall flow if God willith.*

The boys who sang these verses were sailors in training called *grumetes.* These boys often served as cabin boys and pages on their first voyages. The youngest ones helped with the ship's religious ceremonies, singing the blessing every morning and leading the hymns.

Grumetes helped keep the ship on course and seaworthy by maintaining the compass, making caulking materials, sweeping decks, and keeping lookout. Late at night, when the sea was calm and there was little danger, *grumetes* could take the ship's steering wheel. Although some were too small to see over the ship's railing, the *grumetes* learned to keep a steady course for the ship.

On explorer Christopher Columbus's first trip to the Americas, however, he gave orders not to allow *grumetes* to steer. He believed that it was too risky—the ships were too far from home and in unknown waters. Not all the sailors followed these orders. Columbus reported in his log on December 25, "The sailor who was steering the ship decided to go away to sleep and left the [steering] to a ship's boy. . . . The currents of water carried the ship upon one of those banks [coral reefs]." Soon after that collision, the *Santa María,* one of Columbus's ships, sank.

In this unit you will learn more about the adventures of the first Europeans in the Americas, as well as the rich heritage and traditions of the Native American inhabitants. The mingling of European and American cultures would bring dramatic changes to the two continents.

After a crew mutiny in 1611, explorer Henry Hudson, his young son John, and seven others were set adrift in a small boat in the James Bay.

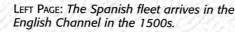

LEFT PAGE: *The Spanish fleet arrives in the English Channel in the 1500s.*
The Granger Collection, New York

◼ CHAPTER 1 ◼
The World Before the Opening of the Atlantic
(Beginnings–1500)

Native Americans had lived in the Americas for thousands of years before the first Europeans arrived after A.D. 1000. In search of land and riches, merchants and adventurers of this time traveled vast distances and met many cultures previously unfamiliar to them. In the 1200s French king Louis IX sent Friar William of Rubrouck on a mission to Asia. William found that meeting distant peoples for the first time was like "stepping into some other world."

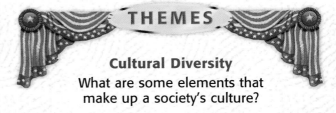

THEMES

Cultural Diversity
What are some elements that make up a society's culture?

Geographic Diversity
In what ways might a group adjust to its environment in order to survive?

Global Relations
How might international trade affect cross-cultural contacts?

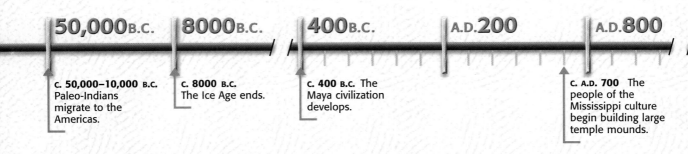

50,000 B.C.	8000 B.C.	400 B.C.	A.D. 200	A.D. 800

c. 50,000–10,000 B.C. Paleo-Indians migrate to the Americas.

c. 8000 B.C. The Ice Age ends.

c. 400 B.C. The Maya civilization develops.

c. A.D. 700 The people of the Mississippi culture begin building large temple mounds.

The Earliest Americans

Reading Focus

How did the first people arrive in the Americas?

What were some aspects of the Aztec and Inca cultures?

What societies existed in North America before European contact, and what were their accomplishments?

Key Terms

archaeology

artifacts

Paleo-Indians

migration

hunter-gatherers

environments

domestication

maize

societies

culture

glyphs

ACCORDING TO SOME NORTHWESTERN *Native American tribes, when the world was young there were only "the trees, the moon, the sun, water, and a few animals." In this emptiness, the lonely Raven walked along the beach and wished for companions. To Raven's surprise, a clam emerged from the sand and released a crowd of tiny people. Raven "sang a beautiful song of great joy," say the northwestern storytellers, for "he had brought the first people to the world." This story represents one of many different ways that people explain how the first humans arrived in the Americas.*

North American raven

IMAGE ON LEFT PAGE: *This ancient manuscript shows the Aztec people and their gods.*

A.D. 900	A.D. 1000	A.D. 1100	A.D. 1200	A.D. 1300	A.D. 1400

C. A.D. 1000 The Vikings land in North America.

A.D. 1099 The crusaders capture Jerusalem.

A.D. 1215 England's King John signs Magna Carta.

A.D. 1368 The Ming Dynasty begins in China.

A.D. 1400 The African kingdom of Mali breaks apart.

The First Migration to the Americas

Many scientists believe that people first arrived in North America during the last Ice Age. At the start of the Ice Age, the global climate became very cold. Water froze into vast moving ice sheets, called glaciers. These glaciers soon covered much of Earth's surface. The glaciers locked up so much water that the ocean levels dropped more than 400 feet lower than they are today. When the ocean levels dropped, a land bridge called Beringia appeared between northeastern Asia and present-day Alaska.

Crossing to the Americas

Historians do not know exactly when people from Asia crossed this land bridge into North America because the travelers left no written records. Historians rely on **archaeology**—the study of the unwritten past—for clues. Archaeologists examine **artifacts**, or remains of objects made by humans, to understand the past. Artifacts indicate that **Paleo-Indians**, or the first Americans, crossed Beringia into Alaska sometime between 50,000 and 10,000 B.C.

This **migration**, or movement of people from one region to another, occurred over a long time. Most archaeologists believe the Paleo-Indians first crossed over in search of game to hunt. One archaeologist described what the land crossing probably looked like at the time of the early migrations:

> **The low lying land bridge was no landscape of gently waving grass. . . . Beringia was a treeless, arctic land, covered with a patchwork of very different types of vegetation.**

Some Paleo-Indians probably crossed into the Americas in small boats. Most Paleo-Indians and their descendants traveled into present-day Canada, the United States, and Mexico. Over many centuries their descendants eventually reached as far as the tip of South America.

The Great Hunters

When Paleo-Indians first migrated into North America, glaciers and cold, treeless plains covered most of what is now Canada and Alaska. Much of the United States and

Migration to America

Learning from Maps Early nomadic people from Asia spread throughout the Americas.

Movement What geographic feature enabled nomads to travel to the Americas?

Mexico had dense forests, tall grasses, and numerous lakes and swamps. Many large animals, including mammoths, saber-toothed tigers, bison, and giant wolves, roamed the continent.

Paleo-Indians were **hunter-gatherers**, people who hunt animals and gather wild plants to provide for their needs. Paleo-Indians made finely crafted stone tools, knives, and spear points for hunting. The Clovis, an early type of stone spear point dating from 10,000 B.C., has been found throughout North America.

★ Adapting to a New Climate

When the Ice Age ended about 8000 B.C., the climate changed around the world. Increasing temperatures caused glaciers to melt. The oceans rose, covering Beringia with water. As late as 1000 B.C., Asian people continued to come over in wooden dugout canoes and animal hide boats to Alaska.

America's Geography

The temperature change at the end of the Ice Age created many new **environments**—climates and landscapes that surround living things. North America's eastern regions remained humid and rich with forests and many kinds of plants and animals. However, in some western regions the previously well-watered land turned into dry plains and harsh deserts.

In addition, short grasses replaced the taller grasses that had supported giant mammals such as the mammoth. These animals died out naturally or may have been hunted to extinction by Native Americans, but large herds of buffalo, caribou, antelope, and deer thrived on the plentiful supply of short grasses.

Hunter-Gatherer Societies

Paleo-Indians adapted to the environmental changes by hunting smaller mammals and birds, and by relying more on seeds, berries, nuts, and edible leaves and roots. Paleo-Indians created many new hunting and fishing tools during this period, including snares and traps, hooks, lines, and nets. To process and store the plants they gathered, Paleo-Indians made grinding stones and baskets.

Agrarian Societies

The earliest agricultural societies in the Americas developed in Mesoamerica, or "middle" America, and South America. Mesoamerica includes present-day Mexico and portions of Central America. People in this region learned to grow what had been wild plants, breeding them to produce food crops. This process of breeding plants and animals, such as dogs, to meet specific human needs is called **domestication**.

Archaeologists in Mexico have found evidence of the first **maize**, or corn, grown by humans. Maize was the most useful crop grown in North

Many early Americans depended on growing maize for survival.

Discovering the Distant Past

In 1956 British scientist Kathleen Kenyon faced a room full of distinguished archaeologists and gave them some stunning news. She presented evidence that farming had begun thousands of years earlier than experts had previously believed. This evidence greatly affected ideas about ancient history. Her discovery was made possible by a new scientific technique called carbon-14 dating.

American scientist Dr. Willard Libby discovered carbon-14 dating in 1947. Before he introduced this test, archaeologists had to use often unreliable and inconsistent methods to guess the age of artifacts. Carbon-14 dating is much more accurate. Archaeologists soon began using carbon-14 dating to fix incorrect age estimates and to test new finds.

Carbon 14 is a form of carbon atom that decays over time. In living beings, carbon 14 from the air replaces the carbon 14 lost to decay, and therefore the amount remains constant. However, the carbon 14 in a dead plant or animal decays without being replaced. Half the carbon 14 in a sample decays about every 5,000 years. After 50,000 years almost all the carbon 14 is gone. Knowing this, archaeologists can measure the amount of carbon 14 left in a fossil or artifact and figure out its age. In 1960 Dr. Libby won the Nobel Prize in chemistry for his work.

Today a more advanced kind of carbon-14 dating, called AMS, lets scientists date even tiny pieces of once living things with great accuracy. To date objects beyond carbon 14's 50,000-year limit, archaeologists use a method called potassium-argon dating. This method can date some objects that are millions of years old.

The use of these dating techniques has revolutionized archaeology. Modern archaeologists use everything from computers to chemistry to explore the past. They can find out what kind of plants used to grow around ancient villages or what the weather was like then. They can also determine what people ate, how they made things, and many other interesting facts. Using new technology and ideas, archaeologists are improving our understanding of what life was like in the distant past.

A scientist performs a test to determine the age of an ancient artifact.

Understanding What You Read

1. Who developed the carbon-14 dating technique?

2. How do scientists use carbon 14 to determine the age of artifacts?

3. What kinds of information can scientists learn about ancient civilizations by using carbon-14 dating?

America and Mesoamerica because it was highly nutritious. People in Mesoamerica also grew beans, peppers, pumpkins, and gourds as early as 7000 B.C. Knowledge about agricultural techniques and crops spread north to Native Americans living in present-day New Mexico by about 3500 B.C. In the eastern woodlands of North America, Native Americans domesticated their own seed plants, such as sunflowers and squashes, by about 2000 B.C. Native Americans in the Andes, a mountain range in South America, relied more on root crops, such as sweet potatoes.

The development of agriculture allowed many Native American groups to settle in one place for long periods of time. It also led to the development of more complex **societies**. A society is a group that shares a common **culture**. A society's culture is made up of its common values and traditions—such as language, government, and family relationships. Like all societies around the world, Native American societies changed over time.

 ## Early Mesoamerican Civilizations

Some of the first American civilizations developed in Mesoamerica. The Olmec, one of the earliest of these civilizations, has been called the Mother Culture because it highly influenced most later civilizations in the area.

The Olmec and the Maya

The Olmec developed along the Mexican Gulf coast among lowland jungles, grasslands, and swamps. There they built large ceremonial and commercial centers between about 1200 and 400 B.C. During that time Olmec priests developed number and calendar systems, as well as a writing system that used **glyphs**, symbols and images that represent ideas.

Some scholars believe that the Olmec later migrated southeast. There they may have contributed to the rise of the Maya civilization around 400 B.C. The Maya built more than 100 ceremonial centers throughout much of Mesoamerica. These places contained magnificent stone structures, such as temple pyramids, palaces, baths, and

This artifact shows the Maya glyph system of writing, which was similar to that of the Olmec.

bridges. One center, Tikal, housed 3,000 of these structures.

The Maya are also known for their intellectual achievements. They created seven different types of calendars, as well as mathematical and astronomical systems and an advanced form of glyph writing that represented both ideas and sounds. About A.D. 900 the Maya civilization started to decline, and people abandoned some of the great ceremonial centers.

The Toltec and the Aztec

While the Maya civilization was declining, a chieftain named Mixcoatl, or Cloud Serpent, led the Toltec south into central Mexico. The Toltec were master builders and artists who designed pyramids and palaces with beautifully painted walls. They built many of these grand buildings in the city of Tula.

Toltec artists crafted gold and silver objects, while other specialists further improved glyph writing. This rich culture began to decline after numerous fires and droughts. Droughts frequently led to poor harvests that caused famine, or mass starvation.

Around A.D. 1168 Aztec invaders from the north moved into central Mexico. The center of Aztec civilization, Tenochtitlán (tay-NAWCH-tee-TLAHN), was located where present-day Mexico City now stands. The Aztec built Tenochtitlán in the middle of a huge lake, with bridges connecting the city to the mainland. Archaeologists estimate that 300,000 people lived in this great city.

The Aztec created a large empire by conquering most of the groups living in central Mexico. These conquests helped the Aztec maintain a trading network in which they exchanged goods such as gold, silver, jade, corn, and cocoa. Despite their great wealth, Aztec leaders acknowledged that

An Inca knife

their society might not always be so successful. The following Aztec poem expresses this belief:

> ❝ **Truly do we live on earth?**
>   **Not forever on earth; only a little while here.**
>   **Although it be jade, it will be broken,**
>   **Although it be gold, it is crushed. . . .**
>   **Not forever on earth; only a little while here.** ❞

⭐ The Inca

While the Aztec culture was thriving, in South America the Inca developed their own complex civilization. The Inca originally held territory around Cuzco (KOO-skoh), a city high in the Andes. In the A.D. 1400s they began to conquer surrounding lands. Eventually, the Inca controlled an area that stretched from present-day Colombia to central Chile.

The Inca controlled their vast empire by building a 64,000-mile network of roads. These roads allowed armies and messengers to move quickly throughout the empire. The Inca built palaces and temples in their capital city of Cuzco. Decorated with gold and silver, the palaces had beautiful gardens and bathrooms with running water. After they were conquered, most Inca subjects lived in villages where they kept their own land, chiefs, and customs. Families worked together to dig irrigation canals and farm crops—such as potatoes, tomatoes, squash, and maize—to help feed the Inca Empire.

⭐ Early North American Societies

Although less populated than South America and Mesoamerica, North America produced several complex farming cultures. These cultures had to adapt to different environments.

Southwestern Civilizations

In the southwestern region of the present-day United States, Native Americans developed advanced agricultural practices. This enabled many groups to create permanent settlements. Two of the first southwestern peoples to develop agriculture were the Mogollon and Hohokam, centered in present-day Arizona. Because they lived in a dry climate, the Hohokam developed irrigation systems to water their crops of maize, beans, squash, tobacco, and cotton. Both of these groups built pit houses three to four feet into the ground for protection against extreme hot or cold temperatures.

Another group, commonly called the Anasazi (ahn-uh-SAHZ-ee), lived among the high flat-topped hills and deep canyons of the Four Corners region where present-day Utah, Colorado, Arizona, and New Mexico meet. The Anasazi built pueblos, above-ground dwellings made mostly of cut stone or adobe—sun-baked clay and straw. While some pueblos were single-story, many were multistory buildings with ladders connecting the different levels. Pueblo Bonito in New Mexico's Chaco Canyon has five stories and 800 rooms. The Anasazi built their pueblos on mesas—flat-topped hills—and later, around A.D. 1200, into cliffsides for defense. By the next century, some Anasazi began to abandon the larger pueblos, possibly because of drought or internal conflicts.

Southwestern Indian tribes built cliff dwellings, like this one in Mesa Verde, Colorado, to protect them from bad weather and enemy attacks.

The Mound Builders

In eastern and midwestern North America, sophisticated cultures developed between 1200 B.C. and A.D. 1250. In the Ohio River valley, the Adena formed a culture that included a complex religion focusing on death and the afterlife. The Adena constructed dome-shaped mounds to bury honored individuals along with their wealth. Even though they were primarily hunter-gatherers, the Adena maintained large settled villages until their culture's decline around A.D. 200.

Another mound-building culture, the Hopewell, arose about 300 B.C. The Hopewell dominated a large area along the Mississippi, Ohio, and Missouri River valleys. They had higher burial mounds than the Adena, some reaching 30 to 40 feet. The Hopewell supported their large populations with agriculture and trade. However, by about A.D. 700, the Hopewell no longer dominated the region for reasons which archaeologists have not yet been able to discover.

The Mississippi Culture

Like the Adena and Hopewell cultures, the Mississippi culture had important religious practices honoring the dead. From about A.D. 700 to the early 1600s, the people of the Mississippi culture

The ancient mound builders constructed the Great Serpent Mound near what is now Hillsboro, Ohio.

lived along the Ohio and Mississippi Rivers. There they built pyramid mounds out of solid earth. Priests held religious ceremonies in temples built on these pyramids. The largest of these is Monks Mound, near Cahokia (kuh-HOH-kee-uh), Illinois. Monks Mound covers 18 acres, stands 100 feet tall, and may have held a population as high as 30,000. In addition to building mounds, the people of the Mississippi culture were farmers who grew maize, beans, squash, pumpkins, and tobacco. They traded extensively with other peoples in North America and Mesoamerica.

SECTION 1 REVIEW

Identify and explain the significance of the following:
- archaeology
- artifacts
- Paleo-Indians
- migration
- hunter-gatherers
- environments
- domestication
- maize
- societies
- culture
- glyphs

Locate and explain the importance of the following:
- Beringia
- Mesoamerica

Reading for Content Understanding

1 **Main Idea** How do archaeologists think the Paleo-Indians got to the Americas?

2 **Main Idea** What were unique aspects of the Aztec and the Inca Empires?

3 **Geographic Diversity** *Region* What were some of the early societies in North America, and where were they located?

4 **Writing** *Describing* Imagine that you are a visitor to the Mississippi culture. Write a letter to a friend describing the society you encounter.

5 **Critical Thinking** *Drawing Conclusions* Why do you think that growing maize was important to many early Native American civilizations?

Culture Areas in North America

Reading Focus

How did the environment influence Native Americans' ways of obtaining food?

What types of housing did Native Americans build?

What were various traits of Native Americans in different culture areas?

Key Terms

kayaks   longhouses

igloos   Iroquois League

totems

potlatches

kivas

wigwams

NATIVE AMERICANS DEVELOPED many customs based on their close relationship with the land. Many farming tribes in the American Southwest held dances and festivals that celebrated the importance of sun and rain to their life in the desert. One Native American song called the Southwest "a House Made of Dawn . . . made of pollen and of rain." The Inuit of the far north, whose homelands were too cold to grow crops, created ceremonies to help them catch wild game and to show respect for the animals they hunted. From the fiery desert to the frozen north, Native Americans across the continent adapted their lifestyles and traditions to their surroundings.

Native American pottery

⭐ The Far North

The far north of North America has long, cold winters and short summers. Few plants grow there because the ground is always frozen. In the more southern areas, thick forests of pine, spruce, and fir trees grow along numerous lakes and rivers.

The Arctic

Researchers describe ancient Native American tribes by culture areas—the geographic locations that influenced their societies. The far north is divided into the Arctic and Subarctic culture areas. The Inuit and the Aleut lived in the Arctic region. Both groups shared many cultural features, including language. The Inuit lived in present-day northern Alaska and Canada, an area stretching from the Pacific Ocean to the Atlantic. The Aleut lived in southwestern Alaska. Both groups survived by fishing and hunting large mammals. The Inuit and Aleut depended on dogs to sniff out seals beneath the ice, to track herds of caribou, and to pull their many sleds.

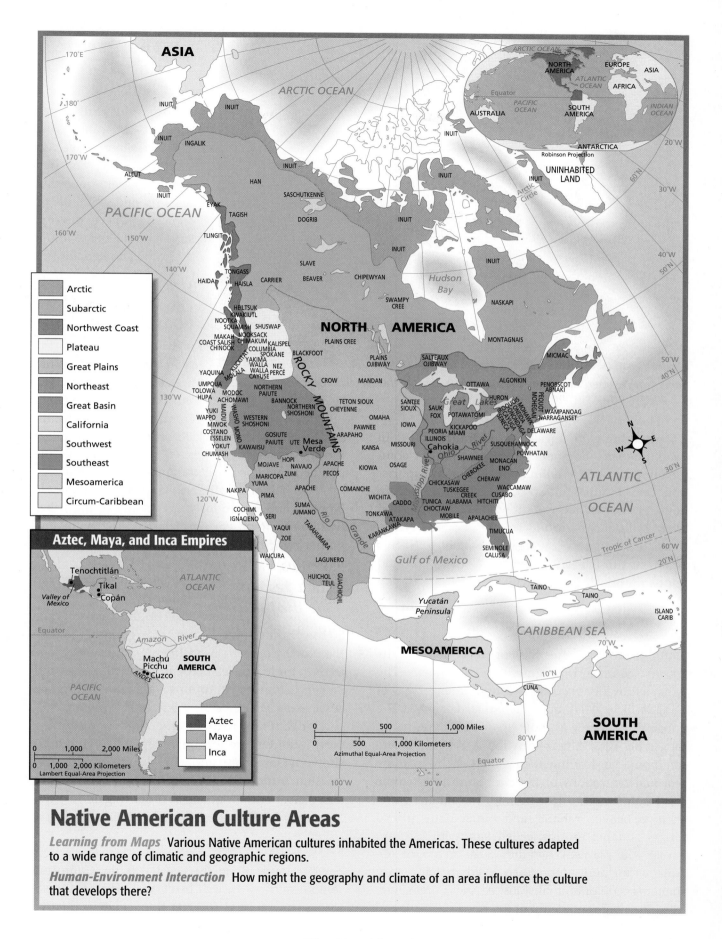

Native American Culture Areas

Learning from Maps Various Native American cultures inhabited the Americas. These cultures adapted to a wide range of climatic and geographic regions.

Human-Environment Interaction How might the geography and climate of an area influence the culture that develops there?

Some Native Americans in the present-day Pacific Northwest still practice the ancient art of making totem poles.

Unlike peoples of the Arctic and Subarctic, Native Americans along the Pacific coast lived in a mild climate. The rich supply of game animals, sea life, and wild plants allowed people to develop large populations without depending on agriculture.

The Northwest Coast

Native Americans of the Northwest Coast culture area lived along the 2,000-mile shoreline stretching from present-day southern Alaska to northern California. Thick evergreen forests and many types of animals and edible plants thrived because of the wet, mild climate.

The Tlingit, Salishan, Chehalis, Tillamook, Nootka, and Skokomish were some of the tribes living in the Northwest. They survived by fishing, gathering, hunting, and trading. Their most important resource was salmon, although they also hunted sea otter and whale from large dugout canoes. Made from red cedar logs, some of these canoes were as long as 70 feet and carried some 50 rowers and three tons of trade goods. People in the Northwest also used the abundant evergreen trees to build houses made of wooden planks and to carve images of **totems**—ancestor or animal spirits—on tall poles.

With these fishing and timber resources, Northwest culture groups prospered. Individuals showed their wealth and earned social standing by holding **potlatches**, events at which hosts gave away most of their goods in order to gain respect.

California

Farther south along the coast was the California region, which varied from wet, dense forests to dry, hot deserts to river-filled valleys. Native

In addition to dogsleds, the Inuit and Aleut used **kayaks**—one-person canoes almost completely enclosed by animal skins—for transportation. Some Inuit built wooden, stone, or earthen houses partly underground, while other Inuit and Aleut built above-ground wooden houses. Where trees or driftwood were unavailable, Native Americans in the Artic used blocks of ice to build **igloos** for housing in the winter.

The Subarctic

South of the Arctic lies the Subarctic, home to the Athapascan and Algonquian peoples. The Athapascan inhabited the western, inland areas of Canada. The Algonquian lived farther east. The Subarctic climate was more hospitable than that of the Arctic. Most Athapascan and Algonquian were seminomadic, leaving their homes to follow the seasonal migrations of the caribou. These people also hunted moose, deer, buffalo, and smaller game such as beaver, rabbits, and birds. Both groups formed smaller groups, called bands, to fish and gather wild plants. When they went on a hunt, the Athapascan and Algonquian lived in temporary shelters made of animal skins. At other times they lived in villages made up of log houses.

American Arts

Totems

Images of ravens, wolves, bears, beavers, fish, frogs, and even people are figures carved into the totem poles found in southeastern Alaska and western British Columbia. The Tlingit, Tongass, Haida, Kwakiutl, Nootka, and Makah are some of the Native American groups that still make these striking artforms today. These cultures' totems dramatically show both tribal and personal or family stories.

The figure of the raven appears on many totem poles. This bird's image is recognizable through its straight beak, wings, and claws. Totem carvers frequently included the raven because it commonly appears in tribal stories. According to some of these tales, the raven created humans, introduced daylight to the world, put rivers and lakes on Earth, and constantly participated in jokes and tricks.

In the early 1800s the fur trade brought new wealth to the region. In addition, members of the tribes began to use axes with metal blades. This enabled local tribes to carve taller poles, sometimes exceeding 60 feet in height. Some of these poles still stand in front of houses today.

To create the poles, first the artist listened to the story or stories that the purchaser of the poles wanted to show. These tales were usually of family deeds or accomplishments. Then the artist would design the work and supervise others employed to do the bulk of the carving. The artist personally carved the most demanding details. After the totem pole's completion, the owner would host a potlatch to dedicate it and hoist it into place. During the potlatch, singers and actors would often perform the pole's story.

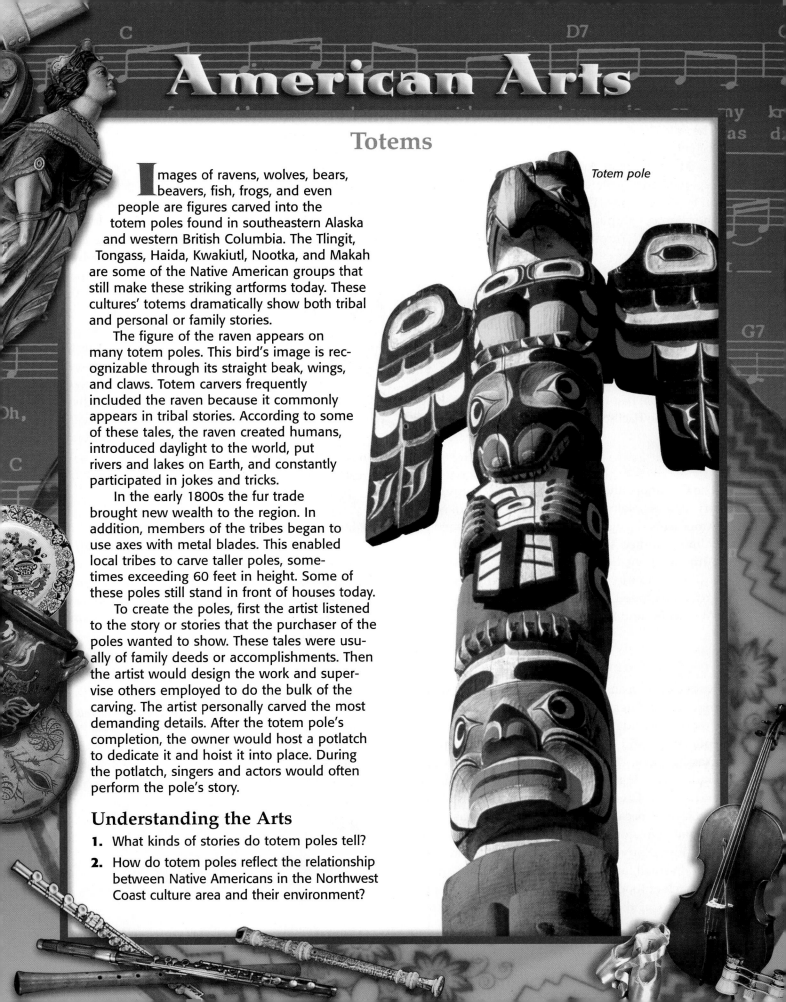

Totem pole

Understanding the Arts

1. What kinds of stories do totem poles tell?
2. How do totem poles reflect the relationship between Native Americans in the Northwest Coast culture area and their environment?

Americans in this area had many food sources available year-round without having to farm. The primary food plant for California culture groups was acorns, which they ground into a coarse flour. They also hunted deer and small game, and fished for salmon and trout.

Most Native Americans in the California region lived in isolated family groups or villages of 50 to 300 persons. These groups—which included the Pomo, Hupa, Chumash, Miwok, Maidu, Cochimi, and Yurok—spoke more than 100 different languages.

 ## The West and Southwest

Native Americans of what is now the interior West and Southwest of the United States lived in an area with less rainfall than the far West. As a result, these people had fewer resources than their neighbors on the Pacific coast.

The Plateau

The Columbia and Fraser Rivers flow through the dry, treeless plain of the Columbia Plateau. Native Americans living near these rivers fished for salmon, hunted small game, and gathered plants. Although they did not practice agriculture, groups in this region lived in permanent villages. These groups included the Nez Percé, Flathead, Modoc, Wenatchee, and Shuswap.

The Great Basin

Native Americans faced more difficulties surviving in the Great Basin because it is primarily desert. They adapted to the harsh environment by collecting and eating mice, lizards, snakes, grasshoppers, crickets, and ants. They also gathered seeds, dug roots, and trapped birds, ducks, and rabbits. Great Basin culture groups highly valued rabbits because they provided meat, as well as fur and skins for blankets and clothing.

Most Native Americans of the Great Basin lived in small family groups that constantly moved in search of food. Most groups in this region spoke variations of the same language. These groups included the Paiute, Shoshoni, and Ute.

The Southwest

Native Americans of the Southwest also had to adjust to a dry environment, but this region's landscape varied from deserts to evergreen forests. Southwestern culture groups included the Pueblo, Navajo, Apache, Papago, Pima, Yaqui, and Karankawa. Many of the groups were agricultural peoples who irrigated their land to grow crops such as maize, beans, squash, and tobacco. Other tribes—including the Navajo and Apache—hunted game, gathered food plants, and raided the villages of agricultural groups such as the Pueblo.

The people of the Pueblo culture group may have descended directly from earlier Southwestern peoples—the Zuni from the Mogollon, and the Hopi from the Anasazi. The Pueblo people had many religious ceremonies, rituals, and festivals. These events focused on the two life-giving forces of Pueblo existence—rain and maize. Pueblo men spent a lot of time in religious activities that were held in **kivas**—circular ceremonial rooms, first built by the Mogollon and used by later Pueblo groups.

 ## The Great Plains

The vast Great Plains region stretches south from Canada into Texas and west from Iowa to the Rocky Mountains. The Plains consisted mainly of grassland, on which millions of buffalo grazed in herds. Deer, elk, antelope, and other game also thrived there.

The Mandan and Pawnee lived in the northern Plains, where they grew crops such as maize,

Native Americans in the Great Plains relied heavily on the buffalo for many needs.

American Museum of Natural History

squash, beans, and pumpkins. Like some other tribes, the Pawnee society was matrilineal. This means that people traced their ancestry through their mothers, rather than their fathers. In addition, when a couple married, the husband moved into the wife's household.

Other agricultural societies lived farther south, on the Red, Arkansas, Canadian, and Brazos Rivers. Native American groups in this region included the Wichita, Caddo, Tonkawa, and Waco. Using pole frames and grass for roofs and siding, they constructed dome-shaped dwellings of 30 to 50 feet in diameter.

Several Native American groups lived in the southern Plains, hunting buffalo on foot and gathering seeds, tubers, nuts, and berries. These groups included the Lipan Apache, who depended almost completely on the buffalo for food, shelter, and clothing. They also used dried buffalo dung to fuel their fires.

Many other Native Americans—including the Kiowa, Comanche, Blackfoot, Crow, Teton Sioux, Cheyenne, and Arapaho—lived on the eastern or western borders of the Plains. These groups had yearly buffalo hunts in which hunters sometimes made many kills by chasing buffalo over steep cliffs.

A European observer drew this image of a young northeastern warrior in the 1600s.

The East

Unlike the Great Plains, the East was rich in resources. Although it was primarily wooded, the region also contained coastal plains, saltwater marshes, the Mississippi River flood plain, and the Everglades, a vast swamp in what is now Florida. The climate of the Southeast is mild during much of the year.

The Southeast

Native Americans of the Southeast included the Cherokee, Choctaw, Chickasaw, Creek, Seminole, and Natchez. The Natchez were direct descendants of the ancient Mississippi culture mound builders.

Southeastern tribes lived in villages along river valleys. They relied primarily on agriculture but also hunted game, gathered plants, fished, and traded. Each of these groups was matrilineal and was organized under village councils. The Natchez groups were ruled by religious leaders.

The Northeast

Northeastern tribes lived in a broad area stretching east from the Atlantic Ocean to the Mississippi Valley and southeast from the Great Lakes to present-day Virginia. The Algonquian people, who were related to those in the Subarctic area, and the Iroquois were the two main groups in the Northeast.

Some Algonquian, such as the Chippewa, Penobscot, and Menomini, lived north of the Great Lakes. These seminomadic bands could not farm all year round because the climate was too cold. They survived by hunting and by gathering edible plants. Other Algonquian peoples, including the Wampanoag, Narragansett, and Pequot, lived farther south. In the warmer climate they farmed, hunted, gathered plants, and fished in rivers and the ocean. They lived in permanent villages and built a variety of housing structures, such as large multi-family lodges and small **wigwams**, which are circular huts. To the east of the Algonquian were the Iroquois, the only Native American people controlled economically by women. Women owned the material possessions and had the responsibility for most aspects of community life—from raising children to planting and harvesting. Men were responsible for hunting and trading.

The Iroquois relied primarily on agriculture, although they also hunted, fished, gathered plants, and traded with other tribes. Neighboring tribes feared the Iroquois because of their military skills and success in warfare. The Iroquois lived in **longhouses**, rectangular dwellings made from logs and bark. Longhouses ranged from 50 to 100 feet long and housed 8 to 10 families each. Fences of pointed stakes surrounded longhouses for defense.

The Iroquois also developed the **Iroquois League**, a unique political confederation made up of the Seneca, Oneida, Mohawk, Cayuga, and

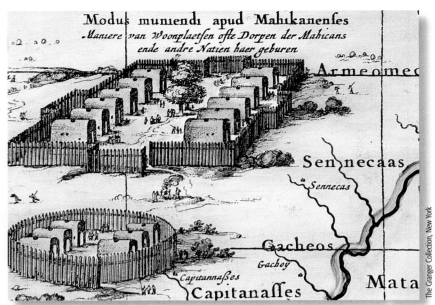

This early American drawing illustrates an Iroquois village where residents lived in longhouses protected by an outside fence. The Iroquois were known for their ability to defend themselves from enemies.

Onondaga tribes. The league was responsible for waging war and making peace with non-Iroquois peoples. Women selected the male members of the league council. Women could overrule decisions made by the council and could remove its members. Under the guidance of the league council, the Iroquois were one of the most powerful peoples in North America.

SECTION 2 REVIEW

Identify and explain the significance of the following:

- kayaks
- igloos
- totems
- potlatches
- kivas
- wigwams
- longhouses
- Iroquois League

Reading for Content Understanding

1 Main Idea How did different Native American groups obtain food, and how was this affected by their environment?

2 Main Idea Make a chart that lists the traits that distinguish the tribes of the different culture groups.

3 Geographic Diversity *Human-Environment Interaction* How did the environment affect the types of housing that different Native American groups built?

4 Writing *Describing* Imagine that you are living in an early Native American society. Write a paragraph describing your life as a member of this group.

5 Critical Thinking *Drawing Conclusions* Why do you think that Native Americans who practiced agriculture were more likely than hunter-gatherers to establish permanent homes?

Europe During the Middle Ages

Reading Focus

What enabled the Vikings to explore new lands, and what is the significance of their voyages?

What was society and daily life like during the Middle Ages?

What events brought about significant change in the late Middle Ages?

Key Terms

colony
Middle Ages
feudalism
manors
Magna Carta

*T*HE BOLD VIKINGS *described their adventures and achievements in sagas—long, heroic stories that blended myth and fact. Erik's Saga tells how Leif Eriksson heard rumors of a land across the sea and decided to search for it in hopes of gaining fame and fortune. He and his crew set sail from his home in Iceland. According to the saga, Eriksson and the Vikings were tossed by the seas before they "finally came upon lands whose existence he [Eriksson] had never suspected." The saga described "fields of flowing wheat there, and vines" with wild grapes. Eriksson, who had landed on the shore of North America, called this site Vinland.*

Viking ship

★ The Viking Explorations

The Vikings were from Scandinavia, which includes the present-day countries of Sweden, Norway, and Denmark. A seafaring people, they developed a unique style of ship with both ends curving identically upward. With these ships, the Vikings rode the rough waves of the North Atlantic more safely and quickly than any other European ship at that time.

The Vikings set out on raids and launched trading expeditions to the British Isles, the northern European coast, and as far away as the Mediterranean and the Black Sea. "Never before had such a terror appeared in Britain," noted English scholar Alcuin in A.D. 793.

Then the Vikings ventured west into the North Atlantic. Much of what historians know about these explorations comes from the Vikings' own sagas. According to the sagas, Norwegian Grímur

Vikings led by Leif Eriksson attack a Native American camp.

Kamban led a group of settlers to Iceland around A.D. 874. A little more than a century later Erik the Red, another Norwegian settler in Iceland, established a **colony**, or settlement, on Greenland.

Leif Eriksson, son of Erik the Red, shared his father's thirst for adventure. Around A.D. 1000 he gathered a crew and launched an expedition, sailing west from Greenland. After a difficult journey, they reached North America, landing in present-day Labrador and Newfoundland, Canada. They then sailed farther south, perhaps as far as New England. According to the sagas, they saw forests, meadows of marsh grass, and rivers that held "larger salmon than they had ever seen." On the coast, Eriksson established a colony called Vinland.

The Vinland colony lasted for only a few years. The Vikings abandoned their settlement because, as one of them reported, "even though the country was richly endowed [gifted] by nature, they would always live in dread" of attacks by Native Americans. In addition, the Vikings may have lacked the ability or the desire to maintain a colony so far across the ocean from Norway. In the 1400s the settlers also abandoned Greenland. However, they maintained the Iceland colony, which was closer to Norway.

⭐ The Middle Ages

The Vikings were not the only raiders who struck at Europe. Beginning in the late A.D. 300s, the great Roman Empire weakened and suffered attacks by Germanic, Slav, and Hun invaders. The vast Roman Empire soon crumbled under the weight of continued invasions, plagues, famines, and economic and political troubles. The empire's collapse marked the beginning of Europe's **Middle Ages**, which started around late A.D. 400s and began to end around A.D. 1350.

The Feudal System

During this time, trade and communication networks broke down, and city populations dropped as people moved into the countryside. Only a few of the biggest cities, such as Constantinople and some Italian port cities, continued as economic and cultural centers. Some Roman law, government structures, and other traditions remained, but much of Europe experienced political conflicts.

The difficult early Middle Ages gradually saw the rise of **feudalism**—a system of government in which people pledged loyalty to a lord in exchange for protection. Feudalism, as historians call it, developed as local rulers sought a defense against repeated invasions.

Nobles

During the Middle Ages, rulers frequently fought with one another for land, riches, and honor. Monarchs and nobles defended their kingdoms and **manors**, or large estates, with the help of loyal vassals. Vassals were soldiers and lords who gave their services in exchange for land, an important step to power and wealth. In his

Many knights in the Middle Ages wore protective armor like this suit.

Peasants like these tended the manor fields.

ceremony to become a vassal, Bernard Atton pledged:

> ❝I swear upon these four gospels of God that I will always be a faithful vassal to thee and to thy successors . . . in all things in which a vassal is required to be faithful to his lord; and I will defend thee, my lord, and all thy successors . . . and the castles and manors and all your men and their possessions against all malefactors [criminals] and invaders, of my own free will.❞

Among these vassals were warriors called knights. To maintain their power, lords needed the loyalty of many knights. Having many knights also demonstrated a lord's wealth, because feeding and equipping knights and their horses was expensive. The military equipment that most knights owned included a lance, an iron helmet, a shield, and a coat of chain mail, which was flexible armor made of interlocking metal rings.

Peasants

Unlike the nobility, peasants—free tenants, serfs, and slaves—farmed the land. Tenants rented land from lords and could leave the manor at the end of their contracts. They paid rent, usually with farm goods or by helping to till the lord's fields.

Serfs lived on a particular manor's land for life in return for the protection of the lord. Serfs farmed but did not own plots of land. They were required to give farm goods or several days of labor each week to their lord. Slaves, who worked as field laborers or domestic servants, were the least powerful members of feudal society. Most slaves in western Europe were freed and eventually became serfs by the A.D. 1000s.

⭐ Life on a Manor

Manors provided most of the necessities for their inhabitants. With little central government, lords ruled their manors without interference. Lords and their families lived in large wooden or stone manor houses or castles, often built with moats and high walls for defense. Noblemen spent their time fighting in battles, organizing their vassals, managing their farmland, and fulfilling their religious duties as Christians. Boys and men were trained in running, swimming, wrestling, dancing, speaking languages, riding, and fencing.

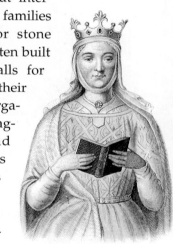

Eleanor of Aquitaine was a powerful noblewoman.

Noblewomen were usually responsible for assuring the household's spiritual well-being through daily prayer. They also maintained the manor house, directed servants, and raised children. In 1190 Richard of Devizes listed some of the qualities of an ideal noblewoman by describing Eleanor of Aquitaine as "beautiful yet virtuous [moral], powerful yet gentle, humble yet keen-witted [intelligent]."

Noblewomen sometimes ruled over feudal lands. When their male relatives were away from the manor or were too young to rule, some noblewomen assumed authority and managed the estates. In the 800s Engelberge, wife of King Louis

This French cathedral built in the 1200s reflects the majesty of medieval Catholic architecture.

II of France, ruled over her husband's court, went on military campaigns with him, and negotiated over territory with his uncles.

Life was very different for peasants. Their houses usually had two rooms, one room in which the family slept and ate and another for farm animals. Male peasants spent a majority of their time plowing fields, planting seeds, harvesting crops, and performing other tasks for the nobility. Women and children tended farm animals, weeded fields, baked and cooked, washed clothes, and planted and harvested fruit trees and vegetable gardens. Women and men worked long days, from before sunrise until after sunset. From an early age, children were expected to work alongside their parents. Children grew up knowing that they would have little chance to advance because a person's birth determined his or her economic and social position in the feudal system.

 ## The Catholic Church

The Catholic Church was the center of religious and social life on manors. Peasants and nobles attended mass, or church services, led by the local priest. Priests also cared for the sick and poor, counseled the rich, and taught the young. Frequent religious festivals offered everyone an opportunity to celebrate and socialize.

Although many religious groups existed during the Middle Ages, most Europeans were Christians. Christianity was an important force that strengthened cultural ties across Europe. The Catholic Church sponsored art and architecture projects such as the Notre Dame cathedral in Paris, France. The Church also gained wealth, land, and power throughout much of Europe. By the late 800s, bishops and priests owned one third of the land in present-day Italy. Bishops also influenced politics. They often personally advised monarchs on spiritual and political matters.

Monasteries

Monasteries were also important during the early Middle Ages. Monasteries were isolated religious communities in which men called monks devoted their lives to practicing Christianity. These places also became centers of education and book production. They often controlled large estates, although individual monks gave up all personal possessions when they joined monasteries. In his *Rules for Monks*, Saint Benedict gave the following advice:

> **Let no one presume [dare] to give or receive anything without the permission of the abbot [director] or to keep anything whatever for his own, neither book, nor tablets, nor pen, nor anything else, because monks should not**

Medieval Catholic wedding

even have their own bodies and wills at their own disposal [use]." 99

Convents

Convents—or religious centers for women called nuns—were similar to monasteries. Nuns who joined convents dedicated their lives to God. Like monks, nuns spent most of their time managing convent estates, reading religious texts, writing, and attending lectures. They also created works of art and earned money by embroidering, sewing, spinning, weaving, and knitting.

Many women joined convents because they wanted to devote their lives to intellectual and spiritual activities rather than get married and have children. In other cases, families forced unmarried female relatives to join convents, which often provided homes for elderly and unmarried noblewomen. Convents not only offered women rare opportunities to pursue an education but also offered abbesses, or convent directors, significant authority. Some nuns wrote history, poetry, and dramatic plays. Hilda, founder and abbess of the Whitby convent in the 600s, received praise from an early writer:

66 **So great was her prudence [good judgment] that not only ordinary folk, but kings and princes used to come and ask her advice in their difficulties and take it.** 99

★ The Rise of Nations

During the mid– and late– Middle Ages, nobles lost power as monarchs expanded their control over vast areas. These growing kingdoms included England and France, which became some of the first nations in the world. In 1066 William of Normandy (an area in present-day France) conquered England. Later, he ordered a survey of the entire realm. The result was the enormous Domesday Book, or Day of Judgment Book. A writer recorded the process of collecting the information:

66 **[William] sent his men over all England into every shire [county] and had them**

Biography

Hildegard of Bingen

Hildegard of Bingen may have taken greater advantage of the opportunities offered by the Catholic Church than any other abbess of the Middle Ages. A nun since about the age of 14, she founded the Rupertsberg convent, near Bingen in present-day Germany. She wrote two books focusing on religious principles and visions. In one of her books, Hildegard wrote that God had come to her in a vision and said: "For the benefit of mankind, do not relinquish [give up] your pen! Write down what your inner eye has seen and your inner ear has heard."

Hildegard also wrote on medicine and science, revealing insights ahead of her time. She also composed a symphony of devotional music. Because of her vast knowledge, popes and monarchs of the 1100s sought her advice.

find out how many hundred hides [one hundred supported one family] there were in the shire, or what land and cattle the king himself had, or what dues [taxes] he ought to have in twelve months from the shire. . . . So very narrowly did he have it investigated, that there was no single hide nor yard of land, nor . . . one ox nor one cow nor one pig was there left out, and not put down in his record. 99

This knowledge helped William establish taxes, distribute land fairly, and determine how many knights and foot soldiers each lord owed in military service.

During the reign of William's great- great-grandson King John, the nobles rebelled against the misuse of royal power. In 1215 they forced John to agree to **Magna Carta**, or the Great Charter. In the charter, John promised to gain the agreement of the nobility before raising new taxes. In addition, the charter established that even monarchs must observe the law. It was also one of the first documents to address the nobility's land rights and to help protect the rights of free individuals.

The early 1200s also brought an increase in local and long-distance trade throughout Europe. Merchants in Italian coastal cities were some of the first Europeans to trade regularly with other countries around the Mediterranean Sea. With the increase in trade, Europeans built new towns and expanded existing cities.

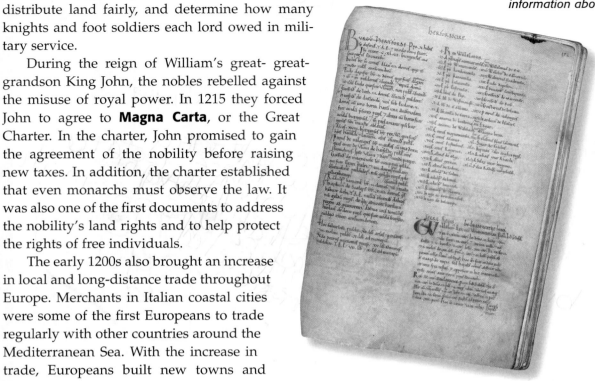

The Domesday Book recorded information about England.

Towns grew even faster when changes in farming led to increased food production and rising populations. These agricultural changes included plowing with horses instead of oxen, fertilizing soil with manure, and rotating crops. As the population grew, landowners cut down trees and drained wetlands to clear more land for farming. To better harness energy, many people began using windmills and watermills for grinding grain, working with metals, and pumping water. With technology, trade, and political power changing, Europe's Middle Ages were coming to a close.

SECTION 3 REVIEW

Identify and explain the significance of the following:
- **Erik the Red**
- **colony**
- **Leif Eriksson**
- **Middle Ages**
- **feudalism**
- **manors**
- **Eleanor of Aquitaine**
- **King William of Normandy**
- **King John**
- **Magna Carta**
- **Hildegard of Bingen**

Reading for Content Understanding

1 Main Idea What was life like during the Middle Ages?

2 Main Idea What actions led to change in the late Middle Ages? What were some of those changes?

3 Geographic Diversity *Movement* What technology enabled the Vikings to explore new lands, and what were the results of their explorations?

4 Writing *Informing* Write a paragraph explaining the role of bishops, monks, and nuns in feudal society.

5 Critical Thinking *Making Conclusions* How were peasants' lives different from those of nobles? How were the two groups similar?

Trade Across Continents

Reading Focus

What was Islam's impact on the Mediterranean region?

What led the Chinese to participate in and then withdraw from international trade?

How did trade influence different regions of Africa?

Key Terms

Crusades
Silk Road

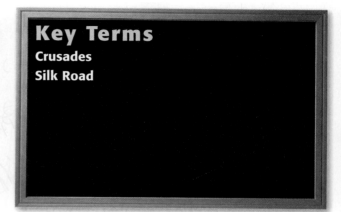

*I*N A.D. 801 THE KING OF PERSIA *gave a white elephant from India to Holy Roman Emperor Charlemagne, who had never before seen such a creature. To bring this gift to France, Charlemagne's ambassador, Isaac, had to struggle through the deserts of North Africa, across the Mediterranean Sea, and over the snow-capped Alps in Italy. Finally, he arrived in France with the elephant, whose name was Abulabaz. The rise of new kingdoms in Europe, Asia, and Africa made journeys like Isaac's more common as trade networks expanded. These networks eventually brought about contact between Native Americans and people from other continents.*

Charlemagne

⭐ The Crossing of Cultures

In A.D. 610 Muhammad, a merchant who lived on the Arabian Peninsula, told of receiving a holy vision that directed him to establish the religion of Islam. He dedicated his life to preaching the message of God, whom he called Allah. After his death, Muhammad's followers recorded these messages in the Qur'an (kuh-RAN), the holy book of Islam. Islam attracted many followers, called Muslims.

Islam spread as Muslims came to control Jerusalem, Syria, the Persian Empire, and Egypt.

Once they controlled the seaports of Syria and Egypt, Muslims built a powerful navy that dominated the entire Mediterranean Sea by the late 600s. With this sea power, they took over areas in North Africa, as well as Sicily and most of the Iberian Peninsula, which includes the present-day countries of Spain and Portugal.

Islamic Scholarship

Trade networks connected many regions, helped spread Islam, and brought new ideas to scholars. From India, Muslim mathematicians learned the numeral system, including the concept of zero. Using this system, they developed algebra.

Muslim scholars based much of their knowledge of medicine, philosophy, astronomy, physics, and mathematics on translations of ancient Greek writings. Muslim doctors improved surgical techniques and knowledge of diseases. They also studied the making of drugs and their effects on the human body. Muslims highly valued learning. One legal and medical scholar gave the following advice to young students: "He who has not endured the stress of study will not taste the joy of knowledge."

The Crusades

Muslims, along with Jews and Christians, showed their religious devotion by visiting the Holy Land. This area included the city of Jerusalem and the region surrounding it. Muslims had taken control of Jerusalem in A.D. 638 but allowed people of other religions to visit. Then in the mid-1000s, Christians began to fear that Muslims would forbid them to enter the city.

In 1095 Pope Urban II called on all Christians to launch a holy war to retake Jerusalem:

❝ Jerusalem is the center of the earth; the land is fruitful above all others, like another paradise of delights. . . . This royal city . . . is now held captive by the enemies of Christ. . . . When an armed attack is made upon the enemy, let this one cry be raised by all the soldiers of God: it is the will of God! It is the will of God!❞

With these words, the pope motivated Christians across Europe to launch the **Crusades**, five wars between 1096 and 1221 for possession of the Holy Land.

Many crusaders were knights, soldiers, and nobles. Eleanor of Aquitaine, queen to King Louis VII of France, enthusiastically joined the crusaders with the women of her court. According to William of Malmesbury, so many Europeans left to join the Crusades that "lands were deserted of their husbands-men, houses of their inhabitants, even whole cities migrated."

The crusaders captured Jerusalem in 1099. They controlled it for nearly 90 years. Then in 1187 military leader Saladin, ruler of Egypt, arrived with a massive army. In the battle that followed, he shouted, "To take it [Jerusalem] I am ready to lose both eyes!" At the battle's end, the city was back in Muslim hands.

★ Empires in Asia

While the last crusaders were fighting in the Holy Land, Genghis Khan was leading the Mongols, nomadic warriors from Central Asia, in an invasion of China. By 1279 his grandson Kublai Khan (KOO-bluh KAHN) ruled an empire that stretched 4,000 miles across Asia's central plains, from the Adriatic Sea to China's southern coast.

The Mongols thought that trade was very honorable and important. Kublai Khan used his powerful navy to open trading networks with present-day Sumatra, Sri Lanka, and southern India. In addition, merchants resumed using the **Silk Road**, an overland trade route several thousand miles long, stretching from the Black Sea to China.

In 1368 the Ming dynasty overthrew the Mongol Empire in China. During the conflict the family of Zhu Di, a Ming prince, captured a 10-year-old boy named Zheng He. As he grew older,

Kublai Khan (left) built a powerful empire in China.

Global Connections

The Silk Road

In 138 B.C. Chinese emperor Wu Ti sent officer Chang Ch'ien west on a secret mission of exploration. On the journey the powerful Hsiung-nu attacked Chang's party and took them captive. About 13 years passed before Chang returned to Wu Ti's court. Chang created a sensation with his tales of lands rich with valuable gems and fast, strong horses.

Wu Ti ordered more expeditions west, and China opened up trade routes. Merchants began sending goods to Europe on the great highway known as the Silk Road, which stretched nearly 5,000 miles from eastern China to the Black Sea. The Silk Road wove through harsh deserts and forbidding mountains. Some travelers froze to death and others died of thirst. All feared the attacks of bandits. One desert traveler wrote:

> " *There are no flying birds above, no roaming beasts below. It would be impossible to know the way but for dead men's decaying bones, which show the direction [to go].* "

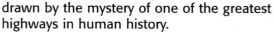
Trader in the Middle Ages

The promise of wealth kept traders on the Silk Road. By the first century A.D., one large caravan was leaving western China every month. The great Roman Empire eagerly bought Chinese silk, a fabric rare in the West. Merchants sent other items as well, such as furs, ivory, ceramic, jade, and cinnamon. Caravans returning to China carried valuables like gold, glass, and wool and linen fabrics. Trade along the Silk Road slowed in the 800s and did not pick up again for another 400 years. Despite this revival, by the 1600s China had cut off all contact with the West. Cities along the route became ruins buried in sand. Today adventurers still explore the Silk Road, drawn by the mystery of one of the greatest highways in human history.

Understanding What You Read

1. What were some goods that were traded along the Silk Road?
2. What was the Silk Road's importance?

Zheng He became Zhu Di's most loyal servant and a skilled military commander. He was a large man, standing nearly seven feet tall. According to his family records, he had

> " **glaring eyes, teeth as white and well-shaped as shells, and a voice as loud as a huge bell. He knew a great deal about warfare and was well accustomed to battle.** "

In 1402 Zhu Di seized the Ming throne. He built a large fleet of ships to exchange silk and porcelain for spices and other goods in India, Arabia, and Africa. Zheng He commanded this treasure fleet, which included 317 brightly painted ships and more than 27,000 men. Using star maps and sailing charts to navigate, Zheng He led the fleet on seven voyages over nearly 30 years. These trips brought wealth and knowledge of other cultures to China.

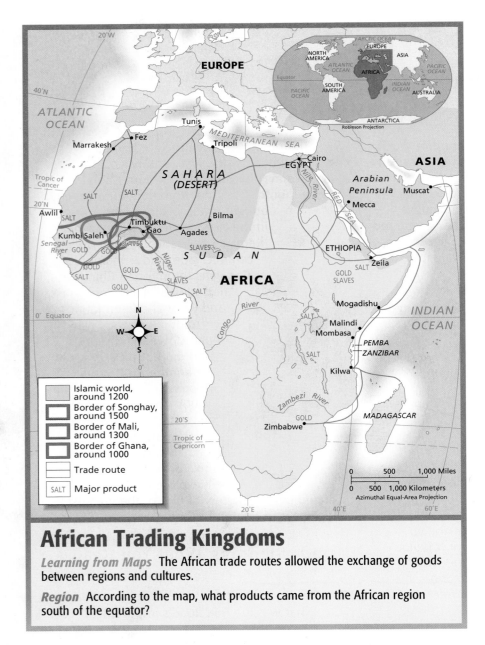

African Trading Kingdoms

Learning from Maps The African trade routes allowed the exchange of goods between regions and cultures.

Region According to the map, what products came from the African region south of the equator?

After Zheng He's death, the Ming dynasty reduced its long-distance ocean trade. By the mid-1400s, political conflicts, a lack of tax money, and other events led China to refocus on internal affairs and to abandon its command of the seas.

⭐ African Trading Kingdoms

When China was actively involved in trade, many Chinese merchants traveled to African kingdoms. By participating in long-distance trading networks, some African kingdoms had grown very wealthy.

East Africa

Several kingdoms existed in the upper Nile River valley region between 1000 B.C. and A.D. 800. One kingdom, called Kush, dominated the region in the 700s B.C. Kushite rulers conquered Egypt and adopted Egyptian religion, writing, language, and culture.

Another African kingdom, Aksum, developed in present-day Ethiopia. Aksum gained much of its wealth by trading with India at port cities along the Red Sea, which separates Africa from Southwest Asia. Aksum's most important trade good was ivory from the tusks of elephants. Many Aksumites converted to Christianity after North African and Asian Christians introduced the religion. The Aksum kingdom declined in the early A.D. 700s because of overuse of farmland and a loss of trade.

Farther down the East African coast, Arab traders exchanged goods with Bantu-speaking peoples. Bantu and Arab traders developed market centers that grew into about 30 separate city-states, including Mogadishu (mahg-uh-DISH-oo), Mombasa (mahm-BAHS-uh), and Kilwa. Each of these city-states had its own ruler and competed for control of the southern Africa gold trade. The mixture of Bantu and Arab influences developed into a unique culture. The people shared a common religion, Islam, and a new language, Swahili (swah-HEE-lee).

West Africa

Long-distance trading networks also developed in West Africa. Starting about A.D. 100, Berbers—nomads from North Africa and the northern Sahara—began using camels to carry goods across the desert. They brought salt south and gold north. Many people desired salt because it could be used to prevent food from spoiling quickly.

Several kingdoms grew wealthy and powerful by participating in these trading networks. Ghana (GAHN-uh) ruled an area between the Niger (NY-juhr) and Senegal Rivers to the south and the Sahara to the north. Most of Ghana's wealth came from trading gold, which Arab merchants carried north to traders in the Mediterranean.

Mali

Mali emerged in the early 1200s after Ghana's collapse. The region Mali controlled stretched from Africa's west coast to more than 1,000 miles inland. The kingdom of Mali included the important trading city of Timbuktu (tim-buhk-TOO). Traveler Ibn Battuta noted:

This image of Mansa Musa comes from an atlas made for a European king.

❝ [The Malians] are seldom unjust, and have a greater horror of injustice than other people. Their [ruler] shows no

mercy to anyone who is guilty of the least act of it. There is complete security in their country. Neither traveler nor inhabitant in it has anything to fear from robbers or men of violence. ❞

In the late 1200s North African traders brought Islam to Mali and to the large eastern region of Sudan. Mali's kings embraced Islam, and Timbuktu became a center of Islamic culture and learning. One of the greatest Malian leaders, Mansa Musa, impressed Arabs with his wealth and power when he went on a pilgrimage to the Islamic holy city of Mecca in 1324.

The large Songhay (SAWNG-hy) Empire also had great influence in the region. Songhay's Muslim rulers encouraged the spread of Islamic culture throughout their vast territory. The Songhay Empire remained wealthy and powerful until the late 1500s.

SECTION 4 REVIEW

Identify and explain the significance of the following:
- Muhammad
- Silk Road
- Crusades
- Kublai Khan
- Zheng He
- Mansa Musa

Locate and explain the importance of the following:
- Mogadishu
- Timbuktu

Reading for Content Understanding

1 **Main Idea** How was Islam spread throughout the Mediterranean region? What new ideas did Muslim scholars bring to the Mediterranean?

2 **Main Idea** Why did Kublai Khan open trading networks with other countries? What led to the decline of Chinese participation in international trade?

3 **Cultural Diversity** How did trade influence the development of East and West African kingdoms?

4 **Writing** *Classifying* Write a paragraph explaining how early global trade affected international relations.

5 **Critical Thinking** *Identifying Cause and Effect* How did trade between different empires affect their economic development?

CHAPTER 1 REVIEW

Chapter Summary

Many scientists believe that humans first arrived in North America during the last Ice Age. After their arrival, many culture groups and civilizations developed throughout the Americas. Around the period of the Middle Ages in Europe, many other civilizations in Asia and Africa were exploring and trading in lands beyond their own. ■

On a separate sheet of paper, complete the following activities.

Identifying People and Ideas

Describe the historical significance of the following:

1. archaeology
2. domestication
3. kayaks
4. Erik the Red
5. feudalism
6. manors
7. Crusades
8. Eleanor of Aquitaine
9. Silk Road
10. Zheng He

Internet Activity

go.hrw.com
SA0 Africa and Asia

Search the Internet through the HRW Web site for information about what life is like today in one of the African or Asian nations mentioned in Section 4. You should find out the nation's population, its religions, its economy, and its agriculture. Compile this information in a short report.

Understanding Main Ideas

1. How did Paleo-Indians adapt to the environmental changes when the Ice Age ended?
2. Where was the center of Aztec civilization, and what was it like?
3. What was the environment like in the California region? Why did Native Americans there not have to farm?
4. What role did women play in the Iroquois society?
5. How did the Aksum kingdom gain much of its wealth? What led to its decline?
6. What was the Catholic Church's role in the Middle Ages?
7. Why did Pope Urban II call on Christians to launch a crusade?
8. Who were the Berbers, and how did they transport trade goods?

Using the Time Line

Number your paper from 1 to 5. Match the letters on the time line below with the following events.

1. Leif Eriksson, son of Erik the Red, sails west from Greenland with his crew. After a difficult journey they reach North America.
2. The Maya Empire develops.
3. Members of the Mississippi culture begin building large temple mounds.
4. The Ming dynasty overthrows the Mongol Empire.
5. King John agrees to Magna Carta.

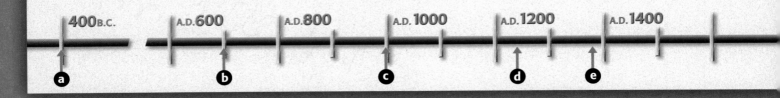

400 B.C. A.D. 600 A.D. 800 A.D. 1000 A.D. 1200 A.D. 1400

a   b   c   d   e

Reviewing Themes

1. **Cultural Diversity**   What characteristics do historians and archaeologists use to group Native American societies into culture areas?

2. **Geographic Diversity**   What types of housing did Native Americans build? Explain why they built the types of houses they did.

3. **Global Relations**   What intellectual contributions did Mesoamerican civilizations make to North American ones? What contributions did Muslim scholars make to their trading partners?

Thinking Critically

1. **Making Comparisons**   In what ways were the early Native American groups in North America different from and similar to one another?

2. **Identifying Cause and Effect**   How did the development of agriculture change the way Native Americans lived?

3. **Supporting a Point of View**   Do you think that all members of society benefited from the feudal system? Use examples to support your answer.

Writing About History

1. **Expressing**   Imagine that you are a trader in an East African village between 800 B.C. and A.D. 800. Write a diary entry describing a typical day. Be sure to include thoughts about trade with other African people as well as Arab merchants.

2. **Informing**   Imagine that you are a Native American from the Southeast culture area who has attended a meeting of the Iroquois League. Write a paragraph to explain the differences and similarities between the Iroquois culture and your own.

Linking Geography and History

1. **Human-Environment Interaction**   Why did many people of the Southwest build their homes high in cliffs?

2. **Movement**   Where did the Vikings land in North America? Why did they leave?

Building Your Portfolio

Complete the following activities individually or in groups.

1. **Manor Life**   You are in charge of putting together a newspaper article about life on a manor during the Middle Ages. Your article should contain a detailed map of the region in which the manor is located, images of life on the manor, and brief reports on its different groups.

2. **Creation Story**   In Section 1 you read a short creation story that explains how the first people came to the world. Write your own such story on a topic of your choice. You might choose to write on how gymnasiums got their name, on why birds fly, or on why trees lose their leaves in the fall. Illustrate your story with a drawing or picture. You may wish to share your story with the class.

History Skills Workshop

Using Visual Resources Study the image to the right, which is a picture of Inca ruins at Machu Picchu, Peru. Briefly describe the image. Then explain what the ruins tell you about Inca society.

▪ C H A P T E R 2 ▪
The Age of Exploration
(1350–1550)

As Europe faced famine, war, and disease throughout the mid-1300s, Italian scholar Petrarch (PEE-trahrk) wished that "we [had] been born far earlier or far later. There was once, and there may be again, a happier time." Before long, Europeans witnessed a dramatic series of changes that affected every area of European society. Some people wondered if these changes would bring the "happier time" that Petrarch wanted.

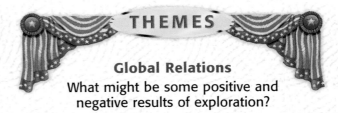

THEMES

Global Relations
What might be some positive and negative results of exploration?

Economic Development
How might global trade affect a country's economic development?

Geographic Diversity
What might be some geographic challenges to exploring new lands?

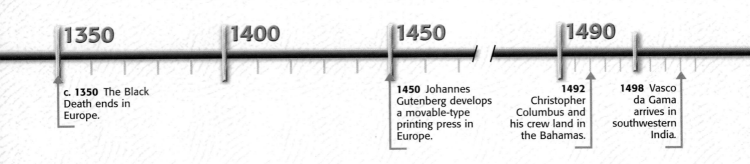

1350

1400

1450

1490

c. **1350** The Black Death ends in Europe.

1450 Johannes Gutenberg develops a movable-type printing press in Europe.

1492 Christopher Columbus and his crew land in the Bahamas.

1498 Vasco da Gama arrives in southwestern India.

Europeans Set Sail

Reading Focus

How did the Commercial Revolution and the Renaissance change Europe?

Why did Europeans seek direct trade with Asia?

What were some of the consequences of early Portuguese explorations?

Key Terms

Black Death

Commercial Revolution

capital

joint-stock companies

Renaissance

astrolabe

monopoly

caravel

IN THE YEAR 1299 *the city of Arras in present-day France was famous for its wealthy merchants. The local Crespin family was so rich that it loaned money to cities, bishops, and even monarchs. The rise of the Crespins and other merchants to such power represented a change in society that worried some Europeans. "Money is too much worshipped here," wrote poet Adam de la Halle about Arras. Others welcomed the changing economy, however, because it provided opportunities for workers to make money and improve their social status. When Baude Crespin died in 1316, his tombstone read, "Pray for his immortal spirit then, Laborers and working men."*

European moneylenders and borrowers in the 1300s

IMAGE ON LEFT PAGE: *A map of the Americas from the late 1500s*

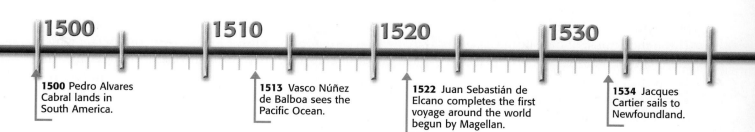

1500

1510

1520

1530

1500 Pedro Alvares Cabral lands in South America.

1513 Vasco Núñez de Balboa sees the Pacific Ocean.

1522 Juan Sebastián de Elcano completes the first voyage around the world begun by Magellan.

1534 Jacques Cartier sails to Newfoundland.

The Age of Exploration **31**

⭐ The Commercial Revolution

The European economy and trade with Asia grew steadily during the 1100s and 1200s, as did the population. Then in the mid-1300s, Europe's prosperity suffered serious blows from famine and a horrible disease.

The Black Death

The Black Death carved on a French tombstone

Italian merchants returning from Asia in 1347 were unaware that aboard their ships were rats infested with the bubonic plague, a deadly disease that had killed many people in Asia. During the **Black Death**, an epidemic that swept through Europe from 1348 to about 1350, the bubonic plague killed perhaps as many as 75 million people, which was about one third of Europe's population. One Italian merchant described the horror that resulted when the plague spread throughout his city:

> 66 **In many places in Siena great pits were dug and piled deep with the multitude of dead. And I . . . buried my five children with my own hands.** 99

The Economy Grows

Eventually, Europe recovered from the Black Death. The reduced population created a labor shortage in Europe, which caused wages to increase. In the 1400s the economy revived during the **Commercial Revolution**—a period of economic development that dramatically changed the way many merchants conducted business. Throughout most of the Middle Ages, merchants had set their prices according to what the local community agreed was fair. During the Commercial Revolution, however, merchants and craftspeople became more aggressive about raising or lowering prices to make a profit.

The seal of a trade union in the Netherlands

Landlords encouraged farmers on rented lands to specialize in crops or goods that could be sold at a profit in distant markets. For example, large areas in France and Italy concentrated on producing wine for export, while parts of England focused on exporting wool.

Many cities—particularly those in Italy and the lower part of the Rhine River, in the present-day countries of the Netherlands and Belgium—grew wealthy during the Commerical Revolution. Some cities specialized in certain crafts. In Italy, for example, Florence became famous for dying fabrics, while Venice was known for its glassmaking. Venice and many other cities also became prosperous trade centers by dealing in rare goods brought from faraway lands.

Banks and Bankers

In the expanding European economy, social status and influence were increasingly tied to wealth. As Spanish poet Juan Ruiz humorously observed in the mid-1300s:

> 66 **Money can do much; it should be held in high esteem [regard]. It turns a tramp into a respected and honorable man. . . . The more money a man has, the more worthy he becomes, while the man who is penniless cannot call himself his own master. . . . Money makes hard things easy.** 99

As merchant families in Europe grew wealthier, they began to think of ways to get **capital**—money or property that is used to earn more money. Merchant families such as the Medici (MED-ee-chee) of Florence began establishing banks that loaned money to monarchs, nobles, and other merchants. The borrowers repaid these loans with interest, which earned additional money for the bankers. The Medici and other bankers became influential throughout Europe. Merchants also began creating **joint-stock companies**, businesses in which a group of people jointly invest and share in the profits and losses. This type of investment helped raise money for new ventures and reduced the individual risk of starting a business.

⭐ The Renaissance

The expanding economy and an increase in trade gave some Europeans the wealth needed to pursue education and the arts. This change contributed to the **Renaissance,** a grand rebirth of European interest in the arts and learning of ancient Greece and Rome. The Renaissance began in the mid-1300s in Italy and spread across Europe, lasting until the early 1600s.

Education and Ideas

The Renaissance combined the rediscovery of ancient Greek and Roman works with new ideas about art, society, science, and technology. Teachers stressed to students the importance of combining a knowledge of the classic scholars with strong moral values. In his book *The Courtier*, Baldassare Castiglione (kahs-teel-YOH-nay) described what an ideal gentleman should learn:

❝ **He should have a knowledge of Greek as well as Latin [and] he should be very well acquainted with the poets, and no less with the orators and historians, and also skilled at writing both verse and prose.** ❞

Many Renaissance thinkers also argued that human beings were superior to all other creatures. "To you is given a body more graceful than other animals . . . to you wit, reason, [and] memory," wrote one scholar. This attitude encouraged people to believe that human beings could accomplish anything. It also motivated Europeans to explore the rest of the world.

Science and Technology

Arab scholars had helped preserve the works of many ancient Greek writers and made their own

A Portuguese astrolabe used to navigate at sea

impressive contributions to fields such as mathematics, astronomy, and medicine. In the 1100s and 1200s European scholars translated these texts from Arabic into Latin. As these ideas spread, they helped start the Renaissance and improved scholars' knowledge of many areas of study.

Sailors put ancient astronomical knowledge to practical use by combining it with tools such as the magnetic compass and the **astrolabe**. The astrolabe allowed navigators to determine their ship's position by charting the position of the stars. With more accurate charts and instruments, sailors could navigate in the open sea without any landmarks to guide them.

One of the most significant developments of the Renaissance was Johannes Gutenberg's invention of movable type for European printing presses around 1450. The printing press made it much easier and less expensive to create multiple identical copies of a book. By 1500, European printers had produced between 15 and 20 million books. As one Italian writer exclaimed, "What did the Greeks and Romans ever invent that could be compared to the printing press?" Books helped spread the science and literature of the Renaissance throughout Europe.

The Growth of the Arts

The Renaissance led to a renewed interest in the arts, particularly in Italy. Artists blended their fascination with ancient Greek and Roman sculpture and architecture with new ideas about painting styles and techniques. Artists such as Italy's Leonardo da Vinci (lay-oh-NAHR-doh dah VEEN-chee) combined art with an interest in many other subjects. Da Vinci, who painted the *Mona Lisa,* also studied architecture,

Leonardo da Vinci completed the Mona Lisa *in 1506.*

From Printing Press to Desktop

Until the mid-1400s, scribes and scholars produced all books and manuscripts by writing them out by hand. Around 1450, however, Johannes Gutenberg, a German printer, revolutionized book production when he developed printing with movable metal type.

Within 50 years of Gutenberg's invention, Europe had more than 1,000 printers. The printing press allowed the spread of new ideas throughout Europe and contributed to the great changes that took place during the Renaissance. Printing techniques remained essentially the same for the next four centuries. Then in the late 1800s, inventors developed machines that made it easier for printers to set type.

Even greater improvements followed the printing press. In the mid-1980s printing and publishing again underwent revolutionary changes as desktop publishing became widely available to anyone who owned a computer, a laser printer, and the appropriate software. Today, individuals produce newsletters, magazines, and even entire books in their own homes or offices. According to one reporter for the *New York Times*, "Armed with a few articles [and] a desktop publishing program . . . almost anyone can become a publisher."

The Granger Collection, New York

Early printing presses produced books on art, science, and religion.

Understanding What You Read

1. How have printing techniques changed over time?

2. What benefits and drawbacks does the greater ease of publishing have for society today?

---

astronomy, biology, geology, and machinery. "A painter is not admirable unless he is universal," he wrote.

Michelangelo Buonarroti (mee-kay-LAHN-jay-loh bwaw-nahr-RAW-tee) was another gifted Italian Renaissance artist. He created the sculpture *David* and painted the beautiful artwork on the ceiling of the Sistine Chapel in the Vatican in Rome. Rich merchants and public officials were eager to buy the work of talented artists such as da Vinci and Michelangelo. Wealthy people also hired artists, writers, musicians, and poets to create works of art that celebrated their prosperity.

Trade with Africa and Asia

Much of the prosperity of the Commercial Revolution came through trade. While trade within Europe was important, the greatest profits came from trading with distant lands such as Asia. An extensive network of merchants, bankers, and trade towns brought prized goods from Africa and Asia to Europe's markets in the Mediterranean.

Trade Risks and Rewards

In Africa, trade networks were built around the exchange of gold, ivory, slaves, and salt, which was used to preserve foods. From Asia came silk and spices. Skilled European tailors turned silk fabric into elegant clothing for wealthy merchants and nobles. Cooks used expensive spices to flavor food, as in this English recipe for fruit pie: "[Add] powdered pepper, cinnamon, cloves, mace, powdered ginger, pines, raisins or currants, saffron, and salt." Most of these spices grew only in Asia.

Although merchants usually carried silk and spices in small quantities, the trade was extremely profitable. In the 1400s one ton of pepper could be worth more than the ship that carried it across the Mediterranean Sea. Crossing the Mediterranean was only the last leg of the journey, however. To reach the Mediterranean, traders traveled long overland routes, such as the Silk Road that stretched from China to the shores of the Black Sea. These lengthy journeys were very dangerous because of the risk of attack by bandits.

Trade goods passed through the hands of many different merchants before reaching their destination. To make a profit, each merchant raised the price of the goods when selling to the next trader. The result was higher prices for European consumers.

The Search for a Sea Route

The countries of western Europe—such as Portugal, Spain, France, and England—wanted to

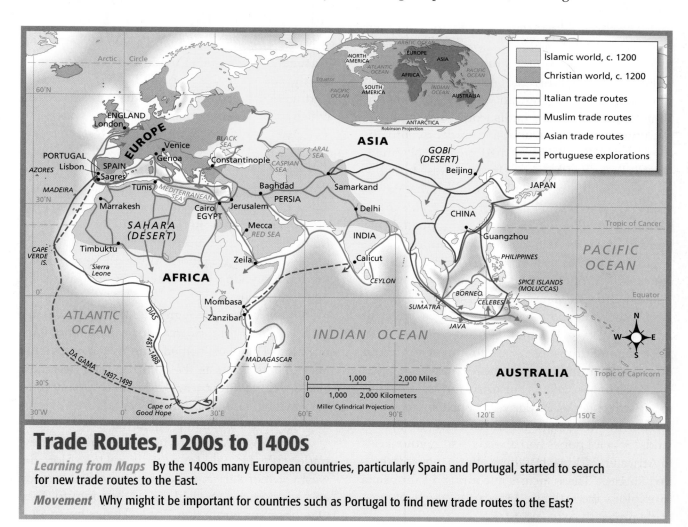

Trade Routes, 1200s to 1400s

Learning from Maps By the 1400s many European countries, particularly Spain and Portugal, started to search for new trade routes to the East.

Movement Why might it be important for countries such as Portugal to find new trade routes to the East?

Technology of the Middle Ages

INVENTION	PLACE OF ORIGIN	BENEFIT TO EUROPE
Astrolabe	Europe	Enabled sailors to determine their north-south position on Earth—that is, their degree of latitude—by using the location of the stars
Compass	China	Enabled people to determine their direction of travel even when the stars were hidden
Heavy plow	Europe	Enabled farming in the hard soils of northern Europe
Horse collar	Central Asia	Enabled horses to pull the heavy plow
Paper	China	Served as a cheap replacement for parchment
Printing	China	Johannes Gutenberg refined Asian printing techniques, which allowed the quick and cheap printing of large quantities of material.

find an alternate sea route to Africa and Asia for several reasons. First, they wanted to have their own access to the wealth of these continents. The Italian city of Venice had a **monopoly** on, or sole economic control of, the Asian products that reached the Mediterranean. With its monopoly, Venice could keep merchants from other countries from participating in the Asian trade. Eventually, even Venetian merchants had trouble obtaining Asian goods and spices as trade routes started to collapse. By the early 1400s political changes in Asia and an increasing threat of bandit raids made it more difficult to use the Black Sea route to bring trade goods from Asia to the markets of Europe.

In addition to wealth from Asian trade, many educated Europeans had become interested in Asian cultures. Marco Polo's *Description of the World*, his book about his travels in Asia, was still quite popular in Europe long after his death in 1324. Many Europeans hoped to learn more about this wondrous land.

Religion, as well as curiosity, turned attention to Africa and Asia. Many Europeans hoped to spread the teachings of Christianity to distant lands. Several popes had already sent missionaries to Africa and China, but these efforts met with limited success. These factors encouraged Europeans to explore the Atlantic Ocean in search of new trade routes to Asia and Africa.

The Portuguese Explore Africa

Portugal became one of the leaders in exploration in the early 1400s. Located west of Spain, Portugal's long coastline faces the Atlantic Ocean, which encouraged exploration of those waters.

Portugal Takes to the Seas

Prince Henry, known as the Navigator, greatly aided Portugal's exploration efforts. Born in 1394, Prince Henry inherited his love for astronomy from his mother, Queen Philippa, who showed him books on navigation. Although he was not a sailor, as a young man Henry became fascinated by exploration.

In the town of Sagres (SAH-greesh), Henry gathered the finest mapmakers, sailors, and ship-builders. There he helped improve navigational instruments, such as the compass. His designers also developed the **caravel**, a small ship built to be very maneuverable and fast. One Italian called caravels "the best ships that sailed the seas."

Henry was willing to take risks to find a new trade route. He paid for expeditions to explore the west coast of Africa, which had a profitable trade and seemed the most likely water route to Asia. One observer wrote that Prince Henry believed if he did not send explorers to this region, "No mariners [sailors] or merchants would ever dare to attempt it." By the time Prince Henry died in 1460, the Portuguese were successfully exploring the west coast of Africa.

In 1487 Portuguese navigator Bartolomeu Dias led an expedition southward along the African coast. A storm blew the ships out to sea. When Dias finally sighted land again, he discovered that his ships had safely passed the southern tip of Africa. He named this point the Cape of Good Hope. Dias wanted to continue the voyage, but according to him the crew was "terrified by the great seas through which they had passed . . . [and demanded] that they proceed no farther." The long voyage also had left them low on supplies, so Dias returned to Portugal.

A bronze flute player from Benin, West Africa

The Slave Trade

As the Portuguese explored the African coast, they established small trading posts from present-day Mauritania, in northwest Africa, to present-day Angola, in the southwest. The Portuguese used these posts to supply their ships. They also bargained with local rulers and merchants for gold and ivory.

In many places along the African coast the Portuguese also were interested in trading for African slaves. Usually they went to African merchants who already had access to people who had been enslaved through war or raiding. As the slave trade grew, so did the warfare among the kingdoms of West Africa. The slave trade had a terrible effect on African communities, breaking up many families. In 1444 a Portuguese record-keeper witnessed the capture and enslavement of Africans:

> " Mothers would clasp [hold] their infants in their arms, and throw themselves on the ground to cover them with their bodies . . . so that they could prevent their children from being separated from them. "

The Portuguese sent many of these enslaved Africans to work in other Portuguese colonies, where they endured hard labor and terrible living conditions. For these Africans, the European explorations had disastrous results.

SECTION 1 REVIEW

Identify and explain the significance of the following:

- **Black Death**
- **Commercial Revolution**
- **capital**
- **joint-stock companies**
- **Renaissance**
- **astrolabe**
- **monopoly**
- **caravel**
- **Henry the Navigator**
- **Bartolomeu Dias**

Reading for Content Understanding

1 **Main Idea** What are some of the changes that occurred in the areas of education, science, technology, and the arts during the Renaissance?

2 **Main Idea** Why was a sea route to Asia important to Europeans?

3 **Economic Development** How did the Commercial Revolution affect trade practices, banking, and the production of goods?

4 **Writing** *Describing* Imagine that you are exploring the west coast of Africa on one of Prince Henry's ships. Write a journal entry describing why you have joined the crew and how you think your explorations will affect Europe and the communities you encounter.

5 **Critical Thinking** *Drawing Conclusions* Why do you think the printing press was such an important invention? What modern invention might be of similar importance? Explain your answer.

Voyages to the Americas

Reading Focus

What was Christopher Columbus's goal, and why did Spain support it?

What happened on Columbus's first voyage?

How did Europeans react to Columbus's voyages?

Key Terms

Reconquista
viceroy
convert
Line of Demarcation
Treaty of Tordesillas

*I*N 1488 CHRISTOPHER COLUMBUS *came to Lisbon, Portugal, to meet with King John II. The Italian explorer hoped that the king would provide the money and ships to sail west to find a sea route to Asia. On a previous trip, King John had called Columbus "a big talker . . . full of fancy and imagination." This time, though, King John seemed more interested in Columbus's idea. Just as Columbus arrived in Lisbon, however, he saw Bartolomeu Dias's ships sailing into port. After Dias brought news of his trip around the southern tip of Africa, King John decided that reaching Asia by way of Africa was better than Columbus's plan. The king lost interest in Columbus, who left Lisbon bitterly disappointed.*

The Metropolitan Museum of Art

Christopher Columbus

⭐ Columbus's Bold Idea

Christopher Columbus was an Italian sailor from the town of Genoa. During his travels and studies he decided to find a new water route to Asia.

A Grand Dream

Historians still debate many of the details of Columbus's early life. He claimed to have sailed to Iceland and to West Africa as a young man.

According to some reports, the young Columbus survived a shipwreck and washed ashore in Portugal. Some historians believe that Columbus learned about advances in navigation technology from Portuguese sailors.

Columbus also read travelers' tales, such as Marco Polo's *Description of the World*. Polo's story of great kingdoms and fabulous wealth in Asia captured Columbus's imagination. He became convinced that he could reach Asia by sailing west across the Atlantic Ocean, rather than by sailing around Africa as the Portuguese were attempting.

Columbus's theory was a very daring idea at the time. No one knew the size of the great ocean to the west of Europe. Some scholars claimed that it was more than 10,000 miles from Europe to the Indies, a common European name for the lands of Asia. This seemed an impossible distance to travel considering the challenges of navigation and of keeping months' worth of food and water from spoiling on long voyages. Columbus, however, was convinced that the Atlantic Ocean was much smaller than many people thought. He based his argument largely on the writings of a few scholars. He also made an error in calculating the earth's circumference. Despite his confidence, Columbus had difficulty convincing others that his theory was correct.

In early August 1492, King Ferdinand and Queen Isabella of Spain said goodbye to Columbus as he began his voyage across the Atlantic.

Columbus in Spain

Eventually, Columbus went to the court of King Ferdinand and Queen Isabella of Spain. When Columbus arrived in Spain, the king and queen were busy fighting the kingdom of Granada. Granada was the last territory in present-day Spain held by the Moors, North African Muslims who had conquered the area in the early Middle Ages. Ferdinand and Isabella did not give Columbus an answer for six years because they were trying to capture Granada. In the meantime, he tried without success to get support from the leaders of other European countries.

Finally, in January 1492, Granada surrendered, ending the **Reconquista** (re-kawng-KEE-stah), the centuries-long struggle to drive the Moors from Spain. King Ferdinand and Queen Isabella then agreed to fund Columbus's voyage because a new sea route to the Indies, if found, would help Spain compete with Portugal. Ferdinand and Isabella ordered him to bring back any "Pearls, Precious Stones, Gold, Silver, Spiceries, and other Things and Merchandise of whatever kind, name or description that may be." Columbus promised to claim for Spain any lands that he explored. In return, Columbus would become **viceroy**, or royal governor, of the lands he found. Columbus also would receive one tenth of all gold sent back to Spain from any lands that he claimed and one eighth of the profits from trade.

★ Crossing the Ocean

On August 3, 1492, just before sunrise, Columbus's small fleet of three ships set sail on its journey. The *Niña* and the *Pinta* were caravels, each carrying about 20 crew members. Columbus sailed in the larger *Santa María*, a cargo ship that carried more than 30 crew members. The cramped ships carried a year's worth of supplies for the trip.

Columbus sailed first for the Canary Islands off the west coast of Africa. From there he caught a favorable wind that blew his ships west across the Atlantic Ocean. The tiny fleet made good progress. Soon, however, the ships passed the limits of Columbus's maps, sailing into an unknown ocean. The crew became increasingly nervous after a month passed with no sight of land. "Here the people could stand it no longer, and complained of the long voyage," wrote Columbus in his journal. According to one Spaniard of the time:

> " **The Admiral [Columbus] cheered them as best he could, holding out good hope of the benefits they would have. And he added that it was useless to complain since he had come to find the Indies, and so had to continue until he found them.** "

Queen Isabella

Queen Isabella I was born in 1451, the daughter of the ruler of the powerful kingdom of Castile (kas-TEEL.) At the age of 18, she married Ferdinand, the heir to the throne of Aragon, another powerful Spanish kingdom. Their marriage united the houses of Aragon and Castile. Isabella became queen of Castile in 1474.

During her reign, Isabella financed and helped direct Castile's military operations. She also supported the arts and supervised the kingdom's religious affairs. When Christopher Columbus came to the royal court, it was Isabella who became interested in his proposed voyage and whose support proved essential to his cause. When she died in 1504, Spain was on the brink of becoming one of the most powerful nations on Earth.

Just a few days later, the crew began to see signs, such as sticks floating in the water, that land was near. Columbus promised to give a reward "to him who first sang out that he saw land." On October 12, 1492, a lookout cried "Land! Land!" The journey from the Canary Islands had taken 33 days.

★ The First Explorations

Exactly where Columbus landed is a mystery. It could have been on any one of several islands in the Bahamas. Whichever island it was, Columbus called it San Salvador, which means "Holy Savior."

First Encounters

When Columbus landed on San Salvador, he thought that he was in the fabled Indies, somewhere near the coast of China or the islands of Japan. He did not realize that he had actually found a different continent.

In search of riches, Columbus explored other islands, including one he called Hispaniola. Expecting to find Chinese or Japanese princes, Columbus instead met the Taino (TEE-noh). He called these people Indians because he believed that he had landed in the Indies. Columbus described the Taino as "very well built, with very handsome bodies and very good faces." He also noted that the Taino were "so generous . . . that no one would believe it who has not seen it. They never refuse [to give] anything which they possess, if it be asked of them."

The Taino had a thriving culture on the islands, living in small farming communities. The great differences between Taino and European culture and the fact that neither side spoke the other's language led to misunderstandings. For example, some Europeans, including Columbus, saw the peaceful ways of the Taino as signs of weakness.

Looking for Gold

For the most part, Columbus had little curiosity about the Tainos' culture. He and his crew were more interested in discovering gold. "There may be many things that I don't know," he wrote in his journal, "but I do not wish to delay but to discover and go to many islands to find gold." On each island, Columbus sent out search parties to look for gold and ask the Taino if they knew of any wealthy rulers, gold mines, or great palaces. He had very little success collecting gold, but he and his crew saw many natural

A pair of golden compasses from the mid-1500s

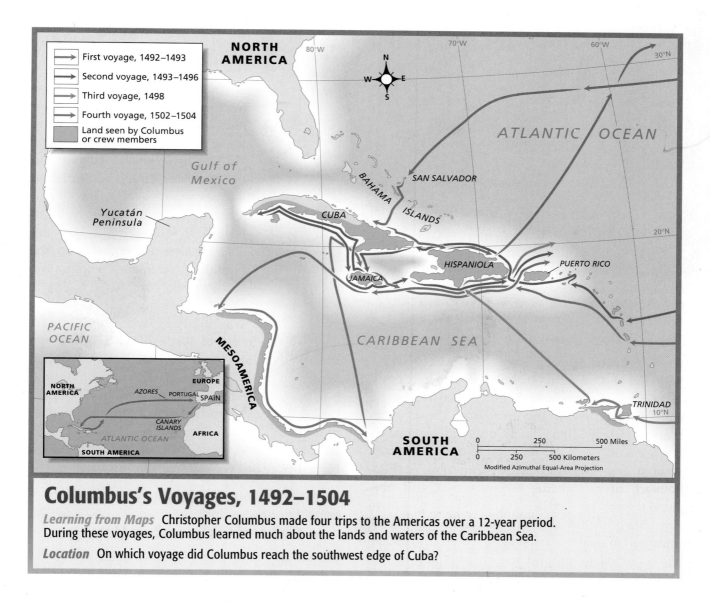

NORTH AMERICA

ATLANTIC OCEAN

Gulf of Mexico

Yucatán Peninsula

BAHAMA ISLANDS

SAN SALVADOR

CUBA

HISPANIOLA

PUERTO RICO

JAMAICA

PACIFIC OCEAN

CARIBBEAN SEA

MESOAMERICA

NORTH AMERICA

EUROPE

AZORES PORTUGAL SPAIN

CANARY ISLANDS

ATLANTIC OCEAN

AFRICA

SOUTH AMERICA

TRINIDAD

SOUTH AMERICA

0   250   500 Miles
0   250   500 Kilometers
Modified Azimuthal Equal-Area Projection

Columbus's Voyages, 1492–1504

Learning from Maps Christopher Columbus made four trips to the Americas over a 12-year period. During these voyages, Columbus learned much about the lands and waters of the Caribbean Sea.

Location On which voyage did Columbus reach the southwest edge of Cuba?

wonders, as Columbus described in a letter back to Spain:

> 66 **All [these islands] are beautiful, of a thousand shapes, and all are accessible [reachable] and filled with trees of a thousand kinds and tall, and they seem to touch the sky.** 99

After more than two months of exploring, Columbus decided that he had gathered enough gold and local treasures to return to Spain. Before they left the area, however, the *Santa María* struck a coral reef and slowly sank. There was not enough room to carry the ship's crew on the *Niña* and *Pinta*, so Columbus decided to build a small colony on the north coast of Hispaniola. He called

this colony *La Navidad*, the Spanish word for Christmas, because it was built with wood from the *Santa María*, which sank on Christmas Day. Columbus left about 20 of his men there and promised to return for them soon. He then transferred his command to the *Niña* and set sail for Spain in January 1493.

 ## Europe Learns of Columbus's Voyage

After a stormy return trip, Columbus finally reached Spain. He was certain that he had succeeded in reaching Asia on his journey, so he wrote a letter to King Ferdinand and Queen Isabella boasting of the wealth that lay across the ocean.

Columbus—accompanied by half a dozen Taino—meets Ferdinand and Isabella on his return to Spain in March 1493.

Spain's Reaction

Ferdinand and Isabella were very excited when they heard Columbus's news. They were even more pleased when he appeared before them with gold nuggets, exotic treasures from the tropical islands, and six Taino whom Columbus planned to teach Spanish and use as interpreters on a return voyage. Isabella believed that Columbus should **convert**, or change the religious beliefs of, the Taino interpreters so they also could serve as missionaries on future voyages. Although Columbus promised to treat the Taino as he would Christians, he continued to support the enslavement of the Taino people.

Ferdinand and Isabella issued a proclamation in which they granted Columbus the titles of admiral and governor, as they had promised to do if he found a sea route to the Indies:

> ❝ **We, considering the risk and danger to which you have exposed yourself for our service . . . [award you] the said offices of Admiral of the said Ocean Sea, . . . and of viceroy and governor of the said islands and mainland.** ❞

Columbus began preparing almost immediately for a second voyage across the Atlantic Ocean, this one with a much larger fleet. He hoped to find greater amounts of treasure. Columbus also expected that he would eventually find the fabulous kingdoms of Asia.

Territorial Conflict

News of Columbus's achievement spread outside of Spain. To secure Spain's right to lands unclaimed by other Europeans, Ferdinand persuaded Pope Alexander VI to make a bold ruling. The pope granted to Spain "all islands and mainlands . . . found one hundred leagues about [300 miles] west and south of the Azores"—a group of islands west of Europe. This created the **Line of Demarcation**, the boundary of Spain's exploration and monopoly rights.

The Portuguese king, John II, was unhappy with this arrangement. In the **Treaty of Tordesillas** (tawrd-uh-SEE-uhs), signed in June 1494, Spain and Portugal agreed to move the Line of Demarcation around 800 miles farther west of the Azores. This gave Portugal more opportunity to claim lands unexplored by other Europeans. It also placed Bartolomeu Dias's route around the Cape of Good Hope firmly under Portuguese control.

★ Columbus's Later Voyages

Columbus made three more voyages across the Atlantic, all of which proved difficult. When he returned to *La Navidad* on his second voyage, he found that the colony had been destroyed and all the sailors had been killed. Disappointed but not discouraged, he began creating new settlements on the islands.

On Columbus's third voyage he became the first European to see South America. Here, according to his journal, Columbus saw "freshness in the land . . . green and pleasant trees . . . sweet streams of water." Columbus also wrote in

A letter believed to have been written by Columbus and signed by him in code

The coat of arms granted to Columbus

his journal that he believed he had found paradise on Earth, "for all men say that [Paradise] is at the end of the Orient."

Although he was the royal governor of these new Spanish territories, Columbus was much happier exploring the sea and searching for gold than he was leading a colony. While Columbus was busy exploring, the conditions in the colonies declined in part because colonists were unable to grow European crops in the tropical climate. The starving Spaniards began moving to American Indian settlements. Columbus also fought many small battles with the Taino and enslaved the defeated Indians, despite Queen Isabella's instructions not to do so.

Ferdinand and Isabella were unhappy with Columbus's actions as governor. In 1500 they removed him from his post, much to his disappointment. Upon his return to Spain, Columbus begged the monarchs for permission to make one last voyage to the Americas. They consented and

he set sail in 1502, with his 13-year-old son, Hernando, serving as a cabin boy. This voyage ran into terrible weather off the coast of Central America and ended in shipwreck on the Caribbean island of Jamaica. There Columbus wrote in his journal that the sailors had "nothing to look forward to but death." The Spanish spent a year on Jamaica, before some Taino helped a Spaniard row a small boat to Cuba, from which a Spanish rescue party was dispatched. In 1504 Columbus returned to Spain a broken man.

Columbus lived for two more years in very poor health. His share of the royal income from the Caribbean had made him wealthy. However, he was too sick to participate in the royal court, where his oldest son, Diego, represented him. Columbus often complained to family and friends that those he had served had forgotten him. In 1506 "the Admiral of the Ocean Sea died unnoticed and unsung," according to one modern historian. It would be years before Europeans realized how dramatically Columbus had changed their world.

SECTION 2 REVIEW

Identify and explain the significance of the following:

- **Christopher Columbus**
- **Ferdinand and Isabella**
- *Reconquista*
- **viceroy**
- **convert**
- **Line of Demarcation**
- **Treaty of Tordesillas**

Locate and explain the importance of the following:

- **Canary Islands**
- **San Salvador**

Reading for Content Understanding

1 **Main Idea** Why did Christopher Columbus want to sail the Atlantic Ocean? Why did Spain agree to fund his voyage?

2 **Main Idea** How did Europeans respond to news of Columbus's first voyage?

3 **Cultural Diversity** Who were the Taino, and what were they like?

4 **Writing** *Informing* You are a royal official recording Columbus's first voyage to the Americas. Write a two-paragraph entry describing the voyage, where the crew landed, and what they found.

5 **Critical Thinking** *Supporting a Point of View* Do you think Columbus's voyages were a success or a failure? Explain your answer.

The Race for Trade Routes

Reading Focus

What areas of the world did Portugal explore, and what was the result of the Portuguese voyages?

Why did Europeans continue to explore across the Atlantic Ocean?

What did Ferdinand Magellan's voyage achieve?

Key Terms

strait
circumnavigate

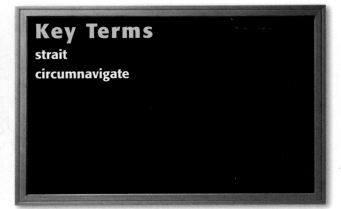

*C*HRISTOPHER COLUMBUS ALWAYS BELIEVED *that he had landed just off the coast of China. He knew, however, that many people did not believe his claims. "Because everything [the wealth of the Indies] did not appear immediately, I was held up to abuse," he wrote. King Manuel, who replaced King John II of Portugal in 1495, was one of those who did not trust Columbus's reports. The Treaty of Tordesillas encouraged Manuel to look eastward for a route to Asia, rather than westward as Columbus had done.*

A decorative bowl made in Asia in the 1200s

★ Portugal Takes the Lead

The race was still on to find a sea route to the Indies. King Manuel believed that the best route to Asia would follow Bartolomeu Dias's course around the southern tip of Africa. Manuel chose Vasco da Gama, a minor noble and skilled sailor, to command another expedition around the Cape of Good Hope.

Voyages to Asia

Da Gama spent two years preparing a large fleet for the task. He left Lisbon in July 1497 and arrived in southwestern India in May 1498. Two Muslim traders greeted da Gama as he sailed into the Indian port of Calicut. Surprised at seeing the Europeans, they cried out in Portuguese, "A lucky venture, a lucky venture! Plenty of rubies, plenty of emeralds! You owe great thanks to God, for having brought you to a country holding such riches!" One of da Gama's crew members wrote, "We never expected to hear our language spoken so far away from Portugal."

The Portuguese soon realized that they were dealing with a culture that had traded with Muslim and Italian merchants for centuries. When the king of Calicut became angry at da Gama for not bringing the traditional gifts, da Gama replied that his ships had come to Asia "merely to make discoveries." Da Gama later reported:

> 66 **The King then asked what it was he [da Gama] had come to discover: stones or men? If he came to discover men, as he said, why had he brought nothing?** 99

After his triumphant return to Portugal, da Gama made two trips back to India, where he governed a small Portuguese colony. Portugal had won the European race for a sea route to the wealth of Asia.

Vasco da Gama and his crew arrive on the southwest coast of India in 1498.

Brazil

The other great Portuguese exploration of the time came by accident. A terrible storm blew Pedro Alvares Cabral's fleet far off course while it was trying to follow da Gama's route to India. Instead of rounding the Cape of Good Hope, Cabral's ships drifted westward for weeks before finally reaching South America in 1500.

Cabral landed somewhere along the coast of present-day Brazil. He claimed the land for Portugal, not knowing at the time that he had landed on the coast of a continent rather than a large island. Cabral was not the first European to explore South America. Its eastern shore was on Portugal's side of the Line of Demarcation, however. This gave the Portuguese a legal claim to land in the Americas, much to Spain's regret. Portugal later founded forts, trading posts, and colonies on this land.

⭐ Other Early Explorations

The promise of wealth, knowledge, and adventure lured other Italian explorers besides Columbus to take to the seas. Like Columbus, they explored for foreign countries searching for a western water route to Asia.

John Cabot

Giovanni Caboto, or John Cabot—the English version of his name—was another talented Genoese sailor. Cabot was in Spain when Columbus returned from crossing the Atlantic in 1493. Cabot wanted to find his own sea route to Asia, and he knew just who to ask for support. King Henry VII of England, who earlier had refused to sponsor Columbus, was now concerned about falling behind in the European race to explore the globe. Cabot offered to pay for his own expedition if Henry would grant him a royal charter to any lands Cabot found. The king agreed, and Cabot made voyages of discovery in 1497 and 1498.

King Henry told Cabot "to seeke out, discover, and finde . . . countreyes, regions or provinces . . . whiche before this time have beene unknowen to all Christians." Cabot hoped to sail north of the lands that Columbus had explored and continue on to Asia. What Cabot found instead was the coast of North America. Cabot left very few records of his journey, but it is most likely that he traveled along the coast of present-day Newfoundland.

Cabot did not find the passage to the Indies that he had hoped for, but he gave England a claim to land in North America. Henry VII rewarded Cabot for his achievement and sent him on another voyage to find a way to Asia. Cabot and his fleet disappeared mysteriously on this expedition. Historian Polydore Vergil wrote at the time that Cabot "found his new lands only in the ocean's bottom, to which he and his ship are thought to have sunk."

Amerigo Vespucci

Italian explorer Amerigo Vespucci (vuh-SPOO-chee) was born in Florence, where he worked as a

Images of the Americas

In the 1500s few Europeans had the opportunity or courage to venture to the Americas. Many were curious, however, about this distant and wondrous land. For information about the Americas, Europeans listened to and read explorers' tales. Occasionally, images would accompany these stories and help stimulate people's imaginations. Maps were also a good source of information. Often illustrated, maps recorded where explorers went, what lands they sighted, and what people they encountered.

Made in 1558, the map shown here includes Brazil and West Africa, both areas that Portugal could claim according to the Treaty of Tordesillas. As well as including landmasses and names of places, the map shows people, animals, and the physical environment.

Understanding the Arts

1. What do you learn about Brazil and West Africa from the map?

2. Why do you think the artist used these particular images on the map?

A map of the southern Atlantic Ocean by Portuguese mapmaker Diego Homem, showing Portugal's possessions on both sides of the water

business agent for the powerful Medici family. When the Medici were expelled from Florence in 1494, Vespucci became an exile in Spain. In 1501 he sailed with a Spanish expedition that reached the coast of present-day South America. Vespucci was amazed by the animals he saw in South America, which were quite different from those in Europe:

❝ What should I tell of the multitude of wild animals, the abundance of pumas, of panthers, of wild cats not like those of Spain . . . ; of so many wolves, red deer, monkeys . . . and many large snakes? ❞

Vespucci and his crew also encountered American Indians, about whom he wrote many exaggerated stories that captured the imaginations of European readers.

The contents of some of Vespucci's letters were copied and published by Martin Waldseemüller, a

German mapmaker. Waldseemüller printed a book containing a large map in which he labeled the continents across the ocean "America" in honor of Vespucci's accomplishments. The book and map became popular throughout Europe, and as a result Europeans soon began using the names North America and South America.

Balboa Reaches the Pacific

As Europeans began to accept the idea that America was a pair of continents, it became clear that Columbus had not found a sea route to Asia as he had thought. Some Spanish explorers began to search for a water passage around or through the lands in the Americas that they were claiming for Spain.

One of these explorers was Vasco Núñez de Balboa (NOON-yays day bahl-BOH-uh). After failing as a farmer in a Spanish colony in the Caribbean, Balboa stowed away on a ship traveling to a new Spanish settlement in present-day Panama. Once in Panama, he took control of the colony away from its struggling governor. Balboa improved the living conditions of the colonists and made peace with local Indians. While negotiating with a powerful tribe, Balboa heard some fascinating news. Peter Martyr, a historian from the time, wrote that the son of an Indian leader stood up and told the Spaniards:

❝ I will shewe [show] you a region flowing with golde, where you may satisfie your ravening [hungry] appetites. . . . When you are passing over [the] mountains . . . you shall see another sea, where they sayle [sail] with shippes as bigge as yours. ❞

Balboa wanted to know if such stories were true, so he gathered almost 200 men and a large group of Indian guides to search for this ocean. Balboa's expedition traveled for weeks through thick jungle and across deadly swamps, fighting with Indians they encountered. In 1513, after an exhausting and dangerous journey, Balboa finally reached the top of a mountain near the coast. From there he saw a great blue sea stretching out as far as his eyes could see. "Behold the much-desired ocean!" he exclaimed to the members of his expedition. Balboa decided to name these waters the "Southern Ocean."

Although there was no way for ships to cross Panama to reach these waters, Balboa's report offered hope that Spain could join in the rich trade with Asia by finding a way into the "Southern Ocean." As he prepared a fleet to explore this ocean, however, Spanish authorities captured Balboa and had him executed for overthrowing the governor of Panama.

⭐ Sailing Around the World

News of Balboa's discovery captured the interest of other European explorers who were seeking a sea route west to the Indies. One of those interested in finding a way to the "Southern Ocean" was Ferdinand Magellan (muh-JEL-uhn), a Portuguese captain.

Balboa reached the west coast of Panama in 1513. He named the sea in front of him the Southern Ocean, but a few years later, another explorer renamed it the Pacific Ocean.

Magellan's Plan

Magellan had spent many years sailing and fighting in Africa and India. These experiences taught him about the seas of Southeast Asia and also shaped Magellan's personality. Antonio Pigafetta, an Italian merchant who sailed along with Magellan, later wrote that "among the other virtues which he possessed, he was always the most constant [reliable] in greatest adversity [danger]." A fellow captain described Magellan simply as being "tough, tough, tough."

Ferdinand Magellan left behind a wife and a six-month-old son when he left Spain in 1519—never to return.

When news reached Magellan about Balboa's "Southern Ocean," he became convinced that he could sail west to Asia as Columbus had planned. Magellan learned that other explorers had found an opening to a possible sea passage. He believed this passage went through South America and into the "Southern Ocean." Portugal already had Vasco da Gama's eastern route to India, but Spain was still looking for a westward passage. Magellan therefore went to Spain with his idea. At first, the Spanish were suspicious of this Portuguese sailor. Magellan's experience and confidence persuaded the royal advisers, however, and Spain agreed to provide him with five ships for the trip.

Voyage to America

Magellan set sail in September 1519. From the start, he had trouble. Several of the captains assigned to his voyage did not trust or respect him. Magellan also angered his officers by refusing to share the location of the possible sea passage. When asked, he shouted, "Follow me and don't ask questions!"

Magellan was stunned when he discovered that the passage was actually the mouth of a huge river—the present-day Río de la Plata, between Argentina and Uruguay. He traveled south, searching desperately for a channel through the continent. The weather grew colder, and supplies began to run low. In the midst of these difficulties, Magellan and his supporters had to put down a mutiny led by the Spanish officers, one of whom was Juan Sebastián de Elcano (el-KAHN-oh).

Then the fleet of ships found a **strait**—a narrow, winding sea passage—through the coastal cliffs. It took them more than a month to pass through the strait, battling fierce winds and avoiding jagged rocks. Finally, as Pigafetta wrote, "The men . . . reported that they had seen the cape and the open sea. The captain-general [Magellan] wept for joy." The passageway at the southern tip of South America became known as the Strait of Magellan.

An Incredible Journey

By this point, Magellan had lost two of his five ships. Magellan and the other remaining captains thought that they could reach Asia in a few weeks. Instead, the journey took more than 100 days, and the ships quickly ran out of supplies. Pigafetta described the terrible conditions:

66 **We were three months and twenty days without getting any kind of fresh food. We ate . . . powder of biscuit swarming with worms. We drank yellow water that had been putrid [spoiled] for many days. . . . Often we ate sawdust.** 99

The Voyage of Magellan and Elcano, 1519–1522

Learning from Maps After Ferdinand Magellan died, Juan Sebastián de Elcano became the fleet's leader.

Place What is the last ocean Magellan crossed?

The weather was so calm during the entire trip that the crew renamed the "Southern Ocean" the Pacific, or peaceful, Ocean.

Navigating by instinct and skill, Magellan crossed the world's largest ocean and reached the Indies. While searching for islands that Portugal had not claimed, Magellan landed in the present-day Philippines. Although he succeeded in converting a local ruler to Christianity, Magellan was later killed in a battle with another Philippine kingdom.

Magellan's crew decided to continue sailing west, hoping to reach Spain. Sailing through waters that were unknown to the Spaniards, the remains of Magellan's fleet had to avoid Portuguese seaports and pirate ships while trying to find their way

One of Magellan's crew sketched this scene of two crew members sailing a boat, off the present-day island of Guam, in March 1521.

home. Only one of the three remaining ships made it back. Captained by the one-time mutiny leader Juan Sebastián de Elcano, it returned to Spain with a cargo of cloves in September 1522. The sale of the cloves paid for the expense of the entire voyage, as well as producing a profit for the Crown, crew, and the original investors. This profit came at a terrible cost, however. Only 18 of the fleet's approximately 240 original crew members had survived the long journey.

These 18 surviving sailors were the first people to **circumnavigate**, or sail completely around, the world. Their 40,000-mile journey had taken them across three oceans, and they had found the all-water route to Asia that Columbus and others had searched for since 1492.

SECTION 3 REVIEW

Identify and explain the significance of the following:
- **Vasco da Gama**
- **Pedro Alvares Cabral**
- **John Cabot**
- **Amerigo Vespucci**
- **Vasco Núñez de Balboa**
- **Ferdinand Magellan**
- **strait**
- **circumnavigate**

Reading for Content Understanding

1. **Main Idea** What areas of the world did Vasco da Gama and Pedro Alvares Cabral explore, and what did these voyages accomplish for Portugal?

2. **Main Idea** Why did Spain continue to sponsor voyages of exploration?

3. **Geographic Diversity** *Location* Where is the passageway known as the Strait of Magellan?

4. **Writing** *Creating* Imagine that you are preparing to interview the survivors of Magellan's voyage. Write five questions that you will ask about the importance of their journey. Then write answers that you imagine the crew would give, using information found in the section.

5. **Critical Thinking** *Supporting a Point of View* Do you think America should have been named after Amerigo Vespucci? Explain your answer.

The Opening of the Atlantic

Reading Focus

How did new trade routes affect Europe?

What was the significance of the Columbian Exchange?

Why were some countries searching for a Northwest Passage?

Key Terms

Columbian Exchange

Northwest Passage

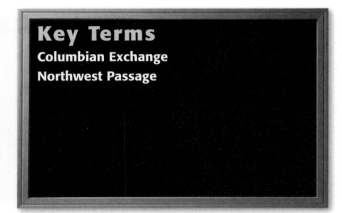

THE VOYAGES OF COLUMBUS, da Gama, Magellan, and others changed the Atlantic from an uncharted ocean to a gateway to Africa, India, and the Americas. Exploration shifted world trade patterns and had a great impact on the nations of western and northern Europe. As one Spaniard explained, "Formerly we were at the end of the world; now we are in the middle of it, with an unprecedented [never before experienced] change in our fortunes."

A saffron plant from India

 A Shift in Trade

The discovery of sea routes to Africa and Asia helped focus Europe's attention on the Atlantic Ocean as a pathway for trade. The return journey from India around the Cape of Good Hope and through the Atlantic Ocean to Portugal was faster than older routes and saved Portuguese traders the expense of dealing with middlemen. As a result, during the 1500s traditional trade routes became less important. Portugal and then Spain grew stronger while Venice declined, having lost its monopoly of European trade with Asia.

In the 1500s the Portuguese controlled as much as 75 percent of the spice trade between Europe and Asia, and made profits of nearly 90 percent on each round-trip trading voyage. Spain benefited from Magellan's discovery of a western route to Asia across the Atlantic and Pacific Oceans. Spain established an outpost in the Philippines as a base for its China trade. The influence of both Portugal and Spain in European affairs increased as a result of their explorations.

The explorations and the riches gained from trade drew the attention of other European nations—such as England, France, and the Netherlands—that had easy access to the Atlantic. Not wanting to be left behind as Europe began expanding its influence around the world, these countries turned their exploration efforts toward the Atlantic Ocean. Each hoped to find its own sea route to the wealth of India, China, and Japan.

Europeans also began to see the Atlantic Ocean as more than just a way to reach Africa and Asia. Explorers reported that the lands on the other side of the Atlantic were more than a few large islands. The Americas were continents that promised to be full of wealth. Columbus and Vespucci reported that the Americas were full of lush forests, clear streams, and many natural resources. In the 1500s some Europeans already were using some of these resources. For example, Spanish, Portuguese, English, and French fishermen began traveling across the northern Atlantic to catch cod off the coast of present-day Newfoundland.

The Columbian Exchange

In the process of exploration, plants, animals, and diseases were transferred between the "Old World" of Europe, Africa, and Asia and the "New World" of the Americas. This transfer, known as the **Columbian Exchange** because it was a result of Columbus's explorations, dramatically changed the world.

Plants and Animals

European explorers in the Americas found many species of plants and animals that were different from those back home. "All the trees were as different from ours as day from night," Columbus noted in his journal.

American plants proved particularly valuable to Europeans. Explorers saw American Indians

Inca pottery in the shape of corn, chiles, and other foods

growing rich harvests of corn and decided to bring the plant back to Europe to use as animal food. In addition, the American tomato became quite a popular ingredient in European cooking, particularly in the Mediterranean countries. In the late 1600s some Europeans began to cultivate the potato, a vegetable popular among

Lisbon, Portugal, benefited greatly from the expansion of trade that followed the explorations of Dias, da Gama, and Cabral.

South American Indians. Potatoes became a common food source, and European settlers later introduced them to North America. Europeans also saw Indians using tobacco and cocoa. These became luxury items when merchants introduced them to the European population.

European settlers and explorers also brought plants and animals from Europe, Africa, and Asia to the American continents. Horses, cattle, and pigs soon ran wild in the Americas. These animals supplied transportation and improved the diet of Native Americans. European farmers also brought grains such as wheat and barley, which thrived in cool climates, and rice and bananas, which grew in warmer parts of the Americas.

The Spread of Disease

Along with new plants and animals, the explorers also unintentionally brought diseases such as smallpox, measles, and typhus. These sicknesses were common in Europe. Most adult Europeans had survived one or more of these diseases and had developed immunity, or natural resistance, to them. The Indians, however, had never encountered these illnesses before and had no immunity to them. As a result, large numbers of American Indians became terribly sick. Chilam Balam, an

Verrazzano and Cartier

In 1524 France sent Italian captain Giovanni da Verrazzano (vayr-raht-SAHN-oh) on a voyage to find the Northwest Passage. Verrazzano traveled along the coast of North America from present-day Georgia to Maine but did not find a passageway to Asia.

Jacques Cartier (kahr-TYAY), a French sailor, was the leader of France's next major exploration of North America. In 1534 he sailed to Newfoundland, in present-day Canada. He returned in 1535 with a larger fleet, this time sailing into the St. Lawrence River and traveling all the way to present-day Montreal. Cartier's crew then spent the winter near present-day Quebec. On these journeys, Cartier encountered the Huron Indians, who called the area he was exploring Canada. Cartier also wrote about strange animals, including a bear "as big as a cow and white as a swan," and large seabirds that "bit even as [like] dogs."

Champlain

Nearly 70 years later, French sailor Samuel de Champlain began exploring North America. In the preface to his journal, Champlain wrote:

> 66 **Through [exploration] we gain knowledge [of] different countries, regions and kingdoms; through it we attract and bring into our countries all kinds of riches; through it . . . Christianity [is spread] in all parts of the earth.** 99

Champlain pursued his passion for exploration for many years. He followed Cartier's old paths and made repeated journeys along the St. Lawrence River. In 1615 Huron Indian guides led him to the Great Lakes. On these inland explorations, Champlain learned that Indian canoes were much better at river travel than European boats.

Champlain's voyages became the basis of French claims to much of Canada. He also

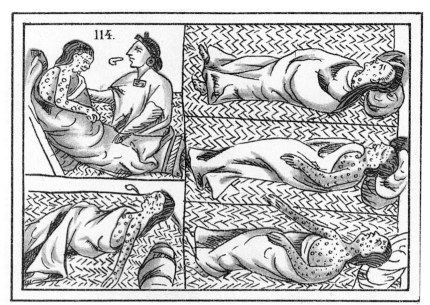

This illustration from a history of New Spain written in the 1500s shows the effects of smallpox on the Aztec of Mexico.

Indian from the Yucatán Peninsula, recalled the days before the Europeans arrived:

> 66 **There was then no sickness; they had then no high fever; they had then no smallpox; they had then no burning chest. . . . The foreigners made it otherwise when they arrived here.** 99

No one is certain how many Indians died from diseases brought to America by Europeans, but the loss of life was staggering. Spanish historian Fernández de Oviedo wrote in 1548 about the destruction of the Indians of Hispaniola. He reported that of the estimated 1 million Indians who had lived on the island in 1492, "there are not now believed to be at the present time . . . five hundred persons [left]."

⭐ Searching for a Northwest Passage

With Spain and Portugal busy exploring Central and South America, other European nations concentrated their searches in North America. There they hoped to find a **Northwest Passage**, a path around or through North America that would allow ships to sail from the Atlantic to the Pacific.

founded a small colony on the St. Lawrence River that he named Quebec. In the end, however, neither Cartier nor Champlain ever found a Northwest Passage.

Dutch and English Exploration

The Dutch entered the race to explore North America by hiring English captain Henry Hudson to search for a Northwest Passage. In 1609 Hudson sailed the ship *Half Moon* to present-day New York. There he traveled past the island of Manhattan and up the river that would later be named in his honor.

In 1610 Hudson returned to North America, this time sailing under the English flag. Traveling farther north than earlier explorers, he reached a strait that he hoped would lead to the Pacific Ocean. Instead, it led into a huge bay, later named Hudson Bay. There Hudson and his crew spent a hungry, freezing winter. "The cold was so extreme that it lamed [crippled] most of our company," wrote one of Hudson's crew. Hudson's desire to continue exploring in the spring led to a mutiny among the crew. The mutineers put Hudson and

This map from the 1540s shows French explorations and settlements in North America. The map was drawn upside-down, so Canada is at the bottom and Florida is in the upper-right corner.

those who would not join them into a small boat, which they set adrift. The mutineers remained in the area for a day or so, "in all which time we saw not the [boat]," said one crewman, "nor ever saw her after." Hudson never returned from his final voyage. Although he and others failed in their attempts to find a Northwest Passage, their explorations increased European interest in North America.

SECTION 4 REVIEW

Identify and explain the significance of the following:
- **Columbian Exchange**
- **Northwest Passage**
- **Giovanni da Verrazzano**
- **Jacques Cartier**
- **Samuel de Champlain**
- **Henry Hudson**

Reading for Content Understanding

1 **Main Idea** What were some of the positive and negative results of the Columbian Exchange?

2 **Main Idea** Which explorers attempted to find a Northwest Passage? What were the results of their explorations?

3 **Global Relations** What effect did the success of Portuguese trade have on other European nations and on the Italian city of Venice?

4 **Writing** *Creating* Write a two-paragraph ending to a story describing what Henry Hudson's fate may have been after being set adrift on his last voyage.

5 **Critical Thinking** *Determining the Strength of an Argument* Do you think that Samuel de Champlain's voyages to Canada gave France the right to claim the land as its possession? Explain your answer.

CHAPTER
2 REVIEW

Chapter Summary

The Commercial Revolution and the Renaissance brought changes to the way that Europeans lived and conducted business. In searching for direct trade routes to Asia, Europeans found what later became known as North and South America. In the process of these explorations, Europeans began an enormous exchange of goods across the Atlantic. Unfortunately, they also brought disastrous diseases to the Americas. ■

On a separate sheet of paper, complete the following activities.

Identifying People and Ideas

Describe the historical significance of the following:

1. joint-stock companies
2. astrolabe
3. Leonardo da Vinci
4. Ferdinand and Isabella
5. Henry Hudson
6. Treaty of Tordesillas
7. Pedro Alvares Cabral
8. strait
9. circumnavigate
10. Christopher Columbus

Internet Activity go.hrw.com
SA0 Columbus

You are planning a museum exhibit on Christopher Columbus's voyages to the Americas. Search the Internet through the HRW Web site to find information for your exhibit. This may include images, facts, or news about documentaries of the events. Use this information to create a plan for your exhibit that you might show to the board of directors of the museum.

Understanding Main Ideas

1. How did the Commercial Revolution bring wealth to many towns and cities?
2. Why was Portugal so interested in finding a sea route to Asia?
3. What did Christopher Columbus promise King Ferdinand and Queen Isabella in exchange for funding his voyage? What did the king and queen promise him?
4. How did Portugal come to claim the land later known as Brazil?
5. Why did John Cabot, Amerigo Vespucci, and Vasco Núñez de Balboa set out on explorations across the Atlantic Ocean?
6. Which native American plants were valued by Europeans?
7. Why were England, France, and the Netherlands interested in finding the Northwest Passage?

Using the Time Line

Number your paper from 1 to 5. Match the letters on the time line below with the following events.

1. **Vasco Núñez de Balboa becomes the first European to see the Pacific Ocean.**
2. **Johannes Gutenberg invents movable type for the printing press.**
3. **Thinking that they have landed in Asia, Christopher Columbus and his crew land in the Americas.**
4. **After sailing around the Cape of Good Hope and through the Indian Ocean, Vasco da Gama arrives in southwestern India.**
5. **The Black Death, an epidemic that killed about one third of Europe's population, ends.**

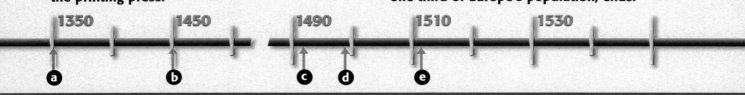

1350   1450   1490   1510   1530

a   b   c   d   e

Reviewing Themes

1. **Global Relations**   What were the positive and negative effects of the Columbian Exchange?
2. **Economic Development**   What effect did global trade have on the economic development of Spain, Portugal, and Venice?
3. **Geographic Diversity**   What difficulties did Europeans face in their explorations?

Thinking Critically

1. **Identifying Cause and Effect**   What were the cause and effects of the Black Death?
2. **Evaluating**   Select one explorer and evaluate his contributions by creating a report card that examines his leadership, fulfillment of expectations, treatment of American Indians, and other actions.

Writing About History

1. **Describing**   Imagine that you are an American Indian and are meeting a European for the first time. Write a speech to give to your tribal council about how you think Europeans will affect your community.
2. **Informing**   Write a paragraph that explains which trade goods were most prized by Europeans.

Linking Geography and History

1. **Movement**   Why did the Portuguese and the Spanish establish outposts around the world?
2. **Human-Environment Interaction**   What did Columbus and his crew do in order to survive on Hispaniola?

History Skills Workshop

Using Visual Resources   Look at this painting, which shows the first contact between Columbus's crew and Native Americans. Choose at least five elements in the painting and explain how they represent aspects of exploration or the interaction between Europeans and Native Americans.

Building Your Portfolio

Complete the following activities individually or in groups.

1. **Trade Today**   Do some research to compile a list of 10 goods that the United States buys from other countries and 10 goods that the United States sells to other nations. Then prepare a map of the world that shows trade patterns between the United States and other countries. Draw symbols on the map to show the goods that the United States buys and sells to foreign nations.

2. **European Renaissance**   Create a booklet of at least three pages on the Renaissance. The title of your booklet is "The European Renaissance" and the titles of your chapters are "Education and Ideas," "Science and Technology," and "Art." Use the library to find information for your booklet. Make sure that your booklet has images and descriptions of the time period.

The Columbian Exchange

On the morning of October 12, 1492, a lookout aboard the Pinta, one of Christopher Columbus's three ships, sighted land. The next day Columbus and his crew landed on an island in the Bahamas and began the European settlement of the Americas. Columbus's landing also started a long process known today as the Columbian Exchange. In this process, plants and animals from the Eastern Hemisphere—Europe, Africa, and Asia—have been exchanged with many species from the Western Hemisphere—the Americas. ■

New Plants and Animals

This Columbian Exchange began as explorers brought plants and animals from Europe, Africa, and Asia along on their voyages to the Americas. These same explorers often returned home with American plants and animals, which spread from Europe to both Africa and Asia.

Geographic Origins of Plants and Animals Involved in the Columbian Exchange

	WESTERN HEMISPHERE—AMERICAS	EASTERN HEMISPHERE—EUROPE, AFRICA, AND ASIA
FOOD CROPS	corn, potatoes, cassava, sweet potatoes, tomatoes, pumpkins, squash, beans (navy, lima, kidney, string), peppers (bell, chili), pineapples, peanuts, pecans, cashews, avocados, papayas, cocoa beans, vanilla beans, wild rice	wheat, oats, barley, Asian rice, sugarcane, soybeans, radishes, lettuce, onions, okra, chickpeas, olives, grapes, peaches, pears, oranges, lemons, coffee, watermelons, bananas
OTHER PLANTS	cotton, tobacco, marigolds	dandelions, crabgrass, bluegrass, roses, daisies
ANIMALS AND INSECTS	turkeys, hummingbirds, rattlesnakes, gray squirrels, guinea pigs, muskrats, potato beetles	cows, horses, goats, sheep, pigs, chickens, elephants, house cats, Mediterranean fruit flies, Japanese beetles, sparrows, mice, rats

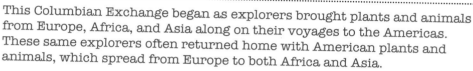

Geography Skills
Reading Tables

1. What was the only major grain crop that originated in the Western Hemisphere?

2. What animal that is now a popular pet in the United States originated in the Eastern Hemisphere?

Economic Results of the Columbian Exchange

U.S. income in 1994 from food crops originally native to Europe, Africa, and Asia

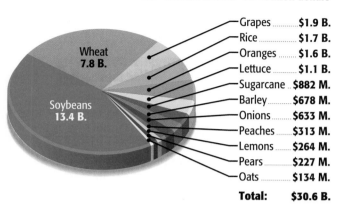

M. = million dollars   B. = billion dollars

Wheat 7.8 B.
Soybeans 13.4 B.

Grapes .... $1.9 B.
Rice .... $1.7 B.
Oranges .... $1.6 B.
Lettuce .... $1.1 B.
Sugarcane .. $882 M.
Barley .... $678 M.
Onions .... $633 M.
Peaches ...... $313 M.
Lemons ...... $264 M.
Pears .... $227 M.
Oats .... $134 M.

Total: $30.6 B.

U.S. income in 1994 from livestock originally native to Europe, Africa , and Asia

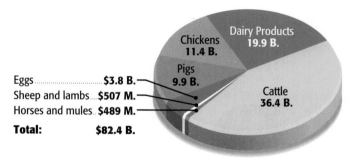

Dairy Products 19.9 B.
Chickens 11.4 B.
Pigs 9.9 B.
Cattle 36.4 B.

Eggs .... $3.8 B.
Sheep and lambs .... $507 M.
Horses and mules .. $489 M.
Total: $82.4 B.

Source: *Statistical Abstract of the United States*

History Note 1

The Columbian Exchange that began more than 500 years ago has had important consequences for the way we live, eat, and work today. Raising and producing plants and animals that were originally from Europe, Africa, and Asia is a huge industry in the United States. Many Americans earn their livings from the production, processing, or sale of these products.

Geography **Skills**
Reading Pie Graphs

1. According to the graph, which two products make up more than two thirds of the total food crop value?
2. What animal accounts for more than one third of the total value of animal products?
3. What is the value of the largest food crop? What is the value of the largest animal product? How many times greater is the value of the largest animal product than the food crop?

Origins of Food Crops

When Columbus returned to the Americas in 1493, he brought seeds and clippings from a number of plants, including wheat, chickpeas, melons, onions, radishes, grape vines, and sugarcane. By 1550, people were growing many of these foods throughout the Americas. European explorers also took home some plants raised by American Indians, such as corn, cassava (a root plant), potatoes, peanuts, and many types of beans.

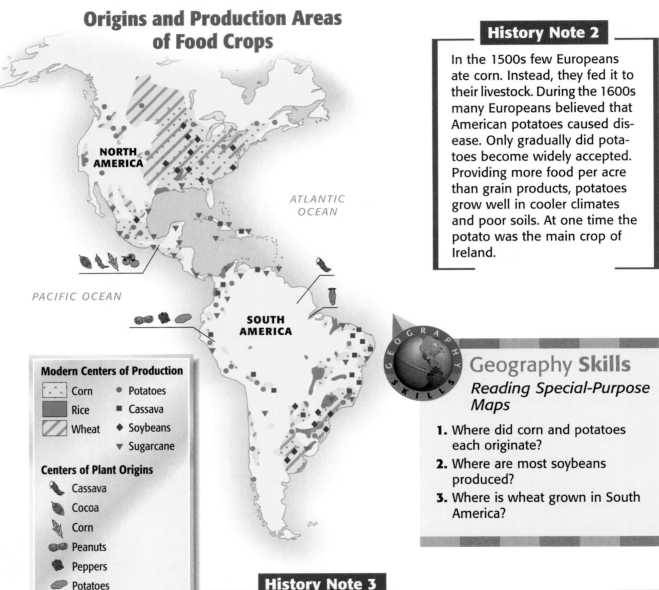

Origins and Production Areas of Food Crops

NORTH AMERICA

ATLANTIC OCEAN

PACIFIC OCEAN

SOUTH AMERICA

Modern Centers of Production

- Corn
- Potatoes
- Rice
- Cassava
- Wheat
- Soybeans
- Sugarcane

Centers of Plant Origins

- Cassava
- Cocoa
- Corn
- Peanuts
- Peppers
- Potatoes
- Sweet Potatoes
- Tomato
- Yams

History Note 2

In the 1500s few Europeans ate corn. Instead, they fed it to their livestock. During the 1600s many Europeans believed that American potatoes caused disease. Only gradually did potatoes become widely accepted. Providing more food per acre than grain products, potatoes grow well in cooler climates and poor soils. At one time the potato was the main crop of Ireland.

Geography **Skills**

Reading Special-Purpose Maps

1. Where did corn and potatoes each originate?
2. Where are most soybeans produced?
3. Where is wheat grown in South America?

History Note 3

Although Columbus brought cocoa beans to Spain in 1496, the recipe to make chocolate from the beans did not arrive in Europe for another 30 years. The Spanish kept the recipe secret for nearly a century until Princess Anna of Austria, who had grown up in Spain, revealed it to the French. The French became famous for their chocolate and shared it with the world.

Origins and Production Areas of Food Crops

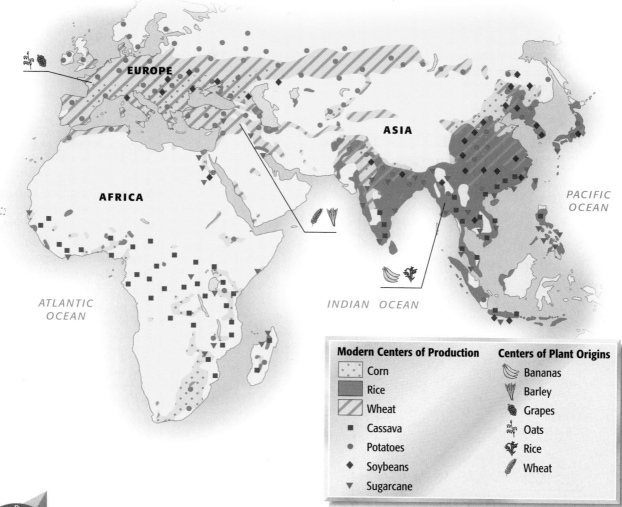

Modern Centers of Production

- Corn
- Rice
- Wheat
- ■ Cassava
- ● Potatoes
- ◆ Soybeans
- ▼ Sugarcane

Centers of Plant Origins

- Bananas
- Barley
- Grapes
- Oats
- Rice
- Wheat

Geography Skills

Reading Special-Purpose Maps

1. Where did rice and oats originate?
2. Which continent has the least amount of land dedicated to growing cereal grains?
3. Which continent has the most areas of potato production?

History Note 4

No spaghetti sauce, pizza, or lasagna? Italian food without tomatoes? Until the 1800s, Europeans thought that American tomatoes were poisonous. Today the tomato is essential to much popular southern Italian cooking, just as the American chili pepper, an ingredient in curry spice, is important to many dishes from India.

Origins of Animals

On his second voyage to the Americas in 1493, Columbus brought a variety of domesticated animals, including dogs, horses, pigs, cattle, chickens, sheep, and goats. Later colonists brought even more livestock, and animal populations boomed because many species had few natural enemies in the Americas. In return, North and South America offered Europe, Africa, and Asia fewer types of animals, such as the turkey and the llama, which were of lesser economic importance.

Origins of Various Animals and Livestock Production Areas

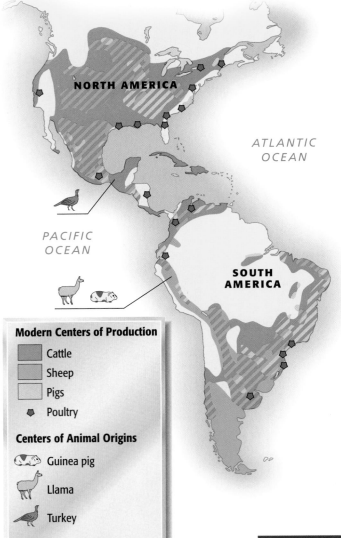

Modern Centers of Production
- Cattle
- Sheep
- Pigs
- Poultry

Centers of Animal Origins
- Guinea pig
- Llama
- Turkey

History Note 5

During the 1500s and 1600s, Spanish colonists raised horses throughout the Americas. Runaway horses multiplied and formed wild herds. Gradually, horse herds spread throughout the grasslands of central and northern South America and from the plains of Mexico all the way north to Canada. American Indians of the western Great Plains learned to train and ride these horses in the 1600s and made horses a part of their culture.

Geography Skills
Reading Special-Purpose Maps

1. Where did turkeys originate?
2. Which continent raises more sheep?
3. Which types of animals are most common to the east coast of South America?

History Note 6

Pigs had the easiest time adapting to the hot, wet climate of the Caribbean and present-day southeastern United States. It even became common practice for explorers to leave pigs behind on islands as food for future expeditions.

Origins of Various Animals and Livestock Production Areas

Modern Centers of Animal Production

- Cattle
- Sheep
- Pigs
- ◆ Poultry

Centers of Origins

- Cow
- Horse
- Chicken
- Pig
- Goat
- Sheep
- Goose

Geography Skills
Reading Special-Purpose Maps

1. Which animals originated in Europe?
2. Which animal originated in both Europe and Asia?
3. In what area are most pigs raised?

History Note 7

The Africanized, or "killer," bee is an example of how the Columbian Exchange continues today. In the 1950s research scientists brought African honeybees to Brazil. African bees accidentally escaped from Brazilian laboratories and mixed with American bees to produce the killer bee. These bees then began to spread north. Today swarms of killer bees live in both Texas and California.

History Skills

WORKSHOP

Reading Maps

Questions about both history and geography can often be answered by consulting maps. Maps communicate a wealth of historical and geographic information through colors, lines, symbols, and labels. To read and interpret maps, you must be able to understand their language and symbols.

Types of Maps Types of maps include *physical maps, political maps,* and *special-purpose maps.* Physical maps show the landforms that mark Earth's surface. Political maps illustrate political units such as states and nations. Special-purpose maps present specific information such as the routes of explorers, the outcome of an election, population density, or battles and troop movements.

Map Features A map's title tells you what the map is about. The legend, or key, explains any special symbols, colors, or shadings used on the map. Labels designate things such as political and geographic place-names as well as physical features like mountain ranges, oceans, and rivers.

Most maps in this textbook have a *compass rose,* or directional indicator. The compass rose indicates the four cardinal points: *N* for north, *S* for south, *E* for east, and *W* for west. Many maps in this textbook also include a scale, showing both miles and kilometers, to help you find the distance between any two points on the map.

The *absolute location* of any place on Earth is given in terms of latitude. Latitude is the number of degrees north or south of the equator, a line of 0° latitude running east and west around the center of Earth. Longitude is the number of degrees east or west of the prime meridian, a line of 0° longitude that runs north and south through western Europe and Africa.

How to Read a Map

1. **Determine the focus of the map** Read the map's title and labels to determine the map's focus—its subject and the geographic area it covers.
2. **Study the map and the legend** Read the legend and familiarize yourself with any special symbols, lines, colors, and shadings used on the map.
3. **Check directions and distances** Use the directional indicator and scale to determine direction, location, and distance.
4. **Check the grid lines** Refer to lines of longitude and latitude.
5. **Study the map** Study the map's basic features and details. If it is a special-purpose map, study the specific information given.

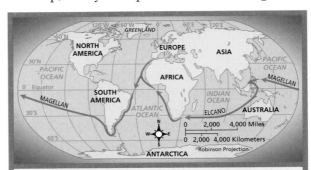

The Voyage of Magellan and Elcano, 1519–1522

Practicing the Skill

Study the map above. Then answer the following questions.

1. In what direction did the Magellan-Elcano expedition sail?
2. About how many total miles did the Magellan-Elcano expedition sail?
3. Is this map an example of a physical map, political map, or special-purpose map? Explain your answer.

History in Action

UNIT PORTFOLIO

American History

Living History Park

Complete the following activity in small cooperative groups.

Your task is to create living history exhibits for a Living History Park of Early Civilizations in the Americas. A living history park is an outdoor museum that re-creates life in another time as accurately as possible. Guides in a living history park take on the roles of people who lived in that time—dressing as people did then, using the tools from that time and place to plant crops or to make things, and speaking about the topics that concerned people of that time. As a designer of the park, you must create a visual model of life for one of the following culture groups or civilizations: Paleo-Indians, the Maya, the Inca, the Aztec, the Anasazi, or the Mogollon and Hohokam. Next, you will create a demonstration to inform park visitors of a special feature of that culture.

Materials To complete this activity, you will need a large piece of paper, a variety of drawing/painting materials, clay, unspun cotton or wool, and dull sculpting utensils.

Parts of the Project Do the following steps to complete your project:

1. **The Visual Model** Simulated environments could take the form of background murals, diagrams, or picture maps. The visual model should illustrate how people met their needs for food, clothing, shelter, and artistic or spiritual expression. Include in your visual model a detailed map of where your group lived. Give your display a catchy title.

2. **The Demonstration** The demonstration should either show how the culture met a basic survival need or focus on a particular achievement of the culture. For example, one group might demonstrate how an advanced form of glyph writing developed among the Maya and relate its importance to humankind.

3. **Introduction** Introduce your demonstration with a brief discussion of the culture, including the following elements: (1) a map showing the location of the culture and how geography affected its development, (2) how basic needs were met, (3) how the society was organized, (4) how the culture used art and religion to give meaning to life, and (5) lasting legacies of the culture.

Practice giving your demonstration when your group has finished its visual model. Set up your exhibit on presentation day, and give a demonstration to the visitors to your park. After each group has given its demonstration, create a chart of basic human needs—food, clothing, shelter, and artistic or spiritual expression—for each exhibit.

Students visit the Alamo in San Antonio, Texas.

UNIT 2
Colonies in the Americas
(1500–1760)

Young People
IN HISTORY
Young American Indians

Among the eastern woodlands of North America, teenagers from different Indian tribes shared similar responsibilities and experiences. Girls learned how to grow and harvest corn, squash, and beans, both in the private gardens near their homes and in the larger community fields. They also collected wild plants for food and medicine and took care of household chores, such as collecting firewood and making clothing. Boys learned how to hunt and fish. To reinforce these lessons, the Lenape of present-day New York required their teenage boys to stay alone in the woods for several days. These boys had to depend on their skills in woodcraft and hunting to find food and build shelter.

Life for young American Indians was not all about work, however. Many tribes in eastern North America played ball games similar to lacrosse and soccer. The Cherokee of the Southeast liked a game called *anetsa,* in which players used netted sticks to carry a ball and throw it toward a goal. This game was rough and physical. Only the most athletic young men played *anetsa,* and many suffered broken bones. Every village had a team, and the Cherokee believed that enormous honor and good fortune would come to the winner.

By their early teenage years, most American Indians were considered adults. Among the Powhatan, who lived around the Chesapeake Bay, boys took part in a special coming-of-age ritual. The ceremony required the most promising boys between the ages of about 10 and 15 to leave their homes and go into the woods for several months. There they were tested with hardships and fasting. Those who proved their strength and bravery were declared worthy as future leaders. Virginia colonist Robert Beverly explained that the intention of the ritual was educational, to encourage the boys' progress into adulthood. He observed, "They unlive their former lives, and commence [become] men, by forgetting that they ever had been boys."

In this unit you will learn about the Native Americans who lived in North America when Europeans first began to build their empires. These two groups increasingly came into conflict as European settlements grew.

Young American Indians like this boy, Ah-No-Je-Nange, often played sports similar to ones today, such as lacrosse.

LEFT PAGE: *In October 1764, British colonists met with American Indian leaders in what is now Ohio.*
The Granger Collection, New York

◼ CHAPTER 3 ◼
New Empires in the Americas

(1500–1700)

In the 1500s nations in western Europe sent people to explore and conquer the mainland of North and South America. These explorers encountered peoples and places that they had never before dreamed of seeing. "I cannot describe one hundredth part of all the things which could be mentioned . . . ," wrote one Spaniard, "for we who saw them with our own eyes could not grasp them with our own understanding."

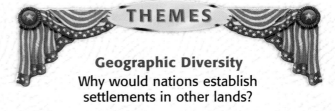

THEMES

Geographic Diversity
Why would nations establish settlements in other lands?

Citizenship and Democracy
In what ways might nations govern their colonies?

Cultural Diversity
Why might different groups' religious beliefs vary?

1500	1520	1540	1560	1580

1517 Martin Luther posts 95 theses criticizing the Catholic Church.

1521 Juan Ponce de León prepares a second expedition to Florida.

1542 Cabeza de Vaca publishes an account of his travels in North America.

1585 Sir Walter Raleigh sends an expedition to establish a colony on Roanoke Island.

The Conquistadores

Reading Focus

What events led to the fall of the Aztec and Inca Empires?

What happened to Spanish conquistadores in Florida?

Why did the Spanish explore the American Southwest?

Key Terms

conquistadores

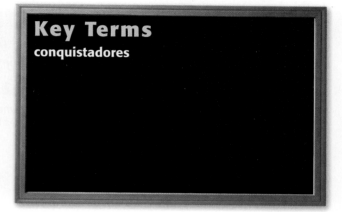

THE RECONQUISTA WAS A PERIOD *of constant warfare in Spain. From this struggle* emerged a Spanish warrior class experienced in fighting but without much land or money. There was little work for these soldiers in the newly united Spain. As military leader Hernán Cortés explained: "Since this harsh land will yield us no living, we must rely on our swords and lances. For the same reason, we must move on." In the 1500s many Spanish soldiers chose to "move on" to the Americas to seek their fortune.

Hernán Cortés

IMAGE ON LEFT PAGE: *Conquest of Tenochtitlán*

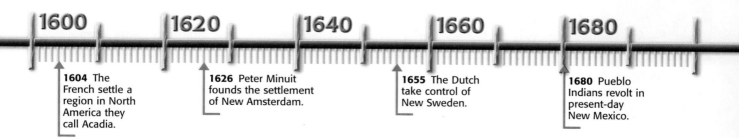

1600　　**1620**　　**1640**　　**1660**　　**1680**

1604 The French settle a region in North America they call Acadia.

1626 Peter Minuit founds the settlement of New Amsterdam.

1655 The Dutch take control of New Sweden.

1680 Pueblo Indians revolt in present-day New Mexico.

★ The Conquistadores

The **conquistadores** (kahn-kees-tuh-DAWR-eez) were Spanish soldiers and explorers who led military expeditions in the Americas. The Spanish began their conquest with Cuba, Puerto Rico, and Jamaica. The conquistadores soon turned to the American continents, however.

Cortés on the March

Hernán Cortés was a conquistador sent in 1519 to present-day Mexico by the governor of Cuba. Cortés's mission was to search for a lost Spanish expedition and possibly seek trade. After landing on the Mexican coast, however, he heard stories of a wealthy land to the west ruled by a king named Moctezuma (MAWK-tay-soo-mah) II. "I decided to go and see him [Moctezuma] wherever he might be . . . ," wrote Cortés. "I would take him alive in chains or make him subject to [the King of Spain]." To prevent his soldiers from turning back, Cortés sank their ships and then marched inland in search of Moctezuma and riches.

Moctezuma's kingdom was the Aztec Empire. The Aztec ruled several million people and had a rich civilization with great buildings, thriving agriculture, and fine arts and crafts. The Aztec had thousands of warriors, while Cortés had only about 500 soldiers, 16 horses, and some guns. Cortés hoped that his superior weapons would bring him victory. The Spaniards' horses provided another advantage because the Aztec had never before seen horses and found them frightening. "These 'horses' . . . make a loud noise when they run . . . as if stones were raining on the earth," Aztec messengers told Moctezuma.

In addition, Cortés received help from an Indian woman named Malintzin (mah-LINT-suhn), also known as Malinche, who served as a guide and interpreter.

This mural shows Aztec officials giving gifts to Hernán Cortés and his interpreter, Malintzin.

Moctezuma II

She advised him about the Aztec and their enemies, many of whom the Aztec had conquered. These enemies played a crucial role in aiding Cortés against the Aztec. Cortés also may have benefited from Aztec legends about Quetzalcoatl (ket-SAHL-kwaht-uhl). In some Aztec historians' accounts, Quetzalcoatl was a god who the Aztec believed would return to them from beyond the sea, and in other accounts he was a mythical king. Images of him showed a man with pale skin and dark hair. Aztec historians wrote that when Moctezuma first heard of Cortés, "It was as if he thought the new arrival was our prince Quetzalcoatl."

The Fall of Tenochtitlán

Not sure who—or what—Cortés was, Moctezuma sent him gifts of gold and other valuables, hoping to keep Cortés away from the Aztec capital, Tenochtitlán. However, these signs of great wealth only encouraged Cortés, who arrived in Tenochtitlán in November 1519. Conquistador Bernal Díaz recorded his first impressions of the city, which sat in the middle of a great lake:

> ❝**We were astounded. These great towns and temples and buildings rising from the water, all made of stone, seemed like an enchanted vision.**❞

Moctezuma was friendly to the Spanish, but the suspicious Cortés took him prisoner. With

Moctezuma under guard, Cortés was confident that he could conquer the Aztec. When the governor of Cuba learned of Cortés's unauthorized actions, he sent Pánfilo de Narváez (PAHM-fee-loh day nahr-BAH-ays) to Mexico with an army to capture Cortés. Cortés marched back to the eastern coast, where he defeated Narváez.

While Cortés was away, the Aztec rebelled and took back their city. The outnumbered Spanish fought their way out of Tenochtitlán with heavy losses. Moctezuma died during the fierce battle. Refusing to accept defeat, Cortés continued to fight for several months around the city. He then gathered thousands of Indian soldiers from other groups, built a small fleet armed with cannons, and attacked Tenochtitlán again. The brutal fighting for the city lasted three weeks. By the time it ended, Tenochtitlán lay in ruins. Cortés later wrote that he regretted destroying the city, "which was the loveliest thing in the world." An Aztec poet wrote, "Broken spears lie in the roads; we have torn our hair in our grief. The houses are roofless now, and their walls are red with blood."

Other Aztec communities also fell to Cortés. In addition to fighting Cortés and his Indian allies, the Aztec suffered from terrible diseases that were brought by the Spanish to Mexico. Illnesses such as smallpox caused hundreds of thousands of deaths in a very short time and quickened the fall of the Aztec Empire.

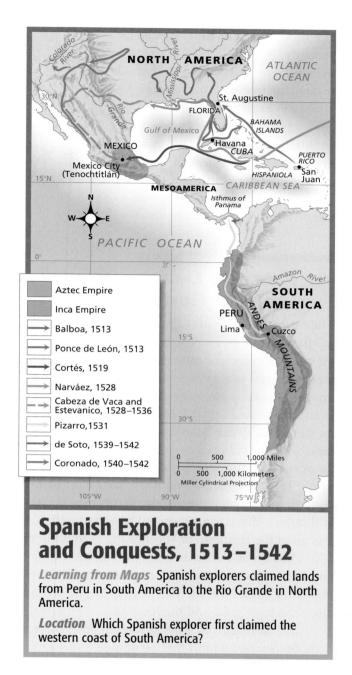

Spanish Exploration and Conquests, 1513–1542

Learning from Maps Spanish explorers claimed lands from Peru in South America to the Rio Grande in North America.

Location Which Spanish explorer first claimed the western coast of South America?

 Pizarro's Conquest of Peru

Cortés had conquered a territory larger than Spain. His achievement gained fame back home and inspired other conquistadores, including Francisco Pizarro (puh-ZAHR-oh), one of the Spanish officers who had arrested Núñez de Balboa. Pizarro heard rumors of golden cities in the Andes mountains of South America. In 1531 he landed with a small army on the coast of what is now Peru. After marching for several weeks, he reached the frontier of the Inca Empire.

The Inca ruled over a vast territory that stretched from what is now central Chile to Colombia. The Inca ruler, Atahuallpa (ah-tuh-WAHL-puh), heard about the Spanish but was unconcerned. Strangers with a force numbering less than 200 did not seem to be much of a threat. Like the Aztec, however, the Inca had no weapons that could match the conquistadores' swords and guns. The Inca had also been weakened by smallpox, which had killed almost 200,000 people, and by an ongoing civil war between Atahuallpa and his half-brother.

After reaching the Andes, Pizarro invited Atahuallpa to dinner and then kidnapped him, killing thousands of his escorts. Atahuallpa promised to fill a large room full of gold and silver as a ransom. After the Inca delivered 13,000 pounds of gold and 26,000 pounds of silver, Pizarro decided to kill Atahuallpa instead of freeing him. Joining with several powerful Inca leaders who had opposed Atahuallpa during the civil war, Pizarro and his forces conquered the Inca Empire by 1534. The second great empire of the Americas had fallen.

Ponce de León searched throughout Florida for gold and the mysterious Fountain of Youth.

Ponce de León Lands in Florida

The possibility of finding another wealthy empire lured many other conquistadores to the Americas. Juan Ponce de León (PAWN-say day lay-AWN) was a conquistador who explored the island of Puerto Rico in 1508–09 and later served as its governor. Peter Martyr, a historian from this time, wrote that Ponce de León heard stories about "a spring of running water of such marvellous virtue [value], that the water thereof being drunk . . . makes old men young again." To Ponce de León and others, this spring sounded like the European legend of the Fountain of Youth. King Ferdinand of Spain had given Ponce de León the right to explore and settle the mainland of North America. The conquistador decided that while exploring he would also search for gold and the fountain.

After sailing from Puerto Rico in 1513, Ponce de León reached a land that he named Florida. He met, and often battled with, many groups of American Indians during his travels along Florida's east and west coasts. None, however, knew of a Fountain of Youth or possessed the gold that Ponce de León had hoped to find. After failing to find any treasure, he gave up and sailed home.

Although Ponce de León no longer believed in the Fountain of Youth, he still wanted to found a settlement in Florida. In 1521 he prepared another expedition. Upon his arrival, Ponce de León and his conquistadores once again fought local Indians, and Ponce de León was wounded by an arrow. His crew sailed to Cuba, hoping to find someone to treat him, but he died from his injury.

The Travels of Cabeza de Vaca

Despite Ponce de León's failure, the Spanish remained interested in Florida. In 1527 Pánfilo de Narváez sailed from Spain with an expedition to explore Florida's west coast. When he arrived in 1528, Narváez decided to divide his forces. He sent the ships ahead and led about 300 soldiers north through the swamps. This decision proved disastrous. The ships lost contact with Narváez and eventually returned home.

Meanwhile, Narváez and his conquistadores faced illness, hostile Indians, and bad weather. By the time they realized that the ships had left, the Spanish were out of food. Desperate, they built simple boats and tried to sail west across the Gulf of Mexico. Most of the boats sank or wrecked along the shore, and only a few people survived. Among these were Álvar Núñez Cabeza de Vaca (kah-BAY-sah day BAH-kah), two other Spaniards, and a Moor named Estevanico (e-stay-bah-NEE-koh). In 1528 they landed on the coast of what is now Texas. Captured by local Indians, they managed to escape and began a journey across Texas to what is now New Mexico. Cabeza de Vaca recalled this time as "years during which I wandered lost and naked through many and very strange lands." He and his companions often came near death, but survived by their wits and luck.

For eight years Cabeza de Vaca lived with various Indian tribes while searching for a Spanish settlement. He worked as a servant, a trader, and a healer—once even saving a warrior's life by removing an arrowhead lodged deep in his chest. Cabeza de Vaca wrote that this act "gave us fame among [the Pueblo Indians]." This respect probably helped the conquistadores survive. So did Estevanico, who according to Cabeza de Vaca, "talked with them [Indians] constantly, found out about the ways we wanted to go . . . and the things we wished to know."

Finally, in 1536 Cabeza de Vaca met a group of Spanish soldiers "who were thunderstruck to see me so strangely dressed and in the company of Indians." Cabeza de Vaca traveled on to Mexico and from there returned to Spain in 1537. He published the story of his travels in 1542 as *The Narrative of Álvar Núñez Cabeza de Vaca.*

★ The Quest for Gold

While in Spain, Cabeza de Vaca described his adventures to Hernando de Soto, a conquistador who had fought with Pizarro in Peru. De Soto became convinced that Florida held a kingdom as rich as the Inca Empire.

Hernando de Soto

De Soto and about 600 other conquistadores set sail for Florida in 1539. After arriving, de Soto led the group north in search of gold. Once he reached what is now North Carolina, de Soto traveled west to present-day Arkansas, becoming the first European to cross the Mississippi River. An expedition member described the river as "[more than a mile] wide . . . of great depth and of very strong current."

De Soto traveled through many American Indian lands on his journeys, meeting thriving cultures with rich farms and large populations. Despite the opportunities for trade or settlement, de Soto kept moving. One conquistador wrote about de Soto:

❝His object [being] to find another treasure like that of [Atahuallpa], . . .

[he] would not be content with good lands nor pearls, even though many of them were worth their weight in gold.❞

On his journey, de Soto stole food from and fought with many Indian groups. The constant fighting wore down the conquistadores, as did their disappointment at not finding any gold. De Soto decided to return home in 1542, but he caught an illness on the way and died near the mouth of the Mississippi River. The other conquistadores rafted down the river and eventually reached Spanish settlements in Mexico in 1543.

The Seven Cities of Cíbola

Meanwhile, Cabeza de Vaca's fellow adventurer Estevanico returned to New Mexico as part of an expedition led by Friar Marcos de Niza. Their goal was to find the legendary Seven Cities of Cíbola, rumored to possess great wealth. Estevanico had gone ahead to greet Indians he had met on his past travels. Instead, however, he encountered and angered some Zuni Indians, who killed him. Learning of his fate, the rest of the expedition returned to Mexico, where de Niza told the viceroy that he had seen the Seven Cities of Cíbola and that they were full of gold and gems.

These reports lured the conquistador Francisco Vásquez de Coronado to New Mexico. Finding a Zuni town called Cíbola, Coronado captured it by force. Zuni legends later described the Spanish: "They wore coats of iron . . . and carried for

The stories told by Cabeza de Vaca inspired numerous other expeditions.

The Granger Collection, New York

The Granger Collection, New York

Estevanico was part of a group searching for the Seven Cities of Cíbola.

weapons short canes that spit fire and made thunder." Instead of the gold he wanted, Coronado found adobe buildings and many bushels of corn.

Coronado sent an angry message to the governor of Mexico, saying that "[Marcos] has not told the truth in a single thing that he has said." Despite this great setback, Coronado sent out scouting parties in search of the Seven Cities. One group of the explorers reached the Grand Canyon, while Coronado traveled northeast, encountering, in addition to the Zuni, other Pueblo Indians such as the Hopi. Coronado's demands for food and clothing angered many Pueblo, who fought to drive him away.

After battling the Pueblo Indians for weeks, Coronado traveled all the way to present-day Kansas. There he discovered that his Indian guide had purposely "[taken] us to a place where we and our horses would starve to death." Coronado and his conquistadores managed to survive, returning home in 1542 without any treasure.

Juan Rodríguez Cabrillo

That same year, Portuguese explorer Juan Rodríguez Cabrillo (kah-BREE-yoh) sailed 1,200 miles up the coast of what is now California, hoping to find gold or a new sea route to China. Crew member Bartolomé Ferrer described the northern coast: "There are mountains which seem to reach the heavens. . . . It appears as though they would fall on the ships." On the journey, Cabrillo heard stories from Indians that "in the interior, men like us [other Spanish explorers] were traveling about, bearded, clothed, and armed."

Cabrillo never returned from his voyage, dying of sickness during the winter in 1543. He had failed to find wealth, but his journey provided useful information for mapmakers. In addition, it established a Spanish claim to the Pacific coast of North America.

SECTION 1 REVIEW

Identify and explain the significance of the following:

- conquistadores
- Hernán Cortés
- Moctezuma II
- Malintzin
- Francisco Pizarro
- Juan Ponce de León
- Pánfilo de Narváez
- Álvar Núñez Cabeza de Vaca
- Hernando de Soto
- Juan Rodríguez Cabrillo

Locate and explain the importance of the following:

- the Andes
- Mississippi River

Reading for Content Understanding

1 **Main Idea** What role did Hernán Cortés play in the fall of Tenochtitlán and the rest of the Aztec Empire?

2 **Main Idea** What happened to the expeditions to Florida led by Juan Ponce de León, Pánfilo de Narváez, and Hernando de Soto?

3 **Geographic Diversity** *Place* Why did Friar Marcos de Niza and Francisco Vásquez de Coronado want to find the Seven Cities of Cíbola?

4 **Writing** *Informing* Write a two-paragraph essay about the fall of the Inca Empire in the 1530s.

5 **Critical Thinking** *Identifying Cause and Effect* What effect do you think Spanish explorations of the Americas had on mapmakers?

Spanish America

Reading Focus

How did Spain organize and govern its empire in the Americas?

Why did the Spanish settle in the borderlands?

How was the economy and society of New Spain structured?

Key Terms

Council of the Indies

pueblos

missions

presidios

encomienda system

plantations

borderlands

El Camino Real

B Y THE MID-1500S, *conquistadores such as Cortés and Pizarro had conquered for Spain a territory in the Americas larger than that held by any other European nation. However, as Francisco López de Gómara wrote at the time, "Without settlement there is no good conquest." The challenge for Spain changed from conquering new lands to settling and controlling an empire many times its size from across the ocean.*

A statue of the Virgin Mary brought from Spain to America in the 1600s

⭐ The Spanish Empire

Spain's monarchy ruled this vast American empire through a system of royal officials. At the top was the **Council of the Indies**, established in 1524. Based in Spain, the Council of the Indies oversaw government in Spanish America. It was responsible for writing laws, appointing officials and reviewing their conduct, and judging legal cases.

Beneath the council were two viceroys, or royal governors. One of them held the viceroyalty of Peru, the other the viceroyalty of New Spain.

The viceroyalty of Peru stretched from what is now Chile to Colombia in South America. The viceroyalty of New Spain extended from Mexico to California to Florida in North America. It also included several Caribbean islands and the Philippine Islands in the Pacific Ocean.

Each viceroyalty consisted of several territories run by officials selected by the viceroy. These local officials often acted without any actual supervision because of the viceroyalties' enormous size. Similarly, the great distance between Spain and the Americas often allowed the viceroys to disregard

The Spanish built many missions across the Southwest. This one, San Jose Mission, is in present-day Texas.

royal laws without punishment. As one concerned Spaniard wrote:

> 66 **Our people, transported across an ocean . . . leave [Spain] meeker than lambs, [but] change as soon as they arrive there [America] into wild wolves, forgetting all the royal commands.** 99

Some of the most densely settled Spanish territories were in the former Aztec and Inca Empires, located in Mexico and the Andes. These areas possessed great mineral wealth, which was mined and then shipped to Spain each year. From 1503 to 1660, Spain received 200 tons of gold and 18,600 tons of silver from its American colonies. In addition, central Mexico and Peru produced large quantites of crops to help support Spain's growing empire. By contrast, few Spaniards settled in northern New Spain or in Peru's rain forests because these areas had less mineral wealth and harsher climates.

Spanish coin

★ Governing New Spain

The Spanish organized a system to govern the spread-out territories of New Spain. They established three types of settlements to handle economic, religious, and military concerns.

Spanish Settlements

The first type of settlements were **pueblos**, or towns. In what is now the southwestern United States, many Indian villages became the sites of Spanish towns. A pueblo usually had a central plaza surrounded by homes, a church, and perhaps some businesses. Farms lay outside the town. Pueblos served as trading posts and sometimes as centers of local government.

Missions were settlements established by priests to convert local Indians to Catholicism. Priests and Indians would build a mission compound around a central church, with farmlands and homes typically lying on the outskirts. Missions in frontier areas often had fortifications. **Presidios**, or military bases, were another type of settlement. Most presidios were in remote frontier areas, particularly in Florida and Texas. The Spanish also built presidios to protect existing towns and missions.

There were several large Spanish cities in the Americas. For example, in the early 1600s the mining center at Potosí in what is now Bolivia had a population of around 100,000. Some cities quickly developed features similar to those of urban Spain. By the 1550s Mexico City had a university, a printing press, fine mansions, and wide streets laid out in European fashion. Spain had established a solid foothold in the Americas.

The Church and the State

The Catholic Church played an important role in the settlement of the Americas. When the first conquistadores explored new lands, they usually brought priests with them. In 1573 King Philip II issued the Royal Orders for New Discoveries. This document stated that "preaching the holy gospel . . . is the principal purpose for which we order new . . . settlements to be made." In many of the frontier areas, dedicated priests established the first Spanish settlements.

The Royal Orders commanded priests to offer religious instruction and to teach American Indians "the use of . . . bread, silk, linen, horses, cattle, tools, and weapons, and all the rest that Spain has had." Some Indians accepted this new way of life, often combining European customs with their own cultural practices. Other Indians rejected European ideas completely.

★ The Economy of New Spain

Many settlers in New Spain depended on the labor of American Indians. Luis de Velasco, a viceroy, complained that "no one comes to the Indies to plow and sow, but only to eat and loaf."

Spanish America, c. 1650

Learning from Maps The Spanish built many towns and settlements and established missions to convert American Indians to Christianity.

Place What was the capital of the viceroyalty of Peru?

The *Encomienda* System

To reward settlers for their service to the Crown, Spain established the **encomienda** (en-koh-mee-EN-duh) **system**. This system gave Spanish settlers known as *encomenderos* (en-koh-muhn-DE-rohs) the right to tax local Indians or to demand labor from them. In exchange, these settlers were supposed to convert the local Indians to Christianity, protect them from attack, and teach them various skills.

Settlers were not supposed to enslave Indians under the *encomienda* system. In practice, however, the Spanish in many areas forced Indians to grow crops, mine for precious metals, and watch over herds of cattle. The working conditions were often very harsh, and many Indians died of disease and exhaustion.

A few Spaniards spoke out against this mistreatment. Bartolomé de Las Casas was an *encomendero* who later became a Catholic priest and protested the *encomienda* system. In his written works, Las Casas defended Indians' rights:

> **The natural laws and rules and rights of men are common to all nations . . . whatever their sect [religious faith], law, state, color, and condition, without any difference.**

Las Casas wrote several books and many letters to Spanish officials demanding an end to the *encomienda* system. While he did not achieve this goal, he did trigger some reforms. Las Casas's efforts helped persuade Spain to limit the *encomienda* system and to free Indians from the system after one generation. However, many settlers violated this law and continued to force Indians to work for them.

Plantations like this one on the island of Grenada became quite common throughout the Caribbean.

Slave Labor

In areas such as Florida and the Caribbean, the Spanish found that Indian resistance and high death rates from disease made the *encomienda* system less successful. As a result, the Spanish began in 1517 to bring enslaved Africans to work in New Spain. Eventually, thousands of enslaved Africans worked on **plantations**, large farms that usually specialized in growing one kind of crop, such as sugar. Sugar plantations were particularly common on the Caribbean islands.

Bartolomé de Las Casas tried to get the Spanish government to treat Indians more fairly.

At first, even Las Casas was in favor of using enslaved Africans rather than Indians for labor. However, after watching the slave trade grow and witnessing the harsh conditions under which enslaved Africans lived, he changed his mind. Las Casas wrote in his *History of the Indies* that Africans were "unjustly and tyrannically [ruthlessly] reduced to slavery." Despite his objections, the African slave trade continued.

★ Expanding into the Borderlands

During the Spanish Empire's first 100 years, most settlers in New Spain went where they could gain the greatest wealth. Few Europeans lived in the region that historians call the **borderlands**, which included northern Mexico, Florida, and parts of present-day Arizona, California, New Mexico, and Texas. Spain's expansion into the borderlands took place over several centuries.

Florida and Georgia

The Spanish had long dreamed of finding riches in Florida. However, after the deaths of several explorers, the Spanish government questioned whether colonizing Florida was worth the risk. Then officials in New Spain discovered that the French had settled on Florida's east coast. Spain's King Philip II sent Pedro Menéndez de Avilés (may-NAYN-days day ah-BEE-lays) to "cast them out by the best means . . . possible." In 1565 Menéndez destroyed a French town and established the fort of St. Augustine in eastern Florida. From this base, the Spanish hoped to protect the fleets that carried treasures from the Americas back to Spain.

Further Spanish settlement in Florida occurred very slowly because of sickness, hostile Indians, and pirate attacks. The colony gradually expanded as priests established missions in eastern Florida and what is now Georgia.

The Southwest

The first serious Spanish settlement in New Mexico began in 1598, when Juan de Oñate (ohn-YAH-tay) set out from Mexico City to explore and to start a colony. After fighting the Acoma and other Pueblo Indians, Oñate helped found the town of Santa Fe around 1609–10. Santa Fe soon became the most important Spanish settlement in New Mexico and one of the most important in the borderlands. Priests also founded missions in New Mexico and neighboring Texas to help spread Catholicism to Indians. In New Mexico these missions and other Spanish settlements depended on the Pueblo Indians to provide them with food and labor. Beginning in 1660, Pueblo Indians also experienced crop failures and raiding by other Indian tribes.

The abuses by the Spanish eventually pushed the Pueblo to revolt in 1680. Led by Popé (poh-PAY), the various Pueblo tribes united and drove the Spanish out of New Mexico. According to Pueblo Indian Pedro Naranjo, Popé told the rebels "to plunge into the rivers and wash themselves" of all Spanish influence. However, Popé could not keep the Pueblo communities united, and in 1692 the Spanish reconquered New Mexico.

Many survivors of the Pueblo revolt fled to El Paso, site of the first mission in what is now Texas. Founded in 1659, the mission was the main Spanish settlement in Texas until the 1700s, when Spanish officials began hearing reports of French forts in Louisiana. In a letter from Texas, Francisco Hidalgo warned the viceroy of New Spain that "[the French] are slipping behind our backs in silence, but God sees their intentions." The Spanish responded to the French threat by establishing more missions and forts. Father Eusebio Kino (ow-SAYB-yoh KEE-noh) helped establish many missions in present-day Arizona.

Spanish settlers also built **El Camino Real**, or "the King's Road," to connect communities in New Spain. Different road networks ran for many hundreds of miles from Mexico City up to Santa Fe, New Mexico, and later stretched to new Spanish settlements in California.

California

California was one of the last borderland areas settled by the Spanish. In 1769 missionary Junípero Serra (hoo-NEE-pay-roh SER-rah) traveled to California. Serra helped persuade the viceroy of New Spain to support further expansion into the region. Serra led his friars and local Indians in building San Francisco and eight other missions along the Pacific coast before his death in 1784.

Finding settlers willing to start new homes on the frontier was often difficult, particularly when

The skilled artisans among the Pueblo Indians made beautifully decorated blankets and pottery.

American Literature

"World, in Hounding Me"
Sor Juana Inés de la Cruz

Juana Inés de Asbaje defied women's traditional role in New Spain by pursuing an education and literary interests. Born in 1651, she showed a lively intelligence, quickly learning to read and write. At age 16 she joined the viceroy's court, where she impressed everyone with her intelligence and charm. After spending two years at court, she decided to enter a convent.

Sor Juana Inés
de la Cruz

She took the name Sor Juana Inés de la Cruz and spent much of the next 25 years writing and studying—collecting a large library and many scientific instruments in the process. Some of her religious superiors criticized her activities, particularly a letter she wrote to a Catholic bishop on women's right to education, independence, and careers. In the last years of her life, she gave away her books and concentrated on religious devotions. She died in 1695 after catching a disease from sick nuns whom she had been treating. In the following poem she defends her decisions in life.

World, in hounding me, what do you gain?
How can it harm you if I choose, astutely*,
rather to stock my mind with things of beauty,
than waste its stock on every beauty's claim?
    Costliness and wealth bring me no
      pleasure;
the only happiness I care to find
derives from setting treasure in my mind,
and not from mind that's set on winning
      treasure.
    I prize no comeliness*.
All fair things pay to time, the victor, their
      appointed fee and
treasure cheats even the practiced eye.
    Mine is the better and the truer way:
to leave the vanities of life aside,
not throw my life away on vanity.

Understanding Literature

1. How does Sor Juana Inés de la Cruz use double meanings in her poem for words such as *stock*?

2. What choices has the poet made in life?

3. In what ways is the history of the 1600s reflected in the poem?

---

*wisely   *beauty

---

there seemed to be better opportunities in Mexico and Peru. As a result, there were fewer than one thousand Spanish settlers in California by 1790.

 ## Colonial Class Structure

By 1650 the vast Spanish Empire in the Americas had between 3 and 4 million inhabitants. About 80 percent of the population were American Indians.

The rest were whites, Africans, and people of mixed racial background.

Spanish law divided this diverse population into social categories based on birthplace and race. The *peninsulares* (pah-neen-soo-LAHR-es), white Spaniards born in Spain, held the most important political offices in Spanish America. Just below the *peninsulares* in status were the *criollos* (kree-OHL-yohs), Spanish people born in the Americas. Next came the *mestizos* (me-STEE-zohs), who were born to Spanish and Indian parents. Mestizos were the largest group of European descent in Spanish America. They often worked as laborers or craftspeople for *criollos*. American Indians had their own rights and restrictions. Enslaved Africans, who made up yet another category, endured terrible living and working conditions and had little or no legal protection.

Few *peninsulares* lived in the borderlands, leaving talented people of other groups to reach a higher status. This was particularly true among soldiers on the frontier. "What does it matter to the [king] whether the one who serves him well be white or black?" asked one official.

Women in each social class usually had fewer opportunities than men, even though they helped start settlements and shared the difficult work of frontier living. Unlike in many European countries, married women in Spanish America could own private property and pass it on to their children. Widow Juana Luján (loo-HAHN), for example, owned a large house, farmlands, livestock, and a

Spanish colonists in America, like these residents of St. Augustine, tried to maintain Spanish customs in their new home.

walled orchard in New Mexico. The high death rates for men often left female relatives and widows such as Luján with added responsibilities.

Most men and women in Spanish America received little or no formal education. However, children of the upper classes received some education. Once they were old enough, children generally had to share in the work. Most people in the borderlands learned what they needed to know by struggling through the hardships of frontier life.

SECTION 2 REVIEW

Identify and explain the significance of the following:
- **Council of the Indies**
- **pueblos**
- **missions**
- **presidios**
- ***encomienda* system**
- **Bartolomé de Las Casas**
- **plantations**
- **borderlands**
- **Juan de Oñate**
- **El Camino Real**

Locate and explain the importance of the following:
- **St. Augustine**
- **Santa Fe**

Reading for Content Understanding

1 **Main Idea** How did the organization of Spanish America help viceroys rule?

2 **Main Idea** Why did Spain establish three types of settlements in the Americas?

3 **Geographic Diversity** *Location* What present-day states make up the region that historians call the borderlands?

4 **Writing** *Classifying* Write a paragraph explaining the *encomienda* system and the Spanish colonial class structure. Create a diagram to show how these systems were organized.

5 **Critical Thinking** *Synthesizing Information* What were the pros and cons for Spain of having such a large empire in the Americas?

Religious and Political Changes in Europe

Reading Focus

What was the Protestant Reformation, and how did it change Europe?

Why did Spain and England go to war in the late 1500s?

What led to the end of Spain's "Golden Age"?

Key Terms

Protestant Reformation
Protestants
sea dogs
Spanish Armada
inflation

ON OCTOBER 31, 1517, *a priest named Martin Luther nailed a paper to the door of Castle Church in Wittenberg, Germany. The paper contained 95 theses criticizing some common practices of the Catholic Church. He also attacked what he saw as the corruption of the church. He charged that the church was too wealthy and abused its great power. When Charles V, emperor of the Holy Roman Empire, asked Luther to give up his views, he replied, "I cannot and will not recant [take back] anything. . . . On this I take my stand. I can do no other."*

Martin Luther

 ## The Protestant Reformation

Luther and others started the **Protestant Reformation**, a religious movement that began as an effort to reform the Catholic Church. These reformers became known as **Protestants** because they protested the Catholic Church's practices. Many Protestants believed that the Bible described a simple religion, unlike that of the Catholic Church. Protestants also objected to the great power possessed by the pope. The Protestant

Reformation began in German towns in the 1520s, and soon spread to the Netherlands, Switzerland, England, France, and other parts of Europe.

The printing press played an important role in spreading and expressing the ideas of the Protestant Reformation. Protestants printed short essays explaining their ideas. Printing presses also produced large numbers of Bibles, allowing more people to read and interpret the Scriptures for themselves, rather than relying on the interpretation of a priest.

Many Catholics believed that Protestants were breaking church laws and defying the authority of the pope without good reason. In turn, Protestants believed that the Catholic Church could not tell them how to worship God. Throughout Europe fighting broke out between Catholics and Protestants, often leading to civil war. Political issues also became mixed up with these religious struggles. During the late 1500s there were constant wars in France between Catholics and the French Protestants, known as Huguenots (HYOO-guh-nahts). Other parts of Europe also experienced widespread violence and destruction. One German writer, angry about royal threats against Protestants, wrote that

" **the emperor may be the most powerful man on earth, but everyone knows there is a majesty in heaven [God] that excels [is greater than] all human and earthly majesty.** "

In England, King Henry VIII founded the Church of England, or the Anglican Church, a Protestant religion that observed many Catholic ceremonies, such as mass. By becoming the head of the Anglican Church in 1534, Henry defied the authority of the pope and angered many Catholics.

★ Conflict Between Spain and England

In the late 1500s King Philip II used Spain's wealth to lead the fight against the Protestant Reformation. Historians call this effort the Catholic Reformation, or the Counter Reformation, which also focused on reforming the Catholic Church.

Queen Elizabeth I

As a devout Catholic, King Philip wanted to drive the Protestants out of England just as Ferdinand

Global Connections

Civil War in the Netherlands

In the mid-1500s a civil war started in the Netherlands between Protestants and Catholics. At the time Spain, a Catholic nation, ruled the Netherlands. When some of the Dutch people became Calvinists—followers of Protestant leader and writer John Calvin—Spanish king Philip II responded by removing the Dutch nobility and putting Catholics in power. The new ruler, Ferdinand Álvarez de Toledo, passed strict new laws and raised taxes.

The Protestants launched a rebellion. Their leader, William of Orange, explained the Protestants' reasons for rebelling:

" *I cannot approve of princes attempting to rule the consciences of their subjects and wanting to rob them of the liberty of belief.* "

However, Philip also remained determined. In response he declared the Dutch to be rebels:

" *To negotiate with these people is so pernicious [harmful] to God's service . . . that I have preferred to expose myself to the hazards of war.* "

The civil war finally ended in 1609 with a Dutch victory, but at the cost of many thousands of lives.

Understanding What You Read

1. How did Philip II try to maintain control of the Netherlands?

2. What do you think is the significance of William of Orange's statement?

Elizabeth I

Elizabeth was an intelligent and well-educated leader who could read Greek and speak Latin, French, and Italian. However, when the 25-year-old Elizabeth became queen in 1558, many people did not want a woman to rule England, no matter what her qualifications.

Scottish philosopher John Knox wrote that it was unnatural "that a woman should reign [rule] and bear empire above men." Despite such prejudices, Elizabeth became one of England's most popular rulers during her 45 years as queen. "I am of her own country," wrote the playwright Thomas Dekker, "and we adore her."

After gaining the throne, Elizabeth tried to improve England's economy and supported the arts. She led her country through troubled political and religious times without the civil wars that raged through many European countries. By the time her long reign ended in 1603, England had become a world power.

and Isabella had driven the Moors out of Spain. Standing in the way of his plans was Queen Elizabeth I, the daughter of Henry VIII. Although she was a Protestant, Elizabeth promoted peace between England's Protestants and Catholics.

One of Elizabeth's most difficult challenges was to maintain England's influence in Europe. This struggle was complicated by Philip's fight against Protestants in the Netherlands. Elizabeth did not want to appear weak or to abandon fellow Protestants, but she also feared officially allying with the Netherlands because of Spain's power.

The Sea Dogs

To fight Spain without officially declaring war, Elizabeth relied on the "**sea dogs**," a group of English sailors whom Elizabeth encouraged to raid Spanish treasure ships. By taking some of Spain's wealth from the Americas, the English gained treasure and hurt Spain's economy. When Philip protested the sea dogs' capturing of Spanish ships, Elizabeth pretended that England had nothing to do with their activities.

The most successful sea dog was Sir Francis Drake, captain of the *Golden Hind*. Drake grew up poor but became well known for leading many daring attacks on Spanish ships. His motto was "Great things from small beginnings." In 1577 Drake sailed through the Strait of Magellan and attacked the west coast of Peru and New Spain. The Spanish were completely unprepared for Drake's attack because they did not expect any English ships to pass through the strait. In addition to raiding Spanish settlements and ships, Drake explored part of the coast of California, landing just north of present-day San Francisco. He then turned west and sailed back to England, becoming the first English person to circumnavigate the world.

★ The Spanish Armada

King Philip decided that the English sea dogs and England's efforts to help the Protestants in the Netherlands had gone too far. He began assembling a huge invasion fleet that became known as the **Spanish Armada**.

The Great Fleet

The Armada included about 130 ships and 30,000 sailors and soldiers. Philip planned to send this mighty fleet to invade England and to overthrow both Queen Elizabeth and the Anglican Church.

From the beginning the Spanish faced problems. The Armada's commander, Philip's cousin the duke of Medina-Sidonia, was not qualified to lead the fleet. He explained his worries to Philip, writing that "it would not be right for a person like myself, possessing no experience of seafaring or war, to take charge of [the Armada]." Philip insisted that the duke remain in command. Then, while the ships were in the Spanish port of Cadiz (kuh-DIZ), Sir Francis Drake raided their supplies, delaying the Armada for several months.

This map shows an artist's version of one of Francis Drake's voyages.

Even with the delays and poor leadership, the Armada was a strong fighting force. In contrast, England's navy had fewer than 40 ships. To try to even the odds, sea dogs, merchants, and fishermen all contributed their ships to England's defense. The English ships had the advantages of speed, mobility, and improved cannons. These ships could outmaneuver the larger Spanish vessels while firing at them from a distance. The Spanish, on the other hand, had to sail close to English ships and then board them with soldiers. Charles Howard, who led England's fleet, was fortunate to have experienced sailors such as Drake commanding ships.

Battles on the Sea

Bad weather caused more delays, but finally the Armada was ready for battle. In late July 1588 the Spanish Armada and the English fleet met near England's coast. There was a series of battles in which the quick English ships damaged but could not destroy the Armada. Then the English surprised the Spanish at night by sending ships loaded with explosives into the fleet. These fireships exploded in the middle of the Armada, causing the Spanish to scatter. The next day the English fleet defeated the disorganized Armada in a huge battle.

News of the Armada's destruction did not reach England immediately. Queen Elizabeth gave a stirring speech to an army of English soldiers preparing to face the Spanish:

 I know I have but the body of a weak and feeble woman; but I have the heart and stomach of a King, and a King of England, too; and I think it foul scorn [pride] that . . . Spain . . . should dare to invade the borders of my realm. 99

While the soldiers cheered for the queen, the Armada struggled home to Spain. Storms sunk many of the ships on their voyage, allowing fewer than half the ships to make it back safely. King Philip's plan to conquer England had failed.

⭐ The Decline of the Spanish Empire

The Armada's defeat shocked Spain, which had been experiencing a Golden Age of prosperity and power. The Spanish Empire controlled vast territories in Europe and the Americas, and its armies were the strongest in Europe. Spain also had impressive achievements in the arts. Philip oversaw the construction of the Escorial, a great complex that included a monastery and palace. He told the architects to "[use] simplicity of form . . . [and] nobility without arrogance [self-importance]."

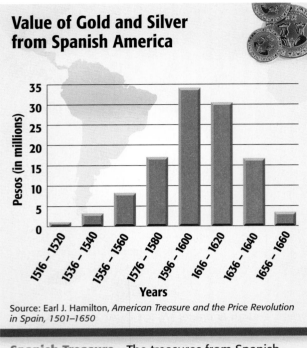

Value of Gold and Silver from Spanish America

Pesos (in millions)

Years: 1516 - 1520, 1536 - 1540, 1556 - 1560, 1576 - 1580, 1596 - 1600, 1616 - 1620, 1636 - 1640, 1656 - 1660

Source: Earl J. Hamilton, *American Treasure and the Price Revolution in Spain, 1501–1650*

Spanish Treasure The treasures from Spanish America were mostly gold and silver. During which time period did Spain receive the greatest amount of treasure from the Americas?

El Greco, a Greek painter who had moved to Spain, gained great admiration for his religious art in the late 1500s. Spain also had respected poets and playwrights such as Lope de Vega, who sailed with the Spanish Armada. Spanish writers produced romantic novels that celebrated the courage of Spanish nobles and conquistadores. Miguel de Cervantes, whose novel *Don Quixote* made fun of European knights, also began writing during this period.

Gradually, however, Spain's Golden Age came to an end, partly because the country's leaders had overlooked major economic problems at home. The large amounts of silver that Spain received from the Americas caused high **inflation**—an increase in the amount of money in circulation and in the price of goods. Rather than purchase high-priced local goods, most Spaniards bought food and manufactured items from other countries. As a result, Spain produced few of its own necessities. However, when the country grew less wealthy, Spaniards could no longer afford many of the goods they needed from other countries. Nor were they prepared to produce goods and food for themselves, which further weakened the economy.

The English defeat of the Spanish Armada showed that Spain's navy was not unbeatable. In addition, the weakened Spanish navy could no longer protect its distant empire in the Americas. As a result, countries such as England, France, and the Netherlands began challenging Spanish power overseas.

SECTION 3 REVIEW

Identify and explain the significance of the following:
- **Martin Luther**
- **Protestant Reformation**
- **Protestants**
- **Henry VIII**
- **Philip II**
- **Elizabeth I**
- **sea dogs**
- **Sir Francis Drake**
- **Spanish Armada**
- **inflation**

Reading for Content Understanding

1 **Main Idea** What complaints did Protestants have about the Catholic Church?

2 **Main Idea** Why did Philip II of Spain want to drive Protestants out of England, and how did Queen Elizabeth I respond to Spain's aggression?

3 **Cultural Diversity** What problems arose as a result of disagreements between Catholics and Protestants?

4 **Writing** *Creating* Write a poem of 6 to 10 lines about the events that led to the end of Spain's Golden Age.

5 **Critical Thinking** *Evaluating* How did the sea dogs help England?

The Race for Empires

Reading Focus

Why were the French and the Dutch interested in colonizing North America?

What common problems did the French, Dutch, and Swedish colonies face?

What happened to the first English settlements in North America?

Key Terms

charter

WHEN FRENCH EXPLORER *Jacques Cartier sailed to North America in 1534, he recorded many strange sights. These included animals such as walruses and thousands of seabirds, which he said "nest [on the islands] as a field is covered with grass." Cartier also reported fish populations so plentiful that he and his crew could catch around 100 cod in an hour. However, one of the most unexpected sights was a French fishing boat! French fishermen had begun traveling to the north coast of North America in the early 1500s to catch the huge schools of fish found there. These French fishermen built temporary settlements to trade with local Indians and to preserve the fish by packing them in salt.*

Jacques Cartier

 ## Early French Settlement

Although Cartier explored the north coast of North America, France established its first official settlement much farther south, in Florida. There, French Huguenots started a few small colonies in 1565. The Spanish, who claimed the land and opposed the Huguenots for religious and political reasons, soon destroyed these settlements and drove out the French.

French Colonies

Religious wars in France delayed further French efforts to colonize North America. When the wars ended, the French established settlements in the north, where the explorations of Cartier and Samuel de Champlain had given France a claim to much of present-day eastern Canada.

In 1604 the French settled in a region they called Acadia, which included what is now Nova Scotia, New Brunswick, and parts of Maine. There

New Empires in the Americas **85**

they established farming communities inland and fishing villages along the coast. One year later Champlain founded Port Royal on the coast of Nova Scotia. Champlain then explored the interior, including the St. Lawrence River and the Great Lakes. He founded the town of Quebec on the St. Lawrence in 1608. He also explored areas in present-day New York and Vermont, where Lake Champlain was named after him.

The Fur Trade

The Great Lakes region proved valuable to France because of the fur trade. Europeans used animal furs, particularly beaver pelts, to make expensive hats. The French traded tools, jewelry, and cloth with Indians in exchange for furs, and then shipped them back to France. Montreal, founded by Paul de Chomedey de Maisonneuve (mez-OH-nehv) in 1642, became a center for the fur trade.

Fur traders often had to travel deep into the wilderness to meet with their Indian trading partners. The traders usually traveled by river, braving the dangers of white-water rapids. "I never saw any stream of water to fall down with such force," wrote Champlain after his first encounter with rapids. French traders used Indian birchbark canoes, which were light enough to carry.

Fur traders lived far from French settlements for long periods of time. Many traders adopted local Indians' clothing and practices to survive. One observer in the mid-1700s wrote:

" It is inconceivable [unbelievable] what hardships the people of Canada must undergo on their hunting journeys. . . . They often suffer hunger, thirst, heat, and cold, and are bitten by . . . dangerous animals and insects. . . . None of them fears danger or hardships. Many of them settle among the Indians far from Canada, marry Indian women, and never come back again. "

A French officer also noted that the fur traders who came back to French towns "Eat, Drink, and Play . . . as long as the Goods [furs] hold out."

The Expansion of the French Empire

In the late 1600s French fur traders, explorers, and missionaries began spreading out from the Great Lakes region. Many headed south toward the lands of New Spain.

Louisiana

In the 1650s French missionaries reported stories about "a beautiful river, large, broad, and deep" that American Indians said ran south of the Great Lakes. In 1673 explorer Louis Jolliet (jahl-ee-ET) and missionary Jacques Marquette set out to find this great river, the Mississippi. They reached the river and traveled downstream as far as present-day Arkansas before turning back to avoid angering the Spanish. Nine years later, René-Robert de La Salle followed the Mississippi River to the Gulf of Mexico. He claimed the Mississippi Valley for King Louis XIV of France and named it Louisiana.

In 1684 La Salle tried to return to Louisiana from the south through the Gulf of Mexico. He hoped to found a colony and drive out the nearby Spanish with the help of local Indians, who La Salle said had "a deadly hatred for the Spaniards." He got lost, however, and ended up on the coast of Texas, where he built a fort. For the next four years, La Salle continued to seek the entrance to the Mississippi so he could go north along the river and reach Canada. Meanwhile, the Spanish

Louis Jolliet and Jacques Marquette traveled along the Mississippi River in 1673.

searched for his settlement. According to officer Alonso de León, when the Spanish found the fort they observed

"books and papers [scattered] throughout the patios, broken chests and bottle cases, and more than a hundred broken harquebuses [guns]."

La Salle's own men had lost confidence in his leadership and killed him, after which Indians burned the fort. Despite La Salle's problems, the French remained interested in the region.

A farm in New Sweden in the mid-1600s

American Swedish Historical Museum, Philadelphia, Pennsylvania

Growth in New France

The French eventually called their North American territory New France. Starting in the early 1700s the French founded forts—such as Detroit, St. Louis, and New Orleans—on the Great Lakes and along the Mississippi. The population of most towns in New France was quite small. Detroit, for example, had fewer than 100 people in 1708. France had trouble attracting settlers to North America, so for a while the government helped pay the travel costs for interested colonists. Despite such efforts, by 1688 there were only about 12,000 French settlers in New France.

New France's small population and the importance of the fur trade encouraged French settlers to ally with local Indians. The French established strong alliances with the Algonquian and Huron Indians but became bitter enemies of the Iroquois. In general, the French regarded Indians with more respect than did many other European settlers.

★ New Netherland and New Sweden

The possibility of trading with American Indians for valuable furs or of farming good land attracted several European nations. The Netherlands and Sweden were two other nations that established settlements in North America.

Trade motivated the Dutch, who had merchant fleets around the world, to come to America.

Explorer Henry Hudson's first voyage to North America had given the Dutch claim to the land between the Delaware and Connecticut Rivers. This area, which they called New Netherland, included parts of present-day Connecticut, Delaware, New Jersey, and New York. In 1624 the newly formed Dutch West India Company—which traded in Africa, the Caribbean, and the Americas—sent about 30 families to settle in New Netherland. Two years later Peter Minuit purchased Manhattan Island from a local Indian tribe and founded the settlement of New Amsterdam.

To encourage more settlers to go to America, the Dutch government established the patroon system. A patroon, or wealthy landlord, received a large grant of land to rent to other settlers and was responsible for helping them. The system failed to attract a large number of settlers. With few Dutch settlers, the Dutch West India Company eventually allowed other Europeans to settle in New Netherland. The Dutch practiced religious toleration, which also attracted colonists. Missionary Isaac Jogues (ZHAWG) wrote in 1646 that in New Amsterdam "there may well be four or five hundred men of different sects [religious groups] and nations."

Peter Minuit, who had resigned from the Dutch West India Company, joined the Swedish in founding New Sweden, located along the Delaware River. He also helped them choose the colony site for Fort Christina, built in 1638. There the Swedish established farms and traded with local Indians for furs. Swedish settlers were among the first in North America to build log cabins.

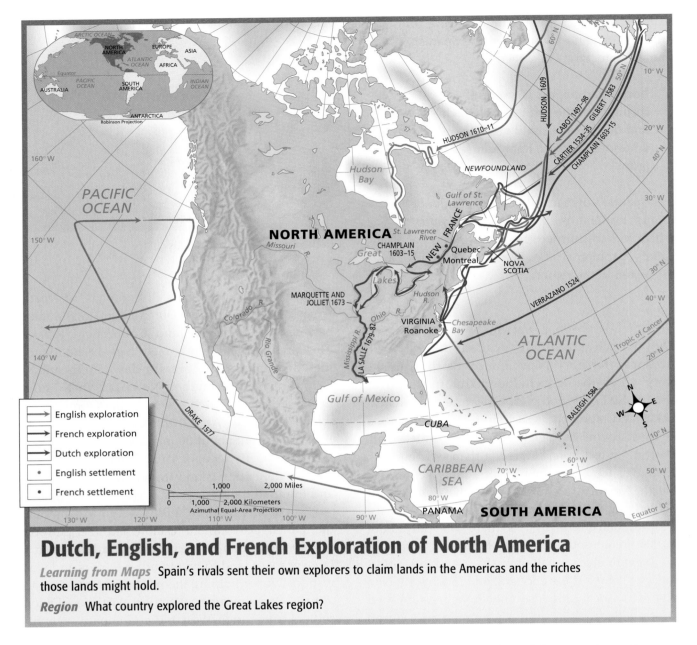

Dutch, English, and French Exploration of North America

Learning from Maps Spain's rivals sent their own explorers to claim lands in the Americas and the riches those lands might hold.

Region What country explored the Great Lakes region?

New Sweden, like the French and Dutch colonies, had difficulty attracting settlers. Few women joined the colony, which forced many men to take on more responsibilities. "Here one must himself cook and bake, and himself do all the things that women do, which I am not accustomed to, and it is difficult for me," wrote soldier Johan Papegoja.

Some women also took on expanded responsibilities. Armegot Printz, the daughter of colonial governor Johan Printz, stayed on his lands when he returned to Sweden, and at times acted "as attorney for her father," according to the legal records. Although New Sweden was small, the Dutch felt that the Swedish were intruding on Dutch lands and fur trading. After a few battles the governor of New Netherland, Peter Stuyvesant (STY-vi-suhnt), seized New Sweden in 1655.

 English Settlements

New Sweden and New Netherland were not the only European settlements along the northern and mid-Atlantic coasts of North America. Aware of the growing French and Spanish settlements, in the late 1500s England decided to begin its own colonization efforts.

Early Efforts

English fishermen, like their French rivals, were building temporary villages on the northeast coast of North America before their country started any official colonies. Then in 1578 Sir Humphrey Gilbert obtained a **charter**, a document granting permission to establish a colony, from Queen Elizabeth. Gilbert launched an expedition to Newfoundland, a region claimed by England as a result of John Cabot's explorations. Gilbert hoped to establish a colony there, but his plans failed when he drowned on a second trip to America in 1583. However, his efforts encouraged his half-brother, Sir Walter Raleigh, to request a charter for another colony in North America.

Raleigh funded an expedition that landed in present-day Virginia and North Carolina. He named the entire area Virginia, and in 1585 he sent another expedition to found a colony on Roanoke Island. The English colonists found life difficult. They fought with local Indians and had trouble finding or growing food. They were forced, according to one account, "to live on rootes and Oysters" and "soup made of sassafras leaves, a food which nobody had ever tried before." In 1586 Sir Francis Drake stopped at Roanoke after a raid on New Spain and agreed to take the remaining settlers home to England.

The Mystery of Roanoke

John White resettled the Roanoke colony in the spring of 1587. White, who was a talented artist and botanist, painted pictures of many American plants and animals. His works are among the earliest known European visual records of North American wildlife. In addition, White's granddaughter, Virginia Dare, became the first English child born in the present-day United States.

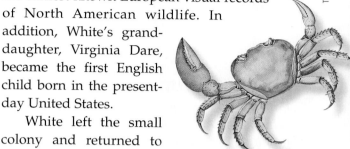

This watercolor of a crab is one of many by John White.

White left the small colony and returned to England at the end of the summer to get more supplies. The threat of the Spanish Armada prevented him from returning to Roanoke until 1590. When White returned, he found the colony's buildings still standing but deserted. Carved into a post was the word *CROTOAN*, which may have been the name of a nearby island inhabited by Indians. White searched for the settlers and his granddaughter. Years later he recalled his efforts: "And thus we [stopped] seeking our Colony, that was never any of them found, nor seen to this day." England's first attempts to settle in North America had failed.

SECTION 4 REVIEW

Identify and explain the significance of the following:
- **Louis Jolliet and Jacques Marquette**
- **René-Robert de La Salle**
- **charter**
- **Sir Walter Raleigh**
- **John White**

Locate and explain the importance of the following:
- **Quebec**
- **Great Lakes**
- **Roanoke**

Reading for Content Understanding

1 **Main Idea** What common problems did many European colonists face?

2 **Main Idea** Briefly describe England's efforts to colonize North America.

3 **Economic Development** Which countries founded settlements in North America, and what were their motivations for settlement?

4 **Writing** *Creating* Write a half-page short story about what might have happened to the settlers at Roanoke.

5 **Critical Thinking** *Making Comparisons* How were the French settlements different from and similar to the Spanish settlements?

CHAPTER 3 REVIEW

Chapter Summary

In the 1500s Spanish conquistadores began to settle in the Americas, destroying the Aztec and Inca Empires in the process. In Europe, a priest named Martin Luther started a religious movement called the Protestant Reformation. This led eventually to war between Spain and England. As Spain's influence declined, other European countries began to establish settlements in North America. ▪

On a separate sheet of paper, complete the following activities.

Identifying People and Ideas

Describe the historical significance of the following:

1. Moctezuma II
2. Álvar Núñez Cabeza de Vaca
3. Juan Rodríguez Cabrillo
4. Council of the Indies
5. inflation
6. plantations
7. Elizabeth I
8. Bartolomé de Las Casas
9. Louis Jolliet and Jacques Marquette
10. charter

Internet Activity
go.hrw.com
SAO French Explorers

Search the Internet through the HRW Web site for more information about one of the conquistadores or French explorers mentioned in the chapter. Then use this information to create a map showing the path he took to the Americas and the places he explored.

Understanding Main Ideas

1. What events led to the fall of the Aztec and Inca Empires?
2. What was Ponce de León looking for in Florida?
3. Why did the Spanish bring African slaves to New Spain?
4. Why did Popé lead a revolt against the Spanish in New Mexico?
5. How did Catholics react to Protestants?
6. Who was Sir Francis Drake?
7. What challenges did fur traders face in the Americas?

Reviewing Themes

1. **Geographic Diversity** Why did the French and the Dutch establish settlements in the Americas?
2. **Citizenship and Democracy** How did Spain organize and govern its American colonies?

Using the Time Line

Number your paper from 1 to 5. Match the letters on the time line below with the following events.

1. **Sir Walter Raleigh sponsors an expedition to establish a colony on Roanoke Island.**
2. **Popé leads the Pueblo Indian revolt, which drives the Spanish out of New Mexico.**
3. **Martin Luther criticizes some practices of the Catholic Church by publicly posting his 95 theses.**
4. **The Dutch in New Netherland take control of the New Sweden colony.**
5. **Juan Ponce de León dies from an injury received during a battle with Indians while exploring Florida.**

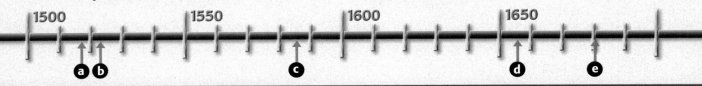

3. **Cultural Diversity**   Why did Martin Luther and his followers start the Protestant Reformation?

Thinking Critically

1. **Synthesizing Information**   What impact did the colonies in Spanish America have on Spain? Explain your answer.

2. **Identifying Cause and Effect**   How did the *encomienda* system affect the daily lives of American Indians?

3. **Drawing Conclusions**   How did the Protestant Reformation affect European colonization of America in the 1600s? Explain your answer.

Writing About History

1. **Informing**   The Spanish monarch has sent you on a fact-finding mission to New Spain. Write a letter to the monarch about the area's economy and society.

2. **Persuading**   Imagine that you are a member of the Spanish Armada or the English navy. Create a flyer to encourage others to join your fleet.

Building Your Portfolio

Complete the following activities individually or in groups.

1. **Settling the Americas**   Create a newspaper titled *Settling the Americas.* Devote one page each to the colonies of Spain, France, Sweden, and the Netherlands. Your newspaper should contain maps, two or more feature stories, an editorial, and a biography of an important person.

2. **Art in Spain**   Create a bulletin board display of artistic and cultural achievements in Spain or New Spain during the Golden Age. Select one painter, poet, playwright, and writer who was popular in Spain or New Spain. Find or re-create examples of each person's work to put in your display. Also write a biographical sketch of each person to accompany his or her work.

Linking Geography and History

1. **Location**   Why do you think that the French, Dutch, Swedish, and English established their early settlements mainly along the Atlantic coast and not the Pacific coast of North America?

2. **Human-Environment Interaction**   How did contact between American Indians and Europeans affect both groups?

History Skills Workshop

Reading Maps   Study the map below, which shows early Dutch, English, French, and Swedish settlements in North America. Then answer the following questions: (a) In what present-day state was New Amsterdam located? (b) What river connected Fort Orange and the New Amsterdam settlements? (c) How far was Quebec from Montreal?

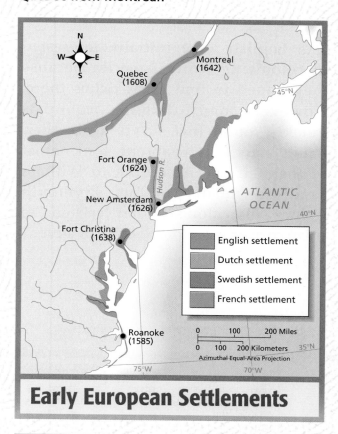

Early European Settlements

■ CHAPTER · 4 ■
The English Colonies
(1605–1752)

The English were initially interested in colonizing North America because they hoped to find great riches there. However, many English colonists quickly found that surviving in their harsh new environment took most of their efforts. According to William Bradford, leader of the Plymouth Colony, his colonists soon learned "to prize corn as more precious than silver."

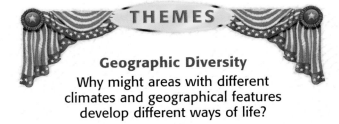

THEMES

Geographic Diversity
Why might areas with different climates and geographical features develop different ways of life?

Economic Development
How might a growing colony develop its economy?

Global Relations
How might people react to a lack of religious freedom in society?

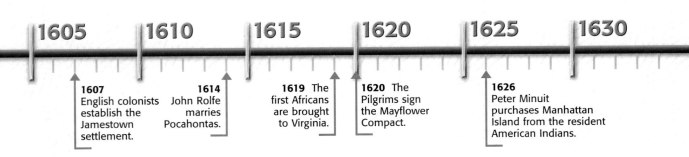

1605	1610	1615	1620	1625	1630

1607 English colonists establish the Jamestown settlement.

1614 John Rolfe marries Pocahontas.

1619 The first Africans are brought to Virginia.

1620 The Pilgrims sign the Mayflower Compact.

1626 Peter Minuit purchases Manhattan Island from the resident American Indians.

SECTION 1

The Virginia Colony

Reading Focus

Why were people in England interested in founding or joining a colony in America?

How did the Jamestown colonists depend on American Indians, and how did their relationship change over time?

What was Virginia's most important crop, and who worked to produce it?

Key Terms

Powhatan Confederacy
headright
indentured servants
House of Burgesses
Bacon's Rebellion

IN 1605 A COMPANY of English merchants asked the Crown for the right to found a settlement and search for gold in North America. The area they wanted to settle was part of the region called Virginia, which at the time extended from present-day Maine to South Carolina. King James I granted the request, promising the London Company the rights to "all the lands, woods, soils, grounds, . . . ports, rivers, mines, minerals, . . . [and] commodities" along a section of the Virginia coast. The company's efforts, wrote King James, "may in time bring . . . a settled and quiet government."

London Company advertisement

IMAGE ON LEFT PAGE: *Puritan colonists building a settlement in New England*

1635	1640	1645	1650	1700	1730
1636 Roger Williams establishes the town of Providence.		**c. 1647** George Fox helps establish the Society of Friends, or Quakers.		**1702** England unites East and West New Jersey into a single royal colony.	**1733** James Oglethorpe helps found Savannah, Georgia.

★ The Drive to Colonize

The failure of Sir Walter Raleigh's Roanoke colony led the London Company to take a different approach to settlement. Instead of relying on the wealth of one person, investors formed a joint-stock company, so that several people shared the cost and risk of establishing the colony. Sir Thomas Smith helped organize the company.

To attract investors and settlers, the London Company printed advertisements praising Virginia. One report boasted:

> **The land yields . . . [an] abundance of fish, infinite store [endless supply] of deer, and hares, with many fruits and roots. . . . There are hills and mountains making a sensible proffer [offer] of hidden treasure, never yet searched.**

The promise of such wealth attracted adventurers and people who were suffering economic hardship in England. During the late 1500s landowners in England had begun fencing in their land, converting farmland into sheep pastures to produce wool for the developing cloth trade. This process of enclosure had left many tenant farmers without land. During the same period the population of England had increased in size, and unemployment levels had risen. English leaders hoped that a colony in America would offer new opportunities for these growing numbers of homeless and unemployed people.

★ Settlement in Jamestown

On April 26, 1607, the first three ships sent by the London Company arrived at the Virginia coast. The fleet brought 105 male colonists to found a settlement in America and to search for riches.

A Rough Start

The ships sailed into Chesapeake Bay and up the James River. About 50 miles upstream, the colonists established their first settlement, which they named Jamestown after the king.

The Jamestown colonists were ill-prepared for the challenges of starting a settlement. Most of them were adventurers interested in making their fortune and returning to England. No families came to the colony, and very few colonists had farming experience or useful skills such as carpentry. One of the colonists, Captain John Smith, complained that "ten good workmen would have done more substantial work in a day than ten of these [colonists] in a week." Most of the adventurers spent their time and energy searching for gold.

The colonists had also picked a poor site for the settlement. Jamestown was surrounded by swamps filled with disease-carrying mosquitoes, and the river water was too salty to drink safely. These conditions were deadly for colonists weakened by a long sea voyage. By the time winter arrived, two thirds of the original colonists were dead, and the survivors were starving and sick.

The situation in Jamestown temporarily improved after Smith gained control of the colony in September 1608. He forced the settlers to plant crops and build better housing, which reduced the number of deaths from starvation and exposure.

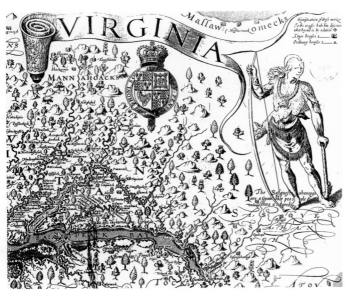

Captain John Smith's book The Generall Historie of Virginia *included this map of the area surrounding the colony.*

The Powhatan Confederacy

The colonists also received help from the powerful **Powhatan Confederacy**—an alliance of Algonquian Indians under the leadership of Wahunsonacock (wah-huhn-SUH-nuh-kahk). The

English colonists meeting the chief of the Powhatan Indians

Powhatan traded with the colonists, bringing food to exchange for the colonists' manufactured English goods. The Powhatan also taught the colonists how to grow North American crops such as corn.

The relationship between the Powhatan and the Virginia colonists was not peaceful, however. On repeated occasions the colonists took food from the Powhatan by force. These actions led Wahunsonacock to address John Smith:

66 **Why will you take by force what you may obtain by love? Why will you destroy us who supply you with food? What can you get by war? . . . We are unarmed, and willing to give you what you ask, if you come in a friendly manner.** 99

The Starving Time

In 1609 around 400 more settlers arrived in Jamestown. John Smith, who had been injured in an accident, returned to England, leaving the settlers without a strong leader. That winter, disease and famine once again struck the colony, leading to what the colonists called the starving time. By the summer of 1610, only 60 colonists were still alive.

By 1611 a new governor, Sir Thomas Gates, and Deputy Governor Sir Thomas Dale had arrived with another group of colonists. Dale established strict laws with harsh punishments and required colonists to work hard. However, high death rates continued in the colony.

★ Growing Tobacco

The Jamestown colony had survived but still had not made a profit for the London Company. Colonist John Rolfe helped solve this problem in 1612. Smoking tobacco had become a popular pastime in England starting in the 1560s. Tobacco grew well in Virginia, but the local variety grown by the Powhatan was too bitter for European tastes. Rolfe

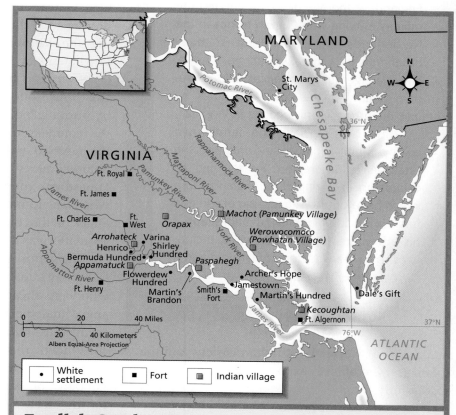

English Settlement in the Chesapeake, 1607–1675

Learning from Maps English colonies in the Chesapeake Bay area were often located near Indian villages. The contact between the two cultures was sometimes cooperative but often turned violent.

Location What Indian village was located across the James River from the English settlement of Martin's Brandon?

The Granger Collection, New York

John Smith

Captain John Smith was a man of great physical and mental strength. Smith was born in 1580 to a farming family in Alford, England. At the age of 17, he entered the military, serving with English troops in the Netherlands. He later fought in many other military campaigns across Europe. These dangerous experiences helped prepare Smith for the great difficulties he and the other colonists faced in Virginia.

After helping save the Jamestown colony, Smith explored and mapped the Chesapeake Bay region. He also led an expedition exploring New England, from which he returned with a cargo of fish and furs. Smith later published books about his adventures in North America, including *The Generall Historie of Virginia* and *A Description of New England*.

introduced a sweeter West Indian variety, and the colonists were able to export tobacco to England successfully.

Not everyone approved of the new tobacco trade. King James I declared that smoking was "a custome loathsome [disgusting] to the eye, hatefull to the Nose, harmefull to the braine, [and] dangerous to the Lungs."

Despite the king's objections, the tobacco trade proved profitable for the Jamestown colony. As colonist John Pory wrote in 1619, "All our riches for the present doe consiste in Tobacco."

★ War in Virginia

John Rolfe also helped the Jamestown colony temporarily achieve more peaceful relations with the Powhatan when he married Pocahontas, Wahunsonacock's daughter, in 1614. However, Pocahontas died in 1617 in England and Wahunsonacock died in 1618. By that time, the colonists no longer depended on the Powhatan for food and had lost interest in allying with their Indian neighbors. Many colonists also wanted to grow tobacco on Indian lands. The resulting expansion of colonial settlement brought the Powhatan and the Virginia colonists into increasing conflict. Governor Francis Wyatt spoke for many colonists when he said the Powhatan "were but as thornes in our sides."

In 1622, colonists killed a Powhatan leader. Opechancanough (OH-puh-chan-kuh-noh), the brother of Wahunsonacock, responded by attacking the Virginia settlers that same year. The Powhatan killed about 350 men, women, and children—around half the colony. Among the dead was John Rolfe. The angry survivors responded by burning Indian villages, and fighting between the colonists and the Powhatan continued for the next 20 years. "Neither fair war nor good quarter [mercy] is ever to be held," declared the Jamestown council. In 1644 Opechancanough—who was around 100 years old—led another large attack on the colonists. He was captured and killed soon afterward, and by 1646 the war was over.

The war in Virginia demonstrated the London Company's inability to help its colonists. Settlers who were already running short of supplies were angry that the London Company failed to send them any military support. These problems convinced the English Crown to cancel the London Company's charter in 1624. From that point on, Virginia became a royal colony under the authority of a governor appointed by the king.

Pocahontas had this portrait made when she visited England with John Rolfe in 1616.

Greater numbers of women began arriving in Jamestown in 1619.

 Daily Life in Virginia

In early Virginia, people lived on scattered farms rather than in towns. With easy access to river transportation, settlers did not need towns for trade.

Tobacco Culture

Tobacco farmers soon began establishing mid-sized or large farms called plantations. These plantations were made possible in part by the **headright** system, set up by the London Company in 1618. Under this system, each colonist who paid his or her own way to Virginia received 50 acres of land plus 50 more acres for every additional person brought from England. The system allowed wealthy colonists to gain large plots of land by bringing servants or relatives to Virginia.

Those who brought relatives over discovered that raising a family was difficult in colonial Virginia. The first large group of single women did not arrive in Jamestown until 1619, and during the early years of settlement, men outnumbered women seven to one. The London Company tried to recruit more women to the colony by offering them land grants and promises of marriage. Colonists who did start families often saw loved ones fall to deadly diseases such as malaria.

Colonial families in Virginia focused on providing the basic necessities for themselves. Most colonists made food, shelter, eating utensils, tools, furniture, and clothing by hand. Parents provided lessons in reading and religion at home because there were no schools and few churches.

Labor Problems

For 40 years, colonists in Virginia continued to face a harsh life and to suffer very high death rates. These deaths led to labor shortages in Virginia and the need for more colonists to maintain and increase the population. However, most people wishing to move to Virginia could not afford to pay their travel costs. They often became **indentured servants**, signing an indenture, or contract, to work from four to seven years for those who paid their ship fare to America. Of the early Virginia colonists, around 75 percent had been under indenture. In one such contract, Margarett Williams promised to work for plantation owner Richard Smyth for four years. In exchange, Smyth promised

> **“to pay for her [ocean] passing, and to find and allow [provide] her meate, drinke, apparrel [clothes] and lodging. . . . And at the end of said term to pay unto her one Ax, one Hoe, double apparel, fifty acres of land [and] one years provision [supplies].”**

Large numbers of indentured servants died before their term was over because of poor living conditions and disease. One servant wrote to his parents, “I have eaten more in a day at home than I have [had] here for a week.” However, servants who survived their period of indenture gained their freedom and were able to claim land.

Colonial indenture contract

Africans in Virginia

In addition to laborers from Europe, the first Africans in Virginia arrived on board a Dutch ship in 1619. Some Africans were indentured servants, while others had been enslaved. African indentured servants worked and lived side by side with white indentured servants and had similar contracts. Some of them, such as Anthony Johnson, became successful farmers at the end of their contracts.

At first most white farmers brought over indentured servants rather than buy expensive slaves, because workers died so quickly in Virginia. Once these death rates declined and slave prices dropped, however, many farmers preferred slaves to indentured servants, who had to be set free at the end of their contracts. By the mid-1600s most Africans in Virginia were kept in lifelong slavery. The widespread use of slave labor created much wealth for tobacco plantation owners but at a great cost in human life and liberty.

The first enslaved Africans to arrive in the English colonies were brought in the early 1600s.

Bacon's Rebellion

By the late 1600s Virginia governor William Berkeley was complaining about the large number of "Poore, Indebted, Discontented and Armed" settlers in the colony. Poor colonists began protesting that the members of the **House of Burgesses**, Virginia's elected assembly, raised taxes only to pay themselves higher salaries. Poor colonists also complained about the lack of available farmland. Many of them began building farms in American Indian territory, ignoring treaties between the government and local Indians.

In 1676 Nathaniel Bacon, a wealthy relative of the governor and a frontier farmer, led a group of slaves, freed slaves, and former servants in an attack against some friendly American Indians. When Governor Berkeley tried to calm Bacon and his angry followers, they attacked and burned Jamestown. At one point during **Bacon's Rebellion**, as it was called, Bacon controlled most of the colony. Bacon died of fever, however, and Berkeley caught and hanged 23 of the remaining rebels. After the rebellion, the Virginia colonists found it difficult to make peace with American Indians. In addition, farmers began to use more slave labor because they feared another rebellion by former indentured servants. This contributed further to the growth of slavery in Virginia.

SECTION 1 REVIEW

Identify and explain the significance of the following:
- **John Smith**
- **Powhatan Confederacy**
- **John Rolfe**
- **Pocahontas**
- **headright**
- **indentured servants**
- **House of Burgesses**
- **Nathaniel Bacon**
- **Bacon's Rebellion**

Reading for Content Understanding

1 **Main Idea** What changes in England helped motivate colonists to settle in North America?

2 **Main Idea** How did American Indians help the Jamestown colonists? What caused conflicts between the Powhatan and the colonists?

3 **Economic Development** Why were indentured servants and enslaved Africans important for the colonial economy?

4 **Writing** *Informing* Write a paragraph explaining why tobacco became Virginia's most important crop.

5 **Critical Thinking** *Synthesizing Information* Why do you think that people were willing to come to the colonies as indentured servants? List the benefits and disadvantages of being an indentured servant in a chart, and then explain your answer.

The Pilgrims' Experience

Reading Focus

Why did the Pilgrims want to leave England?

What was the Mayflower Compact, and why was it important?

What was life like in Plymouth?

Key Terms

Puritans
sect
Separatists
Pilgrims
immigrants
Mayflower Compact

ENGLAND'S KING JAMES I held a conference in 1604 to meet with Protestant leaders. They wanted to reform the Church of England, also known as the Anglican Church. As these leaders presented their complaints, which were critical of the power held by Anglican bishops, the king grew increasingly restless. Finally, he interrupted one of the reformers and began shouting furiously, "While I am in England I will have bishops to govern the Church." As for those who continued to demand reform, James declared, "I will make them conform themselves [become Anglicans] or I will harry [drive] them out of this land."

King James I

 Puritans and Pilgrims

Religious tension in England remained high after the Protestant Reformation. A Protestant group called the **Puritans** wanted to reform, or purify, the Church of England. Puritans believed that the Church of England had kept too many Catholic traditions. The Puritans also thought that the leaders of the Church of England, such as bishops and priests, had too much power over church members. Puritan leaders argued that the Bible was the most reliable source of authority within the church.

The most extreme **sect**, or religious group, of Puritans wanted to separate from the Church of England entirely rather than simply reform it. These **Separatists** developed their own churches and cut all ties with the Church of England. English authorities responded by persecuting Separatists.

One Separatist sect that faced such treatment became known as the **Pilgrims**. Eventually, the Pilgrims decided to escape this persecution. In 1607 the Pilgrims left England and moved to the Netherlands, becoming **immigrants**—people who have left the country of their birth to live in another country. Dutch officials welcomed the Pilgrims and allowed them to practice their religion freely.

Henry Bacon's painting Landing of the Pilgrims

The Founding of Plymouth

The Pilgrims were glad to be able to practice their faith. They were displeased, however, that their children were learning the Dutch language and culture and forgetting their English traditions. The Pilgrims were also unhappy that they were mostly limited to unskilled work in the Netherlands.

These issues motivated the Pilgrims to move from the Netherlands to America. They established a joint-stock company with some merchants and returned to England to apply for permission to settle in Virginia. Before setting out on their journey, the Pilgrims received a letter from their spiritual leader, Reverend John Robinson. Unable to join the colonists, Robinson advised them about the need to stand together:

❝ **You are many of you strangers, as to the persons, so to the infirmities [weaknesses] one of another, . . . which does require at your hands much wisdom and charity for the . . . preventing of incident [accidental] offenses.** ❞

On September 16, 1620, the ship *Mayflower* left England with more than 100 men, women, and children as passengers. Not all of these colonists were Pilgrims, but Pilgrim leaders such as William Bradford were in command of the expedition. The Pilgrims also hired Captain Miles Standish to help organize the defense of their colony.

After two months of rough ocean travel, the Pilgrims sighted land. Soon they realized that they were far north of the current boundaries of Virginia. This put them outside the lands of their English charter. Knowing that they would not be under the authority of the Virginia colonial government, the Pilgrims decided to create and write down the basic laws and social rules that would govern their colony. On November 21, 1620, the 41 male passengers on the *Mayflower* signed this legal contract, which they called the **Mayflower Compact**. In it they agreed to create "such just and equal laws, . . . as shall be thought most meet [fitting] and convenient for the general good of the colony." The Mayflower Compact represented one of the first efforts at self-government in the English colonies.

The Pilgrims chose to land along the shore at Plymouth Rock in present-day Massachusetts. Bradford wrote that once ashore, "They [the Pilgrims] fell upon their knees and blessed the God of Heaven who had brought them over the vast and furious ocean." The *Mayflower* stayed with the colonists until April while they struggled through the winter to build the Plymouth settlement. Exhausted from their journey, nearly half the Pilgrims died during this first winter from sickness and the freezing weather.

William Bradford

Pilgrims and American Indians

European fishing boats had already visited the area around Plymouth before the arrival of the Pilgrims. These Europeans had brought new diseases to the region that had killed most of the local American Indians, such as the Pawtuxet.

Samoset and Squanto

For some time the Pilgrims met no Indians, coming across only a few deserted Indian villages and abandoned cornfields. The Pilgrims used these empty fields in the spring to plant the next year's crop. Then, according to Bradford, in March 1621 an American Indian walked boldly into the colonists' settlement and "spoke to them in broken English, which they could well understand, but marveled at it." This Indian was Samoset, who was from a Pemaquid tribe that lived in the area. He had learned some English from the crews of fishing boats. Samoset gave the Pilgrims useful information about the peoples and places surrounding Plymouth, and he later introduced them to a Pawtuxet Indian named Squanto.

Squanto had been kidnapped by English explorers in 1615 and sold in Spain as a slave. He escaped from his captors and made his way to England, finally returning to North America. He gradually found his way back to his homeland in 1619, only to discover that everyone in his tribe had died from disease while he was gone.

Squanto was not only fluent in English but also willing to help the colonists. According to one observer, he showed the settlers

❝how to set [plant] their corn, where to take [catch] fish, . . . and was also their pilot [guide] to unknown places.❞

From Squanto the Pilgrims also learned how to fertilize the soil on their farms with fish remains. In addition, Squanto helped the Pilgrims establish peaceful relations with Massasoit, the chief of the local Wampanoag Indians. This peaceful relationship helped the Pilgrims in their early years of settlement.

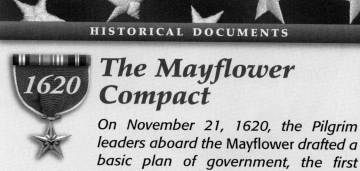

HISTORICAL DOCUMENTS

The Mayflower Compact
1620

On November 21, 1620, the Pilgrim leaders aboard the Mayflower drafted a basic plan of government, the first such document created in the colonies. This excerpt from the Mayflower Compact describes the principles of the Pilgrim colony's government.

❝We whose names are underwritten, [written below] . . . having undertaken, for the glory of God, and advancement of the Christian faith, . . . a voyage to plant the first colony in the northern parts of Virginia, do by these presents [this document] solemnly and mutually in the presence of God, and one of another, covenant [promise] and combine ourselves together into a civil body politic [group organized for government] for our better ordering and preservation and furtherance of the ends aforesaid [mentioned above]; and by virtue [authority] hereof, to enact, constitute, and frame such just and equal laws, ordinances [regulations], acts . . . as shall be thought most meet [fitting] and convenient for the general good of the colony unto which we promise all due . . . obedience.❞

Understanding Primary Sources
1. Who had the signers of the document promised to serve?
2. Why do you think the colonists felt the need to establish a government?

Squanto showed the Pilgrims how to plant and grow corn in New England.

Thanksgiving

The peaceful relationship with the Wampanoag allowed the Pilgrims to grow and harvest their first crops in safety. When harvest time arrived, William Bradford recalled that the Pilgrims began

> 66 **to fit up their houses and dwellings against winter, being all well recovered in health and strength and had all things in good plenty.** 99

To celebrate their harvest, the Pilgrims invited Chief Massasoit and 90 other Wampanoag guests to what became known as the first Thanksgiving. The Pilgrims killed wild turkeys for the occasion, and the Wampanoag contributed venison. For three days the two groups feasted with each other. This event marked the Pilgrims' surviving their first year in the new colony.

★ The Pilgrim Community

Although the Pilgrims overcame many misfortunes, their small settlement continued to struggle. However, they trusted that hard work and a strong religious community would help them survive.

Trade

The Pilgrims had hoped to earn a living by fishing and fur trading. Few of the settlers had any fishing or hunting experience, however. Some colonists participated in a fishing trade with American Indians. The Pilgrims were also able to trade extra corn with the Abenaki Indians for beaver furs. However, most Pilgrims became farmers.

Back in England, the non-Pilgrim merchants who had invested in the Plymouth Colony were unhappy with its slow economic growth. They sold their shares of land to the Pilgrim leaders in 1626. The Pilgrims then distributed this land evenly among the original families who had founded the colony.

The Importance of Family

More than 20 years passed before the Pilgrims raised enough money from fishing and fur trading to pay off the money they had borrowed to buy their lands. However, the Pilgrims were more successful in establishing a strong community than in making a profit.

A wild turkey

Unlike in Virginia, families were common in the Pilgrim settlement. After the first difficult winter during which so many Pilgrims died, colonists quickly adopted orphaned children and raised them as family members. Pilgrim families educated their children and trained their indentured servants. Families also served as the centers of religious faith, health care, and community well-being.

A Pilgrim boy's leather shoes

Peabody & Essex Museum, Salem, Massachusetts

All family members participated in the work required for survival during this time. Women generally cooked, spun and wove wool, sewed clothing, made soap and butter, carried water, dried fruit, and cared for livestock. Men spent most of their time repairing tools, working in the fields, chopping wood, and building and maintaining shelters for people and animals. Most Pilgrims hoped to have large families, partly because children were greatly needed to help with this work.

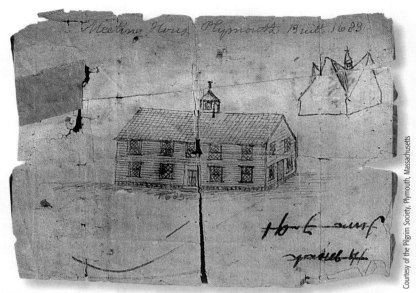

The Pilgrims built a new meetinghouse in Plymouth Colony in 1683, adding glass windows and a church bell.

Courtesy of the Pilgrim Society, Plymouth, Massachusetts

Pilgrim Women

In Plymouth, women had more legal rights than they did in England, where they were not allowed to make contracts, bring lawsuits, or own property. Pilgrim women had the right to sign contracts and to bring some cases before local courts. Widows could also own property. A widow typically received one third of her family's land and belongings. In addition, married and widowed women gained licenses to run inns and sell liquor.

Occasionally, local courts recognized the business contributions of women to the community.

Widow Naomi Silvester received a large share of her husband's estate because the court considered her "a frugal [thrifty] and laborious [hardworking] woman in the providing of the said estate." Widow Elizabeth Warren's business talent convinced colonial officials to appoint her as a purchaser for the colony in place of her late husband. The hard work of Silvester, Warren, and other women helped the Plymouth Colony to survive the difficult times during its founding.

SECTION 2 REVIEW

Identify and explain the significance of the following:
- **Puritans**
- **sect**
- **Separatists**
- **Pilgrims**
- **immigrants**
- **William Bradford**
- **Mayflower Compact**
- **Squanto**

Reading for Content Understanding

1 **Main Idea** Why did the Pilgrims move from England to the Netherlands? Why did they then decide to move to America?

2 **Main Idea** How were the Pilgrims able to survive their first years in Plymouth, and what was the colony like once it was more established?

3 **Cultural Diversity** What kind of relationship did the Pilgrims have with the American Indians near Plymouth?

4 **Writing** *Persuading* Imagine that you were one of the Pilgrims who came to Plymouth on the *Mayflower*. Write a letter to someone back in England describing the Mayflower Compact and explaining why your group felt that it was necessary.

5 **Critical Thinking** *Making Comparisons* How were the experiences of the Pilgrims similar to those of the first Jamestown settlers?

The New England Colonies

Reading Focus

What was the Great Migration, and why did it occur?

What role did religion and the church play in the Massachusetts Bay Colony?

How did the Puritans respond to dissenters?

Key Terms

dissenters
Great Migration
covenant
town meeting
Fundamental Orders of Connecticut

*I*N THE EARLY 1600S *John Winthrop wrote to his beloved wife, Margaret, that "this land [England] grows weary of her inhabitants." As an Englishman, John Winthrop was fond of his country and his work as a lawyer. As a Puritan, however, he believed that the members of his church were no longer welcome in England. Winthrop believed that the time was coming when they would have to leave their comfortable life behind. As he later wrote, his followers had to seek a new home "so that ourselves and our posterity [children] may be better preserved from the common corruptions [sins] of this evil world."*

The Granger Collection, New York

John Winthrop

 ## The Great Migration

During the 1620s and 1630s an economic downturn put many people out of work in England. The English king, Charles I, made the situation worse by raising taxes. When the English legislature challenged the king's authority, he dissolved the body in 1629, causing a political crisis. At the same time, William Laud, head of the Church of England, began to make life difficult for the Puritans because they were **dissenters**. Dissenters are people who disagree with official religious or political opinions. Laud would not allow Puritans to hold positions in Anglican churches or England's universities. He also ensured that authorities harshly punished any Puritan who wrote pamphlets attacking the Church of England.

These problems led to a mass movement called the **Great Migration**. Between 1629 and 1640 at least 80,000 English men, women, and children left England. About 40,000 English immigrants moved to other nations in Europe. Another 40,000 or so

The first settlers of the Massachusetts Bay Colony arrived in New England in 1630 aboard the Arbella, Talbot, and Jewell.

immigrated to English colonies in the Caribbean and New England.

Most Puritans stopped emigrating when the English Civil War began in 1642. At that time, Oliver Cromwell led an army of Puritans and opponents of the monarchy against the forces of King Charles I. Cromwell's army defeated the king's troops in 1646, and Cromwell became head of state in 1649.

The Massachusetts Bay Colony

At the start of the Great Migration, a group of Puritans and merchants planned a Puritan colony in North America. In 1629 King Charles I granted the group a company charter allowing it to set up its colony in the area known as New England. The members formed the Massachusetts Bay Company and put Puritans in charge of the colony.

In 1630 a fleet of ships carrying Puritan colonists left England for Massachusetts. There they hoped to have the freedom to establish their own religion. While on board the flagship *Arbella*, the colony's governor, John Winthrop, wrote:

❝ **We must delight in each other, make others' conditions our own and rejoice together, mourn together, labor and suffer together, always having before**

our eyes . . . our community. . . . For we must consider that we shall be like a City upon a Hill; the eyes of all people are on us. ❞

Winthrop's speech reflected the Puritan belief that they had made a **covenant**, or sacred agreement, with God to build an ideal Christian community.

The Puritans arrived in New England well prepared to start their colony, with large supplies of tools and livestock. They also benefited from trade with the established colony of Plymouth, which supplied them with animals and grain. Like the Pilgrims, the Puritans faced little resistance from local American Indians, whose population had been drastically reduced by an epidemic. In addition, the Massachusetts region, unlike coastal Virginia, had a healthy climate. Thus, relatively few Puritans died from disease. These advantages helped the Puritan colony prosper after it survived the first harsh winter, which took many lives.

By the end of 1630, more ships had arrived in the Massachusetts Bay Colony, carrying about 1,000 men, women, and children. These colonists soon established the towns of Salem, Mystic, Newton, Watertown, Dorchester, and Boston, which became the colony's chief city and capital. Colonists also settled to the north, in present-day New Hampshire. In 1680 New Hampshire became a royal colony.

Colonial Williamsburg Foundation

Colonial woodworking tools

⭐ The New England Way

Through its charter, the Massachusetts Bay Company received the right to govern its colony. As a company colony, Massachusetts had to obey English laws but had more independence than a royal colony such as Virginia. The Puritan colonists created a General Court, in which each town was represented by two or three deputies. The General Court elected the governor and his assistants. In 1644 the General Court became a two-house legislature. All decisions required a majority in each house.

Politics and religion were closely linked in Puritan New England. Government leaders were also church members and ministers often had a great deal of authority in Puritan communities. Reverend John Cotton explained the Puritan point of view: "It is better that the commonwealth [colony] be fashioned [fitted] to . . . God's house . . . than to accommodate [bend] the church frame to the civil state."

White male church members were the only colonists who could vote. Colonists achieved full membership in the church by becoming what the Puritans called God's "elect," or chosen. Achieving this status was a difficult process that required individuals to pass a public examination to prove the strength of their faith. Toward the end of the 1600s, however, the colony began allowing church members who were not among the elect to vote. These voters were required to own a minimum amount of property.

The focus of local New England politics was the **town meeting**. In town meetings each settlement discussed and decided issues of local interest, such as support of schools and regulations on timber cutting or cattle grazing.

⭐ Daily Life and Customs

Life in New England was centered around religion, family responsibilities, and public duties. The Puritans' religion strongly shaped everyday life in colonial New England. Every Sunday, Puritan colonists usually heard two sermons, one in the morning and one in the afternoon. Puritans looked forward to these weekly church gatherings because they brought all members of the community together. As a result of such shared beliefs and the presence of families, many New England communities were more stable and structured than those in Virginia. As one New England song explained,:

> **But bring both a quiet and contented
> mind,
> And all needful blessings you surely
> will find.**

The Economy

While colonists in Virginia tended to be either wealthy or poor, most colonists who migrated to New England were somewhere in between. Many New England colonists were skilled workers or experienced farmers. Others quickly became successful in fishing enterprises or fur trading.

New England farmers focused on growing food rather than crops such as tobacco, which was unsuitable for the climate. Most New England farms were owned and operated by families. In addition to raising crops in the field, family members tended vegetable gardens, raised cows, and

The Granger Collection, New York

*A Puritan couple walking to a church
meeting at night*

produced cream, butter, and cheese to trade or sell. Hogs and corn were the most common farm products sold and traded. Most New Englanders had comparably long lives because of the variety of foods in their diet and the healthy climate of the region.

Family Life

Most colonists either came to New England in family groups or quickly formed families once they arrived. New England men usually married around age 26, and women married around age 22. Couples tended to have many children to help run the family farm. Most couples raised between five and seven children to adulthood.

Parents helped choose their children's marriage partners in colonial New England, in part because marriage involved a transfer of property from one family to another. Puritans thought that women had three main duties in marriage: to obey their husbands, to have children, and to manage

the household. One father carefully instructed his daughter, "Let your Dress, your Conversation and the whole Business of your life be to please your husband and to make him happy." Husbands were expected in turn to treat their wives "with the greatest love, gentleness, kindness, [and] tenderness." Puritan law punished those who behaved badly toward their family.

Education

The first public law regulating education in Massachusetts was passed in 1647. Mothers and fathers in New England wanted their children to be able to read the Bible. The law required parents to provide instruction for their children so that they could "read and understand

Colonial butter churn

American Literature

"To My Dear and Loving Husband"
Anne Bradstreet

When John Winthrop's flagship, the Arbella, *set sail for Boston in 1630, the Bradstreet family was on board. Twenty years later, Anne Bradstreet became the first published American poet with her collection* The Tenth Muse Lately Sprung Up in America. *Despite the demands of living in a new settlement and raising eight children, she continued writing and produced some of her finest poetry, including the following personal poem to her husband, Simon Bradstreet.*

If ever two were one, then surely we.
If ever man were loved by wife, then thee;
If ever wife was happy in a man,
Compare with me, ye women, if you can.
I prize thy love more than whole mines
  of gold

Or all the riches the East doth hold.
My love is such that rivers cannot quench,
Nor ought but love from thee, give
  recompense.
Thy love is such I can no way repay,
The heavens reward thee manifold I pray.
Then while we live, in love let's so
  persevere
That when we live no more, we may
  live ever.

Understanding Literature

1. What value does Bradstreet place on her marriage?

2. What lines in the poem suggest the type of marriage that Bradstreet had and her feelings about it?

the principles of religion and the capital laws of the country." This was one of the first public education laws in Europe or the Americas.

As a result of the new law all towns in New England with 50 or more households were required to appoint someone to teach both male and female children to read and write. In small communities most teachers were female church members. Larger towns also had schools run by male teachers and that were attended only by boys. To serve the colony's need for higher education, colonist John Harvard and the General Court founded Harvard College to teach ministers in 1636. By 1700 about 70 percent of men and 45 percent of women in New England could read and write. These figures were much higher than those for colonists in Virginia, where fewer people were concerned about education.

★ Dissent in Massachusetts

In 1636 minister Thomas Hooker and his followers left Massachusetts partly because of religious disagreements and founded Connecticut, another New England colony. In 1639 Hooker established the **Fundamental Orders of Connecticut**, a set of principles defining the powers of colonial government. These allowed more men to vote in elections than did Massachusetts laws.

Williams and Rhode Island

Roger Williams, another minister who disagreed with the leadership of Massachusetts, also left the colony. After staying in Plymouth with the Pilgrims for two years, Williams returned to Massachusetts in 1633. He then began calling for a complete separation of his church from the other New England congregations. Williams also said that the General Court had no authority in spiritual matters, and he criticized it for taking land from Indians without paying them. Puritan officials felt that these criticisms threatened the colony.

To punish Williams for his actions, the leaders of the colony forced him to leave Massachusetts, never to return. Williams took some of his supporters to southern New England, where they purchased land from the Narraganset Indians in 1636. On this land they established a new settlement called Providence, which later became the New England colony of Rhode Island. Williams eventually received a charter for his small settlement in 1644. In Providence, Williams supported the separation of the church from politics, religious tolerance for all members of the community, and fair dealings with Indians.

HISTORICAL DOCUMENTS

Fundamental Orders of Connecticut

1639

This excerpt describes the structure of the government created by the citizens of Connecticut in 1639.

❝It is ordered . . . that there shall be yearly two general assemblies or courts: . . . The first shall be called the Court of Election, wherein shall be yearly chosen . . . public officers . . . which choice shall be made by all that are admitted freemen and have taken the oath of fidelity [faithfulness]. . . . It is ordered . . . that . . . [each town] shall have power . . . to send four of their freemen as their deputies to every general court; . . . which deputies shall have the power of the whole town to give their votes and allowance to all such laws and orders as may be for the public good, and unto which the said towns are to be bound.❞

Understanding Primary Sources

1. Who elected the public officials in Connecticut?
2. How are the people represented in the General Court?

Roger Williams gains the aid of the Narraganset Indians after being banished from Massachusetts.

The Trial of Anne Hutchinson

Shortly after Williams established Providence, more colonists began openly disagreeing with several Puritan beliefs. Some of these people moved to Williams's community, while others continued speaking out in Massachusetts.

In Boston, Anne Hutchinson soon angered authorities by publicly discussing religious ideas that some leaders thought radical. For example, Hutchinson and other dissenters thought that people's relationship with God did not require guidance from the clergy. Nor did she believe that the performance of good deeds on Earth was a sign of being one of God's elect. Hutchinson began to attract a number of followers, including important community members, who met regularly at her home for religious discussions.

Hutchinson's teachings alarmed Puritan leaders such as John Winthrop. Puritan officials were greatly offended that Hutchinson dared to speak out, in part because women were supposed to follow only the teachings of men in Puritan society. Winthrop told her, "We do not mean to discourse [discuss] with your sex."

Hutchinson was put on trial for her beliefs. When the General Court questioned her, she said that God

66 did open unto me . . . and upon this he [God] did discover [reveal] the ministry unto me and ever since . . . he hath let me see which was the clear ministry and which the wrong. 99

Hutchinson said she had learned these ideas through "an immediate revelation" from God. This private revelation particularly troubled the court, because Puritans believed that God's teachings were in the Bible, not in later revelations. The court decided to banish her from the colony.

With a group of followers, Hutchinson helped to found the new colony of Portsmouth on Aquidneck Island, in Rhode Island. Eventually, she moved to a Dutch settlement on Long Island, in present-day New York, where she was killed by American Indians in a 1643 attack.

⭐ The Salem Witch Trials

Community conflict peaked in New England with the Salem witch trials of 1692. Many colonists had brought a belief in witches with them to America from Europe. Fearful citizens held witchcraft trials in much of New England, particularly in the late 1690s. However, the largest number of cases appeared in Salem, Massachusetts, when the local

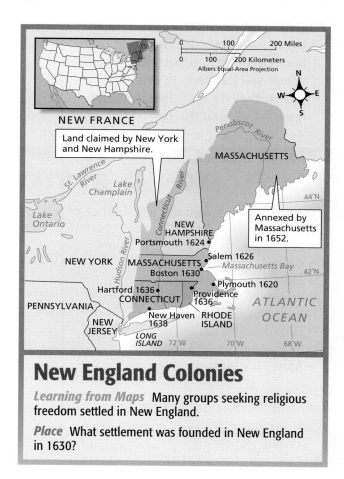

New England Colonies

Learning from Maps Many groups seeking religious freedom settled in New England.

Place What settlement was founded in New England in 1630?

doctors suspected witchcraft after the daughter and niece of Salem's minister began suffering from fits. Authorities blamed these fits on an enslaved girl, Tituba, who had supposedly entertained the girls by telling their fortunes.

Soon a group of girls began accusing many women and a few men in the community of casting spells on them. A special court was organized to decide these cases. During the trial the young girls often screamed and fainted when someone accused of witchcraft entered the room. Witnesses claimed to have seen witches speaking with the devil. One seven-year-old girl claimed that her mother was a witch who had visited her in the form of a cat. When asked by the judges, "How did you know that it was your mother?" the girl replied, "The cat told me so."

The courts frequently pressured the suspected witches to confess. One woman found guilty of witchcraft in Andover, Massachusetts, protested against this treatment:

Colonist George Jacobs, shown kneeling, was one of the few men convicted of witchcraft and hanged as a result of the Salem witch trials.

❝There was no other way to save our lives . . . but by our confessing. . . . Some time after, when we were better composed [calmed], . . . we did profess [insist] that we were innocent and ignorant of such things.❞

More than 100 colonists, including people living outside of Salem, were accused of witchcraft. The trials eventually resulted in the execution of 19 people. By the next year many of the local officials and clergymen involved in the witchcraft trials began to regret their participation. Judge Samuel Sewell became one of the first to apologize publicly for his role in the injustices of the Salem court. The Salem witch trials represented another kind of danger facing the Puritans as they tried to create their ideal colony.

SECTION 3 REVIEW

Identify and explain the significance of the following:
- dissenters
- Great Migration
- John Winthrop
- covenant
- town meeting
- Fundamental Orders of Connecticut
- Roger Williams
- Anne Hutchinson

Reading for Content Understanding

1 **Main Idea** What role did religion and the church play in New England?

2 **Main Idea** Why did Puritan leaders expel Roger Williams and Anne Hutchinson from Massachusetts?

3 **Global Relations** Why did about 80,000 people leave England between 1629 and 1640? Why did some of them come to America?

4 **Writing** *Persuading* Imagine that you are a Puritan living in Massachusetts. Write a letter to your cousins in England, persuading them to move to America.

5 **Critical Thinking** *Drawing Conclusions* Why do you think the Puritans were so harsh with those accused of witchcraft?

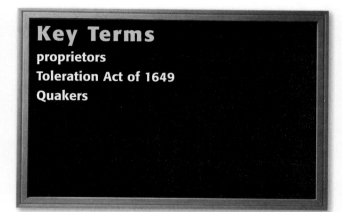

SECTION 4

The Southern and Middle Colonies

Reading Focus

Why did Lord Baltimore establish Maryland, and how did it differ from the other colonies?

How did the middle colonies develop?

For whom was the colony of Georgia originally established?

Key Terms

proprietors
Toleration Act of 1649
Quakers

S THE ENGLISH SHIP the Ark sailed into Chesapeake Bay, one passenger—Father Andrew White— looked out in wonder. He called the Potomac the "greatest river I have seene, so that the Thames is but a little finger to it. There are no marshes or swampes about it." The Ark and its sister ship, the Dove, landed along the banks of the Potomac in March 1634. The colonists on board—primarily Catholics—felt great relief at the end of their long voyage. On the riverbank, Father White and another priest, Father John Altham, led these colonists in making a cross out of a large tree to celebrate their first Catholic mass in North America.

Maryland's St. Ignatius Church, established in 1641

⭐ Tolerant Maryland

Many English Catholics came to America for the same reason as many Puritan immigrants—to escape religious persecution. Catholics in England were not allowed to worship freely because they opposed England's separation from the Roman Catholic Church. English leaders also feared that English Catholics would ally with foreign Catholic nations such as France and Spain. In the 1620s George Calvert, the first Lord Baltimore, asked King Charles I for a charter establishing a new

colony in America for Catholics. By the time Charles issued the charter in 1632, however, Calvert had died. Calvert's son, Cecilius—the second Lord Baltimore—took over the planning of the southern colony, which he called Maryland in honor of England's queen Henrietta Maria. (Mary is the English form of Maria.)

Maryland was a proprietary colony, meaning that **proprietors**, or owners, controlled the government. This colony was located just north of Virginia in the Chesapeake Bay area. In 1634 about 200 colonists arrived in Maryland. They bought

The English Colonies **111**

land from American Indians and built a fort, a storehouse, and a chapel.

About 25 of the first colonists were wealthy landowners, while the rest were servants, craftspeople, and farmers. Having learned from the experience of the Jamestown colonists, settlers in Maryland focused on raising corn, cattle, and hogs so that they would have enough to eat. Before long, however, many colonists devoted their energies to growing tobacco for profit. Because most of the colonists were men, there was initially little family life in Maryland.

Although Catholics established Maryland, an increasing number of Protestants began moving there in the 1640s. Soon religious conflicts arose between Catholics and Protestants in the colony. To ease these rising tensions, Lord Baltimore presented the colonial assembly with a bill that became the **Toleration Act of 1649**. The act, which made restricting the religious rights of Christians a crime, was the first law supporting religious tolerance passed in the English colonies. The act stated:

> **❝ No person or persons whatsoever within this province . . . professing [claiming] to believe in Jesus Christ shall . . . be any ways troubled, molested [persecuted], or . . . any way compelled [forced] to the belief or exercise of any other religion against his or her consent. ❞**

While the Toleration Act did not prevent religious conflict, it did represent an effort to provide some religious freedom for minority groups and to protect their rights.

★ The Carolinas

In 1663 Charles II—whom the English legislature invited to restore the monarchy after the death of Oliver Cromwell—gave much of the land between Virginia and Spanish Florida to eight of his supporters. These colonial proprietors named this new southern colony Carolina, which is a Latin form of the name *Charles*. At first Carolina was a single colony made up of two widely separated areas of settlement, which colonists came to call North and South Carolina. As a result of the distance between the two regions, the proprietors allowed each area to have its own governor. In 1729 North and South Carolina finally became separate colonies.

Most of the colonists in North Carolina were poor farmers who had moved south from Virginia. Many of these farmers raised just enough food to feed their families, while some traded small amounts of tobacco and corn with New England merchants. Unlike Virginia, there were few plantations. North Carolina had no towns or churches until the town of Bath was founded in 1704 by French Huguenots.

The Granger Collection, New York

The port of Charles Town, South Carolina, in 1739

Colonial settlement in South Carolina began in 1670 when three ships arrived from London with about 100 settlers. The colonists soon founded the port of Charles Town, which later became Charleston. Colonists who paid their own way to South Carolina received grants of land, some of which were very large. South Carolina attracted many settlers from other English colonies, particularly those in the British West Indies. The Caribbean colonists brought enslaved Africans with them. South Carolina became one of the first colonies to rely on slave labor.

During the first 20 years of settlement colonists in South Carolina struggled to grow enough food for themselves. Some colonists thought that rice might thrive in South Carolina's hot, humid lowland swamps, but they had little experience growing the crop. Many historians believe that African laborers taught the colonists how to raise rice successfully in the 1690s. By the 1700s wealthy farmer James Glen declared, "the only Commodity of Consequence [importance] produced in South Carolina is Rice."

Rice production required many workers. Plantation owners chose to meet their growing labor needs by expanding slavery in South Carolina. By 1730, almost 20,000 enslaved Africans were living in the colony, compared to only 10,000 whites. South Carolina was the only mainland colony with a higher population of enslaved Africans than free whites.

By that time the Carolinas had become royal colonies. In 1729 the English government officially bought the colonies from the proprietors, whose poor management had failed to satisfy the colonists.

 ## Diversity in New York and New Jersey

In 1664, the year after the eight proprietors received their charter for the Carolinas, the English sought control of the Dutch colony of New Netherland. The Dutch had founded New

Dutch governor Peter Stuyvesant lost his right leg during his years as a soldier.

The Wrath of Peter Stuyvesant, painting by Asher B. Durand from the Collection of the New York Historical Society.

Netherland in 1624 as a trading post for exchanging furs with the Iroquois.

Life in New Netherland

The center of the fur trade in New Netherland was the town of New Amsterdam, located on Manhattan Island. Colonists in New Amsterdam were mainly fur traders and farmers. Generous land grants and religious tolerance soon brought Jews, French Huguenots, Puritans, and others to the colony. A small number of Africans came to work as domestic servants and laborers, while others were brought by European colonists as slaves.

Director General Peter Stuyvesant (STY-vi-suhnt) took control of the colony beginning in 1645. Stuyvesant was an old soldier with a wooden leg who ruled the colony as a dictator. He openly broke the law by selling guns to the local American Indians, and he raised taxes and jailed colonists who could not pay them. Colonists wrote to the Netherlands to complain about Stuyvesant's abuses, including his manner of insulting people "in foul language better fitting the fishmarket than the council board." Despite these problems, Stuyvesant helped the colony by leading the capture of a Swedish fort in 1655. This action increased New Netherland's land and security.

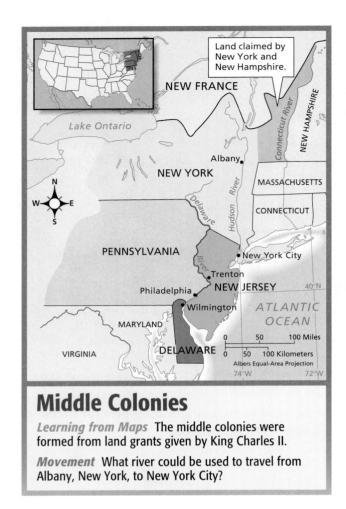

Middle Colonies

Learning from Maps The middle colonies were formed from land grants given by King Charles II.

Movement What river could be used to travel from Albany, New York, to New York City?

The Establishment of New York

In 1664 the English challenged the Dutch claim to the territory occupied by New Netherland. Peter Stuyvesant tried to rally the colonists to defend Dutch control. However, a large English force organized by Charles II's brother, the Duke of York, arrived in New Amsterdam's harbor. The fleet forced Stuyvesant to surrender before any shots were fired.

New Netherland became an English colony and was renamed New York, in honor of the duke. New York became the first of the middle colonies. Most Dutch settlers remained in the colony. Their contributions to colonial society include Dutch words that remain in the American vocabulary, such as *boss, cookie, crib, stoop,* and *kill*.

The Establishment of New Jersey

Shortly after the conquest of New Netherland in 1664, the Duke of York granted lands between the Hudson and Delaware Rivers to Sir George Carteret and Lord John Berkeley. They became proprietors of New Jersey, another middle colony. The colony had a diverse population, including Dutch, Swedes, Finns, and Scots.

Eventually, Carteret and Berkeley were joined by other proprietors and divided New Jersey into an eastern and western province. England united East and West New Jersey into a single royal colony in 1702.

★ Experiments in Pennsylvania

The Society of Friends, or the **Quakers**, made up one of the largest groups in New Jersey. The Quakers were a Protestant sect founded by George Fox and other religious leaders around 1647 in England. Quakers believed that all people were worthy of divine salvation and were guided by an "inner light," or goodness, that could be developed. They rejected formal religious practices and dressed plainly.

The Quakers believed in the equality of the sexes before God, religious tolerance for all peoples, and nonviolence. Many Quakers, such as John Woolman, also felt "that Liberty was the natural Right of all Men equally." Holding such beliefs shocked most Christians. As a result,

Colonial Quakers attending a meeting

Quakers were persecuted in both England and America.

One proprietor of the New Jersey colony was a Quaker named William Penn. Penn's father was a retired naval officer who had loaned large amounts of money to King Charles II. When Penn became dissatisfied with the other leaders of New Jersey and wished to found a larger colony under his personal control, he went to the king for help. In 1681 Charles II agreed to pay off his debts to Penn's father by granting Penn a charter to begin a colony west of New Jersey.

This middle colony, known as Pennsylvania, grew rapidly because Penn advertised throughout Europe for colonists and offered generous amounts of land. Penn wrote that he wanted "people . . . concerned about the future. They both understand and promote good discipline and just government." In addition, Penn's colony offered religious freedom to all Christians and a government that Penn hoped would "secure [protect] the people from the abuse of power . . . for liberty without obedience is

Courtesy of the Pennsylvania Academy of the Fine Arts, Philadelphia. Gift of Mrs. Sarah Harrison (The Joseph Harrison, Jr. Collection)

Pennsylvania proprietor William Penn signs a peace treaty with local Indians on one of his trips to America.

slavery." His system offered colonists benefits such as government care for the poor.

Some of the largest groups to arrive in the colony were Welsh and Irish Quakers. Another major group were Germans, who became known as the Pennsylvania Dutch, after the word

Linking Past to Present

Public Schools

Modern American classrooms are filled with young men and women learning together about many different subjects, such as English, math, history, and science. Students might also learn a foreign language or how to play a musical instrument. Job-related skills are also taught in some classes, such as how to sew, repair cars, or use computers.

In 1683—more than 300 years ago—Quaker officials in Pennsylvania passed laws requiring all children in the colony to learn how to read and write. Quaker leaders also decided to provide free schooling for poor children.

William Penn, founder of Pennsylvania, also supported the teaching of "useful knowledge," or work skills, in schools. Although Quaker Thomas Budd thought that all children should be given job training,

he believed that males and females should attend separate classes and learn very different skills. According to Budd, boys should be instructed in a trade, such as "the making of mathematical instruments, . . . the making of clocks and watches, weaving, [and] shoe-making." Girls, thought Budd, should learn the "spinning of flax and wool, and knitting of gloves and stockings, sewing, and making of all sorts of useful needlework."

Understanding What You Read

1. Why do you think Budd believed that young men and women should learn different skills?

2. What kind of learning did Penn advise for young people?

Deutsch, meaning "German." Most of these colonists became farmers and helped create a peaceful and stable society in Pennsylvania. Few proprietors ever visited their colonies. Penn was an exception. He treated local American Indians with respect, learning the language of the local Delaware Indians so he could speak with them more effectively.

Penn built the capital of his colony—a city he named Philadelphia, or City of Brotherly Love—between the Delaware and Schuylkill Rivers. Penn designed Philadelphia himself, laying it out in a checkerboard pattern that became a model used by city planners in other colonies. Pennsylvania expanded in 1682 when the Duke of York sold Penn a region to the south of Pennsylvania called Delaware. Delaware remained part of Pennsylvania, sharing the same governor, until it separated in 1776, becoming the fourth middle colony.

⭐ The Ideal of Georgia

The English also established the southern colony of Georgia. In 1732 King George II granted a charter to James Oglethorpe and other trustees to found a colony for poor English citizens, such as those who had been jailed for debt. The king hoped that Georgia would serve as a buffer between South Carolina and Spanish Florida.

In 1733 Oglethorpe and 120 other colonists from England founded the settlement of Savannah near the mouth of the Savannah River. Oglethorpe carefully designed the town as a series of squares divided into lots for houses and farms. Many of the early colonists in Georgia were German, Swiss, and Welsh Protestants. Jewish settlers also moved to Savannah. Accompanying Oglethorpe was Methodist minister John Wesley, who wanted to preach to the colonists and to convert American Indians living in the area. Oglethorpe had high hopes for the Georgia settlement. He wrote:

❝ **The examples of other colonies**

Founding the Colonies

	COLONY	DATE OF SETTLEMENT	REASON FOR FOUNDING
NEW ENGLAND COLONIES	Massachusetts: *Plymouth*	1620	Religious freedom
	Massachusetts Bay	1630	Religious freedom
	New Hampshire	1623	Farming
	Connecticut	c. 1633	Trade; farming; religious freedom
	Rhode Island	1636	Religious freedom
MIDDLE COLONIES	New York	c. 1624	Trade (originally settled by the Dutch; became an English colony in 1664)
	Delaware	1638	Trade (originally settled by the Swedish; became part of the English colonies in 1664; was part of the Pennsylvania colony from 1682 until 1776)
	New Jersey	1660	Religious freedom; farming (originally settled by the Dutch; became an English colony in 1664)
	Pennsylvania	1643	Religious freedom (originally settled by the Swedish; land granted to William Penn in 1681; first Quaker colony established in 1682)
SOUTHERN COLONIES	Virginia: *Jamestown*	1607	To establish a permanent colony; search for riches
	Maryland	1634	Religious freedom; farming
	Carolinas	1669	Trade; farming
	Georgia	1733	Relief for poor people; buffer against Spanish Florida

suggest that the new colony will succeed. . . . Georgia is even more likely to succeed than either Virginia or Pennsylvania were.❞

Oglethorpe was determined that Georgia would develop differently from the other southern colonies, which had large plantations ruled by a few wealthy individuals. He hoped that the colony would fill with poor farmers who had some skills. To accomplish this goal, Oglethorpe outlawed slavery and limited the size of land grants to 500 acres each. He also gave each colonist free passage to Georgia, as well as cattle, land, and food until they could provide for themselves. Oglethorpe defended his actions by arguing that "the good discipline established by the people who govern the colony will reform the lives of the settlers."

Soon, however, the settlers grew unhappy with Oglethorpe's strict rules. Many settlers wanted to develop large plantations worked by slaves. Colonists were also unhappy that Georgia's

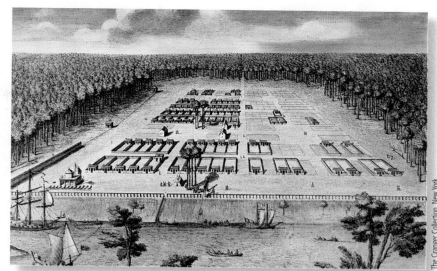

James Oglethorpe carefully planned the town of Savannah, Georgia.

The Granger Collection, New York

colonial government had outlawed the importing of rum and other liquor.

The colonists' dissatisfaction grew. In 1752 the trustees of Georgia gave up their charter. The English government then made Georgia a royal colony. Many of Oglethorpe's restrictions were eliminated. Coastal Georgia soon filled with vast rice plantations worked by thousands of slaves, while elsewhere in the colony poor farmers struggled to survive.

SECTION 4 REVIEW

Identify and explain the significance of the following:
- **Cecilius Calvert**
- **proprietors**
- **Toleration Act of 1649**
- **Peter Stuyvesant**
- **Quakers**
- **William Penn**
- **James Oglethorpe**

Reading for Content Understanding

1 **Main Idea** Why did many Catholics leave England and settle in Maryland?

2 **Main Idea** How were the colonies of New York and New Jersey created?

3 **Geographic Diversity** *Movement* What colony did William Penn found? Why did many Europeans move there?

4 **Writing** *Creating* Make a poster that James Oglethorpe might have used to attract settlers to Georgia. Your poster should list reasons why people would want to settle in the colony.

5 **Critical Thinking** *Synthesizing Information* Of the colonies described in this chapter, where do you think that you would have most liked to live? Where would you have least liked to live? Explain your answer.

CHAPTER 4 REVIEW

Chapter Summary

In 1607 a group of English colonists established a settlement in Virginia. At first they were aided by the Powhatan Indians, but conflicts later arose between the two groups. Many people came to America hoping to make their fortunes. Other groups—such as the Puritans, Quakers, and Catholics—left England to escape religious persecution. Each group established its own colony and grew its own crops for food and trade. ■

On a separate sheet of paper, complete the following activities.

Identifying People and Ideas

Describe the historical significance of the following:

1. John Rolfe
2. headright
3. House of Burgesses
4. sect
5. William Bradford
6. Squanto
7. covenant
8. John Winthrop
9. Toleration Act of 1649
10. Anne Hutchinson

go.hrw.com
SA0 Jamestown
Newspaper

Internet Activity

Search the Internet through the HRW Web site to find information about John Smith, Pocahontas, or John Rolfe. Then use that information to write an obituary for the person that might have appeared in a Jamestown newspaper.

Understanding Main Ideas

1. Why did the Jamestown colonists frequently clash with the Powhatan?
2. What caused Bacon's Rebellion?
3. In what ways did American Indians help the Pilgrims survive in Plymouth?
4. What role did religion play in shaping Puritan life in New England?
5. Why did John Winthrop banish Anne Hutchinson from Massachusetts?
6. How were each of the Carolina colonies different from Oglethorpe's Georgia colony?

Reviewing Themes

1. **Geographic Diversity**   How did climate and geography affect the colonies' development?
2. **Economic Development**   Why were indentured servants and enslaved Africans important to the southern colonies' economy?
3. **Cultural Diversity**   Why did Catholics, Puritans, and Quakers immigrate to America?

Using the Time Line

Number your paper from 1 to 6. Match the letters on the time line below with the following events.

1. Roger Williams establishes Providence, the first permanent settlement in present-day Rhode Island.
2. The Pilgrims sign the Mayflower Compact.
3. James Oglethorpe and 120 other colonists from England found Savannah, Georgia.
4. George Fox founds the Society of Friends.
5. A small group of colonists arrive in Virginia and establish the Jamestown colony.
6. The first Africans in Virginia arrive on board a passing Dutch ship.

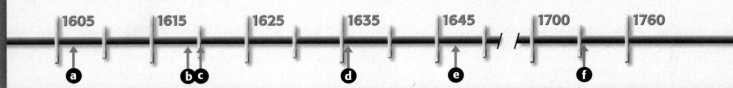

1605   1615   1625   1635   1645   1700   1760

a   b c   d   e   f

Thinking Critically

1. **Making Comparisons** How did Roger Williams and William Penn differ from many other colonists in their dealings with American Indians?

2. **Drawing Conclusions** Why might the Quaker faith have attracted colonial women? Explain your answer.

3. **Identifying Cause and Effect** What conditions contributed to the differences between the Jamestown and Plymouth settlements?

Writing About History

1. **Expressing** Imagine that you are John Smith. Write a description for a London journal about your experiences in America.

2. **Informing** Write a paragraph explaining how religious conflicts in England affected the settlement of Maryland.

Building Your Portfolio

Complete the following activities individually or in groups.

1. **Settling a New Land** The first Jamestown settlers lacked the skills necessary for survival. Some were goldsmiths, while others were jewelers. Imagine that you are putting together a group of colonists to settle in America. Decide how many people to take with you, what kinds of occupations they should have, and where to settle. Make sure you explain the reasons for each choice. Then write a short play about your first month in the settlement. You may wish to perform your play for the class.

2. **The Thirteen Colonies** You are an English merchant traveling through all the thirteen colonies to find new trade goods. Create a travel journal of your trip through the colonies. Include a map showing your route; descriptions of the people, places, and types of goods you encounter; and perhaps drawings of interesting things you see along the way. Your journal should have at least one entry for each colony.

Linking Geography and History

1. **Location** Why did the early colonists in America establish colonies near rivers and the Atlantic Ocean?

2. **Region** Why would slavery and indentured servitude have been more important in the southern colonies than in New England?

History Skills Workshop

Reading Maps Study the map below. Then answer the following questions: (a) Which colonies are known as the New England colonies? (b) Which colonies are known as the southern colonies? (c) Which colonies are known as the middle colonies? (d) Which group of colonies contained the most major seaports?

The Thirteen Colonies

▪ CHAPTER 5 ▪
Life in the English Colonies
(1630–1760)

In 1743 Benjamin Franklin remarked, "The first Drudgery [dull work] of Settling new Colonies, which confines the attention of People to mere necessaries, is now pretty well over." While earlier colonists had focused much of their energy on struggling to survive, in the 1700s colonists could spend more time improving their standard of living.

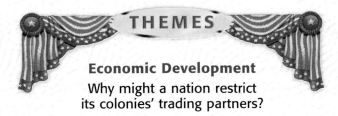

THEMES

Economic Development
Why might a nation restrict its colonies' trading partners?

Geographic Diversity
How might geography affect a region's economy?

Science and Technology
What effect might scientific discoveries have on a society?

1630   1650   1670   1690

1636 Harvard College is founded.

1660 Parliament passes a Navigation Act requiring the colonies to sell certain goods only to England.

1686 The Dominion of New England is established.

Forms of Government

Reading Focus

In what ways did the colonists exercise control in their local governments and courts?

Why did James II establish the Dominion of New England, and how did the colonists react?

How did the Glorious Revolution affect the colonies?

Key Terms

Privy Council
Parliament
bicameral legislature
libel
Dominion of New England
Glorious Revolution

ONE BRIGHT SEPTEMBER MORNING, *William Byrd II rose at 5 A.M., said his prayers, and began the business of running his Virginia plantation. After a few hours, he met Colonel Bassett and rode with him to Williamsburg. In the busy colonial capital, Byrd met with several members of the Council—the core of the colony's government. Having been persuaded to become a member of the Council, Byrd agreed to be sworn in that day. It was an important step in his political career. He wrote in his diary, "God grant I may distinguish myself with honor and good conscience."*

William Byrd II

IMAGE ON LEFT PAGE: *The growing colonial city of Philadelphia*

1710 **1730** **1750**

1700 Samuel Sewall publishes an essay arguing against slavery.

1730 John Smibert holds the first art exhibition in America.

1738 George Whitefield arrives in the colonies.

1752 Benjamin Franklin proves that lightning is a form of electricity.

1733 John Peter Zenger publishes criticisms of the royal governor of New York.

Life in the English Colonies **121**

The Virginia House of Burgesses meeting in the 1600s

★ Governing the Colonies

When founded, each of the original thirteen English colonies in America had established its own form of government. These colonies operated independently of one another. Depending on who held their charter, the colonies fell into three categories: proprietary, company, or royal. The power to grant charters belonged to the English monarch, who owned all of the American colonies. A group of royal advisers called the **Privy Council** set policy for the thirteen colonies.

Organization

Although the Privy Council established English colonial policies, the colonies mostly governed themselves. For example, Rhode Island's 1644 charter contained the requirement that all laws should "be conformable to [agree with] the Laws of England," but also stated that the colonists had "full Power and Authority to rule themselves."

Each colony had a governor, who served as head of the colony's government. In royal colonies the English monarch appointed the governors. A few colonies, such as Connecticut, elected their governors. Most colonial governors were assisted by advisory councils that were either appointed by the governor or elected by the colonists.

Colonial Assemblies

In some cases, colonists elected representatives to an assembly that made laws and set policy. The colonies' assemblies were modeled on the English **Parliament**, or national legislature. Parliament has a **bicameral legislature**—a law-making body made up of two houses, or groups.

The first assembly formed in the thirteen colonies met in 1619 in Jamestown, Virginia. The governor's council and the Virginia Company chose members for the Council of State, one house of the assembly. The colony's 1621 charter stated that the House of Burgesses—the assembly's second house—should consist of "two Burgesses [representatives] out of every town, . . . to be respectfully chosen by the inhabitants." The Plymouth and Massachusetts Bay Colonies also established elected assemblies in the early years of settlement.

Colonial assemblies generally submitted legislation to the colonial governor for approval. Then the Privy Council reviewed the colonial laws to ensure that they followed the laws of England.

At times, assemblies and governors struggled for control of the colonies. Governors had the authority to carry out English policy, set by Parliament, and English colonial policy, set by the Privy Council. However, the assemblies could influence governors' actions by refusing to pay their salaries. Colonial assemblies also had the power to raise taxes, organize local governments, and control the military. One member of the House of Burgesses noted the power the assembly held over the governor:

    66 **Our government . . . is so happily constituted [designed] that a governor must first outwit us before he can oppress us. And if he ever squeezes money out of us he must first take care to deserve it.** 99

Despite such conflicts, the Privy Council allowed most colonies to run their own affairs.

Linking Past to Present

Town Meetings

Watertown, Massachusetts, which held its first meeting in the 1630s, is known as the "cradle of the town meeting." In New England communities like Watertown, people gathered to discuss issues such as dividing up land, planning roadways, or raising taxes. Town meetings continue to be a popular form of local government in New England.

Today the term *town meeting* refers to any meeting, even on a national level, that is open to the public to discuss community issues. For example, a series of town meetings allowed Virginians to voice their concerns about health care, leading to recommendations for the state's improvement of community services. The U.S. government also has organized town meetings to share information with Americans and to let citizens voice their opinions about issues such as the future of nuclear science and community improvements.

In recent years, presidential candidates have held town meetings across the country to give American voters the chance to ask questions and make their views known. Candidates also have held electronic town meetings to give more Americans the opportunity to participate. During such an electronic town meeting, the candidate typically appears on television before a live audience, and Americans can phone in with questions and issues. As one of President Bill Clinton's appointees noted:

66 *The whole notion of town meetings has caught on. Everyone wants to have one. The town meeting movement seems to me to be a magnificent opportunity to catch the whole country up in a common effort.* 99

Citizens gather at the annual town meeting in Hebron, Maine, to discuss local issues.

Understanding What You Read

1. How are electronic town meetings held?
2. Do you think town meetings are an effective means of political participation?

Town Meetings

In addition to having legislatures, New England colonies developed a tradition of holding annual town meetings. All the men in the community would meet to decide important town issues and to select a group of officials who would carry out the town's decisions. Town meetings were less common in the southern colonies because people tended to live farther away from one another. For this reason, many decisions were made at the county level. The middle colonies used both of these methods in their decision-making processes.

Colonial Courts

Colonial courts made up another important part of colonial governments. While royal officials could have a strong influence on colonial courts, the courts generally reflected the interests and beliefs of their local communities. For example, many laws in Massachusetts enforced the Puritans' religious beliefs. Laws based on the Bible, rather than on English common law, set the standard for the community's conduct.

Sometimes colonial courts also protected individual freedoms. For example, a court case involving John Peter Zenger established colonists' right to freedom of the press. In 1733 Zenger published criticisms in his newspaper of the royal governor of New York. Officials accused Zenger of **libel**, a false written statement that damages a person's reputation. He was then arrested and charged with libel against a public official.

At his trial Zenger's attorney, Andrew Hamilton, argued that Zenger had the right to publish whatever he wished, as long as it could be proven to be true. The chief justice of the court disagreed with this argument, explaining to the jury that "nothing can be worse to any government than to have people attempt to create distrust and dislike of the management of it." The jury declared Zenger not guilty, agreeing with Hamilton's defense that a person had the right to print harmful information if it was true. The jury's decision showed its dislike of the royal governor and its belief that colonists had a right to voice their opinions openly. Whenever possible, colonists used the courts to extend their control over local affairs.

The Dominion of New England

In 1685 James II became king of England after the death of his brother Charles II. James was determined to take more control over the English government, both in England and in the colonies. James and other English leaders believed that the colonies had too much independence—from one another and from England—and therefore were too difficult to manage. The king began suspending the colonies' original charters. In 1686 he united the New England colonies under one government called the **Dominion of New England**.

The Dominion eventually included New Hampshire, Massachusetts, Maine, Connecticut, and Rhode Island, as well as the middle colonies of New York and New Jersey. James appointed a royal governor and council to rule the Dominion. The king's actions greatly upset the colonists, particularly because, as one colonist grumbled, the Dominion was "without any liberty for an Assembly."

James appointed Sir Edmund Andros, a former governor of New York, to be governor in chief of the Dominion. Andros proved to be very unpopular with the colonists. One angry colonist explained:

> 66 **Sir Edmund Andros arrived as our governor; who besides his power, with the advice and consent of his Council, to make laws and raise taxes as he pleased, had also authority by himself to muster and employ all persons residing in the territory. . . . And several companies of soldiers were now brought from Europe to support what was to be imposed upon us.** 99

When a number of the residents of Ipswich, Massachusetts, protested Andros's taxation policy, they were arrested and jailed. To prevent further protests, Andros used his royal authority to limit the powers of town governments.

A plate picturing King James II

Although unpopular with colonists, Sir Edmund Andros was a favorite official of King James II.

The Glorious Revolution

James II's attempts to centralize power were just as unpopular in England as they were in the colonies. His policies—particularly his efforts to change England from a Protestant nation back to a Catholic nation—threatened Parliament's power. As a result, Parliament asked the rulers of the Netherlands—James's Protestant daughter Mary and her Dutch husband, William of Orange—to lead England. When William landed in England with his army in the fall of 1688, James fled the country. The overthrow of James II became known as the **Glorious Revolution**.

When residents of the Dominion learned that James had been overthrown, they removed Andros from his post as governor. The delighted colonists sent Andros to England to answer for his actions. The colonies in the Dominion quickly formed new assemblies and sent declarations of support for William and Mary's new government. In time, the monarchs issued new charters for the colonies. The governments of the Dominion colonies were essentially restored.

The new charters differed very little from the original ones, except in Massachusetts. In that colony, the governor became appointed by the Crown rather than elected by the colonists.

Protestant colonists celebrated the crowning of King William and Queen Mary with songs and pictures.

In addition, property ownership, instead of full church membership, became the requirement for men to vote. The colony also grew in size with the addition of Plymouth to its territory.

The political ideas of the Glorious Revolution led to several acts of Parliament, including the English Bill of Rights of 1689. As a result of such acts, the powers of the English monarchy declined significantly during the reign of William and Mary. The resulting increase in Parliament's powers, at the expense of the Crown, greatly interested American colonists. As time went on, the colonists increasingly valued their own right to elect representatives to decide local issues.

SECTION 1 REVIEW

Identify and explain the significance of the following:

- **Privy Council**
- **Parliament**
- **bicameral legislature**
- **John Peter Zenger**
- **libel**
- **Dominion of New England**
- **Edmund Andros**
- **Glorious Revolution**

Reading for Content Understanding

1 **Main Idea** What responsibilities did assemblies and colonial governors have in the colonies?

2 **Main Idea** Explain why James II established the Dominion of New England, and describe the colonists' reactions.

3 **Citizenship and Democracy** Explain the importance of town meetings and colonial courts in the American colonies.

4 **Writing** *Informing* Imagine that you are a colonist who has just been informed of the overthrow of James II. Write an editorial for a newspaper announcing the Glorious Revolution and its effect on the Dominion of New England.

5 **Critical Thinking** *Determining the Strength of an Argument* Do you think people should be able to publish whatever they wish so long as it is true or do you think further limits should be placed on the press? Explain your answer.

The Growth of Trade

Reading Focus

What were the Navigation Acts, and how did they affect the colonies?

What were some of the colonial trade networks, and what was their importance to the colonial economy?

What was life like for enslaved Africans during the Middle Passage?

Key Terms

mercantilism

balance of trade

imports

exports

Navigation Acts

duties

triangular trade

Middle Passage

T HE BEAT OF A DRUM *signaled the beginning of trade at the slave market. According to former enslaved African Olaudah Equiano (oh-LOW-DUH ek-wee-AHN-oh), the buyers then rushed in to "make choice of the parcel they liked best." African slaves stood terrified amid the noise of the buyers. Cries were heard from Africans who were separated from their families and friends. "Why are parents to lose their children, brothers their sisters, or husbands their wives?" asked Equiano. The answer was money. In the colonial trade network, the buying and selling of African slaves had became an important part of the economy.*

Olaudah Equiano

⭐ The Navigation Acts

Much of the colonies' trade benefited England. One of England's main interests in establishing and controlling its American colonies was economic profit. As one English official argued in 1689, England's North American colonies made up

66 **a full third part of the whole Trade and Navigation of England . . . a great nursery of Our Sea Men and the King's Customs depend mightily thereon.** 99

Regulating Trade

In the late 1600s most western European nations, including England, followed the practice of **mercantilism**—creating and maintaining wealth by carefully controlling trade. English officials wanted to create profits for their country by establishing a favorable **balance of trade**. This meant having fewer **imports**—goods purchased from other countries, than **exports**—goods sold to other countries. As a mercantile power, England concentrated on importing from and exporting to its colonies, although it still traded with foreign nations.

Between 1650 and 1696 Parliament passed a series of **Navigation Acts** to regulate trade with the colonies and to increase England's profits. These acts supported the principles of mercantilism because they required the colonists to do much of their trading with England.

The Navigation Act of 1660 forbade colonists from trading "enumerated articles"—specified items England needed but could not produce—with any country other than England. These goods included sugar, tobacco, and cotton. The act also required colonists to use English ships for transporting goods. Parliament later passed other acts that required all trade goods to pass through English ports, where **duties**, or import taxes, were added to the items. Duties were also added to some goods traded among the English colonies.

Ports, such as the one shown here, were kept busy shipping goods to and from the American colonies.

Materials for Manufactures

Under the mercantilist system, the colonies enjoyed some benefits. The colonies had a protected market, or a guaranteed outlet for their goods. High taxes on imports from outside the colonies made it difficult for foreigners to sell their products in England. The American colonies sold raw materials—such as furs, tobacco, and lumber—and some finished products, such as ships, to England. The colonists bought finished English products such as hardware, machinery, and household items.

English officials argued that the advantages enjoyed by the colonies under the mercantilist system offset most of the disadvantages of the Navigation Acts. Some colonists disagreed, noting that England profited most from the relationship. For example, English demand determined the market price of colonial goods. Sometimes the colonies produced more of a good, such as tobacco, than the English market could absorb. However, under the Navigation Acts the colonies could not directly sell their goods to foreign nations as an alternative market. At times, such restrictions negatively affected colonial economies.

★ American Smugglers

Some colonists complained about the hardships caused by the Navigation Acts. Virginia governor Sir William Berkeley said the acts were "mighty and destructive" to the colony's economy. Despite such complaints, English trade restrictions continued into the 1700s. Smuggling, or the illegal trade of goods, increased as a result of these restrictions. Traders routinely smuggled sugar, molasses, and rum into the colonies from the non-English Caribbean. Parliament's Molasses Act of 1733 required colonists to pay duties on these items. In practice, however, customs officials rarely carried out this law.

While smuggling meant that England collected less money from the colonies, smugglers did not threaten English power. They were therefore often overlooked by customs officials who lacked the desire or ability to enforce trade regulations. One colonial official in Massachusetts complained that he could only enforce the law "with great delay and too many difficulties and discouragements to be easily overcome."

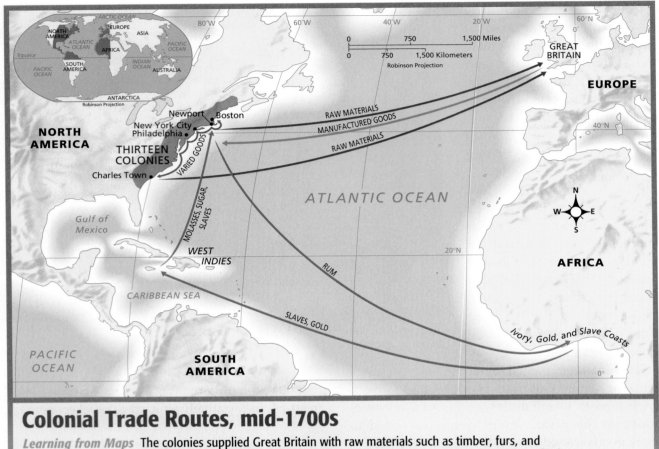

Colonial Trade Routes, mid-1700s

Learning from Maps The colonies supplied Great Britain with raw materials such as timber, furs, and tobacco. They also supplied the West Indies with food, importing molasses and sugar in return. The colonists made these products into rum, which they then exported to Africa, bringing back enslaved Africans.

Region What did Great Britain export to the colonies?

 ## Trade Networks

In 1707 English power expanded with the Act of Union between England and Scotland, which created the United Kingdom of Great Britain. By this time, Great Britain had established trade networks around the world. The British West Indies were very important in the colonial trade network. The colonies sold products—including fish, grain, beef, and horses—to plantation owners in the West Indies. In exchange, the colonists received sugar, molasses, and slaves. Some goods were then shipped to Britain. This pattern developed into a so-called **triangular trade** that involved the colonies, the West Indies, and Britain.

There were several variations on the triangles in colonial trade patterns. For example, some New England traders exchanged rum for slaves on the West African coast. Traders then transported the enslaved Africans to the West Indies and returned to New England with products such as molasses, which was made into rum. Many New England colonists participated in the slave trade. Some of the slave ships were built in New England and owned by New England merchants. Newport, Rhode Island, was a major port for slave ships.

 ## The Middle Passage

The slave trade involved the transport of around 13 million Africans across the Atlantic Ocean to be sold as slaves in North and South America. This terrifying and often deadly voyage was called the **Middle Passage**.

The journey could last as long as three months. Ship captains packed enslaved Africans as tightly as possible, chaining them by the neck and legs.

Enslaved Africans lived between the upper and lower decks of the ship, on the "'tween decks"—in a space hardly three feet high. One ship captain reported that the slaves "had not so much room as a man in his coffin, either in length or breadth. It was impossible for them to turn or shift with any degree of ease." Slave traders fit as many slaves as possible on board to increase profits.

Olaudah Equiano, who was sold into slavery at about the age of 11, described his experiences on the Middle Passage:

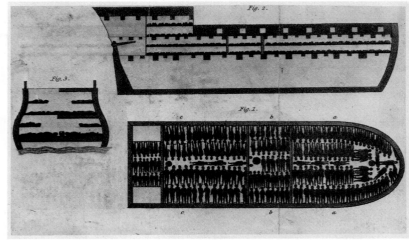

On slave ships like this, each African was confined in a space only about 16 inches wide and 5 1/2 feet long.

❝I was soon put down under the decks, and there I received such a salutation [smell] in my nostrils, as I had never experienced in my life; so that, with the loathsomeness [disgusting quality] of the stench, and crying together, I became so sick and low that I was not able to eat. . . . The shrieks of the women, and the groans of the dying, rendered [made] the whole a scene of horror almost inconceivable [unbelievable].❞

Thousands of captives died during the voyage either from diseases—such as smallpox, dysentery, and malaria—or from being thrown overboard when they became ill.

Some colonists opposed the slave trade. In 1688, Quakers in Germantown, Pennsylvania, made the first recorded colonial protest against slavery. One Quaker declared: "To bring men hither [here], or to rob and sell them . . . we stand against."

Samuel Sewall, a Massachusetts merchant and judge, publicly opposed slavery in 1700 in his pamphlet called *The Selling of Joseph*. Despite these few early protests, slavery existed in all of the colonies. Slave labor and the slave trade had become important parts of the colonial economy.

SECTION 2 REVIEW

Identify and explain the significance of the following:
- mercantilism
- balance of trade
- imports
- exports
- Navigation Acts
- duties
- triangular trade
- Middle Passage
- Olaudah Equiano

Reading for Content Understanding

1 **Main Idea** What effect did the Navigation Acts have on the colonies' economy?

2 **Main Idea** Describe some of the colonial trade networks, and explain why they were important to the colonies.

3 **Economic Development** What advantages did mercantilism give to the colonies? What were the system's disadvantages for the colonies?

4 **Writing** *Creating* Imagine that you are a Quaker in Pennsylvania in 1750. Create a handbill calling for an end to the slave trade. Be sure to describe the living conditions of Africans during the Middle Passage and how those conditions have affected your opposition to the slave trade.

5 **Critical Thinking** *Synthesizing Information* Why did the British allow smuggling to continue in the colonies?

The Colonial Economy

Reading Focus

How did climate and geography affect each region's colonial economy?

What was the labor source in each region, and why did it develop differently?

What roles did women play in the colonial economy?

Key Terms

cash crops
slave codes
apprentices
staple crops

AS LEONARD CALVERT, *the governor of Maryland, lay dying in 1647, he asked that Margaret Brent be brought to his bedside. Brent, who had emigrated from England in 1638 to escape religious persecution, owned a Maryland plantation. Before witnesses, Governor Calvert said to Brent, "I make you my sole executrix [person who carries out a will]. Take all and pay all." The governor trusted Brent to manage his estate wisely because of her considerable business skills and her good reputation for managing plantations.*

Margaret Brent speaking to colonial officials in Maryland

★ The Southern Economy

Large plantations, like Brent's, were common in the southern colonies—Maryland, Virginia, the Carolinas, and Georgia. The southern economy relied on agriculture and raw materials. The southern colonies exported raw materials for building ships, particularly timber, to overseas markets and to its northern neighbors. The region also developed a profitable naval stores industry, producing pitch, turpentine, and tar. Deerskins were another valuable southern trade item.

Agriculture

Small farms as well as large plantations supported the southern agricultural economy, which benefited from a warm climate and long growing season. While the growing conditions were good, they did not meet Virginia governor Robert Beverley's exaggerated claim in 1705 that the colonists "live in so happy a Climate, and have so fertile a Soil, that no body is poor enough to beg, or want Food."

The southern colonies based their agricultural economy on the production of **cash crops**—crops grown mainly to be sold for profits. The primary

This 1670 painting shows enslaved Africans working in the tobacco sheds on a colonial tobacco plantation.

cash crops were tobacco, rice, and indigo. Colonists rarely grew cotton because harvesting it was too difficult and expensive. Some colonies specialized in growing certain crops. For example, Virginia grew tobacco, and South Carolina grew rice and indigo. Indigo was a crop introduced by plantation manager Eliza Lucas (later known as Eliza Lucas Pinckney after her marriage).

Plantations and Slavery

William Byrd II's diary contains a description of a typical day of a plantation owner:

> " I said my prayers and ate milk for breakfast. I walked out to see my people [slaves] at work at the ditch. I read a little geometry. I ate mutton [sheep] for dinner. I walked to the ditch again. In the evening I said my prayers. "

Most of the labor on Byrd's plantation was done by slaves.

The southern colonies' cash crops required a great deal of difficult work and a large labor force. By the 1700s enslaved Africans were the main labor force, rather than indentured servants as was the case in the early years of the colonies. Unlike indentured servants, who could leave after their contracted period of service, enslaved Africans and their children had to work for life.

Slaves worked hard tending fields and performing the skilled labor that was necessary to keep a plantation running. On some plantations, slaves did many of their tasks unsupervised. When a job was finished, slaves were sometimes allowed to do their own work. Some slaves were able to earn enough money to buy their freedom, although this became more difficult as slavery laws became harsher.

Slave Codes

Most of the colonies passed **slave codes**, or laws to control slaves. Slave codes were most extensive in colonies where there were large numbers of slaves, such as South Carolina. This colony's code did not permit slaves to hold meetings or to own weapons, because slaveholders feared that slaves would revolt. Some colonies made it illegal for slaveholders to free their slaves. Members of the Virginia Assembly expressed concern that runaway slaves would commit "injuries to the inhabitants of this dominion [colony]." The Assembly then passed a law allowing people to kill a runaway slave resisting capture.

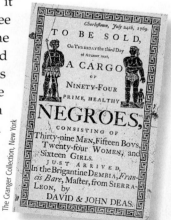

Slave auction poster

Eliza Lucas Pinckney and Indigo

During the colonial period, people used various plants and shellfish to make dyes for fabrics. Blue was one of the most popular dye colors. The finest blue dyes came from an Asian plant called indigo, which Spanish and Portuguese explorers introduced to Europe in the 1600s.

In the early 1700s most indigo came from South Asia or the West Indies. George Lucas was a British plantation owner who had moved his family from the West Indies to South Carolina. While away on military service, he asked his daughter Eliza to raise an indigo crop on the family's plantation.

In 1740 Eliza Lucas (later Eliza Lucas Pinckney) began trying to grow indigo. She also experimented with different ways of removing the valuable blue dye ingredient from the thin, greenish plants. The first attempt at this difficult process ruined an early crop. Despite the many challenges, Lucas remained confident. "I [have] no doubt Indigo will prove a very valuable Commodity [item] in time," she wrote her father. After several years of trial and error, she achieved success and grew a marketable crop.

Removing the blue compounds from indigo was a lengthy process. First, workers packed fresh indigo plants into large outdoor vats and soaked them in water for half a day. Then they drained the liquid into other vats and whipped it with wooden paddles for hours until the bluish "indigo mud" settled to the bottom. This was strained and dried into blue indigo cakes the size of soap bars. It took around 100 pounds of indigo plants to make a single four-ounce indigo bar! Plantation owners relied on skilled slave labor to carry out the time-consuming and numerous steps of indigo production.

Although making indigo bars was a long and complicated process, it was quite profitable. Eliza Lucas Pinckney helped spread indigo throughout the colony. She gave away indigo seeds to many people and helped explain the processing method. By 1747 South Carolina produced more than 135,000 pounds of indigo for export. Eliza Lucas Pinckney went on to perform other agricultural experiments and was a respected figure in colonial society.

Understanding What You Read

1. Why was indigo a valuable crop?

2. How did Eliza Lucas Pinckney contribute to indigo production in the colonies?

3. How were indigo plants turned into bars of indigo?

The Granger Collection, New York

Enslaved Africans on colonial plantations processed indigo in large outdoor vats to remove the valuable dye.

★ The New England Economy

The economy of New England—Connecticut, Massachusetts, New Hampshire, and Rhode Island—was very different from that of the southern colonies. Most New England farmers faced a more difficult agricultural environment. The New England climate was harsh, the soil was rocky, and the few rivers were unsuitable for navigation. For these reasons, few New England farms produced cash crops. They therefore had little demand for large numbers of farm laborers. As a result, slavery as a labor system did not become as important to this region, although it existed throughout New England. Most farming families used their own labor to plant and grow the crops and raise the animals that they needed to survive.

A master potter teaches his craft to a young apprentice, who helps him with the work.

The Granger Collection, New York

The Ocean's Riches

Rich fishing waters and abundant timber made fishing and shipbuilding two of the leading industries in New England. One of the earliest settlers in Massachusetts exclaimed, "Here is a good store of fish, if we had boats to go 8 or 10 leagues to sea to fish in." The waters off New England's coast served as home to a wide variety of fish, including cod, mackerel, and halibut. Dried fish became a major export for merchants in the northern colonies. In addition, whaling provided valuable oil for lighting, and whale meat joined fish as an important and common ingredient in the colonial diet. The demand for shipbuilding grew partly out of the expanding colonial fishing industry in the northern Atlantic.

The extensive commercial activity of the New England seaports also stimulated the building of merchant ships. Shipyards were developed at Boston and Gloucester, Massachusetts, in Portsmouth, New Hampshire, and throughout other New England towns.

Colonial shipyards had a great reputation for building high-quality vessels. Ships made in the colonies brought such high prices that shipowners sometimes told their captains to sell not only their cargo but also the ship itself when they reached their overseas destination.

Merchants and Trade

Merchants in New England also exported other local products such as pickled beef and pork. In addition, the fur trade was an important source of income. The diverse northern economy demanded the labor of many skilled craftspeople, such as blacksmiths, weavers, shipwrights (shipbuilders), and printers. Much of this labor was provided by the domestic population. Because farms typically were too small to divide among all of the sons, families often sent younger sons to learn skilled trades.

The young boys who learned these trades were known as **apprentices**. During their apprenticeships, the boys lived with a master craftsman who taught them the trade. In exchange for their training, the boys performed basic tasks. Gabriel Ginings, an apprentice in Portsmouth, Rhode Island, received "sufficient food and raiment [clothing] suitable for such an apprentice," as his 1663 contract noted.

The Granger Collection, New York

Tremendous labor went into manufacturing sailing ships. This New England shipyard of the 1700s has three vessels in various stages of construction.

Farmers in the middle colonies grew large quantities of food for people and animals. Here colonial farmers in Delaware are harvesting hay.

staple crops, or crops that are continuously in demand, included wheat, barley, and oats. The middle colonies also raised and exported livestock.

Slaves were a more important part of the labor force in the middle colonies than they were in New England. In addition to laboring on farms, slaves worked in cities as skilled laborers, such as printers, tailors, and carpenters. Many other slaves also worked on board ships and in the growing shipbuilding industry.

★ The Middle Colonies

The middle colonies—New York, New Jersey, Pennsylvania, and Delaware—combined the economic characteristics of the New England and southern colonies, developing both commerce and agriculture for export. With a good growing season and plenty of fertile land, the middle colonies produced surpluses of foodstuffs. These

However, indentured servants largely filled the middle colonies' growing labor needs. Between 1700 and 1775, nearly 100,000 indentured servants came to the middle colonies from Britain, and around 35,000 more came from Germany. About half of these immigrants moved to Pennsylvania, rapidly expanding its population. By the late 1700s Philadelphia's population of 30,000 made it the largest British colonial city. Other cities in the middles colonies, such as New York City, also began to grow faster than older colonial cities, such as Boston, which had once been the leader in colonial commerce.

Merchants in Philadelphia and New York City exported colonial goods to their primary markets in Britain and the West Indies. These products included wheat from New York and wheat and flour from Pennsylvania and New Jersey. Although the colonial merchants could potentially make high profits, these were not won without hard work. A Philadelphia merchant wrote to his brother in 1768:

❝ It takes all my industry [hard work] . . . to live well, but [I] have not been able to lay up such a Stock, as would maintain me without daily labor. ❞

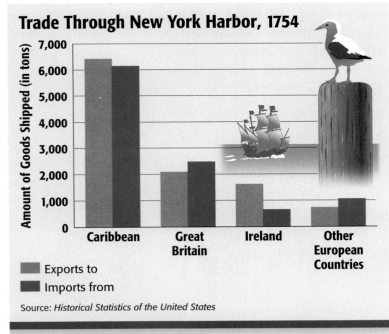

Trade Through New York Harbor, 1754

Amount of Goods Shipped (in tons)

■ Exports to
■ Imports from

Source: *Historical Statistics of the United States*

Trade with the Colonies The colonies used ports like New York Harbor to import and export raw materials and manufactured goods. About how many tons of goods were exported to Ireland in 1754?

★ Women and the Economy

Throughout the colonies, women contributed to the economy in a variety of roles. They could be found running farms and businesses, such as clothing and grocery stores, bakeries, and drugstores. A few female shopkeepers used their business status to demand a voice in colonial politics. One group of women wrote to a New York paper in 1733:

❝ **We are House keepers, Pay our taxes, carry on Trade, and most of us are she Merchants, and as we in some measure contribute to the Support of Government, we ought to be Intitled to some of the Sweets of it.** ❞

In addition to working in shops, some women also practiced medicine. Women were more likely than men to work as nurses, doctors, and midwives. These skills developed out of women's role in caring for the family.

However, colonial laws restricted women's economic activities. Typically, a married woman could not work outside the home without her husband's permission. A husband also had the right to keep his wife's wages.

Courtesy of the Free Library of Philadelphia

Colonial woman spinning wool for local use

Most colonial women worked in the home. Married women raised children and managed households. Women generally had the central role in the household economy, either by selling products such as butter and services such as laundering, or by providing these to their own family. Virginian Devereux Jarrett recalled that his clothing was "altogether my mother's manufacture." Female indentured servants and slaves worked both in and outside the home, also making a large contribution to the colonial economy.

SECTION 3 REVIEW

Identify and explain the significance of the following:
- **cash crops**
- **Eliza Lucas Pinckney**
- **slave codes**
- **apprentices**
- **staple crops**

Reading for Content Understanding

1 **Main Idea** What were the colonies' labor forces, and why did they differ by region?

2 **Main Idea** Give at least three examples of how women contributed to the colonial economy.

3 **Geographic Diversity** *Region* What effect did the environment and climate have on the types of economies that developed in the New England, middle, and southern colonies?

4 **Writing** *Expressing* Imagine that you are an apprentice living in one of the thirteen colonies. Write a diary entry describing your typical day and your role in the colonial economy.

5 **Critical Thinking** *Making Comparisons* Make a chart showing the different products of each colonial region. Judging from your chart, would you say that, overall, the colonies were more dependent on agriculture or commerce? Explain your answer.

The Great Awakening

Reading Focus

What was the message of the Great Awakening?

How did the colonists respond to the Great Awakening?

How did the Great Awakening help bring colonists together?

Key Terms

revivals
Great Awakening

A CONNECTICUT FARMER *and his wife dropped their work one morning in 1741 when they heard that George Whitefield would soon be preaching in a nearby town. Fearing that they would be too late to hear the sermon, the couple rushed to complete the 12-mile journey. Still three miles from the meeting site, they met a continuous line of horses carrying fellow travelers. Each horse appeared, to the farmer, "to go with all his might to carry his rider to hear news from heaven for the saving of souls." Inspired by Whitefield's message, the farmer joined others who had experienced a religious conversion. "I was born on Feb 15th 1711 and born again Octo 1741," he later wrote in the first line of his autobiography.*

George Whitefield

A Revival of Faith

In the early 1700s many church leaders feared that many colonists' dedication to their religion was declining and that the religious commitment of previous generations had been lost. In the late 1730s individual ministers tried to renew an enthusiasm for religion through emotional and inspiring sermons. Ministers began holding **revivals**, public church gatherings where masses of people came together to hear a minister's sermons. These revivals were often held in open fields.

As a result of these ministers' efforts, colonists from Georgia to New England experienced what historians have called "a great awakening" in their religious lives during the 1730s and 1740s. This **Great Awakening** was an unorganized but widespread movement of evangelical Christian sermons and church meetings. It changed religious, as well as social and political, life in the colonies.

Jonathan Edwards was one of the most important leaders of the Great Awakening. Born in Connecticut, he entered Yale College when he was a young teenager and graduated at the head of his class in 1720. After graduating, Edwards served as the head tutor, or president, of the college for several years. He then replaced his grandfather as pastor of the Congregational Church in Northampton, Massachusetts. Edwards's dramatic sermons emphasized that sinners must ask forgiveness for their sins or face eternal punishment.

Revival meetings, such as the one shown here, could draw crowds of thousands who were eager to hear a preacher's words.

In 1738 British minister George Whitefield came to America and began a series of revivals in Georgia and Virginia. In all, Whitefield made seven trips to the colonies, touring from the South on through New England. His revivals drew crowds of thousands. Boston minister Benjamin Colman said that people at Whitefield's revivals told him that never before had they felt "such an awaken'd Sense of the Danger of putting off the grand Concern of their Souls."

Nathan Cole, a New England farmer, wrote about his own emotional revival experience:

❝When I saw Mr. Whitefield come upon the scaffold [platform], he looked almost angelical. . . . And my hearing how God was with him everywhere as he came along, it solemnized [made serious] my mind and put me into a trembling fear before he began to preach; for he looked as if he was clothed with authority from the Great God . . . and my hearing him preach gave me a heart wound. By God's blessing, my old foundation was broken up, and I saw that my righteousness [moral correctness] would not save me.❞

Jonathan Edwards's sermon, "Sinners in the Hands of an Angry God"

As one of the most popular ministers of the Great Awakening, Whitefield inspired many thousands of colonists to join the new evangelical movement. These people promised to renew their faith in Christianity.

⭐ Words of the Great Awakening

The ministers of the Great Awakening preached that salvation could only be gained through the acceptance of God's grace and the confession of sins. This message often took on a threatening tone, as in Jonathan Edwards's 1741 sermon, "Sinners in the Hands of an Angry God":

❝The God that holds you over the pit of hell, much as one holds a spider, or some loathsome [disgusting] insect, over the fire, abhors [hates] you, and is dreadfully provoked [angered].❞

Edwards and other ministers of the Great Awakening preached that all people, regardless of their social status, were born sinners. In

Life in the English Colonies **137**

sermons such as "The Nature and Necessity of our New Birth," Whitefield explained that everyone also had an equal chance to be saved. This emphasis on equality influenced the social and political beliefs of many colonists.

⭐ Old and New Lights

The Great Awakening stirred many, but not all, colonists. As a result of these differences, the congregations of some established churches in the colonies divided into traditionalists and those who followed the new evangelical ministers.

New Beliefs

In New England the traditionalists were called the "Old Lights," while the followers of the Great Awakening were called the "New Lights." Old Light ministers, such as Charles Chauncy of Boston's First Church, did not believe that the enthusiasm of the Great Awakening could truly awaken one's spirituality. Enthusiasm, as Chauncy defined it, was "an *imaginary*, not a *real* inspiration." He thought that anyone who believed in the revivals of the Great Awakening "mistakes the workings of his own passions for divine communications," and "is under no other influence than that of an over-heated imagination." Chauncy thought that this excited form of religion was an inappropriate way to gain individual salvation.

The Great Awakening also had a great effect on the Presbyterian Church in the middle colonies. Presbyterian minister

The First Baptist Church of Providence, Rhode Island

Gilbert Tennent, a leader of the evangelical movement, published a pamphlet called *The Danger of an Unconverted Ministry*. In this work, Tennent attacked the traditionalists. As a result, the Presbyterian Church split into two groups. The "Old Sides" opposed the Great Awakening, while the "New Sides" followed Tennent's preaching. In the middle and southern colonies, particularly Virginia, the Great Awakening inspired a tremendous growth in church membership. Much of this growth took place among groups such as the Baptists and Methodists.

Faith on the Frontier

The Great Awakening eventually swept west to the frontier. Itinerant preachers—those who traveled the country delivering sermons—took the message of the Great Awakening to small communities. They held revival meetings wherever they could gather a group of people willing to listen. These ministers were important to settlers because there were few established churches on the frontier.

Traditional and evangelical ideas were in conflict even in these remote frontier regions. Frontier missionary Charles Woodmason tried to fight the changes brought about by the Great Awakening. He expressed his frustration with the followers of the evangelical movement within the rural population:

❝ **If I give out [announce] to be at such a Place at such a Time, three or four of these fellows [evangelical ministers] are constantly at my Heels—They either get there before me, and hold forth—or after I have finish'd, or the next Day, or for days together. Had I an hundred Tongues, or as many Pairs of Legs, I could not *singly* oppose such a Numerous Crew.** ❞

⭐ The Great Awakening and Society

Despite the religious differences created by the Great Awakening, this widespread and popular movement attracted many people of different classes and races. Women, members of minority groups, and poor people frequently participated. Women were particularly responsive to the message of the Great Awakening. Many women sought spiritual renewal around the time of childbirth, when their lives were often at risk. One woman explained that her faith "would wear off again 'till the time of my first Lying in [labor]; and then I was . . . brought to the very brink of eternity."

Some African Americans, both free and enslaved, found the Great Awakening's message of acceptance and spiritual equality appealing. Despite this message of equality, most revivals were separated by race.

The Great Awakening also affected colonial politics. Ministers from different colonies began communicating with one another. This communication represented one of the few intercolonial exchanges other than trade. Such efforts helped

A group of New Lights sings religious songs as they walk into their church.

bridge some of the differences between colonists from various regions. The large outdoor meetings were also popular places for colonists to discuss politics and social issues as well as religion. Furthermore, some historians believe that by questioning traditional church practices, the Great Awakening may have eventually encouraged colonists to demand greater political equality.

SECTION 4 REVIEW

Identify and explain the significance of the following:
- revivals
- Great Awakening
- Jonathan Edwards
- George Whitefield
- Charles Chauncy
- Gilbert Tennent

Reading for Content Understanding

1 Main Idea What message did ministers of the Great Awakening preach to their listeners?

2 Main Idea How did the ideas of the Great Awakening affect individual colonists, and why did some ministers oppose the movement?

3 Cultural Diversity How did the Great Awakening help to bring different groups of people together?

4 Writing *Describing* Imagine that you have attended one of George Whitefield's revivals. Write a short newspaper article describing what you have seen and heard at the revival as well as the effect that Whitefield's sermon might have on your life in the future.

5 Critical Thinking *Drawing Conclusions* Why might the teachings and spirit of the Great Awakening have led to a movement for greater democracy?

American Culture

Reading Focus

How did the Scientific Revolution affect Enlightenment philosophy?

What was education like in the colonies?

What contributions did colonial scientists, writers, and artists make to American culture?

Key Terms

Scientific Revolution
scientific method
Enlightenment

NIGHT AFTER NIGHT in 1609 Italian scientist Galileo Galilei observed the sky. He began to think that there was something wrong with the idea that Earth was the center of the universe. Focusing his newly built telescope on Jupiter, Galileo saw that this planet was surrounded by several small moons. This discovery suggested that everything in the universe did not have to revolve around Earth. Galileo was soon joined by other scientists who thought that many ideas about the natural world—ideas that people had believed for centuries—should be changed.

Galileo's telescope

 The Scientific Revolution

During the 1600s western Europeans began to re-examine their world. Scientific experiments and discoveries in Europe provided new information about the fundamental laws that govern nature. These dramatic explanations about the workings of the universe began what is known as the **Scientific Revolution**. The revolution began in mathematics and astronomy and eventually affected all areas of natural science.

Galileo and Newton

Galileo Galilei was one of the leading figures in the Scientific Revolution. He confirmed Nicholas Copernicus's theory that the planets revolve around the sun. In the late 1600s Sir Isaac Newton also contributed greatly to people's understanding of the universe. His most famous work, *The Mathematical Principles of Natural Philosophy*, became the foundation for physics for the next 200 years and formed the basis for the methods that scientists use today. Newton's theories about motion and gravity explained the behavior of objects on Earth and in the sky and proved that the same laws govern both.

The Scientific Method

One of the most valuable achievements of the Scientific Revolution was the development of the **scientific method**. This process involves carefully examining natural events and then forming theories from the experiments and observations. These theories can then be used to predict other behaviors or events. As new data becomes available, scientists retest their theories. Science as it is known and practiced today is based on the methods and discoveries developed during the Scientific Revolution.

Sir Isaac Newton

★ The Enlightenment

By the 1700s the Scientific Revolution had greatly changed people's understanding not only of the natural sciences but also of human activity. This change in thought is usually referred to as the Age of Reason, or the **Enlightenment**. Like scientists, Enlightenment thinkers applied reason and logic to the study of human nature and the improvement of society. As a result, philosophers developed new theories about how government should work to best serve the people.

Some Enlightenment philosophers began to claim that there was a social contract, which required rulers to have the consent of the governed. These philosophers, particularly John Locke, believed that people had rights to equality and liberty. Locke argued that in the social contract, people voluntarily obeyed their rulers only when the state fulfilled its responsibility to protect people's life, liberty, and property. In addition to Locke, Jean-Jacques Rousseau (roo-soh), Voltaire, and Baron de Montesquieu (MOHN-tes-kyoo) were among the most important thinkers during the Enlightenment.

★ Colonial Education

Some colonists learned about the Scientific Revolution and the Enlightenment through communication with Europeans or travel to Europe. Colonists rarely learned about these movements in school because few colonists could afford a formal, advanced education at this time.

Elementary Schools

The availability of education varied widely throughout the colonies. In New England, colonists valued the ability to read the Bible and wanted to educate a ministry for future generations. Therefore, they established town schools that were paid for by communities. Students most often used the *New England Primer* to learn to read. The *Primer*'s rhymed alphabet went from A for Adam to Z for "Zachheus, he Did climb the tree, Our Lord to See." Every letter and word of the *Primer* taught children about the Bible and the religious values of the community.

In the middle and the southern colonies, schools were not as widespread as in New England. For those who lived far from towns, education was often available only through parents or by hiring a private tutor.

Throughout the thirteen colonies, most children did not go to school past the elementary level. Instead, some colonial boys became apprentices to learn a particular trade, such as printing or blacksmithing. Boys and girls also worked on family farms. In New England and the middle colonies, some girls left home to become domestic servants for other families.

A page from the early schoolbook, the New England Primer

Higher Education

Some colonists did have the opportunity to get a higher education. English colonists founded nine

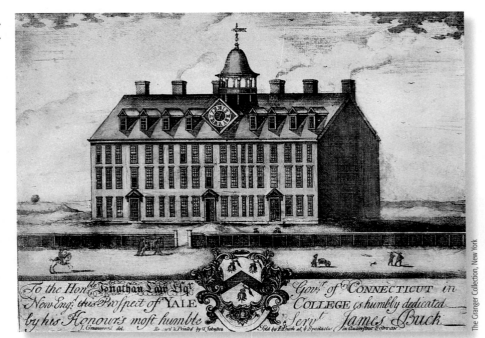

Yale College in New Haven, Connecticut, was founded in 1701.

colleges, the majority of which were located in the middle colonies and in New England. In 1636 Harvard College, located in Massachusetts, was the first college founded in the original thirteen colonies.

Courses in many of these colleges focused on religion. Education at these schools was not available to women because women were not allowed to become ministers. Some young men who wanted an education in the sciences or law, went to universities in Europe. Others went to a colonial college to study and then practiced with a professional in their field to receive additional training.

★ Colonial Scientists

Although few colonial schools taught science, several talented scientists emerged from the colonies. These scientists taught themselves through careful observation of the world around them.

Philadelphia became the most important colonial center for the study of science. In 1743, scientists in Philadelphia established the American Philosophical Society, the first organization in the colonies with a mission to study science. The purpose of the society, as one member explained, was to maintain communication among colonial scientists.

David Rittenhouse, a clockmaker in Philadelphia, served as one of the first presidents of the American Philosophical Society. Rittenhouse also designed a variety of mathematical and astronomical instruments and surveyed boundaries for more than half of the

colonies. In 1767 Rittenhouse constructed the most accurate orrery, a model displaying the planetary system, produced up to that time in the colonies. His skills were so impressive that Virginian Thomas Jefferson wrote:

> ❝ We have supposed Mr. Rittenhouse second to no astronomer living: that in genius he must be the first, because he is self-taught. ❞

Rittenhouse in turn thought highly of fellow astronomer and surveyor Benjamin Banneker, who lived in Maryland. The astronomical calculations made by this free African American included the accurate prediction of an eclipse in 1789. Banneker included these calculations, as well as his comments on social problems, in a popular almanac that he wrote and published yearly.

In the colonial tradition of self-education through close observation, botanist John Bartram traveled extensively throughout the colonies studying plants. He maintained contact with many British scientists, exchanging plants and information. Bartram also

Scientist and surveyor Benjamin Banneker

The Granger Collection, New York

American Literature

Benjamin Franklin's *Autobiography*

For many, Benjamin Franklin's Autobiography *is the first great work of American literature. It had simple, clear writing and popularized the autobiography as a literary form. It also emphasized one of the values closely associated with the American character—self-reliance. In the following passage, Franklin shares his strategy for a successful life.*

It was about this time that I conceiv'd [thought] the bold and arduous [difficult] Project of arriving at moral Perfection. . . . As I knew, or thought I knew, what was right and wrong, I did not see why I might not *always* do the one and avoid the other. But I soon found I had undertaken a Task of more Difficulty than I had imagined. . . . I therefore contriv'd [developed] the following Method. . . . I included after . . . Names of Virtues all that at that time occurr'd to me as necessary or desirable, and annex'd [attached] to each a short Precept [rule]. . . .

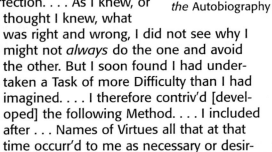

An early edition of the Autobiography

1. **Temperance** *Eat not to Dulness. Drink not to Elevation.*
2. **Silence** *Speak not but what may benefit others or your self. Avoiding trifling [unimportant] Conversation.*
3. **Order** *Let all your Things have their Places. Let each Part of your Business have its Time.*
4. **Resolution** *Resolve to perform what you ought. Perform without fail what you resolve.*
5. **Frugality** *Make no Expense but to do good to others or yourself: i.e. [that is] Waste nothing.*
6. **Industry** *Lose no Time. Be always employ'd in something useful. Cut off all unnecessary Actions.*
7. **Sincerity** *Use no hurtful Deceit. Think innocently and justly; and, if you speak, speak accordingly.*
8. **Justice** *Wrong none, by doing Injuries or omitting the Benefits that are your Duty.*
9. **Moderation** *Avoid extremes. Forbear [keep from] resenting Injuries so much as you think they deserve.*
10. **Cleanliness** *Tolerate no Uncleanness in Body, Clothes or Habitation.*

Understanding Literature

1. What is Franklin trying to achieve?
2. What does this plan reveal about him?

---

established the first colonial botanical garden in Philadelphia.

Benjamin Franklin

Philadelphia was also home to Benjamin Franklin, one of the most significant thinkers of his time. Franklin was born in Boston, where he worked first in his father's soap shop and later as an apprentice in his brother's printing shop. When he was 17 Franklin moved to Philadelphia. In his mid-20s, he started his own newspaper, the *Pennsylvania Gazette*, which quickly became the most successful paper in the colonies.

Franklin published his witty *Poor Richard's Almanack* between 1732 and 1757. Writing under the made-up name of Richard Saunders, Franklin came up with many sayings, some of which are still heard today: "As Poor Richard says . . . There are no Gains, without Pains." Franklin also wrote, "Early to Bed, and early to rise, makes a Man healthy, wealthy and wise." In another suggestion for gaining wealth, Poor Richard cautioned his readers:

> **If you would be wealthy, think of Saving as well as of Getting: The Indies have not made Spain rich, because her *Outgoes* [expenses] are greater than her *Incomes.*"**

Among Franklin's many contributions to American culture and society are his founding of the first circulating library in the colonies and an academy in Philadelphia that later became the University of Pennsylvania. Franklin also helped found the American Philosophical Society and served as its president from 1769 until his death in 1790.

Franklin conducted numerous scientific experiments and developed many useful inventions. His contributions symbolize a central idea of the Enlightenment—that reason could be used to improve people's quality of life. In his most famous experiment, Franklin flew a kite during a thunderstorm in 1752 to prove that lightning is a form of electricity. He also identified the positive and negative charges in electricity. These discoveries gained him widespread fame—both in the colonies and in Europe.

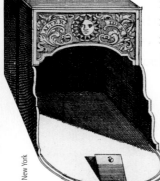

The Granger Collection, New York

A Franklin stove, which was used to heat homes

Franklin's many inventions include the lightning rod, which reduced the risk of fire from electrical storms; the Franklin stove, which heated homes more efficiently; and bifocals— eyeglasses with lenses that correct for both far- and nearsightedness. Franklin explained that he chose not to patent his many inventions because all people enjoy the advantages of others' inventions. It was his opinion, therefore, that "we should be glad of an opportunity to serve others by any invention of ours."

Biography

Phillis Wheatley

Educated by the Boston family that bought her as a slave in 1761, Phillis Wheatley became one of the first African Americans to have her work published. She wrote most of her poetry while still a teenager. Wheatley's first published poem was written in 1770 and took the form of an elegy, or a poem of sorrow, as did much of her other poetry. In 1773 the Wheatleys gave Phillis her freedom so that she could go to England to improve her poor health. While in England she published *Poems on Various Subjects, Religious and Moral*. Wheatley returned to America, however, when she learned that Mrs. Wheatley was gravely ill. In her later years she led a difficult life. After both of the Wheatleys died, Phillis married John Peters. She became a servant in a boardinghouse and died in childbirth in 1784.

 Colonial Writers and Artists

Scientists were not the only self-taught intellectual figures to emerge from the colonies. Several gifted authors and artists made important contributions to colonial American culture.

Colonial Verse

Religious speech, usually in the form of sermons, provided the most artistic form of language in the colonies. Colonial preachers such as John Cotton, Jonathan Edwards, and Cotton Mather created a new American style of preaching with their dramatic sermons. Another significant writer of the time was Robert Beverley, who wrote the *History of the Present State of Virginia*.

New England poet Anne Bradstreet used her talent to write about her love for her family and her dedication to her faith. Her poetry was published in *The Tenth Muse* in London in 1650. Like Bradstreet, Phillis Wheatley used religious language and imagery throughout her poetry. In her poem "On Being Brought from Africa to America," Wheatley described the impact of Christianity on her life.

Robert Feke's portrait of Mrs. James Bowdoin

when a few European painters, including John Smibert, came to paint and teach in America. In 1730 Smibert held an art exhibition in Boston—the first art exhibition in the English colonies. One of his pupils, portrait artist Robert Feke, is among the first widely respected American-born painters. Feke's skillful drafting and sense of color won him much praise. The majority of colonial artists were also portrait painters because that was the only art that most American colonists were interested in buying.

During the 1700s both colonial architecture and household furnishings improved in style and quality. The houses of the wealthiest colonists were also often constructed out of brick rather than wood, usually in elaborate British styles. Inside the homes of the wealthy, elegantly crafted furniture often displayed the work of highly skilled local carpenters and cabinetmakers. These changes reflected the general increase in the colonists' standard of living.

Artists and Craftspeople

The fine arts were not well developed in the colonies. This began to change in the early 1700s,

SECTION 5 REVIEW

Identify and explain the significance of the following:
- Galileo Galilei
- Scientific Revolution
- Sir Isaac Newton
- scientific method
- Enlightenment
- David Rittenhouse
- Benjamin Banneker
- Benjamin Franklin
- Anne Bradstreet
- Phillis Wheatley

Reading for Content Understanding

1 **Main Idea** What effect did the Scientific Revolution have on Enlightenment philosophy?

2 **Main Idea** Describe the types of colonial schools, and explain who attended them.

3 **Cultural Diversity** Describe the achievements in science, literature, or the arts of at least five well-known colonial Americans.

4 **Writing** *Informing* Write a biographical sketch describing Benjamin Franklin's life and explaining his contributions to American society.

5 **Critical Thinking** *Drawing Conclusions* As the colonies became established, why might colonists have begun to develop more cultural pursuits and acquire more material possessions than they had in earlier years?

CHAPTER 5 REVIEW

Chapter Summary

The thirteen colonies were separate communities along the Atlantic coast from New England to Georgia. The colonies' governments and economies were tied to Britain. Colonial trade and the planting of cash crops brought many African slaves to the colonies. The Great Awakening revived colonists' religious enthusiasm. During the Scientific Revolution and Enlightenment, people re-examined their world. ■

On a separate sheet of paper, complete the following activities.

Identifying People and Ideas

Describe the historical significance of the following:

1. bicameral legislature
2. Sir Edmund Andros
3. mercantilism
4. Middle Passage
5. cash crops
6. slave codes
7. Jonathan Edwards
8. revivals
9. scientific method
10. Anne Bradstreet

Internet Activity

go.hrw.com
SAO Trade Goods

Search the Internet through the HRW Web site to find information on some of the goods produced today in the states that made up the original thirteen colonies. Use the information to create a map showing the states, and use special symbols for trade goods. When you have finished, write a short paragraph explaining how these states' economies have changed or remained the same since the colonial period.

Understanding Main Ideas

1. How did England govern the thirteen colonies in the early and mid-1600s?
2. What roles did governors, assemblies, courts, and town meetings play in colonial governments?
3. What were women's economic roles in the colonies?
4. How did the economies of the New England, middle, and southern colonies differ?
5. Why did church leaders believe that many people were in need of a "great awakening"?
6. Who were the most important writers and artists of the colonial period, and what were some of their accomplishments?

Using the Time Line

Number your paper from 1 to 5. Match the letters on the time line below with the following events.

1. **Sir Edmund Andros becomes the royal governor of the Dominion of New England.**
2. **John Smibert holds the first colonial art exhibition in Boston.**
3. **The Puritans establish Harvard College in order to train ministers.**
4. **Benjamin Franklin discovers the connection between lightning and electricity.**
5. **Minister George Whitefield first arrives in Georgia.**

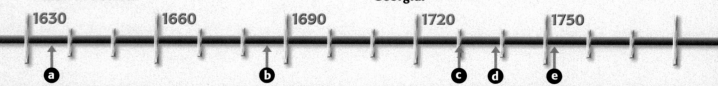

1630   1660   1690   1720   1750

a   b   c d   e

Reviewing Themes

1. **Economic Development** What was the purpose of the Navigation Acts?

2. **Geographic Diversity** How did each region's geography affect the economic development of the New England, middle, and southern colonies?

3. **Science and Technology** What were some of the technological advances made by colonists, and what was their impact on the colonies?

Thinking Critically

1. **Synthesizing Information** How were religion and education related in the colonies?

2. **Drawing Conclusions** If slave labor was more important to the southern economy, why was so much of the slave trade conducted through northern ports?

Building Your Portfolio

American History

Complete the following activities individually or in groups.

1. **Benjamin Franklin** Use your textbook or the library to gather information about Benjamin Franklin. You may wish to begin by looking at Benjamin Franklin's *Autobiography*. Then use this information to write a four-page biography of his life. Your biography should include some drawings of important events or inventions. Decide what events you will focus on, what drawings you will use, and what to title your biography.

2. **Life in Colonial America** Imagine that you were a teenager in colonial America during the 1660s. Choose where you might have lived and what your family would have been like. Then create a journal spanning one year in the colony. You may wish to divide your journal into 12 months. Include a map of your colony, illustrations of your school or workplace and home, and descriptions of people you know and meet.

Writing About History

1. **Persuading** Imagine that you are a colonial leader. Write a letter to King James II explaining why you think the Dominion of New England should be abolished.

2. **Informing** Write a paragraph explaining the importance of apprentices to the colonial economy.

Linking Geography and History

1. **Region** What characteristics did the middle colonies have in common with the southern colonies and the New England colonies?

2. **Movement** How did trade networks affect the colonial economy?

History Skills Workshop

Using Visual Resources Study the image below, which is a picture of African slaves harvesting sugarcane in Brazil. (Brazil was the first country to use African labor in its large-scale sugar plantations.) Based on the picture, what do you think work in the sugar fields was like for enslaved Africans? Explain your answer in a paragraph.

Colonial Economies

Many settlers came to the American colonies for economic opportunities. Colonists often were able to improve their standard of living. As the English colonies grew, they became a rich source of agricultural products and exported tobacco, rice, and wheat to Britain. As plantation owners expanded production in the South, they imported many enslaved Africans to work their plantations—clearing land, putting up buildings, and tending crops. Supplying furs for trade with Europe was also an important part of the growing economies in both the British and French colonies.

Europeans explored north and west, going deeper into the interior of the North American continent to look for new sources of furs. The British expanded their colonies and settlements as they explored new regions. These new settlers increasingly came into conflict with American Indians. ■

Colonial Trade and Industry

The British colonies produced a variety of goods for sale around the world. Most exports went to Britain, but markets in the West Indies and Europe were also important shipping destinations.

Colonial Products, 1700s

N
W E
S

St. Lawrence River
Lake Ontario
Lake Erie

Portsmouth
Albany
Boston
Newport
New Haven
New York City
Philadelphia
Baltimore

ATLANTIC OCEAN
40°N
70°W

Jamestown
Norfolk

New Bern
35°N

Wilmington

Charles Town
75°W

Savannah
30°N

0   100   200 Miles
0   100   200 Kilometers
Albers Equal-Area Projection

Legend:
- Tobacco
- Wheat, flour, bread
- Rice
- Fish
- Indigo
- Rum
- Timber
- Furs
- Extent of settlement

Geography Skills

Reading Special-Purpose Maps

1. What important ocean port towns are shown on the map?
2. In what area of the colonies was tobacco an important product?
3. Where were rice and indigo important products?

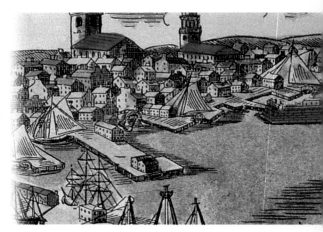

Colonial Boston Harbor

British Colonial Exports, 1770

Percentage of total value of exports from the thirteen colonies by destination

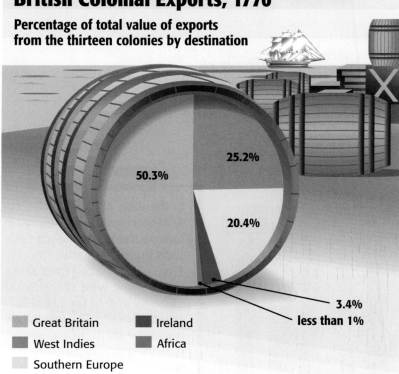

25.2%

50.3%

20.4%

3.4%
less than 1%

- Great Britain
- West Indies
- Southern Europe
- Ireland
- Africa

Source: *Historical Statistics of the United States*

History Note 1

In the 1700s, most exports from the thirteen colonies went to Britain. In recent years, however, Britain has ranked only fourth as a destination for exports from the United States. Most U.S. trade stays closer to home. Canada was first among the destinations for U.S. exports in 1995. Japan, Mexico, and South Korea ranked second, third, and fifth. The value of U.S. imports from Canada was higher than the value of imports from any other country. Japan and Mexico ranked second and third in imports; Britain ranked seventh.

Geography **Skills**
Reading Pie Graphs

1. What percentage of the total value of British colonial exports from the thirteen colonies went to Britain in 1770?
2. Which destination received the smallest percentage of the value of colonial exports?
3. Rank each destination, from the one with the highest percentage to the one with the lowest percentage of the value of exports. Why do you think the colonists traded the most with the top two destinations?

History Note 2

Which colony's settlers were wealthiest? One way to compare the general level of wealth among regions is to look at the average net worth per person in each area. A person's net worth equals the total value of his or her property, cash and financial assets, and all other possessions of value. In 1774 the average net worth of a free settler in the southern colonies was about two and a half times that of a free settler in the middle colonies. A southern settler's net worth was about four times that of a free settler in New England.

The Fur Trade

The fur trade was an important part of the British colonial economy. The total value of fur exports varied from year to year, usually depending on whether British relations with American Indians and the French were friendly or hostile. The lure of the fur trade drew trappers and traders into the interior of North America, where they built forts and trading depots and established important trade routes.

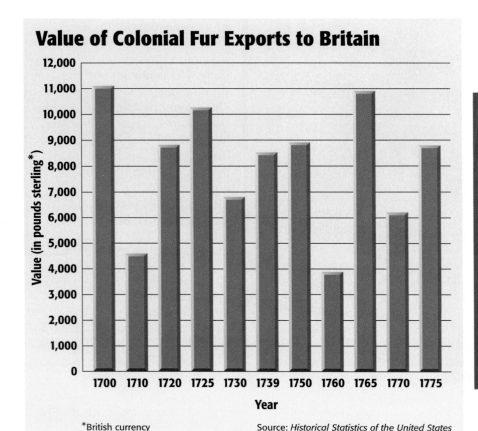

Value of Colonial Fur Exports to Britain

Value (in pounds sterling*)

Year: 1700, 1710, 1720, 1725, 1730, 1739, 1750, 1760, 1765, 1770, 1775

*British currency   Source: *Historical Statistics of the United States*

Geography **Skills**

Reading Bar Graphs

1. When was the value of colonial fur exports to Britain the highest?
2. What was the value of colonial fur exports to Britain in 1760? in 1765?
3. During what years did the value of colonial fur exports to Britain exceed 10,000 pounds sterling?

A fur trader

The Growth of the Fur Trade in North America

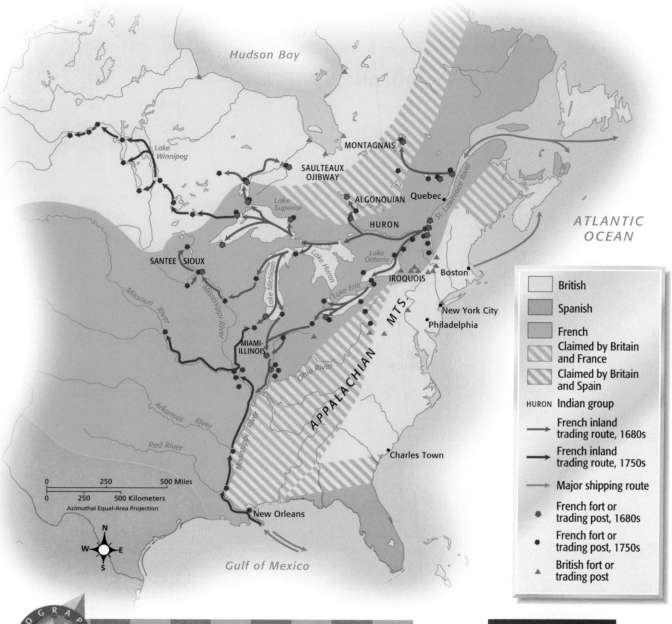

Map legend:
- British
- Spanish
- French
- Claimed by Britain and France
- Claimed by Britain and Spain
- HURON Indian group
- → French inland trading route, 1680s
- → French inland trading route, 1750s
- → Major shipping route
- French fort or trading post, 1680s
- French fort or trading post, 1750s
- ▲ British fort or trading post

Map labels: Hudson Bay, Lake Winnipeg, MONTAGNAIS, SAULTEAUX OJIBWAY, Lake Superior, ALGONQUIAN, Quebec, HURON, St. Lawrence River, ATLANTIC OCEAN, SANTEE SIOUX, Lake Huron, Lake Michigan, Lake Ontario, Lake Erie, IROQUOIS, Boston, Missouri River, Mississippi River, New York City, Philadelphia, APPALACHIAN MTS., MIAMI-ILLINOIS, Ohio River, Arkansas River, Red River, Charles Town, Mississippi River, New Orleans, Gulf of Mexico

Scale: 0 — 250 — 500 Miles; 0 — 250 — 500 Kilometers; Azimuthal Equal-Area Projection

Compass: N W E S

Geography Skills
Reading Special-Purpose Maps

1. Which nation's trading posts were located the farthest north?

2. What lake was closest to the westernmost French trading post?

3. What was the French town located farthest south? What British town was farthest south? How did the location of each of these towns make them important to the French and the British?

History Note 4

Many French traders and explorers in North America used light Indian canoes to travel the inland waterways. Using these rivers, the French dominated trade in the region west of the Appalachian Mountains. They even established trade as far west as the Spanish town of Santa Fe in present-day New Mexico.

Agriculture and the Slave Trade

Colonial settlers in the Americas imported many enslaved Africans to clear land and plant crops. Slaves were particularly important in the southern British colonies, where tobacco, rice, and indigo were grown on large plantations.

The Atlantic Slave Trade

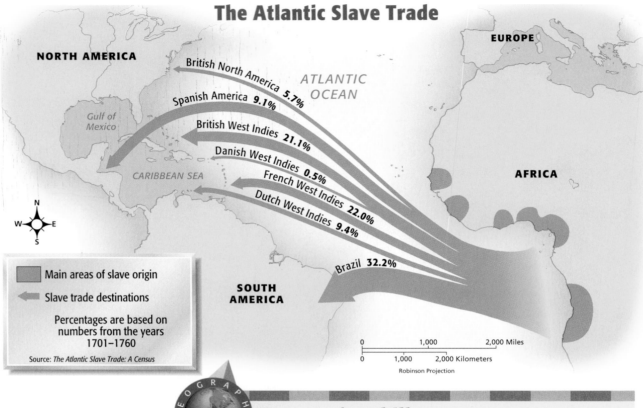

NORTH AMERICA

EUROPE

British North America **5.7%**

ATLANTIC OCEAN

Gulf of Mexico

Spanish America **9.1%**

British West Indies **21.1%**

Danish West Indies **0.5%**

CARIBBEAN SEA

French West Indies **22.0%**

Dutch West Indies **9.4%**

AFRICA

Brazil **32.2%**

SOUTH AMERICA

W N E S

Main areas of slave origin

Slave trade destinations

Percentages are based on numbers from the years 1701–1760

Source: *The Atlantic Slave Trade: A Census*

0   1,000   2,000 Miles
0   1,000   2,000 Kilometers
Robinson Projection

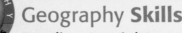

Geography **Skills**
Reading Special-Purpose Maps

1. Which destination received the highest percentage of slaves?
2. What percentage of slaves went to British North America during this period?
3. In what part of Africa did most slave trading take place?

African slave market

History Note 5

Millions of Africans were taken as slaves to the Americas between the 1500s and 1800s. Enslaved Africans were the main labor force for large plantations in the West Indies, South America, and North America. Gradually, opposition to slavery began to grow in the mid-1700s. Many important thinkers and religious leaders of the time argued that slavery was wrong because it violated a human being's basic right to liberty. Britain, once one of the world's largest traders in slaves, abolished the slave trade in 1807. The United States banned the importing of slaves in the same year. However, the United States did not end slavery for another 60 years.

American Indians used tobacco for ceremonial purposes long before Europeans arrived in the Americas. Explorers to the Americas returned to Europe with tobacco in the 1500s, and gradually, Europeans began the practice of smoking. The harmful effects of tobacco were not yet realized, and it became an important agricultural product in Spanish Cuba, Portuguese Brazil, and other European colonies in the Americas. Some English plantation owners in the southern colonies made great fortunes in tobacco. However, growing the crop required more labor than was available in the colonies, and enslaved Africans were brought to work on the southern plantations.

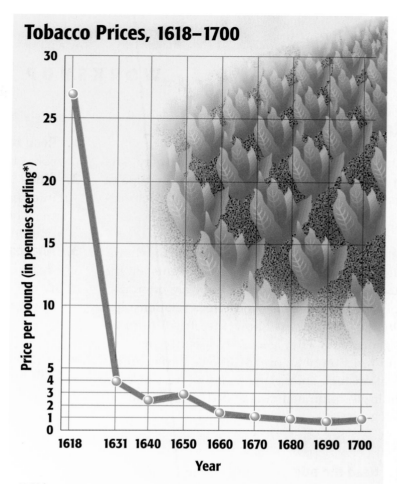

Tobacco Prices, 1618–1700

Price per pound (in pennies sterling)* vs **Year**

*British currency

Source: *Historical Statistics of the United States*

Geography **Skills**
Reading Line Graphs

1. When were tobacco prices highest?

2. What date represents the lowest tobacco prices between 1618 and 1700?

3. How would you describe the trend in tobacco prices between 1618 and 1700?

Tobacco on the way to market

NEW YOR

History Skills

WORKSHOP

Reading Charts and Graphs

Charts and graphs categorize and display data in a variety of ways, depending on the type of chart or graph being used and the subject matter of the data.

Charts   There are various types of charts. *Flowcharts* show a sequence of events or the steps involved in a process. They are often useful in showing cause-and-effect relationships. *Organizational charts* show the structure of an organization. They generally identify the rank and function of an organization's parts and the relationships among them. *Tables* are single- or multiple-columned charts that present data in categories.

How to Read a Chart

1. **Read the title**   Read the title to identify the focus or purpose of the chart.
2. **Study the chart's parts**   Read the chart's headings, subheadings, and labels to identify the categories used.
3. **Analyze the data**   When reading quantities, note increases or decreases in amounts presented in the chart. When reading dates, note intervals of time. When viewing an organizational chart, follow directional arrows or lines.

Graphs   There are several different types of graphs. A *line graph* often plots changes in quantities over time. A line graph has a horizontal axis and vertical axis. A *bar graph* can also be used to display changes in quantities over time. Most often, however, bar graphs compare quantities within categories. A *pie graph*, or *circle graph*, displays proportions by showing sections of a whole as if they were slices of a pie, with all sections of the circular image totaling 100 percent.

How to Read a Graph

1. **Read the title**   Read the title to identify the subject and purpose of the graph.
2. **Study the labels**   To identify the type of information presented in the graph, read the labels that define each of its axes, bars, or sections.
3. **Analyze the data**   Note increases or decreases in quantities presented in the graph. Look for trends, relationships, and changes in the data.

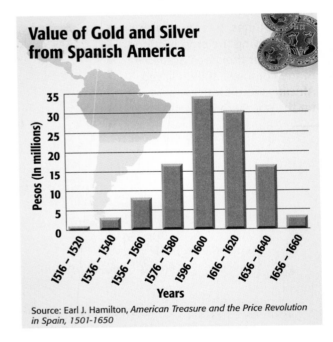

Value of Gold and Silver from Spanish America

Source: Earl J. Hamilton, *American Treasure and the Price Revolution in Spain, 1501-1650*

Practicing the Skill

Study the graph above. Then answer the following questions.

1. During which years did Spain receive the most treasure from the Americas?
2. What was the value of gold and silver that Spain received from 1556 to 1560?
3. What generalizations or conclusions can you draw about Spanish America from the information in this graph?

History in Action

UNIT PORTFOLIO

American History

Television Talk Show: Life in the American Colonies

Complete the following activity in small cooperative groups.

You work as a journalist for the Historical Broadcasting Network, the only television company with a time machine. Today you are going to produce a talk show about life in the American colonies from 1688 to 1750. Guests on the talk show should include important members of the colonies such as Sir Edmund Andros, Olaudah Equiano, Sir William Berkeley, Eliza Lucas Pinckney, Jonathan Edwards, Anne Bradstreet, Cotton Mather, Benjamin Franklin, and Phillis Wheatley. Audience members will be from the thirteen colonies.

Materials To complete this activity, you will need large sheets of butcher paper for creating backdrops and for creating a chart or graph. You will also need a videocassette recorder and blank tapes if the show is to be videotaped.

Parts of the Project The class will be divided into three teams as follows:

1. **Hosts** One team of two or three students will serve as the hosts of the talk show. The talk show hosts will design the set, select the theme music, and prepare the introduction and wrap-up for the show. Hosts should also create cue cards to use during the enactment of the show.

2. **Guests** One team will serve as talk show guests, each of whom will talk about his or her work and the daily and economic life of the colonies. Guests will research the background of the person they are supposed to be and the colony in which he or she lives. They will discuss such issues as law and government, religion, culture, education, and slavery. Guests should prepare at least one graph or chart to support their statements.

3. **Audience** The rest of the class will serve as audience members. This group will include American Indians, farmers from the southern and middle colonies, people who participated in the Great Awakening, enslaved persons, students, scientists, and colonial writers and artists. Audience members should prepare questions to ask the guests and should be ready to tell a little about themselves and their views.

Teams should do their research, write their questions, experiment with costumes and characterization, and practice their presentation. The class should practice several times before the talk show is taped or presented so that the whole show runs as one smooth 45-minute program.

Students making a news program

UNIT 3 The Colonies Break Free

(1675–1783)

Young People

IN HISTORY

Young Patriots

Jonathan Nickerson had quite a story to tell. At age 14, he volunteered to fight the British in the Revolutionary War. Years after serving his country, he recalled an event that happened outside of White Plains, New York, in 1782. The incident began when approximately 80 British cavalry approached a group of American soldiers, including Nickerson. As Nickerson recounted, the British demanded, "Surrender, you . . . rebels, surrender!" Outnumbered, Nickerson and several American patriots laid down their muskets to surrender, but the British wanted blood and attacked the unarmed men. Nickerson was knocked to the ground, trampled by a horse, and struck repeatedly in the head and body with a sword. He recalled a soldier asking, "Shall we kill him?" and the British commander replying, "No, let him alone. He will die soon himself." Proving the British captain wrong, Nickerson recovered from his wounds and lived to relate this dramatic brush with death.

Young battlefield drummers like this boy (left) helped boost soldiers' morale during the American Revolution.

Among those who bravely contributed to the revolutionary struggle was 16-year-old Sybil Luddington. In April 1777 Luddington rode 30 miles through the night to warn American colonists that British forces had landed at Danbury, Connecticut. These colonists escaped capture because of Luddington's heroic effort.

Another teenager to fight for American independence was 16-year-old Michael Smith. Smith's regiment served on a gunboat near Bergen Point on the Hudson River in New York. The gunboat crew was ordered to protect Americans living in the area from British raiding parties. When a British warship approached the shore to land its raiding party, the gunboat's crew opened fire. The cannon volley fired by Smith and two of his fellow crew members successfully turned the British away, easing the threat to Americans. Smith and his crew were declared heroes.

In this unit you will learn more about American colonists from all walks of life who bravely fought for their independence from Great Britain. These individuals helped give life to a new and proud nation—the United States of America.

LEFT PAGE: *Patrick Henry speaking in the Virginia legislature*

Patrick Henry Before the Virginia House of Burgesses (1851) by Peter F. Rothermel. Red Hill, The Patrick Henry National Memorial, Brookneal, Virginia

■ CHAPTER 6 ■
Conflicts in the Colonies
(1675–1774)

In 1748 Swedish scientist Peter Kalm traveled through the British colonies, which he said "have increased so much in their number of inhabitants, and in their riches, that they almost vie [compete] with Old England." Kalm also noted that the colonists were very independent, and that British trade laws caused them "to grow less tender for their mother country." The tensions that Kalm saw increased as the colonies and Great Britain grew further apart.

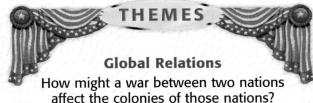

THEMES

Global Relations
How might a war between two nations affect the colonies of those nations?

Cultural Diversity
What can happen when people move onto land that is already occupied?

Citizenship and Democracy
What problems might be caused when a nation taxes people who feel they are not represented in government?

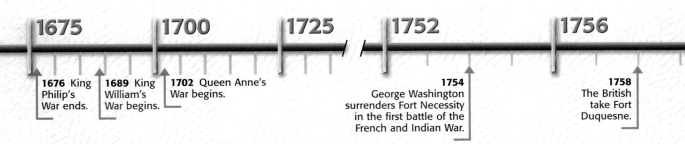

1675 | **1700** | **1725** | **1752** | **1756**

1676 King Philip's War ends.

1689 King William's War begins.

1702 Queen Anne's War begins.

1754 George Washington surrenders Fort Necessity in the first battle of the French and Indian War.

1758 The British take Fort Duquesne.

Trouble on the Frontier

Reading Focus

What were relations like between English colonists and American Indians?

Why were French and English colonists often at war with each other?

How did the French and Indian War affect the British colonies?

Key Terms

militia
Albany Plan of Union
casualties

CHIEF MASSASOIT of the Wampanoag Indians made a peace agreement in 1621 with the Pilgrims that lasted throughout his lifetime. By the 1670s, however, Massasoit's son Metacomet had begun to distrust and dislike the English colonists, charging that they treated their Indian neighbors poorly and were greedy for more land. Metacomet insisted that the colonial authorities treat him with respect. He finally told the colonists, "Your governor is but a subject. I shall treat [negotiate] only with my brother [equal], King Charles of England."

Chief Massasoit with a Pilgrim leader

IMAGE ON LEFT PAGE: *Baltimore in the mid-1700s*

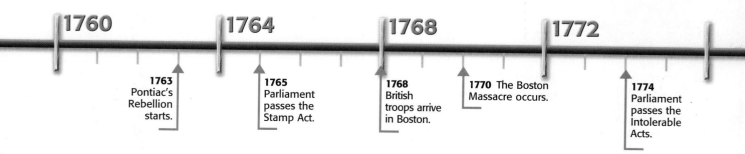

1760

1764

1768

1772

1763 Pontiac's Rebellion starts.

1765 Parliament passes the Stamp Act.

1768 British troops arrive in Boston.

1770 The Boston Massacre occurs.

1774 Parliament passes the Intolerable Acts.

Conflicts in the Colonies **159**

Relations with American Indians

The English settlers called Metacomet King Philip because he compared himself to their king, Charles II. The colonists feared that Metacomet's determination to protect Wampanoag lands was part of a plot to destroy the English colonies.

King Philip's War

In 1675 the tension between the Wampanoag and the colonists finally erupted into a conflict that the English called King Philip's War. Sparked by the death of three Indians, the fighting soon spread across New England as other Indian tribes sided with Metacomet. The colonial **militia**—civilians serving as soldiers—prepared for war. Both sides attacked each other's settlements, killing men, women, and children. Colonist Mary White Rowlandson was captured during one such raid. Caught by surprise, the townspeople were "like a company of sheep torn by wolves," she later wrote.

The colonists were fortunate that some of their long-time Indian trading partners agreed to fight against Metacomet and his allies. After some of these Indian forces defeated part of Metacomet's army, colonial troops led by Captain Benjamin Church captured Metacomet's wife and son. When Metacomet heard the news, he is said to have cried out, "My heart breaks; now I am ready to die." Colonial soldiers later ambushed and killed Metacomet, but the fighting continued for months. When the war finally ended in 1676, around 600 colonists and about 3,000 Indians were dead.

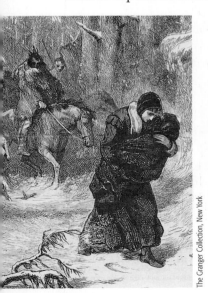

American Indians captured Mary White Rowlandson and her children during King Philip's War.

Trade Alliances

The alliance between Indian groups and the colonists during King Philip's War displayed how some Europeans and American Indians depended on one another. Military alliances often were based on trade. The English and French both wanted American furs, which they could sell for large profits in Europe. Indian leaders wanted tools, weapons, and other goods that Europeans could provide. French colonists traded and allied with the Algonquian and Huron Indians; English colonists traded and allied with the Iroquois League, a union of American Indians from five different tribes: the Cayuga, Mohawk, Oneida, Onondaga, and Seneca.

The French better maintained their allies' trust, partly because the small French settlements were less threatening to American Indians than the rapidly growing English colonies. Indian leaders were careful to retain their independence when forming alliances, as Garangula, an Onondaga, explained:

❝We are born free, We neither depend upon [the governor of New France] nor [the governor of New York]. We may go where we please, and carry with us whom we please, and buy and sell what we please.❞

Nonetheless, American Indians found themselves drawn into European conflicts in the Americas.

Conflicts with France

Beginning in the late 1600s France and England fought to become the dominant European and colonial power in a series of wars in Europe and America. The first of these conflicts was known in the colonies as King William's War, which lasted from 1689 to 1697. This war and those that followed were fought mainly along the frontier border between the English and French colonies. King William's War ended in a treaty that left the boundaries of colonial America unchanged.

Next came Queen Anne's War in 1702, which England fought against France and Spain. In America, English and French forces, each with Indian allies, carried out raids on frontier towns in northern New England, Canada, and south of the Carolinas. During Queen Anne's War the English captured Port Royal in Canada and burned the

Spanish settlement of St. Augustine in Florida. In the 1713 treaty that ended the war, England received present-day Newfoundland, Nova Scotia, and Hudson Bay from France. King George's War, which lasted from 1740 to 1748, had little impact on North America.

Forts in the Ohio Valley

Britain and France both were interested in the Ohio Valley and the Great Lakes region. The French wanted to protect their profitable fur trade, while the British wanted part of the fur trade and room for their colonies to expand. To protect their fur trade, the French began to build a series of forts along important rivers near the Great Lakes. When the French built three forts in the Ohio Valley—on

land claimed by Virginia—the colony's lieutenant governor, Robert Dinwiddie, sent a messenger to instruct the French to leave.

George Washington, a 21-year-old militia officer, volunteered for the job. He set out in October 1753. When Washington reached the Ohio Valley, he received a firm reply to Dinwiddie's warning. The French said they would not leave "no matter what your instructions may be." Washington returned with the news that the French were determined to stay in the region. War seemed increasingly likely.

The French and Indian War

The French and British began making plans for another war. Each side had certain advantages.

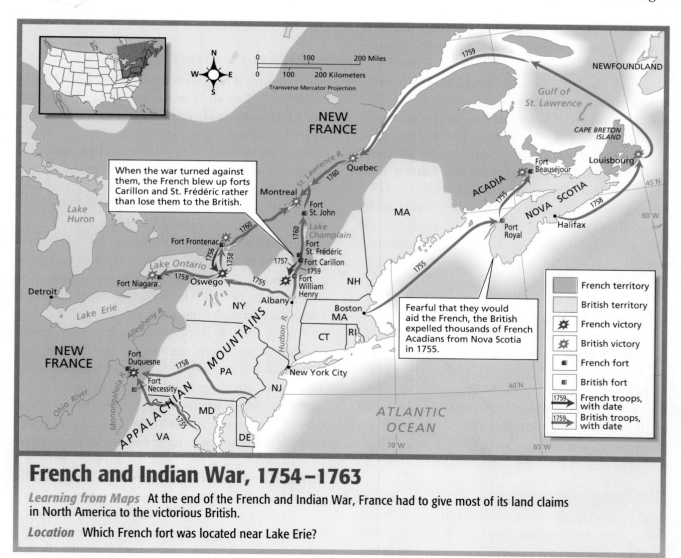

When the war turned against them, the French blew up forts Carillon and St. Frédéric rather than lose them to the British.

Fearful that they would aid the French, the British expelled thousands of French Acadians from Nova Scotia in 1755.

French territory
British territory
French victory
British victory
French fort
British fort
1759 French troops, with date
1759 British troops, with date

French and Indian War, 1754–1763

Learning from Maps At the end of the French and Indian War, France had to give most of its land claims in North America to the victorious British.

Location Which French fort was located near Lake Erie?

George Washington in his Virginia militia uniform

The French had a strong central government, strategically placed forts, extensive alliances with American Indians, and around 6,600 well-trained troops. The British had a much larger colonial population, a superior navy, an alliance with the Iroquois, and a stronger economy. They did not, however, have a strong united government in the colonies.

Many British colonists recognized that their lack of unity was a dangerous weakness. In 1754 seven colonies sent delegates to Albany, New York, to discuss ways of cooperating in times of crisis. Over several weeks, Pennsylvania delegate Benjamin Franklin helped write the **Albany Plan of Union**. This plan called for the colonies to unite for the first time under a president general and a grand council, both of which would report to the Crown. Franklin noted that the Iroquois had formed a union. The colonists, he said, should be able to do the same:

> **It would be a strange thing . . . if [an Iroquois-] like union should be [impractical] for ten or a dozen English colonies.**

However, the colonial governments did not want to give up their individual authority. They rejected the Albany Plan.

Fort Necessity

While colonial delegates were meeting in Albany, George Washington and his troops were fighting the French in the Ohio River valley. The British had tried to build a fort at the fork of the Ohio River, but the French drove off the British troops and built Fort Duquesne on the site. When Washington arrived with a small force of colonial militia, he found that the French already had gained control of the area.

Washington had his troops build a small, crude fort that he named Fort Necessity. Surrounded by French forces, Washington's troops suffered many **casualties**—people who are killed, wounded, captured, or missing in a war. Washington finally surrendered on July 4, 1754, after which the French commander allowed Washington and his militia to return home. The fighting at Fort Necessity was the first battle of what the colonists called the French and Indian War. Europeans called it the Seven Years' War, during which France and Britain once again fought for control of colonies and trade routes.

Braddock's Defeat

King George II sent General Edward Braddock to command British forces in North America. Braddock used traditional British military tactics, in which the opposing troops would line up across from each other in neat rows and then begin the battle. Some colonial militia members thought this sort of fighting was unreasonable. "[It] greatly surprised me, to think that I must stand still to be shot at," wrote 16-year-old David Perry.

Braddock lacked confidence in the poorly trained, unprofessional colonial militia, under the command of George Washington. Nevertheless, in the summer of 1755, Braddock decided to attack Fort Duquesne. As his forces drew near the fort, marching in line through the forest with music playing, they were ambushed by French and American Indian troops. "The Enemy kept behind Trees, and cut down our Troops, as fast as they could advance," wrote one survivor. The surprised British fired aimlessly into the woods. Braddock rode to the front, shouting at his troops to fight. "We would fight, if we could see anybody to fight," replied some soldiers. Braddock was badly wounded while trying to rally his troops.

Washington later recalled that in the confusion he tried to convince the British to stay and fight "the enemy in their own way," but the British "broke and ran as sheep pursued by dogs." Washington helped Braddock escape during the retreat, but the general died a few days later. In the battle, the British suffered almost 500 casualties, while the French and Indians had lost only 50.

The Fight for Canada

The British suffered more defeats during the first few years of the war, but gradually the French lost some of their Indian allies as the British gained some. In one victory in 1758, the British captured Fort Duquesne and renamed it Fort Pitt after William Pitt, the official who was in charge of British foreign and military affairs. The site later became the present-day city of Pittsburgh, Pennsylvania.

General Braddock and his army in retreat in July 1755

The turning point of the war came when British general James Wolfe prepared a daring attack on Quebec, the capital of French Canada. "A vigorous blow struck by the Army at this juncture

Global Connections

Spain and the Seven Years' War

During the 1700s, kings from the Bourbon family ruled both France and Spain. These nations signed the Family Compact of 1761, which stated that "whoever attacked one crown, attacked the other." In 1762 this alliance drew Spain into the conflict with Britain.

Some British colonies in North America that were close to Spanish territory, such as Georgia, feared Spain's entrance into the war. However, these colonies saw little military action because Britain won the Seven Years' War within a year of Spain's involvement.

Spain paid a high price for its participation in the war. The British navy had seized both Havana, Cuba, and Manila in the Philippines. In the Treaty of Paris, Britain returned these territories to Spain in exchange for Florida. Britain had become Spain's primary rival in

Colonial sea battle

North America, and Spain was determined to limit its rival's power in the future.

Understanding What You Read

1. Why did Spain enter the Seven Years' War?
2. What effect did Spain's participation in the war have on North America?

may determine the fate of Canada," Wolfe noted. Quebec was located on top of rocky cliffs above the St. Lawrence River. French general Louis-Joseph de Montcalm had several thousand troops guarding the city. Wolfe fooled the French by sailing his army across the river at night and leading them along a narrow path up the cliffs. The next morning, the surprised French saw Wolfe's troops in position on the Plains of Abraham near the city. In the battle that followed, Wolfe and Montcalm were shot while leading their troops, and both men soon died from their wounds. However, the British captured Quebec, giving Britain the advantage in the war.

 ## The Peace Treaty

Britain and France continued to fight for four more years, with the British winning most of the important battles. Finally, in 1763 the warring countries

A medallion minted in memory of General Wolfe and the British victory at Quebec

signed the Treaty of Paris, officially ending the war. The beginning of the treaty stated that the war "had spread trouble in the four parts of the world." Now the leaders wanted "to diffuse [spread] the spirit of union and concord [peace]" by settling their differences and ending this global conflict. In the process, they redrew the political map of the world.

Under the treaty, Britain gained Canada and all French lands east of the Mississippi River. From Spain, which had allied with France in 1762, Britain received Florida. (In an earlier treaty, Spain received Louisiana, the land that France had claimed west of the Mississippi River.) The Treaty of Paris drastically changed the balance of power in North America. Britain had a claim to all land east of the Mississippi River (except New Orleans), and Spain was now its only major European competitor in North America.

SECTION 1 REVIEW

Identify and explain the significance of the following:
- **Metacomet**
- **militia**
- **George Washington**
- **Albany Plan of Union**
- **casualties**
- **Edward Braddock**
- **James Wolfe**

Locate and explain the importance of the following:
- **Fort Duquesne**
- **Fort Necessity**
- **Quebec**

Reading for Content Understanding

1 **Main Idea** What factors affected the relationship between English colonists and American Indians?

2 **Main Idea** What caused King William's, Queen Anne's, and King George's Wars?

3 **Cultural Diversity** Why were the French more successful than the British at forming trade alliances with American Indians?

4 **Writing** *Informing* Imagine that you are a British official and have received word that the Treaty of Paris has been signed. Write a memo to the British colonists that explains the terms of the treaty.

5 **Critical Thinking** *Synthesizing Information* How do you think the wars discussed—from King Philip's War to the French and Indian War—shifted the balance of power in North America?

Consequences of the French and Indian War

Reading Focus

Why did colonists expand onto the frontier?

What caused Pontiac's Rebellion?

What was the Proclamation of 1763, and how effective was it?

Key Terms

backcountry
pioneers
Pontiac's Rebellion
Proclamation of 1763

IN 1759 BRITISH MINISTER *Andrew Burnaby, fresh out of Cambridge University, decided to visit the American colonies to observe their culture. The colonies were in the midst of the French and Indian War when Burnaby made his two-year trip. He kept a journal including observations on the frontier. He wrote that families "will gradually retire [move] westward and settle upon fresh lands, which are said also to be more fertile." Some of the colonies, Burnaby noted, "are not confined within . . . [set] limits, but extend to the westward indefinitely."*

A covered wagon from the 1700s

The Granger Collection, New York

The Frontier

The first settlers in the British colonies built communities and farms close to the Atlantic coastline or to major rivers. To the west of these early settlements was the vast frontier, where fur traders and scattered forts were often the only signs of European presence among the many American Indians who lived there.

The Backcountry

European settlers gradually moved into the Virginia and Carolina **backcountry**, the frontier region between the coastal settlements and the Appalachian Mountains. These **pioneers**—people who first settle an area—found a hilly region with heavy forests. Backcountry settlements were in danger of attacks from American Indians who resisted this intrusion in their territory.

The frontier slowly shifted westward as more people followed the pioneers and settled in the backcountry. However, just beyond the Appalachian Mountains, in present-day Tennessee and Kentucky, there was little European settlement until the 1770s.

West of the Appalachians

Some pioneers crossed the Appalachian Mountains farther north, moving into the Ohio River valley in the 1750s. Pioneers in the Ohio Valley found large forests of oak, maple, and hickory. The soil in the valleys near the Ohio River and on the plains to the west was good for farming. The region was also good for hunting. The Ohio River valley was full of wild game such as turkey and deer.

Although these were promising conditions, British settlements in that region remained small and isolated. Then in the 1760s, settlers began going across the Appalachian Mountains in greater numbers. The British victory in the French and Indian War had reduced pioneers' concerns about Indian raids and renewed interest in settling in the western lands.

Wild honeysuckle was one of the many colorful plants that greeted European pioneers in the Ohio Valley in the 1700s.

Pontiac's Rebellion

Learning from Maps American Indians under the leadership of the Ottawa chief Pontiac enjoyed some successes, but their inability to capture key forts caused the rebellion to eventually fail.

Location What fort, located west of Lake Michigan, was captured by Indians?

Conflict in the Ohio River Valley

After the Treaty of Paris, Britain replaced France as the European power in the Ohio River valley. This change caused confusion as British and Indian leaders struggled to deal with each other.

Rising Tensions

The French had used gifts of trade goods to earn the trust and cooperation of Indian leaders. During the French and Indian War, British officials such as Sir William Johnson had followed a similar policy with their Iroquois allies. After the war,

Biography

Daniel Boone

Thousands of the settlers who went west across the Appalachians followed a path made by Daniel Boone called the Wilderness Road. Boone was a frontier explorer born in Pennsylvania in 1734. When he was young, his parents moved to North Carolina, where Boone became an excellent hunter and a blacksmith. During the French and Indian War, Boone took part in General Braddock's failed attack on Fort Duquesne. After the war, Boone decided "to wander through the wilderness of America." Boone helped settle present-day Kentucky, founding in 1775 the fort that later became the small town of Boonesborough. A book describing his role in the settlement of Kentucky made Boone's early adventures famous to readers in America as well as Britain. Boone served in the local militia and spent time as a public official, but then returned to his first love, exploring the frontier. He made it as far west as present-day Missouri, where he died in 1820.

however, the British changed their tactics. General Jeffrey Amherst declared, "I do not see why the Crown should be put to that expense."

The ban on gifts angered many American Indians. So did the movement of British settlers onto Indian lands. While the French had not been interested in farming and settlement, the British wanted to settle in the Ohio River valley. The British assumed that when they acquired France's North American territory, it included all Indian lands, such as those in the Ohio River valley and the Great Lakes region. Indian leaders who had neither signed treaties with Britain nor agreed to give up their land disagreed with British claims. Chippewa leader Minavavana reminded a trader in 1761, "Englishman, although you have conquered the French, you have not yet conquered us!"

Pontiac's Rebellion

In the 1760s Indian tribes such as the Ottawa, Miami, Huron, Shawnee, and Delaware began to join together against the British. Chief Pontiac of the Ottawa emerged as the leader of this force. Pontiac followed the teachings of an Indian known as the Delaware Prophet, who called on Indians to drive out the white settlers and give up all European practices. In 1763 Pontiac shared these ideas with a gathering of Indians:

" **How comes it that you suffer the whites on your lands? . . . Drive them out, make war [on] them! . . . They are my enemies and the enemies of your brothers!** "

In May 1763 Pontiac and his allies began **Pontiac's Rebellion** by attacking British forts on the frontier. Within a month, Pontiac's forces had destroyed or captured seven forts and damaged several others. Pontiac then personally led the attack on Fort Detroit, Britain's political and trading center in the Great Lakes region. Despite the best efforts of Pontiac and his allies, the British defenders held out for months. Eventually, the Indian warriors following Pontiac grew tired of attacking the fort without results, so they returned to their villages.

Chief Pontiac led a rebellion against British settlements in the Ohio Valley.

An Indian attack on the important British position at Fort Pitt also failed after many casualties on both sides. After this defeat, more Indians left Pontiac's alliance, leading him to surrender in 1766. He remained an important Indian leader until his death in 1769.

★ The Proclamation of 1763

Pontiac's Rebellion caused great concern in the British government. Leaders feared that more fighting would take place on the frontier if colonists continued to move onto Indian lands. To avoid more loss of life, the British issued the **Proclamation of 1763**. The Proclamation banned any further British colonial settlement west of the Appalachian Mountains, creating a dividing line between colonial and Indian lands. The document stated:

> ❝ It is just and reasonable and essential to our interest and the security of our colonies that the several nations or tribes of Indians with whom we are connected, and who live under our protection should not be . . . [attacked] or disturbed. ❞

King George III ruled Britain from 1760 to 1820.

The Proclamation also ordered colonists who had already moved to the upper Ohio River valley "to remove themselves from such settlements." Many colonists hated the Proclamation. Some felt that Britain should allow the colonies to expand rapidly following France's defeat.

The Proclamation proved difficult to enforce and was ignored by most people who wanted to settle or trade in the Ohio River valley. Colonial settlement expanded as explorers such as Daniel Boone led people west of the Appalachians. The Proclamation and the colonial reactions to it showed that colonists and British officials had different ideas about what was best for the colonies.

★★★★★★ SECTION 2 REVIEW

Identify and explain the significance of the following:
- backcountry
- pioneers
- Pontiac
- Pontiac's Rebellion
- Proclamation of 1763
- Daniel Boone

Locate and explain the importance of the following:
- Ohio River
- Fort Detroit

Reading for Content Understanding

1. **Main Idea** Why did American Indians in the Ohio River valley unite and join Pontiac in fighting the British?

2. **Main Idea** What was the purpose of the Proclamation of 1763? How did most colonists react to it?

3. **Geographic Diversity** *Location* Why was Fort Detroit one of the most important British forts in the Great Lakes region?

4. **Writing** *Creating* Make a poster that might have been used to encourage individuals and families to move to the frontier in the 1700s.

5. **Critical Thinking** *Synthesizing Information* If you were a settler in the late 1700s, would you have moved to the backcountry or to the Ohio River region? Explain your answer.

Trouble over Taxes

Reading Focus

Why did Britain create new taxes for the colonies?

Why did colonists dislike the new tax laws?

How did colonists challenge these new taxes?

Key Terms

Sugar Act
Committees of Correspondence
boycott
Stamp Act
Sons of Liberty
repeal

RIME MINISTER GEORGE GRENVILLE *was determined to find ways to pay Great Britain's heavy debts from the French and Indian War. After taking office in 1763, he spared no one in his search for revenue, not even King George III. "When he has wearied me for two hours,"* said the king of his many meetings with Grenville, *"he looks at his watch to see if he may not tire me for an hour more." Grenville knew that the British people were already overwhelmed with high taxes, so he turned his attention to the colonists in America, who paid far less.*

Paper money from the mid-1700s

★ Raising Revenue

Even though Britain had won the French and Indian War, Parliament still had to pay for it. In addition, Britain maintained a standing army in North America to protect the colonists against Indian attacks.

To help pay for this standing army, Parliament decided to raise money by taxing the colonists. In 1764 Parliament passed the **Sugar Act**, which set duties, or taxes, on molasses and sugar imported by colonists. The Sugar Act was the first law passed by Parliament that was designed specifically to raise money in the colonies.

In another law, the Currency Act, Parliament banned the colonies from printing their own money. This act was meant to prevent colonists from paying taxes or debts in colonial currency, which the British considered unreliable. However, official British currency was in short supply in America, so the act contributed to economic problems in the colonies.

In addition to creating new taxes and currency regulations, Parliament cracked down on colonial

Conflicts in the Colonies **169**

James Otis defends the rights of local merchants before the British Vice-Admiralty Court in Boston.

smugglers. The British required colonial merchants to make lists of all the trade goods they carried on board their ships. Officials had to approve these lists before ships could leave colonial ports, making it more difficult for traders to avoid paying duties on their cargoes. The British navy also began stopping and searching ships for smuggled goods. Traders caught smuggling could have their cargo and ships seized.

Parliament also changed the colonies' legal system by granting broader powers to the Vice-Admiralty courts, which tried smugglers. In these courts, which had no juries, the judges assumed that suspected smugglers were guilty until proven innocent. In regular British courts, the accused was presumed to be innocent until proven guilty.

★ Taxation Without Representation

Parliament's actions upset many colonists. They had grown used to being quite independent—much more independent than people in Britain. Many colonial merchants thought the taxes were unfair and bad for business. Some people believed that Britain did not have the right to tax the colonies at all without their consent.

James Otis, a lawyer from Boston, was one of the first colonists to discuss the issue of unfair taxation. In early 1764 Otis wrote an essay attacking the Sugar Act. He argued that neither the Crown nor Parliament could "take from any man any part of his property, without his consent in person or by representation." No one in Britain had asked the colonial governments if they wanted to be taxed, and there were no representatives for the colonies in Parliament. Therefore, he concluded, the tax was unjust and violated colonists' rights.

At a Boston town meeting in May 1764, local leader Samuel Adams agreed with Otis that Parliament could not tax the colonies without their permission. Adams said that consenting to the tax would be a dangerous first step:

❝ For if our trade may be taxed, why not our lands? Why not the produce of our lands and, in short, everything we possess or make use of? ❞

Colonists soon adopted the ideas of Otis and Adams, and the slogan "No taxation without representation" could be heard throughout the colonies.

To help unite protesters, the Massachusetts House of Representatives approved the creation of **Committees of Correspondence**. Each committee contacted other towns and colonies to share ideas and information about the new British laws and ways to challenge them. A popular method of protest was the **boycott**, or refusal to buy certain goods. Starting in Massachusetts, merchants agreed not to buy British clothing and other items until Parliament eliminated the

The Stamp Act required colonists to display this stamp on nearly all paper documents.

new duties. Colonial women joined in the boycott, and in many households they were responsible for finding or making substitutes for boycotted goods. The boycott soon spread to New York and other colonies. Colonial merchants hoped that their boycott would hurt the British economy and, therefore, would convince British officials to end the new taxes.

★ The Stamp Act

By early 1765 Prime Minister Grenville had heard the complaints about the Sugar Act. He responded by asking the colonists if they had a better plan for paying their share of military expenses.

A New Tax

When the colonists failed to suggest any suitable ideas, Grenville proposed the **Stamp Act**, which Parliament passed in March 1765. The act affected most colonists. It required them to pay for an official stamp, or seal, whenever they bought paper items such as newspapers, pamphlets, licenses, legal documents, and playing cards. Tax collectors sold the stamps and turned the proceeds over to the British government. Colonists who refused to buy stamps could be tried in the hated Vice-Admiralty courts.

Grenville thought the stamp tax was "the easiest, the most equal, and the most certain that can be chosen." After all, in Britain, people already paid taxes such as this one, to cover the cost of wars and other government expenses. The colonists, however, saw the Stamp Act as the first law of Parliament that directly taxed the colonists, not just trade goods, to raise money. Even colonists who had supported Parliament's right to tax foreign trade goods were upset by this new tax on everyday items produced in the colonies.

Colonists Organize

Colonists began protesting the Stamp Act almost immediately. James Otis wrote:

> ❝ **One single Act of Parliament [the Stamp Act] has set people a-thinking in six months more than they had ever done in their whole lives before.** ❞

In several colonies, such as New York and Massachusetts, colonists formed secret societies called the **Sons of Liberty**. These groups often used violence to frighten tax collectors. In Boston, the Sons of Liberty told tax collector Andrew Oliver that "his house would be destroyed and his life [would be] in continual danger" unless he quit his job, which he did. Many colonial courts shut down when people refused to buy the stamps required for legal documents, while many businesses openly ignored the law by not buying stamps.

In Virginia, Patrick Henry presented a series of resolutions to the House of Burgesses in May 1765. These stated that the Stamp Act violated the rights of the colonists as British citizens. The leader of the House, John Robinson, interrupted Henry's speech by crying, "Treason! Treason!" "If this be

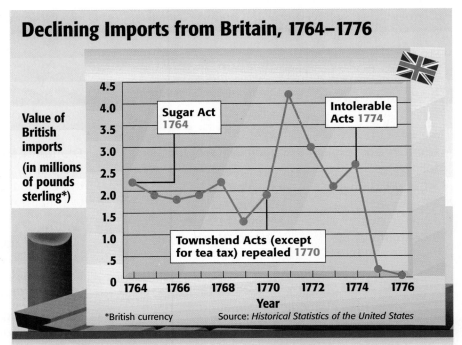

Declining Imports from Britain, 1764–1776

Value of British imports (in millions of pounds sterling*)

Sugar Act 1764

Townshend Acts (except for tea tax) repealed 1770

Intolerable Acts 1774

Year

*British currency   Source: *Historical Statistics of the United States*

British Imports Fall The colonists used boycotts to fight British tax increases. How did British laws affect imports to the colonies?

Conflicts in the Colonies **171**

treason," reportedly replied Henry, "make the most of it!" Although he had been a delegate only 10 days, Henry's speech convinced the House of Burgesses to support some of his resolutions.

Word of Virginia's action reached Boston, where the members of the Massachusetts legislature called for a Stamp Act Congress. In October 1765, delegates from nine colonies met in New York and issued a declaration that claimed the Stamp Act violated their rights and liberties. They then asked Parliament to **repeal**, or abolish, the act.

This cartoon celebrates the repeal, or "death," of the Stamp Act in 1766. Members of Parliament are shown grieving at the act's "funeral."

★ Repealing the Stamp Act

Pressure to repeal the Stamp Act began building on both sides of the Atlantic Ocean. A group of London merchants complained that their trade with the colonies was suffering terribly—as a result of colonial boycotts—and asked Parliament to repeal the Stamp Act. Benjamin Franklin, serving as an official agent for Pennsylvania, assured Parliament that the colonies would buy British goods again after the repeal of the stamp tax.

William Pitt, an influential member of Parliament, also believed that the Stamp Act was unjust. When Prime Minister Grenville asked why

the colonies should be freed from their financial responsibility to Britain, Pitt replied, "I desire to know when they [the colonies] were made slaves [of Britain]." Under Pitt's leadership, Parliament repealed the Stamp Act in March 1766.

The members of Parliament still were disturbed that colonists had challenged Britain's right to tax the colonies. Thus, Parliament issued the Declaratory Act. This act stated that Parliament had the authority to make laws for the colonies "in all cases whatsoever." Parliament declared that Britain, not the colonies, made the rules and that the colonists could expect future acts of Parliament, including more taxes.

SECTION 3 REVIEW

Identify and explain the significance of the following:

- **George Grenville**
- **Sugar Act**
- **James Otis**
- **Committees of Correspondence**
- **boycott**
- **Stamp Act**
- **Sons of Liberty**
- **Patrick Henry**
- **repeal**

Reading for Content Understanding

1 **Main Idea** Why did Britain attempt to raise money from the colonies?

2 **Main Idea** Why did colonists dislike the Sugar Act and the Stamp Act?

3 **Economic Development** How did British merchants' reaction to the boycotts reflect the economic importance of the colonies to Britain?

4 **Writing** *Persuading* Imagine that you are a colonist upset by new taxes. Write a newspaper editorial persuading colonists to protest these new taxes and Parliament to repeal them.

5 **Critical Thinking** *Determining the Strength of an Argument* Do you think the British were justified in their taxation policies? Explain your answer.

New Taxes and Tensions

Reading Focus

How did colonists respond to the Townshend Acts?

How did the Boston Massacre and the Boston Tea Party demonstrate the colonists' willingness to defy British authority?

What was the purpose of the Intolerable Acts?

Key Terms

Townshend Acts

writs of assistance

Daughters of Liberty

Boston Massacre

propaganda

Tea Act

Boston Tea Party

Intolerable Acts

*P*EOPLE IN CITIES *throughout the colonies celebrated the repeal of the Stamp Act with fireworks displays and grand banquets. In Boston, citizens built "a magnificent Pyramid" lit by 280 lamps, and wealthy Bostonians paid for all debtors to be released from jail. The Massachusetts legislature sent King George III a declaration of its gratitude and a pledge of loyalty. Despite the celebrations and kind words, however, the repeal of the Stamp Act did not resolve the strong disagreements between Parliament and the colonies.*

Colonial pottery

⭐ The Townshend Acts

In June 1767 Parliament passed the **Townshend Acts**, which placed duties on imported glass, lead, paints, paper, and tea. The Crown used the revenue from these duties to pay military expenses and the salaries of colonial governors.

The Colonists Respond

To enforce the Townshend Acts, British customs agents used **writs of assistance**. These writs were special search warrants that allowed tax collectors to search for smuggled goods. Britain had been unable to control the smuggling that was common throughout the colonies. The law also created new Vice-Admiralty courts in which to try smugglers. Many colonists thought that the Townshend Acts took too much power away from colonial courts and legislatures and gave it to royal officials. Colonists feared that the royal officials would not be accountable to colonial authorities and did not have the best interests of the colonies at heart.

WILLIAM JACKSON,
an IMPORTER; at the
BRAZEN HEAD,
North Side of the TOWN-HOUSE,
and Opposite the Town-Pump, in
Corn-hill, BOSTON.

It is desired that the SONS and
DAUGHTERS of LIBERTY,
would not buy any one thing of
him, for in so doing they will bring
Disgrace upon themselves, and their
Posterity, for ever and ever, AMEN
PROSCRIBING AN IMPORTER.¹

The Sons of Liberty call for a boycott against a Boston merchant.

The colonists responded to the Townshend Acts with another large-scale boycott of British goods. Women continued to play a key role in the boycotts by making cloth and other necessary goods at home instead of buying British goods. Groups calling themselves the **Daughters of Liberty** met to sew, support the boycotts, and discuss political issues like the Townshend Acts. A leader of one branch of the Daughters of Liberty wrote:

> ❝I hope [we] would sooner wrap ourselves in sheep and goatskin than buy English goods of a people who have insulted us in such a scandalous way.❞

Trouble in Boston

The colonial legislatures also protested the Townshend Acts. In February 1768 Samuel Adams wrote a letter arguing that the Townshend Acts violated the legal rights of the colonists. The Massachusetts legislature sent this letter to other colonial legislatures, asking for their support. Within a few months the legislatures of New Hampshire, New Jersey, Connecticut, and Virginia had voted to join Massachusetts in opposition to the Townshend Acts.

Meanwhile, tax collectors in Massachusetts seized the ship *Liberty* on suspicion of smuggling. The ship's owner, Boston merchant John Hancock, argued that the tax collectors were really trying to punish him for opposing the Townshend Acts. The Sons of Liberty supported Hancock and began attacking the houses of customs officials in protest, once again demanding "no taxation without representation." In response, Governor Francis Bernard requested troops to help restore order. He also disbanded the Massachusetts legislature. The British soldiers that he requested arrived in Boston in October 1768.

★ The Boston Massacre

Many Bostonians saw the presence of British troops as a threat by the British government against its critics in Massachusetts. Some colonists agreed with local leader Samuel Adams, who said, "I look upon [British soldiers] as foreign enemies." The soldiers knew that they were not welcome. Both sides resented each other, and name-calling, arguments, and fights between Bostonians and the soldiers were common.

The tension finally exploded on March 5, 1770. A lone British sentry standing guard in the snow on King Street near Boston's Custom House got into an argument with a civilian and struck him. As word spread, a crowd gathered around the soldier, throwing snowballs and shouting insults. When he loaded his gun, the mob yelled, "You coward, you dare not fire!" Soon a small company of troops arrived to protect the sentry. The soldiers stared nervously at the mob as it grew louder and angrier by the moment. Suddenly, the soldiers fired into the crowd, killing African American sailor Crispus Attucks, sailor James Caldwell, Irish immigrant Patrick Carr, ropemaker Samuel Gray, and apprentice Samuel Maverick.

Bostonians referred to the killings as the **Boston Massacre**. Samuel Adams and other protesters quickly began using the incident as **propaganda**—stories and images designed to support a particular point of view—against the British. Silversmith Paul Revere made an engraving of the incident that was distributed throughout New England.

Amidst the public uproar, the soldiers involved in the shooting and their commanding officer, Thomas Preston, faced charges of murder. Two respected Boston lawyers, Josiah Quincy and John Adams—Samuel Adams's cousin—agreed to defend the soldiers, arguing that they had acted in self-defense during a riot. The Boston jury found Preston and six soldiers not guilty, but convicted two other soldiers of accidentally killing people in the crowd. The two were

The Granger Collection, New York

Samuel Adams

branded on the hand and then released. The trial helped prevent further violence by quieting the unrest.

★ A Tax on Tea

To reduce tension further in the colonies, Parliament repealed the Townshend Acts but kept the tax on tea. Although Parliament wanted peace in the colonies, it kept the tea tax to show that it still claimed the right to tax the colonists.

The Tea Act

British officials estimated that despite the continuing boycott, colonists bought several million pounds of tea each year, much of it smuggled into the colonies. These purchases attracted the interest of the British East India Company, which asked Parliament for permission to sell its tea directly to the colonies. Company officials pointed out that they could charge the lowest prices even after consumers paid the tea tax. These prices would persuade colonists to buy the East India Company's tea, generating more tax revenue and helping the company pay its debts.

Parliament agreed and passed the **Tea Act** in 1773. Many colonial merchants and smugglers opposed the Tea Act, however, out of fear that the British East India Company's cheap tea would put them out of business. Other colonists were concerned that if the British East India Company gained a monopoly on the tea trade, other British companies would follow its example and threaten colonial businesses. Colonists united in opposition to the Tea Act.

The Boston Tea Party

Three ships loaded with British tea arrived in Boston Harbor in November 1773. The Sons of

American Arts

Engraving

Colonial engravers often created works of art that showed what life was like in the colonies. Some art even made political statements. For example, in 1770 Paul Revere made an engraving of the Boston Massacre that showed British soldiers attacking unarmed colonists. Advertised in the Boston *Gazette* as "A Print containing a Representation of the late horrid Massacre in King St," Revere's engraving became a symbol of Britain's injustice in the colonies.

Understanding the Arts

1. Why did Paul Revere circulate this engraving?
2. In looking at Revere's engraving of the Boston Massacre, would you say that it accurately represents the event? Explain your answer.

Paul Revere's engraving of the Boston Massacre of 1770

Battling British Acts

ACT	COLONIAL RESPONSE	BRITISH REACTION
The **Molasses Act (1733)** placed duties on rum, sugar, and molasses imported from foreign countries.	Colonists protested the act and smuggled goods to avoid paying duties.	The act was not strictly enforced.
The **Sugar Act (1764)** replaced the Molasses Act and was aimed specifically at raising revenues from the colonies.	Colonists protested the act and called for a boycott on items with duties.	After asking colonists for a plan to pay military expenses and not receiving one, Prime Minister proposed the Stamp Act. Colonial government strictly enforced duties.
The **Stamp Act (1765)** required colonists to purchase a stamp for newspapers, pamphlets, legal documents, and other items.	Colonists formed Sons of Liberty, boycotted goods, and used violence to frighten tax collectors; Stamp Act Congress asked Parliament to repeal the act.	Parliament repealed the Stamp Act in March 1766, then issued the Declaratory Act.
The **Quartering Act (1765)** required colonists to supply British forces in the colonies with housing, bedding, and other needs.	Colonists defied the act.	The act was allowed to expire in 1770.
The **Townshend Acts (1767)** placed duties on imported glass, lead, paints, paper, and tea; made it easier for tax collectors to get writs of assistance.	Colonists used boycotts, colonial legislatures circulated a letter protesting the acts, and the Sons of Liberty attacked homes of tax collectors.	Soldiers were sent to Boston, October 1768; colonists were killed in Boston Massacre, March 5, 1770; most of the acts were repealed by Parliament, March 5, 1770; troops removed from Boston; soldiers involved in Boston Massacre were tried in court.
The **Tea Act (1773)** kept in place duties on imported tea and allowed the British East India Company to export directly to the colonies.	Colonists used boycotts and propaganda, held the Boston Tea Party, and destroyed tea shipments in some colonies.	Parliament passed the Intolerable Acts.
The **Intolerable Acts (1774)** closed Boston Harbor; canceled Massachusetts's charter; moved trials of colonial officials to Britain; allowed new Quartering Act and Quebec Act, which gave Canada control of the Ohio region.	Colonists called for large-scale boycotts, published propaganda, and convened the First Continental Congress.	The act was repealed in 1778.

Liberty demanded that the ships leave without unloading their cargoes. Thomas Hutchinson, governor of Massachusetts since 1771, ordered that the ships unload their tea. The captains, afraid to offend the governor and afraid to anger the Sons of Liberty, decided to lay their ships at anchor in the harbor for weeks.

On the night of December 16, a group of colonists disguised as Indians crept onto each of the three tea-filled ships. Participant George Hewes recalled of the incident:

❝**In about three hours from the time we went on board, we had . . . broken and thrown overboard every tea chest to be found in the ship. . . . No attempt was made to resist us.**❞

After dumping 90,000 pounds of tea into Boston Harbor, the colonists headed home to remove their disguises. As word of this **Boston Tea Party** spread, the streets echoed with shouts of "Boston harbour [is] a teapot tonight!"

⭐ The Intolerable Acts

When Lord North, the new British prime minister, heard about the Boston Tea Party, he was furious. "Can we remain in this situation long?" he asked Parliament. Another member of Parliament supposedly declared that "the town of Boston ought to be knocked about their ears and destroyed."

As punishment for the Boston Tea Party, in the spring of 1774 Parliament passed the Coercive Acts, which colonists called the **Intolerable Acts**. The first of these four laws shut down Boston Harbor until Boston paid the cost of the destroyed tea. The second law canceled Massachusetts's charter and gave the colony a legislature that met only when and where the governor commanded. The third law moved the trials of royal colonial officials to Britain, where they would get a more sympathetic judge and jury. The fourth measure was called the Quartering Act, which required colonists to quarter, or house and supply, British soldiers. Meanwhile, General Thomas Gage replaced

Mercy Otis Warren

Thomas Hutchinson as governor of Massachusetts. The British hoped that these steps would restore royal authority in the colonies by making an example of Massachusetts.

Some colonists wrote pamphlets, editorials, and plays to criticize the British government's actions. Mercy Otis Warren wrote critical essays, poems, and plays such as *The Defeat*, *The Group*, and *The Blockheads*. In *The Group*, Warren gave British sympathizers nicknames such as "Brigadier Hateall" and "Hum Humbug" to make them look foolish.

While Warren and other writers criticized British officials, colonial leaders in Boston tried to organize a complete boycott of British goods in the colonies. There was not strong support for this tactic from the other colonies, where merchants and farmers did not want to lose money. However, there was a growing movement for a gathering of representatives from each colony. Together these delegates could discuss the problems facing the colonies and try to determine an appropriate response to British abuses of colonial rights.

SECTION 4 REVIEW

Identify and explain the significance of the following:

- **Townshend Acts**
- **writs of assistance**
- **Daughters of Liberty**
- **Crispus Attucks**
- **Boston Massacre**
- **propaganda**
- **Tea Act**
- **Boston Tea Party**
- **Intolerable Acts**
- **Mercy Otis Warren**

Reading for Content Understanding

1 **Main Idea** What were the colonists' reactions to the Townshend Acts?

2 **Main Idea** How were the Boston Massacre and the Boston Tea Party significant to the colonists' struggle against British authority?

3 **Global Relations** How did the four Intolerable Acts reflect the worsening relationship between Britain and its colonies?

4 **Writing** *Creating* Sketch a political cartoon expressing an opinion on one of the events in Boston in the 1770s. Include a one-paragraph caption with your cartoon.

5 **Critical Thinking** *Synthesizing Information* How did conflicts with Britain draw colonists together?

CHAPTER 6 REVIEW

Chapter Summary

A series of wars beginning in the late 1600s between France and Britain left Britain as the major European power in North America. As colonists began to move onto the frontier, tensions rose between the settlers and American Indians. Then a series of protests erupted when Britain created new taxes that colonists did not want to pay. ■

On a separate sheet of paper, complete the following activities.

Identifying People and Ideas

Describe the historical significance of the following:

1. Albany Plan of Union
2. James Wolfe
3. boycott
4. Proclamation of 1763
5. casualties
6. Stamp Act
7. Committees of Correspondence
8. Patrick Henry
9. writs of assistance
10. Mercy Otis Warren

Internet Activity go.hrw.com
SA0 Colonial Wars

Search the Internet through the HRW Web site to find information about significant battles of the French and Indian War. Then create a detailed time line with at least five entries that show these events and the progression of the war.

Understanding Main Ideas

1. What events led to King Philip's War?
2. What were the terms of the Treaty of Paris?
3. How did the British government try to control colonial expansion?
4. How did Parliament attempt to reduce the number of colonial smugglers who dodged the tax laws?
5. How did the Sons of Liberty challenge the Stamp Act?
6. What criticisms did colonists have of the Townshend Acts?
7. Why did Parliament pass the Intolerable Acts?

Reviewing Themes

1. **Global Relations** Why did Britain and France go to war in 1754 in North America? What was the result of this war?
2. **Geographic Diversity** What caused Pontiac's Rebellion?
3. **Economic Development** How did colonists respond to new taxes passed by Parliament?

Using the Time Line

Number your paper from 1 to 6. Match the letters on the time line below with the following events.

1. In an attempt to drive out white settlers, Pontiac attacks British forts on the frontier.
2. Parliament passes the Intolerable Acts to punish Massachusetts for the Boston Tea Party.
3. Britain begins fighting France and Spain in Queen Anne's War.
4. British soldiers fire into a crowd in the event that becomes known as the Boston Massacre.
5. The British capture Fort Duquesne and rename it Fort Pitt, the present-day site of Pittsburgh.
6. Surrounded by the French, George Washington and his troops surrender at Fort Necessity.

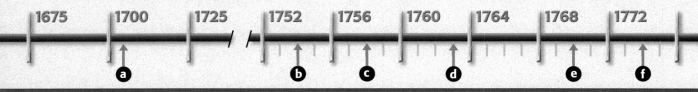

Thinking Critically

1. **Synthesizing Information**   Imagine that you are an American Indian at the time of the French and Indian War. Would you prefer to support the side of the British or the French, or to remain neutral? Explain your answer.

2. **Drawing Conclusions**   Why do you think British leaders felt the need to reassert their authority over the colonies?

3. **Identifying Cause and Effect**   How did events in Boston affect the relationship between Britain and the colonies?

Writing About History

1. **Creating**   Imagine that you are the Wampanoag leader Metacomet. Write a five-line poem about King Philip's War.

2. **Expressing**   Imagine that you are one of the British soldiers accused of the murder of the colonists in the Boston Massacre. Write a letter to your family back in Britain telling them your side of the story.

Linking Geography and History

1. **Location**   Where was the backcountry located, and why did settlers move there?

2. **Region**   Why did Britain and France want to control the Ohio River valley?

History Skills Workshop

Reading Graphs   Study the graph at right, which shows the amount of money Great Britain spent on the French and Indian War and answer the following questions: (a) What was the difference between Britain's tax revenue and its military costs in 1760? (b) How had the relationship between these two numbers changed by 1770?

Building Your Portfolio

American History

Complete the following activities individually or in groups.

1. **Colonial Protests**   Imagine that you are attending a meeting of the Sons of Liberty or the Daughters of Liberty. Write a skit that explains why you are upset with the British government and what actions you might take. Have at least one character in the skit urge the group to proceed with caution. If time permits, videotape a performance of your skit.

2. **The French and Indian War**   Prepare a map showing the major battles of the French and Indian War. Make your map large enough to display in the classroom. Decide how to distinguish between British, French, and Spanish forces and be sure to show troop movements. Then show which country controlled various areas in North America following the Treaty of Paris.

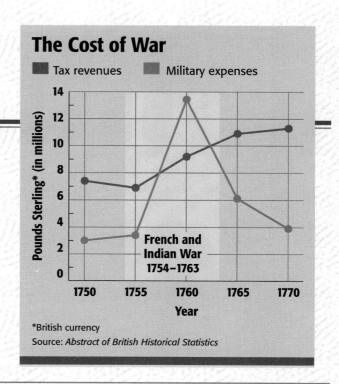

The Cost of War

■ Tax revenues   ■ Military expenses

French and Indian War 1754–1763

*British currency

Source: *Abstract of British Historical Statistics*

A Shift in Power

New-York Historical Society

The British colonies in North America grew rapidly in the late 1600s and 1700s. Although New France grew more slowly, the French remained a significant threat to British settlements and their future expansion, particularly in Canada and the area west of the thirteen colonies.

The two colonial powers fought a number of wars during the period. British victories helped Britain gain political power and control of much of North America by the late 1700s.

During this same time, another shift in power was taking place in North America. American Indians fought to keep their lands, but they were gradually losing them as the European colonies grew. As more Europeans settled in North America, American Indians found themselves being pushed farther and farther west. ■

Conflict with American Indians

Like many of the American colonies, the colonies of New England grew rapidly. Chief Metacomet of the Wampanoag Indians, called King Philip by the settlers, led a war against colonists in New England in 1675. That war and other conflicts helped slow colonial growth, but could not stop it.

Rate of New England Population Growth, 1660–1750

(Bar graph: y-axis "Percent of growth in non-Indian population" from 0 to 60; x-axis "Year" showing 1660, 1670, 1680, 1690, 1700, 1710, 1720, 1730, 1740, 1750)

Source: *Historical Statistics of the United States*

Geography **Skills**

Reading Bar Graphs

1. During what 10-year period was New England's percentage of population growth greatest?
2. During what period was the percentage of population growth slowest?

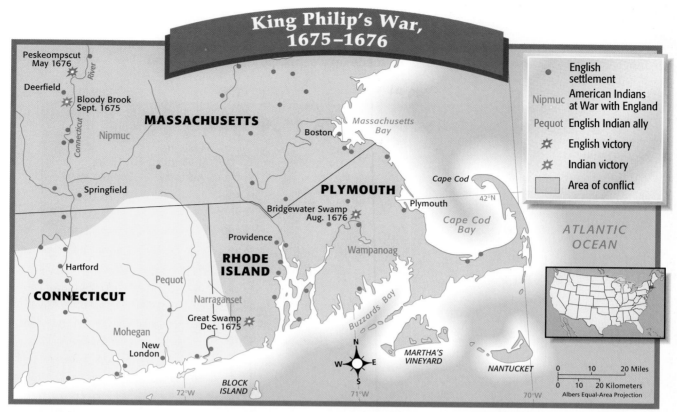

King Philip's War, 1675–1676

Peskeompscut
May 1676 ✸

Deerfield

Bloody Brook
Sept. 1675 ✸

MASSACHUSETTS

Nipmuc

Massachusetts Bay

Boston

Springfield

PLYMOUTH

Cape Cod

Plymouth
42°N

Bridgewater Swamp
Aug. 1676 ✸

Providence

Cape Cod Bay

Hartford

Pequot

RHODE ISLAND

Wampanoag

ATLANTIC OCEAN

CONNECTICUT

Narraganset

Buzzards Bay

Great Swamp
Dec. 1675 ✸

Mohegan

New London

MARTHA'S VINEYARD

NANTUCKET

BLOCK ISLAND

72°W   71°W   70°W

Legend:
- • English settlement
- Nipmuc — American Indians at War with England
- Pequot — English Indian ally
- ✸ English victory
- ✸ Indian victory
- ▢ Area of conflict

0   10   20 Miles
0   10   20 Kilometers
Albers Equal-Area Projection

Geography Skills

Reading Special-Purpose Maps

1. Where and when did American Indians win a victory in King Philip's War?

2. What colonies were involved in the conflict?

3. What western river saw the most fighting?

Metacomet, King Philip

History Note 1

As the colonies grew, officials required American Indians to accept colonial authority. In New England in 1675, American Indians rejected this authority. When Plymouth Colony convicted three Wampanoag Indians of murder, their group attacked colonial settlements in the bitter conflict called King Philip's War. Many people on both sides were killed, and the defeated American Indians had to accept both colonial authority and the loss of more land.

History Note 2

Historians' estimates of the number of American Indians living in North America when the first European settlers began arriving in the 1500s range from 1.2 million to 18 million. Experts believe that European diseases, as well as wars with European settlers, reduced the American Indian population greatly. By 1890 the American Indian population was down to 250,000.

Colonial Settlement

Colonial settlements and population grew rapidly from 1660 to 1780. In the 1700s increasing numbers of enslaved Africans made up a significant part of the total population.

British Colonial Population in America, 1660–1780

■ Population of African Ancestry ■ Total Population

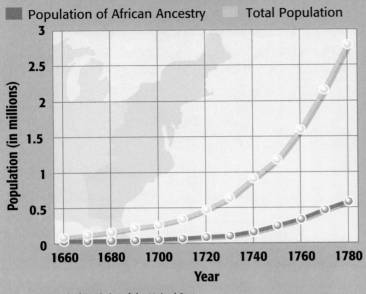

Year	Population of African Ancestry	Total Population
1660	2,920	75,058
1670	4,535	111,935
1680	6,971	151,507
1690	16,729	210,372
1700	27,817	250,888
1710	44,866	331,711
1720	68,839	466,185
1730	91,021	629,445
1740	150,024	905,563
1750	236,420	1,170,760
1760	325,806	1,593,625
1770	459,822	2,148,076
1780	575,420	2,780,369

Source: *Historical Statistics of the United States*

Geography Skills

Reading Line Graphs and Charts

1. What was the population of the American colonies in 1660? in 1760?
2. How many of the people living in the colonies were of African ancestry in 1660? in 1760?
3. When did the population of the British colonies begin to increase at the fastest rate?

History Note 3

Virginia—the most populous colony by the mid-1700s—grew rapidly after the 1730s. This growth came from settlement in the colony's interior. Settlers spread west beyond Virginia's tidewater area near the coast into the valleys of the Piedmont or foothills, region. Western land was less expensive and settlers could afford to support large families by farming.

History Note 4

The population in the colonies grew much more rapidly than the population in Britain. The colonial population increased more than 400 percent, to nearly 1.2 million, between 1700 and 1750. During that same period, Britain's population grew by only 14 percent. Immigration from Europe along with the many enslaved Africans brought to the colonies caused the colonial boom. Another contributor to the growth was that more women married in the colonies than in Britain—often at a younger age—and had more children.

Non-Indian Population in Eastern North America, 1760

Estimated non-Indian population: 1,704,325

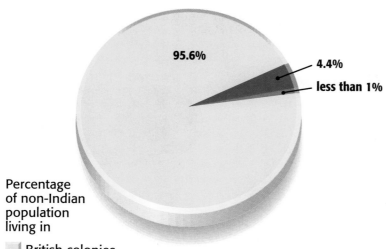

95.6%

4.4%

less than 1%

Percentage of non-Indian population living in

- British colonies
- New France
- Spanish Florida

Sources: *Encyclopedia of the North American Colonies; Historical Statistics of the United States*

Geography **Skills**

Reading Pie Graphs

1. What was the estimated non-Indian population in eastern North America around 1760?
2. What percentage of that population lived in the British colonies?
3. What percentages of that population lived in New France and in Spanish Florida?
4. How do you think the population distribution affected the struggles for power in North America?

History Note 5

The small French population in North America centered around Quebec, which lay along the St. Lawrence River in the north and around New Orleans, located at the mouth of the Mississippi River, in the south. This gave the French access to two great waterways leading to the continent's interior. There the French built forts and widely scattered settlements to promote their fur trade with American Indians.

History Note 6

In eastern North America, colonists from Spain settled first in Florida. However, their population there was never great, numbering only about 3,200 in 1760. In the late 1500s in western North America, the Spanish began moving north from Mexico into the areas that make up present-day Texas, New Mexico, Arizona, and California. By the late 1700s there were about 20,000 Spanish-speaking settlers living in New Mexico. Still, the population of these Spanish settlements never approached the size of the British colonies.

Mission Santa Barbara in California

Changing Empires

In a series of colonial wars beginning in the late 1600s and ending in 1763, the British, French, and Spanish empires in North America experienced great changes. France's empire practically ceased to exist, and Spain lost some lands while gaining others. The British empire saw the most change. After winning the French and Indian War in North America, Britain gained large territories and great power.

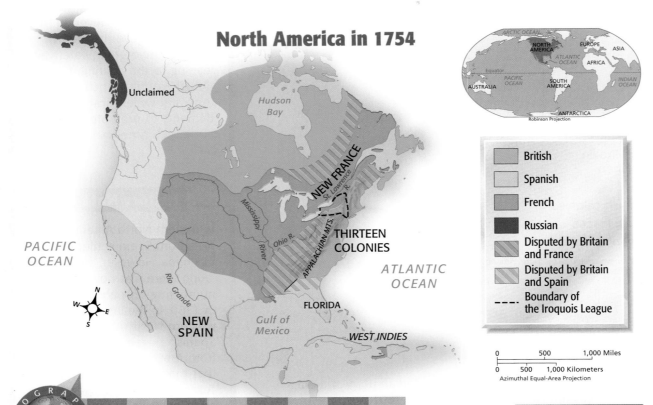

North America in 1754

Legend:
- British
- Spanish
- French
- Russian
- Disputed by Britain and France
- Disputed by Britain and Spain
- Boundary of the Iroquois League

```
0        500      1,000 Miles
0    500    1,000 Kilometers
Azimuthal Equal-Area Projection
```

Geography Skills
Reading Political Maps

1. Describe the general locations of the European colonial empires in North America in 1754.
2. Over which areas of North America did European powers dispute control?
3. Which European powers appeared to control the largest parts of the present-day United States?

History Note 7

In 1739 Britain tried to take Florida from Spain in the so-called War of Jenkins' Ear. The war was sparked in part by a British sailor's claim that a Spanish captain had stopped his ship in the Caribbean and cut off his ear. The war was a defeat for the British. Spanish troops—and tropical diseases such as yellow fever—beat back British forces who invaded Florida and South America.

History Note 8

Many U.S. place-names today reflect the colonial influences of France and Spain. The name of Terre Haute, Indiana, means "high land," and the name of Des Moines, Iowa, means "some monks" in French. Louisiana was named after French king Louis XIV. Florida is Spanish for "land of flowers." In the Southwest, Spanish names include the Rio Grande, or "great river," and Los Angeles, the "city of angels."

North America in 1763

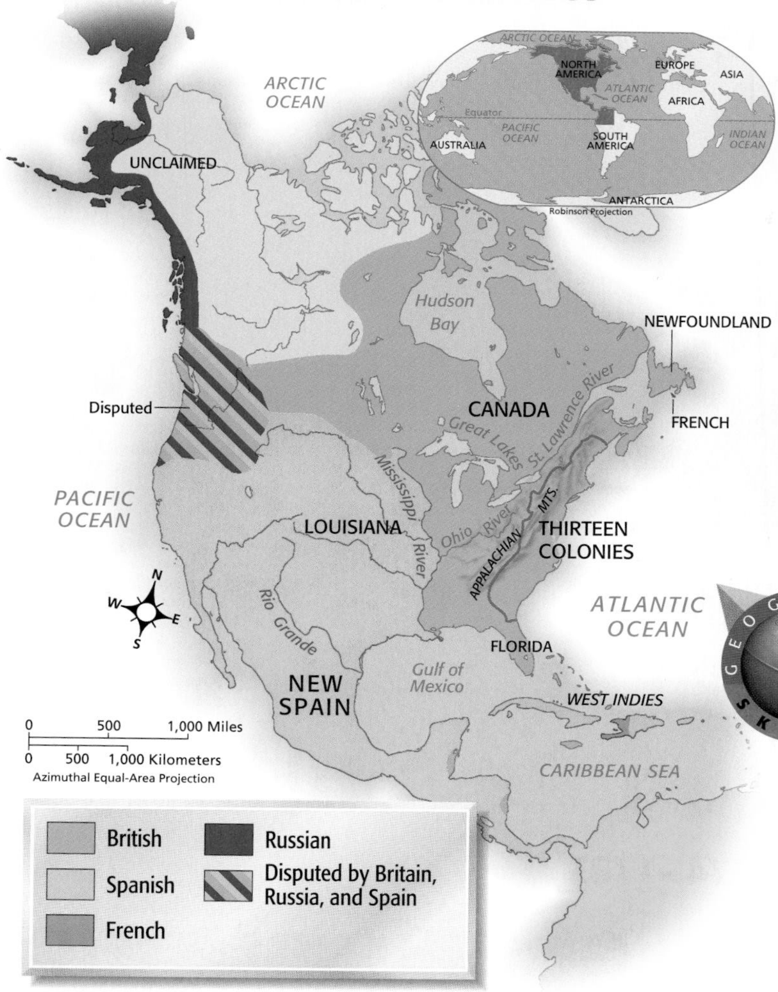

ARCTIC OCEAN

UNCLAIMED

Hudson Bay

Disputed

CANADA

NEWFOUNDLAND

FRENCH

PACIFIC OCEAN

LOUISIANA

Great Lakes

St. Lawrence River

Mississippi River

Ohio River

APPALACHIAN MTS.

THIRTEEN COLONIES

ATLANTIC OCEAN

Rio Grande

FLORIDA

NEW SPAIN

Gulf of Mexico

WEST INDIES

CARIBBEAN SEA

| 0 | 500 | 1,000 Miles |

| 0 | 500 | 1,000 Kilometers |

Azimuthal Equal-Area Projection

- British
- Spanish
- French
- Russian
- Disputed by Britain, Russia, and Spain

(Inset globe: Robinson Projection — ARCTIC OCEAN, NORTH AMERICA, EUROPE, ASIA, AFRICA, SOUTH AMERICA, AUSTRALIA, ANTARCTICA, PACIFIC OCEAN, ATLANTIC OCEAN, INDIAN OCEAN, Equator)

History Note 9

In the 1700s, settlers moved into the lands west of the Appalachian Mountains and south of the Ohio River. These lands in present-day Kentucky and Tennessee were claimed by Virginia and North Carolina, but were beyond the reach of colonial authority. Because they needed law and order in these new lands, some settlers established their own governments and negotiated land deals with the area's American Indians.

Geography Skills
Reading Maps

1. Which European powers possessed which areas in North America in 1763?
2. What areas of North America were disputed or unclaimed?
3. Look at the map of North America in 1754 on page 184. How did the control of North American territory change between 1754 and 1763?

History Note 10

France surrendered Louisiana to Spain in 1762, but the Spanish never really exercised control over the huge territory west of the Mississippi River. Spanish officials generally worked to form trading relationships with American Indians in the region. French influence remained strong in the area, and the territory was returned to France in 1800.

Fort St. Marie de Gannentaha, Onondaga Lake, New York

NEW YOR

▪ CHAPTER 7 ▪
The American Revolution
(1774–1783)

"The land of Liberty! how sweet the sound!" declared Eliza Wilkinson in 1782. Just a few years earlier Wilkinson—a young widow from Charleston, South Carolina—had shown little interest in politics. Soon, however, she was swept up in a movement against British rule. By 1782 Wilkinson, a once loyal British subject, was among the many people proudly calling themselves Americans.

THEMES

Citizenship and Democracy
Why might a country's citizens revolt against their government?

Constitutional Heritage
What does it mean for a country to be founded on the idea of liberty?

Global Relations
Why might some nations support a revolution in another country?

1774   1775   1776   1777   1778

SEPT. The First Continental Congress meets.

APRIL Fighting at Lexington and Concord marks the beginning of the American Revolution.

JULY The Declaration of Independence is signed.

OCT. The Patriots win a major victory at the Battle of Saratoga.

MAY Congress approves a treaty of alliance with France.

The Revolution Begins

Reading Focus

How did the First Continental Congress and the fighting at Lexington and Concord affect the colonies' conflict with Britain?

What tasks did the Second Continental Congress accomplish?

How did geography influence the early battles of the war?

Key Terms

First Continental Congress

Minutemen

Redcoats

Second Continental Congress

Continental Army

Olive Branch Petition

siege

Battle of Bunker Hill

BY THE FALL OF 1774, *the colonists had to decide how to resolve their conflict with Great Britain. Cousins John and Samuel Adams were among those active in the debate. Samuel Adams was the rebel who had organized the Boston Tea Party, while John Adams was the thoughtful attorney who had defended British soldiers accused of firing on colonists in the Boston Massacre. Both cousins agreed that the time had come for colonial leaders to respond to British actions, and the colonies soon scheduled an assembly in Philadelphia. As the Adamses set out on their journey there from Boston, neither one knew what would result from the upcoming meeting.*

The Granger Collection, New York

Swords from the Revolution

IMAGE ON LEFT PAGE: *The Battle of Lexington*

1779

FEB. George Rogers Clark's forces recapture Vincennes.

1780

AUG. The British wipe out most of the Patriot forces stationed at Camden, South Carolina.

1781

OCT. The British surrender at Yorktown secures the American victory in the war.

1782

1783

SEPT. The Treaty of Paris of 1783 formally ends the war.

The American Revolution **187**

The First Continental Congress

In September 1774 the Adams cousins were among 56 colonial delegates who met in Philadelphia for the **First Continental Congress**. Georgia was the only colony not represented. Many people who had been involved in protest groups attended, including John Dickinson of Pennsylvania and Patrick Henry of Virginia.

The delegates debated the best way to respond to the crisis in Massachusetts and what they felt were abuses by British authorities. Many agreed with John Dickinson, who argued that the colonists should find a way to make peace with Britain in order to avoid any more bloodshed. Other delegates, such as Patrick Henry, argued that the conflict would end only through violence. "Arms [weapons] are a resource to which we shall be forced," declared Henry.

In the end the delegates compromised. They recommended that colonists continue to boycott British goods and that they warn their militias to be prepared in case violence did break out. Meanwhile, the delegates assembled a carefully worded list of 10 resolutions to present to King George III. This Declaration of Resolves spelled out what the Congress considered to be the colonists' rights, including the rights to "life, liberty, and property." The delegates agreed to meet again in May 1775 if the king did not acknowledge these rights.

When King George III received the resolutions from the delegates, he refused to consider their demands. Instead, British leaders ordered troops in the colonies to prepare to seize the colonial militias' weapons.

The "Shot Heard Round the World"

Tensions were particularly high in and around Boston, Massachusetts, the center of colonial protests. The British became concerned when local militia units seemed to be actively preparing for armed conflict. These militia members called themselves **Minutemen** because they were ready to fight on a minute's notice.

In mid-April 1775 British general Thomas Gage received his orders to take action. He decided to seize the local militia's weapons, which were stored in Concord, a town about 20 miles west of Boston. Gage tried to keep the British plans a secret, however, spies informed some members of the Sons of Liberty that the British were preparing to move. Unsure of when and how the British might attack, Sons of Liberty member Paul Revere arranged for his informants to signal him from the Old North Church in Boston. They were to display one lantern if the British were coming by land, two if they were coming by sea.

Lexington

On the evening of April 18, 1775, Revere and William Dawes received word that the British were crossing the Charles River to march toward Concord. The two men hopped on their horses and rode through the countryside, warning Minutemen that "the British are coming!" Isaac Davis was one of the Minutemen who heard the

Paul Revere alerts the countryside of Massachusetts about the arrival of British troops. This warning led the Minutemen to prepare for an attack.

warning. His wife later described his response to Revere's call:

❝ **The alarm was given early in the morning, and my husband lost no time in making ready to go to Concord with his company. . . . [He] said but little that morning. He seemed serious and thoughtful; but never seemed to hesitate. . . . He only said, 'Take good care of the children.'** ❞

On the morning of April 19, fewer than 70 Minutemen met a much larger force of British troops at the Lexington village green, near Concord. The colonial commander shouted to his men, "Don't fire unless fired upon. But if they mean to have a war, let it begin here!" The two sides stared at each other for several moments.

Suddenly, a shot rang out. To this day, no one knows who fired this "shot heard round the world," but once the soldiers heard it, the fight began. The battle was over in minutes. When the smoke cleared, the badly outnumbered colonists had suffered 8 dead and 10 wounded.

Concord

The British marched on to Concord, where militia members had supposedly stored their muskets. The British did not find many weapons, because the colonists had already hidden them elsewhere. In anger, some British

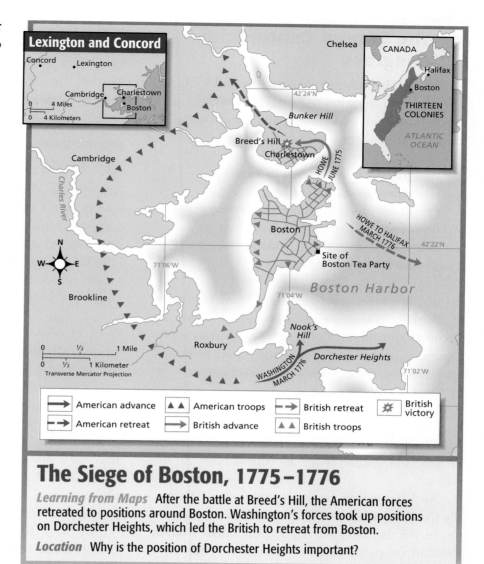

The Siege of Boston, 1775–1776

Learning from Maps After the battle at Breed's Hill, the American forces retreated to positions around Boston. Washington's forces took up positions on Dorchester Heights, which led the British to retreat from Boston.

Location Why is the position of Dorchester Heights important?

A powder horn from the Revolutionary War

troops set fire to a few buildings. When one of the colonists shouted, "Will you let them burn the town down?" Isaac Davis responded, "No, I haven't a man who is afraid to go," and the Minutemen charged forward.

As the British retreated back to Boston, the Minutemen fired upon them from behind trees and buildings. The British soldiers' bright red uniforms with straps that formed an "X" across each soldier's chest made ideal targets. The colonists called the British soldiers **Redcoats** because of these uniforms.

By the time the British reached Boston, they had suffered more than 250 casualities, compared to fewer than 100 for the colonists. Isaac Davis, the Minuteman who "never seemed to hesitate" when called, was among the colonists killed that day.

The Second Continental Congress

As word of the fighting at Lexington and Concord spread, many colonists responded with shock and anger. In one small Massachusetts town, Dr. James Thacher noted:

> " This tragical event seems to have electrified all classes of people. . . . Expresses [messengers] are hastening from town to town, in all directions through the country . . . rousing the people *To Arms! To Arms!* "

In May 1775, representatives from twelve of the thirteen colonies met in Philadelphia for the **Second Continental Congress**. The leaders of the Congress gathered to decide how to act now that open hostilities had taken place. They decided not to break away from Britain, but made plans to organize and fund a **Continental Army** to defend the colonies. They chose Virginian George Washington, a well-respected veteran of the French and Indian War, as commander of the Army.

As Washington began organizing his troops, the Congress tried one final time to restore peace. On July 5 the delegates signed the **Olive Branch Petition**, a peace request named for the olive branch, a traditional symbol of peace. As representative Richard Penn set off to deliver the petition to King George III, the fighting spread. Before Penn reached the king in the fall, the fighting had become so fierce that the king rejected the petition.

Early Battles

Soon after the first session of the Second Continental Congress, word began to spread that a group of colonists had won a victory against the British in northern New York. The capture of Fort Ticonderoga in May 1775 was a great accomplishment for the colonists.

Fort Ticonderoga

Strategically located in northeastern New York, the British-held Fort Ticonderoga controlled access to Lake Champlain, a waterway leading into Canada. Colonel Benedict Arnold was supposed to lead the assault. However, the Green Mountain Boys, a group of men from present-day Vermont, insisted that they would take their guns and go home rather than follow anyone besides their leader. Ethan Allen. Arnold and Allen compromised, agreeing to lead the assault together.

On May 10 the colonists sneaked up on the British under cover of a fierce early morning rainstorm and quickly took the fort. The attack also secured a large supply of British weapons, including cannons, for the colonial forces.

Bunker Hill and Breed's Hill

After the battle at Concord, the British withdrew to Boston, where Minutemen surrounded the city. Once reinforcements arrived, the colonial forces held Boston under **siege**—a military blockade of a city or fort.

In mid-June 1775 the British prepared to secure Charlestown, which overlooks Boston from across its northern harbor. Warned of the plan, colonial forces dug defensive trenches atop nearby Bunker Hill and Breed's Hill. When the British awoke on the morning of June 17, they were shocked to see that the colonial soldiers had secured the hills. Nevertheless, the Redcoats mounted a frontal

Ethan Allen awakens the British commander and demands the surrender of Fort Ticonderoga.

The Granger Collection, New York

assault against the colonists. The colonial commander ordered his troops, who were low on gunpowder, not to fire on the British soldiers "until you see the whites of their eyes."

Most of the fighting took place on Breed's Hill. After turning back several assaults, the outnumbered colonists retreated when they ran out of ammunition. Although the British gained control of the hill, they had suffered more than 1,000 casualties compared to some 400 for the colonists. Despite their retreat, the **Battle of Bunker Hill** was a moral victory for the colonists. It demonstrated that, despite superior British firepower, they could withstand a frontal assault from the British army.

Dorchester Heights

Shortly after the Battle of Bunker Hill, General Washington arrived to command the Continental Army's siege of Boston. To drive the British from the city, Washington knew that he would need heavier guns. In November he put officer Henry Knox in charge of transporting the captured cannons from Fort Ticonderoga to Boston. Knox successfully brought the heavy guns over 300 miles of rough terrain in the middle of winter.

In March 1776 Washington positioned the cannons on Dorchester Heights, a hill that overlooks

The Granger Collection, New York

Hand-to-hand combat in the Battle of Bunker Hill

Boston from the south. Using the heavy artillery, Washington's troops fired down on the British.

The British guns were no match for the colonists' well-positioned cannons. "The rebels have done more in one night than my whole army could do in months," declared British general William Howe. On March 7 Howe ordered a retreat from Boston to Canada. The birthplace of the rebellion was back in colonial hands.

SECTION 1 REVIEW

Identify and explain the significance of the following:

- **First Continental Congress**
- **Minutemen**
- **Redcoats**
- **Second Continental Congress**
- **Continental Army**
- **George Washington**
- **Olive Branch Petition**
- **siege**
- **Battle of Bunker Hill**

Locate and explain the importance of the following:

- **Lexington**
- **Dorchester Heights**

Reading for Content Understanding

1 **Main Idea** How did the battles at Lexington and Concord affect the colonists' feelings toward Britain?

2 **Main Idea** Describe the actions taken by the Second Continental Congress.

3 **Geographic Diversity** *Human-Environment Interaction* How did geography influence the colonists' strategy in the war's early battles?

4 **Writing** *Persuading* Imagine that you are a supporter of either John Dickinson or Patrick Henry at the First Continental Congress. Write a speech persuading others to support your position.

5 **Critical Thinking** *Making Comparisons* What were the differences between the First and the Second Continental Congresses?

Declaring Independence

Reading Focus

How did *Common Sense* influence the colonies?

In what way did the Enlightenment affect the Declaration of Independence?

What issues were and were not addressed in the Declaration of Independence?

Key Terms

Common Sense
Declaration of Independence
Patriots
Loyalists

I N JANUARY 1776, *a 47-page pamphlet appeared on the streets of Philadelphia. The author was 37-year-old Thomas Paine, a self-educated British Quaker. Several years before, Paine had met Benjamin Franklin—then one of the colonial agents living in London—and impressed the colonial inventor with his sharp mind. In 1774 Franklin had helped Paine immigrate to Philadelphia, where he became a writer. Less than two years later, Paine produced a work that changed the course of American history.*

Thomas Paine, *author of* Common Sense

★ Paine's *Common Sense*

News of Paine's pamphlet **Common Sense**, which argued for breaking away from Great Britain, spread throughout the thirteen colonies. Within three months, colonists had bought around 120,000 copies. Eventually, sales throughout the colonies and Europe reached some 500,000 copies.

Common Sense achieved such popularity because of both its message and its style. Most pamphlets of the time were written by lawyers—such as John Dickinson—who typically wrote in a style that only well-educated people could understand. Paine wrote as a common man to common people. He therefore reached a wider audience than most other pamphlet writers of his day.

In *Common Sense*, Paine wrote that the system of monarchy in European countries such as Britain was unnatural and wrong. Instead, he said, countries should be ruled by laws made by the people. At the time, this claim was quite radical, or extreme, because monarchies ruled most of the world. Paine wrote:

> ❝ **A government of our own is our natural right; and when a man seriously reflects on the precariousness [uncertainty] of human affairs, he will become convinced that it is . . . wiser and safer to form a constitution of our own.** ❞

This controversial proposal soon gained many supporters, and the publication of *Common Sense* became a turning point in changing many colonists' attitudes toward Britain. As the fighting continued, some members of the Continental Congress decided it was time to make the idea of independence a reality.

★ The Declaration of Independence

In June 1776 the Continental Congress, influenced by the suggestion of Richard Henry Lee of Virginia, appointed a five-person committee to write a document declaring the colonies' independence. The committee included John Adams, Thomas Jefferson, Benjamin Franklin, Roger Sherman, and Robert R. Livingston. Jefferson was the primary author of the document.

The **Declaration of Independence** defined what colonists believed to be their rights, spelled out their complaints against Britain, and declared that the colonies were free and independent. The Declaration captured the spirit of Thomas Paine's ideas by strongly criticizing King George III for depriving the colonists of trial by jury, imposing taxes without the colonists' consent, dissolving colonial charters and legislatures, and committing two dozen other alleged crimes.

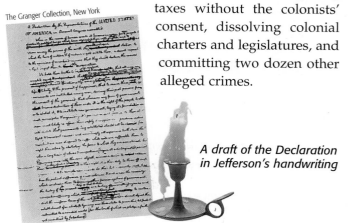
The Granger Collection, New York

A draft of the Declaration in Jefferson's handwriting

The committee assembled to write the Declaration of Independence presents a draft to John Hancock, president of the Second Continental Congress.

The writers of the document also drew inspiration from Enlightenment philosophers who thought that government was a social contract between people and their ruler. The best governments, these philosophers said, were those that respected the "natural rights" of individuals—basic rights such as "life, liberty, and the pursuit of happiness." Britain's John Locke had added that if the people determined that their ruler or form of government was corrupt, the people had a right to overthrow it. Thus, the authors of the Declaration claimed that King George III was "unfit to be the ruler of a free people" and said it was "their duty, to throw off such Government." On July 4, 1776, members of the Continental Congress approved the Declaration of Independence, dissolving all allegiance to the British Crown and creating the United States of America.

★ Choosing Sides

The signing of the Declaration made the rebellion a full-scale revolution against Britain. Those who supported the Revolution would be considered traitors to their mother country. Even many colonists who believed in Enlightenment ideals were hesitant to take such a step. John Dickinson, for example, refused to sign the Declaration because he believed the colonies were not yet prepared to break away from Great Britain.

Those who chose to fight for independence became known as **Patriots**. Tories, who were called **Loyalists** after the hostilities began, were

Abigail Adams

Abigail Adams was born in Massachusetts in 1744. She was educated at home by her parents, and by a young age had read most of the classic writers of Europe. She even taught herself French. From this upbringing she gained a love of reading and writing that led her to become what some historians have called "one of the great letter writers of all time."

She married John Adams in 1764, and they had five children. After John attended the First Continental Congress in 1774, political events prevented him from returning home for many years, except for short visits. During this time, Abigail Adams took control of all her husband's business affairs, including the family farm. Long after the war, she continued to run most of the family's business and to advise her husband on numerous political issues. Since her death in 1818, the many letters she wrote to her husband, family, and friends have served as an important record of the early American republic.

colonists who considered it their duty to remain loyal to, and to side with, Britain. Once the Declaration was signed, Loyalists found it particularly difficult to remain in the colonies because of persecution by Patriots. More than 50,000 Loyalists fled the colonies during the Revolution. Most went to Canada.

Many Loyalists shared the feelings of Samuel Curwen of Salem, Massachusetts. He was a successful merchant who generally stayed out of political affairs that did not affect his business. He believed that British rule was the best way to maintain peace and prosperity in the colonies and could not imagine a nation without a monarch.

Although Curwen considered the fighting at Lexington and Concord "an unhappy affair," he refused to join colonists who blamed the conflict entirely on the British. Targeted as a Loyalist, he fled his home to avoid "the looks, words, and actions of the mad rabble [masses]" of Patriots. Even Thomas Fairfax, one of George Washington's closest friends, had to flee to Britain because he was a faithful Loyalist. Divided allegiances tore apart families as well as friendships—the great Patriot Ben Franklin became separated from his Loyalist son William. Such divisions were yet another price of the war.

★ Other Reactions

Some people pointed out that the Declaration excluded many colonists. While it declared that "all men are created equal," the document failed to mention women or the people held in the most unequal of situations—slaves.

Patriots pull down a statue of King George III in New York.

Women

Although many women worked for the Patriot cause, the Declaration did not address their rights. One critic who voiced concern over this exclusion was John Adams's wife, Abigail. She appealed to her husband to protect the rights of women, advising him in a letter:

> 66 **Remember the Ladies, and be more generous and favorable to them than your ancestors. Do not put such unlimited power into the hands of the Husbands. . . . If particular care and attention is not paid to the Ladies we are determined to foment [start] a Rebellion, and will not hold ourselves bound by any Laws in which we have no voice, or Representation.** 99

Abigail Adams did not start a revolution, however, even though the Declaration did not address women specifically.

African Americans

Abigail Adams was also concerned about the rights of African Americans, another group left out of the Declaration. In his original draft of the Declaration, Thomas Jefferson—a slaveholder himself—had included a passage that condemned

Mum Bett, a Massachusetts slave, believed that the words "all men are created equal" should apply to her and other slaves. She successfully sued for her freedom in 1781.

the slave trade. However, when southern delegates objected to the passage it was removed from the final version.

In July 1776 slavery was legal in all of the colonies, but the Revolution began to stir debates about the existence of slavery within a society that valued liberty. Some political writers who compared living under British rule to living under slavery could not ignore the conflict between the ideals of liberty and the practice of slavery. Some colonists believed that the principle "all men are created equal" should apply to everyone, regardless of gender or race.

Massachusetts slave Mum Bett made this argument when she successfully sued for her freedom in 1781. Massachusetts courts formally abolished slavery in that state two years later. By 1784 the rest of New England also had taken steps to end slavery. Even so, the unresolved conflict between liberty and slavery would continue to haunt the nation long after the Revolutionary War had ended.

SECTION 2 REVIEW

Identify and explain the significance of the following:
- **Thomas Paine**
- ***Common Sense***
- **Declaration of Independence**
- **Thomas Jefferson**
- **Patriots**
- **Loyalists**
- **Abigail Adams**

Reading for Content Understanding

1 Main Idea Why did colonists find the arguments in *Common Sense* so persuasive?

2 Main Idea How did the authors of the Declaration of Independence justify breaking away from British rule?

3 Citizenship and Democracy How did ideas from the Enlightenment influence the people who wrote the Declaration of Independence?

4 Writing *Expressing* Imagine that you are a woman or a slave living in the colonies in 1776. Write a paragraph expressing your reaction to the Declaration of Independence.

5 Critical Thinking *Drawing Conclusions* How might the British have viewed colonists who wanted to break away from Britain? Explain your answer.

Thomas Jefferson wrote the first draft of the Declaration in a little more than two weeks.

In the first paragraph, the signers state that it is important to justify why the colonists must break their political ties with Britain.

impel: force

endowed: provided

"Laws of Nature" and "Nature's God" refer to the belief common in the Scientific Revolution that certain patterns are constant and predictable and that they come from a supreme being. Natural or "unalienable" rights (the rights to life, liberty, and the pursuit of happiness) cannot be taken away. The English philosopher John Locke had argued that people created governments to protect their natural rights. If a government abuses its powers, it is the right as well as the duty of the people to do away with that government.

usurpations: wrongful seizures of power

despotism: unlimited power

THE
DECLARATION
of
INDEPENDENCE

In Congress, July 4, 1776
The unanimous Declaration of the thirteen
united States of America,

When in the Course of human events, it becomes necessary for one people to dissolve the political bands which have connected them with another, and to assume among the Powers of the earth, the separate and equal station to which the Laws of Nature and of Nature's God entitle them, a decent respect to the opinions of mankind requires that they should declare the causes which impel them to the separation.

Natural Rights

We hold these truths to be self-evident, that all men are created equal, that they are endowed by their Creator with certain unalienable Rights, that among these are Life, Liberty, and the pursuit of Happiness. That to secure these rights, Governments are instituted among Men, deriving their just powers from the consent of the governed,

That whenever any Form of Government becomes destructive of these ends, it is the Right of the People to alter or to abolish it, and to institute new Government, laying its foundation on such principles and organizing its powers in such form, as to them shall seem most likely to effect their Safety and Happiness. Prudence, indeed, will dictate that Governments long established should not be changed for light and transient causes; and accordingly all experience hath shown, that mankind are more disposed to suffer, while evils are sufferable, than to right themselves by abolishing the forms to which they are accustomed. But when a long train of abuses and usurpations, pursuing invariably the same Object evinces a design to reduce them under absolute Despotism, it is their right, it is their duty, to throw off such Government, and to provide new Guards for their future security.—

LEFT: *Revolutionary War hero Paul Revere*

Colonists' Complaints Against the King

Such has been the patient sufferance of these Colonies; and such is now the necessity which constrains them to alter their former Systems of Government. The history of the present King of Great Britain is a history of repeated injuries and usurpations, all having in direct object the establishment of an absolute Tyranny over these States. To prove this, let Facts be submitted to a candid world.

He has refused his Assent to Laws, the most wholesome and necessary for the public good.

He has forbidden his Governors to pass Laws of immediate and pressing importance, unless suspended in their operation till his Assent should be obtained; and when so suspended, he has utterly neglected to attend to them.

He has refused to pass other Laws for the accommodation of large districts of people, unless those people would relinquish the right of Representation in the Legislature, a right inestimable to them and formidable to tyrants only.

He has called together legislative bodies at places unusual, uncomfortable, and distant from the depository of their Public Records, for the sole purpose of fatiguing them into compliance with his measures.

He has dissolved Representative Houses repeatedly, for opposing with manly firmness his invasions on the rights of the people.

He has refused for a long time, after such dissolutions, to cause others to be elected; whereby the Legislative Powers, incapable of Annihilation, have returned to the People at large for their exercise; the State remaining in the mean time exposed to all the dangers of invasion from without, and convulsions within.

He has endeavored to prevent the population of these States; for that purpose obstructing the Laws of Naturalization of Foreigners; refusing to pass others to encourage their migration hither, and raising the conditions of new Appropriations of Lands.

He has obstructed the Administration of Justice, by refusing his Assent to Laws for establishing Judiciary Powers.

He has made Judges dependent on his Will alone, for the tenure of their offices, and the amount and payment of their salaries.

He has erected a multitude of New Offices, and sent hither swarms of Officers to harass our people, and eat out their substance.

He has kept among us, in times of peace, Standing Armies without the Consent of our legislature.

He has affected to render the Military independent of and superior to the Civil Power.

He has combined with others to subject us to a jurisdiction foreign to our constitution, and unacknowledged by our laws; giving his Assent to their Acts of pretended legislation:

tyranny: oppressive power exerted by a government or ruler

candid: fair

Here the Declaration lists the charges that the colonists had against King George III. How might the language in the list appeal to people's emotions?

relinquish: release, yield
inestimable: priceless
formidable: causing dread

Why do you think the king had his colonial legislatures meet in places that were hard to reach?

annihilation: destruction

convulsions: violent disturbances

naturalization of foreigners: the process by which foreign-born persons become citizens

appropriations of land: setting aside land for settlement

tenure: term

a multitude of: many

Name five acts that the Declaration states have been committed by the king and the British Parliament.

quartering: lodging, housing

What was the colonists' rallying cry to protest the king's tax policies?

The "neighboring Province" that is referred to here is Canada.

arbitrary: not based on law

render: make

abdicated: given up

foreign mercenaries: soldiers hired to fight for a country not their own

perfidy: violation of trust

insurrections: rebellions

petitioned for redress: asked formally for a correction of wrongs

Notice that the Declaration has 18 paragraphs beginning with "He has" or "He is." What is the effect of this repetition?

unwarrantable jurisdiction: unjustified authority

magnanimity: generous spirit

conjured: urgently called upon

consanguinity: common ancestry

acquiesce: consent to

For quartering large bodies of armed troops among us:

For protecting them, by a mock Trial, from Punishment for any Murders which they should commit on the Inhabitants of these States:

For cutting off our Trade with all parts of the world:

For imposing taxes on us without our Consent:

For depriving us in many cases, of the benefits of Trial by Jury:

For transporting us beyond Seas to be tried for pretended offences:

For abolishing the free System of English Laws in a neighboring Province, establishing therein an Arbitrary government, and enlarging its Boundaries so as to render it at once an example and fit instrument for introducing the same absolute rule into these Colonies:

For taking away our Charters, abolishing our most valuable Laws, and altering fundamentally the Forms of our Governments:

For suspending our own Legislature, and declaring themselves invested with Power to legislate for us in all cases whatsoever.

He has abdicated Government here, by declaring us out of his Protection and waging War against us.

He has plundered our seas, ravaged our Coasts, burnt our towns, and destroyed the lives of our people.

He is at this time transporting large armies of foreign mercenaries to complete the works of death, desolation and tyranny, already begun with circumstances of Cruelty & perfidy scarcely paralleled in the most barbarous ages, and totally unworthy the Head of a civilized nation.

He has constrained our fellow Citizens taken Captive on the high Seas to bear Arms against their Country, to become the executioners of their friends and Brethren, or to fall themselves by their Hands.

He has excited domestic insurrections amongst us, and has endeavored to bring on the inhabitants of our frontiers, the merciless Indian Savages, whose known rule of warfare, is an undistinguished destruction of all ages, sexes and conditions.

In every stage of these Oppressions We have Petitioned for Redress in the most humble terms: Our repeated Petitions have been answered only by repeated injury. A Prince, whose character is thus marked by every act which may define a Tyrant, is unfit to be the ruler of a free People.

Nor have We been wanting in attention to our British brethren. We have warned them from time to time of attempts by their legislature to extend an unwarrantable jurisdiction over us. We have reminded them of the circumstances of our emigration and settlement here. We have appealed to their native justice and magnanimity, and we have conjured them by the ties of our common kindred to disavow these usurpations, which, would inevitably interrupt our connections and correspondence. They too have been deaf to the voice of justice and of consanguinity. We must, therefore, acquiesce in the necessity, which denounces our

Separation, and hold them, as we hold the rest of mankind, Enemies in War, in Peace Friends.

An Independent United States

We, therefore, the Representatives of the united States of America, in General Congress, Assembled, appealing to the Supreme Judge of the world for the rectitude of our intentions, do, in the Name, and by Authority of the good People of these Colonies, solemnly publish and declare, That these United Colonies are, and of Right ought to be Free and Independent States; that they are Absolved from all Allegiance to the British Crown, and that all political connection between them and the State of Great Britain, is and ought to be totally dissolved; and that as Free and Independent States, they have full Power to levy War, conclude Peace, contract Alliances, establish Commerce, and to do all other Acts and Things which Independent States may of right do. And for the support of this Declaration, with a firm reliance on the Protection of Divine Providence, we mutually pledge to each other our Lives, our Fortunes and our sacred Honor.

rectitude: rightness

In this paragraph, the signers state their actual declaration of independence. What rights would the new United States of America now have as an independent nation?

John Hancock
President of
Massachusetts

GEORGIA
Button Gwinnett
Lyman Hall
George Walton

NORTH CAROLINA
William Hooper
Joseph Hewes
John Penn

SOUTH CAROLINA
Edward Rutledge
Thomas Heyward, Jr.
Thomas Lynch, Jr.
Arthur Middleton

MARYLAND
Samuel Chase
William Paca
Thomas Stone
Charles Carroll of
   Carrollton

VIRGINIA
George Wythe
Richard Henry Lee

Thomas Jefferson
Benjamin Harrison
Thomas Nelson, Jr.
Francis Lightfoot Lee
Carter Braxton

PENNSYLVANIA
Robert Morris
Benjamin Rush
Benjamin Franklin
John Morton
George Clymer
James Smith
George Taylor
James Wilson
George Ross

DELAWARE
Caesar Rodney
George Read
Thomas McKean

NEW YORK
William Floyd
Phillip Livingston
Francis Lewis
Lewis Morris

NEW JERSEY
Richard Stockton
John Witherspoon
Francis Hopkinson
John Hart
Abraham Clark

NEW HAMPSHIRE
Josiah Bartlett
William Whipple
Matthew Thornton

MASSACHUSETTS
Samuel Adams
John Adams
Robert Treat Paine
Elbridge Gerry

RHODE ISLAND
Stephen Hopkins
William Ellery

CONNECTICUT
Roger Sherman
Samuel Huntington
William Williams
Oliver Wolcott

Congress adopted the final draft of the Declaration of Independence on July 4, 1776. A formal copy, written on parchment paper, was signed on August 2, 1776.

The following is part of a passage that the Congress took out of Jefferson's original draft: "He has waged cruel war against human nature itself, violating its most sacred rights of life and liberty in the persons of a distant people who never offended him, captivating and carrying them into slavery in another hemisphere, or to incur miserable death in their transportation thither." Why do you think the Congress might have wanted to delete this passage?

Dark Hours

Reading Focus

What were the Patriots' advantages and disadvantages at the beginning of the Revolutionary War?

How did different groups contribute to the war effort?

What problem did the Patriots face in Canada and New York?

Key Terms

mercenaries

Lord Dunmore's Proclamation

GENERAL GEORGE WASHINGTON faced a challenging task when he took charge of the Continental Army. The Patriots were up against a mighty enemy in the British forces. Washington wrote to his wife, Martha, that he was uncertain whether he would succeed in building a strong army. "I shall hope that my undertaking is designed to answer some good purpose," he said. He also promised, "I shall feel no pain from the toil or the danger of the campaign." In the early part of the war, this promise proved difficult to keep.

Martha Washington

Courtesy of the Mount Vernon Ladies' Association

★ Comparing Advantages and Disadvantages

At the beginning of the war, Britain seemed to have a huge advantage over the colonies. British financial resources were much greater than those of the thirteen colonies. Britain maintained a large, mighty military force, whose soldiers were mostly well-trained professionals. The country also had what one historian has called "the most powerful navy in the history of the world." In contrast, at the beginning of the war, the colonists had no navy and no organized army, except for poorly trained local militias.

Despite these challenges, the colonists had some advantages over the British. Most of the civilian population supported the Revolution throughout the war, even when enduring great hardship. This meant that the British army faced citizens who were mostly hostile to its presence. The British also had to ship supplies across the Atlantic Ocean, which slowed down their war effort.

Finally, the Patriots were fighting for a cause in which they believed. Some British soldiers, on the

A soldier in the Continental Army

other hand, were **mercenaries**, or hired foreign soldiers.

⭐ Raising Troops

One of General Washington's first tasks as the Continental Army's commander in chief was to raise troops. During the war, more than 230,000 soldiers served in the Continental Army and another 145,000 enlisted in local militias.

The volunteers came from a variety of backgrounds. Many were teenagers, such as 14-year-old James Forten, who fetched gunpowder for sailors in the Continental Navy. While some army leaders, including Washington, had fought in the French and Indian War, few of the volunteers had combat experience. However, General Charles Lee, for one, had high hopes for the volunteers:

❝ **They are admirable—young, stout, healthy, zealous [eager], good-humored and sober [serious]. . . . I really believe a very little time and pains would render [make] 'em the most invincible [unbeatable] army that have appeared.** ❞

One issue Washington faced was whether to recruit African American soldiers. Many African Americans, including some slaves, were already serving in local militias. Some African Americans, such as Peter Salem and Salem Poor, had fought in important battles. However, many southerners opposed using black soldiers in the army, though they relied heavily on slave labor to fund the war. Shortly after taking command, Washington issued an order that prohibited African Americans from serving in the Continental Army.

A British soldier, also known as a Redcoat because of his uniform

When her husband was wounded in 1778, Molly Pitcher took his place in the cannon crew.

The British reacted quickly. On November 7, 1775, the royal governor of Virginia, Lord Dunmore, issued a statement promising freedom to any slave who fought for the British. **Lord Dunmore's Proclamation** drew to the British side thousands of slaves willing to fight in exchange for their freedom. In response, the Continental Army changed its policy and allowed free African Americans to enlist.

⭐ Other Sources of Help

Although American Indian groups fought on both sides during the war, the British were more successful than the Patriots in convincing Indians to join their side. The British had many Indian allies, while the Patriots worked hard to persuade American Indians to remain neutral in the war. This effort was particularly important in battles on the frontier.

One of the most important allies for the British was Mohawk leader Thayendanegea (thah-yuhn-dah-ne-GAY-uh), also known as Joseph Brant. He persuaded many of the Iroquois in New York to support the British.

Many women helped the Patriot side, running farms and businesses while male relatives served in the army. Other women helped the troops directly with tasks such as cooking, cleaning, and

Science and Technology

The Long Rifle

Most members of the American rifle corps were excellent marksmen from the frontier. They used a weapon unfamiliar to both the British and most eastern colonists. This weapon, known as the long rifle or Kentucky rifle, was an important technological advance.

A rifle is a type of gun with a grooved barrel designed to spin the ball, or bullet, as it is shot. This spinning makes the ball travel farther and with greater accuracy than one shot from a regular musket. Europeans used rifles for big-game hunting but rarely for military fighting. Military leaders thought rifles took too long to reload. The guns also lacked bayonets used in hand-to-hand combat.

Pennsylvania gunsmiths developed the long rifle in the early 1700s. The gunsmiths were responding to requests by people on the frontier for a more accurate and powerful weapon than traditional muskets or rifles. To create the long rifle, the gunsmiths lengthened the barrel of a German rifle, narrowed and improved its rifling grooves, and added a grease patch, making the gun easier to reload.

By the time of the American Revolution, many colonists from the frontier had hunted regularly with the long rifle. In several early battles, British officers were impressed by the ability of the Patriot rifle corps to fire and reload fairly rapidly.

Muskets still could be loaded faster and thus get off more shots than the long rifle, however. Muskets were also more common, and the Patriots' use of the long rifle remained limited. General Washington assigned most riflemen to light infantry units that conducted special missions, such as sharpshooting and scouting. By the end of the war, the long rifle was well known. Over the next 100 years it would become one of the most common weapons in North America.

The long rifle

Understanding What You Read

1. How were rifles different from traditional muskets?

2. Why did European military leaders prefer muskets to rifles?

3. What role did rifle units play during the Revolutionary War?

---

sewing. Some female Patriots served as nurses, spies, or messengers. A few women, such as Deborah Sampson, disguised themselves as men to fight in the war. Perhaps the most famous woman to serve in the war, however, was Mary Ludwig Hays. She earned the nickname "Molly Pitcher" by bringing water to thirsty Patriot troops. In 1778, when her husband was wounded in battle, Hays quickly stepped in and took his place loading cannons.

Most women aided the American cause from behind the scenes. For example, women raised money for supplies and organized sewing groups to make clothing. A Massachusetts man noted:

" At every house Women & children [are] making Cartridges, running Bullets . . . baking Biscuit . . . & at the same time animating [encouraging] their Husbands & Sons to fight for their Liberties. "

George Washington and the Continental Army retreat from Long Island in late August 1776.

Because the Patriots lacked many supplies the contributions of these women were greatly needed.

⭐ Crushing Blows

In part because the army was short on supplies, many Patriot leaders favored fighting a defensive war. However, other military leaders wanted to invade British-controlled Canada and make it the "14th colony."

Canada

In September 1775, Patriot troops led by General Richard Montgomery attacked British forces at St. Johns, Canada, near Montreal. Patriot forces seized the town two months later. Shortly thereafter, Montgomery captured Montreal.

The next major target after Montreal was the city of Quebec. Benedict Arnold, having been promoted to general, led his troops north through what is now Maine. He reached Quebec around the same time that Montreal fell and then waited until General Montgomery's troops arrived before launching an attack. On New Year's Eve, during a fierce blizzard, the Patriots tried to advance but were quickly turned back by the British. The Americans suffered a crushing defeat, with almost half of their troops killed, wounded, or captured. The year 1776 had begun poorly for the Continental Army.

New York

Farther south, General Washington had moved his troops to New York. In late June 1776, Patriots spotted British ships approaching New York Bay. Led by General William Howe, the British forced the Continental Army to abandon Long Island. In late August, Washington's troops retreated to Manhattan Island to avoid complete destruction.

The results were still disastrous. The Patriots suffered more than 1,000 casualties in the campaign. The British, meanwhile, suffered fewer than 400 casualties. After several months of fighting, the British drove the Patriots from Manhattan Island. Howe's revenge for his retreat from Boston was complete.

SECTION 3 REVIEW

Identify and explain the significance of the following:
- **mercenaries**
- **Peter Salem**
- **Salem Poor**
- **Lord Dunmore's Proclamation**
- **Thayendanegea**
- **Deborah Sampson**
- **Molly Pitcher**
- **William Howe**

Reading for Content Understanding

1. **Main Idea** Why did the Patriots' invasion of Canada fail?

2. **Main Idea** What was the outcome of the British attack on New York?

3. **Cultural Diversity** What roles did young men, African Americans, American Indians, and women play in supporting the Patriots during the American Revolution?

4. **Writing** *Classifying* Write a brief paragraph listing the military advantages and disadvantages of the British and the Patriots.

5. **Critical Thinking** *Drawing Conclusions* Why do you think American Indians might have supported the British rather than the Patriots?

SECTION 4

New Hopes

Reading Focus

What was the Patriots' strategy at Trenton and Princeton?

How did the Battle of Saratoga affect foreign aid to the Patriots?

How did the Americans carry out the naval war?

Key Terms

Battle of Trenton
Battle of Princeton
Battle of Brandywine Creek
Battle of Saratoga

*I*N NOVEMBER 1776 GENERAL HOWE *took the last Patriot fort on Manhattan Island. Patriot Alexander Graydon was among those captured. He later recalled a British officer rounding up the prisoners and warning, "Young men, ye should never fight against your king!" Then another British officer rode up and yelled, "What? Taking prisoners? Kill them! Kill every man of them!" The prisoners were spared, but they feared the British were getting close to complete victory in the war.*

General William Howe

 ### Victory in New Jersey

Confident after British victories in Canada and New York, General Howe sent troops to secure New Jersey in November 1776. Certain that the war would soon be over, Howe decided to give his troops a rest for the Christmas and New Years period. He delayed a planned offensive toward Philadelphia and settled in New York City for the holidays. He left New Jersey in the hands of Hessians—mercenaries from the German state of Hesse hired to fight for the British.

Trenton

Had Howe continued on to Philadelphia, the war might have ended there. However, his decision to break for the holidays allowed Washington to move more troops from Canada and attack the Hessians at Trenton, New Jersey. He reasoned that the Hessians could be taken by surprise while celebrating the holiday season. At this time Washington's troops were "half-starved, half-clothed, half-armed, [and] discontented," according to one Loyalist. The Patriots needed a victory to sustain their morale.

On Christmas night in 1776, Washington and 2,400 soldiers silently crossed the icy Delaware River. The troops were short on supplies. Many were without shoes. Continental Army officer Alexander Hamilton observed that despite these obstacles, Washington's soldiers seemed "ready . . . to storm . . . [the] battlements in the night."

Washington and his men crossed the Delaware River on December 25, 1776. The next morning they launched a surprise attack on the Hessian troops guarding Trenton, New Jersey.

After landing in the early morning of December 26, the Patriots marched toward Trenton. The surprise attack worked. The **Battle of Trenton** lasted less than two hours. The Patriot forces captured more than 900 Hessians at the cost of 5 American casualties. The victory boosted the spirits of the colonial forces.

Princeton

Washington was unwilling to settle for just one victory. As British general Charles Cornwallis prepared a counterattack, Washington decided to move on Princeton, a town a few miles northeast of Trenton.

On the night before the battle, Washington's troops carried out a plan to fool the British. The Patriots left their campfires burning, while the bulk of their forces sneaked out of camp under cover of darkness and circled the British troops to attack them from behind the next morning. An 85-year-old civilian described the battle that took place on January 3:

 The guns went off so quick and many together that they could not be numbered. We presently went down into the cellar to keep out of the way of the shot. There was a neighbour woman down in the cellar with us that was so affrighted [frightened] that she imagined that the field was covered with blood. "

The **Battle of Princeton** was hard fought, but the Patriots successfully drove back the British forces.

As the colonists watched the Redcoats flee, Washington cheered, "It is a fine fox chase, my boys!"

⭐ A New British Strategy

The defeats at Trenton and Princeton embarrassed the British authorities. In the spring of 1777, British military leaders proposed an offensive campaign to cut New England off from the rest of the colonies. The plan called for General John "Gentleman Johnny" Burgoyne's troops in Canada to retake Fort Ticonderoga, then march south. Meanwhile, a second force would march east from Lake Ontario. General Howe's troops in New York City would move north, and all three forces would combine at Albany, New York.

Burgoyne recaptured Fort Ticonderoga by early July. However, he found it difficult to carry out the rest of the British plan. His route across New York cut through dense forest, and colonists chopped down large trees across his path to hamper his progress.

Brandywine Creek

Upon hearing of the British victory at Fort Ticonderoga, General Howe thought that Burgoyne no longer needed his help. Instead of marching toward Albany, Howe moved to attack Philadelphia. On September 11, 1777, the British met Washington's troops at the **Battle of Brandywine Creek**.

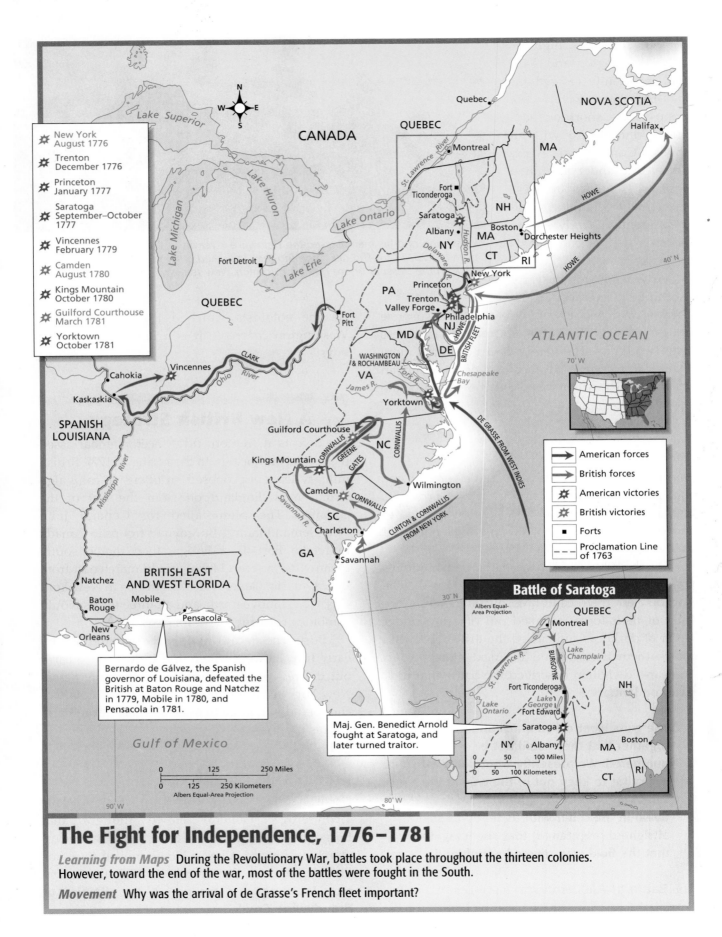

Key (battles):

- New York — August 1776
- Trenton — December 1776
- Princeton — January 1777
- Saratoga — September–October 1777
- Vincennes — February 1779
- Camden — August 1780
- Kings Mountain — October 1780
- Guilford Courthouse — March 1781
- Yorktown — October 1781

Bernardo de Gálvez, the Spanish governor of Louisiana, defeated the British at Baton Rouge and Natchez in 1779, Mobile in 1780, and Pensacola in 1781.

Maj. Gen. Benedict Arnold fought at Saratoga, and later turned traitor.

Map legend:

- American forces
- British forces
- American victories
- British victories
- Forts
- Proclamation Line of 1763

Battle of Saratoga

Albers Equal-Area Projection

0   50   100 Miles
0   50   100 Kilometers

The Fight for Independence, 1776–1781

Learning from Maps During the Revolutionary War, battles took place throughout the thirteen colonies. However, toward the end of the war, most of the battles were fought in the South.

Movement Why was the arrival of de Grasse's French fleet important?

Miscommunication among the American troops led to a victory for Howe's forces. The Patriots suffered almost twice as many casualties as the British. Howe could have crushed the Continental Army completely, but he allowed it to retreat. Once again, Howe's hesitation offered the Patriots a chance to reorganize.

Saratoga

Burgoyne did not know that Howe was bogged down in Pennsylvania or that the force from western Canada had been delayed. As Burgoyne made his way through New York, his badly outnumbered troops clashed with the Patriots at the **Battle of Saratoga**. Burgoyne suffered a major defeat to Patriot troops under Generals Horatio Gates and Benedict Arnold.

On October 17, 1777, Burgoyne formally surrendered to Gates. Saratoga marked the greatest victory up to that point for the American forces. Patriot James Thacher recorded in his diary, "This event will make one of the most brilliant pages of American history."

★ Foreign Allies

The victory at Saratoga boosted foreign countries' support for the Patriots. Britain's longtime enemy France had been pleased to see the Revolution break out and had been secretly supplying the American forces with weapons. After the Patriot victory at Saratoga, the French formally declared their support for the Americans. In May 1778 the Continental Congress approved a treaty of alliance with France.

Individual French citizens already had been fighting for the Patriots. In the summer of 1777 the Marquis de Lafayette arrived from France to help the Americans. Lafayette, a 20-year-old who spoke little English, lacked combat experience. Nonetheless, his passion for the Patriot cause impressed General Washington. Lafayette believed that "the welfare of America is closely bound up with the welfare of mankind."

The Marquis de Lafayette

In his first battle, at Brandywine Creek, Lafayette received a wound in the leg. Throughout the course of the war, his military skills grew stronger, as did his loyalty to the Patriots. The wealthy aristocrat even gave some $200,000 of his own money to support the Revolution.

Spain officially allied with France in 1779. Spain had been a bitter enemy of Britain since the Seven Years' War and was eager to hurt the British cause, particularly in Europe. Like the French, the Spanish had been secretly aiding the Patriots. Much of this help was on the Mississippi River and in the western frontier. Bernardo de Gálvez, the governor of Spanish Louisiana, was particularly helpful to the Patriots.

Individual officers from other countries contributed their military experience to the Continental Army as well. Thaddeus Kosciusko (kahs-ee-UHS-koh) and Casimir Pulaski came from Poland. Kosciusko brought army engineering skills to the Patriot cause, while Pulaski specialized in organizing and training cavalry units.

The Granger Collection, New York

British general John Burgoyne surrenders his army to Patriot general Horatio Gates at Saratoga, New York, in late 1777.

Winter at Valley Forge

The entry of foreign allies into the war could not have come at a better time for the Patriots. They were running terribly low on all supplies. After the victory at Saratoga, Washington settled his troops at Valley Forge, Pennsylvania. Over the harsh winter of 1777–78, one fourth of the hungry and poorly clothed soldiers stationed there died of disease and malnutrition.

The Marquis de Lafayette declared that "the situation of the Americans had never been more critical." By the end of the winter, the troops were growing increasingly restless and frustrated. The chant "No pay, no clothes, no provisions [supplies]" could be heard among them.

In February 1778 an experienced Prussian army officer, Baron Friedrich von Steuben, came to Washington's rescue. Von Steuben, who spoke little English, led with a combination of respect and fear. He started training the American troops, focusing on basic military drills. Von Steuben's tactics paid off. Soon he turned the disorganized Continental Army into a finely tuned fighting force. One historian has called von Steuben's feat "perhaps the most remarkable achievement in rapid military training in the history of the world."

The Naval War

The entry of the French navy into the war greatly aided the Americans on the high seas. Many people had thought that the mighty British navy would crush the much smaller American fleet. However, the British failed to use their powerful navy effectively during the war.

Building a Navy

In the fall of 1775, the Continental Congress made plans to build four American warships. Soon afterward the Congress formally established the marines and the Continental Navy. By adapting

Global Connections

Helping the Patriots

One important foreign ally for the Patriots was Bernardo de Gálvez, the governor of Spanish Louisiana. Gálvez arrived in the area in July 1776 and quickly established himself as an important friend of the Patriot cause.

Gálvez gave the Americans the advantage on the Mississippi River by opening the port of New Orleans to all Patriot vessels. At the same time he ordered the seizure of all British merchant ships in the area.

After Spain officially allied with France in 1779, Gálvez led Spanish forces in several

Bernardo de Gálvez

successful engagements against British forts located along the Mississippi River and in Florida. Largely because of his efforts to help the Patriots during the Revolutionary War, after the war Spain retained control of all of Florida, the mouth of the Mississippi, and the Gulf of Mexico. In addition, Galveston, a port city in present-day Texas, was named in honor of Gálvez.

Understanding What You Read

1. How did Bernardo de Gálvez help the Patriots before 1779?

2. How did Gálvez's actions aiding the Patriots help Spain's position in North America after the war?

merchant vessels, the navy had eight fighting ships ready for combat by February 1776.

That month the tiny American navy launched a major offensive to damage the operating ability of the British fleet located around the Carolina coast. Rather than attack the Carolina fleet directly, the Patriots went after the British supply base on Nassau, in the Bahamas.

The marines hit the beach and seized the main supply fort on the island. They then raised the newly created flag of the American Revolution over Nassau. After that campaign, the American navy focused on seizing British supply ships and weakening their naval forces in the West Indies.

John Paul Jones

The Patriots owed much of their success on the water to naval hero John Paul Jones. Jones had once been considered an outlaw. He was born John Paul in Scotland and began working on ships at a young age. After accidentally killing the leader of a mutiny, he fled to America and added "Jones" to his name.

When the war broke out Jones volunteered his services to the newly created navy. He quickly established himself as a brave and clever sailor. Considered a pirate by the British, Jones captured many British supply ships. The French greatly admired Jones. When France entered the war in 1778, French leaders presented him with a small fleet of seven vessels to command. He named

The flag of the Continental Navy

The Granger Collection, New York

his flagship *Bonhomme Richard* ("Gentleman Richard") in honor of Benjamin Franklin's *Poor Richard's Almanac*.

One of Jones's most famous victories was the capture of the British warship *Serapis* on September 23, 1779. Early in the battle, the British knocked out the heaviest artillery on the *Bonhomme Richard*. Captain Richard Pearson of the Serapis then called out to Jones, "Has your ship struck [surrendered]?" Jones replied, "I have not yet begun to fight!" The battle continued for more than two hours. Finally, the Americans wore down the British, who surrendered at 10:30 P.M. Captain Pearson described fighting against Jones:

> " Long before the close of the action, it became clearly apparent that the American ship was dominated by a command will . . . and there could be no doubt that the intention of her commander was, if he could not conquer, to sink alongside. "

The Patriots used fewer than 100 of their own ships over the course of the war. Nevertheless, the British lost more than 200 ships to the small but effective American sea forces.

SECTION 4 REVIEW

Identify and explain the significance of the following:
- **Battle of Trenton**
- **Battle of Princeton**
- **John Burgoyne**
- **Battle of Brandywine Creek**
- **Battle of Saratoga**
- **Marquis de Lafayette**
- **Bernardo de Gálvez**
- **Friedrich von Steuben**
- **John Paul Jones**

Reading for Content Understanding

1 **Main Idea** What was Washington's strategy for capturing Trenton and Princeton?

2 **Main Idea** Why can the Battle of Saratoga be considered a turning point in the American Revolution?

3 **Global Relations** Why did France and Spain decide to support the Patriot cause?

4 **Writing** *Describing* Write a brief report describing how the Patriots carried out the war on the high seas.

5 **Critical Thinking** *Drawing Conclusions* How did poor information affect British strategy during the war?

Independence

Reading Focus

How did geography affect the Patriot strategy in the West?

How did the war progress in the southern colonies?

What events finally ended the war?

Key Terms

Battle of Vincennes

guerrilla warfare

Battle of Yorktown

Treaty of Paris of 1783

*I*N THE BACKCOUNTRY *of the western Appalachian Mountains lived a group of colonists whose ancestors originally came from Scotland. In the early 1600s King James I of England had forced them to move to present-day Northern Ireland, where they developed a unique culture. In the 1700s many of these Scots-Irish immigrated to North America. They never forgot the poor treatment they had received from the English government, however. As the Revolutionary War moved to the western frontier, the Scots-Irish seized the chance to strike back against their longtime enemy.*

Frontiersmen trade furs for Kentucky rifles.

★ The War in the West

The Scots-Irish were not the only settlers on the western frontier. Despite the Proclamation of 1763, which prohibited white settlement beyond the Appalachians, several scattered settlements had been established in present-day Kentucky and Tennessee.

George Rogers Clark

The Patriot forces in the western frontier were very disorganized at first. Most of their early battles were small clashes with British-allied Indian tribes. A few Patriot leaders discussed trying to take Fort Detroit, but this was never carried out. Then a young frontiersman named George Rogers Clark stepped forward to organize the Patriots' western campaign.

Clark had begun his career as a surveyor, exploring and mapping the lands along the Ohio and Kentucky Rivers. By the time the war broke out, he was a skilled frontiersman who knew the land of the Midwest better than most of the other colonists of his day. He proposed a plan for capturing some small forts and Indian villages throughout the frontier. Clark hoped to weaken the British support systems in the area before beginning an assault on Fort Detroit.

To carry out his plan, Clark traveled far and wide, building up a western force from the scattered settlements. One of the best-known groups he organized was the Over Mountain Men, a band of mostly Scots-Irish fighters from the Tennessee region beyond the Appalachian Mountains.

Victory in the West

Clark decided to target the British trading villages of Kaskaskia and Cahokia, which were located along the Mississippi River. Describing the importance of Kaskaskia, he noted:

> **“ The remote situation of this town . . . enables [the British] to furnish the different [Indian] nations, and . . . keep up a strict friendship with the Indians. . . . If it was in our possession it would distress the garrison [soldiers] at Detroit for provisions [supplies], it would fling the command of two great rivers [Mississippi and Ohio] into our hands, which would enable us to get supplies of goods from the Spaniards, and to carry on trade with the Indians. ”**

In June 1778 Clark and 175 soldiers set out toward Kaskaskia. To surprise the enemy, they did not take the easiest route, along the Mississippi River. Instead, they followed the Ohio River, where they at one point had to ride some river rapids during a total eclipse of the sun. Clark considered the eclipse a good sign, however. After arriving at the mouth of the Tennessee River, they set out on foot for a 120-mile overland trek to Kaskaskia. The journey took Clark's troops through all kinds of terrain, from dense forests to open prairies.

On July 4, 1778, when Clark's group was almost upon the village, Kaskaskia's leaders learned of the planned attack and surrendered without firing a shot. At the same time, a second Patriot group took Cahokia without a fight.

When news of Clark's peaceful capture of these villages spread, the residents of the mostly French town of Vincennes, along the Wabash River, surrendered as well. The western Patriots were still surrounded by many British-allied Indian groups, however. To weaken this support, Clark organized a series of meetings with Indian leaders to persuade them to be neutral in the war.

The British quickly recaptured the poorly defended Vincennes without a fight. However, they soon lost the support of their Indian allies in the region. In late February 1779 Clark launched an offensive to retake the village. The bloody fighting at the **Battle of Vincennes** put the site back in Patriot hands. Clark was never able to take Fort Detroit, but his numerous campaigns severely weakened the British support systems in the West.

★ The War in the South

After the American victory at Saratoga, the British shifted their focus more toward the southern colonies. General Charles Cornwallis led the British campaign in the South.

George Rogers Clark accepts the surrender of Vincennes in 1779.

After their disastrous defeat at Camden, American forces rallied to defeat the British at Cowpens, South Carolina, in late 1780.

British Success

The British efforts to attract slaves to their side paid off when the fighting moved south. In Georgia a slave named Quamino Dolly showed the British a secret trail that allowed them to sneak up on the Patriots and capture the port city of Savannah. Next, the British attacked the major port of Charleston, South Carolina. After months of hard-fought battles, the Continental Army there surrendered on May 12, 1780. The British took more than 5,000 prisoners of war in the process.

As the British marched through the South, they destroyed property that might aid the Patriots. When the British took Charleston, for example, they seized the plantation of indigo developer Eliza Lucas Pinckney. They stole all of her valuable goods, destroyed her crops, and killed all of her farm animals.

One of the most serious Patriot losses was at Camden, South Carolina, in August 1780. Patriot forces led by Horatio Gates launched an offensive to secure the area. The decision to attack showed poor judgment, however. Gates mistakenly thought he had almost twice as many troops as he did. In addition, most of the troops he had were poorly nourished and exhausted from the march. To keep up the troops' spirits, Gates fed them large quantities of molasses and cornmeal, which made many of them ill.

As the weakened Patriots faced off against the British forces, a large group of Americans panicked and retreated soon after the shooting started. The Patriot offensive quickly fell apart. By the time the fighting was over, the British army had crushed Gates's forces. Only about 700 of the approximately 4,100 American troops made it to safety. The Patriots now faced the difficult task of rebuilding their southern army.

Guerrilla Warfare

Although the southern army had been destroyed, the Patriots did not stop fighting in the South. Instead, they switched to **guerrilla warfare**—swift, hit-and-run attacks. They engaged in many attacks on British supplies. No Patriot was better at this style of fighting than Francis Marion, who organized Marion's Brigade, a secret group of guerrilla warriors who led repeated attacks against the British.

For the rest of the war, Marion's Brigade upset the British forces by launching surprise attacks designed to disable their communications and supply systems. Despite great effort by the British, Marion and his men were always able to avoid capture. This led one frustrated British general to remark of the guerrilla leader, "As for this . . . old fox, the devil himself could not catch him." From that point on, both Patriots and Redcoats referred to Marion as "The Swamp Fox."

Francis Marion and his troops cross the Pee Dee River in South Carolina.

American Literature

Sentiments of an American Woman

The Continental Army received aid from female Patriots led by Esther DeBerdt Reed and Sarah Franklin Bache, the daughter of Benjamin Franklin. In 1780 these women organized a campaign that raised $300,000 for soldiers' clothing. The following pamphlet, written by the campaign's leaders, announced the campaign.

On the commencement [start] of actual war, the Women of America manifested [presented] a firm resolution to contribute . . . to the deliverance of their country . . . . Our ambition is kindled by the fame of those heroines of antiquity [ancient times], who . . . have proved to the universe, that . . . if opinion and manners did not forbid us to march to glory by the same paths as the Men, we should at least equal, and sometimes surpass them in our love for the public good. I glory in all that which my sex has done great and commendable [praiseworthy]. I call to mind with enthusiasm and with admiration, all those acts of courage, of constancy and patriotism, which history has transmitted to us. . . .

A female spy passes news to a colonial officer.
The Granger Collection, New York

So many famous sieges where the Women have been seen . . . building new walls, digging trenches with their feeble hands, furnishing arms to their defenders, they themselves darting the missile weapons on the enemy, resigning the ornaments of their apparel, and their fortune, to fill the public treasury, and to hasten the deliverance of their country; burying themselves under its ruins; throwing themselves into the flames rather than submit to the disgrace of humiliation before a proud enemy.

Born for liberty, disdaining [refusing] to bear the irons of a tyrannic [unjust] Government, we associate ourselves . . . [with those queens] who have extended the empire of liberty, and contented [determined] to reign by sweetness and justice, have broken the chains of slavery, forged by tyrants.

Understanding Literature

1. What do the writers "call to mind" in asking women to join the Patriot's cause?

2. With whom do the writers associate themselves?

 ## Victory at Yorktown

In early 1781 the war was going badly for the Patriots. They were low on money, and the entry of their foreign allies had not ended the war quickly. Morale dropped further when one of their most distinguished military leaders, Benedict Arnold, turned to the British side because he was angry at the Continental Congress's treatment of him. In addition, the British controlled most of the South.

Wanting to further increase his hold on the southern colonies, General Cornwallis moved his forces into Yorktown, Virginia. Yorktown lies on a peninsula bounded by the Chesapeake Bay and the York and James Rivers. From the Virginia towns, Cornwallis was preparing to attack a small southern Patriot force led by the Marquis de Lafayette. Lafayette, along with Generals Friedrich von Steuben and Anthony Wayne, waited for the British to make a move.

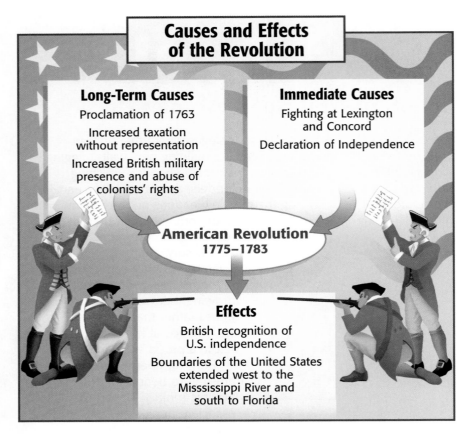

Causes and Effects of the Revolution

Long-Term Causes

Proclamation of 1763

Increased taxation without representation

Increased British military presence and abuse of colonists' rights

Immediate Causes

Fighting at Lexington and Concord

Declaration of Independence

American Revolution 1775–1783

Effects

British recognition of U.S. independence

Boundaries of the United States extended west to the Misssissippi River and south to Florida

---

Meanwhile, General Washington was in New York planning strategy with a French general, the Comte de Rochambeau (roh-sham-BOH). Rochambeau had recently arrived in New York with a large French force. In addition, his son supplied welcome news. At Washington's request, a French fleet under the command of the Comte de Grasse was sailing from the West Indies and heading to Chesapeake Bay. This fleet was prepared to challenge the mighty British navy and to prevent any British ships from entering Chesapeake Bay. The Continental Army was therefore free to take bold action.

Washington and Rochambeau quickly moved their troops south to join Lafayette's forces in Virginia. In September the Patriots and their French allies surrounded Cornwallis's army with at least 16,000 soldiers, more than double the number of British forces opposing them. The Patriots held Yorktown in a state of siege for weeks. Cornwallis continued to expect help from the British navy, but the French fleet led by de Grasse kept the British ships from providing aid. The French navy also prevented any rescue of Cornwallis's army from the seige at Yorktown.

In early October the Patriots prepared for an attack on General Cornwallis's weakened troops. Fearing a bloody defeat, Cornwallis surrendered on October 19, 1781, as a British band reportedly played "The World Turned Upside Down."

Sarah Osborn witnessed the **Battle of Yorktown** and described the surrender:

“ **The British officers rode right on before the army, who marched out beating and playing a melancholy [sad] tune, their drums covered with black handkerchiefs. . . . The British general at the head of the army was a large, portly man, full face, and the tears rolled down his cheeks as he passed along. ”**

When Lord North, the British prime minister, received word of the Yorktown surrender, he declared, "It is all over!"

★ The Treaty of Paris

With Cornwallis's surrender at Yorktown, the Patriots had captured the largest British force on the continent. A few battles occurred after that, but all were minor. In June 1781 a committee from the Continental Congress began serious peace negotiations with the British. The American delegates were John Jay, John Adams, Henry Laurens, and Benjamin Franklin, who had played a crucial role in winning French support during the war. It took more than two years to work out a treaty, but the two nations finally signed a peace agreement.

The **Treaty of Paris of 1783** established British recognition of the United States. The treaty also laid out the new nation's borders: the Great Lakes to the north, the Mississippi River to the west, and

31° north latitude to the south. (A separate treaty between Britain and Spain resulted in the return of Florida to Spanish control.) In addition, the British formally accepted American rights to settle and trade west of the original thirteen colonies. As a result, movement to the frontier rose dramatically after the end of the Revolutionary War.

With the war over, Patriot soldiers could return to their homes and families. The strength and loyalty of soldiers and civilians alike in the long, difficult war had made the Patriot victory possible. As General Washington disbanded the Continental Army, he reflected on the triumph his new country had achieved. "The citizens of America," he declared, "are . . . acknowledged to be possessed of absolute freedom and independency."

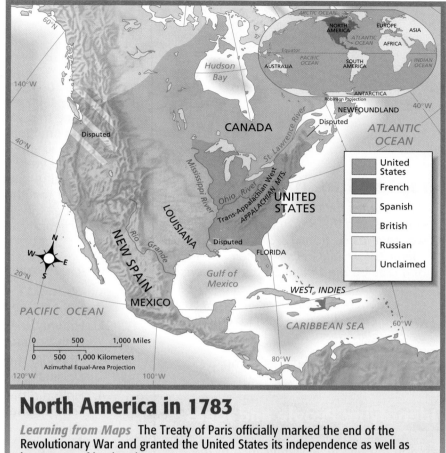

North America in 1783

Learning from Maps The Treaty of Paris officially marked the end of the Revolutionary War and granted the United States its independence as well as large areas of land to the west.

Location Which country claimed the area west of the United States?

SECTION 5 REVIEW

Identify and explain the significance of the following:

- **George Rogers Clark**
- **Battle of Vincennes**
- **Horatio Gates**
- **guerrilla warfare**
- **Francis Marion**
- **Comte de Rochambeau**
- **Battle of Yorktown**
- **Treaty of Paris of 1783**

Locate and explain the importance of the following (see map on page 206):

- **Kaskaskia**
- **Cahokia**
- **Camden**

Reading for Content Understanding

1 **Main Idea** What role did geography play in the war in the West?

2 **Main Idea** What were the major events of the war in the South?

3 **Geographic Diversity** *Location* How did the location of Yorktown help the Patriots win the war?

4 **Writing** *Creating* Make a pamphlet announcing the war's end and outlining the conditions of the Treaty of Paris of 1783. You may want to decorate your pamphlet to attract readers' attention.

5 **Critical Thinking** *Evaluating* How did the war on the western frontier and in the southern colonies affect the outcome of the Revolution?

CHAPTER 7 REVIEW

Chapter Summary

The disputes between the North American colonists and the British government led to a war that lasted from 1775 to 1783. In 1776 the colonists formally declared their independence and created the United States of America. Despite having fewer resources and less military experience, the American forces successfully defeated the British and created a new, democratic nation. ■

On a separate sheet of paper, complete the following activities.

Identifying People and Ideas

Describe the historical significance of the following:

1. Second Continental Congress
2. George Washington
3. *Common Sense*
4. Abigail Adams
5. Lord Dunmore's Proclamation
6. Marquis de Lafayette
7. John Paul Jones
8. Francis Marion
9. Battle of Yorktown
10. Treaty of Paris of 1783

go.hrw.com
SA0
Revolutionary
War

Internet Activity

Imagine that you are a travel agent planning an educational tour. Search the Internet through the HRW Web site for information either on historical sites that were important in the Revolution or on historical re-enactments of Revolutionary War battles. Put together a one-page travel brochure that describes the sites or various re-enactments that your clients could visit on their tour.

Understanding Main Ideas

1. What did the First and Second Continental Congresses achieve?
2. How did *Common Sense* affect the struggle with Britain?
3. How did the Enlightenment help shape the Declaration of Independence?
4. How did the Patriots achieve their victories at Trenton and Princeton?
5. What were some effects of the Battle of Saratoga?
6. What was the Patriots' main focus in the West and in the South?

Reviewing Themes

1. **Citizenship and Democracy** Why did the colonists declare their independence from Britain?

Using the Time Line

Number your paper from 1 to 6. Match the letters on time line below with the following events.

1. The Battle of Vincennes takes place on the western frontier.
2. Thomas Jefferson drafts the Declaration of Independence.
3. An unknown person fires the "shot heard round the world."
4. Delegates gather in Philadelphia for the First Continental Congress.
5. British and American officials sign a peace treaty.
6. The Patriots gain a much-needed ally when France formally enters the war.

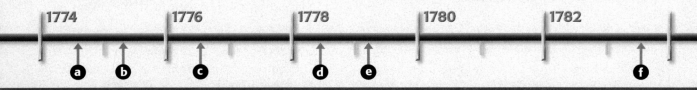

1774   1776   1778   1780   1782

a   b   c   d   e   f

2. Constitutional Heritage What are some important ideas in the Declaration of Independence?

3. Global Relations Why did foreign countries such as France and Spain help the Patriots?

Thinking Critically

1. Determining the Strength of an Argument Historians have argued that the Patriots' devotion to their cause helped make up for their lack of supplies and experience. Using specific examples from the chapter, explain why you agree or disagree with this statement.

2. Identifying Cause and Effect Why do you think most American Indians on the frontier chose to support the British? How did this affect the war?

3. Drawing Conclusions Why do you think the British wanted to separate New England from the rest of the colonies?

Writing About History

1. Expressing Imagine that you are a Loyalist or a Patriot. Write a letter to a friend explaining why you chose the side you did.

2. Describing Write a newspaper article describing life at Valley Forge during the winter of 1777–78.

Linking Geography and History

1. Movement How did Britain's distance from the colonies influence the war?

2. Location What was significant about Bunker Hill, Fort Ticonderoga, Cahokia and Kaskaskia, and Yorktown?

History Skills
Workshop

Using Visual Resources Study the image to the right, which is a recruitment poster for the Continental Army. Explain why you think the artist might have designed the poster in this way. Then draw your own poster encouraging young colonists to join the army.

Building Your Portfolio

Complete the following activities individually or in groups.

1. The Patriot Armies Imagine that you are a soldier or sailor fighting with one of four groups (a) George Washington's army in the Northeast, (b) George Rogers Clark's troops in the West, (c) Francis Marion's brigade in the South, or (d) John Paul Jones's forces at sea. Create a journal describing your experiences throughout the war. You may wish to include maps of troop movements, illustrations of triumphs and hardships your chosen group has encountered, and an indication of why you have become a Patriot.

2. Supporting the Revolution Imagine that you are the leader of a civilian organization that wants to aid the war effort. Design a plan for how you will help the Continental Army and the Congress. Create one or more posters and pamphlets encouraging others to support your plan. Be sure to include information that would attract support from people of various nationalities and backgrounds.

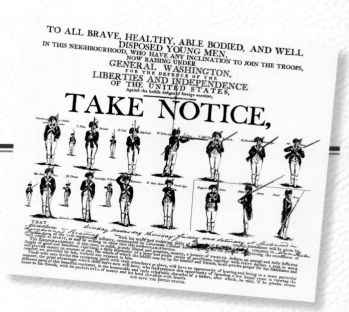

History Skills

WORKSHOP

Organizing Information

Whenever you write an essay or report or are working on a portfolio project, one of the biggest challenges you face is how to organize your information. While researching a topic, you usually record many details, but not necessarily in any type of order. You will have to decide on the best way to organize specific details around central ideas. A good method for doing this is to create a visual representation.

Cluster Diagram A cluster diagram is used to organize specific details around more general concepts. The diagram is a group of ovals with connecting lines between them. A cluster diagram is a great way to make sense of ideas when you are brainstorming a topic with others.

Example Suppose you are asked to come up with important events of the American Revolution. Your list might include:

    Treaty of Paris of 1783 negotiations
    Battle of Trenton
    battles
    First Continental Congress
    meetings
    Battle of Camden
    Second Continental Congress

Your cluster diagram might look like this:

Sequencing Flowchart A sequencing flowchart is a series of boxes with arrows showing their connections. Use sequencing flowcharts when you are trying to determine the order in which certain events occurred.

Example Suppose you were asked to explain how the colonists declared their independence from Great Britain. You might come up with some ideas like:

- Parliament taxed the colonists without their agreement.
- The Second Continental Congress drafted the Declaration of Independence.
- British troops clashed with colonists at Lexington and Concord.
- Colonists staged protests, such as the Boston Tea Party.

You could then turn this list into a clear sequence of events:

> Parliament taxed the colonists without their agreement.
>
> ⮟
>
> Colonists staged protests, such as the Boston Tea Party.
>
> ⮟
>
> British troops clashed with colonists at Lexington and Concord.
>
> ⮟
>
> The Second Continental Congress drafted the Declaration of Independence.

Practicing the Skill

1. Brainstorm some important events from the French and Indian War, and write the list on your paper.

2. Create a cluster diagram showing rough groupings of your ideas.

3. Select one category from your cluster diagram and use a sequencing flowchart to organize the information.

History in Action

American History

The Road to Independence Board Game

Complete the following activity in small cooperative groups.

You and your associates have been hired by W & H Entertainment, Inc. to create a new board game called "The Road to Independence" for ages 12 to adult. The executives at W & H were not very specific on what the game should look like or exactly how it should be played. They have left these decisions up to you. They do want the game to require players to correctly answer historical questions about Americans' struggle for independence from Great Britain. If players answer the game's questions correctly, they get to move around the game board. The first player to cross the finish line is the winner. Your job is to design all the components of this new game, including question cards, the game board, game pieces, and the rule book.

Materials To complete the activity, you will need index cards, posterboard, scissors, pens, pencils, markers, and your textbook.

Parts of the Project Before you turn in your portfolio project, make sure you have included the following components:

1. **Question Cards** Choose five categories from American history between 1763 and 1783 that relate to the colonists' struggle for independence. Possible categories include famous leaders, significant battles, and important meetings.

For each category, come up with at least 10 questions and answers. Write this information on one side of the index cards. Color code the other side of each index card according to category. Use the skills you learned in the History Skills Workshop to help you organize your information while thinking of questions.

2. **Game Board and Pieces** Design and illustrate a board for your game that will allow players to move forward as they correctly answer questions. Design game pieces for the different players, and provide some way to move (dice, spinner, number cards). Make your board and game pieces as attractive as possible. Remember, you want to impress the executives at W & H.

3. **Rule Book** Write a set of rules to accompany your game. The rules should be clear and thorough.

When you have finished creating your game, play a practice round to make sure it works properly. Go back and make any revisions to the rules or design if necessary. Be prepared to present your game to W & H (the class).

Students playing a board game

UNIT 4

A New American Nation

(1777–1800)

Young People
IN HISTORY
Young Americans

The lives of young citizens in the newly independent United States were largely shaped by where they lived and what their parents did for a living. Young people who grew up on the frontier could expect a life of hard work—planting and harvesting crops, tending the farm animals, or helping keep the house in order.

Two girls from the early American Republic study geography.

Many young people on the frontier either did not go to school or spent only a few weeks in school each year. There were few free schools in the early United States, and most parents could not afford to send their children to a private school. Most parents believed that the purpose of education was to teach young people how to work and help support their families. As one writer said, "We seldom see a person fond of labour in old age, who has lived an idle [easy] life when young."

Children from wealthy families could expect a more formal education, although boys usually received more education than girls. A girl was not expected to learn more than reading, writing, and some basic math. Any well-educated boy, however, also learned Greek and Latin.

Most African American youths, particularly in the South, could expect to spend their lives working, either as slaves or domestic servants. Slave children also helped their families in tending the family garden and gathering berries, nuts, and herbs for cooking.

Almost all teenagers, from whatever region or social background, spent some time playing. Sometimes they flew kites, or played leapfrog and marbles. In some places, young people played tag—the same game played today. One teacher during this time period described his students' play, "They all find places of Rendesvous [meeting places] so soon as the Beell [bell] rings, and all seem to choose different sports!" Many young Americans spent their time looking after their pets, which ranged from squirrels to dogs and cats.

In this unit you will find out how Americans worked to establish a new form of government in the United States. You will also learn more about what life was like for people of all ages in the new republic.

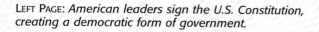

LEFT PAGE: *American leaders sign the U.S. Constitution, creating a democratic form of government.*

The Granger Collection, New York

▪ CHAPTER 8 ▪
Forming a Government
(1777–1791)

In 1787 Benjamin Franklin sat watching the last members of the Constitutional Convention sign the new Constitution of the United States. He noticed the back of the convention president's chair, on which was painted a large sun. Franklin told the other delegates that during the meetings he had thought of the United States as that sun, but "without being able to tell whether it was rising or setting. . . . Now . . . I have the happiness to know that it is a rising and not a setting Sun."

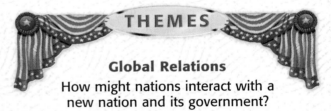

THEMES

Global Relations
How might nations interact with a new nation and its government?

Citizenship and Democracy
What might a nation do to prevent its government from misusing power?

Constitutional Heritage
Why might a nation add a bill of rights to its constitution?

1777   **1779**   **1781**   **1783**

NOV. 1777 The Continental Congress approves the Articles of Confederation.

MAR. 1781 The Articles of Confederation go into effect after being ratified by all the states.

JULY 1783 The British close the West Indies to U.S. shipping.

The Articles of Confederation

Reading Focus

What ideas and traditions provided the basis for American governments?

What powers did the central government have under the Articles of Confederation?

How did the Confederation Congress provide for the entry of new states?

Key Terms

natural rights
constitution
republic
Virginia Statute for Religious Freedom
suffrage
Articles of Confederation

ratification
Land Ordinance of 1785
Northwest Ordinance of 1787
Northwest Territory

IN THE FIRST YEAR OF THE *Revolutionary War, a young professor moved to New Hampshire, where he began teaching at Dartmouth College. Soon after, without revealing his name, he published a short essay calling for the newly independent states to establish representative governments. However, he warned that the American people needed to take great care when building their new governments. "They [the people] are now planting a seed," he stated. This seed, he predicted, would grow into a tree whose branches would "shelter the liberty of succeeding ages." Many Americans agreed with the professor, and hoped that a strong representative democracy could be created in America.*

The bald eagle, symbol of the United States

IMAGE ON LEFT PAGE: *Delegates at the Constitutional Convention*

1785

1787

1789

1791

SEPT. 1786
Shays's Rebellion breaks out.

SEPT. 1787
The final draft of the Constitution is signed.

JUNE 1788
The Constitution goes into effect.

SEPT. 1789 James Madison submits recommended amendments to the Constitution.

DEC. 1791 The Bill of Rights becomes part of the Constitution.

★ Ideas Behind Government

The American colonies had taken a bold step in declaring their independence from Britain in July 1776. The next political challenge was the creation of new governments. To do so, the American people drew from a wide range of political ideas.

English Laws

Revolutionary leaders looked for inspiration to the tradition of English law. One such law, Magna Carta, or "Great Charter," was drawn up by English nobles in 1215 during the reign of King John. The document limited the powers of monarchs by establishing a contract between them and their lords. In later years, Parliament used this contract to press for greater political rights.

Another English document that influenced American Revolutionary leaders was the English Bill of Rights, which Parliament had passed in 1689. This legislation established a limited monarchy. It did so by stating that the king or queen had to follow the law and by giving Parliament supreme legal power. Thus, the English Bill of Rights had given people's representatives the strongest voice in government. Many years later Americans wished to do something similar in the new United States.

Enlightenment Influences

In declaring their independence, Americans had drawn inspiration from the political philosophies of the Enlightenment. These ideas also played an important role in the establishment of American governments. Many Enlightenment philosophers emphasized a faith in human goodness and reason. Patriot Thomas Paine, the author of *Common Sense,* hoped that Americans would become better citizens by adopting Enlightenment ideas. He once said "the mind once enlightened cannot again become dark."

Political leaders and other educated Americans were particularly inspired by the political philosophies

Enlightenment philosopher John Locke of England

of John Locke. Locke believed that a social contract, or agreement, existed between political leaders and the people they governed. Part of this contract included the government's duty to protect the people's **natural rights**, or fundamental rights, such as religious liberty and equality before the law. Locke argued that if leaders did not rule with the consent of the governed, citizens could justly overthrow them. The rule of law, wrote Locke, was more important than the authority of any individual:

> 66 **Whoever in authority exceed the power given him by the law . . . may be opposed as any other man who by force invades the right of another.** 99

Americans also looked to the ideas of French philosopher Baron de Montesquieu. In his 1748 work *The Spirit of Laws,* Montesquieu argued that the only way people could achieve liberty was through the separation of governmental powers. He wrote that "when the legislative and executive powers are united in the same person, . . . there can be no liberty."

American Political Models

Not all ideas on government came from Europe. American leaders also looked to their own traditions for inspiration. One model was the New England town meeting, which had been held since the early days of settlement. At these meetings, colonists gathered to express their views and make decisions on important issues affecting the local community. In addition, Americans looked to the Virginia House of Burgesses as a model of an effective legislative government.

Americans also had written documents that incorporated the ideas of self-government. For example, in 1620 the Pilgrims had drafted and signed the Mayflower Compact to govern themselves at Plymouth Colony. Nearly 20 years later, in 1639, the colonists of Connecticut drew up their own detailed plan of representative government. The

The state seals of North Carolina, New York, and Massachusetts

result was called the Fundamental Orders of Connecticut, the first written **constitution**—a set of basic principles and laws that determine the powers and duties of the government—in the English colonies.

⭐ The State Constitutions

Having declared independence from Britain, the Second Continental Congress recommended that the colonies establish new state governments that would guarantee the freedom and safety of their citizens. Thus, during the American Revolution, nearly every colony produced a state constitution. Some of these remained quite similar to the old colonial charters. Many colonies elected governors to replace royal governors appointed by the king. Two colonies, Connecticut and Rhode Island, saw no need to abandon their colonial charters, which already promoted and protected liberty. Officials in these states merely removed all references to the British Crown, and the states continued to live under their charters until the 1800s.

Government by the People

The writers of the first state constitutions moved toward democratic rule, organizing each state government like a **republic**. A republic is a type of government in which the head of state is elected and the people hold the political power.

Most Americans wanted to prevent individual leaders from gaining too much power. Thus, all state constitutions restricted the governor's authority, often by separating government powers. For example, many states made their courts independent from the governor's control. Most states also denied their governor the ability to veto bills passed by the state legislature. Only Massachusetts, New Hampshire, and New York gave their governors any significant authority.

Protecting Natural Rights

To protect the natural rights of citizens, each state constitution included a bill of rights—a document describing the civil liberties, or individual rights, that a government promises its citizens. For example, Virginia's Declaration of Rights, written by George Mason, included a bill of rights that established, among other things, humane punishments for crimes, a state militia, and freedom of the press. In addition, Thomas Jefferson supported the idea of freedom of religion when he wrote in 1779 that "no man shall be compelled [forced] to . . . support any religious worship . . . . All men shall be free to profess [speak] . . . their opinion in matters of religion." In 1786 Jefferson's ideas became incorporated into the **Virginia Statute for Religious Freedom**. Other states passed similar legislation for religious freedom. By 1833 no state allowed its government to establish an official church.

Voting Rights

Many states' constitutions expanded **suffrage**, or voting rights. As one Virginian wrote, "The spirit of independence was converted into equality, and every one who bore arms, esteems [views] himself upon a footing with his neighbors." Some states allowed any white man who was a taxpaying citizen to vote. Other states gave the vote only to white men who owned property. Most states made property ownership a requirement for holding an elected position.

A few of the first state constitutions gave voting rights to free African American men. In Massachusetts and New Hampshire, free African American men could vote until the 1860s. They

The Virginia Declaration of Rights

New Jersey's state constitution of 1776 gave both male and female property owners the right to vote.

want to give away their states' powers to a central authority. After all, they had revolted against Britain partly to end the abuse of authority by Parliament.

Origins of the Articles

On June 12, 1776, the Continental Congress appointed a Committee of Thirteen, one member from each colony, to create a constitution for the Union. The Committee of Thirteen met for a month to discuss and draft the new document, called the **Articles of Confederation**. The Articles created a central government with limited powers.

Revolutionary leader John Dickinson, who headed the Committee of Thirteen, emphasized that under the Articles the United States was primarily "a firm league of friendship." If the states accepted the Articles of Confederation, they would be governed by a Confederation Congress composed of representatives from each state. On November 15, 1777, after much debate, the Second Continental Congress approved the Articles of Confederation.

could also vote in Maryland until 1810, in North Carolina until 1835, in Pennsylvania until 1838, and in New Jersey until 1844. In New York, free African American men could vote, but the state imposed certain restrictions on them in 1832. New Jersey was the only state that allowed white women to vote after the Revolutionary War, but it took away this right in 1807. American women continued to participate in the political process by petitioning state governments on a variety of issues, but more than 100 years passed before women gained the right to vote in every state.

⭐ Forming a Union

The Second Continental Congress recommended the creation of a permanent national government to oversee the new state governments. Although the Congress had brought the thirteen colonies, which were now states, together under one national government for the first time, it did not have a framework for this new government. However, some Revolutionary leaders were cautious because they did not

Ratifying the New Government

After approving the Articles, the Second Continental Congress sent them to each state legislature for **ratification**, or formal approval. All 13 states had to ratify the Articles before the new national government could take effect.

Conflicts over western land claims delayed the ratification process. Many states claimed territory as far west as the Mississippi River. Virginia and New York had some of the largest land claims. States that claimed western territory hoped to sell this land to settlers and use the revenue to pay off their war debts. States without western land claims believed that these territories should belong to the new national government, even though the Articles stated that no state should be deprived of its western lands for the benefit of the United States.

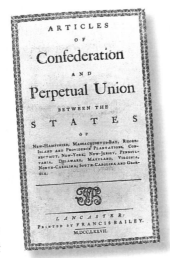

An early copy of the Articles of Confederation

American Arts

American Portrait Painters

Four American painters—Benjamin West, John Singleton Copley, Charles Willson Peale, and Gilbert Stuart—had achieved great success by the end of the 1700s. Each of these painters developed his own particular style and strongly influenced painting in both the United States and Europe. For example, West helped found the Royal Academy of Arts in Britain. In his paintings, West showed people dressing in clothing of the period while other painters at the time usually clothed heroes in ancient Roman or Greek dress. In a letter to Thomas Jefferson, George Washington wrote, "The taste, which has been introduced in painting by West is received with applause, and prevails [is used] extensively."

Benjamin West's painting The Death of General Wolfe *(1770) shows British soldiers dressed in the clothing of the time period.*

Copley emphasized setting to give his portraits the proper mood. Women usually appeared with fine furnishings, while men were painted either outside or surrounded by books and tools.

Peale paid careful attention to detail, providing viewers a fairly accurate picture of colonial America. He also popularized a portrait style that showed the subject engaged in a scene from his or her life.

Stuart's work communicated the character of his subjects. As West said of his former pupil, Stuart "*nails* the face to the canvas." Stuart developed a plain portrait style for his American subjects, in keeping with the democratic spirit of the new country. This style is best seen in the paintings he created of George Washington in the 1790s. The paintings show a simple image of the president without any sign of Washington's military rank or political office. Stuart's first three lifelike portraits of Washington proved so popular that Stuart eventually painted more than 100 copies to satisfy the public demand. You can see a likeness of one of Stuart's paintings today on the $1 bill.

Portrait painting was in great demand among Americans in the late 1700s. Early works show what colonists wore, ate, and read, and how they wanted to be remembered. Many artists also painted American political leaders and figures. Paul Revere, John Hancock, Samuel Adams, Mercy Otis Warren, Thomas Jefferson, Benjamin Franklin, and the Marquis de Lafayette all were popular subjects.

Understanding the Arts

1. What did portraits painted by Peale, Stuart, and Copley tell about life in early America?

2. Why do you think Benjamin West painted General Wolfe and the soldiers in clothing of the period?

3. Why do you think so many Americans liked Stuart's portraits of Washington?

the states. Congress also could ask states for money and soldiers but could not force the states to contribute them. There was no federal executive, such as a president, and no national court system.

Author Noah Webster was one of many who criticized the new national government's limited authority:

> **Congress must have the same power to enact laws and compel [force] obedience throughout the continent, as the legislatures of the States have in their respective jurisdictions [areas of authority].**

Foreign observers also found much to criticize in the government created by the Articles. For example, one London newspaper dismissed the Confederation Congress as "feeble and ineffectual [ineffective]."

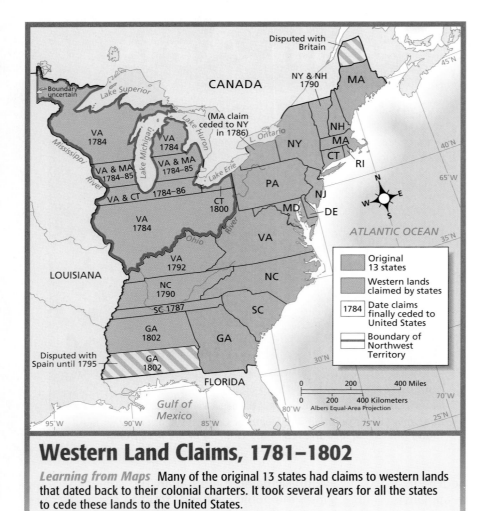

Western Land Claims, 1781–1802

Learning from Maps Many of the original 13 states had claims to western lands that dated back to their colonial charters. It took several years for all the states to cede these lands to the United States.

Location Which states had no claims to western lands?

Despite pressure from Congress, Maryland refused to ratify the Articles until other states gave up their western land claims. In 1780 New York gave up its claims. The next year Virginia agreed to transfer its claim to lands north of the Ohio River to the national government, which received the land in 1784. In March 1781 Maryland finally ratified the Articles of Confederation, putting the first national government of the United States into effect.

Powers of the New Government

Under the Articles of Confederation, the national government consisted only of the Confederation Congress, in which each state had one vote. Congress could coin and borrow money, negotiate and make treaties with foreign nations and American Indians, and resolve conflicts between

★ Western Lands

The new Congress had several issues to address. For example, it had to raise money and organize the western lands that Virginia and other states had ceded, or surrendered, to the national government. Because Congress's ability to raise money from the states was limited, it decided to raise revenue by selling these lands. In May 1785 Congress passed the **Land Ordinance of 1785**, which called for surveys and the

This compass and other surveying tools belonged to George Washington.

division of these public lands. The surveys divided the lands into townships of 36 square miles. The townships, in turn, were divided into 36 lots of 640 acres each. The new ordinance required each township to set aside one lot of land for a public school and four lots for Revolutionary War veterans. The other lots were for sale to the public, but a minimum of one lot had to be purchased at the price of $1 per acre. Land companies, rather than individual farmers, bought most of this land because it was sold only in such large sections.

Many settlers, like these from Connecticut, entered the Northwest Territory in the late 1700s.

To establish a political structure for the region, Congress also passed the **Northwest Ordinance of 1787**, based in part on an earlier proposal by Thomas Jefferson. The ordinance established the **Northwest Territory**, a vast region that included present-day Illinois, Indiana, Michigan, Ohio, and Wisconsin. The Northwest Ordinance also created a system of limited self-government for the settlers living in the territory. It said that when a portion of the Northwest Territory had at least 60,000 free inhabitants, these settlers could draft their own constitution and petition Congress to be admitted to the Union as a state. In addition, the ordinance contained a bill of rights and required that public education be provided for the citizens of the region. Finally, the Northwest Ordinance stated that "there shall be neither slavery nor involuntary servitude [forced labor] in the . . . territory." This last condition, which banned slavery in the Northwest Territory, would become an increasingly controversial issue in the years ahead as new territories were formed.

SECTION 1 REVIEW

Identify and explain the significance of the following:
- **natural rights**
- **constitution**
- **republic**
- **Virginia Statute for Religious Freedom**
- **suffrage**
- **Articles of Confederation**
- **ratification**
- **Land Ordinance of 1785**
- **Northwest Ordinance of 1787**
- **Northwest Territory**

Reading for Content Understanding

1 **Main Idea** On what political ideas and traditions—from both sides of the Atlantic Ocean—did Americans base their state and national governments?

2 **Main Idea** How could new states enter the Union under the Northwest Ordinance?

3 **Geographic Diversity** Why did some states want to hold on to their western land claims?

4 **Writing** *Informing* Imagine that you are a member of the Committee of Thirteen. Write a brief report for the citizens of your state explaining the powers given to the central government under the Articles of Confederation.

5 **Critical Thinking** *Drawing Conclusions* Why might different states have had different suffrage requirements?

Magna Carta

In 1215 a group of English nobles forced King John to agree to Magna Carta. While this document did not protect the rights of individual citizens, it did limit the monarchy's power and provide an example of constitutional government for future generations. The following is an excerpt.

1. That the English Church shall be free, and shall have her whole rights and her liberties inviolable [safe from sudden change]. . . .

12. No scutage [tax for military purposes] nor aid [tax paid by a vassal to a lord] shall be imposed in our kingdom, unless by the common council of our kingdom. . . .

38. No bailiff, for the future, shall put any man to his law upon his own simple affirmation, without credible witnesses produced for that purpose [there must be a witness, rather than just personal belief, for a person to be arrested]. . . .

39. No freeman shall be seized, imprisoned, dispossessed [deprived of his land], outlawed, or exiled, or in any way destroyed; nor will we proceed against or prosecute him except by the lawful judgment of his peers [equals], or by the law of the land.

40. To none will we sell, to none will we deny, to none will we delay right or justice. . . .

42. It shall be lawful to any person . . . to go out of our kingdom, and to return.

Understanding Primary Sources

1. What rules does Magna Carta set for taxation?

2. What is the importance of the right specified in section 42?

The English Bill of Rights

After the Glorious Revolution, Parliament passed the English Bill of Rights to make sure that Parliament, not the monarchy, was the supreme authority in government. Many similar rights are also in the U.S. Constitution and Bill of Rights.

1. Whereas . . . that the pretended power of suspending of laws or the execution of laws by regal [royal] authority without consent of Parliament is illegal; . . .

4. That levying money [raising taxes] for or to the use of the crown by pretense of prerogative [right] without grant of Parliament . . . is illegal;

5. That it is the right of the subjects to petition the king, and all commitments and prosecutions for such petitioning are illegal.

6. That . . . raising or keeping a standing army within the kingdom in time of peace, unless it be with consent of Parliament, is against law. . . .

8. That election of members of Parliament ought to be free;

9. That the freedom of speech and debates or proceedings in Parliament ought not to be . . . questioned in any court or place out of Parliament;

10. That excessive bail ought not to be required, nor excessive fines imposed, nor cruel and unusual punishments inflicted.

11. That jurors ought to be duly impaneled [selected] . . . .

12. That all grants and promises of fines and

forfeitures [loss of property] of particular persons before conviction are illegal and void;

13. And that, for redress of [to make up for] all grievances and for the amending, strengthening, and preserving of the laws, Parliaments ought to be held frequently.

Understanding Primary Sources

1. What parts of this document deal with concerns similar to those addressed in Magna Carta?

2. How does this document protect Parliament's power?

The Virginia Statute for Religious Freedom

Thomas Jefferson wrote a proposal for religious freedom that, after much debate, the state passed as the Virginia Statute for Religious Freedom. Jefferson hoped that by separating church and state, this law would allow Virginians to practice their religion—whatever it might be—freely.

January 16, 1786

I. Well aware that Almighty God has created the mind free; that all attempts to influence it by temporal [civil] punishments or burdens or by civil incapacitations [lack of fitness for office], tend only to . . . [produce] habits of hypocrisy and meanness and are a departure from the plan of the Holy Author of our religion, who . . . chose not to propagate [spread] it by coercions [force] . . . that to compel [force] a man to furnish contributions of money for the propagation of opinions which he disbelieves is sinful and tyrannical [unjust]; that even . . . forcing him to support this or that teacher of his own religious persuasion [belief] is depriving him of the comfortable liberty . . . ; that our civil rights have no dependence on our religious opinions any more than [on] our opinions in physics or geometry. . . . And, finally, that truth is great and will prevail if left to herself . . . and has nothing to fear . . . [for] errors [cease] to be dangerous when it is permitted freely to contradict them.

II. Be it enacted by the General Assembly that no man shall be compelled to frequent or support any religious worship, place, or ministry whatsoever, nor shall be enforced, restrained, molested, or burdened in his body or goods, nor shall otherwise suffer on account of his religious opinions or belief; but that all men shall be free to profess, and by argument to maintain, their opinion in matters of religion, and that the same shall in no wise diminish, enlarge, or affect their civil capacities.

III. And though we well know that this assembly . . . [has] no power to restrain the acts of succeeding assemblies . . . we are free to declare, and do declare, that the rights hereby asserted [stated] are of the natural rights of mankind, and that if any act shall hereafter be passed to repeal the present or to narrow its operation, such act will be an infringement [violation] of natural rights.

Understanding Primary Sources

1. What reasons does this document give for protecting religious freedoms?

2. Why do you think section III was included?

Problems in the New Nation

Reading Focus

How did other nations treat the new government of the United States?

What economic problems arose under the Articles of Confederation?

What were the causes and consequences of Shays's Rebellion?

Key Terms

tariffs
interstate commerce
creditors
debtors
depression
Shays's Rebellion

O N JUNE 7, 1786, THOMAS AMIS *sailed his ship down the Mississippi River to transport trade goods, as he had done many times before. But this day was different. Amis was violating a new Spanish decree that severely restricted U.S. citizens' navigation rights along the lower part of the river. The Spanish troops at Natchez captured Amis and then stripped him of all his cargo, including 53 pots and 50 barrels of flour. Amis lost a valuable load, but the U.S. government could do little to help him.*

Early American iron pot and flour barrel

 International Relations

Americans had established the national government in part to protect citizens like Thomas Amis against foreign threats. Under the Articles of Confederation, however, Congress could not force states to provide soldiers for an army. Without an army, the national government had little power to protect its citizens or to enforce international treaties.

For example, Congress could do little to enforce the Treaty of Paris of 1783, particularly the part that called for the British to turn over "with all convenient speed" their forts on the U.S. side of the Great Lakes. The United States wanted to gain control of these British forts because they protected valuable land and fur trade routes. Britain was slow to withdraw from the area as agreed, but Congress had few options to enforce the treaty. One British official warned that if the United States tried to seize the forts by force, it would face the thousands of former British soldiers who had settled in Canada after the Revolution "who are ready to fly to arms at a moment's warning."

International Trade with Britain

The new nation also faced difficulties involving international trade with Britain. After the Treaty of

Paris was signed, Britain closed many of its ports to American ships. The closure of ports in the British West Indies in July 1783 was particularly hard on the United States. Before the Revolutionary War, colonial ships had traded heavily with these islands and stopped in the British West Indies on their way to other destinations. The British also banned U.S. ships from bringing trade goods to Canada. In addition, Britain forced American merchants to pay high **tariffs**—taxes on imports or exports—in order to sell goods such as rice, tobacco, tar, and oil in Britain.

Trade with Spain

During this same period, Spain also took advantage of the weakness of the United States. In 1784, Spanish officials closed the lower Mississippi River to U.S. shipping. Western farmers were infuriated by this act because it shut down their only effective way to transport goods to New Orleans, from which trade ships sailed to eastern markets.

John Jay, the newly appointed secretary of foreign affairs, started negotiations with a Spanish diplomat, Don Diego de Gardoqui, for a commercial treaty that included reopening the lower Mississippi to American merchants. Gardoqui offered to resolve a territorial dispute with the United States if it would accept Spanish authority over the Mississippi. Gardoqui's proposal was not acceptable to a majority of nine members in Congress, as required by the Articles of

Confederation. As a result, treaty negotiations with Spain ended in 1786.

John Jay

Many state leaders began to criticize harshly the weaknesses of the national government under the Articles. Representatives from Rhode Island wrote to Congress that "our federal government is but a name; a mere shadow without any substance." Representatives from North Carolina believed that Spain might have offered the United States greater access to the Mississippi if the new nation had a strong military. For these political leaders, the United States's inability to gain a satisfactory treaty with Spain signaled a need to expand the national government's powers.

★ The Impact of Closed Markets

Under the weak central government of the Articles of Confederation, the United States was unable to gain many favorable trade agreements with foreign countries. In particular, the closing of markets in the British West Indies dramatically affected the U.S. economy. In 1785 a writer for the *Massachusetts Sentinel* reported that these trade restrictions were resulting in the "entire ruin of our ship-builders, blacksmiths, ropemakers . . . [and] sailmakers." James Madison of Virginia also wrote about this crisis, exclaiming:

66 **The Revolution has robbed us of our trade with the West Indies. . . . In every point of view, indeed, the trade of this country is in a deplorable [terrible] condition.** 99

The British fort and trading post of Oswego, New York, was one of many frontier outposts that Britain refused to evacuate after the Treaty of Paris.

Important trading ports, such as this one in Bermuda were closed to American merchant ships after the Revolutionary War.

their own commerce rather than on cooperating to improve the trade position of the country as a whole. In 1785 the situation led a British magazine to refer to the new nation as the "Dis-United States."

As a result of the trade problems with Britain, American merchants began pursuing other new markets, including Asia. In August 1784 the ship *Empress of China* reached Canton, opening U.S. trade with China. The United States also made trade gains with France and the Netherlands. Despite such attempts to find new international markets, Britain remained the United States's most important trading partner.

Those farmers who exported their products were also hurt by these trade restrictions. They could no longer trade their goods to the British West Indies. In addition, new British laws forced farmers to transport their products in British ships if they wanted to sell their goods in Britain. This was very expensive. Samuel Adams wrote to his cousin John Adams that "our merchants are complaining bitterly that Great Britain is ruining their trade and there is good reason to complain."

While American exports declined, British goods flowed freely into the United States. In 1784 alone, the United States imported almost five times the amount of goods from Britain as it exported to Britain. This unfavorable trade imbalance created serious economic problems for the new nation. British merchants could sell manufactured products in the United States at much lower prices than locally made items, which hurt American businesses.

The Confederation Congress was powerless to correct the imbalance because it had no authority to establish tariffs. The states could offer little help because if one state passed a tariff, the British could simply sell their goods in another state. In addition, many states focused more on improving

★ Internal Problems

In addition to international trade issues, trade among the states became a major problem. The Confederation Congress had no power to regulate **interstate commerce**, which is trade conducted between two or more states. Without such regulation, states adopted trade policies that were beneficial to their own interests. As a result, trade laws varied from state to state, making it difficult for merchants whose businesses crossed state lines.

The ability of the states to issue their own money created additional problems. After the Revolutionary War, most states faced great difficulty in trying to pay off war debts and collect overdue taxes. In an attempt to ease the economic hardships of this period, some states began issuing large amounts of paper money. The result was inflation— increased prices for goods

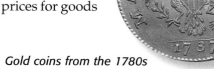
Gold coins from the 1780s

and services combined with the reduced value of money. Congress had no power to stop states from issuing more paper money and could do little to stop inflation.

As a result of this inflation, planters in North Carolina soon were selling tobacco to the state government at double the regular price. Although the tobacco planters received twice as much money, the paper currency used to pay them was worth almost nothing. In Rhode Island a similar problem arose when the state legislature issued large sums in paper money and declared it the legal exchange for payment of debts. Hundreds of **creditors**—people who lend money—fled Rhode Island to avoid accepting worthless currency in payment of debts owed to them. In many states, such as Rhode Island and North Carolina, inflation helped **debtors**—people who owe money—because they were able to pay off debts with currency that had lost value since they had borrowed it.

 Shays's Rebellion

Each state handled its economic problems differently. For example, Massachusetts refused to issue any paper money and tried to pay its war debts by levying taxes on land. This policy, combined with British trade restrictions, created a **depression**—a steep drop in economic activity.

Financial Problems for Farmers

Farmers were particularly hard hit by the economic policy of Massachusetts. As landowners, they had to pay the new taxes. With little gold or silver and no paper money, however, farmers had trouble paying their debts. Massachusetts courts began forcing people who could not pay their debts to sell their property, serve terms in debtors' prison, or sell themselves into indentured servitude. Increasing numbers of farmers suffered foreclosures—legal proceedings in which an indebted person's property is seized. People soon began demanding change. In one petition farmers pleaded for reform:

66 **We beg leave to inform your Honors that unless something takes place more favorable to the people, in a little time at least, one half of our inhabitants in our opinion will become bankrupt [financially ruined]. . . . Sirs, in this situation what have we to live on?** 99

Biography

Daniel Shays

Daniel Shays, for whom Shays's Rebellion was named, was born around 1747 to a poor family in Massachusetts. He worked as a laborer until he eagerly volunteered to serve in the Revolutionary War. During the war, Shays married Abigail Gilbert. He soon became an officer and fought in the battles at Bunker Hill, Ticonderoga, and Saratoga.

After the war, the Confederation Congress did not have enough money to pay most soldiers the salaries that were owed to them. Shays angered his fellow soldiers when he sold a sword given to him by the Marquis de Lafayette to pay for his own food and housing. Nonetheless, Shays proudly retired from the military and decided to settle in Pelham, Massachusetts, where he eventually became the leader of the rebellion named after him. Following the rebellion, Shays returned to Pelham, where he died a poor man in 1825.

However, many government officials in Massachusetts were unsympathetic to the difficulties of farmers and the poor because these politicians were creditors themselves.

Attacking the Government

In September 1786, two months after the Massachusetts legislature finished its yearly meetings without offering to issue paper money for debt relief, farmers in three western counties erupted into revolt. Bands of angry citizens armed with pitchforks and other farm tools closed down courts in western Massachusetts. Their reasoning was simple—with the courts shut down, no one's farm could be foreclosed.

This uprising became known as **Shays's Rebellion** because Daniel Shays, a poor farmer and Revolutionary War veteran, was its most

Rebels led by Daniel Shays met state militiamen outside Springfield, Massachusetts, in early 1787. After the state troops fired a few cannon shots, the rebels scattered.

prominent leader. The Massachusetts government ordered the farmers to stop the revolt and threatened death to any captured rebel. However, these threats only made Shays and his followers more determined. Shays encouraged other citizens to support the rebellion when he wrote, "The seeds of war are now sown. . . . Our cause is yours. Don't . . . let us die here."

Having successfully forced the court in the town of Springfield to close, the rebels tried to capture the federal arsenal, or weapons storehouse, located there. Governor James Bowdoin had sent 600 militiamen to protect the court and the arsenal. In a brief engagement in January 1787, the state troops defeated and scattered the rebels.

Most of the rebels scattered throughout the forests of western Massachusetts, where many of them surrendered or were arrested. Daniel Shays escaped to Vermont, but before long he too was captured. The judge who tried the case against the rebels stated that they were driven by "restless, malevolent [evil], destructive" feelings in trying to overturn the government. Even Revolutionary radical Samuel Adams criticized the farmers as "wicked and unprincipled [dishonest] men."

At first many of the rebels were sentenced to death. However, the state soon granted lighter sentences or even freed most of the participants, including Shays. State officials knew that many citizens in Massachusetts sympathized with the rebels and their economic troubles.

The Impact of Shays's Rebellion

The rebellion greatly disturbed many political leaders. George Washington exclaimed:

66 **I am mortified [embarrassed] beyond expression that in the moment of our . . . independence we should by our conduct . . . render [show] ourselves ridiculous . . . in the eyes of all Europe.** 99

Not everyone saw these events in a negative light, however. Shays's Rebellion actually pleased some of the new nation's leaders. Thomas Jefferson, serving as ambassador to France, wrote: "A little rebellion, now and then, is a good thing. . . . The tree of liberty must be refreshed from time to time with the blood of patriots and tyrants."

In the end, Shays's Rebellion provided a blunt reminder of the weakness of the Confederation government and led some Americans to admit that the Articles of Confederation were not working. When Massachusetts had asked the national government to help put down Shays's Rebellion, Congress could offer no assistance. More Americans began calling for a stronger central government that would be able to protect the nation in times of crisis.

Alexander Hamilton was born on the island of Nevis in the British West Indies. He moved to New York in the 1770s.

★ A Push for Change

In 1786 the Virginia legislature called for a national conference to discuss economic issues and possible revisions to the Articles of Confederation. Virginia proposed that the meeting take place in Annapolis, Maryland—which was centrally located—in September 1786. Only five states sent delegates to this Annapolis Convention, however. The New England states were unrepresented, as were the Carolinas and Georgia. Even Maryland refused to send delegates because its leaders believed that holding this convention violated the authority of the Confederation Congress.

Those who did attend the Annapolis Convention—including James Madison of Virginia and Alexander Hamilton of New York—drafted an address that scolded the absent states for not attending. They called on all 13 states to appoint delegates to attend another convention, at Philadelphia, in May 1787. At this convention, it was hoped, representatives from each state would discuss ways to make "the constitution of the Federal Government adequate to the exigencies [needs] of the Union." This Annapolis Address, as it was called, was sent to the Confederation Congress and the governors of each state. Delegates hoped that others would look on the address favorably and support the call for a larger convention the following spring.

SECTION 2 REVIEW

Identify and explain the significance of the following:
- **tariffs**
- **interstate commerce**
- **creditors**
- **debtors**
- **depression**
- **Daniel Shays**
- **Shays's Rebellion**

Reading for Content Understanding

1 **Main Idea** What trade issues arose under the Articles of Confederation?

2 **Main Idea** What problems plagued the new nation's economy?

3 **Global Relations** In what ways did Great Britain and Spain take advantage of the United States's weaknesses?

4 **Writing** *Describing* Write a short newspaper article explaining the causes and consequences of Shays's Rebellion.

5 **Critical Thinking** *Evaluating* Do you think the "Dis-United States" was an appropriate name for the new nation in 1785? Explain your answer.

The Constitution

Reading Focus

Why did delegates meet for the Constitutional Convention?

What were some of the main issues debated at the Constitutional Convention?

How is the federal government balanced under the U.S. Constitution?

Key Terms

Constitutional Convention
Virginia Plan
New Jersey Plan
Great Compromise
Three-Fifths Compromise

federalism
legislative branch
executive branch
judicial branch
checks and balances

*I*N 1786 A PENNSYLVANIA *newspaper reported rumors that John Adams, ambassador to Britain, was receiving his salary from the French because the U.S. government could not afford to pay him. "Ought we not to blush . . . that the ambassadors of the states are . . . depending on foreign charity for their support?" asked the newspaper's editors. John Adams's wife, Abigail, agreed. She felt that running an embassy with very little money was an embarrassment. She noted that "with the present salary and the present temper of the English no one need envy the embassy." Such problems led some Americans to seek a more effective national government.*

John Adams

The Granger Collection, New York

⭐ The Constitutional Convention

By the mid-1780s many American political leaders were alarmed by the variety of problems that had arisen under the Articles of Confederation. The U.S. government could do little in response to humiliating treatment by Britain and Spain. Cooperation among the states was almost non-existent, as shown by the poor turnout at the Annapolis Convention. Most political leaders agreed that changes to the central government were essential for the survival of the United States.

Meeting in Philadelphia

In February 1787 the Confederation Congress invited each state to send delegates to a convention in Philadelphia. These delegates planned to discuss the much needed revision of the Articles of Confederation. This **Constitutional Convention** was held in May in Philadelphia's Old State House, called Independence Hall, where Americans had officially declared their independence.

Congress said in its invitation that the convention was for

> **"the sole and express purpose of revising the Articles of Confederation, to render [make] the federal constitution adequate to the exigencies [needs] of government, and the preservation of the Union."**

The delegates decided to keep the proceedings and debates a secret until they had accomplished their task. They agreed that they would work more effectively without further public input.

Twelve states sent a total of 55 delegates to participate in the Constitutional Convention. Only Rhode Island refused to send a delegation. The delegates were a remarkable group. Many were college educated, and most were well read in history, law, and political philosophy. More than half had served in Congress, and most of the others had served in state legislatures.

James Madison proved to be one of the most important delegates to the convention. He had thought carefully about the different ways that Americans could construct a government that preserved the powers of the states within a strong union. Madison saw the convention as an important turning point because the delegates "were now to decide the fate of republican government."

Madison participated actively in the convention, taking detailed notes and contributing to discussions. He also helped persuade George Washington, the hero of the Revolutionary War, to participate and lend his authority to the proceedings. The delegates quickly and unanimously elected Washington—who headed the Virginia delegation—to be president of the convention. Other active delegates included Virginia Declaration of Rights author George Mason, Roger Sherman of Connecticut, and James Wilson of Pennsylvania, one of the most skilled lawyers in the country.

James Madison

This engraving advised women that their proper place was in the home. The message reflected the attitudes of many men and women in the early days of the republic.

Absent Voices

Several important leaders did not attend the convention. John Adams was serving as ambassador to Great Britain, while Thomas Jefferson was serving as ambassador to France. Others, such as Revolutionary heroes Samuel Adams and Patrick Henry, chose not to attend because they opposed holding such a convention.

Congress did not invite women, African Americans, or American Indians to participate in the convention. Members of these groups did not yet have the rights of full citizens, including the right to represent other citizens in government.

⭐ The Great Compromise

Several issues divided the delegates to the Constitutional Convention. Some members of the convention thought the Articles of Confederation simply should be revised, while others thought they should be completely rewritten. This situation was further complicated because those who favored rewriting held different points of view regarding the approach to take. For example, small and large states had different concerns about representation. States also differed over regional issues, including economic concerns, that separated northerners from southerners, and easterners from westerners. In addition, some delegates supported a strong national government, while others supported a less centralized, weaker national government.

Both the Declaration of Independence and the Constitution were signed in Philadelphia's Independence Hall.

The Virginia Plan

After the delegates had met for four days, Edmund Randolph of Virginia presented a plan for government—called the large-state plan or **Virginia Plan**—which James Madison had mainly drafted. It offered a new federal constitution that would give sovereignty, or supreme power, to the central government. The Virginia Plan provided for three branches of national government—executive, judicial, and legislative. The legislature in this plan would be a bicameral, or two-house, legislature with representatives chosen in proportion to state populations. Delegates from the smaller states strongly objected to Madison's plan to have population determine representation in both legislative houses.

The New Jersey Plan

The delegates discussed the Virginia Plan for two weeks. New Jersey delegate William Paterson then presented the small-state or **New Jersey Plan**, which proposed keeping the existing organization of Congress. It called for a unicameral, or one-house, legislature with each state entitled to an equal number of votes. This arrangement was meant to ensure that even states with small populations would have an equal voice in the federal government.

The New Jersey Plan proposed that all acts ratified by Congress "shall be the supreme law of the respective States . . . and the Judiciary of the several States shall be bound thereby in their decisions." The plan also gave the federal government the power to tax citizens in all states and allowed the

government to regulate commerce. Delegates from the large states objected to this plan, arguing that representation based on population was more fair.

Compromise

In June, after much debate, the delegates were still unable to agree on how states should be represented in the proposed Congress. Eventually, the convention formed a committee to address this matter. Roger Sherman was among those on the committee who proposed a compromise, which some historians call the **Great Compromise**. To satisfy supporters of the New Jersey Plan, every state, regardless of its size, would have an equal vote in the upper house of the legislature. For those who preferred the Virginia Plan, the Great Compromise proposed that in the lower house each state would receive one representative for every 40,000 inhabitants. This compromise did not solve all the conflicts over representation, however.

The Three-Fifths Compromise

The debate over representation also involved regional differences. Southern delegates wanted slaves to be counted as part of their state populations so they would have more representatives in Congress. Northerners thought that slaves should be counted in deciding a state's taxes but not in determining representation.

To resolve this problem, Edmund Randolph and James Wilson proposed that three fifths of the slaves in each state be counted as part of that state's population when allotting representatives to the lower house. New York delegate Gouverneur Morris spoke passionately against this proposal, arguing:

❝ **The admission of slaves into the Representation [in any way at all] comes to this: that the inhabitant of [a state] who goes to the coast of Africa and in defiance of the most sacred laws of humanity tears away his fellow creatures from their dearest connections and damns them to the most cruel bondage, shall have more votes in a Government instituted [established] for protection of the rights of mankind, than the citizens of [a state] who view with . . . horror, so nefarious [evil] a practice.** ❞

Despite Morris's speech against it, the delegates voted to accept this proposal, which they called the **Three-Fifths Compromise**.

Another controversial issue involved the foreign slave trade. Some of the delegates—such as George Mason of Virginia and John Dickinson of Delaware—wanted the federal government to ban, or stop, the slave trade altogether.

Delegates opposed to a constitutional ban on the slave trade, such as Charles Pinckney of South Carolina, quickly responded that the economies of South Carolina and Georgia would suffer greatly without importing slaves. John Rutledge, also of South Carolina, added, "The people of these States will never be such fools as to give up so important an interest." Many of these southern delegates then threatened to oppose the new constitution and withdraw from the Union if an immediate ban on the slave trade was made part of the document.

To resolve this conflict, delegates reached another compromise.

Northern delegates agreed to let the slave trade continue without interference for 20 years. In exchange, southern delegates agreed to drop their demand that laws in Congress be passed with a two-thirds majority vote.

The delegates omitted, or left out, the word *slavery* or *slave* in the Constitution. They referred instead to "free Persons" and "all other persons." Oliver Ellsworth summed up the view of many delegates when he said, "The morality or wisdom of slavery . . . are considerations belonging to the states themselves."

★ Our Living Constitution

The delegates to the Constitutional Convention worked hard to strengthen the national government without allowing it to become too powerful. The delegates wanted to address not just the shortcomings of the Articles of Confederation but also to correct some of the imbalances that had appeared in the new state constitutions. To ensure that the new national government avoided problems that the states had encountered, the delegates proposed to balance the powers within the national government.

This antislavery painting shows the goddess "Liberty" extending knowledge to newly freed slaves.

The Library Company of Philadelphia

The Articles of Confederation and the Constitution

ARTICLES	CONSTITUTION
EXECUTIVE BRANCH	
No executive to administer and enforce legislation; Congress has sole authority to govern. Executive committee to oversee government when Congress is out of session	President administers and enforces federal laws.
LEGISLATIVE BRANCH	
A unicameral (one-house) legislature Each state had one vote, regardless of population. Nine votes (of the original 13) to enact legislation	A bicameral (two-house) legislature Each state has equal representation in the Senate; each state is represented according to population in the House of Representatives. Simple majority to enact legislation
JUDICIAL BRANCH	
No national court system Congress to establish temporary courts to hear cases of piracy	National court system, headed by the Supreme Court Courts to hear cases involving national laws, treaties, and the Constitution as well as cases between states, between citizens of different states, or between a state and citizen of another state
OTHER MATTERS	
Admission to the Confederation by 9 votes (of 13) Amendment of the Articles by unanimous vote The states retained independence.	Congress to admit new states; all must have a republican form of government Amendment of the Constitution by two-thirds vote of both houses of Congress or by national convention, followed by ratification by three fourths of the states The states accept the Constitution as the supreme law of the land.

Checks and Balances

The balanced government that the delegates designed was based on the idea of **federalism**. Federalism is the distribution of governmental power between a central authority and the states or provinces that make up the nation.

The federal government is organized under three branches. The first is the **legislative branch**, or Congress, which is responsible for proposing bills and passing them into laws. Congress is made up of two houses. The Senate, or upper house, is composed of two members from each state. In the House of Representatives, or lower house, each state is represented according to its population. The second branch of the federal government is the **executive branch**, which includes the president and the administrative departments of the government. The third branch is the **judicial branch**, which is made up of all the national courts. This branch is responsible for interpreting laws, punishing criminals, and settling disputes between states. (For the full text of the U.S. Constitution, see page 266.)

The framers of the Constitution established **checks and balances**, a system to prevent any branch of government from becoming too powerful. For example, the framers gave Congress power to propose and pass bills into law, but also gave the president the power to veto congressional legislation. In later years, people interpreted the Constitution as providing the judicial branch with its own check—the Supreme Court's power to determine whether a law passed by Congress is unconstitutional.

Balancing Power

Another key to the balance of power established by the Constitution is the federal government's authority to enforce federal laws in the states. Article VI of the Constitution states:

> " **This Constitution and the Laws of the United States . . . which shall be made, under the Authority of the United States, shall be the supreme Law of the Land; and the Judges in every State shall be bound thereby, any Thing in the Constitution or Laws of any State to the Contrary notwithstanding.** "

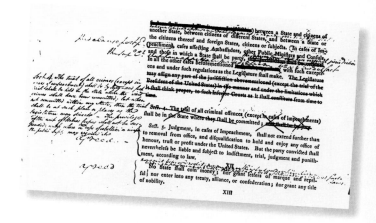

Part of an early draft of the Constitution, with comments written in the margin by George Washington

This means that as a part of the Union, each state is committed to the authority of the federal government's laws over state laws. In addition, the article notes that state legislators, officials, and judges are committed "by Oath . . . to support this Constitution." The federal government has the power to enforce its laws through the use of troops under the command of the president.

While the federal government's power was strengthened under the new Constitution, states kept sovereign, or independent, control over certain government functions. The states kept control over local government, education, the chartering of corporations, the development and administration of civil and criminal law, the supervision of religious bodies, and the general oversight of the welfare of their citizens.

Although the delegates realized that the Constitution was not a perfect document, they believed that they had created a strong government through the balance of powers. In September 1787, after 16 weeks of exhausting, sometimes fiery debates and discussions, delegates signed a final draft of the Constitution and sent it off to Congress. The Congress then sent the document to the states for ratification.

SECTION 3 REVIEW

Identify and explain the significance of the following:

- **Constitutional Convention**
- **James Madison**
- **Virginia Plan**
- **William Paterson**
- **New Jersey Plan**
- **Roger Sherman**
- **Great Compromise**
- **Three-Fifths Compromise**
- **federalism**
- **legislative branch**
- **executive branch**
- **judicial branch**
- **checks and balances**

Reading for Content Understanding

1 **Main Idea** Why was the Constitutional Convention called? Name two important delegates to the convention as well as two important people who did not attend.

2 **Main Idea** What issues divided delegates at the convention?

3 **Citizenship and Democracy** Why did the framers of the Constitution establish a system of checks and balances?

4 **Writing** *Describing* Write a paragraph describing how the system of checks and balances provides the basis for the federal government.

5 **Critical Thinking** *Drawing Conclusions* Why do you think the issue of slavery was controversial when framing the Constitution?

Ratification of the Constitution

Reading Focus

Why did some people oppose the new Constitution?

What arguments for the Constitution did the *Federalist Papers* present?

Why did some people want a bill of rights?

Key Terms

Antifederalists

Federalists

Federalist Papers

amendments

Bill of Rights

OHN DUNLAP AND DAVID CLAYPOOLE *stayed up well into the night on September 17, 1787, resetting type and filling all four pages of their newspaper. They had begun to work only hours after the Constitutional Convention ended. The next morning, the weary printers proudly presented the first printed copies of the U.S. Constitution to the people of Philadelphia. Soon other papers throughout the country also printed copies of the Constitution. For months people carried these newsprint copies with them, arguing over the document's benefits and drawbacks. No one knew whether the states would accept or reject this new form of government.*

An early printed copy of the Constitution

★ Federalists and Antifederalists

When the Constitution was made public, it sparked a heated debate among Americans. Some people feared that the new national government would take too much power away from the states and would not protect the rights of individual citizens. Benjamin Franklin, who supported the Constitution, tried to calm Americans' concerns

about the new federal government. He declared in a speech at the end of the Constitutional Convention:

❝ I consent . . . to [support] this Constitution because I expect no better . . . . I hope therefore that for our own sakes as a part of the people, . . . we shall act heartily and unanimously in recommending this constitution.❞

Franklin had urged convention delegates to sign the document even if they did not agree with all parts of it. He feared that the Union would crumble if the states rejected this Constitution.

Of the 42 delegates who remained at the convention, 39 signed the Constitution. Of the three delegates who refused to sign it—Elbridge Gerry of Massachusetts and George Mason and Edmund Randolph of Virginia—two thought that the Constitution needed a bill of rights and another preferred his own, different plan for government.

These people who opposed the Constitution were called **Antifederalists**. Some Antifederalists thought that the convention delegates had exceeded their authority in creating an entirely new government. Others did not like the Constitution because they thought it gave too much power to the central government. For some Antifederalists, the most critical problem was the Constitution's lack of a bill of rights.

Many Antifederalists were small farmers and debtors, but some were wealthier people. Some Revolutionary heroes—such as George Mason, Richard Henry Lee, Samuel Adams, and Patrick Henry—were also firm Antifederalists. In a letter to the Massachusetts state legislature, Gerry explained:

66 **My principal objections to the plan are, . . . that some of the powers of the Legislature are ambiguous [unclear], and others . . . dangerous; that the Executive . . . will have undue [too much] influence over the Legislature; that the judicial department will be oppressive [unjust] . . . and that the system is without the security of a bill of rights.** 99

Other Antifederalists, such as farmer Amos Singletary, thought that the supporters of the new Constitution "expect to get . . . all the power . . . into their own hands." Like Singletary, many of these Antifederalists feared that the Constitution was undemocratic and created special privileges for a limited few.

Elbridge Gerry

Antifederalists were challenged by many Americans who argued that the Constitution was necessary. Supporters of the Constitution, such as James Madison, George Washington, Benjamin Franklin, Alexander Hamilton, and John Jay, called themselves **Federalists**. Most Federalists believed that the Constitution provided a good balance of power and reflected a careful compromise between a variety of political opinions. Many Federalists were wealthy planters, farmers, merchants, and lawyers, although many poor urban laborers, craftspeople, and traders also supported the Constitution.

★ The *Federalist Papers*

One of the most influential defenses of the Constitution appeared in a series of essays that became known as the *Federalist Papers*. Although these essays were written anonymously under the name Publius, historians are now aware that of the 85 essays, Alexander Hamilton wrote either 50 or 51, James Madison wrote either 30 or 29, and John Jay wrote the other 5.

The Granger Collection, New York

Title page from a collection of the Federalist Papers

The authors of the *Federalist Papers* reassured Americans that the states would not be overpowered by the new federal government. In *Federalist Paper* "No. 10," Madison argued that the diversity of the United States would prevent any single group from dominating the government. He said that in a large country,

66 **you take in a greater variety of parties and interests; you make it less probable that a majority of the whole will have a common motive to invade the rights of other citizens.** 99

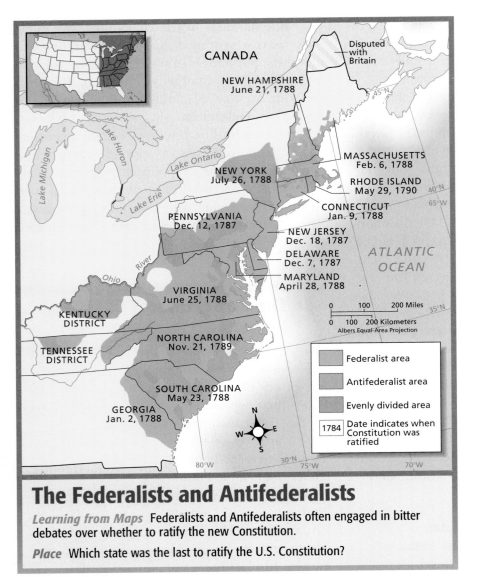

Rhode Island held special state conventions, which gave ordinary citizens the opportunity to discuss and vote on whether the Constitution should be ratified.

Impressions of the Constitution

At the Massachusetts ratifying convention, farmer Jonathan Smith expressed his support for the Constitution. He explained:

❝ **I am a plain man, and get my living by the plough. I am not used to speak in public, but I beg your leave to say a few words to my brother ploughjoggers [farmers] in this house. . . . I formed my own opinion, and was pleased with this Constitution. . . . I don't think the worse of the Constitution because lawyers, and men of learning, and moneyed men, are fond of it.** ❞

The Federalists and Antifederalists

Learning from Maps Federalists and Antifederalists often engaged in bitter debates over whether to ratify the new Constitution.

Place Which state was the last to ratify the U.S. Constitution?

The *Federalist Papers* were widely reprinted as the debate over the Constitution continued. George Washington's and Benjamin Franklin's endorsement of the Constitution also encouraged citizens to support the document. However, the true test of the Constitution came in the states' process of ratification. Unlike the Articles, which had required unanimous state approval, the Constitution would go into effect as soon as nine states had ratified it.

★ The Ratification Fight

Debates took place throughout the states over ratification of the Constitution. Each state except

Paul Revere, a hero of the Revolution and a Boston silversmith, served on a committee supporting ratification. He wrote of the Constitution, "The proposed . . . government, is well calculated to secure the liberties, protect the property, and guard the rights of the citizens of America." Revere and his fellow craftspeople urged the Massachusetts ratifying convention to support the Constitution.

A cast-iron plow from the late 1700s

Antifederalists also spoke out in state ratifying conventions. In New York one citizen said, "It appears that the government will fall into the hands of the few and the great. This will be a government of oppression." At the Virginia ratifying convention, Patrick Henry voiced the opinions of many Antifederalists when he said, "There will be no checks, no real balances, in this government." Although many Federalists believed that the Constitution's checks and balances were adequate, Antifederalists such as Henry thought that more controls were needed to guarantee that the federal government would not abuse its power.

Residents of New York hold a parade to celebrate their state's ratification of the Constitution in July 1788.

The Final Votes

In December 1787 Delaware became the first state to ratify the constitution. Throughout the remainder of 1787 and the first half of 1788, other states ratified the Constitution in the following order: Pennsylvania, New Jersey, Georgia, Connecticut, Massachusetts, Maryland, South Carolina, and New Hampshire. The only four states that had not yet ratified the Constitution were Virginia, New York, North Carolina, and Rhode Island. The Constitution went into effect in June 1788, after

Linking Past to Present

Printing Money

The U.S. Constitution states, "The Congress shall have Power . . . to coin Money." This passage gives the federal government alone the right to issue legal currency, or money, for the nation. However, until the mid-1800s, many state banks could print bank notes. These notes could be exchanged at the bank that issued them for their value in gold or silver coins.

As a result, there were many types of bank notes but little regulation of them. Banks often refused to accept or to honor the value of other banks' notes. The issuing of so many types of bank notes disrupted economic transactions. The federal government, therefore, stopped the states' issuing of bank notes and developed a national currency in the mid-1860s.

In the past 100 or so years, the government has made some changes to the money it issues. The U.S. Treasury discontinued printing the $500, $1,000, and $10,000 bills and introduced the $2 bill and the Susan B. Anthony dollar coin. The Treasury also has worked on redesigning paper money to make it harder to counterfeit. These new bills feature larger portraits than the older bills did. As *Time* magazine writes of the new $100 bill, Benjamin Franklin "now dominates the bill like a movie star in a newspaper advertisement."

Understanding What You Read

1. Why might having many different types of bank notes cause problems in the American economy?

2. How does the creation of a national currency demonstrate the powers of federalism?

Federalism

POWERS DELEGATED TO THE NATIONAL GOVERNMENT	POWERS SHARED BY NATIONAL AND STATE GOVERNMENTS	POWERS RESERVED TO THE STATES
Declare war	Maintain law and order	Establish and maintain schools
Maintain armed forces	Levy taxes	Establish local governments
Regulate interstate and foreign trade	Borrow money	Set corporate laws
Admit new states	Charter banks	Regulate business within the state
Establish post offices	Establish courts	Make marriage laws
Set standard weights and measures	Provide for public welfare	Provide for public safety
Coin money		Assume other powers not delegated to the national government or not prohibited to the states
Establish foreign policy		
Make all laws necessary and proper for carrying out delegated powers		

New Hampshire became the ninth state to ratify it. In July 1788 Congress declared the new Constitution ratified. With much public excitement and celebration, Congress arranged for the first presidential and congressional elections under the new government of the United States.

However, the ratification fights continued in the remaining four states. Political leaders throughout the Union knew that the new government would not succeed without the support of Virginia and New York, because Virginia had the largest population in the nation and New York was an important center for business and trade.

In Virginia, the debate over ratification was long and bitter. Ratification was particularly difficult because some of the most respected Antifederalists—such as Patrick Henry, George Mason, and Richard Henry Lee—lived in Virginia. They declared that under the Constitution the president would become a monarch. Eventually, however, James Madison and other Virginia Federalists convinced the delegates to the convention to ratify the Constitution in late June 1788.

In New York, citizens faced a similar battle over ratification. Many wealthy landowners in New York opposed the Constitution because they feared they would face heavier taxes under this new government. Some Federalist New Yorkers,

including John Jay and Alexander Hamilton, finally threatened that if the state did not ratify, New York City would break away and join the new government. This convinced the state's delegates to ratify the Constitution in July 1788. (North Carolina ratified the Constitution in November 1789 and Rhode Island ratified in May 1790.)

★ Demanding a Bill of Rights

Several states had ratified the Constitution only after the assurance that a bill of rights would be added. Many Antifederalists did not think that the Constitution adequately protected personal liberties. Mercy Otis Warren, a respected writer and Antifederalist, expressed this concern in Boston's *Columbian Patriot:* "There is no provision [requirement for] a bill of rights" to guard against abuses of power, and "the whole constitution . . . appears a perversion [abuse] of the rights of particular states, and of private citizens."

In the first session of the new Congress, some Federalists expressed the opinion that a federal bill of rights was unnecessary because people already were promised these rights under state constitutions. Many Federalists also believed that the entire Constitution was itself a bill of rights

This 1788 print by Amos Doolittle shows George Washington surrounded by the seal of the United States (at top) and the seals of the 13 states.

Courtesy of the John Carter Brown Library at Brown University

A DISPLAY of the UNITED STATES of AMERICA

because it was designed to ensure liberty for all U.S. citizens.

James Madison, on the other hand, was determined to make the creation of a bill of rights one of the new government's first priorities. Responding to a letter from Madison, Thomas Jefferson wrote that "a bill of rights is what the people are entitled to against every government on earth, . . . and what no just government should refuse."

In Congress's first session, Madison encouraged the legislators to put together a bill of rights. These rights would be added to the Constitution as **amendments**—official changes, corrections, or additions. To construct a list of possible amendments, the legislators gathered suggestions from the state ratifying conventions and the rights described

in the Virginia Declaration of Rights. Madison reviewed for Congress nearly 200 amendments that people had sent to him for consideration.

In September 1789, after three months of debate, Congress proposed 12 amendments and sent them to the states for ratification. By December 1791, 10 of these proposed amendments had been ratified by the required three fourths of the states. These first 10 amendments to the U.S. Constitution are known as the **Bill of Rights**. (For a full discussion of the Bill of Rights, see Chapter 9.)

These 10 amendments added to the strength and flexibility of the Constitution. They also established a clear example of how to amend the Constitution in the future to fit the needs of a changing nation. As one leader said, the Constitution was a remarkable document because it was a careful mixture of "definiteness in principles with elasticity in details." The flexibility of the U.S. Constitution has allowed it to survive as the oldest functioning written constitution in the world.

SECTION 4 REVIEW

Identify and explain the significance of the following:
- **Antifederalists**
- **Federalists**
- *Federalist Papers*
- **Mercy Otis Warren**
- **amendments**
- **Bill of Rights**

Reading for Content Understanding

1 **Main Idea** What arguments did some people make for rejecting the U.S. Constitution?

2 **Main Idea** What arguments were made in support of the Constitution?

3 **Constitutional Heritage** Why did some people insist that a bill of rights be added to the Constitution?

4 **Writing** *Creating* Write a half-page dialogue of a debate between a Federalist and an Antifederalist.

5 **Critical Thinking** *Determining the Strength of an Argument* If you had been a citizen during the ratification process, would you have been a Federalist or an Antifederalist? Explain your answer.

CHAPTER 8 REVIEW

Chapter Summary

America faced the challenge of creating its own government after declaring independence. The government's weakness under the Articles of Confederation led to serious national problems. The 13 states drew up a new plan of government, writing and then ratifying the Constitution. Later, the Bill of Rights was added to protect individual rights and freedoms. ▫

On a separate sheet of paper, complete the following activities.

Identifying People and Ideas

Describe the historical significance of the following:

1. Virginia Statute for Religious Freedom
2. Articles of Confederation
3. federalism
4. interstate commerce
5. Daniel Shays
6. Great Compromise
7. Three-Fifths Compromise
8. Northwest Ordinance of 1787
9. *Federalist Papers*
10. Mercy Otis Warren

go.hrw.com
**SA0
Constitution
Bios**

Internet Activity

Search the Internet through the HRW Web site for information about someone who attended the Constitutional Convention. Then write a biographical sketch about that person's life and contribution to U.S. history. Include an image or sketch of that person with your biography.

Understanding Main Ideas

1. What English laws did Americans draw from when creating their new government?
2. What did the Land Ordinance of 1785 accomplish?
3. Why was interstate commerce difficult to conduct under the Articles of Confederation?
4. What were the terms of the Great Compromise?
5. How is the federal government organized under the Constitution?
6. What arguments did Benjamin Franklin make in support of the Constitution? What arguments did Elbridge Gerry make in opposition to the Constitution?

Reviewing Themes

1. **Global Relations** How did the Articles of Confederation affect the new national government's ability to negotiate and conduct foreign policy, particularly with Great Britain?

Using the Time Line

Number your paper from 1 to 6. Match the letters on the time line below with the following events.

1. **The British close their ports to U.S. shipping.**
2. **The Constitution goes into effect after New Hampshire ratifies it.**
3. **The first 10 amendments are officially added to the Constitution.**
4. **Daniel Shays leads a rebellion of farmers in Massachusetts.**
5. **Delegates sign a final draft of the Constitution.**
6. **The Articles of Confederation go into effect.**

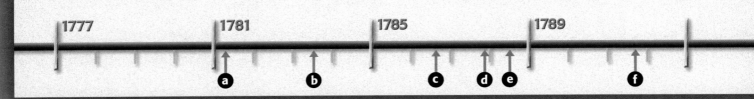

1777   1781   1785   1789
a   b   c   d e   f

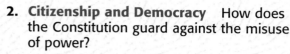

2. **Citizenship and Democracy** How does the Constitution guard against the misuse of power?

3. **Constitutional Heritage** Why did many Americans want a federal bill of rights?

Thinking Critically

1. **Synthesizing Information** How did the Articles of Confederation reflect Americans' fears of a powerful federal government?

2. **Supporting a Point of View** Imagine that you are a poor Massachusetts farmer in 1786. Explain why you will, or will not, join Shays's Rebellion.

Writing About History

1. **Persuading** Imagine that you are a Constitutional Convention delegate. Write a short speech explaining why the Three-Fifths Compromise goes against the spirit of the Declaration of Independence.

2. **Creating** Create a poster supporting or opposing the ratification of the Constitution. Make sure to include specific reasons

Building Your Portfolio

American History

Complete the following activities individually or in groups.

1. **Constitutional Convention** Imagine that you are attending the Constitutional Convention. Think of an issue that was not addressed in the original Constitution (for example, suffrage for all Americans or the ending of slavery). Write a one-act play about the discussion that takes place at the convention surrounding your issue. If possible, perform your play for the class by using actors and props.

2. **The Federal Government** Clip current magazine and newspaper articles on the activities of the three branches of the federal government. Then create a bulletin board display that shows the issues that each branch of the government tackles today.

why your state should or should not vote for ratification.

Linking Geography and History

1. **Region** Why did southerners want slaves to be counted when deciding a state's population? Why did northerners argue against this plan?

2. **Place** Why was it important for New York and Virginia to ratify the Constitution?

History Skills Workshop

Using Primary Sources Dr. Benjamin Rush was an American physician and educator. He signed the Declaration of Independence and was a member of the Pennsylvania constitutional ratification convention. In 1786 he presented a plan for schools in Pennsylvania, recommending instruction for all members of society. Read the following excerpt from his "A Plan for the Establishment of Public Schools." Then answer the following questions:

(a) According to Rush, why is education important for religion? (b) Do you agree with Rush's statement that freedom can exist only with an educated population? Explain your answer.

❝I shall point out, in a few words, the influence and advantages of learning upon mankind.
1. It [education] is friendly to religion inasmuch as it assists in . . . promoting just notions of the Deity [God]; in enlarging our knowledge of His works.
2. It is favorable to liberty. Freedom can exist only in the society of knowledge. Without learning, men are incapable of knowing their rights.❞

The Living Constitution

The present government of the United States began operation in 1789 and is based on a written Constitution that was adopted by the 13 original states. The United States has remained strong through many crises because its Constitution established a government in which the people choose their leaders to make their laws. The Constitution's principles and methods of governing have been strong enough to enforce its authority, but flexible enough to adapt to great changes over more than 200 years.

Today the original nation of 13 states—which housed fewer than 4 million people—has grown to 50 states and some 265 million people. The United States now stretches across the continent, from the Atlantic Ocean to the shores of the Pacific, and includes Alaska in the north and the faraway islands of Hawaii in the West. ■

The Union

The Northwest Ordinance was adopted by Congress in 1787 under the old Articles of Confederation, before the Constitution was written. It set out a method for admitting new states to the Union that remains in place today. The last states admitted to the Union were Alaska and Hawaii in 1959.

The Northwest Ordinance: Becoming a State

CANADA

Lake Superior

WISCONSIN
1848

Mississippi River

Lake Michigan

Lake Huron

MICHIGAN
1837

Lake Ontario

NEW YORK

Lake Erie

NORTHWEST TERRITORY

PENNSYLVANIA

LOUISIANA

ILLINOIS
1818

INDIANA
1816

OHIO
1803

MD.

Ohio River

VIRGINIA

KENTUCKY

N W E S

0   125   250 Miles
0   125   250 Kilometers
Albers Equal-Area Projection

STEPS TO STATEHOOD

Congress specifies that three to five territories will be carved out of the Northwest Territory.

For each territory, Congress appoints a governor, a secretary, and three judges.

When a territory's population reaches 5,000 free male inhabitants of voting age, it elects a territorial legislature and sends a nonvoting delegate to Congress.

Once a territory's population increases to 60,000 free inhabitants, it becomes eligible for statehood and can draft a state constitution.

Congress approves the state constitution, and the territory becomes a state.

Sources: *Record of America; The Oxford Companion to American History*

Geography **Skills**

Reading Political Maps

1. How many people had to be living in a territory for it to be eligible for statehood?

2. Who, or what, has to approve a territory's proposed constitution before the territory becomes a state?

3. In what order did the states of the Northwest Territory join the Union?

Joining the Union

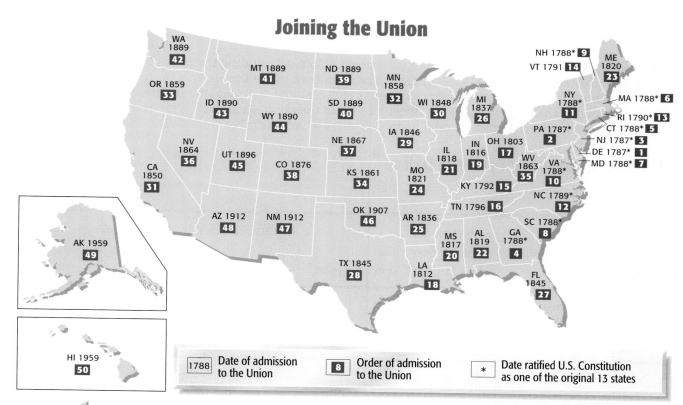

WA 1889 **42**
OR 1859 **33**
MT 1889 **41**
ND 1889 **39**
MN 1858 **32**
NH 1788* **9**
VT 1791 **14**
ME 1820 **23**
ID 1890 **43**
WI 1848 **30**
MI 1837 **26**
NY 1788* **11**
MA 1788* **6**
WY 1890 **44**
SD 1889 **40**
IA 1846 **29**
PA 1787* **2**
RI 1790* **13**
CT 1788* **5**
NV 1864 **36**
UT 1896 **45**
NE 1867 **37**
IL 1818 **21**
IN 1816 **19**
OH 1803 **17**
WV 1863 **35**
VA 1788* **10**
NJ 1787* **3**
DE 1787* **1**
MD 1788* **7**
CA 1850 **31**
CO 1876 **38**
KS 1861 **34**
MO 1821 **24**
KY 1792 **15**
NC 1789* **12**
AZ 1912 **48**
NM 1912 **47**
OK 1907 **46**
AR 1836 **25**
TN 1796 **16**
SC 1788* **8**
MS 1817 **20**
AL 1819 **22**
GA 1788* **4**
TX 1845 **28**
LA 1812 **18**
FL 1845 **27**
AK 1959 **49**
HI 1959 **50**

1788 Date of admission to the Union	**8** Order of admission to the Union	***** Date ratified U.S. Constitution as one of the original 13 states

Geography **Skills**

Reading Special-Purpose Maps

1. Which three states ratified the Constitution first?
2. What were the original 13 states?
3. What states were admitted to the Union in the 1900s?

History Note 2

Not all states went through the territory stage before admission to the Union. Texas was an independent country before it became a state. California went directly to statehood because of its rapidly growing population. Kentucky, Maine, Vermont, and West Virginia started out as parts of other states.

History Note 1

Congress established the method for admission of new states to the Union in the Northwest Ordinance of 1787. Before that, however, people in the northeastern portion of present-day Tennessee made the first attempt to create a new state. This proposed state of "Franklin," named after Benjamin Franklin, appealed to Congress for statehood. Franklin's application for statehood came in 1784 after North Carolina turned over the Tennessee territory to the new United States government. Before Congress acted on Franklin's statehood, North Carolina decided to reclaim the region. For a brief time both the state of North Carolina and the proposed state of Franklin tried to enforce laws in the region. Finally, in 1790 North Carolina again turned over control of the region to the national government. Six years later the proposed state of Franklin became part of the new state of Tennessee.

Rocky Mount, capitol for the first territorial government of Tennessee

The Representatives

The Constitution sets the requirements for federal officials, including the president and vice president, Supreme Court justices, and members of the Senate and House of Representatives. House members represent congressional districts that are distributed among the states based on a census count of the population. The average population size of each congressional district has grown remarkably since 1789.

Requirements for Federal Office

	OFFICE	REQUIREMENTS	TERM	SELECTION
	President Vice President	• 35 years old • Natural-born citizen • Live in United States 14 years	4 years	Elected by electoral college
	Supreme Court Justice	• None	Life	Appointed by president and approved by Senate
	Senator	• 30 years old • U.S. citizen 9 years • Live in state where elected	6 years	Originally chosen by state legislature (per Constitution); Currently elected by voters (per Seventeenth Amendment)
	Representative	• 25 years old • U.S. citizen 7 years • Live in state where elected	2 years	Elected by voters of district

Geography Skills

Reading Charts

1. What are the age requirements for federal officials?
2. Are House members required to live in the congressional districts they represent?
3. What are the terms of the federal officials listed?

1996 presidential inauguration

Growth of Congressional Districts

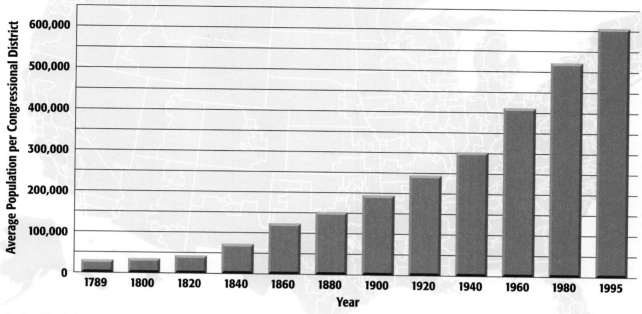

Average Population per Congressional District (vertical axis): 0, 100,000, 200,000, 300,000, 400,000, 500,000, 600,000

Year (horizontal axis): 1789, 1800, 1820, 1840, 1860, 1880, 1900, 1920, 1940, 1960, 1980, 1995

Source: *Historical Statistics of the United States; 1997 World Almanac and Book of Facts*

History Note 4

Until 1912 Congress increased the number of U.S. House districts as the number of states and the nation's population grew. There were 106 congressional districts after the 1790 census, and that number increased until the 1912 election. Since then Congress has kept the number of U.S. House districts at 435.

Geography Skills
Reading Bar Graphs

1. What was the average population of each congressional district in 1800? in 1900?
2. During what 20-year period during the 1800s did the average population of a congressional district increase the most?
3. What is the average population of each congressional district today?

U.S. Capitol

History Note 5

Congressional districts within each state have generally equal populations, but the size of the districts sometimes varies among states. If all congressional districts were of equal size, each would have about 570,000 people (1990 population size divided by 435). However, three states in 1990 had populations of less than 570,000, yet the Constitution requires that every state have at least one member in the U.S. House of Representatives. The U.S. Census Bureau uses a special formula to apportion, or distribute, congressional districts among the states. In 1990 Wyoming, with a population of only 453,589, received one congressional district. Montana, with nearly 800,000 people, also received just one district.

The Citizens

The percentage of the U.S. population eligible to vote has increased greatly over time.

The Expanding Electorate

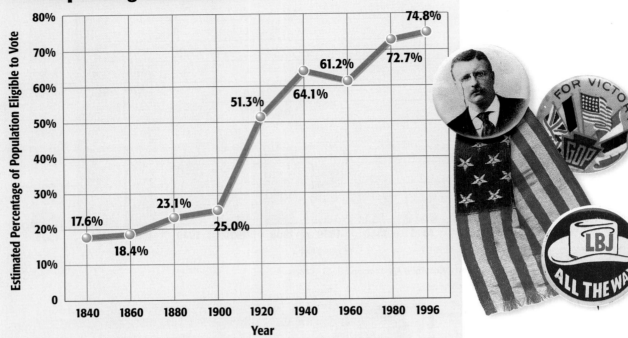

Estimated Percentage of Population Eligible to Vote

- 17.6%
- 18.4%
- 23.1%
- 25.0%
- 51.3%
- 64.1%
- 61.2%
- 72.7%
- 74.8%

Year: 1840, 1860, 1880, 1900, 1920, 1940, 1960, 1980, 1996

Sources: *Historical Statistics of the United States;* Federal Election Commission; *Congressional Quarterly's Guide to U.S. Elections; Datapedia of the United States, 1790-2000: America Year by Year*

History Note 6

The Constitution generally gives states the right to decide who is eligible to vote in elections. Over the years, however, constitutional amendments have extended the right to vote to more and more people. The Fifteenth Amendment, ratified in 1870, protects the right of people of any race to vote. The Nineteenth Amendment, passed in 1920, gives women the right to vote in all states. The Twenty-sixth Amendment, passed in 1971, lowered the minimum voting age from 21 to 18.

Geography Skills
Reading Line Graphs

1. What three years show the largest increases in the percentage of the U.S. population eligible to vote?
2. What amendments to the Constitution help explain the large increases in those years?

History Note 7

In the early and mid-1800s, male immigrants who were not citizens could vote in most states. This was partly to encourage immigration to the United States. However, in the late 1800s attitudes changed, and many people called for limits on immigration. Many states passed laws that restricted the vote to citizens.

Voter Turnout

Voter Turnout

Percentage of Electorate Who Voted (y-axis: 0% to 90%)

Presidential Election Years (x-axis: 1789, 1804, 1820, 1836, 1852, 1868, 1884, 1900, 1916, 1932, 1948, 1964, 1980, 1996)

Sources: Walter Dean Bunham's "The Turnout Problem"; *Historical Statistics of the United States;* Federal Election Commission

Geography **Skills**
Reading Line Graphs

1. In general, during what period was the voter turnout rate highest in the United States?

2. Describe voter turnout after 1964.

3. After 1820 what two periods have experienced the lowest turnout rates?

History Note 8

Voter turnout is greater in years that have presidential elections than in years that have mid-term congressional elections. Mid-term elections come in the middle of a president's four-year term. Those elections are for all 435 seats in the House of Representatives and for one third of the seats in the Senate. Less than 39 percent of eligible voters cast ballots in congressional elections in 1994.

History Note 9

Presidential winners must gain a majority of the votes from the electoral college. When people vote for a presidential candidate, they are actually casting ballots for presidential electors who are pledged to a particular candidate. The electors win the election in a state and then cast their electoral vote for their candidate. Until the 1820s, many states had their legislators—not voters—vote for state electors. The result was people saw little reason to vote, and the turnout rate for presidential elections was very low.

NEW YORK

▪ CHAPTER 9 ▪
Citizenship and the Constitution

(1787–Present)

Thomas Jefferson admired the ideas of ancient Greek philosophers such as Aristotle. "Liberty and equality," wrote Aristotle, "will be best attained [reached] when all persons alike share in the government." Some 2,000 years after Aristotle, U.S. leaders began the process of creating a democratic system of government. Today most Americans can participate in the political process.

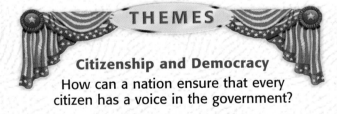

THEMES

Citizenship and Democracy
How can a nation ensure that every citizen has a voice in the government?

Constitutional Heritage
How does a government's organization affect the distribution of power?

Cultural Diversity
What contributions have different groups and individuals made to the nation's formation and government?

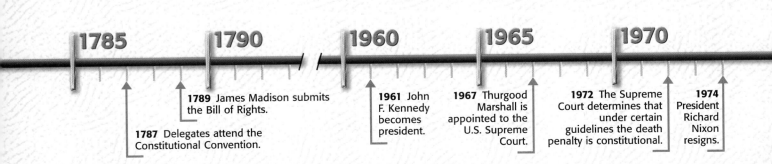

1785

1790

1960

1965

1970

1789 James Madison submits the Bill of Rights.

1787 Delegates attend the Constitutional Convention.

1961 John F. Kennedy becomes president.

1967 Thurgood Marshall is appointed to the U.S. Supreme Court.

1972 The Supreme Court determines that under certain guidelines the death penalty is constitutional.

1974 President Richard Nixon resigns.

Understanding the Constitution

Reading Focus

How did the framers of the Constitution address concerns about the balance of state and federal powers?

What are the three branches of the federal government?

How is power divided among the three branches of government?

Key Terms

delegated powers

elastic clause

reserved powers

concurrent powers

representative democracy

apportionment

impeach

veto

executive orders

pardons

cabinet

TODAY A SIGN *on the Justice Department building in Washington, D.C., reads, "No Free Government Can Survive That Is Not Based on the Supremacy of Law." This idea is central to the U.S. Constitution. Antifederalists opposed the Constitution for fear that the government it created would be too powerful and thus endanger the rights of the people. Federalists such as James Madison assured them that a system grounded in law was the best safeguard of the people.*

The Constitution

The Granger Collection, New York

IMAGE ON LEFT PAGE: *Students view historic artwork in Washington, D.C.*

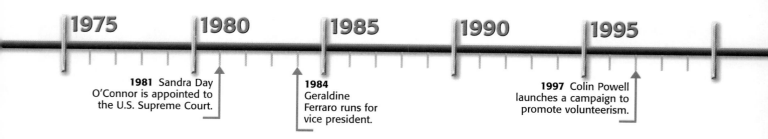

1975 1980 1985 1990 1995

1981 Sandra Day O'Connor is appointed to the U.S. Supreme Court.

1984 Geraldine Ferraro runs for vice president.

1997 Colin Powell launches a campaign to promote volunteerism.

The Federal System

The Antifederalists opposed the Constitution because they wanted a limited national government—one that would not have too much power. To address Antifederalist concerns, in 1787 the writers of the Constitution established the separation of powers between the states and the federal government.

Delegated powers, those granted to the federal government, include coining money, running the country's postal system, regulating interstate and international trade, providing for the nation's defense, declaring war, and conducting diplomacy. These powers allow the national government to protect citizens and to assure a more uniform economic system throughout the country.

The **elastic clause** of the Constitution, found in Article I, Section 8, allows Congress to stretch its delegated powers

The seal of the U.S. Congress

to address issues that the nation's founders could not have foreseen. For example, the Constitution gives the federal government the power to run the postal system, which was the main form of long-distance communication when the Constitution was written. Today the government also regulates modern forms of long-distance communication technology, such as telephones and computers.

The powers retained by the state governments or by citizens are **reserved powers**. These powers include conducting elections, regulating trade within each state, establishing local governments, and regulating education. The federal and state governments also share powers. These **concurrent powers** include taxing, borrowing money, enforcing laws, and providing for citizens' welfare.

The Legislative Branch

The legislative branch makes the nation's laws. "Members of Congress are the human connection between the citizen and . . . government," noted one member of Congress. The founders discussed

the legislative branch in Article I of the Constitution to emphasize that the United States would be a **representative democracy**, or government by representatives of the people.

The House and Senate

The House of Representatives is the larger of the two houses of Congress. Currently it has 435 members (originally it had 65). To maintain the current total, Congress decided that no state can gain a representative unless another state loses one. The number of representatives for each state is based on the U.S. census, a population count taken every 10 years. Congress examines changes in the population to determine the **apportionment**, or distribution, of representatives. After the 1990 census, for example, Texas gained three additional seats in the House while New York lost three.

House members represent a particular district of voters in a state. House members must be at least 25 years old, U.S. citizens for seven or more years, and residents of the state from which they are elected. They do not have to live in the district they represent, however.

Senators represent their entire state. They must be at least 30 years old, U.S. citizens for nine or more years, and residents of the state they represent. Each state has two senators. The one who has served longer is the state's senior senator.

The term for a House member is two years and for a Senate member is six years. No law limits the number of times someone may be elected to Congress. However, in recent years many Americans have supported imposing term limits to restrict the number of terms a member can serve.

Organization

Congress holds regular sessions, or meetings, every year beginning on January 3. During a time of national emergency the president may call a congressional meeting after the regular session has already ended. For example, President Abraham

Newt Gingrich became Speaker of the House in 1995.

American Literature

Federalist Paper "No. 51"
James Madison

During the debates over the ratification of the Constitution, New York newspapers printed a series of essays supporting ratification and countering Antifederalist arguments. The Federalist Papers *were written by Alexander Hamilton, John Jay, and James Madison. In this excerpt from essay "No. 51," Madison discusses the means by which the separation of powers among the various branches of government would be preserved.*

In order to lay a due [proper] foundation for . . . the different powers of government, . . . it is evident that each department should have a will of its own; and should be so constituted [set up] that the members of each should have as little agency [power] as possible in the appointment of the members of the others. Were this principle rigorously adhered to [strictly followed], it would require that all the appointments for the supreme executive, legislative, and judiciary magistracies [offices] should be drawn from the same fountain of authority, the people, through channels having no communication . . . with one another. . . .

But the great security against a gradual concentration of the several powers in the same department consists in giving to those who administer each department the necessary constitutional means and personal motives to resist encroachments [advances] of the others. The provision for defense must . . . be made commensurate [equal] to the danger of attack. . . . It may be a reflection on human nature that such devices should be necessary to control the abuses of government. But what is government itself but the greatest of all reflections on human nature? If men were angels, no government would be necessary. If angels were to govern men, neither external nor internal controls on government would be necessary. In framing a government which is to be administered by men over men, the great difficulty lies in this: you must first enable the government to control the governed; and in the next place oblige [force] it to control itself.

Understanding Literature

1. What is the "fountain of authority"?
2. According to the excerpt, who should the government govern?

Lincoln called Congress into a special session during the Civil War.

The political party with the most members in each house of Congress is called the majority party. The party with fewer members is the minority party of that house. The leader of the House of Representatives is the Speaker of the House. House members select the Speaker, who is usually from the majority party. The vice president of the United States serves as the President of the Senate.

The vice president does not join in Senate debates and can cast a vote only if there is a tie. When the vice president is absent, the president pro tempore, usually the longest-serving senator of the majority party, leads the Senate.

Congress carries out most of its work in committees that examine every proposed bill. Currently the Senate has 16 standing, or permanent, committees and the House has 19. Each committee specializes in certain types of legislation.

For example, all bills relating to taxes originate in the House Ways and Means Committee.

 ## The Executive Branch

Article II of the Constitution specifies the powers of the executive branch, which is responsible for enforcing the laws approved by Congress. The president, as head of the executive branch, is the most powerful elected official in the country.

Becoming President

To become president, one must be a native-born U.S. citizen, at least 35 years old, and have been a resident of the United States for at least 14 years. All presidents have been white men. However, in recent years, candidates have become more diverse, with African Americans such as Shirley Chisholm and Jesse Jackson seeking the presidency. Geraldine Ferraro became the first woman on the ticket of a major political party when she ran as the Democratic nominee for vice president in 1984. No non-Christian has yet been president. When John F. Kennedy took office in 1961, he became the first Roman Catholic president.

Americans elect a president and vice president every four years. The president determines the vice president's responsibilities, which often include representing the president at official functions. Franklin D. Roosevelt, who won four presidential elections, has been the only president to serve more than two terms. The Twenty-second Amendment, ratified in 1951, prevents anyone from serving more than two terms as president. If the president dies, resigns, or is removed from office, the vice president becomes president.

The Constitution gives the House of Representatives the authority to **impeach**, or bring charges against, a president suspected of committing a crime or of violating the essential presidential duties. The Senate tries all impeachment cases. If a president is found guilty, Congress can remove him or her from office. In 1867 Andrew Johnson became the only president ever to be impeached. By one vote, the Senate decided the case in Johnson's favor. In 1974 Richard Nixon became the first president to resign rather than be impeached.

Presidential Duties

The president has many duties, which involve overseeing all aspects of the government. The system of checks and balances often sets the president against Congress, particularly when the president's party is different from that of the majority party in Congress. First Lady Eleanor Roosevelt once noted, "It isn't really possible under our system, I fear, for the Executive and the Legislative to get along well."

Despite their differences, the executive and legislative branches must cooperate for the system to work. As President Lyndon Johnson observed:

❝ **What a President says and thinks is not worth five cents unless he has the people and Congress behind him. Without the Congress I'm just a six-feet-four Texan. With Congress I'm President of the United States in the fullest sense.** ❞

Although Congress passes laws, the president can influence legislation by encouraging members to approve or reject certain bills. The president also has the power to **veto**, or cancel, legislation. Congress can override a president's veto, but doing so is very difficult because it requires a two-thirds majority vote.

"Thanks—Thanks a lot—Thanks again—can I lean back now?"

President Lyndon Johnson was famous for praising members of Congress, or patting them on the back, so that they would pass his legislation.

The Executive Departments

DEPARTMENT OF STATE
• conducts foreign relations
• protects U.S. citizens abroad
• issues passports and visas

DEPARTMENT OF THE TREASURY
• prints coins and issues money
• collects taxes and pays bills
• manages government funds

DEPARTMENT OF JUSTICE
• investigates violations of federal laws
• prosecutes cases before courts
• administers naturalization laws
• enforces immigration laws

DEPARTMENT OF THE INTERIOR
• controls public lands
• maintains public parks
• supervises American Indian reservations
• controls water resources

DEPARTMENT OF AGRICULTURE
• conducts studies to help farmers
• manages food stamp and school
   lunch programs
• helps farmers raise and market crops
• directs soil conservation programs

DEPARTMENT OF COMMERCE
• sets standards for weights and measures
• encourages and regulates foreign trade
• publishes reports on business and trade

DEPARTMENT OF LABOR
• determines standards of labor
• publishes employment information
• directs public employment services

DEPARTMENT OF DEFENSE
• maintains U.S. armed services
• conducts military studies
• operates military bases

**DEPARTMENT OF HEALTH
AND HUMAN SERVICES**
• directs public health services
• sees that foods and medicines are safe

**DEPARTMENT OF HOUSING
AND URBAN DEVELOPMENT**
• helps urban-housing programs
• helps cities plan traffic control
• helps cities plan mass transportation
• cooperates with metropolitan-area planners

DEPARTMENT OF TRANSPORTATION
• helps develop the nation's transportation
   policy
• supervises federal-aid highway program
• promotes transportation safety

DEPARTMENT OF ENERGY
• helps develop the nation's energy policy
• promotes conservation of energy
• regulates energy resources

DEPARTMENT OF EDUCATION
• sets guidelines for granting financial
   aid to schools
• conducts research on educational subjects
• administers federally sponsored
   educational programs

DEPARTMENT OF VETERANS AFFAIRS
• administers medical and disability benefits
   to veterans and their families
• provides pensions and death benefits
   for veterans

After Congress passes a law, federal agencies and departments usually determine how to put it into effect. To carry out laws that affect administrative matters or executive policy, the president sometimes issues **executive orders**, nonlegislative directives that have the force of law. In an emergency the president may issue an executive order that stretches the definition of laws enacted by Congress.

The president, although a civilian, is also commander in chief of the armed forces. Although the president can send U.S. troops into emergency situations, only Congress can declare war. The president's many other responsibilities include carrying out foreign relations through both diplomatic ties and the negotiation of treaties. The president also has the power to grant **pardons**, or freedom from punishment, for persons convicted of federal crimes or who are facing criminal charges.

Executive Departments

Numerous departments carry out most of the work of the executive branch. Currently there are 14 executive departments. The heads of these departments make up the **cabinet**, which advises

Sandra Day O'Connor

Sandra Day O'Connor was born in El Paso, Texas, in 1930. She attended college and law school at Stanford University in California. She began her legal career working as a deputy county attorney in California. Later she moved to Arizona, where she served as the assistant state attorney general and then as a state legislator. In 1973 she became the majority leader for the Arizona state senate before being appointed a judge on the state's second-highest court.

In 1981 President Ronald Reagan appointed O'Connor to the Supreme Court. Although she was appointed by a Republican president, O'Connor has at times opposed Republican policies when deciding cases. Her decisions illustrate how Supreme Court justices often can be free from party politics once appointed. When asked how she hoped to be remembered, O'Connor replied that she would like her tombstone to read simply, "Here lies a good judge."

the president. Some departments, such as the State Department, handle foreign-policy issues. Others, such as the Department of Education, focus on domestic issues.

The Judicial Branch

The third branch of the government is the judicial branch, which consists of a series of federal courts headed by the U.S. Supreme Court. Article III of the Constitution defines the duties of the courts.

The Federal Court System

The president appoints all judges on each level of the federal court system for life. Each of these judges receives the appointment for life to ensure that he or she will make decisions free from the influence of a particular party. Federal judge Shirley Wohl Kram explains her duties, "It is the judge's role to resolve grievances and the role of the legislature to supply the answers for the social and economic problems facing the community."

The lower courts in the federal system are divided according to the types of cases over which they have jurisdiction, or authority. Each state has at least one district court to handle federal cases.

States with large populations usually have more than one district court. Currently there are 94 U.S. districts courts.

Above the lower courts are 13 courts of appeals, which make sure that cases are tried properly in the lower courts. Someone convicted of a crime who believes that his or her rights were violated in the original trial can appeal the case to the higher court.

The courts of appeals do not use juries. Instead, a panel of judges decides whether the lower court handled the original case properly. If the judges uphold, or accept, the lower court's decision, then the case's original outcome remains. If they feel that the case was handled improperly, they usually send it back to the lower court for a new trial. The courts of appeals have the final say in most of the cases they review. Sometimes, however, the U.S. Supreme Court chooses to review decisions of the courts of appeals.

The Supreme Court

Most cases presented to the Supreme Court originate in lower courts. However, some cases—such as those that involve international diplomats or disputes between states—go directly to the Supreme Court.

Congress determines how many justices sit on the Court; typically that number is fixed at nine. The chief justice of the United States leads the Supreme Court. Unlike for the president and members of Congress, the Constitution sets no specific requirements for being a Court justice. So far, however, every justice has been an attorney. William Howard Taft is the only person to have been both president (1909–13) and a Supreme Court chief justice (1921–30).

In the last 50 years the Supreme Court has become more diverse. In 1967 Thurgood Marshall became the first African American justice; the second was Clarence Thomas in 1991. Currently two women sit on the high court, Ruth Bader Ginsburg and Sandra Day O'Connor, who became the first female Court justice after her 1981 appointment by President Ronald Reagan. Each justice contributes greatly to the Court. As O'Connor explained:

Supreme Court Justice Ruth Bader Ginsburg speaks to a group of students.

❝ **The Court benefits from broad and diverse experiences of its members. My own experience in all three branches of state government gave me a background which differed from a majority of my colleagues. It undoubtedly has helped me understand and appreciate the importance and value of the federal system designed by the Framers of the Constitution.** ❞

O'Connor and other Supreme Court justices have time to review around 100 of the thousands of cases appealed to them every year. The justices carefully choose which cases to hear. Generally, cases heard by the Court must involve an important constitutional or public interest issue. If the Court refuses to hear a case, the decision of the court of appeals is final. If the Court finds a law unconstitutional and Congress disagrees with the ruling, lawmakers can begin the process of amending the Constitution.

SECTION 1 REVIEW

Identify and explain the significance of the following:

- delegated powers
- elastic clause
- reserved powers
- concurrent powers
- representative democracy
- apportionment
- impeach
- veto
- executive orders
- pardons
- cabinet
- Sandra Day O'Connor

Reading for Content Understanding

1 **Main Idea** How are the state and federal powers balanced in the Constitution?

2 **Main Idea** List the three branches of the federal government, and explain how power is divided among them.

3 **Citizenship and Democracy** How does a state's population affect that state's representation in the House and Senate?

4 **Writing** *Describing* Write a two-paragraph essay that explains how the judicial system is structured.

5 **Critical Thinking** *Synthesizing Information* Do you think the three branches of government share power equally? If not, which branch do you think has the most power, and why?

THE CONSTITUTION

"WE THE PEOPLE OF THE UNITED STATES, IN ORDER TO FORM A MORE PERFECT UNION, ESTABLISH JUSTICE, INSURE DOMESTIC TRANQUILITY, PROVIDE FOR THE COMMON DEFENCE, PROMOTE THE GENERAL WELFARE, AND SECURE THE BLESSINGS OF LIBERTY TO OURSELVES AND OUR POSTERITY, DO ORDAIN AND ESTABLISH THIS CONSTITUTION FOR THE UNITED STATES OF AMERICA."

*Parts of the Constitution that have been ruled through are no longer in force or no longer apply because of later amendments.

Preamble
The short and dignified Preamble explains the goals of the new government under the Constitution.

Independence Hall, Philadelphia

ARTICLE I

Section 1. All legislative Powers herein granted shall be vested in a Congress of the United States, which shall consist of a Senate and House of Representatives.

Section 2. The House of Representatives shall be composed of Members chosen every second Year by the People of the several States, and the Electors in each State shall have the Qualifications requisite for Electors of the most numerous Branch of the State Legislature.

No Person shall be a Representative who shall not have attained to the Age of twenty five Years, and been seven Years a Citizen of the United States, and who shall not, when elected, be an Inhabitant of that State in which he shall be chosen.

Representatives and direct Taxes shall be apportioned among the several States which may be included within this Union, according to their respective Numbers, which shall be determined by adding to the whole Number of free Persons, including those bound to Service for a Term of Years, and excluding Indians not taxed, three fifths of all other Persons. The actual Enumeration shall be made within three Years after the first Meeting of the Congress of the United States, and within every subsequent Term of ten Years, in such Manner as they shall by Law direct. The Number of Representatives shall not exceed one for every thirty Thousand, but each State shall have at Least one Representative; and until such enumeration shall be made, the State of New Hampshire shall be entitled to chuse three; Massachusetts eight; Rhode Island and Providence Plantations one; Connecticut five; New York six; New Jersey four; Pennsylvania eight; Delaware one; Maryland six; Virginia ten; North Carolina five; South Carolina five; and Georgia three.

When vacancies happen in the Representation from any State, the Executive Authority thereof shall issue Writs of Election to fill such Vacancies.

The House of Representatives shall chuse their Speaker and other Officers; and shall have the sole Power of Impeachment.

Section 3. The Senate of the United States shall be composed of two Senators from each State, chosen by the Legislature thereof, for six Years; and each Senator shall have one Vote.

Immediately after they shall be assembled in Consequence of the first Election, they shall be divided as equally as may be into three Classes. The Seats of the Senators of the first Class shall be vacated at the Expiration of the second Year, of the second Class at the Expiration of the fourth Year, and of the third Class at the Expiration of the sixth Year, so that one third may be chosen every second Year; and if Vacancies happen by

---

Legislative Branch

Article I explains how the legislative branch, called Congress, is organized. The chief purpose of the legislative branch is to make the laws. Congress is made up of the Senate and the House of Representatives. The decision to have two bodies of government solved a difficult problem during the Constitutional Convention. The large states wanted the membership of Congress to be based entirely on population. The small states wanted every state to have an equal vote. The solution to the problem of how the states were to be represented in Congress became known as the Great Compromise.

The number of members each state has in the House is based on the population of the individual state. Each state has at least one representative. In 1929 Congress permanently fixed the size of the House at 435 members. Today, if each member of the House were to represent only 30,000 Americans, the House would have more than 8,600 members.

Every state has two senators. Senators serve a six-year term. Every two years, one third of the senators reach the end of their terms. In any election, at least two thirds of the senators stay in office. This system ensures that there are experienced senators in office at all times.

~~Resignation, or otherwise, during the Recess of the Legislature of any State, the Executive thereof may make temporary Appointments until the next Meeting of the Legislature, which shall then fill such Vacancies.~~

No Person shall be a Senator who shall not have attained to the Age of thirty Years, and been nine Years a Citizen of the United States, and who shall not, when elected, be an Inhabitant of that State for which he shall be chosen.

The Vice President of the United States shall be President of the Senate, but shall have no Vote, unless they be equally divided.

The Senate shall chuse their other Officers, and also a President pro tempore, in the Absence of the Vice President, or when he shall exercise the Office of President of the United States.

The Senate shall have the sole Power to try all Impeachments. When sitting for that Purpose, they shall be on Oath or Affirmation. When the President of the United States is tried, the Chief Justice shall preside: And no Person shall be convicted without the Concurrence of two thirds of the Members present.

Judgment in Cases of Impeachment shall not extend further than to removal from Office, and disqualification to hold and enjoy any Office of honor, Trust or Profit under the United States: but the Party convicted shall nevertheless be liable and subject to Indictment, Trial, Judgment and Punishment, according to Law.

Section 4. The Times, Places and Manner of holding Elections for Senators and Representatives, shall be prescribed in each State by the Legislature thereof; but the Congress may at any time by Law make or alter such Regulations, except as to the Places of chusing Senators.

~~The Congress shall assemble at least once in every Year, and such Meeting shall be on the first Monday in December, unless they shall by Law appoint a different Day.~~

Section 5. Each House shall be the Judge of the Elections, Returns and Qualifications of its own Members, and a Majority of each shall constitute a Quorum to do Business; but a smaller Number may adjourn from day to day, and may be authorized to compel the Attendance of absent Members, in such Manner, and under such Penalties as each House may provide.

Each House may determine the Rules of its Proceedings, punish its Members for disorderly Behaviour, and, with the Concurrence of two thirds, expel a Member.

Each House shall keep a Journal of its Proceedings, and from time to time publish the same, excepting such Parts as may in their Judgment require Secrecy; and the Yeas and Nays of the Members of either House on any question shall, at the Desire of one fifth of those Present, be entered on the Journal.

The only duty that the Constitution assigns to the vice president is to preside over meetings of the Senate. Modern presidents have usually given their vice presidents more responsibilities.

The House charges a government official with wrongdoing, and the Senate acts as a court to decide if the official is guilty.

Congress decided that elections will be held on the Tuesday following the first Monday in November of even-numbered years. The Twentieth Amendment states that Congress shall meet in regular session on January 3 of each year. The president may call a special session of Congress whenever it is necessary.

Congress makes most of its own rules of conduct. The Senate and the House each have a code of ethics that members must follow. It is the task of each house of Congress to discipline its own members. Each house keeps a journal, and a daily, unofficial publication called the *Congressional Record* details what happens in congressional sessions. The general public can learn how their representatives voted on bills by reading the *Congressional Record.*

Neither House, during the Session of Congress, shall, without the Consent of the other, adjourn for more than three days, nor to any other Place than that in which the two Houses shall be sitting.

Section 6. The Senators and Representatives shall receive a Compensation for their Services, to be ascertained by Law, and paid out of the Treasury of the United States. They shall in all Cases, except Treason, Felony and Breach of the Peace, be privileged from Arrest during their Attendance at the Session of their respective Houses, and in going to and returning from the same; and for any Speech or Debate in either House, they shall not be questioned in any other Place.

No Senator or Representative shall, during the Time for which he was elected, be appointed to any civil Office under the Authority of the United States, which shall have been created, or the Emoluments whereof shall have been encreased during such time; and no Person holding any Office under the United States, shall be a Member of either House during his Continuance in Office.

Section 7. All Bills for raising Revenue shall originate in the House of Representatives; but the Senate may propose or concur with Amendments as on other Bills.

Every Bill which shall have passed the House of Representatives and the Senate, shall, before it become a Law, be presented to the President of the United States; If he approve he shall sign it, but if not he shall return it, with his Objections to that House in which it shall have originated, who shall enter the Objections at large on their Journal, and proceed to reconsider it. If after such Reconsideration two thirds of that House shall agree to pass the Bill, it shall be sent, together with the Objections, to the other House, by which it shall likewise be reconsidered, and if approved by two thirds of that House, it shall become a Law. But in all such Cases the Votes of both Houses shall be determined by yeas and Nays, and the Names of the Persons voting for and against the Bill shall be entered on the Journal of each House respectively. If any Bill shall not be returned by the President within ten Days (Sundays excepted) after it shall have been presented to him, the Same shall be a Law, in like Manner as if he had signed it, unless the Congress by their Adjournment prevent its Return, in which Case it shall not be a Law.

Every Order, Resolution, or Vote to which the Concurrence of the Senate and House of Representatives may be necessary (except on a question of Adjournment) shall be presented to the President of the United States; and before the Same shall take Effect, shall be approved by him, or being disapproved by him, shall be repassed by two thirds of the Senate and House of Representatives, according to the Rules and Limitations prescribed in the Case of a Bill.

The framers of the Constitution wanted to protect members of Congress from being arrested on false charges by political enemies who did not want them to attend important meetings. The framers also wanted to protect members of Congress from being taken to court for something they said in a speech or in a debate.

The power of taxing is the responsibility of the House of Representatives. The framers felt that because members of the House are elected every two years, representatives would listen to the public and seek its approval before passing taxes.

The veto power of the president and the ability of Congress to override a presidential veto are two of the important checks and balances in the Constitution.

The framers of the Constitution wanted a national government that was strong enough to be effective. This section lists the powers given to Congress. The last sentence in Section 8 contains the famous "elastic clause"—so called because it has been stretched (like elastic) to fit many different circumstances. The clause was first disputed when Alexander Hamilton proposed a national bank. Thomas Jefferson said that because the Constitution did not specifically give Congress the power to establish a bank, it could not do so. Hamilton argued that the bank was "necessary and proper" in order to carry out other powers of Congress, such as borrowing money and regulating currency. This argument was tested in the courts in 1819 in the case of *McCulloch* v. *Maryland,* when Chief Justice Marshall ruled in favor of the federal government. Powers given to the government by the elastic clause are called implied powers.

Section 8. The Congress shall have Power To lay and collect Taxes, Duties, Imposts and Excises, to pay the Debts and provide for the common Defence and general Welfare of the United States; but all Duties, Imposts and Excises shall be uniform throughout the United States;

To borrow Money on the credit of the United States;

To regulate Commerce with foreign Nations, and among the several States, and with the Indian Tribes;

To establish an uniform Rule of Naturalization, and uniform Laws on the subject of Bankruptcies throughout the United States;

To coin Money, regulate the Value thereof, and of foreign Coin, and fix the Standard of Weights and Measures;

To provide for the Punishment of counterfeiting the Securities and current Coin of the United States;

To establish Post Offices and post Roads;

To promote the Progress of Science and useful Arts, by securing for limited Times to Authors and Inventors the exclusive Right to their respective Writings and Discoveries;

To constitute Tribunals inferior to the supreme Court;

To define and punish Piracies and Felonies committed on the high Seas, and Offences against the Law of Nations;

To declare War, grant Letters of Marque and Reprisal, and make Rules concerning Captures on Land and Water;

To raise and support Armies, but no Appropriation of Money to that Use shall be for a longer Term than two Years;

To provide and maintain a Navy;

To make Rules for the Government and Regulation of the land and naval Forces;

To provide for calling forth the Militia to execute the Laws of the Union, suppress Insurrections and repel Invasions;

To provide for organizing, arming, and disciplining, the Militia, and for governing such Part of them as may be employed in the Service of the United States, reserving to the States respectively, the Appointment of the Officers, and the Authority of training the Militia according to the discipline prescribed by Congress;

To exercise exclusive Legislation in all Cases whatsoever, over such District (not exceeding ten Miles square) as may, by Cession of particular States, and the Acceptance of Congress, become the Seat of the Government of the United States, and to exercise like Authority over all Places purchased by the Consent of the Legislature of the State in which the Same shall be, for the Erection of Forts, Magazines, Arsenals, dock-Yards, and other needful Buildings;—And

To make all Laws which shall be necessary and proper for carrying into Execution the foregoing Powers, and all other Powers vested by this

Constitution in the Government of the United States, or in any Department or Officer thereof.

Section 9. ~~The Migration or Importation of such Persons as any of the States now existing shall think proper to admit, shall not be prohibited by the Congress prior to the Year one thousand eight hundred and eight, but a Tax or duty may be imposed on such Importation, not exceeding ten dollars for each Person.~~

The Privilege of the Writ of Habeas Corpus shall not be suspended, unless when in Cases of Rebellion or Invasion the public Safety may require it.

No Bill of Attainder or ex post facto Law shall be passed.

No Capitation, or other direct, Tax shall be laid, unless in Proportion to the Census or Enumeration herein before directed to be taken.

No Tax or Duty shall be laid on Articles exported from any State.

No Preference shall be given by any Regulation of Commerce or Revenue to the Ports of one State over those of another: nor shall Vessels bound to, or from, one State, be obliged to enter, clear, or pay Duties in another.

No Money shall be drawn from the Treasury, but in Consequence of Appropriations made by Law; and a regular Statement and Account of the Receipts and Expenditures of all public Money shall be published from time to time.

No Title of Nobility shall be granted by the United States: And no Person holding any Office of Profit or Trust under them, shall, without the Consent of the Congress, accept of any present, Emolument, Office, or Title, of any kind whatever, from any King, Prince, or foreign State.

Section 10. No State shall enter into any Treaty, Alliance, or Confederation; grant Letters of Marque and Reprisal; coin Money; emit Bills of Credit; make any Thing but gold and silver Coin a Tender in Payment of Debts; pass any Bill of Attainder, ex post facto Law, or law impairing the Obligation of Contracts, or grant any Title of Nobility.

No State shall, without the Consent of the Congress, lay any Imposts or Duties on Imports or Exports, except what may be absolutely necessary for executing its inspection Laws: and the net Produce of all Duties and Imposts, laid by any State on Imports or Exports, shall be for the Use of the Treasury of the United States; and all such Laws shall be subject to the Revision and Controul of the Congress.

No State shall, without the Consent of Congress, lay any Duty of Tonnage, keep Troops, or Ships of War in time of Peace, enter into any Agreement or Compact with another State, or with a foreign Power, or engage in War, unless actually invaded, or in such imminent Danger as will not admit of delay.

Although Congress has implied powers, there are also limits to its powers. Section 9 lists powers that are denied to the federal government. Several of the clauses protect the people of the United States from unjust treatment. For example, Section 9 guarantees the writ of *habeas corpus* and prohibits bills of attainder and *ex post facto* laws.

Section 10 lists the powers that are denied to the states. In our system of federalism, the state and federal governments have separate powers, share some powers, and are each denied other powers.

ARTICLE II

Section 1. The executive Power shall be vested in a President of the United States of America. He shall hold his Office during the Term of four Years, and, together with the Vice President, chosen for the same Term, be elected, as follows.

Each State shall appoint, in such Manner as the Legislature thereof may direct, a Number of Electors, equal to the whole Number of Senators and Representatives to which the State may be entitled in the Congress: but no Senator or Representative, or Person holding an Office of Trust or Profit under the United States, shall be appointed an Elector.

~~The Electors shall meet in their respective States, and vote by Ballot for two Persons, of whom one at least shall not be an Inhabitant of the same State with themselves. And they shall make a List of all the Persons voted for, and of the Number of Votes for each; which List they shall sign and certify, and transmit sealed to the Seat of the Government of the United States, directed to the President of the Senate. The President of the Senate shall, in the Presence of the Senate and House of Representatives, open all the Certificates, and the Votes shall then be counted. The Person having the greatest Number of Votes shall be the President, if such Number be a Majority of the whole Number of Electors appointed; and if there be more than one who have such Majority, and have an equal Number of Votes, then the House of Representatives shall immediately chuse by Ballot one of them for President; and if no Person have a Majority, then from the five highest on the List the said House shall in like Manner chuse the President. But in chusing the President, the Votes shall be taken by States, the Representation from each State having one Vote; A quorum for this Purpose shall consist of a Member or Members from two thirds of the States, and a Majority of all the States shall be necessary to a Choice. In every Case, after the Choice of the President, the Person having the greatest Number of Votes of the Electors shall be the Vice President. But if there should remain two or more who have equal Votes, the Senate shall chuse from them by Ballot the Vice President~~.

The Congress may determine the Time of chusing the Electors, and the Day on which they shall give their Votes; which Day shall be the same throughout the United States.

No Person except a natural born Citizen~~, or a Citizen of the United States, at the time of the Adoption of this Constitution~~, shall be eligible to the Office of President; neither shall any Person be eligible to that Office who shall not have attained to the Age of thirty five Years, and been fourteen Years a Resident within the United States.

In Case of the Removal of the President from Office, or of his Death, Resignation, or Inability to discharge the Powers and Duties of the said Office, the Same shall devolve on the Vice President, and the Congress

Executive Branch

The president is the chief of the executive branch. It is the job of the president to enforce the laws. The framers wanted the president's and vice president's term of office and manner of selection to be different from those of members of Congress. They decided on four-year terms, but they had a difficult time agreeing on how to select the president and vice president. The framers finally set up an electoral system, which varies greatly from our electoral process today. The Twelfth Amendment changed the process by requiring that separate ballots be cast for president and vice president. The rise of political parties has since changed the process even more.

In 1845 Congress set the Tuesday following the first Monday in November of every fourth year as the general election date for selecting presidential electors.

The youngest elected president was John F. Kennedy; he was 43 years old when he was inaugurated. (Theodore Roosevelt was 42 when he assumed office after the assassination of McKinley.) The oldest elected president was Ronald Reagan; he was 69 years old when he was inaugurated.

may by Law provide for the Case of Removal, Death, Resignation or Inability, both of the President and Vice President, declaring what Officer shall then act as President, and such Officer shall act accordingly, until the Disability be removed, or a President shall be elected.

The President shall, at stated Times, receive for his Services, a Compensation, which shall neither be increased nor diminished during the period for which he shall have been elected, and he shall not receive within that Period any other Emolument from the United States, or any of them.

Before he enter on the Execution of his Office, he shall take the following Oath or Affirmation:—"I do solemnly swear (or affirm) that I will faithfully execute the Office of President of the United States, and will to the best of my Ability, preserve, protect and defend the Constitution of the United States."

Section 2. The President shall be Commander in Chief of the Army and Navy of the United States, and of the Militia of the several States, when called into the actual Service of the United States; he may require the Opinion, in writing, of the principal Officer in each of the executive Departments, upon any Subject relating to the Duties of their respective Offices, and he shall have Power to grant Reprieves and Pardons for Offenses against the United States, except in Cases of Impeachment.

He shall have Power, by and with the Advice and Consent of the Senate, to make Treaties, provided two thirds of the Senators present concur; and he shall nominate, and by and with the Advice and Consent of the Senate, shall appoint Ambassadors, other public Ministers and Consuls, Judges of the supreme Court, and all other Officers of the United States, whose Appointments are not herein otherwise provided for, and which shall be established by Law: but the Congress may by Law vest the Appointment of such inferior Officers, as they think proper, in the President alone, in the Courts of Law, or in the Heads of Departments.

The President shall have Power to fill up all Vacancies that may happen during the Recess of the Senate, by granting Commissions which shall expire at the End of their next Session.

Section 3. He shall from time to time give to the Congress Information of the State of the Union, and recommend to their Consideration such Measures as he shall judge necessary and expedient; he may, on extraordinary Occasions, convene both Houses, or either of them, and in Case of Disagreement between them, with Respect to the Time of Adjournment, he may adjourn them to such Time as he shall think proper; he shall receive Ambassadors and other public Ministers; he shall take Care that the Laws be faithfully executed, and shall Commission all the Officers of the United States.

Emolument means "salary, or payment." In 1969 Congress set the president's salary at $200,000 per year. The president also receives an expense account of $50,000 per year. The president must pay taxes on both.

The oath of office is administered to the president by the chief justice of the U.S. Supreme Court. Washington added "So help me, God." All succeeding presidents have followed this practice.

The framers wanted to make sure that an elected representative of the people controlled the nation's military. Today, the president is in charge of the army, navy, air force, marines, and coast guard. Only Congress, however, can decide if the United States will declare war. This section also contains the basis for the formation of the president's cabinet. Every president, starting with George Washington, has appointed a cabinet.

Most of the president's appointments to office must be approved by the Senate.

Every year the president presents to Congress a State of the Union message. In this message, the president introduces and explains a legislative plan for the coming year. This clause states that one of the president's duties is to enforce the laws.

ARTICLE III

Section 1. The judicial Power of the United States, shall be vested in one supreme Court, and in such inferior Courts as the Congress may from time to time ordain and establish. The Judges, both of the supreme and inferior Courts, shall hold their Offices during good Behaviour, and shall, at stated Times, receive for their Services, a Compensation, which shall not be diminished during their Continuance in Office.

Section 2. The judicial Power shall extend to all Cases, in Law and Equity, arising under this Constitution, the Laws of the United States, and Treaties made, or which shall be made, under their Authority;—to all Cases affecting Ambassadors, other public Ministers and Consuls;—to all Cases of admiralty and maritime Jurisdiction;—to Controversies to which the United States shall be a Party;—to Controversies between two or more States;— between a State and Citizens of another State;— between Citizens of different States;—between Citizens of the same State claiming Lands under Grants of different States, and between a State, or the Citizens thereof, and foreign States, Citizens or Subjects.

In all Cases affecting Ambassadors, other public Ministers and Consuls, and those in which a State shall be Party, the supreme Court shall have original Jurisdiction. In all the other Cases before mentioned, the supreme Court shall have appellate Jurisdiction, both as to Law and fact, with such Exceptions, and under such Regulations as the Congress shall make.

The Trial of all Crimes, except in Cases of Impeachment, shall be by Jury; and such Trial shall be held in the State where the said Crimes shall have been committed; but when not committed within any State, the Trial shall be at such Place or Places as the Congress may by Law have directed.

Section 3. Treason against the United States, shall consist only in levying War against them, or in adhering to their Enemies, giving them Aid and Comfort. No Person shall be convicted of Treason unless on the Testimony of two Witnesses to the same overt Act, or on Confession in open Court.

The Congress shall have Power to declare the Punishment of Treason, but no Attainder of Treason shall work Corruption of Blood, or Forfeiture except during the Life of the Person attainted.

ARTICLE IV

Section 1. Full Faith and Credit shall be given in each State to the public Acts, Records, and judicial Proceedings of every other State. And the

Judicial Branch
The Articles of Confederation did not set up a federal court system. One of the first things that the framers of the Constitution agreed upon was to set up a national judiciary. With all the laws that Congress would be enacting, there would be a great need for a branch of government to interpret the laws. In the Judiciary Act of 1789, Congress provided for the establishment of lower courts, such as district courts, circuit courts of appeals, and various other federal courts. The judicial system provides a check on the legislative branch; it can declare a law unconstitutional.

Congress has the power to decide the punishment for treason, but it can punish only the guilty person. "Corruption of Blood" means punishing the family of a person who has committed treason. It is expressly forbidden by the Constitution.

Congress may by general Laws prescribe the Manner in which such Acts, Records and Proceedings shall be proved, and the Effect thereof.

Section 2. The Citizens of each State shall be entitled to all Privileges and Immunities of Citizens in the several States.

A Person charged in any State with Treason, Felony, or other Crime, who shall flee from Justice, and be found in another State, shall on Demand of the executive Authority of the State from which he fled, be delivered up, to be removed to the State having Jurisdiction of the Crime.

~~No Person held to Service of Labour in one State, under the Laws thereof, escaping into another, shall, in Consequence of any Law or Regulation therein, be discharged from such Service or Labour, but shall be delivered up on Claim of the Party to whom such Service or Labour may be due~~.

The States
States must honor the laws, records, and court decisions of other states. A person cannot escape a legal obligation by moving from one state to another.

Section 3. New States may be admitted by the Congress into this Union; but no new State shall be formed or erected within the Jurisdiction of any other State; nor any State be formed by the Junction of two or more States, or Parts of States, without the Consent of the Legislatures of the States concerned as well as of the Congress.

The Congress shall have Power to dispose of and make all needful Rules and Regulations respecting the Territory or other Property belonging to the United States; and nothing in this Constitution shall be so construed as to Prejudice any Claims of the United States, or of any particular State.

Section 4. The United States shall guarantee to every State in this Union a Republican Form of Government, and shall protect each of them against Invasion; and on Application of the Legislature, or of the Executive (when the Legislature cannot be convened) against domestic Violence.

Section 3 permits Congress to admit new states to the Union. When a group of people living in an area that is not part of an existing state wishes to form a new state, it asks Congress for permission to do so. The people then write a state constitution and offer it to Congress for approval. The state constitution must set up a representative form of government and must not in any way contradict the federal Constitution. If a majority of Congress approves of the state constitution, the state is admitted as a member of the United States of America.

ARTICLE V

The Congress, whenever two thirds of both Houses shall deem it necessary, shall propose Amendments to this Constitution, or, on the Application of the Legislatures of two thirds of the several States, shall call a Convention for proposing Amendments, which, in either Case, shall be valid to all Intents and Purposes, as Part of this Constitution, when ratified by the Legislatures of three fourths of the several States, or by Conventions in three fourths thereof, as the one or the other Mode of Ratification may be proposed by the Congress; Provided that ~~no Amendment which may be made prior to the Year One thousand eight hundred and eight shall in any Manner affect the first and fourth Clauses in the Ninth Section of the first Article; and that~~ no State, without its Consent, shall be deprived of its equal Suffrage in the Senate.

The Amendment Process
America's founders may not have realized just how enduring the Constitution would be, but they did set up a system for changing or adding to it. They did not want to make it easy to change the Constitution. There are two ways in which changes can be proposed to the states and two ways in which states can approve the changes and make them part of the Constitution.

National Supremacy
One of the biggest problems facing the delegates to the Constitutional Convention was the question of what would happen if a state law and a federal law conflicted. Which law would be followed? Who would decide? The second clause of Article VI answers those questions. When a federal law and a state law disagree, the federal law overrides the state law. The Constitution and other federal laws are the "supreme Law of the Land." This clause is often called the supremacy clause.

ARTICLE VI

All Debts contracted and Engagements entered into, before the Adoption of this Constitution, shall be as valid against the United States under this Constitution, as under the Confederation.

This Constitution, and the Laws of the United States which shall be made in Pursuance thereof; and all Treaties made, or which shall be made, under the Authority of the United States, shall be the supreme Law of the Land; and the Judges in every State shall be bound thereby, any Thing in the Constitution or Laws of any State to the Contrary notwithstanding.

The Senators and Representatives before mentioned, and the Members of the several State Legislatures, and all executive and judicial Officers, both of the United States and of the several States, shall be bound by Oath or Affirmation, to support this Constitution; but no religious Test shall ever be required as a Qualification to any Office or public Trust under the United States.

ARTICLE VII

The Ratification of the Conventions of nine States, shall be sufficient for the Establishment of this Constitution between the States so ratifying the Same.

Done in Convention by the Unanimous Consent of the States present the Seventeenth Day of September in the Year of our Lord one thousand seven hundred and Eighty seven and of the Independence of the United States of America the Twelfth. In witness whereof We have hereunto subscribed our Names,

George Washington—
President and deputy from Virginia

NEW HAMPSHIRE
John Langdon
Nicholas Gilman

DELAWARE
George Read
Gunning Bedford, Jr.
John Dickinson
Richard Bassett
Jacob Broom

MASSACHUSETTS
Nathaniel Gorham
Rufus King

MARYLAND
James McHenry
Daniel of St. Thomas Jenifer
Daniel Carroll

CONNECTICUT
William Samuel Johnson
Roger Sherman

NEW YORK
Alexander Hamilton

VIRGINIA
John Blair
James Madison, Jr.

NEW JERSEY
William Livingston
David Brearley
William Paterson
Jonathan Dayton

NORTH CAROLINA
William Blount
Richard Dobbs Spaight
Hugh Williamson

PENNSYLVANIA
Benjamin Franklin
Thomas Mifflin
Robert Morris
George Clymer

Thomas FitzSimons
Jared Ingersoll
James Wilson
Gouverneur Morris

SOUTH CAROLINA
John Rutledge
Charles Cotesworth
* Pinckney*
Charles Pinckney
Pierce Butler

GEORGIA
William Few
Abraham Baldwin

Attest:
William Jackson, Secretary

THE AMENDMENTS

Articles in addition to, and Amendment of the Constitution of the United States of America, proposed by Congress, and ratified by the Legislatures of the several States, pursuant to the fifth Article of the original Constitution.

[The First through Tenth Amendments, now known as the Bill of Rights, were proposed to the states for ratification on September 25, 1789, and declared in force on December 15, 1791.]

First Amendment

Congress shall make no law respecting an establishment of religion, or prohibiting the free exercise thereof; or abridging the freedom of speech, or of the press; or the right of the people peaceably to assemble, and to petition the Government for a redress of grievances.

Second Amendment

A well regulated Militia, being necessary to the security of a free State, the right of the people to keep and bear Arms, shall not be infringed.

Third Amendment

No Soldier shall, in time of peace, be quartered in any house, without the consent of the Owner, nor in time of war, but in a manner to be prescribed by law.

Fourth Amendment

The right of the people to be secure in their persons, houses, papers, and effects, against unreasonable searches and seizures, shall not be violated, and no Warrants shall issue, but upon probable cause, supported by Oath or affirmation, and particularly describing the place to be searched, and the persons or things to be seized.

Fifth Amendment

No person shall be held to answer for a capital, or otherwise infamous crime, unless on a presentment or indictment of a Grand Jury, except in cases arising in the land or naval forces, or in the Militia, when in actual service in time of War or public danger; nor shall any person be subject for the same offence to be twice put in jeopardy of life or limb; nor shall be compelled in any criminal case to be a witness against himself, nor be deprived of life, liberty, or property, without due process of law; nor shall private property be taken for public use, without just compensation.

Sixth Amendment

In all criminal prosecutions, the accused shall enjoy the right to a speedy and public trial, by an impartial jury of the State and district wherein the

Bill of Rights
One of the conditions set by several states for ratifying the Constitution was the inclusion of a bill of rights. Many people feared that a stronger central government might take away basic rights of the people that had been guaranteed in state constitutions. If the three words that begin the preamble—"We the people"—were truly meant, then the rights of the people needed to be protected.

The First Amendment protects—among other freedoms—freedom of speech—and forbids Congress to make any "law respecting an establishment of religion" or restraining the freedom to practice religion as one chooses.

A law enforcement official may enter a person's home with a search warrant, which allows the law official to look for evidence that could convict someone of committing a crime.

The Fifth, Sixth, and Seventh Amendments describe the procedures that courts must follow when trying people accused of crimes. The Fifth Amendment guarantees that no one can be put on trial for a serious crime unless a grand jury agrees that the evidence justifies doing so. It also says that a person cannot be tried twice for the same crime.

The Sixth Amendment makes several guarantees, including a prompt trial and a trial by a jury chosen from the state and district in which the crime was committed. The Sixth Amendment also states that an accused person must be told why he or she is being tried and promises that an accused person has the right to be defended by a lawyer.

The Seventh Amendment guarantees a trial by jury in cases that involve more than $20, but in modern times, usually much more money is at stake before a case is heard in federal court.

The Ninth and Tenth Amendments were added because not every right of the people or of the states could be listed in the Constitution.

The Twelfth Amendment changed the election procedure for president and vice president. This amendment became necessary because of the growth of political parties. Before this amendment, electors voted without distinguishing between president and vice president. Whoever received the most votes became president, and whoever received the next highest number of votes became vice president.

crime shall have been committed, which district shall have been previously ascertained by law, and to be informed of the nature and cause of the accusation; to be confronted with the witnesses against him; to have compulsory process for obtaining witnesses in his favor, and to have the Assistance of Counsel for his defence.

Seventh Amendment

In Suits at common law, where the value in controversy shall exceed twenty dollars, the right of trial by jury shall be preserved, and no fact tried by a jury, shall be otherwise re-examined in any Court of the United States, than according to the rules of the common law.

Eighth Amendment

Excessive bail shall not be required, nor excessive fines imposed, nor cruel and unusual punishments inflicted.

Ninth Amendment

The enumeration in the Constitution, of certain rights, shall not be construed to deny or disparage others retained by the people.

Tenth Amendment

The powers not delegated to the United States by the Constitution, nor prohibited by it to the States, are reserved to the States respectively, or to the people.

Eleventh Amendment

   [Proposed March 5, 1794; declared ratified January 8, 1798]
The Judicial power of the United States shall not be construed to extend to any suit in law or equity, commenced or prosecuted against one of the United States by Citizens of another State, or by Citizens or Subjects of any Foreign State.

Twelfth Amendment

   [Proposed December 9, 1803; declared ratified September 25, 1804]
The Electors shall meet in their respective states, and vote by ballot for President and Vice-President, one of whom, at least, shall not be an inhabitant of the same state with themselves; they shall name in their ballots the person voted for as President, and in distinct ballots the person voted for as Vice-President, and they shall make distinct lists of all persons voted for as President, and of all persons voted for as Vice-President, and of the number of votes for each, which lists they shall sign and certify, and transmit sealed to the seat of the government of the United States, directed to the President of the Senate;—The President of the Senate shall, in the presence of the Senate and House of Representatives, open all the certificates and the votes

shall then be counted;—The person having the greatest number of votes for President, shall be the President, if such number be a majority of the whole number of Electors appointed; and if no person have such majority, then from the persons having the highest numbers not exceeding three on the list of those voted for as President, the House of Representatives shall choose immediately, by ballot, the President. But in choosing the President, the votes shall be taken by states, the representation from each state having one vote; a quorum for this purpose shall consist of a member or members from two-thirds of the states, and a majority of all the states shall be necessary to a choice. ~~And if the House of Representatives shall not choose a President whenever the right of choice shall devolve upon them, before the fourth day of March next following, then the Vice President shall act as President, as in the case of the death or other constitutional disability of the President.~~ —The person having the greatest number of votes as Vice-President, shall be the Vice-President, if such number be a majority of the whole number of Electors appointed, and if no person have a majority, then from the two highest numbers on the list, the Senate shall Choose the Vice-President; a quorum for the purpose shall consist of two-thirds of the whole number of Senators, and a majority of the whole number shall be necessary to a choice. But no person constitutionally ineligible to the office of President shall be eligible to that of Vice-President of the United States.

Thirteenth Amendment

[Proposed January 31, 1865; declared ratified December 18, 1865]

Section 1. Neither slavery nor involuntary servitude, except as a punishment for crime whereof the party shall have been duly convicted, shall exist within the United States, or any place subject to their jurisdiction.

Section 2. Congress shall have power to enforce this article by appropriate legislation.

Although some slaves had been freed during the Civil War, slavery was not abolished until the Thirteenth Amendment took effect.

Fourteenth Amendment

[Proposed June 16, 1866; declared ratified July 28, 1868]

Section 1. All persons born or naturalized in the United States, and subject to the jurisdiction thereof, are citizens of the United States and of the State wherein they reside. No State shall make or enforce any law which shall abridge the privileges or immunities of citizens of the United States; nor shall any State deprive any person of life, liberty, or property, without due process of law; nor deny to any person within its jurisdiction the equal protection of the laws.

Section 2. Representatives shall be apportioned among the several States according to their respective numbers, counting the whole number of per-

In 1833 the Supreme Court ruled that the Bill of Rights limited the federal government but not the state governments. This ruling was interpreted to mean that states were able to keep African Americans from becoming state citizens: if African Americans were not citizens, they were not protected by the Bill of Rights. The Fourteenth Amendment defines citizenship and prevents states from interfering in the rights of citizens of the United States.

sons in each State, ~~excluding Indians not taxed~~. But when the right to vote at any election for the choice of electors for President and Vice President of the United States, Representatives in Congress, the Executive and Judicial officers of a State, or the members of the Legislature thereof, is denied to any of the ~~male~~ inhabitants of such State, ~~being twenty-one years of age,~~ and citizens of the United States, or in any way abridged, except for participation in rebellion, or other crime, the basis of representation therein shall be reduced in the proportion which the number of such ~~male~~ citizens shall bear to the whole number of ~~male~~ citizens ~~twenty-one years of age~~ in such State.

Section 3. No person shall be a Senator or Representative in Congress, or elector of President and Vice President, or hold any office, civil or military, under the United States, or under any State, who, having previously taken an oath, as a member of Congress, or as an officer of the United States, or as a member of any State legislature, or as an executive or judicial officer of any State, to support the Constitution of the United States, shall have engaged in insurrection or rebellion against the same, or given aid or comfort to the enemies thereof. But Congress may by a vote of two-thirds of each House, remove such disability.

Section 4. The validity of the public debt of the United States, authorized by law, including debts incurred for payment of pensions and bounties for services in suppressing insurrection or rebellion, shall not be questioned. But neither the United States nor any State shall assume or pay any debt or obligation incurred in aid of insurrection or rebellion against the United States~~, or any claim for the loss of emancipation of any slave~~; but all such debts, obligations and claims shall be held illegal and void.

Section 5. The Congress shall have power to enforce, by appropriate legislation, the provisions of this article.

The Fifteenth Amendment extended the vote to African American men.

Fifteenth Amendment
[Proposed February 27, 1869; declared ratified March 30, 1870]

Section 1. The right of citizens of the United States to vote shall not be denied or abridged by the United States or by any State on account of race, color, or previous condition of servitude.

Section 2. The Congress shall have power to enforce this article by appropriate legislation.

Sixteenth Amendment
[Proposed July 12, 1909; declared ratified February 25, 1913]

The Congress shall have power to lay and collect taxes on incomes, from whatever source derived, without apportionment among the several States, and without regard to any census or enumeration.

Seventeenth Amendment

[Proposed May 13, 1912; declared ratified May 31, 1913]

The Senate of the United States shall be composed of two Senators from each State, elected by the people thereof, for six years; and each Senator shall have one vote. The electors in each State shall have the qualifications requisite for electors of the most numerous branch of the State legislatures.

When vacancies happen in the representation of any State in the Senate, the executive authority of such State shall issue writs of election to fill such vacancies: *Provided,* That the legislature of any State may empower the executive thereof to make temporary appointments until the people fill the vacancies by election as the legislature may direct.

~~This amendment shall not be so construed as to affect the election or term of any Senator chosen before it becomes valid as part of the Constitution.~~

> The Seventeenth Amendment requires that senators be elected directly by the people instead of by the state legislature.

Eighteenth Amendment

[Proposed December 18, 1917; declared ratified January 29, 1919; repealed by the Twenty-first Amendment December 5, 1933]

~~**Section 1.** After one year from the ratification of this article the manufacture, sale, or transportation of intoxicating liquors within, the importation thereof into, or the exportation thereof from the United States and all territory subject to the jurisdiction thereof for beverage purposes is hereby prohibited.~~

~~**Section 2.** The Congress and the several States shall have concurrent power to enforce this article by appropriate legislation.~~

~~**Section 3.** This article shall be inoperative unless it shall have been ratified as an amendment to the Constitution by the legislatures of the several States, as provided in the Constitution, within seven years from the date of the submission hereof to the States by the Congress.~~

> Although many people felt that the Eighteenth Amendment was good for the health and welfare of the American people, it was repealed 14 years later.

Nineteenth Amendment

[Proposed June 4, 1919; declared ratified August 26, 1920]

The right of citizens of the United States to vote shall not be denied or abridged by the United States or by any State on account of sex.

Congress shall have power to enforce this article by appropriate legislation.

> Abigail Adams was disappointed that the Declaration of Independence and the Constitution did not specifically include women. It took almost 150 years and much campaigning by groups for women's suffrage to finally achieve voting privileges.

Twentieth Amendment

[Proposed March 2, 1932; declared ratified February 6, 1933]

Section 1. The terms of the President and Vice-President shall end at noon on the 20th day of January, and the terms of Senators and Representatives

In the original Constitution, a newly elected president and Congress did not take office until March 4, which was four months after the November election. The officials who were leaving office were called lame ducks because they had little influence during those four months. The Twentieth Amendment changed the date that the new president and Congress take office. Members of Congress now take office on January 3, and the president takes office on January 20.

at noon on the 3d day of January, of the years in which such terms would have ended if this article had not been ratified; and the terms of their successors shall then begin.

Section 2. The Congress shall assemble at least once in every year, and such meeting shall begin at noon on the 3d day of January, unless they shall by law appoint a different day.

Section 3. If, at the time fixed for the beginning of the term of the President, the President elect shall have died, the Vice-President elect shall become President. If a President shall not have been chosen before the time fixed for the beginning of his term, or if the President elect shall have failed to qualify, then the Vice-President elect shall act as President until a President shall have qualified; and the Congress may by law provide for the case wherein neither a President elect nor a Vice-President elect shall have qualified, declaring who shall then act as President, or the manner in which one who is to act shall be selected, and such person shall act accordingly until a President or Vice-President shall have qualified.

Section 4. The Congress may by law provide for the case of the death of any of the persons from whom the House of Representatives may choose a President whenever the right of choice shall have devolved upon them, and for the case of the death of any of the persons from whom the Senate may choose a Vice-President whenever the right of choice shall have devolved upon them.

~~Section 5. Sections 1 and 2 shall take effect on the 15th day of October following the ratification of this article.~~

~~Section 6. This article shall be inoperative unless it shall have been ratified as an amendment to the Constitution by the legislatures of three-fourths of the several States within seven years from the date of its submission.~~

Twenty-first Amendment

[Proposed February 20, 1933; declared ratified December 5, 1933]

Section 1. The eighteenth article of amendment to the Constitution of the United States is hereby repealed.

Section 2. The transportation or importation into any State, Territory, or possession of the United States for delivery or use therein of intoxicating liquors, in violation of the laws thereof, is hereby prohibited.

~~Section 3. This article shall be inoperative unless it shall have been ratified as an amendment to the Constitution by conventions in the several States, as provided in the Constitution, within seven years from the date of the submission hereof to the States by the Congress.~~

The Twenty-first Amendment is the only amendment that has been ratified by state conventions rather than by state legislatures.

Twenty-second Amendment

[Proposed March 21, 1947; declared ratified February 26, 1951]

Section 1. No person shall be elected to the office of the President more than twice, and no person who has held the office of President, or acted as President, for more than two years of a term to which some other person was elected President shall be elected to the office of the President more than once. ~~But this Article shall not apply to any person holding the office of President when this Article was proposed by the Congress, and shall not prevent any person who may be holding the office of President, or acting as President, during the term within which this Article becomes operative from holding the office of President or acting as President during the remainder of such term.~~

~~**Section 2.** This article shall be inoperative unless it shall have been ratified as an amendment to the Constitution by the legislatures of three-fourths of the several States within seven years from the date of its submission to the States by the Congress.~~

From the time of President Washington's administration, it was a custom for presidents to serve no more than two terms of office. Franklin D. Roosevelt, however, was elected to four terms. The Twenty-second Amendment made into law the old custom of limiting a president to no more than two terms.

Twenty-third Amendment

[Proposed June 16, 1960; declared ratified March 29, 1961]

Section 1. The District constituting the seat of Government of the United States shall appoint in such manner as the Congress may direct:

A number of electors of President and Vice-President equal to the whole number of Senators and Representatives in Congress to which the District would be entitled if it were a State, but in no event more than the least populous state; they shall be in addition to those appointed by the States, but they shall be considered, for the purposes of the election of President and Vice-President, to be electors appointed by a State; and they shall meet in the District and perform such duties as provided by the twelfth article of amendment.

Section 2. The Congress shall have power to enforce this article by appropriate legislation.

Until the ratification of the Twenty-third Amendment, the people of Washington, D.C., could not vote in presidential elections.

Twenty-fourth Amendment

[Proposed August 27, 1962; declared ratified January 23, 1964]

Section 1. The right of citizens of the United States to vote in any primary or other election for President or Vice-President, for electors for President or Vice-President, or for Senator or Representative in Congress, shall not be denied or abridged by the United States or any State by reason of failure to pay any poll tax or other tax.

Section 2. The Congress shall have power to enforce this article by appropriate legislation.

Twenty-fifth Amendment
[Proposed July 6, 1965; declared ratified February 10, 1967]

The illness of President Eisenhower in the 1950s and the assassination of President Kennedy in 1963 were the events behind the Twenty-fifth Amendment. The Constitution did not provide a clear-cut method for a vice president to take over for a disabled president or upon the death of a president. This amendment provides for filling the office of the vice president if a vacancy occurs, and it provides a way for the vice president—or someone else in the line of succession—to take over if the president is unable to perform the duties of that office.

Section 1. In case of the removal of the President from office or of his death or resignation, the Vice-President shall become President.

Section 2. Whenever there is a vacancy in the office of the Vice-President, the President shall nominate a Vice-President who shall take office upon confirmation by a majority vote of both Houses of Congress.

Section 3. Whenever the President transmits to the President pro tempore of the Senate and the Speaker of the House of Representatives his written declaration that he is unable to discharge the powers and duties of his office, and until he transmits to them a written declaration to the contrary, such powers and duties shall be discharged by the Vice-President as Acting President.

Section 4. Whenever the Vice-President and a majority of either the principal officers of the executive departments or of such other body as Congress may by law provide, transmit to the President pro tempore of the Senate and the Speaker of the House of Representatives their written declaration that the President is unable to discharge the powers and duties of his office, the Vice-President shall immediately assume the powers and duties of the office as Acting President.

Thereafter, when the President transmits to the President pro tempore of the Senate and the Speaker of the House of Representatives his written declaration that no inability exists, he shall resume the powers and duties of his office unless the Vice-President and a majority of either the principal officers of the executive department or of such other body as Congress may by law provide, transmit within four days to the President pro tempore of the Senate and the Speaker of the House of Representatives their written declaration that the President is unable to discharge the powers and duties of his office. Thereupon Congress shall decide the issue, assembling within forty-eight hours for that purpose if not in session. If the Congress, within twenty-one days after receipt of the latter written declaration, or, if Congress is not in session, within twenty-one days after Congress is required to assemble, determines by two-thirds vote of both Houses that the President is unable to discharge the powers and duties of his office, the Vice-President shall continue to discharge the same as Acting President; otherwise, the President shall resume the powers and duties of his office.

Twenty-sixth Amendment

[Proposed March 10, 1971; declared ratified July 5, 1971]

Section 1. The right of citizens of the United States, who are eighteen years of age or older, to vote shall not be denied or abridged by the United States or by any State on account of age.

Section 2. The Congress shall have power to enforce this article by appropriate legislation.

Twenty-seventh Amendment

[Proposed September 25, 1789; declared ratified May 7, 1992]

No law, varying the compensation for the services of the Senators and Representatives, shall take effect, until an election of Representatives shall have intervened.

The Voting Act of 1970 tried to set the voting age at 18. However, the Supreme Court ruled that the act set the voting age for national elections only, not state or local elections. This ruling would make necessary several different ballots at elections. The Twenty-sixth Amendment gave 18-year-old citizens the right to vote in all elections.

Separation of Power and Checks and Balances

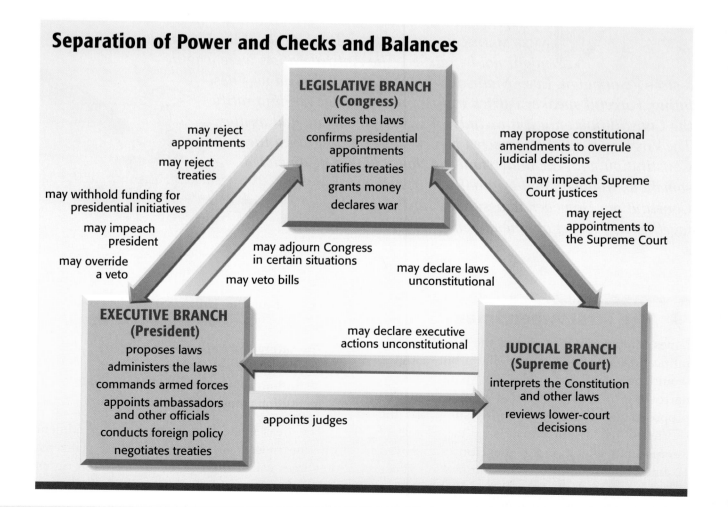

LEGISLATIVE BRANCH (Congress)
writes the laws
confirms presidential appointments
ratifies treaties
grants money
declares war

may reject appointments
may reject treaties
may withhold funding for presidential initiatives
may impeach president
may override a veto

may propose constitutional amendments to overrule judicial decisions
may impeach Supreme Court justices
may reject appointments to the Supreme Court

may adjourn Congress in certain situations
may veto bills

may declare laws unconstitutional

EXECUTIVE BRANCH (President)
proposes laws
administers the laws
commands armed forces
appoints ambassadors and other officials
conducts foreign policy
negotiates treaties

may declare executive actions unconstitutional

JUDICIAL BRANCH (Supreme Court)
interprets the Constitution and other laws
reviews lower-court decisions

appoints judges

The Bill of Rights

Reading Focus

What are the main freedoms of the First Amendment, and why are they important?

Which constitutional amendments reflect issues with pre-Revolutionary War British officials, and how do the amendments address those concerns?

What rights do the amendments give to people accused of crimes?

Key Terms

petition

search warrant

due process

indict

double jeopardy

eminent domain

*J*AMES MADISON WAS WORRIED. *It looked as if the Constitution might not be ratified. The Antifederalists were waging a strong campaign. Even Madison's home state of Virginia was hesitating. Forceful speaker Patrick Henry proposed that Virginia ratify the Constitution only if it included 40 amendments he had written. The Virginia legislature rejected Henry's list, but approved the Constitution with the understanding that it would be amended somehow. Madison had originally opposed amending the Constitution. However, to assure its ratification, he put together its first set of amendments.*

Madison's quill pen

⭐ The First Amendment

James Madison helped secure the Constitution's ratification with the promise that a bill of rights would be added to it. In 1789 Madison began narrowing down the huge list of more than 200 proposed amendments. He then submitted the shortened list of amendments to the House of Representatives. Of those, the House approved 12 amendments, and the states ratified 10. Those 10 amendments, called the Bill of Rights, represent the essential protection of individual liberties

for citizens of the United States. As Madison explained:

❝ **The safety and happiness of society are the objects at which all political institutions aim and to which all such institutions must be sacrificed.** ❞

The ideas spelled out in the First Amendment form the most basic rights of all U.S. citizens. Sometimes called the five freedoms, these rights include freedom of religion, speech, the press, assembly, and petition.

Freedom of Religion

The First Amendment begins by declaring that "Congress shall make no law respecting an establishment of religion, or prohibiting the free exercise thereof." This means that the government cannot support a religion or interfere with any American's decision to practice a religion or not.

At the time the Constitution was written, most nations had a state religion, a system of religious beliefs supported by the government. For example, the Church of England was the state religion of Great Britain. After the Revolution, some Americans supported the separation of church and state, which would keep the government from establishing an official religion and from favoring any religion over others.

Freedom of Speech and of the Press

The importance of the second and third freedoms in the First Amendment is reflected in an idea expressed by former congresswoman Margaret Chase Smith. "The key to security," she once said, "is public information." Everyone in the United States is guaranteed the freedom of speech. Americans have the right to express their own ideas and opinions and to hear the ideas and opinions of others.

Freedom of speech does not mean that people can say anything they want to, however. The Supreme Court has ruled that speech presenting a serious threat to public safety, such as falsely shouting "Fire!" in a crowded theater, is not protected by the First Amendment. Justice Oliver Wendell Holmes explained:

> **❝The question in every case is whether the words used are used in such circumstances and are of such a nature to create a clear and present danger that . . . Congress has a right to prevent.❞**

Another kind of unprotected speech is slander, or the intentional telling of lies that damages someone's reputation.

Intentionally writing a lie that harms another person is called libel. In protecting Americans' freedom of the press, the founders recalled the

The Granger Collection, New York

Biography

James Madison

James Madison was born in Virginia in 1751. He attended the College of New Jersey, now Princeton University, before entering Virginia politics. Early in his career Madison became a strong supporter of religious freedom.

Madison served in Congress until 1797. He continued to influence politics from his family plantation, where he remained a slaveholder despite his belief in individual liberty. In 1801 Madison became secretary of state. He served as president from 1809 to 1817 and continued to be active in politics up until his death in 1836. Madison is often called the Father of the Constitution because of his central role in framing the document and adding the Bill of Rights.

case of John Peter Zenger. The publisher of *New York Weekly Journal*, Zenger had gone on trial in 1735 for printing a factual article that criticized New York's royal governor. The jury found Zenger not guilty, establishing that "the truth is a defense against libel."

Freedom of Assembly and Petition

Another freedom Americans have is that of assembly, or of holding meetings. Anyone may gather with anyone else to discuss issues or to conduct

These students express their freedom of speech and of assembly by organizing an Earth Day celebration.

business. As long as those people gather peacefully and are not involved in any illegal activity, the government cannot interfere.

The right to **petition**, or make a request of, the government is another right of the American people. Any American can present a petition, or formal request, to a government official. The right of petition enables Americans to express their dissatisfaction with current laws or to suggest new ones.

★ Protecting Citizens

The Second, Third, and Fourth Amendments all relate to concerns that grew out of the colonists' disputes with British officials before the Revolution. These amendments continue to affect American life today.

Militias

The Second Amendment deals with state militias. As the conflict with Great Britain increased before the Revolution began, colonial militias prepared for war. The "shot heard round the world" that started the Revolutionary War came when British troops tried to seize the weapons of the Massachusetts militia.

The founders believed that the states needed to continue to maintain militias for emergencies. Today the National Guard has replaced state militias. National Guard members can be called to serve in wars and to help restore order during crises, such as in the event of a natural disaster.

Many people have debated the Second Amendment's intent regarding firearms. Some people argue that gun control laws violate the Second Amendment's declaration that "the right of the people to keep and bear arms shall not be infringed [violated]." In 1939 the Supreme Court approved restrictions for nonmilitary firearms. Years later, a U.S. court of appeals ruled that gun control laws do not violate the Second Amendment. The Supreme Court let that ruling stand in 1983.

Quartering and Search and Seizure

The Third Amendment prohibits the military from forcing citizens to provide housing for soldiers, an idea that may seem odd today. Before the Revolution, however, the British government pressured the colonies to provide food and shelter for British soldiers.

British authorities also issued writs of assistance, which empowered law officials to search colonists' property for illegal goods without first establishing a probable cause of illegal activity. Anger over such actions resulted in the Fourth Amendment's restriction against "unreasonable

These members of the National Guard are helping local citizens prevent a river from flooding.

Judges issue search warrants like this one to allow law enforcement officials to search a suspected criminal's home.

searches and seizures." To conduct a search reasonably, authorities usually must first obtain a **search warrant**. This warrant is a judge's order that authorizes the search because the property in question seems likely to contain evidence relating to a crime.

Authorities do not always need a warrant to conduct a search. Under certain circumstances, such as when a suspect is trying to destroy evidence or conceal a weapon, police can conduct an emergency search. This helps to protect both the officers and any evidence necessary to prove illegal activity.

 ## Protection of the Accused

The Fifth, Sixth, Seventh, and Eighth Amendments establish guidelines for trying people accused of a crime. The goal of these amendments is to protect the rights of the accused. No one may be punished for a crime without **due process**, or the fair application, of the law.

Due Process

According to the Fifth Amendment, a court cannot try someone for a serious crime unless a grand jury decides that enough evidence exists to **indict**, or formally accuse, the person. The Fifth Amendment also protects people being forced to testify in their own trial in a criminal case. To refrain from testifying, the defendant "pleads the Fifth." Anyone found not guilty in a criminal trial cannot face **double jeopardy**, or be tried again for the same crime.

Linking Past to Present

Freedom of Assembly

When Congress first debated what to include in the Bill of Rights, some members thought that guaranteeing citizens' right to meet and speak together was too minor to be a federal issue. Others, however, wanted to make sure that political groups in power did not try to stop rival groups from organizing meetings. Thus, the freedom to assemble became part of the First Amendment.

Over the years Americans have used the right to assemble in many ways, ranging from parades to protests. Citizens have gathered to privately and publicly express their opinions on issues such as civil rights, education, the environment, public policy, and religion. Even in wartime, opponents of U.S. policy have marched to the Capitol and peacefully protested government actions.

Americans do not have unlimited right of assembly, however. Citizens have the right to gather on any public property under guidelines that protect public safety. Parades, for example, usually require a local permit so that traffic flow can be managed during the parade time. Such restrictions are not supposed to be used to prevent people or groups with unpopular beliefs from publicly expressing their opinions.

Understanding What You Read

1. What types of activities might students participate in that are guaranteed under the freedom of assembly?

2. Should all groups—even those whose ideas are unpopular or controversial—have the freedom of assembly? Explain your answer.

Amending the U.S. Constitution

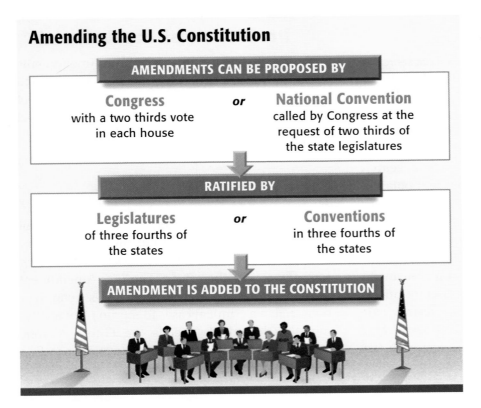

AMENDMENTS CAN BE PROPOSED BY

Congress	or	National Convention
with a two thirds vote in each house		called by Congress at the request of two thirds of the state legislatures

RATIFIED BY

Legislatures	or	Conventions
of three fourths of the states		in three fourths of the states

AMENDMENT IS ADDED TO THE CONSTITUTION

The final clause of the Fifth Amendment states that no one will be deprived of property "without due process of law." The one exception involves the government's power of **eminent domain**, or the right to take personal property to further the public's interest. This would include, for example, the seizing of private lands to build a public road. However, the government must pay the owners a fair amount of money for the property unless the citizens obtained it through illegal activities, such as selling drugs.

Trials

The Sixth Amendment states that someone who is indicted for a crime must have a prompt, public trial by a jury. The accused has the right to know what crime he or she is charged with and to hear and to question the prosecution witnesses. The accused also has the right to an attorney. Today the government pays for the attorney if the person cannot afford legal services.

The accused has the right to refuse any of his or her Sixth Amendment rights. For example, some defendants refuse the services of an attorney, while others choose to have a trial in front of a judge alone instead of before a jury. In many cases, defendants can bypass the trial by agreeing to a plea bargain—pleading guilty to a lesser charge rather than risk being convicted of a crime that may carry a greater sentence.

The Seventh Amendment establishes that juries can decide civil cases. These cases usually involve disputes over money or property. If a person harms another person without breaking the law—for example, by refusing to pay back a debt—the injured party may sue in civil court.

Bail and Punishment

The Eighth Amendment establishes that people accused of a crime have a method of getting out of jail until their trial is over. Defendants gain their release in exchange for bail, money paid to the court to guarantee that they will show up for trial. Whoever pays the bail gets his or her money back at the end of the trial only if the defendant has attended court. If the defendant does not show up for trial, the court keeps all the bail money and issues a warrant for the immediate arrest of the defendant.

The Eighth Amendment prevents courts from setting bail amounts that are too high. How much bail is "too high" depends on the crime. People accused of serious crimes such as murder usually have very high bail. For some people accused of extremely serious crimes or who seem likely to flee if released, the judge may refuse to grant bail.

The Eighth Amendment also prohibits inflicting "cruel and unusual punishments" against a person convicted of a crime. For many years, Americans have debated the meaning of "cruel and unusual punishments." In 1972 the Supreme Court ruled that the death penalty, as it was carried out by most states at the time, was cruel and unusual. The Court also found that the processes by which many states sentenced people to death were unfair. However, the Court did not rule that all executions are cruel and unusual. All states that use the death penalty must follow guidelines spelled out by the Supreme Court.

These students benefit from free public education, which many people now consider a right of citizenship.

⭐ Other Rights of the People

The final two amendments in the Bill of Rights provide a general protection for other individual rights and reserve some governmental powers for the states and for the people. The Ninth Amendment states that listing specific rights in the Constitution does not mean that citizens do not have additional rights. This amendment gives the courts and Congress the ability to determine other fundamental rights of citizens.

Education is one right that was not included in the Constitution but which most Americans consider a fundamental right. "Education is not just another consumer item. It is the bedrock [foundation] of our democracy," explained educational leader Mary Hatwood Futrell. Today state governments provide free education—from elementary to high school—to all citizens.

The Tenth Amendment grants to the states and the people any powers that the Constitution does not specifically give to Congress or prohibit from the states. Recently a group of governors used this amendment to challenge a federal law that required states to pay for and carry out a federal information program. The courts agreed, stating that this requirement interfered with the states' rights, implied under the Tenth Amendment, to determine their own budget priorities. Thus, the last amendment in the Bill of Rights continues to protect the rights of citizens and to balance power between the federal and state governments.

SECTION 2 REVIEW

Identify and explain the significance of the following:
- **James Madison**
- **petition**
- **search warrant**
- **due process**
- **indict**
- **double jeopardy**
- **eminent domain**

Reading for Content Understanding

1 **Main Idea** What are the five main freedoms guaranteed to U.S. citizens under the First Amendment, and why are they important?

2 **Main Idea** How do the Second, Third, and Fourth Amendments address concerns from the Revolutionary period?

3 **Citizenship and Democracy** How does the Ninth Amendment protect people's rights and individual freedoms?

4 **Writing** *Expressing* What rights of the accused are protected by the Constitution? Do you agree or disagree with protecting these rights? Explain your answer in one or two paragraphs.

5 **Critical Thinking** *Evaluating* What do you think are the three most important ways that the Bill of Rights influences our lives today? Explain your answers.

Rights and Responsibilities of Citizenship

Reading Focus

How can a person become a U.S. citizen?

What are some of the most important responsibilities of citizenship?

Why is it important for citizens to be involved with their community and government?

Key Terms

naturalization

deport

draft

political action committees

*P*ATRICK HENRY ARGUED *that the United States should be open for all people who wanted to become citizens. "Let . . . Liberty stretch forth her fair hand toward the people of the old world," he said "—tell them to come, and bid them welcome." Many people desiring liberty have become U.S. citizens. Jozef Patyna immigrated to the United States in the early 1980s to flee an unjust government in Poland. "The idea of freedom and democracy is what the people have an instinctive need for," explained Patyna.*

The Statue of Liberty

Becoming a Citizen

The Constitution protects the rights of all U.S. citizens. People can become U.S. citizens in many ways. Anyone born in the United States or a territory it controls is a citizen. People born in Puerto Rico, for example, are citizens because that island is a commonwealth that remains a U.S. territory.

People born in a foreign country can become U.S. citizens if one of their parents is a citizen. People born in a foreign country whose parents are not U.S. citizens can become citizens only if they move to the United States and undergo a long process in gaining citizenship called **naturalization**. The U.S. Immigration and Naturalization Service (INS) oversees this process.

Foreign-born people who permanently move to a new country are called immigrants. In the United States, legal immigrants have many of the same rights and responsibilities as citizens. They cannot vote or hold public office, however. In some states they cannot hold some government jobs either. The U.S. government also has the right to **deport**, or send back to the country of origin, any immigrant who breaks the law or who is in the country illegally.

Only legal immigrants can begin the process of naturalization. All legal immigrants have to be able to support themselves financially or have someone sponsor them and assume that financial responsibility. After living in the United States for five years, legal immigrants over the age of 18 may petition for naturalization. At that point the INS sets a hearing to test the immigrants' qualifications. The immigrants must prove that they are law-abiding and that they support the U.S. Constitution. They must also take a series of tests to prove that they can read, write, and speak English, and that they have a basic understanding of U.S. history and government.

After the immigrants pass this hearing, the INS conducts a background check on them to make sure they have not hidden any information about themselves. Finally, they go before a naturalization court, where they take an oath of allegiance to the United States and then receive their certificate of naturalization. At that point all young children of the newly naturalized citizens also become citizens.

Becoming a naturalized citizen takes dedication and effort. An elderly Japanese immigrant wrote a poem to celebrate her naturalization:

 Going steadily to study English,
Even through the rain at night,
I thus attain [acquire],
Late in life,
American citizenship. "

Naturalized citizens and resident immigrants contribute a great deal to the United States. Many famous Americans, such as scientist Albert Einstein and Secretary of State Madeleine Albright, have been naturalized citizens. The only distinctions between naturalized and native-born citizens are that naturalized citizens can lose their citizenship and they cannot become president or vice president.

This Asian immigrant is taking the oath of allegiance to become a U.S. citizen.

★ Duties of Citizens

In addition to having certain rights, American citizens have responsibilities to themselves, their government, and other citizens. For the system of representative democracy to work, Americans need to fulfill their civic responsibilities. "The stakes . . . are too high for government to be a spectator sport," explained former Texas congresswoman Barbara Jordan.

Obeying Authority

Citizens elect officials to make laws for them. In turn, citizens must obey the laws passed by those officials. If citizens disagree with a law, they can try to get it changed in a variety of ways, such as by speaking with their local representative, challenging the law in court, petitioning, or voting for elected officials who oppose the law.

Obeying the law includes knowing what the laws are. Thus, citizens need to stay informed of and be aware of changes to laws that affect them. Ignorance of a particular law will not prevent a person from being punished for breaking it.

Citizens also have an obligation to respect the rights of others and to respect people in authority. These people, including parents, teachers and police officers, have been entrusted with looking out for the welfare of others. Parents, for example, have a responsibility to provide for their children's basic needs, including food, clothing, shelter, and education. In return, children have a responsibility

Consumers like this teenager pay sales tax when they buy goods.

sometimes the state, government. The amount of income tax that a person has to pay depends on the level of his or her income.

Income taxes and property taxes are progressive—they collect a higher percentage of money from those with higher incomes and greater wealth. Regressive taxes, such as sales taxes, are taxes that apply equally to all Americans. If a person buys a product, he or she pays the same amount of sales tax on the item regardless of his or her individual income.

to obey their parents. Government authorities may step in to protect any children whose parents do not take proper care of them.

Paying Taxes

Benjamin Franklin once claimed, "In this world, nothing is certain but death and taxes." Paying taxes is a necessary part of being a good citizen. The government relies on taxes to pay for the many services it provides. If Americans did not pay taxes, the government might be unable to provide public roads, police and fire departments, or even public schools.

People pay many kinds of taxes, such as sales taxes, excise taxes, and tariffs. For example, consumers often pay sales taxes when buying items at a store. Sales tax rates vary from place to place because most sales taxes are set and collected by state and local governments.

Property taxes are taxes people pay based on the value of the property they own. The tax amount owed is a certain percentage of the value of the property. Most school funding comes from property taxes.

April 15 of every year is income tax day. By that day all Americans who earned money the year before must give a certain percentage of their income from that year to the federal, and

Serving in the Military

Citizens also have the duty to protect and defend the nation from harm. This means that if a war breaks out, citizens should try to help in the war effort. U.S. citizens have had to go to war a number of times in the nation's history. In some war situations the federal government has issued a **draft**, or requirement of military service, to raise the needed number of soldiers.

Upon turning 18, every male U.S. citizen must fill out a card like this one to register for a potential draft.

The United States has maintained an all-volunteer armed forces since 1973. However, young men are required to register with the government when they turn 18. This registration provides the government with a record of potential draftees in case a war breaks out. Women are not required to register for the draft, although many women serve in the armed forces.

Serving on Juries

All citizens can be called for jury duty, which involves listening to a court case and reaching a verdict on it. It is important for citizens to serve when called for jury duty, otherwise fulfilling each person's Sixth Amendment right to a trial by jury would be difficult.

Americans also have a duty to testify in court if needed. If a person were to witness a crime, for example, he or she should be willing to testify about the event. Judges may issue subpoenas, or orders to appear in court, to force people to testify.

⭐ Citizens and Elections

Elections form the basis of representative democracy in the United States. Voting in elections is crucial to maintaining the country's democratic system. Through free elections, U.S. citizens choose who will lead the government. Not all countries allow their citizens to participate in elections.

An active voter should be an informed voter. Citizens should try to find out as much as they can about the issues and candidates before voting. Much of this information is available through newspapers, television, and other forms of media. However, informed voters should watch out for propaganda, or material that is slanted deliberately to support or harm a cause.

Voting is not the only way that Americans participate in elections. Many become involved by campaigning for a particular candidate or issue. Anyone can help campaign, even if he or she is not eligible to vote. Citizens can also contribute money to a candidate directly or through **political action committees** (PACs), organizations that collect money to distribute to candidates who support the same issues as the contributors.

Voters in the United States must be at least 18 years old. Many people younger than 18 can help campaigns by handing out pamphlets, making signs, or otherwise encouraging citizens to vote. Some schools have clubs, such as the Teen-Age Republicans and the Young Democrats, that allow teenagers to get involved in party politics.

High school student Janet Benson's active participation in the Teen-Age Republicans shaped her career goals. "Some people want a career in science or sports," she noted. "For me, it's politics. I love it." Many active members of political clubs get to know political leaders well. Some continue to be active in politics as adults.

⭐ Citizens and Government

Being involved in elections is just one of the many ways in which citizens can participate in their government. Even after an election, people can influence officials by letting them know what the citizens want done.

Some citizens join interest groups, organizations designed to lobby politicians on behalf of particular issues. People form many kinds of interest groups, and most groups represent the views of a particular segment of society. The American Farm Bureau Federation, for example, is an interest group made up of farmers. It lobbies to get aid for farms—for example, financial assistance to help when a natural disaster destroys crops or to maintain prices of farm products.

Other groups, called public interest groups, lobby for issues that affect all Americans. Mothers Against Drunk Driving (MADD) and Students Against Drunk Driving (SADD) are two public interest groups that work to end drunk driving, which kills thousands of Americans each year. MADD began in 1980 after a drunk driver killed 13-year-old Cari Lightner.

These students are helping run a candidate's campaign during a local election.

These members of Students Against Drunk Driving visited Washington, D.C., to speak out against drinking and driving.

If public officials do not know how citizens feel about an issue, they cannot represent them effectively.

★ Citizens and Their Communities

Being part of a representative democracy does not mean that citizens hand over all the responsibility for society to their elected leaders and government. Indeed, a successful democratic society requires the involvement of all citizens in improving the communities in which they live.

Just as there are many interest groups that help U.S. citizens lobby for new legislation, there are numerous groups that organize citizens for community service. Some small communities whose local governments have limited budgets rely on volunteers to provide many public services, such as fire protection. Other volunteer groups assist

These volunteers are helping their neighbor by repainting a fence.

Her mother, Candy Lightner, found out that under her state's law, drunk driving was not a serious crime and that the driver would probably not spend any time in prison. Lightner founded MADD to change that policy. In explaining her motivation, she said:

> ❝ I believe that for every problem there is a solution. . . . I believe in the rights of victims. And I do feel that if you believe in something badly enough, you can make a difference. ❞

MADD began to lobby for tougher laws against drunk drivers. As a result, every state strengthened its laws against drunk driving. MADD and SADD also work to educate people about the dangers of drunk driving. "We are changing the way people think about drinking and driving," said Lightner. "But more than that, we have caused people to change their behavior, and that is saving lives."

Citizens do not have to join a group to influence political leaders. Individuals can and should let officials know how they feel about certain issues by writing letters and by going to public meetings. Attending city council meetings is a good way to learn about and influence local issues.

Colin Powell launches an effort to increase volunteerism throughout the country.

citizen patrols usually have lower crime rates than those that do not.

Other groups help do jobs in place of the government. The American Red Cross helps citizens in times of natural disasters or other emergencies. Habitat for Humanity helps to build houses for lower-income families. The Boy Scouts and Girl Scouts organize numerous projects to improve the environment, such as planting trees.

The country's leaders expect all citizens to try to do something to serve others in their communities. Service projects do not have to be big to have an effect. They can include simple acts to improve the appearance of a community, such as picking up trash or painting over graffiti. They may also help individuals—perhaps by volunteering to serve food in a homeless shelter or by visiting an elderly person in a retirement home.

Every day many people in the community need assistance. The nation is strengthened when all citizens do their part to help the country and their fellow citizens. As former general Colin Powell declared when he launched a campaign to promote volunteerism in 1997:

❝ **This is the time for each and every one of us . . . to look into our own community, to find someone who is in need . . . to lift up a fellow American and put him on the road to success in this wonderful country of ours.** ❞

government-sponsored agencies, including police departments. For example, Citizens on Patrol and the Neighborhood Watch organize volunteers to walk their neighborhoods and inform police of any possible criminal activity they observe in the area. Neighborhoods with

SECTION 3 REVIEW

Identify and explain the significance of the following:
- naturalization
- deport
- draft
- political action committees

Reading for Content Understanding

1 **Main Idea** How can someone become a U.S. citizen?

2 **Main Idea** What responsibilities do citizens have to their country?

3 **Cultural Diversity** What rights do citizens have that immigrants do not?

4 **Writing** *Creating* Write a short poem that might be used to encourage people to volunteer in their communities or to become involved in the government.

5 **Critical Thinking** *Identifying Cause and Effect* Write about a problem within your community—its causes and effects—and give examples of possible ways to get people more involved in correcting the problem.

CHAPTER
9 REVIEW

Chapter Summary

To ensure a system of checks and balances, the framers of the Constitution divided the government into three branches—legislative, executive, and judicial. Leaders later added the Bill of Rights to protect individual liberties. Citizens have certain rights and responsibilities that must be carried out for representative democracy to work. ▪

On a separate sheet of paper, complete the following activities.

Identifying People and Ideas

Describe the significance of the following:

1. representative democracy
2. impeach
3. Sandra Day O'Connor
4. James Madison
5. search warrant
6. due process
7. double jeopardy
8. naturalization
9. draft
10. political action committees

Internet Activity

go.hrw.com
SA0 Executive Departments

The cabinet consists of the heads of the 14 executive departments and any other officials the president chooses. Search the Internet through the HRW Web site to find the names of the heads of the 14 executive departments. Then give a brief description of each department's responsibilities and how these have developed over time.

Understanding Main Ideas

1. What are the three branches of the federal government, and what are their primary responsibilities?
2. What are delegated powers, reserved powers, and concurrent powers?
3. Why did the founders add the Bill of Rights to the Constitution?
4. Which amendments focus on the rights of people accused of crimes? What rights do these amendments guarantee?
5. What are the only differences between the rights of naturalized citizens and the rights of native-born citizens?
6. What are the duties and responsibilities of citizenship?

Using the Time Line

Number your paper from 1 to 7. Match the letters on the time line below with the following events.

1. Delegates from 12 of the 13 states meet to create a new system of government.
2. Geraldine Ferraro becomes the first woman to run for vice president on a major-party ticket.
3. Richard Nixon becomes the first president to resign rather than risk impeachment.
4. President Ronald Reagan appoints Sandra Day O'Connor as the first female justice on the Supreme Court.
5. Thurgood Marshall becomes the first African American justice appointed to serve on the Supreme Court.
6. The Supreme Court rules that the death penalty is not cruel and unusual.
7. John F. Kennedy becomes the first Catholic U.S. president.

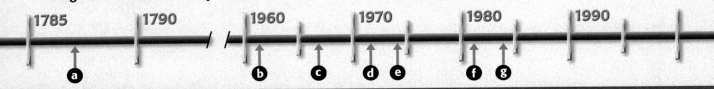

1785 1790 1960 1970 1980 1990

a   b   c   d e   f g

Reviewing Themes

1. **Citizenship and Democracy** Why is voting an important responsibility in a representative democracy?
2. **Constitutional Heritage** How does the Constitution prevent any one branch of the federal government from becoming too powerful?
3. **Cultural Diversity** Why might it be said that the United States is a nation of immigrants?

Thinking Critically

1. **Determining the Strength of an Argument** Recall the qualifications for becoming president. Why do you think the framers of the Constitution put these in place?
2. **Synthesizing Information** How were some amendments to the Bill of Rights influenced by Americans' experiences before and during the Revolution?

Building Your Portfolio

American History

Complete the following activities individually or in groups.

1. **Freedom of Petition** Think about something in your community that is important to you, such as the existence of crosswalks, parks, or holiday parades. Write a letter to a local official about this element of your community. Make sure the letter explains to the official why you are writing and what you want to be done. Then organize a campaign to get others to sign your letter. Support your campaign by creating signs, letters, flyers, and other items.

2. **The Supreme Court** Use your library or other resources to find out information about the nine Supreme Court justices sitting on the bench today. Then create a detailed time line showing the names of each justice, what year he or she was confirmed, and which president nominated him or her. In addition, include some brief biographical information on each justice.

3. **Identifying Cause and Effect** Serving on juries is required by law and is an important responsibility of citizenship. What problems might arise if people were unwilling to fulfill this responsibility?

Writing About History

1. **Expressing** Imagine that you have immigrated to the United States. Write a letter to a friend back home explaining why you have done so.
2. **Informing** Write a two-paragraph essay explaining how the Constitution guarantees that the federal government considers minority rights while honoring majority rule.

Linking Geography and History

1. **Movement** How might movements of large numbers of people from one part of the country to another affect states' representation in Congress?
2. **Human-Environment Interaction** What actions can people take to physically improve their communities?

History Skills Workshop

Using Primary Sources On February 28, 1963, President John F. Kennedy gave a speech to Congress in support of a civil rights bill. He also took the opportunity to discuss the importance of voting rights for African Americans. Read the following excerpt of his speech. Then explain in a paragraph what Kennedy meant by this passage.

66 The right to vote in a free American election is the most powerful and precious right in the world—and it must not be denied on the grounds of race or color. It is a potent [powerful] key to achieving other rights of citizenship. 99

▪ CHAPTER 10 ▪
Launching the Nation
(1789–1800)

After the Constitution was ratified, the United States began a critical stage in its history. Some Americans, such as Patrick Henry, feared that the new federal government would abuse its power. "Your President may easily become king," he warned. Other people, such as George Washington, celebrated the creation of the republic. "No country upon earth ever had it more in its power to attain [achieve] . . . blessings than united America," he claimed.

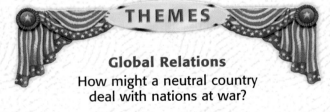

THEMES

Global Relations
How might a neutral country deal with nations at war?

Constitutional Heritage
How might conflict arise over different interpretations of the U.S. Constitution?

Economic Development
In what ways might a new nation strengthen its economy?

1789

1791

1793

JULY The French Revolution begins.

APR. George Washington is elected president.

FEB. Congress charters the Bank of the United States.

JULY The site for the new national capital is chosen and named Washington.

APR. President Washington presents the Neutrality Proclamation to Congress.

NOV. Great Britain and the United States sign Jay's Treaty.

Laying the Foundations of Government

Reading Focus

Why was George Washington chosen as the first president of the United States?

What was life like in the United States when Washington took office?

What steps did Congress and the president take to organize the government?

Key Terms

electoral college

precedent

Judiciary Act

ONCE THE STATES HAD RATIFIED the Constitution, George Washington looked forward to retiring from public life and living quietly on his Virginia farm. However, his friends soon drew him into politics as a presidential candidate. When Washington hesitated, fellow politician Gouverneur Morris told him, "Should the idea prevail [win] that you would not accept the presidency, it should prove fatal . . . to the new government." Morris concluded confidently, "Of all men, you are the best fitted to fill that office."

Courtesy of the Free Library Of Philadelphia

"Hail, Columbia," was composed for Washington's inauguration.

IMAGE ON LEFT PAGE: *American ships salute George Washington as he arrives in New York City for his inauguration in 1789.*

1795

1797

1799

AUG. Indian confederation leaders sign the Treaty of Greenville.

NOV. John Adams is elected president of the United States.

NOV. Thomas Jefferson and Aaron Burr tie for president.

Choosing the President

Although he had led his nation to victory in the Revolutionary War, Washington was not eager to become president. He was concerned that his age and lack of political experience might make him a poor president. In addition, he knew that he would be drawn into political conflicts.

Despite Washington's uneasiness, Americans believed that his character, honesty, and patriotism made him an excellent candidate. In January 1789 the 11 states that had ratified the Constitution sent electors to vote in the presidential election. The winner of the presidential election was not determined by the votes of the public, but rather by the votes of the **electoral college**. This group was selected by the state legislatures to represent the popular vote, though the electors could vote for different candidates if they felt the public had chosen poorly. This was not an issue in the first election. On April 6, 1789, Congress declared that the electoral college had selected Washington unanimously, with John Adams as his vice president.

Washington accepted the presidency because he felt it was his duty "to render [give] service to

Cheering crowds greeted Washington as he passed through small towns on the way to his inauguration.

The Granger Collection, New York

my country in obedience to its call." As he traveled to New York City to be sworn into office, thousands of Americans gathered along the roads to cheer him. When Washington arrived in New York City, people lined up by the thousands to celebrate. Ships in the harbor flew colorful flags and fired their cannons in salute as Washington passed. His challenge would be to make sure the new government lived up to Americans' expectations.

After taking office, Washington and his family found that the presidency brought many changes to their lives. Martha Washington had to constantly entertain guests and attend social functions with her husband. "I have not had one half-hour to myself since the day of my arrival," she wrote to a niece after just two weeks in New York. Just as George Washington brought dignity to his role as president, Martha Washington ran the presidential household with grace and style. Abigail Adams wrote that "I found myself much more deeply impressed [by Martha Washington] than I ever did before their majesties of Britain."

Republican Motherhood

Abigail Adams, Judith Sargent Murray, and other women hoped to play a larger role in the new nation than Martha Washington did. Murray wrote newspaper essays that stressed the need for young women to receive an education. "I would give my daughters every accomplishment which I thought proper," wrote Murray. "Independence should be placed within their grasp."

Some politicians, such as Dr. Benjamin Rush, also supported women's education because educated mothers would "[instruct] their sons in the principles of liberty and government." Republican Motherhood, the idea that women played an important role in teaching their children to be good citizens, became more widespread in the young nation. Some promoters of Republican Motherhood, such as Rush, did not expect women to participate in politics or business. Other people, however, hoped that Republican Motherhood would lead to greater opportunities for women in society, business, and politics. "I expect to see our young women forming a new era in female history," wrote Murray.

Republican Motherhood was only a small step toward enabling women to participate equally in society. Many Americans resisted equal rights for women. Only a few families were willing to provide much education for their daughters, and adult women rarely had the time or money they needed to get an education later in life. Most women in the early republic faced long days managing their households and working inside or outside the home to support their families. As a Maine woman wrote in her diary:

Martha Washington spent much of her time as First Lady hosting social functions for political leaders.

66 **A womans work is never Done as the Song says and happy shee whose strength holds out to the end of the rais [race].** 99

⭐ Life in the New Republic

Hard work also lay ahead for the members of the new government. The United States was home to almost 4 million people in 1790, many of whom had never thought of themselves as citizens of a united nation.

Most citizens wanted the federal government to protect their liberty and to improve the national economy. The vast majority of Americans lived in the countryside in 1790, and only two U.S. cities—New York and Philadelphia—had populations greater than 25,000. Most people worked on farms, while others worked in towns as merchants, craftspeople, or laborers. Many farmers wanted fair tax laws and the right to settle new lands to the west. As more Americans began to buy and sell goods and services in markets across the country and around the world, trade laws also grew increasingly important. Merchants were interested in simpler trade laws controlled by a unified government. American manufacturers hoped that the new republic would pass laws protecting them from foreign competition.

In many ways New York City, which served as the first capital of the United States, represented the spirit of the new nation. Badly damaged by the British during the Revolutionary War, the city had already begun recovering. Citizens got rid of the signs of British rule, changing Crown Street to Liberty Street, for example. International trade was more active than before the war, increasing business activity throughout the city. A French visitor to New York noted:

66 **Everything in the city is in motion; everywhere the shops resound [ring out] with the noise of workers . . . one sees vessels arriving from every part of the world.** 99

By 1790 the city's population had topped 33,000 and was growing rapidly. To many officials, this vibrant city reflected the potential of the future nation. Thus, it served as a fitting place for the new administration to plan for the country's future.

⭐ Setting Precedents

The new federal government faced a series of critical decisions about policies and procedures. As President Washington noted in a letter to James Madison, "The first of everything in our situation will serve to establish a precedent." A **precedent** is an action or decision that later serves as an example.

Washington's Cabinet

Organizing the government's executive branch was one of Congress's first tasks. Congress created several executive departments, each specializing in a different area of national policy. Washington appointed the leaders of these branches, selecting Alexander Hamilton as secretary of the treasury, Thomas Jefferson as secretary of state, Henry Knox as secretary of war, and Samuel Osgood as the postmaster general. Hamilton was a gifted economic planner, Jefferson had served as ambassador to France, Knox had helped Washington run the Continental Army, and Osgood had government experience.

President Washington began meeting with the department heads as a group, which became known as the cabinet. The cabinet members advised the president and debated important issues with one another. By 1792 cabinet meetings were common practice.

Establishing the Federal Courts

The judicial branch also needed organizing, because the Constitution did not specify how many federal courts there should be, where they should be located, or how many federal judges would be required. To address these issues, Congress passed the **Judiciary Act** in September 1789, creating a federal court system with three

levels. At the lower level were the district courts. The courts of appeals, at the next level, reviewed decisions of the district courts. At the top level was the Supreme Court, which had six justices. Washington appointed John Jay to be the first chief justice of the United States and chose Edmund Randolph as attorney general.

Washington wrote to the justices of the Supreme Court to explain the importance of their positions. "The happiness of the people of the United States . . . depend[s] in a considerable degree on the interpretation and execution of its laws." With the parts of the federal government in place, officials could begin addressing the problems that faced the young nation.

President Washington with some of his advisers (left to right): Washington, Henry Knox, Alexander Hamilton, Thomas Jefferson, and Edmund Randolph

SECTION 1 REVIEW

Identify and explain the significance of the following:
- **George Washington**
- **electoral college**
- **Martha Washington**
- **Judith Sargent Murray**
- **precedent**
- **Judiciary Act**

Reading for Content Understanding

1 **Main Idea** Why did Americans elect George Washington as president?

2 **Main Idea** Where did the majority of people in the new republic live? What kind of work did they do?

3 **Citizenship and Democracy** How did the new government organize the executive branch and the federal courts?

4 **Writing** *Describing* Imagine that you are a newspaper columnist at the time of George Washington's inauguration. Write an article describing the inauguration. Make sure to include your thoughts about Martha and George Washington, New York City, and the feelings of the people.

5 **Critical Thinking** *Synthesizing Information* How did Republican Motherhood reflect the ideals of the Revolution?

Hamilton and National Finances

Reading Focus

How did Alexander Hamilton deal with the national and state debts?

In what ways did Hamilton and Thomas Jefferson differ in their attitudes toward democracy?

What disagreement did Hamilton and Jefferson have about the national bank?

Key Terms

national debt

bonds

speculators

protective tariff

strict construction

loose construction

Bank of the United States

PRESIDENT WASHINGTON *was soon asking for advice on how to pay back the money owed by the new government. He took his concerns to Robert Morris, the Philadelphian who had helped fund the Revolution. "What are we to do with this heavy debt?" Washington asked. Morris replied, "There is but one man in the United States who can tell you; that is Alexander Hamilton." Morris's faith in Hamilton was quickly put to the test. Within days of Hamilton's appointment as secretary of the treasury, Congress ordered him to prepare a plan to improve the national economy.*

Robert Morris

 ## Settling the Debt

Alexander Hamilton had a natural gift for financial matters. Growing up in the British West Indies, he had helped run a shipping company when he was just a teenager. After impressing people with his intelligence and desire to learn, he left the West Indies for New York in 1773. There he continued to learn about economics and law while attending college. As secretary of the treasury, Hamilton's biggest challenge was paying off the **national debt**—the amount of money owed by the United

States to various creditors. Hamilton calculated that the United States owed about $11.7 million to foreign countries such as France, and around $40.4 million to American creditors.

Some of the domestic debt was in the form of **bonds**, certificates that represent money owed by the government to private citizens. The U.S. government had raised money during the Revolutionary War by selling these bonds, promising that at a later date it would buy them back at a higher price. This would allow the bondholders to make a profit. The problem was that the

A government bond

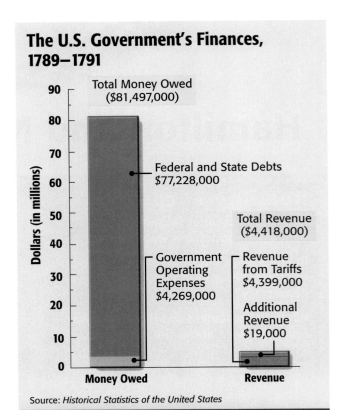

The U.S. Government's Finances, 1789–1791

Total Money Owed ($81,497,000)

Federal and State Debts $77,228,000

Total Revenue ($4,418,000)

Government Operating Expenses $4,269,000

Revenue from Tariffs $4,399,000

Additional Revenue $19,000

Dollars (in millions)

Money Owed   Revenue

Source: *Historical Statistics of the United States*

Financial Difficulties George Washington's administration had to deal with the federal government's financial problems. What were the government's operating expenses from 1789 to 1791?

government could not afford to buy back the bonds. Eventually, investors began to doubt that the government would repay them. As a result, many bondholders who needed money decided to sell their bonds at a fraction of the original value to **speculators**—investors who buy items at low prices in the hope that the value will rise later.

Hamilton knew that the federal government would lose the trust of foreign countries, state governments, and American citizens if it could not start paying off the national debt. He also believed that the government would lose the trust of the American people if it did not buy back the bonds at a fair price. He therefore proposed that the federal government pay the foreign debt as soon as possible and gradually repay the full promised value of all bonds. This second part of his plan became controversial.

Hamilton defended his plan by writing that "he [the speculator] paid what the commodity [bond] was worth in the market and took the risks." Thus, it was only fair, in Hamilton's opinion, for the speculator to make a profit along with those original bondholders who had kept their bonds. Thomas Jefferson strongly opposed this plan. He believed that Hamilton's proposal cheated the original bondholders who had sold their bonds at low prices out of necessity. Jefferson wrote, "Immense sums were thus filched [stolen] from the poor and ignorant."

Representative James Madison suggested a plan that would repay full value only to the original bondholders, giving speculators a lesser amount. However, a majority in Congress agreed with Hamilton's argument and approved his plan. In early 1790 the government started exchanging the old bonds for new, more reliable ones whose value was guaranteed.

⭐ The States' Debts

The second part of Hamilton's economic plan, called debt assumption, was also controversial. He wanted the federal government to assume, or pay, $21.5 million of the $25 million owed by the states for Revolutionary War expenses.

Debt Assumption

Hamilton believed that debtor states would show greater support for the federal government in the future if they received help with their debts. He also thought that the assumption of states' debts by the national government would help the national economy by improving business and trade in debtor states such as Massachusetts and Connecticut. Debt assumption, Hamilton wrote, "will be a measure of sound policy and substantial [sizable] justice."

Southern states such as Virginia and North Carolina had few war debts, however, and their representatives did not believe that they should help the federal government pay the debts of other states. Patrick Henry did not even believe that the Constitution gave Congress the power to assume state debts. Hamilton knew that without the support of southern representatives, he did not have enough votes in Congress to get his plan approved.

A New Capital

While some northern officials wanted debt assumption by the federal government, southern officials wanted a new national capital. Many southerners were concerned that having the capital in New York gave the northern states too much influence over national policy. However, a majority of northerners in Congress wanted to keep the capital in New York City or move it to Philadelphia, Pennsylvania.

The original 1792 plan of the city of Washington shows its distinctive diagonal streets and the location of major public buildings.

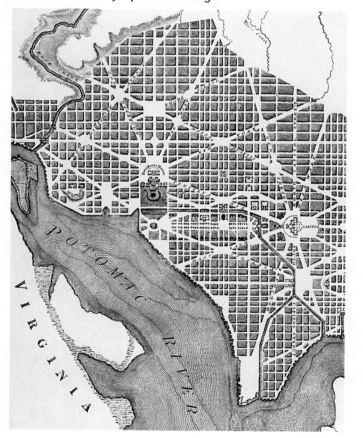

Hamilton and Jefferson decided to compromise on these issues. They met with influential representative James Madison in June 1790. Hamilton promised to persuade New Englanders to support moving the capital to a site along the Potomac River between Virginia and Maryland, while Jefferson and Madison agreed to persuade southern representatives in Congress to vote for debt assumption. The compromise worked.

In July the House of Representatives approved the debt assumption plan and chose the site of present-day Washington, D.C., as the new national capital. Philadelphia served as the temporary seat of government while surveyors such as Benjamin Banneker measured the land for architects to begin designing the new capital city.

 Hamilton Versus Jefferson

Hamilton and Jefferson did not cooperate for long. Soon their political differences put them on opposite sides in Washington's new cabinet.

The Power of the People

The differences between the two men were long-standing. Hamilton believed in a strong central government, while Jefferson wanted to protect the powers of the states. Their conflict went deeper than this, however, for it reflected fundamental differences in their opinions about democracy. Although he came from humble beginnings, Hamilton had little faith in the common person. He once said that "the people are turbulent [disorderly] and changing; they seldom judge or determine right." Hamilton wanted a strong central government that balanced power between the "mass of the people" and wealthier citizens by appealing to the greed and self-interest of both. As he explained:

❝ **We must take man as we find him, and if we expect him to serve the public, [we] must interest his passions in doing so. A reliance on pure patriotism has been the source of many of our errors. . . . One great error is that we suppose mankind more honest than they are.** ❞

American Arts

American Architecture and Classical Revival

After the American Revolution, the new nation became increasingly interested in the arts of the classical world of ancient Greece and Rome. Soon Greek, Roman, and classical revival had become national architectural styles.

Thomas Jefferson started this trend in 1785 when he designed Virginia's capitol building, which was inspired by Roman architecture's use of domes, columns, and white stone. Architects designed banks, churches, colleges, and even the new U.S. Capitol Building in a similar style. Architect Benjamin Latrobe [luh-TROHB] explained that the Greek revival was trying to re-create "the glories of the Greece of (ancient Greek leader) Pericles in the woods of America."

When Latrobe took over construction of the Capitol Building in 1803, the exterior had already been completed, so he put his artistic genius to work on the inside. He drew inspiration from classical styles and the young nation itself. Latrobe's imaginative designs included sculptures, carvings, skylights, and columns. In tribute to the young nation's economy, he had some of these columns decorated with elaborate carvings of corn and tobacco plants. Latrobe also made plans for a column decorated with a cotton plant. Latrobe's columns drew great praise from the United States's new leaders.

Understanding the Arts

1. Why did architects in the United States become interested in classical arts in the late 1700s and early 1800s?

2. How does the Bank of Pennsylvania in the image below reflect Roman revival styles?

The Granger Collection, New York

This painting of the Bank of Pennsylvania shows some of the common elements of the classical revival style.

Women work on a farm in the early republic. Jefferson supported an agricultural economy.

Hamilton believed that his practical approach would protect everyone's liberties while keeping the people from having too much power.

Jefferson disagreed strongly with Hamilton on the average citizen's ability. While he admitted that "the people can not be all, and always, well informed," Jefferson firmly defended the right of the people to rule the country:

❝ **It is my principle that the will of the Majority should always prevail [win]. . . . [I am] convinced that on their good sense we may rely with the most security for the preservation of . . . liberty.** ❞

Manufacturing and Agriculture

Hamilton and Jefferson also fought over what direction the country should take as it grew in size and population. Hamilton wanted to promote the growth of manufacturing and commerce so that America would have a more diverse economy. In his "Report on Manufactures" of 1790, Hamilton suggested that the government hand out prizes to American companies "to reward some particular excellence or superiority" in their products. In addition, he wanted to establish a **protective tariff**, a duty, or tax, on imported goods to raise the prices of foreign products in order to protect domestic products. Hamilton hoped that this price increase on foreign goods would make U.S. goods a better bargain for American consumers.

Jefferson, on the other hand, worried about depending too much on a business and manufacturing economy. He wrote, "Our governments will remain virtuous [pure] for many centuries; as long as they are chiefly agricultural." Jefferson also believed that farmers made the best citizens. In his opinion, farmers—who did not depend too much on other people's work to make a living—were self-reliant enough to be independent voters. Over time Hamilton's and Jefferson's ideas each attracted a large following.

⭐ The Debate over the Bank

Hamilton's and Jefferson's differences came to the public's attention in early 1791. Hamilton's proposal for a national bank brought out the two leaders' different views of the federal government's powers under the Constitution.

The Bank Controversy

Hamilton hoped that establishing a national bank would provide a safe place to deposit government funds and would serve as a reliable source of loans for the government and businesses. Hamilton also proposed that the United States create a national mint and begin issuing its own money. To limit the national bank's power, Hamilton recommended a 20-year charter, at the end of which Congress could vote whether to keep or close the bank. He also encouraged the individual states to charter their own banks to prevent the national bank from having a monopoly.

Despite Hamilton's recommendations to limit the powers of the national bank, his ideas greatly concerned James Madison and Thomas Jefferson. They both questioned whether the U.S. Constitution gave Congress the power to start a national bank. The argument used by Hamilton and his allies to defend the bank depended on

The U.S. Mint made its first coins in 1792.

After Hamilton won his long struggle to create a national bank, the First Bank of the United States was built in Philadelphia, Pennsylvania.

the clause in Article I, Section 8 of the Constitution. This clause states that Congress has the right "to make all laws . . . necessary and proper" for running the nation.

Strict Versus Loose Construction

Jefferson did not agree with Hamilton's interpretation of the Constitution. In a letter to President Washington, Jefferson wrote, "The Constitution allows only the means which are 'necessary,' not those which are merely 'convenient.'" Jefferson

believed in a **strict construction** of the Constitution—that the federal government could do only what the Constitution specifically said it could do. Jefferson believed that the part of Article I, Section 8, which became known as the elastic clause, was to be used only under limited circumstances.

Hamilton, on the other hand, argued for **loose construction**, meaning that the federal government could take reasonable actions that the Constitution did not specifically forbid it from taking. According to this interpretation, the Constitution, particularly the elastic clause, was intended to be flexible so that the government could react appropriately to change.

In the case of a national bank, President Washington and Congress supported Hamilton's argument because they hoped a bank would provide more security for the national economy. In February 1791, Congress chartered the **Bank of the United States**, Hamilton's planned national bank, for a period of 20 years. The stability provided by the Bank played an important role in improving the U.S. economy.

SECTION 2 REVIEW

Identify and explain the significance of the following:

- Alexander Hamilton
- national debt
- bonds
- speculators
- Thomas Jefferson
- protective tariff
- strict construction
- loose construction
- Bank of the United States

Reading for Content Understanding

1 **Main Idea** How did Alexander Hamilton propose the federal government handle the national and state debts?

2 **Main Idea** Why did Hamilton support a strong central government? Why did Thomas Jefferson disagree with him?

3 **Economic Development** How did Hamilton hope to diversify and strengthen the U.S. economy? Why did Jefferson disagree with Hamilton on this issue?

4 **Writing** *Creating* Write a one-page dialogue that might have occurred between Alexander Hamilton and Thomas Jefferson regarding the bank controversy. Be sure to present both points of view clearly in your dialogue.

5 **Critical Thinking** *Supporting a Point of View* Do you believe in a strict or loose construction when interpreting the U.S. Constitution? Explain your answer.

SECTION 3

Troubles Abroad

Reading Focus

How did Americans respond to the French Revolution?

What was President Washington's foreign policy?

How did the United States settle its differences with Great Britain and Spain?

Key Terms

French Revolution
Neutrality Proclamation
privateers
Jay's Treaty
right of deposit
Pinckney's Treaty

---

*O*N JULY 14, 1789, *the citizens of Paris, France, rose up to challenge their corrupt government by attacking the Bastille, a fortress and prison that held the enemies of the French Crown. Soldiers defending the walls were shocked "to see the people arrive in a crowd, armed with muskets . . . swords . . . and shouting. 'We want the Bastille! Down with the troops.'" After hours of fighting, the crowd captured the fortress. The fall of this mighty symbol of royal power stunned the nation.*

French citizens storm the Bastille.

 The French Revolution

The storming of the Bastille was one of the first acts of the **French Revolution**, a rebellion in which the people of France overthrew the French monarchy and replaced it with a republican government. The principles of the French Revolution, written down in the Declaration of the Rights of Man, were "liberty, equality, and fraternity [brotherhood]." News of the Revolution spread rapidly throughout Europe and across the Atlantic Ocean to the United States. In 1789 Thomas Jefferson, who was still serving as U.S. ambassador to France, witnessed the early days of the Revolution. He wrote that the changes in France were "the first chapter of European liberty."

Many Americans supported the French Revolution because they believed France was establishing a republic based on the ideals of the Enlightenment—just as the United States had done. Americans celebrated French independence by burning huge bonfires and singing patriotic French songs. Jefferson wrote to a friend, Maria Cosway, that he was fortunate "to see in the course of fourteen years two such revolutions as were never before seen."

Launching the Nation **311**

Global Connections

America and the French Revolution

Many French citizens had sympathized with the Patriots during the Revolutionary War. One French city official told John Adams:

> ❝[I]could not avoid sympathizing with every sincere friend of Liberty . . . to feel for the Sufferers in the Cause of Liberty, because [I] had suffered many Years in that cause myself.❞

Stories of revolutionary heroes such as Benjamin Franklin and the Marquis de Lafayette increased French interest in the Revolutionary War. Translations of Thomas Paine's *Common Sense* and the U.S. Declaration of Independence appeared in Paris, where they were eagerly read by many people.

In 1784 one French journalist wrote:

> ❝They [Europeans] will see here a country [the United States], a government, where the desires of their hearts have been realized, a land which speaks to them in their own language.❞

King Louis XVI addresses the members of the French legislature in 1789.

In 1789, less than a decade after Americans won their independence from Great Britain, the French began their own revolution against their monarchy.

Understanding What You Read

1. Why might the Revolutionary War have inspired the French to revolt against the monarchy?

2. Why might Americans have supported the French Revolution?

Some Americans were not as enthusiastic. They were particularly concerned about the French Revolution's violent riots and the increasing attacks on all forms of traditional authority. Gouverneur Morris, who served as an ambassador to France, wrote to Secretary of State Jefferson that the French people were dangerously out of control. When revolutionaries beheaded King Louis XVI in January 1793, the act shocked many Americans.

The question of whether the United States should support the new French republic became even more complex a few months later, when France declared war on Great Britain. Spain and the Netherlands soon joined Britain against France. The United States and France had signed a treaty in 1778 that made them allies. Some Americans wanted the United States to honor this treaty and join the French against the British. Other Americans were pro-British or opposed

involvement in a European war. While France did not ask the United States to declare war on Britain, the French did request the continued sale of food for French armies, use of American seaports for French warships, and help in raising an army to drive the Spanish out of Louisiana.

 ## The Neutrality Proclamation

The debate over U.S. foreign policy soon divided both Congress and President Washington's cabinet. The national government was split into pro-French and pro-British groups.

Avoiding Entanglements

In the cabinet, Jefferson and Randolph supported the French, while Hamilton and Knox supported the British. Neither side wanted to compromise. After considering these opposing viewpoints, Washington presented his stand on April 22, 1793. Speaking to Congress, Washington declared:

> **The duty and interest of the United States require that they should with sincerity and good faith adopt and pursue a conduct friendly and impartial [unbiased] towards the belligerent [fighting] powers.**

This **Neutrality Proclamation** stated that the United States would remain neutral toward all nations at war in Europe, a plan that the president thought the safest and most reasonable.

Citizen Genet

Newspaper editors and the general public criticized Washington for his neutral position on the war. James Madison even wrote that Washington had no right to issue the proclamation without Congress's approval. Into this awkward situation stepped Edmond Genet (zhuh-ne), France's new minister, or representative, to the United States. Citizen Genet, as the American papers called him, was convinced that the American people wanted to join France's revolutionary wars. After landing in South Carolina, Genet did not head directly to the national capital as diplomats normally did. Instead, he spent weeks traveling across the country recruiting supporters for France. Genet persuaded several American sea captains to command **privateers**—private ships authorized by a nation, in this case France, to attack its enemies. By the time he reached the capital, Genet had become a celebrity.

President Washington warned Genet that recruiting privateers on American soil violated U.S. neutrality. Then Genet threatened to appeal to the people of the United States to overrule Washington, which stunned even the pro-French Jefferson. He described Genet as "hot-headed, all imagination, no judgment," and agreed with the rest of the cabinet that France should remove Genet as minister.

Edmond Genet

Jefferson Resigns

Despite his support for the removal of Citizen Genet, Jefferson was still upset by the U.S. policy toward France. He also felt that Hamilton was influencing the president's opinions about foreign policy issues and thus interfering with Jefferson's role as secretary of state. As the feud between Jefferson and Hamilton worsened, Jefferson decided that he could not continue serving in Washington's cabinet.

In December 1793 Jefferson resigned his position as secretary of state. This decision disappointed Washington, who wrote Jefferson that he had the highest opinion "of [Jefferson's] integrity [honesty] and talents." Although he disagreed with some of Washington's policies, Jefferson also had great respect for the president. Years later, he wrote:

 General Washington was himself sincerely a friend to the republican principles of our Constitution. . . . He repeatedly declared to me that he . . . would lose the last drop of his blood in its support. "

★ Jay's Treaty

In addition to the problem of Genet's disrespect for the Neutrality Proclamation, Washington had to deal with British violations of U.S. neutrality. These violations threatened the peace he was trying to maintain.

British Abuses

In late 1793 the British decided to seize all ships carrying food to the French West Indies in the Caribbean. In the process, the British seized hundreds of neutral American merchant ships, imprisoning many of the crews or leaving them stranded on island shores. In addition, there were widespread rumors that the officers in British forts on the western frontier were encouraging American Indians to fight against the United States. The British had agreed to abandon these frontier forts under the Treaty of Paris, and their slowness to do so made many Americans suspicious. Now it appeared that the British were going to help Indians fight a frontier war against American settlers.

Even Alexander Hamilton recognized that the United States might be on the path to war. Washington and Hamilton still wanted to avoid war, however, so they sent Chief Justice John Jay to London to negotiate a peaceful resolution.

Negotiating a Treaty

Jay had a difficult time in London, partly because the British were unconcerned about U.S. threats of war or a boycott. The British knew that the United States lacked a strong navy and that many American businesses relied on trade with Britain.

At the same time, however, the British did not want to fight another war in America. After months of negotiations, the two sides signed an agreement in November 1794. In **Jay's Treaty** the British agreed to pay damages for U.S. ships that they had seized, to abandon their forts on the western frontier, and to allow small American merchant ships to continue trading certain items in the Caribbean. In exchange, the United States promised to pay the debts it owed to British merchants from before the Revolutionary War.

When the treaty came before Congress for approval, many leaders argued that it did not accomplish much. Critics pointed out that the treaty did not address Britain's continued capture of large U.S. ships, its support of American Indians on the frontier, or its refusal to return slaves whom the British had freed during the Revolutionary War. Although Washington disliked the treaty, he felt that it was the best that the United States could do under the circumstances. At Washington's urging, Congress passed the treaty.

★ Pinckney's Treaty

American settlers faced additional problems along the frontier with Spanish Florida and Louisiana. The Spanish disputed the border between the

Critics of Jay's Treaty burned figures representing diplomat John Jay.

United States and Florida, and in 1784 Spain had closed the port of New Orleans to all U.S. trade. All goods traveling down the Mississippi River to destinations in the East or overseas had to pass through New Orleans, which lay at the mouth of the river. Without access to New Orleans, settlers on the western frontier were cut off from their most important link with the outside world.

Washington sent U.S. ambassador Thomas Pinckney to Spain to ask the Spanish to reopen New Orleans to U.S. trade. Washington also told Pinckney to request **right of deposit** at the port of New Orleans. Right of deposit would allow American boats to transfer their goods at New Orleans without paying fees on their cargo.

At first, Spanish minister Manuel de Godoy (goh-DOY) tried to delay an agreement, hoping that Pinckney would grow desperate and sign a treaty favorable to the Spanish. This tactic backfired, however, for Pinckney was patient. Godoy became concerned that the United States and

The Mississippi River and the port of New Orleans were vital to the livelihood of Americans settling on the western frontier.

Detail from the original, courtesy of the Historic New Orleans Collection

Great Britain might join together against Spain after they signed Jay's Treaty. In **Pinckney's Treaty**, signed in October 1795, Spain agreed to change the Florida border, to reopen the port at New Orleans to U.S. shipping, and to provide right of deposit. Unlike with Jay's Treaty, Washington and most other Americans considered Pinckney's Treaty a great success, for it opened the frontier to further expansion.

SECTION 3 REVIEW

Identify and explain the significance of the following:
- **French Revolution**
- **Neutrality Proclamation**
- **Citizen Genet**
- **privateers**
- **John Jay**
- **Jay's Treaty**
- **right of deposit**
- **Pinckney's Treaty**

Reading for Content Understanding

1 **Main Idea** Why did some Americans support the French Revolution? Why did other Americans oppose it?

2 **Main Idea** What was President Washington's plan for dealing with events in Europe? What difficulties did he face?

3 **Global Relations** What conflicts did the United States have with Great Britain and Spain? How did the United States settle these conflicts?

4 **Writing** *Classifying* Imagine that you are Thomas Jefferson and that you have decided to resign as secretary of state. Write your resignation letter to give to President George Washington, explaining your reasons for leaving office.

5 **Critical Thinking** *Synthesizing Information* If you had been a U.S. citizen in the late 1700s, would you have supported or opposed the French Revolution? Explain your answer.

Challenges at Home

Reading Focus

Why did American Indians in the Northwest Territory go to war with the United States?

What caused the Whiskey Rebellion, and what was the president's response?

What advice did Washington give the United States in his Farewell Address?

Key Terms

Battle of Fallen Timbers
Treaty of Greenville
Whiskey Rebellion

*I*N NOVEMBER 1786 *Mohawk leader Joseph Brant, or Thayendanegea, stood before a great council of Indian tribes from the Ohio Valley "The interests of any one [Indian] nation should be the welfare of all the others," he said. If Indians of all tribes acted with one mind and one voice, Brant continued, they could stop U.S. settlers from taking their land. Action was vital if Indians were to stop being pushed farther west. The councilmembers agreed and voted to form a confederation of tribes. The members promised to stop selling land to settlers and to demand a new treaty from the U.S. government.*

Joseph Brant

 ## Conflict in the Northwest Territory

American Indian leaders such as Joseph Brant tried to prevent U.S. citizens from buying more Indian land or settling in Indian territory. Despite these efforts, American settlers continued to enter the Northwest Territory in large numbers. As a result, Indians were being forced off their lands and into the lands of other Indians farther west. Many Indians in the Northwest Territory therefore faced conflicts with settlers on their lands or with Indian tribes to the west.

Little Turtle

After the U.S. government rejected their treaty offers in 1788, Indian leaders in the Northwest told American officials, "You have extinguished the council fire." This meant the end of treaty talks, and fighting soon swept through the Northwest Territory. British traders supplied Indians with guns and ammunition. In 1790 a force from the Indian confederation under the leadership of Miami Indian chief Little Turtle soundly defeated U.S. forces. The next year Arthur St. Clair, the governor of the Northwest Territory, led more than 2,000 troops against the Miami.

At dawn on November 4, 1791, Little Turtle's warriors attacked St. Clair's army. A soldier described the fighting:

“It seems like a wild, horrid dream in which whites and [Indians] . . . were all mixed together in a mad confusion . . . melting away in smoke, fire, and blood amid groans, shouts, yells, shrieks—the flashing of steel and crackling of firearms.”

Little Turtle's forces won the battle, killing more than 600 soldiers and sending St. Clair's troops fleeing. When he received the news, President Washington was outraged. He accused St. Clair of allowing the army "to be cut to pieces . . . by surprise, the very thing that I guarded [warned] him against."

The Battle of Fallen Timbers

Washington replaced St. Clair with General Anthony Wayne, known to his troops as "Mad Anthony." Wayne had been a successful officer during the Revolutionary War, and the president trusted him to improve the discipline of the army. When Wayne led his trained soldiers against the Indian confederation in 1794, Little Turtle asked his British allies for support. After the British refused his request, he warned other Indian leaders against fighting the U.S. Army: "The trail has been long and bloody; it has no end. The [whites] . . . are many. They are like the leaves of the trees."

When other Indian leaders ignored Little Turtle's caution, he decided not to remain in command. The confederation forces fought Wayne's troops in the **Battle of Fallen Timbers** on August 20, 1794.

Wayne's forces defeated their Indian opponents and then burned the Indians' villages and fields. After these losses, Indian confederation leaders realized that they could not defeat Wayne's new army or his aggressive tactics. In August 1795 the Indian leaders signed the **Treaty of Greenville**. This gave the United States access to some Indian lands in the Northwest Territory and guaranteed safe travel for U.S. citizens crossing Indian lands in that region.

★ The Whiskey Rebellion

The United States faced further problems on the frontier when Congress passed a tax on U.S.-made whiskey and other alcohol in March 1791. Alexander Hamilton had proposed the tax as a

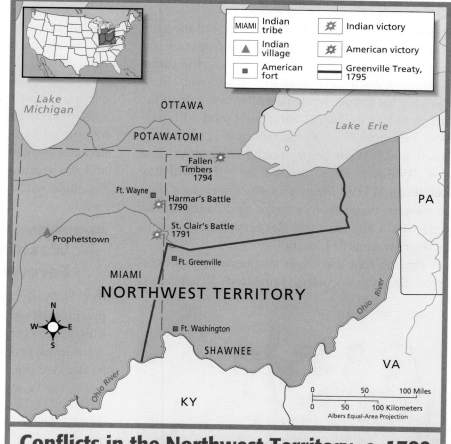

Conflicts in the Northwest Territory, c. 1790

Learning from Maps Many American Indian groups formed alliances to prevent the loss of their lands but were unable to stop the flood of settlers to the region.

Location What geographic feature served as the southern boundary for most of the Northwest Territory?

George Washington

George Washington entered the presidency with a tremendous sense of responsibility to the country. He wanted to be both a proper, dignified leader and a president who listened to the needs of the people. Washington was sometimes trapped between the importance of his office and his wish to be treated like an ordinary citizen. At his inauguration, for example, Washington told the officer of his military guard, "The affection of my fellow citizens is all the guard I want." However, he decided that the escort was necessary to maintain the dignity of the presidency.

While his desire to live up to the people's expectations helped make Washington an excellent first president, the pressure of those expectations often made life difficult for him. Washington was very sensitive to attacks made against him in the press, leading Thomas Jefferson to write, "I think he feels those things [criticisms] more than any person I ever met." Washington retired in 1797, but had little time to enjoy it, because he died in 1799.

way to help pay off the national debt, but the government had trouble collecting taxes from farmers who made small amounts of whiskey for trade. These farmers argued that they could not afford the tax. One farmer wrote that after being fined for failing to pay the tax, "I felt myself mad with passion. I thought $250 would ruin me. . . . I felt my blood boil." What began as the complaints of a few "Whiskey Boys" turned into the **Whiskey Rebellion** in 1794. Many protesters in regions such as western Pennsylvania tarred and feathered tax collectors. Other farmers declared themselves to be the new Sons of Liberty.

Fearing that the rebels threatened the federal government's security, President Washington declared that he could "no longer remain a passive [inactive] spectator of the contempt [disrespect] with which . . . [the laws] are treated." He ordered several states to call out their militia, assembling an army of more than 10,000 soldiers. In November 1794 Washington and Hamilton led this army toward western Pennsylvania. Most of the rebels fled into the countryside as the troops approached, and the army of Washington ended the Whiskey Rebellion without a battle.

 ## Washington's Farewell Address

In 1796 Washington faced the prospect of another presidential election. Although no rule prevented him from serving again and a majority of Americans probably would have voted for him, he decided not to run for a third term.

Stepping Down

The years of dealing with crises at home and overseas had begun to weaken Washington's health. He wrote to a friend that "no man was ever more tired of public life, or more devoutly [strongly] wished for retirement than I do." Washington also believed that by stepping down he would remind Americans

Pennsylvania opponents of the Whiskey Tax tar and feather a tax collector.

The Granger Collection, New York

Washington's Farewell Address

1796

On September 19, 1796, President George Washington's Farewell Address first appeared in a Philadelphia newspaper. Washington was 64 when he wrote the address and had served his country well. He advised the nation on its economy, political parties, and foreign policy.

In contemplating [considering] the causes which may disturb our Union, it occurs as matter of serious concern that any ground should have been furnished for characterizing parties by geographical discriminations: Northern and Southern, Atlantic and Western; whence designing men may endeavor [try] to excite a belief that there is a real difference of local interests and views....

I have already intimated [told] to you the danger of parties in the state, with particular reference to the founding of them on geographical discriminations. Let me now take a more comprehensive [complete] view and warn you in the most solemn manner against the baneful [destructive] effects of the spirit of party generally....

It is important, likewise, that the habits of thinking in a free country should inspire caution in those entrusted with its administration to confine themselves within their . . . constitutional spheres, avoiding in the exercise of the powers of one department to encroach [trespass] upon another.... If, in the opinion of the people, the distribution or modification of the constitutional powers be in any particular wrong, let it be corrected by an amendment....

Of all the dispositions and habits which lead to political prosperity, religion and morality are indispensable [necessary] supports....

Promote, then, as an object of primary importance, institutions for the general diffusion [spreading] of knowledge.... As the structure of a government gives force to public

George Washington

opinion, it is essential that public opinion should be enlightened.

As a very important source of strength and security, cherish public credit. One method of preserving it is to use it as sparingly as possible, . . . avoiding likewise the accumulation of debt, . . . not ungenerously throwing upon posterity [future generations] the burden which we ourselves ought to bear....

Observe good faith and justice toward all nations. Cultivate [seek] peace and harmony with all....

The great rule of conduct for us, in regard to foreign nations, is in extending our commercial relations to have with them as little political connection as possible. So far as we have already formed engagements, let them be fulfilled with perfect good faith. Here let us stop....

It is our true policy to steer clear of permanent alliances with any portion of the foreign world. . . . There can be no greater error than to expect, or calculate [plan], upon real favors from nation to nation. It is an illusion which experience must cure, which a just pride must discard.

Understanding Primary Sources

1. What was President Washington's most important advice?

2. Do you think Washington's advice is still important today? Explain your answer.

that he was their president, not their king, and that the people were the true leaders of the nation.

Advice to the Nation

With the help of Alexander Hamilton and James Madison, Washington wrote his Farewell Address, which was published in several newspapers. Washington described the address as "the disinterested [unbiased] warnings of a parting friend." In the address he spoke about what he believed were the greatest threats to the American republic: public debt, dangerous foreign alliances, and political divisions at home. Washington recommended that the government seldom borrow money and avoid "the accumulation of debt." This, said Washington, would prevent the nation from "throwing upon posterity [future generations] the burden which we ourselves ought to bear."

Washington also warned the nation against developing permanent alliances with other countries because choosing sides could draw the United States into war. Instead, he recommended that the United States

" **observe good faith and justice toward all nations. Cultivate [encourage] peace and**

Many Americans saw George Washington as a champion of liberty, represented as a woman in this painting.

harmony with all. . . . The nation which indulges [allows] toward another an habitual [regular] hatred or an habitual fondness is in some degree a slave."

Washington hoped that by following this advice, the United States could avoid many of the diplomatic problems it had faced during his presidency. It could then remain independent of foreign influences while growing into a powerful nation.

Washington was also concerned about disagreements between political groups within the United States. His experiences with the feud between Hamilton and Jefferson and the unrest in Pennsylvania had convinced Washington that political unity was important for national success. Disputes between political groups, he wrote, "enfeeble [weaken] the public administration. It agitates [upsets] the community with ill-founded jealousies and false alarms." Washington ended his presidency by advising the nation to resolve its internal differences and protect its independence from the rest of the world.

SECTION 4 REVIEW

Identify and explain the significance of the following:

- **Little Turtle**
- **Anthony Wayne**
- **Battle of Fallen Timbers**
- **Treaty of Greenville**
- **Whiskey Rebellion**

Reading for Content Understanding

1 **Main Idea** What events led to the Whiskey Rebellion? How did George Washington respond to it?

2 **Main Idea** What arguments for unity and for neutrality did President Washington make in his Farewell Address?

3 **Cultural Diversity** Why did the United States and the Indian confederation under Chief Little Turtle go to war? What was the outcome of this war?

4 **Writing** *Persuading* What do you think was Washington's greatest achievement as president of the United States? Explain your answer in a paragraph.

5 **Critical Thinking** *Drawing Conclusions* Why do you think Washington chose to personally lead the army that put down the Whiskey Rebellion? What was he afraid might happen as a result of the Whiskey Rebellion?

John Adams's Presidency

Reading Focus

What role did political parties play in the presidential election of 1796?

What foreign-policy problems did John Adams face during his presidency?

What were the main issues in the election of 1800, and what were some of its outcomes?

Key Terms

political parties
Federalist Party
Democratic-Republican Party
XYZ affair
Alien and Sedition Acts
Virginia and Kentucky Resolutions
Twelfth Amendment

W*HEN TWO-TIME VICE PRESIDENT John Adams learned that President Washington was retiring, he asked his wife, Abigail, for advice on his political career. She replied, "I would be second unto no Man but Washington," and suggested that he either run for president or retire from politics. John Adams chose to campaign for the presidency, knowing he was not very popular in the South or the West. The couple had decided that the people would support his campaign "as soon as they have had time to . . . consider and reflect [think about]" his years of loyal service to the nation.*

John Adams campaign button

⭐ The Election of 1796

The election of 1796 began a new era in U.S. politics. For the first time, a presidential campaign included more than one candidate.

The Role of Political Parties

Another new aspect of this election was the important role played by **political parties**, groups that

organize to help elect government officials and to influence government policies. Political parties had begun to form during Washington's presidency, as people became divided over issues such as Alexander Hamilton's economic programs, the French Revolution, and the Whiskey Rebellion. In his Farewell Address, Washington advised against supporting the "continual mischiefs of the spirit of party." Despite his warnings, two parties dominated the 1796 election.

The **Federalist Party**, which was most popular in New England, wanted to strengthen the federal government and to promote industry and trade. One of the Federalist Party's most important members was Alexander Hamilton, who shaped party policy. However, instead of nominating Hamilton for president, the Federalists chose former vice president John Adams and Thomas Pinckney from South Carolina.

The **Democratic-Republican Party**, or the Republicans for short, was started by such leaders as Thomas Jefferson and James Madison, who wanted to preserve the power of the state governments. (It is not related to the modern Republican Party.) It was most popular in the South and along the western frontier. Other states, such as New York, tended to be divided in their support for the two political parties. The Republicans chose Thomas Jefferson and New Yorker Aaron Burr as their candidates.

An Election Plot

Both sides in the 1796 campaign criticized each other harshly. Madison called the Federalists the British Party, and Republican campaign posters asked "whether the Republican Jefferson, or the Royalist Adams, shall be President of the United States." The Federalists responded that the Republicans were influenced by the French.

Some Americans were afraid that the competition between the Federalists and Republicans would tear apart the foundation of the U.S. government.

One critical Federalist wrote that Jefferson was "fit to be a professor in a College, President of a Philosophical Society, or even Secretary of State, but certainly not" president. Abigail Adams wrote to her son about the style of the campaign, "I fear America will never go through another Election without Blood Shed. We have had a paper War for six weeks past."

Hamilton, who did not like Adams, complicated matters by trying to sabotage Adams's campaign and get Pinckney elected instead. The plan failed, and Adams narrowly defeated Jefferson, receiving 71 electoral votes to Jefferson's 68 votes. Under the rules of the Constitution at that time, the second-place finisher in a presidential election became vice president even if that person was not of the same political party as the president. So after months of running against each other, Adams and Jefferson were elected to office together.

★ President Adams

At first glance, John Adams did not appear well suited to the presidency. He wrote that "by my Physical Constitution I am but an ordinary Man." He also lacked Washington's dignity or Jefferson's charm. Adams was uncomfortable around strangers and struck most people as cold and distant. "There are very few People in this World, with whom I can bear to converse [talk]," he confessed. In spite of his limited social skills, Adams had many people's respect, including opponents such as Jefferson. They recognized Adams's intelligence, trusted him, and admired his tremendous work ethic, which led him to rise on most days at 4 A.M. and work until after 10 P.M.

Adams had a long political career before being elected president. He was a leading Patriot during the Revolution, and at its beginning he sat on many committees and ran the war department. Adams later served as a diplomat in France, Britain, and the Netherlands before returning to the United States to serve as vice president from 1789 to 1796.

Adams was eager to become president but was nervous about the difficulties involved in the job. At the presidential inauguration he looked nervously at a relaxed George Washington. Adams thought that Washington's expression seemed to say "I am fairly out and you fairly in! See which of us will be happiest." Adams made his own situation more difficult by allowing the members of Washington's cabinet to remain in office. Adams had intended to be unbiased by rewarding their experience, but these officials were more loyal to Adams's rival, Hamilton, than to the new president.

The XYZ Affair

One of Adams's first goals as president was to improve the relationship between the United States and France. The French had been using privateers to attack American ships. Adams sent a diplomatic team to Paris to repair the damage caused by Jay's Treaty and the Citizen Genet affair.

A Secret Offer

After arriving in France, the three U.S. diplomats—Thomas Pinckney, John Marshall, and Elbridge Gerry—discovered that French foreign minister Charles Talleyrand would not speak with them. Instead, they were visited in secret by French agents, who said that Talleyrand would discuss a treaty only in exchange for a $250,000 bribe and a loan of $12 million to the French government. Shocked, the diplomats refused to meet his demand and told President Adams in March 1798 that their mission had failed.

Adams was angry at the French insult, but he hesitated to reveal the full details of the incident to Congress. When he finally gave Congress papers describing the French terms, he substituted the letters X, Y, and Z for the names of the French agents. Upon hearing the news, Federalists in Congress called for war with France.

Soon the story of the **XYZ affair**, as the bribe offer was called, spread across the country. "Millions for defense, but not one cent for tribute!" became the rallying cry of the American people. Fearing war, Adams urged Congress to strengthen the navy by approving the creation of a small fleet.

This cartoon of the XYZ affair shows France as a monster attempting to bribe honest American diplomats.

The Granger Collection, New York

He also supported maintaining a peacetime army of several thousand troops. Congress approved both measures.

Adams Pursues Peace

Despite his efforts to improve the U.S. military, Adams did not ask Congress to declare war on France. He believed that many people in the United States and France were opposed to war. He was also concerned about the expense of a war. So while American and French ships fought each other in an undeclared naval war, Adams tried to reopen peace talks with France.

Other Federalists were stunned by Adams's decision to pursue peace. "The federal party were thunderstruck," wrote a British minister staying in the American capital. Many Federalists insulted their own president in speeches or essays, and Hamilton worked hard to undermine Adams's authority. Adams refused to change his mind, and in 1800 the United States and France signed a treaty that restored the peace and ended the undeclared war on the seas. Adams then forced two members of his cabinet to resign for trying to block his peace efforts and for carrying on a secret correspondence with Hamilton.

President John Adams increased the size of the U.S. military, including the navy. In 1800, workers began building new warships such as the Philadelphia.

⭐ The Alien and Sedition Acts

Although Adams faced attacks from fellow Federalists during his administration, the harshest attacks came from the Republicans. Their complaints grew loudest when Adams strengthened the military following the XYZ affair.

Silencing Critics

Republicans such as Jefferson and Madison strongly criticized Federalist support for war with France. Many Federalists saw this criticism not as a difference of opinion but as disloyalty to the U.S. government. Claiming that the nation needed protecting from treasonous ideas and actions, the Federalist-controlled Congress passed the **Alien and Sedition Acts** in the summer of 1798. The Alien Act allowed the president to expel foreign citizens from the United States if he concluded that they were involved "in any treasonable or secret machinations [plots] against the government." The Sedition Act stated that U.S. citizens could not participate in any plots "to oppose any measure or measures of the government of the United States." The act also made it illegal to "write, print, utter or publish" any false or hostile words against the government or its policies.

The Federalists used these laws against the largest and the most important Republican newspapers, in some cases arresting their editors. Federalists also arrested Republican representative Matthew Lyon for speaking out against the government. These actions frightened many Republicans into remaining silent and encouraged French citizens living in the United States to leave.

The Republican Response

Jefferson and Madison decided to strike back at the Federalists by writing the **Virginia and Kentucky Resolutions**, passed in 1798 and 1799. Madison wrote the Virginia Resolutions, while Jefferson drafted the Kentucky Resolutions. Madison and Jefferson argued that the Alien and Sedition Acts were unconstitutional because they went beyond the powers granted to the federal government and interfered with the powers of the state governments. Jefferson wrote:

❝ **Whensoever the general government assumes undelegated [unassigned] powers, its acts are unauthoritative [without authority], void, and of no force.** ❞

In 1798 Federalist congressman Roger Griswald attacked Republican Matthew Lyon during a heated debate over the Alien and Sedition Acts.

The USS *Constitution*

To protect American merchant ships from pirates and foreign vessels, in 1797 Congress decided to create a navy. Congress authorized the money to begin constructing a small fleet of new warships. The USS *Constitution* became the most famous ship of this first fleet.

The navy built frigates—medium-sized ships—because the United States could not afford to build large warships. Typical frigates were not very powerful, but American ship designer Joshua Humphreys wanted to make the new U.S. warships faster and stronger than ordinary frigates. He insisted that only the best materials and the greatest care go into their construction.

The *Constitution* had thick wooden planking and a heavily reinforced frame. Skilled carpenters measured, cut, and fit each piece individually. Paul Revere supplied copper plating and fasteners that protected the ship's bottom from wood rot. The *Constitution* carried more cannons than most ships its size. Despite its rugged construction, it was a fast ship.

Shortly after its completion, the *Constitution* played an important role in defeating pirates. Later it achieved fame in two one-on-one duels with British frigates. In one of these victories, sailors claimed to see British cannonballs bounce off the *Constitution*'s thick hull. This led to the ship's popular nickname, "Old Ironsides." The British soon ordered their captains to avoid any more duels with the U.S. "superfrigate."

When the *Constitution* became too old for active duty, the U.S. Navy preserved it for future generations. After 200 years it remains the world's oldest commissioned warship afloat. Tourists now visit Old Ironsides to touch a part of history.

Understanding What You Read

1. Why was the USS *Constitution* built?
2. What made the *Constitution* different from other ships its size?
3. Why do you think Old Ironsides is still a popular tourist attraction today?

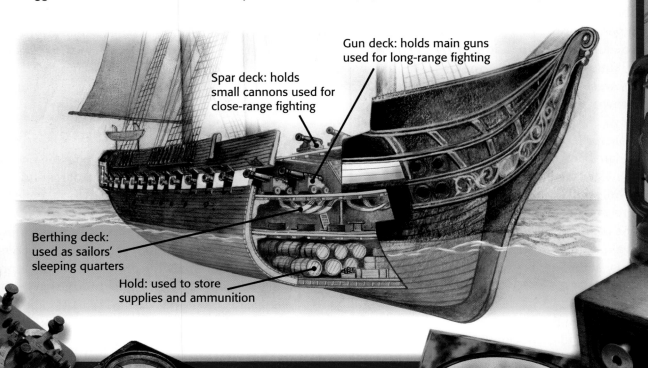

Gun deck: holds main guns used for long-range fighting

Spar deck: holds small cannons used for close-range fighting

Berthing deck: used as sailors' sleeping quarters

Hold: used to store supplies and ammunition

According to this argument, state governments could ignore any federal laws that they found to be unconstitutional. To avoid such a constitutional conflict, the resolutions asked Congress to repeal the Alien and Sedition Acts. Although the Kentucky and Virginia legislatures both approved the resolutions, Congress refused the request for action. The Alien and Sedition Acts remained in effect until a later Congress refused to renew them. The most important impact of the resolutions was their support of the right of the state governments to challenge the federal government. This encouraged future politicians who argued that state governments could declare laws or actions of the federal government to be illegal.

Thomas Jefferson, one of the best-educated American political leaders, wanted to see more schools like this one across the country.

 ## The Election of 1800

Despite the problems his administration had faced, Adams decided to run for re-election. In the presidential election of 1800, Thomas Jefferson and Aaron Burr ran against Adams and Charles Pinckney. During the campaign the Republicans attacked many of the Federalist policies carried out under President Adams. The Republicans challenged the legality of the Alien and Sedition Acts, calling them a biased attack on freedom of the press. They also criticized Adams's creation of a permanent army and the increased taxes needed to support it. In addition, Republicans complained that under Adams the relationship between France and the United States had only grown worse. The nation's leading Republican newspaper declared, "The friends of peace will vote for Jefferson—the friends of war will vote for Adams or for Pinckney."

The Federalists responded as they had done in 1796, accusing Jefferson of being a dangerous pro-French revolutionary whose election would ruin the country. They also claimed that Jefferson, who was deeply interested in science and philosophy, was antireligious. Federalist clergyman William Linn wrote, "The election of any man avowing [holding] the principles of Mr. Jefferson would . . . destroy religion, introduce immorality, and loosen all the bonds of society." Republicans replied that as the author of the Declaration of Independence,

Jefferson could certainly be trusted to protect the liberties of all Americans.

The two presidential candidates played different roles in their individual campaigns. Jefferson was very actively involved, writing letters to his many friends and asking politicians for their support. Adams, however, believed that the people would judge him on his political record and participated very little in his own campaign. Once again Adams faced a challenge from within his own party when Alexander Hamilton made another attempt to sabotage Adams's political career. This time Hamilton published an essay that was highly critical of Adams. Hamilton's actions caused further division among the Federalists and thus damaged the party's chances of winning the election.

A Peaceful Transition

When the final results were in, Jefferson and Burr collected 73 votes each to 65 for Adams and 64 for Pinckney. The Republicans had won the election, but the tie between Jefferson and Burr created a problem under the original system used for presidential elections. There was no way for voters to separate their votes for president and vice president, so technically Jefferson and Burr were both eligible to become president! The matter then went to the House of Representatives to break the tie.

The Federalists in the House refused to vote for Jefferson as president and tried to elect Burr.

The Republicans, meanwhile, voted for Jefferson, resulting in another tie and another vote. This process continued, with the House deadlocking 35 consecutive times. Finally, about half of the Federalists gave up and simply refused to vote for anybody. Hamilton played a part in this decision because he distrusted Burr and thought that Jefferson was the better choice. The Republicans were thus able to elect Jefferson on the 36th vote. The unforeseen problems created by the voting system led Congress in 1803 to propose the **Twelfth Amendment,** which created a separate ballot for president and vice president. The states ratified the amendment in September 1804, in time for the next presidential election.

The loss in the presidential election weakened the Federalists and strengthened the Republicans. Adams, who was deeply wounded by his defeat, retired from public life. Despite the criticisms of his career, he looked back upon his many years of service to his country with a conscience "clear as crystal glass," as he put it. For many years after the election, Adams and Jefferson did not speak to each other. However, their respect for one another finally led them to renew their friendship.

Jefferson saw the transfer of power from one party to another as a kind of peaceful revolution that demonstrated the strengths of the U.S. system

The Granger Collection, New York

A Jefferson campaign banner from the election of 1800

of government. Years later he wrote to a friend about the achievement:

66 **[The election was] as real a revolution in the principles of our government as that of 1776 was in its form; not effected [caused] indeed by the sword, as that [was], but by the rational and peaceable instrument of reform, the suffrage [vote] of the people.** 99

To Jefferson, his victory represented the triumph of the people. In addition, it proved that his faith in the intelligence of the everyday citizen was justified.

SECTION 5 REVIEW

Identify and explain the significance of the following:
- **political parties**
- **Federalist Party**
- **John Adams**
- **Democratic-Republican Party**
- **Charles Talleyrand**
- **XYZ affair**
- **Alien and Sedition Acts**
- **Virginia and Kentucky Resolutions**
- **Twelfth Amendment**

Reading for Content Understanding

1 **Main Idea** Explain how the events of the 1796 election led to John Adams's becoming president.

2 **Main Idea** How did the growth of political parties and the elections of 1796 and 1800 lead to the passage of the Twelfth Amendment to the Constitution?

3 **Global Relations** Why did President Adams want a treaty with France?

4 **Writing** *Persuading* Write a short editorial in which you argue for or against the Alien and Sedition Acts.

5 **Critical Thinking** *Evaluating* Do you think political parties unite or divide U.S. society today? Explain your answer.

CHAPTER 10 REVIEW

Chapter Summary

Americans chose George Washington as their first president. He organized the executive branch and the federal court system. Alexander Hamilton strengthened the nation's finances as U.S. settlement in the Northwest Territory led to conflicts with American Indians. After Washington left office, political parties developed and played an important role in the elections of John Adams and Thomas Jefferson to the presidency. ■

On a separate sheet of paper, complete the following activities.

Identifying People and Ideas

Describe the historical significance of the following:

1. George Washington
2. electoral college
3. Alexander Hamilton
4. protective tariff
5. Citizen Genet
6. right of deposit
7. Little Turtle
8. Whiskey Rebellion
9. John Adams
10. Virginia and Kentucky Resolutions

Internet Activity go.hrw.com SA0 Cabinet

Search the Internet through the HRW Web site for information about the president's cabinet today, including what departments there are and who heads them. Then compare the number of cabinet positions today with the number in the first cabinet. Write a short paragraph discussing how the current cabinet contrasts with that of Washington's presidency.

Understanding Main Ideas

1. What were the major concerns of citizens during Washington's presidency?
2. How did speculators profit when the government paid its debts?
3. How did Americans greet the news of the French Revolution in 1789?
4. Why was President Washington upset with Citizen Genet?
5. What led to the Battle of Fallen Timbers?
6. How did Americans react to the XYZ affair?

Reviewing Themes

1. **Global Relations** How did President Washington deal with conflicts in Europe?
2. **Constitutional Heritage** Why did Alexander Hamilton and Thomas Jefferson disagree about the national bank?

Using the Time Line

Number your paper from 1 to 6. Match the letters on the time line below with the following events.

1. Britain and the United States sign Jay's Treaty.
2. American Indians sign the Treaty of Greenville, giving the United States access to Indian lands.
3. President George Washington proposes the Neutrality Proclamation.
4. George Washington is elected the first president of the United States.
5. Congress charters the Bank of the United States.
6. The House of Representatives chooses the site of the new national capital.

1785   1790   1795

a   b c   d   e f

3. **Economic Development** How did Alexander Hamilton propose handling states' debts and the national debt?

Thinking Critically

1. **Identifying Cause and Effect** How did the tax on whiskey and other alcohol lead to the Whiskey Rebellion?

2. **Evaluating** Do you think John Adams should have pushed for war with France? Explain your answer.

3. **Making Comparisons** What were the main differences between the Federalist and the Democratic-Republican Parties?

Writing About History

1. **Expressing** Write a note to George Washington, thanking him for his years of service to the United States. You may wish to include Washington's accomplishments in the Revolutionary and French and Indian Wars, as well as his later political life.

2. **Creating** Imagine that you are a campaign adviser for the Federalist or the Democratic-Republican Party during the election of 1800. Create a campaign poster for your party's candidates.

Linking Geography and History

1. **Movement** Why was access to New Orleans important for settlers on the western frontier?

2. **Location** Why do you think the House of Representatives chose the site of present-day Washington, D.C., as the new national capital?

Building Your Portfolio

Complete the following activities individually or in groups.

1. **Battle of Fallen Timbers** Use your textbook or the library to research the Battle of Fallen Timbers. Then prepare interviews with members of the armies–both of the Indian confederation and of the United States. Questions and answers should explain why each side fought, describe the battle itself, and explain the results and consequences of the battle. Present your interviews to the class as if they were being reported by a journalist.

2. **U.S. Diplomats** It is 1800 and you have been asked to establish a school to train new U.S. diplomats, who will soon be traveling overseas. Create a four-page instruction manual giving the new diplomats some idea of what they can expect in their new careers. Use examples from the chapter to describe things the diplomats might watch out for when they are on assignment. You may also wish to illustrate your manual with political cartoons or other images.

The Metropolitan Museum of Art, Gift of Edgar William and Bernice Chrysler Garbisch, 1963. (63.201.2)
Photograph © 1983 The Metropolitan Museum of Art

History Skills
Workshop

Using Visual Resources Study the image at right, which is a painting of President George Washington attempting to put down the Whiskey Rebellion in 1794. Then answer the following questions: (a) How is Washington portrayed in this image? (b) Why do you think President Washington personally led the army to put down the rebellion? (c) Do you think the president should actively fight in domestic conflicts? Explain your answer.

History Skills

WORKSHOP

Reading a Time Line

Time lines provide a visual organization of events in chronological order, or the sequence in which the events occurred. Knowing the chronological order of historical events is essential to understanding their significance. Studying a time line involves seeing relationships between events as well as remembering important dates when events occurred.

Sequence in a Time Line Time lines are meant to be read from left to right. The dates on the left are the oldest. The dates on the right are the most recent. The lines of the time line mark the time period between each event. For example, the lines might mark 10-, 5-, or 1-year periods. Each entry lists an important event and when it took place. The entries connect to the time line so that you can see during which time period the events occurred.

B.C. and A.D. Sometimes a time line will contain the abbreviations B.C. or A.D. The abbreviation B.C. stands for "before Christ." The abbreviation A.D. stands for "anno Domini," meaning "in the year of the Lord." There was no year "0." The year 1 B.C. was followed by A.D. 1. Keep these rules in mind when you read dates marked B.C. or A.D.:

- The abbreviation B.C. appears after the year. For example, 100 B.C.
- The abbreviation A.D. appears before the year. For example, A.D. 100.

How to Read a Time Line

1. **Determine its framework** Note the years covered and the intervals of time into which the time line is divided.
2. **Study the sequence of events** Study the order in which the events appear on the time line, noting the length of time between events.
3. **Supply missing information** Think about the people, places, and other events associated with each item on the time line. This lets you "flesh out" the framework.
4. **Note relationships** Ask how an event relates to earlier or later events. Look for cause-and-effect relationships and long-term developments.

Practicing the Skill

Study the time line below, which lists important events in the history of the United States between 1789 and 1795. Then answer the following questions.

1. Into what periods is the time line divided?
2. Judging from the time line, how much time passed between Washington's election and his presentation of the Neutrality Proclamation?
3. What happened in November 1794?
4. Using the information you have just read about time lines, create your own time line of several significant events in U.S. history. Your time line should cover at least five years.

1789   **1791**   **1793**   **179**

JULY The French Revolution begins.

APR. George Washington is elected president.

FEB. Congress charters the Bank of the United States.

JULY The site for the new national capital is chosen and named Washington.

APR. President Washington presents the Neutrality Proclamation to Congress.

NOV. Great Britain and the United States sign Jay's Treaty.

History in Action

American History

Constitutional Mobile

Complete the following activity in small cooperative groups.

Your task is to research factors that our country's founders had to consider while developing the U.S. Constitution. Remember that delegates to the Constitutional Convention had to weigh and balance numerous factors, such as the economy, slavery, individual rights, and centralized government. You will discuss and compare these factors and then create mobiles that represent the relative weight and balance of each factor. When you have finished, you will write a paragraph explaining the importance of one of the mobile's items.

Materials To complete this activity, you will need wooden dowels or semistiff wire as well as posterboard and construction paper. You will also need art supplies, such as paper, twine, glue, ink, paints, or cloth.

Parts of the Project To create your mobile complete the following steps:

1. **Overview** You and the members of your group will be researching, gathering, and creating items for a Constitutional Mobile. Each group member will be responsible for one arm of the mobile, and each arm must include at least five items. Use quotes, letters, news articles, song lyrics, maps, charts, constitutional excerpts, images or illustrations, and items you create yourself to construct your part of the mobile.

2. **Jobs** Here are the different jobs that each group member will need to perform in order to make your project a success:

   - **Researchers:** All members of the group will be responsible for gathering information for your mobiles. Each group member should research at least one topic for the mobile.
   - **Artists:** Each group member will be responsible for designing and constructing one arm of the mobile.
   - **Writers:** Each group member will be responsible for writing a paragraph explaining the importance of his or her arm of the mobile. Paragraphs should be typed or written on posterboard or a transparency.

3. **Evaluation** Once you have completed your research, meet as a group to discuss the importance of each researched topic at the Constitutional Convention. Then decide how to balance each arm of the mobile. The arms of the mobile should be sized and weighted according to their importance in the overall mobile.

When the mobile is complete, create a time line showing the sequence of events leading to the ratification of the U.S. Constitution. Use your textbook or the library to find events to place on your time line.

Student council members learn how to govern.

UNIT 5 Building a Strong Nation
(1800–1840)

CHAPTER 11 **The Expanding Nation** (1800–1815)

CHAPTER 12 **A New National Identity** (1812–1840)

Young People

IN HISTORY

Young Explorers

At age 18, George Shannon was the youngest person chosen to join Meriwether Lewis and William Clark on their 1804 expedition to the western lands of the Louisiana Purchase. Shannon joined Lewis and Clark and several other explorers in the Corps of Discovery, a group described by Lewis as the "best young woodsmen & Hunters in . . . the Countrey." Shannon excelled at his duties early on and was put in charge of part of the expedition.

Young members of the Lewis and Clark expedition relax along the trail.

In late August 1804 Shannon failed to return after a day of hunting in Sioux Indian territory. Lewis and Clark sent a search party for Shannon, but the young explorer was far ahead of the rest of the corps. Shannon, however, believed that he had lagged behind the group, so he continued traveling west as fast as he could. Over time, he used all his bullets and was unable to hunt for food, surviving for a few weeks on plums and grapes. Too weak to keep moving, Shannon sat down on a riverbank in hopes that a trading boat would come by and find him. Instead, his friends rescued him! On September 11, the expedition rounded a bend in the Missouri River and found an exhausted and hungry Shannon.

Shannon was one of the many young adventurers who set their sights west in the 1800s. William Swift and Titian Peale were two 19-year-olds who accompanied Stephen Long in 1819 on his expedition along the Missouri River and into the western plains. Swift was hired to prepare a map of the territory, while Peale went along as an assistant naturalist.

Other teenagers explored the west as fur trappers. When he was about 18, Jim Bridger traveled to the upper Missouri River on a trapping expedition. Two years later, Bridger discovered what looked like a great shallow bay. Tasting the water, he found it salty and declared he had come across an arm of the Pacific Ocean. Soon, however, several other trappers realized that Bridger had seen the Great Salt Lake.

In this unit you will learn more about the many brave people who explored the American West. You will also learn about the political challenges, including another war with Britain, that faced the new nation.

LEFT PAGE: *The Rocky Mountains were among the most beautiful sites in the American frontier.*

The Granger Collection, New York

▪ CHAPTER 11 ▪
The Expanding Nation
(1800–1815)

As the 1800s began the United States was a young country with seemingly limitless opportunities for the future. In his first inaugural address, President Thomas Jefferson described the United States as "a rising nation, spread over a wide and fruitful land, traversing [crossing] all the seas with the rich productions of their industry."

THEMES

Constitutional Heritage
Why might a federal court be given great power?

Geographic Diversity
Why might a nation explore the land outside its boundaries?

Global Relations
What problems might arise along a border between nations?

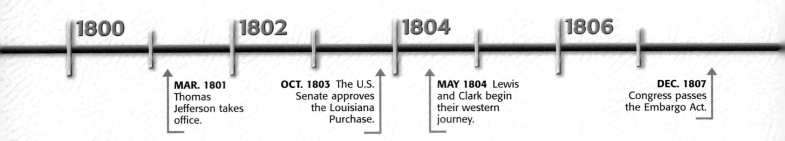

1800

1802

1804

1806

MAR. 1801 Thomas Jefferson takes office.

OCT. 1803 The U.S. Senate approves the Louisiana Purchase.

MAY 1804 Lewis and Clark begin their western journey.

DEC. 1807 Congress passes the Embargo Act.

Jefferson As President

Reading Focus

What issues did Thomas Jefferson discuss in his first inaugural address?

What changes did Jefferson make to the Federalist style of government, and which Federalist ideas did he keep?

Why was *Marbury* v. *Madison* an important court case?

Key Terms

Marbury v. *Madison*
judicial review

Collection of the American
Numismatic Society

HE DAY WAS MARCH 4, 1801, *and Thomas Jefferson was about to be sworn in as president of the United States. While Washington and Adams had worn splendid uniforms and ridden in carriages to their inaugurations, Jefferson chose to walk the few blocks from his boardinghouse to the Capitol Building. A reporter observed, "His dress was, as usual, that of a plain citizen, without any distinctive badge of office." Known by some Republicans as "The People's Friend," Jefferson demonstrated his democratic views on government by not wearing fancy clothes to the inauguration.*

U.S. coins celebrating Jefferson's inauguration

IMAGE ON LEFT PAGE: *Army captain and explorer Zebulon Pike leads an expedition west in 1806.*

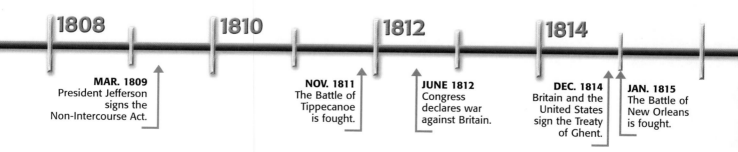

1808

1810

1812

1814

MAR. 1809
President Jefferson signs the Non-Intercourse Act.

NOV. 1811
The Battle of Tippecanoe is fought.

JUNE 1812
Congress declares war against Britain.

DEC. 1814
Britain and the United States sign the Treaty of Ghent.

JAN. 1815
The Battle of New Orleans is fought.

The Republican Victory

Thomas Jefferson's inauguration drew a large crowd. Margaret Bayard Smith, who attended the inauguration, called it "one of the most interesting scenes a free people can ever witness." Those attending the inauguration were celebrating more than just Jefferson's success in the presidential election. Along with his victory, the Republican Party had won control of both houses of Congress from the Federalist Party. This assured Jefferson that he could rely on congressional support for many of his plans.

The victory of Jefferson and his fellow Republicans over the Federalists also represented the first time that one political party had replaced another in power in the United States. Many Americans saw this event as proof that the leadership of the United States could change hands peacefully, a rare accomplishment for many governments during that time. The exchange of power was not entirely smooth, however. Former president John Adams was so upset by his defeat that he left the city before the inauguration.

After taking the oath of office, Jefferson read his carefully written inaugural address in a quiet voice. He spoke about the United States's potential to become a great nation. Jefferson also presented his interpretation of the basic principles of the American republic and the rights of its citizens. He wanted to make it clear that although he supported the will of the majority, he was not in favor of mob rule, as some Federalists had charged.

66 **Though the will of the majority is in all cases to prevail [win], . . . the minority possess their equal rights, which equal law must protect, and to violate [these rights] would be oppression.** 99

In addition to discussing the goals of his new administration, Jefferson tried to reassure the remaining Federalists in the government that he would not let party conflicts interfere with running the government fairly.

66 **We are all Republicans, we are all Federalists. . . . Let us, then, with courage and confidence pursue our . . . attachment to union and representative government.** 99

After delivering his speech, Jefferson walked back down New Jersey Avenue to his boardinghouse to meet with supporters and friends. Copies of his speech were soon printed for those who attended the inauguration.

The New Capital

Jefferson was the first president to be inaugurated in the new capital city of Washington. Although Congress had selected the site for the city 10 years earlier, when Jefferson took office the streets and buildings were still under construction. This proved very inconvenient. On the way to his inauguration, Jefferson had to walk along a stone footpath next to mud streets filled with potholes, and tree stumps. Some members of the federal government were unhappy with the unfinished status of the Capitol

The first Capitol Building in Washington

Treasury Secretary Albert Gallatin

The Granger Collection, New York

Building and the lack of fancy social functions in the town. Republican Albert Gallatin said bluntly that the city of Washington was "hated by every member of Congress without exception of persons or parties." Others in the city complained that it was "a place with a few bad houses, [and] extensive swamps." During the summers, even President Jefferson refused to stay in the capital because of the heat, humidity, and danger of disease.

From these rough beginnings, Washington eventually grew into a large and impressive city. Over the years, the Capitol Building and the executive mansion were joined by other state buildings and monuments that served as symbols of national pride and confidence. Jefferson, who had long dreamed of a new national capital that would be independent of the interests of any one state, was pleased to be a part of this process of building a federal city.

 ## Jefferson in Office

After moving into the executive mansion on Pennsylvania Avenue, Jefferson faced the task of putting his Republican ideas into practice. He soon found that his duties kept him "from 10 to 12 and 13 hours a day at my writing table."

Setting New Policies

President Jefferson first selected the members of his cabinet, including James Madison as secretary of state and Albert Gallatin as secretary of the treasury. Jefferson and his cabinet changed many of the Federalist policies put in place by John Adams

and Alexander Hamilton. The most significant changes involved military spending and taxes. Jefferson decreased military spending, reducing the size of the army and navy to about 3,200 troops and seven active ships. President Jefferson and Treasury Secretary Gallatin hoped that savings from these budget cuts would allow the government to concentrate on repaying the national debt.

To improve the economy, Jefferson also encouraged Gallatin to devise plans to repeal domestic taxes, such as the tax on whiskey, and to abolish the government agency that collected these taxes. The Republican-led Congress passed the laws needed to carry out these measures.

Jefferson did recognize that some Federalist-supported policies—such as the creation of the Bank of the United States—should be kept. Although Jefferson had battled Hamilton over the Bank's constitutionality, as president he agreed to let the Bank function as it had under the Federalists. Explaining his change of mind, Jefferson noted, "What is practicable [practical] must often control pure theory." Whatever its faults, the banking system created by Hamilton seemed practical.

Political Battles

President Jefferson's administration faced a difficult challenge soon after he was sworn into office. While Jefferson had planned to keep many Federalists in their government positions, a large number of Republicans expected the president to replace all the Federalist officials with Republican politicians. "If this should not be the case, for what . . . have we been contending [struggling]?" asked the New York *American Citizen*, a pro-Republican newspaper. Federalists were equally unhappy with Jefferson. They complained about his reduction of military spending, accusing him of endangering the country just to save money.

Under pressure from both parties, Jefferson agreed to replace a number of Federalist officials with Republicans, but he refused to replace all Federalists. He also stuck to his ideas on government spending. In an effort to preserve cooperation between Congress and the presidency, Jefferson kept the members of Congress informed on his opinions and plans through letters, meetings, and his annual State of the Union messages.

Thomas Jefferson

Thomas Jefferson was a man of many talents. "Nature intended me for the tranquil [peaceful] pursuits of science," he once wrote, and he followed these pursuits all his life. Jefferson often put his interests to practical use, as when he designed Monticello, his magnificent plantation in Virginia. Although he was a wealthy slaveholder and a scholar of a variety of subjects—including science, philosophy, architecture, farming, and art—many people were often surprised by Jefferson's down-to-earth personality.

While he possessed many skills, Jefferson lacked some of the qualities that people of the time expected of their political leaders. He was not a good public speaker, both because he was shy and because he mumbled. Jefferson was also well known for his dislike of social snobbery. He made a point of not seating guests at his dinner parties according to their social status.

Jefferson also made an effort to invite most members of Congress, including Federalists, to at least one of these dinners. There guests enjoyed fine conversation and good food, and might sometimes be treated to the display of some new invention or scientific idea. Even his opponents agreed that President Jefferson was an excellent host.

Marbury v. Madison

President Jefferson was concerned that Federalist judges dominated the federal court system. He hoped to change this situation by appointing Republicans to any judicial positions that were available.

The Midnight Judges

The number of Federalist judges had greatly increased only a few months before Jefferson took office in 1801. Before leaving office, President John Adams had appointed dozens of Federalists to fill vacant judgeships and other court offices that had been newly created by Congress. Jefferson accused Adams of filling these numerous positions "till 9 o'clock of the night, at 12 o'clock of which he was to go out of office." Other Republicans soon referred to the individuals appointed by Adams as the "midnight judges."

Several of these Federalist appointees did not receive their signed commissions before the deadline on March 3, 1801. As president, Jefferson took advantage of this detail by ordering Secretary of State James Madison to withhold the commissions. William Marbury, one of the appointees affected by this decision, demanded that the Supreme Court force the executive branch to hand over his commission. Marbury pointed out that under the Judiciary Act of 1789 the Supreme Court had the authority to issue such an order to the executive branch. The Supreme Court, however, had never done so.

Marshall's Precedent

The Chief Justice of the United States was John Marshall, a Federalist appointed by John Adams. Chief Justice Marshall and President Jefferson disagreed about many political issues. When Marshall agreed to hear Marbury's case, Jefferson protested, saying that the Federalists "have retired into the judiciary as a stronghold." He

This document presents the Supreme Court's decision in Marbury v. Madison.

claimed that through Marshall's efforts, "all the works of republicanism are to be beaten down and erased."

The Supreme Court's decision in **Marbury v. Madison** surprised many people, including Jefferson. All the justices agreed that Marbury had a legal right to his judgeship. However, they also agreed that the Supreme Court could not force Madison to give Marbury the position. According to Chief Justice Marshall, in the Judiciary Act of 1789 Congress had incorrectly given the Supreme Court some powers that were, in fact, unconstitutional. Among these was the power to force the federal government to give Marbury his commission.

Marshall's ruling established the principle of what came to be called **judicial review**. This principle means that the Supreme Court has the right to declare an act of Congress to be unconstitutional and therefore without any legal authority. Marshall defended this right of the Court forcefully in his written decision:

> 66 **It is, emphatically [absolutely], the province and duty of the Judicial Department to say what the law is. . . . The Constitution is superior to any ordinary act of the legislature.** 99

Chief Justice John Marshall greatly increased the power of the judicial branch with his ruling in Marbury v. Madison.

Marshall's decision took away some powers of the Supreme Court. However, by introducing the concept of judicial review, he greatly increased the Court's legal authority. As a result, the Supreme Court gained tremendous power in the national government.

SECTION 1 REVIEW

Identify and explain the significance of the following:
- **Thomas Jefferson**
- **William Marbury**
- **John Marshall**
- **Marbury v. Madison**
- **judicial review**

Reading for Content Understanding

1 **Main Idea** What did Thomas Jefferson speak about in his first inaugural address?

2 **Main Idea** What changes to the Federalist style of government did President Jefferson make? What

Federalist-supported institution did he leave in place?

3 **Constitutional Heritage** How did John Marshall's ruling in *Marbury v. Madison* change the power of the Supreme Court?

4 **Writing** *Describing* Imagine that you are a resident of Washington during Jefferson's first term in office. Write a letter to a friend in another part of the country describing what life is like in the city.

5 **Critical Thinking** *Drawing Conclusions* Why do you think Jefferson wanted such a simple inauguration?

The Louisiana Purchase

Reading Focus

Why was Napoleon unable to re-establish France's North American empire?

Why did President Jefferson want the United States to control New Orleans?

What was the purpose of the Lewis and Clark expedition, and what were the conditions like on the journey?

Key Terms

Louisiana Purchase
Lewis and Clark expedition

AS SPAIN'S POWER *over its American empire declined, Spanish minister Manuel de Godoy struggled to protect his nation's interests. One of his great concerns was how to defend the Spanish territory of Louisiana from the growing number of American settlers. "You can't put doors on open country," he said in despair. Despite years of effort, Godoy failed to strengthen Spain's position. Under a secret treaty he traded Louisiana to France, thereby passing the problem on to someone else. When the Spanish military was told to withdraw, one officer said, "I can hardly wait to leave them [the Americans] behind me."*

The flag of Spain

 ## Napoleon and Louisiana

In 1800 France was under the control of General Napoleon Bonaparte (nuh-POH-lee-uhn BOH-nuh-pahrt), whose ambition and military genius inspired fear throughout Europe. In addition to conquering neighboring countries, Napoleon dreamed of rebuilding France's empire in North America. Napoleon hoped that by occupying Louisiana the French would replace the Spanish as the key European power in western North America.

Standing in the way of Napoleon's plan was a rebellion in the French colony of Saint Domingue (present-day Haiti) on the Caribbean island of Hispaniola. Enslaved Africans had risen and overthrown the local government in the 1790s, gaining their freedom in the process. Former slave Toussaint L'Ouverture (TOO-sahn loo-vuhr-TOOHR) assumed leadership over the island. Slaveholders throughout the Caribbean and the United States, including Thomas Jefferson, were alarmed by this successful slave revolt.

Toussaint L'Ouverture played a key role in the founding of the nation of Haiti.

The Granger Collection, New York

Napoleon wanted to regain control of the island to use as a supply base before occupying Louisiana. In 1802 he sent a French army to recapture Saint Domingue. To Napoleon's surprise, L'Ouverture and his troops successfully fought the French forces. The French managed to capture L'Ouverture, but his followers continued to fight. An outbreak of deadly yellow fever also weakened French forces. The French failed to retake the island, further frustrating Napoleon's plans to send troops to Louisiana.

★ The Mississippi Region

When U.S. leaders learned that France had regained ownership of Louisiana, they began watching Napoleon's actions with suspicion. President Jefferson knew that a French-occupied Louisiana could block the future westward expansion of the United States. Furthermore, the French could interfere with vital U.S. trade along the Mississippi River by controlling the seaport of New Orleans. As Jefferson explained:

 There is on the globe one single spot, the possessor of which is our natural and habitual enemy. It is New Orleans, through which the produce of three-eighths of our territory must pass to market. ⟩⟩

The busy seaport of New Orleans had a rich cultural heritage and was of growing economic importance. Founded by the French in 1718, the city came under Spanish rule in 1762 and remained Spanish until returning to French control some 40 years later. Its busy docks were filled with settlers' farm products brought downriver, manufactured goods headed upriver, and valuable furs gained from trade with American Indians. Many of these cargoes were then sent to Europe. A variety of languages and cultures—including African, American Indian, English, French, and Spanish—contributed to the rich diversity of New Orleans. This diverse community, which had been under the rule of several different nations, soon became the focal point of Jefferson's foreign policy.

★ Purchasing the Territory

Although President Jefferson wanted to keep the French from controlling New Orleans, he did not want to start a war. He hoped that the United States would be able to buy the port city from France and thus solve the problem peacefully.

A Surprising Offer

Jefferson instructed the U.S. ambassador to France, Robert Livingston, to try to purchase New Orleans as well as Florida from the French government. Livingston met with French minister Charles Talleyrand to discuss the offer. James Monroe, sent by Jefferson to help Livingston negotiate, had arrived in Paris by the time Talleyrand replied. Talleyrand began by saying that without New Orleans "the rest [of Louisiana] would be of little value" to France. Then he asked Livingston what the United States would "give for the whole." The stunned Americans realized that the French were offering to sell all of Louisiana to the United States.

Napoleon was willing to sell Louisiana for a number of reasons. About to go to war with Britain, Napoleon did not want to fight the United States and Britain at once. In addition, the French had no troops in Louisiana because they had been busy fighting in Saint Domingue. Instead of North American land that he could not protect,

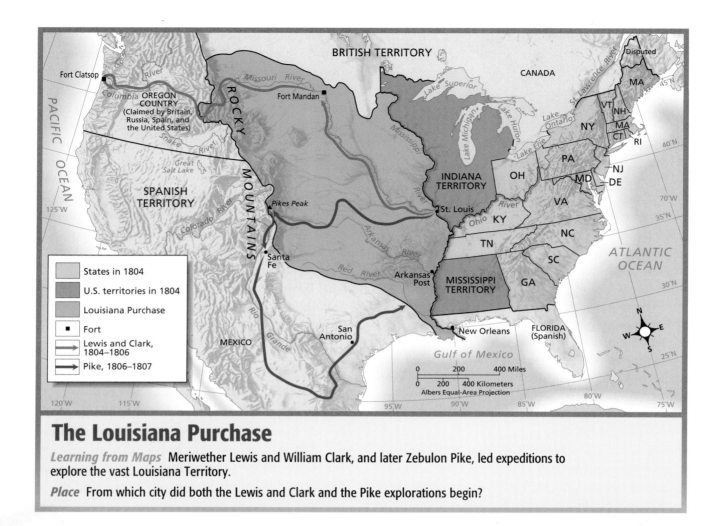

The Louisiana Purchase

Learning from Maps Meriwether Lewis and William Clark, and later Zebulon Pike, led expeditions to explore the vast Louisiana Territory.

Place From which city did both the Lewis and Clark and the Pike explorations begin?

Napoleon now wanted money to buy supplies for his armies in Europe. In addition, Napoleon hoped that by selling Louisiana to the United States, he would create a challenge to Britain's power in North America. He boasted to his friends, "I have given England a rival who, sooner or later, will humble her pride."

The U.S. diplomats were eager to take advantage of this opportunity. Congress had only authorized them to spend $10 million. Nevertheless, they agreed to buy Louisiana from France for $15 million and signed a treaty on May 2, 1803. Livingston wrote, "This business has cost me much pains and anxiety, but I think our country will be essentially served."

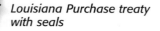

Louisiana Purchase treaty with seals

Expanding the Nation

When President Jefferson learned about France's offer to sell all of Louisiana, he understood the great enthusiasm of Livingston and Monroe. Nonetheless, as a strict constructionist Jefferson did not believe that the Constitution granted the federal government's executive branch, which directed the diplomats, the power to bring territories such as Louisiana into the United States. Livingston and Monroe, however, feared that the French would withdraw their offer and urged the president to act quickly. Jefferson did what he thought was best for the country and supported the deal. On October 20, 1803, the Senate approved the treaty with France and made the **Louisiana Purchase** official.

The Louisiana Purchase doubled the size of the United States. Although the boundaries of the Louisiana Territory were not yet clearly defined, it was a huge region of land stretching west from the

This 1803 painting of New Orleans celebrates the purchase of the city by the United States.

 Mississippi River all the way to the great Rocky Mountains. In 1804 historian David Ramsay wrote that with the exception of the American Revolution and the U.S. Constitution, the Louisiana Purchase provided

> " such important benefits, at so moderate [fair] a price, and under such favorable circumstances . . . [that] the acquisition [gaining] of Louisiana is the greatest political blessing ever conferred on [provided to] these states. "

President Jefferson was pleased that the land offered so much opportunity for agricultural expansion. He said proudly that the Louisiana Purchase expanded "the empire of liberty" and provided "a widespread field for the blessings of freedom."

★ The Lewis and Clark Expedition

Long before the Louisiana Purchase—before he even became president—Jefferson had been trying to send an expedition of explorers west of the Mississippi River. U.S. citizens knew little about western American Indians or the land they occupied. Jefferson wanted to learn more about both the West's people and its land. In addition, he wanted to see if there was a river route that could be taken to the Pacific Ocean.

Preparations

In January 1803 President Jefferson convinced Congress to fund a small western expedition. To lead this mission, he chose former army captain Meriwether Lewis, who had served as his presidential assistant. Jefferson described Lewis as "brave, prudent [careful], habituated [used] to the woods, and familiar with Indian manners and character." Lewis chose Lieutenant William Clark to be the coleader of the expedition. Jefferson told Lewis and Clark to explore the Missouri River and to establish peaceful relations with American Indians they encountered. In addition, the president asked them to study

> " the soil and face of the country, its growth and vegetable productions . . . the animals of the country . . . the mineral productions of every kind . . . [and the] climate. "

These instructions meant that Lewis had to spend weeks studying with experts about botany, surveying, and other subjects that he would need to know to take careful notes on what he saw. He also gathered supplies for the journey. Lewis and Clark carefully selected the members of this Corps of Discovery, filling the group with experienced frontiersmen. One of the group's members, York, is believed to be the first person of African descent to cross the continent. After being delayed by problems with equipment and poor weather, the members of the **Lewis and Clark expedition** set out on their epic journey in May 1804 from a spot near St. Louis, in present-day Missouri.

Crossing the Plains

Lewis and Clark traveled up the Missouri River to the lands of the Mandan and the Sioux. Each time the expedition encountered a new tribe, Lewis told the tribal leaders through interpreters that the United States now owned the land on which the Indians lived. He then handed out a few presents from the expedition's limited supplies. Lewis and Clark tried to appear confident and powerful to

An illustrated page from William Clark's journal

these Indian leaders, but they depended a great deal on the goodwill and help of the Indians they met. Some of the most important help came from Sacagawea (sak-uh-juh-WEE-uh), the wife of a French fur trader who lived in a Mandan camp. Sacagawea, a Shoshoni originally from the Rocky Mountains, offered to help Lewis and Clark as they headed across the Great Plains.

Lewis and Clark kept journals describing the people, places, and animals that they encountered. Their journal entries are filled with wonder at things they saw for the first time. After reaching the Great Plains, Lewis wrote:

> **❝I had a most delightfull view of the country, the whole of which except the vally formed by the Missouri is void of [without] timber or underbrush, exposing to the first glance of the spectator immense herds of Buffaloe, Elk, deer, and Antelopes feeding in one common and boundless pasture.❞**

On other occasions, the journals revealed the many dangers of the journey, including sickness, conflicts with Indians, and natural hazards such as raging rivers, steep mountains, and terrible storms.

To the Pacific and Back

After Lewis and Clark crossed the Plains, they came to the Rocky Mountains. The sight of this tremendous snow-capped mountain range filled Lewis with concern as well as awe, for he realized "the difficulties which this snowy barrier would most probably throw in my way to the Pacific." Fortunately, when Lewis and Clark met the Shoshoni who lived in the area, they learned that the tribe's leader was Sacagawea's brother. The Shoshoni provided horses and a guide to lead the expedition across the mountains. The journey was dangerous and difficult. An exhausted Lewis wrote, "We suffered everything Cold, Hunger, and Fatigue could impart [give]."

Lewis and Clark gladly left the mountains behind and continued their journey. They followed the Columbia River to where it emptied into the Pacific, on the border of present-day Washington and Oregon. Along the way they encountered the powerful and friendly Nez Percé Indians, who provided the expedition with food and horses to continue its journey. Sacagawea's skill as a guide and interpreter helped the expedition travel safely through these lands. On November 7, 1805, Clark saw the Pacific Ocean, writing in his journal, *"Ocian in view!* O! the joy." The expedition stayed in the Pacific Northwest during the rough winter, trading with the Clatsop and Chinook Indians and exploring the coast.

In March 1806 Lewis and Clark set out on the long trek home. The party arrived by canoe in St. Louis in late September 1806. Hundreds of people from this trading town lined up along the river to greet the expedition members with cheers. Clark happily wrote, "Every person . . . seemed to express great pleasure at our return, and acknowledged themselves much astonished."

Although they had not discovered a river route across the West to the Pacific Ocean, Lewis and Clark provided useful information on western lands and paths across the Rockies. The explorers

Sacagawea helped Lewis and Clark travel through the Rockies and on to the Pacific Northwest.

also established contact with many Indian tribes and collected a great deal of valuable scientific information on the plants and animals of the region. Lewis went on to become governor of the new Louisiana Territory, while Clark later became governor of the Missouri Territory.

One of several journals kept by Lewis and Clark, bound in elk skin

Pike's Exploration

While Lewis and Clark were traveling across the West in 1805, Zebulon Pike, a young army officer, was sent on another mission of exploration. He was ordered to find the starting point of the Red River, which runs through Louisiana and along some of the northern border of present-day Texas. The United States claimed that the Red River formed the Louisiana Territory's western border with New Spain. Pike may also have had instructions to spy on Spanish outposts and forts in the Southwest.

Pike led his small expedition to the Rocky Mountains in present-day Colorado, where he tried to climb the mountain known today as Pikes Peak. Then in 1807 he headed south with a few expedition members into present-day New Mexico. They

struggled across mountains in the bitter winter before reaching the Rio Grande. Although he had passed into Spanish-held lands, Pike continued exploring, following the course of the river until a group of Spanish cavalry arrested him. When stopped, Pike pointed to the Rio Grande and asked, "What, is not this the Red River?"

The Spanish suspected Pike of being a spy and imprisoned him. When he was finally released, he returned to the United States and reported on his trip. Despite his imprisonment, he praised the opportunities for doing business with the Spanish in the Southwest.

SECTION 2 REVIEW

Identify and explain the significance of the following:

- **Napoleon Bonaparte**
- **Toussaint L'Ouverture**
- **Louisiana Purchase**
- **Meriwether Lewis**
- **William Clark**
- **Lewis and Clark expedition**
- **Sacagawea**
- **Zebulon Pike**

Locate and explain the importance of the following:

- **New Orleans**
- **Mississippi River**
- **Missouri River**
- **Rocky Mountains**
- **Columbia River**
- **Pikes Peak**
- **Red River**
- **Rio Grande**

Reading for Content Understanding

1 **Main Idea** What stood in the way of Napoleon's plan of rebuilding France's empire in North America?

2 **Main Idea** Why did President Jefferson want to keep the French from controlling New Orleans?

3 **Geographic Diversity** *Movement* What was the purpose of Zebulon Pike's expedition? What did Pike report about the West?

4 **Writing** *Expressing* Imagine that you are a soldier on the Lewis and Clark expedition. Write a diary entry expressing what the group's mission is and describing a specific adventure on the trip.

5 **Critical Thinking** *Synthesizing Information* What instructions did President Jefferson give Lewis and Clark? Why do you think he was interested in gaining this information?

The Coming of War

Reading Focus

How were American ships affected by the war between France and Britain?

What did Tecumseh want to accomplish, and how successful was he?

Why did the United States declare war on Britain in 1812?

Key Terms

impressment
embargo
Embargo Act
Non-Intercourse Act
Battle of Tippecanoe
War Hawks

IN THE FALL OF 1793 *Samuel Calder wrote a desperate letter to the U.S. government. "I am very sorry to inform you of my present situation . . . I was taken by an Algerian Cruzier [ship]." Calder went on to say that he and other Americans were being held prisoner by Algerian pirates. "We was immediately put into Chains and put to hard Labor," he wrote in despair. Calder begged for $100 so he could pay his ransom and be free again.*

Algerian slave ship

Merchants and Pirates

After the Revolutionary War, American merchant ships traveling through the Mediterranean Sea were at the mercy of pirates. The small North African kingdoms of Algiers, Morocco, Tunis, and Tripoli—known as the Barbary States—operated these pirate fleets. Like many European nations, the United States decided to pay the Barbary States a yearly tribute, or fee, to keep them from capturing American ships. Thomas Jefferson opposed this arrangement, arguing that hero "[John] Paul Jones with a half dozen frigates would totally destroy their [the pirates'] commerce . . . cutting them to pieces." Once Jefferson became president, he was able to take action.

In 1801 Tripoli demanded a higher tribute than normal. When the United States refused, Tripoli declared war. In response, Jefferson sent a small fleet to patrol the Mediterranean. Without enough ships to catch the pirates on the open sea, however, this fleet struggled to achieve its mission. A Tripolitan ship captured the USS *Philadelphia* and its crew, holding the sailors hostage for ransom and threatening to use the ship against the rest of the U.S. fleet.

In 1803 the situation began to change when more U.S. warships arrived in the Mediterranean. Naval officer Stephen Decatur made a daring night raid in 1804 into Tripoli's harbor to destroy the *Philadelphia* and prevent the enemy from using it. The USS *Constitution* then bombarded the city of Tripoli. In 1805 a combined force of U.S. Marines and some mercenaries marched hundreds of miles through the desert to surprise and capture another Tripolitan town. Faced with these defeats, the ruler of Tripoli signed a peace treaty. He also agreed not to demand any more tribute and returned his American hostages. The other Barbary States, however, remained a threat to American shipping until 1815.

 ## Conflict with Europe

The Barbary States were a minor threat compared to the mighty navies of Great Britain and France. When war broke out between these two European powers in 1803, the United States found itself once again caught in the middle of the bloody conflict.

The Law of the Sea

Both Britain and France decided that to win the war they needed to prevent neutral countries such as the United States from supplying war materials to the enemy. In 1804 and 1805 Britain passed a series of laws allowing it to search and seize ships carrying war supplies to France. The French quickly struck back by declaring that no country could ship goods to Britain. Lured by the desire to make high profits during the war, many American merchants ignored these foreign laws and carried goods to both sides.

The British navy captured hundreds of American merchant ships that were trying to reach France. British officials also searched these merchant ships for sailors who had deserted from the British navy. The officials then forced any suspected deserters to serve on British warships. European nations called this practice of pressing, or forcing, people to serve in the army or navy **impressment**. In the process of searching for deserters, the British also impressed thousands of American citizens, despite the many protests of the U.S. government.

One widely publicized example of this impressment took place in June 1807 when the British ship *Leopard* stopped the U.S. Navy ship *Chesapeake* and tried to remove four of its sailors. When the *Chesapeake*'s captain refused, the British opened fire and took the sailors by force. The *Chesapeake* incident outraged many Americans. Attorney General Caesar A. Rodney declared that it "has excited the spirit of '76 and the whole country is literally in arms."

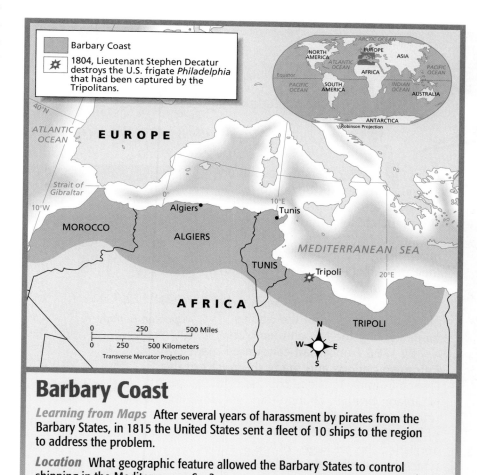

Barbary Coast

Learning from Maps After several years of harassment by pirates from the Barbary States, in 1815 the United States sent a fleet of 10 ships to the region to address the problem.

Location What geographic feature allowed the Barbary States to control shipping in the Mediterranean Sea?

A Trade War

Debates raged about how the United States should respond to Britain's violations of U.S. neutrality. Some citizens wanted to go to war. Others, such as a writer for the Boston *Chronicle*, argued, "Our trade is the most powerful weapon we can use in our defense." These people favored an **embargo**, or the banning of trade, against Britain.

President Jefferson and his fellow Republicans supported the idea of an embargo. In December 1807 Congress passed the **Embargo Act**, which in effect prohibited trade with all foreign nations. Although the intent of the law was to punish Britain and France and to protect American ships from capture, the act most affected U.S. merchants, who lost a great deal of business. The economies of New England and New York, which relied heavily on trade, were particularly hard hit by the embargo.

The popularity of the Federalist Party rose, and Jefferson's declined as the embargo continued. By December 1808 Jefferson had received 199 separate petitions from citizens asking him to repeal the Embargo Act. Meanwhile, the act did not have the desired effect on Britain and France. Many American merchants smuggled goods to Europe. The British also increased their trade with South America to replace lost U.S. trade. The U.S. minister in Paris claimed, "Here it [the embargo] is not felt, and in England . . . it is forgotten."

The problems with the Embargo Act led Congress to repeal the unpopular law and replace it with the **Non-Intercourse Act** in 1809. This act went into effect just before newly elected President James Madison took office. Unlike the Embargo Act, the Non-Intercourse Act banned trade only with Britain and France. It also stated that the United States would renew trade with the first side that stopped violating U.S. neutrality. Congress hoped that the Non-Intercourse Act would be less harmful to American merchants and that it would pressure Britain and France into changing their policies.

Global Connections

The Spread of French Revolutionary Ideas

In 1792 France's revolutionary armies began to conquer other nations, spreading French ideas of political reform throughout Europe. The French urged their neighbors to overthrow their monarchies and embrace liberty. When Napoleon Bonaparte took power six years later, he continued to attack the privileges of the nobles while fighting the Napoleonic Wars.

Napoleon Bonaparte

By 1808 France had conquered many European nations and made them part of the French Empire. To these conquered territories, Napoleon brought change—land reforms, tax reforms, new institutions, and a new code of law. Most countries in the French Empire abolished the privileges of the aristocracy, which eventually led to greater social equality and individual freedoms. The ideas and changes that Napoleon spread across the continent had long-lasting effects. As one Greek patriot said:

❝ The French Revolution and the doings of Napoleon opened up the eyes of the world. . . . Through this present change it is more difficult to rule the people. ❞

Understanding What You Read

1. What changes did Napoleon bring to countries that France conquered?

2. What effect did the spread of French ideas have on other Europeans?

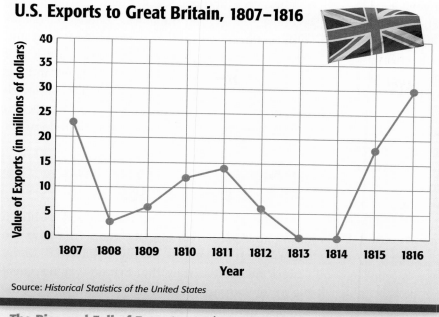

U.S. Exports to Great Britain, 1807–1816

Source: *Historical Statistics of the United States*

The Rise and Fall of Exports In the early 1800s the United States greatly restricted trade to Great Britain. What was the value of U.S. exports to Great Britain in 1808?

⭐ Trouble on the Frontier

The disagreements between Britain and the United States went beyond the neutral rights issue. In the West, the British, American Indians, and American settlers once again came into conflict over land.

The Struggle over Land

Throughout the early 1800s, thousands of American settlers poured into the Northwest Territory, where they established farms and settlements. The Treaty of Greenville provided the federal government with much of the land settled by these pioneers.

Britain wanted to contain the rapid western expansion of the United States and to protect its interests in Canada. British leaders did not want to fight the United States, however. The British government therefore provided military aid to Indian nations in the Northwest Territory. These nations were angry over the terms of the Treaty of Greenville—which many of them had not signed—and over American settlement of lands beyond those that were not in the U.S. territory included in the treaty.

Tecumseh

One of the most influential and talented Indian leaders of this period was Tecumseh, a Shawnee chief. A skilled warrior and a brilliant speaker, Tecumseh warned other tribes about the dangers they faced from settlers:

> ❝ Where [today are] the Narranganset, the Mohican, the Pokanoket and many other once powerful tribes of our people? They have vanished before the avarice [greed] and oppression [domination] of the white man, as snow before a summer sun. ❞

Tecumseh's dream was to unite the American Indians of the Northwest Territory, the South, and the eastern Mississippi Valley into a single confederation to oppose the American settlers. Tecumseh and his brother, a religious leader some Indians called the Prophet, began uniting these different Indian groups and gathering followers. Tecumseh founded a village for his followers near the Wabash and Tippecanoe Rivers.

Tecumseh and William Henry Harrison disagreed violently about treaties between the United States and American Indian nations.

William Henry Harrison, the governor of the Indiana Territory, believed that Tecumseh was a serious threat to American power, calling him "one of those uncommon geniuses which spring up occasionally to . . . overturn the established order." In 1810 Tecumseh informed Harrison of the Indians' anger over the treaty.

The next year Tecumseh met face to face with Harrison, who asked if the Indian leader would follow the treaties that had been signed. Tecumseh replied, "The white people have no right to take the land from the Indians, because the Indians had it first." No single chief, he insisted, could sell land that belonged to all the Indian groups who used it. In response, Harrison warned Tecumseh not to resist the power of the United States.

The Battle of Tippecanoe

In 1811 Tecumseh left his brother in charge while he traveled south to ask the leaders of the Creek nation to join his Indian confederation. Harrison decided to take advantage of Tecumseh's absence and lead an army against the Indian confederacy. Harrison's forces marched close to the Indians, provoking an attack.

The **Battle of Tippecanoe** began when Indians attacked Harrison's camp in the early morning hours of November 7, 1811. The Indians broke through the army's lines, but Harrison maintained

The Battle of Tippecanoe broke the power of Tecumseh's Indian confederation.

The Granger Collection, New York

a "calm, cool, and collected" manner, according to one observer. During the all-day battle, Harrison's soldiers forced the Indian warriors to retreat and then destroyed Tecumseh's village. Said Chief Shabbona, "With the smoke of that town and the loss of that battle, I lost all hope." Although Tecumseh was safe, he lost the support he needed to create his dream of a great Indian confederation.

★ The War Debate

After the Battle of Tippecanoe, one Republican newspaper declared angrily that "the war on the Wabash [River] is purely BRITISH." Many Americans were certain that Britain was responsible for encouraging American Indians to fight the U.S. forces in the West.

The War Hawks

The **War Hawks** were members of Congress who believed the only answer to Britain's insults was to declare war. They were strongest in the West and the South, where they were led by congressmen such as Henry Clay of Kentucky and John C. Calhoun of South Carolina. The War Hawks believed that Britain was trying to prevent the United States from becoming a powerful nation and that the only response to these bullying tactics was force. "If we submit," Calhoun warned, "the independence of this nation is lost." Philadelphia newspaper editor John Binns echoed Calhoun by insisting, "The honor of the Nation . . . will be sacrificed if war be not declared."

Some War Hawks also believed that war would provide an opportunity to increase the size of the nation. Speaking to the House, Tennessee representative Felix Grundy predicted:

“This war, if carried on successfully, will have its advantages. . . . I . . . feel anxious [eager] not only to add the Floridas to the South, but the Canadas to the North of this empire.”

The Opposition

The strongest opponents of the War Hawks were Federalists from New England. Although these states were hurt by British trade restrictions and impressments, they were more interested in renewing friendly business ties with Britain than in fighting another war. Other politicians, such as John Randolph of Virginia, argued that war would accomplish nothing. Challenging the War Hawks in the House, Randolph asked:

> ❝ But is war the true remedy? Who will profit by it? . . . A few lucky merchants . . . and contractors. Who must suffer by it? The people. It is their blood, their taxes, that must flow to support it. ❞

Other antiwar politicians feared that the United States was not yet ready to fight a powerful opponent such as Britain. Senator Obadiah German of New York pointed out that the U.S. Army and Navy were still small and poorly equipped. German pleaded with the War Hawks

U.S. Army private in the 1810s

to be patient: "Prior to any declaration of war . . . my plan would be, and my first wish is, to prepare for it—to put the country in complete armor."

Declaring War

President James Madison, a Republican, faced both the difficulty of continuing the trade war and the increasing pressure from the War Hawks. Speaking to Congress on June 1, 1812, Madison described Britain's impressment of American sailors and its violation of U.S. neutrality. He concluded that Britain was in "a state of war against the United States." The president asked Congress to decide what to do about this situation.

A few days later, the southern and western states voted for war, while New England and New York, New Jersey, and Delaware voted for peace. When the votes were counted, the War Hawks had won. For the first time in U.S. history, Congress declared war. A few months later, Madison was elected to a second term in office and served as commander in chief during the War of 1812.

SECTION 3 REVIEW

Identify and explain the significance of the following:

- impressment
- embargo
- Embargo Act
- Non-Intercourse Act
- Tecumseh
- Battle of Tippecanoe
- War Hawks
- James Madison

Reading for Content Understanding

1 **Main Idea** How did the war between France and Britain affect the United States?

2 **Main Idea** What was Tecumseh's dream, and did he accomplish it?

3 **Global Relations** Why did the United States go to war with the Barbary States?

4 **Writing** *Informing* Write a short memo announcing the United States's declaration of war against Britain. Be sure to include the reasons why the United States declared war.

5 **Critical Thinking** *Drawing Conclusions* Do you think that President Jefferson's foreign policy was successful? Explain your answer.

The War of 1812

<table>
<tr>
<td>

Reading Focus

How did the war progress at sea and in the Great Lakes region?

How did actions by American Indians aid the British during the war?

What strategy did the British pursue during the war, and how did the war come to an end?

</td>
<td>

Key Terms

Battle of Lake Erie
Battle of the Thames
Battle of Horseshoe Bend
Battle of New Orleans
Hartford Convention
Treaty of Ghent

</td>
</tr>
</table>

ON AUGUST 19, 1812, the USS Constitution *met the British frigate* Guerrière *off the coast of Nova Scotia. The crews on both ships scrambled across the decks and the rigging as the vessels circled one another. An observer said the* Constitution's *first cannon blast rocked the* Guerrière *"as though she had received the shock of an earthquake." When the British returned fire, a U.S. sailor saw a cannonball bounce off the side of the* Constitution. *"Huzza, her sides are made of iron!" he cried. The British ship was no match for the American one, and soon "Old Ironsides" won one of the first battles of the War of 1812.*

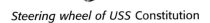

Steering wheel of USS Constitution

The War at Sea

The *Constitution*'s triumph over the *Guerrière* shocked many observers, most of whom expected the British to sweep the U.S. Navy from the seas. At the start of the War of 1812, the British navy had hundreds of ships stationed around the world. The U.S. Navy, by comparison, had fewer than 20 ships, and none as powerful as the greatest British warships. Figures such as these had led Republican Adam Seybert to declare, "We cannot contend [compete] with Great Britain on the ocean."

Despite being severely outnumbered, the United States did have some advantages at the start of the war. The American government licensed privately owned ships called privateers to attack British merchant ships. These privateers did not cost the government as much money to equip or operate as building more naval ships would. One Republican leader called the privateers "our cheapest & best Navy." The privateers captured hundreds of British ships. A London newspaper complained, "On the ocean, and even on our own coasts, we have been insulted."

The crew of the USS *Constitution* *celebrates their victory over the British* Guerriére.

These problems became painfully obvious when the invasion failed. In July 1812 the British joined with Indians led by Tecumseh to defeat one American army and capture Fort Detroit. The other two American armies retreated after state militia troops refused to cross the Canadian border and fight on foreign soil. By the end of 1812, Britain controlled the strategic Great Lakes region. Treasury Secretary Albert Gallatin wrote:

> **The series of misfortunes exceeds [goes beyond] all anticipations made even by those who had least confidence in our inexperienced officers and undisciplined men.**

Most of the British navy's ships were scattered around the globe and could not be called away to fight the United States. Although small, the U.S. Navy had well-trained sailors. Its superfrigates, such as the *Constitution*, were also more powerful than most British ships of the same size. U.S. captains proved this point several times early in the war by defeating British ships in one-on-one duels. Such victories embarrassed the British and raised American morale.

Eventually, the British brought more ships to the American coast and began patrolling in large groups that the U.S. Navy could not confront. The British blockaded American seaports and captured American merchant ships.

⭐ The Canadian Border

U.S. Army leaders hoped to equal the early success of the U.S. Navy. Army commanders planned to invade Canada with three separate armies and quickly end the war.

Early Setbacks

Many Americans expected that French Canadians would rather welcome U.S. troops than fight for Britain. According to former president Thomas Jefferson, conquering Canada would be "a mere matter of marching [there]." What Jefferson and others overlooked was the fact that the U.S. Army was poorly equipped and unprepared for war.

Perry's Victory

The United States tried in 1813 to regain the ground it had lost. Vital to this effort was breaking Britain's control of Lake Erie. The navy gave this task to Captain Oliver Hazard Perry, who oversaw the construction of a small fleet. He sailed out to meet the British on September 10, 1813, flying a flag inscribed "Don't give up the ship!" The **Battle of Lake Erie** lasted for more than three hours and resulted in heavy casualties for both sides. Finally, the British surrendered. Perry immediately sent a message to General William Henry Harrison: "We have met the enemy and they are ours." Perry's victory forced the British to withdraw and gave the U.S. Army new hope.

Captain Oliver Hazard Perry leads his forces in the brutal Battle of Lake Erie.

The Frontier War

Harrison took advantage of Perry's victory by pursuing the British and their Indian allies, led by Tecumseh, into Canada. Rather than stand and fight, British general Henry Proctor retreated and looked for reinforcements.

The Battle of the Thames

Tecumseh was furious with Proctor for retreating so quickly and abandoning his Indian allies who remained in the Great Lakes region. Tecumseh convinced Proctor to make a stand by the Thames River in southern Canada. U.S. troops under General Harrison caught up with the British there in early October 1813.

In the **Battle of the Thames**, Harrison boldly ordered a cavalry charge directly into the British defenses, breaking them apart. The Indians continued to fight the U.S. soldiers on foot and took heavy casualties. Eventually, the Indian forces retreated. The American victory in the Battle of the Thames broke British power in the Northwest and secured the border with Canada. In addition, Tecumseh was killed during the battle. The death of this powerful leader weakened the Indian-British alliance around the Great Lakes.

The Creek War

In 1813 the Creek Indians that Tecumseh had visited two years earlier finally decided to take up arms against the United States. Led by Chief Red Eagle, Creek forces destroyed Fort Mims in present-day Alabama, killing more than 500 soldiers and settlers. When this news reached Andrew Jackson, a general in the Tennessee militia, he led his soldiers south to fight the Creek.

Each side had victories in several bloody battles. Jackson also led attacks against Creek villages. Then in the spring of 1814, Jackson attacked the Creek's main base, a small fort on the Tallapoosa River in Alabama. The **Battle of Horseshoe Bend** was an overwhelming victory for Jackson and his troops against the Creek. Days later, Red Eagle came into Jackson's camp and surrendered. The Indian leader said wearily: "I have done the white people all the harm I could; . . . if I had an army, I would yet fight, and contend [struggle] to the last." Jackson's victory ended the Creek War and led to a treaty that forced the Creek to give up millions of acres of their land.

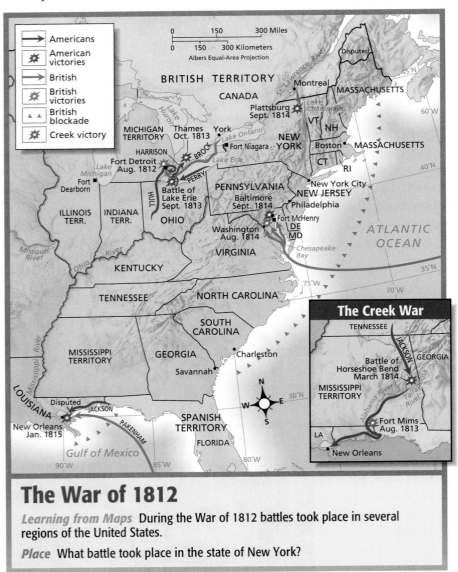

The War of 1812

Learning from Maps During the War of 1812 battles took place in several regions of the United States.

Place What battle took place in the state of New York?

Much of the city of Washington burned after the attack by British forces.

Britain on the Offensive

Although the fighting was going well for the United States on the western and southern frontiers, the situation in the East was growing worse. Having defeated France in April 1814, the British sent more troops to America and more ships to strengthen their blockade of eastern seaports.

The British used these reinforcements to attack the nation's capital. President Madison and most of his cabinet went to the front lines to defend Washington, but were forced to flee when the British broke through the defenses. In the White House, First Lady Dolley Madison heard about the British advance. Despite the danger, she stayed and saved a famous portrait of George Washington before escaping. The British marched into the city and set fire to the White House and other government buildings. This destruction was in response to the Americans' earlier burning of the British capital in Canada. After the British had left Washington, an American observer of the ruins wrote that all that was left of the president's home were "unroofed, marked walls, cracked, defaced [damaged], blackened with the smoke of fire."

First Lady Dolley Madison

The British sailed on to Baltimore, Maryland, which was guarded by Fort McHenry. The British fleet bombarded the fort and its defenders for two solid days. A reporter for the *Salem Gazette* witnessed the scene:

> 66 **The attack on Fort McHenry . . . was distinctly seen from Federal Hill, and from the tops of houses which were covered with men, women, and children. The night . . . presented the whole awful spectacle of shot and shells, and rockets, shooting and bursting through the air.** 99

The Americans refused to surrender Fort McHenry, forcing the British to retreat before American reinforcements could arrive.

Ending the War

After the attack on Washington, the British launched an offensive from their Caribbean bases against New Orleans. They hoped to capture the city and thus take control of the Mississippi River.

The Battle of New Orleans

Andrew Jackson was in command of the U.S. forces around New Orleans. When news arrived that British troops were seven miles away from the city, the startled Jackson ordered his troops to make a stand behind a quickly constructed wall of earth and logs. There the troops—a mix of regular soldiers, state militia, and even a group led by pirate Jean Lafitte—waited for the attack.

The **Battle of New Orleans** began on the morning of January 8, 1815, when 5,300 British troops attacked Jackson's force of 4,500. The British began marching toward the American defenses under the cover of a thick morning fog. As they drew near, the air cleared and exposed them to heavy fire from American riflemen and artillery. Caught on an open field, the British were cut down with frightening speed. A militia member recalled: "The field was entirely covered with . . . bodies. In some places they were lying in piles of several, one on top of the other."

In about half an hour more than 2,000 British soldiers had been killed or wounded, compared to fewer than 100 U.S. casualties. Although Jackson had won the most convincing victory of the war for the United States, Americans soon found out that the two sides had actually signed a peace treaty two weeks before the battle.

The National Anthem

By September 1814 the British were ready to attack Fort McHenry outside of Baltimore. That month, American Francis Scott Key boarded a British warship docked in Chesapeake Bay. Key went to ask for the freedom of Dr. William Beanes, a friend of his who was being held prisoner. Key convinced the British to let Beanes go free, but the two Americans were not allowed to leave right away—the British were about to launch their assault on the American fort.

From the ship's deck, Key could see the American flag flying over Fort McHenry as the battle began. He anxiously waited on deck as the British shot their cannons throughout the night. At 7 A.M. the mist and smoke finally cleared, and Key saw that the American flag still flew above Fort McHenry. The British had lost the battle. Years later, he described his feelings at the moment he noticed the flag was still flying:

The sheet music for "The Star-Spangled Banner"

The Granger Collection, New York

❝ *Through the clouds of the war the stars of that banner still shone in my view. . . . Then in that hour of deliverance and joyful triumph, my heart spoke; and 'Does not such a country and such defenders of their country deserve a song?' was its question.* ❞

Key was so moved with joy that he wrote a poem to express his feelings. He set the verses of his poem to the melody of a popular song. Copies of the song were presented to the soldiers at Fort McHenry. The song also circulated throughout Baltimore, where citizens sang it at home, in the streets, and on stage. Soon Key's composition was published under the title "The Star-Spangled Banner." Just a few months later, Americans played "The Star-Spangled Banner" at the Battle of New Orleans.

Key emphasized that his song honored the American victory at Fort McHenry as well as the brave soldiers who fought for it. He later declared,

❝ *Let the praise, then, if any be due, be given, not to me, who only did what I could not help doing, not to the writer, but to the inspirers of the song!* ❞

For some time, "The Star-Spangled Banner" was simply one of many patriotic American songs, such as "Yankee Doodle." However, "The Star-Spangled Banner" grew in popularity and was played in the Civil War, the Spanish-American War, and World War I. In 1931 it became the national anthem of the United States.

Understanding the Arts

1. How did Key know the Americans had won the battle?

2. Why do you think "The Star-Spangled Banner" became instantly popular?

British forces charge the walls built by Andrew Jackson's troops in the Battle of New Orleans.

The Hartford Convention

While Jackson was preparing to fight at New Orleans, Federalists from New England were gathering at Hartford, Connecticut, to protest the war. Some delegates to the **Hartford Convention**, as it was called, demanded that New England withdraw from the United States entirely. More moderate members convinced the convention to send a delegation to meet with President Madison. These delegates offered to support the war if measures were taken to increase the power of the states versus the federal government.

Before this delegation reached Washington, however, news reached North America that the war had ended. Delegates to the Hartford Convention were laughed at by some Republicans and accused of treason by others. Discredited, the Federalists lost much of their political power. However, they did set a precedent for states to challenge the policies of the federal government.

The Treaty of Ghent

The peace agreement that neither the Federalists nor Jackson knew about was the **Treaty of Ghent**, signed in Belgium on December 24, 1814. After months of frustrating negotiations, U.S. and British diplomats finally decided to end the war. All conquered territory was restored, but the diplomats found no solutions to the problems of impressment or trade embargoes.

Although it did not solve the problems facing Britain and the United States, the Treaty of Ghent was a relief for two nations tired of war. Both sides agreed that future negotiations could address the remaining issues once there was peace. For the United States, the War of 1812 was a narrow escape from potential disaster. However, the fact that the young nation had stood up to the mighty British opponent inspired a sense of pride among many Americans.

SECTION 4 REVIEW

Identify and explain the significance of the following:
- **Oliver Hazard Perry**
- **Battle of Lake Erie**
- **Battle of the Thames**
- **Red Eagle**
- **Battle of Horseshoe Bend**
- **Andrew Jackson**
- **Battle of New Orleans**
- **Hartford Convention**
- **Treaty of Ghent**

Locate and explain the importance of the following:
- **Fort Detroit**
- **Fort Mims**
- **Washington**
- **Baltimore**

Reading for Content Understanding

1 **Main Idea** What events occurred in the fighting at sea and near the Great Lakes?

2 **Main Idea** How did the war progress after the Great Lakes campaign, and how did it finally come to an end?

3 **Cultural Diversity** How did Indians aid Britain during the War of 1812?

4 **Writing** *Informing* Imagine that you are in Washington when it was burned by the British in 1814. Write a letter to your family in another part of the country, explaining the events that took place in the capital.

5 **Critical Thinking** *Synthesizing Information* Why could the War of 1812 be called the "Second War for American Independence"?

CHAPTER 11 REVIEW

Chapter Summary

After Thomas Jefferson became president, he made some changes to the Federalist style of government. The United States bought the Louisiana Territory from France. Disputes over land led to war between American Indians and the U.S. government. Conflicts between the United States and Great Britain erupted into the War of 1812. ▮

On a separate sheet of paper, complete the following activities.

Identifying People and Ideas

Describe the historical significance of the following:

1. John Marshall
2. judicial review
3. Toussaint L'Ouverture
4. Lewis and Clark expedition
5. Sacagawea
6. impressment
7. Tecumseh
8. War Hawks
9. Oliver Hazard Perry
10. Battle of Horseshoe Bend

Internet Activity
go.hrw.com
SA0 Washington, D.C.

Search the Internet through the HRW Web site for information on the construction and history of one of the famous buildings of Washington, D.C., such as the White House or the Capitol. Use the information to create the text of a historical plaque that might hang outside the building.

Understanding Main Ideas

1. Describe the city of Washington at the time of Jefferson's inauguration.
2. What decision of the Federalists did President Jefferson leave in place?
3. Why were New Orleans and the Mississippi River important to the United States?
4. What dangers did American ships and sailors face at sea during the early 1800s?
5. What did Tecumseh do to organize the Indians of the Northwest Territory, the South, and the Mississippi Valley?
6. Why did some Americans believe that the U.S. Navy could not compete with the British navy? What advantages did the U.S. Navy have?
7. What was the significance of Captain Oliver Hazard Perry's naval victory in the Battle of Lake Erie?

Using the Time Line

Number your paper from 1 to 6. Match the letters on the time line below with the following events.

1. Andrew Jackson leads his troops to victory in the Battle of New Orleans.
2. Under pressure from the War Hawks, Congress declares war against Britain.
3. The U.S. Senate approves the Louisiana Purchase.
4. The Battle of Tippecanoe begins between American Indians and U.S. forces led by William Henry Harrison.
5. Thomas Jefferson is sworn in as president.
6. Congress passes the Embargo Act.

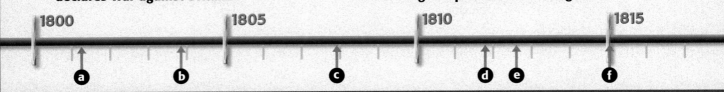

1800 — a — b — 1805 — c — 1810 — d — e — f — 1815

Reviewing Themes

1. **Constitutional Heritage** What was the significance of *Marbury* v. *Madison*?

2. **Geographic Diversity** Why did President Jefferson send Lewis and Clark to explore the West? What important information did they bring back about the area?

3. **Global Relations** What conflicts arose between the United States and American Indians along the western frontier?

Thinking Critically

1. **Evaluating** Do you think that Thomas Jefferson was right to purchase the Louisiana Territory despite his concerns that doing so was unconstitutional? Explain your answer.

2. **Drawing Conclusions** Why do you think the Creek War threatened the United States?

3. **Supporting a Point of View** Imagine that you are a member of Congress debating whether to declare war on Britain in 1812. Present your argument for or against declaring war.

Building Your Portfolio

Complete the following activities individually or in groups.

1. **Tecumseh** Write and perform a play on Tecumseh. Prepare and present scenes with Tecumseh in different roles. Show Tecumseh (a) meeting with General Harrison (b) discussing the Indian confederation with the Prophet (c) asking leaders of the Creek nation to join his confederation and (d) meeting with the Prophet after the Battle of Tippecanoe. You may wish to use props and wear appropriate clothing for your performance.

2. **The USS *Constitution*** Research the role of the USS *Constitution* ("Old Ironsides") in the War of 1812. Use this information to build a model or make a sketch of the warship. Then use your model or sketch as a visual aid in a short oral report that you present to the class.

Writing About History

1. **Creating** Draw a political cartoon evaluating Jefferson's presidency from a Federalist point of view. Be sure to include a one-paragraph caption to accompany your cartoon.

2. **Describing** Imagine that you are a resident of New Orleans in 1815. Write a diary entry describing the Battle of New Orleans and its significance.

Linking Geography and History

1. **Location** Why were the Great Lakes an important strategic location?

2. **Region** In which region of the country was the War of 1812 very unpopular, and why?

History Skills Workshop

Using Primary Sources "The Star-Spangled Banner," written by poet Francis Scott Key, describes the scene as the British attacked Fort McHenry in 1814. Read the words of "The Star-Spangled Banner." Then answer the following questions: (a) What allowed Key to see the flag at night? (b) How does Key describe the United States and the American people?

> **"**Oh, say, can you see, by the dawn's early light,
> What so proudly we hailed at the twilight's last gleaming,
> Whose broad stripes and bright stars through the perilous fight,
> O'er the ramparts we watched were so gallantly streaming?
> And the rockets' red glare, the bombs bursting in air,
> Gave proof through the night that our flag was still there.
> Oh, say, does that star-spangled banner yet wave
> O'er the land of the free, and the home of the brave?**"**

Expanding National Borders

In 1790 the United States was a new nation. Although the 13 states were located on the eastern coast of North America, pioneers had begun to move west beyond the Appalachian Mountains. In 1803 more land was opened to them when the United States bought vast western lands from the French. This Louisiana Purchase stretched all the way from the Mississippi River to the Rocky Mountains and nearly doubled the size of the country.

During the 1800s settlers streamed west into new territories. They pushed aside the American Indian inhabitants and turned forests and hunting grounds into farms and pastures. While the United States remained primarily a nation of farmers, much of the young country's wealth was based on trade and commerce with foreign nations. ■

The New Nation

In 1790 the United States housed nearly 4 million people and stretched from the Atlantic Ocean in the East to the Mississippi River in the West. Much of the new nation's push toward westward settlement came from farmers in the eastern regions looking for cheaper lands.

Abby Aldrich Rockefeller Folk Art Center

THE RESIDENCE OF DAVID TWINING 1787.

Farming in the late 1700s

History Note 1

The United States in 1790 was primarily a rural nation, with the vast majority of people living on farms. Only 24 U.S. cities had a population of more than 2,500. Philadelphia—the largest U.S. city at that time—and New York City were the only American urban areas with more than 25,000 residents.

The United States, 1790

Legend:
- U.S. territory
- Spanish territory
- British territory
- Disputed territory
- Northwest Territory
- Spanish settlements and missions
- UTE Native American tribe

0   250   500 Miles
0   250   500 Kilometers
Albers Equal-Area Projection

History Note 2

By 1790 most states had given up their claims to western lands beyond their borders. Virginia gave up its claim to Kentucky, which made it possible for Kentucky to become a state in 1792. North Carolina turned over its claim to present-day Tennessee to the federal government in 1790. After a period as a territory, Tennessee became a state in 1796.

Geography Skills
Reading Political Maps

1. Which nation's lands bordered the United States to the south and west?
2. What major American Indian peoples still populated U.S. territory in 1790?
3. In what parts of the present-day United States were many Spanish settlements located?
4. Where was British territory located?

History Note 3

Many American Indians in the West strongly and violently resisted the movement of settlers into their regions, but gradually most tribes lost their lands. By the 1790s treaties opened to settlement areas throughout the Trans-Appalachian West, including lands in New York, North Carolina, Georgia, and present-day Tennessee. After a series of battles, two thirds of present-day Ohio was opened for settlement by a 1795 treaty.

Immigrants to the United States in 1820

Total number of immigrants: 8,385

Places of origin:

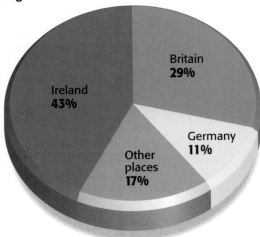

Britain
29%

Ireland
43%

Germany
11%

Other places
17%

Source: *Historical Statistics of the United States*

History Note 4

As American settlers moved westward, the abundance of land and other resources helped support large families. In fact, the average American household was significantly larger than households in Europe. An average free household in the United States had 6 members compared to an average of 4.5 persons in British homes. A higher birthrate and standard of living in the United States helped explain this difference in size.

Geography Skills
Reading Pie Graphs

1. In 1820, about how many immigrants came to the United States from Ireland? Germany?
2. Why do you think British immigration to the United States slowed after the American Revolution?

History Note 5

Immigration has always been an important contributor to the U.S. population. The original thirteen colonies that became the United States were mostly populated by immigrants from Great Britain, with sizable numbers from Germany. More than 130,000 people came between 1763 and 1775. After the Revolutionary War, overall immigration slowed. By 1820 more people were coming from Ireland than from Great Britain.

The Granger Collection, New York

Crossing the Appalachian Mountains

The Growing Republic

The territory and population of the United States expanded greatly between 1790 and 1820. The nation's economy generally expanded with increased agricultural production and more foreign trade. However, the growth of trade and commerce sometimes varied wildly with the ups and downs of international disputes and wars.

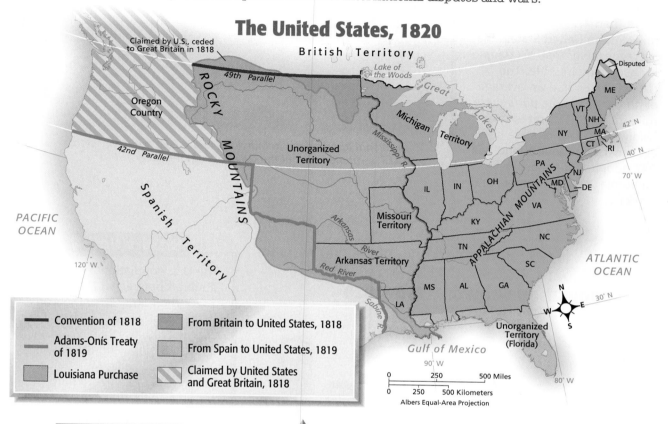

The United States, 1820

Claimed by U.S., ceded to Great Britain in 1818

British Territory

49th Parallel

ROCKY MOUNTAINS

Oregon Country

42nd Parallel

Spanish Territory

PACIFIC OCEAN

120° W

Unorganized Territory

Lake of the Woods

Great Lakes

Mississippi R.

Michigan Territory

Disputed

ME

VT NH

NY MA

CT RI

42° N

40° N

70° W

Arkansas River

Missouri Territory

IL IN OH

PA

NJ

MD DE

VA

KY

TN

NC

SC

APPALACHIAN MOUNTAINS

ATLANTIC OCEAN

30° N

Red River

Arkansas Territory

MS AL GA

Sabine R.

LA

Gulf of Mexico

90° W

Unorganized Territory (Florida)

80° W

Legend:
- — Convention of 1818
- — Adams-Onís Treaty of 1819
- Louisiana Purchase
- From Britain to United States, 1818
- From Spain to United States, 1819
- Claimed by United States and Great Britain, 1818

0 250 500 Miles
0 250 500 Kilometers
Albers Equal-Area Projection

History Note 6

By 1820 the United States had negotiated with Spain and Britain to clearly define its national borders. The United States and Britain agreed in 1818 to jointly occupy Oregon Country for 10 years. This joint occupation actually lasted until 1846. In addition, the two nations agreed to a common boundary in the northern areas of the Louisiana Purchase. In 1819 the United States and Spain set a boundary along the Sabine, Red, and Arkansas Rivers for their territories in the Southwest.

Geography Skills
Reading Political Maps

1. What state west of the Mississippi River had been admitted into the Union by 1820?
2. Which two nations shared control of Oregon Country after 1818?
3. What effect did the Convention of 1818 have on the border between the United States and British Territory north and west of the Mississippi River?
4. What treaty established the border between the United States and Spanish territory in 1819?

The National Road began in Maryland in the East and connected with U.S. territories west of the Ohio River in the early 1800s.

History Note 8

The U.S. population more than doubled between 1790 and 1820. The number of Americans in the West grew particularly fast. In 1790 less than 3 percent of the U.S. population lived west of the Appalachian Mountains, but by 1820 this figure had grown significantly.

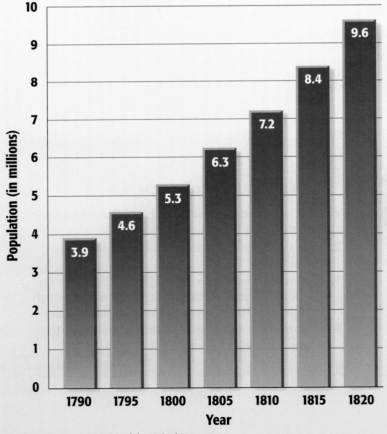

U.S. Population Growth, 1790–1820

Population (in millions)

Year	Population
1790	3.9
1795	4.6
1800	5.3
1805	6.3
1810	7.2
1815	8.4
1820	9.6

Source: *Historical Statistics of the United States*

Geography Skills
Reading Bar Graphs

1. What was the population of the United States in 1790?
2. How much did the U.S. population increase between 1790 and 1820?
3. During which two five-year periods did the U.S. population increase the most?

History Note 9

Between 1790 and 1820 international conflicts sometimes made foreign trade difficult. For example, in 1808 the value of U.S. exports declined by $86 million because Congress had passed the Embargo Act in 1807. That act tried to punish Britain and France for interfering with U.S. trade by halting exports to them. Foreign trade declined for a long period. Exports began rising again after 1808, but by 1820 they still had not reached their previous peak of 1807.

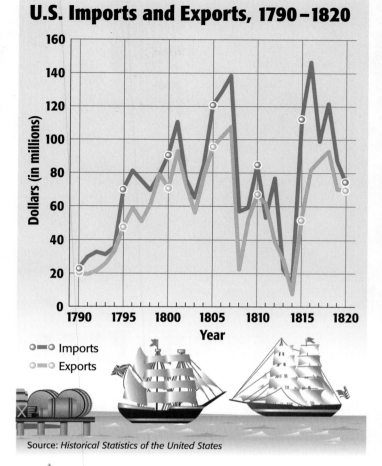

U.S. Imports and Exports, 1790–1820

Dollars (in millions) / Year

○—○ Imports
○—○ Exports

Source: *Historical Statistics of the United States*

Said snow DEBBY, 140 tons
burthen, 4 months old.   *April 20.*
              FOR SALE,
On board the Brig JAMES, opposite No 67, South-
              side Long-Wharf.
    400 hhds Lisbon SALT afloat, &
a quantity of excellent LEMONS; only 35 days
from Lisbon.   *april 20.*
     Brig ____ 's Cargo, from Trinidad.

Early American trade goods

Geography Skills

Reading Line Graphs

1. Did the values of U.S. exports and imports generally rise or fall between 1790 and 1820? Was the change smooth? Explain your answer.

2. When were the values of U.S. exports and imports lowest? Why do you think exports and imports were so low at that time?

3. Was the value of U.S. exports usually higher or lower than the value of imports from 1790 to 1820? How did this affect the U.S. economy?

History Note 10

Although the United States had defeated Britain in the American Revolution, the British remained important trading partners of the new nation. In 1790 more than a third of U.S. exports went to Britain.

NEW YORK

■ CHAPTER 12 ■
A New National Identity
(1812–1840)

By the early 1800s more Americans were expressing pride in their country through music. American folk music of the period reflected the unique culture and views of the growing nation. One of the most popular songs of the era was "Hunters of Kentucky," which celebrated the Battle of New Orleans and became an anthem for a new spirit of nationalism in the United States.

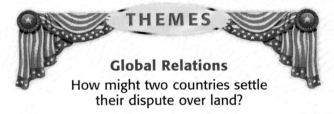

THEMES

Global Relations
How might two countries settle their dispute over land?

Citizenship and Democracy
What might lead a state to ignore a federal law?

Constitutional Heritage
How might a Supreme Court decision affect people's rights?

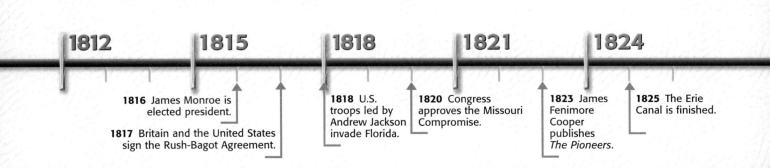

1812 **1815** **1818** **1821** **1824**

1816 James Monroe is elected president.

1817 Britain and the United States sign the Rush-Bagot Agreement.

1818 U.S. troops led by Andrew Jackson invade Florida.

1820 Congress approves the Missouri Compromise.

1823 James Fenimore Cooper publishes *The Pioneers.*

1825 The Erie Canal is finished.

The Rise of Nationalism

Reading Focus

Why was James Monroe's presidency called the Era of Good Feelings?

How did the United States settle its land disputes with Britain and Spain?

Why did President Monroe issue the Monroe Doctrine, and what were its main points?

Key Terms

Rush-Bagot Agreement
Convention of 1818
Adams-Onís Treaty
Monroe Doctrine

ALTHOUGH JAMES MONROE *greatly admired the French republic, he believed that the United States had the potential to become the greatest republic ever. He shared these views with his daughter Eliza while they walked through the streets of Paris. Eliza noted, however, that the French had superior roads. Monroe replied, "That's true, our country may be likened to a new house. We lack many things, but we possess the most precious of all—liberty!"*

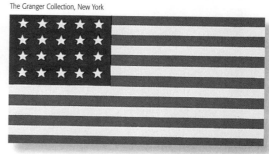

The Granger Collection, New York

U.S. flag, 1818

IMAGE ON LEFT PAGE: *A country dance during the early 1800s*

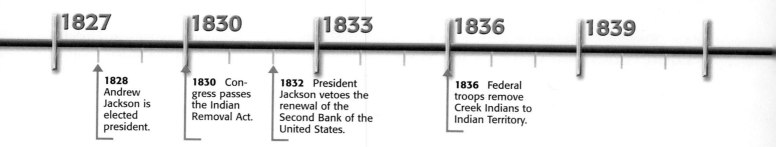

1827	1830	1833	1836	1839

1828 Andrew Jackson is elected president.

1830 Congress passes the Indian Removal Act.

1832 President Jackson vetoes the renewal of the Second Bank of the United States.

1836 Federal troops remove Creek Indians to Indian Territory.

A New National Identity **367**

★ The Era of Good Feelings

After the War of 1812, the United States experienced a period of relative peace and national pride. When James Monroe was elected president in 1816, journalists wrote that the nation was entering the "Era of Good Feelings." Monroe, a Republican, had soundly defeated the Federalist candidate, Rufus King, by a margin of 183 electoral votes to 34. Monroe also easily won re-election in 1820. During Monroe's presidency, members of his administration resolved ongoing conflicts with foreign powers. Two long-term disputes involved the northern and southern borders of the United States.

Conflict with Canada

Most Americans were pleased with the Treaty of Ghent, which had ended the War of 1812. One issue left unresolved by the treaty, however, was control of the waterways between the United States and Canada. American and British leaders both wanted to maintain fishing rights and navies on the Great Lakes.

James Monroe

In the spring of 1817, the two sides compromised with the **Rush-Bagot Agreement**. The treaty limited naval power on the Great Lakes for both the United States and British Canada. To address other issues, the two sides then signed the **Convention of 1818**. This treaty gave the United States fishing rights off parts of the Newfoundland and Labrador coasts and established the border between the United States and Canada at the 49th parallel, as far west as the Rocky Mountains. Both countries also agreed to a joint occupation of the Pacific Northwest.

Conflict with Spain

The United States also had a dispute with Spain over Florida. Some Americans wanted to move into Florida, particularly since Spain no longer had many soldiers there. Many southerners also were upset by the actions of the Seminole Indians in Florida. The Seminole often helped runaway slaves and sometimes raided U.S. settlements.

By early 1818 Secretary of State John Quincy Adams was

An 1881 treaty divided Patagonia between Chile and Argentina.

Latin American Nations in 1830

Learning from Maps Many countries in Latin America became independent in the early 1820s.

Place Which nations became independent before 1820?

negotiating with Spanish diplomat Luis de Onís to allow Americans to settle in Florida. President Monroe had also sent U.S. troops under General Andrew Jackson to secure the U.S. border with Spanish Florida. In April 1818 Jackson's troops invaded Florida to capture Seminole raiders. Jackson's invasion began the First Seminole War between U.S. and Seminole forces. During the war, Jackson seized most of Spain's important military posts and overthrew the governor of Florida, although he did not have authorization to do so from President Monroe. Jackson also ordered the execution of two British citizens whom he suspected of aiding the Seminole raiders against the United States.

Both British and Spanish leaders protested Jackson's actions. "We can hardly believe that any thing so offensive to public decorum [proper behavior] could be admitted, *even in America!*" reported one London journal. Most Americans, however, supported Jackson. One newspaper reported, "Among the people of the West, his popularity is unbounded [unlimited]."

With Jackson already in Florida, Spanish officials decided to resolve all U.S.-Spanish border disputes. With the **Adams-Onís Treaty** of 1819, Spain gave Florida to the United States. In return, the United States gave up its claims to present-day Texas and agreed to take responsibility for up to $5 million of U.S. citizens' claims against Spain.

HISTORICAL DOCUMENTS

The Monroe Doctrine

1823

On December 2, 1823, President James Monroe issued what became known as the Monroe Doctrine. The following is an excerpt from the doctrine, which has had a significant effect on U.S. foreign policy.

We ... declare that we should consider any attempt on their [European powers'] part to extend their [political] system to any portion of this hemisphere as dangerous to our peace and safety.

With the existing colonies or dependencies of any European power we have not interfered and shall not interfere. But with the governments who have declared their independence and maintained it, and whose independence we have ... acknowledged, we could not view any interposition [interference] for the purpose of oppressing [unjustly ruling] them, or controlling in any other manner their destiny, by any European power in any other light than as the manifestation [realization] of an unfriendly disposition toward the United States....

Our policy in regard to Europe ... remains the same, which is, not to interfere in the internal concerns of any of its powers. But in regard to those continents [the Americas], circumstances are ... different. It is impossible that the allied powers should extend their political system to any portion of either continent without endangering our peace and happiness....

It is equally impossible, therefore, that we should behold such interposition in any form with indifference.

Understanding Primary Sources

1. What warning did Monroe give to the European powers in the Monroe Doctrine?

2. What do you think is most important about this document?

★ The Monroe Doctrine

At the time of the treaty, Spain was involved in numerous military struggles in its colonies farther south. By the early 1820s most of Latin America—the countries of Central and South America—had declared independence from Spanish rule. Revolutionary fighter Simón Bolívar, nicknamed "the Liberator," led many of these fights for independence. Most American officials sympathized with these revolutions, seeing them as similar to the American Revolution. In 1818 one Tennessee politician offered this toast:

" *The patriots of South America*: palsied [paralyzed] be the arm that would wrest [take] from them the standard of liberty for which thay have so nobly struggled. Six cheers!"

After neighboring Mexico broke free from Spain in 1821, President Monroe became increasingly concerned that rival European powers might try to take control of the Latin American countries. Britain was also interested in restraining other European nations' influence in the Americas. This was because Britain had formed close trade ties with most of the independent Latin American countries. Britain wanted to issue a joint statement with the United States that warned Europe not to interfere with Latin America.

Simón Bolívar

Instead, Secretary of State Adams planned a brilliant diplomatic move. Adams and President Monroe put together a statement, delivered on December 2, 1823, warning European powers not to interfere with the Americas. This statement, which became known as the **Monroe Doctrine**, declared that North and South America were off limits to future colonization by any foreign power. Monroe further declared that the U.S. government would consider any European country's attempt to colonize or interfere with the independent Latin American countries to be a hostile act. He also warned that the United States would not ignore such an act.

Some Europeans responded by strongly criticizing the Monroe Doctrine. Austria's leading statesman called Monroe's speech "indecent declarations." The French foreign minister declared that the doctrine "ought to be resisted by all the powers having commercial or territorial interests in the hemisphere." Despite such threats, few European nations challenged the Monroe Doctrine. Mainly they feared Britain, which had the world's most powerful navy. In the years since Monroe issued the doctrine, it has played a significant role in shaping U.S.–Latin American relations.

SECTION 1 REVIEW

Identify and explain the significance of the following:

- James Monroe
- Rush-Bagot Agreement
- Convention of 1818
- Adams-Onís Treaty
- Simón Bolívar
- Monroe Doctrine

Reading for Content Understanding

1 Main Idea Why did Monroe's presidency get the name the Era of Good Feelings?

2 Main Idea What did the president declare in the Monroe Doctrine, and why did some European leaders criticize it?

3 Global Relations What caused a dispute between the United States and Spain during Monroe's presidency? How was this dispute settled?

4 Writing *Informing* Write two paragraphs explaining how the United States settled its conflict with Britain over Canada, and why resolving the issue was important to both nations.

5 Critical Thinking *Evaluating* Do you think Monroe's presidency was really an Era of Good Feelings? Explain your answer.

Expansion and Improvements

Reading Focus

What regional issues did the Missouri Compromise attempt to address?

How did improvements in transportation affect the United States?

Why was the 1824 presidential election controversial?

Key Terms

Missouri Compromise
American System
Cumberland Road
Erie Canal

IN THE EARLY 1800S *many Americans continued to move west looking for land and opportunity.* "The western country continues to rise in population and importance with unabated [unstopping] rapidity," wrote one Ohio migrant in 1816. The writer offered as an example the town of Mount Pleasant, Ohio, which grew from a population of 7 families to about 90 families in just 10 years. As more Americans pushed west, however, debates arose over what laws would govern the newly settled lands.

Covered wagon

★ The Missouri Compromise

A major regional conflict emerged in 1819, when Congress considered Missouri's application to enter the Union as a slave state. At the time there were 11 free states and 11 slave states. The free states, which had more representatives because of the North's greater population, controlled the House. To protect the power of the free states, the House passed an amendment accepting Missouri as a slave state only if the further importation of slaves into the state was prohibited. The law also required all children of Missouri slaves to be set free when they reached the age of 25.

In the Senate, where slave states and free states had an equal number of votes, the amendment was rejected. Some senators, such as Rufus King of New York, opposed any expansion of slavery. "The existence of slavery impairs [harms] the industry and the power of a nation," he argued. North Carolina senator Nathaniel Macon wanted to continue admitting slave states. "Why depart from the good old way, which has kept us in quiet, peace, and harmony?" he asked.

Henry Clay

To settle this dispute, Kentucky representative Henry Clay proposed the **Missouri Compromise**, in which Missouri would enter the Union as a slave state while Maine joined as a free state. The agreement also declared that slavery would be prohibited in any new territories or states formed north of the 36°30' line, which ran along Missouri's southern border.

Another Kentucky representative, Benjamin Hardin, urged support for this compromise, warning that regional differences over slavery threatened national unity:

❝It is north and east against the south and the west. It is a great geographical line that separates the contending [competing] parties. And those parties, when so equally divided, shake mighty empires to their center, and break up the foundations of the great deep, that sooner or later, if not settled, will rend in twain [break in two] this temple of liberty, from the top to the bottom.❞

Congress approved the Missouri Compromise in 1820. However, slavery remained a controversial issue for the nation.

★ The American System

Henry Clay proposed the Missouri Compromise in an attempt to keep the country unified. He believed that the key to avoiding regional conflicts was to create a national economy that linked the country together. To encourage the development of such an economy, in 1816 he had supported a bill to charter the Second Bank of the United States. Then in 1824 Clay proposed a protective tariff to boost domestic industries and to discourage Americans from buying foreign goods.

Clay wanted the federal government to use the tariff's proceeds for internal improvements such as better roads and canals, or artificial waterways. These improvements would link the regions of the country, making trade easier. This plan for using high tariffs to pay for internal improvements became known as the **American System**.

Many people supported the idea of unifying the country through internal improvements. "I believe the time [is] not very distant," predicted a western citizen in 1816, "when the wealth and resources of the western country will be brought almost to your door, by means of an extensive inland navigation system through the lakes." Some members of Congress, however, opposed Clay's plan, arguing that the Constitution did not authorize the federal government to spend money on internal improvements. Clay countered that the benefits to the country justified federal action.

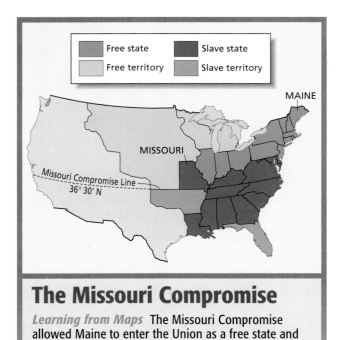

| Free state | Slave state |
| Free territory | Slave territory |

MAINE

MISSOURI

Missouri Compromise Line 36° 30' N

The Missouri Compromise

Learning from Maps The Missouri Compromise allowed Maine to enter the Union as a free state and Missouri as a slave state.

Region After the Missouri Compromise, how many slave states were there? How many free states?

★ Internal Improvements

Although Congress approved a protective tariff, many Americans were reluctant to use the money for internal improvements. As Congress debated the issue, many state governments and private citizens were already investing in improving the country's internal transportation systems.

Rough Roads

In the early 1800s most roads in the United States were made of dirt, making land travel difficult. British actress Frances ("Fanny") Kemble described one New York road she traveled on during a visit in the 1830s:

> **"The wickedest road, I do think, the cruellest, hard-heartedest road, that ever [a] wheel rumbled upon. Through bog and marsh, and ruts, wider and deeper than any . . . ruts I ever saw, with the roots of trees protruding [sticking out] across our path . . . ; and, more than once, a half-demolished trunk or stump lying in the middle of the road."**

Some people built roads made of planks or logs, but these efforts just tended to make the roads bumpier. A Pennsylvania company built an improved 66-mile toll road paved with stone and gravel between Philadelphia and Lancaster. Once the road was completed, the company charged users a toll, or fee, to travel on it. This type of road, called a turnpike, soon became common in the United States.

The **Cumberland Road** was the first federal road project. It ran from Cumberland, Maryland, to a town on the Ohio River called Wheeling, in present-day West Virginia. Construction began in 1815, and by 1818 the road reached Wheeling. The economic downturn after the Panic of 1819 temporarily halted further expansion. Construction began again in the 1820s. This National Road, as it was called, stretched to Columbus, Ohio, in 1833 and to Vandalia, Illinois, by 1850.

Canal Fever

Water transportation was usually quicker, easier, and cheaper than overland travel, but many areas of the country did not have rivers to connect them to other towns. Some Americans tried to make water transportation easier by building canals. During the early 1800s canal construction increased dramatically in the United States, particularly in the Northeast.

One of the largest projects was the **Erie Canal**, which ran from Albany to Buffalo, New York. Because Albany is located on the Hudson River—which feeds into New York Bay—and Buffalo is on Lake Erie, the canal opened up transportation between all towns on the lake and New York City. The Great Lakes region now had easier access to the nation's largest port city. One supporter hailed the canal as a triumph of technology, noting: "They have built the longest canal in the world, in the least time, with the least experience, for the least money and to the greatest public benefit."

The project was as much a triumph of human determination as of technology. New York governor DeWitt Clinton worked for many years to get approval for the project. Begun in 1817 and completed in 1825, the canal cost about $7 million to build. New York's citizens paid the majority of this expense through taxes.

The success of the Erie Canal encouraged states and private citizens to build more canals. South Carolina governor George McDuffie sponsored a canal project in hopes of making Charleston the center of southern Appalachian trade—what he called "the New York of the South."

The Granger Collection, New York

Travel by wagon could be very difficult in the 1800s because of poor road conditions.

Building the Erie Canal

In the early 1800s most American roads were in terrible condition. Wagons often sank deep in mud, and delays were common. These factors made shipping goods by land more time-consuming and expensive than shipping goods by water.

New York governor DeWitt Clinton urged the state to build a canal to connect Buffalo, on Lake Erie, to Albany, on the Hudson River, which flows south to New York City. The state began construction in 1817. Constructing such a large canal was an amazing engineering feat. Much of the land from Buffalo to Albany was hilly, so engineers used locks to raise or lower the boats.

A lock is a section of a canal with large gates at either end. After a boat enters a lock, operators close the gate behind it. Then they raise or lower the water level inside the lock by opening smaller gates. When the water reaches the desired height, the forward gate is opened, and the boat continues on its way. Engineers used more than 80 locks in the Erie Canal to raise the water level a total of more than 600 feet.

When finished in 1825, the Erie Canal was 363 miles long, 40 feet wide, and 4 feet deep. Many of the thousands of workers who built the canal lost their lives during construction. Despite its tragic cost in human life, the Erie Canal was a tremendous success and earned a profit for its investors. The cost of shipping cargo to areas served by the canal dropped dramatically. The canal also shortened travel times. The towns along the canal grew rapidly as a result of the increased traffic.

The success of the Erie Canal helped start a canal-building boom across the country. It also became part of American folklore, inspiring songs such as "Fifteen Miles on the Erie Canal." The canal is still in use today, more than 170 years since its completion.

Understanding What You Read

1. What challenges did engineers overcome in building the Erie Canal?

2. Describe the major benefits provided by the Erie Canal. Do you think they are still important today?

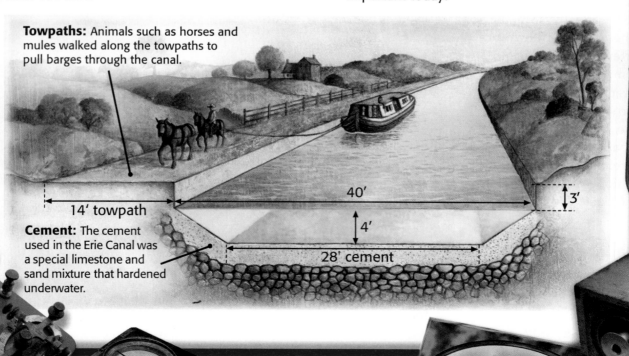

Towpaths: Animals such as horses and mules walked along the towpaths to pull barges through the canal.

Cement: The cement used in the Erie Canal was a special limestone and sand mixture that hardened underwater.

14' towpath

40'

3'

4'

28' cement

The Election of 1824

Some of the nation's domestic concerns during the previous four years were reflected in the heated presidential election of 1824. The five presidential candidates in the election all ran as Republicans, including Secretary of State John Quincy Adams and Andrew Jackson, who had become a senator from Tennessee. The campaign revealed growing regional divisions in the nation.

Jackson received the most popular votes but did not have enough electoral votes to win office. Under the Constitution, the House of Representatives had to determine the winner. Speaker of the House Henry Clay influenced the vote by backing Adams.

When the House chose Adams as president, Jackson's supporters claimed that Adams had made a "corrupt bargain" with Clay. These accusations increased after Adams appointed Clay as secretary of state. "Corruptions and intrigues at Washington . . . defeated the will of the people," declared Jackson.

The election controversy further weakened Adams's congressional and public support during his presidency. He was already unpopular in the slaveholding South. This support declined even more after he took office and introduced proposals to expand federal funding of roads, canals, scientific research, and education. Congress rejected

As president, John Quincy Adams supported higher education and tried unsuccessfully to establish a national university.

most of these proposals but agreed to fund some road and canal projects. Although one historian has called Adams "one of the most intelligent, courageous, experienced, and public-spirited of all our Presidents," he was far less effective as president than he had been as a secretary of state.

SECTION 2 REVIEW

Identify and explain the significance of the following:
- **Henry Clay**
- **Missouri Compromise**
- **American System**
- **Cumberland Road**
- **Erie Canal**
- **John Quincy Adams**

Reading for Content Understanding

1 **Main Idea** Why did Missouri's application for admission to the Union spark a controversy?

2 **Main Idea** How was the outcome of the 1824 election determined, and what reactions did it bring?

3 **Geographic Diversity** *Movement* How did new transportation systems affect the nation, particularly the western states?

4 **Writing** *Expressing* Write a letter to Henry Clay, agreeing or disagreeing with the Missouri Compromise.

5 **Critical Thinking** *Evaluating* Which of the 1824 presidential candidates, Adams or Jackson, would you have chosen? Explain your choice.

The Age of Jackson

Reading Focus

How did Jacksonian Democracy represent a change in U.S. politics?

What led to the nullification crisis, and how did President Jackson respond?

Why did President Jackson oppose a national bank, and how did this opposition affect the economy?

Key Terms

nominating conventions

Democratic Party

spoils system

kitchen cabinet

Tariff of Abominations

states' rights

nullification

McCulloch v. *Maryland*

Whig Party

Panic of 1837

JOHN QUINCY ADAMS *once described himself as "a man of reserved, cold . . . and forbidding [threatening] manners." To many citizens, Adams represented an old, upper-class culture that was out of touch with the nation's needs. Although his personality was not much different from that of previous presidents, political rallies of the 1820s indicated that the people wanted a more lively candidate. Journalists were particularly amazed by the wild gatherings held by Andrew Jackson's supporters. One writer noted that Jackson's popularity proved there "must be a new order of things."*

Medallions from the 1824 election

 ## Jacksonian Democracy

Changes in voting rights meant that many more Americans could vote for the first time in the 1820s and 1830s. More white men gained suffrage when many states began eliminating property ownership as a requirement for voting. In addition, some political parties began holding public **nominating conventions**—meetings to select a party's presidential and vice presidential candidates—to allow more voter input. These measures helped voters become more active in politics and increased their influence over who was elected president. Historians call this democratic expansion "Jacksonian Democracy."

However, not everyone gained greater political power. In 1807, women had lost their right to vote in New Jersey—the only state that had granted them suffrage after the Revolution. In addition, several states that had previously allowed free African Americans to vote took away that right when they expanded suffrage for white men.

Andrew Jackson

Andrew Jackson's nickname "Old Hickory" reflected his reputation for being extremely tough, like the hard wood of a hickory tree. In addition to his military service, Jackson was known for dueling and physically fighting with his enemies. American politician Thomas Hart Benton, who survived one such encounter with the Tennessean, admitted proudly afterward, "I had a fight with Jackson. A fellow was hardly in the fashion who didn't."

Although his opponents often pointed to these incidents as examples of Jackson's hot temper, many of his supporters believed that they reflected his high sense of honor. For example, in his most famous duel, Jackson took a bullet near his heart. Others argued that Jackson was just following the advice of his mother, who is said to have once told him, "Never sue for assault or slander; settle [those] cases yourself." Although Jackson avoided physical fights while he was president, many critics believed that his quick temper harmed his ability to work with Congress and with his cabinet.

Adams Versus Jackson

Andrew Jackson's supporters, who were mostly farmers and southern slaveholders, saw their candidate as someone who would defend the rights of the common people and the slave states. Many of these Americans believed that a "corrupt bargain" had stolen the 1824 election from Jackson. These supporters organized to ensure that Jackson would become the next president.

The Election of 1828

Jackson's supporters, who included many poor citizens and frontier settlers, began to identify themselves as Democrats and became the **Democratic Party**. Many people who backed President Adams began calling themselves National Republicans. In the presidential election of 1828, Adams ran as a National Republican and Jackson as a Democrat.

The 1828 campaign focused heavily on the candidates' personalities. Jackson's campaigners contrasted his image as a war hero—who was born poor and rose to success through his own determination—with the image of Adams, the Harvard-educated intellectual whose father had been the second U.S. president. Some of Jackson's supporters also described Adams as being unfamiliar with everyday people. Even an Adams admirer admitted that his personality was as "cold as a lump of ice." In turn, Adams's supporters accused Jackson of being hot-tempered, crude, and ill-equipped to be president. When the votes were counted, however, Jackson and his vice presidential running mate, John C. Calhoun, had won a majority of both the popular and electoral votes.

Jackson's Style

Jackson's supporters saw his victory as a win for the common people. One Kentucky newspaper editor declared, "It was a proud day for the people. General Jackson is *their own* president." To emphasize this point, a crowd of Jackson voters threw a huge party on the White House lawn to celebrate his inauguration. The party caused a great deal of property damage, and some people feared that the mob at the White House signaled an unstable era to come. Observer Margaret Bayard Smith recalled the inauguration party:

❝ **What a scene did we witness! . . . a rabble, a mob, of boys, . . . women, children, scrambling, fighting, romping. . . . But it was the people's day, and the people's President, and the people would rule.** ❞

Political Conventions

Before the 1830s, U.S. presidential candidates were selected by caucuses, or groups of lawmakers from each political party's members in the U.S. Congress. In the election of 1832, the three major parties—the Democrats, the National Republicans, and the Anti-Masons—held national conventions to choose their candidate for president.

According to one New Hampshire lawmaker, the object of these conventions was

“ *not to impose on the people, as candidates for either of the two first offices of the government, any local favorite; but to concentrate the opinions of all the states.* ”

Delegates—the people who select the presidential candidate—came from the states that participated in these first conventions. There were no established convention practices, so each of the parties made up its own rules. For example, the National Republicans' convention introduced the keynote address, the nominating speech, and the seconding speech, all of which are standard convention practices today.

In the party conventions held in 1831 and 1832, each state held a convention to choose its delegates to the national meeting. In the early 1900s, however, parties began using a variety of methods to pick delegates, including selection by party officials and election by voters.

Other important changes have also taken place over the years. For example, the number of delegates attending conventions has risen significantly as the population has increased. In 1831 only 116 delegates attended the first convention, but in 1996 the Democratic National Convention had 5,500 delegates. Both the Democratic and Republican Parties have increased their number of delegates in order to include more women, minority group members, and younger people in their conventions. An important goal of both parties is the equal representation of men and women, to better reflect the population.

In recent years, improvements in telecommunications have influenced conventions as well. The 1996 Democratic National Convention was the first to use the Internet to keep delegates informed of events. A technical director called it "one of the most technically advanced conventions ever." Among other things, delegates were able to "talk" with each other through computer chat lines and receive information on the convention in both audio and video formats.

The 1996 Democratic National Convention

Understanding What You Read

1. How were presidential nominees chosen before the 1830s?

2. How have political nominating conventions changed over time?

Jackson rewarded some of his supporters with government jobs—a practice known as the **spoils system**, after the saying "to the victor go the spoils [possessions] of the enemy." However, Jackson did not change many government positions—he replaced only 9 percent of federal officeholders. Secretary of State Martin Van Buren was one of Jackson's strongest allies in his official cabinet. President Jackson also relied heavily on an informal group of trusted advisers, called the **kitchen cabinet** because they often met in the White House kitchen.

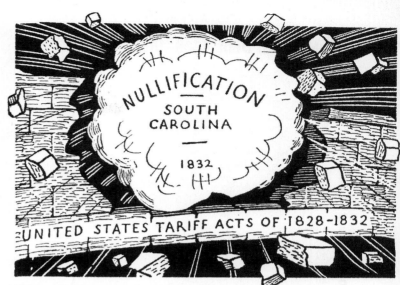

This political cartoon shows how nullification attempted to tear down the nation's protective tariffs.

A Threat to the Union

As Jackson placed more trust in the kitchen cabinet, he came to mistrust Vice President Calhoun. The dispute between the two widened during a national conflict over tariffs. Southerners opposed protective tariffs because the region had little industry and relied heavily on imported goods.

When Congress passed a new tariff in 1828, southerners grew very angry. Opponents nicknamed the law the **Tariff of Abominations** (an abomination is something that is hateful). Some southern leaders saw the tariff as another example of the federal government's power over the states.

Siding with the southern opposition, Calhoun wrote a statement in support of **states' rights**, or the belief that state power should be greater than federal power. In what was known as the idea of **nullification**, Calhoun declared that the states had the right to nullify, or not to obey, any federal law with which they disagreed. "If there be no protective power in the reserved rights of the states, they must in the end be forced to rebel," he warned in 1830. Other Americans agreed with Senator Daniel Webster of Massachusetts, who opposed nullification. Webster vowed, "Liberty *and* Union, now and forever, one and inseparable!"

Andrew Jackson stated his opposition to nullification in this letter to Martin Van Buren.

South Carolina then tested the nullification theory after Congress passed a new tariff in 1832. Calhoun resigned from the vice presidency to support his home state of South Carolina in its fight for nullification. Van Buren became the new vice president when Jackson was re-elected president in November 1832. That same month, the South Carolina state legislature passed a resolution declaring the 1828 and 1832 tariffs "null, void . . . nor binding upon this State, its officers or citizens."

Jackson responded by strongly condemning nullification. "I consider, then, the power to annul [cancel] a law of the United States . . . incompatible with [contrary to] the existence of the Union," he said. Jackson threatened to send U.S. troops into South Carolina to enforce federal laws. However, such measures were not necessary because the two sides reached a compromise. Congress agreed to gradually lower the tariffs over several years. South Carolina leaders agreed to enforce the tariffs, although they continued to insist that nullification was legal.

The Second Bank of the United States

Although President Jackson upheld federal authority in the nullification crisis, he did not always support the expansion of federal power. For example, he opposed the Second Bank of the United States, which Congress had established in 1816.

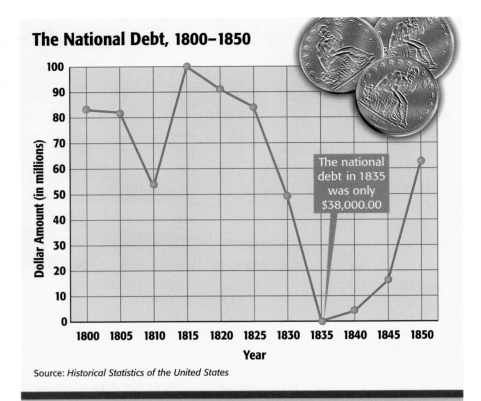

The National Debt, 1800–1850

The national debt in 1835 was only $38,000.00

Source: *Historical Statistics of the United States*

Lowering the Debt   Around 1830 President Jackson was able to lower the national debt by using profits made from the sale of public lands. According to the graph, during which year was the national debt highest?

McCulloch v. Maryland

Many states also opposed the Bank and took action against it. For example, Maryland tried to impose a tax that would restrict the Bank's operations. The Bank refused to pay the tax, and the case went to the U.S. Supreme Court. The Court, led by Chief Justice John Marshall, made two important rulings in **McCulloch v. Maryland**. The Court supported the Bank's constitutionality, using the argument that the elastic clause allowed Congress to establish the Bank. This Court ruling was a broad interpretation of the implied powers of Congress. The Court also ruled that because federal law was superior to state law, Maryland could not tax, or otherwise interfere with, the Bank.

Jackson's War on the Bank

Nicholas Biddle, the Bank's director, decided to make the Bank a presidential issue. Rather than waiting until its charter expired in 1836, Biddle pushed for a bill to renew the Bank's charter in 1832. Jackson campaigned strongly for its defeat.

"I will kill it," he promised. Jackson vetoed legislation to renew the charter. He issued a strongly worded statement arguing that the Bank allowed the wealthy to influence the government:

❝ **It is to be regretted that the rich and powerful too often bend the acts of government to their selfish purposes. . . . By attempting to gratify their desires, we have in the results of our legislation arrayed [positioned] section against section, interest against interest.** ❞

Congress could not get the two-thirds majority needed to override Jackson's veto. Although the Bank's existing charter was not due to expire until 1836, Jackson weakened the Bank's power by moving most of its funds to state banks, which his opponents nicknamed "pet banks." In many cases, these banks used the funds to offer credit to people buying land. While this helped spur expansion in the West, it also led to inflation. To slow inflation, in August 1836 Jackson ordered Americans to use only gold or silver to buy government-owned land. Although this policy did not help the national economy as he had hoped, Jackson did improve the economy by lowering the national debt.

★ Van Buren's Presidency

Jackson was still very popular with voters in 1836. His actions, however, had

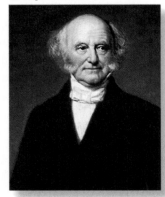

Martin Van Buren gained the presidency largely because of his loyalty to Andrew Jackson.

angered members of Congress, who believed he had abused his presidential powers. In 1834 a group of Jackson opponents had formed a new political organization known as the **Whig Party**. Many Whigs supported the idea of a weak president and a strong legislature. In 1836 the Whigs nominated four candidates for president against the democratic candidate Martin Van Buren. With strong support from Jackson, Van Buren won the election.

The people never embraced Van Buren the way they had Jackson. Shortly after Van Buren took office, the country experienced a financial crisis, called the **Panic of 1837**, which led to a severe economic depression. The policies of the "pet banks" and Jackson's plan to curb inflation had helped lead to the panic, but Van Buren received the blame for it.

The financial crisis hurt President Van Buren's re-election campaign in 1840. The Whigs ran William Henry Harrison, the hero of the Battle of Tippecanoe, as their candidate. He and John Tyler, his running mate, used the slogan "Tippecanoe and Tyler too." The Whigs characterized Van Buren as a friend of the rich, while showing

The Granger Collection, New York

William Henry Harrison's years as governor of Indiana Territory led Whig supporters to show him as a rugged frontiersman during the 1840 campaign.

Harrison as the friend of the common people. The Whigs' emphasis on Harrison's war record and log-cabin roots—even though he had actually been born to a wealthy family—seemed to compare him to Jackson. Over 75 percent of the voters turned out for this election. Although the popular vote was close, Harrison won in a electoral landslide, with 234 electoral votes to Van Buren's 60. The Whigs had gained the presidency.

SECTION 3 REVIEW

Identify and explain the significance of the following:

- **nominating conventions**
- **Democratic Party**
- **Andrew Jackson**
- **John C. Calhoun**
- **spoils system**
- **kitchen cabinet**
- **Tariff of Abominations**
- **states' rights**
- **nullification**
- *McCulloch* v. *Maryland*
- **Whig Party**
- **Martin Van Buren**
- **Panic of 1837**
- **William Henry Harrison**

Reading for Content Understanding

1 **Main Idea** Why did southerners oppose protective tariffs, and how did this opposition lead to the nullification crisis?

2 **Main Idea** Why did President Jackson veto the Bank of the United States, and what effect did this have on the economy?

3 **Citizenship and Democracy** Why did Jackson's supporters see his election to the presidency as a victory for the common people?

4 **Writing** *Describing* Write a newspaper editorial describing the rise of Jacksonian Democracy.

5 **Critical Thinking** *Drawing Conclusions* Why do you think Jackson used the spoils system, and how do you think this system affected American politics?

Indian Removal

Reading Focus

Why did the U.S. government begin an American Indian removal policy?

How did the American Indians resist being forced off their lands?

What were the results of the Trail of Tears and the Second Seminole War?

Key Terms

Indian Removal Act
Indian Territory
Bureau of Indian Affairs
Treaty of Dancing Rabbit Creek
Worcester v. Georgia
Trail of Tears

Black Hawk

T*HE STAGE WAS SET for a major conflict. As American settlers sought more Indian land, tribal leaders debated the best way to deal with the migrants. Keokuk, a Sauk leader from Illinois, supported compromise with the settlers to avoid war. However, another Sauk leader named Black Hawk believed that U.S. officials had bribed Keokuk and other tribal leaders to gain their support. Black Hawk would not be bribed. He vowed to resist all attempts to take Indian lands, even if it meant going to war.*

★ The Black Hawk War

In 1827 the government of Illinois decided to end years of conflict between American Indians and American settlers by ordering the removal of all Indians from the state. Black Hawk and his followers ignored the removal policy and refused to accept the idea of land ownership. As he explained:

❝ My reason teaches me that land cannot be sold. The Great Spirit gave it to his children to live upon. So long as they occupy and cultivate it they have the right to the soil. Nothing can be sold but such things as can be carried away. ❞

When the Sauk Indians returned to their village of Saukenuk after a winter hunt in 1829, they found white settlers had set up camp there. Black Hawk and his followers remained, but as more settlers arrived Governor John Reynolds became determined to remove the Sauk. In the spring of 1831 the militia destroyed Saukenuk and drove out the Sauk. When Black Hawk returned the next year, President Jackson ordered federal troops to join the militia.

In May 1832 Black Hawk and around 40 other Sauk observed a force of about 275 militia approaching their camp. Black Hawk sent a peace delegation under a white flag. The militia ignored the flag and attacked the Sauk delegates, killing three. Black Hawk's followers then attacked so fiercely that the troops retreated.

Black Hawk's victory inspired other Indian tribes to resist removal. Many Indian groups began to raid American settlements and fight against the U.S. Army. However, by August the Sauk forces were running out of food and supplies. The Black Hawk War ended when U.S. Army troops attacked the Sauk as they were attempting to retreat west across a river. The army had 20 casualties, while the Sauk lost about 300 lives. When Black Hawk surrendered in late August, he agreed to give up leadership of the Sauk.

⭐ The Indian Removal Act

After the Black Hawk War, Indians in the Northwest Territory no longer physically resisted white settlement on their lands. By 1846 the government had completed Indian removal northeast of the Mississippi River. Meanwhile, conflict over removal of American Indians from the Southeast increased.

Conflict over Land

American Indians had long thrived on the fertile lands of the Lower South, with settlements stretching from Georgia to Mississippi. President Jackson and other political leaders decided to clear the land for American farmers. The government wanted Indians in the Southeast to move to lands in the West.

Under steady pressure from Jackson, in 1830 Congress passed the **Indian Removal Act**, which authorized the removal of Indians who lived east of the Mississippi River. Congress then established **Indian Territory**, an area containing most of present-day Oklahoma, as a new homeland for removed tribes. Some supporters of this plan, like John C. Calhoun, argued that removal to Indian Territory would protect Indians from further conflicts with American settlers. "One of the greatest evils to which they are subject is that incessant [constant] pressure of our population," he noted. "To guard against this evil . . . there ought to be the strongest . . . assurance that the country given [to]

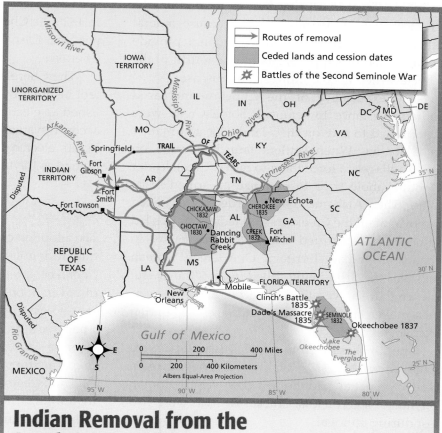

Indian Removal from the Southeast, c. 1830s

Learning from Maps The Indian Removal Act of 1830 allowed the president to exchange land west of the Mississippi River for lands owned by American Indians in the Southeast. American Indians were forced from their homes and marched hundreds of miles to the new Indian Territory.

Place From what present-day state were the Seminole removed?

them should be theirs." To oversee the federal policy toward American Indians, Congress also created the **Bureau of Indian Affairs**.

Removal

The Choctaw were the first Indians sent to Indian Territory. After the Mississippi legislature abolished the government of the Choctaw, some Choctaw leaders signed the **Treaty of Dancing Rabbit Creek**. This treaty gave more than 10 million acres of their land to the state. The Choctaw then made the journey from Mississippi to Indian Territory during the winter of 1831–32. The trek was disastrous in part because federal officials in charge of the move did not provide enough food or supplies. About one fourth of the Choctaw died of cold, hunger, and disease.

The experience of the Choctaw increased Indian resistance to removal. Some Creek were determined to stay on their lands, located mainly in Alabama. When settlers launched raids on Creek villages to force them to move, Creek leader Opothleyaholo tried to organize an armed resistance. Then Alabama officials ordered the forced removal of all the Creek. In 1836 federal troops led some 14,500 captured Creek Indians, many in chains, to Indian Territory. One Creek woman recalled the trip being filled with "the awful silence that showed the heartaches and sorrow at being taken from the homes and even separation from loved ones."

The Chickasaw, from upper Mississippi, were removed west in 1837–38. They had negotiated a treaty for better supplies on their trip to Indian Territory. Nevertheless, Chickasaw lives were also lost during removal.

★ The Cherokee Nation

American Indians resisted removal in various ways. The Cherokee, for example, sought justice through the U.S. court system.

Sequoyah created a written version of the Cherokee language.

The Granger Collection, New York

Cherokee Society

Many Cherokee believed that they could avoid conflict with settlers by adopting practices similar to those of white society. For example, in the early 1800s, the Cherokee invited missionary societies to establish schools in their towns. In these schools, Cherokee children learned how to read and write English.

Although American Indian cultures had complex spoken languages, none had a written language. In 1821 a Cherokee named Sequoyah produced a writing system that used 85 characters to represent Cherokee syllables. In 1828 the Cherokee began publishing a newspaper, the *Cherokee Phoenix*, in both English and Cherokee.

The Cherokee also created a government system inspired by the U.S. Constitution. They established an election system, a bicameral council, and a court system, all headed by a principal chief. Voters elected John Ross, a successful plantation owner, as the first principal chief.

A Court Challenge

The adoption of white culture did not protect the Cherokee after gold was discovered on their land in Georgia. Ignoring the Cherokee's treaty rights, Georgia officials began preparing for the removal. After the Cherokee refused to move, the Georgia militia began attacking Indian towns.

The tribe sued the state, arguing that the Cherokee were an independent nation and did not have to follow state laws. In March 1831 the

Cherokee children used this primer in school to learn how to read and write in Cherokee.

Supreme Court rejected the claim, saying that Indian tribes were "domestic dependent nations." This ruling meant that American Indians were neither a foreign nation nor U.S. citizens. They could not sue in federal court, but they still had to obey federal laws. Although the justices implied that Georgia was not treating the Cherokee fairly, they issued no order to stop the state's actions.

The Cherokee and their supporters continued to argue the issue. Samuel Worcester, a missionary who worked with the tribe, was arrested for failing to take an oath of allegiance and to obey a Georgia militia order to leave the Indians' lands. Worcester sued, charging that Georgia had no legal authority on Cherokee lands. In 1832 the Supreme Court agreed. In **Worcester v. Georgia** the Court ruled that the Cherokee Nation "is a distinct community, occupying its own territory, . . . in which the laws of Georgia can have no force." This decision agreed with the Court's earlier ruling that the Cherokee tribe was a domestic dependent nation. The Court also ruled that only the federal government, not the states, had authority over the Cherokee.

The Court ruling made Georgia's actions illegal. However, with Jackson's support, Georgia defied the Court's ruling. "John Marshall has made his decision; now let him enforce it," Jackson declared. By not enforcing the Court's decision, Jackson was violating his presidential oath to uphold the laws of the land. However, most members of Congress and the American people chose not to take serious issue over Indian Removal and Jackson's method of accomplishing it.

★ The Trail of Tears

With President Jackson refusing to enforce the Supreme Court's decision, many Cherokee saw removal as unavoidable. Elias Boudinot, editor of the *Cherokee Phoenix*, wrote, "I cannot tell (my people) that we will be reinstated in [given back] our rights when I have no such hope." To silence further criticism, the Georgia militia destroyed the *Phoenix*'s printing press.

In the spring of 1838, U.S. troops began to force the removal of all Cherokee to Indian Territory. While a few managed to escape and hide in the mountains of North Carolina, most were captured. An army private recalled the scene:

66 **Chief Ross led in prayer and when the bugle sounded and the wagons started rolling many of the children . . . waved their little hands good-bye to their mountain homes.** 99

Georgia took the Cherokee's farms, businesses, and property after they were removed.

The Cherokee's 800-mile forced march, known as the **Trail of Tears**, lasted from 1838 to 1839. Almost one fourth of the 18,000 Cherokee died from disease, hunger, and harsh weather.

★ The Second Seminole War

Unlike the Cherokee, the Seminole of Florida resisted removal with armed force. In 1832 some Seminole leaders were forced to sign a treaty promising to leave Florida within three years and agreeing that any Seminole of African ancestry would be considered a runaway slave. This last condition concerned the Seminole because they had a tradition of harboring runaway slaves. Many escaped slaves had married into the tribe,

The removal of the southeastern Indian tribes often had tragic results. Many American Indians died on journeys such as the Trail of Tears, shown here.

becoming accepted as family members of the Seminole.

The Seminole ignored the treaty and refused to leave Florida. Federal officials then pressed for a new removal agreement. A Seminole leader named Osceola refused to sign the new treaty. He called upon the Seminole to resist removal by force:

> ❝When the Great Spirit tells me to go with the white man, I go, but he tells me not to go. I have a rifle, and I have some powder and some lead. I say, we must not leave our homes and lands.❞

Indian removals forced many of the Seminole to abandon villages like this one in the Florida Everglades.

Osceola's followers rallied behind him, and the Second Seminole War began.

Initially, the Seminole won many battles against the U.S. forces. One of their greatest victories was on New Year's Eve, 1835, when an outnumbered Seminole force surprised and defeated some 800 Florida militia and U.S. Army troops at the Withlacoochee River. Then in 1837, U.S. forces captured Osceola. He died in prison the next year, but the Seminole continued to fight against the United States.

By 1842 the U.S. Army had captured and removed some 3,000 Seminole and killed hundreds of others. In the process, some 1,500 U.S. soldiers lost their lives. After spending millions of dollars, U.S. officials decided to give up the fight. The Seminole had not been defeated.

Some Seminole eventually chose to migrate to Indian Territory. One such Seminole was Wildcat, a warrior who had fought against removal for years. He said, "I am about to leave Florida forever and have done nothing to disgrace it. It was my home; I loved it, and to leave it is like burying my wife and child." Several hundred Seminole remained carefully hidden in the Florida Everglades, where they continued to maintain their culture. The Seminole still live on tribal lands in Florida today.

SECTION 4 REVIEW

Identify and explain the significance of the following:

- Black Hawk
- Indian Removal Act
- Indian Territory
- Bureau of Indian Affairs
- Treaty of Dancing Rabbit Creek
- Sequoyah
- John Ross
- *Worcester* v. *Georgia*
- Trail of Tears
- Osceola

Reading for Content Understanding

1 **Main Idea** Why did U.S. officials support an Indian removal policy?

2 **Main Idea** How did Indian groups in the Midwest and Southeast resist removal?

3 **Constitutional Heritage** How did the Cherokee use the courts to resist removal from their lands? What was the outcome of their legal challenge?

4 **Writing** *Expressing* Imagine that you are reporting about a Cherokee Indian who is on the Trail of Tears and about a Seminole who is fighting in Florida. Write a short article about both people.

5 **Critical Thinking** *Drawing Conclusions* Why do you think the U.S. government had difficulty defeating the Seminole?

American Culture

Reading Focus

How did popular writers reflect growing American nationalism?

What was the focus of the Hudson River school?

Why did ancient styles of architecture become popular in the United States?

Key Terms

Hudson River school

*I*N 1817 VIRGINIA POLITICIAN *William Wirt published a popular biography of Revolutionary leader Patrick Henry. Wirt spent years researching his book but found that Henry was not as exciting as he had hoped. "The incidents of Mr. Henry's life are extremely monotonous [boring]," Wirt told a friend. "It is all speaking, speaking, speaking." To make the book more exciting, Wirt exaggerated certain events, leading some critics to charge that the author was changing history. Despite these complaints, Wirt's book made Patrick Henry a hero for a whole new generation of Americans.*

Patrick Henry

★ American Tales

The success of William Wirt's biography of Patrick Henry reflected several developments in American society, including a public fascination with the Revolutionary era. Wirt represented a growing number of writers who wrote about the heroes of the Revolution to encourage American pride. Unlike Wirt, however, most of these writers used fictional characters to represent American ideals.

One of the first American writers to gain international fame was Washington Irving. Born in 1783, he was named after George Washington.

Irving's written works often told about American history in a humorous way, using a form of writing called satire. Through humor, Irving showed why Americans should learn from the past and be cautious about the future.

Irving expressed this idea in one of his best-known short stories, "Rip Van Winkle." In this story a man falls asleep during the time of the American Revolution and wakes up 20 years later to a society he does not recognize. Irving published this story in an 1819–20 collection that included another of his well-known tales, "The Legend of Sleepy Hollow."

Washington Irving's character, Rip Van Winkle (left), commented on the dramatic changes in the United States following the Revolutionary War.

Irving was one of the first American writers to gain respect in Europe, partly because his humorous style was heavily influenced by European writers. Irving believed that the United States should not abandon European traditions altogether. He said, "We are a young people . . . , and we must take our examples and models in a great degree, from the existing nations of Europe."

★ Historical Fiction

In some of his most popular works, Irving combined European influences with settings and characters that were uniquely American. In this way, his work served as a bridge between European traditions and a new breed of American writers who were hopeful about the country's future.

James Fenimore Cooper

The best known of these new writers was James Fenimore Cooper, who was born to a wealthy New Jersey family in 1789. Although Cooper never saw the American frontier, he was fascinated by stories that he heard about the West and the American Indians who lived there. These subjects became the focus of his most popular works. Cooper's first book was not very successful, but his next novel, *The Spy*, was a huge success. Published in 1821, it was an adventure story set during the Revolution. It appealed to American readers' patriotism and desire for an exciting, action-filled story.

In 1823 Cooper published *The Pioneers*, the first of five novels featuring the heroic character Natty Bumppo. This collection of books, called the "Leatherstocking Tales," focused on settling the western frontier, with Bumppo representing a frontiersman who finds truth in nature. Most of the stories involved historical events, such as *The Last of the Mohicans*, which takes place during the French and Indian War. By placing fictional characters in a real event, Cooper popularized a genre, or type, of writing called historical fiction.

Some critics complained that Cooper's characters were uninteresting—particularly the women in his stories, who seemed to be included only to get rescued by the hero. Poet Russell Lowell complained,

❝ **The women he draws from one model don't vary,**
All sappy as maples and flat as a prairie.❞

Despite such criticism by Lowell and others, Cooper's "Leatherstocking Tales" became bestsellers that remain popular today.

Catharine Maria Sedgwick

Although Cooper's female characters seemed dull to some observers, other authors of historical fiction, such as Catharine Maria Sedgwick, created interesting heroines. In 1822 Sedgwick published her first novel, *A New England Tale*, which focused on the landscape and culture of her society.

Another popular Sedgwick book, *Hope Leslie*, was a historical novel set in Massachusetts in the 1600s. To make this 1827 novel realistic, Sedgwick conducted extensive research into the culture of the Mohawk Indians, who had lived in the area at the time. Some readers complained that her

The Last of the Mohicans
James Fenimore Cooper

James Fenimore Cooper, one of the nation's first novelists, helped create the myth of the frontier and the American hero who thrived in it. Natty Bumppo, also called Leatherstocking and Hawkeye, is the hero of the five novels in the "Leatherstocking Tales." Chingachgook, a Mohican Indian, is also an important character in the popular stories. Cooper's experience with Indians and the frontier was limited to the books he read and the stories his father told. Nevertheless, Cooper's novels brought the frontier to life. They had a wide audience in America and Europe and have remained popular since his death in 1851. In the following passage from The Last of the Mohicans, *set during the French and Indian War, Chingachgook tells Hawkeye about the Mohicans' recent history.*

James Fenimore Cooper, shown here in 1831, became one of the most popular American writers of the early 1800s.

"The first pale-faces who came among us spoke no English. They came in a large canoe, when my fathers had buried the tomahawk [made peace] with the redmen around them. Then, Hawkeye," he continued, betraying his deep emotion . . . "then, Hawkeye, we were one people, and we were happy. The salt lake gave us its fish, the wood its deer, and the air its birds. We took wives who bore us children; we worshipped the Great Spirit; and we kept the Maquas [their enemy] beyond the sound of our songs of triumph! . . ."

"The Dutch landed, and gave my people the fire-water [alcoholic beverages]; they drank until the heavens and the earth seemed to meet, and they foolishly thought they had found the Great Spirit. Then they parted with their land. Foot by foot, they were driven back from the shores, until I that am a chief and a sagamore [a lesser chief of the Algonquian], have never seen the sun shine but through the trees, and have never visited the graves of my fathers! . . ."

"Where are the blossoms of those summers!–fallen, one by one: so all of my family departed, each in his turn, to the land of spirits. I am on the hill-top, and most go down into the valley; and when Uncas follows in my footsteps, there will no longer be any of the blood of the sagamores, for my boy is the last of the Mohicans."

Understanding Literature

1. What has happened to the Mohican Indians?

2. What does Chingachgook mean by going down into the valley, and how is this significant for the Mohicans?

description of the Pilgrims included unflattering aspects of their society, such as their superstitions and intolerance. She defended her description, saying that it accurately showed both the strengths and weaknesses of early Americans:

❝ **These were the vices [bad habits] of their age. . . . They had a most generous and self-devoting zeal [energy] to the cause of liberty, so far as they understood it, but they were still in the thraldom of [believed in] . . . superstition.** ❞

Sedgwick hoped that reading about the experiences of the Pilgrims would teach Americans to remain open to new ideas.

Sedgwick wrote six books and was the most successful female author of her time. Through her work, she also challenged commonly held prejudices about women. For example, in *Married or Single?* the never-married Sedgwick rejected the notion that all women had to get married. She said

Catharine Maria Sedgwick used her knowledge of New England to create vivid stories about the region's history.

that she hoped the novel would "lessen the stigma [disgrace] placed on the term, old maid."

⭐ A New Style of Art

Inspired by the writings of Irving and Cooper, a group of painters began to draw landscapes that glorified the history of America and the beauty of its landscape. Before the Jacksonian era, most American painters like John Singleton Copley focused on painting portraits. By the 1830s a new group of artists had emerged called the **Hudson River school**. These artists primarily painted landscapes. They received their name because many of their paintings focused on images from the Hudson River valley, such as the scenic wonder of the Catskill Mountains.

The leader of the group, Thomas Cole, had immigrated to the United States from Britain in 1819. At age 17 he recognized the unique qualities of the American landscape. As his work gained fame, he encouraged other American artists to show the beauty of nature. "To walk with nature as a poet is the necessary condition of a perfect artist," Cole once recorded. Observer William Bryant said of Cole's work:

❝ **[It] carried the eye over scenes of wild grandeur peculiar to our country, over our aerial mountain tops with their mighty growth of forests never touched by the axe, along the bank of streams never deformed by culture and into the depth of skies bright with the hues [colors] of our own climate.** ❞

By the 1840s more artists were trying to combine images of the American landscape with the people who lived on it. For example, George Caleb Bingham's

Painters belonging to the Hudson River school created images like this one that focused on the beauty of the American landscape.

The Granger Collection, New York

most famous painting, *Fur Traders Descending the Missouri*, captures the rugged, lonely existence of traders in the West.

American Architecture

American artistry extended to the way in which people designed buildings. Before the Revolution, most American architects followed the "Georgian" style used in Britain. This style featured square or rectangular brick and wood buildings, with ornamented flat roofs and impressive fronts.

After the Revolution, many American leaders such as Thomas Jefferson called for Americans to model their architecture after the style used in ancient Greece and Rome. Many Americans admired these ancient civilizations because they contained some of the same ideals as the new American nation. Ancient Greek and Roman buildings, usually made out of marble or other stone, featured large, stately columns.

A few Americans rejected the idea of using older architectural models. Thomas Paine argued that Americans should create a unique style to show that the United States was a better republic than the ancients. As time went by, however, more architects followed Jefferson's ideas than Paine's. Westward expansion and economic prosperity

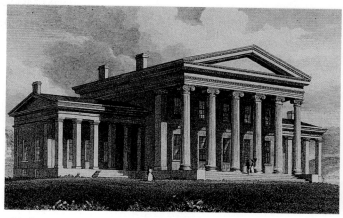

This home in Massachusetts reflects the architecture of the early 1800s, which used ancient Greek and Roman styles.

created a building boom in the Jacksonian era. Almost all of these new buildings used Greek and Roman styles, though some mixed them with other styles to create a more original look.

Such styles extended even to private homes and public buildings in small towns. An increase in reading helped spread common architectural styles. Many carpenters throughout the country read books like Asher Benjamin's *Practical House Carpenter*, which showed them how to construct buildings with the new methods. As the nation grew, these new types of architecture, as well as the developments in literature and art contributed to the creation of a new national American identity.

SECTION 5 REVIEW

Identify and explain the significance of the following:
- **Washington Irving**
- **James Fenimore Cooper**
- **Catharine Maria Sedgwick**
- **Hudson River school**
- **Thomas Cole**
- **George Caleb Bingham**

Reading for Content Understanding

1 **Main Idea** What themes did Washington Irving, James Fenimore Cooper, and Catharine Maria Sedgwick write about, and what does their work say about American culture at the time?

2 **Main Idea** What subjects did Thomas Cole and the Hudson River school artists paint?

3 **Cultural Diversity** Why did some leaders call for a new architectural style after the American Revolution?

4 **Writing** *Creating* Write a short story of historical fiction about events you have studied so far in U.S. history.

5 **Critical Thinking** *Drawing Conclusions* Why do you think most of the new buildings constructed during the Jacksonian era were modeled after Greek and Roman styles?

CHAPTER 12 REVIEW

Chapter Summary

James Monroe's presidency ushered in what many called the Era of Good Feelings. Nationalism and democracy were on the rise. Andrew Jackson, who was elected president in 1828, dealt with issues such as the Bank of the United States and Indian removal. American culture began to break away from European styles and form its own unique traditions. ■

On a separate sheet of paper, complete the following activities.

Identifying People and Ideas

Describe the historical significance of the following:

1. James Monroe
2. Monroe Doctrine
3. Henry Clay
4. American System
5. Democratic Party
6. William Henry Harrison
7. Bureau of Indian Affairs
8. Sequoyah
9. Catharine Maria Sedgwick
10. Hudson River school

Internet Activity

go.hrw.com
SA0 American Architecture

Search the Internet through the HRW Web site for images of American buildings constructed in the early 1800s. Choose one example and write a short paragraph describing what architectural style or styles the building represents.

Understanding Main Ideas

1. What led to the Missouri Compromise?
2. What effect did the revolutions in Latin America have on U.S. foreign policy?
3. Why did President Jackson veto the rechartering of the Second Bank of the United States?
4. What caused the Panic of 1837?
5. How did American Indians resist removal to Indian Territory?
6. How did Catharine Maria Sedgwick's book *Married or Single?* challenge common notions about women?
7. Why did Thomas Jefferson call for a revival of classical architecture in the United States?

Reviewing Themes

1. **Global Relations**   How did the United States settle its conflicts over land with British Canada and Spain?
2. **Citizenship and Democracy**   What events led Vice President John Calhoun to resign?

Using the Time Line

Number your paper from 1 to 6. Match the letters on the time line below with the following events.

1. **Congress approves the Missouri Compromise, allowing Missouri to enter the Union as a slave state while Maine joins as a free state.**
2. **The Rush-Bagot Agreement is signed.**
3. **James Fenimore Cooper publishes *The Pioneers.***
4. **James Monroe is elected president, beginning the Era of Good Feelings.**
5. **President Jackson vetoes the renewal of the Second Bank of the United States.**
6. **The Erie Canal is finished, costing $7 million.**

1815   1820   1825   1830   1835

a b   c   d e   f

3. **Constitutional Heritage** What did the Supreme Court decide in *Worcester* v. *Georgia*?

Thinking Critically

1. **Evaluating** Do you think that Jackson's use of the spoils system was a good way to run the federal government? Explain your answer.

2. **Identifying Generalizations and Stereotypes** How did U.S. citizens' views of Indians influence the government's Indian policy?

3. **Synthesizing Information** Why do you think many people wanted to develop an "American" culture in the 1820s? What were some examples of this culture?

Writing About History

1. **Informing** Use your textbook or the library to gather information about the life of Simón Bolívar. Then write a two-paragraph tribute to Bolívar that might have appeared in a newspaper at the time of the Latin American revolutions.

Building Your Portfolio

Complete the following activities individually or in groups.

1. **Regional Differences** Select a region of the country (either the South, the Northeast, or the Midwest). Then create a brochure that might be used to attract settlers or immigrants to that region in the 1830s. Your brochure should focus on the region's economy, culture, and historical points of interest.

2. **American Literature** Read Washington Irving's "Rip Van Winkle" or "The Legend of Sleepy Hollow." Then write a report summarizing the story and explaining how it fulfills Irving's desire to create American myths and legends. Finally, create a visual representation of the story you have read. For example, you may choose to draw a cartoon strip detailing important events in the story.

2. **Creating** Reread the section on Andrew Jackson's 1828 presidential campaign. Then create a newspaper advertisement announcing the expansion of suffrage.

Linking Geography and History

1. **Region** Why did protective tariffs hurt southerners more than northerners?

2. **Movement** What effect did the construction of the Erie Canal have on those who lived along the Hudson River and Lake Erie?

History Skills Workshop

Reading Charts Study the chart below, which examines public land sales by the U.S. government between 1820 and 1845. Then answer the following questions: (a) In what year was the most land sold? (b) How many acres were sold that year? (c) What 1830 act affected public land sales for the next 10 years?

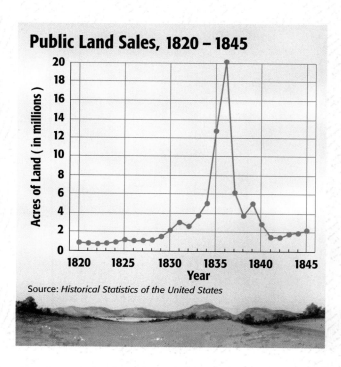

Public Land Sales, 1820 – 1845

Source: *Historical Statistics of the United States*

History Skills

WORKSHOP

Identifying Cause and Effect

Identifying and understanding cause-and-effect relationships is crucial to the study of history. To investigate why an event took place the way that it did, and what else may have happened as a result of that event, historians often ask questions such as: What were the immediate activities that may have triggered the event? What was the background leading up to the event? Who were the people involved?

How to Identify Cause and Effect

1. **Look for clues** Certain words and phrases are immediate clues that may reveal the existence of a cause-and-effect relationship in history. Note some examples of such "clue" words or phrases on the following chart:

Clue Words and Phrases

Cause	Effect
because	aftermath
brought about	as a consequence
gave rise to	as a result of
inspired	depended on
led to	originating from
produced	outcome
provoked	outgrowth
spurred	proceeded from
the reason	resulting in

2. **Identify the relationship** Read carefully to identify how historical events may be related. Writers do not always state the link between cause and effect. Sometimes a reader of history has to infer, or draw a conclusion about, the cause or the effect of a particular event or action.

3. **Check for complex connections** Beyond the immediate cause and effect, check for other, more complex connections. Note, for example, whether (1) there were additional causes of a given effect, (2) a cause had multiple effects, and (3) these effects themselves caused further events.

Example The following diagram presents an important cause-and-effect relationship among the events leading up to Shays's Rebellion. In the late 1700s the Massachusetts legislature passed a law that imposed a heavy tax on land. If a landowner did not pay his or her taxes, the state would foreclose on that landowner's property. Outraged at this law, farmers started Shays's Rebellion.

Cause
The Massachusetts legislature imposes a heavy tax on land.

Effect/Cause
If a landowner did not pay the tax when required, the state would seize that landowner's property.

Effect
In what became known as Shays's Rebellion, angry farmers shut down debtor courts and stopped property auctions in Massachusetts.

Practicing the Skill

Reread Chapter 11, Section 3, in your textbook, which discusses the causes of the War of 1812. Draw a diagram like the one above, showing the relationships between the actions and the outcomes of important events leading up to the War of 1812.

History in Action

American History

Building a Strong Nation Crossword Puzzle

Complete the following activity in small cooperative groups.

You and the members of your group will be creating a crossword puzzle covering the issues, people, and events that influenced U.S. history from 1801 to 1830. This project will be completed in four stages. First, your group will create a list of words relating to the assigned topic. Second, your group will arrange these words into a crossword puzzle and write related clues. Third, your group will draw a large-scale model of your crossword puzzle on heavy butcher paper. Finally, your group will complete another group's crossword puzzle.

Materials To complete this activity, you will need a dictionary, a thesaurus, a large rectangular piece of butcher paper or some other heavy paper, rulers, yardsticks, pencils, and markers or felt-tipped pens.

Parts of the Project The class will be divided into three groups as follows:

1. **Age of Jefferson** You and the other members of your group will create a crossword puzzle covering Thomas Jefferson's presidency. Each clue and answer in the crossword puzzle should relate to this topic, or focus. You might include names of people, places, treaties, events, groups, and issues or important concerns of the time. Your final list should include at least 40 terms, 20 each for across and down.

2. **War of 1812** You and the other members of your group will create a crossword puzzle covering the War of 1812. Include names of people, places, battles, treaties, and events. Your final list should include at least 40 terms, 20 each for across and down.

3. **A New National Identity** You and the other members of your group will create a crossword puzzle covering the growth of nationalism and patriotism in the United States following the War of 1812, the expansion of the United States's boundaries between 1801 and 1830, revolutions in Latin America during this period, and James Monroe's presidency and the Era of Good Feelings. Include names of people, places, battles, treaties, events, groups, and issues or important concerns of the time. Your final list should include at least 40 terms, 20 each for across and down.

When your group has finished compiling the list of terms you will use in your crossword puzzle, create a blank, large-scale version of the puzzle. In addition, provide an answer key for your puzzle. The key should be a small-scale completed version of the puzzle. Next, exchange your crossword puzzle with another group and complete their puzzle. Finally, make a cause-and-effect diagram showing the actions and outcomes of some event related to your topic. Then write a paragraph that explains the connections.

Students work a crossword puzzle.

UNIT 6 A Changing Nation

(1790–1860)

Young People

IN HISTORY

Young Workers

By the mid-1800s teenage girls throughout New England, whether they lived in the city or the country, were working and earning money of their own. Girls in rural areas usually worked out of their homes, weaving cloth, braiding hats, or stitching together shoes. Girls in cities often did needlework or found work as housekeepers or cooks.

In Fitzwilliam, New Hampshire, for example, many young women made hats to be sold at the local store. They were usually not paid in money, but in store credit. Martha Alexander was 18 years old when she began making hats. Over about the next four years she braided 341 hats, and with the credit she bought teacups, saucers, and plates for her upcoming marriage.

Other New England girls worked in textile mills. About half of the young women who worked in mills in Lowell, Massachusetts, were between the ages of 15 and 19 when they first arrived. Despite the long hours, many girls

Young workers in a New England textile mill in the 1830s

The Granger Collection, New York

enjoyed their work in the mills. It brought them independence and relieved the loneliness of farm life. Girls used their hard-earned money in many ways. Some sent it home to their families, while others saved for their future or spent their money on clothes and recreation, such as plays and concerts.

Some teenagers found that life at the mills opened up a bright, new future for them. Lucy Larcom worked in the Lowell mills while she was a teenager. She recalled those days:

> "And I was every day making discoveries about life, and about myself. . . . I found that the crowd was made up of single human lives, not one of them wholly [entirely] uninteresting, when separately known. . . . I defied the machinery to make me its slave. Its incessant discords [constant noise] could not drown the music of my thoughts. . . . I know that I was glad to be alive, and to be just where I was."

In this unit you will learn more about the changes that took place in the United States in the late 1700s to mid-1800s. As the economy of the nation shifted, so did many Americans' way of life.

LEFT PAGE: *These young workers from a shoe factory in Lynn, Massachusetts, went on strike in 1860.*
The Granger Collection, New York

The Granger Collection, New York

◼ CHAPTER 13 ◼
Industrial Growth in the North
(1790–1860)

In the 1800s new ideas and inventions transformed the way people lived and worked in the northern United States. Massachusetts senator Daniel Webster wrote enthusiastically in 1847, "It is an extraordinary era in which we live. It is altogether new. The world has seen nothing like it before." What most impressed Webster was "the application of this scientific research to the pursuits of life."

THEMES

Global Relations
How might new technologies spread from one nation to another?

Technology and Society
In what ways might new technology change people's lives?

Economic Development
How might changes in transportation technology affect a nation's economy?

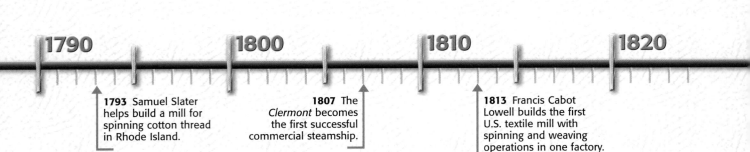

| 1790 | 1800 | 1810 | 1820 |

1793 Samuel Slater helps build a mill for spinning cotton thread in Rhode Island.

1807 The *Clermont* becomes the first successful commercial steamship.

1813 Francis Cabot Lowell builds the first U.S. textile mill with spinning and weaving operations in one factory.

The Industrial Revolution and America

Reading Focus

How did the Industrial Revolution affect the way people worked?

Why did the U.S. textile industry get its start in New England?

What ideas did Eli Whitney contribute to the Industrial Revolution in the United States?

Key Terms

Industrial Revolution
textiles
technology
interchangeable parts
mass production

IN 1761 THE BRITISH SOCIETY OF ARTS *issued an advertisement, searching for "the best invention of a machine that will spin six threads of wool . . . or cotton, at one time." The society also asked that the machine "require but one person to work and attend it." In exchange the advertisement offered a cash reward. No one had a good idea of what such a machine would look like or just how it would work, but many inventors nevertheless tried to solve the problem. The society's advertisement was only the start of a growing demand for new machinery to meet industrial needs.*

The Granger Collection, New York

Women in the 1700s preparing wool for spinning

IMAGE ON LEFT PAGE: *One of the first American locomotives, c. 1830*

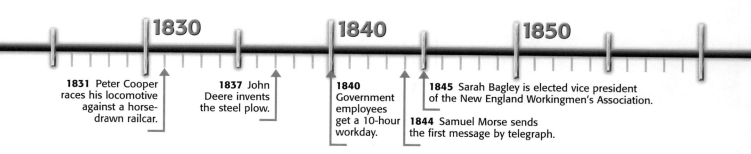

1830

1840

1850

1831 Peter Cooper races his locomotive against a horse-drawn railcar.

1837 John Deere invents the steel plow.

1840 Government employees get a 10-hour workday.

1845 Sarah Bagley is elected vice president of the New England Workingmen's Association.

1844 Samuel Morse sends the first message by telegraph.

★ The Industrial Revolution

At the beginning of the 1700s most people in Europe and the United States were farmers. Many families made their own clothing and other basic necessities at home. The job of making clothing usually fell to female family members. First, they spun raw materials such as cotton or wool into thread by using a simple spinning wheel. They then used a hand loom to weave the thread into cloth. Textile merchants paid some families to make extra cloth and then sold it at a profit. In towns, a few skilled artisans—such as blacksmiths, carpenters, and shoemakers—made small numbers of manufactured goods by hand in their shops. This way of life had worked for generations.

By the mid-1700s, however, Britain underwent a series of changes. Improvements in agriculture, the growth of cities, better roads, expanding overseas trade, and rapid population growth all combined to increase the demand for manufactured goods. Merchants found that their traditional, small-scale manufacturing methods could not keep up with this demand. People began looking for ways to use machines to produce items more quickly and efficiently than could be done by hand. These changes led to the **Industrial Revolution**, a period of rapid growth in the use of machines in manufacturing and production.

The first of many breakthroughs of the Industrial Revolution took place in the manufacture of **textiles**, or cloth. The speed at which cloth was made was limited by the fact that spinning thread took much longer than weaving it into cloth. It took several spinners to make enough thread to supply a single weaver. In 1764 Englishman James Hargreaves designed a small, inexpensive machine called the spinning jenny. This new hand-powered spinning wheel allowed a worker to make eight threads at the same time, and later versions increased this number. Soon the spinning jenny was being used in homes across Britain.

Five years later another Englishman, Richard Arkwright, brought a more dramatic change to the textile industry when he invented the water frame, a large spinning machine. Powered by a waterwheel, Arkwright's water frame could create dozens of long, strong cotton threads at one time. The introduction of the water frame lowered the cost of cotton cloth and further increased the speed of production.

Richard Arkwright's water frame revolutionized the textile industry.

Arkwright's invention also changed the lives of many textile workers. His machines were too large to fit in people's homes and needed to be located near streams that could supply waterpower. To address these needs, merchants built large textile mills filled with water frames. Instead of paying families for cloth produced in their own homes, mill owners began paying people to go to work in the first factories.

James Hargreaves's spinning jenny increased the speed of textile production by allowing one worker to spin large amounts of thread.

The Granger Collection, New York

★ Slater and His Secrets

The machines that ran the new textile mills gave Britain an economic advantage over other countries. To prevent this valuable equipment from falling into foreign hands, Parliament passed laws making it illegal for machines, plans, or skilled mechanics to leave the country.

One of these skilled mechanics was Samuel Slater, who had

begun working in an Arkwright textile mill as a young man. Slater immigrated to the United States in hopes of making his fortune. Soon after he arrived, Slater sent a letter to New England businessman Moses Brown, whose family was trying to mechanize its textile business. Slater wrote confidently:

The textile mill built by Samuel Slater in Pawtucket, Rhode Island, used nearby waterfalls to turn waterwheels that powered the mill machinery.

 I flatter myself that I can give the greatest satisfaction, in making machinery, making good yarn . . . [as good] as any that is made in England. **"**

Slater promised that if he could not build machines that lived up to his claims, he would accept no pay and "throw the whole of what I have attempted over the bridge."

Slater's letter interested Brown, who arranged for one of his workers to test Slater's knowledge of machinery. Slater passed the test easily, and Brown's son Smith Brown and son-in-law William Almy agreed to form a partnership with Slater.

In 1793 the partners built their first mill in Pawtucket, Rhode Island. Slater ran the mill and the machinery, while the partners Almy and Smith Brown sold the thread that the mill produced. Families still did most of the actual weaving of thread into cloth at home or in small shops. Hannah Slater, Samuel's wife, contributed to the business's success. She invented a type of cotton thread used not for weaving but for sewing. This product became a popular item both in the United States and Europe.

The Pawtucket mill overcame several mechanical and financial problems. Gradually, Almy, Slater, and Brown expanded their business and built more mills. Their success encouraged other American businesspeople to build similar textile mills. Most of these early mills were concentrated in the Northeast, particularly New England, which had some important advantages for the young textile industry. As one New England mill owner observed, "Our thousand rivers and streams afford [provide] an inexhaustible [everlasting] supply of . . . power." New England merchants also had the willingness and the money needed to invest in building new mills.

★ A Manufacturing Breakthrough

While the use of machinery had revolutionized the textile industry, most other kinds of manufacturing were still being done by hand. The existing **technology**, or tools used to produce goods or to do work, was simply not advanced enough to improve the manufacturing process.

Whitney's Idea

Eli Whitney was an inventor whose designs had affected business and gained him great respect. He had earned few financial rewards from his efforts, however. In 1798 Whitney saw an opportunity to improve his luck by applying his knowledge of technology to a new challenge. Concerned about the possibility of war with France, the U.S. government wanted more muskets to equip the army. However, U.S. gun makers could not produce the muskets quickly enough because skilled workers made the parts for each weapon by hand. No two parts were exactly alike, and carefully fitting all the pieces together for each individual musket took time and skill.

Whitney wrote to U.S. government officials and suggested that they try an entirely different

Industrial Espionage

For centuries, countries have conducted industrial espionage—the use of unlawful methods, especially spying, to obtain business or technological information. As early as the A.D. 500s, Persian monks smuggled precious silkworms out of China, thus bringing silk production to the Mediterranean region for the first time.

In 1789, the United States obtained technological information that Britain did not want to share. Determined to protect Britain's valuable monopoly on manufactured cloth, Parliament tried to prevent any textile machines or knowledge of the machines from leaving the country. However, Americans were just as determined to learn these industrial secrets. Many American businesspeople began offering rewards for working models of British machinery. These offers attracted the interest of Samuel Slater, a skilled mechanic who had worked in British textile mills for many years. After carefully memorizing the designs of several mill machines, Slater posed as a farmworker, boarded a ship, and set sail for the United States. Once there he assembled the machinery from memory, helping found the cotton textile industry in the United States.

Today industrial espionage occurs throughout the world. Industrial spies have stolen all sorts of different products and ideas—Brazilian rubber trees, automobile makers' designs, toothpaste marketing plans, even cookie recipes. Aerospace, microelectronics, and computer companies around the world have been prime targets for high-tech industrial espionage.

Companies and national governments turn to industrial espionage because it can be very profitable.

In the words of a former director of France's secret service, industrial espionage allows companies to discover processes that "might have taken years and possibly millions of francs to invent or perfect."

For this reason, governments at times send spies to foreign countries, seeking top-secret industrial information. Even countries that are political allies have been known to spy on each other. Experts estimate that industrial espionage may cost U.S. companies billions of dollars each year. As one European said of the United States, "We are allied, but in the economic competition, in the technological competition, we are competitors."

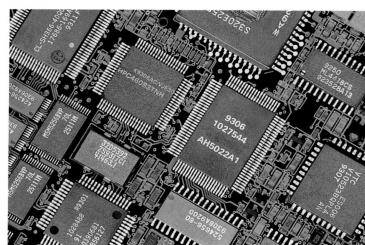

Modern businesses like the one that produced this microchip can be harmed by industrial espionage.

Understanding What You Read

1. What happened as a result of Samuel Slater's bringing technological secrets into the United States?

2. What kinds of secrets have been learned through industrial espionage over the centuries?

3. Why do you think high-tech companies are prime targets for industrial espionage?

approach to making the guns they needed. He said simply:

> **I am persuaded that machinery moved by water [and] adapted to this business would greatly reduce the labor and facilitate [speed] the manufacture of this article.**

Whitney promised to build 10,000 muskets in two years, an incredible number for those days. The federal government gave Whitney a contract for the guns and funds to begin building his factory.

Early artisans had to create and fit together each part of a machine by hand, a time-consuming process that required great skill.

Interchangeable Parts

In addition to using machines, Whitney's plan relied on a new concept called **interchangeable parts**—each vital part that went into making the product would be made exactly the same. Thus, if Whitney made 100 muskets, the parts from any one musket would be interchangeable with those from another musket. Whitney explained the system:

> **One of my primary objects [goals] is to form the tools so the tools themselves shall fashion [make] the work and give to every part its just proportion.**

Whitney believed that this idea was a "new principle" in manufacturing. With interchangeable parts, workers could more easily assemble muskets and replace any defective part quickly.

Whitney's Influence

Despite Whitney's confidence, designing the machines and training the workers to put his system into practice took him much longer than he had expected. At the end of two years, he had not delivered a single musket. To answer his critics, in 1801 Whitney arranged a daring demonstration in Washington. In front of President John Adams and Vice President Thomas Jefferson, Whitney placed an assortment of lock parts for 10 muskets on a table. He then completed the locks with parts chosen at random and quickly assembled them into the muskets. Whitney repeated the process several times to the amazement of the onlookers. Witness Elizur Goodrich said that "all Judges & Inspectors unite in a declaration that they [the muskets] are superior to any" made in the United States or Europe. Despite the success of this demonstration, Whitney was never able to fulfill his musket contract or put his plans into full effect.

Other businesses tried **mass production**, or the efficient production of large numbers of identical goods, with greater success. For example, Eli Terry began mass-producing thousands of inexpensive clocks for American families in the early 1800s. Whitney's work also showed that American inventors could keep up with and improve upon the new ideas and machines coming out of Britain.

One of Eli Whitney's early machines for making musket parts

★ Manufacturing's Slow Start

Despite the hard work of people such as Samuel Slater, manufacturing in the United States grew slowly. In 1810 Secretary of the Treasury Albert Gallatin suggested some reasons why there were few factories in the United States:

  ❝the superior attractions of agricultural pursuits [farming], . . . the abundance of land compared with the population, the high price of labor, and the want [lack] of sufficient capital [investment].❞

Gallatin reasoned that few people would choose to work in a factory if they could own their own farm instead. Many more people were able to buy farms in the United States than in Britain, where land was scarce and expensive. British factory workers generally were willing to work for lower wages than factory workers in the United States. This low cost of labor combined with British workers' technical skills allowed British manufacturers to produce goods less expensively than most American businesses could. The lower British prices made it difficult for many U.S. manufacturers to compete. This in turn discouraged American investors from spending

This scene from an early New England textile mill shows the growing use of machinery in industry.

the money needed to build new factories and machinery.

These circumstances began to change around the time of the War of 1812. The embargo and later blockade during the war prevented American consumers from buying British goods. This gave U.S. manufacturers a chance to sell their goods, make profits, and expand their factories. At the same time, the war demonstrated to many U.S. officials and businesspeople that their country was too dependent on foreign nations for manufactured goods. If the United States could not take care of its own needs, it would be weak and open to attack.

SECTION 1 REVIEW

Identify and explain the significance of the following:
- **Industrial Revolution**
- **textiles**
- **James Hargreaves**
- **Richard Arkwright**
- **Samuel Slater**
- **technology**
- **Eli Whitney**
- **interchangeable parts**
- **mass production**

Reading for Content Understanding

1 **Main Idea** How did changes in technology, manufacturing, and production affect working people?

2 **Main Idea** In what ways did interchangeable parts and mass production affect industry in the United States?

3 **Geographic Diversity** *Location* Why was New England an ideal place to build factories?

4 **Writing** *Persuading* Imagine that you are a member of the British Parliament in the early 1800s. Write a short speech to persuade the other members of Parliament that Britain either should or should not share its important industrial secrets with other nations.

5 **Critical Thinking** *Determining the Strength of an Argument* Do you agree or disagree that it was important for the United States to develop its own manufacturing industries? Explain your answer.

Changes in Working Life

Reading Focus

What were conditions like for early mill workers?

What role did women play in factory work in the early 1800s?

Why did factory workers organize in the early 1800s, and what methods did they use to bring about change?

Key Terms

trade unions

strike

MITH WILKINSON WAS A BOY *in Pawtucket, Rhode Island, when Samuel Slater started his first textile mill there. "I was then in my tenth year,"* remembered Wilkinson, *"and went to work with him [Slater], and began attending the breaker [a machine]." It was common in the early 1800s for children even younger than Wilkinson to work in the textile mills for up to 12 hours a day. Wilkinson spent much of his life working in mills and eventually ran one himself.*

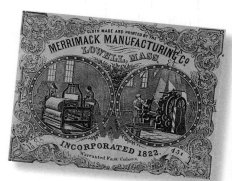

Cloth label for a textile company

★ Factory Families

Many mill owners in the United States found it difficult to attract people to work in factories. At first, Samuel Slater and his two partners used apprentices. However, young men often grew bored with the repetitive, simple jobs they were given in the mills, such as feeding cotton into machines or cleaning the mill equipment. Apprentice James Horton ran away from Slater's mill complaining, "Mr. Slater . . . keep me always at one thing and I might have stayed there until this time and never knew nothing." Eventually, explained Slater's son

Horatio, "Mr. Slater was obliged [forced] to seek families, and induce [persuade] them to emigrate to Pawtucket."

By hiring entire families to come work in the mills, Slater could fill his labor needs at a low cost. The machines made many tasks in the mill simple enough for children to perform. Mill owners also paid children less than adults, who usually earned as much in a day as most children were paid in a week. It was traditional in many farming families for children to work, and few people complained when this practice switched from farms to factories. H. Humphrey, an author of books on raising

Industrial Growth in the North **405**

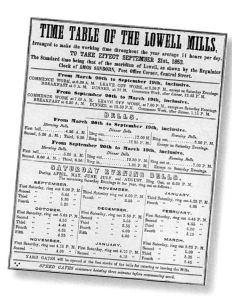

The daily work schedule for the Lowell mills. On most days, workers began at 6:30 A.M. and stopped work at 6:30 P.M.

children, told parents that it was necessary for children to be useful. Humphrey wrote, "If he [a child] will not study, put him on to a farm, or send him into the shop, or in some other way provide regular employment for him."

Slater's approach of hiring families and dividing factory work into simple tasks became known as the Rhode Island system and was copied by mill owners throughout the United States. Owners placed advertisements such as "Men with growing families wanted" and sent recruiters out to poor communities to find new workers.

⭐ The Lowell System

Not all mill owners followed Samuel Slater's system. A very different kind of factory system emerged under the guidance of New England businessman Francis Cabot Lowell. Before the War of 1812, Lowell had traveled to Britain on business and toured several factories. He returned to the United States with two ideas that revolutionized the textile industry in the Northeast.

First, Lowell decided to build a water-powered loom based on a machine he had seen in Britain. He knew from observing the British factories that a textile mill using this loom could weave and spin under one roof. This would allow Lowell's mills to

make cloth instead of simply producing thread, like Slater's mills. Lowell's other new idea was to employ young unmarried women from local farms instead of hiring entire families to work in his factories. He wanted to avoid creating the terrible conditions that existed in the British mills and mill towns. Lowell's combination of employing young women and of spinning and weaving in one mill became known as the Lowell system.

To build his factory, Lowell gathered a group of financial backers known as the Boston Manufacturing Company. They built the first textile mill using the Lowell system in Waltham, Massachusetts, in 1813. Lowell's factory was an immediate success. "From the first starting of the first power loom there was not hesitation or doubt about the success of this manufacture," wrote one investor.

In 1823 the Boston Manufacturing Company built a larger mill in a town later named Lowell, Massachusetts. Visitors to Lowell were dazzled by the machinery, the clean factories, and the neatly kept boardinghouses for the workers.

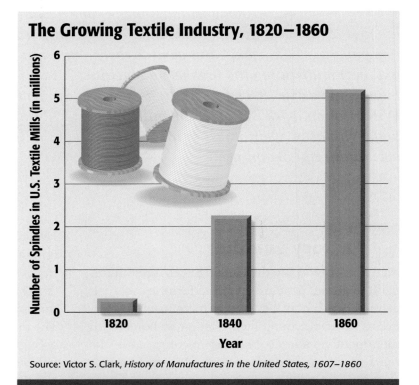

The Growing Textile Industry, 1820–1860

Number of Spindles in U.S. Textile Mills (in millions)

Year

Source: Victor S. Clark, *History of Manufactures in the United States, 1607–1860*

Making Thread Spindles twist and wrap thread and yarn on spools. The number of spindles a factory used was directly related to its level of output. About how many spindles were being used in U.S. textile factories in 1840?

Women and children heading to work at a textile factory

The Lowell Girls

Visitors to the Lowell mills were also impressed by the young women who worked there. These mill workers soon became known in the press as "Lowell girls."

New Opportunities

The Lowell mills paid their workers between $2 and $4 a week, with $1.25 deducted for room and board. Because these wages were much better than those that women could earn teaching or doing domestic work, the Lowell mills were able to attract young women from across New England. Many women welcomed the opportunity to earn money in the mills instead of working on the family farm and earning nothing. "I am most [of] 19 years old," wrote one young woman. "I must of course have something of my own before many more years have passed over my head." The typical female employee worked at the Lowell mills for about four years.

Workers at the Lowell mills used their free time to take classes, form women's clubs, and even write their own magazine, the *Lowell Offering*. Lucy Larcom, who started working at Lowell at age 11, wrote as an adult about the positive influence of her fellow workers:

> **I regard it as one of the privileges of my youth that I was permitted to grow up among those active, interesting girls, whose lives . . . had principle and purpose distinctly their own.**

A Hard Day's Work

For many women, however, the disadvantages of mill work outweighed the positive aspects. At Lowell, daily life was carefully regulated, with ringing bells to tell workers when to go to breakfast or lunch. Mill owners steadily increased the size and speed of their machines throughout the 1800s, and they forced employees to work harder and faster to keep pace with the equipment.

A newspaper reporter commented on the working conditions at Lowell in 1846:

> **Each girl usually attends three looms. Doing so requires constant attention. The atmosphere of the room is full of cotton filaments [fibers] and dust, which we were told are very harmful to the lungs.**

Mill machinery was also dangerous, with moving parts that could tear hair and injure limbs.

Working under such difficult conditions for 12–14 hours a day exhausted the mill workers. Lucy Larcom wrote that the pace at Lowell finally drove her to quit. As she was collecting her final wages, the paymaster asked her, "Going to where you can earn more money?" Larcom replied, "I am going where I can have more time."

Workers Organize

Factories continued to spread in the 1800s. The changes caused by factory labor greatly concerned skilled craftspeople.

Rough Times

While the growth of factories brought new opportunities to unskilled workers, it also threatened the livelihoods of many craftspeople who made goods by hand. To compete with the factories' ability to produce low-priced goods quickly, shop owners

American Arts

The *Lowell Offering*

Many Lowell girls shared an interest in improving themselves through education. Some women studied at evening schools, while others pooled their money to hire tutors in subjects such as German or music. Many Lowell girls took up writing as a pastime, forming clubs in which members could read their work to one another.

Interest in these writings eventually led to the first publication of the *Lowell Offering* in 1840. This monthly magazine featured poems, stories, essays, and editorials about the lives of mill workers. Its cover featured the proud banner "A REPOSITORY [storehouse] OF ORIGINAL ARTICLES, WRITTEN BY FACTORY GIRLS."

In many ways the *Lowell Offering* presented an unrealistic view of mill life. This can be seen by studying the cover for the *Lowell Offering* for December 1845, the last year the magazine was published. The setting looks more like a garden than a factory community, with the mill and the women's boardinghouses seen only in the background. The mill worker pictured seems happy and content, taking time out of her day to go for an afternoon stroll and to read the book she holds in her right hand. The only hint of the rapid pace of mill life is that the Lowell girl is gazing at a beehive. This object serves as a reminder to her that she is supposed to be a hardworking laborer, just like the worker bees in a hive.

The artist who created the cover apparently ignored several harsh realities of mill

Cover page from the Lowell Offering
The Granger Collection, New York

life, which was magazine policy. By the 1840s mill workers labored an average of 75 hours a week. The Lowell girls spent the majority of their time either in the mill or in the boardinghouse, with only a few hours of free time before evening curfew at 10:00 P.M. This left little or no opportunity for a relaxing daylight walk or socializing.

In addition, the open space and rural countryside suggested by the cover was beginning to disappear in the 1840s. New buildings were contracted in space that was once preserved for parks. The town of Lowell was becoming more crowded with buildings, stores, and residences.

Harriet Farley, the editor of the *Offering*, tried in 1844 to explain the image of Lowell shown in the magazine:

> **“**If in our sketches, there is too much light, and too little shade, ... we have not thought it necessary to state . . . that our life was a toilsome [difficult] one.**”**

Understanding the Arts

1. What activities did Lowell girls take up to further their education?

2. How does the *Offering* cover inaccurately represent life in the Lowell mills?

3. What might an *Offering* cover that accurately reflected the working conditions look like?

The arrival of large numbers of immigrants like this group increased competition for jobs in the 1840s.

had to hire more workers and pay them less money. As shoemaker William Frazier explained in the mid-1840s:

" **Where we have to sit on our seats from twelve to sixteen hours per day, to earn one dollar, it must be apparent [clear] to all that we are in a sad condition.** "

Increased competition for factory jobs in the 1840s also drove down or froze wages for many factory workers. Whereas few people were willing to work in the mills in the early 1800s, a massive wave of immigration in the 1840s brought many families willing to take factory jobs at low pay. Eventually, these immigrants replaced the Lowell girls, who often returned to their family farms or refused to continue laboring in the mills when pay decreased and working conditions worsened. In addition, increased competition came from workers who had lost their jobs during the Panic of 1837. More than 50,000 workers lost their jobs in New York City alone.

Forming Unions

In the 1830s and 1840s low wages, long hours, and the fear of losing their jobs led many workers in skilled trade to begin forming new **trade unions**—organizations created by workers to improve working conditions. In time, factory workers also formed trade unions. Most employers and factory owners did not want their workers to organize and join unions. A group of New York employers expressed a typical business owner's opinion when they stated in 1836:

" **We consider such associations [unions] illegal because they are harmful to trade and prevent us from competing successfully with manufacturers of similar goods in our neighboring towns and cities.** "

Employers often refused to hire workers whom they knew or suspected of being union members.

To persuade business owners to listen to them, union members sometimes staged a **strike**—the refusal to work until employers meet union demands. Most early strikes were not very successful, because courts and police usually supported companies against striking union members.

These problems led unions to become politically active in an effort to get the laws changed. One union warned its members, "Do not vote for proud members of the upper class who cannot subscribe to the precepts [rules] and principles of the workers." Instead, the group advised workers to support candidates more sympathetic to working people. "Only through them [such candidates] can we secure the passage of just laws," the labor organization concluded.

Banner for a New York City labor union

⭐ Labor Reform Efforts

One of the strongest voices in the union movement belonged to Sarah Bagley, who founded the Lowell Female Labor Reform Association in 1844. Bagley and her companions worked hard to publicize the struggles of factory laborers.

Workers join a parade to show support for hundreds of female workers who went on strike for improved working conditions in Lynn, Massachusetts.

The 10-hour-day crusade drew support from many working men and women, despite opposition from business owners. An anonymous worker in the Lowell mills encouraged her friends to "circulate the 'Ten Hour Petition' among all classes . . . ; may you continue on in courage." In 1845 Sarah Bagley was elected vice president of the New England Workingmen's Association and put in charge of the 10-hour-day reform effort. This election made her the first woman to hold such a high-ranking position in the American labor movement.

The 10-Hour Day

One of Bagley's causes was the fight for shorter working hours. In 1840 President Martin Van Buren had granted a 10-hour workday to government employees. Bagley and other reformers such as Huldah Stone and Seth Luther wanted to extend this protection to employees of private businesses. At the time, most working men and women put in 12 to 14 hours, six days a week. Stone, who like Bagley worked in a textile mill, attacked this practice as unfair. She wrote, "Call ye this *life*—to labor, eat, drink and die?"

Limited Reform

Although union members made their voices heard, factory workers' long hours remained unchanged in many states. The unions achieved some legal victories, as New Hampshire, Maine, Pennsylvania, Ohio, Connecticut, and a few other states passed 10-hour-day laws. However, company officials often managed to avoid such laws by requiring workers to sign special contracts agreeing to work longer hours. Despite their setbacks, union supporters continued to fight for work reforms, speaking out against long days and poor working conditions. This struggle to gain better treatment continued throughout the 1800s.

SECTION 2 REVIEW

Identify and explain the significance of the following:
- **Francis Cabot Lowell**
- **trade unions**
- **strike**
- **Sarah Bagley**

Reading for Content Understanding

1 **Main Idea** Why were women like the Lowell girls recruited to work in factories?

2 **Main Idea** Explain why workers joined unions, and give two methods that workers used to bring about change.

3 **Technology and Society** What was the Rhode Island system, and why did many mill owners copy it?

4 **Writing** *Informing* Imagine that you are a writer for the *Lowell Offering*. Write a brief article that examines the life of factory laborers in the early 1800s.

5 **Critical Thinking** *Synthesizing Information* Imagine that you are a mill owner and choose whether you will use the Rhode Island system or the Lowell system. Explain your answer.

The Transportation Revolution

Reading Focus

How did the Transportation Revolution change life in the United States?

What was the impact of the steamboat on the U.S. economy?

What were the advantages and disadvantages of early American railroads?

Key Terms

Transportation Revolution
Clermont
clipper ship

IN 1805 INVENTOR ROBERT FULTON *returned to America. Neither the French nor the British had shown much interest in funding his inventions. However, Fulton was determined to continue with his work. Two years later, in August 1807, he took his boat, known by some doubters as "Fulton's Folly," out on the Hudson River. It traveled up the river, passing sailboats along the way. Instead of ending in disaster, "Fulton's Folly" was a success. Faster than sailboats and powered without sails, Fulton's boat revolutionized water transportation.*

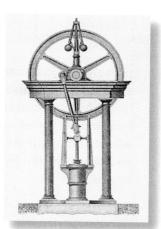

A steam engine design

 New Ways to Travel

In addition to the Industrial Revolution, during the 1800s the United States experienced a **Transportation Revolution**—a rapid growth in the speed and convenience of transportation. The Transportation Revolution helped create a boom in business across the country, particularly by speeding travel and reducing shipping time and shipping rates between the East and the West. As one foreign observer declared in 1835, "The Americans . . . have joined the Hudson to the Mississippi, and made the Atlantic Ocean communicate with the Gulf of Mexico."

In 1817 it took almost two months to ship cargo from Cincinnati, Ohio, to New York City. By the early 1850s the same trip took only a week. Along with trade goods, people and information traveled from town to town and state to state with new speed and efficiency. The growth in communication, trade, and travel encouraged the development of new towns and businesses.

These improvements were made possible by the expansion of roads and canals and the invention of two new forms of transportation: the steamboat and the railroad. Both methods relied on steam engines to supply power. Together they increased the pace of American life.

⭐ Steam and Sails

One of the first breakthroughs of the Transportation Revolution occurred with water transportation. While canals were being built in the Northeast, new, faster boats were changing travel and trade on rivers and oceans.

The Steamboat

The invention of the steamboat changed water transportation.

Steamboats on the Mississippi River

Although several inventors in the United States and Europe had developed steam-powered boats in the late 1700s, the most successful was American Robert Fulton. Fulton was an artist by trade, but the idea of harnessing steam power to run a ship caught his imagination. He tested his first steamboat design in 1803 while in France. A French newspaper recorded the event:

> 66 **[Fulton] put his boat in motion . . . and for an hour and a half afforded [provided] the curious spectacle of a boat moved by wheels like a cart, these wheels being provided with paddles . . . and being moved by a fire [steam] engine.** 99

Several more years passed before Fulton was ready to test a full-sized commercial steamboat in the United States. Fulton's odd-looking vessel was called the **Clermont**. On August 9, 1807, the *Clermont* traveled up the Hudson River without any trouble. There was immediate demand for a steamboat ferry service, and within a few months Fulton and his partners had earned back all the money spent building the vessel.

The steamboat was well suited to river travel because it could move quickly against the current and did not rely on uncertain winds. At times, steamboat travel could be dangerous because the coal-fueled engines could explode. Despite such risks, steamboats were soon a common sight on the Mississippi River, with more than 500 in use by 1840. The new steamboats shaved months

off the time it had previously taken to travel from New Orleans to Pittsburgh, Pennsylvania.

The steamboats also lowered prices by as much as 90 percent for upstream travel and 75 percent for trips downstream. These savings in time and money made it much easier and more economical for westerners to ship goods such as grain and lumber to eastern markets. Eastern companies also found it easier to ship their goods to western buyers. The boom in trade and easier transportation encouraged more settlers to move to the Midwest.

Clipper Ships

Although steamboats became popular for travel on rivers and along coastlines, the early versions could not carry enough fuel to make long voyages across the ocean. To fill the need for fast ocean shipping, Americans introduced the **clipper ship** in the 1840s. These sleek, tallmasted sailing ships used many sails and had narrow hulls that sliced through the water at great speed.

Clipper ships such as *America* and *Flying Cloud* carried small cargoes of valuable goods from the East Coast to places such as California and China. The ships became famous for their beautiful design and record-breaking voyages. By the 1850s, however, the age of the clipper ship was coming to an end as new technology enabled steamboats to begin making ocean voyages at high speed while carrying more cargo than clipper ships could. When speed was not important, huge sailing ships continued to carry bulk cargo until the 1900s.

⭐ American Railroads

What the steamboat did for water travel, the train did for overland travel. First developed in Britain in the early 1800s, steam-powered trains did not become popular in the United States until the 1830s. One of the earlier locomotives was Peter

The Age of Steam

Before the Industrial Revolution began, people had to rely on natural sources of energy to do work. Muscle power from animals or humans, waterpower from rivers, and wind power were the only options available. This limited suitable factory locations and the speed of transportation.

With the development of steam power, a new source of energy became available. The first steam engines were built in the early 1700s in Europe. The early steam engines were large and heavy with three main parts: the boiler, the cylinder, and the condenser. In the boiler a fuel such as wood or coal burned to heat water and produce steam. The steam then entered the cylinder, where it built up enough pressure to push a piston up and down. The condenser increased the engine's power by pulling steam out of the cylinder, thus speeding up the piston.

Other machinery converted the piston's powerful up-and-down motion into energy that could turn the paddlewheel of a steamboat, the wheels of a train, or the belts on a machine. These early "low-pressure" steam engines produced steady, reliable power for transportation and industry.

American Oliver Evans helped develop a more powerful steam engine. Evans designed a smaller engine, without a condenser, that used steam at much higher pressure. Although it required more fuel to operate, Evans's high-pressure steam engine was simple to maintain. Its power was ideal for steamboats running on the Mississippi or trains racing across the American countryside.

Steam power was often dangerous. As engineers on steamboats or steam trains tried to get the most power out of their engines, the high-pressure boilers often exploded, injuring or killing people. Engineers continued to use and improve steam engines throughout the 1800s. Eventually, factories began to use steam power, allowing them to be built in areas that did not have access to waterpower.

Understanding What You Read

1. How did early steam engines work?
2. How do you think steam engines changed the way people lived and worked?

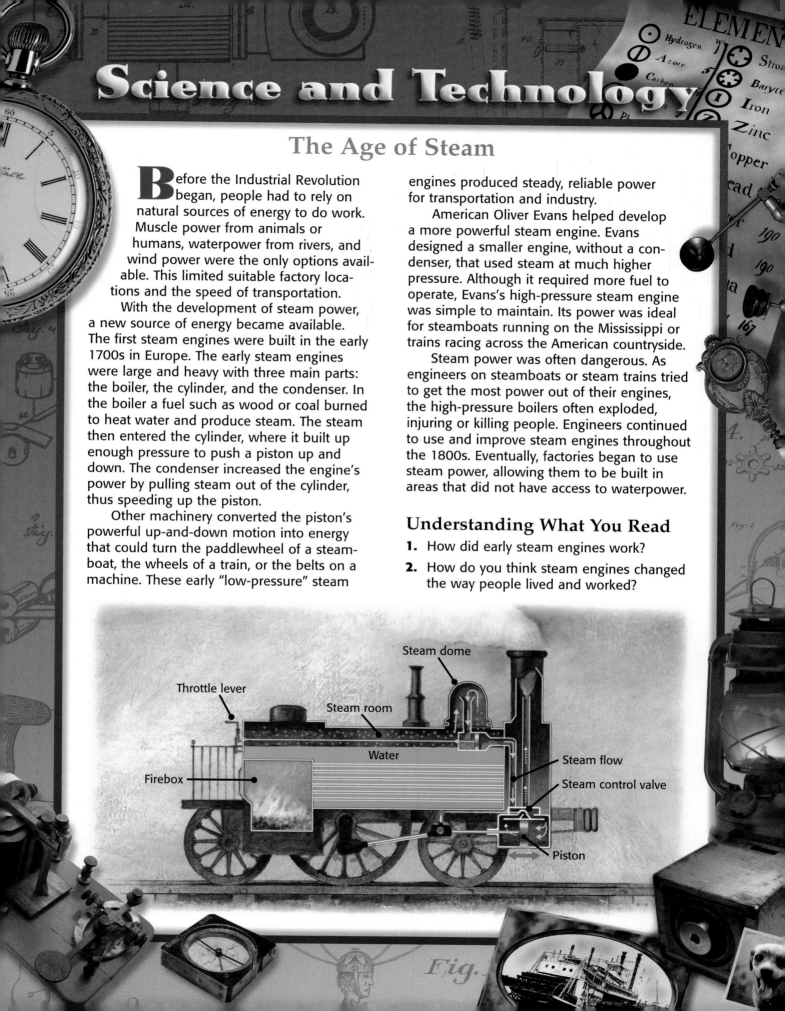

Steam dome · Throttle lever · Steam room · Water · Firebox · Steam flow · Steam control valve · Piston

Cooper's *Tom Thumb*. Around 1830 Cooper decided to race *Tom Thumb* against a horse-drawn railcar. Eyewitness John Latrobe later described the race, in which *Tom Thumb* had a slow start and fell behind. Latrobe wrote, "The pace increased, the passengers shouted, the engine gained on the horse . . . then the engine passed the horse, and a great hurrah hailed the victory." Unfortunately for Cooper, victory was spoiled when *Tom Thumb* broke down and lost the race near the end. Despite the defeat, the contest demonstrated the power and speed of even a small locomotive.

Railroad fever soon spread across the country. Railroad companies laid about 2,800 miles of track by 1840—some 1,000 more miles of track than existed in all of Europe. French economist Michel Chevalier observed, "The Americans have a perfect passion for railroads."

In this rapid building process, engineers and mechanics overcame many unique challenges. Most British railroads, for example, ran on straight tracks across flat ground. In the United States, however, many railroads had to run up and down steep mountains, around tight curves, and over swift rivers. Railroad companies also built the tracks quickly and often with the least-expensive materials available.

To make these feats possible, engineers and mechanics built heavier, faster, and more powerful steam locomotives. With the growing demand for more rail connections and faster travel, the pace of railroad construction continued to increase. By 1860 there were around 30,000 miles of railroad linking almost every major city in the eastern United States. American locomotives hauled more freight than any other country in the world. Thus, the railroads transported many of the goods produced by factories during the Industrial Revolution. The railroad companies that ran these lines became some of the most powerful businesses in the nation.

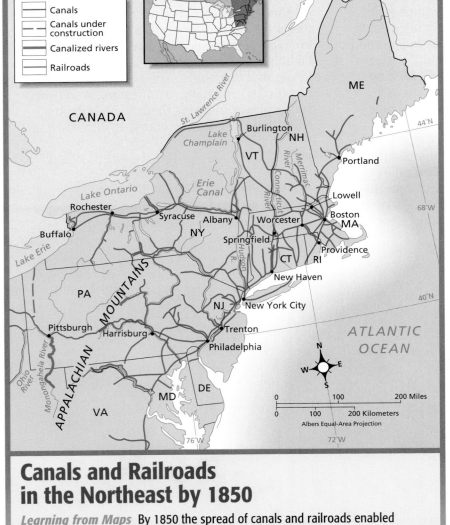

Canals and Railroads in the Northeast by 1850

Learning from Maps By 1850 the spread of canals and railroads enabled goods to be moved faster between many northeastern cities.

Place Which port cities were connected to inland cities by canals?

⭐ Traveling by Train

In addition to their tremendous economic impact, the railroads made a powerful impression on the senses of passengers and observers. Trains were one of the fastest forms of transportation most people had ever experienced. Locomotives averaged around 20 miles per hour while wagons often traveled less than

10 miles per hour. Writer George Templeton Strong of New York City described the thrill of a steam train passing by in the night:

❝whizzing and rattling and panting, with its fiery furnace gleaming in front, its chimney vomiting fiery smoke above, and its long train of cars rushing along behind like the body and tail of a gigantic dragon—. . . and all darting forward at the rate of twenty miles an hour. Whew!❞

Transportation Methods of the Mid 1800s

TYPE OF TRANSPORTATION	AVERAGE SPEED	SHIPPING COSTS
Roads	2 miles per hour by wagon 6–8 miles per hour by stagecoach	$0.12 per ton per mile
Canals	1.5–5 miles per hour	$0.045 per ton per mile
Steamboats	around 20 miles per hour	$0.007 per ton per mile
Clipper Ships (Ocean Travel)	11.5–17 miles per hour (depending on weather)	$10.00 per ton for trans-Atlantic shipment
Railroads	around 20 miles per hour (including stops)	$0.06 per ton per mile

Source: George Rodger Taylor, *The Transportation Revolution, 1815 to 1860*

Riding on the early trains was often an adventure and sometimes dangerous. John Latrobe wrote that "to ride in a railroad car in these days was, literally, to go thundering along."

Train wrecks were common because engineers tried to stay on schedule by traveling too fast on hastily built tracks. Englishman Charles Richard Weld was on a railroad car only minutes before he realized he and other travelers "were on the eve of a smash." The train did wreck, flying off the tracks and injuring several people. To Weld's amazement, however, the other passengers did not complain about the accident. Instead, they praised the engineer for trying to stay on time.

Passengers were willing to take these risks because the railroads reduced travel time dramatically. Railroads also helped tie communities together. Senator Daniel Webster spoke for many in the United States when he declared in 1847 that the railroad "towers above all other inventions of this or the preceding [earlier] age."

SECTION 3 REVIEW

Identify and explain the significance of the following:
- **Transportation Revolution**
- **Robert Fulton**
- *Clermont*
- **clipper ship**
- **Peter Cooper**

Reading for Content Understanding

1. **Main Idea** How did the Transportation Revolution affect the movement of goods, information, and people?

2. **Main Idea** What were the disadvantages of railroad travel, and why were people willing to travel by railroad anyway?

3. **Economic Development** How did railroads and steamboats affect the U.S. economy?

4. **Writing** *Creating* Imagine that you are in charge of producing a newspaper advertisement for a railroad company. List advantages of traveling by train, and write an ad that encourages Americans to use the railroad.

5. **Critical Thinking** *Drawing Conclusions* If you had lived during the early 1800s, which mode of transportation would you have chosen to visit another part of the country? Explain your answer.

More Technological Advances

 N MAY 24, 1844, SAMUEL MORSE *sat down before his newly invented device in the Supreme Court chamber of the Capitol Building in Washington. To test his invention, he had his friend Annie Elsworth think of and then write down a message on a slip of paper. He then read her message and used the device to send it instantly to Baltimore, Maryland, 37 miles away. His associates in Baltimore quickly sent back the message—"What hath God wrought?"—to Morse. An exchange that would have taken hours if delivered by train had taken place in only a minute. A new age in communications had begun.*

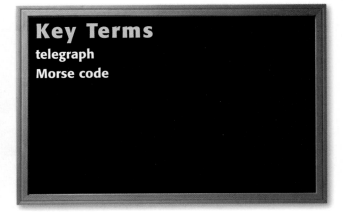

A telegraph key

★ Messages by Wire

Samuel Morse's invention was known as the **telegraph**. The telegraph worked by sending pulses of electric current through a wire. These pulses were converted into sound at the other end of the line. The telegraph operator controlled the length of each pulse by tapping a bar called a telegraph key; short pulses are called dots, and longer pulses are called dashes. Combinations of dots and dashes represent each letter of the alphabet according to a system developed by Morse, known as **Morse code**. For example, in Morse code *dot*

dot dot, *dash dash dash*, *dot dot dot* represents the universal distress call SOS, or "Save our ship." By tapping very quickly and by listening carefully to the Morse code signals, skilled telegraph operators could send and receive many words a minute.

Morse did not discover the principles behind the telegraph, but he put them together in a practical machine in 1837. Several years passed before he could successfully connect two distant locations with telegraph wires, however. Even then people doubted his machine. Some critics claimed that Morse was just making lucky guesses rather than reading messages sent from miles away.

The telegraph combined with trains and steamboats to increase greatly the speed of communication in the 1800s.

The Granger Collection, New York

Biography

Samuel Morse

Like steamboat creator Robert Fulton, American Samuel Morse began his career as an painter rather than an inventor. Morse first became interested in sending messages electronically while talking to another passenger on board a steamship in 1832. Morse's wife, Lucretia, had died several years earlier, and he was struggling to raise his three children alone. Morse hoped that an invention such as the telegraph would earn him enough money to support his family and his art. It took him 12 years and all his savings to achieve this goal. Royalties from the telegraph made Morse extremely wealthy, and he was famous across the United States before he died in 1872.

Morse's biggest break came in the 1844 presidential campaign, when his telegraph sent information about events at the Democratic convention in Baltimore, Maryland. Almost immediately after the party chose its presidential nominee, a telegraph wired that news to politicians in Washington. The response from the politicians was "Three cheers for the telegraph!" Telegraphs were soon sending and receiving information for the government, newspapers, businesses, and private citizens.

The telegraph grew side by side with the railroad. Telegraph companies strung telegraph lines on poles alongside old and new railroads across the country and established telegraph offices in many train stations. By 1854 more than 15,000 miles of telegraph cable connected cities throughout the United States, with thousands of miles being added each year.

 ## New Factories

As the Industrial Revolution progressed, more factory owners turned to steam instead of water-power to run their machinery. While waterwheels remained popular in many areas, the use of steam engines allowed business owners to build factories in places that did not have suitable streams or waterfalls. Companies that built their factories closer to cities and transportation centers lowered the price of labor and reduced shipping costs.

Improvements in power were joined by steady improvements in machine design. Mechanics invented tools capable of more precise cutting, stamping, and shaping of wood, metal, and other materials. When Englishman Joseph Whitworth wrote a report on U.S. manufacturing in 1854, he noted that Americans

❝ **call in the aid of machinery in almost every department [area] of industry. Wherever it can be introduced as a substitute for manual labor, it is universally and willingly resorted [turned] to.** ❞

Industrial Growth in the North **417**

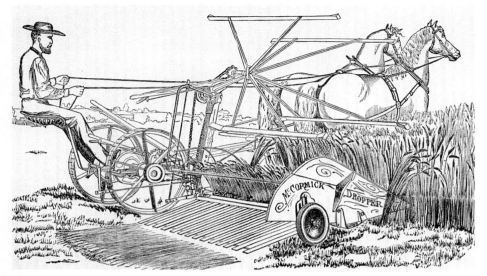

The *London Times* *described Cyrus McCormick's odd-looking reaper as* "*a cross between a flying machine [and] a wheelbarrow.*"

In the 1840s precision machinery finally allowed gun-makers at the federal Springfield Armory in Massachusetts to achieve Eli Whitney's dream of interchangeable parts and mass production.

⭐ Better Farm Equipment

During the 1830s technology began transforming the farm as well as the factory. In 1837 blacksmith John Deere saw the problems that his farming friends in Illinois were having plowing the rich, thick soil, which stuck to their iron plows. Deere thought that a steel blade, like one he had seen in a sawmill, might slice through the earth without getting stuck. His steel plow design was a success, and by 1846 Deere was selling 1,000 plows a year. His business continued to prosper as more farmers moved west.

Deere's plow made it easier to plant wheat, but harvesting it was time-consuming and difficult. At about the same time that Deere was working on his new plow, Cyrus McCormick was developing a mechanical reaper to cut down wheat much

An advertisement for plows and other new farming tools

more quickly and efficiently. McCormick, who encountered many difficulties designing the device, later recalled, "I was often advised by my father and family to abandon [the invention]."

Despite these setbacks, McCormick continued to improve his design. In the 1840s he began selling models of his machine, later entering it in international competitions, where it achieved great success. McCormick soon began mass-producing his reapers in a large factory in Chicago, Illinois. This factory was one of the first to use the new improvements in steam engine technology, running its many saws and other machines on steam power. McCormick overcame competition from other inventors on his way to becoming a millionaire.

The combination of Deere's plow and McCormick's reaper made it possible for midwestern farmers to plant and harvest huge wheat fields cheaply and in far less time than was previously required. It took 20 hours to harvest an acre of wheat in 1830. McCormick's farm machinery eventually reduced that to one hour per acre. By 1860 there were more than 2 million farms in the United States together, producing 839 million bushels of corn and 173 million bushels of wheat a year.

⭐ Changing Life at Home

Not all inventions of the Industrial Revolution involved manufacturing or transportation. Many devices were simply intended to make life easier. Alexis de Tocqueville identified what he called the particularly American desire

❝to be always making life more comfortable and convenient, to avoid trouble, and to satisfy the smallest wants without effort and almost without cost.❞

The sewing machine was one of many such conveniences that was invented during the Industrial Revolution. In Lowell, Massachusetts, factory apprentice Elias Howe invented the sewing machine. Isaac Singer made improvements on it and made a fortune selling the machines. Starting in the 1850s, his Singer sewing machines became increasingly popular, combining a clever design with simple operation. Early advertisements claimed, "Even a child can run it." Many women bought sewing machines to try to earn a living out of their homes by sewing clothing for large companies. In some households, more elegant sewing machines became symbols of progress and prosperity.

Other household advances were basic improvements on everyday items. In the 1830s iceboxes cooled by large blocks of fresh ice became available, allowing families to store fresh food safely for longer periods of time. Iron cookstoves began replacing cooking fires and stone hearths. Companies also applied improved production methods to old inventions such as the clock, mass-producing them cheaply and enabling many families to buy one. A clock that cost $50 in 1800 was selling for only $1.50 by the 1850s.

As more cities developed public water systems, a few wealthy families were able to install water pumps inside their houses instead of relying on public pumps on street corners. However, even in

By the late 1800s many American homes had sewing machines.

these homes it was extremely rare to have any kind of plumbing above the first floor. Hotels were often the first buildings in a city to feature such plumbing advances.

Other useful inventions of the period included matches, introduced in the 1830s, and the safety pin, invented in 1849. All of these inventions helped make life at home more convenient for an increasing number of Americans.

SECTION 4 REVIEW

Identify and explain the significance of the following:
- **Samuel Morse**
- **telegraph**
- **Morse code**
- **John Deere**
- **Cyrus McCormick**
- **Isaac Singer**

Reading for Content Understanding

1. **Main Idea** How did Morse code affect the spread of information throughout the United States?

2. **Main Idea** Make a chart listing new technologies in the home and showing how they made life easier by the mid-1800s.

3. **Technology and Society** What technological advances made farming easier and more efficient?

4. **Writing** *Creating* Invent your own Morse code system. Then send a short message that another inventor may have sent to announce his or her new invention.

5. **Critical Thinking** *Evaluating* Which of the devices that began appearing in homes in the mid-1800s do you think was the most important? Explain your answer in a paragraph. Also note if the invention is still used today or if it was the basis for an invention in use today.

CHAPTER 13 REVIEW

Chapter Summary

Between 1790 and 1860 life in the United States changed dramatically because of the Industrial and Transportation Revolutions. The Industrial Revolution introduced factories, changing the way people worked. The Transportation Revolution brought railroads and steamboats, which allowed people and goods to travel faster and quicker. Other technological advances in the 1800s improved communications and farming. ■

On a separate sheet of paper, complete the following activities.

Identifying People and Ideas

Describe the historical significance of the following:

1. Industrial Revolution
2. Samuel Slater
3. mass production
4. technology
5. trade unions
6. Sarah Bagley
7. Transportation Revolution
8. clipper ship
9. telegraph
10. Cyrus McCormick

Internet Activity go.hrw.com
SA0 Products

Search the Internet through the HRW Web site to find information about a product that was invented between 1790 and 1860 to make home life easier. Then create an advertisement that might have appeared in a magazine at that time to sell the item.

Understanding Main Ideas

1. What ideas did Eli Whitney contribute to manufacturing in the United States?
2. What was the benefit of the spinning jenny?
3. Explain the differences between the Rhode Island system and the Lowell system.
4. What were working conditions like in early factories?
5. What were some advantages and some disadvantages of railroads?
6. Why was the McCormick reaper important?

Reviewing Themes

1. **Global Relations** How did Britain's industrial technology reach the United States?
2. **Technology and Society** In what ways did the Industrial Revolution change where and how people worked?
3. **Economic Development** How did railroads and steamboats boost the U.S. economy?

Using the Time Line

Number your paper from 1 to 6. Match the letters on the time line below with the following events.

1. **Francis Cabot Lowell introduces the Lowell system at his first textile mill.**
2. **Government workers receive a 10-hour workday.**
3. **Samuel Morse successfully tests the telegraph.**
4. **Sarah Bagley is elected vice president of the New England Workingmen's Association.**
5. **After seeing the problems that farmers were having with iron plows, blacksmith John Deere invents the steel plow.**
6. **The *Clermont* travels along the Hudson River.**

Thinking Critically

1. **Evaluating** Considering that many factories paid better wages than workers received in other jobs, do you think workers were justified in their demands for reform? Explain your answer.

2. **Synthesizing Information** How do you think the concept of interchangeable parts affected farm equipment, household items, and industries such as railroads?

3. **Identifying Cause and Effect** Create a chart listing what you think are the five most important inventions in the early 1800s and what effect they had on American life.

Writing About History

1. **Expressing** Imagine that you live on a farm in the Midwest in the 1800s and have just purchased your first Deere plow or McCormick reaper. Write a journal entry describing the events of that day.

2. **Describing** Imagine that you are a magazine writer in 1831 and are at the race between the locomotive *Tom Thumb* and the horse-drawn railcar. Write a short article on the event and the reactions of the audience to the race.

Linking Geography and History

1. **Location** Why were early factories established in the Northeast?

2. **Human-Environment Interaction** Why did new inventions make it easier for farmers to plant and harvest their crops?

History Skills Workshop

Using Primary Sources By the 1830s many factory owners were forcing their employees to work 13 to 15 hours per day in order to increase company profits. Read the following excerpt, which is from testimony that was given before the Massachusetts House of Representatives in 1845 during hearings on working conditions in the factories. Then answer the following questions: (a) What complaints did Eliza Hemmingway have about the factory? (b) What time did work begin, and what time did it end? (c) Why did women miss work?

Building Your Portfolio

American History

Complete the following activities individually or in groups.

1. **The *Lowell Offering*** Imagine that you are in charge of writing a two-page issue of the *Lowell Offering*. In your magazine, include two articles about life in the factories and the boardinghouses, an article about the movement to improve working conditions, an editorial, an editorial cartoon, images of work and daily life in Lowell, and a biographical sketch of at least two people.

2. **Transportation Revolution** Prepare a bulletin board or multimedia display to show the impact of the Transportation Revolution in the United States. Your display should show major rivers, canals, roads, and railroads by 1860.

66 The first petitioner who testified was Eliza R. Hemmingway. She had worked 2 years and 9 months in the Lowell factories. . . . Her employment is weaving-works by the piece. . . . She complained of the hours for labor being too many, and the time for meals too limited. In the summer season, the work is commenced [begins] at 5 o'clock, a.m., and continued til 7 o'clock, p.m., with half an hour for breakfast and three quarters of an hour for dinner. . . . The air in the room she considered not to be wholesome [healthful]. . . . [She] thinks that there is no day when there are less than six of the females out of the mill from sickness. 99

Detail of John Antrobus, *Plantation Burial*, (1860) oil on canvas, The Historic New Orleans Collection

▪ CHAPTER 14 ▪
Agricultural Changes in the South
(1790–1860)

The South in the early 1800s was many things to many people. To Virginia-born slave Delia Garlic, it was a cruel culture that was built on the abuse of African Americans. Garlic recalled her life as "nothin' except . . . work." To Susan Dabney Smedes, it was a culture filled with men like her father, a plantation owner who was "well assured of the contentment and well-being of his slaves."

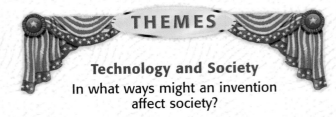

THEMES

Technology and Society
In what ways might an invention affect society?

Economic Development
How might increased demand for raw materials affect society?

Cultural Diversity
How might slavery shape a region's culture?

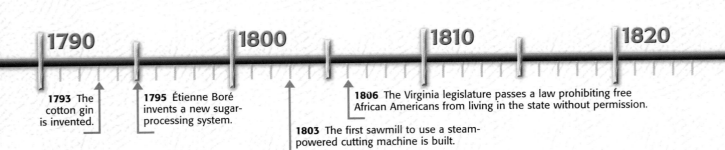

1790   1800   1810   1820

1793 The cotton gin is invented.

1795 Étienne Boré invents a new sugar-processing system.

1803 The first sawmill to use a steam-powered cutting machine is built.

1806 The Virginia legislature passes a law prohibiting free African Americans from living in the state without permission.

The Growth of Cotton

Reading Focus

How did changes in agriculture affect slavery immediately after the American Revolution?

What effect did the cotton gin have on the South and slavery?

How did the cotton boom affect the South's economy?

Key Terms

cotton gin

planters

cotton belt

scientific agriculture

O N AN AUGUST DAY IN 1770, *slaveholder Landon Carter rode out to view his tobacco crops.* He was pleased by the thick, healthy plants he saw. Carter was one of the most successful plantation owners in Virginia. He and his neighbors believed that the ability to produce good crops reflected a person's good character. "I know in this neighborhood people are very fond of speaking meanly of their neighbor's Crops," he noted. "However, when I ride out, I declare I do not see any so good [as mine]."

Fan used by a wealthy southerner

Colonial Williamsburg Foundation

IMAGE ON LEFT PAGE: *Slaves conduct a funeral at night.*

1830

1831 Nat Turner's Rebellion occurs.

1840

1839 A new way of drying tobacco is developed in North Carolina.

1850

1848 Joseph R. Anderson becomes owner of the Tredegar Iron Works.

1860 Two thirds of all cotton grown in the United States is produced in the South.

The South's Agricultural Economy

Since 1612, when John Rolfe introduced a high-grade tobacco that could be grown in Virginia, agriculture had played a central role in the southern economy and culture. Tobacco became one of the cash crops produced by plantations and the slaves who labored on them.

An Agricultural Tradition

Successful plantation owners like Landon Carter took great pride in their agricultural techniques. To them, the cultivation of crops such as tobacco was an art to be passed down from generation to generation.

Carter expressed great disappointment, for example, when he found out that his son was following the practice of other tobacco growers by not having the plants primed, or prepared before harvesting. "I will venture a wager that a plant primed and topped [cut] to 10 leaves should be thicker and weigh more than one of these unprimed plants," Carter wrote. Carter boasted, "I dare bet anything that none of the Tobacco tended as they have done can be thick as mine."

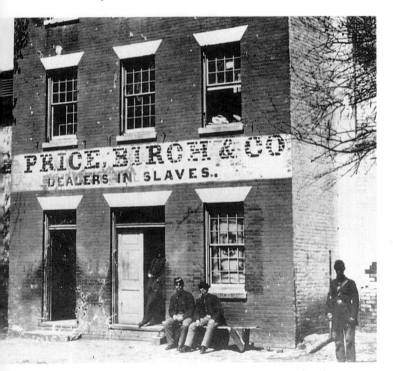

This business in Alexandria, Virginia, specialized in selling slaves.

Such competition among farmers was quite common in the South, where residents prided themselves on their ties to the land. Many southerners believed that the entire future of the United States rested on agriculture. Thomas Jefferson wrote around 1782:

> **Those [independent white farmers] who labor in the earth are the chosen people of God. . . . Corruption of morals in the mass of cultivators is a phenomenon [happening] of which no age nor nation has furnished an example.**

When Jefferson wrote these words, however, southern agriculture was going through a decline. After the American Revolution, the South's three major cash crops—tobacco, rice, and indigo—greatly decreased in price.

Slavery in the New Nation

Around the time that southern agriculture was declining, reliance on slavery also seemed to be decreasing in parts of the country. Some Revolutionary leaders believed that a nation founded on the ideal of liberty could not justify enslaving people. After the Revolution, northern states gradually began to declare slavery illegal.

Some southern plantation owners also freed their slaves in the years following the Revolution. A few were like Richard Randolph, who came to view slavery as "the most lawless and monstrous tyranny [injustice]." Randolph, who had inherited many of his slaves, instructed them all to be freed in his 1797 will, "to impress my children with just horror at a crime so enormous," he said. Other slaves also gained their freedom this way during the years immediately after the Revolution, leading to predictions that slavery would someday die out as a labor system in the United States.

The ideal of liberty was not the only factor behind the freeing of some slaves during this period. The drop in tobacco, indigo, and rice prices in the late 1700s led many landowners to scale back production or experiment with other crops, such as wheat, that required less labor. As a result, many landowners needed fewer workers than before. Because the lack of demand for laborers caused the price of slaves to drop, it was cheaper for some slaveholders to free their slaves than to keep them. Soon, however, the development of a new southern cash crop—cotton—changed this situation.

⭐ Whitney and the Cotton Gin

When southern agriculture declined in the late 1700s, some southerners thought that cotton might be a cash crop that would boost the economy. The expanding British and U.S. textile industries relied on cotton to make their cloth. However, U.S. farmers had difficulty keeping up with the demand for raw cotton because growing and processing the crop was difficult.

Types of Cotton

Farmers had been growing small amounts of cotton in the South since 1682. One type of southern cotton originated in China. This type of cotton, which was yellow in color, grew well in the backcountry of the Carolinas and Georgia, but never became popular as a large-scale cash crop.

Many farmers experimented with long-staple, or black-seed, cotton a type imported from the West Indies in 1785. The advantage of long-staple cotton was its long white fibers, which could be removed from the seed easily. Farmers had the most success growing long-staple cotton on the Sea Islands off of South Carolina.

Short-staple, or green-seed, cotton grew best in the South, but its short white fibers were difficult to remove from its tough green seed. It usually took a worker an entire day to remove the seeds from just one pound of such cotton. To remedy the problem, people began trying to build a machine that could more easily remove the seeds from the short-staple cotton and thus saved on production time.

Short-staple, or green-seed, cotton plants grew well throughout the South.

Whitney's Machine

Northerner Eli Whitney finally developed such a machine for removing cotton seeds in 1793. Whitney had never even seen cotton until 1792, when he visited a Georgia plantation owned by his friend Catherine Greene. Noticing Whitney's interest in technology, Greene asked for his help in improving a machine that workers were using to remove the seeds from long-staple cotton. This machine had never worked well on the short-staple cotton because it tended to grind the seeds into the fibers rather than separate them.

Eli Whitney

By the spring of the following year, Whitney had perfected a machine for removing short-staple seeds from cotton fibers. This rather simple device, called a **cotton gin**, consisted of a cylinder filled with rows of wire teeth. Workers spun the cylinders by turning a crank. As the cotton passed through the gin, or "engine," the wire spikes on the rotating cylinders pulled the fibers away from the seeds.

Whitney described how his invention would improve the cotton business:

> ❝One man will clean ten times as much cotton as he can in any other way before known and also clean it much better than in the usual mode [method]. This machine may be turned by water or with a horse, with the greatest ease, and one man and a horse will do more than fifty men with the old machines.❞

Whitney's gin revolutionized the cotton industry and gave new life to the southern agricultural economy. **Planters**—large-scale farmers who owned more than 20 slaves—built gins that could process tons of cotton quickly. Some southerners, like William McCreight of South Carolina, created successful businesses making gins for other people.

The Cotton Boom

Whitney's cotton gin sparked a boom in the growing of cotton. Short-staple cotton was easy to grow just about anywhere in the South. In theory, all a person needed in order to start raising cotton was land and labor. Increasingly, large-scale cotton growers came to depend on slave labor.

The Cotton Belt

By 1860 the South, east of the Mississippi River, was producing two thirds of all cotton grown in the United States. Cotton accounted for more than half of all U.S. exports, worth millions of dollars. Many farmers who were eager to profit from the cotton boom headed west to find land on which to grow cotton. Most of the South from South Carolina to east Texas had formed what is known as the Cotton Kingdom, or **cotton belt**, the region that grew most of the country's cotton crop.

As the cotton belt spread, farmers continued trying to improve the crop. In the 1830s diseases began to affect the short-staple cotton, wiping out entire crops in many areas. By crossbreeding the short-staple cotton with some varieties of Mexican cotton, agricultural scientists like Dr. Rush Nutt produced stronger types of cotton that were soon grown throughout the cotton belt.

Nutt and others who experimented with cotton production were part of a larger movement throughout the South that promoted **scientific agriculture**, or the use of scientific techniques to improve crop production. During the early 1800s publications such as the *Farmer's Register* began to inform farmers about the latest advances in agricultural research.

One concern of the scientists who studied the cotton belt was how to protect the land used for growing cotton. The crop's main drawback was that it pulled large amounts of nutrients from the soil. When a farmer planted cotton over and over again on the same piece of land, the soil wore out quickly. Virginia farmer Edmund Ruffin published numerous articles calling for better use of fertilizers and other products to protect the soil. Other scientific agriculturists advised farmers to rotate crops—to periodically change the types of crops grown on a particular piece of land—in order to help the soil. They also supported research to help people better understand how soil chemistry works.

The Growth of Slavery

Growing and harvesting cotton required many field hands. Other southern crops, such as Louisiana sugarcane, also took many laborers to cultivate and process. Rather than hire workers through a wage-labor system, planters began to rely more heavily than ever on the slave system.

Although the importation of slaves into the United States became illegal in 1808, the growing demand for slaves led to an increase in the domestic slave trade. Many

The Cotton Kingdom

| Extent of cotton growing by 1820 |
| Extent of cotton growing by 1860 |

Learning from Maps The growth of the textile industry caused a large demand for cotton. To meet this demand, farmers dramatically increased the area devoted to growing cotton between 1820 and 1860.

Place What states were growing cotton in 1820?

slaveholders from states like Virginia and Maryland profited by selling slaves to cotton or sugar planters from states farther south.

⭐ Dreams of Wealth

Desire for profits fueled the southern economy. Cotton had many advantages as a profitable cash crop. Besides being easy to grow, it was also inexpensive to market. Unlike food staples, harvested cotton did not perish over time if it was stored properly. Cotton was also lighter than other staple crops, so it did not cost much to transport long distances. All these factors meant that most cotton farmers who could produce a healthy crop stood to earn a significant amount of money.

Many cotton farmers started out like Ferdinand Steel in Mississippi, who grew cotton with his brother. Steel worried that he had made a bad decision by focusing on cotton instead of food crops. "I do not think that it is a good plan to depend so much on cotton," he wrote in his diary. "It takes up all our time. . . . I at this time think that we had better raise corn and let cotton alone."

Although Steel continued to grow cotton, he never earned tremendous wealth from it. Other cotton farmers had better luck. Thomas Dabney was one such farmer. For many years Dabney was a successful farmer in Virginia, growing staple

The Granger Collection, New York

Large cotton gins like this one processed tons of cotton in a short amount of time.

crops such as wheat, corn, rye, and tobacco. In the 1820s and 1830s, however, he suffered several financial setbacks. Wanting to start a new life, in 1835 he moved to Mississippi to become a cotton farmer. Within a few years he was one of the wealthiest men in the area. Success stories such as Dabney's encouraged other planters to turn to cotton as a cash crop.

SECTION 1 REVIEW

Identify and explain the significance of the following:
- **Eli Whitney**
- **cotton gin**
- **planters**
- **cotton belt**
- **scientific agriculture**

Reading for Content Understanding

1 **Main Idea** What happened to the southern agricultural economy and to southern slavery after the American Revolution?

2 **Main Idea** How did the cotton gin affect southerners' ability to grow cotton and their reliance on the slave system?

3 **Geographic Diversity** *Location* Which states made up the Cotton Kingdom?

4 **Writing** *Informing* Write a paragraph explaining cotton's advantages as a cash crop. Also explain cotton's economic impact on the South.

5 **Critical Thinking** *Synthesizing Information* How did the ideas of the American Revolution influence some southern slaveholders?

SECTION 2

The Southern Economy

Reading Focus

How did trade affect the southern economy?

Why were crops other than cotton important to the southern economy?

What kinds of factories were located in the South?

Key Terms

factors

Tredegar Iron Works

I N AN 1858 SPEECH *before the U.S. Senate, South Carolina politician James Henry Hammond declared, "Cotton is King." Southern senators listened closely. Like many of them, Hammond was a planter who believed that the expansion of the cotton trade had given the region global power and even protection from foreign attacks. The importance of the South's cotton in global trade networks led Hammond to predict that any threat to the southern crop would topple the world economy. "No power on earth dares to make war upon it," he declared. "Who can doubt . . . that cotton is supreme?"*

Cotton bales

 ## The Cotton Trade

James Henry Hammond was not the only southerner who shared this view about cotton. Southerner David Christy declared, "KING COTTON is a profound [learned] statesman, and knows what measures will best sustain his throne." Statements such as this reflected the importance of the cotton trade, which connected the South to many other nations and people.

Trading Centers

Many countries bought cotton and other southern staple products, but Great Britain was the South's main foreign trading partner. The importance of international and domestic trade to the southern economy led to the growth of major port cities such as Charleston, South Carolina; Savannah, Georgia; and New Orleans, Louisiana. Important northern port cities, such as New York, also participated in the cotton trade as southerners provided

Some plantations, like this one on the Mississippi River, grew sugarcane instead of cotton.

tons of cotton to the growing textile industry in the northern states.

Within the southern port cities, crop brokers called **factors** managed the trade between planters and their customers. Small farmers sold their cotton to merchants, who then negotiated with factors. Merchants and factors also arranged loans for farmers to get supplies and often advised them on how to invest any profits they made.

Cotton factors like William Washington Gordon Jr. and Godfrey Barnsley, both of Savannah, helped their towns grow into thriving commercial cities. So many factors opened offices along Bay Street near Savannah's port that the citizens nicknamed the street "Factor's Walk."

Getting to Market

Once the farmers got their cotton to the port cities, the factors arranged transportation aboard a trading ship. Getting their crops to the ports was a problem for many farmers. Most southern farmers relied on the region's many navigable rivers for transportation. In the southern interior, farmers used the Ohio and Mississippi Rivers. For many years, flatboats carried cotton and other products to port. With the invention of the steam engine, however, steamboats became the main method of transportation. New Orleans became the major port city of the interior region as hundreds of steamboats traveled up and down the mighty Mississippi River.

Farmers who did not live near navigable rivers, however, faced many challenges. For example, overland transportation was very difficult in the South. The few major road projects were limited to the Southeast.

Southern states were also slow to adopt the canal system. Although Maryland built the Chesapeake and Ohio Canal and Virginia had invested in the James and Kanawha Canal, few other southern states could find supporters for canal projects. By 1850 the South possessed only about 14 percent of the country's total canal mileage.

★ Other Agricultural Products

Not all southern leaders supported the expanding cotton trade. Some southern leaders were concerned about the region's economic dependence on cotton. Journalist James D. B. De Bow and others urged southerners to try a variety of crops and investments, rather than relying so much on cotton. De Bow noted that cotton was wearing out the South's soil. In addition, he warned that the international cotton trade was making the South dependent on foreign products, because

Hogs were the most common type of livestock raised in the South in the early 1800s.

Global Connections

The Cotton Trade

Colonists in Jamestown grew cotton as early as 1607. However, cotton did not become an important southern crop until after Eli Whitney invented the cotton gin in 1793. Southern planters quickly began switching from other crops to cotton. By the mid-1820s the South, known as the Cotton Kingdom, was the largest supplier of cotton in the world.

One Mississippi farmer noted 20 years later that

> *planters crowded every spot of their fields with cotton plants. . . . You might have travelled all day without seeing a corn field of any importance.*

During the late 1840s the South exported more than 900 million pounds of cotton—almost 2 million bales—a year. To supply its textile mills, Great Britain bought around half of all cotton grown in the South. Many other European countries, particularly France, also bought thousands of bales of cotton.

This success made the South confident of its important position in the global economy. In 1859 one owner of a cotton factory expressed the thinking of many southerners: "This country does now, and probably for ever will, possess

Cotton merchants from India gather at a marketplace in Bombay.

the monopoly of raw cotton." However, cotton-growing countries such as Egypt, India, China, Brazil, and Russia were becoming significant competitors.

Understanding What You Read

1. Why did Britain purchase so much of the South's cotton?

2. How do you think increased international competition in cotton production might have affected the southern economy?

southerners generally traded cotton for British manufactured goods. In an 1847 article, De Bow wrote:

> **This is the great evil under which the southwest labors. She is yearly wearing out her soil in the production of one great staple, which has become ruinously low in price by reason of its great supply: she parts with this staple at prime cost,**

> **and purchases almost all her necessary appliances of comfort from abroad, not at prime cost.**

Food Crops

Some farmers were already following De Bow's advice. Although cotton was certainly the most important crop for the southern economy, it was never the only crop that southerners grew. Corn

Rice fields like this one were very common in the Southeast.

continued to be the most important southern food crop. By the late 1830s the top three corn-growing states in the nation were all in the South. Tennessee was the leader, producing some 45 million bushels of corn in 1839. Kentucky and Virginia ran close behind. Some farmers, such as Ferdinand Steel, grew both corn and cotton.

Sweet potatoes, wheat, rice, and sugarcane were also common southern food crops. Maryland and Virginia led the region in wheat production. High demand for flour in Britain increased the value of southern wheat. Many London bakers particularly liked a special type of flour made from Alabama wheat. This flour was of such high quality that bakers could use less of it than other types of flour to make bread, resulting in higher profits.

Louisiana was the capital of the U.S. sugar industry. Sugar had been a major product of the West Indies for many years. The French introduced sugarcane to Louisiana around 1700. However, the crop never became very popular until after 1795, when Étienne Boré (ay-tyen bohr-AY) invented a new sugar-processing system.

Using techniques from the sugar plantations of the Caribbean, Boré perfected a way of processing Louisiana sugarcane into granulated sugar. This method was cheaper than others used at the time. Boré began a campaign to persuade Louisiana farmers to grow sugar. Slaves performed the harsh labor required to grow and process sugarcane. The crop soon became so important to the state's economy that many white southern planters began to refer to Boré as the "savior of Louisiana."

Nonfood Crops

Some nonfood crops also continued to be important to southern agriculture. Tobacco had been the South's first major cash crop. Tobacco production, however, was very time-consuming. Most farmers prepared their harvested tobacco for market by curing, or drying, it in small barns. In 1839 a slave who worked as a blacksmith in North Carolina discovered a way to speed up this process by curing tobacco with heat from burning charcoal. This method boosted tobacco farming, but tobacco still took much longer to process than other crops.

In parts of Kentucky and Tennessee, hemp and flax became major cash crops partly as a result of the cotton boom. The fibers of these plants were used to make rope and sackcloth. Farmers in the cotton belt used lots of Kentucky and Tennessee rope to bundle the cotton into bales.

Southern Factories

The rope and sackcloth industries were typical of many southern businesses that provided for the needs of farmers. Kentucky and Tennessee in particular supplied products for other southerners. In addition to providing rope and sackcloth, the states also raised horses, mules, and other animals put to work by farmers. These animals thrived on the hearty bluegrass that grew wild in western Kentucky and parts of Tennessee.

Another important business that served southerners was the lumber industry, which was greatly aided by new technology. In 1803 a sawmill owner from Donaldsonville, Louisiana, built the nation's first mill that used cutting machines powered by steam engines.

Although mechanization did not spread throughout the South as rapidly as it did in the Northeast, it did have an effect on the southern economy. Most of the first factories in the South

Few industries such as this textile mill in Columbus, Georgia, existed in the South before 1860.

were built to process staple crops. The task of turning sugarcane into sugar, for example, involved a series of machines. Writer Mark Twain once described a southern sugar-processing factory as "a wilderness of tubs and tanks and vats and filters, pumps, pipes, and machinery."

Some southerners, however, felt that the South needed even more industries. Writer Hinton Rowan Helper warned that the region was falling behind the modern world by not industrializing. He wrote:

> ❝We should . . . keep pace with the progress of the age. We must expand our energies, and acquire habits of enterprise and industry; we should arouse ourselves from the couch of lassitude [fatigue], and inure [condition] our minds to thought and our bodies to action.❞

Few southerners followed Helper's advice, however. One exception was Joseph R. Anderson, who took over the **Tredegar Iron Works** in Richmond, Virginia. This was the only large factory in the South that made iron products. Anderson was a graduate of the military academy at West Point who had worked as an engineer for the U.S. Army in the 1830s. He became the owner of the iron works factory in 1848. By 1860 he had turned it into one of the most productive iron works in the nation, making locomotives, boilers, cables, naval hardware, and cannons for the government, as well as other products.

SECTION 2 REVIEW

Identify and explain the significance of the following:
- factors
- Étienne Boré
- Joseph R. Anderson
- Tredegar Iron Works

Reading for Content Understanding

1 **Main Idea** Why did some people urge southern farmers to plant a variety of crops?

2 **Main Idea** What were some of the first factories in the South?

3 **Global Relations** How did international trade affect the South's economy and its major port cities?

4 **Writing** *Classifying* If you were a southern farmer in the 1800s, which food and nonfood crops would you plant? Which would you not plant? Write a paragraph explaining your answers.

5 **Critical Thinking** *Drawing Conclusions* What might be some drawbacks of an economy like the South's that was so heavily dependent on agriculture?

SECTION 3

Southern Society

Reading Focus

What was life like for southern planters and small farmers?

What was the urban South like?

What challenges did free African Americans face in the South?

Key Terms

yeomen

SOUTHERN WRITER AND BUSINESSWOMAN Anne Newport Royall loved to travel. She published several popular collections of her observations about people throughout the United States. In one, she ranked the citizens of different southern states by their tendency to show off their wealth, which to her demonstrated a lack of honor. "I find the Tennesseeans are a very plain people, and have a very high sense of honor," she noted. "The North Carolinians next; the South Carolinians and Georgians, next; and the Virginians the most ostentatious [showy] of any."

The Granger Collection, New York

Southern furniture

 The Planters

Popular fiction often gave the impression that all white southerners were residents of large plantations. However, the majority of white southerners did not live on plantations or own slaves. In the first half of the 1800s, about one third of white southern families owned slaves. Fewer still owned plantations and large numbers of slaves. Despite their small numbers, planters had a powerful influence over the South because many served as political leaders. As the wealthiest members of the society, they also greatly influenced the economy.

Although some planters showed off their wealth by living in beautiful mansions, many others lived quite simply. A visitor to wealthy planter Alexander Stephens's estate described it as "an old wooden house" surrounded by weeds. Some planters saved all their money to reinvest in more land and slaves.

Male planters focused primarily on raising crops and left the running of the plantation household to their wives. Although this task was physically much easier than the work of most farm wives, it was still a large responsibility. The planter's wife oversaw the raising and education

Children of a wealthy plantation owner

of her children, the work of all slaves within the household, and the social duties of the family. Most southern politicians were planters who often discussed policy issues at the dances and dinners hosted by their wives.

Economic and political issues were so important to planter families that they often arranged marriages for their children based on business concerns. Lucy Breckinridge, daughter of a wealthy Virginia planter, greatly dreaded the thought of such an arranged marriage. She wrote in her journal in 1862:

> **" A woman's life after she is married, unless there is an immense amount of love, is nothing but suffering and hard work. I never saw a wife and mother who could spend a day of unalloyed [pure] happiness and ease. "**

Breckinridge failed to escape her family's desires, however. She entered into an arranged marriage in January 1865. Her married life was cut short, however, when she died six months later of typhoid fever.

★ Small Farmers

Breckinridge's life was much different from that of the average white southern woman, who was more likely to be married to a small farmer than a wealthy planter. Although most white southern farmers owned few or no slaves, many small farmers hoped one day to become planters.

Yeomen

Most white southerners were **yeomen**, or small landowning farmers. By 1860 about 80 percent of all southern farmers owned their own land, with a typical farm averaging about 100 acres. These yeomen took great pride in their work. A young Georgia man expressed this pride in an 1849 letter to a southern magazine: "I desire above all things to be a 'Farmer.' It is the most honest, upright, and sure way of securing all the comforts of life." Most yeomen families had few material comforts and typically worked long days at a variety of tasks. "My life is one of toil," wrote yeoman Ferdinand Steel in 1839, "but blessed be God that it is as well with me as it is."

Some yeomen earned enough money to buy a few slaves. Unlike the planters, however, yeomen generally worked side by side with slaves. Some white southerners like D. R. Hundley complained that yeomen treated their slaves too much like equals, "making so little distinction between master and man." Most planters believed that their domination over slaves reflected the planters' superior social and racial status.

On small southern farms, everyone in the family helped raise and gather crops, sometimes working alongside slaves.

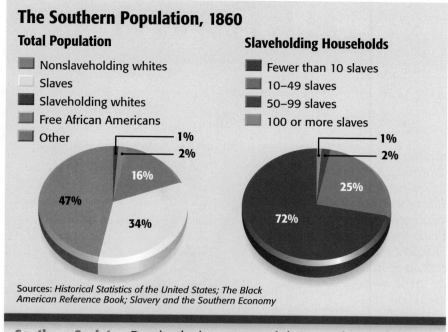

The Southern Population, 1860

Total Population

- Nonslaveholding whites
- Slaves
- Slaveholding whites
- Free African Americans
- Other

1%
2%
16%
47%
34%

Slaveholding Households

- Fewer than 10 slaves
- 10–49 slaves
- 50–99 slaves
- 100 or more slaves

1%
2%
25%
72%

Sources: *Historical Statistics of the United States; The Black American Reference Book; Slavery and the Southern Economy*

Southern Society Despite the importance of slavery to the South's agricultural economy, most southerners held no slaves. Which group made up the largest section of the southern population? What percent of slaveholding households had 100 or more slaves?

Poor Whites

Although most white southerners owned land, a few very poor, landless whites did live in the region. Other white people often looked down on these poorest of white southerners, who never amounted to more than about 10 percent of the white southern population.

Most very poor whites lived on lands unsuitable for producing cash crops. Many of them survived by hunting, fishing, raising small gardens, and doing odd jobs for money.

★ White Southern Culture

There were wide-ranging differences in the economic status and background of white southerners. However, they did share some common cultural characteristics.

Religion

Religion was central to southern social life. Because so many farm families were isolated from one another, people often saw their neighbors only at special church functions, such as revivals or socials. Rural women were particularly involved in church activities. Though not allowed to become ministers, women often took on important volunteer roles.

Other wealthy white southerners used religion to justify not only their position in society but also the institution of slavery. They argued that God created some people, like themselves, to rule over others. This belief set them at odds with those northern Christians who believed that God opposed slavery.

Literature

Some southern writers tried to increase national awareness of southern culture through literature. Charleston, South Carolina, attracted many writers who gathered to discuss their poems, short stories, and essays. Hugh Swinton Legaré, the leader of this so-called Charleston School, published many of the group's works in a literary magazine called the *Southern Review*.

Most white southern writers greatly romanticized southern life, focusing on what they saw as its unique traditions. Baltimore writer John Pendleton Kennedy reflected this style in his 1832 book *Swallow Barn*, which was the first plantation novel—a book that glorifies the life of planter families. After the publication of Kennedy's book, there was a booming market in plantation novels, particularly among readers wishing to justify the slave system that supported the planters' lifestyle.

Caroline Howard Gilman was a popular southern writer in the early 1800s.

American Literature

Life on the Mississippi
Mark Twain

Samuel Langhorne Clemens, better known as Mark Twain, was born in 1835 in Missouri. One of America's most humorous writers, Twain enriched his works by using local color—writing that expresses the culture and language of a particular region. In the following passage from Twain's book Life on the Mississippi, *he recalls a lesson from Mr. Bixby, a steamboat pilot who taught him to pilot a riverboat on the Mississippi River.*

In the course of time . . . my self-complacency [overconfidence] moved to the front once more. Mr. Bixby was all fixed, and ready to start it to the rear again. He opened on me after this fashion—

"How much water did we have in the middle crossing at Hole-in-the-Wall, trip before last?"

I considered this an outrage. I said—

"Every trip, down and up, the leadsmen [workers who measure the water's depth] are singing through that tangled place for three quarters of an hour on a stretch. How do you reckon I can remember such a mess as that?"

"My boy, you've got to remember it. You've got to remember the exact spot and the exact marks the boat lay in when we had the shoalest [most shallow] water, in every one of the five hundred shoal places between St. Louis and New Orleans; and you mustn't get the shoal soundings and marks [measurements of water depths] of one trip mixed up with the shoal soundings and marks of another, either, for they're not often twice alike. You must keep them separate."

When I came to myself again, I said—

"When I get so that I can do that, I'll be able to

Writer Mark Twain, shown here aboard a steamboat, was fascinated by the Mississippi River.

raise the dead, and then I won't have to pilot a steamboat to make a living. I want to retire from this business. I want a slush-bucket and a brush; I'm only fit for a roustabout [laborer on a boat]. I haven't got brains enough to be a pilot; and if I had I wouldn't have strength enough to carry them around, unless I went on crutches."

"Now drop that! When I say I'll learn [teach] a man the river, I mean it. And you can depend on it, I'll learn him or kill him."

Understanding Literature

1. What point is Twain making in the next-to-last paragraph?

2. Why is this passage funny?

The Urban South

Southern writers' novels about the South generally focused on rural whites. Few writers focused on southern African Americans or white southerners who lived in cities. Although most southern cities' economies were closely tied to the plantations, cities housed a variety of businesses, social organizations, and people. Southern urban residents often took on many roles in their communities. James A. Cowardin of Richmond, Virginia, was a typical urban business leader. He headed a brokerage firm and edited one of the first "penny press" newspapers, the Richmond *Daily Dispatch*. He also was on the city's Board of Trade, was vice president of the Virginia Mechanics' Institute, and served as a member of the state legislature.

In many ways, southern cities were like northern cities. City governments provided services to improve life—for example, public water systems, well-maintained streets, and, in some places, public education. Southern urban leaders wanted their cities to appear as modern as possible to the international visitors who came there to do business. In addition, many wealthy urban residents donated large sums of money to charities, from orphanages to public libraries.

Much of the work in southern cities was done by slaves. A greater percentage of urban whites were slaveholders than rural white southerners.

Many urban business leaders owned slaves or hired them out from nearby plantations. Slaves worked in mills, in shipyards, in skilled jobs, and as domestic servants. Free African Americans also found similar work in southern cities.

Free African Americans

By 1860 more than half of all free African Americans lived in the South. Some who were born free were the descendants of slaves who had been freed after the American Revolution. Others were the descendants of refugees from the Haitian Revolution led by Toussaint L'Ouverture. Still others were once enslaved but had obtained their freedom mainly by running away.

Some free African Americans had to wear badges like this one to prove they were free.

Work

Free African Americans who lived in southern cities worked in a variety of jobs, mostly as skilled artisans. Some, like barber William Johnson of Natchez, Mississippi, became fairly successful in their businesses. Free African Americans who lived in rural areas often hired out their services to plantations. A few of them were quite financially successful, such as William Ellison, a maker of cotton gins who eventually became a wealthy planter.

Urban Life

Some free southern African Americans, particularly those in the cities, were able to form loose social and economic ties. Churches frequently served an important function as the center of their social life. Although free African Americans and slaves rarely

Southern cities were often the region's centers of trade, attracting a diversity of people and businesses.

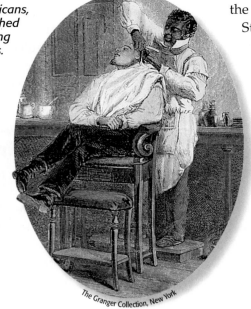

Some free African Americans, like this barber, established successful businesses serving other free African Americans.

The Granger Collection, New York

attended the same churches, in the early 1800s free African Americans and slaves in Charleston established an independent church movement. However, such movements were rare because they were discouraged by white southerners.

Discrimination

Free African Americans faced constant discrimination from white southerners who feared they would try to encourage rebellions among slaves. Many cities and states passed laws limiting the rights of free African Americans. Most could not vote, travel freely, or hold certain types of jobs. In some places, free African Americans had to have a white person represent them in any business transaction they conducted.

In 1806 the Virginia legislature passed a law prohibiting any former slaves from residing in the state without special permission. A free African American woman named Jemima Hunt petitioned

the legislature to grant her husband, Stephen, permission to stay in the state. She had only recently purchased his freedom. In her petition to the legislature, Hunt asked the representatives not to break up her family, writing:

❝**Your petitioner [Hunt] farther states that she has a numerous family of Children by the said Stephen, who are dependent upon the daily labor of herself & husband for a support, & without the assistance of her husband Stephen they must suffer.**❞

Many white southerners, however, argued that free African Americans could not take care of themselves. "A *free* negro is an anomaly [exception]—a violation of the . . . laws of nature," wrote one white Mississippian. "The status of slavery is the only one for which the African is adapted," he continued. To many white southerners, free African Americans threatened the institution of slavery because they proved that African Americans could live outside of the slave system.

SECTION 3 REVIEW

Identify and explain the significance of the following:
• **yeomen**
• **Caroline Howard Gilman**

Reading for Content Understanding

1 **Main Idea** How were the lives of planters different from and similar to the lives of small farmers?

2 **Main Idea** What was life like in southern cities?

3 **Cultural Diversity** What kind of discrimination did free African Americans face in the South?

4 **Writing** *Creating* Write a short story about life in a rural or urban area in the South in the early 1800s. Make sure your characters include at least one planter, one yeoman, one slave, and one free African American.

5 **Critical Thinking** *Drawing Conclusions* Why do you think that novels about the lives of southern planters were popular?

The Slave System

Reading Focus

What were work and daily life like for most slaves?

How did slaves' family, religion, and other aspects of their culture help them cope with the slave system?

How did enslaved African Americans challenge the slave system?

Key Terms

folktales

spirituals

Nat Turner's Rebellion

HARRIET JACOBS, WHO WAS *born into slavery in 1813, asked, "Why does the slave ever love?" She was working in a doctor's household when she fell in love with a free African American man who wanted to buy her freedom and marry her. Her owner refused and ordered her never to see the young man again. "If I catch him lurking [sneaking] about my premises, I will shoot him as soon as I would a dog," he threatened. Jacobs advised her admirer to move north while she made plans to run away and join him someday. She never saw him again.*

Slave auction poster

Slaves and Work

Although treatment of enslaved African Americans varied, most slaveholders tried to get as much work as they could out of slaves. Enslaved people on small farms usually did a wide variety of jobs. On large plantations most slaves were assigned to specific jobs, with the majority working in the fields. Some plantations hired men called drivers to make sure that slaves followed orders and to carry out punishments. On many plantations the driver was also a slave.

Most plantation field hands worked in "gang" systems, whereby everyone worked on the same task at the same time, usually from sunup to sundown. Former slave Harry McMillan, who had worked on a plantation in South Carolina, recalled that the field hands usually did not even get a break to eat lunch: "You had to get your victuals [food] standing at your hoe."

Women and men usually did the same work, as did children over the age of about 10. Hardly anything, including illness and poor weather, stopped the work. "The times I hated most was picking cotton when the frost was on the bolls [seed pods]," recalled former Louisiana slave Mary Reynolds. "My hands git sore and crack open and bleed."

Some slaves worked as cooks, nurses, or butlers around the planter's home. These slaves usually received better food and clothing than field hands but often worked longer hours. They were at the service of the planter's family 24 hours a day. Slaves who usually worked in the house also could be sent to work in the fields during a critical time in the agricultural season.

On larger plantations, some slaves worked in skilled jobs such as blacksmithing or carpentry. Sometimes the planters allowed these slaves to hire out their services to other people. In this way, some skilled slaves earned enough money to buy their freedom. For example, William Ellison purchased his freedom by hiring out his services as a cotton gin maker. It took him several years working late at night and on Sundays to raise the needed funds. Eventually, he also purchased the freedom of his wife and daughter.

Slave auctions like this one often resulted in the division of slave families.

This slave worked as a maid for a wealthy plantation family in the 1840s.

⭐ Life Under Slavery

Generally, the people who profited from slavery viewed slaves only as property, not as people. Most slaveholders were constantly trying to maximize profits and exert their control over slaves. Slaves were bought, worked, and sold to make a profit. Some dishonest slave traders would even kidnap free African Americans from the North and sell them into slavery down south. Solomon Northup, for example, was kidnapped in Washington. He later described spending 12 years as a slave—"shut out from the sweet light of liberty"—before he could prove his identity and gain his release.

Conditions

Most slaves received very poor clothing and shelter. Their housing usually consisted of dirt-floor cabins, which often had leaky roofs and few furnishings. Clothing for the field hands was usually simple and made out of rough fabric. Delia Garlic recalled that her slave clothing "was made out of the cheapest cloth that could be bought—unbleached cloth, coarse, but made to last." Some slaves tried to brighten up their clothing by using discarded scraps of material to sew designs on the fabric. In this way, they tried to individualize the clothing assigned to them by the planters.

Likewise, many slaves did what they could to improve their food rations. Every morning on the way to the field, Delia Garlic received her food ration for the day. "That piece of cornbread was all [we] had for breakfast, and for supper, [we] had the same," she recalled. Some planters allowed slaves to keep their own gardens for vegetables, and chickens for eggs. Other slaves were able to add a little variety to their diet by using what little time they had to themselves to catch fish or pick wild berries.

Slaves like these often tended the fields under the supervision of an overseer.

Control

Some planters offered rewards of food or better conditions to encourage slaves' obedience. However, most slaveholders relied more heavily on fear of punishment. Some slaveholders would severely punish one slave in front of all the others as a warning to the entire group. Former slave Harry McMillan recalled some of the typical punishments he witnessed:

> ❝ **The punishments were whipping, putting you in the stocks [frames to lock people in] and making you wear irons and a chain at work. They had a collar to put round your neck with two horns, like cows' horns, so that you could not lie down. . . . This also kept you from running away for the horns would catch in the bushes. Sometimes they dug a hole like a well with a door on top. This they called a dungeon keeping you in it two or three weeks or a month, or sometimes till you died in there.** ❞

Often just witnessing such severe mistreatment was enough to frighten most slaves into obeying the planter's or overseer's orders.

Many southern communities also passed strict slave codes to limit what slaves could do. For example, some laws prohibited slaves from traveling very far from their owner's home or from learning to read or write.

 ## Slave Culture

Despite the harsh realities of daily life, many slaves found comfort through their community and their culture. After working an exhausting day of 12–14 hours in the fields or in the planter's house, most slaves made time for some social activity to relieve the hardship of their lives.

Community

Slaves worked hard to maintain strong ties to one another and to their heritage. The most important unit of slave communities was the family. More than any physical punishment, most slaves feared being sold to another plantation and separated from their families. Josiah Henson never forgot the day that he and his family were all sold at a slave auction. His mother begged her new owner to buy Josiah so that she would have at least one of her children with her. The slaveholder refused, and Henson's entire family was separated. "I must have been then between five or six years old," he recalled years later. "I seem to see and hear my poor weeping mother now."

To make sure that the children never forgot their heritage, enslaved parents told them stories passed down from earlier generations. Some

Slaves made crafts, such as this quilt showing stories from the Bible, that reflected their culture and spiritual beliefs.

stories would tell family history, and some would reflect the customs and traditions of life in Africa. Slaves also told **folktales**, or stories with a moral, which taught lessons about how to survive under slavery. These folktales often involved animals, particularly a clever character called a trickster who usually defeated a stronger creature by outwitting it.

Most tricksters represented slaves. The lesson of the folktales was usually that slaves could survive by outsmarting the slaveholder, who was represented by a predatory animal such as a fox. In some folktales, however, the stronger creature was the trickster, which reflected how slaveholders sometimes tried to deceive slaves. These stories served as a warning that slaves should never trust the slaveholders.

Religion

Another important aspect of slave culture was religion. By the early 1800s many slaves were Protestant. White ministers often tried to use religion to support the institution of slavery, preaching that God wanted slaves to obey slaveholders. However, slaves themselves noted that the Bible also implied that all people are equal in the eyes of God. They came to see themselves as God's chosen people, much like the Hebrew slaves in ancient Egypt, who had faith that they would someday live in freedom.

Some slaves expressed their religious beliefs through the singing of **spirituals**, emotional Christian songs that blended African and European traditions. Many spirituals, such as "The Heavenly Road," reflected slaves' belief in their equality in the eyes of God:

> 66 **Come, my brother, if you never did pray,**
> **I hope you may pray tonight;**
> **For I really believe I'm a child of God**
> **As I walk in the heavenly road.** 99

Some historians have referred to slave religion as "the invisible institution," because worship was sometimes carried out in secret, out of the watchful eye of the slaveholder. Slaves' style of worship blended many aspects of traditional African religions with those of Christianity.

The Granger Collection, New York

Biography

Nat Turner

Nat Turner always believed he was called by God to do something important. As a child on a Virginia plantation, he gained a reputation among the other slaves for his religious beliefs and intelligence. He impressed others when he learned to read and write at a young age.

Turner grew up to be a well-respected minister among the local slave community. In 1827 he even baptized a white overseer. Not long after, Turner reported seeing a vision: "I saw white spirits and black spirits engaged in battle, and the sun was darkened—the thunder rolled in the Heavens, and blood flowed in streams." Turner then interpreted a solar eclipse in 1831 as a sign that the time had come to start a revolt.

★ Challenging Slavery

Maintaining their own religious beliefs and practices was only one way in which slaves resisted slaveholders' attempts to control them completely. In small ways, on a daily basis, slaves rebelled against the slave system and tried to gain a measure of control over their lives. Sometimes this meant working slower to protest increased hours in the fields. Other times it meant running away for a few days to avoid an angry slaveholder.

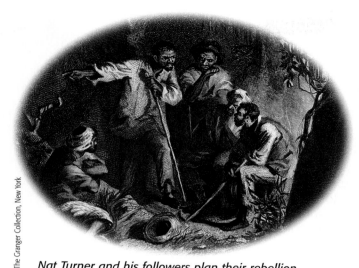

Nat Turner and his followers plan their rebellion.

The most violent slave revolt in the United States occurred in 1831. Nat Turner, a slave from Virginia, believed that God had called on him to overthrow slavery. **Nat Turner's Rebellion** began on an August night in 1831, when Turner led a group of slaves in a plan to kill all of the planter families in their county. They started with the family that held Turner as a slave and had soon killed almost 60 white people in the area.

More than 100 slaves were killed in an attempt to put down the rebellion. A posse finally caught up with the group, but Turner escaped. However, he was caught within weeks and sentenced to hang. Before the trial, he made a confession in which he expressed his belief that the revolt was justified and worth losing his own life. "I am willing to suffer the fate that awaits me." He was executed on November 11, 1831. After this rebellion many states strengthened their slave codes to increase control over slaves, as the slave system continued to spread.

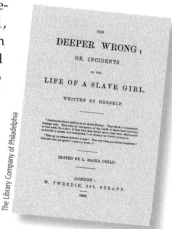

Runaway Harriet Jacobs published a book about her life experiences.

Although some slaves ran away permanently, most left for only short periods of time, often to see relatives. They usually returned voluntarily. It was difficult to escape all the way to the North, although thousands of enslaved people like Harriet Jacobs did succeed.

While violent slave revolts were rare, planters lived in fear that such a revolt would occur. Two planned slave rebellions—one led by Gabriel Prosser near Richmond in 1800 and one led by Denmark Vesey in Charleston in 1822—were stopped before they could be carried out. Authorities executed most of those involved in planning the Charleston rebellion.

SECTION 4 REVIEW

Identify and explain the significance of the following:
- **Harriet Jacobs**
- **folktales**
- **spirituals**
- **Nat Turner's Rebellion**

Reading for Content Understanding

1 Main Idea What was a typical day like for slaves?

2 Main Idea What ways did slaves find to challenge the slave system?

3 Geographic Diversity *Region* Why was slavery mostly concentrated in the South?

4 Writing *Describing* Imagine that you are a newspaper journalist in the mid-1800s. Write a half-page article on how slaves cope with the slave system. Make sure your article includes the role of religion and family.

5 Critical Thinking *Identifying Cause and Effect* How do you think Nat Turner's uprising affected the lives of southern slaves who did not take part in the rebellion?

CHAPTER 14 REVIEW

Chapter Summary

The invention of Eli Whitney's cotton gin in 1793 made growing cotton extremely profitable in the South. The growth of the Cotton Kingdom also affected southerners' economic and social life, and led to the expansion of slavery. Although slaves suffered under terrible conditions, they maintained a rich culture.

On a separate sheet of paper, complete the following activities.

Identifying People and Ideas

Describe the historical significance of the following:

1. Eli Whitney
2. cotton gin
3. cotton belt
4. factors
5. Étienne Boré
6. planters
7. yeomen
8. Nat Turner
9. Harriet Jacobs
10. spirituals

Internet Activity go.hrw.com
SA0 Southern Economy

Search the Internet through the HRW Web site to find information on the southern economy today, including what the major industries are and what role agriculture plays in the region. Then use this information to write a short essay about how the southern economy has changed since the early 1800s.

Understanding Main Ideas

1. Why did cotton production increase in the 1790s?
2. Why did slavery seem to decline after the American Revolution, and why did it increase again in the 1800s?
3. What kinds of factories existed in the South in the 1800s?
4. What role did religion play in the social life of rural southerners?
5. How did religion and family ties help enslaved African Americans cope with the slave system?

Reviewing Themes

1. **Technology and Society** How did Eli Whitney's cotton gin lead to an increased demand for slave labor?
2. **Economic Development** How did the growth of industrialization affect the South?

Using the Time Line

Number your paper from 1 to 5. Match the letters on the time line below with the following events.

1. The nation's first sawmill that uses steam-powered cutting machines is built.
2. Nat Turner leads the most violent slave revolt ever in the United States.
3. Northern inventor Eli Whitney develops the cotton gin.
4. Joseph R. Anderson takes over the ownership of the Tredegar Iron Works factory in Richmond, Virginia.
5. Using techniques from the sugar plantations of the Caribbean, Étienne Boré invents a new sugar-processing system.

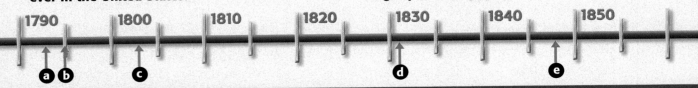

3. **Cultural Diversity**   How did slavery influence African American culture in the 1800s?

Thinking Critically

1. **Identifying Cause and Effect**   How did the cotton gin benefit southern farmers and northern cloth manufacturers? How did the cotton gin make life more difficult for slaves?

2. **Making Comparisons**   How were the lives of free southern African Americans different from and similar to the lives of slaves?

3. **Determining the Strength of an Argument** What were some of the weaknesses of the arguments made by slaveholders to justify slavery?

Writing About History

1. **Informing**   Imagine that you are a newspaper reporter during Nat Turner's Rebellion. Write an article about the events and consequences of the rebellion.

2. **Creating**   Write a folktale that a slave might have told his or her children. You might want to include a trickster in your story.

Linking Geography and History

1. **Human-Environment Interaction**   What types of crops did southern farmers grow between 1790 and 1860?

2. **Place**   What role did agriculture play in the development of southern port cities?

Building Your Portfolio

Complete the following activities individually or in groups.

1. **The Southern Economy**   Prepare a written argument on the debate topic that follows. Resolved: the focus on cotton was or was not good for the southern economy in the early 1800s. Use the library and your textbook to research reasons why dependence on one staple crop such as cotton may or may not have been good for the economy. Then use this information to write a persuasive essay on your arguments. If time permits, hold a class debate.

2. **Oral History**   Write the script for an oral historical account that an enslaved African might have told to his or her children. The account should cover the lives of several generations and could trace the family's heritage back to Africa. Be sure to include important aspects of slave culture, such as religion and family ties, in your account. When you have finished your script, relate your account to the rest of the class.

History Skills Workshop

Using Visual Resources   Study the image to the right, which is a Currier & Ives painting titled *Cotton Plantation on the Mississippi*. Currier & Ives paintings often show a romantic, unrealistic view of life in the South. Briefly describe what is happening in this painting. Then write two or three sentences explaining why this painting is a romanticized view of slave life.

The Granger Collection, New York

A Growing Economy

From 1790 to 1860, the economy of each region of the United States grew and developed in very different ways. The regional economies of the West and the South were based largely on agriculture, while the economy of the North was increasingly focused on industry. In some ways these differences worked together to help the nation grow. The South provided some raw materials, such as cotton, to northern factories. The West provided large supplies of food for the growing number of people living in northern cities.

The growth of American manufacturing in the late 1700s and early 1800s was made possible by the invention and development of new technologies. Improved waterpower systems and new machines such as the spinning jenny and the water frame increased the speed of textile production. At the same time, expanded railroad networks moved goods rapidly and inexpensively to and from market. ■

The North

The North developed an industrial economy partly because of its geography and superior transportation system. Since farmland in the North was not generally suited for large-scale commercial agriculture, industrial development was necessary for the region's economic growth.

Water Power and Early Industry

Industrial centers along the Fall Line

0   100   200 Miles
0   100   200 Kilometers
Albers Equal-Area Projection

History Note 1

Many early industrial centers, particularly in the North, were located along the imaginary line called the Fall Line. There river waters began flowing downhill, descending from the uplands to the lowlands. This fast-moving water formed waterfalls and rapids that were often used to power factory machines.

Geography Skills

Reading Special-Purpose Maps

1. What geographical formation lies west and north of the Fall Line in the eastern United States?
2. What were some industrial centers located along the Fall Line?

Industry in the North, 1860

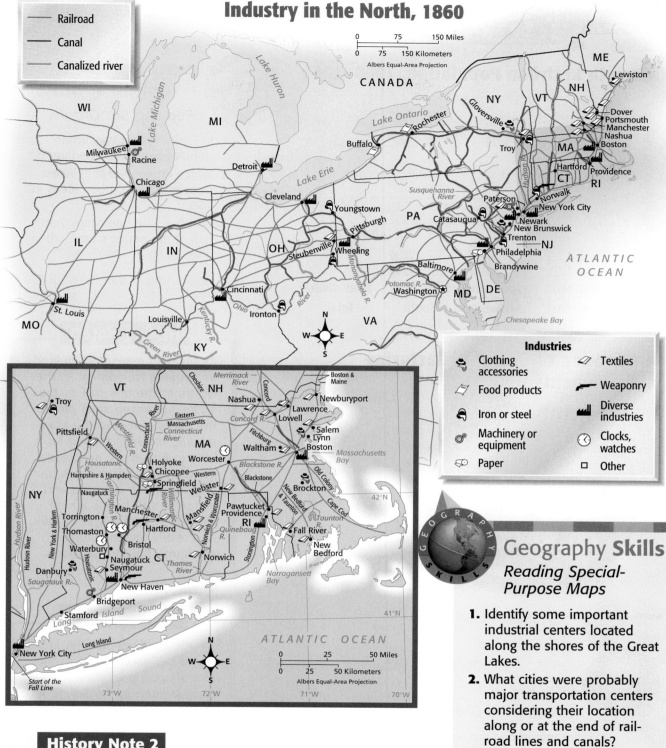

Railroad
Canal
Canalized river

0   75   150 Miles
0   75   150 Kilometers
Albers Equal-Area Projection

Industries

- Clothing accessories
- Food products
- Iron or steel
- Machinery or equipment
- Paper
- Textiles
- Weaponry
- Diverse industries
- Clocks, watches
- Other

Geography Skills

Reading Special-Purpose Maps

1. Identify some important industrial centers located along the shores of the Great Lakes.

2. What cities were probably major transportation centers considering their location along or at the end of railroad lines and canals?

3. Where were some textile centers located?

History Note 2

Improved transportation networks in the North encouraged industrial expansion. Businesses shipped goods on rivers, the Great Lakes, and the growing networks of canals and railroads. The New England states of Connecticut, Massachusetts, and Rhode Island provide good examples of the important relationship between the growth of industry and the expanded transportation networks in the first half of the 1800s.

Growth in Urban Population, 1800–1860

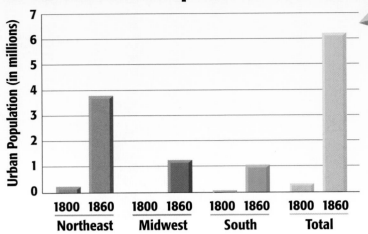

Urban Population (in millions)

7
6
5
4
3
2
1
0

| 1800 1860 | 1800 1860 | 1800 1860 | 1800 1860 |
| Northeast | Midwest | South | Total |

Source: *Historical Statistics of the United States*

Distribution of U.S. Manufacturing Establishments, 1860

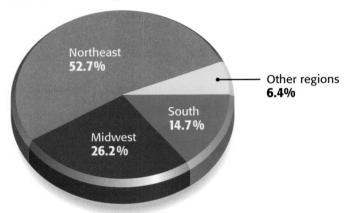

Northeast
52.7%

Other regions
6.4%

South
14.7%

Midwest
26.2%

Source: *Encyclopedia of American History*

Geography **Skills**

Reading Pie Graphs

1. What region had the largest percentage of the nation's manufacturing establishments in 1860?
2. What was the percentage of manufacturing establishments located in the South?
3. What was the combined percentage of manufacturing establishments located in the Midwest and other regions in 1860?

Geography **Skills**

Reading Bar Graphs

1. In which region was urban population growth the largest?
2. Which region had the fewest people living in urban areas in 1860?
3. Which region had more than half of the nation's total urban population in 1860?

History Note 3

Changes in agriculture helped industrial development in the North. In the first half of the 1800s, improved steel plows, the cotton gin, and the grain-reaping machine helped farmers produce more agricultural goods. These goods were then shipped along railroads and waterways to towns where meatpacking plants, flour mills, and textile factories turned them into finished products.

History Note 4

By 1860 only about one in seven U.S. factories and other manufacturing establishments were located in the South. As industry increased in the North, so did the region's urban population. Cities, particularly those in the Northeast and Midwest, grew larger as factories provided more and more jobs. In the South, which had fewer factories, urban growth was much slower.

The South

While industry in the North grew, agriculture in the South boomed. The invention of the cotton gin in 1793 encouraged spectacular growth in southern cotton production. However, as that region's economy grew, so did disapproval in the North and the West of the South's use of slave labor.

Agriculture and Slavery in the South, 1860

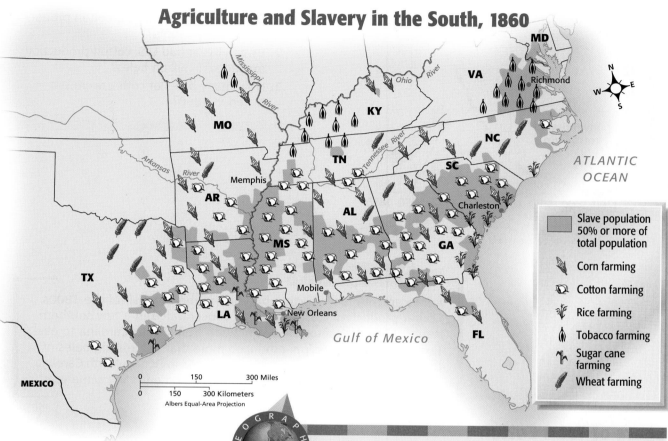

Legend:
- Slave population 50% or more of total population
- Corn farming
- Cotton farming
- Rice farming
- Tobacco farming
- Sugar cane farming
- Wheat farming

Slave census

Geography Skills
Reading Special-Purpose Maps

1. What agricultural products were grown in nearly all southern states by 1860?
2. Where was tobacco an important agricultural product?
3. In what states were sugarcane and rice cultivated?
4. Slavery was more common in areas that grew what product?

History Note 5

Before the invention of the cotton gin, growers in coastal Georgia and South Carolina cultivated a warm-weather long-staple cotton whose fibers were easily pulled from its seeds. However, it was difficult and expensive to separate the fiber of the hardier short-staple cotton. The cotton gin pulled the seeds out with metal teeth and made it practical to grow short-staple cotton throughout the South.

U.S. Cotton Production, 1790-1860

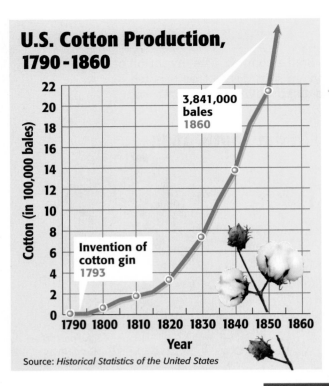

3,841,000 bales 1860

Invention of cotton gin 1793

Cotton (in 100,000 bales)

Year: 1790 1800 1810 1820 1830 1840 1850 1860

Source: *Historical Statistics of the United States*

Geography **Skills**
Reading Bar Graphs

1. During what decades did cotton production almost double?
2. By what year had U.S. cotton production exceeded 1 million bales?
3. How many bales of cotton were produced in 1860?

History Note 6

American cotton production boomed in the first half of the 1800s. Cotton production was particularly concentrated in a few southern states called the cotton belt, which ran from South Carolina to east Texas. In 1860 Mississippi produced more than 1.2 million bales of cotton—more than all of the cotton produced in Florida, North Carolina, South Carolina, Tennessee, and Virginia combined in the same year.

Share of Total Cotton Production by State in 1860

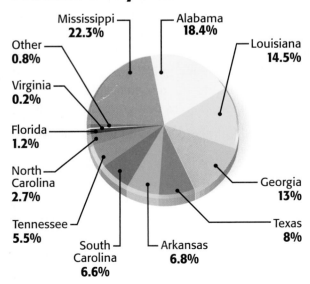

Mississippi 22.3%
Other 0.8%
Virginia 0.2%
Florida 1.2%
North Carolina 2.7%
Tennessee 5.5%
South Carolina 6.6%
Arkansas 6.8%
Texas 8%
Georgia 13%
Louisiana 14.5%
Alabama 18.4%

Source: *Historical Statistics of the United States*

Geography **Skills**
Reading Pie Graphs

1. What state accounted for nearly one quarter of cotton production in 1860?
2. Study the percentages in the pie graph and locate each state on the map on page, XX in the front of your textbook. From the percentages shown here, what states formed the cotton belt by 1860?
3. Which three southern states produced the least cotton in 1860?

U.S. Cotton and Tobacco Exports, 1790-1860

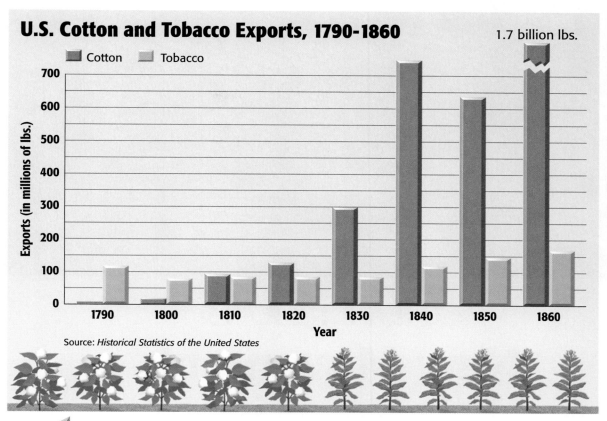

1.7 billion lbs.

Cotton ■ Tobacco

Exports (in millions of lbs.)

700
600
500
400
300
200
100
0

1790 1800 1810 1820 1830 1840 1850 1860

Year

Source: *Historical Statistics of the United States*

Geography **Skills**

Reading Bar Graphs

1. By what year had the amount of cotton exports overtaken the amount of tobacco exports?
2. Describe the general growth of tobacco exports between 1790 and 1860.
3. By what year had the amount of cotton exports become more than double that of tobacco exports?

History Note 7

States that produced smaller amounts of cotton often produced larger amounts of other agricultural products. In 1860 Virginia produced less cotton than any other southern state, but produced nearly 30 percent of the nation's tobacco. South Carolina produced nearly two thirds of the nation's rice in that year. Georgia's agriculture was more diverse, producing 13 percent of the nation's cotton and more than 28 percent of its rice in 1860.

Southern cotton plantation

▫ CHAPTER 15 ▫
New Movements in America

(1815–1850)

In 1831, after visiting the United States, Frenchman Alexis de Tocqueville commented that "Americans of all ages, all conditions, and all dispositions [types], constantly form associations. . . of a thousand . . . kinds." Between 1790 and 1850, life in the United States changed significantly as a new revival movement swept the nation, and many people joined new associations to challenge long-standing ideas and institutions.

THEMES

Cultural Diversity
What changes in society might lead people to start a new form of community?

Geographic Diversity
Why might people immigrate to another nation?

Citizenship and Democracy
How might citizens try to bring equal rights for all people?

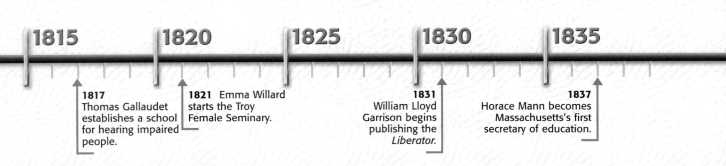

1815	1820	1825	1830	1835

1817 Thomas Gallaudet establishes a school for hearing impaired people.

1821 Emma Willard starts the Troy Female Seminary.

1831 William Lloyd Garrison begins publishing the *Liberator.*

1837 Horace Mann becomes Massachusetts's first secretary of education.

America Stirs to New Ideas

Reading Focus

How did the Second Great Awakening affect Americans?

What were the transcendentalists' views of American society?

What were some ideas of the romantic movement?

Key Terms

Second Great Awakening
transcendentalism
utopian community

EARLY IN HER TEENS, *New Yorker Huldah Baldwin began thinking seriously about her spiritual life. When she became deathly ill, she asked relatives and friends to come to her bedside out of concern for the state of their souls. "Oh beloved parent, my tender brothers, my affectionate sisters, my dear friends . . . ," she pleaded as death grew near. "O live for him [God] that we may meet hereafter and enjoy a blessed eternity together." Such deep religious beliefs were increasingly common in the early 1800s in New York, particularly among young women like Baldwin.*

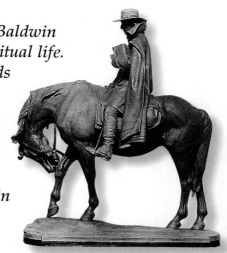

Traveling minister

IMAGE ON LEFT PAGE: *Revivals like this one attracted huge crowds in the early 1800s.*

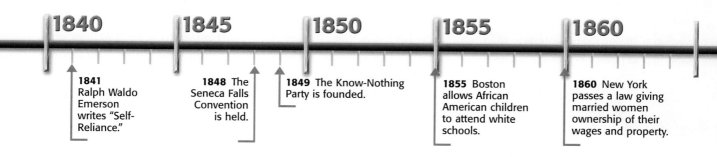

1840	1845	1850	1855	1860
1841 Ralph Waldo Emerson writes "Self-Reliance."	**1848** The Seneca Falls Convention is held.	**1849** The Know-Nothing Party is founded.	**1855** Boston allows African American children to attend white schools.	**1860** New York passes a law giving married women ownership of their wages and property.

New Movements in America **453**

The Second Great Awakening

During the 1790s the **Second Great Awakening**—a period of widespread evangelism—began to emerge in towns across upstate New York and in the Ohio River valley. By the 1820s and 1830s this new religious devotion had spread throughout New England, the Appalachians, and the South.

Charles Grandison Finney was one of the most important leaders of the Second Great Awakening. After experiencing a dramatic religious conversion in 1821, Finney left his career as a lawyer and began preaching. Speaking in a forceful and direct style, Finney challenged traditional Protestant beliefs by telling congregations that each individual was responsible for his or her own salvation and that sin was avoidable. He held prayer meetings that lasted for days, during which time many people were converted. Finney called on converts to perform good deeds in their communities to prove their faith. The popular minister claimed that the religious revival signaled "nothing else than a new beginning of obedience to God."

In 1794 Richard Allen (inset) founded the Bethel African American Episcopal Church in Philadelphia.

Finney angered some traditional ministers. Boston preacher Lyman Beecher used vivid imagery to warn Finney away from the city:

❝ **I know your plan and you know I do. You mean to come into Connecticut, and carry a streak of fire to Boston. But if you attempt it, as the Lord liveth, I'll meet you at the State line, and call out all the artillery-men, and fight every inch of the way to Boston.** ❞

Despite these challenges, the popularity of Finney and other revival ministers grew. As a result, church membership nationwide increased dramatically during the Second Great Awakening. The movement appealed particularly to women.

African Americans were also drawn to the new religious movement. Many of them joined congregations, and others became Baptist, Methodist, and Presbyterian ministers. Branches of the African Methodist Episcopal Church, for example, spread throughout the Middle Atlantic states. By 1820 there were about 4,000 African American Methodists in Philadelphia alone. Although the movement had begun in the Northeast, the Second Great Awakening renewed Americans' religious faith throughout the country.

Transcendentalism

Some New England writers and thinkers found spiritual inspiration from **transcendentalism**—the idea that people could transcend, or rise above, the material things in life. Important figures in this group include Ralph Waldo Emerson, Margaret Fuller, and Henry David Thoreau.

Emerson's essay "Self-Reliance," written in 1841, discusses his concerns about society. Emerson criticized Americans' reliance on institutions and traditions and encouraged people to look within themselves for guidance. "What I must do is all that concerns me, not what the people think," he wrote.

Fuller edited the transcendentalist publication *The Dial*. In 1845 she wrote a book called *Woman in the Nineteenth Century*. In it, she argued for what she called women's universal sacred right to develop their individual natures. This idea also earned her a reputation as a champion of women's rights. Fuller and other transcendentalists encouraged people to follow their personal beliefs, rely more on their own judgment, and live simply, without regard to wealth and possessions.

Thoreau also believed in self-reliance and distrusted institutions. He recorded many of his ideas in *Walden, or Life in the Woods*, published in 1854. In *Walden*, Thoreau drew upon his experience of living alone for two years in a small cabin on Walden Pond in Massachusetts. Explaining his experiment with isolation, Thoreau wrote:

Brook Farm, a utopian community in Massachusetts, attracted many famous writers such as Ralph Waldo Emerson.

> **❝ I went to the woods because I wished to live deliberately [purposefully], to front [experience] only the essential facts of life, and see if I could learn what it had to teach, and not, when I came to die, discover that I had not lived. ❞**

 Utopian Communities

Some transcendentalists experimented in community living at Brook Farm, Massachusetts, in the 1840s. Brook Farm did not last very long, however. This **utopian community**—a group of people working to establish a perfect society on Earth—was one of many such experiments that took place in the early 1800s.

Americans founded some utopian communities as an extension of their religious beliefs, while other communities were based on social philosophies. In 1774 Ann Lee started a community of Shakers, an American religious sect so called because of their tendency to shake their bodies during worship. By the 1840s this group had about 6,000 members living in various communities. The Shakers banned private ownership of property and lived an extremely plain lifestyle. Their simple approach to life is reflected in the furniture they made.

Other societies, particularly those influenced by English social reformer Robert Owen, established themselves on secular, or nonreligious,

principles. Owen came to the United States and started a utopian community in New Harmony, Indiana, in 1825. There members jointly owned all property and worked together on an equal basis.

Many utopian communities emphasized equality between men and women. Mary Paul, a member of a utopian community in Redbank, New Jersey, explained that she was not "confined to one kind of work but could do almost anything." Paul added that in the community "both men and women have the *same pay* for the *same* work." Such utopian communities allowed people to pursue spiritual and cooperative lifestyles that were unavailable in the larger society. However, only a few of these communities were able to sustain any long-term success. Most failed to get their members to cooperate and work together well enough for the community to survive.

The Shakers were well known for their handcrafted furniture.

 The American Romantics

Ideas about spiritual renewal, simplicity, and nature also influenced painters and writers in the early 1800s. The romantic movement, which began in Europe, drew upon the idea that each individual brings a unique perspective to the world that is best expressed by emotion rather than reason.

Romantic Artists

Thomas Cole was a leading romantic painter and part of the Hudson River school. Artists of this school painted the countryside of the Catskill Mountains and the Hudson River valley. Their landscape paintings showed the beauty and innocence of nature in the United States. This contrasted with what many thought to be the corrupt civilizations of Europe. Other artists such as George Caleb Bingham painted frontier scenes that celebrated westward expansion and showed the spaciousness of the North American continent.

Novels

Many female authors, such as Ann Sophia Stephens, wrote romantic novels that became enormously popular during the mid-1800s. This period also brought some of the earliest literature to be recognized as distinctly American in its style and content. One British critic in the mid-1800s commented that American writers "Edgar [Allan] Poe, Nathaniel Hawthorne, [and] Herman Melville are assuredly no British offshoots [imitators]; nor is Emerson."

One of the best-known examples of romantic literature is New Englander Nathaniel Hawthorne's first novel, *The Scarlet Letter*, which examined Puritan society in the 1600s. Hawthorne wrote that the novel's moral was "Be true! Be true! Be true! Show freely to the world, if not your worst, yet some trait whereby the worst may be inferred [known]!" In this way he encouraged his readers not to hide their faults from themselves or others.

Hawthorne's friend Herman Melville was a former sailor who wrote tales of the sea such as *Moby Dick* and *Billy Budd*. While Melville did not achieve great popularity during his lifetime, many people consider *Moby Dick*—a novel about a tragic

American Literature

"This Is My Letter to the World"
Emily Dickinson

Emily Dickinson

Born in 1830, Emily Dickinson led a quiet life in Amherst, Massachusetts. Few people realized that she was one of the country's greatest poets because only two of her poems were published during her lifetime—both anonymously. Dickinson used strong images rather than rhyme to express her ideas. Her use of punctuation and meter was also unique. After her death in 1886, Dickinson's family discovered hundreds of her poems, some written on loose scraps of paper. Her first published collection of poetry included the following selection.

This is my letter
to the World
That never wrote to Me—
The simple News that Nature told—
With tender Majesty

Her Message is committed
To Hands I cannot see—
For love of Her—Sweet—countrymen
Judge tenderly—of Me.

Understanding Literature

1. What does Dickinson mean by her "letter to the world"?

2. What might the second line of the poem say about her life?

3. What is she asking the reader?

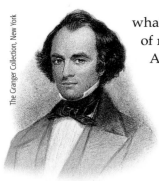

whaling voyage and the power of nature, to be one of the finest American novels ever written.

Short Stories and Poems

Nathaniel Hawthorne

In addition to novels, American romantic writers also composed many famous short stories and poems. Edgar Allan Poe, for example, is best known for his short stories and poetry. Poe also created the modern detective story, in which the hero uses logic to solve a mystery. The most famous of Poe's works published during his lifetime was the haunting poem "The Raven," which begins with the following verse:

> " **Once upon a midnight dreary,**[1]
>   **while I pondered,**[2] **weak and weary**
> **Over many a quaint and curious**
>   **volume of forgotten lore**[3] **—**
> **While I nodded, nearly napping,**
>   **suddenly there came a tapping,**

---

[1] [gloomy], [2] [thought] [3] [legends]

> **As of some one gently rapping,**
>   **rapping at my chamber door—**
> **'Tis some visiter,' I muttered,**
>   **'tapping at my chamber door—**
> **Only this and nothing more.'** "

The United States produced several other gifted poets during this period, including Henry Wadsworth Longfellow, Walt Whitman, Emily Dickinson, and John Greenleaf Whittier. Whittier spoke out against slavery in works such as *Poems Written During the Progress of the Abolition Question*, published in 1838. Dickinson saw only two of her poems published during her lifetime, yet her work had a strong impact on later poets. Longfellow was the most popular poet of the mid-1800s. His long, sweeping story-poems, such as *Hiawatha*, the *Courtship of Miles Standish*, and *Tales of a Wayside Inn* became favorites in many American households.

Walt Whitman's simple, unrhymed poetry celebrated both American individualism and democracy. His work *Leaves of Grass*, published in 1855, is noted for its distinct style. "Americans of all nations at any time upon the earth have probably the fullest poetical nature," Whitman wrote in the preface to *Leaves of Grass*. "The United States themselves are essentially the greatest poem."

SECTION 1 REVIEW

Identify and explain the significance of the following:

- **Second Great Awakening**
- **Charles Grandison Finney**
- **transcendentalism**
- **Ralph Waldo Emerson**
- **Margaret Fuller**
- **Henry David Thoreau**
- **utopian community**
- **Thomas Cole**
- **Nathaniel Hawthorne**
- **Edgar Allan Poe**
- **Emily Dickinson**
- **Walt Whitman**

Reading for Content Understanding

1 Main Idea What criticisms did Ralph Waldo Emerson, Margaret Fuller, and Henry David Thoreau have of American society?

2 Main Idea What was the romantic movement, and who were some of its important artists and writers?

3 Cultural Diversity What effect did the Second Great Awakening have on religious life in America?

4 Writing *Creating* Write a poem on a subject of your choice based on the style of the romantics. Be sure that your poem appeals to readers' emotions.

5 Critical Thinking *Evaluating* What might be some advantages and disadvantages of living in an isolated society such as one of the utopian communities?

Immigrants and Cities

Reading Focus

Why did so many Irish and German immigrants come to the United States in the 1840s and 1850s?

How did some Americans react to immigrants?

What benefits and problems came along with the growth of U.S. cities?

Key Terms

nativists

Know-Nothing Party

middle class

tenements

*I*RISH IMMIGRANTS TO THE UNITED STATES *traveled in tightly packed sections of ships, which received little air or light. Herman Melville, the cabin boy aboard the merchant ship* **Highlander,** *later recalled the terrible effects of fever on one voyage across the Atlantic Ocean. As people died from sickness, he wrote, "By their own countrymen, they were torn from the clasp [embrace] of their wives . . . and with hurried rites [ceremonies], were dropped into the ocean." Of the millions of immigrants who left their homes hoping for better lives in the United States, not all made it safely across the Atlantic.*

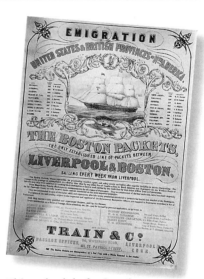

Ship schedule for immigrants

⭐ Waves of Immigrants

In the mid-1800s waves of immigrants crossed the Atlantic Ocean from Europe to begin new lives in the United States. More than 4 million immigrants settled in the United States between 1840 and 1860, with more than 3 million of them arriving from Ireland and Germany. Many immigrants were fleeing from economic or political troubles in their native countries.

Fleeing the Irish Famine

Most immigrants from the British Isles during this period were Irish. In the 1840s a potato blight, or disease that causes rot, left many families in Ireland with little food. Thomas Francis Meagher, an Irish leader, sadly commented, "One business alone survives! . . . That fortunate business . . . is the Irish coffin-maker's." More than 1 million Irish people died of starvation and disease. Even more fled to the United States.

Most Irish immigrants were very poor. Many settled in towns and cities in Massachusetts, New Jersey, New York, and Pennsylvania. Those who did not live in cities often worked on building canals and railroads or labored in mines. Many Irish women worked as domestic servants for wealthy families, laboring 16 hours or more a day. Irish men in the cities could usually find only unskilled work. In 1849 a Boston health committee reported that such labor paid low wages, forcing most Irish immigrants to live in "wretched, dirty and unhealthy conditions." The same report added that the homes of many poor immigrants allowed "no cleanliness, privacy, or proper ventilation, and little comfort."

Nevertheless, many immigrants enjoyed a new feeling of equality. Patrick Dunny wrote home to his family, "People that cuts a great dash [style] at home . . . think it strange [in the United States] for the humble class of people to get as much respect as themselves." Other immigrants sent letters home about the abundance of good food. For example, Alice Barstow wrote:

66 **There is no want [lack] of meat and drink here. . . . Tell little Adam, if he was here, he would get puddings and pies every day.** 99

A Failed German Revolution

Many Germans also immigrated to the United States during this period. In 1848 the German people had staged a revolution. Some educated Germans fled to the United States to escape persecution during this revolt. Many others came for economic reasons. After the revolution failed, working-class Germans began to emigrate as well, many searching for new economic opportunity and freedom from government control. While most Irish immigrants were Catholics, German immigrants included Catholics, Jews, or Lutherans.

Germans were more likely than the Irish to become farmers and to live in rural areas where there was more land available, particularly in midwestern states such as Michigan, Ohio, and Wisconsin. A large percentage of German immigrants arrived in the United States with money in hand. German immigrants—like the Irish—often were forced to take low-paying jobs, despite their skills. The Chicago *Daily Tribune* rejoiced that the German immigrant population was "fitted to do the cheap and ingenious [clever] labor of the country."

Some Occupations of Irish and German Immigrants in New York, 1855

OCCUPATION	TOTAL NUMBER OF WORKERS	FOREIGN-BORN WORKERS	IRISH	GERMAN
Bakers	3,692	3,323	861	1,987
Blacksmiths	2,642	2,159	1,339	530
Cabinetmakers/upholsterers	3,517	2,917	408	2,153
Leatherworkers	1,386	980	416	391
Tobacco workers	1,996	1,535	100	1,227
Jewelers	1,705	1,037	177	483
Carpenters	7,531	4,863	2,230	1,664
Bricklayers/masons	3,634	2,870	2,203	336
Clerks	13,929	5,921	2,135	2,249
Dressmakers/seamstresses	9,819	6,606	4,559	935
Shoemakers/tailors	19,354	18,600	6,292	10,430
Domestic servants	31,749	29,470	23,386	4,493
Food dealers	8,300	5,274	1,817	3,045
Merchants	6,299	1,705	278	627
Physicians	1,469	566	113	228
Printers	2,077	1,151	519	237
Retail shopkeepers	2,646	1,835	916	442

Source: Robert Ernst, *Immigrant Life in New York City, 1825–1863*, 1949

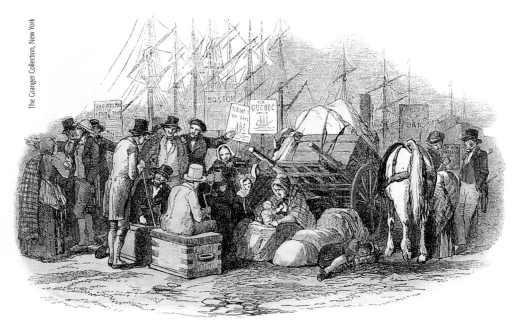

Irish citizens crowd the docks as they prepare to immigrate to the United States.

The Nativist Response

Industrialization and the waves of newcomers from Europe greatly changed the U.S. labor force. Immigrants filled the need for cheap labor in many towns and cities. These new laborers in turn fueled the local economies, creating new jobs for supervisors, merchants, clerks, and other professional workers. Such changes often made it possible for native-born workers to move out of their unskilled jobs and into better ones.

Nevertheless, many native-born citizens felt threatened by the immigrants' different cultural and religious backgrounds and the economic competition they presented. Prior to the arrival of many new Catholic immigrants, most people living in the United States were Protestants. Long-standing conflicts between Catholics and Protestants in Europe made American Protestants suspicious of Catholic immigrants. In addition, many native-born citizens feared losing their jobs to immigrants, who would often

work for a lower wage. Americans who held such views and who opposed immigration were called **nativists**.

One of the leading nativists of the 1830s was inventor Samuel Morse, who wrote a popular book entitled *Conspiracy Against the Liberties of the United States*. In the book Morse outlined the ways he believed immigrants were harming the country. In the 1840s and 1850s some nativists became politically active. One of their main goals was to try to stir up anti-immigrant feeling. An 1844 election flyer described different groups of immigrants as

❝**thieves and vagabonds [tramps], roaming about our streets . . . monopolizing [taking] the business which properly belongs to our own native and true-born citizens.**❞

In 1849 nativists founded a political organization that became known as the **Know-Nothing Party** because when asked questions by outsiders, its members answered, "I know nothing." The

A protest by a nativist group led to this Philadelphia riot in 1844. Similar riots took place elsewhere in the country.

Know-Nothings wanted to exclude Catholics and immigrants from public office and to require immigrants to live in the United States for 21 years before they could become citizens. Know-Nothing politicians had some success, winning several state elections during the 1850s and briefly gaining control of the Massachusetts legislature.

★ The Growth of Cities

The Industrial Revolution led to the creation of many new jobs in the United States. Job opportunities helped encourage immigration as well as the migration of rural inhabitants to the cities. As a result, U.S. cities grew rapidly during the mid-1800s, particularly in the Northeast and Middle Atlantic states, where three quarters of the country's manufacturing jobs were located.

Free African Americans were among the many people who migrated from rural areas to the cities. In the cities, African Americans faced many restrictions and strong opposition from white workers, who feared competition for jobs. Though most free African Americans worked as common laborers, others found work in a wide variety of occupations. They worked as builders, machine operators, druggists, grocers, engravers, photographers, and tailors.

The rise of industry and growth of cities offered new opportunities for people who owned their own businesses or worked in skilled occupations. Located primarily in the Northeast, the families of these merchants, manufacturers, professionals, and master craftspeople made up a growing social class. This **middle class** was a social and economic level between the wealthy and the poor. However, the population was still largely made up of the working class.

In the growing cities, people found entertainment and an enriched cultural life in places such as libraries and clubs. Writing about his visit to New Orleans in 1818, British surgeon Henry Bradshaw Fearon described "markets, shops, theatre, circus, and public ball-rooms" available for public entertainment. In the early 1800s people attended urban theaters, where they often got caught up in the excited atmosphere of the performance. American author Washington Irving compared the audience

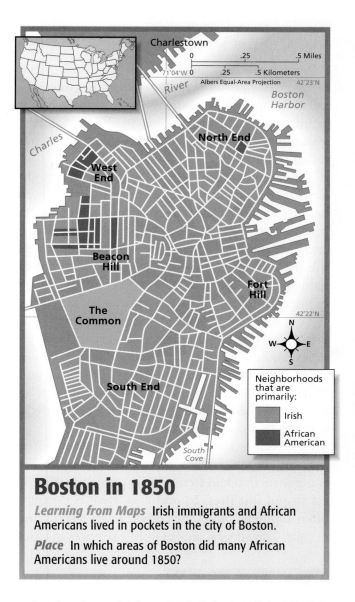

Boston in 1850

Learning from Maps Irish immigrants and African Americans lived in pockets in the city of Boston.

Place In which areas of Boston did many African Americans live around 1850?

noise "to that which prevailed [existed] in Noah's ark; for we have an imitation of the whistles and yells of every kind of animal." Popular pastimes, such as bowling and playing cards, also provided recreation for urban residents.

Cities during this period were compact and crowded. Many people lived within walking distance of where they worked. Wagons transported goods down streets paved with stones, making a noisy, bustling scene. One visitor from Maine complained that the noise in Boston made it too hard to sleep. The fast pace of city life affected people's attitudes as well. One observer remarked that the clerks and businesspeople on Broadway Avenue in New York City always carried themselves with a "knitting of the eyebrows and compression of the lips . . . and a hurried walk."

New Movements in America **461**

⭐ Urban Problems

American cities in the early and mid-1800s faced many challenges as a result of their rapid development. Many urban residents—particularly immigrants—could only afford to live in dirty, overcrowded, and poorly built housing structures called **tenements**.

Diseases spread easily in the unsanitary conditions of the tenements. Epidemics were common because cities lacked clean water, public health regulations, or sanitary ways to dispose of garbage and human waste. These problems posed perhaps the greatest risks for poor immigrants. The cholera epidemics of 1832 and 1849 in New York City, for example, hit Irish immigrants particularly hard.

Other factors besides disease made urban life dangerous. As populations rose, urban communities became centers of criminal activity. Most cities—including New York, Boston, and Philadelphia—had no permanent police force to fight crime. Instead, they relied on volunteer night watches that provided inadequate protection.

Fire protection was also usually poor. The majority of cities were served by volunteer fire companies that had to use hand-pumps and buckets to put out fires. In addition, rival companies often competed with each other when responding to calls. The general lack of public services in cities

During the 1800s poor city residents often lived in overcrowded tenement neighborhoods like this one.

also extended to sanitation workers and road maintenance crews. These shortages created significant health and safety problems for many urban residents.

SECTION 2 REVIEW

Identify and explain the significance of the following:
- **nativists**
- **Know-Nothing Party**
- **middle class**
- **tenements**

Reading for Content Understanding

1 **Main Idea** Why did nativists fear immigration?

2 **Main Idea** Provide at least three positive and three negative aspects of the rapid growth of American cities in the mid-1800s.

3 **Global Relations** What types of economic and political problems encouraged more than 3 million people from Germany and Ireland to immigrate to the United States between 1840 and 1860?

4 **Writing** *Informing* Write a half-page newspaper article explaining why American cities grew so quickly in the mid-1800s.

5 **Critical Thinking** *Identifying Generalizations and Stereotypes* What stereotypes did nativists form about immigrants? How were these stereotypes inaccurate, and how did they make life more difficult for immigrants?

Reforming Society

Reading Focus

What factors led to the growth of the reform movement?

Why did reformers start the temperance movement?

How did Americans' educational opportunities change during the early 1800s?

Key Terms

temperance movement
common-school movement

I N 1841 DOROTHEA DIX *visited a jail in Cambridge, Massachusetts, to teach a Sunday school class. What she saw there shocked her. Mentally ill women were jailed alongside common criminals in filthy cells. Outraged at the conditions she found there and in other Massachusetts jails, Dix began a campaign to improve care of mentally ill people throughout the country. She joined many other women who became reformers in the early and mid-1800s.*

Dorothea Dix

The Origins of Reform

The Second Great Awakening led many Americans to try to improve social conditions in the United States. Often it was members of the growing middle class who became the leaders of these reform efforts. Middle-class women were particularly active in reform movements during this period. Many of these women did not work outside the home, and some had domestic servants to help maintain their households. This gave them more time to become involved in reform associations.

Helping Mentally Ill People

Dorothea Dix was a middle-class reformer who helped change the prison system in the United States. Dix investigated jails throughout Massachusetts. She found terrible conditions and poor treatment of mentally ill people, who were often imprisoned. She reported her findings to the state legislature in a fiery speech, pleading for the lawmakers to

❝ **hasten to the relief of the victims of legalized barbarity [cruelty]. I come to**

New Movements in America **463**

Reformers wanted to help prison inmates become productive citizens. These inmates are learning to make hats.

present the strong claims of suffering humanity . . . the miserable, the desolate [deserted], the outcast . . . to call your attention to the present state of insane persons confined within this Commonwealth, in *cages, closets, cellars, stalls, pens! Chained, naked, beaten with rods, and lashed* into obedience. "

The government of Massachusetts responded to Dix's criticism by creating special facilities for mentally ill people, separating them from criminals. Dix's reform efforts extended across the nation and resulted in the establishment of more than 100 state hospitals where mentally ill people could receive more professional treatment.

Helping Disadvantaged Youth

In addition to housing people with mental illness, prisons during the early 1800s held debtors as well as children who had no other place to live, such as runaways and orphans. These children, who often had been forced to beg or steal to stay alive, were treated the same as adult criminals.

This nun accepts a boy without parents into an orphanage.

A prison reformer from New England named Josiah Quincy asked that young offenders be given different punishments than adults. Many reformers also tried to prevent prison overcrowding and improve the inhumane conditions there. In the 1820s several state and local governments established the first houses of correction and reform schools. These institutions sought to change prisoners' behavior through education rather than through punishment alone. Children in reform schools attended classes, worked at tasks where they could learn useful skills, and lived together under strict rules.

★ Campaigning Against Alcohol

A number of reformers also turned their efforts toward preventing alcohol abuse. Many people believed that Americans were consuming liquor at an alarming rate in the early and mid-1800s. During the 1830s the average alcohol consumption per person was more than seven gallons a year.

In 1842 Abraham Lincoln, an Illinois lawyer, remembered that in his youth, liquor was an "angel of death, commissioned [employed] to slay, if not

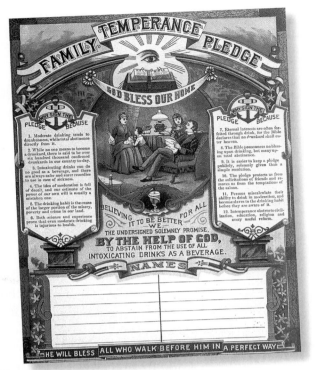

Temperance posters like this one urged people to stop drinking to help their families.

the first, the fairest born in every family." Many reformers considered alcohol abuse to be responsible for social problems such as family violence, poverty, and criminal behavior.

Americans' concerns about the negative effects of alcohol led to the growth of a **temperance movement.** This social reform effort encouraged people to use self-discipline to stop drinking hard liquor and to drink beer and wine only in small amounts. Reformers established the American Temperance Society and the American Temperance Union to spread this message. Minister Lyman Beecher preached widely about alcohol's evil effects. He lectured that people who drank alcohol were disobeying God's laws and "neglecting the education of their families—and corrupting their morals."

The temperance movement was popular and widespread. However, some people, such as Neal Dow of Maine, came to believe that temperance would not go far enough in solving the social problems caused by alcohol

abuse. These people wanted to outlaw the sale of alcohol. Dow's efforts resulted in the Maine Law of 1851, which made selling alcohol illegal in the state. Banning the sale of alcohol became a major goal of reformers. By 1855 twelve other states had passed laws similar to the one in Maine.

The Common-School Movement

One of the most important reform campaigns in the early 1800s was the movement to improve the education of young Americans. As the immigrant population grew, reformers argued that only better education could provide Americans with the skills necessary to become productive workers and responsible citizens.

Limited Education

While most families in the United States considered education to be important, they did not expect their children to receive a great deal of schooling. Many children worked in factories or on farms to

A teacher in 1857 instructs students in a one-room schoolhouse. There were many schools like this one across the country.

New Movements in America **465**

help support their families. Parents generally wanted their children to be able to read the Bible, to write, and to do simple calculations. The availability of education varied considerably throughout the United States. New England maintained the most schoolhouses, while the South and the West maintained the fewest.

Schoolteachers often were untrained young men who taught for a few years before becoming farmers or practicing another trade. They worked in small, poorly built schoolhouses teaching students of many ages and abilities. As reformer Horace Mann wrote, the students ranged from "infants just out of their cradles" to "men . . . enrolled in the militia."

The textbook most often used in public schools in the mid-1800s was the McGuffey's *Reader*. Compiled by William Holmes McGuffey, an educator and Presbyterian minister, these books were made up mostly of British and American literary selections. As well as introducing students to literature and teaching them to read, the textbooks were used to teach moral and social values.

Education varied considerably among people from different backgrounds in the United States. Wealthy people could educate their children in private schools or with private tutors, while poor children could attend only the public school that existed in their community. Girls could attend school, but parents kept them home more often than boys. The result was that fewer girls learned to read.

School Reform

The **common-school movement** got its name from the effort to have all children, regardless of their class or background, educated in a common place. Horace Mann, the leading voice for educa-

PICTORIAL PRIMER

Mary reciting her Lesson.

Mary had learned to read and spell from the "Pictorial Primer" well. Could sew and knit a little too, and many other things could do, while her mother ever kind, would study to improve her mind, and in hymns of praise and love taught her to lift her heart above.

The Granger Collection, New York

Reformers fought to get schools to use common textbooks like the American Pictorial Primer, *a page of which is shown here.*

tional reform in the mid-1800s, explained this philosophy:

 It is on this common platform that a general acquaintanceship [friendship] should be formed between the children of the same neighborhood. It is here that the affinities [bonds] of a common nature should unite them together. ”

Mann was appointed as the first secretary of education for Massachusetts in 1837. The former lawyer and state legislator worked tirelessly—traveling, speaking, and writing—to help encourage the improvement of children's education. His accomplishments included doubling the school budget of Massachusetts, substantially increasing teachers' salaries, extending the school year, and establishing the first school for teacher training.

Mann's writings and ideas on education spread throughout the United States, and to Latin America and Europe as well. He won over many other educators with his argument that "the common school, improved and energized, may become the most effective . . . of all the forces of civilization." His work set the standard for educational reform throughout the nation.

★ Women's Education

The educational reform movement also created greater opportunities for women. Before the 1820s few women in the United States could obtain an education beyond grade school. Catharine Beecher, daughter of Lyman Beecher, became one of the most effective women's educational reformers during the early 1800s.

Beecher based her campaign on the belief that women had a superior ability to teach the moral lessons that made good citizens: "Let every woman become so . . . refined in intellect that her taste and judgment will be respected." Beecher established an all-female academy in Hartford, Connecticut, and wrote several influential essays including *An Essay on the Education of Female Teachers.*

In 1821 the citizens of Troy, New York, asked educator Emma Willard to establish a college-level institution for women—the first in the United States. At Willard's Troy Female Seminary, women took classes in a variety of subjects ranging from mathematics to philosophy. More than 12,000 women attended the school between 1821 and 1872.

In 1837 Oberlin College in Ohio—a school founded by a group of ministers during the Second Great Awakening—became the first co-educational college in the United States. This meant that the school admitted both men and women. Several women's colleges also opened in the 1830s, including Mount Holyoke Seminary in Massachusetts, founded by educator Mary Lyon in 1837. Lyon responded to critics of her efforts to educate women by saying, "I am doing a great work, I cannot come down." As a 16-year-old, Emily Dickinson described her rigorous classes at Mount Holyoke:

❝ **You cannot imagine how trying they [the exams] are, because if we cannot** **go through them all in a specified time, we are sent home.** ❞

Dickinson and her classmates took advantage of the new opportunities available for women in higher education.

★ African American Schools

Free African Americans also enjoyed some benefits of educational reform. Although their educational opportunities expanded, African Americans usually attended separate schools from white students. The New York African Free School, which had opened in New York City in 1787, grew considerably and educated hundreds of children in the 1820s. Many of them, such as Henry Highland Garnet, went on to become brilliant scholars and important African American leaders.

The people of Philadelphia also supported the development of African American education and operated seven schools by the year 1800. In 1820 Boston opened a separate elementary school for African American children, but by 1855 the city began allowing African Americans to attend white schools.

James Thomas, a free African American in Tennessee, described the irregular education that many received in the 1830s:

❝ **School was kept occasionally. It was regarded a great favor to have it allowed at any time. Each pupil or scholar paid one dollar per month. Often there was no school because there was no teacher.** ❞

African Americans rarely attended college because only a few higher-education institutions would accept them. In 1835 Oberlin became the first to do so. It was later joined by schools such as Harvard and

Many young women received higher educations at Mount Holyoke Seminary, one of the country's best schools for women.

Dartmouth. Black colleges also began to be founded in the 1840s. In 1842 the Institute for Colored Youth opened in Philadelphia, and Avery College, also located in Pennsylvania, was founded in 1849. In the North and the Midwest, free African Americans did have some opportunities to attend school. In the South, however, fewer free African Americans were able to obtain an education. In addition, laws in the South prevented most slaves from receiving any education, even at the primary-school level.

Henry Highland Garnet

Americans. In 1831 Howe opened a school for people with visual impairments called the Perkins Institute, located in Massachusetts. He trained the school's staff to address the particular needs of the students. He also traveled to 17 other states to speak out on behalf of educating visually impaired people. Howe ran the Perkins Institute for 45 years, during which time he demonstrated that people with visual impairments could lead economically and socially productive lives.

In his attempt to improve the education and lives of hearing impaired people, Thomas Gallaudet went to France for two years to study methods of teaching such students. When he returned to the United States in 1817, Gallaudet established the first free American school for people with hearing impairments, in Hartford, Connecticut. He served as the school's principal until 1830. Thus, the efforts of school reformers touched the lives of people in many parts of American society throughout the early and mid-1800s.

★ Teaching People with Disabilities

Efforts to improve education extended to people with special needs. In addition to his efforts in education reform, prison reform, and care for mentally ill people, Samuel Gridley Howe significantly improved the education of visually impaired

SECTION 3 REVIEW

Identify and explain the significance of the following:
- **Dorothea Dix**
- **temperance movement**
- **Lyman Beecher**
- **Horace Mann**
- **common-school movement**
- **Catharine Beecher**
- **Emma Willard**
- **Mary Lyon**
- **Samuel Gridley Howe**
- **Thomas Gallaudet**

Reading for Content Understanding

1 **Main Idea** Why were middle-class Americans, particularly women, active in reform movements during the 1800s? What aspects of American society did the reformers hope to change?

2 **Main Idea** What societal problems did many reformers blame on the use of alcohol?

3 **Geographic Diversity** *Region* Which region of the United States had the most schools? In what region did African Americans and women have the greatest educational opportunities?

4 **Writing** *Describing* Write a paragraph describing the ways in which many more Americans gained the opportunity to receive an education in the early and mid-1800s.

5 **Critical Thinking** *Making Comparisons* How do you think some of the reform movements of the early and mid-1800s are similar to or different from reform efforts today? Explain your answer.

The Movement to End Slavery

Reading Focus

Why did some Americans become abolitionists, and what did they hope to achieve for enslaved African Americans?

How did abolitionists spread the movement's message?

Why did some Americans oppose abolition?

Key Terms

abolition
emancipation
American Colonization Society
Liberator
American Anti-Slavery Society
Underground Railroad

URING THE MID-1800S *John Fairfield helped enslaved African Americans escape to freedom in the North. Fairfield traveled throughout the South under different disguises, posing as a slaveholder, or a trader, or a peddler. On one occasion he led 28 slaves to freedom by disguising them as part of a funeral procession. Although most antislavery activists did not take risks such as Fairfield's, they all contributed to a movement that gathered enormous strength in the mid-1800s.*

Antislavery medallion

★ Abolition

During the 1830s Americans who had opposed slavery for years began organizing a movement to support **abolition,** or a complete end to slavery, in the United States. Some abolitionists sought immediate **emancipation,** or freedom from slavery, for all enslaved African Americans.

Different Beliefs

Abolitionists came from a variety of backgrounds and opposed slavery for different reasons. The Quakers were among the first groups, starting in colonial times, to challenge slavery on religious grounds. Some ministers of the Second Great Awakening, such as Charles Finney and Theodore Weld, also believed that slavery was morally wrong. These ministers inspired many of their followers to take up the cause of abolition. Other abolitionists noted that the Declaration of Independence supported equality.

Many antislavery reformers, however, disagreed about the degree of equality that African Americans should have in the United States. While some abolitionists thought that African Americans should be treated the same as white Americans, other abolitionists strongly opposed slavery without supporting full social and political equality for African Americans.

The Colonization Movement

Some abolitionists wanted to send freed African Americans to Africa to start new colonies there. They thought that such colonization would prevent conflicts between different races in the United States. Many Americans supported this view. J. C. Galloway of North Carolina wrote, "It is impossible for us [whites] to be happy, if . . . they [freed African Americans] are to remain among us."

In 1817 a minister named Robert Finley started the **American Colonization Society**. The society established the colony of Liberia on the west coast of Africa in 1822. Although 12,000 African Americans eventually settled in Liberia, many abolitionists who had once supported colonization later turned against it. African Americans such as David Walker soon became some of the most vocal opponents of the African colonization

This engraving shows ships bringing freed slaves to Liberia in 1832.

movement. In his 1829 essay, *Appeal to the Colored Citizens of the World,* Walker declared:

> " **The greatest riches in all America have arisen from our blood and tears: And they [whites] will drive us from our property and homes, which we have earned with our blood.** "

Global Connections

British Abolitionists and the Ottoman Empire

In the early 1800s abolitionists in Britain began working to end slavery in the British Empire. After outlawing the slave trade in 1807, Parliament finally abolished all slavery in the British Empire in 1833. British abolitionists then turned their attention to fighting slavery in the rest of the world. One of their first targets was the Ottoman Empire, where slavery had existed for hundreds of years.

In 1840 the British and Foreign Anti-Slavery Society organized the World Anti-Slavery Convention in London. Participants discussed the need for worldwide abolition. The subject of Ottoman slavery was raised by a recent visitor to that part of the world:

> " *There [in the Ottoman Empire] slavery is the great impediment [obstacle] to civilization, to the march of instruction, to the introduction and the progress of civil liberty.* "

The members of the convention unanimously voted to urge Britain to assist "in obtaining such declarations . . . as are likely to lead to the entire suppression [ending] of Slavery." In 1846 Britain persuaded the Ottoman Empire to join in ending the slave trade. This action opened the door for future British influence on Ottoman slave policy.

Understanding What You Read

1. What was the goal of many British abolitionists?

2. How might the ending of the slave trade in the Ottoman Empire have helped the abolitionist cause?

Spreading the Abolitionist Message

Abolitionists used speaking tours, newspapers, and pamphlets to further their cause. Editor Horace Greeley became a strong voice in the movement through the *New York Tribune*. Others, like John Greenleaf Whittier, spread the abolitionist message through their poetry and literature.

Sarah (left) and Angelina (right) Grimké were southerners who spoke out against slavery.

Northern Abolitionists

William Lloyd Garrison, one of the most outspoken and controversial leaders in the abolitionist movement, began publishing his antislavery newspaper, the **Liberator**, in 1831. In the first issue, Garrison wrote:

> **❝ I *will* be as harsh as truth, and as uncompromising [inflexible] as justice. On this subject, I do not wish to think, to speak, or write, with moderation [caution]. . . . I will not retreat a single inch—AND I WILL BE HEARD. ❞**

In 1833 Garrison helped found, and later became president of, the **American Anti-Slavery Society**. This group demanded immediate emancipation and racial equality for African Americans. The society appealed to Americans' sense of religious principles and conscience, rather than resorting to violence. However, some critics, even fellow abolitionists, accused Garrison of having extreme views.

Both the *Liberator* and the Anti-Slavery Society relied on the support of free African Americans. Members of the society spread antislavery literature throughout the North and the Midwest. They also petitioned Congress to end all federal support of slavery. Then in 1840 the American Anti-Slavery Society split between abolitionists who favored immediate emancipation and equal participation for women in the movement, and those who supported gradual emancipation and a limited role for women.

William Lloyd Garrison's banner announcing "I WILL BE HEARD"

Southerners Against Slavery

Two white southern women, Angelina and Sarah Grimké, became some of the best-known antislavery activists of the 1830s. Although they were members of a slaveholding family in South Carolina, the sisters rejected their parents' support of slavery and moved to Philadelphia to join the abolition movement.

Angelina Grimké attempted to bring other white southern women to the antislavery cause through her pamphlet *Appeal to the Christian Women of the South*, published in 1836:

> **❝ I know you do not make the laws, but . . . if you really suppose you can do nothing to overthrow slavery, you are greatly mistaken. . . . Speak to your relatives, friends, acquaintances. . . . Try to persuade your husband, father, brothers and sons that slavery is a crime *against God and man.* ❞**

As a result of this essay's popularity in the North, the Grimké sisters became the first female members of the Anti-Slavery Society. The sisters toured New England, delivering lectures and forming dozens of female antislavery societies. After they retired from public speaking, the sisters became teachers and concentrated on writing. In 1839 they joined Angelina's husband—abolitionist leader Theodore Weld—to produce one of the most important antislavery publications of the period, *American Slavery as It Is*. The sisters continued to remain active in both antislavery and women's causes.

New Movements in America **471**

African Americans Fight for Abolition

Many former slaves were very active in the antislavery movement. These freed African Americans told powerful stories of their lives in slavery.

Frederick Douglass

Frederick Douglass, who escaped from slavery at the age of 20, became one of the most important African American leaders of the 1800s. Douglass had secretly learned to read and write as a boy. In addition, his public-speaking skills so impressed the members of the Anti-Slavery Society that in 1841 they asked him to give regular lectures.

Douglass quickly became one of the best-known speakers in the United States. He had a rich voice, which he used to describe vividly the horrors of slavery and racial injustice. Speaking at a Fourth of July celebration in 1852, he captured the audience's attention by saying:

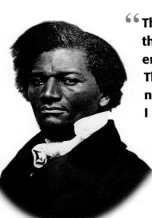

Frederick Douglass

66 **The blessings in which you, this day, rejoice, are not enjoyed in common. . . . This Fourth of July is *yours,* not *mine.* You may rejoice, I must mourn.** 99

In addition to his many speaking tours in the United States and in Europe, Douglass published a newspaper called *The North Star* and wrote several autobiographies.

Other Strong Voices

Former slaves such as Henry Highland Garnet and Sojourner Truth also contributed to the abolitionist cause. Garnet, a Presbyterian minister, called for a national African American community and a slave rebellion. Truth became legendary in the antislavery movement for her dramatic and fiery speeches. Charles Remond was another powerful spokesperson for abolition. In 1842 he asked the Massachusetts legislature to abolish racial discrim-

ination in the state: "It is JUSTICE I stand here to claim, and not FAVOR for either complexion [skin color]," he declared.

Other African Americans wrote slave narratives about their experiences. In 1857 Harriet Jacobs wrote *Incidents in the Life of a Slave Girl,* one of the few slave narratives written by a woman. William Wells Brown also wrote an antislavery play, as well as a personal slave narrative, a novel called *Clotel.* These writers and many other African Americans contributed significantly to the abolitionist cause.

The Underground Railroad

By the 1830s a loosely organized group of free African Americans, former slaves, and white abolitionists had begun helping slaves escape from the South to northern states and Canada. They created what became known as the **Underground Railroad**, a network of people who arranged transportation and hiding places for fugitives, or escaped slaves.

African American businessman Robert Purvis, one of the leading organizers of the Underground Railroad, concentrated his efforts on building a network in Pennsylvania. Many fugitives escaped into Pennsylvania, partly because it was one of the free states bordering the South and because of the large number of abolitionists there who supported the Underground Railroad.

Harriet Tubman (far left) helped many African Americans, including this group, escape slavery on the Underground Railroad.

Often wearing disguises, fugitives moved along the "railroad" at night, guided by the North Star. They stopped to rest during the day at various "stations," which were the homes of abolitionists known as conductors. The conductors hid the fugitives in barns, attics, and other secret locations. Someone "conducting" a group of escaping slaves would then send word to the next station farther north that they were on the way.

The most famous and daring conductor on the Underground Railroad was Harriet Tubman, an escaped slave who helped other fugitives to freedom. When she escaped in 1849, she had left behind her husband, parents, sisters, and brothers. Tubman returned to the South 19 times and succeeded in leading her family and more than 300 other slaves to freedom while never losing a fugitive. At one time the reward for Tubman's capture climbed to $40,000. She credited her faith in God for sustaining her through the many dangerous journeys she made, saying, "I always told God, I'm going to hold steady on to you, and you've got to see me through." Although it is impossible to know today exactly how many slaves used the Underground Railroad to reach freedom, many thousands escaped between 1810 and 1850.

★ Opposition to Abolition

At the same time that abolitionists fought for emancipation, many white people in both the North and the South strongly supported slavery. Some had economic reasons while others held racist beliefs.

Northern Opposition

Many white northerners did not believe in equal treatment for African Americans. As Frederick Douglass recalled, free African Americans in the North were "routinely denied the privileges and courtesies common to others." White northern industrial workers believed the warnings of newspaper editors and politicians that freed slaves would move north and take jobs from white laborers. Abolitionists angered many northerners, some

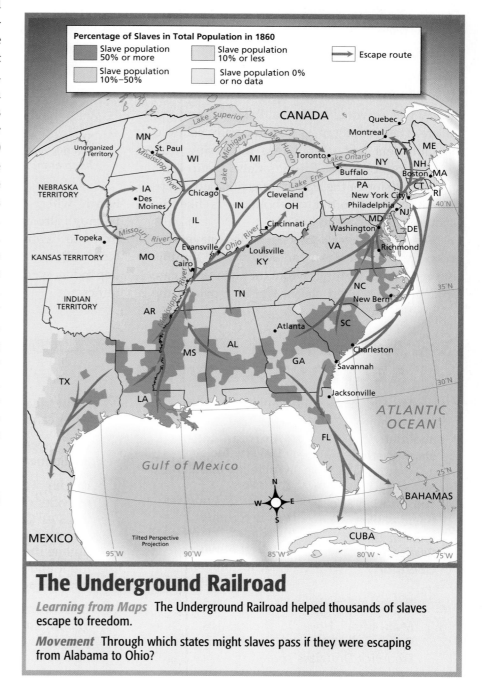

Percentage of Slaves in Total Population in 1860

- Slave population 50% or more
- Slave population 10%–50%
- Slave population 10% or less
- Slave population 0% or no data
- Escape route

The Underground Railroad

Learning from Maps The Underground Railroad helped thousands of slaves escape to freedom.

Movement Through which states might slaves pass if they were escaping from Alabama to Ohio?

of whom joined violent mobs that attacked African Americans, burned antislavery literature, and threatened the movement's leaders. Such a mob killed abolitionist editor Elijah Lovejoy in 1837.

The federal government also stood in the way of the abolitionist movement. Between 1836 and 1844 the U.S. House of Representatives used a "gag rule" to prohibit discussion of the thousands of antislavery petitions sent to Congress. This rule violated the First Amendment right to petition. Southern congressmen opposed debate about slavery, while many northern congressmen simply wanted to avoid the issue.

Southerners Defend Slavery

Many white southerners thought the institution of slavery was essential to the South's economy and culture. These southerners also generally believed that outsiders had no business interfering with their affairs. After Nat Turner's Rebellion in 1831, open discussion of the slavery question had disappeared in the South and abolitionists like the Grimké sisters chose to leave.

Some white southerners justified slavery as necessary to protect African Americans. Virginia lawyer George Fitzhugh wrote that unable to care for themselves, freed slaves would move to the

SLAVERY AS IT EXISTS IN AMERICA.

SLAVERY AS IT EXISTS IN ENGLAND.

THE ENGLISH ANTI-SLAVERY AGITATOR.

The Granger Collection, New York

Southern defenders of slavery used images like this one to argue that American slaves were happier than most British factory workers.

North where they would "freeze or starve." Fitzhugh also argued that slaves in the South lived in better comfort than wage earners in the North. Racism, fear, and the South's economic dependence on slavery made emancipation very difficult.

SECTION 4 REVIEW

Identify and explain the significance of the following:
- **abolition**
- **emancipation**
- **Robert Finley**
- **American Colonization Society**
- **David Walker**
- **William Lloyd Garrison**
- *Liberator*
- **American Anti-Slavery Society**
- **Angelina and Sarah Grimké**
- **Frederick Douglass**
- **Underground Railroad**
- **Robert Purvis**
- **Harriet Tubman**

Reading for Content Understanding

1 **Main Idea** How did abolitionists such as David Walker, William Lloyd Garrison, and Frederick Douglass spread their message?

2 **Main Idea** For what reasons did many Americans support slavery?

3 **Geographic Diversity** *Place* Why did abolitionists establish Liberia?

4 **Writing** *Creating* Imagine that you are a member of one of the antislavery societies in 1840. Create a poster announcing your group's next meeting. Your poster should outline the goals of the abolitionist movement and explain why Americans should become active in the movement.

5 **Critical Thinking** *Synthesizing Information* What do you think motivated people to take part in the Underground Railroad?

SECTION 5

Women's Rights

Reading Focus

How did the abolition movement affect the women's rights movement?

What were some goals of the women's rights movement?

What was the purpose and the significance of the Seneca Falls Convention?

Key Terms

Seneca Falls Convention
Declaration of Sentiments

*I*N FEBRUARY 1838, *Angelina Grimké nervously prepared to speak before the Massachusetts legislature. "I never was so near fainting under the tremendous pressure of feeling," she wrote her future husband. "My heart almost died within me." Grimké planned to present antislavery petitions, but she felt a great weight of responsibility being the first woman to speak before a legislature in the United States. As she spoke before 1,500 people, Grimké courageously addressed both the issue of slavery and the question of women's role in politics.*

An antislavery speech

⭐ The Influence of Abolition

Many women who participated in the abolition movement, such as the Grimké sisters and Sojourner Truth, also became active in the women's rights movement of the mid-1800s. These women had discovered that they had to defend a woman's right to speak in public—particularly when their audiences contained both men and women. Members of the press, the clergy, and even some male abolitionists criticized the Grimké sisters for giving public speeches and for going beyond traditional female roles. The Grimkés replied to these critics that women had a moral obligation to provide leadership in the antislavery movement.

Some abolitionists who defended women's role in the antislavery movement also supported equal rights for women. In 1838 Sarah Grimké published a pamphlet called "Letters on the Equality of the Sexes and the Condition of Women." She wrote:

❝**I ask no favors for my sex. . . . All I ask our brethren [brothers] is, that they will take their feet from off our necks, and permit us to stand upright on that ground which God designed us to occupy.**❞

Sarah Grimké also argued for equal educational opportunities, identified laws that negatively affected women, and passionately demanded equal pay for equal work.

Sojourner Truth was another extremely effective speaker for both abolition and women's rights. Author Harriet Beecher Stowe said of Truth that she had never spoken "with anyone who had more of that silent and subtle [complex] power which we call personal presence than this woman." A former slave, Truth stood six feet tall and spoke in an aggressive style. At one women's rights convention in 1851, she challenged the audience members to reconsider their perception of women as the weaker sex:

Sojourner Truth

66 **That man over there says that women need to be helped into carriages and lifted over ditches, and to have the best place everywhere. Nobody ever helps me into carriages or over mud puddles, or gives me any best place. And ain't I a woman? . . . I could work as much and eat as much as a man—when I could get it—and bear the lash as well. And ain't I a woman?** 99

Truth and other supporters of the women's movement were determined to be heard.

⭐ Women's Rights

In the 1830s and 1840s more women than ever before came together to organize and speak out against their social inequality. As they worked together in various efforts to improve society, many women found that they had common concerns about their rights.

Increased Involvement

Publications about women's rights first appeared in the United States shortly after the American

Activist Victoria Woodhull protested the lack of women's voting rights by trying to vote in a local election.

Revolution. It was not until women began participating in the reform and abolition efforts, however, that women's concerns were first addressed as a national issue.

With improved education and the experience of working together in reform associations, women gained some of the skills and tactics necessary to organize themselves effectively. Some men also became active in the struggle for women's rights. Many activists were concerned that women could not vote or sit on juries and that married women in many states had little or no control over their own property.

Opposition to Women's Rights

Many people, both men and women, opposed some of the goals of the women's rights movement. Some critics believed that women should try to influence society in the home, not in public. "Let her not look away from her own little family circle for the means of producing moral and social reforms," wrote T. S. Arthur in a popular women's magazine called *The Lady at Home*.

In addition, many women believed that they did not need any new rights because they were not unequal to men, only different. Some ministers joined the criticism, writing in a group letter that when a woman

66 **assumes the place and tone of man as a public reformer . . . she yields the power which God has given her for her**

protection, and her character becomes unnatural. "

Some people also thought that women needed protection because they lacked the physical or mental strength to survive without men's assistance. People with this viewpoint believed that a woman needed to be married and that her husband should control her property. Such vocal criticism did not prevent women from pursuing their goals of greater rights.

The Seneca Falls Convention

In 1840 twenty-five-year-old Elizabeth Cady Stanton attended the World Anti-Slavery Convention in London, England, while on her honeymoon. Stanton had to watch the meeting separately from her husband, however, because the convention voted to exclude women from participating. Women sat in a separate gallery of the assembly hall, hidden from men's view by a curtain. In protest, abolitionist William Lloyd Garrison sat with them, refusing to join a proceeding that did not allow women's equal participation.

As a result of the poor treatment that female abolitionist leaders received at the convention, Stanton and her new acquaintance, Lucretia Mott, "resolved to hold a convention as soon as we returned home, and form a society to advance the rights of women," Stanton later wrote. Eight years passed before Stanton and Mott sent out a notice announcing the **Seneca Falls Convention**, to be held on July 19, 1848, in Seneca Falls, New York. This two-day convention launched the organized women's rights movement. It was the first public meeting about women's rights to be held in the United States.

To present their case, the organizers of the convention wrote a **Declaration of Sentiments** modeled on the language of the Declaration of Independence. At the convention, 100 people signed the document, which detailed their beliefs about social injustice against women.

More than 300 people attended the Seneca Falls Convention, including some men such as Frederick Douglass. Most of these reformers were

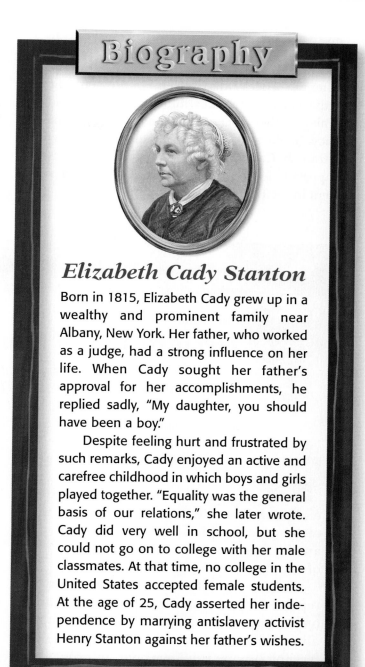

Biography

Elizabeth Cady Stanton

Born in 1815, Elizabeth Cady grew up in a wealthy and prominent family near Albany, New York. Her father, who worked as a judge, had a strong influence on her life. When Cady sought her father's approval for her accomplishments, he replied sadly, "My daughter, you should have been a boy."

Despite feeling hurt and frustrated by such remarks, Cady enjoyed an active and carefree childhood in which boys and girls played together. "Equality was the general basis of our relations," she later wrote. Cady did very well in school, but she could not go on to college with her male classmates. At that time, no college in the United States accepted female students. At the age of 25, Cady asserted her independence by marrying antislavery activist Henry Stanton against her father's wishes.

also involved in the temperance and antislavery movements. In addition, several women who worked in nearby factories participated in the convention as well. Nineteen-year-old Charlotte Woodward signed the Declaration of Sentiments because she was tired of making gloves for pitiful wages—pennies that she then had to turn over to her father anyway. Although women had spoken out for their rights earlier, the Seneca Falls Convention and the Declaration of Sentiments marked the first time that women organized for their rights as a group.

The Continuing Struggle

After the Seneca Falls Convention, women's rights activists met with many difficulties on the road to achieving their goal of greater equality for women. Lucy Stone and Susan B. Anthony, along with Elizabeth Cady Stanton, emerged as the most important leaders of the women's rights movement in the United States.

Lucy Stone was a well-known speaker for the Anti-Slavery Society. She also championed the cause of women's rights, stating at the beginning of her speaking career:

> **“I mean to plead not for the slave alone but for suffering humanity everywhere. Especially do I mean to labor for the elevation of my sex.”**

HISTORICAL DOCUMENTS

The Seneca Falls

1848

Declaration of Sentiments

On July 19 and 20, 1848, people gathered in Seneca Falls, New York, to discuss women's rights. Organizers Elizabeth Cady Stanton and Lucretia Mott helped write the Declaration of Sentiments. Signed by 100 people, it helped shape the future of the women's rights movement.

We hold these truths to be self-evident: that all men and women are created equal; that they are endowed [provided] by their Creator with certain inalienable [permanent] rights; that among these are life, liberty, and the pursuit of happiness. . . .

The history of mankind is a history of repeated injuries and usurpations [seizures] on the part of man toward woman, having in direct object the establishment of an absolute tyranny [unjust rule] over her. To prove this, let facts be submitted to a candid [fair] world.

He has never permitted her to exercise her inalienable right to . . . [the vote]. . . .

He has taken from her all right in property, even to the wages she earns. . . .

He has monopolized nearly all the profitable employments, and from those she is permitted to follow, she receives but a scanty remuneration [payment]. He closes against her all the avenues to wealth and distinction which he considers most honorable to himself. . . .

He has denied her the facilities for obtaining a thorough education, all colleges being closed against her. . . .

He has endeavored [tried], in every way that he could, to destroy her confidence in her own powers, to lessen her self-respect, and to make her willing to lead a dependent and abject [hopeless] life. . . .

Resolved, That woman is man's equal—was intended to be so by the Creator, and the highest good of the race demands that she should be recognized as such.

Understanding Primary Sources

1. What are some of the injustices that the declaration describes?

2. How is the Declaration of Sentiments modeled after the Declaration of Independence?

3. Are the rights demanded in the declaration granted to women in the United States today? Explain your answer.

During the early years of the women's rights movement, Stone earned a reputation as a powerful speaker. Stanton said that Stone was "the first who really stirred the nation's heart on the subject of women's wrongs."

Stone became one of the first women's rights activists to suggest changing the institution of marriage. At her wedding to Henry Blackwell, the couple refused to follow the "present laws of marriage" and vowed that theirs would be an "equal and permanent partnership." Furthermore, Stone resolved to keep her maiden name, to continue to be known as Lucy Stone rather than Mrs. Blackwell. For decades to come, married women who kept their maiden names were known as Lucy Stoners.

Susan B. Anthony brought outstanding administrative abilities to the women's rights movement. Raised in a Quaker household by a father who supported equality between men and women, she turned the fight for women's rights into a political movement. Women's economic difficulties were of particular interest to Anthony because, as a single woman, she supported herself. She argued that

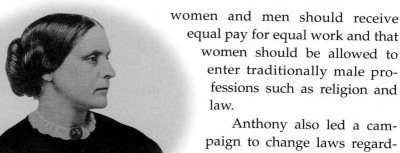

Susan B. Anthony

women and men should receive equal pay for equal work and that women should be allowed to enter traditionally male professions such as religion and law.

Anthony also led a campaign to change laws regarding women's property rights. She understood that no woman could be free without "a purse of her own," as she wrote in her diary, "and how can this be so long as the Wife is denied the right to her individual and joint earnings."

Organizing a network to cover every area of New York State, Anthony collected more than 6,000 signatures to petition for a new property rights law. In 1860 the state legislature finally passed a law giving married women ownership of their wages and property. Other states in the Northeast and Midwest followed with similar laws. Despite this success, other major reforms, such as the right to vote, were not achieved at this time. One of the movement's greatest accomplishments was that more American women than ever before became actively involved in women's rights issues.

SECTION 5 REVIEW

Identify and explain the significance of the following:
- **Sojourner Truth**
- **Elizabeth Cady Stanton**
- **Lucretia Mott**
- **Seneca Falls Convention**
- **Declaration of Sentiments**
- **Lucy Stone**
- **Susan B. Anthony**

Reading for Content Understanding

1 Main Idea Why did many female abolitionists also become active in the women's rights movement?

2 Main Idea What were the main goals of the women's rights movement?

3 Citizenship and Democracy Why did Elizabeth Cady Stanton and Lucretia Mott organize the Seneca Falls Convention, and who participated in it?

4 Writing *Expressing* Write a half-page letter to the leaders of the women's rights movement, congratulating them for the work they did to improve the lives of women in the mid-1800s. Include examples of modern-day gains that women have made as a result of these leaders' work.

5 Critical Thinking *Drawing Conclusions* Why do you think some women opposed the women's rights movement of the mid-1800s?

CHAPTER
15 REVIEW

Chapter Summary

By the 1820s the Second Great Awakening had sparked a renewed interest in religion in much of the United States. A famine in Ireland and a political uprising in Germany led millions of people to immigrate to the United States in the early and mid-1800s. Also during this time, reformers struggled for temperance, educational reform, the abolition of slavery, and women's rights. ◼

On a separate sheet of paper, complete the following activities.

Identifying People and Ideas

Describe the historical significance of the following:

1. utopian community
2. tenements
3. Emma Willard
4. Seneca Falls Convention
5. common-school movement
6. American Anti-Slavery Society
7. Harriet Tubman
8. Frederick Douglass
9. Horace Mann
10. Susan B. Anthony

Internet Activity go.hrw.com
SAO Reform

Search the Internet through the HRW Web site to find information about reform movements that have recently taken place in other countries. Create a graphic organizer showing how these movements are similar to and different from the reform movements of the mid-1800s.

Understanding Main Ideas

1. What did Charles Finney preach?
2. Who were some of the most important artists and authors of the romantic period?
3. How did the Industrial Revolution and immigration affect U.S. cities?
4. What educational reforms did Horace Mann try to establish?
5. Why did some abolitionists want to send freed African Americans to Africa?
6. How did former slaves help the abolitionist cause?
7. What were the major issues of the women's rights movement?

Reviewing Themes

1. **Cultural Diversity**   For what reasons did people try to establish utopian communities between 1820 and 1850? Name one utopian community and its purpose.

Using the Time Line

Number your paper from 1 to 6. Match the letters on the time line below with the following events.

1. **William Lloyd Garrison begins publishing the antislavery newspaper the *Liberator*.**
2. **Horace Mann becomes secretary of education for Massachusetts.**
3. **Women's rights leaders hold the Seneca Falls Convention.**
4. **Nativists form the Know-Nothing Party.**
5. **Emma Willard begins a women's higher-education institution in Troy, New York.**
6. **Ralph Waldo Emerson writes "Self-Reliance," an essay about society's principles and values.**

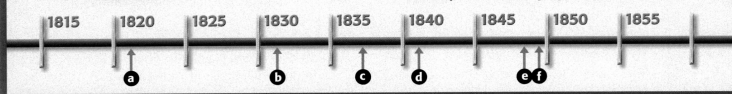

1815   1820   1825   1830   1835   1840   1845   1850   1855

ⓐ   ⓑ   ⓒ   ⓓ   ⓔⓕ

2. **Geographic Diversity**   Why did millions of Irish and Germans immigrate to the United States between 1840 and 1860?

3. **Citizenship and Democracy**   Choose three of the following people and explain how they worked to end slavery: Robert Finley, David Walker, William Lloyd Garrison, Angelina and Sarah Grimké, Frederick Douglass, and Harriet Tubman.

Thinking Critically

1. **Evaluating**   What impact did the Second Great Awakening have on the various reform movements of the 1800s?

2. **Identifying Generalizations and Stereotypes**   Why did nativists want to restrict immigration to the United States?

3. **Drawing Conclusions**   Why is it important to educate all members of a democratic society?

Writing About History

1. **Creating**   Design your own ideal community using the ones described in this chapter as a model. Then make a list of at least seven rules for members of your new utopian community.

Building Your Portfolio

Complete the following activities individually or in groups.

1. **Reform**   Select an issue that you think is important to society today and plan a campaign to heighten public awareness of the issue. You should design a poster and a flyer to inform others about the issue. Also prepare the script for a speech you might give at a public meeting.

2. **Women's Rights**   Create a collage of women's roles in society today. Use images from old magazines and newspapers to complete your project. When you have finished, write a short paragraph explaining why you chose the particular images on your collage.

2. **Persuading**   Imagine that you support temperance. Write a half-page editorial explaining why people should limit their consumption of alcohol.

Linking Geography and History

1. **Region**   How would you describe U.S. cities from the 1840s to the 1860s?

2. **Location**   Why was Pennsylvania important in the success of the Underground Railroad?

History Skills Workshop

Reading Graphs   Study the "Immigration to the United States in 1840 and 1850" graph below. Then answer the following questions: (a) How many thousands of Irish immigrants came to the United States in 1850? (b) How many times higher was the number of German immigrants in 1850 than in 1840? (c) How did the number of "other" immigrants who arrived in 1850 differ from the number in 1840?

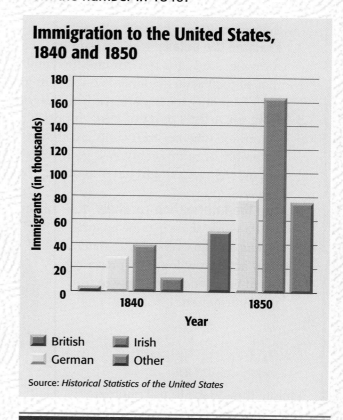

Immigration to the United States, 1840 and 1850

Source: *Historical Statistics of the United States*

History Skills

WORKSHOP

Using Visual Resources

This textbook contains photographs as well as reproductions of famous paintings and other artwork. Gathering information from these sources is a key strategy to understanding history. Visual resources can provide a better understanding of how people in the past behaved, dressed, thought, and communicated with one another. Images can also provide an accurate record of historical events.

Gathering Information from Art

To effectively gather information from art, follow these steps.

1. **Determine the subject of the work** Study the people, objects, and actions that are present in the art. Check the title or caption to determine the art's focus.
2. **Examine the details** If it is a painting or drawing, study the background. Remember that *all* the visual evidence is important to understanding the historical event or period.
3. **Note the artist's point of view** If possible, determine whether the events are shown favorably or unfavorably. Ask yourself what impact the work might have on other viewers.
4. **Use the information carefully** Remember that a work of art may be an artist's *interpretation* of an event. Try to determine how accurately the art represents the event before deciding how to use the information.

Using Photographs as Primary Sources

Follow these steps to use photographs as primary sources.

1. **Study the subject** Identify the person, event, or location in the photograph.
2. **Check for details** Note the expression, action, or setting. Look closely at the style of clothing and other details.
3. **Do not be misled** Remember that many scenes are posed and exclude more than they include. Also keep in mind that early photography took such a long time for the exposure that subjects had to remain still and often appear unnaturally stiff.

Practicing the Skill

Study the image below, which is a painting showing the duel between Vice President Aaron Burr and Alexander Hamilton on July 11, 1804. The weapons shown are dueling pistols of the period. After studying the image, answer the following questions.

1. Describe what each person in the painting is doing.
2. What, in your opinion, is the artist's point of view about the subject of the painting?
3. Do you feel this painting is a fairly accurate representation of the duel? Explain your answer.

BURR AND HAMILTON DUEL.

History in Action

UNIT PORTFOLIO

American History

Coming to America One-Act Play

Complete the following activity in small cooperative groups.

Imagine that you and your family are newly arrived immigrants to the United States from Germany or Ireland in 1855. You and your group members will write and perform a one-act play about your trip to the United States and your current living and working conditions. In addition, your group will create a visual representation of one aspect of your family's life.

Materials To complete this activity, you will need art supplies to create your visual representation and backgrounds or props for your performance. In addition, you will need costumes or clothes that look like those worn by an immigrant family in the 1850s.

Parts of the Project Complete the following steps as you prepare your play.

1. **Research** Use the library and your textbook to gather information about the experiences of Irish and German immigrants to the United States in the 1850s. You will also need to do research on what life was like in the city where your play will be set. For further research, you might also consult your community's local historical museum. There you might find letters or diaries of people who immigrated to the United States in the 1850s. You may also wish to interview people in your community who are recent immigrants or who remember stories about grandparents, parents, or other relatives who immigrated to the United States.

2. **Writing** Once you have gathered enough information, write the script of your play. Remember that your play must have a conflict, a climax and resolution; characters; and a setting. Add stage directions to show how the characters speak and move. Give your play an appropriate title. Make sure each member of the group works on the play.

3. **Rehearsal and Production** Once the play is written, decide who will direct it and who will play each of the characters. Prepare the props and costumes that you will use in the performance. Then create a visual representation of one aspect of your family's new life in the United States. (You may wish to use a photograph, either real or staged.) Make sure you use this drawing or photograph in your performance. Finally, rehearse your play several times.

Perform your play once you have completed rehearsals. You may want to use special lighting or music to enliven your performance.

Students perform a play.

UNIT 7

The Nation Expands West

(1790–1860)

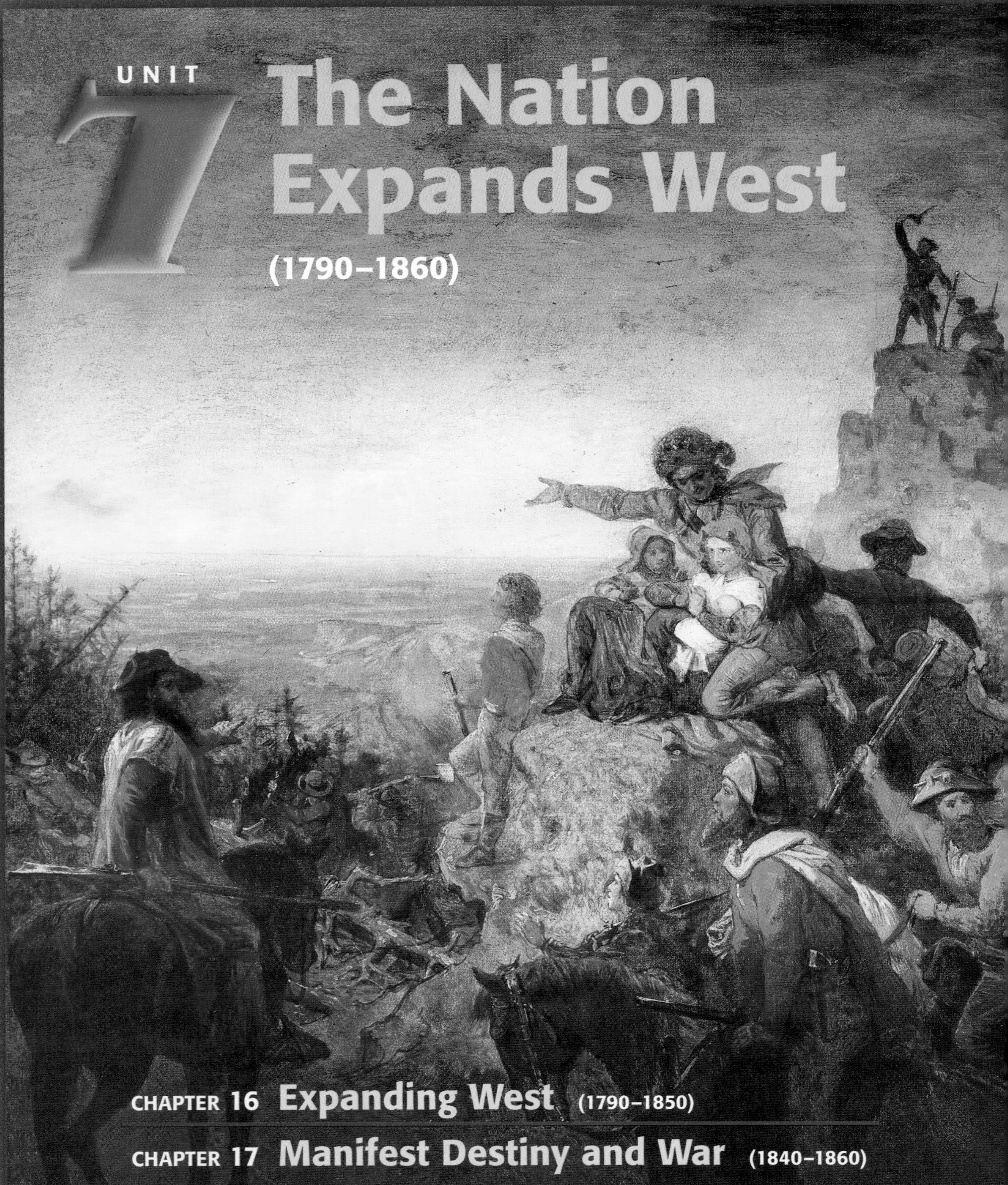

CHAPTER 16 **Expanding West** (1790–1850)

CHAPTER 17 **Manifest Destiny and War** (1840–1860)

Young People

IN HISTORY

Young Pioneers

The young pioneers who set out for the West with their families in the 1840s and 1850s showed great courage along the uncertain and dangerous journey. They knew that hardship and possible death lay ahead on the trail. Martha Gay, who traveled to Oregon in the 1850s when she was a teenager, remembered, "We often saw human skulls bleached by sun and storms lying scattered around."

Many teenagers were willing to push ahead, no matter what the conditions. Young Nancy Kelsey was one of the first group of pioneers to head for California in 1841. When the group's horses began to tire, Kelsey and the others left their wagons at the Great Salt Lake. She remembered:

Young pioneers travel across the western frontier in the 1800s.

> ❝We had a difficult time to find a way down the [Sierra Nevada] mountains. . . . We were then out of provisions [supplies], having killed and eaten all our cattle. I walked barefeeted until my feet were blistered and lived on roasted acorns for two days.❞

Not long after, Kelsey arrived in California. When another group of pioneers known as the Donner party got stranded in the Sierra Nevada in the winter of 1847, twelve-year-old Lemuel Murphy was among those who tried to climb out of the mountains and send back a rescue party.

Young pioneers worked hard every day to keep their families healthy and safe. Older boys watched the livestock. Even boys as young as 12 took turns standing guard to protect the wagon train. Teenage girls often took care of their younger siblings and helped with domestic chores.

Teenagers still found ways to have fun during the trip. They played music and danced in the evenings. Fifteen-year-old Mary Margaret Hezlep stitched patch blocks for a quilt during her trip to California. The blocks tell the story of her journey. Other young pioneers brought along books like *The Life of Daniel Boone,* *Pilgrim's Progress,* and *Robinson Crusoe* to read, and many kept diaries.

In this unit you will learn more about those Americans who traveled across the North American continent to Texas and the Far West. These courageous pioneers led the way for settlement of the United States from sea to shining sea.

LEFT PAGE: *In the mid-1800s Emanuel Gottlieb Leutze painted this image of the frontier, called* Westward the Course of Empire Takes its Way.

Albert Bierstadt, "Emigrants Crossing the Plains," 1867, Oil on Canvas, A.011.1T: National Cowboy Hall of Fame, Oklahoma City, OK.

■ **CHAPTER 16** ■

Expanding West

(1790–1850)

In the early 1800s American settlers and traders continued to push westward. Pioneer Moses Austin recalled a typical conversation with hopeful early settlers: "Have you any [land]? No, but I expect I can get it. . . . Did you ever see the country? No, but everybody says it is good land." The settlers' quest for land often brought them into conflict with American Indians and Mexican citizens already occupying much of the West.

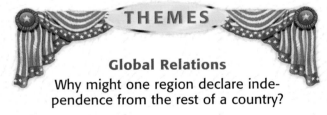

THEMES

Global Relations
Why might one region declare independence from the rest of a country?

Cultural Diversity
What effect might immigration have on a territory?

Geographic Diversity
Why might people move to other lands?

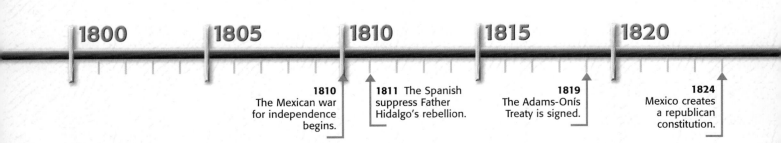

1800	1805	1810	1815	1820

1810 The Mexican war for independence begins.

1811 The Spanish suppress Father Hidalgo's rebellion.

1819 The Adams-Onís Treaty is signed.

1824 Mexico creates a republican constitution.

The Spanish West and Southwest

Reading Focus

What was life like in Spanish California, New Mexico, and Texas?

Why did some of New Spain rebel against Spain, and what was the result?

How did the Mexican war for independence affect California and Texas?

Key Terms

Californios
Tejanos

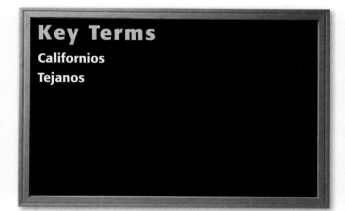

ISHOP PEDRO TAMARÓN Y ROMERAL *visited the town of Santa Fe in 1760 during his tour of northern New Spain. He noted, "This villa [town] of Santa Fe has 379 families of citizens of Spanish and mixed blood, with 1285 persons." Tamarón was particularly interested in the town's churches, which were all built from adobe in the Pueblo Indian style. The bishop's visit showed him how Spanish communities struggled to survive on the northern frontier by combining European and Indian ways of life.*

San Miguel Chapel, Santa Fe

IMAGE ON LEFT PAGE: *Albert Bierstadt's painting* Emigrants Crossing the Plains *shows settlers moving west in the mid-1800s.*

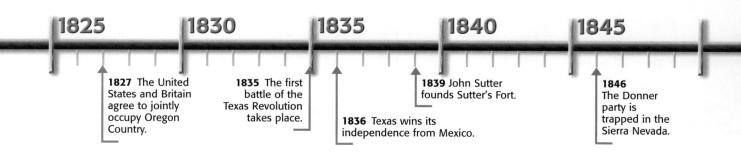

1825	1830	1835	1840	1845

1827 The United States and Britain agree to jointly occupy Oregon Country.

1835 The first battle of the Texas Revolution takes place.

1836 Texas wins its independence from Mexico.

1839 John Sutter founds Sutter's Fort.

1846 The Donner party is trapped in the Sierra Nevada.

Life in Northern New Spain

By the end of the 1700s, Spanish settlements were spread thinly across New Spain's northern frontier. Settlers there faced unique challenges.

California

In California, missions were the center of colonial society. The Spanish built 21 missions in California between 1769 and 1823. Starting in San Diego, the missions stretched north along the coast to San Francisco, each mission one day's travel from the next. Protecting the missions were four presidios, or Spanish military outposts, which guarded against attacks and were meant to discourage the British and Russians from colonizing the region.

The missions had large amounts of land and supported themselves through farming and ranching. Most of the labor was done by American Indians living on mission lands under the control of Franciscan priests. The crowded living conditions in the missions led to outbreaks of disease that killed tens of thousands of mission Indians over the years. As one priest sadly remembered, "They [Indians] live well free but as soon as we reduce them to a Christian and community life . . . they fatten, sicken, and die."

Despite this terrible loss of life, the Spanish continued with the mission system in California.

Missions such as San Diego de Alcala, shown here, controlled much of the land in early Spanish California.

The missions were financially successful into the early 1800s, often selling their goods to local communities. Colonist Guadalupe Vallejo later recalled those early days:

> " **We were the pioneers of the Pacific coast, building towns and Missions while General [George] Washington was carrying on the war of the Revolution.** "

Spanish colonists in California, known as **Californios**, were basically cut off from the rest of New Spain because of the great distance. This isolation was one reason that the Spanish population of California had reached only 3,200 by 1821.

New Mexico

New Mexico was the oldest and most important province on New Spain's northern frontier. Unlike in California, by the mid-1800s missions were no longer the center of life in New Mexico. Settlers lived in small villages scattered across the region. New Mexico's capital was Santa Fe.

Pueblo Indians and Spanish colonists heavily influenced one another. While the Spanish brought tools and new foods such as peaches, the Pueblo introduced the Spanish to foods such as beans and corn. Like Pueblo Indians, the Spanish used adobe in many of their buildings.

Texas

Fewer cultural exchanges took place between Indians and the Spanish in early Texas. The Spanish built nearly 40 missions in Texas, but isolation and Indian resistance prevented the mission system from being as established as it was in California. Frequent attacks by the Indian inhabitants, particularly the Comanche and the Apache, discouraged Spanish settlers during the early 1700s. The Spanish government tried to encourage more settlement by offering land grants to colonists.

By 1755 about 9,000 Spanish settlers, called **Tejanos** (tay-HAH-nohs), were living in present-day southern Texas. Tejanos introduced new breeds of cattle and soon developed a cattle-ranching society on the vast Texas grasslands.

The Comanche and the Apache still controlled much of Texas, however, which limited Spanish expansion. Viceroy Bernardo de Gálvez commented on the situation in the late 1700s, saying, "A bad peace with all the [Indian] tribes which ask for it would be more fruitful [helpful] than the gains of a successful war." The cost of fighting these tribes was too high for the Spanish government to bear.

Father Miguel Hidalgo y Costilla, holding a copy of the Grito de Dolores

The Mexican War for Independence

In September 1810 an army of more than 50,000 Indians and mestizos revolted against Spanish rule in New Spain. Father Miguel Hidalgo y Costilla, a priest in the town of Dolores in northern Mexico, was the first leader of this rebellion. Father Hidalgo and his followers hoped that political independence would lead to better living conditions for the many poor Indians and mestizos living in New Spain. The rallying cry of the revolt was the *Grito de Dolores* (Cry of Dolores), which went: "Long live our Lady of Guadalupe, down with bad government, death to the Spaniards!"

Support grew for Father Hidalgo. As his army marched across Mexico, he began carrying out reforms. He abolished slavery, ended unfair taxes on Indians, and took money from wealthy colonists to give to poorer ones. However, Father Hidalgo was unable to achieve his goal of uniting all the villages. In 1811 the Spanish defeated him and his followers, executing Father Hidalgo.

Father José María Morelos y Pavón continued the revolution and Hidalgo's reforms. Morelos

fought bravely until his capture in 1815. It was not until 1821 that a revolutionary army led by officer Agustín de Iturbide (ee-toor-BEE-day) finally defeated the Spanish. The group quickly declared Mexico an independent country.

Iturbide made himself emperor of Mexico, but he lacked political support. Two and a half years after he took power, the army forced Iturbide to step down from office. A new congress then created the Mexican Constitution of 1824, which declared Mexico a republic. The boundaries of this new republic stretched far beyond those of present-day Mexico. The newly independent Mexican republic included the current U.S. states of Arizona, California, New Mexico, Nevada, Texas, and Utah, as well as parts of Colorado, Kansas, Oklahoma, and Wyoming.

An Independent Mexico

The Mexican government soon changed the old Spanish policies toward the territories of California and Texas. Mexican officials tried to bring these frontier regions into closer contact with the rest of the nation.

Breaking Up the California Missions

In 1833 the Mexican government decided that the mission system had grown too powerful. To take away this power and to encourage different types of settlement, officials ended the mission system and gave mission lands to Californios. This action gave many Indians a chance to leave the harsh conditions of the missions, but life for most American Indians did not improve greatly. American Indians continued to do much of the hard physical labor in California, working mostly on farms or ranches.

The wealthiest Californios were able to acquire huge pieces of land. This allowed a group of about 500 families to create large ranchos, or "ranches." A few Americans who had married into Californio society were part of this group. The largest ranchos had up to 50,000 acres of land and huge herds of cattle.

The Californios developed a reputation for generous hospitality and skilled horsemanship. In his novel *Two Years Before the Mast*, American Richard Henry Dana Jr. described his various encounters with Californio culture. After entering one small town, a local man served Dana and a friend a feast:

The town of San Antonio, founded by the Spanish in 1718, was one of the largest communities in early Texas.

> 66 **The dishes contained baked meats, frijoles [beans] stewed with peppers onions, boiled eggs . . . the most sumptuous [delicious] meal we had eaten since we left Boston. . . . We took out some money and asked him how much we were to pay. He shook his head and crossed himself, saying that it was charity—that the Lord gave it to us.** 99

Changes in Texas

After Mexico's war for independence, Texas became part of the Mexican province of Coahuila (koh-ah-WEE-lah) y Tejas. Fighting between rebels and loyalists during the war had killed or chased away many Tejanos, and only a few thousand were left in 1821. Most of the Tejano population still lived on scattered ranches and in a few towns such as San Antonio.

Mexican officials were concerned that a small population could not protect such a large territory as Texas. They knew that the remaining Tejanos were in danger of Indian attacks and to a possible invasion by Britain or the United States. The Mexican government responded to this threat by once again trying to recruit settlers to help protect the northern frontier.

SECTION 1 REVIEW

Identify and explain the significance of the following:

- Californios
- Tejanos
- Father Miguel Hidalgo y Costilla
- José María Morelos y Pavón
- Agustín de Iturbide

Reading for Content Understanding

1. **Main Idea** What policies did Father Hidalgo and his followers try to institute across Mexico?

2. **Main Idea** Why did the Mexican government break up the mission system in 1833? What replaced this system?

3. **Geographic Diversity** *Region* What issues did newly independent Mexico face regarding Texas, and how did the government try to solve these problems?

4. **Writing** *Describing* Imagine that you are a traveler journeying through Spanish California, New Mexico, and Texas. Record in your journal what you observe about life there.

5. **Critical Thinking** *Supporting a Point of View* Do you think the mission system was a successful way for the Spanish to organize their territories in northern New Spain? Explain your answer.

Texas Gains Independence

Reading Focus

Why did Mexico allow the first American settlers into Texas, and what conditions did the Mexican government establish?

Why did many Texans choose to rebel against Mexico?

What events led Texas to win its independence from Mexico?

Key Terms

empresarios
Alamo
Battle of Goliad
Battle of San Jacinto

IN 1819 ADVENTURER JAMES LONG *persuaded a group of U.S. citizens from Natchez, Mississippi, to settle illegally in Spanish Texas. Long's followers built a fort on Galveston Bay, living there for two years before Mexican troops arrived to arrest them. While her husband was in prison, Jane Long remained in the fort with their two small children. She survived the winter, driving off hostile Indians with the fort's cannon. James Long eventually died in Mexico City, and Jane Long went back to Mississippi, determined that she would someday return to Texas.*

Texas defender
Davy Crockett's rifle

Alamo Collection, photograph courtesy the Daughters of the Republic of
Texas Library, CT97.23

 American Settlers in Texas

In 1821 the new Mexican republic wanted to bring more people into Texas. The government decided to allow foreigners to move to Texas if they agreed to follow certain rules.

The Austin Family

Moses Austin, a U.S. citizen, became one of the first **empresarios**, agents contracted by Mexico to bring settlers to Texas. In exchange for recruiting these settlers, *empresarios* received a large amount of land—as much as 67,000 acres for every 200 families. All of these families had to agree to become Mexican citizens, obey Mexican laws, and support the Roman Catholic Church before they could live in Texas.

Moses Austin died before he could bring any American settlers to Texas, but his son Stephen F. Austin took charge of the expedition. In 1821 Stephen F. Austin selected a colony site on the lower Colorado River and began carefully choosing settlers. The first 300 families that he brought to Texas, which included Jane Long, became known as the Old Three Hundred.

Stephen F. Austin eventually asked his fellow Texans to rise up and fight against the Mexican government.

Austin was a careful and cautious administrator. He tried hard to keep the peace between the Mexican government and Americans arriving in Texas. Although some people criticized his decisions in running the colony, few of them doubted his devotion to Texas.

Settlement Expands

Austin's colony was a success. Other American and Mexican *empresarios*, such as John McMullen and Martín de León, brought many more settlers into Texas. By 1834 more than 20,000 Americans had moved to Texas.

The majority of American settlers came from the southern states. In some parts of the South, the letters *GTT*, which stood for "Gone To Texas," commonly appeared on houses and wagons as a brief explanation of why someone was leaving. The promise of cheap or free land lured most of these families. They could receive 640 acres, with an extra 320 acres for each child in the family. Other grants offered 4,600 acres of free land to every married man. Many southern settlers brought enslaved African Americans with them to work on this land, often growing cotton.

 ## Conflict in Texas

U.S. settlers in Texas often ignored Mexican laws. These immigrants did not want to learn about Mexican culture or become Mexican citizens.

Sources of Tension

Many Texans—Americans and Tejanos alike—believed that Texas was not fairly represented in the Mexican government. These Texans wanted the Mexican Constitution of 1824, which limited the power of the central government, to be more strictly enforced. Some Texans also believed that the Mexican republic gave too much power to appointed officials and military officers rather than elected representatives.

Some Mexican officials complained that Texans did not show enough respect for the authority of the Mexican government. In addition, by 1830, American settlers in Texas greatly outnumbered Tejanos. These settlers often ignored Mexican laws and acted as if they were still in the United States and not on Mexican soil. For example, even though Mexico had banned the importation of slaves, many settlers ignored this law.

To deal with the violation of Mexican laws by American settlers, the Mexican government restricted American immigration and tried to enforce the ban on slavery. This greatly concerned settlers who were slaveholders. Mexico also raised tariffs on U.S. goods and criticized American settlers for not supporting the Catholic Church. To enforce its authority, Mexico sent more soldiers to Texas. One Mexican warned the country's minister of war and navy, "Either the [Mexican] government occupies Texas now, or it is lost forever."

Negotiation Fails

While the Mexican government's crackdown angered many Texans, Stephen F. Austin tried to keep relations peaceful. However, the situation grew worse in 1833, when greater limits were placed on local governments. While in Mexico to show the president a petition asking for more self-government in Texas, Austin was thrown in jail.

Mexican general Antonio López de Santa Anna

When General Antonio López de Santa Anna became the new Mexican leader in 1833, he suspended the constitution.

Austin was released from jail after a year and a half. Soon he sent out a call for all Texans to take up weapons against the Mexican government:

66 **War is our only recourse [option]. There is no other remedy. We must defend our rights, ourselves, and our country by force of arms.** 99

⭐ Fighting for Independence

The first battle of the Texas Revolution took place in the town of Gonzales in October 1835. The Mexican army tried to remove a cannon from the town, while a group of rebels stood next to the gun with a flag reading "Come and take it." In the following battle, the Texans defeated a detachment of Mexican cavalry.

Texans Revolt

A month later a group of Texans met and formed a temporary government, which pledged to overthrow Santa Anna. There was no official Texas army, but Texan volunteers quickly captured the two towns of Goliad and San Antonio. At San Antonio, a group of Texans led by William Travis and Jim Bowie occupied the **Alamo**, an old Franciscan mission. These troops were soon joined by a few volunteers, including frontiersman Davy Crockett and officer Juan Seguín.

Santa Anna, outraged at the news of these defeats, marched rapidly toward San Antonio with his army. Travis ignored orders to retreat and waited for reinforcements. When Santa Anna arrived with around 3,000 soldiers on February 23, 1836, there were only 189 troops at the Alamo.

Defending the Alamo

Santa Anna surrounded the Alamo for 13 days. Before the attack came, Travis sent Seguín on a daring mission through enemy lines to try to get reinforcements. Despite the terrible odds against the defenders, Travis also wrote a bold letter addressed "To the People of Texas and All Americans in the World":

66 **I shall never surrender or retreat. Then, I call on you in the name of Liberty, of patriotism, and everything dear to the American character, to come to our aid with all dispatch [speed]. . . . If this call is neglected I am determined to sustain myself as long as possible and die like a soldier who never forgets what is due his honor and that of his country.**
VICTORY OR DEATH. 99

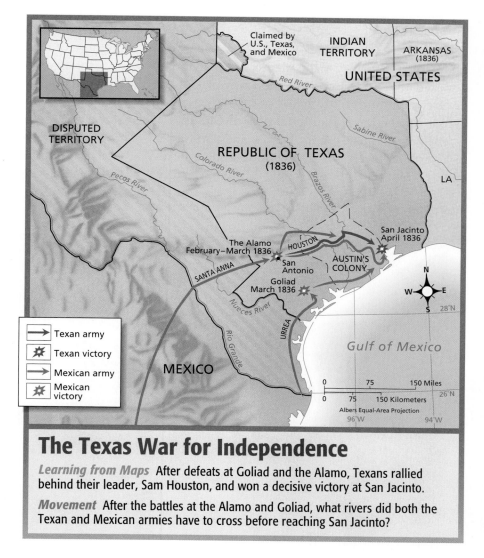

The Texas War for Independence

Learning from Maps After defeats at Goliad and the Alamo, Texans rallied behind their leader, Sam Houston, and won a decisive victory at San Jacinto.

Movement After the battles at the Alamo and Goliad, what rivers did both the Texan and Mexican armies have to cross before reaching San Jacinto?

Susanna Dickinson

The Mexican army launched an attack before dawn on March 6, 1836. The Mexicans suffered heavy losses, including some of their finest troops. Within a short period of time, the Mexican soldiers overwhelmed the Texans, killing Travis, Bowie, Crockett, and all the other defenders. Santa Anna spared the lives of a few people not involved in the fighting, including Susanna Dickinson. Dickinson and others spread the story of the fall of the Alamo throughout Texas, increasing support for the revolution. "Remember the Alamo!" became a rallying cry in Texas and the United States.

The Battle of Goliad

Following the victory at the Alamo, Mexican forces attacked the Texas troops at the town of Goliad. Severely outnumbered, Texas commander James Fannin surrendered after the **Battle of Goliad**.

By Santa Anna's orders, Fannin and almost 400 of his soldiers were charged with treason and executed. This act shocked some of the Mexican troops and outraged many Texans. Francisca Álvarez, a nurse and the wife of a Mexican officer, helped several of Fannin's men escape the firing squads by hiding them. She became known as the Angel of Goliad for this act of mercy.

⭐ Texas Becomes a Republic

Santa Anna's early victories failed to break the spirit of the Texas rebels. While the Mexican army marched across Texas, the rebel leaders worked together to further the cause of independence.

The Convention of 1836

Four days before the Battle of the Alamo, Texas delegates had met to declare independence from Mexico. Within two weeks they had created a Texas constitution. Both Texas's declaration of independence and its constitution were modeled on those of the United States.

However, there were some differences between the Texan and U.S. documents. For example, the Texas constitution specifically legalized slavery, despite the language of liberty used throughout the document. According to the Texas constitution, the president of Texas would serve a three-year term and could not serve consecutive terms. The delegates elected politician David Burnet as temporary president and *empresario* Lorenzo de Zavala as vice president.

San Jacinto

Sam Houston, commander in chief of the newly formed Texas army, quickly began preparations to fight against Santa Anna. Outnumbered and untrained, Houston's troops had to retreat east. Acting president David Burnet criticized Houston for retreating from the Mexicans. "The enemy are laughing at you," he cried.

After a two-week siege, Santa Anna's army overwhelmed the outnumbered defenders of the Alamo.

Houston finally made a stand at San Jacinto, near the present-day city of Houston. Santa Anna, confident of victory, was careless in choosing the site for his camp. As a result, the Mexican army had poor defenses and no way to maneuver. On the afternoon of April 21, 1836, many of the Mexican soldiers were resting. They awoke to the shouts of Houston's forces as the Texans attacked the camp. "Remember the Alamo! Remember Goliad!" The **Battle of San Jacinto** had begun.

Caught by surprise, Santa Anna's troops were driven back and trapped in the surrounding woods. Texas cavalry led by Juan Seguín helped block the Mexican soldiers' escape. One Mexican officer remembered the scene. "I saw our men flying in small groups . . . sheltering themselves behind large trees." The officer tried to rally the troops,

Santa Anna surrenders to the wounded Sam Houston after the Battle of San Jacinto.

❝ **but it was impossible. The enemy's cavalry surrounded the grove, while his infantry penetrated it, pursuing us with fierce and bloodthirsty feelings.** ❞

The crushing defeat destroyed Santa Anna's army and led to his capture. He was forced to recognize the independence of Texas in a treaty and was then released to return to Mexico City. While Texans celebrated Houston's accomplishment, Santa Anna was thrown out of power by angry Mexican citizens upon his return home. Though the fighting was over for the time being, many Mexicans did not accept that Texas had become an independent country.

SECTION 2 REVIEW

Identify and explain the significance of the following:

- **Jane Long**
- *empresarios*
- **Moses Austin**
- **Stephen F. Austin**
- **Antonio López de Santa Anna**
- **William Travis**
- **Alamo**
- **Battle of Goliad**
- **Sam Houston**
- **Battle of San Jacinto**

Locate and explain the importance of the following:

- **San Antonio**
- **Goliad**
- **San Jacinto**

Reading for Content Understanding

1 **Main Idea** Why did Mexico allow U.S. citizens to settle in Texas? What rules did these citizens agree to follow?

2 **Main Idea** Why did some Americans choose to settle in Texas?

3 **Citizenship and Democracy** What complaints did American settlers and Tejanos have against the Mexican government? How did the Mexican government respond to these complaints?

4 **Writing** *Informing* Write an article for either a Texas or a Mexican newspaper, explaining how Texas won its independence from Mexico. Include in your article the fighting at the Alamo and the Battles of Goliad and San Jacinto.

5 **Critical Thinking** *Determining the Strength of an Argument* Do you think Texans had a right to seek their independence from Mexico? Explain your answer.

The Lone Star Republic

Reading Focus

Why did Texas not immediately become part of the United States?

What were the policies of the Republic of Texas toward new immigrants and people already living there?

What were Texas's government policies and the economy like during its time as a republic?

Key Terms

Republic of Texas

annex

I N DECEMBER 1836 *President Andrew Jackson faced a difficult decision as he addressed Congress. Texas had declared its independence from Mexico earlier that year, and Congress had asked Jackson to recognize, or formally accept, the new Texas government. However, Mexico still considered Texas a part of its territory. In his speech, Jackson admitted that the people of Texas "are bound to many of our citizens by ties of friendship and kindred blood." He concluded, however, that it was still too soon to take sides in the dispute between Texas and Mexico.*

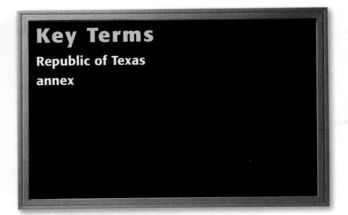

Flag of the Republic of Texas

The Granger Collection, New York

★ The Texas Government

The independent nation of Texas was called the **Republic of Texas**, and its capital was the new town of Houston. Voters elected Sam Houston, former governor of Tennessee and victor at San Jacinto, as president. Mirabeau Lamar was chosen as vice president.

The Annexation Question

One of the issues facing the republic was whether to ask the United States to **annex**, or take control of, Texas. If annexed, Texas would eventually become a U.S. state. Most Texas leaders hoped that President Andrew Jackson would support annexation because he had previously supported efforts to buy Texas from Mexico.

Jackson, however, was concerned that adding Texas as a slave state would upset the balance between free states and slave states. Jackson also did not want to go to war with Mexico over Texas. He decided to recognize Texas as an independent nation in 1837 but avoided the annexation issue during his final year in office. Martin Van Buren followed the same course of action when he succeeded Jackson as president. France recognized the Texas government in 1839, and Britain did so the next year. However, Mexico still refused to agree that its former province had become an independent country.

Texas's Indian Policy

Texas vice president Mirabeau Lamar wanted the republic to expand west and increase its power. President Houston wanted to be more cautious and to continue trying to join the United States. When Lamar succeeded Houston as president in 1838, it meant important changes in Texas policy.

One area that changed was the treatment of American Indians in Texas. As a young man, Houston had lived with the Cherokee in Tennessee and was sympathetic to Indian interests. During his first term as president, from 1836 to 1838, Texas adopted a peaceful approach to Indian negotiations. When Lamar took office, Texan Indian policies became much harsher. Lamar demanded that Indians leave their homelands and follow all Texas laws, or face military action.

Fighting soon broke out with several Indian tribes, such as the Cherokee and the Comanche. Many Texans believed that the Cherokee were plotting with Mexican authorities to overthrow the republic. Comanche raids on Texan settlements also increased. After Houston was re-elected president in 1841, the fighting slowed. By then, however, Texans had forced out most American Indian tribes from the eastern part of the country and had begun occupying many of their rich lands.

Tejanos in the Republic

Another group that suffered under the policies of the republic were Tejanos, who often faced unfair treatment from American settlers. Juan Seguín, hero of the Texas Revolution and mayor of San Antonio, described the problems he faced:

> " At every hour of the day and night, my countrymen [Tejanos] ran to me for protection against the assaults . . . of these [American] adventurers. . . . Were not the victims my own countrymen, friends, and associates? "

Biography

Juan Seguín

Born to an important San Antonio family in 1806, Juan Seguín became a well-known Tejano politician. Seguín was sympathetic to the interests of American settlers arriving in Texas and formed a friendship with Stephen F. Austin. During the Texas Revolution, Seguín served as a captain in the Texas cavalry and led a troop of Tejano cavalry in the victory at San Jacinto.

After the war, he served in the Texas senate and became mayor of San Antonio in 1840. Despite his service during the Texas Revolution, Seguín faced criticism from some Texans for his attempts to keep the peace between Anglos and Tejanos. In 1842 he left the republic he had helped create, moving to Mexico with his family because of rising tensions between the two groups.

These problems angered many Tejanos who had supported and participated in the war for independence from Mexico. Despite losing land, property, and political power, Tejanos and Mexicans maintained a strong physical and cultural presence in south Texas and the Rio Grande valley.

New Immigrants

The Republic of Texas encouraged immigration from the United States and Europe by offering

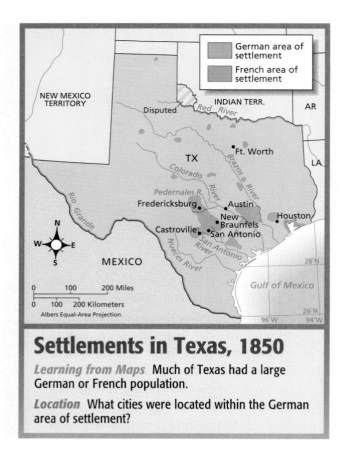

Settlements in Texas, 1850

Learning from Maps Much of Texas had a large German or French population.

Location What cities were located within the German area of settlement?

land grants to settlers. Between 1836 and 1841 the government gave out more than 40 million acres.

Coming to Texas

Texas attracted around 100,000 new residents from 1836 to 1845. By 1845 so many immigrants were arriving daily that they had to wait at ferry crossings for hours. Settlement pushed westward across the republic, beyond the existing Tejano settlement of San Antonio. In 1839, Texans moved the capital from Houston to the more centrally located town of Austin to keep up with these changes.

After the Panic of 1837, many more Americans came to Texas. They settled primarily in the eastern and northern parts of the republic. Many settlers came from nearby southern states, and they often brought enslaved African Americans with them to work the land and to grow cotton. By 1847 there were almost 40,000 enslaved African Americans living in Texas. In 1840 Texas slaveholders helped pass a law banning the few free African Americans

living in Texas from remaining in the republic, though some free African Americans refused to leave their homes.

Arrivals from Europe

Along with the steady flow of U.S. settlers, large numbers of European immigrants came to Texas in the 1840s. The largest group came from various regions of what is now Germany. Germans established farming communities as well as towns such as New Braunfels and Fredericksburg, both in central Texas. German immigrant Gustav Dresel described the rapid growth of Texas in the 1840s:

> ❝There was land in abundance. . . . The lawyers . . . accepted payment in land. The innkeepers received so and so many hundreds of thousands of acres of land for board [food] and lodging from the army officers or big estate owners.❞

By the late 1840s the legislature was publishing the laws in German and English. Some of these Germans opposed slavery. As early as 1840 they protested Texas laws that banned all free African Americans.

★ Struggles of the Republic

Texas faced many challenges as an independent country. Economic, military, and social issues all posed difficulties for the republic.

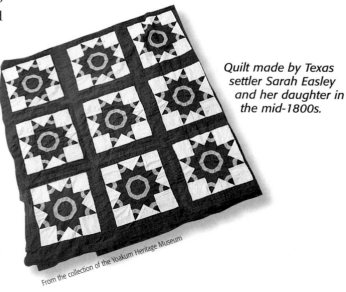

Quilt made by Texas settler Sarah Easley and her daughter in the mid-1800s.

From the collection of the Yoakum Heritage Museum

Ethnic Traditions in Texas

In Texas, a wide range of cultures influence everything from architecture to food to holidays. The Tejanos who founded Texas and the Mexican Americans who settled there afterward have shaped many aspects of Texas society. Holiday celebrations such as *Diez y Seis de Septiembre*—which celebrates the announcement of the *Grito de Dolores* on September 16, 1810—is one of many Texas traditions that date back to the first settlers.

Adding to Texas culture were the thousands of European immigrants who moved to the Republic of Texas in the 1840s. These groups founded towns, raised families, and brought traditions that continue down to the present.

Germans made up the largest group of European immigrants to Texas. Prince Carl of Solms-Braunfels, one of the founders of New Braunfels, told the Germans before they crossed the Atlantic: "Stay together and remain faithful to German culture and habits." They did so, remembering and keeping their language, customs, and traditions alive. One settler wrote to relatives back home, "Be sure to bring all the sheet music that you can collect. . . . And do not fail to bring the complete works of Goethe [a German poet]."

Germans also kept their customs alive through newspapers, theater, and dancing groups. Some of these traditions survive to this day. A modern festival in New Braunfels features oompah music and polka dancing. German singing societies throughout the state still participate in the Sängerfest, or "singers' festival."

About 2,000 colonists from the Alsace-Lorraine region in present-day France settled in Castroville, Texas, in 1844. They built houses in a rural French style that are still visited by tourists. Castroville also honors its heritage with the St. Louis Day celebration, which has been held every year since 1882. It features traditional folk dancing and authentic French food.

Texans love to celebrate the state's rich cultural background. Every year the Institute of Texan Cultures hosts the Folklife Festival, a four-day celebration honoring the traditions and crafts of ethnic groups in Texas. Texans from 70 counties representing different backgrounds participate in the fun.

Texas children participate in Wurstfest, a traditional German celebration.

Understanding What You Read

1. What current celebrations honor the ethnic traditions of Texas?

2. In what other ways do you think newcomers to Texas may have kept their heritage alive?

3. Why do you think people might enjoy attending ethnic celebrations?

The Economy

In the mid-1800s only four Texas towns—Galveston, Houston, New Braunfels, and San Antonio—had more than 1,000 inhabitants. Travel between the newer settlements was slow, difficult, and often dangerous. The Texas economy was still based largely on agriculture and ranching, with very little manufacturing.

Although the republic was rich in resources, particularly land, it had little cash. Taxes on imports and property failed to bring in much additional revenue, leaving the new nation almost bankrupt. The public debt rose from $2 million to $7 million between 1838 and 1841, while the value of Texas paper money fell from $1 to 12 cents.

Problems with Mexico

Money problems and the sheer size of Texas made it difficult for the young nation to defend its borders. The congress organized the Texas Rangers to guard the frontier against Mexican and Indian attacks after President Houston disbanded the army in May 1837.

The second president of the republic, Mirabeau Lamar, took an aggressive stance toward Mexico. When he took office, Lamar declared, "If

The Texas Rangers guarded the vast Texas frontier against raids by Mexican and American Indian forces.

peace can only be obtained by the sword, let the sword do its work." In 1841 he authorized a military attack against Santa Fe, New Mexico, without the approval of the Texas congress. The invasion failed miserably, and most of the participants were taken prisoner.

Worse still, the Santa Fe incident prompted Mexican counterattacks against Texas. Santa Anna returned to power and sent an army into Texas that recaptured San Antonio on two occasions. After Sam Houston returned to the presidency in 1841, he tried to end the fighting, finally signing a peace agreement with Santa Anna in 1844.

SECTION 3 REVIEW

Identify and explain the significance of the following:
- **Republic of Texas**
- **annex**
- **Mirabeau Lamar**
- **Juan Seguín**

Locate and explain the importance of the following:
- **Houston**
- **Austin**

Reading for Content Understanding

1 **Main Idea** How did the Republic of Texas encourage settlers to move there?

2 **Main Idea** What economic and political challenges did the Republic of Texas face?

3 **Citizenship and Democracy** Why did President Jackson oppose the annexation of Texas?

4 **Writing** *Expressing* Imagine that you are either a Tejano or one of Austin's colonists. Write a diary entry comparing and contrasting your life under Mexican rule to that under the Republic of Texas.

5 **Critical Thinking** *Making Comparisons* How did Republic of Texas presidents Sam Houston and Mirabeau Lamar differ in their policies toward American Indians?

Oregon and the Far West

Reading Focus

How did the economics of the fur trade affect mountain men?

Why did U.S. settlers travel to Oregon Country?

What was life like on the Oregon Trail?

Key Terms

mountain men
rendezvous
Oregon Trail

FUR TRAPPER MANUEL LISA *was one of the earliest explorers of the Rocky Mountains. Writing to the famous explorer William Clark, Lisa once said, "I go a great distance while some are considering whether they will start today or tomorrow." In 1807 Lisa led an expedition up the Missouri River into the middle of present-day Montana, braving dangerous river rapids and freezing weather. In the winter, he stopped at the Little Bighorn River, where he built Lisa's Fort. Lisa's accomplishment set the stage for more expeditions into the Rockies and to the Pacific coast that blazed trails for future generations.*

A mountain man

 The Fur Trade

Most of the first non-Indians who traveled to the Rocky Mountains and the Pacific Northwest were fur traders and trappers hired by eastern companies. These frontier hunters and merchants were known as **mountain men**.

Exploring the Frontier

In the early 1800s mountain men traveled to the Rocky Mountains and beyond in search of the furs of beaver and other animals. Merchants in the East and in Europe bought these furs to make hats and other articles of clothing. John Jacob Astor's American Fur Company, based in St. Louis, Missouri, was one of the largest businesses that bought furs from trappers.

Mountain men lived an often isolated and dangerous lifestyle, trapping animals on their own and trading with Indians for more furs. People such as Jedediah Smith, Manuel Lisa, and Jim Bridger survived many hardships during their search for wealth and adventure. In the process of surviving on the frontier, many mountain men adopted Indian customs and clothing. It was also common

This 1841 drawing of Fort Walla Walla in Oregon Country shows fur trappers and American Indians meeting to trade with one another.

for mountain men to marry Indian women. A married trapper's success often depended largely on the knowledge and hard work of his wife.

The Rendezvous

Once a year the mountain men met to trade and socialize in an event known as the **rendezvous**. At the rendezvous, mountain men and Indian trappers would sell their furs to fur company agents. One trapper described the participants of a typical rendezvous in 1837 as

> 66 **Americans and Canadian French with some Dutch, Scotch, Irish, English, . . . and full blood Indians, of nearly every tribe in the Rocky Mountains.** 99

Trapper Joseph Thing wrote that the rendezvous had "as crazy a set of men as I ever saw."

Although the rendezvous was filled with celebrating and storytelling, it was also about business. Western artist Alfred Jacob Miller described the beginning of trade in the rendezvous camp:

> 66 **The Fur Company's great tent is raised; the Indians erect their picturesque [beautiful] white lodges; the accumulated furs of the hunting season are brought forth and the Company's tent is a . . . busy place.** 99

The Decline of the Fur Trade

The stories and rugged lives of the mountain men captured the American imagination, but the era of American fur trading in the Pacific Northwest lasted for only a few decades. By the 1840s the demand for beaver pelts decreased as clothing fashions changed. Overtrapping had also greatly reduced the supply of beaver.

Some mountain men who had succeeded in the fur business moved back east to retire. Others began guiding farmers, miners, and ranchers to the West. In the 1840s these new settlers replaced the mountain men on the frontier.

★ Oregon Country

In 1811 American merchant John Jacob Astor founded Astoria, a fur-trading post at the mouth of the Columbia River in the Pacific Northwest. This small outpost was one of the earliest American settlements in the region that became known as Oregon Country.

At the beginning of the 1800s Oregon Country was occupied by Indian tribes such as the Flathead, the Nez Percé, the Cayuse, and the Shoshoni. Spain, Russia, Britain, and the United States also claimed ownership of this land. The United States based its claim to the region on the exploration of merchant captain Robert Gray, who had reached the mouth of the Columbia River in 1792.

In 1819 Spain and the United States settled their claims over ownership of Oregon Country in the Adams-Onís Treaty. Spain agreed to give up all claims to land beyond the northern border of present-day California. Russia then agreed in a treaty in 1824 to withdraw its claims in the region north to the southern border of present-day Alaska. This left the United States, Britain, and American Indians as the remaining rivals for the Pacific Northwest.

In 1827 the United States and Great Britain agreed to extend an 1818 treaty that called for a joint occupation of Oregon Country. The agreement did not specify how long this shared ownership would last. Both sides wanted to maintain access to the Columbia River and its surrounding land, but neither country was willing to start a war over the territory.

The British were interested in the Pacific Northwest primarily for the fur trade. Relatively few settlers from Canada or Britain moved into the area. In the late 1830s and early 1840s, however, many Americans began making the difficult journey across the Great Plains to Oregon Country.

★ Missionaries and Settlement

Missionaries such as Marcus and Narcissa Whitman played an important role in the settlement of Oregon Country. As the Second Great Awakening brought a new religious spirit to the northeastern United States, some churches began looking for ways to spread Christianity to American Indians in the Far West. The Whitmans went to the Pacific Northwest in 1836 to convert Indians. Narcissa Whitman and a fellow missionary's wife were the first two white women known to have crossed North America.

Upon arriving in Walla Walla in present-day Washington State, the Whitmans established a mission called Waiilatpu. The Whitmans had limited success converting the local Cayuse Indians, in part because the missionaries believed that the Cayuse needed to give up their traditional customs. Narcissa Whitman found pioneer life not only difficult but also lonely, even though she adopted many children. She wrote to her sister in 1846, "My health has been so poor, and my family has increased so rapidly, that it [frontier life] has been impossible."

Despite the challenges the Whitmans encountered on the frontier, Marcus Whitman wrote letters and took trips back East to encourage settlers to move out West. "I have no doubt our greatest work is . . . to aid the white settlement of this country," he wrote his parents. Returning from one such recruiting trip in 1843, Whitman even helped guide a wagon train across the Great Plains.

Waiilatpu became a frequent stopping point for many settlers arriving in Oregon Country, with the Whitmans providing rest and shelter for weary travelers. Some of the settlers who stayed at the Whitman mission carried diseases to which the Cayuse had never before been exposed. In 1847 a measles epidemic broke out among Cayuse children, killing many of them. Indian leaders became angry at the Whitmans for guiding the settlers who brought sickness and took Cayuse lands. A group of Cayuse attacked Waiilatpu, killing the Whitmans and more than 10 others. News of the massacre increased U.S. government concerns about the safety of settlers in Oregon Country.

Narcissa Whitman

★ The Oregon Trail

Many of the settlers moving to Oregon Country and other western areas followed the **Oregon Trail**. Stretching more than 2,000 miles across the northern Great Plains and the Rocky Mountains, the Oregon Trail challenged the endurance and determination of these pioneer families.

Hitting the Trail

Following the economic hardships of the Panic of 1837, many Americans looked to the West as a place to improve their lives. Some newspapers

As more pioneers came to Oregon Country, they began founding settlements such as Oregon City, built in the early 1800s along the Willamette River.

The Granger Collection, New York

Expanding West **503**

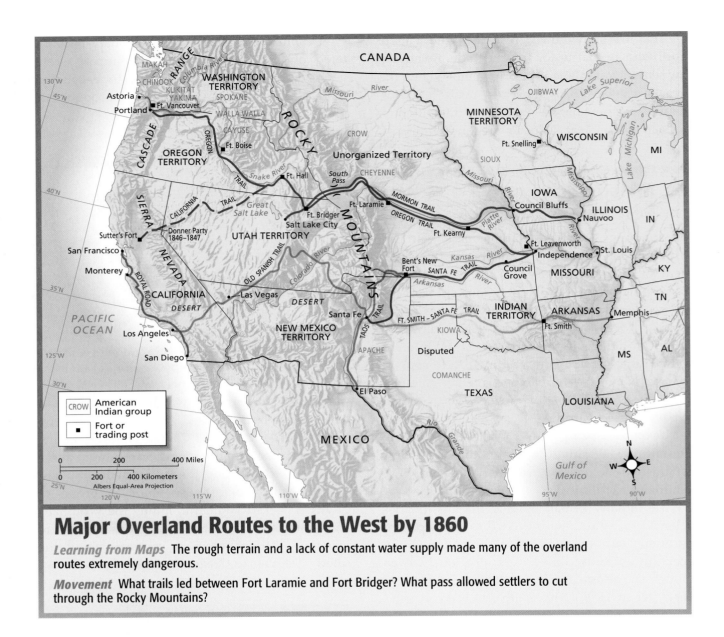

Major Overland Routes to the West by 1860

Learning from Maps The rough terrain and a lack of constant water supply made many of the overland routes extremely dangerous.

Movement What trails led between Fort Laramie and Fort Bridger? What pass allowed settlers to cut through the Rocky Mountains?

encouraged people to move by printing glowing descriptions of Oregon Country. In May 1843 the *Ohio Statesman* newspaper reported, "The Oregon fever is raging in almost every part of the Union." Pioneers started on the Oregon Trail in Independence or St. Joseph, Missouri, or Council Bluffs, Iowa. The trail followed the Platte and Sweetwater Rivers over the Plains, crossed the Rockies, and then forked. The northern branch led to the Willamette Valley in Oregon, while the other branch went to California.

The pioneers' journey usually began in late spring, once the rainy season ended, and lasted for six to eight months. A family of four needed about $600 to buy the supplies necessary for making the trip. This was a lot of money at a time when laborers made around $1.50 per day. Most of the groups were young families who gathered in wagon trains ranging from 10 wagons to several dozen on some of the early trips.

Challenges on the Trail

Families on the trail faced great obstacles. Shortages of food, water, and supplies were a constant problem for many wagon trains. Pioneers also faced rough weather and natural barriers such as rivers and mountains. Travelers often got confused over the best route to take. Lucy Hall Bennett, who was 13 years old when her family set out on the trail, remembered her family's struggles:

Thousands of settlers like the members of this wagon train journeyed across the Oregon Trail.

66 **The road we took had been traveled by the Hudson Bay Fur traders, and while it might have been alright for pack horses, it was certainly not adapted to immigrants traveling by ox train. The water was [so] bad . . . you could hardly drink it. There was little grass and before long our cattle all had sore feet from traveling over the hard sharp rocks. . . . Several of our party died.** 99

Pioneers also encountered American Indians from many different tribes along their journey. Indians often helped pioneers by acting as guides or by supplying food in exchange for trade goods.

The Long Journey West

Pioneers walked much of the way on the trail. They did this to conserve their animals' strength and to keep space in the wagons free for provisions, household goods, and the sick. The pioneers kept up a tiring pace, traveling from dawn until dusk. Settler Jesse Applegate recalled the advice he received from an experienced Oregon pioneer: "Travel, *travel*, TRAVEL. . . . Nothing is good that causes a moment's delay."

At the end of each day's journey, much work remained to be done. Women unpacked wagons, cooked dinner, cleaned up, washed and mended clothes, and tended to children. Men looked after livestock, hunted for food, and scouted the trail ahead. Martha Ann Morrison recalled that when most of the men were away hunting or scouting, "the women helped pitch the tents, helped unload, and helped yoking up the cattle."

The settlers who arrived safely in Oregon and California found generally healthy and pleasant climates and fertile valleys for farming. By 1845 about 5,000 settlers occupied the Willamette Valley, with thousands more settlers from the United States willing to brave the dangers of the Oregon Trail in order to find new opportunities in the West.

SECTION 4 REVIEW

Identify and explain the significance of the following:
- **mountain men**
- **rendezvous**
- **John Jacob Astor**
- **Marcus and Narcissa Whitman**
- **Oregon Trail**

Reading for Content Understanding

1 **Main Idea** What led to the rise and the fall of the fur trade, and how did these changes affect traders and trappers?

2 **Main Idea** What difficulties did settlers on the Oregon Trail face?

3 **Geographic Diversity** *Movement* How were missionaries important in the settlement of Oregon Country?

4 **Writing** *Creating* Make a flyer that might have been used to encourage U.S. settlers to travel to Oregon Country. Your flyer should describe the reasons why people should head west.

5 **Critical Thinking** *Supporting a Point of View* Do you think that moving to Oregon was worth the difficulties of the journey? Explain your answer.

California and the Southwest

Reading Focus

What challenges did travelers face on the trails to California and the Southwest, and what was life like for the settlers once they arrived?

How did the Mexican territories and the United States become more closely connected?

Why did artists travel to the West?

Key Terms

California Trail
Donner party
Sutter's Fort
Santa Fe Trail

I N 1835 AMERICAN RICHARD HENRY DANA *arrived in San Francisco Bay on board a merchant ship. Looking around at the large harbor and the forested hills, Dana admired the climate, calling it "as near to being perfect as any in the world." He also praised the nearby town of Yerba Buena, which supplied traders and whaling ships with food. After spending a few days ashore, Dana and the crew set sail for more destinations on the California coast. As he glanced up at the hills while leaving the bay, Dana predicted, "If California ever becomes a prosperous country, this bay will be the center of its prosperity."*

Mexican coin used in California

Collection of the American Numismatic Society

 California Trails

Under Mexican rule, California became a meeting ground for merchants from Mexico and the United States in the 1830s and 1840s. Both coastal and inland trade increased during this period.

The Road to California

The main route to California split off from the Oregon Trail once it reached the Snake River in present-day Idaho. While most settlers continued following the Oregon Trail north, a few took the southern branch, which became known as the **California Trail**.

American immigrants and traders following the California Trail tried to avoid the first snows in the Sierra Nevada. The travelers were not always able to get through the mountain range in time, however. The **Donner party** was perhaps the most tragic example of a group of western travelers with bad luck and poor judgment. This group of families began its journey west in the spring of 1846. While attempting to take a shortcut, George

Donner and the other leaders left the main trail and got lost. By the time the Donner party reached the Sierra Nevada, winter had arrived early, trapping their wagons in heavy snows. Donner party member Virginia Reed later wrote her sister about the party's struggles to survive in their winter camp:

❝ There was 15 in the cabin we was in and half of us had to lay a [in] bed all the time there was 10 starved to death. . . . It snowed and would cover the cabin all over so we could not get out for 2 or 3 days. ❞

The members of the Donner party found themselves trapped by high snows in the Sierra Nevada.

Tinted drawing courtesy of the California History Room, California State Library, Sacramento, California.

A rescue party found the starving and freezing group in February 1847. Of the original 87 members of the party, 40 had died.

Life in California

Despite the increase in traffic along the California Trail, California was still inhabited mainly by Mexicans and American Indians. U.S. merchants were usually more interested in trading manufactured goods for hides, tallow (animal fat), and gold dust than in settling in the region. In addition, Mexican officials did not want to let large numbers of Americans settle in California as they had done in Texas. In 1839 Swiss immigrant John Sutter received permission to start a colony called **Sutter's Fort**, near the Sacramento River.

Sutter's Fort soon became a popular destination for many U.S. immigrants. These new arrivals praised Sutter's generosity and hospitality. The Mexican government was less pleased with his actions. By the mid-1840s some of the Anglo-Californians were publishing guide books encouraging other settlers to move west to the Mexican territory.

★ Other Trails West

Other major western trails were used primarily as trade routes to the Southwest, formerly the northern frontier of New Spain. Under Spanish rule, the province of New Mexico had been closed to Americans. Once Mexico gained independence in 1821, however, American merchants were allowed to enter New Mexico. These traders soon established the **Santa Fe Trail**, which ran from Independence, Missouri, to Santa Fe, New Mexico. American traders loaded wagon trains with cloth and other manufactured goods and later exchanged these products for horses, mules, and silver from Mexican merchants in Santa Fe.

The long trip across the desert and mountains was difficult and dangerous, but the lure of high profits encouraged traders to take the trail. The U.S. federal government helped protect traders by sending troops and money to ensure Indian cooperation.

In 1847 Susan Shelby Magoffin became one of the first white women to travel on the Santa Fe Trail when

Sutter's Fort, a popular stopping point on the California Trail, was located on the site of present-day Sacramento, California.

The Granger Collection, New York

American Arts

George Catlin

Early western pioneers had few sources of information about the Great Plains and the western lands of California and Oregon. What information they did receive came from descriptions from American Indians, traders, and explorers. Often the first images of the West that these settlers and other people in the United States saw were paintings by western artists such as George Catlin.

Catlin explored much of the Americas and is best known for his paintings of American Indians. From 1830 to 1836, Catlin traveled throughout the western Plains to create a visual documentary of the Indian tribes who lived there. He painted portraits of chiefs, spiritual leaders, and warriors from the major tribes in the region. Catlin also painted important events such as buffalo hunts and religious ceremonies. His hundreds of paintings provide a valuable record of American Indian culture.

After Catlin finished his travels, he brought his paintings back East for exhibition. This "Indian Gallery" visited New York, Washington, Baltimore, and Boston before Catlin took it to Europe. One New York newspaper carried the following advertisement for the show:

❝ *There will be several hundred Portraits exhibited, as well as Splendid Costumes—Paintings of their villages—Dances—Buffalo Hunts—Religious Ceremonies, etc. . . . Mr. Catlin will be present at all of these exhibitions, giving illustrations and explanations in the form of a Lecture.* ❞

People eagerly came to see Catlin's paintings and to hear his tales about the great beauty of the West.

Audiences crowded Catlin's exhibitions and thousands viewed his widely distributed paintings. For many of these people, Catlin's landscapes were the only images they would ever see of the West.

Understanding the Arts

1. How did pioneers heading west get information about the lands to which they were traveling?

2. Why do you think Catlin's Indian Gallery was popular with people in the East?

George Catlin's Buffalo Dance

she accompanied her husband with a load of trade goods. At one point there was a terrible crash as her wagon plunged into a gully:

" **To see the wreck of that carriage now with the top and sides entirely broken to pieces, [one] could never believe that people had come out of it alive.** "

El Camino Real, or "King's Road," still connected Santa Fe to Mexico City. Another Mexican road, known as the Old Spanish Trail, reached from Santa Fe to the California coast and other distant outposts of the old Spanish Empire. By the mid-1800s the traders traveling along the Old Spanish Trail were likely to be American traders taking goods to southern California.

 Frontier Artists

Stories of the people and scenery in the West inspired some artists to travel with explorers to the frontier. George Catlin gave up a career as a portrait painter in Philadelphia to go west and paint scenes of American Indians. He painted more than 500 such images on his journeys throughout the West. In 1840 he wrote, "I have visited forty-eight tribes . . . containing in all 400,000 souls."

John Mix Stanley's Buffalo Hunt on the Southwestern Prairies

Artist Alfred Jacob Miller traveled through the Rocky Mountains, painting striking images of the landscape as well as portraits of the mountain men who hunted and trapped in remote regions. Other artists such as John Mix Stanley and Seth Eastman contributed to the gallery of portraits of Indians and the western environment. Not all of these artists had great talent, and their paintings often exaggerated the things that they saw. Together, however, the work of these artists added to the visual record of the West. The work of such artists became extremely popular in the East and in Europe. It captured imaginations and shaped people's ideas about the West.

SECTION 5 REVIEW

Identify and explain the significance of the following:

- **California Trail**
- **Donner party**
- **Sutter's Fort**
- **Santa Fe Trail**
- **George Catlin**
- **Alfred Jacob Miller**

Locate and explain the importance of the following (see map on page 504):

- **Snake River**
- **Sierra Nevada**
- **Santa Fe**
- **Independence, Missouri**

Reading for Content Understanding

1 **Main Idea** Why were the journeys along the California and Santa Fe Trails difficult?

2 **Main Idea** What motivated artists like George Catlin and Alfred Jacob Miller to travel to the West?

3 **Global Relations** What linked the Mexican territories more closely with the United States?

4 **Writing** *Classifying* If you were planning on settling in California or in the Southwest in the mid-1800s, what five items do you think would be most important to bring with you? Explain your choices in a paragraph.

5 **Critical Thinking** *Evaluating* How might the work of frontier artists have encouraged more people to move to the West?

CHAPTER 16 REVIEW

Chapter Summary

In 1821 Mexico won its independence from Spain. The Mexican government then allowed foreigners to move to Texas if they agreed to follow certain rules. However, tensions between the Mexican government and American settlers developed. This led to the Texas Revolution, after which Texas became an independent republic. Pioneers continued to move to Texas, while others set out in increasing numbers for Oregon Country and California. ■

On a separate sheet of paper, complete the following activities.

Identifying People and Ideas

Describe the historical significance of the following:

1. Tejanos
2. Father Miguel Hidalgo y Costilla
3. Stephen F. Austin
4. Battle of San Jacinto
5. Republic of Texas
6. Juan Seguín
7. mountain men
8. Marcus and Narcissa Whitman
9. California Trail
10. George Catlin

Internet Activity

go.hrw.com
SA0 Early Settlement

Choose one of the early settlements in Texas or California, such as San Antonio, Houston, San Diego, or San Francisco. Search the Internet through the HRW Web site to find information on historical places, events, or exhibits today that reflect the city's early history. Using this information, write a paragraph on what a visitor to the city might expect to learn about the city's past.

Understanding Main Ideas

1. Why did Father Hidalgo lead a revolt against the Spanish government?
2. Why did Mexican officials want to close down the northern missions?
3. What concerns did President Jackson have about annexing Texas?
4. How did the fur trade help to open up the West to American settlers?
5. Why did people travel to Oregon Country?
6. What did Alfred Jacob Miller accomplish?

Reviewing Themes

1. **Global Relations**   Describe the events that led Texans to declare their independence from Mexico.
2. **Cultural Diversity**   How did German immigrants affect the Republic of Texas?

Using the Time Line

Number your paper from 1 to 5. Match the letters on the time line below with the following events.

1. Lawmakers draft the Mexican constitution.
2. General Santa Anna is captured and forced to sign a treaty accepting Texas as an independent country.
3. Swiss immigrant John Sutter receives permission from the Mexican government to build a colony called Sutter's Fort in California.
4. Spain and the United States settled their land claims over Oregon Country in the Adams-Onís Treaty.
5. An army of some 50,000 Indians and mestizos revolt against Spanish rule in New Spain.

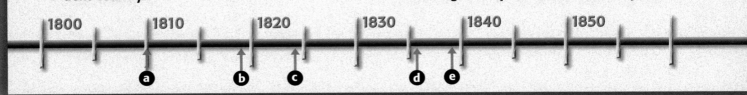

| 1800 | 1810 | 1820 | 1830 | 1840 | 1850 |

a   **b**   **c**   **d**   **e**

3. **Geographic Diversity** Why did missionaries travel to Oregon Country?

Thinking Critically

1. **Making Comparisons** How was life in New Spain different from that in the northern United States?

2. **Determining the Strength of an Argument** Do you think the Mexican government made a good decision in limiting the number of immigrants to Texas? Explain your answer.

3. **Identifying Cause and Effect** What effect did the Panic of 1837 have on westward settlement?

Building Your Portfolio

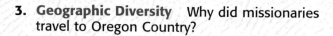

Complete the following activities individually or in groups.

1. **Heading West** Imagine that you are the leader of a wagon train preparing to head west to Oregon Country or California. Prepare a set of guidelines for your wagon train instructing people on what things they need to bring and what they should expect to find on the trail and in their new homes. Also create a simple map indicating the route you will take on your journey West.

2. **Art of the American West** Select an artist of the American West and write a critique of one or more of that person's works. Artists may include, but are not limited to, the following: George Catlin, Karl Bodmer, Frederick Remington, Charles Russell, Alfred Jacob Miller, John Mix Stanley, Paul Kane, Seth Eastman, George Caleb Bingham, Carl Wimar, Albert Bierstadt, and Frank Marryat. Use your textbook and the library to research your artist and find examples of the person's work. Your critique should examine the artist's point of view, use of color, and choice of subject matter. Your critique should also include your own interpretation of the possible meaning or significance of at least one of the artist's works.

Writing About History

1. **Expressing** Imagine that you are Stephen F. Austin in 1834. Write a short speech to give to the Mexican government in which you explain the feelings of Texans about the conflicts with Mexico.

2. **Describing** Write a paragraph describing how immigration changed life in the territories of northern Mexico.

Linking Geography and History

1. **Human-Environment Interaction** What difficulties did travelers on the Oregon Trail face?

2. **Movement** What trails did American traders and immigrants take to reach California and the Southwest? What lands did they cross, and what were some of the dangers?

History Skills
Workshop

Using Primary Sources On February 23, 1836, a large Mexican army surrounded the defenders of the Alamo, who were led by William Travis. Read the following excerpt from a letter Travis wrote and answer the following questions: (a) What is Travis's situation at the Alamo? (b) What will happen if Travis does not surrender? (c) Why do you think Travis addresses his letter to all Americans and not just to Texans?

Commandancy of the Alamo Bejar,

Feb. 24, 1836

To the People of Texas & all Americans in the world Fellow Citizens & Compatriots:

I am besieged, by a thousand or more of the Mexicans under Santa Anna. I have sustained [withstood] a continual bombardment & cannonade for 24 hours & have not lost a man. The enemy has demanded a surrender at discretion [without conditions], otherwise the garrison is to be put to the sword, if the fort is taken.

■ CHAPTER 17 ■
Manifest Destiny and War
(1840–1860)

In 1845 the editors of the Washington *Union*, a Democratic newspaper, urged Americans to acquire Texas and expand westward. "Let the great measure of annexation [of Texas] be accomplished," the editors wrote. "The road to California will be open to us." As more Americans began settling in the West, conflicts arose between expansionists, antiexpansionists, and the many cultures already living in the region.

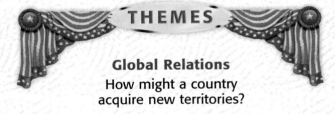

THEMES

Global Relations
How might a country acquire new territories?

Cultural Diversity
What conflicts might arise when different groups come into contact for the first time?

Geographic Diversity
How might a large group of people organize a long migration?

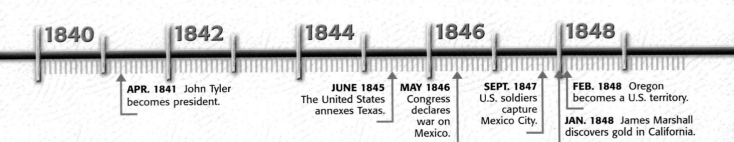

1840　　**1842**　　**1844**　　**1846**　　**1848**

APR. 1841 John Tyler becomes president.

JUNE 1845 The United States annexes Texas.

MAY 1846 Congress declares war on Mexico.

SEPT. 1847 U.S. soldiers capture Mexico City.

FEB. 1848 Oregon becomes a U.S. territory.

JAN. 1848 James Marshall discovers gold in California.

Manifest Destiny and Expansion

Reading Focus

How did Americans' belief in manifest destiny affect western expansion?

How did the United States acquire Oregon and Texas?

What events led to the Mexican War?

Key Terms

manifest destiny

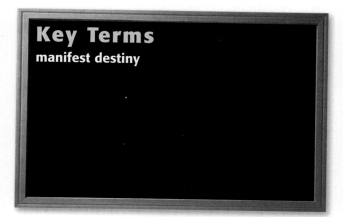

I N A SPEECH TO CONGRESS, *South Carolina senator John C. Calhoun described the great changes he had witnessed during his lifetime. "In the period of thirty-two years which have elapsed [passed] since I took my seat . . . [the] frontier has receded [moved] 1,000 miles to the west," he noted proudly. Looking to the future, he declared, "Our population is rolling toward the shores of the Pacific with an impetus [force] greater than what we realize." Calhoun believed that if the United States was patient and avoided unnecessary wars, it would eventually become the strongest nation in the world.*

One of several magazines that supported western expansion

IMAGE ON LEFT PAGE: *U.S. soldiers entering Mexico City in 1847*

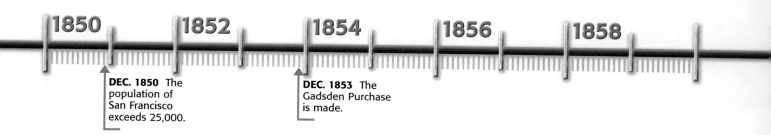

1850 | 1852 | 1854 | 1856 | 1858

DEC. 1850 The population of San Francisco exceeds 25,000.

DEC. 1853 The Gadsden Purchase is made.

★ America Expands

By the 1840s many Americans shared Senator Calhoun's belief that the United States was meant to expand across the continent to the Pacific Ocean and that nothing could stop this growth from taking place. This expansionist idea became known as **manifest destiny**, from an article by John O'Sullivan, a New York editor. O'Sullivan declared:

> ❝The American claim is by the right of our manifest destiny to overspread and to possess the whole of the continent which Providence [fate] has given us for the development of the great experiment of liberty.❞

He added, "We are the nation of human progress, and who will, what can, set limits to our onward march?"

Belief in manifest destiny encouraged many Americans to build settlements beyond the boundaries of the United States, in places such as California, Oregon, and Texas. One woman, for example, recalled the stories told by an Oregon pioneer. "He said: 'Friends, you are traveling to the garden of Eden, a land flowing with milk and honey.'" People who favored expansion hoped that this movement of people to the West would prevent crowding in the eastern cities by allowing the growing population there to find new opportunities on the frontier.

Painting of the Rocky Mountains, which settlers had to cross on their way to Oregon Country

Most supporters of manifest destiny ignored the fact that thousands of American Indians and Mexicans had been living in the West for centuries. Many Americans believed that taking western land against the will of its inhabitants was acceptable because, as they saw it, the region had not been fully developed with agriculture. Supporters of manifest destiny such as Missouri senator Thomas Hart Benton argued that American settlers would also improve the West by spreading democracy to the peoples they conquered.

★ The Election of 1844

President John Tyler helped make western expansion a critical issue in the election of 1844. Elected as William Henry Harrison's vice president in 1840, Tyler became president when Harrison died in April 1841. Tyler was a pro-slavery Whig from Virginia who wanted to extend the political power of the southern slave states. He believed that the annexation of Texas would help the South by adding another slave state to the nation.

Tyler's ideas about Texas sparked a national debate. Many Whigs disagreed with his expansionist beliefs, and as a result, he was too unpopular within his own party to run in the 1844 election. Instead, the Whigs selected Senator Henry Clay of Kentucky as their candidate. Clay began his presidential campaign by opposing the annexation of Texas. After being pressured by southern voters, however, he decided half-heartedly to support annexation. His decision angered many of his original backers.

The Democratic Party chose former Tennessee governor James K. Polk as its presidential candidate. Polk campaigned aggressively for the annexation of both Texas and Oregon. The election was further complicated by a third-party candidate and rumors that the Republic of Texas might abolish slavery and ally itself with Great Britain. When the results had been tallied, Polk defeated Clay by a very narrow margin. Clay believed that he had lost the election as a result of "a most extraordinary combination of adverse [bad] circumstances." Polk, on the other hand, insisted that his victory was a sign that the American people supported his aggressive views on westward expansion.

James K. Polk

James K. Polk was born into a wealthy Tennessee farming family in 1795. After graduating from college, Polk practiced law before serving in the House of Representatives. He later became governor of Tennessee. Despite his accomplishments, Polk was not well known nationally when the Democratic Party nominated him as its presidential candidate. He did not let this discourage him during the campaign, however. He promised voters that as president he would make every effort to annex Texas and acquire Oregon. As president, Polk considered himself "the hardest working man in this country."

 Acquiring New Territory

President Polk quickly set out to fulfill his campaign promises. He was confident that he could bring Oregon and Texas into the United States.

The Dispute over Oregon

In the 1810s and 1820s, Russia and Spain had given up their claims to Oregon Country. Britain and the United States had meanwhile agreed to jointly occupy the region. As more Americans settled there they began to insist that Oregon become part of the United States. Polk wanted to protect these settlers' interests. Other politicians noted that Oregon Country would provide a Pacific port for the growing U.S. trade with China.

Britain disagreed strongly with the United States over where in Oregon to draw the U.S.-Canada border. War between the two countries seemed possible. American expansionists cried "Fifty-four forty or fight!" referring to the contested northern boundary of Oregon Country. However, neither side truly wanted a conflict in the region. Congressman Robert C. Winthrop told Congress, "This question, from its very nature, is . . . one for negotiation, compromise, and amicable [friendly] adjustment."

In 1846 Britain and the United States signed a treaty that gave the United States all Oregon land south of the 49th parallel. This treaty established the present-day border between Canada and the United States. Oregon became a U.S. territory in February 1848.

Texas Becomes a State

Polk and his supporters also wanted to acquire Texas. By March 1845 Congress had already approved annexation and needed only the support of the Republic of Texas. Many Americans continued to move to Texas, and Texas politicians hoped that joining the United States would help solve the republic's financial and military problems. Editor John O'Sullivan spoke for the expansionists when he wrote, "It is time . . . for common sense to give in to what is inevitable." Texas voters approved annexation in June, and Texas became a U.S. state in December 1845. This action angered the Mexican government, which considered Texas a "stolen province."

Democrats celebrated their victory over their Whig opponents when Congress voted to annex Texas in March 1845.

★ War Along the Border

Mexico reacted to the annexation of Texas by cutting off all diplomatic relations with the United States. In addition, Mexican officials ordered the removal of American settlers from California and banned further American immigration there. In addition, Mexico continued to reject the Texas and U.S. claim that the Rio Grande marked the southern border of Texas. "Why not declare the limits of the rebel state [Texas] extended to . . . the capital [of Mexico]?" asked one Mexican official sarcastically. The Mexican government insisted instead that the real border lay along the Nueces River, many miles to the north.

In June 1845 Polk ordered General Zachary Taylor to take U.S. troops into the disputed border region. Polk claimed that this force was intended to protect Texas from a possible Mexican invasion. Around the same time, Polk sent diplomat John Slidell to Mexico City to try to negotiate the Texas boundary dispute. Polk also instructed Slidell to offer to buy California and New Mexico from the Mexican government for $30 million. However, when Slidell arrived in Mexico City, officials there

General Zachary Taylor

refused to speak to him. Slidell angrily reported back to Polk that negotiations with the Mexican government were no longer possible.

In March 1846 General Taylor marched his troops to the Rio Grande, across from Mexican forces stationed near the town of Matamoros, Mexico. In April the Mexican commander warned that "arms and arms alone must decide the question" if General Taylor did not remove the U.S. forces from the region. When Taylor did not move, Mexican soldiers crossed the river and attacked a group of 63 U.S. soldiers, killing 11 of them, wounding 5 others, and capturing the rest.

When the news reached Polk, he quickly prepared a message to give to Congress. Speaking on May 11, 1846, he announced:

> ❝ **Mexico has passed the boundary of the United States, has invaded our territory, and shed American blood upon the American soil. . . . The two nations are now at war.** ❞

Polk's war message had its desired effect. Two days later Congress declared war on Mexico.

SECTION 1 REVIEW

Identify and explain the significance of the following:
- **manifest destiny**
- **John O'Sullivan**
- **John Tyler**
- **Henry Clay**
- **James K. Polk**
- **Zachary Taylor**

Reading for Content Understanding

1 **Main Idea** Why did Great Britain and the United States almost go to war in the 1840s? What were the results of the treaty the two nations signed in 1846?

2 **Main Idea** How did Texas become part of the United States?

3 **Global Relations** What did manifest destiny mean to its American supporters? How did the belief in manifest destiny influence U.S. foreign policy?

4 **Writing** *Informing* Write a brief article announcing Congress's declaration of war on Mexico. Be sure to include the background events that have led to this declaration.

5 **Critical Thinking** *Evaluating* Do you think Mexico should have negotiated with the United States over the Texas border dispute? Explain your answer.

The Mexican War

Reading Focus

How did Americans react to the declaration of war against Mexico?

How did the war progress?

What were the terms of the treaty that ended the Mexican War?

Key Terms

Bear Flag Revolt
Treaty of Guadalupe Hidalgo
Mexican Cession
Gadsden Purchase

THE DAYS FOLLOWING *Polk's war message to Congress were full of angry debate. Some members of the Whig Party believed that the president had intentionally started a conflict with Mexico. Congressman Garrett Davis of Kentucky said bitterly, "It is our own President who began this war." The House of Representatives, however, stood firmly by the president, stating in its declaration of war that the conflict was started "by the act of the Republic of Mexico."*

An American soldier during the Mexican War

★ Responses to War

News of the declaration of war spread across the country. At the beginning of the war, the U.S. Army was greatly outnumbered by Mexican forces. U.S. soldiers had better weapons and equipment, however. To strengthen the army during the Mexican War, the U.S. government called for 50,000 volunteers to enlist.

The New Patriotism

Around 200,000 volunteers answered the call. Many were young men who saw the war as a grand adventure in a foreign land. The Mexican War was the first U.S. war fought primarily on foreign soil. It was also the first U.S. conflict covered by many newspapers. Reporters took advantage of railroads and the newly invented telegraph to send their articles back to the East very quickly. News thus reached American homes much faster than in previous wars. In addition, the war was one of the first to be photographed.

On the homefront many men and women supported the soldiers by collecting supplies or writing patriotic poems and songs. For example, one popular war song encouraged soldiers to "Arm and strike for liberty!"

Manifest Destiny and War **517**

For many Americans, the war strengthened national pride. Many people felt that the war was justified because they believed that it would result in the spread of republican values.

Antiwar Sentiment

Not all Americans supported the war, however. Many members of the Whig Party thought that the conflict was unjustified and unnecessary. A young Whig congressman named Abraham Lincoln questioned whether the fighting had really started on American soil. "If I should claim your land by word of mouth [alone], that certainly would not make it mine," he insisted. The war also upset antiexpansionists and people who were opposed to armed conflict. Transcendentalist writer and philosopher Henry David Thoreau was so upset by the war that he went to jail rather than pay taxes, which he thought would be used to support the fighting in Mexico.

Antiwar political cartoonists made fun of American war volunteers.

The Granger Collection, New York

Northern abolitionists opposed the Mexican War because they were concerned that the southern states would expand slavery into any new lands the United States might acquire in the Southwest if it won the war. Some of the pro-slavery southerners, on the other hand, worried that new territories might instead ban slavery. This concern led southern politicians such as John C. Calhoun to question the goals of the Mexican War.

Thoreau's fellow transcendentalist Ralph Waldo Emerson predicted that these disagreements over the Mexican War would divide Americans:

❝ The United States will conquer Mexico, but it will be as the man swallows the arsenic [a poison], which brings him down in turn. Mexico will poison us. ❞

★ American Victories

While supporters and opponents of the war argued, the fighting had already started. Even before the official declaration of war, General Zachary Taylor's soldiers fought and won battles south of the Nueces River, at Palo Alto and Resaca de la Palma on May 8 and 9, 1846.

Early Battles

Taylor's victories drove the Mexican troops back into Mexico. Taylor then crossed the Rio Grande and occupied Matamoros. While Taylor waited for reinforcements, Polk ordered General Stephen Kearny to attack New Mexico. Kearny followed the Santa Fe Trail into Santa Fe and took the city without a fight in August 1846. After claiming the entire territory of New Mexico for the United States, Kearny prepared to march to California.

Kit Carson, an experienced explorer and army scout, guided Kearny and his western forces toward San Diego. Near San Diego, Kearny's army joined forces with U.S. Navy commodore Robert Stockton. The navy had been sent to blockade Mexican ports on the Pacific coast as well as those on the Gulf of Mexico.

Mexican cavalry charging against U.S. Army cannons in the Battle of Palo Alto

"Civil Disobedience"
Henry David Thoreau

Transcendentalist Henry David Thoreau was one of the many Americans who protested the Mexican War. He even went to jail rather than pay taxes to a government whose actions he strongly opposed. Later his beliefs in peaceful resistance inspired leaders such as Mahatma Gandhi of India and Martin Luther King Jr. of the United States. In the following excerpt from his essay "Civil Disobedience," Thoreau discusses a citizen's individual social responsibility.

I heartily accept the motto, "That government is best which governs least"; and I should like to see it acted up to more rapidly and systematically. Carried out, it finally amounts to this, which also I believe—"That government is best which governs not at all"; and when men are prepared for it, that will be the kind of government which they will have. Government is at best but an expedient [means to an end]; but most governments are usually, and all governments are sometimes, inexpedient. . . . The government itself, which is only the mode [method] which the people have chosen to execute their will, is equally liable to be abused and perverted [twisted] before the people can act through it. Witness the present Mexican war, the work of . . . a few individuals using the standing government as their tool; for, in the outset, the people would not have consented to this measure. . . .

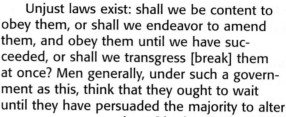

Henry David Thoreau argued for non-violent opposition to the Mexican War.

Unjust laws exist: shall we be content to obey them, or shall we endeavor to amend them, and obey them until we have succeeded, or shall we transgress [break] them at once? Men generally, under such a government as this, think that they ought to wait until they have persuaded the majority to alter them [the laws]. They think that, if they should resist, the remedy would be worse than the evil. But it is the fault of the government itself that the remedy *is* worse than the evil. *It* makes it worse. Why is it not more apt [suitable] to anticipate and provide for reform? Why does it not cherish its wise minority? . . .

If the injustice is part of the necessary friction of the machine of government, let it go, let it go: perchance [maybe] it will wear smooth—certainly the machine will wear out. If the injustice has a spring, or a pulley, or a rope, or a crank, exclusively [only] for itself, then perhaps you may consider whether the remedy will not be worse than the evil; but if it is of such a nature that it requires you to be the agent of injustice to another, then, I say, break the law.

Understanding Literature

1. Under what conditions does Thoreau support breaking the law?

2. Do you agree with Thoreau that it is acceptable to peacefully break a law that is supported by the government? Why or why not?

The Bear Flag Revolt

As General Kearny marched toward southern California in June 1846, a small group of American settlers near the town of Sonoma revolted against the Californios. These rebels declared that California was an independent republic. To represent themselves and the new republic, the rebels created a flag with a single star and a grizzly bear. The **Bear Flag Revolt**, as it was called, soon gained the support of Captain John C. Frémont, a well-known army explorer. Frémont had been leading an expedition across the Sierra Nevada when he heard of the revolt. He quickly declared that he would conquer all of California, although he did not even know that the United States and Mexico were at war!

California Conquered

As American settlers formed the Bear Flag Republic in the north, Commodore Stockton planned the naval invasion of California from the south. With support from Kearny's forces, Stockton captured Los Angeles, San Gabriel, and San Diego. Commodore John Drake Sloat seized the provincial capital of California at Monterey. In August of 1846, Stockton declared that California belonged to the United States. Some Californios continued to resist the U.S. occupation, however.

For a brief period, Stockton took political control of California. He made Frémont governor, despite Polk's having appointed Kearny to the position. Kearny accused Stockton of "doing that for which you have no authority & preventing me from complying with [following] the President's orders." Eventually, Kearny regained control. Frémont, who had supported Stockton, was later court-martialed for his actions, and he resigned from the U.S. Army.

★ The War's End

In Mexico, Taylor finally received his reinforcements. He immediately pushed deep into Mexican territory.

A Change in Command

Taylor's army soon drove the Mexican army farther into the interior, to the heavily fortified city of Monterrey. There the U.S. troops defeated the Mexicans after a hard-fought battle. While both sides spent a few months maneuvering for position, General Santa Anna once again took over Mexico's government. He led his army north in February 1847, clashing with Taylor's forces at Buena Vista.

The Mexican War, 1846–1847

Learning from Maps Within months of declaring war, U.S. forces had captured all the major cities and towns along the coast of California and controlled much of the territory north of Mexico City.

Movement Which military commander led the U.S. forces from Santa Fe to Chihuahua?

Santa Anna sent the outnumbered U.S. soldiers a note demanding their surrender. Officer Thomas L. Crittenden replied, "General Taylor never surrenders." After two days of hard fighting, Santa Anna's men retreated under the cover of darkness. One soldier recalled that in the morning the exhausted U.S. troops began shouting, "The enemy has fled! The field is ours!"

Taylor's success earned him popularity with his troops and made him a war hero back home. Soldiers called him Old Rough and Ready. Taylor's popularity troubled President Polk. Taylor was a Whig rumored to have plans of running against Polk in the presidential election of 1848. Polk was also concerned that Taylor, who was a brave leader but not a great planner, would be unable to win the war. For these reasons, Polk replaced Taylor with General Winfield Scott, known to the troops as Old Fuss and Feathers.

Scott sailed down to the port of Veracruz, which was the strongest fortress in Mexico. He launched a huge attack on the port city, laying siege for eight days. On March 29, after an 88-hour bombardment in which the Americans shelled the city day and night, Veracruz fell to Scott's army. The next part of the strategy was to attack Mexico City.

Mexico Surrenders

Following a route similar to the one taken by Spanish conquistador Hernán Cortés in 1519,

General Winfield Scott's capture of Veracruz was a critical U.S. victory.

Scott's men pushed some 200 miles inland to the heart of Mexico. Santa Anna tried to stop the U.S. forces at Cerro Gordo in mid-April. With a daring uphill attack on the Mexican position, U.S. soldiers won an important victory. By August 1847, U.S. troops were at the edge of Mexico City.

Portraits of the niños heroes *who leaped to their deaths at Chapultepec*

Following a truce that failed to lead to peace negotiations, Scott finally ordered a massive assault on Mexico City. Mexican soldiers and civilians fought fierce battles on the outskirts and in the neighborhoods of the capital. At a military school atop the steep and fortified hill of Chapultepec, young cadets bravely defended their position. Their situation was hopeless, however, and some jumped to their deaths rather than surrender to the invading forces. Huge statues of these heroic cadets were later built at the park that was created on the site. On September 14, 1847, U.S. soldiers captured the Mexican capital. Santa Anna fled the country soon afterward.

⭐ New Territories

During the war, President Polk had assigned State Department official Nicholas Trist to negotiate a peace treaty with Mexico. Trist had little success for months, but he finally got his chance when Scott captured Mexico City.

The Treaty of Guadalupe Hidalgo

Meanwhile, Polk had ordered Trist back to Washington to receive new instructions. Not wanting to lose his chance for a treaty, the diplomat ignored his orders. He remained in Mexico and negotiated the **Treaty of Guadalupe Hidalgo**. Signed in February 1848, this treaty ceded, or turned

Manifest Destiny and War **521**

over, much of Mexico's northern territory to the United States. This land became known as the **Mexican Cession**. The Mexican Cession included the present-day states of California, Nevada, and Utah; most of Arizona and New Mexico; parts of Colorado and Wyoming; and the area claimed by Texas north of the Rio Grande. This totaled more than 500,000 square miles and increased the size of the United States by almost 25 percent.

In exchange for this vast territory, the United States agreed to pay Mexico $15 million and to assume claims of more than $3 million held by American citizens against the Mexican government. The treaty also promised that Mexicans in the Mexican Cession would be "protected in the free enjoyment of their liberty and property, and secured in the free exercise of their religion."

When news of the treaty reached Washington, Polk was so upset with Trist for ignoring his orders that he fired him. The treaty itself sparked a controversy. Some Americans wanted to take all of Mexico. Others—such as Whigs, antislavery and antiwar supporters, and people who thought that Mexicans would not make good republican citizens—opposed the Mexican Cession. Polk responded to these arguments by pointing out that if the treaty were ratified, "there will be added to the United States an immense empire, the value

The Treaty of Guadalupe Hidalgo

of which twenty years hence it would be difficult to calculate." The Senate ratified the treaty in March 1848.

The Gadsden Purchase

After the Mexican War, some Americans wanted to ensure that any southern railroad to California would be completely on American soil. James Gadsden, U.S. minister to Mexico, negotiated with Mexico, leading to the **Gadsden Purchase** in December 1853. Under the terms of the purchase, the U.S. government paid Mexico $10 million in exchange for a strip of land that includes the southern parts of present-day Arizona and New Mexico. With this purchase, the continental boundaries of the United States were finally fixed.

SECTION 2 REVIEW

Identify and explain the significance of the following:

- **Henry David Thoreau**
- **Stephen Kearny**
- **Robert Stockton**
- **Bear Flag Revolt**
- **John C. Frémont**
- **Winfield Scott**
- **Nicholas Trist**

- **Treaty of Guadalupe Hidalgo**
- **Mexican Cession**
- **Gadsden Purchase**

Reading for Content Understanding

1 **Main Idea** How did some Americans support the Mexican War? What reasons did other Americans give for opposing the war?

2 **Main Idea** How did the inland attack on Monterrey, Mexico, followed by an attack on the port city of Veracruz, affect the outcome of the war?

3 **Global Relations** What did each side gain in the Treaty of Guadalupe Hidalgo?

4 **Writing** *Describing* Imagine that you are a reporter covering the events of the Mexican War. Write a short newspaper article describing how the United States gained control of California.

5 **Critical Thinking** *Making Comparisons* How do you think the news coverage of the Mexican War compares with the coverage of modern wars?

More Settlers Head West

Reading Focus

What conflicts did new U.S. settlement cause in the Southwest?

How did various cultures interact in the Southwest?

Who were the Mormons, and what did they accomplish in the West?

Key Terms

Mormons

Mormon Trail

N HER NOVEL **The Squatter and the Don,** *María Amparo Ruiz de Burton described the Californios' struggle to keep their land after the Mexican War. A Californio landowner herself, Burton put her family's anger and despair into the words of her characters, Doña Josefa Alamar and Don Mariano Alamar. "Is it possible that there is no law to protect us; to protect our property?" asked Doña Josefa. "The treaty said that our rights would be the same as those enjoyed by all other American citizens," Don Mariano replied. "[But] we have had no one to speak for us."*

Title page of The Squatter and the Don

Courtesy The Bancroft Library

★ Conflicts over Land

After the Mexican War, longtime residents of the Southwest faced a flood of traders, trappers, settlers, and speculators moving to the region. The legal, economic, and social discrimination faced by most Mexicans, Mexican Americans, and American Indians made asserting their rights difficult. This situation led to a struggle between American newcomers and longtime inhabitants over the control of land and other valuable resources, such as water and minerals.

Legal Disputes

In Article 10 of an early draft of the Treaty of Guadalupe Hidalgo, the United States promised to protect the land rights previously granted by Mexico or Spain to the residents of the Mexican Cession. However, this article was later deleted from the final version of the treaty. The treaty promised to protect residents' property rights, but the differences between Mexican land laws and U.S. land laws led to great confusion. The U.S. government often forced Mexican American landowners to go to court to prove that they had

Manifest Destiny and War **523**

a title to their land. The court costs were often as much as the land was worth and frequently bankrupted landowners. The problem was particularly bad in California. In the 1850s magazine writer John S. Hittell described the situation faced by the Californios after the Mexican War:

A Mexican family during the 1800s making tortillas at home

> **It was not their fault that the Mexican land system differed from the American. . . . It was severe hardship for owners of land under grants from Mexico, that they should be required to sue the government of the United States, or lose their land.** "

In Colorado, New Mexico, and Texas, Mexican and Mexican American landholders faced problems similar to those in California. Mexican legal concepts such as community property or community water rights were usually ignored by new settlers. Conflicts over the ownership of cattle and sheep were also common. Small ranchers often lost their property. Some wealthy Tejanos attempted to protect their land and livestock holdings by marrying into powerful American families.

Southwestern Indians

The steady arrival of additional settlers and the policies of the U.S. government dramatically affected American Indians in the Southwest. In some areas, Indian inhabitants were soon outnumbered by vast numbers of new white settlers, who often tried to take control of valuable water resources and seize grazing land from Indians. Cattle ranchers in California, for example, seized many Indian lands by force. In the process, the new arrivals usually showed little respect for Indian holy places, such as mountain lakes and burial grounds.

Indian tribes such as the Navajo and the Apache tried to protect their land and livestock from the new settlers. Indian raiding parties also took settlers' cattle and sometimes attacked settlements. In response, angry whites often attacked not only the raiding parties but also friendly Indian tribes or villages, thus creating new conflicts. The government responded by building a series of army posts in the Southwest.

★ Cultural Encounters

Despite conflicts over land and resources, Indian, Mexican, and Anglo cultures influenced one another in the Southwest. As American settlers made homes for themselves in the Southwest, they adopted some of the customs and practices of the peoples they encountered.

Language and Customs

In settlements with large Mexican populations, laws were often printed in both English and Spanish. The Spanish language also remained important for trade and daily life throughout California, New Mexico, and Texas. One Texan described the typical scene at San Antonio's Military Plaza:

> " [You could hear] a babble of voices from three or four languages . . . [but] almost everyone spoke Spanish and most of the business was conducted in this common language. . . . The political border [between the United States and Mexico] was at the Rio Grande, but Military Plaza was the commercial and social border between the countries. "

Place-names throughout the Southwest—such as San Antonio, San Diego, and Taos—also reflect the region's Mexican and Indian heritage.

Communities throughout the Southwest regularly celebrated both Mexican and American holidays. *Diez y Seis de Septiembre*, for example, which celebrated the declaration of the *Grito de Dolores*, became a popular holiday in Texas. In addition, American settlers and French and German immigrants in towns such as San Antonio preserved many of their traditional customs.

The Southwestern Economy

Mexican and Indian knowledge and traditions influenced the local economies of many American communities that developed in the Southwest. Mexican Americans taught Anglo settlers about mining in the region's rugged mountains. The ranching communities first developed by Mexican settlers also expanded as new ranchers moved in and new markets became available. In addition, Mexican Americans introduced new types of saddles and other equipment to American ranchers. Adobe, a building material first developed by the Pueblo Indians and then adopted by the Spanish, was commonly used by American settlers in New Mexico and California. In addition, new settlers adopted Mexican and Indian foods such as tamales, tortillas, and beans.

Navajo woman weaving a woolen blanket using traditional methods

Trade also transformed the Southwest and its inhabitants, as even small communities were pulled into the expanding market economy. For example, the Navajo increased their production of handwoven woolen blankets to sell to Americans. The Navajo also developed a reputation as skilled silversmiths. They had learned the craft after being introduced to metalworking by Spanish settlers.

Americans, in turn, brought manufactured goods and capital to the Southwest. The introduction of firearms, other trade goods, and new breeds of animals from elsewhere in the United States gradually changed the economies of many Mexican American and Indian communities in the Southwest.

★ The Mormons

One group of American settlers traveled to the West in search of religious freedom. In 1830 a young man named Joseph Smith founded the Church of Jesus Christ of Latter-Day Saints in western New York. The members of this church became known as **Mormons**. Smith told his followers that he had found and translated a set of golden tablets containing religious revelations. These writings became the *Book of Mormon*.

Joseph Smith

The Mormons emphasized hard work and community, and their church membership grew rapidly. However, some Mormon beliefs and practices made them the target of persecution. For example, some Mormon men practiced polygamy—in which one man is married to several women at the same time.

In the early 1830s Smith and his growing number of converts left New York to form communities first in Ohio and then in Missouri. The first community went bankrupt during the Panic of 1837, while the second was abandoned when the Mormons were chased away by a mob of neighbors. The next settlement, at Nauvoo, Illinois, was quite successful, attracting some 15,000 converts. However, the strong-willed Smith faced challenges from some of his followers and from those who opposed his religion. An anti-Mormon mob murdered Smith in jail in 1844. "I can tell you it is a sorrowful time here at present," wrote Mormon Sarah Scott after Smith's death.

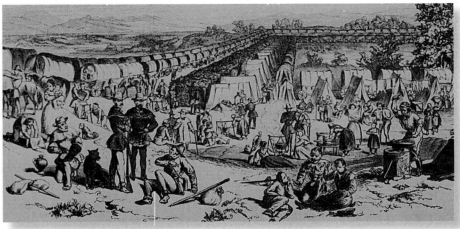
Brigham Young led the first Mormon settlers to the West in a large, well-organized wagon train.

A New Home out West

Following Smith's murder, Brigham Young rose to become the head of the Mormon Church. The Mormons decided to move west to build a new community. Young chose present-day Utah as the destination for his followers. At the time, Utah was still Mexican territory, outside the boundaries of the United States.

Young was a gifted leader who carefully organized the long trek west. An advance party arrived at a pass overlooking the Great Salt Lake in July 1847. Follower Erastus Snow recalled Young's words: "This is the place whereon we will plant our feet." These pioneers began preparing the area for other Mormon immigrants.

Thousands of Mormons took to the **Mormon Trail**, which closely paralleled the Oregon Trail for much of the way west. Many people traveled with heavy handcarts that they pushed or pulled along the rough ground. Mormon pioneer Martha Haven wrote home, "Mother, these western moves are hard . . . on the people." American Mormons fleeing persecution in the East and the Midwest were joined by converts immigrating from Great Britain and Scandinavia.

The Mormons chose a desert valley for their new home. The principal Mormon settlement of Salt Lake City was a carefully planned and prosperous community with broad roads and surrounding farms. Lots were spacious, and streets were organized in a gridlike pattern. Soon after his arrival in 1847, Brigham Young had designated the site for the Mormons' Great Temple, and construction was well under way by 1853. Salt Lake City soon became the center of Mormon settlement. In December 1860 the Mormon population of Utah stood at about 40,000.

Mormon settlers hauling a handcart across the Great Plains

Water Use in the West

The Mormons established a very disciplined community. Brigham Young told one of the first groups of Mormon pioneers, "Those that do not like our looks and customs are at liberty to go where they please." Young made it clear that those who stayed must follow community rules: "If they remain

Linking Past to Present

Water Usage in the West

When the Mormons arrived at the Great Salt Lake in Utah on July 24, 1847, they saw a barren plain. The Mormons, however, considered the place their Promised Land.

They quickly dammed one of the streams that came down from the mountains, flooded the soil, and planted their first crops. Within a few weeks, 1,800 more settlers had arrived.

Brigham Young's welcoming words to the new settlers expressed the Mormons' belief in cooperation to make the best use of their scarce resources:

❝ *[T]here shall be no private ownership of the streams that come out of the canyons, nor the timber that grows on the hills. These belong to the people: all the people.* ❞

The Theodore Roosevelt Dam on the Salt River in Arizona is one of many modern dams controlling water flows throughout the Southwest.

Mormon leaders allowed farmers only enough water to properly irrigate their fields. This leadership and cooperation helped the Mormons build a thriving agricultural community in the Utah desert.

Over the years, as more and more settlers made their way west, the U.S. government helped them meet the demands of the harsh environment. In the 1860s agents from the Department of Agriculture taught farmers on the Great Plains how to dig deep to find water. The department also introduced farmers to planting and harvesting techniques that conserved valuable water resources.

Then in 1902 the government established the Bureau of Reclamation—part of the Department of the Interior—to construct irrigation works. These projects enabled farmers to settle and grow crops on even more western lands. Because water supplies were concentrated in a few areas in the West, the Bureau of Reclamation built dams, reservoirs, and canals to bring additional water to dry regions.

Today the bureau manages all the water in the 17 states west of the Mississippi River. It delivers water to about 10 million acres of land and provides flood control and community assistance during droughts. One of the agency's most important goals is to increase water availability to the millions of people who live in the West. To do so, it uses technology, expertise, and cooperation. In 1997 U.S. Secretary of the Interior Bruce Babbitt announced that water from the Colorado River would be transferred to cities in California, not just to farms. Babbitt was confident that the new plan would benefit everybody. "If we keep at it," he stated, "we will be able to assure that every need will be addressed."

Understanding What You Read

1. Why was cooperation so important to the Mormon settlement in Utah?

2. What laws did the Mormons pass to enable equal water distribution?

3. How might states work together today to share water?

Western settlers used crude machinery and extensive labor to dam rivers during the 1800s.

or decrease the flow of water or change its direction. These restrictions generally prevented landowners from constructing dams, because doing so would infringe upon the water rights of neighbors.

with us they must obey the laws sanctioned [approved] by us." One of the most important laws established by the Mormons involved water rights.

Eastern Water Laws

In the East, water-use laws were intended to protect every person's access to this precious and necessary resource. Laws commonly required owners whose land bordered streams or rivers to maintain a free flow of water downstream. Specifically, such rules stated that landowners could not increase

Western Water Rights

In the generally dry climate of the West, large-scale agriculture was not possible without irrigation. Dams and canals were required to channel the scarce supplies of water to the fields. This need conflicted with the accepted eastern tradition of equal access to water.

Brigham Young established a strict code regulating water rights for the Mormon community. Under this code, the first person to use the water had full rights to its use, provided that the water was used for beneficial purposes such as farming, mining, or manufacturing. In any dispute over water use, the good of the community would outweigh the interests of individuals. Young's approach helped the Mormons make the desert bloom with crops. It also stood as an example for modern water laws throughout the West by its emphasis on the needs of the community.

SECTION 3 REVIEW

Identify and explain the significance of the following:
- Joseph Smith
- Mormons
- Brigham Young
- Mormon Trail

Reading for Content Understanding

1 **Main Idea** What events led Mormons to move to Utah?

2 **Main Idea** Explain the similarities and differences between the kinds of water-rights laws developed in the eastern and the western United States.

3 **Geographic Diversity** *Movement* What conflicts arose between American settlers, American Indians, and Mexican Americans as more settlers moved into the West and the Southwest?

4 **Writing** *Creating* Imagine that you are a traveler to the Southwest. Write a journal entry describing how Mexican, American Indian, and Anglo cultures are mingling in the region.

5 **Critical Thinking** *Drawing Conclusions* Why do you think it was important for U.S. settlers to adopt some of the customs and practices of the people already living in the Southwest?

The Gold Rush

Reading Focus

Why did many people head west to California in 1849, and how did they get there?

How did miners prospect for gold?

What was life like in gold rush mining camps and towns?

Key Terms

California Gold Rush
forty-niners
prospect

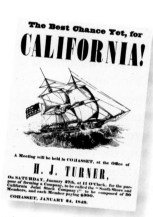

IN 1849 BAYARD TAYLOR traveled west to report on the discovery of gold in California. Taylor spent five months wandering around the gold camps and mines. Mining gold had little appeal to him until he saw the nuggets dug up by one group of miners. "The gold was of the purest quality and most beautiful color," wrote Taylor. Then he admitted, "I confess there was a sudden itching in my fingers to seize the heaviest crowbar and the biggest shovel." Such stories prompted thousands of Americans to race to the gold fields of California in search of a fortune.

Advertisement for travel to California

★ Gold in California

Although the American Indian population of California was declining, in the early 1840s Indians still outnumbered Californios and Americans. On January 24, 1848, James Marshall made a discovery that suddenly changed this situation. Marshall recalled that he was working that day near Sutter's Mill in California when he glanced down:

❝ My eye was caught with the glimpse of something shining in the bottom of the ditch. . . . I reached my hand down and picked it up; it made my heart thump, for I was certain it was gold. The piece was about half the size and of the shape of a pea. ❞

Marshall rushed to tell John Sutter, the owner of the mill. At first, according to Sutter, "I thought something had touched Marshall's brain." When Sutter saw the gold, however, he "was fairly thunderstruck." Both men agreed to keep the discovery a secret, but when they went to examine the work site the next day, they met a Spanish-speaking

Indian worker holding a nugget and shouting, "Oro [gold]! Oro! Oro!"

Sutter's workers soon quit to search for gold. Stories of the discovery spread across the country. President Polk added to the national excitement by confirming the California gold strike in his farewell message to Congress in December 1848.

Newly arrived gold-seekers in San Francisco were forced to live in tent communities on Telegraph Hill as the town struggled to keep up with its rapid growth.

⭐ The Forty-Niners

In 1849 the **California Gold Rush** caused a huge surge in California's population. That year about 100,000 gold-seekers—known as **forty-niners**—came to California hoping to strike it rich. As one Iowa woman who left with her husband to find gold recalled, "At that time the 'gold fever' was contagious, and few, old, or young, escaped the malady [sickness]." Nearly 80 percent of the forty-niners were Americans, while the rest came from all around the world.

Most of the forty-niners braved long and often dangerous journeys to reach California. Many easterners and Europeans took one of two major sea routes. One route wound down the Atlantic and up the Pacific coasts of South America, and the other combined ship and land travel across the Isthmus of Panama or Nicaragua. The trip around Cape Horn at the tip of South America took six to eight months but was fairly safe. The Central American route was much shorter, but travelers had to cross jungles and risk catching deadly diseases such as malaria or yellow fever.

Midwestern gold-seekers usually traveled west in wagon trains along overland routes. Some of these forty-niners took a northern route from Missouri or Iowa through the South Pass of the Rocky Mountains. Others followed a southern trail that went through Santa Fe and the southwestern deserts. With luck a wagon train could cover the roughly 2,000 miles to the gold fields in about three months. Overland travelers were commonly delayed by poor planning, bad weather, and rough terrain, however.

Whatever their method of travel, most forty-niners arrived in San Francisco. Its fine natural harbor and its location not far from the newly-discovered gold strikes made the port town a convenient trade center and a stopping point for travelers. As a result, San Francisco grew more rapidly than any other city in the world, jumping from a population of around 800 in March 1848 to more than 25,000 by 1850.

The Granger Collection, New York

A group of forty-niners searching for gold in a riverbed

⭐ Gold Fever

Few of the forty-niners had any previous gold-mining experience. While some people had quick success, most found the work to be difficult and time-consuming.

Staking a Claim

The forty-niners would **prospect**, or search for gold, along the banks of streams or in shallow surface mines. The early forty-niners worked an area that ran for 70 miles in northern California. Later, the forty-niners began searching for gold farther up into the icy streams of the Sierra Nevada and began carving out mines in the western foothills.

The first person to arrive at a site would "stake a claim." Early miners frequently banded together to prospect for gold. The miners agreed that each would keep a share of whatever gold was discovered. When one group abandoned a claim, more recent arrivals often took it over, hoping for success. Sometimes two or more groups arrived in an area at the same time. In the early gold rush days, before courts were established, this competition led to many arguments, even violent disputes, over claims.

Mining Methods

The mining methods used varied by the time of year and the location of the claim. The most popular method was known as placer mining, which was done along rivers and streams. Placer miners used pans, a rocker/cradle device, or a sluice box to wash gold nuggets out of loose rock and gravel.

Extracting gold from hard rock was much more difficult and expensive. To reach the gold deposits buried in the hills, miners had to dig shafts and tunnels. These tasks were usually pursued by mining companies rather than individual workers. At some locations, miners diverted streams and rivers so that they could search the riverbeds for gold. Sometimes the miners' tree cutting caused soil erosion, and piles of debris washed downstream from mining camps, clogging the rivers.

Striking It Rich

In 1853 California's yearly gold production peaked at more than $60 million. Individual success stories inspired

Mining tools

The California Gold Rush

Learning from Maps California drew national attention after the discovery of gold at Sutter's Mill.

Place What city is located at the junction of three trails and a supply route?

---

many miners. One lucky man pocketed two and a half pounds of gold after only 15 minutes of work. Two African American miners found a rich gold deposit that became known as Negro Hill in honor of their discovery.

The overwhelming majority of gold rush miners did not become rich, however. Forty-niner Alonzo Delano commented that the "lean, meager [thin], worn-out and woe-begone [sorrowful] miner . . . might daily be seen at almost every point in the upper mines." The good luck that made some miners wealthy never came to thousands of gold-seekers who found little but misery and debt.

★ Mining Camps and Towns

Mining camps sprang up wherever enough people gathered to look for gold. These camps had colorful names such as Skunk Gulch, Hangtown, Git-Up-and-Git, and Dry Diggings.

Law and Order

Most mining camps had little local authority, in part because they appeared and disappeared so quickly. Miners also found themselves making money one day and broke the next, as rich claims opened up and other claims died out. Under these circumstances, theft and miscommunication were common, and there were rarely any authorities to provide law and order.

While some early miners tried to establish an informal system of law and order in the camps and to observe Sunday as a day of rest, others lived rowdy and often dangerous lives. When William Perkins visited the notorious Sonora mining camp in 1850, he remarked: "It is surprising how indifferent [uncaring] people become to the sight of violence and bloodshed in this country."

Life in the Camps

Mining camps were often full of miners from many cultural backgrounds. Most of the miners were young, unmarried men. Only around 5 percent of gold rush immigrants were women or children. Some married women did make the journey to California with their husbands, however. These hardworking wives generally made good money by cooking meals, washing clothes, and operating boardinghouses. Catherine Haun recalled her first home in California:

66 **We were glad to settle down and go housekeeping in a shed that was built in a day of lumber purchased with the first fee. . . . For neighbors, we had a real live saloon. I never have received more respectful attention than I did from these neighbors.** 99

Haun's husband, a lawyer, concluded that practicing law was actually more profitable than panning for gold. He was one of many people who found that they could make a good living by supplying miners with food, clothing, equipment, and services. Miners paid high prices for basic necessities because the large amounts of gold in circulation caused severe inflation in California. A loaf of bread, for example, might cost 5 cents back East but sell for 50 to 75 cents in San Francisco. Prices could rise even higher if goods had to be shipped to isolated mining camps.

Enterprising settlers took full advantage of these circumstances. Biddy Mason and her family arrived in California as slaves brought by a Georgia slaveholder during the gold rush years. He quickly discovered, however, that most Californians opposed slavery, particularly in the gold mines. Mason and her family gained their liberty and moved to the small village of Los Angeles, where she eventually managed to purchase some land. Over time Mason's property increased in value from $250 to $200,000—making her one of the wealthiest landowners in California. She became a community leader and a well-known supporter of charities, having found in California an even greater prize than gold—her freedom.

The mining town of Columbia, California, during the height of the gold rush

Early Mining Methods

The forty-niners built much of their equipment from scratch, but they needed the right tools for the job. Axes, shovels, and picks were necessary to chop wood, dig ditches, and break rocks into gravel. Mules and wagons were also important for transporting miners and their equipment from one claim to another.

Very few miners had the time and money it took to dig mine shafts and work underground. Instead, the most popular mining methods used water to wash away lighter rock and dirt, leaving heavier gold particles behind. One common method was panning. A miner filled a shallow pan with dirt and water, then carefully swirled the pan until any gold began to settle at the bottom. The miner continued this process until nothing was left in the pan but a little water and some gold and rocks.

As surface gold became harder to find, miners built better equipment to separate gold from ordinary dirt and gravel. These mining devices included equipment such as rocker/cradles and sluice boxes. Each of these tools included a wooden box with a curved bottom. Miners shoveled dirt into the box, as water washed over it. At the bottom of the box a grooved screen caught gold pieces while allowing lighter dirt to be washed or shaken away. Some miners added mercury to the water to help catch fine particles of gold that would otherwise escape the traps.

Rockers, cradles, and sluice boxes all required a steady flow of water. Miners often made small dams near rivers and dug ditches to direct the water toward their claims.

Understanding What You Read

1. How did miners use water to mine gold?

2. What were some of the tools and equipment used to mine gold?

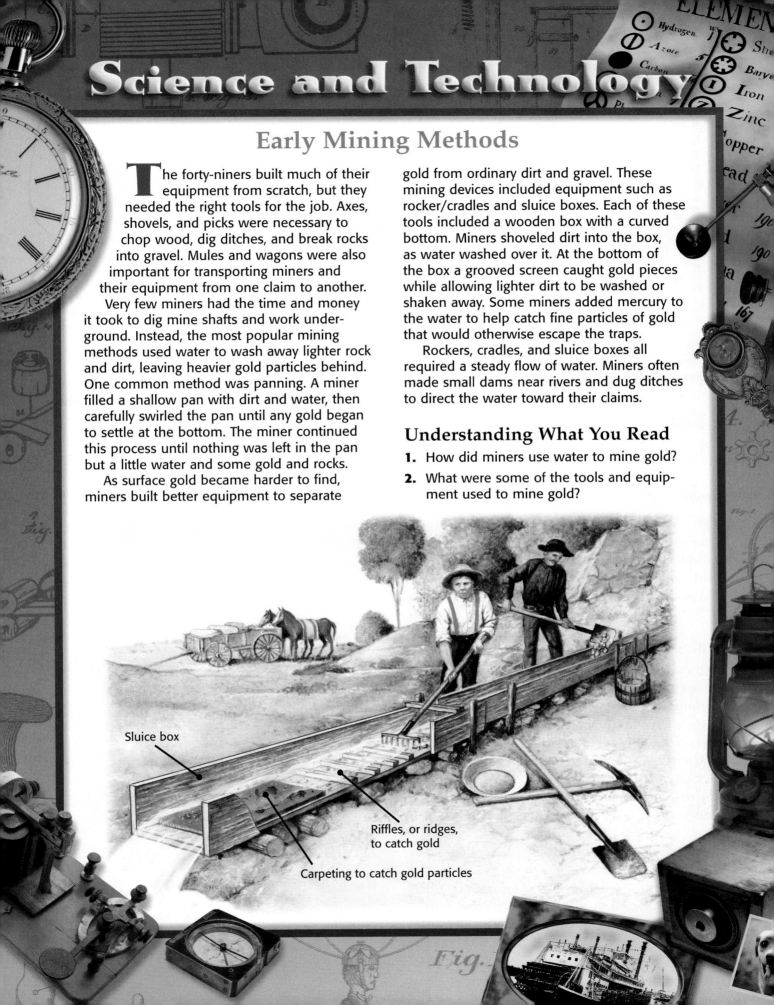

Sluice box

Riffles, or ridges, to catch gold

Carpeting to catch gold particles

California Gold

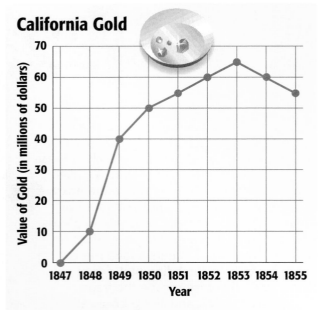

Value of Gold (in millions of dollars)

Source: *Statistical Abstract of the United States*, 1892

Gold! During the first year of the California Gold Rush, miners found $10 million in gold. They found another $270 million in gold over the next five years. About how much more gold was mined in 1853 than in 1848?

Immigrants to California

The lure of gold attracted miners from around the world to California. Many were from nations that had seen few people immigrate to the United States in the past.

Chinese Immigrants

Famine and economic hardships in southeastern China encouraged many Chinese men to seek their fortunes in the American West. These immigrants were known in Chinese as *gam saan haak*, or "travelers to Gold Mountain." Most of them hoped to find great wealth and then return home to China. Between 1849 and 1853, some 24,000 young Chinese men migrated to California. "From far and near we came and were pleased," wrote merchant Lai Chun-Chuen in 1855.

Chinese immigrants soon found that many Americans did not welcome them, however. As a result of anti-Chinese feeling, Chinese immigrants were not allowed to become U.S. citizens. In 1852 California placed a high monthly tax on all foreign

miners. Chinese miners had no choice but to pay this tax if they wished to search for gold in California. Chinese workers were also the targets of violent attacks in the mining camps. The legal system offered little protection, for it often favored Americans over Chinese and other immigrants.

Many Chinese immigrants continued to work in the gold mines, despite such treatment. Others looked for different jobs, often opening their own businesses. A California newspaper reported that Chinese worked as "ploughmen, laundrymen, placer miners, woolen spinners and weavers, domestic servants, cigar makers, [and] shoemakers." Many Chinese opened laundries, which required little initial investment and had numerous steady customers from the mining camps.

Other Gold-Seekers

In addition to those from China, prospectors came to California from Europe, Mexico, and South America. Around 10,000 foreign miners arrived in 1849 alone. Like most American gold-seekers, these new arrivals intended to return back home after they had made their fortunes. However, even when they did not become rich as they had hoped, many decided to stay. Some who remained in California, such as German immigrant Levi Strauss, became successful business owners. Strauss earned his fortune by making durable denim work pants to sell to miners.

Chinese miners faced steep taxes, harsh working conditions, and discrimination in the gold fields.

Courtesy of the California History Room, California State Library, Sacramento, California. Image has been altered.

Mexican American miners separating gold dust from gold-bearing soil using a blanket

East. With luck and hard work, immigrants could build good lives for themselves in the West.

Such a rapid population growth had negative consequences for many Californios and California Indians. As one early observer of the gold rush wrote:

❝ **The Yankee regarded every man but a native American [meaning a white U.S. citizen] as an interloper [trespasser], who had no right to come to California and pick up the gold of 'free and enlightened citizens.'** ❞

Mariano Vallejo, an important Californio, considered California's growing population and said, "The good ones were few and the wicked many."

Without the gold rush, California would probably have continued to grow slowly, becoming a U.S. territory and eventually a state. The California Gold Rush changed this, however, by increasing California's population and making it eligible for statehood only two years after being acquired by the United States. Along with the gold rush came an economic boom that stimulated growth in agriculture and industry.

★ Growth in the West

During the Spanish and then Mexican periods of settlement, California's population had grown slowly. This changed dramatically with the arrival of the forty-niners. Almost overnight, California's economy was transformed by gold mining, trade, and business growth. As the gold rush faded, frontier society became more stable. While great wealth became more difficult to achieve, average wages remained high compared to those in the

SECTION 4 REVIEW

Identify and explain the significance of the following:
- **James Marshall**
- **John Sutter**
- **California Gold Rush**
- **forty-niners**
- **prospect**
- **Biddy Mason**

Reading for Content Understanding

1 **Main Idea** What were some of the different mining methods and equipment that prospectors used to find gold in California?

2 **Main Idea** What difficulties did Chinese miners face in California?

3 **Geographic Diversity** *Movement* What were some of the travel methods that the forty-niners used to get to California?

4 **Writing** *Describing* Imagine that you are a prospector looking for gold in California. Write a letter to your family members back home, telling them about life in the local mining town.

5 **Critical Thinking** *Evaluating* Would you have moved to California in the 1850s from another part of the country? Explain your answer.

CHAPTER 17 REVIEW

Chapter Summary

A belief in manifest destiny encouraged many Americans to establish settlements outside the United States in the early 1800s. In the 1840s the United States acquired Oregon and Texas. The annexation of Texas led to the Mexican War, after which the United States gained more than half of Mexico's northern territory. More American settlers moved west—including Mormons. Many settlers and immigrants moved to California after gold was discovered there in 1848. ■

On a separate sheet of paper, complete the following activities.

Identifying People and Ideas

Describe the historical significance of the following:

1. manifest destiny
2. James K. Polk
3. Henry David Thoreau
4. Bear Flag Revolt
5. Gadsden Purchase
6. Mormons
7. Brigham Young
8. John Sutter
9. forty-niners
10. prospect

Internet Activity

go.hrw.com
SAO China

Search the Internet through the HRW Web site to find information about what conditions were like in China around the time of the California Gold Rush. Use the information to write a short essay explaining why Chinese men were willing to come to California.

Understanding Main Ideas

1. How did the possible annexation of Texas affect the presidential election of 1844?
2. Why did the United States declare war against Mexico?
3. Why did President Polk put General Scott in command of the army sent to capture Mexico City?
4. Why did Mormons move west?
5. How did the gold rush increase the population of California?
6. What discrimination did Chinese miners face?

Reviewing Themes

1. **Global Relations**   How did Texas and Oregon enter the Union?
2. **Cultural Diversity**   How were Mexican, American Indian, and Anglo cultures mingled in the Southwest? What conflicts arose as a result?

Using the Time Line

Number your paper from 1 to 5. Match the letters on the time line below with the following events.

1. **The United States and Mexico go to war.**
2. **Led by General Scott's troops, the United States captures Mexico City.**
3. **John Tyler becomes president after the death of William Henry Harrison.**
4. **While working near Sutter's Mill in California, James Marshall discovers gold.**
5. **Texas is annexed by the United States.**

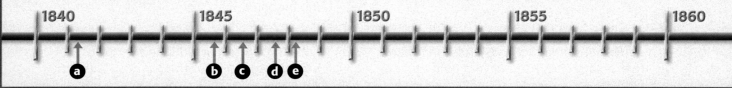

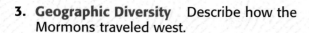

3. **Geographic Diversity** Describe how the Mormons traveled west.

Thinking Critically

1. **Evaluating** Do you think the United States had a good reason for declaring war against Mexico? Explain your answer.

2. **Drawing Conclusions** Several presidents—Jackson, Taylor, and Harrison, for example—were elected partly because of their popularity as military leaders. Do you think military experience is an important qualification for the presidency? Explain your answer.

Writing About History

1. **Informing** Write a newspaper article explaining the events and major outcomes of the Mexican War.

2. **Creating** Make a picture postcard about life in a mining town in the 1850s. On the back, write a two-paragraph note describing life in this mining town.

Building Your Portfolio

Complete the following activities individually or in groups.

1. **Miners' Supplies** Imagine that you are planning to open a general store in a California mining camp. Create a poster showing the layout of your store and labeling the different items you will sell. Make a list of the five items you think will be the best-sellers. For each item, write one or two sentences explaining why you think it will be profitable.

2. **Mexican American Festival** Imagine that your class is holding a Mexican American festival highlighting Mexican contributions to American culture. Complete one of the following activities: select a traditional Mexican dish and prepare it for your class, make a piñata and give an oral report to your class on the history of the piñata; find a Mexican short story on the topic of your choice and read it to the class.

Linking Geography and History

1. **Location** What territory did the United States acquire in the mid-1800s as a result of the Mexican Cession and the Gadsden Purchase?

2. **Region** Why did Brigham Young need to establish a new code regulating water rights after the Mormons moved west?

History Skills Workshop

Reading Maps Study the map below of the major water routes from the East Coast to California in 1849 and answer the following questions: (a) About how many miles did people have to travel if they took the route across the Isthmus of Panama to reach California? (b) About how many miles was the journey for those who traveled all the way around South America?

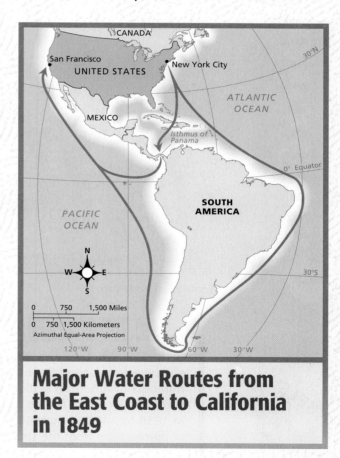

Major Water Routes from the East Coast to California in 1849

Westward Expansion

By the early 1800s the United States stretched from the Atlantic Ocean to the Rocky Mountains. Gradually, American pioneers moved across the Mississippi River, pushing the frontier of farms and settlements farther west.

Oregon Country in the Pacific northwest and Mexico in the Southwest blocked further U.S. expansion. Oregon Country included present-day Washington State and was jointly held by the United States and Britain.

Mexican lands included California, Nevada, Utah, Arizona, New Mexico, and parts of other present-day western states.

In 1846 Britain and the United States agreed on a boundary line dividing Canada and Oregon. The land south of that line became U.S. territory. After a war with Mexico from 1846 to 1848, the United States added California and the Southwest. The Gadsden Purchase in 1853 completed the rapid expansion of the southwestern United States. ■

The Early West

The United States annexed Texas in 1845. However, Mexico bitterly disputed Texas's southern and western boundary claims. Mexican officials insisted that the land in those areas legally belonged to Mexico, not Texas.

Santa Fe, New Mexico

History Note 1

By the mid-1840s about 80,000 Mexicans lived in what is now the southwestern United States (not including Texas). However, growing numbers of American settlers were moving into California and other parts of the region. Texas's population also grew rapidly, from 30,000 in 1836 to 140,000 in 1846. Most of this increase came as a result of immigration from the United States.

The West, 1845

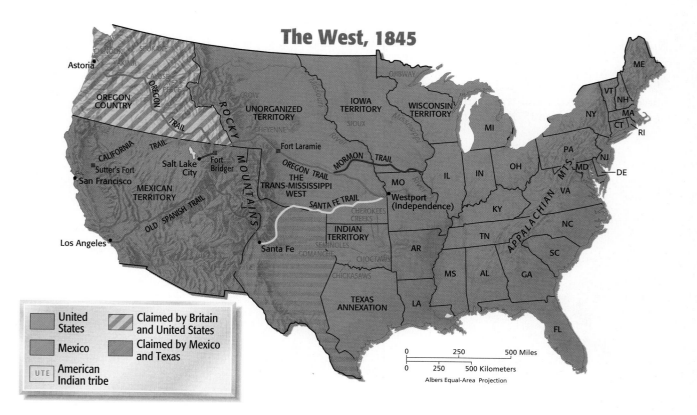

Legend:
- United States
- Mexico
- UTE — American Indian tribe
- Claimed by Britain and United States
- Claimed by Mexico and Texas

0   250   500 Miles
0   250   500 Kilometers
Albers Equal-Area Projection

Geography **Skills**
Reading Special-Purpose Maps

1. Compare this map to the current map of the United States on page 542. What current states occupy land that was Mexican territory in 1845?
2. Over what parts of present-day Texas was territorial control disputed?
3. Which countries claimed Oregon Country in 1845?

History Note 3

New Mexico was the most populated and economically developed of the Mexican territories that became a part of the United States. The Mexican population of the territory had reached about 25,000 by 1800 and 60,000 by the mid-1840s. New Mexicans traded with other Mexican territories to the south and with American Indians. By 1845 the United States was also a major trading partner.

History Note 2

The Texas Constitution of 1836 granted the rights of equal citizenship to nearly all non-Indian residents in Texas at the time of the 1835–36 revolution against Mexico. However, many Mexican Texans, called Tejanos, resettled in Mexico after the revolution. They doubted that they would receive fair treatment in a Texas where Anglo-American settlers from the United States controlled the government and most of the land.

The Effect of the Mexican Cession

After winning the war with Mexico, the United States took control of a vast stretch of territory from west Texas to the Pacific Ocean. Even though this territory had long belonged to Spain and then Mexico, the total number of people there from the United States outnumbered Hispanic residents by 1850.

U.S. Boundaries in 1853

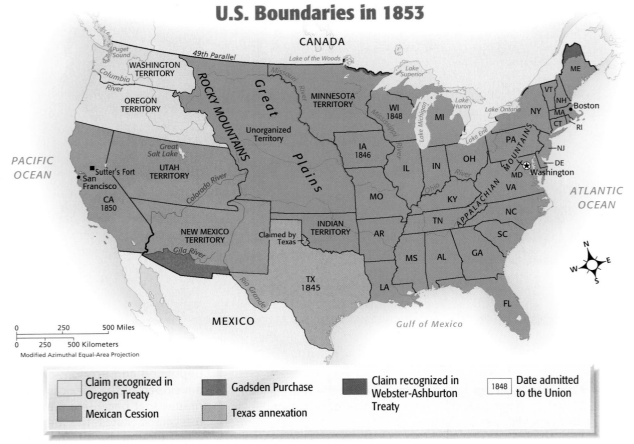

Claim recognized in Oregon Treaty	Gadsden Purchase	Claim recognized in Webster-Ashburton Treaty	1848 Date admitted to the Union
Mexican Cession	Texas annexation		

Geography Skills
Reading Special-Purpose Maps

1. What states and territories were organized in the new U.S. lands by 1853?
2. Compare this map to the current map of the United States on page 542. What two current states include territory from the Gadsden Purchase? What three states were formed from Oregon Territory?
3. What river had become the boundary between Texas and Mexico?
4. By 1853 the boundary between the United States and British Canada, west of the Great Lakes, lay along what line?

History Note 4

The additions of Texas, Oregon Country, the Mexican Cession, and the Gadsden Purchase added more than 1.2 million square miles to the United States between 1845 and 1853—about one third of the entire area of the United States today.

Ethnic Population of California in 1850
(excluding American Indians)
Total population: 93,000

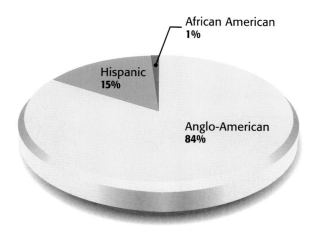

African American
1%

Hispanic
15%

Anglo-American
84%

Source: *Historical Statistics of the United States; The Hispanic Almanac*

Travel on the California Trail

Geography Skills
Reading Pie Graphs

1. How many people did the U.S. census of 1850 count in California?
2. In 1850 what percentage of non-American Indians in California were Hispanic? What percentage were African American?

History Note 5

By 1850 California's population had grown to nearly 100,000. This rapid increase was triggered by the gold rush that began in the late 1840s. People from all over the United States—as well as immigrants from France, Australia, Ireland, and South America—moved to California. As more and more people moved into the area, the percentage of California's Hispanic population declined. In fact, from 1850 to 1860 the percentage of Hispanic Californians declined from about 15 percent to 4 percent.

History Note 6

Anglo-Americans made up most of California's population in 1850. However, most of New Mexico's 62,000 non-Indian residents were Hispanic. In fact, in 1850 almost half of the total population that was not American Indian in the Mexican Cession territories were Hispanic.

Gold miners

The West Today

The southwestern United States has many historical ties with Spain and Mexico that are reflected in the people and culture of the region. The largest concentration of Hispanic Americans is found in the Southwest. Some are descended from families that stayed in the region after 1848. Others have immigrated since then.

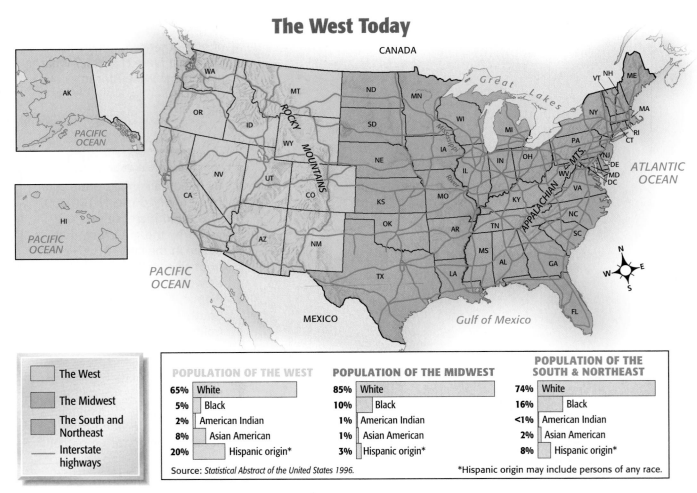

The West Today

Legend
- The West
- The Midwest
- The South and Northeast
- Interstate highways

POPULATION OF THE WEST
- 65% White
- 5% Black
- 2% American Indian
- 8% Asian American
- 20% Hispanic origin*

POPULATION OF THE MIDWEST
- 85% White
- 10% Black
- 1% American Indian
- 1% Asian American
- 3% Hispanic origin*

POPULATION OF THE SOUTH & NORTHEAST
- 74% White
- 16% Black
- <1% American Indian
- 2% Asian American
- 8% Hispanic origin*

Source: *Statistical Abstract of the United States 1996.*

*Hispanic origin may include persons of any race.

History Note 7

According to the 1990 census there were about 16 million Hispanic Americans living in the West, including Texas. Their presence, along with that of more Asian and Pacific Islander Americans, helps give the West the most diverse population of any region in the nation.

Geography Skills

Reading Special-Purpose Maps and Bar Graphs

1. What percentage of the West's population is Hispanic?
2. In which region do Asian Americans make up the third-largest ethnic group?
3. In which region do African Americans make up about 16 percent of the population?

Sources of Immigration to the United States in 1850

Total number of immigrants in 1850: 369,980

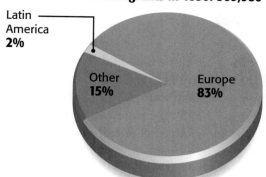

Latin America 2%

Other 15%

Europe 83%

Source: *Datapedia of the United States, 1790–2000: America Year by Year*

Geography Skills
Reading Pie Graphs

1. How many people immigrated to the United States in 1850?
2. What percentage of immigrants came from Latin America?
3. Which region provided most of the immigrants to the United States in 1850?

History Note 8

The West has become a major entry point for immigrants to the United States. More than one quarter of all immigrants to the United States in 1994 were admitted to the country in California. In recent years, people from Latin America, including Mexico, have made up nearly half of all immigrants to the United States.

Chinese American celebration in San Francisco, California

Sources of Immigration to the United States in 1994

Total number of immigrants in 1994: 804,416

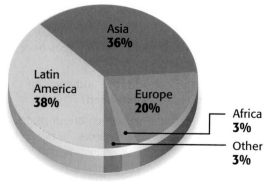

Asia 36%

Latin America 38%

Europe 20%

Africa 3%

Other 3%

Source: *Datapedia of the United States, 1790–2000: America Year by Year*

Geography Skills
Reading Pie Graphs

1. How many people immigrated to the United States in 1994?
2. Which region provided the highest percentage of immigrants to the United States? What percentage of all immigrants came from that region?
3. What percentage of immigrants came from Europe?
4. What percentage of immigrants came from Asia?

NEW YOR

History Skills

WORKSHOP

Using Primary and Secondary Sources

There are many sources of firsthand historical information, including diaries, letters, editorials, and legal documents such as wills and titles. All of these are *primary sources*. Newspaper reports, too, are considered primary sources, although they are generally written after an event has taken place. The same is true for personal memoirs and autobiographies, which are usually written late in a person's life. The paintings, photographs, and editorial cartoons that make up history's visual record also are primary sources. Because they allow a close-up look at the past—a chance to get inside people's minds—primary sources are valuable historical tools.

Secondary sources are descriptions or interpretations of historical events written after the events have occurred by persons who did not participate in or witness the events. History books,

biographies, encyclopedias, and other reference works are examples of secondary sources. Writers of secondary sources have the advantage of knowing the long-range consequences of events. This knowledge helps shape their analyses.

How to Study Primary and Secondary Sources

1. **Study the material carefully** Consider the nature of the material. Is it verbal or visual? Is it based on firsthand information or on the accounts of others? Note the major ideas and supporting details.
2. **Consider the audience** Ask yourself: For whom was this message originally meant? Whether a message was intended, for instance, for the general public or for a specific, private audience may have influenced its style or content.
3. **Check for bias** Watch for certain words or phrases that signal a one-sided view of a person or event.
4. **When possible, compare sources** Study more than one source on a topic if you can. Comparing sources gives you a more complete, balanced account.

Practicing the Skill

1. How are secondary sources different from primary sources?
2. What advantage do secondary sources have over primary sources?
3. Why should you consider the audience for whom the source was intended?
4. Of the following, identify which are primary and which are secondary sources: a newspaper article, a history book, a documentary film, an encyclopedia, a snapshot of a family on vacation, a Web page article about Dred Scott, an autobiography.

History in Action

UNIT PORTFOLIO

American History

U.S. History Hall of Fame

Complete the following activity in small, cooperative groups.

A national historical society is currently developing a U.S. History Hall of Fame. One wing of the museum will be devoted to people who made important contributions to the United States during the years 1790 to 1860. You and your group will create an exhibit highlighting people who you think should be included in this wing. Because space is limited, you must pick only one of the following topics: politics and government leaders, war with Mexico, the Republic of Texas, and westward expansion.

Materials To make your exhibits and plaques, you will need posterboard and construction paper, as well as art supplies such as colored markers, glue sticks, glitter, scissors, balsa wood, paint, cloth, clay, twine, and yarn. You may also wish to use computers and audio- and video-recording equipment in your exhibit.

Parts of the Project To create your exhibit, complete the following tasks:

1. **Planning** Put together a list of people to include in your exhibit. Decide who will research each of the people on your list. You should identify the accomplishments and contributions of the person or people assigned to you.

2. **Selecting Candidates** When you are finished with your research, decide as a group which of the individuals are the best candidates for the U.S. History Hall of Fame. To perform this task, organize your group into pairs. If you have an odd number of members, include a trio. Each pair or trio will select one candidate to sponsor for

The Baseball Hall of Fame

membership. Other students will be voting on which candidate in your exhibit should be included in the U.S. History Hall of Fame. Therefore, you must try to convince them that your candidate is the best choice.

3. **Display** Your display should include a brief biography of your candidate's life. Displays might also include quotes, letters, diary entries, newspaper articles, obituaries, pamphlets, time lines, charts, maps, diagrams, and any other appropriate items.

4. **Set Up** As a group, prepare and set up your exhibit. Each exhibit should include a banner or some other device that indicates the focus of the exhibit. In addition, prepare ballots and a ballot box for your exhibit. Ballots should list each candidate included in the exhibit.

You will vote for one candidate at each exhibit, including your own. Your teacher will count the final votes and announce the winners. Winners' displays will be part of the 1790–1860 wing of the U.S. History Hall of Fame.

UNIT 8 The Nation Breaks Apart

(1848–1877)

Young People

IN HISTORY

Young Soldiers

During the Civil War, 15-year-old Union soldier Thomas Galway described a fierce battle:

Young Union soldiers relax between battles.

> *Now we are close to the enemy. They rise up in the sunken lane and pour deadly fire into us. Our men drop. . . . We go forward on the run, heads downward as if under a pelting rain. . . . We are kneeling in the soft grass and I notice for a long time that almost every blade of grass is moving. For some time I supposed that this is caused by the merry crickets; and it is not until I made a remark to that effect to one of our boys near me and notice him laugh, that I know it is bullets that are falling thickly around us!*

The soldier who wrote this description was one of the thousands of teenage boys who fought in the Civil War.

Although both the North and the South tried to keep boys out of their armies, many teenagers lied about their ages to join. Elisha Stockwell's father would not let his 15-year-old son enlist, so Elisha told his parents he was going to attend a dance in town. Instead, he joined the Union army. Although Stockwell did not return home for two years, he thought of home often, particularly during his first battle, as he crouched on the ground amidst exploding shells. "I thought what a foolish boy I was to run away and get into such a mess as I was in."

Other boys joined the army as drummers. Because the beat of the drum was an important way to communicate orders to soldiers, drummer boys often found themselves the target of enemy fire. Johnny Clem went from drummer boy to fighting soldier during the Battle of Shiloh. After his drum was shattered, 11-year-old Clem picked up a gun and began firing. Within two years, Clem was promoted to sergeant.

In this unit you will learn more about a nation divided by war. The issues that had divided the North and the South for decades erupted into violence and brought tragedy and destruction to much of the country.

LEFT PAGE: *Members of the 54th Massachusetts Infantry attack southern soldiers at Fort Wagner.*
The Granger Collection, New York

▪ CHAPTER 18 ▪
A Divided Nation
(1848–1860)

"'A house divided against itself cannot stand.' . . . I believe this government cannot endure, permanently half *slave* and half *free*," Abraham Lincoln said in 1858. Lincoln stated that he did not expect the "house" to fall—nor did he think the Union would be dissolved. "But I *do* expect it will cease to be divided," he said. "It will become *all* one thing, or all the other."

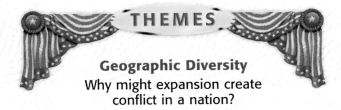

THEMES

Geographic Diversity
Why might expansion create conflict in a nation?

Citizenship and Democracy
How might a Supreme Court decision affect individuals' rights?

Constitutional Heritage
Why might a state want to leave the Union?

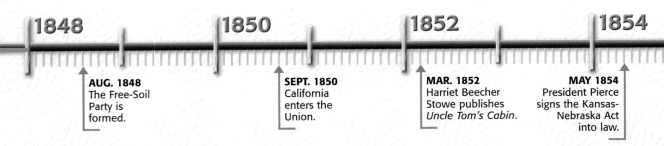

1848	1850	1852	1854
AUG. 1848 The Free-Soil Party is formed.	**SEPT. 1850** California enters the Union.	**MAR. 1852** Harriet Beecher Stowe publishes *Uncle Tom's Cabin*.	**MAY 1854** President Pierce signs the Kansas-Nebraska Act into law.

The Debate over Slavery

Reading Focus

What were the main conditions of the Compromise of 1850, and what reasons did people have for supporting or opposing it?

Why was the Fugitive Slave Act controversial in the North?

What was the impact of *Uncle Tom's Cabin*?

Key Terms

Wilmot Proviso
sectionalism
popular sovereignty
Free-Soil Party
Compromise of 1850
Fugitive Slave Act
Uncle Tom's Cabin

O N AUGUST 8, 1846, *members of the U.S. House of Representatives slowly returned from their dinner break and resumed their discussion of the ongoing war with Mexico. It was one of the hottest nights of the summer; ice water and fans were in heavy demand. As the representatives began to discuss the outcome of the war, a first-term congressman from Pennsylvania asked to be allowed to speak. David Wilmot held the floor for 10 minutes—and showed how the course of American history was changing.*

The U.S. Capitol, 1800s

IMAGE ON LEFT PAGE: *Crowds gathering at the Republican Party's national convention in 1860*

1856	1858	1860

NOV. 1856
James Buchanan wins the presidential election.

MAR. 1857
The Supreme Court issues the *Dred Scott* decision.

AUG. 1858
The Lincoln-Douglas debates begin in Illinois.

OCT. 1859
John Brown seizes the federal arsenal at Harpers Ferry, Virginia.

DEC. 1860
South Carolina votes to secede from the Union.

The Expansion of Slavery

Victory in the Mexican War in 1847 added more than 500,000 square miles to the United States. It also revived the bitter debate over slavery in the western territories. The Missouri Compromise of 1820 had admitted Missouri to the Union as a slave state and divided the remainder of the Louisiana Purchase into free and slave territory. Slavery was prohibited north of latitude 36°30' but was allowed south of that line. In the 1840s President James K. Polk and others recommended extending the 36°30' line to the Pacific coast. This would have divided the Mexican Cession into two regions—one banning slavery and the other allowing it.

The Wilmot Proviso

Some northerners wanted to prohibit slavery in all parts of the Mexican Cession. During the war, Representative David Wilmot proposed a plan known as the **Wilmot Proviso**. It stated that "neither slavery nor involuntary servitude shall ever exist in any part of [the] territory."

The House, which had a northern majority, approved the proviso, but it died in the Senate, where the South had more power. Though the Wilmot Proviso never became law, the debate over it demonstrated the increasing **sectionalism**—a devotion to the interests of one region instead of to the country as a whole—over the issue of slavery.

Popular Sovereignty

Another politician, Senator Lewis Cass of Michigan, hoped to end the controversy over slavery in new territories by using a principle known as **popular sovereignty**. This would allow voters in a territory to decide whether they wanted to ban or permit slavery. They would make their decision by electing antislavery or pro-slavery representatives to their territorial legislatures. Based on the will of the majority, these legislatures then would pass laws to prohibit or promote slavery.

The Free-Soil Party

This debate over slavery in the Mexican Cession played an important role in the presidential election of 1848. The current president, Democrat James K. Polk, was not seeking a second term. Instead, the Democrats nominated Senator Cass, the champion of popular sovereignty, but their platform avoided a definite position on slavery in the West.

The Whigs nominated Zachary Taylor, one of the heroes of the Mexican War. Taylor had never held political office—in fact, until 1848 he had never even voted—but this mattered little to the Whigs. They stressed Taylor's

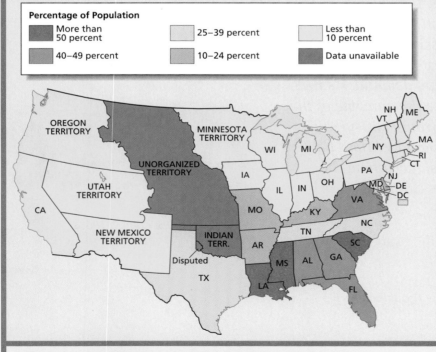

Percentage of Population

- More than 50 percent
- 40–49 percent
- 25–39 percent
- 10–24 percent
- Less than 10 percent
- Data unavailable

African American Population in 1850

Learning from Maps African Americans made up 15 percent of the total U.S. population in 1850. However, in slave states African Americans accounted for a much higher percentage.

Place In what states did African Americans make up more than 50 percent of the population?

Zachary Taylor campaign pin, 1848

war record and tried to avoid the slavery controversy by not producing a party platform.

The Democrats' and the Whigs' refusal to address the slavery issue led thousands of antislavery northerners to create a new political party. In August 1848 in Buffalo, New York, they formed the **Free-Soil Party**. The Free-Soilers endorsed the Wilmot Proviso and chose former president Martin Van Buren of New York as their candidate.

The new party won 10 percent of the popular vote, beating Cass in three northern states. The Free-Soilers' success contributed to Taylor's winning a narrow victory in the electoral college, thus capturing the election.

The California Question

Shortly after the election of 1848, outgoing president James K. Polk announced that gold had been discovered in California. The resulting gold rush rapidly increased California's population, allowing it to bypass the territorial stage and apply directly for admission to the Union. This then raised the question of whether California would be admitted to the Union as a free state or a slave state.

Most Californians did not want slavery. Under Mexican rule, slavery had been illegal in California. In addition, most of the Forty-Niners came from free states and did not want to compete for jobs against slave labor. Although the majority of its residents wanted California to enter the Union as a free state, doing so would upset the balance between free and

slave states that had been maintained since the Missouri Compromise.

This imbalance was unacceptable to many in the South. "We are about permanently to destroy the balance of power between the sections," said Senator Jefferson Davis from Mississippi. He and many other southerners vowed to oppose the admission of California as a free state—even if their actions threatened the future of the Union.

The Compromise of 1850

The same man who had helped settle the Missouri crisis of 1819–20 and the nullification crisis of 1832–33 now stepped forward with another plan of compromise. Senator Henry Clay of Kentucky addressed each issue of sectional disagreement.

Clay's Compromises

Clay's compromise plan had five main parts. First, he urged Congress to admit California to the Union as a free state. Second, he called for the rest of the Mexican Cession—already called New Mexico—to be organized as a federal territory in which popular sovereignty could determine the status of slavery. Third, Clay addressed a border dispute between Texas and New Mexico. He called

The Granger Collection, New York

In 1850 Senator Henry Clay of Kentucky once again urged Congress to compromise on the issue of slavery in the territories.

on Texas to give up its claim to all land east of the upper Rio Grande. In exchange, the federal government would assume the debt that Texas had left over from its days as an independent republic.

Fourth, bowing to a common northern request, Clay called for an end to the slave trade—but not slavery—in the nation's capital. Fifth, meeting the demands of southern slaveholders who claimed to lose many slaves a year to the North, Clay called for a new, more effective fugitive slave law.

Three Perspectives

Almost immediately, Clay's proposed compromise came under fire from those who disliked one or more parts of the plan. Senator William Seward of New York, speaking for abolitionists in the North, demanded the admission of California "directly, without conditions, without qualifications, and without compromise."

Senator John C. Calhoun of South Carolina spoke for much of the South. Near death, Calhoun was so weak that his speech had to be read by another senator. Calhoun claimed that the admission of California as a free state would "destroy . . . the equilibrium [balance] between the two sections" of the country. If that happened, he said, the slave states could not "remain in the Union consistently with their honor and their safety." He asked that they be allowed "to separate and part in peace."

While Calhoun had many supporters, others in the Senate joined Clay in trying to reach a good compromise. Senator Daniel Webster of Massachusetts delivered a stirring speech in support of Clay's compromise plan:

John C. Calhoun

❝ I wish to speak today, not as a Massachusetts man, nor as a Northern man, but as an American. . . . I speak today for the preservation of the Union. Hear me for my cause. ❞

Webster criticized northern abolitionists and scolded southerners who spoke of disunion.

Reaching an Agreement

During the months-long debate in Congress, two of the main people who opposed enacting Clay's compromise plan died. Senator Calhoun died in late March. President Taylor—who opposed the compromise plan partly because he did not get along with Henry Clay—died suddenly in July. Taylor was succeeded by Vice President Millard Fillmore, a New Yorker who favored compromise. When Congress finally passed Clay's plan in September 1850, Fillmore signed each bill.

The **Compromise of 1850** accomplished most of what Clay had wanted. California entered the Union as a free state. The rest of the Mexican Cession was divided into two territories—Utah and New Mexico—in which the status of slavery would be decided by popular sovereignty. Texas agreed to surrender its land claims in New Mexico in exchange for financial assistance from the federal government. Finally, the compromise abolished the slave trade in the nation's capital and produced a new fugitive slave law that replaced the Fugitive Slave Law of 1793.

The Granger Collection, New York

Northern poster protesting the capture of a suspected fugitive slave

⭐ The Fugitive Slave Act

One element of the Compromise of 1850 kept the slavery issue very much on Americans' minds. The **Fugitive Slave Act** made it a federal crime to assist runaway slaves and allowed them to be arrested even in areas where slavery was illegal.

Catching Slaves

Under the new law, slaveholders and their agents could take suspected fugitive slaves before U.S. commissioners and try to prove ownership through documents or the testimony of white witnesses. The accused fugitives could not testify in their own defense. Commissioners who rejected a slaveholder's claim and released a suspected fugitive received $5 for their services. Those who returned a suspected fugitive to his or her owner in the South received $10. Anyone who hid or otherwise assisted a runaway slave faced six months in jail and a $1,000 fine.

Many slaveholders took advantage of the Fugitive Slave Act almost immediately. In September 1850, federal marshals arrested an African American porter named James Hamlet who had lived in New York City for three years and sent him to a slaveholder in Maryland. Several months later, agents seized an African American tailor who had lived in Poughkeepsie, New York, for many years and carried him back to slavery in South Carolina.

In the 10 years after Congress passed this law, 343 fugitive slave cases came before the review of commissioners in the North. The accused fugitive was declared free in only 11 of these cases. Such numbers struck fear into many African Americans living in the North. Thousands of African Americans fled to Canada to avoid the reach of the Fugitive Slave Act.

Helping Fugitives

The Fugitive Slave Act offended many northerners, most of whom were otherwise indifferent to the struggles of slaves in the South. These northerners objected to the lack of a trial by jury and the apparent "bribe" often given to commissioners to encourage them to send a suspected fugitive slave back to the South.

As expected, abolitionists were the most vocal in their opposition to the new law. Some said it was every citizen's duty to make sure that it was "resisted, disobeyed at all hazards." Martin R. Delany, a doctor and a leading African American abolitionist, publicly told the mayor of Pittsburgh, Pennsylvania:

> **66 If any man approaches that house in search of a slave—I care not who he may be . . . if he crosses the threshold of my door, and I do not lay him a lifeless corpse at my feet, I hope the grave may refuse my body a resting place, and righteous Heaven my spirit a home. 99**

Biography

Frederick Douglass

Frederick Douglass was born to a slave family in Maryland in 1817. At the age of 20, he borrowed the identity papers of a free African American and took a train to freedom in the North. In 1841 Douglass began to work full-time speaking and writing for the abolition movement. Four years later, he published the *Narrative of the Life of Frederick Douglass*, an autobiography so detailed that he had to leave the country to avoid being arrested as a fugitive slave.

He returned in 1847 with enough money to buy his freedom and start a newspaper, which he named *The North Star*. In the first issue, Douglass called on other former slaves to join his crusade for freedom. "He who has endured the cruel pangs [pains] of Slavery," he said, "is the man to advocate [support] Liberty."

In general, northerners resisted the Fugitive Slave Act without resorting to violence, but blood was spilled on several occasions. In 1854, for example, the case of Anthony Burns captured the nation's attention. Burns, a fugitive slave from Virginia, was arrested and jailed in Boston. A group of abolitionists in the city stormed the courthouse and tried to rescue Burns by force. A deputy marshal was killed in the attempt, but the abolitionists did not get close enough to Burns to free him. Burns was eventually returned to slavery in Virginia.

American Literature

Uncle Tom's Cabin
Harriet Beecher Stowe

Like Mark Twain, Harriet Beecher Stowe was a local-color writer, concentrating on describing regional culture and language. While she wrote mostly about New England, she is best remembered for Uncle Tom's Cabin, *a powerful novel about slavery. In the following passage, Simon Legree is a northerner who has moved south and become a cruel slaveholder. He has ordered Sambo, a slave driver, to whip Tom in an attempt to learn what Tom knows about the disappearance of two slaves. Tom, one of the main characters of the novel, is a slave who has maintained his religious faith despite the brutality he has witnessed and experienced. The scene shows the consequences of slavery—both to the suffering slave and to the soul of the slaveholder. The criticism on slavery in the first and last paragraph is the author's voice.*

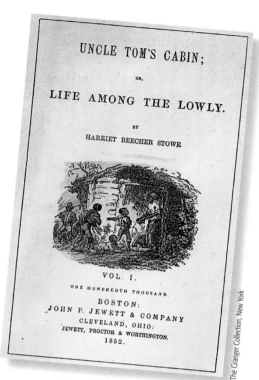

The 100,000th copy of
Uncle Tom's Cabin

Scenes of blood and cruelty are shocking to our ear and heart. What man has nerve to do, man has not nerve to hear. What brother-man and brother-Christian must suffer, cannot be told us, even in our secret chamber, it so harrows up [torments] the soul! And yet, oh my country; these things are done under the shadow of thy laws! O, Christ! thy church sees them, almost in silence! . . . "He's most gone [dead], Mas 'r," [Master] said Sambo, touched, in spite of himself, by the patience of his victim.

"Pay away, till he give up! Give it to him!—give it to him!" shouted Legree. "I'll take every drop of blood he has, unless he confesses!"

Tom opened his eyes, and looked upon his master. "Ye poor miserable crittur!" he said, "there an't no more ye can do! I forgive ye, with all my soul!" and he fainted entirely away.

"I b'lieve, my soul, he's done for, finally," said Legree, stepping forward, to look at him. "Yes, he is! Well, his mouth's shut up, at last,—that's one comfort!"

Yes, Legree; but who shall shut up that voice in thy soul? that soul, past repentance [beyond forgiveness], past prayer, past hope, in whom the fire that never shall be quenched [hell] is already burning!

Understanding Literature

1. In the opening paragraph, whom does Stowe criticize for allowing slavery to occur?

2. How does Simon Legree respond to the death of Tom?

3. What do you think Stowe is asking of the reader?

★ Antislavery Literature

Abolitionists in the North used the stories of fugitive slaves such as James Hamlet and Anthony Burns to further their cause. They also used the slave narrative. Although a few slave narratives were published before 1800, they did not become popular until around 1840. Among the best known were the narratives of Frederick Douglass and Sojourner Truth. The latter differed from other slave narratives in two ways—its central character was a woman, and she had been a slave not in the South but in New York.

However, no other literary work had the impact of **Uncle Tom's Cabin,** a powerful antislavery novel written by Harriet Beecher Stowe. She was born into a religious family in Connecticut and moved to Ohio at the age of 21. There she met with fugitive slaves and learned about the cruelty of slavery. Inspired by slave narratives and angered by the passage of the Fugitive Slave Act of 1850, Stowe decided to write a book that would show northerners what slavery was really like.

Published in 1852, *Uncle Tom's Cabin*'s main character is a kindly old slave named Tom, who is taken from his wife and sold "down the river" in Louisiana. There Tom becomes the slave of a

vicious cotton planter who, in a fit of rage, has Tom beaten to death. The novel sparked outrage in the South. Louisa McCord, one of the most famous southern writers, criticized the "foul imagination which could invent such scenes."

The book also had a powerful impact in the North. As one woman wrote to Stowe:

Harriet Beecher Stowe

> ❝ **I thought I was a thoroughgoing abolitionist before, but your book has awakened so strong a feeling of indignation and of compassion [anger and pity], that I seem never to have had *any* feeling on this subject till now.** ❞

In its first year in print, *Uncle Tom's Cabin* sold 300,000 copies in the United States alone. Within a decade, more than 2 million copies had been sold in the United States, causing one northerner to remark that Stowe and her book had created "two millions of abolitionists."

SECTION 1 REVIEW

Identify and explain the significance of the following:
- **Wilmot Proviso**
- **sectionalism**
- **popular sovereignty**
- **Free-Soil Party**
- **Henry Clay**
- **Daniel Webster**
- **Compromise of 1850**
- **Fugitive Slave Act**
- **Anthony Burns**
- **Uncle Tom's Cabin**
- **Harriet Beecher Stowe**

Reading for Content Understanding

1 **Main Idea** What did the Compromise of 1850 propose, and why did Senator Daniel Webster support it? Why did Senator John Calhoun oppose it?

2 **Main Idea** What point did Harriet Beecher Stowe try to make in *Uncle Tom's Cabin*, and how did Americans react to the novel?

3 **Geographic Diversity** *Region* How did the Mexican Cession lead to renewed tensions between the North and the South?

4 **Writing** *Creating* Imagine that you are a northerner who is opposed to the Fugitive Slave Act. Create a handbill that you would pass out at a town meeting to persuade members of your community to protest the law.

5 **Critical Thinking** *Making Comparisons* How did the Compromise of 1850 differ from the Missouri Compromise?

Trouble in Kansas

Reading Focus

How did different sections of the country react to the Kansas-Nebraska Act?

In what ways did people attempt to settle the conflict over slavery in Kansas?

How did the North and the South react to the beating of Charles Sumner?

Key Terms

Kansas-Nebraska Act
Pottawatomie Massacre

*F*RANKLIN *AND* JANE PIERCE *spent the morning taking a peaceful carriage ride just outside Boston, Massachusetts. On their way back to their hotel in the city, they noticed a horseman racing toward them. When the rider reached the Pierces' carriage, he shouted the news— the Democratic convention in Baltimore, Maryland, had nominated Franklin Pierce for the presidency. Pierce found it hard to believe. Jane Pierce, who did not want to leave her home in New England to live in Washington, promptly fainted.*

Campaign banner for Franklin Pierce

⭐ The Election of 1852

As the Democratic convention opened, there were four leading candidates, including Lewis Cass, who had represented the party in 1848. It soon became clear, however, that none of these four could win a majority of votes. After nearly 50 ballots, the frustrated delegates suddenly turned to Franklin Pierce, a little-known politician from New Hampshire.

Pierce and his party promised to honor the Compromise of 1850 and to enforce the Fugitive Slave Act. Thus, although he was a New Englander,

many southerners considered Pierce "as reliable as Calhoun himself" on the slavery issue.

The Whigs also held their convention in Baltimore in 1852. In previous elections they had nominated a famous soldier for the presidency— William Henry Harrison in 1840 and Zachary Taylor in 1848—and on both occasions the party had won the election. In 1852 the Whigs employed the same tactic and hoped for the same success. They bypassed the current president, Millard Fillmore, and nominated Winfield Scott, a hero from the Mexican War. Scott was born in Virginia but had spent most of his life in the army serving in various parts of the country. Although he was a native of the South, many southerners distrusted Scott because he had failed to come out in complete support of the Compromise of 1850.

In the election, the Democrats won overwhelmingly. Pierce won 27 of the 31 states in the most lopsided victory since 1820. Even Scott's home state of Virginia voted for Pierce. Many Whigs considered it a painful defeat, but Representative Lewis Campbell of Ohio feared the worst. "We are slayed—" he cried, "the party is dead—dead—dead!"

 ## The Kansas-Nebraska Act

In his inaugural address, President Pierce expressed his hope that the slavery issue had been put to rest "and that no sectional . . . excitement may again threaten the durability [stability] of our institutions." Less than a year later, however, a proposal to build a railroad to the West Coast helped revive the slavery controversy and opened a new period of sectional conflict.

Douglas and the Railroad

Ever since entering Congress in the mid-1840s, Stephen Douglas had supported the idea of building a railroad to the Pacific. Douglas favored a line running from Chicago, in his home state of Illinois. The first step toward building such a railroad would be organizing what remained of the Louisiana Purchase into a federal territory. The Missouri Compromise required this land to be free territory and eventually free states.

Southerners in Congress did not support Douglas's plan, recommending instead that the railroad run along a southern route. Their preferred line ran from New Orleans, across Texas and the already organized territory of New Mexico, to southern California. Determined to have the railroad start in Chicago, Douglas asked a few key southern senators to support his plan. They replied that they would abandon their plans for a southern railroad route if the new territory west of Missouri was opened to slavery.

Two New Territories

In January 1854 Douglas introduced what became the **Kansas-Nebraska Act**, a plan that would divide the remainder of the Louisiana Purchase into two territories—Kansas and Nebraska. In each territory, popular sovereignty would decide the question of slavery. Douglas's proposal would eliminate the Missouri Compromise's restriction on slavery north of the 36°30' line.

Antislavery northerners were outraged. Some called the proposal a "gross violation of a sacred pledge" and part of a terrible plot to turn free territory into a "dreary region . . . inhabited by masters and slaves." All across the North, citizens attended protest meetings and sent anti-Nebraska petitions to Congress.

Even so, with strong southern support—and with Douglas and President Pierce pressuring their fellow Democrats to vote for it—the measure passed the Senate in March and the House two months later. The president signed the act into law on May 30, 1854. Lost amid all the controversy over the territorial bill was Douglas's proposed railroad to the Pacific. Congress would not approve the construction of such a railroad until 1862.

At his inauguration on March 4, 1853, Franklin Pierce became the first president to deliver his address without using any notes.

The Granger Collection, New York

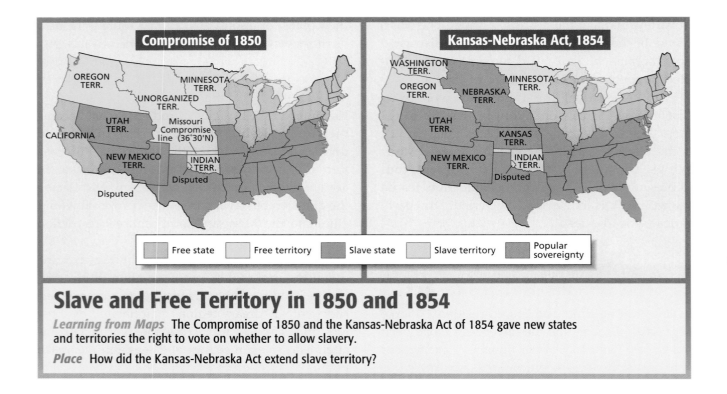

Compromise of 1850

OREGON TERR.
MINNESOTA TERR.
UNORGANIZED TERR.
UTAH TERR.
CALIFORNIA
Missouri Compromise line (36°30'N)
NEW MEXICO TERR.
INDIAN TERR.
Disputed
Disputed

Kansas-Nebraska Act, 1854

WASHINGTON TERR.
OREGON TERR.
NEBRASKA TERR.
MINNESOTA TERR.
UTAH TERR.
KANSAS TERR.
NEW MEXICO TERR.
INDIAN TERR.
Disputed

Free state   Free territory   Slave state   Slave territory   Popular sovereignty

Slave and Free Territory in 1850 and 1854

Learning from Maps The Compromise of 1850 and the Kansas-Nebraska Act of 1854 gave new states and territories the right to vote on whether to allow slavery.

Place How did the Kansas-Nebraska Act extend slave territory?

⭐ Kansas Divided

Antislavery and pro-slavery groups scrambled to get people to Kansas as quickly as possible. Both northern and southern politicians recognized that a contest had begun. "Gentlemen of the Slave States," said Senator William Seward of New York,

“ **since there is no escaping your challenge, I accept it in behalf of the cause of freedom. We will engage in competition for the virgin soil of Kansas, and God give the victory to the side which is stronger in numbers as it is in right.** ”

Abolitionist Eli Thayer soon formed the Massachusetts Emigrant Aid Company to help northern families to move to Kansas. Southern families— some with slaves, but most without—poured into Kansas as well. At first, the majority of settlers were pro-slavery because many came from nearby slave states such as Missouri.

An 1855 advertisement for land in Kansas

Elections to seat a territorial legislature in Kansas were held in March 1855. To ensure a pro-slavery victory, thousands of men crossed the border from Missouri, voted in Kansas, and then returned home, taking advantage of the vague residency requirements of the Kansas-Nebraska Act. As a result, the territorial legislature, located at Lecompton, had an overwhelming pro-slavery majority.

The new legislature passed a series of strict pro-slavery laws. One law made it a crime to question anyone's right to hold slaves, and another made it an offense punishable by death to assist a fugitive slave. In response, antislavery Kansans decided to boycott the new pro-slavery legislature and create their own legislature 30 miles away in Topeka.

⭐ "Bleeding Kansas"

By early 1856 Kansas had two governments and a hostile population that was divided into two armed camps. Many of the pro-slavery settlers had brought guns

Antislavery activist Reverend Henry Ward Beecher

with them to the new territory. The free-soilers—that is, antislavery settlers—had meanwhile requested shipments of weapons from their friends in the East. Abolitionist organizations soon were providing everything from handguns to some small cannons. In New York, Reverend Henry Ward Beecher—the brother of Harriet Beecher Stowe—and his congregation raised enough money to send rifles to Kansas. Free-soilers called these weapons Beecher's Bibles.

With both sides heavily armed, violence soon broke out. In May 1856 a pro-slavery grand jury indicted the leaders of the free-soil government for treason. An 800-member posse rode to Lawrence, where the free-soil leaders lived, to arrest them. Discovering that the leaders had fled, the posse took its anger out on Lawrence, setting fire to some buildings, looting others, and destroying the printing presses used to print free-soil newspapers. One man was killed in the event that became known as the Sack of Lawrence.

Abolitionist John Brown decided that it was his duty to avenge the attack on Lawrence. Brown was a New Englander who had sworn to dedicate his life to the abolition of slavery. He and some of his sons had moved to Kansas in 1855. When he learned of the Sack of Lawrence, he said it was time to "fight fire with fire" and "strike terror in the hearts of the pro-slavery people." On the night of May 24, 1856, Brown led a company of seven—four of whom were

his own sons—along Pottawatomie Creek in eastern Kansas. During the night, they pulled five pro-slavery men from their homes and killed them in the **Pottawatomie Massacre**.

After the Sack of Lawrence and the Pottawatomie Massacre, Kansas collapsed into a state of civil war. Around 200 people were killed in the months that followed. The events in "Bleeding Kansas" became front-page stories in many of the country's newspapers.

★ Violence in Congress

During the same week the Sack of Lawrence took place, Senator Charles Sumner of Massachusetts delivered a speech entitled "The Crime Against Kansas." In it, he criticized the actions of the pro-slavery people in that territory. Sumner also made numerous personal remarks during his speech. For example, he insulted Andrew Pickens Butler, a pro-slavery senator from South Carolina who was not

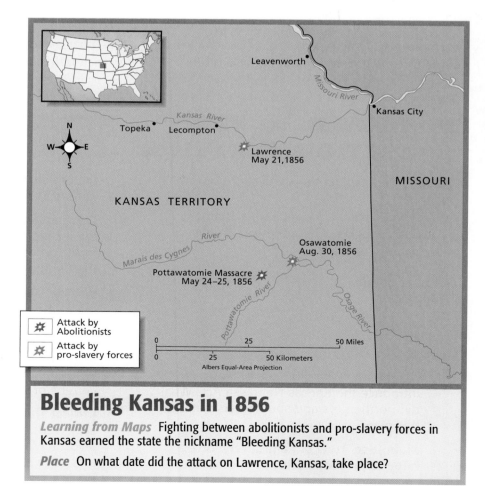

Bleeding Kansas in 1856

Learning from Maps Fighting between abolitionists and pro-slavery forces in Kansas earned the state the nickname "Bleeding Kansas."

Place On what date did the attack on Lawrence, Kansas, take place?

in the Senate chamber at the time of the speech. Many members of Congress were angered by Sumner's words, but none more so than Representative Preston Brooks, a relative of Butler's from South Carolina. On May 22, 1856, Brooks approached Sumner in the Senate chamber and beat him unconscious with a walking cane.

Many white southerners applauded Brooks's action. A newspaper editor in Richmond, Virginia, wrote:

Preston Brooks attacking Charles Sumner on the Senate floor

The Granger Collection, New York

66 **We consider the act good in conception, better in execution. . . . These vulgar abolitionists in the Senate . . . must be lashed into submission. Sumner, in particular, ought to have nine-and-thirty [lashes] early every morning.** 99

Dozens of southerners sent Brooks new canes to replace the one he had broken in his assault.

In the North, many people were outraged over the incident. They nicknamed the attacker "Bully Brooks" and said that his behavior was merely an "illustration of the ferocious southern spirit." A northern attempt to expel Brooks from the House failed; the only punishment Brooks faced was a $300 fine imposed by a federal court. Sumner, on the other hand, never fully recovered from his injuries suffered during the attack.

SECTION 2 REVIEW

Identify and explain the significance of the following:
- **Franklin Pierce**
- **Stephen Douglas**
- **Kansas-Nebraska Act**
- **Pottawatomie Massacre**
- **Charles Sumner**
- **Preston Brooks**

Reading for Content Understanding

1 **Main Idea** Why did Senator Douglas introduce the Kansas-Nebraska Act? What did northerners and southerners think of this plan?

2 **Main Idea** How did antislavery forces hope to prevent slavery in Kansas? How did pro-slavery groups influence the Kansas territorial elections in 1855?

3 **Geographic Diversity** *Location* How did the location of Kansas give pro-slavery forces an advantage in the race to settle the territory?

4 **Writing** *Describing* Imagine that you are a southern or northern newspaper reporter covering the beating of Charles Sumner by Preston Brooks. Write a half-page article describing the events leading up to the beating and the reactions of the citizens of your state.

5 **Critical Thinking** *Drawing Conclusions* Why were southerners so strongly in favor of maintaining a balance of free and slave states?

Political Divisions

Reading Focus

How did the Kansas-Nebraska Act affect U.S. political parties?

Why did Dred Scott sue for his freedom, and how did the Supreme Court rule on his case?

How did Abraham Lincoln and Stephen Douglas differ in their views on slavery?

Key Terms

Republican Party

Dred Scott decision

Lincoln-Douglas debates

Freeport Doctrine

THE CALL WENT OUT across Michigan. Those opposed to the recently passed Kansas-Nebraska Act should meet at the town of Jackson, in the southern part of the state, on July 6, 1854. On that day, hundreds of people took part in the creation of a new political organization. "We will . . . be known as Republicans," they declared in their platform. They promised to uphold the principles of republican government and vowed to fight the spread of slavery "until the contest be terminated." Thus, under a cluster of trees in southern Michigan, a new political party was born.

First national
Republican convention

 New Political Parties

Political unrest led some Whigs, Democrats, Free-Soilers, and abolitionists to join together and form the **Republican Party** in 1854. The main issue uniting these different groups was their opposition to the spread of slavery in the West. This issue had once again been brought into the national spotlight by the Kansas-Nebraska Act of 1854. Democrat Stephen Douglas had predicted that the act would "raise a . . . storm," and he was quickly proven right.

Under pressure from Senator Douglas and President Pierce, nearly 60 northern Democrats had voted for the Kansas-Nebraska bill. They suffered the political consequences for their support. In the next congressional elections, only seven of the northern Democrats who voted for the bill retained their seats in the House.

A number of northern Democrats abandoned their party because of the Kansas-Nebraska controversy. The party was hurt further by the Ostend Manifesto. In this document, three U.S. diplomats laid out a plan to buy the Spanish island of Cuba,

A Divided Nation **561**

Know-Nothings in New York City meet at night in the 1850s.

which allowed slavery. If Spain refused the offer, the diplomats recommended taking the island by force. When the originally secret document was released to the public in March 1855, many northerners criticized the Democrats' attempt to acquire more slave territory.

The Democrats were not the only party in trouble at this time. The Whig Party, still stunned by its disastrous defeat in the presidential election of 1852, fell apart completely over the Kansas-Nebraska Act. Every northern Whig voted against Douglas's bill while most southern Whigs voted for it. Thereafter, northern and southern Whigs refused to work with one another. "The Whig Party has been killed off . . . by that miserable Nebraska business," a senator from Connecticut complained.

★ The Election of 1856

The presidential election of 1856 showed just how divided the country was becoming. Some long-time Whigs and Democrats joined the Know-Nothing Party, which held the first nominating convention of 1856. The party quickly fell apart over the slavery issue. Northern delegates called for a repeal of the Kansas-Nebraska Act, but southerners refused to put this measure in the party platform. The northerners promptly left the convention hall. Many of them eventually joined the

Republican Party. Those Know-Nothings who remained behind chose former president Millard Fillmore as their presidential candidate.

The Democrats realized that they could not nominate anyone closely associated with the Kansas-Nebraska Act, such as President Pierce or Senator Douglas. Instead, they decided to nominate James Buchanan of Pennsylvania, who had had a long political career—10 years in the House, another decade in the Senate, and four years as Polk's secretary of state. Most importantly, he had not been involved in the Kansas-Nebraska controversy because he was serving as ambassador to Great Britain when the debate took place.

At their first presidential nominating convention, the Republicans chose John C. Frémont as their candidate. He was a well-known explorer who had scouted the Oregon Trail and earned the nickname "The Pathfinder." Frémont had much less political experience than his opponent, but he appealed to Republicans because he was strongly opposed to the spread of slavery. Although the Republicans embraced other issues, such as protective tariffs, the public generally viewed them as a "single-issue party." Because they so vocally opposed the spread of slavery, the Republicans had almost no supporters outside of the free states.

Some white southerners even said that they would not accept a Republican victory in the election. "If Frémont is elected there will be a revolution," said the governor of Virginia. A politician from Georgia predicted, "The election of Frémont would be the end of the Union."

On the election day, Buchanan carried 14 of the 15 slave states, while Frémont won 11 of the 16 free states. Fillmore, meanwhile, carried only

Republican poster for the 1856 presidential campaign

one state—Maryland. Buchanan therefore became the new president.

★ The *Dred Scott* Decision

President Buchanan found himself almost immediately in the middle of another sectional dispute, again about slavery. Just two days after Buchanan took office, the Supreme Court issued a decision that threw the country back into crisis.

Suing for Freedom

The Court reviewed a case involving Dred Scott. He was the slave of Dr. John Emerson, an army surgeon who lived in St. Louis, Missouri. In the 1830s Emerson had taken Scott with him on tours of duty in Illinois and the northern part of the Louisiana Purchase. After they returned to Missouri, the doctor died, and Scott became the slave of Emerson's widow. In 1846 Scott sued for his freedom, saying that he had become free when he lived in free territory.

The case reached the U.S. Supreme Court in 1856. The justices—a majority of whom were from the South—had three key issues before them. First, the Court had to rule on whether Scott was a citizen of the United States and thus able to sue in federal court. Second, the Court needed to decide if his time living on free soil made him free. Third, the Court had to determine whether it was constitutional to prohibit slavery in parts of the Louisiana Purchase. This last ruling would affect the Missouri Compromise.

Dred Scott fought unsuccessfully to gain his freedom.

A Controversial Verdict

Chief Justice Roger B. Taney (TAW-nee), himself from a slaveholding family in Maryland, wrote the majority opinion in the ***Dred Scott*** decision in March 1857. First he addressed the issue of Dred Scott's citizenship. Taney said the nation's

Chief Justice Roger Taney shown next to a copy of the controversial majority opinion he wrote for the Dred Scott case

founders believed that African Americans "had no rights which a white man was bound to respect." He therefore concluded that all African Americans, whether slave or free, were not citizens under the U.S. Constitution. Thus, Dred Scott did not have the right to file suit in federal court.

Taney also ruled on the other issues before the Court. As to whether Scott's residence on free soil made him free, Taney flatly said it did not. Because Scott had returned to the slave state of Missouri, the chief justice said, "his *status*, as free or slave, depended on the laws of Missouri."

Finally, Taney declared that the Missouri Compromise restriction on slavery north of 36°30' to be unconstitutional. He pointed out that the Fifth Amendment said no one could "be deprived of life, liberty, or property without due process of law." Because slaves were considered property, Congress could not prohibit someone from taking slaves into a federal territory. Under this ruling, Congress had no right to ban slavery in any federal territory.

Most white southerners cheered the decision. It "covers every question regarding slavery and settles it in favor of the South," reported a Georgia newspaper. Another newspaper, the New Orleans *Picayune*, assured its readers that the ruling put "the whole basis of the . . . Republican organization under the ban of the law."

The ruling stunned many northerners. The Republicans were particularly upset because their platform in 1856 had argued that Congress held the right to ban slavery in the federal territories. Now the nation's highest court had ruled that Congress did not have this right.

Indeed, some northerners feared that the spread of slavery would not stop with the federal territories. Illinois lawyer Abraham Lincoln warned that a future Court ruling, or what he called "the next Dred Scott decision," would prohibit states from banning slavery:

❝ We shall *lie down* pleasantly dreaming that the people of *Missouri* are on the verge of making their state *free;* and we shall *awake* to the *reality,* instead, that the *Supreme* Court has made *Illinois* a *slave* state. ❞

⭐ The Lincoln-Douglas Debates

At the time of the *Dred Scott* decision, Lincoln was little known outside of Illinois. A native of Kentucky, he moved to the Midwest in 1816. Lincoln became involved in politics, serving four terms in the Illinois legislature and one term in Congress. A longtime Whig, he joined the Republican Party in 1856 and supported its efforts to halt the spread of slavery. In 1858 Illinois Republicans nominated him for a U.S. Senate seat.

His opponent was Democrat Stephen Douglas, who had represented Illinois in the Senate since 1847. Douglas was well known for the Kansas-Nebraska Act. In an attempt to take advantage of his opponent's popularity, Lincoln challenged Douglas to a series of debates throughout the state.

Lincoln Attacks Slavery

Thousands of people attended the seven **Lincoln-Douglas debates**, each of which lasted about three hours. In the debates held across Illinois, Lincoln stressed that the central issue in the campaign involved slavery and its future in the West.

Lincoln claimed that the Democrats wanted to spread slavery across the continent. He said his party believed that slavery was wrong and that "one of the methods of treating it as a wrong is to make provision [ensure] that *it shall grow no larger.*" In response to Taney's ruling in the *Dred Scott* decision, Lincoln said that African Americans were "entitled to all the natural rights" listed in the Declaration of Independence—namely, "the right to life, liberty, and the pursuit of happiness."

Lincoln tried to focus primarily on the extension of slavery rather than on the issue of racial equality. However, he was asked about his views on racial equality. He replied that African Americans were not necessarily the political or social equals of whites but that "in the right to eat the bread . . . which his own hand earns, he [an African American] *is my equal and the equal of Judge [Stephen] Douglas.*"

Douglas's Reply

Although Lincoln said he was not in favor of social and political equality for African Americans,

Abraham Lincoln stands to speak during his fourth debate with Stephen Douglas, who is seated to Lincoln's right.

Douglas insisted that Lincoln "thinks that the Negro is his brother. . . . Those of you who believe that the Negro is your equal . . . of course will vote for Mr. Lincoln." Douglas hoped that many white voters would be shocked by these statements and would refuse to vote for Lincoln as a result.

Douglas also criticized Lincoln for saying the nation could not remain "half slave and half free." Douglas said that this statement revealed a Republican desire to make every state a free state. This, he warned, would only lead to "a dissolution [destruction] of the Union" and "warfare between the North and the South."

The Freeport Doctrine

At the second debate, in the northern Illinois town of Freeport, Lincoln pressed Douglas on the apparent contradiction between the Democrats' belief in popular sovereignty and the *Dred Scott* decision. Lincoln asked Douglas to explain how, if Congress could not ban slavery from a federal territory, Congress could allow the citizens of that territory to ban it.

Douglas's response became known as the **Freeport Doctrine**. "It matters not" what the Supreme Court decides about slavery, said Douglas. He argued that

Wooden campaign doll of Stephen Douglas

❝the people have the lawful means to introduce it or exclude it as they please, for the reason that slavery cannot exist a day or an hour anywhere, unless it is supported by local police regulations.❞

The Freeport Doctrine put control of the slavery issue back in the hands of American citizens. The doctrine also helped Douglas win the Senate seat. However, Lincoln had made a strong showing in the debates. He had debated Douglas on even terms and emerged as one of the leaders of the new Republican Party.

SECTION 3 REVIEW

Identify and explain the significance of the following:
- **Republican Party**
- **James Buchanan**
- **John C. Frémont**
- **Dred Scott**
- **Roger B. Taney**
- ***Dred Scott* decision**
- **Abraham Lincoln**
- **Lincoln-Douglas debates**
- **Freeport Doctrine**

Reading for Content Understanding

1 **Main Idea** How was the Democratic Party affected by the passage of the Kansas-Nebraska Act? How did the act affect the Whigs?

2 **Main Idea** On what grounds did Dred Scott sue for his freedom?

3 **Constitutional Heritage** What did the Supreme Court rule in the *Dred Scott* decision? What arguments did Roger B. Taney make in the majority opinion of the case?

4 **Writing** *Informing* Write a paragraph explaining Abraham Lincoln's views on the spread of slavery and describing Stephen Douglas's response during their debates.

5 **Critical Thinking** *Determining the Strength of an Argument* Do you agree with Stephen Douglas's theories put forth in the Freeport Doctrine? Explain your answer.

Secession

Reading Focus

How did Americans react to John Brown's raid on Harpers Ferry?

What factors led to Lincoln's victory in the presidential election of 1860?

Why did some southern states decide to leave the Union?

Key Terms

John Brown's raid
Constitutional Union Party
secession
Confederate States of America

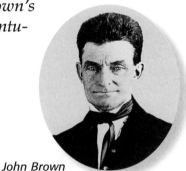

*A*FTER THE POTTAWATOMIE MASSACRE, *John Brown's life was in danger. He left Kansas and eventually returned to New England. There Brown was frustrated by the fact that most abolitionists wanted to end slavery without resorting to violence. "Talk! talk! talk!" he said with disgust after attending a meeting of the New England Anti-Slavery Society. "That will never free the slaves. What is needed is action—action."*

John Brown

★ The Raid on Harpers Ferry

In 1858 John Brown had several plans for aiding the abolitionist cause. One plan involved helping more slaves to escape to freedom. Another was to strike a blow that would rally antislavery Americans to act. Brown decided to follow the latter course of action. He proposed raiding a federal arsenal in Virginia and seizing the weapons stored there. Then he would arm the slaves in the surrounding area. This force would then move south along the Appalachians, creating panic and freeing more slaves as it went. Brown planned to take hostage or kill any white southerner who stood in the way of his grand plan.

He urged his fellow abolitionists to give him enough money to recruit, train, and supply a small army. However, after nearly two years of fundraising and recruiting, Brown's band contained only 22 men—including three of his sons and himself.

The Night Raid

On the night of October 16, 1859, **John Brown's raid** began as Brown and his men entered Harpers Ferry, Virginia, a town on the Potomac River about 50 miles northwest of Washington. After seizing the federal arsenal there, Brown sent several of his men into the countryside to urge slaves to come to Harpers Ferry.

Brown hoped enslaved African Americans would join him but none did—no doubt knowing they would be severely punished if they took part in an uprising. Instead, white southerners from Harpers Ferry and the surrounding communities armed themselves and attacked Brown. Eight of his men and three local men were killed in the exchange of gunfire. Brown and some of his followers retreated to the safety of a firehouse.

Federal troops arrived in Harpers Ferry on the night of October 17. The following morning Colonel Robert E. Lee ordered a squad of marines to storm the firehouse. In a matter of seconds, the marines killed two more of Brown's men and captured the rest—including Brown.

In less than two weeks, Brown was indicted and convicted of treason, murder, and conspiracy to incite slave rebellion—all offenses punishable by death. Some of the others who participated in the raid, such as John A. Copeland—a fugitive slave—received death sentences. On the way to his execution, Copeland said, "If I am dying for freedom, I could not die for a better cause—I had rather die than be a slave!" On November 2, convinced that he would be sentenced to death, Brown delivered a memorable speech:

> **It is unjust that I should suffer such a penalty. . . . I believe that to have interfered . . . in behalf of His [God's] despised poor, is no wrong, but right. Now, if it is deemed necessary that I should forfeit my life for the furtherance of the ends of justice, and mingle my blood . . . with the blood of millions in this slave country whose rights are disregarded by wicked, cruel, and unjust enactments, I say, let it be done.**

As expected, the judge ordered Brown to be hanged. The sentence was carried out a month later, on December 2, 1859.

Global Connections

Reactions to John Brown's Raid

While the raid on Harpers Ferry sparked debate throughout the United States, news of John Brown's actions also stirred up strong emotions across the Atlantic, particularly in Great Britain. Three weeks after Brown's execution, Sarah Parker Remond, an African American from Massachusetts, addressed an antislavery meeting in the British city of Leeds. When she declared that she had no criticism of Brown or of "the means which he took to carry out his great idea," she was interrupted by approving cries of "Hear, hear!"

British politician William Edward Forster said, "Whatever John Brown may have done toward freeing the slaves . . . he has exposed the utter [complete] weakness of the slave system." Other Europeans also praised Brown and the abolitionist cause.

In early 1860 French writer Victor Hugo predicted that Brown's raid would lead to the breakup of the United States. "Between the North and the South stands the gallows of Brown," Hugo wrote. "Union is no longer possible: such a crime cannot be shared."

Understanding What You Read

1. How did the audience in Leeds react to Sarah Parker Remond's show of support for John Brown's raid?

2. Why do you think some Europeans felt so certain that the raid on Harpers Ferry would lead to the end of slavery?

3. Why might French writer Victor Hugo have argued that Brown's raid would lead to the break-up of the Union?

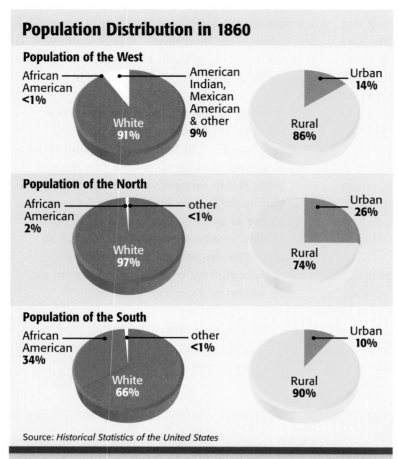

Population Distribution in 1860

Population of the West

African American <1%

American Indian, Mexican American & other 9%

White 91%

Urban 14%

Rural 86%

Population of the North

African American 2%

other <1%

White 97%

Urban 26%

Rural 74%

Population of the South

African American 34%

other <1%

White 66%

Urban 10%

Rural 90%

Source: *Historical Statistics of the United States*

Where People Lived The vast majority of people in each region lived in rural areas. What percentage of the southern population lived in urban areas?

A National Uproar

Many people in the North mourned the death of John Brown. In that part of the country, church bells rang and public buildings were draped in black on the day of his execution. Novelist Louisa May Alcott referred to him as "Saint John the Just." Reverend Henry Highland Garnet, a well-known African American abolitionist, said that Brown gave his life as "a sacrifice for the sake of justice and equal human rights."

Not everyone who opposed slavery felt this way. Some condemned Brown's actions. For example, Abraham Lincoln said that while Brown "agreed with us in thinking slavery wrong, that cannot excuse violence, bloodshed, and treason."

John Brown is led to his execution on December 2, 1859. Writer Henry David Thoreau called Brown "an angel of light."

Most southern whites—slaveholders and nonslaveholders alike—felt threatened. With so many in the North sympathetic to Brown's cause, southerners wondered how long it would be before a "John Brown the Second" attacked another southern target. As one South Carolina newspaper put it, "We are convinced the safety of the South lies only outside the present Union." Another journal from the same state was more blunt: "The sooner we get out of the Union, the better."

★ The Election of 1860

In this climate of distrust, Americans prepared for another presidential election. Politicians and editors across the South, associating the Republican Party with abolitionists and John Brown, warned that a Republican victory in the election would mean disunion. South Carolina and three other states promised to act swiftly should the Republicans win the election.

The Democrats were the first party to try to nominate a presidential candidate in 1860. They met in Charleston, South Carolina, in late April but failed to select a candidate who was acceptable to both the

The Metropolitan Museum of Art

This banner calls for the election of Republican Abraham Lincoln and his vice presidential candidate, Hannibal Hamlin, in 1860.

northern and southern members of the party. They agreed to meet again in Baltimore in six weeks.

When the Democrats assembled in Baltimore in June, they still could not agree on a single candidate, so the party split in two. Northern Democrats nominated Senator Stephen Douglas, while southern Democrats rallied behind the current vice president, John C. Breckinridge of Kentucky. Breckinridge strongly supported the spread of slavery, but he did not believe that a Republican victory in the election would justify dissolving the Union.

Meanwhile, in early May some northerners and southerners—many of them former Whigs—formed a new political party. Called the **Constitutional Union Party**, its platform was simple: it recognized "no political principles other than the Constitution of the country, the Union of the states, and the enforcement of the laws." Members of this new party met in Baltimore, Maryland, and selected John Bell of Tennessee as their presidential candidate. Bell was a slaveholder but had opposed the Kansas-Nebraska Act in 1854.

In mid-May the Republicans held their convention in Chicago. Although Senator William Seward of New York was the leading candidate, many Republicans worried

that his antislavery views made him a poor choice. Thus, Abraham Lincoln won the nomination on the third ballot. Lincoln was a moderate who opposed the spread of slavery but promised not to support abolishing it where it already existed.

The presidential race showed just how divided the country had become. The four-man contest was really a pair of two-man contests. Lincoln challenged Douglas for the North's electoral votes; Bell and Breckinridge competed for those of the South. If they could not win the election themselves, Douglas, Bell, and Breckinridge hoped to win enough votes to prevent Lincoln from winning in the electoral college. Such an outcome would send the vote to the House of Representatives.

In this they failed. Lincoln won the race, taking less than 40 percent of the overall popular vote but winning 180 of the 183 electoral votes in the free states. Breckinridge and Bell split the electoral

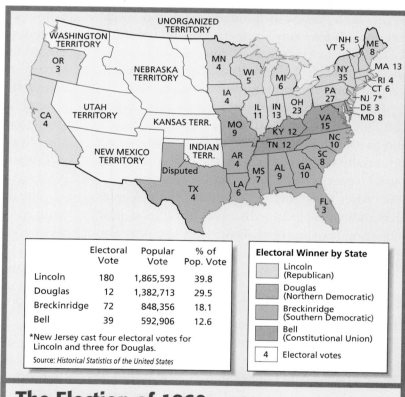

	Electoral Vote	Popular Vote	% of Pop. Vote
Lincoln	180	1,865,593	39.8
Douglas	12	1,382,713	29.5
Breckinridge	72	848,356	18.1
Bell	39	592,906	12.6

*New Jersey cast four electoral votes for Lincoln and three for Douglas.
Source: *Historical Statistics of the United States*

Electoral Winner by State
- Lincoln (Republican)
- Douglas (Northern Democratic)
- Breckinridge (Southern Democratic)
- Bell (Constitutional Union)
- 4 — Electoral votes

The Election of 1860

Learning from Maps The division between North and South was clearly reflected in the election of 1860. Lincoln's victory increased tensions between the regions, and secession soon followed.

Place Which state had the most electoral votes? Which candidate won this state?

votes of slave states, with the exception of Missouri. Despite having the second-highest number of overall popular votes, Douglas won only one state—Missouri—outright and finished with just 12 electoral votes.

The election results angered many southerners. Lincoln did not campaign in their region and did not carry a single southern state, but he would be the next president. This was a strong reminder of how the South was losing its political power on the national level.

Leaving the Union

Many southern whites believed that once in power, Lincoln would move to abolish slavery in the South. They feared this action would destroy the social and economic fabric of the region. Lincoln insisted he would not touch slavery in the southern states. He had said, however, that the institution must be put on a "course of ultimate extinction." That was enough for many southerners, who vowed to act quickly to protect their interests. A man in Mississippi said, "Let us rally . . . before the enemy can make good his promise to overwhelm us."

Just four days after Lincoln's election, South Carolina's legislature called for a special convention to consider the question of **secession**, the act of formally withdrawing from the Union. The convention opened in Charleston on December 17, 1860. After three days of speeches, the delegates unanimously voted to dissolve "the union now subsisting [existing] between South Carolina and other States."

A Constitutional Question

The Constitution does not directly address the issue of secession. Despite this, southern secessionists believed that they had a right to leave the Union. They pointed out that each of the original states had voluntarily joined the Union by holding a special convention that had ratified the Constitution. Surely, they reasoned, states could also leave the Union by the same process—the will of a popular convention—whenever they wished.

Critics of secession thought this argument was ridiculous. President Buchanan said the Union

Representatives in the House

YEAR	SLAVE STATES	FREE STATES
1840	88	135
1860	85	155

was not "a mere voluntary association of States, to be dissolved at pleasure by any one of the contracting parties." President-Elect Abraham Lincoln agreed, saying, "No State, upon its own mere motion, can lawfully get out of the Union." Lincoln added, "They can only do so against [the] law, and by revolution."

The Crittenden Compromise

While the South Carolina secession convention was being held, a plan to save the Union was introduced in Congress. Senator John J. Crittenden of Kentucky proposed a series of constitutional amendments to satisfy the South. One would extend the 36°30' line to the Pacific coast, allowing slavery in all territories "now held, or hereafter acquired" south of this line. Another would use federal funds to reimburse slaveholders who were prevented from recovering their fugitive slaves in the North. Crittenden hoped his plan would address the chief fears of the South and thus prevent secession and civil war.

President-Elect Lincoln strongly disagreed with this plan. He sent a flurry of letters to Republicans in the Senate, urging them to oppose Crittenden's compromise plan. "Entertain no proposition for a compromise in regard to the extension of slavery," Lincoln wrote. "The tug has to come and better now than later." When the Senate voted on the Crittenden Compromise, every Republican present rejected it, as Lincoln had requested.

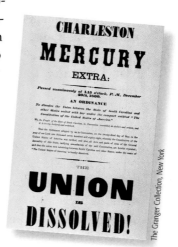

Broadside announcing the secession of South Carolina

The Granger Collection, New York

The Confederate States of America

By February 1, 1861, Mississippi, Florida, Alabama, Georgia, Louisiana, and Texas had followed South Carolina's lead and seceded from the Union. This did not mean that everyone in these states supported secession, however. Some public figures tried to slow or stop the march toward disunion—and promptly suffered the consequences of opposing the public will. In Texas, for example, Governor Sam Houston was removed from office for standing in the way of secession.

On February 4, delegates from the seceding states met in Montgomery, Alabama, to form a new nation—the **Confederate States of America**, also known as the Confederacy. It took the delegates just four days to draft a constitution—mainly because this document closely resembled the U.S. Constitution. Among the key differences was a guarantee of the right to hold slaves.

Next, the assembled delegates elected Jefferson Davis of Mississippi president of the Confederacy and Alexander Stephens of Georgia vice president. Davis was a graduate of West Point and a veteran of the Mexican War. He was secretary of war under President Pierce and served in the Senate until Mississippi left the Union.

With his military background, Davis hoped to be appointed general in chief or secretary of war in the Confederate government. He did not seek the presidency of the Confederacy nor was he initially delighted to receive it. According to his wife, Varina, when he was telegraphed news of his election,

The Granger Collection, New York

" he looked so grieved that I feared some evil had befallen [happened to] our family. After a few minutes' painful silence he told me [what the telegram contained], as a man might speak of a sentence of death. "

Confederate president Jefferson Davis

Davis was a highly intelligent and hardworking politician who was intensely loyal to his friends. However, he also had a habit of involving himself in details that should have been left to his staff. Furthermore, his devotion to his friends—and dislike of his perceived enemies—often tended to cloud his judgment. These personal qualities would later create problems for the Confederate States of America.

SECTION 4 REVIEW

Identify and explain the significance of the following:
- **John Brown's raid**
- **John C. Breckinridge**
- **Constitutional Union Party**
- **John Bell**
- **secession**
- **John J. Crittenden**
- **Confederate States of America**
- **Jefferson Davis**

Reading for Content Understanding

1 **Main Idea** Describe the northern and southern reactions to John Brown's raid on Harpers Ferry.

2 **Main Idea** What led to South Carolina's secession from the Union?

3 **Citizenship and Democracy** How did the four-way race for president help Lincoln win the election of 1860?

4 **Writing** *Persuading* Write a letter to Congress urging members to reject the Crittenden Compromise.

5 **Critical Thinking** *Determining the Strength of an Argument* Do you think South Carolina had a valid reason for seceding from the Union? Explain your answer.

CHAPTER 18 REVIEW

Chapter Summary

The U.S. victory in the Mexican War revived the bitter debate over slavery in the western territories. The Compromise of 1850 failed to settle the slavery debate, and conflict soon broke out in Kansas. After Abraham Lincoln won the 1860 presidential election, South Carolina seceded from the Union. Other southern states followed and formed the Confederate States of America. ■

On a separate sheet of paper, complete the following activities.

Identifying People and Ideas

Describe the historical significance of the following:

1. sectionalism
2. Free-Soil Party
3. Harriet Beecher Stowe
4. Stephen Douglas
5. Republican Party
6. Roger B. Taney
7. John Brown's raid
8. secession
9. Confederate States of America
10. Jefferson Davis

Internet Activity

go.hrw.com
SA0 John Brown

Search the Internet through the HRW Web site for information on John Brown's life. Then write an obituary that might have appeared in a northern or southern newspaper shortly after Brown's execution.

Understanding Main Ideas

1. Why did southerners oppose the Wilmot Proviso?
2. What were the five measures of the Compromise of 1850?
3. How did pro-slavery and antislavery forces oppose each other in Kansas?
4. What effect did the Kansas-Nebraska Act have on the Democratic Party?
5. Who were the four candidates for president in the 1860 election, and which party did each candidate represent?
6. What was one key difference between the Confederacy's constitution and the U.S. Constitution?

Reviewing Themes

1. **Geographic Diversity** Why did the Mexican Cession renew tensions about slavery between northern and southern states? How did the Compromise of 1850 attempt to solve this problem?

Using the Time Line

Number your paper from 1 to 5. Match the letters on the time line below with the following events.

1. The Kansas-Nebraska Act is signed into law.
2. Antislavery northerners form the Free-Soil Party when the Whig Party refuses to address the slavery issue.
3. South Carolina votes to secede from the Union.
4. Abraham Lincoln and Stephen Douglas, competing for a U.S. Senate seat in Illinois, begin a series of seven debates.
5. After much debate about upsetting the balance of free and slave states, California is admitted to the Union as a free state.

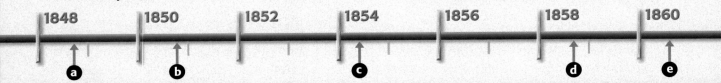

1848 1850 1852 1854 1856 1858 1860

a b c d e

2. **Citizenship and Democracy** What did the Supreme Court decide in the *Dred Scott* case? Why was the decision strongly criticized?

3. **Constitutional Heritage** What event prompted South Carolina and other southern states to secede from the Union? What was their legal argument for secession?

Thinking Critically

1. **Drawing Conclusions** Why do you think slave narratives were used in the abolitionist movement?

2. **Supporting a Point of View** Do you think John Brown was a hero or a criminal? Explain your answer.

3. **Evaluating** Which candidate would you have voted for in the election of 1860? Explain your answer.

Writing About History

1. **Creating** Write a review of *Uncle Tom's Cabin* that might have appeared in a northern newspaper in 1855.

2. **Expressing** Imagine that you are a laborer planning to move to Kansas. Write a short letter to the local newspaper explaining why you oppose the Kansas-Nebraska Act.

Linking Geography and History

1. **Region** Why did many northerners object to the Fugitive Slave Law?

2. **Location** Where is Harpers Ferry located? Why did John Brown choose this place to begin his movement to free slaves?

History Skills Workshop

Reading Maps Study The United States in 1860 map to the right. Then answer the following questions: (a) How many slave and free states were there in 1860? (b) What would the total number of senators have been for the free states and for the slave states in 1860? (c) How might slavery in the territories affect political power?

Building Your Portfolio

Complete the following activities individually or in groups.

1. **New Political Parties** Prepare a chart showing the political parties that were formed from 1848 to 1860. The chart should include information about the year the party was formed (and ended, if applicable), the party's platform, presidential candidates, and region of strongest support. Add appropriate images to your chart. Finally, write a paragraph to accompany your chart, explaining the importance of third parties in political elections.

2. **Abolitionist Literature** Imagine that you are a publisher in the 1850s and have been hired to promote one of the works of abolitionist literature in the northern United States. Create a poster to advertise one these works, such as the *Narrative of the Life of Frederick Douglass,* the *Narrative of Sojourner Truth*, or *Uncle Tom's Cabin.* Be sure that your poster clearly states what the work is about and explains why people should buy and read the book.

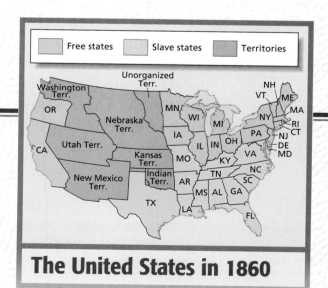

The United States in 1860

■ CHAPTER 19 ■
The Civil War

(1861–1865)

Through the haze and just beyond his reach, Confederate general Jubal Early could see the Capitol's new dome rising only about six miles away. "We haven't taken Washington," Early told his troops, "but we've scared Abe Lincoln." It was the summer of 1864, and the country was entering the fourth year of bloody fighting between the North and the South. Three years earlier, few people had expected such a long-lasting and serious conflict.

THEMES

Technology and Society
What effect might new technology have on how a war is fought?

Economic Development
How might a civil war affect a nation's economy?

Cultural Diversity
In what ways might different groups contribute to a war effort?

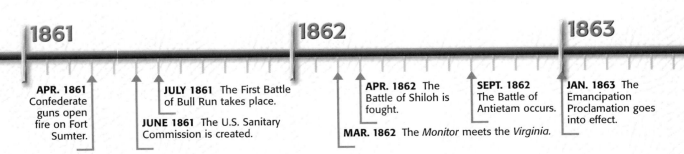

1861

1862

1863

APR. 1861 Confederate guns open fire on Fort Sumter.

JULY 1861 The First Battle of Bull Run takes place.

JUNE 1861 The U.S. Sanitary Commission is created.

APR. 1862 The Battle of Shiloh is fought.

MAR. 1862 The *Monitor* meets the *Virginia.*

SEPT. 1862 The Battle of Antietam occurs.

JAN. 1863 The Emancipation Proclamation goes into effect.

The War Begins

Reading Focus

Why was Fort Sumter so important to both the North and the South?

What was the strategic importance of the border states?

What advantages and strategies did each side have as the war began?

Key Terms

Fort Sumter
border states
cotton diplomacy

LATE ONE FEBRUARY day in 1861, the sound of the "Star Spangled Banner" filled the air at the United States Military Academy at West Point, New York. As the song that later became the national anthem played, cadets began to appear in the windows of their barracks. Suddenly, one cadet let out a cheer for the Union flag. Another responded with a cheer for the Confederate states. A shouting match then erupted among the cadets, drowning out the music. These young men were supposed to become the future leaders of the U.S. Army. Their ranks divided, however, as southern states left the Union in late 1860 and early 1861.

Recruitment poster, the Spirit of '61

IMAGE ON LEFT PAGE: *Fort Sumter being bombarded by Confederate cannons in April 1861*

1864

1865

NOV. 1863 President Lincoln delivers the Gettysburg Address.

JULY 1863 The Union army wins major victories at Vicksburg, Mississippi, and Gettysburg, Pennsylvania.

SEPT. 1864 Atlanta falls to the Union.

APR. 1865 General Lee surrenders at Appomattox Courthouse.

Abraham Lincoln

An amateur inventor himself, Abraham Lincoln loved gadgets and new technology. He collected many models of proposed weapons, and personally tested several inventions on the White House lawn.

Lincoln hoped that the development and use of new weapons technology would help speed the end of the war. As a result, he almost always was willing to listen to someone with a fresh idea. The president was particularly impressed by an inventive naval officer named John Dahlgren. Lincoln often traveled across Washington to witness Dahlgren's experiments with new guns and explosives at the U.S. Navy Yard.

Not every inventor, however, impressed Lincoln. One gentleman said that he could improve military planning by accurately predicting the weather. Lincoln wrote that "he told me three days ago that it would not rain again [for five days]. It is raining now and has been for ten hours."

★ Lincoln Faces a Crisis

Several challenges faced President-Elect Abraham Lincoln before his inauguration in 1861. First, the Republican Party was sharply divided. To ease these tensions, Lincoln later appointed several members of his rival party to his cabinet. For example, he asked William H. Seward, a vocal opponent of slavery, to serve as secretary of state.

A far greater challenge was the breakup of the Union. Before Lincoln took office, seven states had seceded. Hoping to prevent the loss of more southern states, Lincoln pledged in his March 4, 1861, inaugural address that he would not try to abolish slavery in the South. He also promised the South that the federal "government will not assail [attack] you. You can have no conflict without being yourselves the aggressors." However, Lincoln also stated his intention to preserve the Union. Even as Lincoln prepared this address, the Confederacy was seizing federal property in the South. It took control of many federal mints, arsenals, and forts.

One important federal outpost in the South was **Fort Sumter**. Located in South Carolina, the fort controlled the entrance to Charleston Harbor. By early March 1861 the federal troops at Fort Sumter were running low on supplies. Some of Lincoln's advisers recommended that he surrender the fort. Instead, Lincoln decided to resupply the federal troops there. Before the supply ships arrived, however, South Carolina demanded that the troops evacuate the fort. The fort's commander, Major Robert Anderson, refused to leave, saying politely but firmly, "Gentlemen, I will await your fire."

Before sunrise on April 12, 1861, Confederate guns opened fire on Fort Sumter. A witness wrote that the first shots "brought every soldier in the harbor to his feet, and every man, woman, and child in the city of Charleston from their beds." Anderson and his men endured the Confederate bombardment for more than 30 hours before surrendering.

The fall of Fort Sumter stunned the North. Lincoln declared that a state of rebellion existed in the South. He called on the state governors to provide 75,000 militiamen to help put down the rebellion. Mary Boykin Chesnut, whose husband became a Confederate congressman, wrote in her diary during this time:

Secretary of State William H. Seward

❝I did not know that one could live in such days of excitement. . . . Everybody tells you half of something, and then rushes off . . . to hear the last news.❞

★ Choosing Sides

Democratic senator Stephen Douglas, speaking in support of Lincoln's call for troops, declared, "Every man must be for the United States or against it. There can be no neutrals in this war, *only patriots—or traitors.*" While northerners rallied behind the Union, the non-Confederate slave states were choosing which side to support.

The Upper South

The states of the Upper South—North Carolina, Tennessee, and Virginia—joined the Confederacy shortly after Lincoln's request for troops. "The South must go with the South. . . . Blood is thicker than Water," wrote a North Carolinian. Farther west, Arkansas made the same decision.

The Upper South, with its greater population and many factories, provided soldiers and industrial resources to the Confederacy. The Upper South also was the site of the new capital of the Confederacy—Richmond, Virginia—which replaced the former capital of Montgomery, Alabama.

The Border States

Four slave states—Delaware, Kentucky, Maryland, and Missouri—bordered the North. The strategic position of these four **border states** made them vital to both the North and the South. Kentucky and Missouri dominated key stretches of the Ohio and Mississippi Rivers, while Maryland separated the federal capital of Washington from the North.

In Delaware, only a few of the slaveholders supported secession. In Kentucky, Missouri, and Maryland, however, people were deeply divided. Troops from Kentucky and Missouri served in both the Union and the Confederacy. The citizens of Baltimore, Maryland, rioted and attacked Union soldiers marching to the front lines.

Despite these divisions, Kentucky, Maryland, and Missouri eventually voted against secession.

Union recruiting poster

Lincoln sent federal troops into Maryland to help keep order and to discourage secession. He also sent troops into western Virginia. This encouraged the region's largely pro-Union population to resist joining the Confederacy. The new state of West Virginia joined the Union in 1863.

In the border states, members of the same family often joined opposing sides. For example, one of Kentucky senator John Crittenden's sons became a general in the Union army, while another served as a general in the Confederate army. The president's Kentucky-born wife, Mary Todd Lincoln, had four brothers who fought for the Confederacy. Disagreements over secession deeply divided many friends and families.

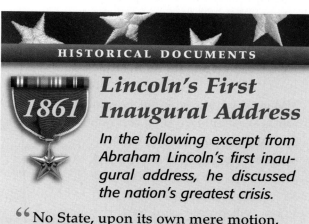

HISTORICAL DOCUMENTS

1861 Lincoln's First Inaugural Address

In the following excerpt from Abraham Lincoln's first inaugural address, he discussed the nation's greatest crisis.

❝No State, upon its own mere motion, can lawfully get out of the Union . . . acts of violence, within any State or States, against the authority of the United States, are . . . revolutionary. . . . There needs to be no bloodshed or violence; and there shall be none, unless it be forced upon the national authority. . . . We are not enemies, but friends. We must not be enemies. Though passion may have strained, it must not break our bonds of affection.❞

Understanding Primary Sources

1. How did Lincoln view secession?
2. Under what circumstances would Lincoln have supported military action?

★ The Volunteer Spirit

Neither side was militarily prepared when the war began. Both sides' armies relied on volunteers to fight the war.

Volunteer Armies

The Union army had only 16,000 troops at the start of the war. The army soon swelled with thousands of volunteers who responded to Lincoln's call for troops. One northern soldier explained why he volunteered:

> ❝[It is] a duty I owe to my country and to my children to do what I can to preserve this government as I shudder to think what is ahead for them if this government should be overthrown.❞

Many southern volunteers shared the view of Thomas Webber of Virginia, who said he wanted to fight "against the invading foe who now pollute the sacred soil of my beloved native state." Early in the war, Union soldiers asked one captured southerner why he was fighting. He replied simply, "I'm fighting because you're down here."

Helping Soldiers

Civilians on both sides helped those in uniform. They raised money, provided aid for soldiers and their families, and ran emergency hospitals. In April 1861 Dr. Elizabeth Blackwell, the first woman to receive a license to practice medicine, started a group that then helped pressure President Lincoln to form the U.S. Sanitary Commission in June 1861. Run by clergyman Henry Bellows, the Sanitary, as

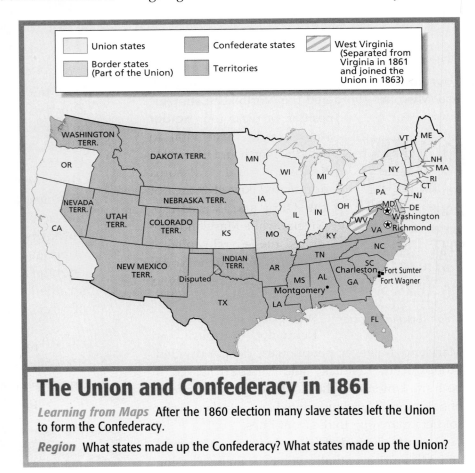

Eleanor S. Brockenbrough Library, the Museum of the Confederacy, Richmond, Virginia, Photography by Katherine Wetzel

A Confederate soldier

it was known, had tens of thousands of volunteers. They sent bandages, medicines, and food to Union army camps and hospitals. In the field, the commission's staff and volunteers worked to prevent disease and improve the health of Union troops.

★ Northern and Southern Resources

The North had several key advantages over the South at the beginning of the war. The North had a much larger population and could recruit more soldiers. Most of the nation's factories also were in the North. In addition, the North's better network of railways allowed for more efficient transportation. The North also had more shipyards to produce naval vessels. Finally, the Union was able to raise more money to spend on the war effort.

The Confederacy had several advantages going into the war. The South's military tradition

Union states
Border states (Part of the Union)
Confederate states
Territories
West Virginia (Separated from Virginia in 1861 and joined the Union in 1863)

The Union and Confederacy in 1861

Learning from Maps After the 1860 election many slave states left the Union to form the Confederacy.

Region What states made up the Confederacy? What states made up the Union?

provided it with a large number of talented officers. In addition, the South needed only to defend itself until the people and the government of the North grew tired of war. The North, on the other hand, faced the difficult task of having to conquer and occupy large amounts of enemy territory.

Women on both sides contributed to the war effort. These women are making gun cartridges.

 ## War Strategies

The Union and the Confederacy took different approaches to winning the war. Each side planned its strategy according to its strengths.

At the start of the war, Union general Winfield Scott developed a plan to defeat the South. He hoped to use a naval blockade to cut off southern seaports and thereby strangle the South's economy. Scott also wanted to gain control of the Mississippi River, dividing the Confederacy and cutting its communications. Scott believed that this strategy would defeat the Confederacy "with less bloodshed than by any other plan." This two-part plan became the basic Union strategy. Knowing that such a strategy would take time to succeed, many northern leaders called for a direct strike on the southern capital of Richmond.

The Confederacy's early strategy was to defend itself against northern attacks and to wear down the Union's will to fight. The Confederate offensive plan focused on seizing Washington. The South also tried to win foreign support, particularly from Britain, through the use of **cotton diplomacy**.

Confederate leaders hoped the British government would support the Confederacy because of southern cotton's importance to Britain's textile industry. One southern paper told planters, "Keep every bale of cotton on the plantation. Don't send a thread . . . till England and France have recognized the Confederacy." The British, however, had a large supply of cotton when the war began and later were able to obtain cotton from India and Egypt.

The strategies of the North and South led to a war that was fought on several land fronts and at sea. The separate regions in which combat took place are known as theaters of war. Many of the best-known battles of the war took place in the eastern theater, which included fighting in Virginia, Maryland, and Pennsylvania.

SECTION 1 REVIEW

Identify and explain the significance of the following:

- **Abraham Lincoln**
- **Fort Sumter**
- **border states**
- **Elizabeth Blackwell**
- **Winfield Scott**
- **cotton diplomacy**

Reading for Content Understanding

1 **Main Idea** Why did the Confederacy want to control Fort Sumter?

2 **Main Idea** What was the North's strategy for winning the war? What was the South's strategy?

3 **Geographic Diversity** *Region* Why was it so important for the Union that the border states not join the Confederacy?

4 **Writing** *Classifying* Make a chart showing the advantages and disadvantages that the North and the South had at the beginning of the war. Based on the chart, write a short paragraph explaining which side would most likely win the war.

5 **Critical Thinking** *Evaluating* Why do you think Lincoln refused to surrender Fort Sumter? What did he hope to achieve?

The War in the East

Reading Focus

What battles occurred when the Union army tried to achieve its main goal in the East?

How did Confederate strategy change once Robert E. Lee took command?

How did the North and the South carry out the war at sea?

Key Terms

First Battle of Bull Run
Seven Days Battles
Second Battle of Bull Run
Battle of Antietam
ironclads

IN THE MONTHS *after the fall of Fort Sumter, the northern public demanded bold action. The* Confederate Congress was due to meet in Richmond on July 20, 1861. *As Union troops massed in Washington during the early summer of 1861, a northern newspaper cried, "Forward to Richmond! Forward to Richmond! The Rebel Congress Must Not Be Allowed to Meet There." Sensitive to public opinion, President Lincoln ordered that plans be drawn up for an offensive against the Confederate capital.*

A Union army drum

⭐ The First Battle of Bull Run

The first major clash of Union and Confederate armies took place in July 1861. President Lincoln ordered General Irvin McDowell to begin the push toward the Confederate capital of Richmond. Many northerners expected an easy victory. Advancing from Washington, McDowell's 35,000 troops were joined by civilians from Washington hoping to witness an afternoon of excitement. McDowell complained that his barely trained soldiers "stopped every moment to pick blackberries or get water; they would not keep in the ranks, order as you pleased."

The Union army finally met its Confederate opposition about 25 miles to the southwest of Washington, near Manassas, Virginia. Some 35,000 Confederates held positions along a creek called Bull Run. At first the Union troops drove the left side of the Confederate line back. Confederate resistance stiffened, however, when a unit under General Thomas J. Jackson held firm. "Look!" one southern officer cried out, "There is Jackson standing like a stone wall! Rally behind the Virginians!" The Confederates rallied, and General "Stonewall" Jackson flung his troops against the northern line. As they charged forward, the Confederates let out their terrifying Rebel Yell.

Northern correspondent Charles Coffin witnessed the battle. He wrote:

> **There is smoke, dust, wild talking, shouting; hissings, howlings, explosions. It is a new, strange, unanticipated experience to the soldiers of both armies, far different from what they thought it would be.**

Fresh southern reinforcements soon arrived, driving the Union army back. Soon it was retreating to Washington. Had the Confederates been less tired and better organized, they might have pursued the northern forces and even captured Washington. In the **First Battle of Bull Run**, the Confederacy dashed Union hopes of winning the war quickly and easily.

general Joseph Johnston was severely wounded in the fighting.

With Johnston unavailable, General Robert E. Lee took charge of the Confederate army in Virginia. Lee was among the most talented officers on either side. The son of a Revolutionary War hero, he had graduated from the U.S. Military Academy at West Point, served in the Mexican War, and led the federal troops that captured John Brown at Harpers Ferry. In 1861 Lee had declined Lincoln's request to take command of Union forces. Although Lee personally opposed slavery and secession, he felt his first loyalty was to his home state. As he told a northern friend, "I cannot raise my hand against my birthplace, my home, my children." Once Virginia seceded, he became a Confederate. Lee resigned from the U.S. Army and

The War in Virginia

Although the defeat at Bull Run had struck a heavy blow to northern pride, Lincoln still wanted to capture Richmond. He sent Union forces back into Virginia in the spring of 1862 under the leadership of General George B. McClellan.

By early April 1862 McClellan was camped with about 100,000 soldiers near Yorktown, Virginia, southeast of Richmond. McClellan delayed attacking, however, because he mistakenly believed that his troops were greatly outnumbered by the Confederates. McClellan's hesitation allowed the Confederates to reinforce Richmond's defenses.

In early May, McClellan finally took Yorktown, forcing the southern army to retreat. At the end of the month, the two armies fought again near Richmond. The Confederate

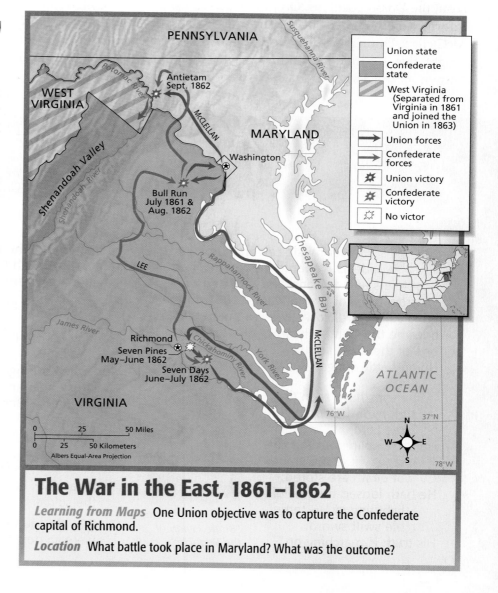

The War in the East, 1861–1862

Learning from Maps One Union objective was to capture the Confederate capital of Richmond.

Location What battle took place in Maryland? What was the outcome?

returned to Virginia, where he became commander of Virginia's military forces.

General Robert E. Lee was widely respected in both the North and the South for his intelligent, bold leadership.

 ## More Southern Victories

During the summer of 1862, General Lee pursued an offensive-defensive strategy in Virginia. He strengthened his positions and then launched attacks in the eastern theater.

The Seven Days Battles

As General McClellan awaited reinforcements, Lee moved to isolate McClellan's army and push it away from Richmond. In preparation for his attack, Lee sent a cavalry unit under General Jeb Stuart to scout the Union positions. On June 26, 1862, using information obtained by Stuart, Lee attacked McClellan. During the next week, the two armies fought five separate times during what became known as the **Seven Days Battles**. Casualties mounted as soldiers on each side bravely charged fortified positions. Confederate general D. H. Hill grimly described one failed attack on the Union line: "It was not war—it was murder." Confederates suffered more than 20,000 casualties but inflicted nearly 16,000 on the Union. More importantly, Lee forced McClellan to retreat from the area around Richmond.

American Arts

Civil War Songs

Civil War music celebrated political ideals, honored heroes, inspired soldiers and civilians, and reflected the sorrow brought by the war. In 1861 northerner Julia Ward Howe wrote a poem that became the "Battle Hymn of the Republic," one of the most popular Union battle songs.

"Mine eyes have seen the glory of the coming of the Lord;
He is trampling out the vintage where the grapes of wrath are stored;
He hath loosed the fateful lightning of His terrible swift sword:
His truth is marching on."

Song sheet for the "Battle Hymn of the Republic"

In the South, "The Bonnie Blue Flag," which referred to South Carolina's new flag, became a national anthem for the Confederacy.

"We are a band of brothers and native to the soil,
Fighting for our liberty, with treasure, blood and toil.
And when our rights were threatened, the cry rose near and far—
Hurrah for the Bonnie Blue Flag that bears a single star."

Understanding the Arts

1. What does each of these songs say are the soldiers' reasons for fighting?

2. Why do you think these battle songs were so popular during the Civil War?

The Second Battle of Bull Run

After McClellan's defeat, Lincoln ordered General John Pope to advance directly on Richmond from Washington. Pope advised his soldiers, "Let us look before us and not behind. Success and glory are in the advance." McClellan disagreed. "Pope will be thrashed . . . and be disposed of," he predicted.

Lee's plan to stop Pope was daring. He sent troops under Stonewall Jackson around Pope's right side to take up a position near the site of the First Battle of Bull Run. With Pope thus distracted, Lee's main force fell upon the Union's left side in what became known as the **Second Battle of Bull Run**. Caught off guard, Pope's army fell apart. By the end of August 1862, Lee had pushed most of the Union forces out of Virginia. He then decided to take the war into the North.

After the hard-fought battle had ended, photographers took pictures of some of the thousands of soldiers killed at Antietam.

 ## The Battle of Antietam

Confederate leaders hoped to follow up General Lee's successes in Virginia with a major victory on Union soil. They believed that such a victory might break northern morale and persuade European powers to aid the South. On September 4, 1862, Lee's forces began crossing into Maryland. The condition of his army was poor, and many of his 40,000 soldiers suffered from hunger and exhaustion. Union soldiers then stumbled across a copy of Lee's battle plan wrapped around some cigars. General McClellan used the information to plan a counterattack against Lee's army.

On September 17, 1862, the Union army met the Confederates along Antietam Creek in Maryland. The **Battle of Antietam** lasted for hours. By the end of the day, the Confederates had suffered more than 13,700 casualties, the Union around 12,500. Trapped by a sunken road, Union officer A. H. Nickerson looked around and recalled, "It seemed that everybody near me was killed." Antietam was the bloodiest single-day battle of the war—and in U.S. military history.

Antietam was an important victory for the Union. Lee lost a large number of his troops, and his northward advance had been stopped. After the battle, President Lincoln ordered McClellan to

"destroy the rebel army, if possible," but the Union general hesitated and allowed Lee to retreat back to Virginia. Confederate general James Longstreet wrote, "We were so badly crushed. . . . But McClellan did not know it." Two months later, tired of McClellan's delays, Lincoln relieved him of command in the eastern theater.

 ## The War at Sea

While the two armies fought for control of the land, the Union controlled the sea. Most naval officers had remained loyal to the Union, and the North kept control of most of its small fleet. Moreover, the North possessed the industrial capacity to build up its navy during the war.

Blockades and Raiders

The Union navy's main task was to blockade the South, hurting the Confederacy's ability to wage war by cutting off its trade. Though effective, the blockade was not easy to maintain. The Union navy had to patrol thousands of miles of coastline from Virginia to Texas.

The South tried to break the blockade with blockade runners. These small, fast vessels could outrun the larger Union warships to reach southern ports as well as ports like Nassau in the Bahamas. The blockade runners could not, however, wholly make up for the South's loss of trade.

Confederate blockade runners delivered important supplies to the South.

Clash of the Ironclads

In an early effort to overcome the Union's superiority at sea, the Confederacy used a new type of warship. Heavily armored with iron, these ships were known as **ironclads**. The Confederates had seized the Union ship *Merrimack* and converted it into an iron-plated steamship. Union sailor A. B. Smith later described the Confederate ironclad as "a huge half-submerged crocodile." Renamed the *Virginia*, the vessel headed north in early March 1862 to Hampton Roads, near Chesapeake Bay, where many Union ships were located. Before

nightfall, the *Virginia* easily sank two of the Union's wooden warships while suffering only minor damage. A Baltimore reporter predicted doom the next day:

❝**There appeared no reason why the iron monster might not clear [the] Roads of our fleet, [and] destroy all the stores [supplies] and warehouses on the beach.**❞

The Union navy had built its own ironclad several months before the *Virginia*'s attack. A Swedish-born engineer named John Ericsson designed the northern ironclad and named it the *Monitor*. His design had unusual new features such as a revolving gun turret. One Confederate observer called the *Monitor* "a tin can on a shingle!" Though small, the Union ironclad carried powerful guns and had thick plating.

When the *Virginia* returned to Hampton Roads on March 9, 1862, the *Monitor* was waiting. After several hours of fighting, in which neither ship was seriously damaged, the *Monitor* forced the *Virginia* to withdraw. This saved the Union fleet and ensured the continuation of the blockade. The clash of the ironclads also signaled a revolution in naval warfare—the days of wooden warships powered by wind were drawing to a close.

SECTION 2 REVIEW

Identify and explain the significance of the following:

- Irvin McDowell
- Thomas "Stonewall" Jackson
- First Battle of Bull Run
- George B. McClellan
- Robert E. Lee
- Seven Days Battles
- Second Battle of Bull Run
- Battle of Antietam
- ironclads

Reading for Content Understanding

1 **Main Idea** What did the First Battle of Bull Run reveal about both the northern and the southern strategies?

2 **Main Idea** Why was the Battle of Antietam important for the Union?

3 **Technology and Society** How did the ironclad change naval warfare?

4 **Writing** *Informing* Imagine that you are a war correspondent. Write an article explaining the South's strategy since Robert E. Lee has taken command of Confederate forces in Virginia.

5 **Critical Thinking** *Drawing Conclusions* Why did northern leaders consider the capture of Richmond to be so important to the Union's war efforts?

The War in the West

Reading Focus

Why did the Union want to control the Mississippi River?

How did the Union pursue its goal of controlling the Mississippi, and what was the outcome?

What fighting took place in the Far West?

Key Terms

Battle of Shiloh
Siege of Vicksburg
Battle of Pea Ridge

IN LATE 1861 *a Union force advanced down the Mississippi River from Illinois. After defeating a small Confederate force near Belmont, Missouri, Union soldiers soon found themselves surrounded by southern reinforcements. Some of the Union officers wanted to surrender, but their commander, General Ulysses S. Grant, told them that "we had cut our way in [to enemy territory] and could cut our way out just as well." And that they did. Although the Union troops later retreated from Belmont, the fighting there established Grant as a strong military leader.*

A mortar, designed for shelling forts

★ Western Strategy

Union strategy in the West focused on gaining control of the Mississippi River. Union leaders knew that by dominating this vital waterway, the North could cut the Confederacy off from important sources of food production in Arkansas, Louisiana, and Texas. In addition, from bases on the Mississippi, the Union army would be able to attack the South's transportation network by striking deep into Tennessee.

The most important figure in the western theater of war was Ulysses S. Grant. A graduate of West Point, Grant had served in the Mexican War. He later resigned from the army and then pursued a variety of business ventures with mixed results. When the Civil War broke out, Grant quickly volunteered for service with the Union army. Grant's determination and aggressiveness in battle set him apart at a time when General McClellan's sluggish leadership in the East frustrated the president. *"I can't spare this man,"* Lincoln said of Grant. *"He fights."*

In February 1862 Grant led a Union army into Tennessee. Grant hoped to capture two important forts—Fort Henry and Fort Donelson. With help

The Civil War **585**

from Union navy gunboats, Grant took Fort Henry on February 6. He captured Fort Donelson 10 days later. When the Confederate commander of Fort Donelson asked to discuss surrender terms, Grant replied, "No terms except an unconditional and immediate surrender can be accepted."

The fall of these two forts—combined with the surrender of Nashville to other northern forces on February 25—secured Union control of Kentucky and much of Tennessee.

Union general Ulysses S. Grant

By the spring of 1862 the Union forces controlled key stretches of the Tennessee and Cumberland Rivers as well as some vital southern railroads.

 ## The Battle of Shiloh

General Grant continued his advance south along the Tennessee River toward the Mississippi state line. Grant followed orders and halted just north of the border. There, near a creek and a church named Shiloh, he awaited reinforcements, unaware that there was a large Confederate force nearby.

On April 6, 1862, the Confederates began the **Battle of Shiloh**, catching Grant by surprise. Pushing Grant's army back, the southerners believed that they were about to achieve a complete victory. Grant, however, ordered his troops to hold their ground whatever the cost. That night, one of Grant's officers found the general under a tree. "We've had the devil's own day, haven't we?" the officer asked. "Yes, yes," Grant replied. "Lick 'em tomorrow [though]," he predicted.

During the night, Union reinforcements arrived, and on April 7, Grant mounted a counterattack. By evening's end, the Confederates were in retreat. Teenage Union soldier John Cockerill looked out in shock at the corpses on the battlefield. "The blue and the gray were mingled together . . . as though they had bled to death

while trying to aid each other," he wrote. Southern nurse Kate Cumming treated the Confederate wounded from Shiloh. "Oh, if the authors of this cruel and unnatural war could but see what I saw there, they would try and put a stop to it!" she wrote. It was among the first major bloody battles of the war. The Union forces were too exhausted to pursue the Confederates. Through their victory at Shiloh, however, they gained the upper hand in the struggle to control the Mississippi River valley.

Fighting for Control of the Mississippi

General Grant and other Union commanders turned their attention to capturing key southern positions along the Mississippi River. First, the Union navy would try to capture New Orleans, the largest city in the South. By taking control of this vital port, the Union could send forces up the Mississippi to join Grant's army advancing from the north. The problem was that two forts guarded the approach to New Orleans from the Gulf of Mexico.

New Orleans

The task of capturing New Orleans fell to Flag Officer David G. Farragut, a daring Union naval leader from Tennessee. When asked to serve the Confederacy at the start of the war, Farragut had

The Confederate cannons at Vicksburg were in an excellent position to shell Union gunboats and ships trying to pass by on the Mississippi.

refused, replying, "Mind what I tell you: You fellows will catch the devil before you get through with this business."

Unable to destroy the two forts guarding the approach to New Orleans, Farragut decided to sail boldly past them. In the predawn hours of April 24, 1862, Farragut ordered his warships to advance. The Confederates fought furiously to halt Farragut's progress. Enduring bombardment from the shore and assaults by southern gunboats, Farragut cleared the forts and pressed ahead. After his ships arrived in New Orleans on April 25, the city surrendered to Farragut's forces.

Following the capture of New Orleans, Farragut next proceeded farther up the Mississippi River, taking Baton Rouge, Louisiana, and Natchez, Mississippi. Only the powerful fortifications at Vicksburg, Mississippi, stood in the way of total Union dominance of the river. Farragut tried to force the city to surrender, but the military governor of the city remained defiant:

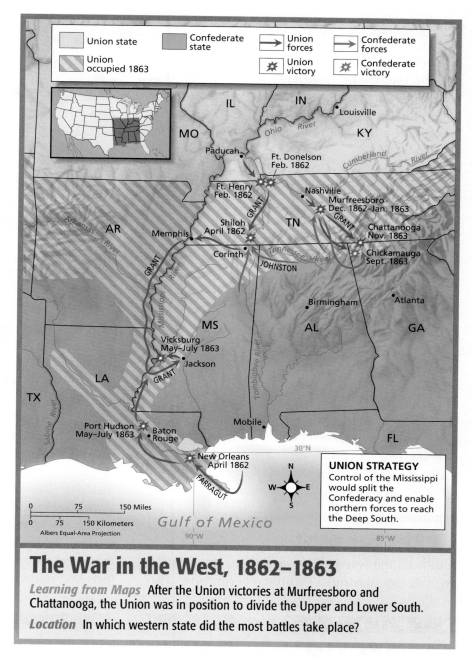

The War in the West, 1862–1863

Learning from Maps After the Union victories at Murfreesboro and Chattanooga, the Union was in position to divide the Upper and Lower South.

Location In which western state did the most battles take place?

66 **Mississippians don't know, and refuse to learn, how to surrender. . . . If Commodore Farragut . . . can teach them, let [him] come and try.** 99

The Fall of Vicksburg

The southern defenders of Vicksburg occupied an advantageous position. The city's high river bluffs allowed Confederate general John C. Pemberton's forces to cover the surrounding area with heavy guns. Previous attempts to take Vicksburg by land and naval assaults had failed.

General Grant then tried a new approach in the spring of 1863. From the Mississippi River, he marched east to Jackson, Mississippi. His attack pinned down southern forces based there and denied reinforcements to Vicksburg. Grant then surrounded Vicksburg with his troops in mid-May.

The **Siege of Vicksburg** lasted around six weeks. As supplies ran out, the residents and Confederate defenders of Vicksburg resorted to eating horses, dogs, and rats. The city's civilian population was driven to despair. "We are utterly [completely] cut off from the world, surrounded by a circle of fire," wrote one woman. "People do nothing but eat what they can get, sleep when they can, and dodge the shells."

The southern soldiers in Vicksburg were no less distressed. In late June a group of them sent Pemberton a letter in which they warned:

❝The army is now ripe for mutiny, unless it can be fed. If you can't feed us, you'd better surrender us, horrible as the idea is.❞

With no real hope of relief and under increasing pressure from his sick and hungry troops, Pemberton surrendered Vicksburg on July 4, 1863.

The capture of Vicksburg gave the Union total control of the Mississippi and was a great blow to the Confederacy. The western states of the Confederacy—Arkansas, Louisiana, and Texas—were cut off from the rest of the South. Grant later claimed that "the fate of the Confederacy was sealed when Vicksburg fell."

General Stand Watie led Cherokee troops in support of the Confederacy.

★ The Far West

Although the war in the western theater focused on the Mississippi, significant fighting also occurred farther west. Union and Confederate troops battled in Arkansas and Missouri, along the Texas coast, and in New Mexico. In August 1861, Confederate forces from Texas marched into New Mexico. Union forces advancing from Colorado defeated the Confederates at Glorieta Pass, near Santa Fe, New Mexico. The Union victory dashed Confederate hopes for control of the Southwest.

Confederate attempts to control Missouri also failed. Union forces turned back a Confederate effort to seize the federal arsenal at St. Louis in the summer of 1861. In March 1862, Union forces drove back the pro-Confederate Missourians and defeated them in the **Battle of Pea Ridge** in northwestern Arkansas. A group of American Indians, mainly Cherokee, fought in this battle on the side of the Confederacy. They hoped that Confederate leaders would grant the Indian nations greater independence than the Union had. Slavery was also legal in Indian Territory, and some Indians who were slaveholders supported the Confederacy. Although the Union victory at Pea Ridge secured northern control over Missouri, pro-Confederate units remained active in the region. They attacked Union forts and raided towns in Missouri and Kansas.

SECTION 3 REVIEW

Identify and explain the significance of the following:

- Ulysses S. Grant
- Battle of Shiloh
- David G. Farragut
- John C. Pemberton
- Siege of Vicksburg
- Battle of Pea Ridge

Reading for Content Understanding

1 **Main Idea** How did Grant secure control of much of Kentucky and Tennessee?

2 **Main Idea** What tactics did Grant use to lay siege to Vicksburg?

3 **Geographic Diversity** *Region* Why was gaining control of the Mississippi River important to the Union?

4 **Writing** *Classifying* Create an annotated time line showing the major events of the war in the West, including the Far West. Include events such as the battles at Shiloh, Pea Ridge, New Orleans, and Vicksburg.

5 **Critical Thinking** *Making Comparisons* How was Grant different from other Union commanders of the time? Use specific examples to support your answer.

Life During the War

Reading Focus

Why did President Lincoln issue the Emancipation Proclamation?

How did African Americans and women contribute to the war effort?

Why did northerners and southerners criticize the war, and how did their governments respond to the criticism?

Key Terms

Emancipation Proclamation
contrabands
54th Massachusetts Infantry
Copperheads
habeas corpus

I*N JULY 1862, while attending a funeral, President Lincoln met privately with Secretary of State William Seward and Secretary of the Navy Gideon Welles. Lincoln wanted to discuss freeing the slaves in the South, a topic of great concern to him. Lincoln felt that slavery continued to strengthen and support the South. "We must free the slaves or be ourselves subdued [defeated]," he explained. Lincoln's cabinet members advised him to wait for a better opportunity to put his plans into action.*

Poster celebrating the Emancipation Proclamation

The Emancipation Proclamation

Many northerners saw more reasons for supporting abolition than just the military advantages discussed by President Lincoln. Blaming southern slaveholders for causing the war, a large number of northerners viewed abolition as an effective means of punishing them. Others argued that unless slavery was ended, future conflict between the North and the South would be unavoidable even if the Union won the current war.

Lincoln's Strategy

Lincoln faced two problems with emancipation, or the freeing of the slaves. First, he feared that northern prejudice against African Americans and northern support of property rights might weaken public support for the war if emancipation became a Union goal. Second, Lincoln lacked the constitutional authority to abolish slavery on his own. As a solution, Lincoln decided to use his power as commander in chief of the armed forces to issue a military order freeing slaves in areas controlled by the Confederacy. Believing that he lacked the

The Civil War **589**

authority to extend emancipation to states that remained in the Union and because he did not want to upset the border states, this order did not affect slaveholding areas in the Union.

Lincoln also waited for a northern victory in the East before announcing his intention to free the South's slaves. He wanted to make the announcement from a position of strength so it would not be seen as an act of desperation. Antietam provided the victory, and on September 22, 1862, President Lincoln issued a preliminary order that called for all slaves in areas rebelling against the Union to be freed. This **Emancipation Proclamation** went into effect on January 1, 1863. While in practice the order did not immediately free all of the Confederacy's slaves, it did encourage enslaved people in the South to escape as soon as they heard that Union troops were nearby. This loss of slave labor severely damaged the southern economy and the Confederate war effort.

After the Emancipation Proclamation went into effect, the Union army began to recruit African American soldiers.

Reactions to the Proclamation

Many African Americans and northerners celebrated the Emancipation Proclamation. Abolitionist Frederick Douglass wrote, "We shout for joy that we live to record this righteous decree." He also called January 1, 1863, "the great day which is to determine the destiny not only of the American Republic, but that of the American Continent." Union officer Regis de Trobriand added, "It was no longer a question of the Union *as it was* that was to be re-established. It was the Union *as it should be*." News of the Proclamation spread overseas, where it received popular support in Britain and France.

Many northern Democrats, however, including General McClellan, believed that the Emancipation Proclamation went far beyond the purpose of the war. They wished only to restore the Union, not to abolish slavery. A few abolitionists, on the other hand, argued that Lincoln had not gone far enough. William Lloyd Garrison complained that the president left "slavery, as a system . . . , still to exist in all the so-called loyal Slave States."

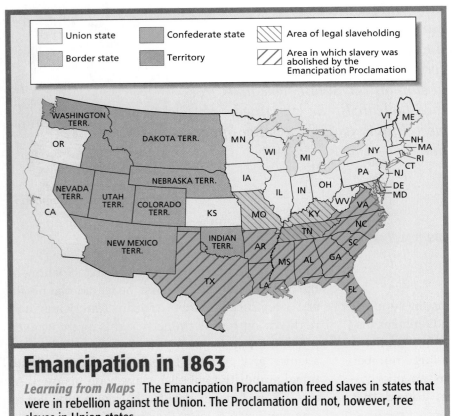

Legend:
- Union state
- Border state
- Confederate state
- Territory
- Area of legal slaveholding
- Area in which slavery was abolished by the Emancipation Proclamation

Emancipation in 1863

Learning from Maps The Emancipation Proclamation freed slaves in states that were in rebellion against the Union. The Proclamation did not, however, free slaves in Union states.

Place Which states were affected by the Emancipation Proclamation?

African Americans and the War

Along with emancipation, the question of whether African Americans should serve in the Union military troubled many northern leaders. Although the Union navy had accepted African American volunteers, African Americans were not initially allowed to serve in the army.

The Right to Volunteer

Since the war began, abolitionists had called for the Union army to take African American recruits. Frederick Douglass said that military service would help African Americans earn equal rights:

❝Once let the black man get upon his person the brass letters, U.S.; . . . and a musket on his shoulder and bullets in his pocket, and there is no power on earth which can deny that he has earned the right to citizenship.❞

Northern leaders also saw a practical reason to grant African Americans the right to serve. With the Union in need of troops, Congress authorized the army to enlist African American volunteers as laborers in July 1862. Meanwhile, Lincoln authorized the enlistment of **contrabands**, or escaped slaves, in South Carolina. Groups of free African Americans in Louisiana and Kansas also began organizing their own regiments.

African American Soldiers

By the spring of 1863, African American regiments were in the field with the Union army. In a Union attack on Port Hudson, Louisiana, in May 1863, two African American regiments showed they could fight as well as any other northern unit. In July 1863 the **54th Massachusetts Infantry**, a

Global Connections

Reactions to the Emancipation Proclamation

Abraham Lincoln's Emancipation Proclamation drew the attention of many people across the Atlantic Ocean. American historian Henry Adams wrote from London that the news of the freeing of the slaves created "an almost convulsive [violent] reaction in our favor all over this country." Workers from Manchester, England, wrote to the president:

Giuseppe Garibaldi

❝We joyfully honor you . . . for many decisive steps toward practically exemplifying [making an example of] your belief in the words of your great founders: 'All men are created free and equal.'❞

Within a few weeks after President Lincoln issued the Proclamation, notable Europeans began to share their views on the Civil War. Great Britain's duke of Argyll praised the Union's high moral purpose in the Civil War. Giuseppe Garibaldi, an Italian leader, hailed Lincoln as "the heir of the aspirations [dreams] of . . . [abolitionist] John Brown."

Understanding What You Read

1. How did some British citizens react to the Emancipation Proclamation?

2. Why do you think that Garibaldi would compare Lincoln to John Brown?

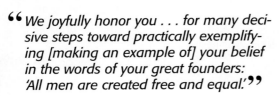

regiment consisting mainly of free African Americans, played a key role in the capture of Fort Wagner in South Carolina. Lewis Douglass, Frederick Douglass's son, fought in and survived the battle. "My regiment has established its reputation as a fighting regiment—not a man flinched," he proudly wrote later. The 54th went on to become the most famous African American regiment of the war.

African American soldiers fought bravely despite facing prejudice on both sides. For most of the war, they received less pay than white soldiers. Confederate troops often killed African American soldiers and their white officers rather than take them prisoner. Captured African American troops were usually enslaved.

In 1864 President Lincoln wrote to a critic of African American soldiers:

66 **Abandon all the posts now possessed by black men, surrender all these advantages to the enemy, and we would be compelled [forced] to abandon the war in three weeks.** 99

In the same year, Lincoln suggested giving African American soldiers the right to vote as a reward for their service to their country. About 180,000 African Americans served with Union forces during the war, and many distinguished themselves in combat.

★ Unrest in the North

The issue of abolition only added to the unrest in the North. The length of the war and the growing number of casualties had already increased northern desires to end the war.

The Copperheads

Northern Democrats who opposed the war called themselves Peace Democrats. Comparing them to a poisonous type of snake, their enemies called them **Copperheads**. Like their leader, Clement L. Vallandigham of Ohio, many Copperheads were midwesterners who sympathized with the South and opposed abolition. They believed the war was

unjustified and called for the North to cease hostilities. Vallandigham asked what the war had accomplished, then said, "Let the dead at Fredericksburg and Vicksburg answer."

Lincoln regarded the Copperheads and their antiwar criticisms as a threat to northern morale. The president tried to silence the Copperheads by suspending ***habeas corpus***—the constitutional protection against unlawful imprisonment. Union authorities could imprison dissenters such as the Copperheads without evidence of a crime and without a trial. Lincoln's actions infuriated Democrats.

The Northern Draft

By 1863 the enlistment periods of many soldiers began expiring, and some of them were returning home. More men had to be enlisted to continue the war effort. In March 1863 Congress passed a new law allowing the forcible draft of men into the army. Few men entered Union ranks through the draft, but the system still was controversial. Wealthy people could legally buy their way out of military service, and critics noted that dishonesty was common in the draft. Other critics, such as the Copperheads, charged that forcing unwilling white men to fight for the sake of African Americans in the South was wrong.

In July 1863 such sentiments led to antidraft riots in New York City. Fearing that free African Americans would come north and compete for jobs, a white mob went on a rampage through African American neighborhoods. Many of the rioters were poor immigrants who feared losing

This 1863 political cartoon shows the Copperheads as snakes attacking the Union.

Soldiers fire upon crowds to stop the antidraft riots in New York City.

their jobs to free African Americans. Rioters damaged much property, even burning an African American orphanage. The New York City riot left more than 100 people dead before Union troops stopped the violence.

 ## Southern Struggles

The South also faced many internal challenges that hampered its war effort. Eventually, southern support for the war effort began to fade.

The Price of War

The North's naval blockade took a heavy toll on southerners. "Every day we grow weaker. . . . Already they [Confederate soldiers] begin to cry out for more ammunition, and already the blockade is beginning to shut it all out," wrote Mary Chesnut. The value of Confederate money dropped as southern exports declined. At the same time, prices of daily necessities such as food, clothing, and medicine rose dramatically as supplies ran out. Basic items such as bread became too expensive for most people to afford.

The severe shortages caused unrest in the South. In the spring of 1863, food riots erupted in several southern cities, including Richmond. Southern authorities ordered local newspapers not to mention the civil unrest. Confederate president Jefferson Davis feared that news of the riots would embarrass the South and encourage the North to continue fighting.

The Southern Draft

As in the North, the draft proved controversial in the South. Passed in 1862, the southern draft excluded those who owned a large number of slaves. This rule led to resentment among poor southerners, who generally held few if any slaves. Confederate private Sam Watkins wrote in his memoirs that the draft law "gave us the blues. . . . There was raised the howl of 'rich man's war, poor man's fight.'" The draft was extremely unpopular in rural areas such as in western North Carolina. Hatred of the draft, combined with some pro-Union sentiment in this region, led to some protests and even armed resistance to Confederate authority.

 ## Daily Life

In both the North and the South, the war effort involved participation at all levels of society. On the battlefield and on the home front, the war affected the lives of most Americans.

The Home Front

People too young or too old for military service performed vital tasks in factories and other areas. When northern farmers and industrial workers left for war, women replaced them at their work. One visitor to Iowa in 1862 reported that he "met more women . . . at work in the fields than men." In the South, women also ran farms and plantations after

It was not uncommon during the war for soldiers on both sides to bring their families to camp with them. This Union soldier is joined by his wife and children.

their husbands and sons went to war. Enslaved African Americans continued to work in towns and on plantations, hoping for a Union victory but uncertain of what the future would bring.

Camp Life

Soldiers spent most of their time dealing with hazards other than battle. For every day of fighting, soldiers spent weeks living in uncomfortable and unhealthy camps. Soldiers there faced bad weather, boredom, disease, and unsafe food. Commenting on the spoiled meat served to his company, a weary Confederate soldier said, "A decent dog would have turned up his nose at it, but a hungry man will eat almost anything." Thousands of soldiers on both sides died of sickness brought on by such conditions. In fact, about twice as many Civil War soldiers died of disease than died in combat.

Women played an important role in improving the medical care received by soldiers on both sides. Headed by Dorothea Dix, more than 3,000 women served as paid nurses in the Union army during the war. Working as a volunteer, Clara Barton organized efforts to gather medicine and supplies and deliver them to Union troops on the battlefield. She often remained at field hospitals to comfort the wounded. Barton's work formed the

Civil War nurse
Clara Barton

basis for what would eventually become the American Red Cross.

Women in the South also provided vital care to sick and wounded soldiers. Sally Louisa Tompkins established a small hospital in Richmond that grew into a major army hospital by the end of the war. Jefferson Davis recognized Tompkins's value to the southern war effort by appointing her a captain in the Confederate army.

Prisoners of War

Military prisoners suffered greatly during the Civil War. Captured soldiers from both sides endured terrible treatment. The worst conditions were at Andersonville, in southwestern Georgia. The thousands of Union soldiers held in this camp had no shelter and little food. Following her visit to Andersonville, southerner Eliza Andrews reported being told that "at one time the prisoners died at the rate of a hundred and fifty a day." In prison camps, in field camps, and on the battlefields, the terrible hardships of the war took the lives of many thousands of soldiers.

SECTION 4 REVIEW

Identify and explain the significance of the following:

- **Emancipation Proclamation**
- **contrabands**
- **54th Massachusetts Infantry**
- **Copperheads**
- **Clement L. Vallandigham**
- ***habeas corpus***
- **Clara Barton**
- **Sally Louisa Tompkins**

Reading for Content Understanding

1 **Main Idea** What were President Lincoln's reasons for issuing the Emancipation Proclamation, and why did it free only those slaves who lived in the Confederate states?

2 **Main Idea** What contributions did African Americans make during the war? How did women aid the war effort?

3 **Citizenship and Democracy** Why did Lincoln suspend the right of *habeas corpus*?

4 **Writing** *Informing* Imagine that you are a foreign journalist reporting on the North and the South. Write a half-page newspaper article with information on the home front, army life, and criticisms of the war.

5 **Critical Thinking** *Supporting a Point of View* Do you think the president should be able to stop people from criticizing the nation's role in times of war? Explain your answer.

The Tide of the War Turns

Reading Focus

Why was the Battle of Gettysburg important?

How did the progress of the war affect the election of 1864?

How did the war finally end, and what were some of the war's consequences?

Key Terms

Battle of Gettysburg
Pickett's Charge
Gettysburg Address
total war

IN MAY 1863 GENERAL LEE *won a stunning victory over a larger Union force near the town of Chancellorsville, Virginia. During the heavy fighting, however, Lee's trusted general Stonewall Jackson was accidentally shot by his own troops while riding at the front lines. Doctors amputated Jackson's left arm in an effort to save him, but his condition worsened. When Lee found out that his trusted general, Jackson, was hurt, he told an aide, "Tell him to . . . come back to me as soon as he can. He has lost his left arm, but I have lost my right." Jackson died just a few days after the battle.*

Stonewall Jackson's grave

★ The Battle of Gettysburg

After his victory at Chancellorsville, General Lee decided to launch another offensive into Union territory. Once again, his goal was to break the North's will to fight and to seize supplies for his army. He also hoped that a victory would encourage other nations to recognize the Confederacy.

A Turning Point

In mid-June 1863 Lee cut across northern Maryland and then advanced into southern Pennsylvania with 65,000 men. By late June, Lee's forces had gathered near a small town called Gettysburg. When a Confederate raiding party advanced on the town in hopes of capturing supplies, the troops came under fire. This event triggered the **Battle of Gettysburg**.

On the first day of battle—July 1, 1863—the Confederates pushed the Union line back to Cemetery Ridge, just south of the town. The Confederate forces occupied nearby Seminary Ridge. On July 2 Lee ordered an attack on the left side of the Union line, but the bold charge of Colonel Joshua Chamberlain's troops at Little

Photography in the Civil War

In 1862 Mathew Brady shocked the people of New York by presenting photographs from the Battle of Antietam. "Mr. Brady has done something to bring to us the terrible reality . . . of the war," a reporter wrote. Brady was the most famous photographer of the Civil War. Before the war he was well known for his photo portraits of public figures, including one of Abraham Lincoln in 1860. When the war started, Brady followed the Union army to record events with his camera. He hired other photographers, including Timothy O'Sullivan and Alexander Gardner, to help cover the war.

Photography was still a new field in the 1860s. Few people could afford cameras, and taking pictures was a complicated process. Camera film was made from plates of glass. Photographers first brushed a plate with a special chemical mixture called collodion. Then they soaked the plate in the chemical silver nitrate just before placing it in the camera.

When the photographer removed the lens cap and exposed the film, light struck the plate and produced a negative image on the glass. The photographer or an assistant then rushed the plate to a darkroom or to a special covered wagon to develop the picture.

This technology limited the kinds of photographs that Brady and others could take. The glass plates were fragile and had to be prepared and developed in the dark. The lenses in the early cameras were crude and could focus only on still objects. The cameras were also bulky and hard to set up quickly. As a result, the photographs of the Civil War were mostly portraits of soldiers, scenes of camp life, and pictures of battlefields after the fighting had stopped.

Understanding What You Read

1. Who were some Civil War photographers?
2. What were the limitations of the cameras used during the Civil War?

The lens allows light to enter the camera and produces an image on a glass plate.

Photographers had to use extreme care when handling the glass plates, which were covered with dangerous chemicals.

The glass plate was rushed to a nearby darkroom wagon to be developed.

Round Top helped turn back the Confederate assault. As General George G. Meade reinforced each end of the Union line, Lee planned to rush the middle of the Union position on July 3.

The task of charging the center of the Union line fell to three divisions of Confederate soldiers, the largest under the command of General George Pickett. In the late afternoon, nearly 15,000 men took part in **Pickett's Charge** up Cemetery Ridge. Confederate lieutenant G. W. Finley was part of the attack. "Men were falling all around us, and cannon and muskets were raining death upon us," he wrote. Fewer than half of Pickett's troops reached the top of the ridge, where many were killed or captured. As the survivors returned to the Confederate rear, Lee ordered Pickett to organize his division for a possible second attack. "General Lee, I *have* no division now," Pickett replied. "The battle was now over," wrote Union lieutenant Jesse Young, "but nobody knew it."

Confederate general George Pickett led thousands of troops (right) in a costly charge against Union forces.

Consequences of Gettysburg

Rain halted Meade's troops, allowing Lee once again to retreat back to Virginia. Nonetheless, Gettysburg represented a key turning point in the war. Lee would never again launch an attack in the North. The Union victory at Gettysburg, combined with Grant's capture of Vicksburg on the same day, renewed northern confidence that the war could be won. The victory at Gettysburg, however, had come at a high price. Union casualties there numbered more than 23,000, while the Confederacy suffered more than 28,000.

President Lincoln expressed the Union's new sense of confidence and commitment in his **Gettysburg Address** of November 19, 1863. The short, moving speech became one of the most famous in American history. Lincoln spoke of what the battle meant to the soldiers who fought it and to the Union they represented. Lincoln dedicated himself and the rest of the Union to winning the war. Lincoln knew that a difficult road still lay ahead for the Union.

 Grant's Drive to Richmond

To win the war, the Union had to advance into the very heart of the Confederacy. Impressed with General Grant's successes in the West, Lincoln transferred him to the critical eastern theater and made him supreme commander of the Union armies. In early 1864 Grant advanced into eastern Virginia, where he forced Lee to fight a series of battles that stretched the number of Confederate soldiers and supplies to their limits.

During the spring of 1864, Grant and Lee fought at places in Virginia such as the Wilderness, Spotsylvania, and Cold Harbor. In these battles, Union forces suffered massive casualties—twice as many as their Confederate opponents. Even so, Grant continued to attack and to slowly but surely press forward. He told another officer, "I propose to fight it out along this line if it takes all summer."

In June 1864 Grant's attack stalled south of Richmond. Grant had hoped to take the key railroad junction at Petersburg, Virginia, but Lee's army formed a solid defense. After the Union army suffered huge casualties, Grant was forced to call off his attack. Instead, he prepared to lay siege to Petersburg. Grant was winning the war, but his failure to capture Richmond was discouraging news for Lincoln.

★ Sherman Sweeps Through the South

Union general William Tecumseh Sherman

Lincoln needed a victory to help his chances for re-election in 1864. The bold campaign of another Union commander provided this vital victory. General William Tecumseh Sherman carried out a Union strategy to destroy southern railroads and industries.

Taking Atlanta

In the spring of 1864, Sherman marched southward from Tennessee with 100,000 troops. His objective was to take Atlanta, Georgia. From May through August, Sherman's army made steady progress through the Appalachian Mountains toward Atlanta. Several times, Sherman maneuvered his forces around defenses set up by Confederate general Joseph Johnston.

In July, as Sherman drew within sight of Atlanta, Confederate president Davis transferred command of Confederate forces in the region to General John Hood. Hood repeatedly attacked Sherman in a last attempt to save Atlanta, but the Union won. The Confederate troops fell back as Sherman held Atlanta under siege.

Atlanta fell to Sherman on September 2, 1864, depriving the South of a vital railroad junction and center of industry. Much of the city lay in ruins because of Sherman's bombardment and because southerners had burned buildings to keep supplies from falling into Union hands. Many civilians had fled, and Sherman ordered the evacuation of those who remained. Responding to his critics, he later wrote, "War is war, and not popularity-seeking."

The capture of Atlanta helped Lincoln's campaign for re-election. Many people in the North had been upset with the long duration of the war. Sherman, however, showed that definite progress was being made toward victory. Union voters re-elected Lincoln in a landslide.

Marching to the Sea

Shortly after the election, General Sherman launched his next offensive. His goal was the port of Savannah, Georgia. In mid-November 1864 Sherman left Atlanta with a force of about 60,000 men. He said he would "make Georgia howl!"

On his March to the Sea, Sherman engaged in **total war**—targeting civilian as well as military resources to destroy an opponent's economy and ability to fight. Sherman ordered his troops to destroy railways, bridges, crops, livestock, and other supplies. Sherman's troops burned plantations and helped liberate slaves. When he reached Savannah on December 10, 1864, his army had left behind a path of destruction 60 miles wide and almost 300 miles long. Georgian Eliza Andrews saw firsthand the effects of Sherman's march: "About three miles from Sparta we struck the 'burnt country,'... and then I could better understand the wrath [anger] and desperation of these poor people."

Sherman believed that his March to the Sea would speed the end of the war. He thought that marching a Union force through the heart of the Confederacy would break the South's will to fight.

Sherman's forces destroyed huge amounts of southern property, particularly railroads such as this junction outside of Atlanta, Georgia.

★ The South Surrenders

In early April, as Sherman closed in on the last Confederate defenders in North Carolina, Grant finally broke through the defenses at Petersburg and forced Lee to retreat. The war was now in its final days.

Appomattox Courthouse

By the second week of April 1865, Grant had sur-rounded Lee's army and demanded its surrender. Lee knew his surrender would mean the end of the Confederate war effort. Trapped to the west of Richmond in the small town of Appomattox Courthouse, Lee concluded that the situation was hopeless. "There is nothing left for me to do but go and see General Grant," Lee said, "and I would rather die a thousand deaths."

The two generals met in the parlor of a private home on April 9, 1865. After Lee received Grant's assurances that Lee's troops would be fed, allowed to keep their horses, and would not be tried for treason, he signed the surrender documents. The long, bloody war had finally ended, but Grant later wrote that he found the scene at Appomattox Courthouse more tragic than joyful:

> **"I felt . . . sad and depressed at the down-fall of a foe who had fought so long and valiantly, and had suffered so much for a cause, though that cause was, I believe, one of the worst for which a people ever fought."**

As Lee returned to his troops, Grant stopped his men from cheering the Union victory. "The war is over," Grant said with relief. "The rebels are our countrymen again."

Lee surrendered to Grant at Appomattox Courthouse on April 9, 1865. Grant agreed to treat the surrendering Confederate troops with dignity and allowed them to return to their homes.

Consequences of the War

The Civil War had deep and lasting effects. Almost 620,000 Americans lost their lives in the four years of fighting, making the Civil War the most costly conflict in American history. Bitterness over the war would linger in both the North and the South for decades.

At war's end, the South faced an uncertain future. The Emancipation Proclamation had led to the end of slavery in much of the South, but the majority of former slaves were without homes or jobs. The southern economy lay in ruins. Ahead lay the enormous task of rebuilding the Union.

SECTION 5 REVIEW

Identify and explain the significance of the following:
- **Battle of Gettysburg**
- **George G. Meade**
- **George Pickett**
- **Pickett's Charge**
- **Gettysburg Address**
- **William Tecumseh Sherman**
- **total war**

Reading for Content Understanding

1 **Main Idea** Why was the Battle of Gettysburg a turning point in the war?

2 **Main Idea** How did the capture of Atlanta help President Lincoln win his re-election campaign?

3 **Geographic Diversity** *Human-Environment Interaction* What was Sherman's March to the Sea? Why did he engage in total war, and what effect did this tactic have on the South?

4 **Writing** *Creating* Imagine that you were present at Appomattox Courthouse. Write an account of General Lee's surrender. Include the events leading up to the surrender and the consequences of the war.

5 **Critical Thinking** *Drawing Conclusions* Why do you think that General Grant agreed to let the Confederates return home after their surrender? Explain your answer.

The Emancipation Proclamation

When the Union army won the Battle of Antietam, President Lincoln felt that the timing was right for a bold move. In late September 1862 he issued a preliminary Emancipation Proclamation. On January 1, 1863, the following official Proclamation went into effect:

A Proclamation by the President of the United States of America

Whereas on the twenty-second day of September, A.D. 1862, a proclamation was issued by the President of the United States, containing, among other things, the following, to wit [namely]:

"That on the first day of January, A.D. 1863, all persons held as slaves within any state or designated part of a state, the people whereof shall then be in rebellion against the United States, shall be then, thenceforward [afterward], and forever free; and the executive government of the United States, including the military and naval authority thereof, will recognize and maintain the freedom of such persons and will do no act or acts to repress [keep down] such persons or any of them, in any efforts they may make for their actual freedom.

"That the Executive will on the first day of January aforesaid, by proclamation, designate the states and parts of states, if any, in which the people thereof, . . . shall then be in rebellion against the United States; and the fact that any state or the people thereof shall on that day be in good faith represented in the Congress of the United States by members chosen thereto at elections wherein a majority of the qualified voters of such states shall have participated shall, in the absence of strong countervailing [opposing] testimony, be deemed [declared] conclusive evidence that such state and the people thereof are not then in rebellion against the United States."

Now, therefore, I, Abraham Lincoln, President of the United States, by virtue of the power in me vested [empowered] as Commander-in-Chief of the Army and Navy of the United States in time of actual armed rebellion against the authority and government of the United States, and as a fit and necessary war measure for suppressing said rebellion, do, on this first day of January, A.D. 1863, and in accordance with my purpose so to do, publicly proclaimed for the full period of one hundred days from the first day above mentioned, order and designate as the states and parts of states wherein the people thereof, . . . are in this day in rebellion against the United States the following, to wit:

Arkansas, Texas, Louisiana (except the parishes of St. Bernard, Plaquemines, Jefferson, St. John, St. Charles, St. James, Ascension, Assumption, Terrebonne, Lafourche, St. Mary, St. Martin, and Orleans, including the city of New Orleans), Mississippi, Alabama, Florida, Georgia, South Carolina, North Carolina, and Virginia (except the forty-eight counties designated as West Virginia, and also the counties of Berkeley, Accomac, Northampton, Elizabeth City, York, Princess Anne, and Norfolk, including the cities of Norfolk and Portsmouth), and which excepted parts are for the present left precisely as if this proclamation were not issued.

And by virtue of the power and for the purpose aforesaid, I do order and declare that all persons held as slaves within said designated states and parts of states are, and henceforward shall be, free; and that the executive government of the United States, including the military and naval authorities thereof, will recognize and maintain the freedom of said persons.

And I hereby enjoin upon [order] the people so declared to be free to abstain [hold back] from all violence, unless in necessary self-defense; and I recommend to them that, in all cases when allowed, they labor faithfully for reasonable wages.

And I further declare and make known that such persons of suitable condition will be received into the armed service of the United States to garrison [defend] forts, positions, stations, and other places, and to man vessels of all sorts in said service.

And upon this act, sincerely believed to be an act of justice, warranted by the Constitution upon military necessity, I invoke [call upon] the considerate judgment of mankind and the gracious favor of Almighty God.

Understanding Primary Sources

1. What authority did Lincoln claim allowed him to issue the Emancipation Proclamation?

2. In what places does Lincoln free slaves?

3. Why do you think Lincoln did not free all slaves?

Abraham Lincoln's

1863 *The Gettysburg Address*

On November 19, 1863, Abraham Lincoln addressed a crowd gathered to dedicate a cemetery at the Gettysburg battlefield. His short speech reminded Americans of the ideals on which the republic was founded.

Four score and seven years ago our fathers brought forth on this continent, a new nation, conceived [created] in Liberty, and dedicated to the proposition that all men are created equal.

Now we are engaged in a great civil war, testing whether that nation, or any nation so conceived and so dedicated, can long endure. We are met on a great battlefield of that war. We have come to dedicate a portion of that field, as a final resting place for those who here gave their lives that that nation might live. It is altogether fitting and proper that we should do this.

But, in a larger sense, we can not dedicate—we can not consecrate [make holy]—we cannot hallow—this ground. The brave men, living and dead, who struggled here, have consecrated it, far above our poor power to add or detract. The world will little note nor long remember what we say here, but it can never forget what they did here. It is for us the living, rather, to be dedicated here to the unfinished work which they who fought here have thus far so nobly advanced. It is rather for us to be here dedicated to the great task remaining before us—that from these honored dead we take increased devotion to that cause for which they gave the last full measure of devotion—that we here highly resolve that these dead shall not have died in vain—that this nation, under God, shall have a new birth of freedom—and that government of the people, by the people, for the people, shall not perish from the earth.

Understanding Primary Sources

1. Why does Lincoln say that he and the other members of the crowd cannot consecrate the battlefield?

2. For what cause does Lincoln say the soldiers at Gettysburg died? Why—at this particular point in the war—do you think that Lincoln decided to remind Americans about this cause and its importance?

CHAPTER 19 REVIEW

Chapter Summary

The Confederate attack on Fort Sumter on April 12, 1861, began the Civil War. As both the North and the South prepared their strategies and armies, many people hoped for a short war. After the First Battle of Bull Run, however, both sides realized that winning the war would not be easy. The war's political and military events hurt the economies of both the North and the South. During the fighting, more than 600,000 Americans lost their lives. ■

On a separate sheet of paper, complete the following activities.

Identifying People and Ideas

Describe the historical significance of the following:

1. Robert E. Lee
2. cotton diplomacy
3. Thomas "Stonewall" Jackson
4. Siege of Vicksburg
5. Ulysses S. Grant
6. Battle of Shiloh
7. Copperheads
8. Clara Barton
9. William Tecumseh Sherman
10. Gettysburg Address

Internet Activity go.hrw.com
SA0 Civil War Generals

Search the Internet through the HRW Web site to find additional information about the life of one of the Union or Confederate generals during the Civil War. Write a short biography of the person's life, describing important events and the general's contribution to the war.

Understanding Main Ideas

1. What advantages and disadvantages did the North and the South each have at the beginning of the Civil War?
2. How did the First Battle of Bull Run change many people's ideas about the war?
3. How successful was the naval blockade of the South? How did southerners attempt to avoid the blockade?
4. Why did the Union want to gain control of the Mississippi River?
5. How did President Lincoln attempt to silence criticism of the Civil War?
6. Why did General Sherman wage total war during his March to the Sea?

Reviewing Themes

1. **Technology and Society** How did ironclads reflect the changes that new technology brought to the war?

Using the Time Line

Number your paper from 1 to 6. Match the letters on the time line below with the following events.

1. **The Emancipation Proclamation goes into effect, granting freedom to all slaves in Confederate territory.**
2. **Confederate guns open fire on Fort Sumter.**
3. **The Union captures Vicksburg, gaining complete control of the Mississippi River.**
4. **The U.S. Sanitary Commission is created to supply and support Union army camps and hospitals.**
5. **General Lee surrenders to General Grant at Appomattox Courthouse.**
6. **Soldiers fight the Battle of Antietam.**

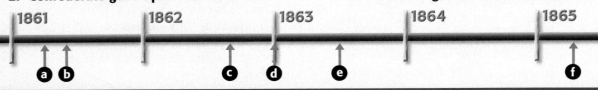

| 1861 | 1862 | 1863 | 1864 | 1865 |

a b   c d e   f

2. **Economic Development** What effect did the war have on the South's economy?

3. **Cultural Diversity** What contributions did African Americans make to the war effort? How did women help with the war effort?

Thinking Critically

1. **Synthesizing Information** Which battle—Vicksburg or Gettysburg—do you think was the most important turning point in the war? Explain your answer.

2. **Identifying Cause and Effect** What effect did Sherman's March to the Sea have in the North? How do you think it affected the residents of Georgia?

3. **Making Comparisons** How were Generals Grant and Lee similar? In what ways were they different?

Writing About History

1. **Informing** In a paragraph, explain the importance of the Battle of Antietam.

Building Your Portfolio

Complete the following activities individually or in groups.

1. **Battles of the Civil War** Create an annotated time line showing the important battles of the Civil War. Include each battle and its significance, as well as Union and Confederate casualties, and important leaders for each side. Illustrate your time line with appropriate images or maps.

2. **Consequences of the War** You are in charge of writing a chapter on the consequences of the Civil War for your textbook. Discuss (a) how the war changed the lives and roles of men, women, and children; (b) the roles of women at home and on the battlefront; (c) the soldiers who died for their cause; (d) the war's effect on former slaves and free African Americans; and (e) the war's effect on American Indians. Include images, maps, or charts in your chapter.

2. **Describing** Imagine that you fought alongside General Grant at the Battle of Shiloh. In your journal, record the details of the battle and its significance for Grant's career.

Linking Geography and History

1. **Region** Why was it important for the Union that the border states not join the Confederacy?

2. **Movement** Why did much of the Union strategy focus on taking control of important southern railroad junctions?

History Skills Workshop

Reading Charts Study the chart below, Lives Lost in the Civil War, 1861–1865. Then answer the following questions: (a) What was the total number of soldiers killed in the war? (b) About how many Union soldiers died from battle causes? (c) About how many Confederate soldiers died from nonbattle-related causes?

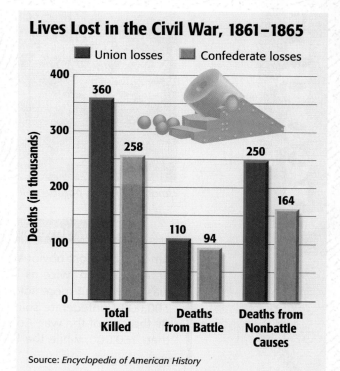

Lives Lost in the Civil War, 1861–1865

■ Union losses   ■ Confederate losses

Deaths (in thousands)

Total Killed: 360 / 258
Deaths from Battle: 110 / 94
Deaths from Nonbattle Causes: 250 / 164

Source: *Encyclopedia of American History*

Theaters of War

Geography played an important role in the development of military strategies during the Civil War. The Confederacy included a large stretch of land from the Atlantic Ocean to west Texas. To achieve military victory, Union leaders had to capture key parts of this large region.

Union leaders planned to gain control of river transportation routes, railroads, and seaports. Union leaders wanted to stop Confederate trade with Europe and the movement of troops and supplies across the South. Disruption of trade and supplies would greatly weaken the Confederate forces, making them easier targets for Union attacks.

Confederate armies did not have to invade and occupy the North to win the war. However, they did have to hold out against overwhelming odds and continue to fight. Their hope was to make the war so costly in Union lives and money that the North would decide that the price of victory was too high, and ask for peace instead. ■

Resources and Strategies

With more people, industry, railroads, and money, the North entered the war with great advantages over the South. Union generals were able to use these advantages in their war strategies.

The Granger Collection, New York

Union soldiers in parade drill

History Note 1

Among the most obvious of the North's advantages was a population more than twice as large as the South's. As a result, the North was able to put more soldiers in the field. In late 1862, an estimated 300,000 Confederate soldiers faced nearly 700,000 Union soldiers. By the end of the war, Confederate soldiers probably numbered less than 160,000, while the Union had about 1 million troops.

Comparing the North and the South, 1860

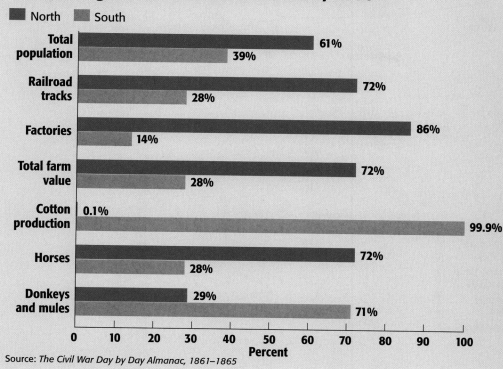

■ North ■ South

Total population	North 61% / South 39%
Railroad tracks	North 72% / South 28%
Factories	North 86% / South 14%
Total farm value	North 72% / South 28%
Cotton production	North 0.1% / South 99.9%
Horses	North 72% / South 28%
Donkeys and mules	North 29% / South 71%

Percent: 0 10 20 30 40 50 60 70 80 90 100

Source: *The Civil War Day by Day Almanac, 1861–1865*

Geography **Skills**
Reading Bar Graphs

1. What percentage of the nation's factories was found in the southern states at the beginning of the war?
2. What resources did the South have more of than the North?
3. Which region's railroad network was largest? Why do you think railroads were important during the war?
4. Which region had the largest number of horses? Union and Confederate armies used horses in cavalry units that could raid or gather information on enemy troops. In what other ways do you think horses were valuable to the armies?

History Note 3

The value of northern exports was far greater than the value of southern exports at the beginning of the war. Leaders of the Confederacy hoped that Britain and France would support them in the war because European textile mills depended on southern cotton. However, European merchants looked elsewhere for cotton. In the end, British and French leaders decided that their need for southern cotton was not great enough to openly support the Confederacy.

History Note 2

The Union also had a great advantage in communications. The North controlled far more miles of telegraph line than the South. The telegraph made Union supply and reinforcement easier because field commanders could communicate quickly with officials in Washington. The South's expansion and repair of telegraph lines was hurt by a shortage of equipment and operators.

A telegraph key

Theaters of War

Legend:
- Eastern theater
- Western theater
- Far Western theater
- → Union war strategy
- ▲▲▲ Union naval blockade
- ✪ Capital city

Union gunboat

Geography Skills
Reading Special-Purpose Maps

1. What southern states were part of both the western theater and far western theater?
2. What river and what southern cities lay along the Union plan of attack in the western theater?
3. In which theater of war were Washington and Richmond, Virginia, located?

History Note 4

Once the Union had gained control of the Mississippi River, Union forces could more easily reach inland Confederate targets. In addition, the loss of New Orleans—near the mouth of the Mississippi River—took away the Confederacy's most important seaport.

History Note 5

Union strategy focused on the western and eastern theaters of war. The Union intended to split the Confederacy into three parts. Union commanders planned to cut off Arkansas, Louisiana, and Texas by taking control of the Mississippi River. Then they would cut off Virginia from the Lower South by sending an army from Tennessee through Georgia to the Atlantic Coast. With the eastern theater separated from the rest of the Confederacy, the Union planned to destroy General Robert E. Lee's army and capture the Confederate capital at Richmond, Virginia.

The Road to Victory

In the summer of 1863 the Union strategy for winning the war began to fall into place. In July the capture of Vicksburg, Mississippi, completed Union control of the Mississippi River and split the Confederacy into two parts. Union troops then began to occupy important southern rail centers in a push toward Savannah, Georgia, and Richmond, Virginia. Southern cities and farms suffered heavy damage as the war moved into the Confederate heartland.

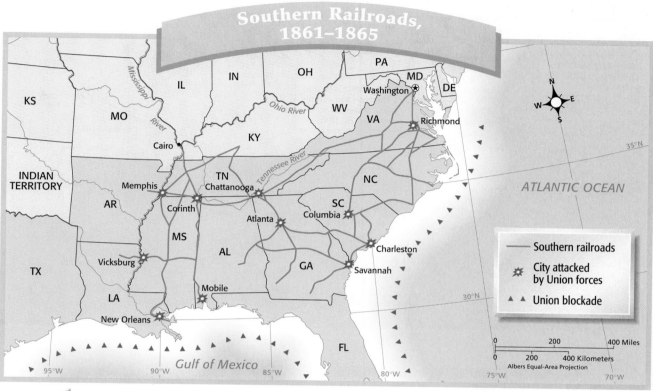

Southern Railroads, 1861–1865

ATLANTIC OCEAN

Gulf of Mexico

Legend:
- Southern railroads
- ✸ City attacked by Union forces
- ▲▲ Union blockade

0   200   400 Miles
0   200   400 Kilometers
Albers Equal-Area Projection

Geography Skills

Reading Special-Purpose Maps

1. What seaport cities were attacked by Union forces?
2. Study the railroad lines through Chattanooga, Tennessee. Why do you think the capture of this city was so important?
3. What other inland cities were attacked by Union forces?

U.S. military railroad engine

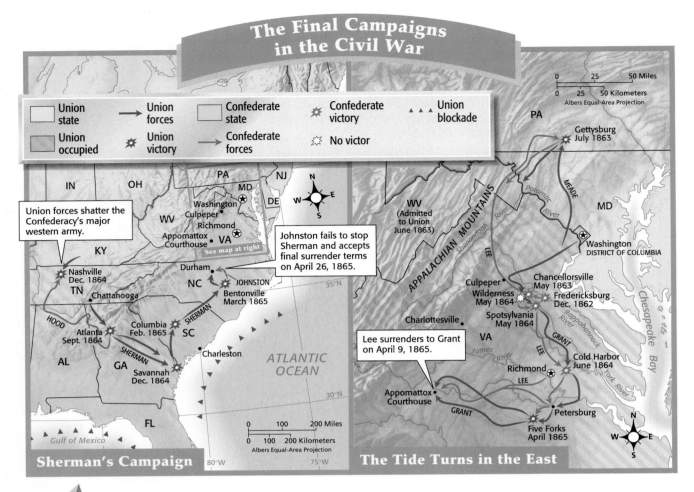

The Final Campaigns in the Civil War

Legend:
- Union state
- Union occupied
- → Union forces
- ✹ Union victory
- Confederate state
- → Confederate forces
- ✹ Confederate victory
- ✰ No victor
- ▲▲▲ Union blockade

0 — 25 — 50 Miles
0 — 25 — 50 Kilometers
Albers Equal-Area Projection

Sherman's Campaign

Union forces shatter the Confederacy's major western army.

Johnston fails to stop Sherman and accepts final surrender terms on April 26, 1865.

IN
OH
PA
NJ
MD
DE
WV
Washington
Culpeper
Richmond
Appomattox Courthouse
VA
See map at right
KY
Nashville Dec. 1864
TN
Chattanooga
Durham
NC
JOHNSTON
Bentonville March 1865
HOOD
Atlanta Sept. 1864
Columbia Feb. 1865
SC
SHERMAN
SHERMAN
Charleston
AL
GA
Savannah Dec. 1864
FL
Gulf of Mexico
ATLANTIC OCEAN
35°N
30°N
80°W
75°W

0 — 100 — 200 Miles
0 — 100 — 200 Kilometers
Albers Equal-Area Projection

The Tide Turns in the East

PA
Gettysburg July 1863
WV (Admitted to Union June 1863)
APPALACHIAN MOUNTAINS
Potomac River
MEADE
Shenandoah River
LEE
MD
Washington DISTRICT OF COLUMBIA
Culpeper
Chancellorsville May 1863
Wilderness May 1864
Fredericksburg Dec. 1862
Rappahannock River
Charlottesville
Spotsylvania May 1864
Chesapeake Bay
VA
GRANT
LEE
Cold Harbor June 1864
James River
Richmond
LEE
York River
Appomattox Courthouse
GRANT
Petersburg
Five Forks April 1865

Lee surrenders to Grant on April 9, 1865.

Geography Skills
Reading Special-Purpose Maps

1. How long after capturing Atlanta did it take General Sherman's forces to reach Savannah?
2. Where did Sherman's army go after taking Savannah?
3. What battles did the armies of Generals Grant and Lee fight from May 1864 to April 1865?

Richmond, Virginia, after the war

History Note 7

Most of the major battles occurred in the eastern and western theaters of the war. Battles on a smaller scale took place in the less-populated far western theater. For example, in 1862 a Confederate force of less than 3,000 troops invaded New Mexico, but was eventually turned back.

Farm Values by Region, 1860 and 1870

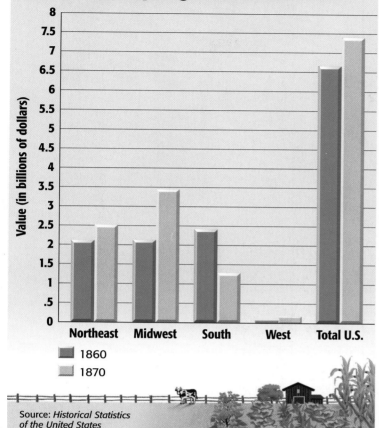

Value (in billions of dollars)

Region	1860	1870
Northeast		
Midwest		
South		
West		
Total U.S.		

■ 1860
■ 1870

Source: *Historical Statistics of the United States*

Geography Skills
Reading Bar Graphs

1. Which region's farms had the highest total value in 1860?
2. Which region's farms had the lowest total value in 1870?
3. Where did farms have the greatest growth in value from 1860 to 1870?

History Note 8

The Civil War left the economies of all the Confederate states badly damaged. In 1870 the total value of farmland and buildings in the South was less than $1.3 billion, down from $2.3 billion just 10 years earlier. Farms in South Carolina and Louisiana lost nearly three quarters of their value between 1860 and 1870. Georgia, which suffered great damage during Sherman's March to the Sea, saw the total value of its farms cut in half.

History Note 9

The production of cotton, sugar, tobacco, and rice—important products in the South's economy—remained below pre–Civil War levels for many years after the war. Cotton production, which had reached nearly 4.5 million bales in 1861, did not pass that mark again until 1875. Fewer than 800,000 bales were produced in 1863 and 1864 combined.

Cotton

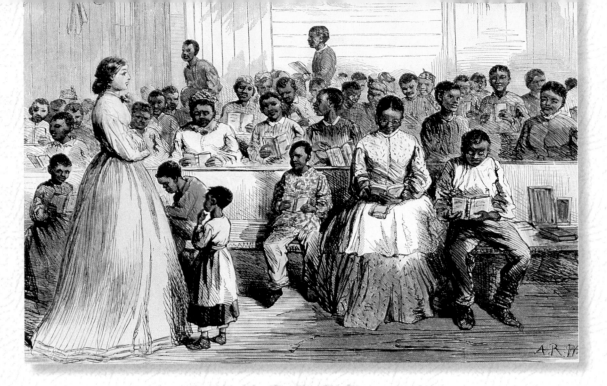

CHAPTER 20

Reconstruction

(1865–1877)

The Civil War was over, but two major issues remained unresolved. First, the federal government had to decide the conditions by which the South could rejoin the Union. Second, the government had to define the rights of the 4 million African Americans freed by the Emancipation Proclamation. As abolitionist Frederick Douglass explained, "The work does not end with the abolition of slavery, but only begins."

THEMES

Constitutional Heritage
How might a nation attempt to rebuild itself following a civil war?

Citizenship and Democracy
Why might a nation's definition of a democratic society change over time?

Cultural Diversity
How might the experiences of a newly freed group affect a nation?

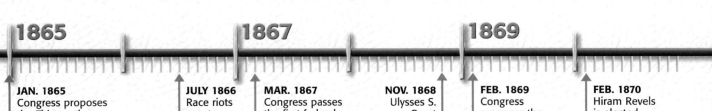

1865

1867

1869

JAN. 1865
Congress proposes the Thirteenth Amendment.

JULY 1866
Race riots erupt in New Orleans.

MAR. 1867
Congress passes the first federal Reconstruction Act.

NOV. 1868
Ulysses S. Grant is elected president.

FEB. 1869
Congress proposes the Fifteenth Amendment.

FEB. 1870
Hiram Revels is elected to the U.S. Senate.

Rebuilding the South

Reading Focus

What effect did the end of the Civil War have on southern life?

How did Lincoln, Congress, and Johnson differ in their views on Reconstruction?

In what ways did the Freedmen's Bureau aid newly freed slaves?

Key Terms

Reconstruction
amnesty
Thirteenth Amendment
Freedmen's Bureau

A SOUTHERNER WHO KEPT A *diary while traveling through Georgia after the Civil War recorded* the destruction he saw: *"Every village and station we stopped at presented an array [group] of ruined walls and chimneys standing useless." When he reached the once prosperous city of Columbia, South Carolina, burnt and empty buildings greeted him. The war had dramatically changed the landscape of the South and the lives of southerners.*

The Museum of the Confederacy, Richmond, Virginia, Katherine Wetzel, Photographer

A Georgia newspaper with news of Robert E. Lee's surrender

IMAGE ON LEFT PAGE: *A school for freedpeople in Vicksburg, Mississippi*

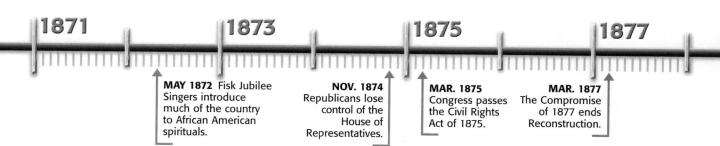

1871   **1873**   **1875**   **1877**

MAY 1872 Fisk Jubilee Singers introduce much of the country to African American spirituals.

NOV. 1874 Republicans lose control of the House of Representatives.

MAR. 1875 Congress passes the Civil Rights Act of 1875.

MAR. 1877 The Compromise of 1877 ends Reconstruction.

The South After the Civil War

After the South's surrender, weary southern soldiers—many permanently disabled—returned home to find their farms destroyed and their cities in ruins. However, the damage went beyond crops and buildings. Former Confederate Josiah Reams reached his home in Tennessee to find:

> 66 **My father and stepmother . . . [had] died. My only brother was killed . . . and a half-brother on the Union side . . . died. So our home was broken up and I was penniless.** 99

Many southerners faced the threat of starvation. The Shenandoah Valley in Virginia, once full of rich farmland, was now battle-scarred and barren. Across the South, harvests of cotton, rice, corn, and other crops were well below normal. Many farm animals had been killed or run away. Food prices, already high because of wartime shortages, remained high.

When food was available, distributing it was difficult. The widespread destruction of railroads by Union troops had disabled transportation and communications throughout the South. Living in Richmond, Virginia, Mary Chesnut wrote in her diary about the isolation: "We are shut in here. . . . All RR's [railroads] destroyed—bridges gone. We are cut off from the world."

Much of Richmond, Virginia, burned in the last days of the war.

In addition, financial institutions, which had begun to collapse during the war, continued to struggle. Banks failed and merchants went bankrupt because few southerners could repay their debts. The Confederate currency they held was now worthless. Former Confederate general Braxton Bragg found that "*all, all* was lost, except my debts."

The Meaning of Freedom

Despite having to suffer through the postwar difficulties, freedpeople, or newly freed slaves, had reason to celebrate as word of emancipation spread slowly through the South. Freedom meant important changes for families. Numerous couples held ceremonies to legalize marriages that had not been recognized under slavery. Many freedpeople searched for relatives who had been sold away from their families years earlier. One man walked 600 miles through Georgia and North Carolina looking for his wife and children. Other freedpeople placed newspaper ads seeking information about their children. Many women began to work at home rather than in the fields.

Now that they could travel without a pass, many freedpeople moved from mostly white counties to places with more African Americans. Some freedpeople in the Upper South tried to find work in Lower South states such as Texas, Florida, and Mississippi, where expanding farms needed new workers. Other freedpeople traveled simply to test their new freedom of movement. A South Carolina woman explained, "I must go, if I stay here I'll never know I'm free."

For most former slaves, freedom to travel was just the first step on a long road toward equal rights and a new way of life. Adults took new last names and began to insist on being called Mr. or Mrs., rather than by their first name or by nicknames.

Most freedpeople, such as Henry Adams, wanted the same rights as whites. Adams said, "If I cannot do like a white man I am not free."

Many African Americans left white-controlled churches and created their own congregations. These new churches became the first large

After the Civil War, African Americans bought and filled out family records such as this one.

organizations run by African Americans. Church members established voluntary associations and mutual aid societies to help those in need.

Many freedpeople wanted their own land to farm. At the end of the Civil War, General William Tecumseh Sherman had issued an order to break up plantations in coastal South Carolina and Georgia. He wanted to divide the land into 40-acre plots and give them to freedpeople as compensation for their forced labor during slavery. Many white planters, however, refused to surrender their land. Some freedpeople pointed out that it was only fair that they receive some of this land, because the labor they had performed as slaves had made the plantations prosper. At this time, many freedpeople were unsure about where they would live, what kind of work they would do, and what rights they had.

Planning Reconstruction

The U.S. government soon stepped in to help freedpeople in the South. The government also faced the task of bringing the defeated southern states back into the Union. **Reconstruction**—the process of reuniting the nation and rebuilding the southern states in the absence of slavery—lasted from 1865 to 1877.

Lincoln's Plan

President Lincoln wanted to reunite the nation as quickly and painlessly as possible. Before the war ended, he proposed a plan for readmitting the southern states. He wanted to offer southerners **amnesty**, or an official pardon, for all illegal acts supporting the rebellion. Those southerners who pledged an oath of loyalty to the United States and accepted a ban on slavery would receive amnesty. Any southern state with at least 10 percent of its voters making this pledge could establish a new state government and be readmitted to the Union. Louisiana and other southern states that had been occupied by Union troops before the war's end quickly elected new state legislatures under this Ten-Percent Plan.

The Wade-Davis Bill

Some politicians believed that Congress had the constitutional authority to admit new states. Thus,

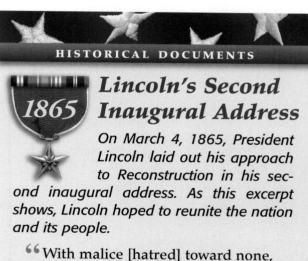

HISTORICAL DOCUMENTS

Lincoln's Second Inaugural Address

On March 4, 1865, President Lincoln laid out his approach to Reconstruction in his second inaugural address. As this excerpt shows, Lincoln hoped to reunite the nation and its people.

66 With malice [hatred] toward none, with charity for all, with firmness in the right, as God gives us to see the right, let us strive on to finish the work we are in, to bind up the nation's wounds, to care for him who shall have borne the battle, and for his widow, and his orphan—to do all which may achieve and cherish a just, and a lasting peace. 99

Understanding Primary Sources
1. What is Lincoln asking of the nation?
2. What issues might have prevented Lincoln's request from being fulfilled?

they argued, Congress should handle the southern states' return to the Union. Many Republican members of Congress simply disagreed with Lincoln's plan for Reconstruction. They shared the views of one senator who said,

> **" The people of the North are not such fools as to . . . turn around and say to the traitors, 'all you have to do [to return] is . . . take an oath that henceforth you will be true to the Government.' "**

Two Republicans—Senator Benjamin Wade and Representative Henry Davis—proposed a stricter alternative to Lincoln's plan. Under the Wade-Davis Bill, a state had to meet two conditions before it could rejoin the Union. First, it had to ban slavery. Second, a majority of adult males in the state had to take the loyalty oath. Furthermore, only southerners who swore that they had never supported the Confederacy would be allowed to vote or to hold office. President Lincoln refused to sign this bill into law, because few southerners could fulfill its requirements.

The Thirteenth Amendment

One thing Republicans agreed on was abolishing slavery. The Emancipation Proclamation had freed slaves only in the Confederate states that had been unoccupied by Union forces. The proclamation allowed slavery to continue in the border states. In addition, many people feared that the federal courts might someday declare the Emancipation Proclamation unconstitutional. On January 31, 1865, at Lincoln's urging, Congress proposed the **Thirteenth Amendment** to the Constitution, which made slavery illegal throughout the United States. The amendment then went into effect on December 18, 1865. Abolitionist William Lloyd Garrison declared that his work was now finished and called for the American Anti-Slavery Society to disband. Frederick Douglass, however, insisted that "Slavery is not abolished until the black man has the ballot [vote]."

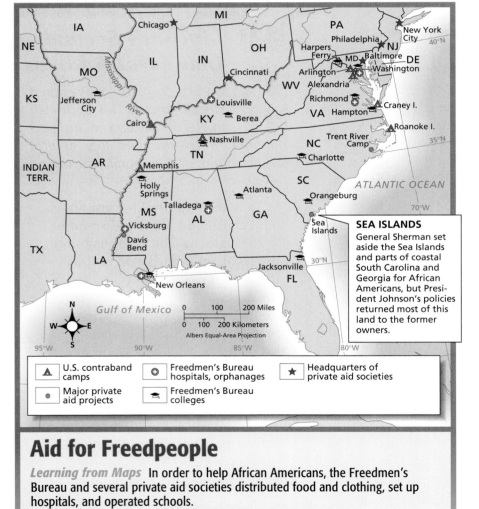

SEA ISLANDS
General Sherman set aside the Sea Islands and parts of coastal South Carolina and Georgia for African Americans, but President Johnson's policies returned most of this land to the former owners.

⚠	U.S. contraband camps
⊕	Freedmen's Bureau hospitals, orphanages
★	Headquarters of private aid societies
•	Major private aid projects
🎓	Freedmen's Bureau colleges

Aid for Freedpeople

Learning from Maps In order to help African Americans, the Freedmen's Bureau and several private aid societies distributed food and clothing, set up hospitals, and operated schools.

Location According to the map, which states had major private aid projects?

★ The Freedmen's Bureau

In addition, in 1865 Congress established the **Freedmen's Bureau** to provide relief for all poor people—black and white—in the South. The bureau had a difficult job. At its high point about 900 agents served the entire South. Bureau commissioner

Historically Black Colleges and Universities

The Freedmen's Bureau, private donors, and religious organizations helped establish colleges for African Americans in the South. In addition to traditional education, many of these schools—now known as historically black colleges and universities—offered training and teaching degrees.

A half century ago, African Americans had few choices when selecting a college because laws in many states prohibited them from attending white schools. Today, however, African American students can choose which schools to attend. Many continue to choose historically black colleges and universities because of their emphasis on African American identity and history.

According to United Negro College Fund president William H. Gray III, students have support from the faculty, administration, and fellow students in such schools. One Howard University graduate noted, "From the minute you walk on campus during freshman orientation, you feel like you finally got to the right place."

Almost 150 years after the founding of the first black college,

African American students study art at Virginia Union University in Richmond, Virginia.

African American enrollment continues to rise at these schools. Many African Americans share the view of one Hampton graduate who said, "I'll always see a need for black colleges. . . . It made me who I am and what I'm going to be."

Understanding What You Read

1. What groups helped establish colleges for African Americans in the South?

2. Why do many African American students choose to attend historically black colleges and universities?

Oliver O. Howard eventually decided to use the bureau's limited budget to distribute food to the poor and to provide education and legal help for freedpeople. The bureau also assisted African American war veterans.

The Freedmen's Bureau played an important role in establishing more schools in the South. Laws against educating slaves meant that most freedpeople had never learned to read or write. Before the war ended, however, northern groups such as the American Missionary Society began providing books and teachers. The teachers were mostly women who were committed to helping freedpeople. One teacher said of her students:

❝ I never before saw children so eager to learn. . . . It is wonderful how [they] . . . can have so great a desire for knowledge, and such a capacity for attaining [reaching] it. ❞

Andrew Johnson

Andrew Johnson had a long political career before becoming president. Born to a poor family in North Carolina, Johnson became a tailor's apprentice. Unhappy with this arrangement, Johnson ran away to Tennessee, where he started his own tailoring business. Eventually, he became a prosperous landowner and entered politics, but he never forgot his humble beginnings. He often criticized wealthy southern planters, calling them a "pampered, bloated, corrupted aristocracy."

Johnson served as governor of Tennessee before becoming a U.S. senator. During the Civil War, he was the only senator from a Confederate state who remained loyal to the Union. Hoping that he would appeal to voters in the border states, Republicans selected Johnson as Lincoln's running mate in the presidential campaign of 1864. He had been vice president for less than six weeks when Lincoln's death elevated Johnson to the presidency.

After the war, some freedpeople organized their own education efforts. For example, Freedmen's Bureau agents found that some African Americans had opened schools in abandoned buildings. Many white southerners continued to believe that African Americans should not be educated. Some whites burned down schools and attacked teachers and students. Despite such opposition, by 1869 more than 150,000 students attended the more than 3,000 schools that had been established. The Freedmen's Bureau also helped establish several colleges for African Americans, including Howard and Fisk.

Students quickly filled the new classrooms. Working adults attended classes in the evening. African Americans made these sacrifices for many reasons, including their desire to learn to read the Bible. They also hoped that education would help them to understand and protect their rights and to enable them to find better jobs. Both black and white southerners benefited from the effort to provide greater access to education in the South.

⭐ A New President

While the Freedmen's Bureau was helping African Americans in the South, the issue of how the southern states would rejoin the Union remained unresolved. Soon, however, a tragic event ended Lincoln's dream of reuniting the country.

Lincoln's Assassination

On the evening of April 14, 1865, a little more than a month after his second inauguration, President Lincoln and his wife attended the play *Our American Cousin* at Ford's Theater in Washington. During the play, John Wilkes Booth—a southerner hostile to Lincoln's policies—sneaked into the president's theater box and shot him.

Lincoln was rushed to a boardinghouse across the street, where he died at about 7:30 the next morning. Secretary of the Navy Gideon Welles was by the president's side. He later wrote that "strong and brave men wept when I met them" with the news of Lincoln's death.

Vice President Andrew Johnson was sworn into office that morning. Reconstruction was now his responsibility. Republicans approved of President Johnson because he seemed to favor a tougher approach to Reconstruction than Lincoln had. Senator Wade spoke for many Republicans when he told the new president, "Johnson, we have faith in you."

Johnson's Reconstruction Plan

Despite his tough talk, Johnson's plan for the re-entry of the southern states into the Union was similar to Lincoln's Ten-Percent Plan. Johnson gave amnesty to all southerners who pledged an oath of loyalty and who promised to support the abolition of slavery. He also returned all property except slaves to southerners who received amnesty. Johnson did add some special restrictions to his plan. Wealthy southerners and former Confederate officials could not receive amnesty without a presidential pardon. In the end, however, this was not as restrictive as it might seem. Johnson shocked Republicans by eventually pardoning almost 7,000 people.

Johnson established a system for setting up new southern state governments. First, he appointed a temporary governor for each state. Then in each state, southerners who had taken the loyalty oath elected delegates to a convention that would revise their state constitution. Voters then elected state officials and representatives to the U.S. Congress. Once a state government was in place, it had to declare that secession was illegal and refuse to pay Confederate debts before the state could be readmitted to the Union. Virginia and three states that had already set up governments using Lincoln's Ten-Percent Plan—Arkansas, Louisiana, and Tennessee—were allowed to keep their governments in place.

By the end of 1865 all the southern states except Texas had created new governments. Johnson approved all these governments and declared that the United States was restored. When the new representatives from each state came to the capital, he asked Congress to allow them to take their seats in the House and Senate.

Lincoln's funeral procession passes through Springfield, Illinois, in April 1865. A month later, Andrew Johnson issued his plan of Reconstruction.

However, Republicans did not approve of the new representatives, many of whom had been military officers and political leaders in the Confederacy. For example, Alexander Stephens, the former vice president of the Confederacy, was elected a U.S. senator from Georgia. Most Republicans did not believe that people like Stephens were loyal to the United States.

Congress therefore refused either to seat the new representatives or to readmit the southern states into the Union. Clearly, the nation was still divided over who should control Reconstruction and what direction it should take.

SECTION 1 REVIEW

Identify and explain the significance of the following:
- **Reconstruction**
- **amnesty**
- **Thirteenth Amendment**
- **Freedmen's Bureau**
- **John Wilkes Booth**
- **Andrew Johnson**

Reading for Content Understanding

1. **Main Idea** How did life in the South change after the Civil War?

2. **Main Idea** What were the various Reconstruction plans, and how did they differ?

3. **Citizenship and Democracy** How did freedpeople express their new freedom?

4. **Writing** *Persuading* Write a one-paragraph editorial that explains the importance of the Freedmen's Bureau for both black and white southerners.

5. **Critical Thinking** *Evaluating* Why might owning farmland have been important for freedpeople?

The Fight over Reconstruction

Reading Focus

How did Black Codes restrict African Americans' freedoms?

Why did Radical Republicans try to impeach President Johnson?

How did Republicans try to protect the civil rights of African Americans?

Key Terms

Black Codes
Radical Republicans
Civil Rights Act of 1866
Fourteenth Amendment
Reconstruction Acts
Fifteenth Amendment

T O TEST HIS NEWFOUND FREEDOM, *in 1865 Henry Adams left the plantation where he had been enslaved. A group of white men stopped Adams on the road and asked who owned him. When Adams replied that he was free, the men beat him. Such incidents of violence were not unusual in the post–Civil War South. Many white southerners opposed African Americans' freedom and feared the consequences of that freedom. This resentment and fear also affected local authorities and state governments.*

A federal soldier protects an African American man from violence.

★ The Black Codes

While Congress debated the rules for restoring the Union, in 1866 the new state legislatures approved by President Johnson began passing laws to deny African Americans' civil rights. "This is a white man's government, and intended for white men only," declared Governor Benjamin F. Perry of South Carolina. Soon every southern state passed **Black Codes**—laws that greatly limited the freedom of African Americans.

Each state had a set of Black Codes, which were usually designed to help white southerners

economically. Black Codes forced African Americans to work on farms or as servants and required them to sign labor contracts that re-created conditions similar to those under slavery. One of South Carolina's Black Codes, for example, stated:

❝ **All persons of color who make contracts for service or labor, shall be known as servants, and those with whom they contract shall be known as masters.** ❞

In most southern states, any African American who could not prove he or she was employed

Under the Black Codes, white southerners could arrest unemployed African Americans and auction off their labor to the highest bidder.

could be arrested and punished with one year of work without pay. Other Black Codes prevented African Americans from owning guns, holding public meetings, or renting property in cities.

African Americans were alarmed by the Black Codes. As one Civil War veteran declared, "If you call this Freedom, what do you call Slavery?" African Americans organized and took action to oppose the codes. One group sent a petition to officials in South Carolina, which had one of the strictest Black Codes:

> ❝We simply ask . . . that the same laws which govern *white men* shall govern *black men*; that we have the right of trial by a jury of our peers; that schools be established for the education of *colored children* as well as white . . . that, in short, we be dealt with as others are—in equity [equality] and justice.❞

Such calls for equality had little effect on the new state governments, however.

⭐ The Radical Republicans

The Black Codes angered many Republicans who felt the South was returning to its old ways. Most Republicans were moderates who wanted the South to have loyal state governments but also believed that African Americans should receive their rights as citizens. Most moderates hoped that the South would not have to be forced to follow the laws passed by the U.S. government.

Another group in Congress, called the **Radical Republicans**, wanted the South to change much more than it had before it could return to the Union. Like the moderates, they considered the Black Codes to be undemocratic and cruel. The Radical Republicans, however, wanted the federal government to be much more involved in Reconstruction, fearing that too many southern leaders remained loyal to the former Confederacy. Thaddeus Stevens of Pennsylvania and Charles Sumner of Massachusetts led the Radical Republicans.

A harsh critic of President Johnson, Stevens was known for his honesty, his sharp tongue, and his interest in economic justice for both African Americans and poor white southerners. Sumner had been a strong opponent of slavery before the Civil War and continued to argue tirelessly for African Americans' civil rights. These included the right to vote and the right to fair laws. Stevens and Sumner both felt that President

Thaddeus Stevens

Johnson's Reconstruction plan was a failure. Although the Radical Republicans did not control Congress, they began to gain support among moderates when President Johnson ignored criticism of the Black Codes. "The same national authority that destroyed slavery must see that this other pretension [the Black Codes] is not permitted to survive," said Sumner.

⭐ Johnson vs. Congress

In early 1866 Congress proposed a bill to increase the powers of the Freedmen's Bureau by allowing it to use military courts to try individuals accused of violating African Americans' rights. Supporters of the bill hoped that these courts would be more fair than local courts in the South. To the surprise of many members of Congress, Johnson vetoed the bill and insisted that Congress could not pass any new laws until the southern states again were represented in Congress. He also argued that the Freedmen's Bureau was unnecessary because he believed that African Americans did not need any special assistance.

Republicans responded with the **Civil Rights Act of 1866**. This act provided African Americans with the same legal rights as white Americans. Republicans believed that without rights for African Americans, the South would never have a strong economy or democracy.

President Johnson once again used his veto, arguing that the act gave too much power to the federal government. He also rejected the principle of equal rights for African Americans, insisting that they did not understand "the nature and character of our institutions." The Republicans overrode Johnson's veto.

⭐ The Fourteenth Amendment

Many Republicans were concerned that the Civil Rights Act might be overturned by Congress once the southern states were readmitted. To protect the new civil rights laws from hostile presidents or legislators, Republicans proposed an amendment to the Constitution in the summer of 1866.

Equal Protection

The **Fourteenth Amendment** guaranteed citizenship and equal protection under the law to all people born or naturalized within the United States with the exception of American Indians. It said that state governments could not "deprive any person of life, liberty, or property, without due process of law."

The amendment also banned many former Confederate officials from holding state or federal offices. In addition, the amendment made state laws subject to federal court review. The final section of the amendment gave Congress the power to pass any laws needed to enforce any part of the amendment. The editors of one black newspaper wrote, "We are entering upon the greatest political contest that has ever agitated [upset] the people of the country."

The 1866 Elections

President Johnson and most Democrats opposed the Fourteenth Amendment. As a result, civil rights for African Americans became a key issue in the 1866 congressional elections. Republican candidates asked Americans to support civil rights by voting for the Republican Party. To help the Democrats, Johnson traveled around the country defending his Reconstruction plan.

Johnson's speaking tour was a disaster and did little to help win votes for the Democratic Party. He got into arguments with spectators and often seemed to wander from the subject. When a spectator at one of his speeches cried out, "Hang Jeff Davis!" Johnson replied angrily, "Why don't you hang Thad Stevens? . . . I can tell you, my countrymen, I have been fighting traitors in the south, and . . . I am prepared to fight traitors at the north, . . . with your help." Such outbursts did not impress many voters.

The Granger Collection, New York

President Johnson traveled to cities such as Philadelphia, Cleveland, and St. Louis when he campaigned for Democratic candidates in 1866.

Southern whites fire on African American demonstrators during the New Orleans riot of 1866.

Violence in the South

Two major riots in the South also hurt Johnson's campaign. On May 1, 1866, a dispute in Memphis, Tennessee, between local police and black Union soldiers turned into a three-day wave of violence against African Americans. To make things worse, police officers joined in the attacks on freedpeople. By the time federal troops restored peace, 46 African Americans were dead.

Three months later, another riot took place in New Orleans when African Americans attempted to hold a peaceful political demonstration. This time 34 African Americans and 3 white Radical Republicans were killed. Again, the local police participated in the violence, and federal troops had to restore order. These widely publicized events convinced many voters that Johnson's Reconstruction plan was failing.

★ Congress Takes Charge

The 1866 elections gave the Republican Party a commanding two-thirds majority in both the House and the Senate. This gave the Republicans the power to override any presidential veto. In addition, the Republicans became united as the moderates joined with the Radicals. Together they called for a new form of Reconstruction.

The Reconstruction Acts

In March 1867 Congress passed the first of several **Reconstruction Acts**. These acts divided the South into five districts that were controlled by military commanders. The acts also required all southern states to create new state constitutions supporting the Fourteenth Amendment before they could be readmitted to the Union. In addition, the states would be required to give African American men the right to vote.

Thaddeus Stevens was one of the new Reconstruction Acts' most enthusiastic supporters. Defending them before Congress, he argued:

> ❝ Have not loyal blacks quite as good a right to choose rulers and make laws as rebel whites? Every man, no matter what his race or color . . . has an equal right to justice, honesty, and fair play with every other man; and the law should secure him those rights. ❞

President Johnson disagreed strongly with Stevens, arguing that African Americans did not deserve the same treatment as white people. He also insisted that the Reconstruction Acts used "powers not granted to the federal government or any one of its branches."

Impeachment

Congress knew that Johnson did not support its Reconstruction policies. To limit his power, Congress passed an act preventing the president from removing cabinet officials without the approval of the U.S. Senate. Johnson defied the new law soon after by firing Secretary of War Edwin Stanton.

The Granger Collection, New York

A ticket to President Andrew Johnson's 1868 trial in the Senate

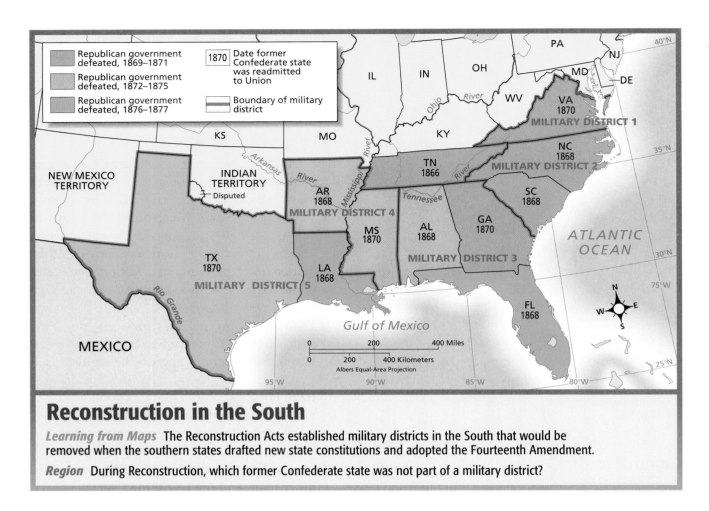

Reconstruction in the South

Learning from Maps The Reconstruction Acts established military districts in the South that would be removed when the southern states drafted new state constitutions and adopted the Fourteenth Amendment.

Region During Reconstruction, which former Confederate state was not part of a military district?

The House of Representatives responded by voting for presidential impeachment for the first time in U.S. history. Impeachment is the process of bringing charges of wrongdoing against a public official. The next step, under Article I of the Constitution, was a trial in the Senate. A two-thirds majority was required to find Johnson guilty and remove him from office.

Although Johnson was unpopular with Republicans, some of them believed he was being judged unfairly. Others did not want to disrupt the balance of powers by interfering with presidential authority over the cabinet. By a single vote, Senate Republicans failed to convict Johnson. Even so, the trial broke his power as president.

★ The Election of 1868

The Democratic Party chose former New York governor Horatio Seymour as its 1868 presidential candidate instead of Johnson. The Republicans chose Ulysses S. Grant. As a war hero, Grant appealed to many northern voters. He had no political experience but supported the congressional Reconstruction plan. He ran under the slogan "Let Us Have Peace."

Shortly after Grant was nominated, Congress readmitted seven southern states: Alabama, Arkansas, Florida, Georgia, Louisiana, North Carolina, and South Carolina. (Tennessee already had been readmitted in 1866.) Under the terms of readmission, these seven states approved the Fourteenth Amendment and agreed to let African American men have the vote. During the election, however, white southerners used violence to keep African Americans from the polls in many states.

Ulysses S. Grant

Despite such tactics, thousands of African Americans voted for Grant and the "party of Lincoln." One black newspaper reported that many freedpeople "see clearly enough that the Republican party [is] their political life boat." African American votes helped Grant win a narrow victory.

This poster—which includes images of African American preachers, soldiers, and students—celebrated the passage of the Fifteenth Amendment.

★ The Fifteenth Amendment

Congressional Republicans wanted to protect their Reconstruction plan, which they believed most African American voters would support. Some Radical Republicans argued that it was not fair that only eight northern states allowed African Americans to vote while all southern states were required to grant suffrage to African American men.

In 1869 Congress proposed the **Fifteenth Amendment**, which gave African American men throughout the United States the right to vote. Abolitionist William Lloyd Garrison praised "this wonderful, quiet, sudden transformation of four

millions of human beings from . . . the auction block to the ballot-box." The amendment, which went into effect in 1870, was one of the last important pieces of Reconstruction legislation passed at the federal level.

The Fifteenth Amendment did not please every reformer, however. Women's rights activists were angry because the amendment did not also grant women the right to vote.

SECTION 2 REVIEW

Identify and explain the significance of the following:
- Black Codes
- Radical Republicans
- Thaddeus Stevens
- Civil Rights Act of 1866
- Fourteenth Amendment
- Reconstruction Acts
- Fifteenth Amendment

Reading for Content Understanding

1 **Main Idea** What was the purpose of the Black Codes?

2 **Main Idea** Why did Radical Republicans want to remove President Johnson from office?

3 **Constitutional Heritage** What did Congress do to guarantee the civil rights of African Americans?

4 **Writing Mastery** *Creating* Make a slogan that might have been used by the Republican or the Democratic Party to appeal to voters in either the 1866 congressional election or the 1868 presidential election.

5 **Critical Thinking** *Making Comparisons* How might a conservative white southerner have viewed the Fourteenth and the Fifteenth Amendments? How might a Radical Republican or an African American have viewed these amendments?

Reconstruction in the South

Reading Focus

What roles did African Americans, northerners, and southern white Republicans play in rebuilding the South?

How did the Ku Klux Klan try to stop Reconstruction?

What factors led to the end of Reconstruction?

Key Terms

carpetbaggers
scalawags
Ku Klux Klan
Panic of 1873
Civil Rights Act of 1875
General Amnesty Act of 1872
Compromise of 1877
Redeemers
poll tax
segregation
Jim Crow laws
Plessy v. *Ferguson*

OVERNMENTS ELECTED with the support of African American votes took control of most southern states. This led planter William Henry Ravenel to express concerns about the future in his daily journal: "The experiment [Reconstruction] is now to be tried. . . . It produces a financial, political, and social revolution [in] the South." Ravenel feared how the actions of the new governments would affect southern society, but he still hoped that God would "bless the effort and make it successful."

William Henry Ravenel

 ## Reconstruction Governments

The Republican Party controlled most southern governments partly because the Fourteenth Amendment banned a large number of former Confederates from holding office. Most of these Republican officeholders were unpopular with the majority of white southerners.

Carpetbaggers and Scalawags

Many white southerners called northern-born Republicans **carpetbaggers**. Most of these northerners

had come South after the war, carrying all their possessions in a bag made from carpeting. Many southerners resented "carpetbaggers," believing that they had moved south to profit from Reconstruction. Southern Democrats were no more fond of white southern Republicans. They referred to them as **scalawags**, which means liars and cheats. Democrats believed that "scalawags" had betrayed the South by voting for the Republican Party.

Despite southern resentment, northerners and white southern Republicans had many reasons for taking part in Reconstruction. Some northerners shared the view of one reformer who strongly believed he "had a Mission with a large M" to help

In this cartoon, the South bears the heavy burden imposed by President Grant, federal troops, and carpetbaggers during Reconstruction.

freedpeople. Others hoped to make money while rebuilding the southern economy. An Illinois man who had moved to Texas explained, "I am going to introduce new ideas here in the farming line." Many southern Republicans were small farmers who had supported the Union during the war. Others, like Mississippi governor James Alcorn, were former members of the Whig Party who preferred to become Republicans rather than join the Democrats. By 1872, about 25 percent of southern whites were Republicans.

African Americans in Politics

African Americans seeking equality overwhelmingly supported Reconstruction and were the largest group of southern Republican voters. During Reconstruction, voters elected more than 600 African American representatives to state legislatures and sent 16 to Congress. Other African Americans held important state offices such as lieutenant governor, treasurer, and secretary of state. Many more held local offices in counties throughout the South. Apart from their regular duties, these politicians helped enforce civil rights laws that white officials often ignored. In Georgia, for example, Justice of the Peace Tunis Campbell arrested some white overseers who

mistreated black workers. One African American called Campbell "the champion of their rights and the bearer of their burden."

African American politicians came from many different backgrounds. Hiram Revels was born a free man in North Carolina. He went to college in Illinois and became a Methodist minister. During the Civil War, he served as a chaplain in the Union army. In 1870 Revels became the first African American in the U.S. Senate when he took over the seat previously held by Jefferson Davis. Blanche K. Bruce was another important African American leader. Bruce grew up in slavery in Virginia and later became a prominent Republican politician in Mississippi. He served one term as a U.S. senator and was active in politics for many years.

Reconstruction Reforms

The Reconstruction governments provided money for many new programs and organizations. These governments helped to establish the first state-funded public school systems in the South and built new hospitals, prisons, and orphanages. Republican governments also passed laws prohibiting discrimination against African Americans.

During this period, southern states spent large amounts of money building or repairing railroads, bridges, and public buildings—improvements intended to help the southern economy recover

The first African American members of Congress: (left to right) Hiram Revels, Benjamin Turner, Robert DeLarge, Josiah Wells, Jefferson Long, Joseph Rainey, and Robert Elliott

from the war. To get the money for these projects, the Reconstruction governments raised taxes and issued bonds.

★ Opposition to Reconstruction

Despite all of these efforts to rebuild the South, the majority of white southerners opposed Reconstruction. Democrats claimed that the Reconstruction governments were unjust and illegal. They also disliked having the federal soldiers stationed in their states. Many white southerners disapproved of African American officeholders. One Democrat noted, "'A white man's government' [is] the most popular rallying cry we have."

In 1866 a group of white southerners in Tennessee created the **Ku Klux Klan**. This secret society opposed African Americans obtaining civil rights, particularly suffrage, and used violence and terror to frighten and discourage them. The Klan's membership grew rapidly as it spread throughout the South. Klan members wore robes and hoods to hide their identities as they attacked—and even murdered—African Americans, white Republican voters, and public officials, usually at night. Charlotte Fowler described her husband's murder by the Klan:

> ❝We still had a little grandchild living with me. . . . I heard somebody by the door. . . . The little child followed its grandfather to the door. . . and just then I heard the report [shot] of a pistol, and they shot him down. And this little child ran back to me before I could get out and says, 'Oh grandma, they have killed my poor grandpappy.'❞

Local governments did little to stop the violence because many officials feared the Klan or

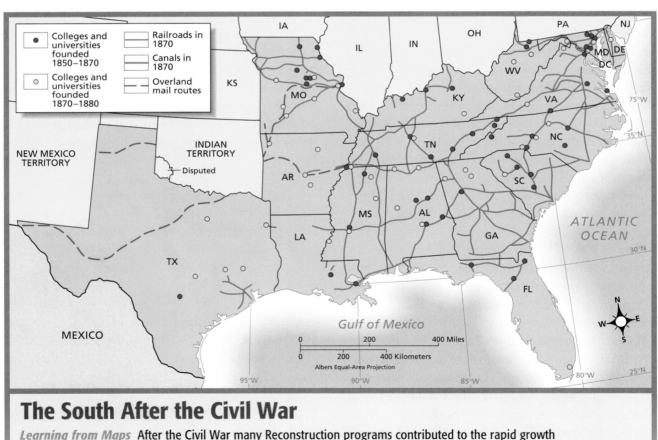

The South After the Civil War

Learning from Maps After the Civil War many Reconstruction programs contributed to the rapid growth in transportation and education in the South.

Place How many colleges and universities were founded in Alabama from 1850 to 1870?

were sympathetic to its activities. In Kentucky a committee of African Americans presented a list of at least 70 murder victims and a formal complaint to the state legislature about the lack of action against the Klu Klux Klan. "We regard them [the Klan] as now being licensed to continue their dark and bloody deeds under cover of the dark night," they wrote.

In 1870 and 1871 the federal government passed a series of laws that made it a federal crime to interfere with elections or deny citizens equal protection under the law. Thus, by the mid-1870s the Klan was no longer an organized threat, although it would re-emerge later. Even with the decline of the Klan, white mobs continued to assault African Americans and Republicans throughout the 1870s. Such actions made federal action and protection necessary for Reconstruction's success.

African American men—one of them a soldier—voting in the South.

The Election of 1876

The violence that took place throughout the South was not the only challenge to Reconstruction. Northerners also grew more critical of the Reconstruction policies during the early 1870s.

Republican Support Fades

Although President Grant was re-elected in 1872, his administration suffered many scandals that upset voters. The financial **Panic of 1873**, which helped cause a severe economic downturn, also hurt the Republican Party. In 1874 the Republicans lost control of the House of Representatives to the Democrats. Nevertheless, Republicans managed to pass one last act—the **Civil Rights Act of 1875**, which allowed African Americans to sue private businesses for discrimination.

Southern and national politics had also changed with the passage of the **General Amnesty Act of 1872**. This act repealed Section III of the Fourteenth Amendment and allowed former Confederates, with the exception of those of high rank, to hold public office. Many of these former Confederates were Democrats. As a result, southern state governments gradually became controlled by the Democratic Party.

Republicans could tell that support for Reconstruction was also fading in the North, where people were growing concerned about economic problems and government corruption. Thus, the Republicans selected for their 1876 presidential candidate Ohio governor Rutherford B. Hayes, who believed the time had come to end federal support of the Reconstruction governments. The Democrats nominated New York governor Samuel J. Tilden.

The Compromise of 1877

During the election, Democrats in the South again used violence at the polls. Senator Blanche K. Bruce of Mississippi described the problem:

❝ In many parts of the State corrupt and violent influences were brought to bear [used] . . . changing the number of votes cast; . . . threats and violence were practiced directly upon the masses of voters . . . to deter [prevent] them from [voting]. ❞

The election between Hayes and Tilden was very close. When the votes from the electoral college came in, Tilden appeared to have won, but Republicans questioned the election returns in three southern states.

The Election Commission hears testimony on disputed returns from the presidential election of 1876.

A special commission of 10 members of Congress and five Supreme Court justices settled the issue. The commission narrowly decided to give all the disputed votes to Hayes. Hayes thus won the election by one electoral vote. In the **Compromise of 1877**, the Democrats agreed to accept Hayes's victory if all remaining federal troops were removed from the South. They also asked for funding for internal improvements in the South and the appointment of a southern Democrat to the president's cabinet. Shortly after he took office in 1877, President Hayes removed the last of the federal troops from the South.

 Turning Back the Clock

Reconstruction ended at different times in southern states, depending on when the Democrats regained control of a particular state government. In general, their first order of business was to eliminate the Reconstruction reforms.

The Redeemers

The individuals behind the Democratic Party's return to power in the South were known as the **Redeemers**. The Redeemers included people from many different backgrounds, such as U.S. senator John T. Morgan of Alabama—a former general in the Confederate army—and newspaper editor Henry Grady of Georgia, who was interested in promoting southern industry. "Never was nobler duty confided [given] to human hands than the uplifting and upbuilding of the…South," said Grady. The Redeemers wanted to reduce the size of state government and limit the rights of African Americans. They lowered state budgets and got rid of social programs. They cut property taxes and reduced public funding for schools. The Redeemers also succeeded in limiting African Americans' civil rights.

In an effort to deny the vote to African Americans, the Redeemers set up the **poll tax**, which required individuals to pay a special tax before they could vote. The poll tax, however, often stopped not only African American men but also some white men from voting. To bypass this result, some states more carefully targeted African American voters by requiring them to pass literacy tests. A "grandfather clause" was usually written into law as well, allowing any man whose father or grandfather could vote before 1867 to avoid poll taxes and literacy tests. This meant that almost every white man could benefit from the clause, but few black men could.

Segregation and Jim Crow

Another change made by the Democratic governments was the introduction of legal **segregation**—the forced separation of whites and African Americans in public places. **Jim Crow laws**—laws that enforced segregation began appearing in southern states in 1881. African Americans had to stay in different hotels than whites, sit in separate theater sections, and ride in separate rail cars. One white southerner described segregated areas as "in every instance . . . the most uncomfortable, uncleanest, and unsafest place[s]."

African Americans challenged these laws in

An African American man is ordered to leave a "whites only" railroad car.

court. In 1883, however, the U.S. Supreme Court ruled that the Civil Rights Act of 1875—and laws like it—was unconstitutional and that the Fourteenth Amendment applied only to the actions of state governments. This allowed private individuals and businesses to practice segregation.

Plessy v. Ferguson

In 1896 the U.S. Supreme Court returned to the issue of segregation in the case **Plessy v. Ferguson**. Homer Plessy was an African American who had purchased a first-class ticket on a Louisiana train. When he tried to sit in the first-class car, he was arrested because Louisiana's Jim Crow laws did not allow African Americans to ride in first class with whites. Plessy and his lawyers argued that this violated the Fourteenth Amendment's guarantee of equal legal treatment.

The Court ruled against Plessy, arguing that it was legal to force African Americans and whites to use separate facilities as long as the facilities were of equal quality. According to the Court, this was fair so long as "separate-but-equal" facilities were provided for African Americans.

The only justice who disagreed with the court's decision was John Marshall Harlan. Justice Harlan explained his concerns in a dissenting, or disagreeing, opinion:

> 66 **In the eye of the law, there is in this country no superior, dominant [controlling], ruling class of citizens. . . . Our Constitution is color-blind, and neither knows nor tolerates classes among citizens. In respect of civil rights, all citizens are equal before the law.** 99

Few white Americans agreed with Justice Harlan in 1896, however. Segregation continued to be widespread both in the South and in the North. In addition, the public schools, libraries, parks, and other areas open to African Americans were usually inferior in quality to

A judge's gavel

those created for whites. Thus, in practice, the "separate-but-equal" facilities usually were "separate-and-unequal."

SECTION 3 REVIEW

Identify and explain the significance of the following:

- carpetbaggers
- scalawags
- Hiram Revels
- Blanche K. Bruce
- Ku Klux Klan
- Panic of 1873
- Civil Rights Act of 1875
- General Amnesty Act of 1872
- Rutherford B. Hayes
- Compromise of 1877
- Redeemers
- poll tax
- segregation
- Jim Crow laws
- *Plessy v. Ferguson*
- John Marshall Harlan

Reading for Content Understanding

1 **Main Idea** What contributions did African Americans, northern whites, and white southern Republicans make to the Reconstruction process?

2 **Main Idea** Why did some white southerners oppose Reconstruction? Why did some of them form the Ku Klux Klan?

3 **Citizenship and Democracy** What was the Compromise of 1877, and how did it lead to the end of Reconstruction?

4 **Writing Mastery** *Persuading* Imagine you are a newspaper editor who opposes the *Plessy* v. *Ferguson* ruling. Write an editorial to convince your readers that the ruling is wrong.

5 **Critical Thinking** *Evaluating* Do you think the civil rights aspects of Reconstruction were a short-term failure but a long-term success? Explain your answer.

The New South

Reading Focus

What problems did some southern farmers face at the end of the Civil War?

Why did some business leaders hope to create a "New South"?

What were some popular forms of southern culture during and after Reconstruction?

Key Terms

sharecropping

AFTER RENTING LAND FOR YEARS, *Charley White and his wife, Lucille, saved enough money to buy their own farm in Texas. Reflecting back on the purchase, Charley White said, "The house wasn't much more than a shack." The fact that it belonged to them made all the difference. "It just set us on fire. We didn't seem to get half as tired, or if we did we didn't notice it." Lucille White told her husband that "even the rocks look pretty." Many other African American farmers, however, were not fortunate enough to share the Whites' accomplishment.*

Farmers used harrows such as this one to smooth their soil.

★ Farming in the South

Throughout most of the South, few African Americans could afford to buy or even rent their own farms and the necessary farm supplies. Moving west also was costly. Thus, many African Americans remained on plantations, while others tried to make a living in the cities.

The Growth of Sharecropping

Those African Americans who stayed on plantations often became part of a system known as **sharecropping**, or sharing the crop. Landowners provided the land, tools, and supplies, and sharecroppers provided the labor. At harvest time, the sharecropper gave most of the crop to the owner. Whatever remained belonged to the sharecropper.

The sharecropping system allowed poor African Americans and poor whites to farm land that they could not afford to rent or buy. The system also enabled small farmers to hire people to work on their land. Many sharecroppers hoped to save enough money from selling their share of the crops to buy a farm. Only a few were able to achieve this dream, however.

A Cycle of Debt

When sharecropping families needed food, clothing, or supplies, they went to the general store. Most families bought goods on credit because they had little money. When the harvest came, sharecroppers hoped to sell their crops and pay off their debt to the store. However, bad weather or low crop prices often prevented them from making as much money as they had hoped.

Many merchants cheated sharecroppers by charging them for items they did not purchase. Some landowners also cheated sharecroppers by taking more than their fair share of the crop. Abolitionist Frederick Douglass complained about the treatment of sharecroppers:

❝ **The merchant puts him [the sharecropper] off with his poorest commodities [goods] at highest prices, and can say to him take these or nothing. . . . By this means the laborer is brought into debt, and hence is kept always in the power of the land-owner. . . . On such a system of fraud and wrong one might well invoke [request] a bolt from heaven.** ❞

As a result of such practices, most sharecroppers found themselves deeper in debt at the end of the harvest than they had been when they planted their crops.

Too Much Cotton

Many farmers saw planting cotton as a sure way to make money. Cotton was one of the South's most important cash crops—crops that farmers grow to sell to others rather than to use themselves. Cotton had a worldwide market and could be sold or stored easily. As a result, numerous landowners and sharecroppers grew cotton, hoping to pay their debts or save money. When too many farmers

The Granger Collection, New York

Children in the South often had to help their parents pick cotton at harvest time.

African American Property Owners in the South, 1860 and 1870

Total number of African American property owners (in thousands)

1860	1870
9	139

*Figures are for former Confederate states.
Source: The Facts of Reconstruction, 1991*

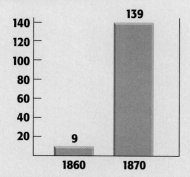

Owning Property The number of African American property owners in the South dramatically increased in the years following the Civil War. How much did this number increase from 1860 to 1870?

planted cotton, however, the supply became too great and the price per bale dropped. One man wrote his father about a drop in the price of cotton: "It nearly ruined us. . . . The farmers are very blue here. But getting ready to plant cotton again."

Even though many farmers understood the drawbacks of planting cotton, they felt too much pressure from banks or landlords to change their ways. "Cotton raising has grown to be a necessity more than a choice," a farmer in Alabama said. Another southern man explained,

❝ **Cotton is the thing to get credit on in this country. . . . You can always sell cotton. You leave home with a wagon load of cotton and you will go home that night with money in your pocket; you load up your wagon with wheat or corn . . . and I doubt some days whether you could sell it.** ❞

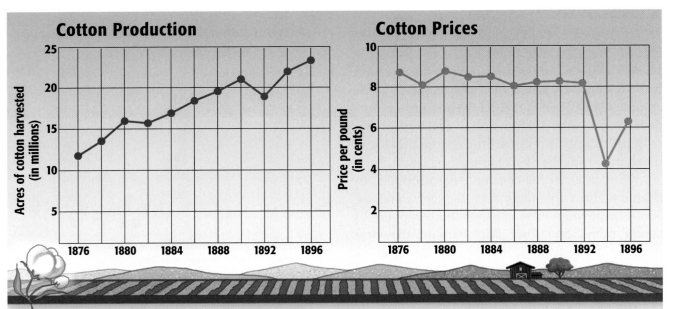

Cotton Production

Acres of cotton harvested (in millions)

1876 | 1880 | 1884 | 1888 | 1892 | 1896

Cotton Prices

Price per pound (in cents)

1876 | 1880 | 1884 | 1888 | 1892 | 1896

King Cotton   During the late 1800s cotton remained a primary crop for many farmers. According to the graphs, what generally happened as cotton production increased?

The "New South" Movement

The southern economy, like the southern farmer, relied on cash crops such as cotton. This created cycles of good and bad years as prices went up or down. Tired of watching the southern economy suffer, some business leaders wanted to create a "New South" that had an industrial base in addition to its agricultural one. They hoped industry would strengthen the southern economy.

Southern Industry

Henry Grady, a newspaper editor in Atlanta, was one of the leaders of the New South movement. "The new South presents a perfect democracy," he wrote, "and a diversified [varied] industry that meets the complex needs of this complex age." Grady and his supporters wanted to take advantage of the South's resources—such as its cotton production and cheap and abundant labor—to build textile mills and other factories.

Grant Hamilton's From Darkness to Light *(1895) shows the New South rising from the destruction of the Civil War.*

They hoped their plans for development would interest investors.

New industries developed in the South, though not as quickly or in as many areas as Grady hoped. One of the great changes after the Civil War was the repair of the old railroads and the growth of new lines as workers laid thousands of miles of railroad track throughout the South. The new railroads allowed companies to ship goods faster and farther than ever before. The telegraph lines that accompanied the railroads also helped bring news to small southern towns.

The most successful industrial development in the South involved textile production. Businesspeople built textile mills that produced cotton fabric in many small towns, drawing hundreds of people from the countryside to work in the mills. While this industry pumped new life into the southern economy, the New South was far from the "perfect democracy" that Grady had claimed. The most important example of this lack of democracy was the cotton mills' refusal to hire African Americans.

Southern Mill Life

Work in the cotton mills appealed to farm families that had trouble making ends meet. As one mill worker explained, "It was a necessity to move and get a job, rather than depend on the farm." Recruiters sent out by the mills promised good wages and steady work.

Entire families often worked in the same mill. One company in South Carolina asked for "whole families with at least three workers for the mill in each family." Mills employed large numbers of women and children. Many children started working around the age of 12; some started earlier than that. Women did most of the spinning and were valued workers, although few women had the opportunity to advance within the company.

Many mill workers were proud of the skills they used, but they did not enjoy their work. One unhappy worker described it as "the same thing over and over again. . . . The more you do, the more they want done." Workers often labored six days a week, 12 hours a day. Cotton dust and lint filled the air, causing asthma and an illness known as brown-lung disease. Fast-moving machinery caused many injuries and some deaths. Despite the long hours and dangerous working conditions, wages were low. However, mill work did offer an alternative to farming.

 ## Southern Literature

While the New South movement sought to modernize the South, many southerners looked to the arts to reinforce their traditions. Southern literature, an important element of southern culture, gained national popularity in the late 1800s. The most famous writer about the South at the end of Reconstruction was probably Mark Twain. Twain, whose real name was Samuel Clemens, wrote *The Adventures of Tom Sawyer* in 1876. Although Twain wrote about many subjects, his novels and stories about the South were among his most admired.

Part of the reason that southern literature gained national attention was that many of these stories involved people and places in the South that seemed exotic to northerners. The popular writer Mary Noailles Murfree, for example, wrote short stories and novels about the people who lived in the mountains of eastern Tennessee. Another writer, George Washington Cable, wrote novels about the African American community in New Orleans. Cable used his writing as an opportunity to protest racial prejudice in the South.

Joel Chandler Harris was one of the most popular southern writers. He wrote short stories about a fictional plantation slave named Uncle Remus, a wise old storyteller who taught lessons by reciting folktales. Another author, William J. Faulkner, brought together many more African American folktales in his book *The Days When the Animals Talked*. Both Harris and Faulkner based their work on stories they were first told by enslaved African Americans and later by freedpeople.

Many white southern writers set their stories in a pre–Civil War South full of beautiful plantations and happy slaves. Unlike these authors who presented romantic images of life on southern plantations, African American writer Charles W. Chesnutt wrote plantation stories that showed the greed and cruelty of the slavery system. Chesnutt was born in Ohio but raised in North Carolina. Many of his short stories are in a book called *The Conjure Woman.*

Mary Noailles Murfree began her writing career by producing short stories, which she read to her family.

A southern dancing party

American Literature

"The Wife of His Youth"
Charles W. Chesnutt

Author Charles W. Chesnutt wrote short stories and novels dealing with problems caused by slavery and racial prejudice. In "The Wife of His Youth," the main character, Mr. Ryder, is courting a young widow, Mrs. Dixon. Ryder's wife, from whom he has been apart for 25 years, appears one day. He must choose between his first wife, a woman he married when he was a slave, and the widow. In the following excerpt, Mr. Ryder tells his friends about his wife.

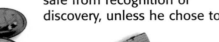

Charles W. Chesnutt
The Granger Collection, New York

"Suppose that this husband, soon after his escape, had learned that his wife had been sold away, and that such inquiries [investigations] as he could make brought no information of her whereabouts. . . . Suppose, too, that he made his way to the North . . . and there, where he had larger opportunities, had improved [himself]. . . . And then suppose that accident should bring to his knowledge the fact that the wife of his youth, . . . was alive and seeking him, but that he was absolutely safe from recognition or discovery, unless he chose to reveal himself. My friends, what would the man do? . . ."

There was something in Mr. Ryder's voice that stirred the hearts of those who sat around him. . . . It was observed, too, that his look rested more especially upon Mrs. Dixon. . . .

She was the first to speak: "He should have acknowledged her." "Yes," they all echoed, "he should have acknowledged her."

"My friends and companions," responded Mr. Ryder, "I thank you, one and all. It is the answer I expected, for I knew your hearts."

He turned and walked toward the closed door of an adjoining room. . . . He came back in a moment, leading by the hand his visitor of the afternoon. . . .

"Ladies and gentlemen," he said, "this is the woman, and I am the man, whose story I have told you. Permit me to introduce to you the wife of my youth.**"**

Understanding Literature

1. How does Mr. Ryder become separated from his wife?

2. Why do you think Mr. Ryder chooses to tell his friends about his wife?

 Southern Music

Southern music also grew in popularity after the Civil War. Popular musical instruments in the South included the violin, the banjo, and the guitar. Fiddle players provided the music for square dancing, a popular pastime. Mary Noailles Murfree described a country dance in "The Dancin' Party at Harrison's Cove:"

"Now and then a guffaw [laugh] mingled with the violin's resonant [loud] strains and the dancers' well-marked pace; the women talked to each other with somewhat more animation [cheerfulness] than was their wont [typical practice], under the stress of the unusual excitement of a dancing party."

One of the most important musical styles of the period was the spiritual. These songs were based on Christian hymns and African music sung in the days of slavery. In these songs the lead singer often called out a verse that the rest of the singers would repeat. Although the lead singer might change the words slightly to reflect current events, the lyrics usually described the sorrows of slavery and the hope for freedom. One of the best-known spirituals, "Swing Low Sweet Chariot," expressed African Americans' longing for "the promised land," where they would be free from slavery:

Many of the original Fisk Jubilee Singers were recently emancipated slaves.

❝ Swing low sweet chariot,
Comin' for to carry me home,
Swing low sweet chariot,
Comin' for to carry me home,
I look'd over Jordan, an' what did I see,
Comin' for to carry me home,
A band of angels comin' after me,
Comin' for to carry me home,
If you get-a there befo' I do,
Tell all of my friends I'm comin' too. ❞

During Reconstruction, the Fisk Jubilee Singers—a group of students from Fisk University in Nashville, Tennessee—traveled widely to earn money for their school. They brought African American music to a national audience. This singing group entertained people with spirituals, touring the United States in 1871 and 1872 and performing in Europe in 1873. Their tours made Fisk University famous and also raised enough money to save the college from financial ruin and build a new campus. Other African American colleges, such as Hampton University in Virginia, formed similar singing groups, which increased the popularity of spirituals.

SECTION 4 REVIEW

Identify and explain the significance of the following:

- **sharecropping**
- **Henry Grady**
- **Mark Twain**
- **Mary Noailles Murfree**
- **Joel Chandler Harris**
- **Charles W. Chesnutt**
- **Fisk Jubilee Singers**

Reading for Content Understanding

1 **Main Idea** What were some of the drawbacks of being a sharecropper in the years after the Civil War?

2 **Main Idea** Why did some business leaders want to develop southern industry?

3 **Cultural Diversity** What types of southern culture were popular throughout the United States?

4 **Writing Mastery** *Describing* Write a paragraph describing what life might have been like in a southern mill.

5 **Critical Thinking** *Making Comparisons* How were the lives of black and white sharecroppers similar? How were they different?

CHAPTER
20 REVIEW

Chapter Summary

After the Civil War, the United States struggled with restoring the southern states to the Union and dealing with the rights of former slaves. Americans differed in their approach to Reconstruction. At the end of Reconstruction, the Union was restored, but African Americans continued to be denied their full citizenship rights. ▣

On a separate sheet of paper, complete the following activities.

Identifying People and Ideas

Describe the historical significance of the following:

1. Thirteenth Amendment
2. Freedmen's Bureau
3. Black Codes
4. Andrew Johnson
5. Hiram Revels

6. Fourteenth Amendment
7. Ulysses S. Grant
8. Ku Klux Klan
9. *Plessy v. Ferguson*
10. sharecropping

Internet Activity go.hrw.com
SA0 Colleges

Search the Internet through the HRW Web site to find information on one of the historically black colleges and universities that was founded during Reconstruction. Then use the information to create a one-page brochure about that school.

Understanding Main Ideas

1. How did the Reconstruction plans of Lincoln, the Radical Republicans, and Johnson differ?
2. What was the Civil Rights Act of 1866? Why did President Johnson veto it, and how did Congress react to his veto?
3. How did the Reconstruction Acts of 1867 protect the rights of African Americans in the South?
4. What roles did African Americans, northerners, and white southern Democrats play in Reconstruction?
5. Why were most white southerners loyal to the Democratic Party?
6. What crisis was resolved by the Compromise of 1877? What were the elements of this compromise?
7. What musical styles were popular in the South after the Civil War?

Using the Time Line

Number your paper from 1 to 5. Match the letters on the time line below with the following events.

1. **Congress proposes the Fifteenth Amendment, giving African American men the right to vote.**
2. **Democrats take control of the House of Representatives.**
3. **Hiram Revels becomes the first African American senator.**
4. **Congress proposes an amendment to make slavery illegal throughout the United States.**
5. **Americans elect Ulysses S. Grant, a Civil War hero, president.**

1865   1868   1871   1874   1877

a   b c   d   e

Reviewing Themes

1. **Constitutional Heritage**   Which three amendments to the Constitution attempted to protect the rights of African Americans? How did these amendments protect those rights?

2. **Citizenship and Democracy**   How did democracy expand during Reconstruction?

3. **Cultural Diversity**   What contributions did African Americans make to southern society, government, and culture?

Thinking Critically

1. **Drawing Conclusions**   Why might southern culture have increased in popularity during the late 1800s?

2. **Synthesizing Information**   If you were a freedperson living in the South in 1870, how would your life have changed after emancipation?

3. **Evaluating**   How might the Redeemers' efforts to limit the rights of African Americans affect poor whites?

Writing About History

1. **Informing**   Imagine that you are a foreign newspaper reporter in Washington. Write a one-paragraph news article on either the assassination of President Lincoln or President Johnson's impeachment trial.

Building Your Portfolio

Complete the following activities individually or in groups.

1. **Travel Journal**   Imagine that you are traveling through the South during Reconstruction. Create a journal describing what you see. You may wish to include maps of the places you have visited and descriptions of the people you have met.

2. **Freedom**   Write a poem or song about an African American who was set free at the end of the Civil War. If you create a poem, find an image to illustrate it. If you write a song, select a musical style in which it would be performed.

2. **Describing**   Imagine that you are a teacher from the North who moved to the South to teach African Americans after the Civil War. Write a letter to your family telling them about your experiences.

Linking Geography and History

1. **Movement**   Why did many freedpeople leave their homes and towns?

2. **Place**   Explain why the Civil War left the South a poor region.

History Skills Workshop

Reading Maps   Study the map below, which shows historically black colleges and universities, and answer the following questions: (a) According to the map, which state had the most African American colleges and universities? (b) Which states located outside the former Confederacy had African American colleges and universities? (c) Why might most African American colleges and universities have been located in the South?

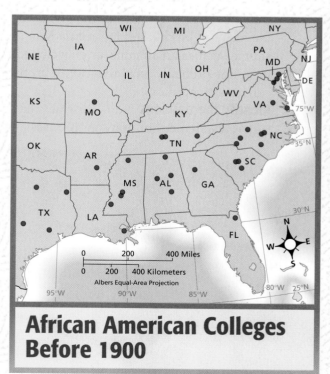

African American Colleges Before 1900

History Skills
WORKSHOP

Distinguishing Fact from Opinion and Identifying Bias

Historical sources may contain both facts and opinions. Sources such as letters, diaries, and speeches usually express personal views. The ability to distinguish facts from opinions is essential to judging the soundness of an argument or the reliability of a historical account.

When reading historical sources, try to identify a writer's *bias*—prejudices or strong feelings—that he or she might have about the subject. Many famous historical people had strong opinions that appear in their writings and speeches. Remember that just because a person is famous does not mean that you must agree with his or her opinions.

How to Distinguish Fact from Opinion

1. **Identify the facts** Ask yourself: Can the statement be proven? Determine whether the idea can be checked for accuracy in a source such as an almanac or encyclopedia. If so, it is probably factual; if not, it probably contains an opinion.
2. **Identify the opinions** Look for clues that signal a statement of opinion: phrases such as *I think* and *I believe*, comparative words like *greatest* and *more important*, and value-filled words like *extremely* and *ridiculous* imply a judgment, and thus an opinion.

How to Identify Bias

1. **Evaluate the information presented** What are the sources of information? How reliable are they? Why might a historical figure have supported one view over another? Be sure to distinguish between provable facts and someone's preferences or opinions.
2. **Make your own judgment** Remember that many of the historical documents you read are created by people who have their own opinions and points of view. It is up to you to read each document critically and to draw your own conclusions.

Practicing the Skill

Read the excerpt below, in which a southern newspaper editor defends Preston Brooks's beating of Senator Charles Sumner. Then answer the questions that follow.

> ❝We consider the act good in conception [thought], better in execution.... These vulgar abolitionists ... must be lashed into submission. Sumner, in particular, ought to have nine-and-thirty [lashes] early every morning.❞

1. Is this excerpt an example of a fact or an opinion? Which words let you know?
2. What bias, if any, does the author express about abolitionists? If you found bias, how did you identify it?

History in Action

UNIT PORTFOLIO

American History

Civil War Scrapbook

Complete the following activity in small, cooperative groups.

You and the members of your group will be researching and creating items for a Civil War Scrapbook. Each group member will be responsible for five scrapbook items, ranging from quotes to poems to letters. Your group's scrapbook should focus on one of the following topics: geography and secession, the North and the South, battles and army life in the East, battles and army life in the West, the Emancipation Proclamation, and the impact of the Civil War.

Materials To complete this activity, you will need butcher paper, posterboard, construction paper, and various raw materials, such as pens, pencils, paper, twine, glue, paints, or cloth for creating scrapbook items.

Parts of the Project To create your scrapbook, complete the following tasks:

1. **Research** Conduct research to find quotes, poems, letters, news articles, obituaries, diary entries, song lyrics, maps, time lines, charts, and images or illustrations that have something to do with your focus. You can gather the items from the library and other sources. Make a list of the items you collect; then discuss which ones would best tie into the focus of your scrapbook. You can also use your imagination to create your own items, but be sure that they are based on historical reality. Each group member should produce at least five items.

2. **Writing** Each group member will write captions to explain his or her items and will relate their significance to the group's topic and to the Civil War. In addition, one or two members of the group will be responsible for writing (and typing, if possible) a table of contents and an introduction for the scrapbook.

3. **Presentation** One or two group members will be responsible for putting the scrapbook together and making a cover.

Display your group's finished scrapbook for the class. Write a paragraph about your scrapbook, identifying facts, opinions, and bias in the items that you have presented.

These young people are part of a reenactment to celebrate the unveiling of the African American Civil War Memorial at Arlington National Cemetery.

UNIT
9 A Growing America
(1850–1920)

Young People

IN HISTORY

Young Cowhands

Cowhands herded Texas longhorn cattle northward across the Great Plains to be sold in Kansas railroad towns. A cattle drive of this distance required working long hours in all kinds of weather. Occasionally, cowhands would encounter problems with cattle thieves known as rustlers, but the greatest danger was a stampede.

Many cowhands began working cattle when they were children. A rancher paid young Cliff Newland 50 cents a day to haul supplies to cattle drivers 75 miles away. From this job, Newland turned to wrangling—the work of herding and caring for livestock. To help him learn to stay in the saddle while training horses, Newland's father tied him onto the seat. By age 13, Newland had already ridden on three cattle drives and had gotten a job training young horses.

Not all young cowhands were boys, however. At age 13, Agnes Morley and her younger brother travelled across 130 miles of harsh New Mexico terrain for days in order to sell some cattle.

Many cowhands left home to work the cattle drives while they were still children. E. C. Abbott, also known as "Teddy Blue," went on his first cattle drive when he was 11 years old. He recalled his trip up the Western Trail in 1879:

Many young cowhands like this female broncobuster gained recognition for their unique skills.

> *That trip up the trail in '79 was my second, but in a way it was the first that counted, because I was only a button [youngster] the other time. I wasn't nineteen years old when I come up the trail with the Olive herd, but don't let that fool you. I was a man in my own estimation and a man in fact.*

Teddy Blue recalled a story he had once heard about a schoolteacher who had asked a Texas cowhand to tell her about life on the trail. She said, "Oh, Mister So-and-So, didn't the boys used to have a lot of fun riding the ponies?" He replied, "Madam, there wasn't any boys or ponies. They was all horses and men."

In this unit you will learn about the people who settled the American West and the many challenges they faced. You will also learn about how great changes in industry transformed the American landscape and people.

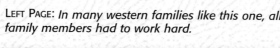

LEFT PAGE: *In many western families like this one, all family members had to work hard.*

CHAPTER 21
The West
(1850–1890)

After the Civil War, Americans witnessed the rapid growth of the U.S. population and the spread of settlements throughout the West. This flood of miners, ranchers, and farmers transformed the western landscape, as did the railroads that carried them westward. Civil War veteran Ely Parker, who was an American Indian, watched this change with concern. "The Indian [tribes]," he wrote, "are more seriously threatened . . . than ever before."

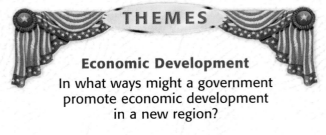

THEMES

Economic Development
In what ways might a government promote economic development in a new region?

Cultural Diversity
How might the actions of one group affect the culture of another?

Geographic Diversity
How might people adjust to living in a different environment?

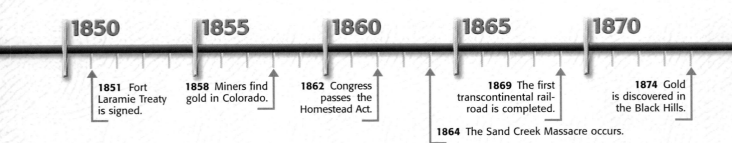

1850 **1855** **1860** **1865** **1870**

1851 Fort Laramie Treaty is signed.

1858 Miners find gold in Colorado.

1862 Congress passes the Homestead Act.

1869 The first transcontinental railroad is completed.

1874 Gold is discovered in the Black Hills.

1864 The Sand Creek Massacre occurs.

SECTION 1

The Wars for the West

Reading Focus

What was life like for American Indians on the Great Plains?

What were the causes and results of conflict between American Indians and U.S. settlers in the West?

How did the reservation system and the Dawes Act affect American Indians?

Key Terms

Fort Laramie Treaty

reservations

Sand Creek Massacre

Bozeman Trail

Treaty of Medicine Lodge

Battle of the Little Bighorn

Long Walk

Ghost Dance

Massacre at Wounded Knee

Dawes General Allotment Act

*L*IKE MANY SIOUX BEFORE HIM, *Standing Bear was eager for his first buffalo hunt. " Watch the buffalo closely. . . . They are very quick and powerful," warned his father. " They can get their horns under your horse and toss him high in the air." When he got close to the buffalo herd, Standing Bear recalled, "I realized how small I was." He brought down a buffalo and rode proudly back to camp to give his mother the buffalo skin. Buffalo hunts were important to American Indians' way of life on the Great Plains.*

The Granger Collection, New York

Cheyenne warrior's shield

IMAGE ON LEFT PAGE: *Plains Indians observe the westward movement of settlers and the railroad in the late 1800s.*

1875	1880	1885	1890

1876 The Sioux defeat the U.S. Army in the Battle of the Little Bighorn.

1881 Helen Hunt Jackson's *A Century of Dishonor* is published.

1887 Congress approves the Dawes General Allotment Act.

1890 The Massacre at Wounded Knee ends the war between the U.S. Army and Plains Indians.

The Great Plains

The Great Plains lie between the Mississippi River and the Rocky Mountains, stretching north into Canada and south into Texas. Early explorers such as Stephen Long thought that the Great Plains, which were dry and barren except for grasslands, were no better than a desert.

Despite their harshness, the Great Plains were home to the Plains Indians. Groups such as the Apache and the Comanche lived on the southern Plains around Texas and present-day Oklahoma. The Cheyenne and Arapaho roamed across the central Plains. The Pawnee occupied parts of Nebraska, while the Sioux spread north across Minnesota to Montana. Plains Indians spoke many languages and used a common sign language to communicate with each other.

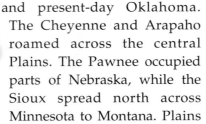

Sioux moccasins

For survival, Plains Indians depended on two animals—the horse and the buffalo. After the Spanish brought horses to America in the 1500s, Plains Indians traveled on horseback and became highly mobile. Indian hunters were able to move onto the Plains year-round, following the herds of buffalo that roamed the land.

Most hunters used a short bow and arrows to shoot the buffalo at close range from horseback. Plains Indians used the buffalo for food, shelter, and tools. Women dried buffalo meat to make jerky. They also made clothing and tepees from buffalo hides and cups and tools from buffalo horns. As one Sioux explained, "When our people killed a buffalo, all of the animal was utilized [used] in some manner; nothing was wasted." With the buffalo providing many of their needs, the Plains Indians prospered. By 1850 some 75,000 American Indians lived on the Plains.

Negotiations and Conflicts

When miners and settlers began crossing the Great Plains in the mid-1800s, U.S. officials sent agents to negotiate treaties with the Plains Indians. The first major agreement was the **Fort Laramie Treaty**, signed with northern Plains tribes in Wyoming in 1851. Two years later, several southern Plains tribes signed a treaty at Fort Atkinson in Kansas.

These treaties accepted Indian claims to most of the Great Plains and allowed the United States to build forts and roads and to travel across Indian homelands. The U.S. government promised to pay for any damages to Indian land. The treaties, however, did not keep the peace for long. After the discovery of gold in present-day Colorado in 1858, thousands of miners came into conflict with the Cheyenne and Arapaho.

In 1861 the U.S. government negotiated new treaties that created **reservations**, areas of federal land set aside for Indians. The Bureau of Indian Affairs operated the reservations. The government expected Indians to stay on the reservations, which made hunting buffalo almost impossible. Many Indians refused to live on reservations. Some continued to fight, while others shared the view of Cheyenne chief Black Kettle. "It is not my intention or wish to fight the whites," he declared. "I want to be friendly and peaceable and keep my tribe so."

He did not get his wish. In November 1864 U.S. Army colonel John M. Chivington led a surprise attack on Black Kettle's camp on Sand Creek

Several African American cavalry regiments served in the western U.S. Army. American Indians nicknamed these African American troops "buffalo soldiers."

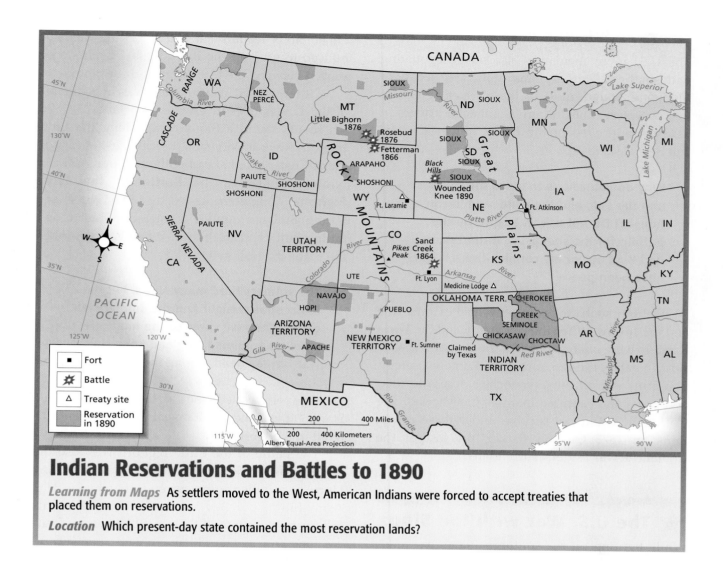

Indian Reservations and Battles to 1890

Learning from Maps As settlers moved to the West, American Indians were forced to accept treaties that placed them on reservations.

Location Which present-day state contained the most reservation lands?

in southeastern Colorado. The Cheyenne raised a white flag and a U.S. flag to show that they were peaceful. Chivington ignored the flags. "Kill and scalp all, big and little," he ordered. The soldiers killed around 200 men, women, and children. Black Kettle was among the Cheyenne who escaped the **Sand Creek Massacre.**

 Fighting on the Plains

News of the Sand Creek Massacre spread across the Great Plains. Along with the news came more pioneers, miners, and conflicts.

The Bozeman Trail

Many miners used the **Bozeman Trail**, a route named after pioneer John M. Bozeman that ran

from Wyoming to Montana. To protect the miners, the U.S. Army built forts along the trail, which went through Sioux hunting grounds. Sioux chief Red Cloud responded to the army's actions with war. In late 1866 warrior Crazy Horse and a group of Sioux lured 82 cavalry troops to their deaths in an ambush.

William Tecumseh Sherman, the famous Civil War general, had been placed in charge of the western armies. He threatened the "extermination [of the Sioux], men, women, and children." The U.S. Army had little success in this effort, however, and asked Red Cloud to negotiate. He replied, "When we see the soldiers moving away and the forts abandoned, then I will come down and talk." In 1868 the U.S. Army closed the Bozeman Trail and abandoned the forts along it. Many Sioux then moved to the Black Hills Reservation in Dakota Territory.

The West **645**

The Comanche

The U.S. government was also busy negotiating with southern Plains Indians. In the 1867 **Treaty of Medicine Lodge**, most of these tribes agreed to live on reservations. Many Comanche leaders in Texas disapproved of the treaty, however. Chief Ten Bears asked:

> 66 **Why do you ask us to leave the rivers, and the sun, and the wind, and live in houses? Do not ask us to give up the buffalo for the sheep. . . . If the Texans had kept out of my country, there might have been peace.** 99

Fighting soon broke out between the Comanche and the Texans. When the U.S. Army and the Texas Rangers were unable to defeat the Comanche warriors in battle, the U.S. forces tried a new strategy. The army cut off the Comanche's access to food and water and captured many of their horses. The Comanche could not survive under these conditions. In 1875 Quanah Parker, the last of the Comanche war leaders, surrendered.

⭐ The U.S. War with the Sioux

While fighting on the southern Plains was ending, new trouble was starting to the north. In 1874 Lieutenant Colonel George Armstrong Custer's soldiers discovered gold in the Black Hills. The U.S. government responded by insisting that the Sioux who lived in the area sell their reservation land in the Black Hills. Sitting Bull, a Sioux shaman, or spiritual leader, protested these new demands:

> 66 **What treaty that the whites have kept has the red man broken? Not one. What treaty that the white man ever made with us have they kept? Not one.** 99

Other Sioux leaders listened to Sitting Bull and refused to give up the Black Hills. Fighting soon started between the U.S. Army and the Sioux.

Custer, a Civil War veteran, was in command of the U.S. Army 7th Cavalry. On June 25, 1876, his scouts found a Sioux camp along the Little Bighorn River in Montana. Leading 264 of his soldiers, Custer raced ahead without waiting for any reinforcements. In the **Battle of the Little Bighorn**, Sioux warriors led by Crazy Horse and Sitting Bull surrounded Custer and his troops. Sitting Bull's cousin Pte-San-Waste-Win described the battle that followed:

> 66 **The soldiers fired many shots, but the Sioux shot straight and the soldiers fell dead. When we came to the hill there were no soldiers living and Long Hair [Custer] lay dead among the rest.** 99

Newspapers called the battle "Custer's Last Stand." It was the worst defeat the U.S. Army suffered in the West.

The Battle of the Little Bighorn was also the Sioux's last major victory. In late 1877 Crazy Horse was killed after surrendering to the U.S. Army. Sitting Bull fled to Canada with a few of his followers. With two of their most important leaders gone, the northern Plains Indians soon surrendered to the U.S. Army.

At the Battle of the Little Bighorn, a troop of the 7th Cavalry suffered a devastating defeat at the hands of Sioux warriors. None of the cavalry troops survived the battle.

Indians in the Southwest and Far West

Far from the Great Plains, other American Indians fought against their relocation to reservations. Their struggles were rarely successful.

The Long Walk

In 1863 the U.S. government ordered the Navajo of present-day Arizona and New Mexico to settle on a reservation. The Navajo refused. Kit Carson, a former scout, led U.S. troops in raids on the Navajo's fields, homes, and livestock. Then he lay siege to the Navajo warriors, who were in a well-defended canyon in northeastern Arizona.

When the Navajo ran out of food and shelter, they started surrendering to the U.S. Army. In 1864 the army led Navajo captives on the **Long Walk**, a 300-mile march across the desert to a reservation at Bosque Redondo, New Mexico. Along the way,

hundreds of Navajo died. At Bosque Redondo the Navajo suffered harsh conditions until 1868, when they negotiated for a new reservation located in Arizona and New Mexico.

The Nez Percé

While the Navajo were moving to their new reservation, the U.S. government was promising to let the peaceful Nez Percé keep their homelands in northeastern Oregon. Within a few years, however, settlers persuaded the government to move the Nez Percé to a reservation in present-day Idaho.

Nez Percé leader Chief Joseph reluctantly agreed to move. Before leaving, a few angry Nez Percé killed some settlers. Fearing revenge, the Nez Percé fled. The U.S. Army chased this band of around 700 Indians across Idaho, Wyoming, and Montana. Although outnumbered, the band defeated or avoided the army for weeks before trying to escape to Canada. Less than 40 miles

American Literature

"I Will Fight No More Forever"
Chief Joseph

Chief Joseph led the Nez Percé from 1871 to 1877. He gave the following speech to the U.S. Army officers who took him prisoner on October 5, 1877. Chief Joseph died in 1904.

Chief Joseph

Tell General Howard I know his heart. What he told me before, I have in my heart. I am tired of fighting. Our chiefs are killed. . . . The old men are all dead. It is the young men who say yes and no. He who led on the young men [Joseph's brother, Alokut] is dead. It is cold and we have no blankets. The little children are freezing to death. My people, some of them, have run away to the hills, and have no blankets, no food; no one knows where they are perhaps freezing to death. I want to have time to look for my children and see how many I can find. Maybe I shall find them among the dead. Hear me, my chiefs. I am tired; my heart is sick and sad. From where the sun now stands I will fight no more forever.

Understanding Literature

1. What repeated word shows Chief Joseph's grief for his people?

2. Why does Chief Joseph want to "fight no more forever"?

Geronimo

Many Apache found it difficult to get along with Geronimo—he had grown bitter after Mexican soldiers killed his wife and children. Despite this bitterness, other Apache admired Geronimo for his intelligence and resourcefulness. "In times of danger he was a man to be relied upon," recalled his cousin.

As a young warrior, Geronimo fought alongside the great Apache leader Cochise. Eventually, Geronimo led his own band of warriors. He was captured several times, but usually managed to escape. Geronimo surrendered to U.S. troops in 1886 and remained a prisoner of war until he died in 1909. His courage and determination to remain free made Geronimo a legend.

from the border, U.S. troops overtook and surrounded the Nez Percé. Chief Joseph surrendered on October 5, 1877, and the U.S. government sent the Nez Percé to a reservation in present-day Oklahoma.

The End of Armed Resistance

By the 1880s most American Indians had stopped fighting. The Apache of the Southwest, however, continued to battle the U.S. Army. The Apache were fierce raiders, known for their ability to survive in the desert. Settlers living illegally on Apache lands feared them. In the 1870s the U.S. Army gathered some Apache on a reservation in San Carlos, Arizona. One Apache called the reservation "nothing but cactus, rattlesnakes, heat, rocks, and insects."

A Chiricahua Apache named Geronimo and his small band of warriors left the reservation and resisted capture until 1884. The next year Geronimo escaped again. When the U.S. Army caught him, he broke free once more on the way to the reservation. "I feared treachery [dishonesty]," he said. This time the army sent 5,000 soldiers to capture Geronimo and 24 of his followers. Finally, in September 1886, he surrendered, ending the Apache armed resistance. The U.S. government sent Geronimo and all Chiricahua Apache to Florida as prisoners of war.

 ### The Ghost Dance and Wounded Knee

Meanwhile, in 1881 Sitting Bull and his Sioux followers returned from Canada after running out of food during the hard winter. "I wish it to be remembered," Sitting Bull said, "that I was the last man of my tribe to surrender my rifle." He joined most of the Sioux on Standing Rock Reservation in Dakota Territory. Black Elk, a Sioux shaman, described the difficulties of reservation life: "All our people now were settling down in square gray houses . . . around them the [whites] had drawn a line to keep them in. . . . The people were in despair."

At this time a religious movement known as the **Ghost Dance** began. Wovoka, a Paiute Indian, predicted the arrival of a paradise in which Indians would live freely and at peace. The buffalo herds would return and the settlers would disappear. This paradise was for those Indians who performed the sacred Ghost Dance.

When the Ghost Dance spread across the Plains, U.S. officials did not understand its meaning. They did, however, fear that it would inspire the Sioux to rebel. While following orders to arrest Sioux leaders, reservation police killed Sitting Bull in 1890. In response, many Sioux left the reservations. Later that year, the U.S. Army found a camp of Sioux near Wounded Knee Creek in South Dakota. When the two groups faced one another, a shot rang out. The U.S. troops began firing and killed at least 150 Indians. This **Massacre at Wounded Knee** marked the end of more than 25 years of war on the Great Plains.

★ Policy and Protest

By the 1870s many American Indian tribes were living on reservations. Indian leaders spoke out against the reservation system, complaining that Bureau agents stole government food and money meant for Indians. In addition, reservation land was usually not suitable for farming or buffalo hunting. As a result, many Indians were starving.

In the late 1870s a Paiute Indian named Sarah Winnemucca became one of the first Indians to call for reform. "Day after day my people were begging me to go east to talk for them," she explained. She eventually pleaded her case in Washington. She also gave lectures on the need to reform the reservation system. After listening to her, "many people were moved to tears," according to one spectator.

Another person pushing for reservation reform was writer Helen Hunt Jackson. In 1881 she published *A Century of Dishonor*, which criticized the federal government's treatment of Indians. She wrote that "it makes little difference where one opens the record of the history of the Indians; every page and every year has its dark stain." The popularity of Jackson's writings helped spread the reform message.

Once the major wars for the West had ended, many reformers believed that Indians would be better off if they adopted the ways of white people. Congress passed the **Dawes General Allotment Act** in 1887 to lessen the tribal influence on Indian society by making land ownership private rather than shared. The Dawes Act split up reservation lands and divided them among individual Indians. Families were supposed to receive 160 acres, single adults 80 acres. The act also promised U.S. citizenship to American Indians.

After it split up the reservations, the government sold the land that remained unassigned. As a result, Indians lost much of the land that they occupied before the Dawes Act. Despite the hopes of reformers, the Dawes Act claimed more land from American Indians than all the wars combined, did not grant them citizenship as promised, and failed to improve their lives.

Sarah Winnemucca

The Granger Collection, New York

SECTION 1 REVIEW

Identify and explain the significance of the following:

- **Fort Laramie Treaty**
- **reservations**
- **Sand Creek Massacre**
- **Bozeman Trail**
- **Treaty of Medicine Lodge**
- **George Armstrong Custer**
- **Sitting Bull**
- **Battle of the Little Bighorn**
- **Long Walk**
- **Geronimo**
- **Ghost Dance**
- **Massacre at Wounded Knee**
- **Sarah Winnemucca**
- **Dawes General Allotment Act**

Reading for Content Understanding

1 **Main Idea** What events started the wars in the West?

2 **Main Idea** What were the consequences of the wars in the West?

3 **Geographic Diversity** *Region* Why were the horse and buffalo important for the Plains Indians?

4 **Writing** *Explaining* Imagine that you are an American Indian who will be affected by the Dawes Act. Write a letter to a member of Congress describing how your life has changed since living on the reservation and how the Dawes Act will impact you.

5 **Critical Thinking** *Evaluating* Why do you think the Ghost Dance was important to American Indians in the West?

Miners and Railroads

Reading Focus

What were some of the challenges of mining in the West?

What obstacles did the builders of the transcontinental railroad face?

How did the transcontinental railroad affect the settlement and development of the West?

Key Terms

Comstock Lode
bonanza
boom towns
Pony Express
transcontinental railroad
Pacific Railway Acts

I N 1859 GREAT EXCITEMENT *swept the United States when news of a gold strike in Colorado reached the East. Traveling west to examine this find,* New York Tribune *editor Horace Greeley announced that the "discovery is . . . the richest and greatest [gold mine] in America." Thousands of prospectors in wagons labeled "Pikes Peak or Bust" raced west to the mining region around Pikes Peak. Most of these "fifty-niners," as they were called, traveled hundreds of miles only to find that the early prospectors had started the rush by filling part of their mine with extra gold.*

Gold ore

The Mining Booms

Many fifty-niners, still full of excitement created by the California Gold Rush, continued to search for strikes. Some miners found gold in other parts of Colorado. Gold rushes also occurred in Idaho in 1862 and two years later in Montana.

The Comstock Lode

The same year that miners rushed to Pikes Peak, prospectors Peter O'Riley and Patrick McLaughlin struck gold and silver in western Nevada. Their good fortune attracted the attention of miner Henry Comstock, who convinced the partners that he owned the water source they were using at the mine. O'Riley and McLaughlin gave Comstock a share in their find to avoid legal trouble. Comstock bragged that he had found the mine, and the discovery became known as the **Comstock Lode**.

Within a year, thousands of California miners arrived, and Virginia City sprang up almost overnight. The Comstock Lode was a **bonanza**—a large deposit of precious ore. In the next 20 years, the Lode produced nearly $400 million worth of gold and silver.

These miners are bringing ore out of a mine shaft along the Comstock Lode in the 1860s.

Mining Companies

Comstock sold his share of the mine to a big corporation for $11,000. Large companies had the funds needed to remove the silver and gold trapped within the quartz rock. To get this quartz, miners dug and blasted tunnels hundreds of feet long into the mountain. Then they loaded the ore onto mining carts and brought it to the surface. The ore was usually shipped by train to a refining center, where powerful stamping mills crushed the ore, and large machines called smelters melted the pieces so that the metal could be separated. Mining became a big business as large companies bought up mining claims from miners who could not afford such expensive equipment.

 ## A Miner's Life

As companies dug bigger and deeper mines in the West, the work became more dangerous. Miners risked their lives every day that they went underground.

Working in the Mines

To ride down into the mines, miners squeezed together on elevator platforms just a few feet wide. These "cages" had no walls, and a careless move or an accident could pin a miner between the wall and the moving cage with deadly results. Down in the poorly lit tunnels, miners used picks, drills, and explosives to get to the gold- and silver-rich rock. In the 1860s miners began using power drills, which produced dust that caused serious lung problems. Unexpected explosions killed or injured many miners. In addition, dynamite explosions sometimes created poisonous gases.

In the deeper tunnels, temperatures often rose above 130°F. An Idaho miner recalled that in the cold winters, "I came off work soaked to the skin, and before reaching home all my clothes were frozen fast on me and I couldn't take them off myself." The hot, stuffy air was often filled with toxic gases. Some tunnels had so little oxygen that candles would not burn. Cave-ins and floods from underground springs sometimes killed miners or trapped them below ground. The threat of fire in the mines was also a great concern. With all these hazards, mining was one of the most dangerous jobs in the country. In the West, concerns about safety and wages led to the creation of several miners' unions in the 1860s.

The Miners

In addition to the dangerous work, miners faced other difficulties. Many Mexican immigrants and Mexican Americans were experienced miners, skilled in assaying, or testing, the contents of valuable ore. Despite their skill, they were often denied the better-paying mining jobs. Chinese immigrants faced similar job discrimination.

People from all over the world worked in the western mines. Some miners came from the eastern United States, while others immigrated from Europe, Central and South America, Asia, and Australia. Some miners hoped to get rich and return to their native countries, but most hoped to stay in the United States.

 ## Mining Towns

Mining booms also produced **boom towns**, communities that grew suddenly when a mine opened and disappeared just as quickly when the mine closed down. Most boom towns had general stores, saloons, and boardinghouses. Business owners charged high prices for goods and services. This was partly to make a big profit and partly because most merchandise had to be shipped west and then transported to the remote mining communities. "The sociable [friendly] man is lost in the money making," admitted one store

Families faced many hardships in the early mining camps.

owner. In his autobiographical work *Roughing It*, Mark Twain described Virginia City during its boom years:

> 66 [It] had grown to be the 'livest' town . . . that America had ever produced. The sidewalks swarmed with people. . . . The streets themselves were just as crowded. . . . Money-getting schemes . . . were . . . in every brain. 99

Boom towns were dangerous places that lacked basic law and order. "To be raised in a mining camp," as one man put it, "means an experience as full of thrills and wounds and scars as going to the war." There were few women or families in most boom towns. In 1860, for example, there were more than 75 men for every woman in Virginia City. Most women who lived in mining towns faced a life of hard work and few friends. "I was never so lonely and homesick in all my life," wrote one young woman.

Women contributed to the local economy by washing, cooking, making clothes, chopping wood, and growing food for the miners. Women also helped turn some mining camps into successful permanent communities by raising families, teaching in schools, and writing for local papers. Such efforts drew more Americans to the West.

⭐ Crossing the Continent

More Americans began moving west, increasing the need to send goods and information between the East and West. The **Pony Express**, established in 1860, used a system of messengers on horseback to carry mail from one relay station to another along a 2,000-mile route. Telegraph lines, which sent messages faster, quickly put the Pony Express out of business.

Some Americans hoped to improve communication and travel across the country by building a **transcontinental railroad** to connect the East to the West. Many business-people and politicians were confident that such a railroad could be built despite the many geographic obstacles and the expensive labor and resources needed.

To help railroad companies overcome these difficulties, the federal government passed the **Pacific Railway Acts** in 1862 and in 1864. These acts gave railroad companies loans and large land grants, which could be sold to pay for construction costs. By 1872 Congress had granted more than 125 million acres of public land to railroad companies. In exchange, the government required the railroads to carry U.S. mail and troops at reduced rates. These acts inspired many companies to begin laying tracks.

Poster advertising the Pony Express

⭐ The Great Race

Two companies, the Central Pacific and the Union Pacific, took the lead in the great race to complete the transcontinental railroad. In February 1863 the Central Pacific began building east from Sacramento, California. At the end of the year, the Union Pacific started in Omaha, Nebraska, and headed west.

Working on the Railroad

To build its railroad, the Union Pacific hired thousands of workers, particularly Irish immigrants.

Global Connections

The Railroads of India

While workers were completing the world's first transcontinental railroad in Promontory, Utah, other nations were building their own massive rail systems. Great Britain was developing one of the world's largest railroad networks in India, which was then part of the vast British Empire.

In the early 1800s Britain wanted to increase trade with India by selling British-made manufactured goods there and by getting raw materials from remote Indian regions. A railroad would make such trade easier. In addition, a rail system would allow the British to strengthen their military control over India and to improve communications.

The British pushed to construct the railroad quickly. Between 1859 and 1869, Indian laborers laid more than 5,000 miles of track. As in the United States, laying track in India posed many challenges to workers and engineers. Large rivers and mountains made the work difficult and dangerous. Two sections of land in the Western Ghats Mountains were so rugged and steep that workers had to build 81 bridges and 38 tunnels for the railroad to get through the mountain range. Despite such obstacles, by 1900 some 25,000 miles of railway stretched across India, making the

Engineers overcame many geographic obstacles to build India's railroads.

Indian rail network larger than any other in Asia.

The railroad carried mail, freight, and passengers. Most of the railroad's business came from transporting passengers. In 1855 the newspaper *Friend of India* noted, "The fondness for traveling by rail has become almost a national passion . . . and it is producing a social change in the habits of general society."

Understanding What You Read

1. Why did the British want to build a rail network in India?

2. What benefits did the railroad system in India have in common with the transcontinental railroad in the United States?

Some laborers were Civil War veterans. Under former brigadier general Jack Casement, "the Casement Army" worked long, hard days laying rails across the Great Plains.

Chinese immigrants made up some 85 percent of the Central Pacific workforce. The railroad's part-owner Leland Stanford praised these Chinese workers as "quiet, peaceful, [and] industrious" but paid them less than white laborers. Chinese crews were also given the most dangerous jobs and were

required to work longer hours than other railroad laborers. Nonetheless, Chinese workers took on the job because the $30 dollars a month that the Central Pacific paid was in some cases 10 times as high as wages in China.

Geographic Obstacles

The Central Pacific workers struggled to cross the Sierra Nevada range in California. Breaking apart

The success of the transcontinental railroad led to the creation of other railroad lines linking the East and the West. Here workers on the Northern Pacific pose for an 1886 photograph.

its rock formations required large amounts of blasting powder and the explosive nitroglycerin. In the winter of 1866, many workers were trapped and killed in snow drifts over 60 feet high. "Many of them we did not find until . . . the snow melted," reported a company official.

Meanwhile, the Union Pacific workers faced harsh weather on the Great Plains. In addition, the company pressured them to work at a rapid pace—at times laying 250 miles of track in six months. Faced with greater geographic obstacles, the Central Pacific took four years to lay the first 115 miles of track. For both lines, providing food and supplies for their workers became more difficult as they pushed into remote areas. The railroad companies often relied on local resources. Professional hunters such as "Buffalo Bill" Cody shot thousands of buffalo to feed workers on the Union Pacific as it crossed the Plains.

The Golden Spike

When the two railroads neared completion, Congress required them to connect at Promontory, Utah. On May 10, 1869, workers and reporters watched the two lines meet for the first time. In a dramatic ceremony, a golden spike was used to

Workers from the Central Pacific and the Union Pacific celebrate the completion of the transcontinental railroad at Promontory, Utah.

connect the railroad tie joining the two tracks. Alexander Toponce witnessed the event:

> ❝ **Governor Stanford, president of the Central Pacific, took the sledge [hammer], and the first time he struck he missed the spike and hit the rail. What a howl went up! Irish, Chinese, Mexicans, and everybody yelled with delight. 'He missed it.' . . . Then Stanford tried it again and tapped the spike. . . . The tap was reported in all the offices east and west.** ❞

The transcontinental railroad had finally united the East and the West. Following its completion, companies continued building railroads until the West was crisscrossed with shining rails.

★ The Impact of the Railroads

The transcontinental railroad increased both economic growth and the population in the West. The railroad companies encouraged settlement by providing better transportation for people and goods and by selling land to settlers.

Time and Cargo

Another benefit of railroads was that they saved time. The Union Pacific advertised that a trip from Omaha, Nebraska, to San Francisco, California,

would take four days—instead of a month by wagon. The Union Pacific also promised greater safety: "Travelers for pleasure, health or business will find a trip over the Rocky Mountains healthy and pleasant."

The new railroads also helped businesses. In time, telegraph lines ran along-side railroads, opening up the West to faster and more convenient communication. Western timber companies, miners, cattle ranchers, and farmers used railroads to ship items to the East. Wood, metals, beef, and grain traveled east in exchange for manufactured products that were shipped west.

Railroad Booms and Busts

Railroad companies encouraged people to invest money in the railroads, sometimes unwisely. Railroad speculation and the collapse of railroad owner Jay Cooke's banking firm helped start the

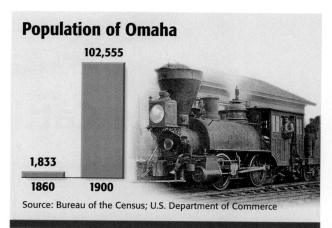

Population of Omaha

102,555

1,833

1860   1900

Source: Bureau of the Census; U.S. Department of Commerce

City on the Rise In 1865 the Union Pacific Railroad laid its tracks through the city of Omaha, Nebraska, causing the population to soar. How much did Omaha's population increase between 1860 and 1900?

Panic of 1873 and the depression that followed. By the 1880s many of the smaller western railroads were deep in debt.

Despite such setbacks, Americans remained interested in railroad investments. By 1890 there were around 199,000 miles of railroad track in operation compared to only about 35,000 miles in 1865. Almost 750,000 Americans worked for railroad companies. Railroads had become one of the biggest industries in the United States and one of the most important in the West.

SECTION 2 REVIEW

Identify and explain the significance of the following:

- **Comstock Lode**
- **bonanza**
- **boom towns**
- **Pony Express**
- **transcontinental railroad**
- **Pacific Railway Acts**
- **Leland Stanford**

Reading for Content Understanding

1 **Main Idea** Why was mining one of the most dangerous jobs in the West?

2 **Main Idea** What were some of the difficulties in building a transcontinental railroad?

3 **Cultural Diversity** Why do you think so few women lived in mining towns?

4 **Writing** *Creating* Write a short song that might have been sung at the celebration of the connection of the Union Pacific and Central Pacific Railroads. Your song should focus on how the railroad will change life in the West or improve communication between family members.

5 **Critical Thinking** *Drawing Conclusions* Why do you think the railroad is still one of the most effective ways of transporting goods across the country, even though faster forms of transportation have been developed?

The Cattle Kingdom

Reading Focus

What factors led to a cattle boom in the 1870s?

What was life like for cowboys?

What caused the decline of the Cattle Kingdom?

Key Terms

Texas longhorn
Cattle Kingdom
open range
range rights
vaqueros
roundup
cattle drive
Chisholm Trail
range wars

*I*N THE MID-1800S *Texas ranchers began gathering up huge herds of wild cattle. Describing these herds, one rancher wrote, "Cattle are permitted to range . . . over a large surface of country, thirty, forty, and even fifty miles in extent [size]." Keeping track of these roaming cattle required great skill. Although the ranch hands who did this work faced many hardships, a rancher wrote that "the young men that follow this 'Cow-Boy' life . . . generally become attached to it." These cowboys and ranchers helped start the cattle-ranching industry in the West.*

A wealthy rancher bought this golden bull clock.

⭐ The Roots of Ranching

Spanish settlers brought their cattle to California and Texas in the 1700s. These cattle later mixed with English breeds to create the **Texas longhorn**, which spread rapidly throughout western Texas. Longhorn cattle were lean and tough, with horns up to five feet across. Many butchers said the longhorn had too little meat, calling it "8 pounds of hamburger on 800 pounds of bone and horn." Nonetheless, settlers preferred to raise longhorns because the animals needed very little water and could survive harsh weather.

The new breed was also resistant to a terrible disease commonly called Texas fever. This sickness, which was transmitted by ticks that infested the cattle, was usually deadly. Unfortunately, healthy longhorns were often carriers, which meant they could endanger other cattle breeds and oxen by giving them the ticks.

In the 1850s ranchers rounded up Texas longhorns and sold them to miners, U.S. soldiers, railroad workers, and American Indians living on reservations. During the Civil War, the cattle herds grew because Texas was isolated from its markets and unable to sell cattle for much of the war.

Ranchers brought their cattle to railroad towns to sell them to buyers, who then shipped the cattle to meatpacking plants farther east.

many of their cattle north to Colorado, Wyoming, Nebraska, and Montana. In 1871 more than 600,000 cattle had been moved from Texas onto the Plains. The many ranches in the land stretching from Texas north to Canada formed the **Cattle Kingdom**. Many ranchers grazed their huge herds on the **open range**, or public land. The U.S. government did not charge ranchers for using this public land that was once occupied by Plains Indians and buffalo herds.

 ## Open-Range Ranching

Following the Civil War, the demand for beef in the East increased as the economy and the population expanded. A cow worth $3 to $6 in Texas could be sold for $38 in Kansas or $80 in New York. Nobody drove the longhorns to eastern markets, however, because of the distance and the danger of transmitting Texas fever to other farm animals.

The Cattle Boom

In 1867 businessman Joseph McCoy had the idea "to establish a market whereat the southern . . . [rancher] and the northern buyer would meet." The creation of new western railroads made this possible. McCoy built pens for cattle in the small town of Abilene, Kansas, which was located on the Kansas Pacific Railroad line. Cattle could be shipped by rail from Abilene straight to processing plants in St. Louis, Missouri. The idea was a great success. When rancher J. F. Ellison sold his cattle in Abilene, his son recalled, "This trip proved to be a profitable one. . . . Father had $9,000 cash, which was a lot of money in those days." Soon many Texas ranchers were making the trip north to sell their herds of cattle.

Around the same time, cattle ranching began to expand onto the Great Plains. Ranchers found that the tough longhorns did well on the Plains and were free of disease. In 1890 it was discovered that the cold winters killed the ticks that carried the Texas fever. Ranchers began taking

The Ranches

One of the people who saw the profits of ranching was Elizabeth Collins. When she and her husband had trouble mining gold, Collins decided "to discontinue the business of mining and engage in that of cattle raising." She moved to the Teton Valley in Montana and started ranching. She was so successful she earned the name "Cattle Queen of Montana."

Collins was just one of many ranchers who became prosperous during the cattle boom. Charles Goodnight started the first ranch in the Texas Panhandle, more than 250 miles from any town or railroad. Speculators in the East and in Europe invested money in ranches the same way that they did in railroads. Some of the resulting ranches were huge, such as the XIT Ranch, which covered more than 3 million acres.

Elizabeth Collins

Most ranchers did not own this much land. Instead, they concentrated on buying the **range rights**, or water rights, to ponds and rivers. This gave them access to scarce water as well as ownership of the land around it. With range rights, ranchers could eliminate competition by stopping farmers and other ranchers from using the water.

Cowboys borrowed many of their methods and equipment from the vaqueros who worked on ranches in California and the Southwest.

The remote locations of many ranches meant that some ranchers were the local authority. Joseph McCoy noted that the cattle rancher considered himself "an independent sovereign [ruler] . . . capable of conducting his affairs in his own way." Isolated ranchers needed to be self-reliant and capable of solving their own problems. Mary Jaques, who lived on a Texas ranch for two years, explained:

❝The ideal ranchman must be butcher, baker, carpenter, . . . blacksmith, plain cook, milker. . . . It is a fact that each of these trades will have to be practiced to some extent sooner or later.❞

★ The Cowboys

The workers who took care of a rancher's cattle were known as cowhands or cowboys. They became symbols of the American West for many people around the world. Cowboys borrowed many of their techniques from the Mexican **vaqueros** (vah-KER-ohs), ranch hands who tended cattle and horses. From the vaqueros came the western saddle, the lariat—a rope used for lassoing cattle—and the leather chaps that cowboys wore over their pants for protection against the thorny brush. The cowboys borrowed the vaqueros'

broad felt hat and changed it into the familiar high-peaked cowboy hat. Cowboys also adopted the bandanna, a cloth that covered the face to protect it from dust and served as a handkerchief or bandage.

Many cowboys were Mexican Americans or African Americans. African American cowboy Nat Love wrote an autobiography in which he described daily ranch life:

❝When we were not on the trail taking large herds of cattle or horses to market to be delivered to other ranches, we were engaged in range riding, moving large numbers of cattle from one grazing range to another, keeping them together, and hunting up strays.❞

Although most cowhands were men, some women worked alongside cowboys. One female rancher explained, "I love to work with my cattle, and have spent a good deal of my time on the range."

Gathering the cattle together was known as the **roundup**. At the spring roundups, cowboys branded young calves and horses. Branding involved burning a ranch's unique mark onto an animal to prevent thieves from stealing horses and cattle and selling them as their own.

Riding the range involved a great deal of hard work as well as danger from cattle thieves, bad weather, and unpredictable livestock. The words to one western song warned potential cowboys,

❝Some boys go up the trail for pleasure, But that's where you get it most
    awfully wrong.
For you haven't any idea of the trouble
    they [the cattle] give us
While we go driving them along.❞

Cowboys worked for low wages, and few were able to make enough money to start their own ranches. Despite these factors, many agreed with Love, who said he enjoyed his days as a cowboy because he had "a genuine love of the free and wild life of the range."

Cowboy Nat Love

Cattle Drives and Cattle Towns

One of the most important and dangerous duties of the cowboy was the **cattle drive**. On these long journeys, cowboys herded cattle to the market or to the northern Plains for grazing. These trips usually lasted several months and covered hundreds of miles.

Riding the Trail

The **Chisholm Trail** was one of the earliest and most popular routes for cattle drives. Blazed by Texas cowboy Jesse Chisholm in 1867, this trail ran from San Antonio, Texas, to the cattle town of Abilene, Kansas. Charles Goodnight blazed a trail leading from Texas to New Mexico Territory that became known as the Goodnight-Loving Trail. The most heavily used route, the Western Trail, headed north from San Antonio, Texas, to Dodge City, Kansas.

Cattle drives usually started in the spring. Some cowboys specialized in cattle drives and took other ranchers' cattle to market for them. These cowboys made several of the long, difficult trips in one year. Cattle driving was rugged and dangerous work. Cowboy James H. Cook described life on the trail:

" **There was plenty of rough country, with creeks and steep-banked rivers to be crossed. We had no tents or shelter of any sort other than our blankets.** "

The cattle were as difficult to deal with as the geographical challenges. During storms they would stampede. Then cowboys would have to track down the strays and round them up again. At night, cowboys had to stand watch over the cattle herds. Cowboy "Teddy Blue" Abbott complained, "There was never enough sleep. . . . I have often sat in my saddle sound asleep." Most cowboys were happy to reach the end of the cattle drive.

Cowboy's spur

The Cattle Towns

A large cattle town such as Dodge City or Abilene was usually at the end of the trail. Small businesses sprang up as more cowboys passed through town. Many of these businesses were owned or operated by women such as Malinda Jenkins, who ran a boardinghouse in Fort Worth, Texas. To get her business started, she traded her sewing machine for the first month's rent and bought a cookstove on credit. Eventually, she paid off her debts and had a successful business.

Boardinghouses, hotels, saloons, and restaurants in cattle towns counted on tired cowboys spending money during the few days they were in town. Most ranchers paid the cowboys in cash when the drive ended. Cowboys spent their money on food, hot baths, and comfortable beds after long weeks on the trail. John Baumann described his cowboy friends in Dodge City:

" **The boys have received their wages; $200 or $300 perhaps, in a lump, and are turning themselves loose. . . . Clean-shaven and [wearing] new store clothes from head to foot, we scarcely recognize each other.** "

During the cattle drive season the large number of rowdy cowboys could make life in cattle towns rough and violent. While there were rarely shoot-outs in the streets, there were

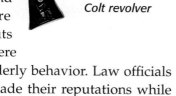
Colt revolver

often fights and disorderly behavior. Law officials such as Wyatt Earp made their reputations while keeping the peace in cattle towns.

The End of the Open Range

In the early 1880s cattle ranching became increasingly profitable. In 1882 Gustavus Swift used the newly invented refrigerator railroad car to carry beef from packing plants to the big eastern cities. This increased the national demand for beef and made cities such as Chicago, Illinois, famous for their meatpacking factories.

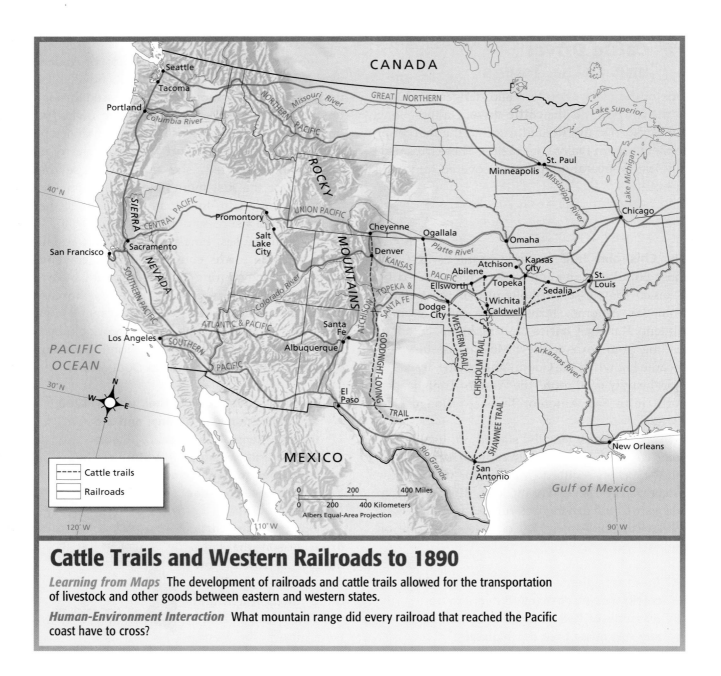

Cattle Trails and Western Railroads to 1890

Learning from Maps The development of railroads and cattle trails allowed for the transportation of livestock and other goods between eastern and western states.

Human-Environment Interaction What mountain range did every railroad that reached the Pacific coast have to cross?

Range Wars

While the cattle business boomed, ranchers faced increased competition for use of the open range. As more settlers came to the Great Plains, farmers began to buy range land where cattle had once grazed. Smaller ranchers also began competing with the large ranches for land. Then in 1873 Joseph Glidden invented barbed wire, which allowed westerners to fence off large amounts of land at a low cost. Westerners had been unable to do this because traditional fencing material, such as stones and lumber, was scarce on the Great Plains.

Large ranchers moved quickly to fence in the open range to keep out farmers and smaller ranchers. Some farmers and small ranchers responded by cutting fences and moving onto the land or stealing cattle. This competition led to **range wars** between large ranchers, small ranchers, and farmers. Although the large ranchers often won these battles, few ranchers could continue to count on letting their cattle roam free on public land.

Cattle ranchers also fought with sheep owners. As the number of sheep increased in the 1880s, so did the competition for grasslands. Sheep chewed the grass down so far that there was nothing left for the cattle. Despite threats and violence against them, sheep ranchers continued to prosper in the West.

The Decline of the Cattle Kingdom

By the 1880s an estimated 7 million cattle roamed the Great Plains. These large numbers drove down cattle prices. To improve prices, ranchers began introducing eastern cattle to the western range. These cattle produced larger amounts of tastier beef than the Texas longhorns but were not well adapted to the conditions on the Plains.

In 1885 and 1886 disaster struck the Cattle Kingdom. The huge cattle herds on the Plains had eaten much of the prairie grass that ranchers depended on for feed. Unusually severe winters in both years made the ranching situation even worse. Thousands of cattle died, particularly the new eastern breeds. Most ranches lost 30 percent of their herd, and some ranchers lost as many as 9 out of 10 cattle. "The prairies were seen thickly dotted with the dead bodies of famished [starved] and frozen animals," according to Elizabeth Collins. Rancher Granville Stuart saw the damage to his herd and vowed,

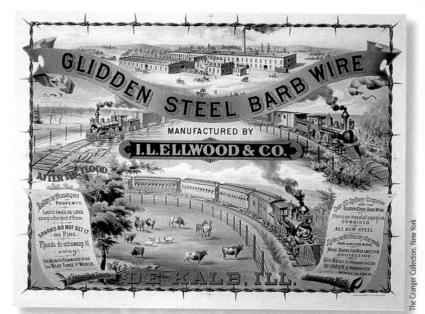

Joseph Glidden's barbed wire made it easier and more affordable to build fences around western ranches and farms, helping lead to the end of the open range.

"I never wanted to own again an animal that I could not feed and shelter."

Many ranchers were ruined financially. To pay their debts, ranchers rushed to sell their cattle, even though the prices were low. Cattle towns were also hard hit. While cattle ranching continued, it became more costly. Ranchers were forced to buy winter feed for their cattle and to raise smaller herds. Low prices, harsh weather, and greater competition for grazing land brought an end to the reign of the Cattle Kingdom.

SECTION 3 REVIEW

Identify and explain the significance of the following:

- **Texas longhorn**
- **Joseph McCoy**
- **Cattle Kingdom**
- **open range**
- **Elizabeth Collins**
- **range rights**
- **vaqueros**
- **Nat Love**
- **roundup**
- **cattle drive**
- **Chisholm Trail**
- **range wars**

Reading for Content Understanding

1 **Main Idea** Why did cattle ranching become profitable in the 1870s?

2 **Main Idea** What factors led to the end of the Cattle Kingdom?

3 **Economic Development** *Region* How did ranching and cattle trails help western economic development?

4 **Writing** *Describing* Imagine that you are a cowboy during the late 1800s. Write a paragraph explaining what your daily life is like. Include some of the problems or mishaps you might face.

5 **Critical Thinking** *Drawing Conclusions* Why might American Indians have become cowboys?

Farming the Great Plains

Reading Focus

Why did settlers move to the Great Plains?

What challenges did farming families face on the Plains?

What was daily life like on the Plains?

Key Terms

Homestead Act
Morrill Act
Exodusters
sodbusters
dry farming

 IN 1879 SCOTTISH WRITER *Robert Louis Stevenson took the transcontinental railroad across the United States. Most of the other passengers were settlers moving to the West. When a passenger began to play the song "Home Sweet Home," all conversation stoppped, "and the faces began to lengthen," noted Stevenson. Then "an elderly, hard-looking man . . . [asked] the performer [to] stop. 'I've heard about enough of that,' he [said]. 'Give us something about the good country we're going to.'" The passengers cheered, and the performer began to play music for dancing. Despite being homesick, most settlers hoped to build a better life in the West.*

Pioneer rail ticket

⭐ Settling the Plains

In 1862 Congress passed two important land grant acts that helped open the West to settlers. The **Homestead Act** gave government-owned land to small farmers. Any adult who was a U.S. citizen or planned to become one could receive 160 acres of land in exchange for a small registration fee and a promise to live on the land for five years. The **Morrill Act** granted more than 17 million acres of federal land to the states. The act required each state to sell this land and use the money to build colleges to teach agriculture and engineering.

The federal government also offered land in the present-day state of Oklahoma that had formerly belonged to Creek and Seminole Indians. In March 1889 officials announced that homesteaders could file claims on these lands starting noon of April 22. Within a month of the announcement, some 50,000 people had rushed to Oklahoma to stake their claim. In all, the settlers claimed more than 11 million acres of former Indian land in the Oklahoma land rush.

Federal land grants encouraged settlers to move west. At first, settlers made this journey in wagons as earlier pioneers had done on the

Before the completion of the transcontinental railroad, pioneers moving west had to travel alone or as part of massive wagon trains that rolled across the Plains.

Oregon Trail. These trips were filled with hard work, boredom, and danger. "I am getting impatient for our journey to come to an end," wrote one pioneer woman. There were dangerous obstacles such as rivers, valleys, and mountains to cross. Rough weather and sickness could also make the trip risky.

The trip west on the railroads was safer and faster. As railroads stretched across the Great Plains, many settlers chose to travel by train. The railroad companies encouraged people to move west by printing posters and pamphlets advertising fertile and inexpensive land. The Union Pacific even promised free houses to settlers on its land in Nebraska. Many railroads also offered lower fares to pioneers.

★ The Homesteaders

The great stretches of land drew pioneers to the Great Plains. The Plains offered pioneers the chance to make a fresh start.

Moving West

People from all over the country chose to move west. One train traveler noted that "they came from almost every quarter. From Virginia, from Pennsylvania, from New York, from far western Iowa and Kansas." People who had already moved to the Great Plains often chose to move again after a few years. All of these settlers hoped to find prosperity on the Plains, usually by starting their own farms. Many farming families moved from areas where farmland was becoming scarce or expensive, such as New England. Others were the descendants of earlier pioneers to the Midwest. Many single women moved west because the Homestead Act granted land to unmarried women, which was unusual for the time.

The promise of land also drew a large group of African Americans west. In 1879 Benjamin Singleton led 20,000 to 40,000 southern African Americans to Kansas. These settlers became known as **Exodusters** because of their exodus, or mass departure, from the South. Many of these Exodusters were sharecroppers such as John Solomon Lewis, who explained his reasons for moving his family:

 I one day said to the man I rented [land] from: 'It's no use, I works hard and raises big crops and you sells it and keeps the money, and brings me more and more in debt, so I will go somewhere else.'

Soon black communities, such as Nicodemus, Kansas, developed, having drawn many African Americans west with land advertisements. Other Exodusters moved west, seeking not only more economic opportunity but also equal rights, which they were denied in the South after Reconstruction.

Many African American families, such as the Shores, moved to the Great Plains.

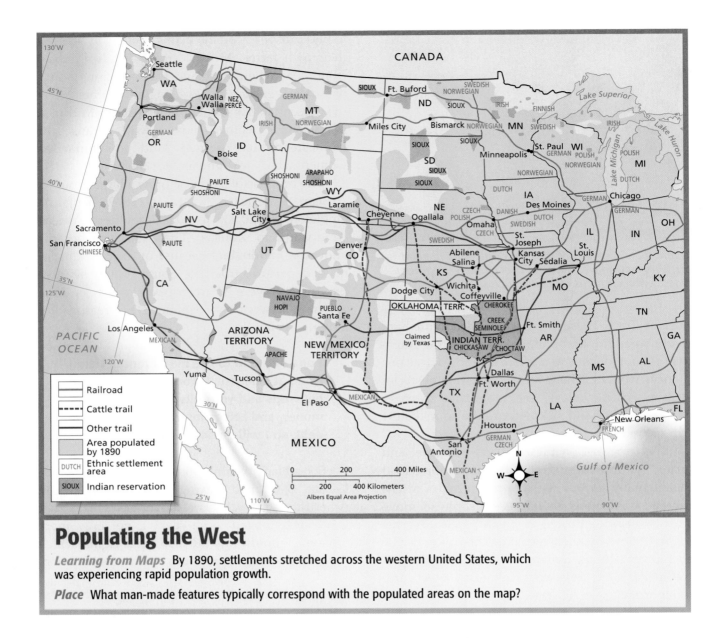

Populating the West

Learning from Maps By 1890, settlements stretched across the western United States, which was experiencing rapid population growth.

Place What man-made features typically correspond with the populated areas on the map?

Immigrants

Western homesteads also appealed to immigrants, who could receive land grants under the Homestead Act if they promised to stay in the United States. Norwegian, Swedish, Danish, German, and Czech immigrants created many small communities on the Great Plains. These groups were looking for economic opportunity. Usually, a relative made the journey to America first and then wrote letters home encouraging family members to come. One immigrant described his good economic prospects to his family, writing "that a farm had been given to him by the government. It was 60 acres of land, [with] good soil."

In addition, thousands of Mennonites, a religious group from Russia, came to the Great Plains. They were some of the first to begin large-scale farming and introduced American farmers to a type of red wheat that grew very well on the Plains.

 Farming on the Plains

Although the inexpensive land and rich soil appealed to settlers, the Great Plains presented unique challenges to farmers. "Whatever I had learned of farming in the East, had to be . . . learned over again here," wrote one pioneer.

The Environment

When settlers came to the Plains, they found a mostly flat landscape covered with grass. On the eastern half of the Great Plains, the prairie grass grew up to eight feet tall. In contrast, the grass in the western part of the Plains was just a few inches tall.

Settlers found that the seasons were extreme on the Plains. In the winter, temperatures on the northern Plains could fall to 40° below zero Fahrenheit, while the scorching summer temperatures could reach 110°. Farmers could not raise the same crops that they had grown in the East because the climate of the Plains was much drier. Settlers also faced the threat of blizzards and tornadoes. The dangerous and unpredictable weather made life difficult for the pioneers.

A Storm of Grasshoppers

In the summer of 1874, many farmers in Kansas and nearby states were expecting a very good harvest. Then one day they saw something startling on the horizon—millions of grasshoppers were swarming toward the fields. Settler Mary Lyon described the strange scene: "They began, toward night, dropping to earth, and it seemed as if we were in a big snowstorm where the air was filled with enormous-size flakes." Mary Roberts, another pioneer woman, said "When they came down, they struck the ground so hard it sounded almost like hail."

The grasshoppers covered the fields in a carpet up to four inches thick. They ate settlers' crops from the fields, the food in their houses, and even their clothing. Lyon recalled that by the time the grasshoppers left, "They [had] devoured every green thing but the prairie grass." The huge swarms returned each year, then suddenly stopped. Swarms occasionally returned in later years but never as dramatically as in the 1870s.

★ New Ways of Farming

Farmers learned to cope with the challenges of the Great Plains by developing new farming equipment and methods. The root-filled sod beneath the

Mechanical farming equipment such as the reaper made it easier for western farmers to harvest huge fields of wheat.

grass was very tough and could actually break the plows that many farmers had brought with them to the Plains. Inventor John Deere's deep steel plow made it possible to break through the sod, allowing the farmers to plant crops in the tough soil. The farmers on the Plains, along with the plows they used, were nicknamed **sodbusters** for the hard work they had in breaking up the sod.

In the 1890s a farmer named Hardy Campbell began to teach farmers on the western Plains a new method called **dry farming**. This method shifted the focus from water-dependent crops such as corn to more hardy crops like red wheat. In addition, farmers left part of their fields unplanted each year so that the soil preserved water. Even on the eastern Plains, which received more rain, farmers discovered that the soil required special care. As one observer noted, they "learned that their lands needed feeding as well as their cattle and hogs." Although imperfect, these dry-farming methods helped farmers make it through drought years.

By the 1880s mechanical farming was becoming increasingly common. Cyrus McCormick made his fortune designing, building, and selling farm equipment to thousands of eager customers. Horse-drawn machines such as McCormick reapers collected wheat stalks, and threshing machines separated the grain from the husk. By using machinery, farmers could work much more quickly on large fields with fewer workers.

Corporate farmers who could afford to invest in the needed land and machinery created huge bonanza farms where they grew thousands of bushels of wheat. Farmer Oliver Dalrymple used "eighty horses, twenty-six breaking plows, forty

Cost of Establishing a Farm in 1870

ITEM	PRICE
Land (per acre)	$3–$12
Team (horses or oxen)	$300
Wagon and yoke or harness	$150
Plow	$25
Cultivator and harrow	$45
Combination reaper and mower	$252
Other hand tools (ax, shovel, fork, rake, and scythe)	$50

Source: The Iowa Railroad Land Company, *Choice Iowa Farming Lands,* 1870

Working the Land In 1870 the average total investment for establishing a farm in Iowa was more than $4,000. This total included the value of land, buildings, livestock, and machinery. By 1900 the total investment had more than doubled. What was the most expensive piece of farm equipment in 1870?

cross plows, twenty-one seeders, [and] sixty harrows [spiked farming tools]" to plant crops on 7,000 acres of a North Dakota farm.

Once they harvested their crops, farmers shipped their harvest east by train. From there, crops were shipped overseas. As farming technology improved, the Great Plains became known as the breadbasket of the world because of all of the grains that the region's farmers produced.

★ Daily Life on the Plains

Settler Gro Svendsen described the challenges of Plains life, "When one begins to farm, it takes a great deal to get started—especially when one must begin with nothing." Building a house was one of the first challenges that settlers faced. With very little wood available, many families built houses from bricks of sod cut out of the ground. Although cheap to build, these sod homes were typically very small and uncomfortable. Pioneer May Avery explained a few of the common problems. "The roof leaked something awful [and inside] we killed a snake or two . . . and several centipedes." For all their faults, however, the small homes did provide necessary shelter.

Once a home was built, daily chores kept pioneer families busy. For example, settlers had to make and mend their own clothes. Without machines to do the work, washing clothes was a tremendous chore that usually took an entire day to complete. Pioneers usually made their wash soap from lye and animal fat. One pioneer woman's list of 11 washday chores started with "build fire in back yard to heat kettle of rain water," and ended with "brew cup of tea, set and rest and rock a spell and count blessings." Women also prepared meals and often grew vegetables, raised chickens, or made butter to earn money for the family.

Farming families raised livestock and worked hard in the fields, plowing and planting. Harvesting a crop such as wheat required reaping, binding, and stacking. In addition, pioneers often had to build or repair most of their farm buildings and machinery.

Children helped with many chores around the farm. Farm families were often large, and everyone had a task. Author Laura Ingalls Wilder was one of four children in a pioneer family that plowed its own fields, built its own homes, and made many of its own clothes. In *The Long Winter*, Wilder described harvesting hay:

❝ **While Pa tossed the hay from the wagon she [Laura] spread it as well as she**

Windmills were used to pump water in the West.

could, walking around and around on the stack to pack it tightly. . . . Laura was proud. Her arms ached and her back ached and her legs ached . . . but she did not tell anyone. "

Wilder's books about settlers' lives on the prairie gained a large readership and are still popular today.

This group of students in Hecla, Montana, posed with their teacher in October, 1893.

Nebraska State Historical Society

 ## Building Communities

Communities were an important part of life on the Plains. Many early settlers found life on their remote farms to be extremely difficult. About her mother's life as a pioneer, Esther Clark explained: "It took [courage] to live twenty-four hours at a time, month in and out, on the lonely and lovely prairie." Farmers developed communities so that they could assist one another in times of need.

One of the first things that many pioneer communities did was establish a local church and a school. Churches served as gathering places for pioneer families. Even small communities made an effort to get schools started. Many communities raised money and ran the schools themselves. One woman recalled proudly, "They [the school board]

and the pupils and I built that school house with our own hands."

Pioneer schools were usually small one-room buildings where children of all ages learned together in one class. Few children had school-books, and many children went to school only part of the year because they had to help with farm-work. Most teachers in these pioneer schools were young women who made little money.

Frontier families worked very hard to provide a community for themselves and for their children. Through these efforts, more people found the West an appealing place to live and raise a family.

SECTION 4 REVIEW

Identify and explain the significance of the following:
- **Homestead Act**
- **Morrill Act**
- **Exodusters**
- **sodbusters**
- **dry farming**
- **Cyrus McCormick**

Reading for Content Understanding

1 **Main Idea** What motivated settlers to move west?

2 **Main Idea** Why was farming on the Plains difficult, and how did that affect pioneers' lives?

3 **Economic Development** What technology helped Plains farmers, and how did it affect the region's economic development?

4 **Writing** *Expressing* Imagine that you are a student on the Plains in the late 1800s. Write a letter to a friend discussing a typical day at your school and on the farm.

5 **Critical Thinking** *Making Comparisons* Do you think it would be easier to be a teenager today or in the West in the 1890s? Explain your answer in a paragraph, using information from the chapter and your personal experiences.

CHAPTER 21 REVIEW

Chapter Summary

When settlers and miners moved west in the mid-1800s, conflicts arose with American Indians. The U.S. government sent Indians to reservations. The discovery of gold, the transcontinental railroad, and offers of free land encouraged more western settlement. The 1870s saw the rise of the Cattle Kingdom. With new farming techniques and inventions, the Great Plains became the breadbasket of the world. ◼

On a separate sheet of paper, complete the following activities.

Identifying People and Ideas

Describe the historical significance of the following:

1. reservations
2. Elizabeth Collins
3. Sitting Bull
4. Comstock Lode
5. Pacific Railway Acts
6. Nat Love
7. Chisholm Trail
8. Exodusters
9. Joseph McCoy
10. Homestead Act

go.hrw.com
SA0 Western
Paintings

Internet Activity

Imagine that you are putting together a documentary guide to western artists. Search the Internet through the HRW Web site to find at least three paintings about the West. For each image, write a few sentences explaining how the image does, or does not, accurately show life in the West in the late-1800s.

Understanding Main Ideas

1. What was life like for the Plains Indians?
2. How did the wars for the West affect American Indians?
3. What factors made mining in the West such a dangerous job?
4. What dangers did cowboys face?
5. Why was there a cattle boom in the 1870s?
6. What effect did the transcontinental railroad have on western settlement?
7. Why did many immigrants move to the West?

Reviewing Themes

1. **Economic Development**   What factors led to the expansion of the economy in the West in the late 1800s?
2. **Cultural Diversity**   What effect did the movement of American Indians to reservations have on their social and economic life?

Using the Time Line

Number your paper from 1 to 5. Match the letters on the time line below with the following events.

1. **A golden spike connects the last railroad tie of the transcontinental railroad.**
2. **The northern Plains Indians sign the Fort Laramie Treaty.**
3. **The Homestead Act grants 160-acre plots of land to people who can pay a small fee and will live on the land for five years.**
4. **Congress passes the Dawes General Allotment Act, which split up reservation lands.**
5. **Helen Hunt Jackson publishes *A Century of Dishonor*, criticizing the treatment of American Indians.**

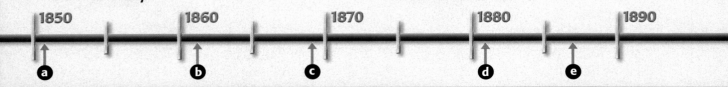

1850   1860   1870   1880   1890

a   b   c   d   e

3. **Geographic Diversity**   In what ways did the environment affect the crops that farmers planted and the farming methods they used?

Thinking Critically

1. **Identifying Cause and Effect**   What effect do you think the invention of cars, trucks, and airplanes has had on the railroad industry?

2. **Evaluating**   List two positive and two negative consequences of economic development in the West.

3. **Making Comparisons**   What similarities and differences were there among mining towns, cattle towns, and farming communities?

Writing About History

1. **Describing**   Imagine that you are in one of the mining boom towns of the late 1860s. Write a two-paragraph letter home to your family back East telling about your life in the West. Describe your work as a miner or a boardinghouse keeper.

Building Your Portfolio

American History

Complete the following activities individually or in groups.

1. **Battle of the Little Bighorn**   Imagine that you are a newspaper reporter from the East who has been assigned to cover the Battle of the Little Bighorn. To help your readers understand more about the event, either write a biographical sketch of two key figures in the battle, prepare a relief map of the battle site, or create an illustration of the battle.

2. **Heading West**   Imagine that your family has decided to move west in 1870. You are in charge of making sure you are prepared for the challenges that lie ahead. Make a list of 10 things you will take with you. Then imagine that you have arrived in your new home. Write a journal entry about how each item on your list has helped you on the frontier. Note if there are items you wish you had chosen to bring, and explain why.

2. **Creating**   Write a four-line stanza for a cowboy song that might have been sung on one of the long cattle drives to the North.

Linking Geography and History

1. **Movement**   Most of the Exodusters came from Kentucky, Tennessee, and Mississippi. Why do you think they moved to Kansas and other parts of the West instead of to the North or the Northeast?

2. **Place**   Describe the physical environment of the Great Plains.

History Skills Workshop

Reading Graphs   Study the graph below and then answer the following questions. (a) How many buffalo (bison) were there in the United States in 1800? (b) How many buffalo were there in the United States in 1889? (c) What was the estimated buffalo population in 1994? (d) What factors led to the decline of the buffalo population?

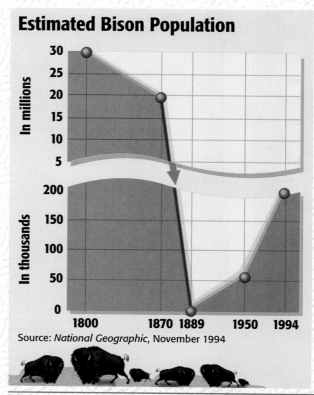

Estimated Bison Population

In millions
30
25
20
15
10
5

In thousands
200
150
100
50
0

1800   1870 1889   1950   1994

Source: *National Geographic*, November 1994

The Economy of the West

In the last half of the 1800s, great numbers of settlers followed the trails of earlier pioneers westward across North America. People moved west for new economic opportunities in mining, ranching, and farming.

Prospectors and miners came to California during the gold rush of 1849. Many continued pursuing the dream of striking it rich and moved throughout the West, chasing later strikes. Cattle drives brought the herds north from Texas, bringing the ranching industry to the northern Great Plains. Growing numbers of farmers also came and planted vast wheat fields where once only buffalo had roamed.

Networks of railroads continued bringing more settlers west. The railroads also connected farmers, ranchers, and miners with markets in the rest of the United States. By 1890 settlement was so extensive throughout the West that the U.S. Census Bureau reported the official end of the frontier. ■

Western Mining

A mining boom in the late 1800s brought thousands of prospectors to the West. Successful strikes in western mining contributed to a huge increase in the amount of gold and silver produced in the United States.

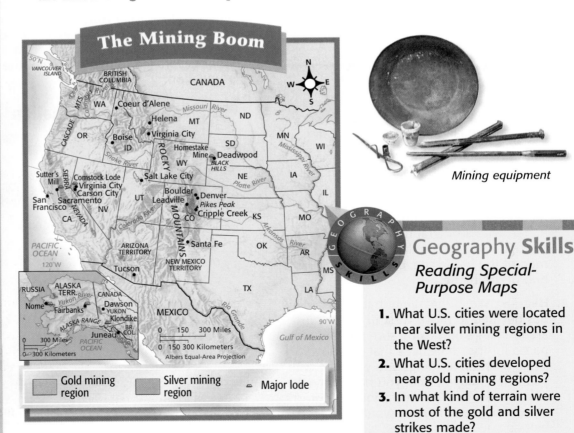

Mining equipment

Geography Skills
Reading Special-Purpose Maps

1. What U.S. cities were located near silver mining regions in the West?
2. What U.S. cities developed near gold mining regions?
3. In what kind of terrain were most of the gold and silver strikes made?

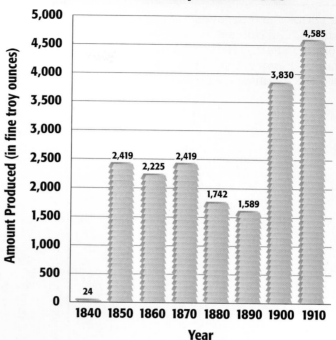

U.S. Gold Production, 1840–1910

Amount Produced (in fine troy ounces) vs. Year

- 1840: 24
- 1850: 2,419
- 1860: 2,225
- 1870: 2,419
- 1880: 1,742
- 1890: 1,589
- 1900: 3,830
- 1910: 4,585

Source: *Historical Statistics of the United States*

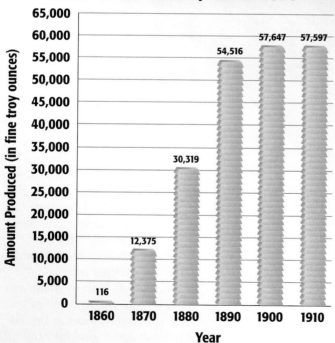

U.S. Silver Production, 1860–1910

Amount Produced (in fine troy ounces) vs. Year

- 1860: 116
- 1870: 12,375
- 1880: 30,319
- 1890: 54,516
- 1900: 57,647
- 1910: 57,597

Source: *Historical Statistics of the United States*

Geography Skills
Reading Bar Graphs

1. What decade saw gold production in the United States increase dramatically? silver production?
2. In what year was gold production highest in the United States?
3. In what year was silver production highest?

History Note 2

Gold and silver have been made into coins since around 700 B.C. These metals continue to be used as currency, but they are also valued as jewelry, ornaments, and art, and are used in electronics and manufacturing. Most gold and silver mined in the United States today still comes from the West.

The Changing West

In the 1860s the U.S. government passed legislation to encourage western settlement. The Homestead Act sold government-owned western lands at a very low cost. The Pacific Railway Acts encouraged railroad construction by giving companies land for every mile of track they laid. By 1900 a network of railroad lines crisscrossed the mountains and farmlands of the increasingly populated West.

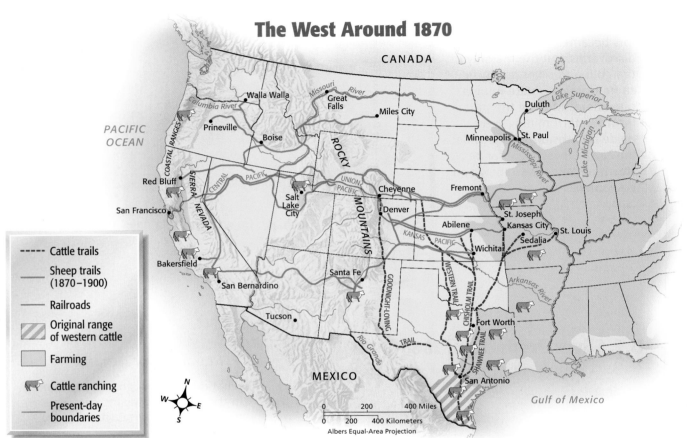

The West Around 1870

Legend:
- ---- Cattle trails
- —— Sheep trails (1870–1900)
- —— Railroads
- Original range of western cattle
- Farming
- Cattle ranching
- —— Present-day boundaries

Albers Equal-Area Projection

Geography Skills
Reading Special-Purpose Maps

1. What towns and cities were served by the Union Pacific and Central Pacific railroad lines by 1870?
2. Where did the cattle trails that ran north to the railroads begin?
3. Why do you think cattle trails ended at towns along railroad lines?
4. What areas in the West were focused on farming by around 1870?

History Note 3

Although many of our images of the West are of cowboys and cattle drives, sheepherders also moved millions of sheep along a network of western trails. Experienced sheepherders were often immigrants from places like Mexico, France, and Spain and helped move large western herds with as many as 7,000 sheep. One of the first great sheep drives in the United States provided food for hungry miners during the California Gold Rush.

The West Around 1900

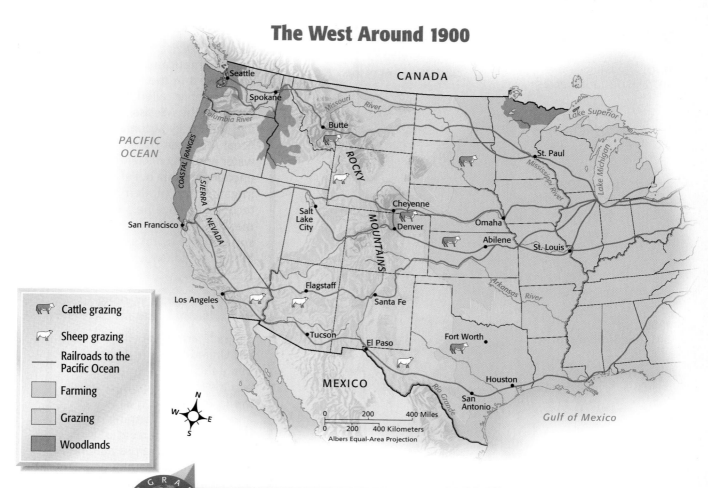

Legend:
- Cattle grazing
- Sheep grazing
- Railroads to the Pacific Ocean
- Farming
- Grazing
- Woodlands

Geography **Skills**
Reading Special-Purpose Maps

1. By 1900 what West Coast cities were linked by railroads to the eastern United States?
2. Where was sheep grazing most common?
3. Compare the map above to the one on page 672. Into what regions of the West had farming expanded between 1870 and 1900?

History Note 4

The construction of railroads in the West contributed much to the settlement of the region and to the industrialization of the U.S. economy. Railroads gave farmers and ranchers a way to get their goods to market in the East, and at the same time opened new markets for eastern industrial goods in the West. The extensive use of steel rails in railroad construction also gave a boost to the nation's young steel industry. In 1880 there were 93,262 miles of steel railroad lines in the United States. By 1900 there were nearly 200,000 miles, with much of the new mileage located in the rapidly growing West.

U.S. Land in Farms

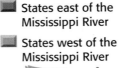

States east of the Mississippi River

States west of the Mississippi River

1870:
407,735,000 total acres

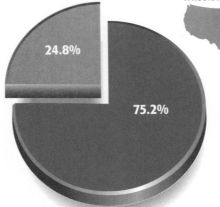

24.8%

75.2%

1900:
841,202,000 total acres

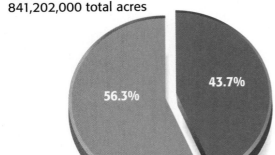

56.3%

43.7%

1995:
972,000,000 total acres

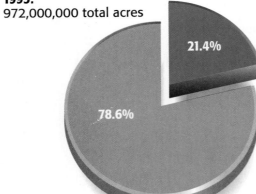

21.4%

78.6%

Source: *Historical Statistics of the United States; 1997 World Almanac and Book of Facts*

Geography **Skills**
Reading Pie Graphs

1. What percentage of total U.S. farmland was located west of the Mississippi in 1870? in 1995?
2. How has the geographical distribution of total farmland in the United States changed between 1870 and 1995?
3. How many acres of farmland were in the United States in 1995?

Western Population Growth, 1860–1900

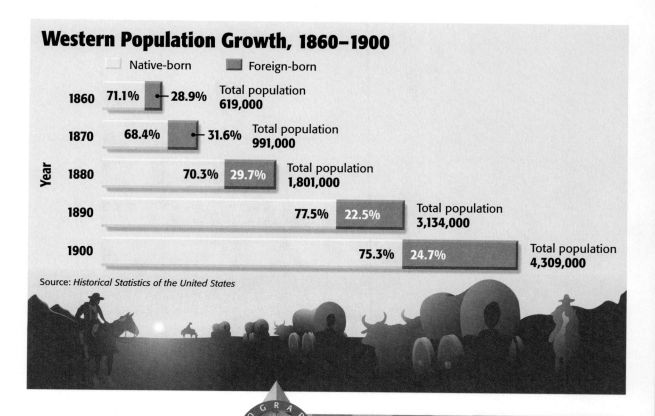

Native-born ☐ Foreign-born ■

Year		
1860	71.1% — 28.9%	Total population 619,000
1870	68.4% — 31.6%	Total population 991,000
1880	70.3% 29.7%	Total population 1,801,000
1890	77.5% 22.5%	Total population 3,134,000
1900	75.3% 24.7%	Total population 4,309,000

Source: *Historical Statistics of the United States*

Geography Skills
Reading Bar Graphs

1. What was the West's population by 1860? By what year had that population almost tripled?
2. In what year was the percentage of foreign-born residents highest?
3. From studying this bar graph, would you say that immigration in the late 1800s was, or was not, an important contributor to population growth in the West? Explain your answer.

History Note 7

San Francisco was California's largest and most economically important city in the 1800s. By 1900 more than 340,000 people lived in San Francisco. Many Asian immigrants, particularly the Chinese workers who had labored building the railroads, entered the United States through San Francisco. Farther south, Los Angeles had a population of only a little more than 100,000 by 1900. Like San Francisco, it also had a busy port. The city has experienced rapid industrial growth in recent years and by the early 1990s had expanded into a city of nearly 3.5 million people.

Chinese American bookkeepers

NEW YORK

The Granger Collection, New York

▪ CHAPTER 22 ▪
An Industrial and Urban Nation
(1876–1900)

To celebrate the United States's 100th birthday, the Centennial Exhibition opened in Philadelphia on May 10, 1876. The Chicago *Tribune* urged Americans to come even "if you have to live six months on bread and water to make up for the expense." During the next six months some 10 million visitors viewed "the results . . . of the best brains of all lands." These new technologies on exhibit were bringing U.S. agriculture and industry into a new era.

THEMES

Technology and Society
How might advances in technology reshape a country's economy?

Economic Development
How might a government respond to economic and industrial expansion?

Cultural Diversity
What effect might increased immigration have on a nation?

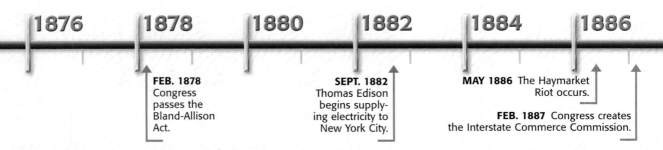

1876   1878   1880   1882   1884   1886

FEB. 1878 Congress passes the Bland-Allison Act.

SEPT. 1882 Thomas Edison begins supplying electricity to New York City.

MAY 1886 The Haymarket Riot occurs.

FEB. 1887 Congress creates the Interstate Commerce Commission.

The Second Industrial Revolution

Reading Focus

How did the Second Industrial Revolution affect the U.S. economy?

What changes occurred in the way that businesses were organized?

Why did some Americans oppose monopolies, and what actions did they take against them?

Key Terms

Bessemer process

patent

Second Industrial Revolution

free enterprise

entrepreneurs

corporations

vertical integration

horizontal integration

trust

Sherman Antitrust Act

THE MOST POPULAR EXHIBIT *at the 1876 Centennial Exhibition was the 700-ton, 40-foot-high Corliss steam engine, which helped power other machines at the exhibition. Fascinated by machines, many spectators stood in awe of the engine's size and power. Author William Dean Howells wrote that those who "would understand its vast and almost silent grandeur [magnificence]" had to see it for themselves. Millions of people did come to see what Howells called "an athlete of steel and iron." For many, the Corliss engine symbolized the ever-improving future that modern machines seemed to promise.*

The Corliss engine ran all the equipment in the exhibition's Machinery Hall.

IMAGE ON LEFT PAGE: *Centennial Exhibition in Philadelphia, 1876*

1888   **1890**   **1892**   **1894**   **1896**   **1898**

SEPT. 1889
Jane Addams and Ellen Gates Starr open Hull House.

JULY 1890
Congress passes the Sherman Antitrust Act.

JUNE 1892
The Homestead Strike begins.

MAY 1894
The Pullman Strike begins, eventually halting midwestern railroad traffic.

An Industrial and Urban Nation   **677**

An Age of Steel

One of the most significant advances in technology occurred in the steel industry. Steel is iron that has been strengthened by heating it and combining it with other metals. Skilled workers originally produced steel in small batches, but it was difficult and expensive to make.

The Bessemer Process

In the 1850s British inventor Henry Bessemer discovered a way to make steel more easily and less expensively than previous methods. Bessemer found that by blasting hot air through melted iron he could remove the impurities quickly. The **Bessemer process** allowed several tons of iron to be made into steel in only 10 or 20 minutes instead of a day or more.

In 1870 U.S. steel production skyrocketed from 77,000 tons to more than 1 million tons in 1879. As production climbed, prices dropped from more than $100 per ton in 1873 to $17 per ton by 1900. At first the demand for steel rails for railroads fed this growth, but soon mills were making steel girders for tall buildings and steel cable for suspension bridges, as well as steel nails, wire, and tubes.

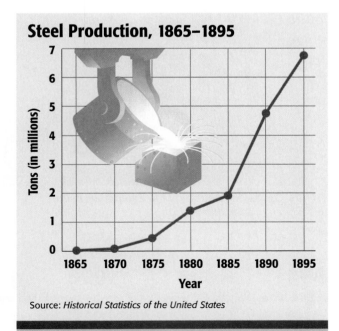

Steel Production, 1865–1895

Source: *Historical Statistics of the United States*

Built of Steel Steel had many uses, which caused its production to skyrocket in the late 1800s. About how much steel was produced in 1890?

Railroads

Steel particularly affected the railroad industry. As steel dropped in price, companies built thousands of miles of new steel track. These stronger, longer-lasting rails were able to carry heavier loads. A network of major railroad lines soon carried heavy freight traffic across the nation. Railroad mileage grew from some 30,000 miles in 1862 to 199,000 by 1900. A popular song of the late 1800s described the expansion of the railroads:

> " Ring out, O Bells! let cannon roar.
>   In loudest tones of thunder,
>   The iron bars, from shore to shore,
>   Are laid and nations wonder,. . .
> And all the world will do its best
>   To keep the cars a-going. "

New technology also made railroad travel faster and safer. Steel locomotive boilers withstood greater steam pressure and thus produced higher speeds. George Westinghouse's and Granville T. Woods's improved air brakes made travel on these heavier, faster trains safer. In addition, sleeping cars designed by George Pullman made long-distance travel more comfortable for passengers.

Other developments helped railroads improve their services. Cornelius Vanderbilt and other owners of large railroad companies began consolidating, or buying smaller companies to form one large company. Consolidation of the many smaller lines improved efficiency and travel time. Whereas in 1860 it had taken two days and 17 line changes to travel from New York City to Chicago, by 1870 passengers could make the trip in 24 hours without changing trains. People could stay on the same railroad line the entire way. Vanderbilt also instituted other ideas such as building large central depots in big cities to centralize railroad services in urban areas. Upon his death one newspaper called Vanderbilt "the great railway king of the country."

The railroads had a huge impact on the U.S. economy and development. Manufacturers and farmers could get their products to market more rapidly than ever by rail. Railroads also promoted western settlement, and large cities grew where major rail lines met. In addition, railroads and their related industries were one of the largest employers in the United States.

This cartoon shows the Illinois Central Railroad connecting rural people to the rest of the world.

Another pair of brothers, Orville and Wilbur Wright, applied motor technology to aviation and put a gasoline engine in a glider. On December 17, 1903, in Kitty Hawk, North Carolina, Orville Wright made the first piloted flight—12 seconds and 120 feet—in a powered plane. Three years later the Wright brothers received a **patent**—an exclusive right to manufacture or sell an invention—for the design of their airplane. Such inventions would change the way that many Americans traveled in the future and increase the demand for oil production.

Power and Communication

Just as railroads affected the nation's development, new energy sources changed the way that the nation was powered. Oil and electricity became two new major sources of power.

Oil

In the late 1850s Dr. Benjamin Silliman Jr. discovered how to refine oil into a fuel called kerosene, which could be used for lighting lamps, cooking, and heating. Suddenly there was a demand for oil. In 1859 retired railroad conductor Edwin L. Drake proved that it was possible to pump oil from the ground. People mockingly referred to his oil well in Pennsylvania as "Drake's Folly," but they stopped laughing when his well began producing 20 barrels per day.

Wildcatters, or oil prospectors, drilled for oil in Ohio, Pennsylvania, and West Virginia. Oil became a big business as these states soon began producing millions of barrels annually. Companies built oil refineries to turn the crude oil into finished products—mostly kerosene.

In the late 1800s people found another use for oil—powering machinery. In 1876 Nikolaus A. Otto invented an engine powered by gasoline, another fuel produced from oil. Gasoline also was used for powering new types of transportation. In 1893 Charles and J. Frank Duryea built the first practical motorcar in the United States.

Electricity

The invention of the electric generator in the mid-1880s meant that electricity could also be used as a power source. The possibilities of electricity increased interest among inventors like Thomas Alva Edison. Edison had started his career as a telegraph operator, but he was always fascinated by how things worked. He designed several improvements to telegraph systems, which earned him enough money to start his own research laboratory in Menlo Park, New Jersey. Edison brought other inventors to Menlo Park, creating what he called a scientific village.

In September 1878, after viewing an experimental electric light source powered by candle heat, Edison bragged that he and his team would soon invent an electric lightbulb. By October 1879 they had succeeded. Edison began supplying electricity to some buildings in New York City in September 1882. The *New York Times* reported that with electric lighting in the newspaper's offices, "it seemed almost like writing by daylight."

A woman uses an early electric-powered vacuum cleaner.

However, electricity could not be transmitted over long distances with direct current (DC). In 1886 George Westinghouse bought inventor Nikola Tesla's patent for an alternating current (AC) generator to replace DC. AC helped electric usage spread rapidly. Electricity had become a power source for both urban households and industry.

An Industrial and Urban Nation **679**

Switchboard operators run one of the many telephone systems created after Alexander Graham Bell (right) invented the telephone.

The Telephone

Just as Edison had started his career by improving telegraph systems, many other inventors tried to improve this important form of communication. In 1861, telegraph wires connected the East and West coasts. Five years later a cable on the Atlantic Ocean's floor successfully connected the United States and Britain. In 1876 Scottish-born professor Alexander Graham Bell invented the "talking telegraph," or telephone. He exhibited it at the Centennial Exposition, where judges called it "perhaps the greatest marvel hitherto [yet] achieved by the electric telegraph."

By the mid-1890s many major American cities such as Boston, Chicago, and New York were linked by telephone lines. The number of telephones in U.S. homes and businesses increased very rapidly, from 54,000 in 1880 to almost 1.5 million in 1900.

★ Economic Changes

Technological advances contributed to what has been called the **Second Industrial Revolution**—a period of explosive growth in U.S. manufacturing in the late 1800s. As a result, the United States became the world's industrial leader by the mid-1890s.

The U.S. government promoted **free enterprise**—business that is free from government involvement. In the late 1800s this policy continued in the form of laissez-faire capitalism, or little government regulation of the economy. However, government did try to promote business through such aid as protective tariffs for manufacturers and land grants to railroads. As a result, **entrepreneurs**—people who organize new businesses—had a great deal of freedom and many opportunities.

To cut costs and increase production, many entrepreneurs organized their businesses as **corporations**—companies that sell shares of ownership called stocks. Corporations are similar to joint-stock companies except that stockholders are not personally responsible for the debts of the business. Stock sales provide a way to combine the assets of many people and to raise large amounts of money. This money was needed to pay for modern factories and machinery. One corporate leader described shares of stock as representing "nothing more than good will and prospective [future] profits."

★ Leaders of Big Business

Many Americans admired wealthy entrepreneurs. Political leaders hailed them as examples of American individualism and success. One lecturer told his audiences, "It is your duty to get rich."

Carnegie and Steel

Andrew Carnegie was one of the most admired business leaders of the late 1800s. Born in Scotland, he came to the United States as a poor immigrant. As a teenager, he took a job with a railroad company and quickly worked his way up to the position of railroad superintendent.

While working as an executive for the Pennsylvania Railroad, Carnegie used personal connections to borrow money and invest in iron mills and bridge-building businesses. In 1865 Carnegie left the railroad to concentrate on his own businesses. Inspired by the new Bessemer process, in 1873 he focused on steelmaking. He bought out his competitors when steel prices were low. By 1900 Carnegie's mills were producing more steel than all of the mills of Britain combined.

The Wizard of Menlo Park

Before he turned 30, Thomas Alva Edison was already a talented inventor. In 1876 he used funding from his inventions to build a new laboratory in Menlo Park, New Jersey. There he was given the nickname "The Wizard of Menlo Park."

Edison designed Menlo Park as an "invention factory." He had a team of skilled specialists to help him. Edison also employed young people who wanted to learn about technology firsthand. Many of them began by working for free. In fewer than six years at Menlo Park, Edison patented more than 400 devices or ideas created by his team. Three of their most important inventions were the carbon telephone transmitter, the phonograph, and the electric lightbulb.

The telephone transmitter came first. Edison improved Alexander Graham Bell's original design in several ways that made it possible to send stronger telephone signals. This greatly improved the sound quality of telephone messages. Today many telephones still use Edison's basic ideas.

His success with the telephone encouraged Edison's team to try recording the human voice. Their experiments resulted in the first phonograph. A person operated this device by speaking into a tube and turning a crank. The vibrations caused by the voice moved a small needle up and down on a tin cylinder. This created a pattern of tiny indentations that formed a groove around the cylinder. The pattern was a record of the person's voice. To play the phonograph, a person touched another needle to the groove and turned the crank again. The indentations caused the needle to vibrate and re-created the sound of the voice through a small speaker.

This invention thrilled the American public. Edison even demonstrated the device to President Rutherford B. Hayes and his wife, Lucy. Eventually, other inventors improved the phonograph and used it to play music.

One of Menlo Park's greatest achievements was the creation of the electric lightbulb. After many failures, Edison's team succeeded in using electricity to heat a filament placed inside a glass bulb with no air in it. The filament would glow brightly and provide a steady source of light.

In the 1880s few buildings had electricity, so Edison tackled the problem of providing it. In 1882 he left Menlo Park and opened an electric power plant in New York City that provided electric lighting for 85 customers. Edison eventually started electric power companies in other cities and built a new, larger laboratory in West Orange, New Jersey. In 1929 a full-scale re-creation of Menlo Park was built in Greenfield Village, Michigan, and it remains a popular tourist attraction.

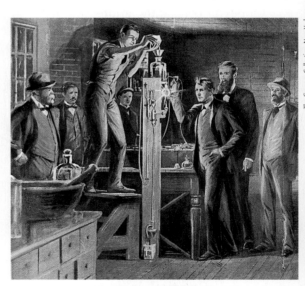

Thomas Edison's team of inventors at Menlo Park work on creating a lightbulb.

The Granger Collection, New York

Understanding What You Read

1. What were some of the inventions created at Menlo Park?

2. How did these inventions change people's lives?

Andrew Carnegie

Andrew Carnegie was born in Scotland in 1835 and immigrated to Pennsylvania at age 13. As a teenager, Carnegie took any job he could get, first working at a textile mill, then as a machine cleaner in a factory. His big break came when he got a job as a railroad messenger, which led to his becoming a telegraph operator and then an assistant to a railroad manager.

Carnegie constantly impressed his employers with his hard work and ability to learn things quickly. One employer, Thomas Scott, loaned Carnegie $600 to make his first investment in a company. Carnegie soon became wealthy by making wise investment choices. Unlike many other successful businesspeople of his era, Carnegie continued to live very simply, warning that "wealth is one of the worst species of idolatry [idol worship]."

Carnegie's businesses succeeded in part through his use of **vertical integration**—owning businesses involved in each step of a manufacturing process. To lower his costs of production, Carnegie purchased the iron ore mines, coal fields, and railroads needed to supply and support his steel mills.

Rockefeller and Oil

John D. Rockefeller was also successful in business consolidation. He began his rise to wealth and power as a bookkeeper. By age 21 he was a partner in a wholesale business and had decided to invest in the booming oil industry. Rockefeller formed an oil-refining company, which seemed more profitable and less risky than drilling for oil.

By 1870 Rockefeller's Standard Oil Company, which had started in Cleveland, Ohio, was the nation's largest oil refiner. Like Carnegie, Rockefeller used vertical integration. Standard Oil made its own barrels and cans and controlled most of the pipelines, tank cars, and storage facilities it used. Many railroads that wanted Standard Oil's valuable shipping business offered lower rates and rebates—partial returns of payment—to Rockefeller. At times he even got railroads to agree not to provide service to his competitors.

Rockefeller's company was also organized through **horizontal integration**—owning all the businesses in a particular field. By 1879 his companies controlled more than 90 percent of the U.S. oil-refining businesses, making them a monopoly. Rockefeller used consolidation as a means of cutting costs. He also formed a **trust**—a legal arrangement grouping a number of companies under a single board of directors. To make higher profits, trusts often tried to eliminate competition and to regulate production, raising prices for consumers in the process. Rockefeller stated, "The day of combination [trusts] is here to stay. Individualism has gone, never to return."

 ## Social Darwinism and Philanthropy

Many businesspeople who supported laissez-faire capitalism also believed in social Darwinism. This idea was based on scientist Charles Darwin's theory of natural selection. He argued that over time, species evolved by adapting to their environments. Social Darwinists argued that societies also developed this way, and that government regulation of businesses threatened the "natural" economic order. John D. Rockefeller Jr. said that "the growth of large business is merely a survival of the fittest . . . the working-out of a law of nature." Some business leaders used social Darwinism to justify practices such as child labor, low wages, and unsafe working conditions. In addition, some leaders argued that they had gained great wealth because they were the fittest members of society.

Other business leaders argued that social Darwinism meant that the wealthy had a duty to take care of the poor, because nature pre-determined who would be poor and who would be rich. They tried to help the poor through philanthropy, or giving money to charities. Andrew Carnegie, among others, called this idea "The Gospel of Wealth." He summed up this philosophy:

> **The man of wealth [is] thus becoming the mere agent and trustee for his poorer brethren [society members], bringing to their service his superior wisdom, experience, and ability to administer, doing for them better than they would or could do for themselves.**

These beliefs led Carnegie to give away much of his fortune. During his lifetime he gave more than $350 million to charity, about $60 million of which went to fund public libraries to expand access to books. Other business leaders, including Rockefeller, also gave large sums of money to various causes. By the late 1800s, charities had received millions of dollars from philanthropists.

★ The Antitrust Movement

Some critics, however, argued that many entrepreneurs earned their fortunes not through natural selection but through unfair business practices. These people believed that monopolistic trusts reduced the competition that was necessary to keep prices low and the quality of goods and services high. Citizens and small businesses demanded government action to control monopolies and restore competition. Although Congress was generally supportive of big business, it could not ignore the voters' concerns. As Senator John Sherman explained, "You must heed their appeal. . . . Society is now disturbed by forces never felt before."

In July 1890 Congress passed the **Sherman Antitrust Act**, which outlawed monopolies and trusts that restrained trade. However, the act did not clearly define what it meant by a monopoly and thus was difficult to enforce.

This magazine used humor to criticize trusts.

SECTION 1 REVIEW

Identify and explain the significance of the following:

- **Bessemer process**
- **Orville and Wilbur Wright**
- **patent**
- **Thomas Alva Edison**
- **Second Industrial Revolution**
- **free enterprise**
- **entrepreneurs**
- **corporations**
- **Andrew Carnegie**
- **vertical integration**
- **John D. Rockefeller**
- **horizontal integration**
- **trust**
- **Sherman Antitrust Act**

Reading for Content Understanding

1 **Main Idea** What effect did new technologies and business growth have on the U.S. economy?

2 **Main Idea** Why did some people oppose business monopolies, and what did they do to prevent them?

3 **Economic Development** How did new forms of business ownership and organization enable business leaders to control their industries?

4 **Writing** *Informing* Imagine that you are an editor of a magazine in the 1880s. Write a short editorial article explaining to your readers what you think the most important invention of the period is and why.

5 **Critical Thinking** *Drawing Conclusions* Why do you think many people admired wealthy business leaders?

Industrial Workers

AT THE BEGINNING OF *the Second Industrial Revolution, skilled workers called puddlers turned hot, liquid iron into steel. One puddler said he felt "like some frantic baker in the inferno kneading a batch of iron bread." Puddlers' skills made them valuable to employers and difficult to replace. However, over time, factory owners began replacing puddlers with machines. Like many other skilled workers, puddlers began losing their jobs as well as their bargaining power with employers.*

Labor union announcement

★ The New Workplace

During the Second Industrial Revolution, machines replaced many skilled workers. These machines could be run by unskilled workers. Because these low-paid workers required little training, they usually could be replaced easily. Therefore, they feared that complaining about wages or working conditions would cause them to lose their jobs.

As machines became more widely used in industries, factories focused on specialization—having workers repeatedly perform a single step in the production process. Specialization lowered costs and increased production. This focus on reducing costs caused managers to value efficiency.

In the early 1880s Frederick W. Taylor, an efficiency engineer with the Midvale Steel Company, performed time-and-motion studies to standardize worker activity. Taylor examined the steps that workers performed to do their jobs and measured the time each step took. He then found ways to do these tasks more efficiently, in order to lower labor costs and make them a measurable, predictable part of production. Taylor explained that "in the past the man has been first; in the future the system must be first."

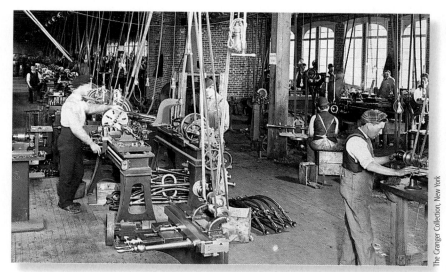

Scientific management encouraged the creation of factories like these, where each worker performed a few specific tasks.

Taylor's ideas became so popular that he left Midvale and became a well-known and successful consultant to many businesses. In 1911 he published *The Principles of Scientific Management* and established efficiency studies as a standard part of U.S. industry.

By focusing on how to reduce the cost of labor, scientific management encouraged managers to see workers as parts of the production process, not as individuals. In factories, managers increasingly ignored working conditions. Managers strictly regulated workers' activities, such as taking a break to get a drink of water. Injuries increased as workers used more machines and were pushed to work at a rapid pace. Companies rarely took responsibility for work-related injuries. As conditions grew worse, workers sought ways to bring about change.

⭐ Labor Unions

To improve working conditions, workers formed labor unions, usually in spite of their employers' objections. Unions increased workers' power because an entire workforce of a business was not as easily replaced as one individual worker. When all workers acted collectively, or together, they had a much greater chance of success. Unions tried to use **collective bargaining**—in which union leaders negotiated for better wages and working conditions on behalf of all workers in a particular factory or industry. Most employers opposed collective

bargaining, sharing the feelings of one company president who said, "I shall never give in. I would rather go out of business."

The Knights of Labor

Founded by Uriah Stephens, the **Knights of Labor** was a union originally organized like a secret society. During a depression in the 1870s, it built a network of local assemblies and sought to, as Stephens said, "include men and women of every creed and color." In 1879 Terence V. Powderly became the leader of the Knights. He eliminated the secrecy surrounding the organization and turned it into the first truly national labor union in the United States. Under Powderly's leadership, the Knights worked for goals such as an eight-hour workday, equal pay for equal work, regulation of trusts, and an end to child labor. Unlike most unions at the time, the Knights welcomed both skilled and unskilled workers as members.

Women not only joined the union but also took an active role in it. Union organizer Mary Harris Jones was called "Mother" Jones by the workers whose rights she fought to protect. Jones organized

The Knights of Labor was one of the few unions to accept African Americans like Frank J. Farrell (left), shown here introducing Terence V. Powderly (center).

many strikes among workers, such as a group of poorly paid Virginia miners whose lives were very difficult. She described their condition:

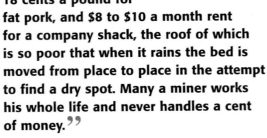
"Mother" Jones

66 **In some of these [company] camps the miners are forced to pay as much as $9 a barrel for sugar, 18 cents a pound for fat pork, and $8 to $10 a month rent for a company shack, the roof of which is so poor that when it rains the bed is moved from place to place in the attempt to find a dry spot. Many a miner works his whole life and never handles a cent of money.** 99

Even though workers faced such problems, Powderly was reluctant to support strikes. Local Knights of Labor chapters, however, supported the great railroad strike of 1877 that affected the nation from coast to coast. Such strikes led the Knights to their greatest strength in the mid-1880s. By 1886 the Knights' membership had increased to 700,000.

The Haymarket Riot

By 1886 other unions were gaining strength. In May thousands of union members in Chicago, Illinois, went on strike to support an eight-hour workday. Two strikers were killed in a clash with police. The next night, workers met at Haymarket Square to protest the killings. When police arrived to break up the crowd, someone threw a bomb that wounded more than 60 officers and killed 8 of them. The police responded by firing into the crowd, killing several people and wounding 100 others. The Chicago *Herald* described the event that became known as the **Haymarket Riot** as "wild carnage [slaughter]."

Eight anarchists—people who oppose all forms of government—were arrested and convicted of conspiracy, although there was no evidence directly linking them to the

bombing. One of the anarchists predicted more violence among union members. "When you shall have hanged us, then—mark my words— they will do the bombthrowing!" he warned.

Although Powderly and the other Knights' leaders never supported the strike or the Haymarket demonstration, several local chapters of the Knights did. One of the convicted anarchists, Albert Parsons, held a Knights of Labor membership card. Public opinion linked the Knights to the Haymarket Riot and its violence. As a result, membership in the Knights declined rapidly.

The AFL

Another union, the **American Federation of Labor** (AFL), fared better than the Knights. Unlike the Knights, the AFL organized individual national unions, such as the mineworkers and the steelworkers unions, into a loose association. Led by Samuel Gompers, the AFL limited its membership to skilled workers, which gave the union great bargaining power but excluded the majority of workers.

Gompers said that the AFL tried to "accomplish the best results in improving the conditions of the working people . . . today and tomorrow" by negotiating for better wages, hours, and working conditions. By 1890 the AFL's membership was larger than that of the Knights, and 10 years later it had more than 500,000 members.

The bombing at Haymarket Square resulted in the deaths of several police officers and a decline in union support.

Strikes Against the Entrepreneurs

Unions continued to use strikes to improve conditions. Workers sometimes struck simply for the right to join a union. In such cases, losing could end the union. Sometimes business owners pushed unions into striking in hopes of gaining the government's support in breaking the union. One such conflict occurred in 1892 at one of Andrew Carnegie's steel plants.

The Homestead Strike

Previously, workers had gotten along well with managers at Andrew Carnegie's Homestead Steel works near Pittsburgh, Pennsylvania. This changed in 1889 when Henry Frick became chairman of the company. In 1892, union members protested Frick's plan to introduce new machinery to the plant, which would cut the number of workers. When an agreement with the union could not be reached, Frick set out to break the union and cut

costs. He announced that the company would negotiate only with individual workers, not the union.

On June 29 the **Homestead Strike** began while Carnegie was out of the country. Frick locked workers out of the plant. He refused to negotiate with the union or allow union members back to work. The workers responded by seizing control of the town of Homestead. Frick then hired private detectives from the Pinkerton agency to break the power of the union by force.

The striking workers were prepared, however. Gunfire erupted on July 6, when the Pinkerton detectives tried to enter the steel works from barges on the Monongahela River. Nine workers and seven Pinkertons were killed in the battle that followed. After a long standoff, the outnumbered and trapped Pinkertons surrendered. They were then marched through the streets and insulted by crowds. Pennsylvania's governor called out the state militia to restore order. Although the strike continued for four more months, the union was eventually defeated. Frick sent a message to

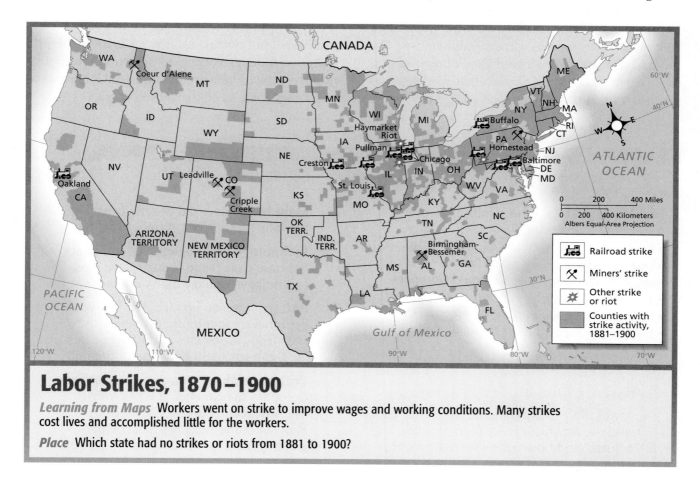

Labor Strikes, 1870–1900

Learning from Maps Workers went on strike to improve wages and working conditions. Many strikes cost lives and accomplished little for the workers.

Place Which state had no strikes or riots from 1881 to 1900?

Carnegie, "Our victory is now complete."

The Pullman Strike

Another major strike occurred among the workers at George Pullman's company. The Pullman Palace Car Company had established the company town of Pullman, Illinois, where most of its workers lived. Workers had to pay higher rents and utility costs than in nearby towns.

During a depression that began in 1893, Pullman laid off nearly half of the company's workers and cut the wages of those who remained by 25–40 percent without lowering rents. On May 11, 1894, workers protesting the wage cuts began the **Pullman Strike**. Support for the strike quickly spread throughout the railroad industry. The American Railway Union, headed by Eugene V. Debs, supported the strikers by refusing to work on trains carrying Pullman cars. By July, traffic on most midwestern rail lines was halted because almost all trains carried Pullman cars. The railroad officials then ordered the Pullman cars to be attached to U.S. mail cars, so that workers who stopped Pullman cars could be charged with the

Pinkertons confront workers during the Homestead Strike.

federal offense of interfering with the U.S. mail.

The federal government backed the railroad companies. Despite the protest of the Illinois governor, President Grover Cleveland sent federal troops to Chicago, the heart of the strike. Cleveland vowed:

> **If it takes every dollar in the Treasury and every soldier in the United States to deliver a postal card in Chicago, that postal card should be delivered.**

The U.S. attorney general broke the strike by securing a court order telling the workers to stop their strike because they were acting in restraint of trade. He used the Sherman Antitrust Act—originally intended to curb big business, not labor—to get the court order and keep the trains rolling. Debs was arrested and later sentenced to six months in jail for violating the court order. Strikes continued, but defeats like the Pullman Strike and the government's continued support of big business over the unions set the industrial labor movement back for several decades to come.

SECTION 2 REVIEW

Identify and explain the significance of the following:
- **Frederick W. Taylor**
- **collective bargaining**
- **Knights of Labor**
- **Terence V. Powderly**
- **Mary Harris Jones**
- **Haymarket Riot**
- **American Federation of Labor**
- **Samuel Gompers**
- **Henry Frick**
- **Homestead Strike**
- **Pullman Strike**

Reading for Content Understanding

1 **Main Idea** Why were the Knights of Labor and the American Federation of Labor formed, and how were they organized?

2 **Main Idea** How did the major strikes of the late 1800s affect American workers?

3 **Technology and Society** What impact did new changes in industry and new technology have on the workplace?

4 **Writing** *Describing* Imagine that you are a newspaper journalist during the Haymarket Riot. Write a short article describing the events and outcome of the riot.

5 **Critical Thinking** *Making Comparisons* Compare the Knights of Labor with the American Federation of Labor. How were the unions similar? How were they different?

Many immigrant families like this one went through the receiving center on Ellis Island.

unskilled jobs were the only work most immigrants could get at first. "Wherever the heat is most . . . scorching, the smoke and soot most choking," wrote one Hungarian immigrant, "there we are certain to find compatriots [countrymen] bent . . . with toil." Entire families often worked to survive. Despite such challenges, many immigrants found opportunities in the United States that they did not have at home.

Many immigrants also worked hard to build communities. Immigrants tended to form neighborhoods with others who shared their nationality. In these neighborhoods, immigrants could hear their own language, eat familiar foods, and preserve their customs. Some immigrant communities formed **benevolent societies** —aid organizations to help others in cases of sickness, unemployment, and death. At that time, there were no national government agencies to provide such aid.

Many immigrant groups established newspapers in their own languages and founded schools, churches, and synagogues to preserve their beliefs and customs. At the same time, many other immigrants eagerly embraced American culture, encouraging their children to learn English and to become familiar with American customs. While immigrants' experiences in the United States were often difficult, they were usually able to build a better future for their families.

★ Opposition to Immigration

Opponents of increased immigration claimed that the new immigrants' poverty and lack of education would negatively affect American society. Nativism, which had started in the 1840s and 1850s with opposition to Irish Catholic newcomers, strengthened in the late 1800s.

Labor unions, particularly in the West, opposed immigration, fearing that immigrants would work for low wages and take jobs away from union members. Some business leaders favored immigration for the opposite reason—they wanted a large supply of low-wage workers to keep labor costs down. One businessman said, "Their home countries have borne the expense of rearing them . . . and then America . . . reaps whatever profits there are" from their work.

Some nativists rioted violently against immigrants. Other nativists worked to stop or limit immigration by lobbying for anti-immigration legislation. In 1882 Congress passed the **Chinese Exclusion Act**, which prohibited Chinese people from immigrating to the United States for the next 10 years. This act was the first time a nationality was prohibited from entering the country. After the ban was extended into the early 1900s, the Chinese American population declined.

To further reduce the flow of immigrants, in 1894 nativists founded a new organization called the **Immigration Restriction League**. The league demanded that all immigrants prove that they could read and write in some

This cartoon shows the attitude of nativists who looked down on the many new immigrants arriving in the United States in the late 1800s.

The Granger Collection, New York

language before being allowed into the country. Congress approved a literacy test for immigrants in 1897, but it was vetoed by President Cleveland.

Despite opposition, the new immigrants played an essential role in industrial growth in the late 1800s. They performed much of the low-wage factory work that drove rapid growth. They also built many of the nation's buildings, highways, and railroads.

The Growth of Urban Communities

During the late 1800s immigrants and native-born Americans alike moved to cities in record numbers. By 1870 there were 168 cities with a population of more than 10,000, and 15 cities' populations exceeded 100,000. Urban population exploded, particularly in many new midwestern cities. Chicago grew from 30,000 residents in 1850 to 1.7 million in 1900.

Although some city residents were businesspeople and skilled workers, many more were poor. Agricultural hardships drove large numbers of rural residents to the cities. There they joined the immigrants in looking for work. Author Henry Blake Fuller described Chicago's new residents as having "come for the common avowed object [declared goal] of making money." At the turn of the century, 40 percent of Americans lived in cities, and the percentage kept climbing.

As groups of people moved to cities, they established a variety of organizations to improve their communities and bring their neighborhoods together. Among urban African American communities, particularly in the South, churches became the centers of social and political life. In the late 1800s African American religious groups emerged as a powerful force to organize and aid their communities. African American ministers often served as political leaders as well as spiritual leaders in black neighborhoods. One report from a Baptist organization described black ministers as "a class of men who . . . have won the confidence, love, and respect of their people."

These ministers were often aided in their work by African American women, who made up the majority of church members and volunteer leaders. Through the churches, black women held power and influence in their communities. One Georgia woman noted that the typical man in her community believed that men should be the leaders in society. She said, "But whenever it comes to church affairs, he quietly puts his hands in his pockets and steps aside leaving it for the women to do."

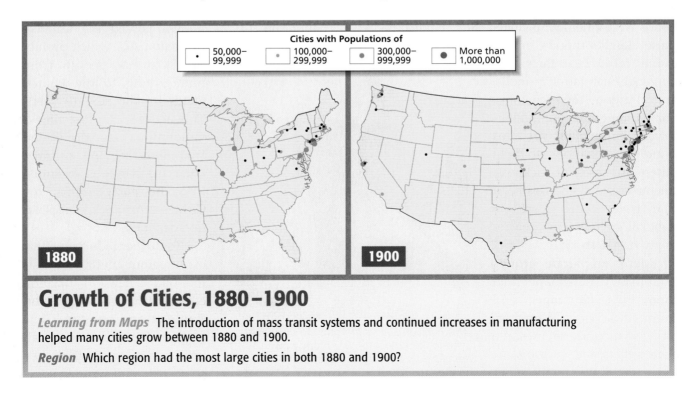

Cities with Populations of

50,000–99,999   100,000–299,999   300,000–999,999   More than 1,000,000

1880

1900

Growth of Cities, 1880–1900

Learning from Maps The introduction of mass transit systems and continued increases in manufacturing helped many cities grow between 1880 and 1900.

Region Which region had the most large cities in both 1880 and 1900?

Large buildings, like this one in New York City, became more common in U.S. cities in the late 1800s.

⭐ Urban Changes and Problems

Organizations like churches and social groups helped make life easier for many city residents. New technologies also brought some improvements to urban centers. Engineers could build increasingly taller buildings by using steel-beam frames for support. Elisha Otis's steam-powered elevators carried people up and down multiple stories. As more of these so-called skyscrapers were built to use limited city space more efficiently, the central part of cities became more densely populated.

In addition, small local stores gave way to department stores, which offered a wider variety and choice of goods in one place than ever before. Cities also offered residents libraries, parks, theaters, museums, and the best schools and hospitals.

However, cities sometimes grew too fast to provide services such as sanitation. In addition, houses could not always be built fast enough. Overcrowding and lack of sanitation often led to disease and poor health. The poor, who often lived in substandard housing, suffered the worst of such problems. Jacob

Riis described the cramped living conditions of poor urban residents in his book *How the Other Half Lives:*

> ❝ **Nine lived in two rooms, one about ten feet square that served as parlor, bedroom, and eating room, the other a small hall room made into a kitchen. The rent was . . . more than a week's wages for the husband.** ❞

Landscape architect Frederick Law Olmsted believed that city life caused people to develop "a peculiarly hard sort of selfishness." New York City hired Olmsted to design Central Park, which he hoped would have a "harmonizing [unifying] and refining influence upon the most unfortunate and most lawless classes of the city." The idea of preserving green areas in cities for recreation caught on, and many cities began building parks.

Some people wanted private space, not just public parks. Many middle-class Americans chose to live in quieter areas where they could own homes. They moved to **suburbs**—residential neighborhoods outside of downtown areas. Mass transit networks of trolleys, subways, and commuter trains made living in the suburbs and working in the cities possible.

Overcrowding caused problems in many cities as the population grew too fast.

Frederick Law Olmsted

Frederick Law Olmsted was one of the first designers to call himself a landscape architect and is best known as the architect in chief of New York City's Central Park. In addition to designing Central Park, Olmsted planned Prospect Park in Brooklyn, New York; South Park in Chicago; the Stanford University grounds in California; the grounds of the Capitol at Washington, D.C.; and the entire Boston park system.

In 1857 Olmsted was appointed superintendent of Central Park, the first major public park in the United States. He designed new plans for the park with designer Calvert Vaux. Although town commons and greens had existed in the United States since the 1600s, the public park, specially designed for recreation, was unknown until the mid-1800s. Olmsted planned Central Park to serve as a rural retreat for city dwellers. He hoped that it would be a place where they could relax while they explored the park's natural landscape. For this reason, he purposefully planned every square foot of the park's surface, every tree and bush, as well as every arch. Olmsted also hoped that the park would offer a place for people to exercise. He wanted to create a setting where people of all social classes might gather outdoors.

Olmsted's designs for Central Park called for three main bodies of water—the Lake, the Meer, and the Pond. To make the Pond area more attractive to visitors, Olmsted planted trees along its edge and lined its path with benches. He purposely placed the Pond near busy streets, hoping that it would attract walkers, if only for a brief period of rest.

South of the Lake is the Children's District. It was designed as a place where parents could bring their children during the hot summer months. Because infant and child deaths

This image from 1870 shows Frederick Law Olmsted's plan for Central Park.

The Granger Collection, New York

in the city sharply increased during hot weather, staying cool was important. "For them," Olmsted said, "the best that can be done is to spend an occasional day or part of a day in the Park."

Central Park provided other activities, such as horseback riding, ice skating, boating, and baseball. Central Park proved extremely popular, attracting an average of 30,000 visitors a day for a total of 10 million in 1871. It remains a popular destination for people today.

Understanding the Arts

1. How did Frederick Law Olmsted design the Pond area of Central Park?

2. What is the Children's District?

3. Why do you think Central Park became such a popular attraction?

The Settlement Houses

Few government programs existed to help the urban poor in the late 1800s. However, many private aid organizations offered assistance. In addition to benevolent societies, there were **settlement houses**—neighborhood centers in poor areas staffed by professionals and volunteers who offered education, recreation, and social activities.

Settlement houses began in Britain but became common in the United States. Janie Porter Barrett established an African American settlement house, the Locust Street Social Settlement, in Virginia. The most famous settlement house was **Hull House**, founded by Jane Addams and Ellen Gates Starr in September 1889. Addams and Starr were among the many upper-class women of their era who received a college education but found few job opportunities open for them. Addams wanted to do work that would help the poor. "I was quite settled in my mind that I should study medicine and 'live with the poor.'" She and Starr bought a run-down building in a poor neighborhood in Chicago and turned it into Hull House, which focused on the needs of families, particularly immigrants.

Addams brought in many other women like herself, who had education and money but desired a useful career. These female social workers lived

Jane Addams poses with children from Hull House.

at the settlement house. Addams believed it was best for the workers to live among the people they hoped to help. She later explained,

> " I gradually became convinced that it would be a good thing to rent a house in a part of the city where many . . . needs are found, in which young women who have been given over too exclusively to study might . . . learn of life from life itself; where they might try out some of the things they have been taught. "

Addams and her staff participated in a variety of activities. They established the first kindergarten and public playground in Chicago. They taught English and U.S. government to help the immigrants become citizens. The staff also worked for reforms such as child labor laws and the eight-hour work day for women. Hull House served as a model for other settlement houses.

SECTION 3 REVIEW

Identify and explain the significance of the following:

- old immigrants
- new immigrants
- steerage
- benevolent societies
- Chinese Exclusion Act
- Immigration Restriction League
- suburbs
- settlement houses
- Hull House
- Jane Addams

Reading for Content Understanding

1 **Main Idea** What kind of work did many of the immigrants in the late 1800s perform? What were immigrants' living conditions like?

2 **Main Idea** Why did cities experience such rapid growth in the late 1800s, and what problems did this growth cause?

3 **Cultural Diversity** How were new immigrants different from old immigrants? Why did nativists oppose immigrants?

4 **Writing** *Persuading* Imagine that you are an immigrant to the United States in 1885. Write a letter to your family back home, telling them about your good and bad experiences. Try to persuade them to join you.

5 **Critical Thinking** *Drawing Conclusions* How do you think a city government might have solved some of the city's problems in the late 1800s?

Populism

Reading Focus

What effects did industrialization have on farmers, and what actions did farmers take to fight for change?

How did farmers want to change the money supply?

What issues did the Populist Party support?

Key Terms

National Grange

Interstate Commerce Act

Interstate Commerce Commission

free coinage

gold standard

Sherman Silver Purchase Act

Farmers' Alliances

Populist Party

IN THE LATE 1800S *many western farmers blamed their economic hardships on the railroads. Frank Norris's 1901 novel,* The Octopus, *shows the farmers' point of view. The octopus in the story is the railroads, which threaten farmers' livelihoods by charging high rates. When farmer Dyke asks a railroad official on what basis the company raised shipping rates, the response is: "All—the—traffic—will—bear." However, the rate increase will leave Dyke with no profit from his harvest. Unless Dyke pays back the money he borrowed to raise his crops, the bank will foreclose on his home. Dyke realizes that "not only would the Railroad devour every morsel of his [Dyke's] profits, but also it would take from him his home."*

Farm family

★ Rural Unrest

From 1860 to 1900, the U.S. population more than doubled, from 31.5 million to 76 million. To feed the growing population, the number of farms tripled, from 2 million to 6 million. Many farmers borrowed money to buy land and machinery, as farming became more mechanized. With modern machines, in 1900, farmers could produce a bushel of wheat almost 20 times faster than in 1830. However, the combination of more farms and greater productivity led to overproduction and lower prices for crops. Many farmers responded to lower prices by increasing crop production, which eventually pushed prices even lower.

As their income decreased, many farmers found it more difficult to pay their bills. Those who could not make their mortgage payments lost their farms and homes. Many became tenant farmers. By 1880 one fourth of all farms were rented by tenants, and the number kept growing. Many Americans could not even afford to rent land and thus became farm laborers. By 1900 there were 4.5 million farm laborers in the United States.

Many farmers blamed businesspeople—wholesalers, brokers, grain buyers, grain elevator operators, and particularly railroad owners—for profiting at their expense. Leonidas Polk, an editor of a North Carolina farm journal, expressed this view when he wrote,

" There is something radically wrong. . . . The railroads have never been so prosperous. . . . The banks have never done a better . . . business. . . . Manufacturing enterprises have never made more money. . . . Towns and cities flourish and 'boom,' . . . and yet agriculture languishes [declines]. "

As economic conditions grew worse for farmers, they began to organize associations—like workers had done—to further their interests.

★ The National Grange

In 1866 clerical worker Oliver Kelley toured the South for the U.S. Department of Agriculture. Kelley saw firsthand how the nation's farmers suffered. After that tour, Kelley and several government clerks founded the National Grange of the Patrons of Husbandry in 1867. The **National Grange** was a social and educational organization for farmers. The Grange wanted to ease the isolation of farm life and improve farmers' living standards. Local chapters, or granges, were quickly established, and membership grew rapidly, to more than 1.5 million by 1874.

Granges formed organizations called cooperatives to buy goods in bulk at lower prices, increasing farmers' buying power. Farmers also formed cooperative societies to sell their crops, hoping that by joining together they could demand higher prices. Unfortunately for farmers, these cooperatives were often run by people who were inexperienced in business. In addition, banks, merchants, and railroads usually organized to oppose these cooperatives. As a result, most of the cooperatives fared poorly.

The Grange then shifted its focus to politics. It campaigned for political candidates who supported farmers' goals and demanded legislation to

This Granger poster shows the group's ideal image of farm life.

regulate rates for the use of railroads and grain elevators. In a few states, Granges managed to enact laws regulating railroads, which farmers relied on to ship their crops.

The issue of railroad regulation came before the U.S. Supreme Court in 1877 in the case of *Munn* v. *Illinois.* The Court ruled that the government did have the right to regulate the railroads and other businesses that affected the public interest. In the 1886 case of *Wabash* v. *Illinois,* the Court clarified that the federal government could only regulate companies that did business across state lines. Regulation of rates for railroad lines within states fell to the state governments.

Congress also tried to exert its authority. In February 1887 it passed the **Interstate Commerce Act** to provide some uniform national regulations over trade between the states. This act created the **Interstate Commerce Commission** (ICC) to ensure that railroads charged fair rates and did not discriminate in favor of big shippers. However, the commission lacked any real power to enforce its regulations, and the courts gave the agency little help when it appealed to them.

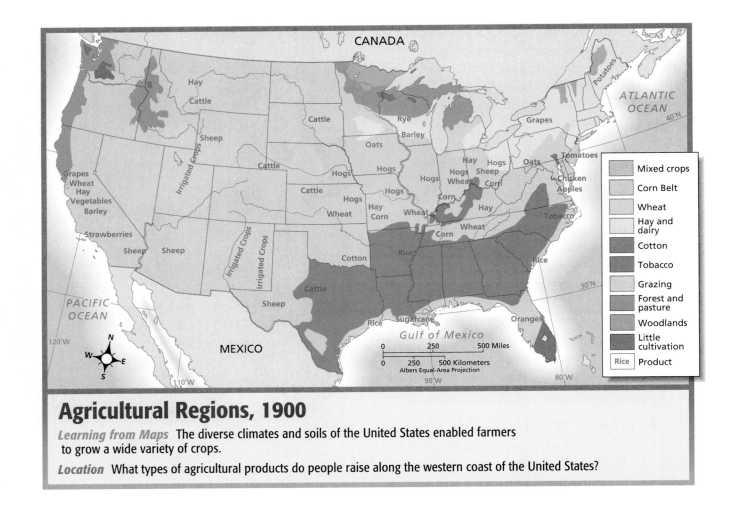

Agricultural Regions, 1900

Learning from Maps The diverse climates and soils of the United States enabled farmers to grow a wide variety of crops.

Location What types of agricultural products do people raise along the western coast of the United States?

⭐ Money Issues

Railroad rates were not the only concern facing farmers. Farmers' problems most often involved money issues, such as debt, credit, and low crop prices. Many farmers thought that assistance would come only from national legislation that affected the money supply.

Farmers for Silver

Since 1792, the United States had allowed free and unlimited coinage. **Free coinage** meant gold and silver were coined and that paper money was worth a specific amount of gold or silver. The Coinage Act of 1873 placed the United States strictly on a **gold standard**—meaning that only gold could back U.S. currency.

1863 silver half dollar

Tied to the gold standard, the money supply tended to grow more slowly than the nation's population. This meant that there were fewer dollars in circulation for each citizen, which resulted in deflation—a shrinking of the money supply and a general lowering of prices. Farmers supported coining silver to create inflation—an increase in the money supply and a rise in prices. With inflation, farmers hoped that prices for farm products would rise, thus increasing their income and allowing them to pay their debts more easily.

Silver Politics

During the late 1870s there was considerable support for free coinage of silver. Many farmers began backing political candidates who supported free silver coinage. One such politician was William Jennings Bryan of Nebraska, who claimed that with

Grover Cleveland

the free coinage of silver all "necessary reforms will be possible." In 1878 Congress passed the Bland-Allison Act, which allowed for limited silver coinage, over President Hayes's veto.

A new political party, the Greenback Party, favored inflating the money supply with paper dollars not backed by gold or silver. In the presidential election of 1880 the Greenback Party nominated Iowa congressman James B. Weaver as its candidate. The two major parties, however, largely ignored the money issue.

The Republicans finally made continued coinage of silver an issue in the presidential election of 1888. President Cleveland, a Democrat, lost the election to Republican Benjamin Harrison, grandson of former president William Henry Harrison. After the election, the Republican Congress passed the **Sherman Silver Purchase Act** to increase the amount of silver purchased for coinage. However, this act did not help farmers economically as much as they had hoped.

 ## Farmers' Alliances

Many farmers formed their own political organizations to increase their power. First locally, then regionally, they organized to elect candidates and to achieve policies favorable to them. These political organizations became known as the **Farmers' Alliances**.

In Texas the alliance started as a frontier farmers' association in 1877 and quickly grew to become the Grand State Alliance in 1879. Other alliances joined, and membership soared, topping 1.5 million in 1890. The Colored Farmers' Alliance had more than 1 million members of its own.

The Farmers' Alliance was more politically active than the

Grange had been. Its goals and proposals put more emphasis on government legislation and action to help farmers. The Alliance called for increased railroad regulation and lower interest rates.

In the 1890 elections the Alliance ran candidates who emerged as a serious political force, particularly in the West and in the South. These candidates won the governorship of Texas and Georgia and gained control of both houses of the Georgia legislature. Alliance candidates also won 38 seats in the U.S. Senate.

The Populist Party

Following their state and local successes, farmers raised their political sights and hopes to the national level. At a conference in Cincinnati, Ohio, in May 1891, Alliance leaders met with representatives from labor and reform organizations. They agreed to organize a new national political party, the People's Party. This organization, better known as the **Populist Party**, was the high point of farmers' political activity.

The Election of 1892

In 1892 the Populist Party held its first national convention in Omaha, Nebraska, where the group decided on a platform of far-reaching reforms. The Populists' goal was to remove the influence of big

The Colored Farmers' Alliance fought for the rights of African American farmers like this family from Virginia.

business on government and to provide all Americans with greater democracy and voice in the government. Populist Mary Lease expressed their sentiments:

> 66 **Wall Street owns the country. It is no longer a government of the people, by the people, and for the people, but a government of Wall Street, by Wall Street, and for Wall Street.** 99

To restore the political power of the common people, the Populist platform called for government ownership of railroads and the telephone and telegraph systems, and it supported the "free and unlimited coinage of silver and gold." To attract votes from industrial workers, the Populists supported the eight-hour workday and immigration restrictions.

In the 1892 presidential election the Democrats nominated Grover Cleveland and the Republicans nominated Benjamin Harrison. The significant issue of the campaign was the Republicans' support for high tariffs. This time, however, Cleveland won. James B. Weaver, the Populist candidate, won an impressive 1 million votes, about 8.5 percent of the total popular vote.

The Panic of 1893

Shortly after Grover Cleveland took office, the Philadelphia and Reading Railroad failed, causing a stock market panic. This triggered the worst economic downturn that Americans had yet experienced. By 1894 millions of Americans

The Granger Collection, New York

In 1895 Mary Lease published her views on populism in a well-known book.

Linking Past to Present

Third Political Parties

Ever since the presidential election of 1796, the United States has had a two-party system. However, at times some Americans have felt that the two major parties did not adequately represent their views. Thus, many Americans formed or joined third political parties, such as the Populist Party.

Dissatisfied with the Democratic and Republican presidential candidates for the 1992 and 1996 elections, Americans supported several new political parties. Ross Perot ran as an independent candidate in 1992. Perot then founded the Reform Party and ran as its candidate in 1996. Each time he campaigned on a platform of government reform. Ralph Nader ran in 1996 for the Green Party, which was formed in 1984. The party had an environmental platform. In 1996 Perot was on the ballot in all 50 states, and Nader was on the ballot in 18 states. Other third parties were formed, but the Reform Party was the strongest of the new parties.

While running as an independent candidate in the 1992 presidential campaign, Perot joined the Republican and Democratic candidates in televised debates. Perot received almost 20 million votes in the election, about 19 percent of the total. Although a third-party candidate has yet to win a presidential election, third parties remain an important part of the democratic process.

Understanding What You Read

1. Why have Americans formed political parties in the past?

2. What role do you think third parties play in the democratic process?

were unemployed and some 690,000 workers went on strike to protest reduced wages.

The depression had multiple causes, but some Americans blamed the money system. Many investors reacted to the downturn by selling their investments in exchange for gold, causing a gold drain. Bank depositors feared a further downturn and exchanged their paper money and silver coins for gold at federal banks. The result was a serious shortage of U.S. gold reserves, which forced the government to sell bonds to increase the gold supply.

Democrat William Jennings Bryan supported many Populist ideas.

The Election of 1896

With the economic panic, many voters began to agree with the Populists' call for reform. In 1896 the Republicans nominated William McKinley for president, and he came out firmly against free coinage of silver. Many Democrats saw this platform as a chance to win Populist and some Republican votes.

At the Democrats' nominating convention their nominee, William Jennings Bryan, swept the crowd with an emotional speech. In support of free coinage of silver he said, "You shall not press down upon the brow of labor this crown of thorns. You will not crucify mankind upon a cross of gold!"

The Democrats had put the Populists in a difficult position by adopting their strongest issue. The Populists had to decide between running their own candidate, and thus splitting the silver vote, or supporting Bryan and possibly being absorbed by the Democrats. The Populists decided to nominate Bryan but chose their own vice president.

The Democrats carried the South and the West, but the Republicans won the election with the strong support of the more heavily populated Midwest and Northeast. The well-financed Republican campaign had convinced many industrial workers in large urban areas that free silver coinage would create high unemployment. McKinley's victory in the election of 1896 marked the end of both the Populist Party and the organized farmers' parties.

SECTION 4 REVIEW

Identify and explain the significance of the following:

- **Oliver Kelley**
- **National Grange**
- **Interstate Commerce Act**
- **Interstate Commerce Commission**
- **free coinage**
- **gold standard**
- **William Jennings Bryan**
- **James B. Weaver**
- **Benjamin Harrison**
- **Sherman Silver Purchase Act**
- **Farmers' Alliances**
- **Populist Party**

Reading for Content Understanding

1. **Main Idea** What problems did farmers face during the late 1800s, and how did they respond?

2. **Main Idea** What issues did farmers support in the National Grange and the Populist Party?

3. **Economic Development** Why did many farmers support the free coinage of silver?

4. **Writing** *Informing* Write a paragraph explaining the goals of the Populist Party and why it did not win the 1896 presidential election.

5. **Critical Thinking** *Making Comparisons* In what ways was the Populist Party different from the Democratic and Republican Parties?

CHAPTER 22 REVIEW

Chapter Summary

The Second Industrial Revolution brought the growth of new industries such as steel and oil, and inventions such as the lightbulb. The Second Industrial Revolution also changed the way that businesses were organized and how people worked. Immigration from European countries increased, which contributed to the rapid growth of cities. Farmers sought to reverse their hard times and increase their political influence through the National Grange and the Populist Party. ■

On a separate sheet of paper, complete the following activities.

Identifying People and Ideas

Describe the historical significance of the following:

1. Bessemer process
2. Thomas Alva Edison
3. free enterprise
4. Andrew Carnegie
5. Pullman Strike
6. Terence V. Powderly
7. benevolent societies
8. suburbs
9. Jane Addams
10. gold standard

Internet Activity

go.hrw.com
SA0 Inventions

Search the Internet through the HRW Web site to find information about one of the many new inventions of the late 1800s. Use the information to create a detailed diagram of the invention. Be sure to label important parts of your diagram and provide a caption explaining its importance both at the time it was invented and today.

Understanding Main Ideas

1. How did Andrew Carnegie use vertical integration to gain control of the steel industry?
2. What was the cause and outcome of the strike at Carnegie's Homestead plant?
3. How did the immigrants coming to the United States after 1880 differ from those who had come earlier? What problems did these new immigrants face?
4. What factors contributed to the growth of U.S. cities in the late 1800s?
5. Why were the years 1860 to 1900 difficult for American farmers?
6. Why did Congress pass the Sherman Silver Purchase Act?

Reviewing Themes

1. **Technology and Society** What effect did the Second Industrial Revolution have on the U.S. economy?

Using the Time Line

Number your paper from 1 to 6. Match the letters on the time line below with the following events.

1. **Hundreds of people are wounded in the Haymarket Riot in Chicago.**
2. **Congress creates the Interstate Commerce Commission to regulate trusts.**
3. **Thomas Edison begins supplying customers in New York City with electrical power.**
4. **Congress passes the Sherman Antitrust Act to stop the growing power of the trusts.**
5. **Jane Addams and Ellen Gates Starr found Hull House in Chicago.**
6. **Congress passes the Bland-Allison Act.**

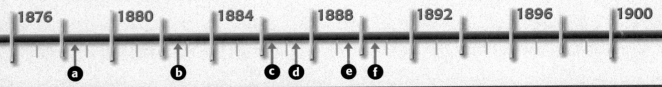

2. **Economic Development** What actions did the federal and local governments take to help big business? What steps did government take to control big business?

3. **Cultural Diversity** How did the growth of immigration in the late 1800s increase the cultural diversity of the United States?

Thinking Critically

1. **Identifying Generalizations and Stereotypes** Why do you think old immigrants were able to become a part of American society more quickly than new immigrants were?

2. **Making Comparisons** How was the Knights of Labor different from and similar to the American Federation of Labor?

3. **Evaluating** Although the Populist Party lost the presidential election of 1892, several reforms listed in the party's platform were later put into effect. Which reform do you think was the most important? Explain your answer.

Building Your Portfolio

Complete the following activities individually or in groups.

1. **Immigrant Communities** Many immigrant communities established during the 1800s still thrive in American cities today. Do some research about an immigrant community today, and create a tourist brochure to attract visitors to that community. Your brochure should include some historical information about the community as well as descriptions and images of current attractions.

2. **Presidential Elections** Research and create a campaign poster for either the 1892 or the 1896 presidential election. Create one poster for each presidential candidate. (Remember that in 1892, the third-party candidate made a strong showing.) Make sure that your poster includes the important issues of that election and the candidate's position on those issues.

Writing About History

1. **Classifying** Which new invention of the Second Industrial Revolution do you think most changed Americans' lives? Which new invention today has had the same type of effect on your life? Explain your answer in a paragraph.

2. **Persuading** Write a newspaper editorial supporting a candidate in the 1896 presidential election.

Linking Geography and History

1. **Location** Why do you think that western cities grew at the intersections of major railroads in the late 1800s?

2. **Movement** For what reasons did many immigrants come to the United States?

History Skills Workshop

Using Visual Resources Study the image below, which is an artist's sketch of troops firing on striking Pullman Company workers. Write one paragraph describing this scene from the point of view of the troops and another paragraph from the point of view of the Pullman Company strikers.

The Granger Collection, New York

The Granger Collection, New York

■ CHAPTER 23 ■
The Spirit of Reform
(1868–1920)

When reformers gathered together in 1912, activist Jane Addams described the mixture of social workers, religious leaders, scholars, and politicians. "Suddenly, as if by magic, the city of Chicago became filled with men and women from every state in the Union who were moved by the same needs and hopes." With the formation of the Progressive Party in 1912, many reformers hoped to create economic and democratic reforms on a national level.

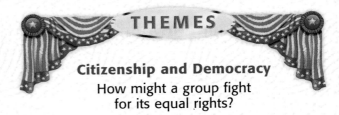

THEMES

Citizenship and Democracy
How might a group fight for its equal rights?

Constitutional Heritage
What effect might a Supreme Court ruling have on workers' rights?

Economic Development
In what ways might a government try to reform business?

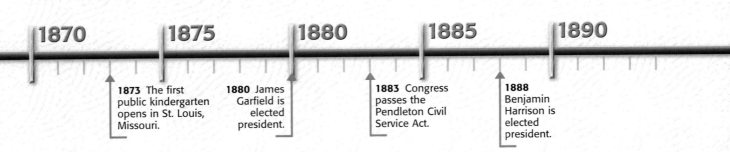

1870 **1875** **1880** **1885** **1890**

1873 The first public kindergarten opens in St. Louis, Missouri.

1880 James Garfield is elected president.

1883 Congress passes the Pendleton Civil Service Act.

1888 Benjamin Harrison is elected president.

The Gilded Age

Reading Focus

What types of systems controlled city and state politics?

What were some of the issues in national government and presidential campaigns during the Gilded Age?

How did the appointment of federal officials change during the late 1800s?

Key Terms

bosses

political machines

mugwumps

Pendleton Civil Service Act

W HEN MAGAZINE EDITOR *Lincoln Steffens visited St. Louis, Missouri, in the early 1900s, he noted the citizens' pride in their city. "The visitor is told of the wealth of the residents, of the financial strength of the banks, and of the growing importance of the industries," Steffens wrote. However, Steffens saw a different side of the city. It had poorly paved streets filled with garbage. The crumbling City Hospital was crowded with the sick. Even in the hotel, liquid mud ran out of the taps of his bath. Steffens's experience highlighted the contrasts that caused people to refer to this period as the Gilded Age.*

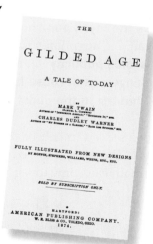

THE

GILDED AGE

A TALE OF TO-DAY

BY
MARK TWAIN
(SAMUEL L. CLEMENS)
AUTHOR OF "INNOCENTS ABROAD," "ROUGHING IT," ETC.
AND
CHARLES DUDLEY WARNER
AUTHOR OF "MY SUMMER IN A GARDEN," "SAUNTERINGS," ETC.

FULLY ILLUSTRATED FROM NEW DESIGNS
BY HOPPIN, STEPHENS, WILLIAMS, WHITE, ETC., ETC.

SOLD BY SUBSCRIPTION ONLY.

HARTFORD:
AMERICAN PUBLISHING COMPANY.
W. E. BLISS & CO., TOLEDO, OHIO.
1874.

The novel The Gilded Age

IMAGE ON LEFT PAGE: *Theodore Roosevelt campaigning for the Progressive Party in 1912*

1895	1900	1905	1910	1915

1895 Booker T. Washington gives his Atlanta Compromise speech.

1901 The New York State Tenement House Law is passed.

1909 The National Association for the Advancement of Colored People is formed.

1913 The Seventeenth Amendment is passed.

1919 The states ratify the Eighteenth Amendment.

1920 The Nineteenth Amendment gives women the vote.

⭐ Corruption in Politics

In 1873 Mark Twain and Charles Dudley Warner published the best-selling novel *The Gilded Age.* Twain believed that American society looked golden from a distance but was merely gilded, or coated with cheap gold paint on the outside. This meant that society, despite its positive appearance, was ugly and corrupt on the inside. Twain argued that the country lived by the motto "Get rich; dishonestly if we can, honestly if we must."

Machine Politics

State and local politics suffered from corruption during the Gilded Age. Powerful organizations used illegal methods to control government and to grow rich from it. The rapid growth of cities in the late 1800s made possible the rise of **bosses**, political leaders who controlled elections through bribery and payoffs. For example, in return for votes and money, a boss might provide jobs, order neighborhood improvements, or allow an illegal business to stay in operation. Author James Bryce explained that the boss

> 66 **rewards the loyal, punishes the mutinous [disloyal], . . . negotiates treaties. He generally avoids publicity . . . and is all the more dangerous because he sits, like a spider, hidden in the midst of his web.** 99

The bosses drew much of their support from immigrants. "There's got to be . . . somebody that any bloke [man] can come to—no matter what he's done—and get help," explained one Boston politician. The boss system offered immigrants both jobs and social mobility—opportunities often denied to them in the larger society.

City bosses developed **political machines**—organizations that guaranteed votes at election time through both legal and illegal methods. The political machine usually printed election ballots listing only the party's candidates. These were often printed on colored paper so the bosses knew how individuals voted. Party organizers also paid citizens for their votes and hired the people who counted the votes. New York City boss William Marcy Tweed declared, "The ballots made no result; the counters made the result." Through their political machines, bosses protected their political positions, controlled the spending of public money, and thus personally profited from their own dishonesty.

Tammany Hall

New York City's political machine, Tammany Hall, became widely known throughout the country. Through corrupt practices, Boss Tweed may have succeeded in stealing nearly $200 million from the city treasury. He was eventually convicted of another crime, however, and died in jail.

Some politicians thought that the political machines were a fair exchange of money, influence, and jobs for working-class votes. For example, after winning the election of 1888, Tammany Hall members provided some 12,000 jobs to their supporters, particularly Irish immigrants.

National Scandals

In the late 1800s political scandals were also common on the national level. The presidency of Republican Ulysses S. Grant—who was elected in 1868 and re-elected in 1872—was widely regarded as corrupt. During his second term, for example, government revenue officials were jailed for their part in the Whiskey Ring. They took bribes from whiskey distillers seeking to avoid paying taxes.

Members of Congress also participated in corrupt activities. In 1872 the *New York Sun* broke the story of a new scandal. The major owners of the Union Pacific Railroad had created a construction

The Granger Collection, New York

Members of Tammany Hall blame each other for stealing public money.

company called Crédit Mobilier of America. The owners gave or sold shares in this company to the members of Congress responsible for awarding federal land grants to the railroads. The congressmen then gave large federal land grants to Crédit Mobilier. These grants increased the value of the company's stock, and both the congressmen who received shares and the railroad owners profited at the public's expense.

The Crédit Mobilier scandal damaged the careers of several Gilded Age politicians, including Schuyler Colfax, Grant's vice president. This sort of political corruption led many angry Americans to question the honesty of the government and of the presidency.

This cartoon shows corrupt officials weighing down the Grant administration.

⭐ Gilded Age Presidents

In 1876 the Democratic presidential campaign called for government reform. Their presidential candidate, Samuel J. Tilden, had already attacked corruption in his own party. He promised to create an honest administration in Washington. The Republicans nominated Rutherford B. Hayes, a moderate reformer who promised "thorough, radical, and complete" changes in the government. Hayes had a reputation for honesty and was a war hero. The House of Representatives declared him the narrow victor over Tilden in a disputed election.

Republicans won another close victory in 1880 with the election of reformer James Garfield and his vice president, Chester Arthur. On July 2, 1881, frustrated government job-seeker Charles Guiteau confronted President Garfield at a Washington railroad station, shouting "Arthur [is] President now," and shot Garfield twice. The president died from his wounds in September, and Vice President Arthur became president.

In the 1884 election, Republicans chose James G. Blaine as their nominee rather than another reform candidate. Blaine's record of association with corruption upset many Republican

reformers, who came to be known as **mugwumps** (the Algonquian Indian word for big chiefs). Dissatisfied mugwumps left the Republican Party and threw their support behind the Democratic nominee, Grover Cleveland, who had a reputation for political honesty. In a campaign full of personal attacks, American voters chose Cleveland over Blaine as president. Cleveland involved himself in all the day-to-day details of the presidency. He worked hard to hire and fire government employees based on their merit rather than their party loyalty.

Four years later, Cleveland once again won the popular vote, but this time lost the electoral vote, and thus the presidential election, to Republican Benjamin Harrison. Harrison controlled inflation and supported the buildup of the U.S. Navy. Cleveland remained popular, however, and in 1892, crowds sang:

66 **Grover, Grover, four more years of Grover— Out they go and in we come and we'll be in the clover.** 99

Police capture Charles Guiteau after the murder of President James Garfield.

Winning both the popular and electoral vote in 1892, Cleveland defeated Harrison and returned to the White House. During his second term the country faced a recession and Cleveland angered many fellow Democrats with his economic policies. In 1896 the Democrats nominated William Jennings Bryan, who lost to Republican William McKinley. The practical, friendly McKinley worked well with Congress and was re-elected in 1900. During his two terms, he helped restore public confidence in the presidency by avoiding the corruption and scandals that had plagued the federal government in the Gilded Age.

 ## Civil Service Reform

Many Americans reacted to the widespread corruption of the Gilded Age by demanding changes in the civil service, or government jobs. The party in control of the government had long taken advantage of the spoils system to award jobs to loyal members, whether they were qualified or not. Every time a new party took power, many current government employees were replaced. This resulted in ruined careers and inefficient administrations. Henry Adams, author and grandson of former president John Quincy Adams, commented on this practice in 1870 by saying that "all my friends have been or are on the point of being driven out of the government."

Reformers wanted a system that used competitive exams to award jobs based on merit. They argued that this system would keep out incompetent and corrupt workers. President Hayes had promoted some reform efforts during his administration in the 1870s. Many Americans also believed that the spoils system was responsible for President Garfield's assassination by an unhappy federal job-seeker in 1881. *The Nation*, a weekly newspaper, commented that "the crime seems to have acted on public opinion very like a spark on a powder-magazine." This reaction led to a movement to pass stronger civil service reform legislation.

A fellow official congratulates Senator George Pendleton on his plan for civil service reform.

The Granger Collection, New York

President Chester Arthur responded to the public's feelings by supporting the **Pendleton Civil Service Act**, which established a merit system under the control of the Civil Service Commission. The act, passed in January 1883, initially only affected about 14,000 out of 130,000 federal jobs. President Cleveland doubled the number of positions covered by the legislation. The act has since been expanded so that it now affects almost 90 percent of government jobs.

SECTION 1 REVIEW

Identify and explain the significance of the following:
- bosses
- political machines
- William Marcy Tweed
- Rutherford B. Hayes
- James Garfield
- Chester Arthur
- mugwumps
- Grover Cleveland
- Benjamin Harrison
- Pendleton Civil Service Act

Reading for Content Understanding

1 **Main Idea** How did scandals and dishonesty affect politics in the Gilded Age?

2 **Main Idea** How did civil service reform affect the appointment of federal officials?

3 **Citizenship and Democracy** How did bosses and political machines control city governments?

4 **Writing** *Classifying* Make a chart that shows the presidents who served during the Gilded Age, their political party, and the year they were elected.

5 **Critical Thinking** *Evaluating* Do you agree with the objectives of the Pendleton Civil Service Act? Explain your answer.

The Progressive Movement

Reading Focus

What were the common goals of most progressives?

How did progressives address the nation's social problems?

How did progressives change government?

Key Terms

progressives

muckrakers

direct primary

Seventeenth Amendment

recall

initiative

referendum

Wisconsin Idea

ONE COLD, SNOWY MORNING in late December 1891, Florence Kelley and her three children arrived on the front steps of Hull House in Chicago. When she knocked on the door, Jane Addams answered. "We were welcomed as though we had been invited," Kelley later wrote. "We stayed." At Hull House, Kelley not only found refuge but also joined the increasingly popular movement for reform and went on to become one of the nation's leading social reformers.

Hull House in Chicago

★ Progressivism

In the late 1800s a group of reformers who became known as the **progressives** began working to improve society. They thought that they could make reforms by studying a problem and developing plans to correct its root cause. Many reforms focused on changing environments, such as those that gave rise to crime, poverty, and disease. Progressives wanted to address the social and political problems caused by rapid industrial and urban growth.

The Progressives

Many progressives were well-educated professionals who lived and worked in cities. During the late 1800s, a rise in the number of new professionals and small-business owners increased the size of the middle class. Many men and women in the progressive movement came from such backgrounds, although some working-class and wealthy people also fought for reforms.

Although progressives often shared goals, they had different ideas about how to solve problems and did not always agree on which

The Spirit of Reform **709**

problems required action. As a result, they focused their efforts in many areas. These included improving health and education in poor neighborhoods, reforming government, and regulating business. Many progressives believed that they could accomplish these goals through government regulation of business, health, and safety issues. Progressives wanted the government to respond to the needs of the nation's citizens to create an atmosphere in which people and government leaders worked together to solve social problems.

Muckrakers

Journalists also became involved in the progressive effort. Reporters began writing about corruption in business and politics, hoping that their articles would lead to public awareness and eventually to reform. These journalists were nicknamed "**muckrakers**" because some people said they "raked up" and exposed the muck, or filth, of society.

Lincoln Steffens exposed scandals in city politics in one of the first muckraking articles, published in 1902 in *McClure's Magazine.* Another muckraker, Ida Tarbell, wrote a series of articles describing the unfair business practices of the Standard Oil Company. "We have the directors of the Standard Oil Company acting as directors on nearly all of the great railways of the country," she noted. Tarbell argued that this control of related industries gave Standard Oil an unfair advantage and ultimately damaged the public good.

Ida Tarbell wrote many muckraking articles for McClure's Magazine.

Muckrakers often focused on poor people such as this Jewish immigrant who lived in a coal cellar.

★ Urban Reform

Reform movements and some political parties had tried to address the problems created by industrialization in the early 1800s. The progressive movement focused much more attention and effort on problems in the cities. Progressive minister Josiah Strong declared that

> ❝the city is the nerve center of our civilization. It is also the storm center. . . . The city has become a serious menace [threat] to our civilization.❞

As many native-born Americans and immigrants moved into U.S. cities looking for work, city officials found themselves unable to keep up with demands for housing and social services. The results were unsanitary, unsafe conditions for thousands of families living in poverty. Many of them crowded into tenements whose owners failed to make needed improvements in living conditions. Progressive Lawrence Veiller described the effects of tenement living on society:

> ❝A child living its early years in dark rooms, without sunlight or fresh air, does not grow up to be a normal, healthy person. . . . It is not of such material that strong nations are made.❞

Progressives addressed these problems in a variety of ways. Veiller successfully campaigned for the 1901 New York State Tenement House Law, which outlawed the construction of dark and airless tenements. The law required new buildings to have better ventilation, toilets, and running water. New York's law became a model for housing reform in other states. Many progressives also established settlement houses patterned after Jane Addams's Hull House in Chicago. These organizations worked in immigrant and poverty-stricken communities to improve education, sanitation, and housing conditions.

Interest in city reform grew so much that in 1909 hundreds of reformers gathered at the first National Conference on City Planning and Congestion. Supporters of city planning proposed to get rid of unsafe housing, to develop more park land, and to improve public transportation. Such reforms were the beginning of local political efforts to control and regulate the growth of cities through the enforcement of building codes, zoning laws, and sanitation standards.

New professions also arose to meet city needs. Engineers played a key role. Civil engineers tried to improve city transportation by paving streets. Sanitation engineers tackled the problem of water supplies, waste disposal, and air pollution. Cities that addressed these problems experienced a dramatic drop in death rates by the end of the century. As more improvements were adopted, urban Americans came to enjoy the highest standards of public services in the world.

⭐ Improving Democracy

In addition to dealing with local issues of public health and city reform, progressives tried to make local and state governments more responsive to people's needs. They did this through election reform, improvements in the structure of city government, and changes in state politics.

Elections

Progressives passed a number of election reforms. Reformers in many cities and states stopped political machines from printing ballots that listed only their own candidates. Governments replaced these ballots with ones that listed all candidates regardless of their party. Beginning in 1888, many states also adopted the secret ballot, patterned after one used in Australia. Reformers broadened political participation by introducing the **direct primary**. This allowed voters to choose candidates directly rather than relying on the choices of party leaders. In addition, the passage of the **Seventeenth Amendment** in 1913 allowed Americans to vote directly for U.S. senators, who had previously been elected by state legislatures.

Some states like Oregon as well as cities like Los Angeles also passed a measure known as the **recall**. Under this measure, if enough voters sign a petition, the public can then vote to remove an elected official from office before the end of his or her term.

Reformers in Oregon and the Midwest also pushed for two reforms that gave voters the chance to directly affect new legislation. The **initiative** gave voters the ability to propose new laws by collecting a certain number of signatures on a petition. If enough signatures were collected, the proposed law would be placed on the ballot for the public to vote on in the next election. A similar measure, the **referendum**, allowed voters to approve or disapprove legislation already proposed by a state or local government.

A New York official voting in 1916

A Philadelphia street in 1897

States

Corrupt city officials such as city bosses often had connections to state politicians. These relationships led some reformers to concentrate their efforts on state governments. In Wisconsin, progressive Republican Robert M. La Follette failed to win his party's nomination for governor in 1896 and 1898. He finally won the nomination and the governor's seat in 1900.

La Follette opposed the power of the party machines, believing that government should be directly responsive to the people. He supported direct primaries and the use of professionals to manage social problems. La Follette's **Wisconsin Idea**—a program of reform to decrease the influence of political machines—became a model for other state governments.

Cities

In many cities, businesspeople and other professionals led the effort to make local government more efficient and less costly. Samuel M. "Golden Rule" Jones, a business leader and mayor of Toledo, Ohio, attacked corruption and waste in public service. He argued that government should not be an instrument "for the purpose of plundering [stealing from] the poor."

Many reformers wanted to replace elected officials with professionals who would run the city more like a business. John Patterson of the National Cash Register Company remarked that the new system would put city government "on a strict business basis." As a result, several cities changed to a council-manager government, in which an elected city council appoints a manager to run the city. This system put power in the hands of professional administrators rather than politicians. However, many urban residents found the new system created a city government that was less responsive to their needs than elected officials had been. Other cities changed to a commission government, in which an elected body manages city agencies.

★ Reforming Society

Progressives such as La Follette had used the scientific method to deal with political problems. Other progressives applied the scientific method to educational reform.

Public Education

Many progressives believed that by improving public education, they could cure social ills and meet the demand from business and industry for better-educated managers. To meet the changing needs of students, high school courses were broadened to include areas such as health, citizenship, and job training. Many progressives started kindergarten programs to serve the needs of poor city residents, particularly immigrants.

Kindergartens taught basic social skills to children between the ages of three and seven. In 1873 reformer Susan Blow opened the nation's first public kindergarten in St. Louis, Missouri. By 1898 more than 4,000 kindergartens had been opened in the United States.

School enrollment greatly increased in the late 1800s, because the push for

Robert M. La Follette created a widely used model for reforming government.

High school students study science in 1900.

educational reform had led to the creation of new public high schools and thousands of public kindergartens.

One supporter of early childhood education, John Dewey, was an important philosopher and educator. As director of the University of Chicago's Laboratory School, Dewey tried to develop teaching methods suited to the interests and needs of students. Two teachers at the school described the classes as based on "the idea of the school-house as a home." The goal was to nurture children and give them critical thinking skills to help them in everyday life. For example, Dewey wanted to teach children problem-solving skills rather than have them simply memorize lessons.

The teaching methods that Dewey designed at Chicago's Laboratory School became the model for progressive education throughout the country.

Progressivism in Medicine

Progressives also tried to improve the education of doctors and other medical professionals. In the late 1800s the United States suffered from a lack of well-trained and professionally organized doctors. For example, researchers had identified the causes of infectious diseases such as malaria, tuberculosis, pneumonia, and yellow fever. However, there were few medical organizations to help spread this knowledge.

Under the leadership of Joseph McCormack, the American Medical Association (AMA)—which brought together local medical organizations—was reorganized in 1901. The AMA joined other progressive groups in support of laws protecting public health. These reform efforts reflected the progressives' ability to unite professionals in using their skills to help improve society.

NOTICE
A Communicable Disease
WHOOPING COUGH
Exists Within — For Your Protection
DO NOT ENTER
Penalty Provided for Violation Thereof
By Order of
HARDING TOWNSHIP BOARD OF HEALTH

Contagious diseases posed serious challenges for American doctors.

SECTION 2 REVIEW

Identify and explain the significance of the following:

- progressives
- muckrakers
- Lincoln Steffens
- Ida Tarbell
- direct primary
- Seventeenth Amendment

- recall
- initiative
- referendum
- Robert M. La Follette
- Wisconsin Idea
- John Dewey
- Joseph McCormack

Reading for Content Understanding

1. **Main Idea** Why were middle-class reformers particularly active in the progressive movement? What issues did they address?

2. **Main Idea** Why did some progressives want to improve public education? How did they work to fight corruption in local and state governments?

3. **Geographic Diversity** *Movement* What problems did U.S. cities face as their populations grew rapidly?

4. **Writing** *Informing* Imagine that you are a muckraking journalist for *McClure's Magazine.* Write a short article describing the conditions of U.S. cities in the early 1900s and explaining the different ways that progressives have addressed these problems.

5. **Critical Thinking** *Drawing Conclusions* Describe John Dewey's teaching methods, and explain why you think they were so popular at the time.

Reforming the Workplace

Reading Focus

What were working conditions like for adults and children during the late 1800s?

Why did progressives want to pass laws to protect workers?

How did the courts react to labor legislation?

Key Terms

capitalism

socialism

Industrial Workers of the World

The Granger Collection, New York

Labor union booklet

EVERY DAY AT 7:00 A.M. 15-year-old Sadie Frowne sat down at her machine in a garment factory in Brooklyn, New York. "The machines go like mad all day, because the faster you work the more money you get," she explained. "Sometimes in my haste I get my finger caught and the needle goes right through it." When her workday ended at 6:00 P.M., she felt exhausted. One of the progressives' main goals was to establish better working conditions for people like Frowne.

 ## Reforming Child Labor

Low wages for unskilled workers in the late 1800s meant that many more children had to work to help support their families. Girls often cooked and cleaned for boarders, and some boys sold newspapers or shined shoes on the streets. Other girls worked with their mothers at home, sewing garments or creating artificial flowers and costume jewelry.

Many children also worked outside the home. In 1900, more than 1.75 million children aged 15 and younger worked in mines, mills, and factories. The situation of these children moved many progressives to action. One wealthy reformer, Marie Van Vorst, posed as a poor woman to investigate conditions in a South Carolina textile mill. She noted that children as young as five years old were working in the mills. She described working with one young child:

> 66 **Through the looms I catch sight of . . . my landlord's little child. She is seven; so small that they have a box for her to stand on. . . . I can see only her fingers as they clutch at the flying spools; her head is not high enough, even with the box, to be visible.** 99

"Tired?" Van Vorst asked the child, who nodded without stopping. The girl received 40 cents a day for her work, providing cheap labor for the manufacturer, and $2.40 a week for her parents.

Florence Kelley, who had raised her own three children under difficult conditions in a settlement house, became the leader of the progressive crusade against child labor. Her strategy was to "investigate, educate, legislate, and enforce." Beginning her career as a social reformer at Chicago's Hull House, Kelley traveled throughout the United States lobbying for labor laws to protect women and children. As a boardmember of the National Consumers' League—the major lobbying group for women's and children's labor issues—Kelley established about 60 local consumer leagues throughout the United States.

Another organization, the National Child Labor Committee, worked with state labor committees to pass laws restricting child labor in many states. Although Congress passed federal child labor laws in 1916 and 1919, the Supreme Court declared them unconstitutional. A later constitutional amendment restricting child labor failed to be ratified.

Progressives wanted to keep companies from using the labor of children, like this young coal miner.

 The Progressives and Labor

Child labor reform was only part of the progressive effort to help American workers. Many wage earners could not earn enough money to escape poverty. In 1910 perhaps one third of the nearly 30 million men and 7.4 million women who worked still lived in poverty.

Some progressives cooperated with labor unions to pass legislation that addressed the low wages, long hours, and unsafe working conditions faced by millions of adult workers. The National Consumers' League led efforts to establish laws to guarantee a minimum wage and to limit the number of hours in the workday. The eight-hour day was an important goal of progressives. Many

states passed minimum-wage laws and maximum-hour laws for women.

Tragic accidents also led reformers to call for safety regulations in the workplace. In 1900 around 35,000 people were killed in industrial accidents, and about 500,000 suffered injuries. In 1911 the Triangle Shirtwaist Factory in New York City was the site of a shocking accident. As a group of about 500 immigrant women prepared to leave their jobs one afternoon, a deadly fire broke out in the 10-story building. The women tried to escape through stairway exits but found that the managers had locked them. Other workers crammed into elevators and jumped into the elevator shafts. Some women leaped hand in hand from the top of the building, falling to their deaths.

By the time firefighters finally brought the deadly blaze under control, 146 women had died. The factory owners, insurance company, and city building and fire departments were all blamed in

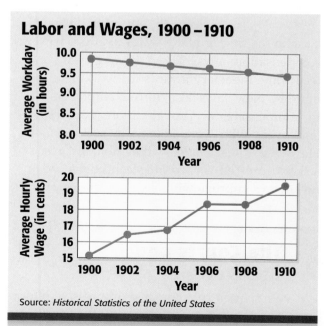

Labor and Wages, 1900–1910

Source: Historical Statistics of the United States

Earning a Living In the early 1900s employees worked fewer hours than before but earned a higher hourly wage. What was the average hourly wage in 1902?

the investigation. No one was convicted on criminal charges, however. At a memorial for the women, union organizer Rose Schneiderman appealed to other workers for action:

66 **This is not the first time girls have been burned alive in the city. Each week I must learn of the untimely death of one of my sister workers. . . . The life of men and women is so cheap and property is so sacred. . . . It is up to the working people to save themselves.** 99

Josephine Goldmark fought to protect the rights of female workers.

Factory accidents such as the tragic Triangle fire encouraged legislation that increased factory safety standards and improved working conditions. State legislatures passed some mine and factory safety laws and new inspection regulations. Labor leaders and progressive reformers fought for workers' compensation laws that would provide benefits to people who were injured on the job. In 1902 Maryland became the first of many states to adopt workers' compensation laws. These laws guaranteed some monetary awards for workplace injuries. New laws also forced employers to compensate, or provide more pay to, employees who were injured in accidents. However, these laws were not always strictly enforced, so working conditions did not always improve with new regulations.

⭐ The Courts and the Workplace

U.S. courts often ruled against progressive reform laws. Some business leaders opposed workforce regulations and believed that the economy should operate without government interference. State and federal courts often upheld these views, arguing that the Fourteenth Amendment protected

businesses against regulations that deprived them of property without due process of law.

Lochner v. *New York*

In an 1898 decision the Supreme Court ruled that states could limit the hours worked by people in particularly dangerous jobs such as mining. The state of New York passed a law that limited bakers to a 10-hour workday. A business owner named Lochner then violated the 10-hour law, and the case eventually went to the Supreme Court. In *Lochner* v. *New York* the Supreme Court ruled that states could not restrict ordinary workers' hours and that the New York law was unconstitutional. Justice Rufus Peckham's opinion stated:

66 **The freedom of master and employee to contract with each other . . . cannot be prohibited or interfered with without violating the Fourteenth Amendment's guarantee of liberty.** 99

Muller v. *Oregon*

The Supreme Court did uphold some laws limiting the hours that women and children worked. In the 1908 case *Muller* v. *Oregon*, the Court upheld laws that limited women's hours. The Court argued that pregnancy and other health factors distinguished female

The Granger Collection, New York

The Triangle Shirtwaist Factory fire shocked the country.

Global Connections

Worker Reforms

In 1911 one German laborer read some U.S. newspapers that detailed "the misery of the workers." Commenting on the story, he said, "What they wrote in those papers was the truth." Europeans had long been aware of labor's concerns because European workers were more successful at organizing themselves than were American workers.

British workers strike in Liverpool.

European workers formed unions and often went on strike to gain increased wages, reduced hours, and improved working conditions. By the mid-1880s strikes had been legalized in industrialized European countries and were a standard union tactic.

Workers in many professions engaged in strikes. National general strikes, in which all the workers in a country go on strike at the same time, occurred in Belgium, the Netherlands, and Sweden. Some strikes resulted in violence, but by 1900 most of the thousands of strikes that occurred annually were peaceful. Collective bargaining also resolved many disputes between workers and their employers.

The labor movement was strongest in Britain, where there were around 4 million union members in 1913. As their standard of living declined in the early 1900s, British workers staged several serious labor protests. A series of transportation strikes paralyzed the nation in 1911. Riots broke out in Liverpool, requiring some 50,000 troops to restore order.

British workers did make some gains during this period. In the early 1900s they won retirement pensions, while British miners gained the eight-hour workday. Parliament also passed the British National Insurance Act, which provided some workers with insurance against unemployment.

Understanding What You Read

1. How did European unions try to bring about changes in the workplace?

2. What gains did British workers make in the early 1900s?

---

workers from males. The justices wrote that a "woman's physical structure and the performance of maternal functions place her at a disadvantage," and therefore her health is a matter of public concern. For the progressives, this was also an important decision because it was the first case successfully argued from social evidence rather than prior legal principle. Progressives and union leaders continued to try to win the same legal protection for male workers.

Labor Unions and Reform

Many workers formed labor unions to secure higher wages and better working conditions. Union membership increased from about 600,000 in 1899 to around 5 million in 1920. Most unions discouraged women from joining, so some female workers organized their own unions. For example, New York reformers started the national Women's Trade Union League (WTUL) in 1903.

The American Federation of Labor (AFL) continued to be one of the leading labor unions, with some 4 million members by 1920. The AFL worked for higher wages, better working conditions, and union recognition. These goals followed AFL president Samuel Gompers's idea of "pure and simple unionism." Gompers and others like him supported the system called **capitalism**, in which private businesses run most industries, and competition determines how much goods cost and how much workers are paid.

Some union members embraced more radical ideas than those supported by the AFL. These workers claimed that capitalism was unfair. Instead, they supported **socialism**, a system in which the government or the workers own and operate a nation's means of production. Socialists hoped that the government would be more sympathetic to workers' concerns than to those of big business.

Some socialists and union leaders founded the **Industrial Workers of the World** (IWW) in 1905. Led by William D. "Big Bill" Haywood, the IWW worked to bring all laborers together into one large industrial union that would work to overthrow capitalism and establish socialism. The IWW unionized many workers who were unwelcome in the AFL, including immigrants, women, African Americans, and migrant workers.

Haywood said that workers and capitalists were engaged in "an irreconcilable [unresolvable]

class struggle." As part of this struggle, the IWW organized a number of successful strikes. The beliefs and actions of the IWW frightened many Americans, particularly those who were rich and powerful. Later political events caused the union to weaken, and it practically disappeared by 1920.

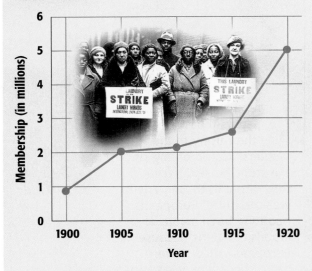

Labor Union Membership, 1900–1920

Source: *Historical Statistics of the United States*

The Growing Unions The nation's industrial growth and the efforts of progressive reformers helped the membership of labor unions grow. During which five-year period was union membership the lowest?

SECTION 3 REVIEW

Identify and explain the significance of the following:
- **Florence Kelley**
- **Rose Schneiderman**
- **capitalism**
- **socialism**
- **Industrial Workers of the World**
- **William D. Haywood**

Reading for Content Understanding

1 **Main Idea** What workplace issues did progressives and labor unions hope to address?

2 **Main Idea** Why did many progressives try to reform labor conditions and practices in the United States?

3 **Constitutional Heritage** What did the Supreme Court decide in *Muller* v. *Oregon* and *Lochner* v. *New York*?

4 **Writing** *Describing* Write a half-page news article about the Triangle Shirtwaist Factory fire in 1911.

5 **Critical Thinking** *Drawing Conclusions* Do you think that the courts should or should not have attempted to regulate the workplace? Explain your answer.

The Rights of Women and Minorities

Reading Focus

Why did many women participate in the progressive movement, and what were their goals?

What reforms did African Americans seek during the Progressive Era?

How was the progressive movement limited?

Key Terms

Woman's Christian Temperance Union

Eighteenth Amendment

National American Woman Suffrage Association

National Woman's Party

Nineteenth Amendment

Atlanta Compromise

National Association for the Advancement of Colored People

URING THE SUMMER OF 1910, *a campaign tour for women's right to vote stopped in Warren, Illinois. The local crowd greeted the female activists with colorful banners and enthusiasm. The activists told Warren's residents that their state representative had opposed the Woman Suffrage bill. The crowd brought the representative forward and demanded to know if he would change his vote and support the bill the next time. "It looks as if I would have to,"* he responded. *To the delight of the crowd, he shouted, "I can't fight against a woman's campaign. I'm for you."*

Suffrage supporter

⭐ Progressive Women

In the late 1800s, women gained access to higher education in record numbers. Several women's colleges had been founded after the mid-1800s, including Vassar, Smith, and Wellesley. Women's colleges were designed "to develop as fully as may be the powers of womanhood," said Sophia Smith, founder of Smith College. In addition, many of the state universities that opened during this period admitted both men and women. Some educators were opposed to the admission of women to college, however. In 1874 Dr. Edward Clarke, a professor at Harvard Medical School, argued that the physical and mental strain of too much thinking would harm a woman's health.

Despite such views, many women seized the opportunity to expand their education. More than 20 percent of college students were women in 1870; that number rose to 40 percent in 1910. After graduation, however, most of these women found that there were few jobs available for them. Jane Addams explained the frustration this caused her and other women, stating that she could "not understand this apparent waste of herself, this elaborate [complex] preparation, if no work is provided for her." Although many female graduates entered fields such as teaching, social work, and library management, they found it much harder to join male-dominated professions such as law and medicine.

Women who were denied access to such careers often found that they could play a central role in the reform movements of the Progressive Era. Many women became publicly active as members of social clubs. Women's clubs fought for dozens of causes, including political reform, child welfare, women's suffrage, and temperance. Charlotte Perkins Gilman, a writer and women's rights activist, rejoiced that

This cartoon shows temperance leader Carry Nation as a warrior.

❝ **the woman's clubs reached almost everyone and brought her out of the sacred selfishness of the home and into the broader contact and relationship so essential to social progress.** ❞

 ## The Temperance Movement

Female progressives were vital to the organization and success of the temperance movement. Temperance reformers had been arguing since the 1840s that alcohol was to blame for many of society's problems. In the 1870s many women renewed the fight against alcohol. They claimed that alcohol disrupted the family and led to crime.

The first temperance crusade of this period began in Hillsboro, Ohio, where women demanded that liquor dealers give up their evil trade "in the name of our . . . ruined lives . . . for the good of the town, in the name of God who will judge you and us, for the sake of our souls." During the 1870s the movement

spread to hundreds of small towns as reformers shut down more than 1,000 saloons. Some followed the example of temperance leader Carry Nation, who stormed into saloons with an ax, chopping bars and smashing liquor bottles and glasses.

In 1874, reformers created the **Woman's Christian Temperance Union** (WCTU), which brought together women from many different backgrounds in the fight against alcohol. Frances Willard, president of the WCTU from 1879 to 1898, created a highly effective organization with 10,000 local branches. The WCTU inspired other temperance organizations such as the Anti-Saloon League, which was particularly active in the early 1900s. As a result of such activities, many state and local governments passed laws restricting the sale of alcohol. In 1919 temperance efforts eventually led to the passage of the **Eighteenth Amendment**, which outlawed the production and sale of alcoholic beverages in the United States.

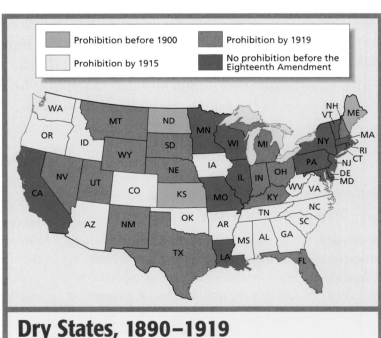

Dry States, 1890–1919

Learning from Maps Before the Eighteenth Amendment became law, many states had taken steps to ban alcohol.

Place Which states had prohibited the use of alcohol before 1900?

★ Suffrage

Women also organized in a renewed effort to gain suffrage during the Progressive Era. The suffrage movement met with many opponents, however. Some people opposed what women might do once they had the vote. For example, political bosses feared women's anticorruption efforts, and many businessmen opposed women's proposals for prohibition and workplace reforms, such as child labor laws and the minimum wage. The vote would give women more power to achieve such reforms. In addition, some people thought that women belonged in the home as homemakers and mothers, rather than in politics. One suffragist leader responded that women

> **must go beyond the house. No longer is home compassed [contained] by four walls. Many of its most important duties lie now involved in the bigger family of the city and state.**

Elizabeth Cady Stanton and Susan B. Anthony began the **National American Woman Suffrage Association** (NAWSA) in 1890 to focus on getting the vote for women. That same year, women gained full suffrage in Wyoming. Colorado, Idaho, and Utah followed in the 1890s.

Carrie Chapman Catt, who had fought successfully for women's suffrage in the West, succeeded Susan B. Anthony as the president of the NAWSA in 1900. Catt mobilized 1 million volunteers for the movement. She promoted the NAWSA's goals in dozens of campaigns and hundreds of speeches. Catt argued that female voters were needed to help bring about progressive reforms. She also pointed out that women deserved to have a voice in creating the laws that affected them.

Some women believed that the efforts of the NAWSA did not go far

enough, however. In 1913 suffragist Alice Paul founded what would become the **National Woman's Party** (NWP), which used methods such as picketing, hunger strikes, and civil disobedience. The NWP campaigned for a constitutional amendment to grant women the vote.

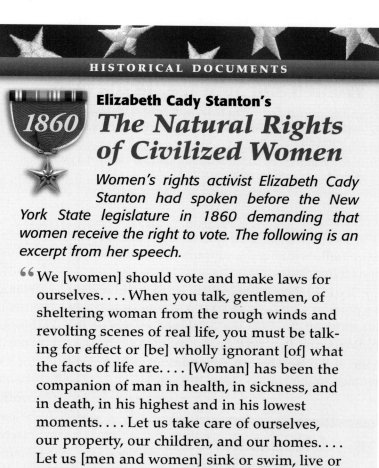

Carrie Chapman Catt waves to supporters.

HISTORICAL DOCUMENTS

Elizabeth Cady Stanton's
1860 *The Natural Rights of Civilized Women*

Women's rights activist Elizabeth Cady Stanton had spoken before the New York State legislature in 1860 demanding that women receive the right to vote. The following is an excerpt from her speech.

> We [women] should vote and make laws for ourselves. . . . When you talk, gentlemen, of sheltering woman from the rough winds and revolting scenes of real life, you must be talking for effect or [be] wholly ignorant [of] what the facts of life are. . . . [Woman] has been the companion of man in health, in sickness, and in death, in his highest and in his lowest moments. . . . Let us take care of ourselves, our property, our children, and our homes. . . . Let us [men and women] sink or swim, live or die, survive or perish together.

Understanding Primary Sources

1. Why does Stanton believe that women should have the vote?

2. What does Stanton think of arguments that women should be protected from politics?

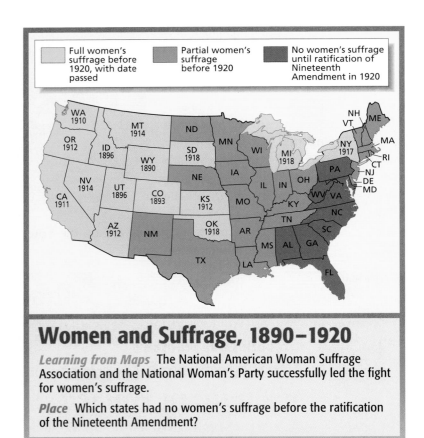

Full women's suffrage before 1920, with date passed

Partial women's suffrage before 1920

No women's suffrage until ratification of Nineteenth Amendment in 1920

Women and Suffrage, 1890–1920

Learning from Maps The National American Woman Suffrage Association and the National Woman's Party successfully led the fight for women's suffrage.

Place Which states had no women's suffrage before the ratification of the Nineteenth Amendment?

The NAWSA also pursued this goal, with Catt eventually winning the support of the president of the United States.

By 1919 there were 26 state legislatures willing to petition Congress to pass a women's suffrage amendment. In 1920 the combined efforts of the NAWSA and the NWP finally resulted in the passage of the **Nineteenth Amendment**, which gave women in the United States the vote.

 ## African Americans Fight for Change

White reformers of the progressive movement often ignored issues such as discrimination. While other areas of life were improving during the late 1800s, racial discrimination and segregation actually increased throughout the nation.

Leadership

Some African American leaders, such as Booker T. Washington, promoted efforts to aid African Americans. Born into the slave system, Washington became a respected educator while in his twenties. In 1881 Washington founded the Tuskegee Institute in Alabama to provide education and training for African American schoolteachers. He argued that African Americans should not spend their efforts fighting discrimination and segregation, but instead should focus on improving their own educational and economic well-being. Washington explained his philosophy in his **Atlanta Compromise** speech of 1895:

❝ **In all things that are purely social we [whites and African Americans] can be as separate as the fingers, yet one as the hand in all things essential to mutual [shared] progress.** ❞

However, other African American leaders of the time, such as journalist Ida B. Wells-Barnett, did not share Washington's philosophy. Wells-Barnett was active in issues such as women's suffrage and an antilynching campaign. She wrote editorials in her Memphis newspaper *Free Speech* to draw national attention to the lynching, or killing by mob, of black men in the South. In 1895 she published the book *Red Record*, which reported lynching statistics for a three-year period. Her work gained her many enemies. Forced to move to the North as a result of death threats, she later helped organize an international crusade against lynching.

W. E. B. Du Bois also took a direct approach to fighting racial injustice. Born in Massachusetts, Du Bois went to Fisk University, and he later earned a doctoral degree from Harvard. He criticized Washington for unfairly making African Americans responsible for

Writer Ida B. Wells-Barnett fought to end lynchings of African Americans.

The Granger Collection, New York

Booker T. Washington (left) wrote his autobiography, Up From Slavery, *in 1901. W. E. B. Du Bois (right) challenged many of Washington's arguments in a collection of essays called* The Souls of Black Folk, *published in 1903.*

correcting racial injustice. Du Bois also disagreed with Washington's emphasis on job training and downplaying of liberal arts education. Du Bois brought attention to cases of racial prejudice and wrote dozens of articles and speeches.

African American Organizations

In 1905 Du Bois and other African Americans committed to immediate action met at Niagara Falls, Canada. Calling themselves the Niagara Movement, the group demanded economic and educational equality, as well as an end to segregation and discrimination. The movement's platform insisted that "to ignore, overlook, or apologize for these wrongs is to prove ourselves unworthy of freedom."

To further the goals of the Niagara Movement, Du Bois helped found the **National Association for the Advancement of Colored People** (NAACP) in 1909. The new organization included many well-known leaders in the progressive movement, such as Jane Addams and John Dewey. Du Bois acted as the director of publicity and research and also as the editor of the NAACP journal, *Crisis*. Opposing the approach of Booker T. Washington, the NAACP worked to bring racial inequality to the attention of white Americans. The organization also attacked racial discrimination through the court system. In 1915 the NAACP won the first of several important Supreme Court decisions in *Guinn* v. *United States*. This decision outlawed the grandfather clause, which had been

widely used in the South to prevent African Americans from voting.

Another important organization, the National Urban League, was formed in 1911. This group helped African Americans—particularly those moving from the South to northern cities—find jobs and housing and adjust to a new life in an urban environment.

⭐ The Limitations of Progressive Reform

Many other members of minority groups did not benefit from the reforms of the progressive movement. This was mainly because the needs of these groups often did not fit into the largely urban reform efforts of the period.

In the 1890s the American Indian population in the United States had declined to about 250,000, its lowest point ever. To address the poverty of American Indians, some leaders founded the Society of American Indians in 1911. Members believed that obeying the Dawes Act and adopting the beliefs and practices of the larger white society was the best solution to American Indians' poverty and unemployment. The organization claimed to speak "for the . . . hopeless of our race." Most of its members, however, did not understand the views of Indians who lived on the reservations and who wanted to preserve traditional Indian culture.

Gertrude S. Bonin helped found the Society of American Indians.

Many Indians saw the breakup of reservations under the Dawes Act as the end of tribal life and culture. In 1912 some 2,000 Cherokee refused to accept their government land allotments, despite living in extreme poverty. Other Indian groups wanted to slow down the allotment process and to allow people to remain on reservations. Eventually, such efforts helped lead to laws that gave Indians the choice of whether to remain on reservations.

Some immigrant groups were also ignored by white progressives. Many Chinese immigrants were men who came to the United States to mine gold and to build railroads. However, Chinese immigration slowed dramatically as a result of the Chinese Exclusion Act of 1882, which made Chinese immigration illegal for a period of 10 years. In 1902 Congress extended the act for an indefinite period of time. The Chinese population dropped because few of those already living in the United States were able to form families.

Chinese Americans often faced violent discrimination, including riots against them in Colorado, Montana, and Wyoming, during the late 1800s. As a result, many Chinese Americans formed their own communities in neighborhoods in cities such as San Francisco. Ing Weh-teh wrote his friend in China that in America he had "to labor, to suffer, floating from one place to another, . . . for more than twenty years."

While Chinese immigration declined, immigration from Mexico increased between 1900 and

Many Mexican immigrants were agricultural workers, like these laborers knocking walnuts out of trees in an orchard.

1930. (Immigrants could move freely across the United States's borders with Mexico and Canada during this time.) Most Mexican immigrants moved to areas that had once been part of Mexico, such as Texas or California. Cities with existing Hispanic communities—such as San Antonio and El Paso, in Texas, and Los Angeles, in California—grew in size as a result. Immigrants often returned to Mexico to encourage other family members and friends to move to the United States. Despite the importance of Mexican immigrants to the economy of the Southwest, many faced discrimination and harsh labor conditions.

SECTION 4 REVIEW

Identify and explain the significance of the following:

- Carry Nation
- Woman's Christian Temperance Union
- Frances Willard
- Eighteenth Amendment
- National American Woman Suffrage Association
- Carrie Chapman Catt
- National Woman's Party
- Nineteenth Amendment
- Booker T. Washington

- Atlanta Compromise
- Ida B. Wells-Barnett
- W. E. B. Du Bois
- National Association for the Advancement of Colored People

Reading for Content Understanding

1 **Main Idea** In what ways did opportunities for women expand during the late 1800s and early 1900s?

2 **Main Idea** How did some women fight for suffrage?

3 **Cultural Diversity** How did some African Americans work to end racial injustice?

4 **Writing** *Informing* Write a short essay explaining the advances and shortcomings of the progressive movement for women and members of minority groups.

5 **Critical Thinking** *Making Comparisons* Compare and contrast the methods of Booker T. Washington and W. E. B. Du Bois.

The Progressive Presidents

Reading Focus

What were the major points of President Roosevelt's progressive policy?

Why did progressives turn against President Taft?

What reforms did Woodrow Wilson accomplish during his presidency?

Key Terms

arbitration	Sixteenth Amendment
Pure Food and Drug Act	Federal Reserve Act
conservation	Clayton Antitrust Act
Bull Moose Party	
Underwood Tariff Act	Federal Trade Commission

HE SUMMER TOUR *following President McKinley's second inauguration in 1901 was filled with friendly crowds eager to shake the president's hand. As McKinley greeted a group of well-wishers in Buffalo, New York, however, anarchist Leon Czolgosz pulled a pistol and shot the president at point-blank range. As he lay dying, the president whispered, "My wife, be careful how you tell her—oh be careful!" A little more than a week later, McKinley was dead.*

The Granger Collection, New York

President William McKinley and Vice President Theodore Roosevelt

★ President Theodore Roosevelt

After the assassination of President McKinley in 1901, Vice President Theodore Roosevelt took the oath of office. Unlike most of the Gilded Age presidents, who saw themselves more as administrators, Roosevelt believed the president should be an active leader. He quickly made his mark on the nation.

The Square Deal

Roosevelt believed that the interests of business, labor, and consumers should be balanced for the public good. He called this policy the Square Deal and demonstrated it in his response to a national coal miners' strike in 1902. He believed that the strike had "become a matter of vital concern to the whole nation," because it threatened to leave the country without heating fuel in the coming winter. Arguing that the president had a responsibility to become involved, Roosevelt brought the strikers and managers together for **arbitration**, a formal meeting to discuss and settle disagreements. To get both sides to agree to arbitration, Roosevelt threatened to have the federal government take over the mines. His actions broke with the tradition of presidential noninvolvement in labor disputes and helped labor to bargain with management. In 1903 he promised:

> 66 **The labor unions shall have a square deal, and the corporations shall have a square deal, and in addition all private citizens shall have a square deal.** 99

Roosevelt used the Square Deal as a slogan in his successful presidential campaign in 1904.

Regulation

President Roosevelt made regulating trusts the most important goal of his first administration. He later recalled, "The absolutely vital question was whether the government had power to control them at all." His belief was that it did. Roosevelt argued that there were "good" trusts, which benefited society, and "bad" trusts, which hurt the public.

The first bad trust that Roosevelt tackled was the Northern Securities Company, an enormous railroad corporation in the Northwest. In 1904 the Supreme Court narrowly upheld the Sherman Antitrust Act and decided in favor of the federal government in its suit against Northern Securities for illegal business practices. The Court's decision sent a warning to large corporations, outraging business leaders while pleasing the public.

Roosevelt's actions gained him a reputation as a trustbuster. Some Americans, however, feared this expansion of the federal government's powers and disapproved of the government's interference in the economic system.

In some cases, President Roosevelt was responding to public pressure. For example, Upton Sinclair's account of the horrors of the meat-processing industry in his 1906 novel, *The Jungle*, led to public outrage. Roosevelt responded by launching an investigation. His report concluded that

> 66 **the stockyards and packing houses are not kept even reasonably clean, and . . . the method of handling and preparing food products is uncleanly and dangerous to health.** 99

Although he was forced to settle for a compromise, Roosevelt persuaded Congress to pass a meat inspection law and the **Pure Food and Drug Act** in 1906. This act prohibited the manufacture, sale, or transportation of mislabeled or contaminated food and drugs sold in interstate commerce. Roosevelt also successfully promoted legislation regulating the railroads and their shipping rates. The public supported Roosevelt's expansion of the regulatory powers of the federal government, and his activism set a standard for later progressive presidents.

THE LION-TAMER

President Roosevelt taming businesses

★ Conservation

Roosevelt joined other progressives in what became known as the **conservation** movement, or the effort to preserve nature and its resources. His love of the outdoors made him the first president to consider conservation an important issue.

During the late 1800s many Americans became concerned that the country was using up all of its natural resources. For the first time, a vocal group of conservationists said that Americans needed to manage the use of these natural resources more efficiently. Gifford Pinchot, chief of forestry,

The Jungle
Upton Sinclair

In 1906 Upton Sinclair published The Jungle, *a muckraking account of the horrible working conditions and unsanitary practices in the Chicago meatpacking industry. The novel is noted for its graphic descriptions of meatpacking plants. In fact, after the novel was released, meat sales sharply declined, and there was popular support for pure food legislation. In the following excerpt from* The Jungle, *members of the Jurgis Rudkus family discuss conditions at one of the Chicago meat plants.*

The family had a first-hand knowledge of the great majority of Packingtown swindles. For it was the custom, as they found, whenever meat was so spoiled that it could not be used for anything else, either to can it or else to chop it up into sausage. . . .

Jonas had told them how the meat that was taken out of pickle [vinegar solution] would often be found sour, and how they would rub it up with soda to take away the smell, and sell it to be eaten on free-lunch counters; also of all the miracles of chemistry which they performed, giving to any sort of meat, fresh or salted, whole or chopped, any color and any flavor and any odor they chose. . . .

It was only when the whole ham was spoiled that it came into the department of Elzbieta. Cut up by the two-thousand-revolutions-a-minute fly-ers, and mixed with half a ton of other meat; no odor that ever was in a ham could make any difference. There was never the least attention paid to what was cut up for sausage; there would come all the way back from Europe old sausage that had been rejected . . . and [it was] made over again for home consumption [eating]. There would be

Upton Sinclair intended for his novel to focus attention on the problems facing immigrants. Instead, it resulted in major reforms in food industries.

meat that had tumbled out on the floor, in the dirt and sawdust, where the workers had tramped and spit uncounted billions of . . . germs. There would be meat stored in great piles in rooms; and the water from leaky roofs would drip over it, and thousands of rats would race about on it. . . . . This is no fairy story.

Understanding Literature

1. What happened to meat that was so spoiled that it could not be used for anything else?

2. What were workers' attitudes toward the meat that they handled?

3. Why do you think *The Jungle* shocked the American public into supporting new health laws?

Theodore Roosevelt

Theodore Roosevelt was born into a wealthy family in New York City in 1858. Despite his privileged upbringing, Roosevelt felt that his success came as a result of his hard work. As a boy, Roosevelt suffered from severe asthma and poor eyesight. "I was nervous and timid," Roosevelt remembered.

At the age of 11, he began improving his health through exercise and outdoor activities. His asthma got better, and he became a strong and confident young man. At the age of 55, he was still adventurous. As he explained about a trip to the jungles of Brazil, "I had just one more chance to be a boy, and I took it!"

argued that forests should not be preserved simply "because they are beautiful" but more importantly because they produced materials necessary to build "prosperous homes." Conservationists also fought to establish national and state parks to preserve lands for public use. Roosevelt said that parks could provide "rest, health, and recreation" for the American people.

By 1870, tens of millions of acres of federal lands had been sold or given to private mining, logging, and railroad companies. Such companies opposed efforts to conserve federal land. Nevertheless, during Roosevelt's administration nearly 150 million acres of public land were placed under the control of the forest service. Roosevelt doubled the number of national parks, created 16 national monuments, and established 51 wildlife refuges.

President Roosevelt meets with conservationist John Muir at Yosemite Valley, California, site of the first national park.

★ Taft Angers the Progressives

Theodore Roosevelt hoped that his secretary of war, William Howard Taft, would take his place as president in 1908. Taft agreed with Roosevelt in opposing socialism and supporting the regulation of corporations and railroads. Much of Taft's professional experience had been as a lawyer and judge, and he would have gladly accepted the position of chief justice of the Supreme Court had it been available. Instead, he followed a path toward the presidency.

Roosevelt helped Taft defeat William Jennings Bryan in the election of 1908. Despite their friendship, Taft and Roosevelt held different ideas about the role of the president. Taft thought that Roosevelt had claimed too much presidential power. Instead, Taft chose to pursue reforms and regulation more cautiously, which upset many progressives. He started twice as many antitrust suits as Roosevelt had, but some progressives such as Bryan and Robert La Follette wanted to destroy the trusts entirely. Roosevelt also argued that Taft should support stricter federal regulation of big businesses. Taft received further criticism from political opponents when he signed the Payne-Aldrich Tariff of 1909, which did not reduce tariffs to as low a level as many Americans wanted.

While he was president, Taft often felt misunderstood by the public but told his wife that "it is not the height of my ambition to be popular." Perhaps the greatest public relations disaster of Taft's administration occurred in his battle with

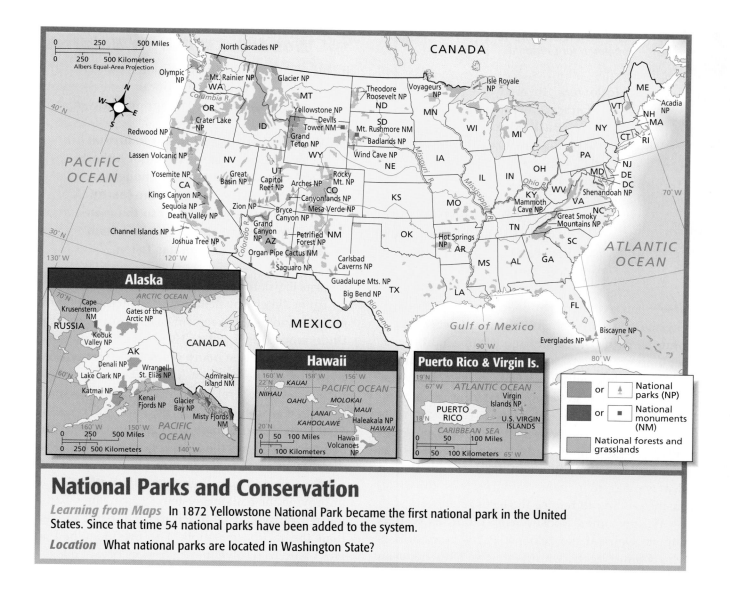

National Parks and Conservation

Learning from Maps In 1872 Yellowstone National Park became the first national park in the United States. Since that time 54 national parks have been added to the system.

Location What national parks are located in Washington State?

Roosevelt's close friend and ally Gifford Pinchot. In 1909 Pinchot accused Secretary of the Interior Richard Ballinger of endangering conservation efforts by siding with the interests of big business and by leasing public lands. Taft decided to fire Pinchot, which upset conservationists and many other progressives, including Roosevelt. Taft defended Ballinger, saying:

> **If I were to turn Ballinger out, in view of his innocence and in view of the conspiracy against him, I should be a white-livered skunk.** "

Taft was unable to win back progressive support, even though he had transferred more land into government reserves than Roosevelt had.

★ The Election of 1912

Disappointed in Taft's administration, Roosevelt told his oldest son in 1911 that the president "has not the slightest idea of what is necessary if this country is to make social and industrial progress." In August of the previous year, Roosevelt had proposed a new progressive plan, which he called the New Nationalism. This program called for a strong executive, more active regulation, and the enactment of more social welfare measures.

Stating that "the bulk of the people wanted a given job done, and . . . wanted me to do that job," Roosevelt decided to again run for president in 1912. He lost the Republican nomination to Taft, however, in a convention controlled by Taft supporters. In response, Roosevelt and his progressive

Items from Roosevelt's 1912 campaign for president

followers formed the Progressive Party. It became nicknamed the **Bull Moose Party** after Roosevelt told a crowd that he was "as strong as a bull moose." The party built its platform around Roosevelt's New Nationalism.

The Democratic Party's nominee for president was Woodrow Wilson. Wilson's reforms as governor of New Jersey had received national attention. Born in Virginia, Wilson earned a doctoral degree from Johns Hopkins University and became a professor. Beginning in 1902 he served as president of Princeton University until he accepted the nomination to become governor of New Jersey in 1910.

Wilson based his presidential campaign on a program called the New Freedom. This program called for government action against monopolies to ensure free competition in the economy. Wilson also wanted to expand opportunities for small businesses and to reduce the tariff rate.

Wilson joined Roosevelt and Taft, as well as Eugene Debs of the Socialist Party, as reformers who wanted to be president. The split between Taft and Roosevelt divided the Republican vote. Although Wilson did not receive a majority of the popular vote, he won the electoral vote by a wide margin and captured the presidency.

⭐ Woodrow Wilson's Reforms

In his inaugural address, Wilson pointed to the terrible social conditions under which many Americans—particularly immigrants—lived:

❝ **We have been proud of our industrial achievements, but we have not hitherto [yet] stopped thoughtfully enough to count the human cost, . . . the fearful physical and spiritual cost to the men and women and children upon whom the . . . burden of it all has fallen.** ❞

Reform legislation was Wilson's top priority, and he immediately pushed for two measures: tariff revision and banking reform. Wilson supported the **Underwood Tariff Act** of 1913, which brought the lowest tariff rates in many years. It also introduced a version of the modern income tax on personal earnings. The federal income tax had only recently become constitutional with the ratification of the **Sixteenth Amendment** in February 1913. This amendment allows the federal government to pass direct taxes, such as the income tax.

President Wilson then turned his attention to improving the banking system. Wilson knew banking reform would be much more difficult to pass than the tariff legislation. The president had to work hard to resolve the differences between legislators who wanted a centralized banking system and those who wanted a decentralized one. The result was a compromise called the **Federal Reserve Act**. Passed in December 1913, the act

Woodrow Wilson entered the presidency with many new ideas and goals for reform.

created a banking system called the Federal Reserve. This system is made up of 12 regional Federal Reserve banks as well as many privately owned banks. The Federal Reserve is overseen by an independent decision-making body that controls banking policy. The Federal Reserve gave the government an opportunity to try to minimize sudden changes between boom and bust in the economy.

President Wilson also pushed for legislation regulating big businesses. The **Clayton Antitrust Act** of 1914 strengthened federal laws against monopolies. Other reforms came through the establishment of the **Federal Trade Commission** in 1914. The commission investigated corporations and could issue restraining orders to prevent "unfair trade practices."

As the presidential race of 1916 approached, Wilson gave increased attention to the needs of farmers, businesspeople, and wage workers. He

President Wilson used antitrust laws to protect small businesses from greedy big businesses.

appointed Louis Brandeis, a progressive lawyer with a reputation for helping people, to the Supreme Court. Brandeis was the first Jewish person to become a Supreme Court justice. The president also helped pass the Keating-Owen Child Labor Act and a law requiring workers' compensation for federal employees. In addition, he supported the Adamson Act, which limited the workday on the nation's railroads to eight hours. Wilson's actions helped him win the people's support and the 1916 election.

President Wilson displayed great skill and determination in guiding his reform programs through Congress. Wilson told a friend in 1913 that legislators followed his lead because "I do know how to put my mind at the service of others for the accomplishment of a common purpose." Wilson's impressive legislative record helped put many progressive reforms into place in the early 1900s.

SECTION 5 REVIEW

Identify and explain the significance of the following:
- **Theodore Roosevelt**
- **arbitration**
- **Pure Food and Drug Act**
- **conservation**
- **William Howard Taft**
- **Bull Moose Party**
- **Woodrow Wilson**
- **Underwood Tariff Act**
- **Sixteenth Amendment**
- **Federal Reserve Act**
- **Clayton Antitrust Act**
- **Federal Trade Commission**
- **Louis Brandeis**

Reading for Content Understanding

1 **Main Idea** What actions did President Roosevelt take against large corporations and railroads?

2 **Main Idea** What reform programs did President Wilson guide through Congress?

3 **Geographic Diversity** *Human-Environment Interaction* Why did conservationists think that America's natural resources should be protected?

4 **Writing** *Persuading* Write one or two paragraphs explaining why some people became angry with President Taft's actions as president.

5 **Critical Thinking** *Synthesizing Information* Why might people have described Theodore Roosevelt as an "activist president"?

CHAPTER 23 REVIEW

Chapter Summary

The progressive movement was a time when many concerned Americans attempted to reform society. The progressives worked to reform such areas as politics, government, the workplace, public schools, and cities. Americans also tried to improve the lives of women, African Americans, American Indians, and other groups. ■

On a separate sheet of paper, complete the following activities.

Identifying People and Ideas

Describe the historical significance of the following:

1. political machines
2. John Dewey
3. Industrial Workers of the World
4. Frances Willard
5. Carrie Chapman Catt
6. Nineteenth Amendment
7. Atlanta Compromise
8. Booker T. Washington
9. Theodore Roosevelt
10. Underwood Tariff Act

go.hrw.com
SAO Federal Reserve

Internet Activity

Search the Internet through the HRW Web site to find information about how the Federal Reserve system works today. Use this information to create a graphic organizer that shows how the Federal Reserve system affects the economy.

Understanding Main Ideas

1. How did bosses use political machines to control local and city governments?
2. How did the Wisconsin Idea give voters more choice in selecting their candidates for public office?
3. What were working conditions like for child laborers and other factory workers in the late 1800s?
4. Why did some women form the Woman's Christian Temperance Union?
5. How did President Roosevelt respond to Upton Sinclair's novel *The Jungle*?
6. What reforms did President Wilson pass during his presidency?

Reviewing Themes

1. **Citizenship and Democracy** Why did women form the National American Woman Suffrage Association? How did Booker T. Washington and W. E. B. Du Bois differ in their approach to fighting for equal rights?

Using the Time Line

Number your paper from 1 to 5. Match the letters on the time line below with the following events.

1. **Grover Cleveland loses the presidency to Benjamin Harrison.**
2. **Susan Blow opens the nation's first public kindergarten in St. Louis, Missouri.**
3. **Leaders of the progressive movement form the National Association for the Advancement of Colored People.**
4. **The New York State Tenement Law outlaws the construction of dark and airless tenements.**
5. **The Pendleton Civil Service Act is passed, establishing a merit system under the control of the Civil Service Commission.**

1870   1880   1890   1900   1910

a   b   c   d   e

2. Constitutional Heritage   What was the significance of the ruling in *Lochner* v. *New York*? How did the Supreme Court's decision in *Muller* v. *Oregon* partially reverse its earlier ruling?

3. Economic Development   What was President Roosevelt's Square Deal? What actions did he take against large corporations and railroads?

Thinking Critically

1. Making Comparisons   How were progressives similar to and different from previous reformers?

2. Evaluating   Which of the progressive presidents do you think was the most successful in reforming American society? Explain your answer.

3. Identifying Cause and Effect   What effect did the growth of big business have on the United States's natural resources?

Building Your Portfolio

American History

Complete the following activities individually or in groups.

1. Muckrakers   If muckrakers were investigating problems in American society today, what do you think would be the top five problems they would address? Find newspaper and magazine articles and images on these topics. Use this information to create a bulletin-board display titled, "Reforming Society Today."

2. Theodore Roosevelt   Use your textbook or the library to find information about the life of Theodore Roosevelt. Focus on the following topics: Roosevelt the Conservationist, Roosevelt the Rancher, Roosevelt the Rough Rider, Roosevelt the Trust Buster, Roosevelt the Family Man, or Roosevelt the President. Use this information to write a biography about several aspects of Theodore Roosevelt's life. You should include some quotes by Roosevelt himself, as well as some quotes from other people talking about Roosevelt.

Writing About History

1. Informing   Imagine that you are writing a section of a history book that explores women's participation in the various reform efforts of the Progressive Era. Write a half-page feature on this topic.

2. Determining the Strength of an Argument Write a letter to Booker T. Washington telling him whether you agree with his Atlanta Compromise speech.

Linking Geography and History

1. Place   What problems did urban areas in the United States face that rural areas did not? What were some reasons for these differences?

2. Human-Environment Interaction   How did President Roosevelt try to protect the nation's environment?

History Skills Workshop

Using Primary Sources   In his book *How the Other Half Lives*, reformer Jacob Riis described the living conditions of many poor people. Read the excerpt below, which is Riis's description of a New York City tenement house, and answer the following questions: (a) What connection is Riis making between tenement houses and the child's illness? (b) Why do you think Riis chose this example to illustrate poor people's living conditions? (c) How do you think readers might have responded to these descriptions?

> 66 Suppose we look into [a tenement] on Cherry Street. . . . Here is a door. Listen! that short hacking cough, that tiny helpless cry—what do they mean? . . . The child is dying of measles. With half a chance it might have lived. But it had none. That dark bedroom killed it. 99

CHAPTER 24

America As a World Power

(1865–1914)

While campaigning for the Senate in 1898, Albert J. Beveridge declared, "If England can govern foreign lands, so can America." Previously the United States had expanded only across the North American continent. However, as the 1800s came to a close, many Americans began to look overseas for a source of new lands. Beveridge summed up this attitude by saying that "the ocean does not separate us from lands of our duty and desire."

THEMES

Geographic Diversity

Why might a nation attempt to expand its boundaries?

Economic Development

For what reasons might a nation want to increase international trade?

Global Relations

How might a nation's overseas territories bring it into conflict with another nation?

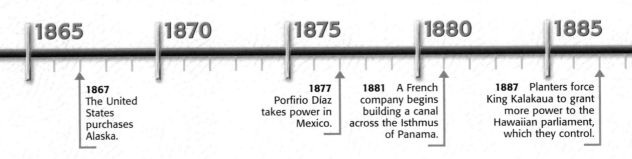

| 1865 | 1870 | 1875 | 1880 | 1885 |

1867 The United States purchases Alaska.

1877 Porfirio Díaz takes power in Mexico.

1881 A French company begins building a canal across the Isthmus of Panama.

1887 Planters force King Kalakaua to grant more power to the Hawaiian parliament, which they control.

The United States Gains Overseas Territories

Reading Focus

Why did some people favor expansion over isolationism?

What events led to the U.S. annexation of Hawaii?

What was the goal of U.S. foreign policy in Japan and China?

Key Terms

imperialism

isolationism

McKinley Tariff

subsidy

spheres of influence

Open Door Policy

Boxer Rebellion

ON THE MORNING OF MARCH 16, 1889, *the crews of one British, three German, and three U.S. warships prepared for a possible battle. At any moment the peace of Apia Harbor—a port in the Pacific island-nation of Samoa—might erupt with blasts of heavy guns. The United States, Germany, and Britain had each sent their ships to gain control of the Samoa Islands. Before the warships could do battle, however, a sudden typhoon swept into the harbor, destroying all the ships except the British vessel. Although the typhoon had prevented hostilities that day, it did not end Western nations' competition for territories around the world.*

Cartoon showing Europeans struggling for power over the Samoans

IMAGE ON LEFT PAGE: *Battle of Manila Bay during the Spanish-American War*

1890

1895

1900

1905

1910

1915

1890 Congress passes the McKinley Tariff.

1895 Cuba revolts against Spain.

1898 The USS *Maine* explodes and sinks.

1900 Hawaii becomes a U.S. territory.

1904 President Theodore Roosevelt presents his corollary to the Monroe Doctrine.

1910 The Mexican Revolution begins.

1914 The Panama Canal is opened.

Imperialism and Isolationism

Powerful Western nations were willing to risk war in such far-off places as Samoa to establish a naval base and to protect shipping routes in the Pacific. By the late 1800s the nations of Europe had become engaged in **imperialism**—the practice of extending a nation's power by gaining territories for a colonial empire. Between 1870 and 1914, Europeans built vast colonial empires, seizing control of most of Africa and much of Southeast Asia.

Several forces drove this wave of imperialism. Nations wanted new and plentiful sources of raw materials, such as copper, tin, and rubber, to maintain their industrial growth. At the same time, businesspeople needed new markets in which to sell their goods. Many people also saw colonies as a source of power and national pride.

The United States, however, had not built an overseas colonial empire like many European nations had. Americans were pursuing a limited policy of **isolationism**—avoiding involvement in the affairs of other nations. In his Farewell Address, President George Washington had advised the United States "to steer clear of permanent alliances" with other nations, particularly in Europe. U.S. leaders had tried to follow this advice by avoiding involvement in conflicts overseas.

Washington's advice had been fairly easy to follow partly because the United States enjoyed the security of a wide ocean separating it from Europe. Good relations with Britain meant that the powerful British navy stood between the United States and possible European enemies. Despite their support of isolationism, many Americans favored expanding the U.S. economy through foreign trade and building a strong military to protect U.S. interests.

Expansion

Many Americans thought that the United States needed to expand its lands to maintain its economic strength. One well-known supporter of expansion was Alfred T. Mahan. In his book *The Influence of Sea Power upon History*, Mahan argued that the United States needed a strong navy to protect its economic interests. Mahan also explained that a strong navy required overseas bases and coaling stations—places where steamships could take on coal for fuel. Senator Henry Cabot Lodge echoed the call for economic expansion through naval power. "Commerce follows the flag," Lodge declared, "and we should build up a navy strong enough to give protection to Americans in every quarter of the globe."

In 1867 the United States greatly expanded its territory when Secretary of State William Seward arranged the purchase of Alaska from Russia for $7.2 million, less than two cents per acre. People laughed at the purchase, calling it "Seward's Folly" and the "Alaskan Icebox." Despite such criticism, Alaska added some 600,000 square miles to the United States—an area more than twice the size of Texas. Alaska contained natural resources such as furs, timber, and mineral wealth. The 1896 Klondike Gold Rush in Canada's Yukon Territory brought many miners to the region. Around 1900, miners found gold in Alaska, bringing more settlers to the region.

Seward believed that the United States "must continue to move on westward," and in 1867 the nation annexed the Midway Islands. The islands' location, about halfway between the U.S. West

Uncle Sam begins to reap the harvest of imperialism.

Alaska's beautiful scenery and natural resources made it a valuable addition to the United States in the long run.

Coast and Japan, made Midway an excellent base and coaling station for the U.S. Navy. The United States also wanted the island group of Samoa for similar reasons, and in 1899 Germany and the United States agreed to divide the Samoa Islands. Britain, interested in territories elsewhere, had given up its part of Samoa to Germany.

 ## Hawaii

Even more appealing than Samoa were the Hawaiian Islands. The Hawaiian people had first come in contact with Europeans in 1778, when British explorer Captain James Cook arrived in the islands.

Economic Interests

Soon after Cook's arrival, Pacific trading and whaling ships from the United States and other countries began stopping in Hawaii for supplies. After the sailors' arrival, American missionaries came to convert the Hawaiians to Christianity. Many of these missionaries remained in the islands, establishing businesses and raising crops such as sugarcane. Some missionary families eventually became wealthy sugar planters.

In 1795 Chief Kamehameha (kuh-may-uh-MAY-huh) had created a monarchy that united Hawaii's eight major islands. In 1839 Hawaii adopted written laws and a constitution based on U.S. and British models.

By the 1840s some 80 percent of the ships arriving in Hawaii were American owned, as were most shops, warehouses, and shipyards. By this time, sugar had become a leading export of the Hawaiian economy. Thousands of workers, particularly Chinese and Japanese, arrived to work on the sugar plantations. An 1875 treaty allowed Hawaiian sugar to be shipped duty-free to the United States. In exchange, Hawaii agreed not to grant territory or special privileges to any nation other than the United States. Hawaiian sugar production boomed, and the planters' influence grew. In 1887 they forced King Kalakaua (kah-LAH-KAH-ooh-ah) to sign a new constitution granting more power to the Hawaiian parliament, which the planters controlled. Many Hawaiians worried that foreigners were becoming too powerful.

Political Control

Sugar planters in Hawaii suffered a severe economic setback when Congress passed the **McKinley Tariff** in 1890. This law allowed all countries to ship sugar duty-free to the United

Pineapple plantations like this one were among the most profitable businesses on the Hawaiian Islands.

Queen Liliuokalani

Liliuokalani was born in Honolulu in 1838 and was educated by American missionaries. In 1887 she traveled across the United States and visited with President Grover Cleveland in Washington.

Liliuokalani became queen in 1891. After the revolt that ended her reign, Liliuokalani continued to work to reclaim her throne. In her autobiography, *Hawaii's Story*, she wrote "that the United States could become a successful rival of the European nations in the race for conquest, and could create a vast military and naval power." She asked, "But is such an ambition laudable [admirable]?" Until her death in 1917 Liliuokalani served as a symbol of Hawaiian pride and a link to the islands' history.

States but gave U.S. sugar producers a **subsidy**, or bonus payment, of two cents per pound. Prices for Hawaiian sugar dropped, and the islands' economy collapsed.

In 1893 Queen Liliuokalani (li-lee-uh-woh-kuh-LAHN-ee), who had taken the throne in 1891, announced a new constitution that returned power to the monarchy. The planters revolted. John L. Stevens, U.S. ambassador to Hawaii, called 150 marines ashore to support the revolt. The revolt succeeded without any shots being fired. The planters established a new government with lawyer Sanford B. Dole as president. Acting without authority from the state department, Stevens recognized the new government and declared Hawaii to be under U.S. control on February 1, 1893. He wrote to the U.S. State Department that "the Hawaiian pear is now fully ripe, and this is the golden hour for the United States to pluck it." On a U.S. speaking tour at the time, Liliuokalani's 17-year-old niece, Princess Kaiulani, asked Americans to oppose annexation:

> " I am strong . . . in the strength of seventy million people who in this free land will hear my cry, and will refuse to let their flag . . . dishonor . . . mine. "

President Grover Cleveland disapproved of the revolt and refused to annex Hawaii. However, he took little effective action to help restore the monarchy. The islands remained an independent republic until July 7, 1898, when Congress annexed the islands. Hawaii became a U.S. territory in 1900 and the 50th state in 1959.

★ The Opening of Japan

By the mid-1800s some European powers had established strong trade ties to much of East Asia—with the notable exception of Japan. The island-nation of Japan had isolated itself from the rest of the world for centuries. In the 1500s Japan was ruled by several competing family groups, some led by warrior-lords called shoguns. After an extended period of civil war, the leader of the Tokugawa family unified the country.

Suspicious of outsiders, the Tokugawa shoguns had expelled all westerners in the early 1600s. Only the Dutch East India Company was allowed to trade, and only at one port. The Tokugawa had also forbidden travel abroad.

Perry in Japan

The United States looked upon Japan as a trade market it could open before Europeans got there. The *Democratic Review* expressed the feelings of many Americans when it wrote that "the opening of commerce with Japan is demanded by reason, civilization, progress and religion." Eager to overcome Japan's isolationism, President Millard Fillmore sent Commodore Matthew Perry to secure "friendship, commerce, a supply of coal and provisions."

On July 8, 1853, an astonished Japanese crowd watched a fleet of four U.S. warships move into Edo (now called Tokyo) Harbor. Perry delivered a letter from President Fillmore suggesting a peaceful trade relationship. Perry's fleet then sailed off, and he returned in February 1854 with seven warships. To show some of the technological gains that trade with the United States would offer, Perry presented Japanese leaders with gifts of a telegraph transmitter and a model train. However, it was mostly the U.S. show of force that persuaded Japanese leaders to sign a treaty opening trade with the United States. Many Japanese leaders also pushed for trade because they believed that their country needed to industrialize.

In 1856 Townsend Harris arrived in Japan as the first U.S. consul general, or chief diplomat. His instructions were to secure a treaty that would open Japan to further trade. This was difficult because, as Harris wrote, "the absence of a man-of-war [warship] . . . tends to weaken my influence with the Japanese." He eventually overcame Japanese opposition and in 1858 negotiated a commercial treaty.

Japan Expands

In 1868, supporters of industrialization came to power in Japan and began a period of modernization known as the Meiji [MAY-jee] Restoration. Over the next 40 years, Japanese leaders invested heavily in industry and in strengthening the nation's military. The government sent Japanese students to Western schools to learn about modern science and technology and Western government. One such student, Yukichi Fukuzawa, realized

❝ **what policy Japan must take to preserve herself among the powers of the**

Global Connections

Japanese Immigrants in Hawaii

Japanese immigrants began arriving in Hawaii in the 1860s but did not immigrate in large numbers until the late 1800s. By 1923 they made up almost 43 percent of the population. They came to meet the labor needs of the islands' many sugar plantations and to find a better life with more opportunities.

Many Japanese were recruited and signed labor contracts to work on the plantations. Life on the plantations was difficult. The workday began at sunrise and ended at sundown. The working conditions were harsh, as workers planted, weeded, fertilized, watered, harvested, and hauled the sugarcane.

Many Japanese immigrants remained in Hawaii once their contracts expired because

Japanese fieldworkers in Hawaii

they could not afford to return to Japan. Some, believing there was a potential market for Japanese products, started their own businesses, such as importing food, clothing, and hardware.

Today people of Japanese descent make up about one fourth of Hawaii's population. They live on all the major islands and work in all occupations, including government, law, and education.

Understanding What You Read

1. Describe the working conditions on Hawaii's sugar plantations.

2. How have Japanese immigrants contributed to Hawaiian society?

world. . . . The final purpose of all my work was to create in Japan a civilized nation as well equipped in the arts of war and peace as those of the Western world.**"**

By the end of the century, Japan was emerging as a major imperial power. Japan's invasion and defeat of China in 1894-95 gave the Japanese the same trade privileges in China as European nations had.

Japan dealt a similar blow to Russia. In 1904 the Japanese attacked Russian forces stationed in China. The Japanese won early victories over the Russians in the Russo-Japanese War. Japan sank an entire Russian fleet in a single battle. In 1905 U.S. president Theodore Roosevelt helped negotiate a peace treaty to end the war. Japan had won the respect it desired and had gained Korea, as well as a lease on Port Arthur in China, and other rights. In less than 50 years Japan had gone from an isolated nonindustrial country to a major world power. Hilary Herbert, U.S. secretary of the navy, said that "Japan has leaped, almost at one bound, to a place among the great nations of the earth."

Asian goods like this fan were popular trade items.

⭐ Foreign Powers in China

Economic interests drew the United States not only to Hawaii and Japan but also to China. There the United States and many European nations engaged in a profitable trade.

Spheres of Influence

Japan's 1894 invasion of China with a modern, well-equipped army had resulted in a swift and surprisingly easy victory. In its defeat, China granted Japan trade privileges, formally accepted Japan's control of Korea, and surrendered Taiwan and other territories.

Other nations quickly took advantage of China's weakness to seize **spheres of influence**—areas where foreign nations control trade and natural resources. Many nations joined in what was called "the carving up of the Chinese melon." Germany took control of a harbor in Shandong Province in November 1897. Other nations followed suit—Russia in the north, Great Britain on the coast opposite Hong Kong Island, and France and Japan in the southern provinces.

The Open Door

The United States feared that it would be closed out of Chinese markets. Some of President William McKinley's advisers called for a U.S.

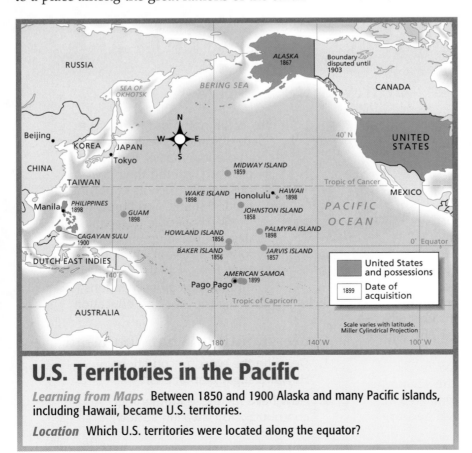

U.S. Territories in the Pacific

Learning from Maps Between 1850 and 1900 Alaska and many Pacific islands, including Hawaii, became U.S. territories.

Location Which U.S. territories were located along the equator?

sphere of influence, but the nation lacked the naval power to accomplish this. Instead, the United States turned to diplomacy.

In 1899 Secretary of State John Hay sent a series of notes to Japan and most European nations outlining what became known as the **Open Door Policy**—that all nations should have equal access to trade with China. The goal of this policy was to protect U.S. trade interests. Japan and the European powers neither accepted nor rejected the Open Door Policy. Hay took advantage of this situation to announce that the policy had been accepted.

Participants in the Boxer Rebellion

The Boxer Rebellion

Within China, there was strong resentment of the power and control held by foreign nations. In 1900 this antiforeign hostility boiled over, producing the **Boxer Rebellion**. The Boxers were Chinese nationalists who were members of the "Fists of Righteous Harmony." The Boxers were angered by foreign involvement in Chinese affairs, mismanagement by the Chinese government, and the hunger and homelessness caused by a series of natural disasters.

In June 1900 the Boxers took to the streets of Beijing, China's capital, and murdered two foreign diplomats. They then laid siege to the walled settlement in which foreigners lived, killing more than 200 people. Knowing the attack was doomed,

the Chinese government did not support the Boxers.

The siege continued for two months until military forces including U.S. Marines fought their way from the port of Tianjin to Beijing. The Boxers were soon defeated. Afterward, China was forced to accept a harsh settlement that included a $333 million cash payment, $25 million of which went to the United States. Secretary of State Hay then sent another Open Door note to Japan and the European nations, restating the U.S. position that all nations should have equal access to Chinese markets. Hay wanted to prevent any European colonization of China that would limit U.S. influence there. The Open Door Policy remained in effect long after the Boxer Rebellion.

SECTION 1 REVIEW

Identify and explain the significance of the following:

- **imperialism**
- **isolationism**
- **William Seward**
- **McKinley Tariff**
- **subsidy**
- **Liliuokalani**
- **Matthew Perry**
- **spheres of influence**
- **Open Door Policy**
- **Boxer Rebellion**

Reading for Content Understanding

1 **Main Idea** What arguments did people make for isolationism and for expansion in the 1800s?

2 **Main Idea** How did Hawaii become a part of the United States?

3 **Global Relations** What did U.S. leaders hope to accomplish in relations with Japan and China?

4 **Writing** *Persuading* Imagine that you are a member of Congress at the time William Seward proposes the purchase of Alaska from Russia. Write a short speech you might give to Congress, explaining why you are voting for or against the proposed purchase.

5 **Critical Thinking** *Making Comparisons* How were China's and Japan's reactions to foreign trade similar? How were they different?

The Spanish-American War

Reading Focus

How did the press affect U.S. involvement in the conflict in Cuba?

What enabled the United States to win the war with Spain?

How did the Spanish-American War affect the Philippines, Cuba, and Puerto Rico?

Key Terms

yellow journalism
Teller Amendment
Anti-Imperialist League
Platt Amendment

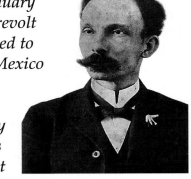

José Martí

OSÉ MARTÍ WAS BORN *in Havana, Cuba, on January 28, 1853. At the age of 15, Martí joined in a revolt against Cuba's Spanish rulers. For his actions, Martí was banished to Spain, where he earned a university degree. He later worked in Mexico as a journalist and in Guatemala as a teacher. Martí returned to Cuba in 1878 but was banished again for his actions. This time, he moved to New York City, where he continued to work tirelessly for Cuban independence. While anxiously watching events in his homeland, Martí waited for the day when he could return to fight the Spanish once again.*

 ## Revolts Against Spain

In the late 1800s only Cuba and Puerto Rico remained of Spain's once-great American empire. In 1868, Cubans revolted, beginning a decade-long struggle for freedom. Spain eventually regained control and forced many members of the Cuban independence movement, like José Martí, to leave the country.

After the revolt, U.S. trade with Cuba grew, and the United States invested some $50 million in Cuba, mostly in sugar and mining. However, in 1894 the Wilson-Gorman Tariff removed Cuban sugar from the list of duty-free products. This made Cuban sugar more expensive in the United States and harmed the Cuban economy.

The next year, Cuba erupted in revolt again, further damaging its trade with the United States. Martí returned to Cuba to fight the Spanish but was killed soon after. He quickly became a Cuban hero. Spain decided to crack down harshly on Cuba, and sent General Valeriano Weyler to crush the rebellion. Because many civilians supported the rebels, Weyler gathered several hundred thousand Cubans into barbed-wire camps, called *reconcentrados*, or reconcentration camps. He reasoned that anyone not in the camps was a rebel. More than 100,000 Cubans died in the camps because of bad and inadequate food and lack of sanitation. Weyler's harsh measures led many Americans to support the rebels.

The Road to War

Many Americans sympathized with the rebels, believing that the Cubans' struggle for liberation was similar to that of the United States in 1776. The conflict was widely reported, even exaggerated, in the American press, further increasing support for the Cubans.

The Press

Two newspapers—Joseph Pulitzer's New York *World* and William Randolph Hearst's *New York Journal*—were particularly critical of the Spanish. Their harsh words and stories were part of a competition between Pulitzer and Hearst to sell the most newspapers. This use of sensational, often exaggerated stories to attract readers is known as **yellow journalism.**

Pulitzer was the first to engage in yellow journalism, but Hearst soon outdid Pulitzer at his own game. Describing General Weyler as "pitiless, cold, an exterminator of men," the *New York Journal* went so far as to create the stories that Hearst wanted. To increase support for U.S. action in Cuba and to sell papers, Hearst hired artist and illustrator Frederic Remington to provide pictures of the conditions on the island. Remington supposedly telegraphed Hearst from Cuba, saying, "Everything is quiet. There is no trouble here. There will be no war." Hearst is said to have replied, "You furnish the pictures and I'll furnish the war."

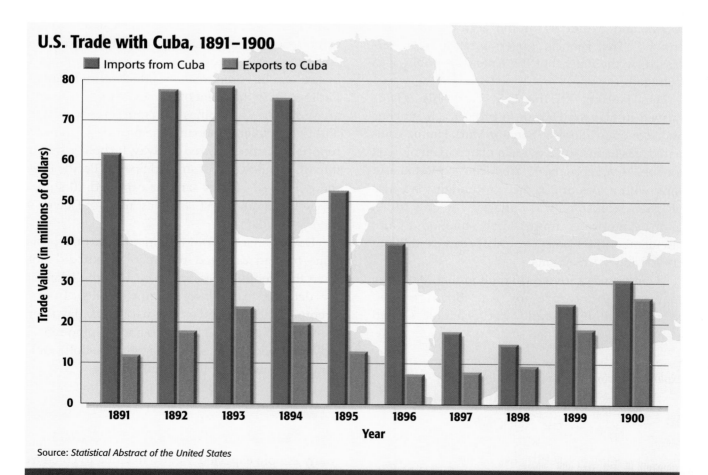

U.S. Trade with Cuba, 1891–1900

Source: *Statistical Abstract of the United States*

The Value of Trade The United States's valuable trade with Cuba was a factor in the decision to go to war with Spain. What was the value of imports from Cuba in 1896?

Political Pressure

Despite growing support for military action, President Cleveland remained strongly opposed to involvement in Cuba. In 1896, however, William McKinley, who supported Cuban independence, was elected president.

Growing international protest over the treatment of Cubans led the Spanish government to recall General Weyler in October 1897. Attempting to end the rebellion, Spain offered to grant Cubans autonomy—self-government without independence. However, Cuban rebels were committed to independence and refused the offer.

"Remember the *Maine*"

Several events soon made the *Journal*'s stories of war come true. On February 9, 1898, Hearst published a letter that Dupuy de Lôme, the Spanish minister to the United States, had written to a friend. In it, Lôme called President McKinley "weak and a bidder for the admiration of the crowd." The Spanish government was embarrassed by the letter, but the American public was outraged.

On January 25 the U.S. battleship *Maine* arrived in Havana Harbor to protect U.S. citizens and economic interests. Senator Mark Hanna compared this action to "waving a match in an oil well for fun." On February 15 the *Maine* exploded and sank with a loss of 260 men. Although the cause of the explosion was unclear at the time, many Americans immediately blamed Spain. "Remember the *Maine*!" quickly became a rallying cry for angry Americans.

Congress approved $50 million that McKinley requested to prepare for war. Spain offered to negotiate but would not consider Cuban independence. Even though Cuba was not a U.S. territory, on April 20 Congress issued a resolution that declared Cuba independent. That same resolution also gave Spain three days to leave the island. Attached to the resolution was the **Teller Amendment**, which declared that the United States had no intention of taking over Cuba. In response to the U.S. resolution, Spain declared war on April 24. The next day, Congress passed and McKinley signed a declaration of war.

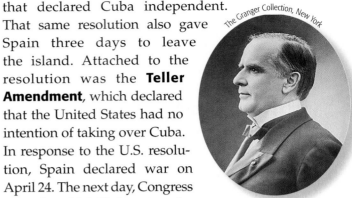
The Granger Collection, New York

President William McKinley

⭐ Fighting in the Pacific

While attention was focused on Cuba, the U.S. Navy won a quick and spectacular victory nearly halfway around the world in the Pacific Ocean. Commodore George Dewey, commander of the American Asiatic squadron at Hong Kong, had orders to be prepared to attack the Spanish Philippines in the event of war. On April 30 Dewey arrived at the Philippines with four large warships and two smaller gunboats. The next day, ignoring reports that mines barred his way, he boldly sailed into Manila Bay and destroyed Spain's Pacific fleet there. Dewey's forces sank or captured 10 ships. While the Spanish lost 381 lives, none of Dewey's men were killed.

Dewey's victory put him in an awkward position—he had defeated the Spanish but did not have the troops necessary to occupy the islands. He decided to wait for reinforcements. Troops eventually arrived and on August 13, one day after the war had ended, U.S. troops and Filipino rebels led by Emilio Aguinaldo (ahg-ee-NAHL-doh) took control of the Philippine capital, Manila.

⭐ The War in the Caribbean

Many people expected victory in Cuba to come as quickly as it had in the Philippines. However, training and supplying thousands of volunteer troops took longer than getting the navy under way.

The New York Journal *announces the explosion aboard the* Maine.

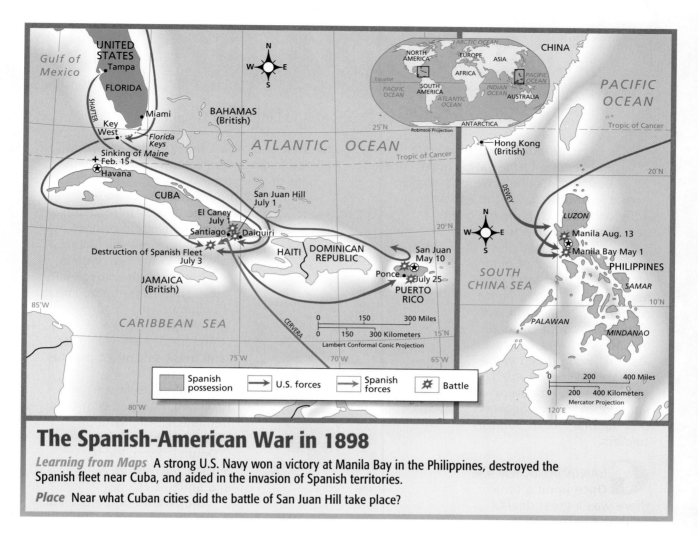

The Spanish-American War in 1898

Learning from Maps A strong U.S. Navy won a victory at Manila Bay in the Philippines, destroyed the Spanish fleet near Cuba, and aided in the invasion of Spanish territories.

Place Near what Cuban cities did the battle of San Juan Hill take place?

The Soldiers

At the start of the war, only about 28,000 soldiers were serving in the regular U.S. Army. The army was unprepared to train and supply the more than 280,000 soldiers who would see active duty. There were shortages of bullets and rifles, and soldiers received warm woolen uniforms to wear in the tropical heat. Once in Cuba, many soldiers were struck by deadly diseases such as yellow fever. For food the army purchased canned meat that one general called "embalmed beef." Of the few thousand U.S. forces who died during the war, only a small percentage died in battle. The rest died from food poisoning, disease, and other causes.

The most colorful group of soldiers in the war were the Rough Riders, the First Volunteer Cavalry commanded by General Leonard Wood. Second in command was Lieutenant Colonel Theodore Roosevelt. Anxious to join the fighting, Roosevelt organized a group of volunteers to fight in Cuba. The Rough Riders came from many walks of life. They included college athletes, miners, American Indians, ranchers, and cowboys.

Newspaper accounts of Roosevelt's charm and the Rough Riders' heroic achievements in battle earned the group the admiration of the American public. Many other U.S. soldiers also served bravely. Four privates of the African American 10th Cavalry rowed through heavy gunfire to rescue 15 members of a U.S. landing party. All four received the Congressional Medal of Honor for their actions.

The Battles

On June 1, 1898, U.S. ships caught the Spanish Caribbean fleet in the harbor of Santiago de Cuba. The more numerous and powerful U.S. Navy blockaded the harbor and made it safe for U.S. troops to land nearby. Set ashore on June 22 and

The War Dispatches of Stephen Crane

Although most people know Stephen Crane for his novel The Red Badge of Courage, *he also worked as a journalist during the Spanish-American War. Only in his twenties, Crane was already such a popular reporter that his editors made a point of putting his name in their front-page headlines to attract more readers. The following war dispatch, "Night Attacks on the Marines and a Brave Rescue," was printed in the* New York World *on July 16, 1898. It is an account of fighting in Cuba between U.S. Marines and Spanish soldiers.*

Stephen Crane
The Granger Collection, New York

GUANTANAMO, July 4.—Once upon a time there was a great deal of fighting between the marines and the guerrillas [Spanish soldiers] here, and during that space things occurred.

The night attacks were heart-breaking affairs, from which the men emerged in the morning exhausted to a final degree, like people who had been swimming for miles. From colonel to smallest trumpeter went a great thrill when the dawn broke slowly in the eastern sky, and the weary band quite cheerfully ate breakfast. . . . Afterward the men slept, sunk upon the ground in an abandon [physical exhaustion] that was almost a stupor [daze].

Lieut. Neville, with his picket [forward group] of about twenty men, was entirely cut off from camp one night, and another night Neville's picket and the picket of Lieut. Shaw were cut off, fighting hard in the thickets [forests]

for their lives. At the break of day the beleaguered [surrounded] camp could hear still the rifles of their lost pickets.

The problem of rescue added anxiety to the already tremendous anxiety of the fine old colonel. . . . The guerrillas were still lurking [sneaking] in the near woods, and it was unsafe enough in camp without venturing into the bush.

Volunteers from Company C were called for, and these seventeen privates volunteered:

Boniface, Conway, Fitzgerald, Heilner, Harmson, Hemerle, Lewin, Mann, Mills, Monahan, Nolan, O'Donnell, Ryan, Riddle, Sinclair, Sullivan, W. A., and Smith, J. H.

They went out under Lieut. Lucas. They arrived in Neville's vicinity just as he and his men, together with Shaw and his men, were being finally surrounded at close range. Lucas and his seventeen men broke through the guerrillas and saved the pickets, and the whole body then fell back to Crest Hill. That is all there is to it.

Understanding Literature

1. How did the soldiers feel after the night attacks?

2. How did Lieutenant Lucas and his men save the pickets?

3. Why do you think the American soldiers from Company C volunteered to help in the rescue of the pickets that were cut off from camp?

4. What effect do you think this war dispatch had on readers in the United States?

aided by Cuban rebels, the U.S. troops moved to capture the hills around the main Spanish forces at Santiago. At the village of El Caney on July 1, some 7,000 U.S. soldiers overwhelmed about 600 Spanish defenders. The main U.S. force under General Hamilton Hawkins then attacked and captured San Juan Hill. A smaller force, including the Rough Riders and the African American 9th and 10th Cavalries, captured nearby Kettle Hill. A journalist on the scene described their charge:

> **It was a miracle of self-sacrifice, a triumph of bulldog courage. . . . The fire of the Spanish riflemen . . . doubled and trebled [tripled] in fierceness, the crests of the hills crackled and burst in amazed roars and rippled with waves of tiny flame. But the blue line [of U.S. soldiers] crept steadily up and on.**

On July 3 the U.S. artillery was within range of the Spanish fleet, so the Spanish commander decided to try breaking through the U.S. blockade. Every Spanish ship was destroyed in the battle, with 474 Spaniards killed and 1,750 others captured. American forces suffered only two casualties. Santiago surrendered on July 17. A few days later, U.S. troops commanded by Nelson Miles invaded Puerto Rico, where they met little resistance. Puerto Rico soon surrendered. Spain asked for peace and signed a cease-fire on August 12, 1898.

 The Peace Treaty

The peace treaty between Spain and the United States placed Puerto Rico, Guam, Cuba, and the Philippines under U.S. control. Groups like the **Anti-Imperialist League**, made up of Americans who opposed the treaty, accused the United States of building a colonial empire. Despite such protests, the treaty was ratified by a vote of 57 to 27, one vote more than the two-thirds majority needed.

The Philippines

Spain surrendered the Philippines in return for a $20 million payment from the United States. Many Americans wondered why the United States

The Rough Riders and the 9th and 10th Cavalries fight to help secure Santiago.

wanted the islands. Some believed that it would be wrong to annex the islands without the consent of the Filipinos. Other people agreed with President McKinley, who said that the United States would benefit from the islands' naval and commercial value, and that annexing the islands would keep Europeans from seizing them.

Filipino rebels, however, had helped U.S. forces capture Manila, and expected to gain their independence after the war. When the United States decided to keep the islands, the rebels began a guerrilla war against the U.S. forces. Some 70,000 U.S. soldiers fought in the Philippines, and hundreds of thousands of Filipinos died, before the war ended more than three years later in 1902.

On July 1, 1902, the U.S. Congress passed the Philippine Government Act. This act provided that the Philippines would be ruled by an appointed governor and a two-house legislature, the lower house of which was elected. In 1946 the United States granted full independence to the Philippines.

Cuba

Although the Teller Amendment had stated that the United States would not annex Cuba, President McKinley established a military government there. McKinley wanted to create stability and increase U.S. trade and influence in the region. He appointed General Leonard Wood as governor, and Wood quickly began building schools and a sanitation system. To combat disease, Dr. Walter

Reed, head of the Army Yellow Fever Commission, was sent to Cuba in 1900. He and his volunteers proved that yellow fever was transmitted by mosquitoes. Getting rid of standing water reduced the mosquito population, which in turn helped health officials to effectively control the disease.

Wood also oversaw the drafting of a Cuban constitution, which also included the **Platt Amendment**. The amendment limited Cuba's right to make treaties, required Cuba to sell or lease land to the United States for naval stations, and authorized the United States to intervene in Cuban affairs. Cuban leaders compared this to

After the United States acquired Puerto Rico, the government built many new schools.

> ❝**handing over the keys to our house so that they [the Americans] can enter it at any time, whenever the desire seizes them, day or night, whether with good or evil design [intentions].**❞

The Cubans reluctantly accepted the Platt Amendment, and U.S. troops withdrew. The amendment remained in force until 1934.

Puerto Rico

Like Cuba, Puerto Rico had hoped for independence after the war. Instead, the U.S. government made the island a territory like the Philippines. On April 12, 1900, the Foraker Act established a civil government that was headed by a governor and included a two-house legislature.

A debate soon arose over the citizenship status of the people of the new territories. Residents of Puerto Rico were considered citizens of the island but not of the United States. In 1917 the Jones Act granted Puerto Ricans U.S. citizenship and made both houses of the legislature elective. However, another 30 years passed before Puerto Ricans could elect their own governor. In 1952 Puerto Rico became a commonwealth. This unique status means that the island has its own constitution and elected officials. As with the 50 states, Puerto Rico can change its constitution as long as it does not conflict with that of the United States.

SECTION 2 REVIEW

Identify and explain the significance of the following:
- **José Martí**
- **Joseph Pulitzer**
- **William Randolph Hearst**
- **yellow journalism**
- **Teller Amendment**
- **Emilio Aguinaldo**
- **Theodore Roosevelt**
- **Anti-Imperialist League**
- **Platt Amendment**

Reading for Content Understanding

1 **Main Idea** How did the American press influence relations between the United States and Spain?

2 **Main Idea** What led to U.S. victory in the Spanish-American War?

3 **Global Relations** How did the war affect the Philippines, Cuba, and Puerto Rico?

4 **Writing** *Expressing* Imagine that you are a soldier during the Spanish-American War. Write a journal entry describing the war and the dangers you face.

5 **Critical Thinking** *Supporting a Point of View* If you had been a U.S. diplomat in Cuba in the 1890s, would you have supported going to war? Explain your answer.

SECTION 3

The United States and Latin America

Reading Focus

What steps did the United States take to build a canal across Panama?

How did U.S. involvement in Latin America change under President Theodore Roosevelt?

How did Presidents Taft and Wilson enforce the Monroe Doctrine?

Key Terms

Hay-Herrán Treaty
Hay–Bunau-Varilla Treaty
Panama Canal
Roosevelt Corollary
dollar diplomacy

$\mathcal{W}$HEN THE SPANISH-AMERICAN WAR *began in 1898 the U.S. battleship* Oregon *was stationed at Puget Sound in Washington State. After receiving its orders, the* Oregon *set out at breakneck speed on a 12,000-mile voyage around the southern tip of South America to join the fighting in Cuba. Newspapers charted the* Oregon's *daily progress while the American public "breathlessly pushed her along." The trip lasted from March 19 to May 24, 1898—67 days!*

The USS Oregon

 The Panama Canal

Despite the best efforts of the *Oregon*'s crew, the ship barely arrived in time to take part in the major battle around Cuba. The delay concerned many people. The United States needed to be able to transfer naval forces between the Caribbean and the Pacific quickly. However, travel around the southern tip of South America took weeks.

Spanish explorer Vasco Núñez de Balboa had crossed the narrow Central American Isthmus of Panama in the early 1500s. Since then, many people

had dreamed of building a canal there to link the Pacific and Atlantic Oceans. In the late 1800s some U.S. leaders began to explore ways to dig a canal across the narrow neck of Central America. Such a canal would cut 8,000 miles off the voyage and join the Atlantic and Pacific naval fleets.

Negotiations

In 1850 the United States and Great Britain had signed the Clayton-Bulwer Treaty, which called for a partnership to build and maintain a canal,

America As a World Power **749**

although nothing was actually built. In 1881 a French company headed by Ferdinand de Lesseps, who had engineered the Suez Canal in Egypt, began work. After spending nearly $300 million and losing some 20,000 lives, the company went bankrupt in 1887. At that time, less than one third of the planned 51-mile canal had been dug.

No one was a stronger supporter of a Central American canal than Theodore Roosevelt, who had become president in 1901 after the assassination of William McKinley. Influenced by the ideas of Alfred Mahan, Roosevelt believed that naval power was essential to U.S. strength and security. Earlier, Roosevelt had written to Mahan, "I believe we should build the [Central American] canal at once, and, in the meantime, . . . we should build a dozen new battleships." In 1901 Secretary of State John Hay completed negotiations with the British for the Hay-Pauncefote Treaty, which replaced the Clayton-Bulwer Treaty. Britain surrendered its interest in building and operating a Central American canal in exchange for a U.S. agreement to keep the canal open to all vessels at all times.

With this agreement settled, Secretary Hay began negotiating with Colombia, because the Isthmus of Panama was part of that country. Hay and Colombian minister Thomas Herrán soon reached an agreement. The United States would pay $10 million plus $250,000 a year for a 99-year lease on a five-mile-wide strip of land across the Isthmus.

This cartoon shows President Theodore Roosevelt digging the canal he wanted and throwing dirt on Colombia.

The Granger Collection, New York

The U.S. Senate ratified the **Hay-Herrán Treaty** in March 1903, but the Colombian senate rejected it in hopes of better terms. The French company's rights would expire in October 1904, and the Colombian government hoped to negotiate for $40 million that the United States would pay to the French. Roosevelt, however, wanted to avoid paying any more money to Colombia. He considered other ways of gaining the Isthmus of Panama, such as seizing it by force.

A New Nation

Phillipe Bunau-Varilla, chief engineer with the French Canal Company, stepped in with an alternative. He informed Roosevelt that a revolution was brewing in the Colombian province of Panama. In fact, Bunau-Varilla was helping to organize the revolt. He learned that the warship USS *Nashville* would arrive at Colón, Panama, on November 2, 1903. The next day an army of 500 Panamanian soldiers plus members of the local fire department launched a revolt.

Colombian forces were unable to reach the province to put down the rebellion. Dense jungle blocked overland routes, and the U.S. ship blocked the sea lanes. The United States formally accepted the new Panamanian government almost immediately. On November 13, though still a French citizen, Bunau-Varilla arrived in Washington as the Panamanian minister to the United States. He met with the Roosevelt administration and five days later signed the **Hay–Bunau-Varilla Treaty**. The terms of this treaty were identical to the Hay-Herrán Treaty, except that the canal zone was widened to 10 miles. The United States was finally ready to build the canal.

Building the Canal

Building the canal proved to be very difficult. The first obstacle to overcome was tropical disease, particularly yellow fever, which had been a serious problem for the earlier French effort. The canal route ran about 51 miles through dense jungles and swamps that were home to many mosquitoes. Having helped Dr. Walter Reed combat disease in Cuba, Dr. William C. Gorgas organized a vast effort to rid the canal route of the mosquitoes that

The building of the Panama Canal was very difficult and took many years to complete.

The Granger Collection, New York

carried malaria and yellow fever. Without his success in slowing down these deadly diseases, digging the canal would have been much more costly.

Although the danger of disease was reduced, the construction work also posed a risk to the workers. Much of the canal had to be blasted out of solid rock. On one occasion, lightning struck a 12-ton explosive charge, setting it off prematurely. Seven workers were killed. In several other incidents, workers died when their shovels struck the cap of an unexploded charge. One West Indian worker recalled, "The flesh of men flew in the air like birds many days."

Another challenging obstacle was the high mountain range of central Panama. The solution was to cut out a narrow, eight-mile-long channel—later known as the Gaillard Cut—through solid rock. Under the direction of chief engineers John Stevens and George W. Goethals, dozens of steam shovels were used in the attempt to cut mountains in half.

In total, some 6,000 lives were lost building the **Panama Canal**, which finally opened to traffic on August 15, 1914. The cost was $367 million on top of the nearly $300 million spent in the failed French effort. In the end, however, the world had its "highway between the oceans."

★ Roosevelt and Latin America

With the building of the Panama Canal, the United States had increased its involvement in Latin America. In 1823 President James Monroe had announced the United States's interest in the region when he had warned European nations not to colonize or otherwise interfere in Central or South America. In what became known as the Monroe Doctrine, he had declared that "the American continents . . . are henceforth not to be considered as subjects for future colonization by any European powers."

This doctrine became a defining principle of U.S. foreign policy. At the time it was declared, however, the United States lacked the military power to enforce the policy. Fortunately for the United States, it had also lacked the need to do so. President Monroe's administration had relied on Britain's large navy as well as British interest in keeping the area free of other European powers to enforce the Monroe Doctrine. This situation changed as the United States grew stronger and expanded its influence, particularly after the Spanish-American War.

U.S. officials gather near the Panama Canal.

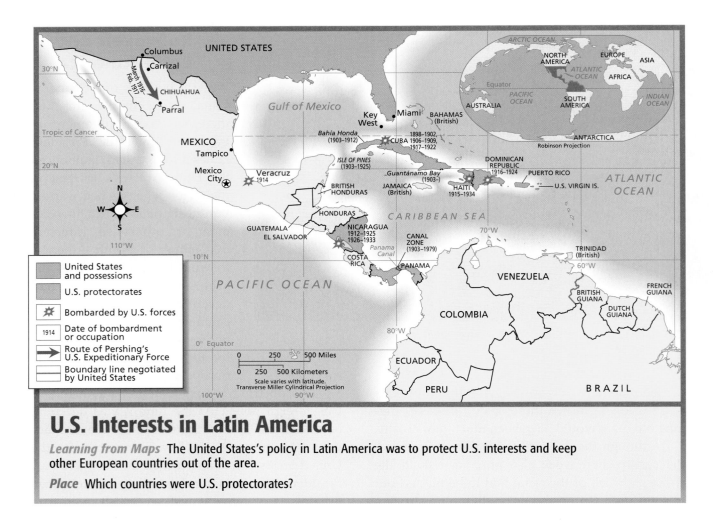

U.S. Interests in Latin America

Learning from Maps The United States's policy in Latin America was to protect U.S. interests and keep other European countries out of the area.

Place Which countries were U.S. protectorates?

A Larger Role

During the late 1800s European banks had invested in, and made loans to, a number of Latin American countries. When some of these nations had difficulty repaying their loans, European nations used force to collect their debts. Venezuela, under the rule of dictator Cipriano Castro, fell deeply in debt to German and British investors. In 1902 the Venezuelan government refused to repay these debts or to have the claims settled by a neutral third party.

European leaders were concerned about the Monroe Doctrine, but President Roosevelt had declared in 1901 that the United States did "not guarantee any State against punishment if it misconducts itself." The only condition Roosevelt set was "that punishment does not take the form of acquisition [taking] of territory by any non-American power." The European nations interpreted this to mean that they could use force to collect their debts. Britain and Germany sent ships

to blockade Venezuela. The Venezuelan dictator then asked Roosevelt to propose having the matter settled by a third party, which the Europeans accepted.

A similar situation developed in the Caribbean nation of the Dominican Republic in 1904. Again, European nations considered using force to collect their debts. This time Roosevelt worried that the foreign forces might not leave afterward. The presence of European forces in the Caribbean would not only have violated the Monroe Doctrine, it could have threatened U.S. control of both the region and the Panama Canal.

The Roosevelt Corollary

President Roosevelt realized that if the United States kept European creditors from collecting their debts, U.S. officials would be obliged to intervene. They would have to force the debtor nations to pay, using military power if necessary. In December 1904

Roosevelt outlined his thinking in what is known as the **Roosevelt Corollary** to the Monroe Doctrine, saying:

❝ **Chronic wrongdoing . . . may in America, as elsewhere, ultimately require intervention [involvement] by some civilized nation, and in the Western Hemisphere the adherence [observance] of the United States to the Monroe Doctrine may force the United States, however reluctantly [unwillingly], in flagrant [strong] cases of such wrongdoing, . . . to the exercise of an international police power.** ❞

This role of the United States as the Western Hemisphere's "police officer" suited Roosevelt's style. He had summed up his ideas in 1900 when he said, "I have always been fond of the West African proverb: 'Speak softly and carry a big stick, you will go far.'" Roosevelt actively enforced the corollary throughout the rest of his presidency.

★ Dollar Diplomacy

When William Howard Taft became president in 1909, he also acted to protect U.S. interests in Latin America. However, instead of Roosevelt's "big-stick" approach of using military force, Taft used a policy known as **dollar diplomacy**, which emphasized using U.S. economic power and business investment to influence Latin American governments. Taft believed he could influence events, encourage stability, and keep European nations out of the region by expanding American businesses there. He explained that dollar diplomacy

❝ **has been characterized as substituting dollars for bullets. It is . . . directed to the increase of American trade . . . [and] the substitution of arbitration and reason for war in the settlement of international disputes.** ❞

Taft supported American businesses overseas and tried to replace European investments in Latin America with U.S. investments. In an agreement signed in June 1911 the United States declared that it would help Nicaragua secure private loans from American banks to pay its national debt. In exchange, Nicaraguan officials gave the United States the right to send troops into their country if U.S. leaders felt it necessary. The United States also signed a similar agreement with Honduras.

Although the U.S. Senate rejected both agreements, the Taft administration informally observed their terms. In July Nicaragua failed to repay a large loan from British investors. Secretary of State Chase Knox helped secure a $1.5 billion loan for Nicaragua from American bankers. In exchange, the bankers received control of the National Bank of Nicaragua and the government-owned railway. Local dissatisfaction over this arrangement soon led to a revolt in Nicaragua. Taft sent in U.S. Marines to protect American interests. The marines remained until 1925, returned the next year, and finally left in 1933.

★ Wilson's Foreign Policies

President Woodrow Wilson, who took office in 1913, rejected the dollar diplomacy of the Taft administration. Wilson disapproved of the role of big business in foreign affairs and said he would not support any "special group or interests." Instead, he sought to protect U.S. interests in Latin America by encouraging the growth of democracy there. He believed the United States had a moral obligation to promote democracy in Latin America.

The Granger Collection, New York

This cartoon shows how President Taft became entangled in many difficult problems, including foreign affairs.

The New York *World* responded to Wilson's policy by writing, "There is . . . not a word [here] to stir the greed of a dictator." Although Wilson opposed imperialist ideas, he sent more troops into Latin America than any president before him in an attempt to bring democracy to the region.

For example, the Caribbean nation of Haiti had long been in financial disorder. The country also suffered a series of political revolutions that threatened people's lives and safety. In 1915 Haitian president Guillaume Sam ordered 167 political prisoners executed. As a result, he was overthrown and assassinated in another revolt. Previously, both Germany and France had temporarily sent troops to Haiti to protect their interests. President Wilson feared that those countries might now try to seize control of Haiti. On July 29, 1915, U.S. Marines landed in Haiti and quickly restored order. The United States took control of collecting customs taxes—to pay Haiti's debts—and installed a new government there.

Similar events occurred in the Dominican Republic. The customs arrangements established by President Roosevelt in 1905 had brought peace and stability to this nation. In 1911, however, political chaos returned when its president was

These U.S. Marines were among the many that President Wilson sent to restore order in Haiti.

assassinated. By threatening to withhold customs revenue, Secretary of State Knox had forced the Dominican Republic to accept a U.S.-supported government.

In 1913 William Jennings Bryan, the new secretary of state, was appointed to oversee the Dominican Republic's finances. In 1916 the Dominican president opposed the appointment of a new financial adviser. Fearing renewed political unrest, President Wilson declared martial law on the island and established a government run by the U.S. Navy. Wilson, like Roosevelt and Taft before him, refused to let internal political unrest threaten U.S. interests in Latin America.

SECTION 3 REVIEW

Identify and explain the significance of the following:

- **Hay-Herrán Treaty**
- **Phillipe Bunau-Varilla**
- **Hay–Bunau-Varilla Treaty**
- **William C. Gorgas**
- **Panama Canal**
- **Roosevelt Corollary**
- **dollar diplomacy**

Reading for Content Understanding

1 Main Idea What was President Theodore Roosevelt's foreign policy in Latin America?

2 Main Idea How were the foreign policies of Presidents Taft and Wilson similar to and different from that of Roosevelt?

3 Technology and Society Describe the steps that led to the completion of the Panama Canal.

4 Writing *Describing* Imagine that you are a worker helping to build the Panama Canal. Write a letter home to your family, describing the difficulties you have encountered during your time in Panama.

5 Critical Thinking *Determining the Strength of an Argument* Do you agree with President Roosevelt that the United States should serve as an international police officer of the Western Hemisphere? Explain your answer.

The United States and Mexico

Reading Focus

Why did the Mexican people revolt against their government in 1911?

Why did President Woodrow Wilson intervene in the Mexican Revolution?

Why did Mexican immigration to the United States increase in the early 1900s?

Key Terms

Mexican Revolution
ABC Powers

*I*N 1910 MEXICO CELEBRATED *the 100th anniversary of Father Miguel Hidalgo's call for revolution,* known as the Grito de Dolores. *Mexican president Porfirio Díaz treated guests from around the world to entertainment and fine food and toasted Mexico's successful revolt against Spain. Another Mexican leader, Francisco Madero, celebrated the* Grito *in a different way, however. He published* a *pamphlet demanding that Díaz resign and calling for free elections. When Díaz refused the demand, Madero began another revolution.*

The Granger Collection, New York

Porfirio Díaz

 The Mexican Revolution

For 34 years, from 1877 to 1911, Porfirio Díaz ruled Mexico. During that time he eagerly welcomed foreign investment. The United States became the biggest investor in Mexico, and by 1913 had invested more than $1 billion in Mexican land, mining, oil, railways, and manufacturing. At the same time, more than 500,000 U.S. citizens lived and worked in Mexico. To open Mexico to foreign investors, however, Díaz had ruled the Mexican people harshly. He imprisoned his opponents and rewarded his supporters. The country's leaders

may have been getting rich, but the people were not. Most of Mexico's 15 million people were landless and living in poverty.

The people found a leader in democratic reformer Francisco Madero, who began the **Mexican Revolution**. After Díaz won re-election in a corrupt campaign in 1910, Madero led a military campaign that captured Ciudad Juárez. Gradually, Madero won support throughout the country and forced Díaz to resign in May. Madero was elected president soon after. The Taft administration quickly recognized, or gave formal approval to, Madero's government.

These women were among the many people who fought in the Mexican Revolution.

Madero wanted to create a democratic government, but he was not as good a president as he had been a revolutionary. A struggle for power continued in Mexico. After revolts and street fighting in Mexico City, General Victoriano Huerta assumed power and had Madero killed in February 1913.

Woodrow Wilson, who was about to take office as the U.S. president, was angered by this violence and refused to recognize the new Mexican government. Wilson defended this action by saying:

> ❝We hold, as I am sure all thoughtful leaders of republican government everywhere hold, that just government rests upon the consent of the governed.❞

Huerta failed to immediately secure his power. When an uprising led by Venustiano Carranza began gathering force, Wilson saw an opportunity. He proposed that the two sides cease fighting and agree to a free election. If they agreed, Wilson said he would help the elected Mexican government secure loans from U.S. banks. However, Wilson insisted that Huerta could not be a candidate in the election because he had seized power by force. Not surprisingly, Huerta refused.

Wilson responded by lifting the arms embargo on Mexico so that weapons could be supplied to the forces opposing Huerta. Wilson also stationed U.S. warships near Veracruz, Mexico, in an attempt to keep Huerta from gaining any outside support. Despite Wilson's

efforts, Huerta continued to strengthen his power. On October 10 Huerta dissolved the Mexican congress, and later that month he was elected president.

★ Struggles for Power

In addition to Carranza's supporters, two other major revolutionary groups—led by Francisco "Pancho" Villa in the north and Emiliano Zapata in the south—were trying to overthrow Huerta. All three of these leaders had fought on Madero's side against Díaz. Zapata was a champion of agricultural reform and a hero to the poor of Mexico. He had broken away from Madero in 1911 when Madero failed to return lands taken from farmers.

Villa had spent much of his early life as a ranch hand, and was known as an excellent horseman. After Madero's assassination Villa had organized a military force called the *División del Norte.* The group operated from the borderlands region of northern Mexico, supporting Carranza's effort to overthrow Huerta. Like Zapata, Pancho Villa was a leader of Mexico's poor.

When the Mexican Revolution began, Venustiano Carranza was governor of the Mexican state of Coahuila. He supported Madero against Díaz, and when Huerta gained power, Carranza fought against him. The relationship between

Pancho Villa (left) and Emiliano Zapata (right) led poor revolutionaries against Victoriano Huerta's government.

Carranza, Villa, and Zapata was best described by the saying "The enemy of my enemy is my friend." They all wanted to overthrow Huerta. However, as rivals each also wanted to be the one to replace him.

 ## The United States Reacts

President Wilson adopted a policy of "watchful waiting" toward Mexico. He strongly disapproved of Huerta and looked for an opportunity to act.

Pressure to Intervene in Mexico

Many American business leaders wanted Huerta out of office immediately, fearing that they would lose all of their financial investments in Mexico. Americans with businesses there had already lost large sums of money, and every day of not recognizing Mexico cost them more. Wilson answered demands for sending American troops to Mexico, by saying that the United States "will never again seek one additional foot of territory by conquest."

The public pressure to intervene continued to grow, however. Many members of Congress demanded military action. Even foreign leaders questioned Wilson's hesitation. The German emperor reflected the opinion of many people, particularly business leaders, when he said, "Morality [is] all right, but what about dividends [profits]?"

The press at home and abroad strongly criticized Wilson's policy toward Mexico. Wilson, however, refused to be swayed by such attacks. He told his secretary,

> ❝I have to pause and remind myself that I am President of the United States and not of a small group of Americans with vested interests [investments] in Mexico.❞

While these criticisms continued, President Wilson continued his policy of watchful waiting.

Tampico

In 1914 an incident occurred that gave Wilson the opportunity for which he had been waiting. The

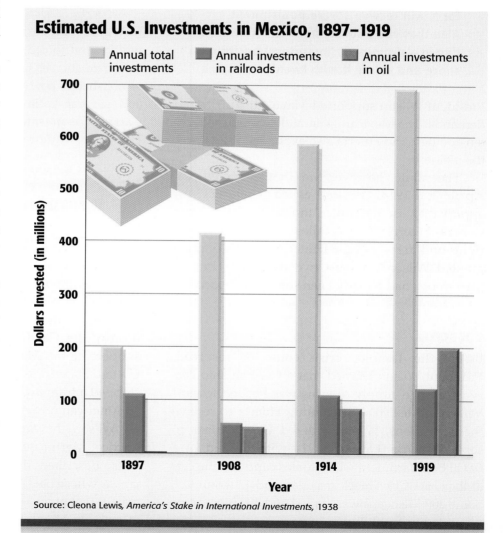

Estimated U.S. Investments in Mexico, 1897–1919

Source: Cleona Lewis, *America's Stake in International Investments*, 1938

Investment Concerns The disorder of the Mexican Revolution gave many Americans concern about money they had invested in Mexico's economy. In which category—railroads or oil—had U.S. investment increased the most by 1919?

U.S. ship *Dolphin* was patrolling in Mexican waters. A group of its sailors went ashore for supplies at Tampico, Mexico, which was under military rule. When the sailors accidentally entered a restricted area, Huerta's troops arrested them.

The sailors were soon released, and the local commander apologized to Admiral Mayo, who was commanding the American fleet. Mayo, however, was not satisfied and without authorization, wrote to the Mexican general in charge of Tampico:

These U.S. Marines served at Veracruz.

> **❝ I must require that you send me . . . [an] apology for the act, together with your assurance that the officer responsible for it will receive severe punishment. Also that you publicly hoist the American flag in a prominent [important] position on shore and salute it with twenty-one guns. ❞**

President Wilson supported Mayo's unauthorized demands. The Mexican general delivered the written apology, and Huerta also expressed regret over the incident.

The salute, however, was not delivered. On April 20, 1914, Wilson asked Congress for approval to use the armed forces "to obtain from General Huerta . . . the fullest recognition of the rights and dignity of the United States." Congress granted Wilson's request two days later, but by then troops had already been sent into Mexico.

Veracruz

Before the Tampico crisis could be resolved, President Wilson learned that a German ship carrying a large supply of arms was headed toward Veracruz, Mexico. Not wanting Huerta to receive these weapons, Wilson ordered U.S. Marines to seize Veracruz. On April 21—with the aid of a naval bombardment—U.S. forces captured the city at the cost of 19 Americans dead and 47 wounded. Some 200 Mexicans were killed and 300 more were wounded in the fighting.

The assault united Mexicans against the United States. Huerta broke off diplomatic relations, and the two nations stood on the brink of war. Then the **ABC Powers**—Argentina, Brazil, and Chile—stepped in and offered to settle the dispute. Wilson gladly accepted their offer.

Huerta rejected the proposed settlement. However, his position of power was declining, which soon forced him to leave office. In August, Carranza and his forces occupied Mexico City and established a new government. The United States and several Latin American nations recognized Carranza as president of Mexico. In November the U.S. troops withdrew from Veracruz.

⭐ Pursuing Pancho Villa

Despite Huerta's overthrow, Pancho Villa and Emiliano Zapata continued their revolt against Carranza's rule. Violence soon spread across the border. Although the United States recognized Carranza as president, in 1916 Villa tried to force U.S. intervention. At the same time he hoped to destroy the Carranza government and win the support of the Mexican people by attacking the United States. In January, Villa and his troops stopped a train at Santa Ysabel, Mexico, and killed 18 American mining engineers on board.

Wilson, however, did not send troops into Mexico. Martín Luis Guzmán, who fought under Villa, described the revolutionary leader as "a jaguar whose back we stroke with trembling hand, fearful that at any moment a paw might strike out at us." On March 9, 1916, the "jaguar" struck, as Villa and his troops attacked Columbus, New Mexico, burning the town and killing 17 U.S. citizens. U.S. Army units stationed at Columbus drove the raiders back into Mexico.

In response, Wilson sent General John J. Pershing and 15,000 soldiers into Mexico. Pershing's forces chased Villa more than 300 miles but failed to capture him. Mexicans greatly resented having U.S. troops in their country. President Wilson eventually agreed to Carranza's repeated demands for withdrawal and recalled the troops.

Wilson still hoped to avoid war. Carranza continued his fight against Villa and strengthened his hold on power. In 1917 Carranza approved a liberal constitution to bring orderly government to Mexico. However, in 1920 he was overthrown and killed by the forces of Álvaro Obregón, one of his former generals.

General John J. Pershing led the failed effort to capture Pancho Villa.

★ Consequences of the Mexican Revolution

The Mexican Revolution resulted in a large-scale Mexican migration to the United States. The disorder of the revolutionary years led many Mexicans to flee the violence and destruction of the war. Others fled to escape political persecution. These immigrants included upper- and middle-class refugees, as well as farmers and urban poor. Mexicans were also drawn to the United States by increasing numbers of industrial jobs.

Between 1905 and 1909 more than 28,000 Mexicans migrated to the United States. The next five years saw the arrival of about three times that number. In 1910 more than 250,000 Mexican immigrants were living in the United States. Between 1910 and 1920 close to 240,000 additional Mexicans immigrated as the revolution continued. Over the years, economic and political motivation has continued to draw Mexican immigrants to the United States.

SECTION 4 REVIEW

Identify and explain the significance of the following:
- **Porfirio Díaz**
- **Francisco Madero**
- **Mexican Revolution**
- **Victoriano Huerta**
- **Venustiano Carranza**
- **Francisco "Pancho" Villa**
- **Emiliano Zapata**
- **ABC Powers**
- **John J. Pershing**

Reading for Content Understanding

1 **Main Idea** Why did Francisco Madero begin the Mexican Revolution?

2 **Main Idea** For what reasons did the United States become involved in the Mexican Revolution?

3 **Cultural Diversity** Why did Mexican immigration to the United States increase during and after the Mexican Revolution?

4 **Writing** *Informing* Write an article that might have appeared in a Mexican newspaper in 1920 about the life of Pancho Villa and the role he played in the Mexican Revolution.

5 **Critical Thinking** *Identifying Cause and Effect* Why might the revolution in Mexico have made U.S. businesspeople uneasy?

CHAPTER 24 REVIEW

Chapter Summary

As the United States's economy grew, so did the desire to secure new foreign markets for its products. In the late 1800s the United States purchased Alaska from Russia, annexed the islands of Hawaii, and tried to open markets in Asia. Victory in the Spanish-American War gave the United States additional territories. Afterward, the United States became increasingly involved in events in Latin America, including the revolution in Mexico.

On a separate sheet of paper, complete the following activities.

Identifying People and Ideas

Describe the historical significance of the following:

1. imperialism
2. Liliuokalani
3. Boxer Rebellion
4. José Martí
5. Teller Amendment
6. Platt Amendment
7. Roosevelt Corollary
8. Francisco Madero
9. ABC Powers
10. John J. Pershing

Internet Activity

go.hrw.com
SAO Panama Canal

Search the Internet through the HRW Web site to find information about the operation of the Panama Canal. Use the information to create a drawing that shows how ships pass through the canal. Be sure to provide a caption with your drawing.

Understanding Main Ideas

1. What did Secretary of State John Hay call for in the Open Door Policy?
2. How did the press help spark U.S. involvement in the conflict in Cuba?
3. How did the outcome of the Spanish-American War affect the United States, Spain, and Cuba?
4. Explain the steps that the United States took to build and control the Panama Canal.
5. Why did President Wilson refuse to recognize General Huerta's government in Mexico?
6. Why did President Wilson order U.S. troops into Mexico?

Reviewing Themes

1. **Geographic Diversity** Why did the United States want control of Pacific islands?
2. **Economic Development** What steps did the United States take to expand trade with China and Japan?

Using the Time Line

Number your paper from 1 to 5. Match the letters on the time line below with the following events.

1. Secretary of State William Seward negotiates the purchase of Alaska from Russia.
2. Revolution breaks out in Mexico.
3. Congress passes the McKinley Tariff, allowing all countries to ship sugar duty-free to the United States.
4. The USS *Maine* explodes and sinks, killing some 260 people.
5. Despite most Hawaiians' opposition to losing their independence, Hawaii becomes a U.S. territory.

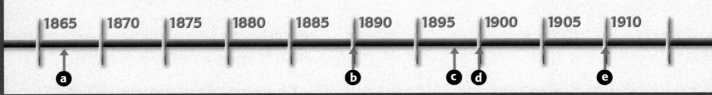

1865	1870	1875	1880	1885	1890	1895	1900	1905	1910

a   b   c d   e

3. **Global Relations** Why did the United States defend Cuba against Spain?

Thinking Critically

1. **Supporting a Point of View** Do you think the United States had good reasons for purchasing Alaska? Explain your answer.
2. **Synthesizing Information** Why did many Americans support gaining more overseas territory?
3. **Identifying Cause and Effect** What effect did the Mexican Revolution have on the people of Mexico?

Writing About History

1. **Creating** Imagine that you are a member of the Anti-Imperialist League. Create a pamphlet that explains your group's position and tell why people should join your organization.
2. **Informing** Imagine that you are a journalist covering the Mexican Revolution. Write a half-page news story explaining the events leading to the revolution, as well as the United States's involvement, and the revolution's outcome.

Linking Geography and History

1. **Human-Environment Interaction** What obstacles stood in the way of building a canal across Panama?
2. **Location** Why did the United States want to acquire the Philippines?

History Skills Workshop

Using Visual Resources Study the image to the right, which is a 1904 cartoon by Joseph Keppler. In this cartoon an American eagle stretches all the way from the United States to the Philippines. What message do you think Keppler was trying to get across to the viewer? Do you agree with his message? Explain your answer.

Building Your Portfolio

Complete the following activities individually or in groups.

1. **Latin America** Choose one of the following Latin American nations: Argentina, Cuba, the Dominican Republic, Haiti, Mexico, Nicaragua, Panama, or Venezuela. Present a short report in class on the country's historical and present-day relationship with the United States. Your report should include appropriate images and a map of the country.

2. **Yellow Journalism** Select an event you have studied recently in class or one that is in the news. Then write two half-page newspaper articles, with headlines, on that topic. One article should report the facts in an unbiased manner, and the other should be written in the style of yellow journalism. Finally, share your news articles with the class. Have the class vote on the article that they think best represents the style of yellow journalism.

The Granger Collection, New York

History Skills

WORKSHOP

Writing a Paragraph

A paragraph is a group of sentences that express an idea. Some paragraphs are bigger than others, and some have more parts than others. Have you ever noticed that some paragraphs can be very short—even a single word or sentence—and that other paragraphs go on and on?

Parts of a Paragraph Paragraphs almost always have a *main idea,* the big picture in the paragraph. The *topic sentence* states the main idea of the paragraph. You may find it at the beginning of the paragraph, in the middle, or even at the end. *Supporting sentences* give details that explain or prove the main idea.

Writing with a Purpose Always keep your purpose for writing in mind as you write your paragraph. That purpose might be to evaluate, to persuade, or to inform. Each different purpose for writing requires its own form, tone, and content.

How to Write a Paragraph

Most writing assignments will have specific directions about what and how to write. The guidelines outlined below can help you plan and improve your writing.

1. **Identify your purpose in writing** Read the directions carefully to identify the intended goal of the assignment.
2. **Collect information** Think and plan before you begin writing your paragraph. Do research if necessary. Your paragraph will be more effective if you have plenty of details at hand.
3. **Create unity and coherence** A paragraph has *unity* when all of the sentences support, or tell something about, the main idea. A

paragraph has *coherence* when readers can tell how and why ideas are connected.

4. **Use good sentence structure** All of your sentences should begin with a capital letter and end with a period, a question mark, or an exclamation point. Avoid sentence fragments (incomplete sentences) and run-on sentences (two or more complete thoughts that run together as if they were one complete thought).

   Example:
   Good: **Sofia's favorite dance is the merengue.**

   Fragment: **The dance, which Sofia learned from her parents.**

   Run-On: **Sofia's favorite dance is the merengue, she learned it from her parents.**

5. **Write a first draft and evaluate it** Your paragraph should express a single main idea or set of related ideas, with details for support. Make sure your sentences support your topic sentence.
6. **Write your final version** Revise and reorganize your draft as needed. Improve sentences by adding appropriate adjectives and adverbs. Check for proper spelling, grammar, and punctuation. Prepare a neat, clean final version.

Practicing the Skill

Follow the steps above to write a paragraph on one of the following topics:

1. a book you have read lately
2. a movie you have seen recently
3. the newest trend in clothes

History in Action

American History

Muckraker Magazine

Complete the following activity in small, cooperative groups.

Imagine that you are a journalist working for the fictitious news publication *Muckraker Magazine* during the early 1900s. Your editor has asked you to prepare a special investigative issue examining the problems and reforms of the Progressive Era. Five teams of reporters will work to put this special issue together. Each team will create one section of the magazine that focuses on a specific topic.

Materials To complete this activity, you will need posterboard, construction paper, or typing paper. You may wish to write your article on a computer. In addition, you will need markers, pens, pencils, and glue, tape, or rubber cement.

Parts of the Project To create your magazine, complete the following tasks:

1. **Planning and Writing** You will work on one of the following topics: urban living conditions; working conditions; politics and government; monopolies, trusts, and big business; and social reform. Meet as a group and decide on the articles to include in your section of the magazine. Then decide who will research and write each article. Remember to keep the articles objective. Journalists are responsible for presenting unbiased facts.

Students prepare their school newspaper.

2. **Editing** When you have completed your article(s), pair off with another member of your group and exchange articles. Edit your partner's article(s) and offer constructive comments. Revise your own article(s) and prepare a final typed draft.

3. **Designing** Meet in your group to plan the design and layout for your magazine section. Decide how to organize the articles, and discuss images, charts, and maps that you might use to improve the layout.

4. **Laying out the Magazine** Next, decide who will be news editors and who will be photographers. News editors will begin laying out the magazine and writing headlines while photographers are selecting or creating images and writing captions. When these tasks have been completed, paste your section together and combine it with other groups' sections to make a complete issue of *Muckraker Magazine*.

Elect someone in the class to design the cover and table of contents for the entire magazine. Display the finished magazine in your classroom or in another area of your school.

▪ E P I L O G U E ▪
Modern America
(1914–Present)

World War I was a global conflict that lasted for four long years, cost millions of lives, and caused massive destruction in Europe. Red Cross worker Florence Harriman remembered the day the war finally ended. "It seemed," she said, "as if everything in the world were possible, and everything was new." This attitude about the future characterized much of the new century.

THEMES

Global Relations
Why might a neutral nation decide to enter an international conflict?

Citizenship and Democracy
What strategies might citizens employ to gain their civil rights?

Economic Development
How might countries work together to encourage economic development?

1910   **1920**   **1930**   **1940**   **1950**

1914 Austrian archduke Franz Ferdinand and his wife are assassinated.

1925 John T. Scopes is arrested for teaching the theory of evolution.

1935 The Works Progress Administration is created.

1944 The Allies launch the D-Day invasion of France.

1949 The North Atlantic Treaty Organization (NATO) is founded.

World War I and the 1920s

Reading Focus

What led to the outbreak of World War I, and what was the war's outcome?

What problems and cultural changes did the United States face after the war?

How did differing ideals among Americans lead to conflicts in the 1920s?

Key Terms

militarism

Selective Service Act

armistice

Treaty of Versailles

Communists

Red Scare

prohibition

Twenty-first Amendment

Jazz Age

Harlem Renaissance

Lost Generation

ON JUNE 28, 1914, *Archduke Franz Ferdinand—heir to the throne of Austria-Hungary—and his wife, Sophie, were visiting Sarajevo, a city in Bosnia. Despite the efforts of the Serbian government to annex the area, Austria-Hungary had annexed Bosnia in 1908, leaving many Serbs in Sarajevo upset. As Ferdinand and Sophie rode through Sarajevo, a Serb assassin stepped out and killed the couple. This incident sparked a war that soon spread throughout the world.*

Soldier and horse wearing gas masks

IMAGE ON LEFT PAGE: *The American space shuttle* Atlantis *docking with the Russian space station* Mir

1960   **1970**   **1980**   **1990**

1954 The U.S. Supreme Court declares segregated schools unconstitutional in *Brown* v. *Board of Education.*

1961 The Berlin Wall is built.

1968 The Tet Offensive is launched.

1979 President Carter negotiates the Camp David Accords.

1987 The Intermediate-Range Nuclear Forces Treaty is signed.

1995 A federal office building in Oklahoma City is bombed, killing 168 people.

Europe at War

World War I resulted from years of growing tensions in Europe. Many European countries were on the brink of war by the early 1900s. Excessive nationalism—a feeling of pride in one's nation, language, or culture above all others—threatened stability in Europe. For example, hostilities between Serbia and Austria-Hungary over control in the Balkan region grew so intense that the area was like a powder keg ready to explode.

Countries came into conflict as they attempted to expand their borders. Many nations wanted to acquire overseas territories as well as to expand their control in Europe. Because of these rivalries, some countries began to adopt a policy of aggressive military preparedness. The countries built up their armed forces and developed new weapons. This policy, along with the belief that military force is a good solution to international problems, is known as **militarism**.

Countries also formed alliances to increase their military strength in case of attack. Austria-Hungary, Germany, and Italy formed the Triple Alliance, while France, Great Britain, and Russia formed the Triple Entente. These alliances threatened peace in Europe. As an American adviser reported about conditions in Berlin in May 1914, "the air seemed full of the clash of arms, of readiness to strike."

This clash became real the following month when Franz Ferdinand and his wife were assassinated. Believing that the Serbian government was behind the assassination, officials in Austria-Hungary, declared war on Serbia a month later. Within a few days, the system of alliances drew most of the major European nations into the war. Austria-Hungary and Germany, and later Bulgaria and the Ottoman Empire, formed the Central Powers. Fighting against them were the Allied Powers, or Allies, which included France, Great Britain, Russia, and later Italy.

Many people expected the war to end quickly. German emperor Wilhelm II told his troops, "You will be home before the leaves have fallen from the trees." However, by winter of 1915 it became clear that this would be a long war. Because of new weapons such as machine guns and poison gas, soldiers could not easily charge their enemy's position or protect themselves from attack. Thus, armies began digging deep trenches for troops to defend their positions.

Two massive systems of opposing trenches stretched several hundred miles across Belgium and northern France in what was known as the western front. Between them was a narrow strip of land covered with the craters of countless artillery shells. As soldiers settled in their trenches, the war became a deadly stalemate—a situation in which neither side is able to win a decisive victory.

The Granger Collection, New York

Trenches were cramped, muddy, and uncomfortable, but they were often the only protection that soldiers had during World War I.

The United States and the War

Most Americans believed that to remain neutral in the conflict was the best policy. Events in the Atlantic Ocean, however, soon drew the United States into the war.

Declaring War

Germany declared the waters around Britain a war zone, leaving any ship that entered these waters open to attack. In May 1915 a German submarine, or U-boat, sank the British passenger liner *Lusitania*. The attack killed 1,198 people

An artist's re-creation of the sinking of the *Lusitania*, based on survivors' memories of the tragic event

on board, including 128 Americans. Submarine warfare continued, and many more unarmed ships were sunk. Then the Germans attacked the *Sussex*, another British ship with American passengers, in March 1916. Under threat from President Woodrow Wilson, Germany issued the *Sussex* pledge, in which it agreed not to sink any more passenger or merchant vessels without warning.

Wilson tried to settle the war in Europe peacefully. He wanted to avoid a situation in which the losing side would seek revenge. "Victory would mean peace forced upon the loser," he said. "Only a peace between equals can last." However, the Allies and the Central Powers refused to negotiate. When the Germans resumed unrestricted submarine warfare on February 1, 1917, Wilson broke off diplomatic relations with Germany.

Although Wilson had maintained U.S. neutrality, he quickly changed his mind upon learning the contents of a telegram from German foreign minister Arthur Zimmermann to the German minister in Mexico. The telegram, known as the Zimmerman note, told of a German proposal for forming an alliance with Mexico against the United States. Declaring that "the world must be made safe for democracy," on April 2, 1917, Wilson asked Congress to declare war on Germany.

Preparing for War

To raise troops, Congress quickly passed the **Selective Service Act**, requiring men between the ages of 18 and 45 to register for the draft. Initially, the draft enlisted only those men between 21 and 30 years of age into the armed forces. More than 4.5 million Americans served in World War I. The more than 350,000 African Americans who enlisted served in segregated units. Thousands of women also served in the army, many as nurses, secretaries, and clerks. Others joined the Red Cross and drove ambulances on the front lines. One driver recalled the dangers she faced on duty one night:

> **❝I had just stopped my engine . . . when shrapnel [shell fragments] whizzed past my head and there was a tremendous crash close beside. . . . Then an ambulance call came and I tore off.❞**

To finance the war, Congress raised taxes and sold bonds. By buying bonds, U.S. citizens were loaning money to their government. Around 9.4 million Americans spent nearly $4 billion purchasing bonds. The federal government also took greater control of the country's resources. The new War Industries Board oversaw the production and distribution of manufactured goods. The Food Administration increased farm production and controlled food prices. It also encouraged Americans to make do with less food by voluntarily observing daily rationing such as "meatless Mondays" and "wheatless Wednesdays."

The U.S. Treasury Department encouraged Americans to buy savings stamps to support the war effort.

Groups of people who had frequently faced employment discrimination in the past found greater opportunity during the war years. Soldiers headed for the war left many jobs needing to be filled at home. More than 1.5 million women took industrial jobs, and thousands of Hispanics and African Americans moved north in search of factory work.

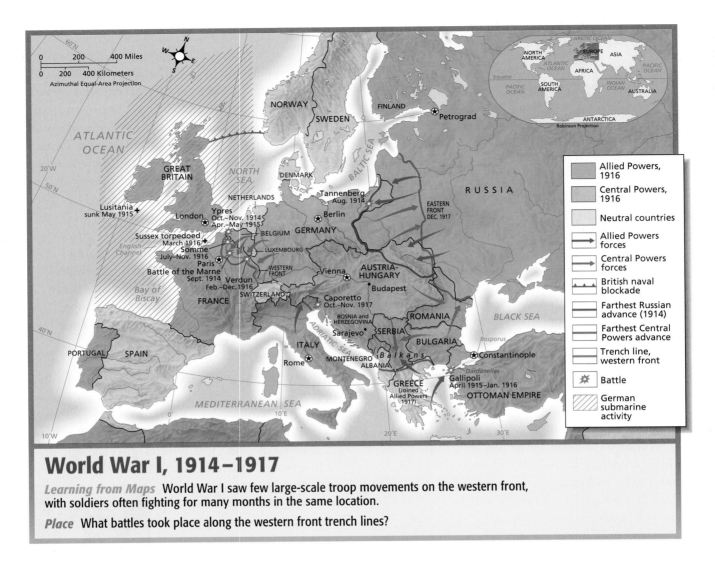

World War I, 1914–1917

Learning from Maps World War I saw few large-scale troop movements on the western front, with soldiers often fighting for many months in the same location.

Place What battles took place along the western front trench lines?

Fighting in Europe

U.S. forces began arriving in France in June 1917. They were shocked at conditions in the trenches. "Men were soaked from one day's end to the other. . . . Water slopped to and fro on the dugout floors," noted Theodore Roosevelt Jr. "At times a bursting German shell would throw to the surface fragments of a long-buried soldier." In the spring of 1918, the Germans launched a brutal attack on the western front. With the help of U.S. soldiers, the Allies held the German army back.

⭐ The Push for Peace

By the fall of 1918 the Allies were on the offensive. On November 11, 1918, Germany signed an **armistice**, or truce, with the Allies. World War I had finally ended. More than 10 million soldiers

had been killed, and twice as many had been wounded. The war had destroyed industry and agriculture in many parts of Europe.

President Wilson knew that it would be difficult to bring a lasting peace to Europe. He proposed a plan, called the Fourteen Points, that outlined a system to avoid future wars. Among other things, it called for the creation of the League of Nations, an international congress of countries whose members would work together to solve international conflict and prevent wars.

In January 1919, leaders of 27 nations attended the peace conference held at the palace of Versailles in France. The European Allies demanded that the Central Powers be punished. Therefore, the final **Treaty of Versailles** arranged for Germany to pay billions of dollars in reparations—payments for the costs and damages of the war. The treaty also included the establishment of the League

Pictured here at the Versailles peace conference, from left to right, are David Lloyd George of Britain, Foreign Minister Giorgio Sonnino of Italy, Georges Clemenceau of France, and Woodrow Wilson of the United States.

of Nations. In the United States, however, some people, including a number of senators, expressed fears that involvement in the League of Nations would drag the country into more international conflicts. Congress rejected the Treaty of Versailles, and the United States did not join the League of Nations.

A Return to Normalcy

After the war, American society saw drastic changes. The nation's industries boomed, and more Americans moved to the growing cities.

Domestic Problems

The war's end brought about certain economic difficulties as industries scaled back on production. The return of some 4.5 million military personnel led to a surplus of workers, forcing many women out of their wartime jobs. Most workers saw their earnings drop, though prices continued to rise. In 1919 more than 4 million workers went on strike to demand higher pay.

Many Americans saw the strikes as a sign that **Communists**—people who believe that there should be no private ownership of property— were attempting to take over the United States. Communists had waged a successful revolution in

Russia in 1917. Soon a powerful wave of anticommunist fear called the **Red Scare** swept the United States.

Gradually, the Red Scare began to die down, but it had fueled a general fear and hatred of foreigners. Such sentiments influenced the trial of Nicola Sacco and Bartolomeo Vanzetti, two Italian immigrants and political radicals who were accused of robbery and murder. Despite serious doubts about their guilt, the two were found guilty and executed.

Republican Leadership

The 1920s brought better times for the United States. By 1920, women had won the right to vote. The first election in which they cast their ballots also began a decade of Republican leadership. President Warren Harding's administration tried to focus on strengthening the economy, but found itself weakened by scandal. When Harding died unexpectedly in 1923, the new president, Calvin Coolidge, promised continued prosperity and declared that "the business of America is business."

As with Harding, most of Coolidge's policies benefited the wealthy. Although the gap between the rich and the poor grew, overall the economy went through a period of prosperity. This economic boom expanded as people purchased consumer products like automobiles.

The Rise of the Automobile

Since 1909, industrialist Henry Ford had been producing a car known as the Model T. Over time, he made his factories more efficient by using the assembly line, a production system in which each worker attached a particular part to machines moving along a series of conveyer belts. The system cut the car's assembly time, and as a result, lowered its price. In the 1920s the car industry became the biggest business in the country, encouraging the growth of related industries such as steel and rubber. By 1929 around 375,000 employees were working for Ford and his competitors.

Americans had purchased some 15 million Model Ts by 1927. The growing automobile craze

Even during the 1920s, traffic jams were common on weekends as families used their cars to visit relatives and to travel to parks.

The Granger Collection, New York

transformed the landscape of the United States. Seemingly overnight, roadside diners, service stations, and motels—or "motor hotels"—sprang up across the country. More people moved to the suburbs, and many businesses moved to the outskirts of towns, where real estate was cheaper. Many other companies copied the advertising and sales techniques of the car industry to market their products. During the 1920s Americans purchased many new products—from radios to electric toasters. Demand for these goods kept business booming.

Changes in Society

The 1920s were also a time of clashing ideals. In 1919 Congress passed the Eighteenth Amendment, which called for **prohibition**—the banning of the manufacture, distribution, and sale of alcohol. However, many Americans ignored the law and continued drinking at home and in clubs that illegally served liquor. Prohibition led to an increase in organized crime as gangsters armed with machine guns fought for control of the illegal alcohol business. Such problems eventually led to passage of the **Twenty-first Amendment**, which ended prohibition in 1933.

Violating prohibition became one of the many ways that young people rebelled against traditions of society in the 1920s. Women called flappers rejected traditional ideas about proper behavior and styles for women. Flappers wore makeup and cut their hair short to show their independence.

Religious ideals also led to national debate during the 1920s. In 1925 Tennessee outlawed the teaching of Charles Darwin's theory of natural selection and evolution, which some people believed conflicted with the biblical story of creation. That year, people across the United States and around the world followed the trial of Tennessee schoolteacher John T. Scopes, who had violated a state law against teaching Darwin's theory. Although Scopes was convicted, this decision was overruled two years later.

Nativism, or strong anti-immigrant feelings, also increased in the 1920s. The U.S. government responded by significantly limiting immigration from all countries except Mexico. Membership in the Ku Klux Klan also grew dramatically as the Klan started striking out against immigrants, Catholics, Jews, and other groups, in addition to its ongoing attacks on African Americans.

The Roaring Twenties

For many Americans, however, the 1920s were more a time of fun than of conflict. While enjoying the economic boom and greater leisure time of the late 1920s, people sought new forms of entertainment. They listened to music and sports on radios, which became more widespread as the decade progressed. Movies also gained in popularity. By 1927, when the first talkie—a movie with sound—appeared, there were 17,000 movie theaters in the United States.

Musical and literary artists also made important contributions to the culture of the 1920s. The decade is often known as the **Jazz Age** because many people listened to jazz, a type of music with its origins in African American culture. Jazz became more popular among white audiences as increasing numbers of African Americans moved to northern cities, bringing this musical style with them. The Harlem neighborhood of New York City soon became the center of African American cultural life. As African American writer and artist Elton Fax said:

The Harlem Renaissance featured popular performers such as singer Bessie Smith (left) and jazz musician Louis Armstrong (right).

❝**Harlem epitomized [symbolized] a kind of freedom that we did not know: 'Once I get to Harlem, I won't need to worry about anything. Nobody's gonna bother me in Harlem.'**❞

This period of African American artistic accomplishment is known as the **Harlem Renaissance**.

A group of writers, known as the **Lost Generation**, responded to the terrible death and destruction of World War I. One of these writers,

Ernest Hemingway, called the war "the most colossal [huge], murderous, mismanaged butchery that has ever taken place on earth." In their work the members of the Lost Generation also expressed their dislike of postwar society. Overall, however, the decade known as the Roaring 20s reflected an era of positive feelings about the future, as expressed by the popular American song "Happy Days Are Here Again."

SECTION 1 REVIEW

Identify and explain the significance of the following:

- **militarism**
- **Woodrow Wilson**
- **Selective Service Act**
- **armistice**
- **Treaty of Versailles**
- **Communists**
- **Red Scare**
- **Calvin Coolidge**
- **prohibition**
- **Twenty-first Amendment**
- **Jazz Age**
- **Harlem Renaissance**
- **Lost Generation**

Reading for Content Understanding

1 **Main Idea** What economic and social problems faced the United States following World War I?

2 **Main Idea** How did prohibition and the Scopes trial show that the 1920s were a time of clashing ideals?

3 **Global Relations** What event sparked World War I? What caused the United States to enter the war in 1917, and how did the war end?

4 **Writing** *Creating* Make a poster that might have appeared in 1917 to encourage Americans to support the war effort. Your poster might be aimed at recruiting people to become soldiers, buy war bonds, or support "meatless Mondays."

5 **Critical Thinking** *Evaluating* Do you agree with those Americans who did not support the United States in joining the League of Nations? Explain your answer.

The Great Depression and World War II

Reading Focus	Key Terms	
What were some of the major causes of the Great Depression?	Great Depression	fascism
	public works	Nazis
How did the depression affect Americans, and what did the federal government do to try to help them?	New Deal	Lend-Lease Act
	Federal Deposit Insurance Corporation	D-Day
What actions did the United States take during World War II, and what was the war's outcome?		Holocaust
	Social Security Act	

ON OCTOBER 29, 1929, *the U.S. stock market had its single worst day in history. As investors desperately tried to sell their increasingly worthless stock, fistfights broke out on the floor of the New York Stock Exchange. Men reportedly lost shoes, glasses, and false teeth. One man even lost his wooden leg in the fighting. Journalist Jonathan Leonard was on Wall Street the day of the crash. "This was real panic," he recalled. "When the closing bell rang, the great bull market was dead and buried."*

The Granger Collection, New York

A newspaper headline the day after the 1929 stock market crash

The Dawn of the Depression

Before the stock market crash, there had been warning signs of financial troubles to come. Despite the general prosperity of the 1920s, industries such as lumber, mining, and agriculture had never recovered from the financial setbacks brought by the end of World War I. The United States also had an unequal distribution of wealth: a few people had a lot of money to spend on goods while other people could afford little. Despite these problems, the U.S. stock market seemed to be on a constant rise. In addition to the wealthy, Americans from homemakers to elevator operators invested in the stock market in hopes of making money.

The Stock Market Crash

Following an all-time high in September 1929, stock prices began to slide downward. On October 29, 1929, nervous investors rushed to sell their stock, causing prices to drop even lower. Losses for that day, which became known as Black Tuesday, totaled around $15 billion. Many investors who had bought their stock on credit lost everything they had.

In the months after the crash, few people realized that the economy was on its way to collapse. Businesses slowed down and laid off workers. As fewer Americans had money to spend on goods, manufacturers decreased production or closed their factories and laid off even more workers. In 1932 unemployment stood at about 25 percent. Banks also failed, partly because investors could not repay their loans. People across the country lost their savings. Everywhere, people were feeling the effects of the **Great Depression**—the severe global economic decline that had begun with the U.S. stock market crash.

Hoover and the Depression

Critics charged that President Herbert Hoover, who had been elected in 1928, acted too slowly to help the economy and the American people. He did cut taxes and increased government spending for **public works**—construction projects to benefit the public. By hiring people for these projects, Hoover hoped to decrease unemployment. He also bought up surplus crops from farmers, hoping this would boost prices. Hoover did not believe in giving direct relief such as food, clothing, shelter, and money, however. He thought that such aid would destroy people's self-reliance. Most suffering Americans saw Hoover's approach as a sign that he did not care about them.

★ Roosevelt Takes Charge

In 1932, voters elected Democrat Franklin D. Roosevelt to the presidency. At his inauguration he promised, "This great nation will . . . revive and will prosper. . . . The only thing we have to fear is fear itself."

Dorothea Lange took this photograph of a migrant mother during the Great Depression.

The New Deal

Roosevelt immediately called a special session of Congress to pass legislation to help the economy. During the first three months of Roosevelt's presidency, Congress passed the proposals that made up the heart of the **New Deal**—Roosevelt's plan for improving the economy. One of Roosevelt's first acts was to save the nation's banks. He declared a "bank holiday," closing every bank in the country and allowing only financially sound ones to reopen. Then he reassured Americans that it was safe to return their money to the banks. Congress also established the **Federal Deposit Insurance Corporation** (FDIC), which insured bank deposits.

Roosevelt also gave direct relief to those in need by creating the Federal Emergency Relief Administration (FERA). At one point nearly 8 million American families survived on public assistance. At the same time, Roosevelt started job programs, employing people to work on federal projects. Returning to work helped many Americans reclaim their self-esteem. New Deal legislation also brought some relief to farmers.

The Second New Deal

In 1935 Roosevelt proposed a new series of reforms to help American businesses as well as the millions of citizens who were still out of work. Congress created a new relief agency, the Works Progress Administration (WPA). The WPA employed around one fifth of the total workforce between 1935 and 1943. WPA workers built public facilities, taught classes, and produced projects in the arts. In 1935 Roosevelt signed what was perhaps the most far-reaching legislation of his administration—the **Social Security Act**. It provided pensions for retired workers and unemployment insurance for workers who lost their jobs. These benefits were later expanded by Congress.

Franklin D. Roosevelt

Born into a wealthy family in 1882, Franklin D. Roosevelt gave up a promising law career for a seat in the New York legislature. After serving as assistant secretary of the navy, he ran on the Democratic ticket for vice president in 1920. Roosevelt modeled his political career on that of his distant cousin Theodore Roosevelt, whose niece Eleanor he married in 1905.

Roosevelt suffered a setback in 1921 when he became ill with polio. Although the disease left both of his legs paralyzed, he fought back and returned to politics. He became New York's governor in 1928 and won re-election two years later.

As president in the midst of the Great Depression, Roosevelt promised to take care of the "forgotten" people in society. He often said that his experience in trying to conquer polio helped him sympathize with others who were struggling through hard times. This ability was one of many factors that made Roosevelt one of the most beloved presidents ever. He is the only U.S. president to have been elected to serve four terms in office.

Hard Times Everywhere

The depression affected almost all Americans. Family life was often disrupted by economic hardships. People relied on the help of family, friends, neighbors, and free meals from soup kitchens during these hard times. Some 20 percent of children suffered from malnutrition. Writer Louise V. Armstrong described this urban scene:

> 66 **One vivid [distinct], gruesome moment of those dark days we shall never forget. We saw a crowd of some fifty men fighting over a barrel of garbage which had been set outside the back door of a restaurant. American citizens fighting for scraps of food like animals!** 99

The Granger Collection, New York

Some people who lost their houses were forced to live on the streets. They set up makeshift shelters made of cardboard boxes. Many farmers lost their land as crop prices fell, leaving them no money to repay their bank loans and mortgages.

First Lady Eleanor Roosevelt

In the midst of the depression, a severe drought hit the Great Plains. As winds blew away the topsoil in huge clouds of dust, the area became known as the Dust Bowl. Unable to grow crops, many farmers headed west, looking for a better life. Once in California, many farmers could find jobs only as migrant workers.

African Americans and Mexican Americans were particularly hard hit by the depression. They were often the first employees to be fired and the last to be hired. Many Mexican immigrants were sent back home to Mexico. Despite these setbacks, African Americans made some advances. President Roosevelt appointed several African Americans to serve in his administration. These officials, as well as First Lady Eleanor Roosevelt, fought vigorously to expand civil rights.

Depression-era programs brought some welcome changes for American Indians. Congress had granted U.S. citizenship to American Indians in 1924, but many still lived under substandard conditions. Congress restored tribal rule and land ownership. It also provided money for education and cultural programs.

The depression had some other positive outcomes. For instance, the New Deal legislation included many acts that favored workers, allowing them to organize unions. Secretary of Labor Frances Perkins encouraged employers to meet the demands of many striking workers. Although the New Deal programs did slowly improve the economy, the nation did not pull out of its slump until the 1940s.

 ## World War II

The Great Depression affected countries throughout the world in the 1930s. As a result of these hard times, many countries turned to new forms of government that promised relief. In the end, however, many of these new governments led their people into war.

The Rise of Dictators

The events that led to World War II began with the Treaty of Versailles. Many political leaders had hoped that the treaty would prevent another global war, but instead some countries were unhappy with the treaty's terms. Italians felt that they should have been awarded more territory. They welcomed new leader Benito Mussolini, even though he established a system of military dictatorship called **fascism**. Mussolini promised to turn Italy into a world power.

The Treaty of Versailles had forced Germany to pay $33 billion in reparations to the countries it had attacked during World War I. As the depression increased this economic hardship, Germans also turned to a new leader. Adolf Hitler and his National Socialist Party, or **Nazis**, appealed to the German people by blaming Jews, intellectuals, and Communists for Germany's difficulties. By 1933 Hitler controlled Germany.

The Start of the War

Hitler violated the Treaty of Versailles by reoccupying the Rhineland in 1936, annexing Austria in 1938, and taking over Czechoslovakia in 1939. At first, European leaders followed a policy of appeasement— giving in to an aggressor to avoid more serious conflict. When the German army invaded Poland on September 1, 1939, however, Britain and France fulfilled their treaty obligations and declared war on Germany. German forces quickly overran much of western and northern Europe, aided by a combination of airplane strikes and massive tank attacks. In 1940 Germany, Italy, and Japan formed an alliance called the Axis Powers. Japan had invaded China in the 1930s and hoped to expand its power throughout Asia. Germany also attacked the Soviet Union in 1941, leading the Soviets to join the Allied Powers, Britain and France.

The United States maintained a policy of neutrality. Once German planes began bombing Britain, however, the U.S. Congress passed the **Lend-Lease Act** in 1941. This act allowed the United States to lend or lease ships, planes, tanks, and guns to Britain. U.S. involvement in the war also grew as U.S. warships helped track German submarines and escorted merchant ships in the Atlantic. When a German submarine shot at a U.S. destroyer in September 1941, Roosevelt warned that if German and Italian forces invaded U.S. waters, "they do so at their own peril [risk]."

Roosevelt also challenged Japan's expansion in Asia by freezing Japanese funds in the United States and by refusing to sell aviation fuel to Japan. On December 7, 1941, Japan responded with a surprise attack on the U.S. naval base at Pearl Harbor, Hawaii. Japan's military leaders hoped that this

U.S. naval power in the Pacific suffered a great blow when Japan attacked Pearl Harbor.

action would destroy the U.S. Pacific Fleet and clear the way for further Japanese expansion into the Pacific. Japanese planes bombed the ships and airfields at the base, disabling all of the battleships and destroying around 150 planes. More than 2,000 soldiers and sailors were killed. The damage would have been even worse if the navy's aircraft carriers had not been away from the naval base on maneuvers.

News of the surprise attack stunned the nation. On December 8, President Roosevelt spoke before a joint session of Congress, declaring December 7 "a date that will live in infamy [disgrace]." Congress declared war on Japan that same day. Germany and Italy, the other major Axis Powers, soon declared war on the United States in support of Japan. American neutrality had ended, and the United States joined the fighting in Europe and Asia.

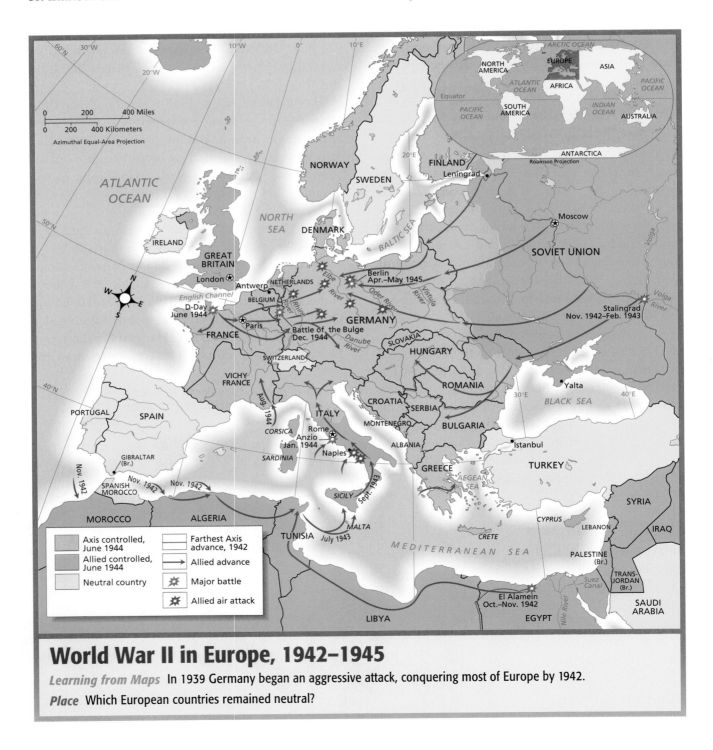

World War II in Europe, 1942–1945

Learning from Maps In 1939 Germany began an aggressive attack, conquering most of Europe by 1942.

Place Which European countries remained neutral?

⭐ The Home Front

Americans quickly rallied to the war effort. Millions of men signed up for military service, as did about 300,000 women. About 6 million women also went to work in factories to help produce war materials. During the 1940s hundreds of thousands of African Americans moved to industrial centers in the North and the West, often finding higher-paying employment. As a result of the war effort, unemployment dropped to an all-time low of 1.2 percent in 1944.

The federal government also became more involved in industrial affairs—rationing many goods, such as tires, meat, and gas. The Office of War Information produced films, posters, and radio broadcasts to remind citizens that their actions at home affected U.S. forces overseas. U.S. citizens responded strongly to the call of duty. One way in which they helped was by buying billions of dollars in bonds. According to the secretary of the treasury, these bonds gave all citizens "an opportunity to contribute toward the defense of . . . democracy."

Despite these patriotic activities, discrimination still affected many U.S. citizens. Racial tensions in Los Angeles led to the arrest and beating of many Mexican Americans, even though some 300,000 Mexican Americans served in the military. About 1 million African Americans served in the military during the war, though they were segregated in training camps and in their units. At home, African Americans often earned less money than whites and worked at lower-level jobs.

Japanese Americans in particular faced much discrimination as the U.S. government came to believe that they posed a threat to national security. During the war years, some 112,000 Japanese Americans, the majority of whom were U.S. citizens, were sent to internment camps. Many

These two young women worked as welders in a war plant. Many women built aircraft and other machinery during the war.

Japanese Americans lost their homes and businesses. Supreme Court justice Frank Murphy called this the "legalization of racism," but other members of the Court upheld the policy. Despite the internment policy, about 33,000 Japanese Americans signed up for military service. Japanese Americans made up the majority of soldiers in the 442nd Division, the most decorated combat force in the U.S. Army.

⭐ Allied Victory

In 1942 the Allies began to turn back the Axis Powers in Europe. The Allies won important victories in the Soviet Union, North Africa, and Italy. They also heavily bombed German cities and supply centers. On June 6, 1944, the Allies launched the **D-Day** invasion of France. By July 2 around 1 million Allied soldiers had landed on the beaches of Normandy. The troops recaptured French towns from the Germans and marched steadily east toward the heart of Germany. At the same time, Soviet forces pushed west toward the German capital of Berlin. With its capital as well as many other cities in ruins, Germany surrendered on May 7, 1945.

Allied troops trying to rest before attacking the beaches of Normandy on D-Day

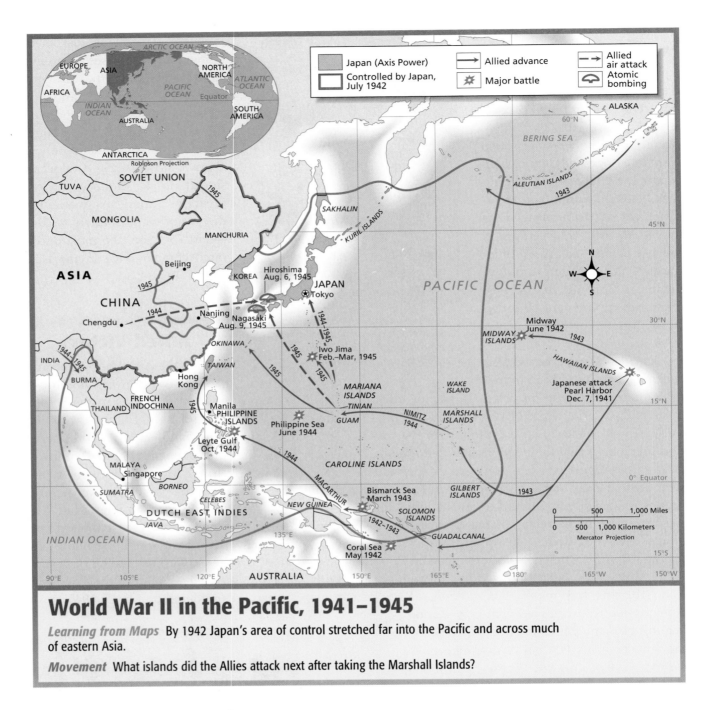

World War II in the Pacific, 1941–1945

Learning from Maps By 1942 Japan's area of control stretched far into the Pacific and across much of eastern Asia.

Movement What islands did the Allies attack next after taking the Marshall Islands?

The war in the Pacific raged on, however. The Japanese had driven back Allied forces early in the war, occupying large areas in Southeast Asia as well as many Pacific islands. This fighting was particularly brutal. In the Philippines, for example, more than 70,000 captured U.S. soldiers were forced to march 65 miles through the jungle while being beaten and starved. Thousands died on what became known as the Bataan Death March.

After a key naval victory at the Battle of Midway in 1942, however, U.S. military forces had gradually begun recapturing strategic islands from the Japanese. In the process, U.S. forces destroyed Japan's naval and air power while moving closer to the Japanese home islands. President Harry Truman—who became president after Roosevelt's death in April 1945—approved the use of a new weapon, the atomic bomb, against Japan. On August 6, 1945, a U.S. plane dropped an atomic bomb on Hiroshima, Japan, killing or injuring more than 160,000 people. Three days later, another U.S. plane dropped a more powerful

More than 1 million people were killed by the Nazis at the Auschwitz concentration camp. These children were among the survivors.

atomic bomb on Nagasaki. Rather than suffer more such devastating attacks, Japan surrendered on August 14 and signed a peace agreement on September 2, 1945.

World War II finally was over, but with great costs. Some 37 million people around the world, including both civilians and soldiers, had lost their lives. More than 400,000 Americans had died as a result of the war. From London to Tokyo, cities and countrysides lay in ruins. Millions of people had lost their homes, and adults and children lived in fear of starvation even after the war had ended.

During the war, the Nazis had systematically murdered people in concentration camps. Around 6 million Jews and 3 million other people were killed during the **Holocaust**. Despite such horror, some people managed to hold onto their hopes for a better future. As Anne Frank, a young Jewish girl who died in a concentration camp, wrote in her diary:

❝It's difficult in times like these: ideals, dreams and cherished hopes rise within us, only to be crushed by grim reality. It's a wonder I haven't abandoned all my ideals, they seem so absurd and impractical. Yet I cling to them because I still believe, in spite of everything, that people are truly good at heart.❞

SECTION 2 REVIEW

Identify and explain the significance of the following:

- **Great Depression**
- **Herbert Hoover**
- **public works**
- **Franklin D. Roosevelt**
- **New Deal**
- **Federal Deposit Insurance Corporation**
- **Social Security Act**
- **Benito Mussolini**
- **fascism**
- **Adolf Hitler**
- **Nazis**
- **Lend-Lease Act**
- **D-Day**
- **Holocaust**

Reading for Content Understanding

1 Main Idea What warning signs showed that the U.S. economy was in trouble in the 1920s? What events contributed to the Great Depression?

2 Main Idea How did the depression affect Americans' daily lives, and how did the government try to solve some of that era's problems?

3 Citizenship and Democracy How did Americans support the war effort on the home front during World War II?

4 Writing *Informing* Imagine that you are a magazine journalist in 1945. Write an article describing the events leading to World War II, U.S. involvement in the war, and the war's outcome.

5 Critical Thinking *Synthesizing Information* How did both the Treaty of Versailles and the Great Depression affect the outbreak of World War II?

Postwar America

Reading Focus

What events characterized the early years of the Cold War?

What changes affected American lifestyles in the 1950s?

How did African Americans work to gain civil rights in the 1950s?

Key Terms

Yalta Conference

United Nations

Cold War

Truman Doctrine

Marshall Plan

North Atlantic Treaty Organization

Warsaw Pact

House Un-American Activities Committee

Brown v. *Board of Education*

Montgomery bus boycott

IN 1956 A POPULAR AMERICAN *magazine conducted a discussion session among several middle-class women whose lives reflected the changes brought about after World War II. Most participants said that they were happy and content with their lives. "I don't think there is one thing I would like to change in the household," said one of the women. "We are all very happy." Such feelings were common among many white middle-class Americans as the country entered an era of peace and prosperity following the struggles of the Great Depression and of World War II.*

A soldier returns home in 1945.

★ Postwar Peace

Even before the end of World War II, President Roosevelt and the Allies began working to lay the foundations for a postwar peace. In February 1945 Roosevelt met with British prime minister Winston Churchill and Soviet leader Joseph Stalin at the **Yalta Conference** to plan how to end the war. They also prepared for the creation of the **United Nations** (UN), an international organization for settling problems between countries.

After Germany's surrender, Churchill, Stalin, and Truman—the new American president—met together at the Potsdam Conference to discuss Germany's immediate future. They divided Germany into four occupation zones, each controlled by one of the four primary Allies: Britain, France, the Soviet Union, and the United States. The Allies also divided up the capital city, Berlin, even though it lay completely within the Soviet zone. In addition, they decided to hold war crimes trials for the Nazi leaders involved in the Holocaust.

The Allies, however, disagreed sharply over the future status of Poland. Stalin wanted a Soviet-friendly government in neighboring Poland, to ensure the security of the Soviet Union. The Western

The Berlin Airlift helped the people of West Berlin endure the Soviet blockade of the city.

nations wanted Poland to have a democratic government. Stalin's refusal to allow free elections to take place in Poland contributed to the growing tensions between the Soviet Union and the West.

 ## The Truman Era

The differences between the United States and the Soviet Union grew as the Soviets came to dominate Eastern Europe after the war. As a result, the two countries became involved in a **Cold War**—a long power struggle for world influence. In 1946 Winston Churchill declared that "an iron curtain has descended across the Continent [of Europe]." The symbol of the iron curtain came to signify the division of Europe between the democratic nations of the West and the communist nations of the East.

The Cold War Abroad

In 1947 President Truman announced the **Truman Doctrine**—a policy stating that the United States would help any country struggling against communism. This policy, also called containment, defined U.S. foreign policy for decades to come.

That same year the United States announced the **Marshall Plan** to offer aid to European countries for their postwar economic recovery. The United States offered around $12.5 billion in aid, both to provide relief and because officials believed that a strong economy would keep Europeans from turning to communism. "Our policy is directed not against any country or

doctrine," said Secretary of State George Marshall, "but against hunger, poverty, desperation, and chaos." However, the Soviet Union and its allies in Eastern Europe refused to accept U.S. aid.

In response to the Marshall Plan and the Western Allies' decision to make the western part of Germany an independent country, the Soviets began to halt all ground traffic to West Berlin. Instead of persuading the Western nations to abandon the city, this blockade "turned Berlin into the heroic symbol of liberty," according to one historian. For more than a year, the United States and Britain conducted the Berlin Airlift, flying more than 7,000 tons of food and supplies to the people of West Berlin every day. The Soviets eventually gave up their blockade in May 1949.

Also in 1949, the United States, Britain, and 10 other countries formed the **North Atlantic Treaty Organization** (NATO). The member countries pledged to defend each other in case of attack. Several years later the Soviet Union and other countries in Eastern Europe signed their own military agreement, the **Warsaw Pact**.

War in Asia

When Communists took over China in 1949, the United States became concerned about the spread of communism in Asia, particularly in Korea. Japan had controlled Korea since 1910, but after World War II the United States and the Soviet Union agreed to temporarily divide the country. A communist, Soviet-backed government soon

The Korean War was the first major conflict fought by the U.S. Army after President Truman integrated the armed services in 1948.

developed in North Korea, and a somewhat democratic, U.S.-backed government developed in South Korea. Each side wanted to unite the country under its own government.

North Korea invaded South Korea in June 1950. Within days the United Nations voted to send troops—most of them American—to defend South Korea. Soon China, fearing that the fighting would cross its border, entered the Korean War by sending thousands of troops to attack UN and South Korean forces. Eventually, the troops reached a standoff, very near the original boundary of the two Koreas. The fighting continued until the summer of 1953, when a truce was signed that divided Korea into two countries.

The Cold War at Home

Cold War tensions sparked a widespread fear of communism among Americans. In 1947 Congress gave new powers to the **House Un-American Activities Committee** (HUAC) and ordered it to investigate U.S. citizens suspected of communist activities. Being accused of such crimes often ruined people's careers and lives. The government began to investigate possible communist ties among federal employees, who were required to sign loyalty oaths. HUAC also distributed anticommunist propaganda to the American public, including millions of pamphlets that gave warnings such as "Where can Communists be found? Everywhere."

The Duck-and-Cover program used cartoon characters such as Bert the Turtle to teach children about civil defense during the 1950s.

During this time, Senator Joseph McCarthy of Wisconsin took advantage of Cold War fears. In 1950 he declared that he had a list of hundreds of Communists who worked in the U.S. government. McCarthy's accusations led to televised hearings. In front of some 20 million viewers, it became clear that McCarthy had no evidence to back up his accusations. Public sentiment turned against him, but not before he had destroyed the reputations of many innocent people.

Eisenhower and the Cold War

American voters elected Dwight D. Eisenhower president in 1952. Eisenhower had led the Allied invasion of Europe in World War II. He was a strong, confident leader and helped bring the Korean War to an end. Eisenhower also pledged to help any Middle Eastern nation threatened by communism. This Eisenhower Doctrine greatly increased U.S. involvement in the Middle East.

During Eisenhower's administration the United States constructed increasing numbers of nuclear weapons. Rather than relying on a large army, the U.S. military's strategy was to maintain an ability to launch a massive nuclear attack on the nation's enemies, particularly the Soviet Union. This policy was known as massive retaliation. The Soviets had already begun constructing their own nuclear weapons. These new weapons—hydrogen bombs—were vastly more powerful than the earlier atomic bombs. People around the globe grew frightened of the massive destruction these weapons could cause.

Eisenhower's foreign policy depended largely on brinkmanship, or the willingness to get as close as possible to full-scale nuclear war. Secretary of State John Foster Dulles explained brinkmanship in an article in *Life* magazine:

> " You have to take chances for peace, just as . . . in war. . . . The ability to get to the verge [edge] without getting into war is the necessary art. . . . If you try to run away from it, if you are scared to go to the brink [edge], you are lost. "

By the mid-1950s President Eisenhower had recognized the need for arms control. In hopes for a "thaw" in the Cold War, in 1959 Vice President Richard Nixon visited the Soviet Union, and Soviet premier Nikita Khrushchev [kroohsh-CHAWF] came to the United States. Eisenhower and Khrushchev planned to meet at a conference in Paris in May 1960 to discuss arms reductions. Two weeks before this conference, or summit, however, the Soviets shot down a U.S. spy plane over their country. This incident embarrassed the United States and angered the Soviets, putting a halt to the negotiations.

In the 1950s popular images such as this family scene often encouraged Americans to buy the latest gadgets and appliances.

The United States and the Soviet Union also competed in a race for space exploration. The Soviets sent *Sputnik*, the first artificial satellite, into space in October 1957. Americans were shocked to find themselves lagging behind the Soviets in space technology. Congress quickly responded by establishing the National Aeronautics and Space Administration (NASA) in July 1958 to advance U.S. space exploration.

 ## A Changing America

The United States's economic growth helped fuel its efforts to win the Cold War. Despite President Truman's fear that the United States would undergo an economic downturn, the postwar years were a time of prosperity for many. Truman had approved a series of reforms to strengthen the economy, which continued to improve under Eisenhower. People had saved their money during the war and were eager to spend it on new goods. Incomes increased, unemployment remained low, and a new era of prosperity was born.

Television Culture

Television greatly influenced American culture in the 1950s. In 1945 few Americans even owned a television set, but by the mid-1950s more than 65 percent of all U.S. homes had one. Americans enjoyed watching many types of shows. In response, critics like Boston University president Daniel Marsh warned that "if the television craze continues with the present level of programs, we are destined to have a nation of morons."

Television contributed to rising consumerism by giving advertisers a unique opportunity to reach the vast public. The stars of television shows encouraged viewers to buy the advertisers' products. Game shows closely blended entertainment and consumerism by awarding prizes to contestants. Game shows were among the most popular television programs.

Changing Populations

Advertisers were trying to influence a workforce that was changing greatly in the 1950s. Many businesses restructured, creating the need for new managers and clerical workers. Companies began moving to the South and the West, creating new employment opportunities. Americans followed these opportunities, moving in great numbers.

The United States also experienced a baby boom after World War II as the number of children increased dramatically. To find more spacious homes, many middle-class Americans moved to the suburbs. Life in the suburbs centered around families. Although popular culture idealized the role of the full-time suburban homemaker, many women had jobs other than taking care of their families.

⭐ Social Critics

Some critics worried about suburban residents' increasing focus on material things. Middle-class families seemed to define their lives by the types of goods they owned. Some observers also complained that the suburbs themselves placed an emphasis on conformity, or fitting in with the larger group. Not only did many houses look alike, almost all of the people who lived in the suburbs by 1960 were white and had middle-class incomes. Harvard professor John Kenneth Galbraith claimed that Americans' desire to consume goods rather than to produce goods reflected their growing selfishness. He believed that suburban families were so caught up in their own lives that they refused to think about problems facing others in society—particularly the urban poor.

A group of poets called the beats condemned this lack of individuality and called on young people to live a more independent lifestyle. The beats never collected a large following, but many teenagers did find ways to rebel. They read books and saw movies that expressed their dissatisfaction with average life. A popular form of rebellion was through music, particularly rock 'n' roll, which drew heavily on African American rhythm and blues. Although teenagers generally loved this music, many adults argued that it sounded awful and contributed to antisocial behavior.

⭐ The Civil Rights Movement Begins

Other groups challenged 1950s society in different ways. After World War II many African Americans were determined to win their civil liberties and fight discrimination. President Truman pledged to support civil rights and desegregated the U.S. armed forces in 1948, but for many African Americans he moved too slowly.

Desegregating the Schools

The NAACP had long struggled to end segregation in education. The Supreme Court had upheld segregation based on the "separate-but-equal" principle, but most black schools received much less funding than white schools and rarely provided equal facilities or opportunities for African American children.

In 1954 Linda Brown—an African American girl living in Topeka, Kansas—went with her father to enroll in her neighborhood school, which was for white children only. When the principal told her that she had to attend the all-black school that was a half-hour bus ride away, her parents joined with the NAACP in filing suit against the Topeka school board. In a historic ruling in 1954, the U.S. Supreme Court declared in **Brown v. Board of Education** that segregated public schools were unconstitutional.

Despite this ruling, by 1957 only four southern states had integrated their schools. The school board of Little Rock, Arkansas, selected nine outstanding black students, nicknamed the Little Rock Nine, to integrate Central High School in the fall of 1957. However, Arkansas governor Orval Faubus ordered National Guard troops to prevent the students from entering the school. Eventually, President Eisenhower sent federal troops to enforce desegregation. In May 1958 Ernest Green became the first African American student to graduate from Central High School. "When they called my name there was an eerie silence. Nobody clapped," Green recalled of his graduation. "But I figured they didn't have to . . . because after I got that diploma, that was it. I had accomplished what I had come there for."

An angry white mob shouts at Elizabeth Eckford, one of the Little Rock Nine, as she walks to school.

Boycotting the Buses

African Americans also fought segregation on public transportation. In 1955 Rosa Parks was arrested for refusing to give up her seat on a Montgomery, Alabama, bus to a white passenger. She explained how years of ill-treatment had led her to take such an action:

❝Having to take a certain section (on a bus) because of your race was humiliating, but having to stand up because a particular driver wanted to keep a white person from having to stand was, to my mind, most inhumane.❞

The local NAACP and other African American groups organized the **Montgomery bus boycott**. Practically all African Americans in the city of Montgomery, who made up more than 75 percent of bus ridership, boycotted the bus system. To get to work, they formed car pools and walked. The boycott of the buses continued for more than a year until December 1956, when the Supreme Court declared Montgomery's segregated bus system to be illegal.

Martin Luther King Jr. posing with his wife, Coretta, and their children

The boycott inspired African Americans in other communities to carry out their own boycotts. It also introduced the nation to a powerful African American leader, Martin Luther King Jr. A young minister and inspiring speaker, King would become one of the most important figures in the ongoing fight for the extension of civil rights to all Americans.

SECTION 3 REVIEW

Identify and explain the significance of the following:

- **Yalta Conference**
- **United Nations**
- **Cold War**
- **Truman Doctrine**
- **Marshall Plan**
- **North Atlantic Treaty Organization**
- **Warsaw Pact**
- **House Un-American Activities Committee**
- **Joseph McCarthy**
- **Dwight D. Eisenhower**
- ***Brown v. Board of Education***
- **Rosa Parks**
- **Montgomery bus boycott**
- **Martin Luther King Jr.**

Reading for Content Understanding

1 Main Idea Make a chart that lists some of the Cold War's main events and policies as well as their outcomes.

2 Main Idea How did African Americans fight segregation in public schools and on city buses? How successful were these efforts to end segregation?

3 Global Relations Explain how the Truman Doctrine and the Marshall Plan were intended to stop the spread of communism.

4 Writing *Informing* Write a paragraph explaining how daily life changed for many middle-class Americans after World War II.

5 Critical Thinking *Evaluating* Do you think that television has had a generally positive or negative effect on American society since it became more widespread in the 1950s? Explain your answer.

Searching for Solutions

Reading Focus

How did Cold War concerns affect the foreign policy of Presidents Kennedy, Johnson, and Nixon?

What were the strategies and achievements of the 1960s civil rights movement?

What domestic problems faced the United States in the early 1970s?

Key Terms

Cuban missile crisis

Great Society

Freedom Rides

Civil Rights Act of 1964

Voting Rights Act of 1965

Gulf of Tonkin Resolution

Tet Offensive

energy crisis

Watergate

National Organization for Women

DONNA SHALALA, who spent her entire career in public service, remembered listening to President John F. Kennedy's inaugural address in which he urged Americans to work for a better country. "The energy, the faith, the devotion which we bring to this endeavor [attempt] will light our country," the president said. "And so, my fellow Americans—ask not what your country can do for you—ask what you can do for your country." Shalala was just one of the many young people who answered this call.

President John F. Kennedy and First Lady Jacqueline Kennedy

Kennedy and Johnson

In the 1960s both ordinary citizens and government officials worked hard to improve social conditions at home. Events overseas, however, also demanded U.S. attention.

The Kennedy Era

When John F. Kennedy was campaigning for the presidency in 1960, he promised to "get the country moving again." After his election, however, his attention soon shifted to foreign affairs. Kennedy supported an invasion by 1,500 Cuban exiles who wanted to retake their country from Soviet-backed communist dictator Fidel Castro. On April 17, 1961, these troops landed at the Bay of Pigs in Cuba, only to be defeated by Castro's forces.

The defeat at the Bay of Pigs was a major embarrassment for the United States in the Cold War. Relations between the United States and the Soviet Union further declined when Soviet leader Nikita Khrushchev ordered the construction of the Berlin Wall in 1961. This barrier divided East and West Berlin, preventing East Germans from escaping to Western Europe.

This political cartoon shows Kennedy's firm response to the Cuban missile crisis.

The most serious crisis took place in October 1962 when U.S. spy planes discovered Soviet missiles in Cuba. Kennedy demanded that the Soviets remove these weapons. For the next week, the world nervously awaited the outcome of the **Cuban missile crisis**. Finally, the Soviets offered to remove the missiles if the United States promised not to invade Cuba. After this crisis, the Soviet Union and the United States worked to improve their relations with each other.

Johnson's Reforms

Americans were shocked when, on November 22, 1963, President Kennedy was assassinated in Dallas, Texas. Within hours, Vice President Lyndon B. Johnson became the new president. He was re-elected in 1964.

President Johnson launched the War on Poverty to help the poor obtain better education and jobs. He also introduced the **Great Society**, a series of programs that he said "demands an end to poverty and racial injustice." The Great Society programs provided more people with health insurance, gave federal money to schools, and reduced the number of Americans living in poverty.

Goals and Changes

During the 1960s the United States achieved many other important goals. As the space race continued, President Kennedy had set a goal that the United States would be the first country to get a human on the moon. The nation launched the Apollo Project to

begin preparing for a moon landing. On July 20, 1969, the world watched as U.S. astronaut Neil Armstrong stepped onto the moon's surface. "That's one small step for a man," he said, "one giant leap for mankind."

Other challenges seemed harder to resolve. The country experienced extreme social conflicts in the late 1960s as younger people rejected many of the beliefs and ideals of the older generation. Some young people rejected society entirely by "dropping out" and forming a new culture, called the counterculture.

★ The Civil Rights Movement

One of the most important movements in the 1960s was the continuing campaign for civil rights. "The Negro and white students, North and South, are seeking to rid America of . . . racial segregation and discrimination," said civil rights leader Ella Baker, "in every aspect of life."

Peaceful Protests

African Americans fought for equal treatment in public places, from lunch counters to bus stations. Beginning in 1960, African American students led sit-ins, refusing to leave segregated restaurants until they were served. Over the next year, more than 50,000 people participated in similar demonstrations.

Following Kennedy's assassination, Lyndon Johnson was sworn in as president aboard Air Force One.

Freedom Riders continued to challenge segregated bus stations in the South despite violent attacks from white southerners.

In 1961, civil rights workers challenged the illegal segregation of bus stations in the South. Black and white riders took part in these **Freedom Rides**, taking a bus from Washington, D.C., through several southern states. When the first bus stopped, angry white mobs met the riders with clubs and firebombs. The riders kept coming, however, and transportation companies and other businesses throughout the South gradually ended their segregation policies.

These successes gave greater hope to the movement. When President Kennedy proposed a new civil rights bill in 1963, civil rights leaders organized the March on Washington to show their support for it. More than 200,000 men, women, and children—black and white—gathered in Washington, D.C., where Martin Luther King Jr. described his hopes for racial harmony in his "I Have a Dream" speech:

> **❝ I have a dream that my four little children will one day live in a nation where they will not be judged by the color of their skin but by the content of their character. ❞**

Congress later passed the **Civil Rights Act of 1964**, banning racial discrimination by administrators of public services and by employers that contract with the federal government.

In the summer of 1964, hundreds of civil rights workers traveled to Mississippi to register African American voters. Throughout the South, such voters were prevented from going to the polls by threats and by unfair laws, such as poll taxes and literacy tests. The volunteers kept working even though they received threats of violence and several of them were murdered. Civil rights leaders organized protest marches in Alabama in support of a voting-rights bill. Over the next several months the police arrested thousands of marchers, even attacking some with dogs and water hoses. Soon afterward, President Johnson signed the **Voting Rights Act of 1965**, which ensured every American's right to vote. Within three years, more than half of all African Americans eligible to vote in the South had registered.

Other Paths

Some African Americans did not follow the path taken by King and other peaceful civil rights organizers. Leaders like Malcolm X and groups like the Black Panthers believed that African Americans needed to be economically independent of white society and to use force if necessary to gain their rights. For some of these African American leaders, the course of progress was too slow.

In the late 1960s, as African Americans continued to face economic inequality, riots took place in cities throughout the country. Some of the most severe rioting followed the assassination of Martin Luther King Jr. in April 1968. A leading figure in the civil rights movement was gone, but many others vowed to carry on the struggle.

Malcolm X was a powerful speaker who called for African American independence.

The Vietnam War

In the early 1960s the nation became increasingly involved in affairs in the Southeast Asian nation of Vietnam. By the middle of the decade, the United States was fighting a full-scale war.

Independence and Civil War

After World War II, Vietnamese nationalist leader Ho Chi Minh, a Communist, organized his forces—known as the Vietminh—to fight for independence from French colonial rule. U.S. leaders helped France oppose the Vietminh because they believed in the domino theory. This theory stated that if one Asian country fell to communism, others would soon follow.

Despite U.S. aid, the French forces failed to stop the Vietminh. After years of fighting, the French finally gave up in 1954. A peace agreement divided Vietnam in two but called for elections to reunite the country in 1956.

North Vietnam had a communist government, while South Vietnam had a U.S.-backed government led by Ngo Dinh Diem (en-GOH DIN de-EM). An ineffective and unpopular ruler, Diem refused to allow the elections of 1956 to take place because he feared that he would lose. As his rule became increasingly harsh, some pro-communist South Vietnamese, known as the Vietcong, began to fight against his government. By the late 1950s South Vietnam was in the midst of a civil war.

In 1963 South Vietnamese military leaders overthrew Diem. The new government wanted to negotiate a peace agreement with North Vietnam, but U.S. officials feared that this might allow communism to spread. In August 1964, after North Vietnamese vessels reportedly attacked a U.S. ship in the Gulf of Tonkin, Congress passed the **Gulf of Tonkin Resolution**. This resolution gave President Johnson the authority

"to take all necessary measures to repel any armed attack against forces of the United States" and to secure peace in Southeast Asia.

U.S. Involvement Grows

Although some U.S. military personnel had been in Vietnam since the 1950s, in 1965 Johnson began to greatly increase U.S. involvement. By 1968 more than 500,000 U.S. soldiers were serving in Vietnam.

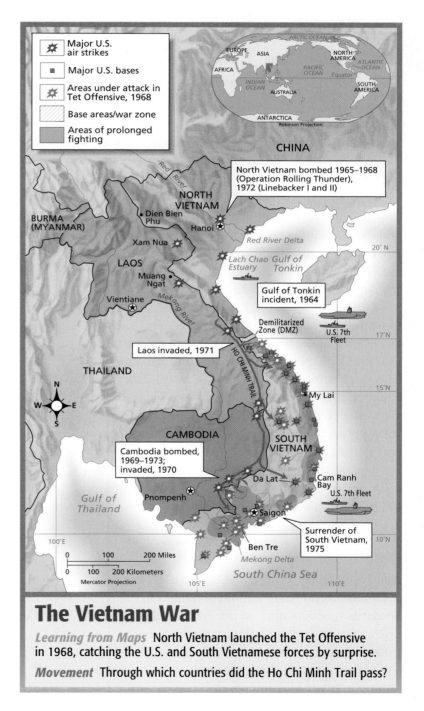

The Vietnam War

Learning from Maps North Vietnam launched the Tet Offensive in 1968, catching the U.S. and South Vietnamese forces by surprise.

Movement Through which countries did the Ho Chi Minh Trail pass?

U.S. Troops in Vietnam, 1964–1972

Number of Troops in Vietnam

Soldiers Killed in Battle

Source: National Archives and Records Administration

The Costly War The number of U.S. troops sent to Vietnam escalated as the United States became more involved in the conflict. In what year did the number of U.S. troops in Vietnam peak?

The fighting was difficult because the Vietcong and North Vietnamese troops launched hit-and-run attacks and knew the dense jungle better than the U.S. forces. Still, U.S. military officials assured the American public of victory.

Public confidence in such claims were shattered in late January 1968, when enemy soldiers launched a major series of attacks that reached into the heart of U.S. defenses, including the American embassy. Although U.S. troops eventually beat back the attacks, this **Tet Offensive** demonstrated that the North Vietnamese still had military strength and would not give up fighting. "To say that we are closer to victory today is to believe, in the face of the evidence, the optimists who have been wrong in the past," declared commentator Walter Cronkite in February 1968.

Americans Against the War

As the fighting progressed, many U.S. citizens began to protest American involvement in the war. Students participated in numerous demonstrations and even closed down many college campuses across the country. Charlotte Keyes, whose son was of draft age, described the people she saw joining antiwar movements in 1966:

❝ **The peaceniks [peace lovers] these days are legion [vast]—they are ninety years old and fifteen, heads of families and housewives with babies, students, [and] young people.** ❞

 ### Ending the War

After the Tet Offensive, some 49 percent of U.S. citizens believed that the United States should never have gotten involved in Vietnam. These negative feelings had a strong effect on the 1968 presidential election. Johnson did not run for re-election. Blaming the Democrats for the war, voters elected Eisenhower's former vice president, Republican Richard Nixon. He promised to bring about "peace with honor."

Nixon began a process that he called Vietnamization, or turning over responsibility for the fighting to the South Vietnamese army. Though he did withdraw U.S. troops, Nixon also tried to weaken the Vietcong by bombing their supply lines in Cambodia and Laos. Finally, on January 27, 1973, U.S. officials reached a peace agreement and withdrew all American forces. Fighting continued between North and South Vietnam until

American and South Vietnamese soldiers waiting to leave Saigon

April 1975, when North Vietnamese forces took South Vietnam's capital, Saigon. The country was reunited under a communist government.

More than 1.5 million Vietnamese soldiers and civilians were killed in the war. In the years after the war, more than 1.5 million refugees fled the country, many coming to the United States. About 58,000 Americans died in the war, while returning veterans faced an often bitter public. Americans also lost some of their faith in their leaders. Since the Vietnam War, U.S. officials have been more cautious about committing troops to foreign wars.

 ## The Early 1970s

In the 1970s the United States faced many domestic challenges. These troubles ranged from economic problems to political scandal.

Nixon and Ford

In the 1970s the United States experienced stagflation—the rising of both inflation and unemployment during a period of little economic growth—for the first time. Although President Nixon enforced wage and price controls, the economy did not recover. The economy worsened when Middle Eastern nations increased the price of their oil. The cost of gasoline and heating oil skyrocketed, leading to the **energy crisis**.

In foreign affairs, Nixon improved relations with China by meeting with Chinese leader Mao Zedong. Nixon was the first president to visit China. He also followed a policy of détente—a lessening of military and diplomatic tensions—

with the Soviet Union. U.S. and Soviet leaders signed a treaty to limit nuclear missiles.

A scandal called **Watergate** soon overshadowed Nixon's successes, however. In June 1972 five men were caught breaking into the Democratic National Committee headquarters at the Watergate apartment-hotel complex in Washington, D.C. Congress investigated the incident, and soon members of Nixon's administration were arrested for involvement in the break-in. They accused Nixon of trying to cover up the incident. President Nixon denied any involvement. However, after the Supreme Court forced him to turn over tape recordings of White House conversations, it became clear that he had lied. He had been deeply involved in the Watergate scandal. To avoid being impeached, Nixon resigned his office on August 8, 1974.

The new president, Gerald Ford, quickly granted Nixon a full pardon for his role in Watergate. Although Ford said that he only wanted to heal "the wounds of the past," this action cost him much public support. Ford faced other domestic problems, such as continued inflation, but he did have some foreign-policy successes. He continued the policy of détente and worked on improving relations with Middle Eastern countries.

Domestic Changes

Americans faced many other challenges in the 1970s, such as the continued fight for equal rights. More African Americans enrolled in college, held professional jobs, and served in public office. The Chicano movement worked to end discrimination and to increase cultural pride among Mexican Americans. César Chávez led the struggle for more rights for Hispanic migrant workers.

An organization that was called the American Indian Movement (AIM) struggled to protect the rights of American Indians. Through-out the 1970s AIM organized protests to increase

César Chávez

Women's movement leaders Gloria Steinem, Bella Abzug, Shirley Chisholm, and Betty Friedan worked to increase women's political influence.

awareness of American Indian issues. Some tribes also successfully sued the U.S. government for land or cash awards to make up for treaty violations.

Women's rights activists formed the **National Organization for Women** in 1966. In 1972 Congress passed the Equal Rights Amendment to guarantee women equal protection under the law, but the necessary number of states failed to ratify it. Women did become more involved in politics and increasingly entered traditionally male professions.

☆ Carter in Office

By the mid-1970s the country was ready for new leadership. In 1976, voters elected Democrat Jimmy Carter, the former governor of Georgia. As the energy crisis and economic problems dragged on, President Carter seemed to offer few solutions.

At first, Carter had more success in foreign policy. Believing that "our commitment to human rights must be absolute," Carter worked to preserve the freedom of peoples in Latin America and Africa. However, he experienced setbacks with the Soviet Union. After the Soviets invaded the Asian nation of Afghanistan, Congress rejected a new arms treaty, and Carter called for a U.S. boycott of the 1980 Summer Olympics in Moscow.

Carter had his greatest success and his worst failure in the Middle East. In 1979 he negotiated the Camp David Accords, a peace treaty between longtime enemies Israel and Egypt. Then in November 1979, Iranians who were angry with Carter's policy of helping their former leader took 53 American hostages in the U.S. Embassy in Iran's capital, Tehran. Although Carter continually tried to gain the release of the hostages, many Americans blamed him for the imprisonment, which lasted 444 days.

SECTION 4 REVIEW

Identify and explain the significance of the following:

- **John F. Kennedy**
- **Cuban missile crisis**
- **Lyndon B. Johnson**
- **Great Society**
- **Freedom Rides**
- **Civil Rights Act of 1964**
- **Voting Rights Act of 1965**
- **Gulf of Tonkin Resolution**
- **Tet Offensive**
- **Richard Nixon**
- **energy crisis**
- **Watergate**
- **Gerald Ford**
- **National Organization for Women**
- **Jimmy Carter**

Reading for Content Understanding

1 **Main Idea** How did President Johnson respond to communist expansion in Southeast Asia? How did the Tet Offensive affect U.S. citizens?

2 **Main Idea** What domestic problems did Presidents Nixon and Carter face?

3 **Citizenship and Democracy** What strategies did African Americans use to gain their civil rights in the 1960s? Why were some frustrated by these strategies?

4 **Writing** *Informing* Write two paragraphs about the foreign-policy issues that Presidents Kennedy and Nixon faced.

5 **Critical Thinking** *Synthesizing Information* How do you think the Cold War policies of the 1950s affected U.S. involvement in Vietnam? Explain your answer.

The Modern Era

Reading Focus

How did Republican presidents in the 1980s respond to communism and the Soviet Union?

What successes and failures did President Clinton see during his two terms in office?

How did nations work together in the 1990s to improve the global economy and the environment?

Key Terms

supply-side economics

Strategic Defense Initiative

Iran-contra affair

War on Drugs

Operation Desert Storm

Contract with America

North American Free Trade Agreement

Earth Summit

*I*NAUGURATION DAY, 1981, *was like no other in American history. Up until the last moment, the outgoing president, Jimmy Carter, was working frantically to ensure the release of the American hostages in Iran. Just moments after Ronald Reagan was sworn in as president, the news came that the hostages were indeed free. As Americans cheered this announcement by their new leader, it was clear that a renewed spirit of hope was emerging in the country.*

1980s bumper sticker

 ## The Reagan Years

Americans looked forward to the 1980s. They believed that they would find solutions to the problems that had been troubling the country.

The Economy

President Ronald Reagan challenged society by insisting that people, not the government, should be responsible for resolving domestic difficulties facing the United States. He scaled back government activity and cut spending on social programs. Reagan's policies were based on the theory of **supply-side economics**, which held that lowering taxes would cause people to invest their savings in business and thus boost the economy.

By 1984 the economy was thriving, but some critics doubted that this boom was helping the nation's poorest citizens. Among those who did benefit from the economy were yuppies, or young urban professionals.

President Ronald Reagan and First Lady Nancy Reagan

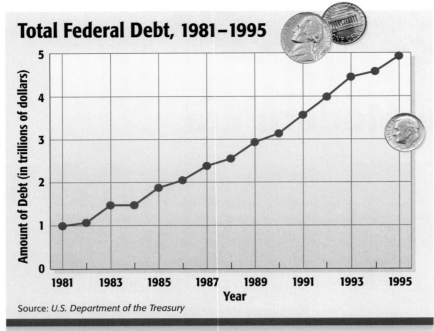

Total Federal Debt, 1981–1995

Amount of Debt (in trillions of dollars)

Year

Source: *U.S. Department of the Treasury*

The Growing Debt   Despite efforts to reduce the federal debt, it continued to rise throughout the 1980s and the 1990s. What was the federal debt in 1992?

Foreign Policy

Believing that the Cold War was a moral struggle of "good versus evil, right against wrong," Reagan took a strong position against communism. The administration spent hundreds of billions of dollars on the military and on arms construction, nearly doubling the defense budget from 1980 to 1985. Such massive spending contributed to a dramatic rise in the federal deficit, or amount of money the government borrows each year. Reagan also urged Congress to fund the **Strategic Defense Initiative** (SDI), an expensive new space technology meant to protect the country from Soviet missiles.

The Reagan administration also provided military assistance to some countries that were trying to defeat communist movements. However, Congress voted to ban aid to Nicaragua's anti-communist forces, known as contras. Despite this ban, some top White House officials continued to fund the contras by illegally selling weapons to Iran. The **Iran-contra affair** was the biggest scandal of the Reagan years.

In the mid-1980s Reagan changed his position on the Soviet Union. As new Soviet leaders allowed greater political and economic openness, U.S.-Soviet relations improved. In 1987 Reagan met with Soviet leader Mikhail Gorbachev, and they signed the Intermediate-Range Nuclear Forces Treaty, which reduced nuclear weapons. Some political observers credit Ronald Reagan's policies with helping to end the Cold War.

★ George Bush's Presidency

Reagan's vice president, George Bush, won the presidency in 1988 by promising to continue the course that Reagan had laid out. "We don't need radical new directions," Bush said. Although he followed President Reagan's agenda, Bush also started several new programs. For example, the **War on Drugs** attempted to stop illegal drugs from entering the United States. President Bush also focused on improving education for children.

The Cold War finally ended during Bush's presidency as many Eastern European countries began to break free from Soviet influence. The Berlin Wall, the most widely recognized symbol of communist rule, was torn down. In 1990 East and West Germany reunited. Then in 1991 the Soviet Union itself broke apart.

Vice President George Bush and his wife, Barbara, at the 1988 Republican convention

While the Cold War was ending, conflict in the Middle East drew the United States into the Persian Gulf War. When the Iraqi army took over the small country of Kuwait in the summer of 1990, the United Nations set economic restrictions on Iraq. When Iraq refused to withdraw its troops from Kuwait, UN forces led by the United States launched **Operation Desert Storm** in January 1991. U.S. general Colin Powell later declared,

> **"I had no doubt we would be successful. We had the troops, the weapons, and the plan. What I did not know was how long it would take, and how many of our troops would not be coming home."**

UN forces waged an intensive, six-week bombing campaign against Iraq, followed by a brief but massive ground assault. After the Iraqis were defeated, President Bush ordered a cease-fire. About 150 U.S. soldiers died in the conflict, compared to more than 100,000 Iraqis. The victory boosted Bush's popularity at home.

 ## Bill Clinton's Policies

By 1992 many Americans were growing concerned over the economy, which was undergoing a recession. President Bush faced two opponents in the 1992 election: Arkansas governor Bill Clinton, a Democrat, and Texas billionaire Ross Perot, an independent candidate. Clinton promised to fix the economy. His central goal was "restoring the hopes of the forgotten middle class." Perot also had a plan for helping the economy, while many voters felt that Bush was ignoring the issue. Clinton won with 43 percent of the popular vote.

President Clinton proposed several programs. His health-care plan, devised in part by First Lady Hillary Rodham Clinton, was designed to make affordable health care available to all Americans. The plan, which sparked much debate, never came to a vote in Congress. Some of its opponents believed it would be too expensive, and others felt it would limit people's ability to make their own health-care decisions.

In 1994, voters elected a Republican-controlled Congress for the first time in 40 years. Earlier,

President Bush (left) discussed issues with 1992 presidential candidates Ross Perot (center) and Bill Clinton (right) in a nationally televised debate.

many Republicans had signed the **Contract with America**, promising to pass a 10-point plan that included a balanced budget, anticrime programs, welfare reform, and tax cuts. The Republicans were only partially successful in pushing these reforms through Congress.

Voters re-elected Clinton in 1996. That year Clinton named former UN ambassador Madeleine Albright as secretary of state. Albright was both the first woman to hold the post and the highest-ranking woman ever to serve in the federal government. In 1997 Congress and the president passed the first balanced federal budget in nearly 30 years. The 1998 budget, also balanced, included plans to improve education and child care. Clinton declared in a White House ceremony:

> **"This budget marks the end of an era, an end to decades of deficits that have shackled [chained] our economy, paralyzed our politics, and held our people back."**

 ## America in the 1990s

With the breakup of the Soviet Union, the United States was the only remaining superpower, and many countries looked to it for help. In the 1990s the United States sent troops and aid to Somalia, which was suffering from famine and civil war, and helped return Haiti's democratically elected leader to power. U.S. involvement in Bosnia helped bring about a peace agreement in the region.

Breakup of the Soviet Sphere, 1989–1992

Learning from Maps By 1992, revolutions had caused the collapse of many communist governments in Eastern Europe.

Place What countries shown above were part of the former Soviet Union?

Peace and Challenges

The United States created better relations with countries around the world, but challenges to security still faced the nation. The United States suffered attacks by terrorists—people who use violence to achieve their goals. In 1993 an Arab group bombed the World Trade Center in New York City. Then in 1995, terrorists bombed a federal office building in Oklahoma City, killing 168 people and injuring hundreds of others. Two U.S. Army veterans were later convicted of this crime.

Race Relations

Tensions between the races continued to be a concern in the 1990s. In 1992, riots erupted in Los Angeles after a jury found four white Los Angeles police officers innocent of using excessive force against an African American motorist. The verdict angered many Americans who had seen the incident, which had been caught on videotape and televised. The riots left some 50 people dead and thousands injured, destroyed more than 1,000 businesses, and caused more than $1 billion in damages. In 1997 President Clinton appointed a special committee to seek solutions to the racial conflicts behind incidents such as the Los Angeles riots.

Growing Up

Young people faced concerns about their futures. A college education became more expensive, but was more necessary for the competitive job market. Tausha Carmack, student-body vice president at the University of Tennessee, voiced the opinion of many young people: "I believe a college degree now is worth about as much as a high school degree was in the '50s and '60s."

Many Americans also worried that, because of poor management, government benefits such as Social Security would be unavailable by the time they retired. As a result, some Americans focused on investing their money for the future. Many people chose to invest in the stock market, which experienced a boom during the 1990s.

⭐ A Changing World

The 1990s brought remarkable new developments as advances in medicine and technology improved people's quality of life. Other advances in communications and transportation made it easier for people and countries to work together.

Technology

By the 1990s people around the world were using the Internet—a global network tying together millions of computers. Computer advances created new jobs and made it easier to work at home. People also used the Internet to do research and share ideas.

The end of the Cold War also led to increasing U.S. cooperation with Russia in space exploration. The two countries made plans to construct a permanent space station, and American astronauts worked aboard the Russian space lab *Mir*. Independently, the United States has sent many probes to study the solar system.

Global Trade

The 1990s also brought more economic interaction between countries. The United States, Mexico, and Canada passed the **North American Free Trade Agreement** (NAFTA) in the early 1990s. This agreement allowed goods, services, and trade to move freely between the three countries. In 1993, the United States and other members of the long-standing international General Agreement on Tariffs and Trade (GATT) agreed to reduce tariffs and eliminate manufacturing quotas. In 1995 the World Trade Organization (WTO) was created to resolve global trade problems.

Environmental Concerns

Worries about the negative effects of human activity on the environment grew in the 1990s as the world population continued to increase rapidly. Scientists also observed holes in the ozone layer, which protects the earth from the sun's harmful radiation. In response to such dangers, many people

Children posing in front of a mural created for the 1992 Earth Summit

tried to conserve natural resources and reduce pollution. International delegates also gathered at the **Earth Summit** in 1992 to discuss how to prevent global warming—the gradual increase in the temperature of the earth's atmosphere.

Americans looked forward to the challenges of the twenty-first century. Poet Maya Angelou expressed these hopes for the future in a poem she read at President Clinton's inauguration on January 20, 1993:

> **Lift up your faces, you have a
> piercing need
> For this bright morning dawning for you
> History, despite its wrenching pain,
> Cannot be unlived, but if faced
> With courage, need not be lived again.**

SECTION 5 REVIEW

Identify and explain the significance of the following:

- **Ronald Reagan**
- **supply-side economics**
- **Strategic Defense Initiative**
- **Iran-contra affair**
- **George Bush**
- **War on Drugs**
- **Operation Desert Storm**
- **Bill Clinton**
- **Contract with America**
- **Madeleine Albright**
- **North American Free Trade Agreement**
- **Earth Summit**

Reading for Content Understanding

1 **Main Idea** What changes in global trade occurred during the 1990s?

2 **Main Idea** What concerns did many people share about the environment? How did they address these concerns?

3 **Global Relations** How did Presidents Reagan and Bush work to improve relations with the Soviet Union?

4 **Writing** *Classifying* What do you think has been Bill Clinton's greatest success and biggest failure as president? Explain your answer in a paragraph.

5 **Critical Thinking** *Evaluating* Reread Maya Angelou's poem at the end of this section. What is she telling Americans? Do you agree with her? Explain your answer.

EPILOGUE REVIEW

Chapter Summary

The United States tried to remain neutral in World War I but joined the fighting in 1917. The war's end led to some economic and social difficulties. The Great Depression began in 1929 and did not end until the United States entered World War II. The war's end saw the start of a Cold War between the United States and the Soviet Union. The postwar years also saw more groups demand equal rights. In the 1990s the Cold War came to an end. ▄

On a separate sheet of paper, complete the following activities.

Identifying People and Ideas

Describe the historical significance of the following:

1. Woodrow Wilson
2. Harlem Renaissance
3. Franklin D. Roosevelt
4. Holocaust
5. Marshall Plan
6. Martin Luther King Jr.
7. John F. Kennedy
8. Cuban missile crisis
9. Ronald Reagan
10. Bill Clinton

Internet Activity go.hrw.com
SA0 Wars

Search the Internet through the HRW Web site to find information on the men and women who served in World War I, World War II, the Korean War, the Vietnam War, or Operation Desert Storm. Then use this information to create a scrapbook about these people's experiences. Be sure to include appropriate images and quotes in your scrapbook. Also be sure to add captions to describe the significance of items in your scrapbook.

Understanding Main Ideas

1. Describe trench warfare during World War I.
2. Who were the members of the Lost Generation?
3. What were some causes of the Great Depression?
4. Explain President Eisenhower's foreign policy toward the Soviet Union.
5. Why did supporters of the civil rights movement hold the March on Washington in 1963?
6. What was the Iran-contra affair?

Reviewing Themes

1. **Global Relations** Why did the United States declare war on Germany in 1917? What incident led the United States to enter the fighting in World War II?

Using the Time Line

Number your paper from 1 to 6. Match the letters on the time line below with the following events.

1. The Supreme Court rules in *Brown* v. *Board of Education* that "separate educational facilities" are unconstitutional.

2. John T. Scopes is arrested for teaching Charles Darwin's theory of evolution.

3. The Tet Offensive is launched, taking U.S. and South Vietnamese forces by surprise.

4. The Berlin Wall is constructed.

5. The Intermediate-Range Nuclear Forces Treaty (INF) is signed.

6. The Works Progress Administration (WPA) is established.

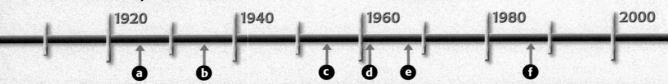

2. Citizenship and Democracy What different strategies did civil rights workers use in the 1950s and 1960s?

3. Economic Development How have some nations tried to strengthen their global economic ties since World War II?

Thinking Critically

1. Making Comparisons Compare how Presidents Hoover and Roosevelt addressed the needs of U.S. citizens during the Great Depression.

2. Evaluating Do you think President Nixon should have been allowed to resign in order to avoid impeachment? Explain your answer.

Writing About History

1. Describing Imagine that you are a reporter in 1941. Write a newspaper article describing the events leading to U.S. involvement in World War II.

Building Your Portfolio

Complete the following activities individually or in groups.

1. Foreign-Policy Time Line Create an illustrated time line of major U.S. foreign-policy events since 1914. Your time line should include descriptions of the significance of each item shown. Choose several time line items to illustrate. Divide your time line into 1-, 5-, or 10-year intervals.

2. Time Capsule Choose one of the decades between the 1920s and the 1990s. Create a time capsule of that decade to show future generations. Make a poster showing what items you would include in your capsule. Items should give people some idea of major events of the decade as well as how people lived at the time. You may want to include things that represent art, literature, or entertainment. When you have finished, write several paragraphs explaining why you chose the items you did for your time capsule.

2. Persuading Select one of the presidents mentioned in the chapter. Then write a paragraph explaining why you think that person did or did not have a successful presidency.

Linking Geography and History

1. Region How was the fighting in the Pacific theater different from fighting in Europe during World War II?

2. Place Why did many people see communist Cuba as a threat to the United States?

History Skills Workshop

Using Primary Sources Langston Hughes was one of the most famous writers of the Harlem Renaissance. Much of his poetry focused on the prejudice facing African Americans. Read his poem "I, Too" and answer the following questions: (a) Who is the speaker in this poem? (b) Compare the opening and closing lines. What word has Hughes changed in the closing line? Why is this change important?

> **I, Too**
>
> I, too, sing America.
>
> I am the darker brother.
> They send me to eat in the kitchen
> When company comes,
> But I laugh,
> And eat well,
> And grow strong.
>
> Tomorrow,
> I'll be at the table
> When company comes.
> Nobody'll dare
>
> Say to me,
> "Eat in the kitchen,"
> Then.
>
> Besides,
> They'll see how beautiful I am
> And be ashamed—
>
> I, too, am America.

American pocket watch

Early American flag

Cotton, an important southern product

The Granger Collection, New York

One of the first American locomotives, c. 1830

James Madison's quill pen

Native American totem pole

Call to
FREEDOM
Beginnings to 1914

REFERENCE

The Statue of Liberty

No
Stamp Act

Colonial pottery
Colonial Williamsburg Foundation

Advertisement for the Pony Express

PONY EXPRESS!
REDUCED RATES!
CHANGE OF TIME!
10 Days to San Francisco!
LETTERS
WILL BE RECEIVED AT THE
OFFICE, 84 BROADWAY,
NEW YORK,
TUESDAY. SATURDAY.

Collection of the American Numismatic Society

U.S. coins celebrating Thomas Jefferson's inauguration

Presidents of the United States

The Official Portraits

1 GEORGE WASHINGTON
Born: 1732   Died: 1799
Years in Office: 1789–97
Political Party: None
Home State: Virginia
Vice President: John Adams

2 JOHN ADAMS
Born: 1735   Died: 1826
Years in Office: 1797–1801
Political Party: Federalist
Home State: Massachusetts
Vice President: Thomas Jefferson

3 THOMAS JEFFERSON
Born: 1743   Died: 1826
Years in Office: 1801–09
Political Party: Republican*
Home State: Virginia
Vice Presidents: Aaron Burr,
    George Clinton

4 JAMES MADISON
Born: 1751   Died: 1836
Years in Office: 1809–17
Political Party: Republican
Home State: Virginia
Vice Presidents: George Clinton,
    Elbridge Gerry

5 JAMES MONROE
Born: 1758   Died: 1831
Years in Office: 1817–25
Political Party: Republican
Home State: Virginia
Vice President: Daniel D. Tompkins

6 JOHN QUINCY ADAMS
Born: 1767   Died: 1848
Years in Office: 1825–29
Political Party: Republican
Home State: Massachusetts
Vice President: John C. Calhoun

7 ANDREW JACKSON
Born: 1767   Died: 1845
Years in Office: 1829–37
Political Party: Democratic
Home State: Tennessee
Vice Presidents: John C. Calhoun,
    Martin Van Buren

* The Republican Party of the third through sixth presidents is not the party of Abraham Lincoln, which was founded in 1854.

8 MARTIN VAN BUREN
Born: 1782 **Died:** 1862
Years in Office: 1837–41
Political Party: Democratic
Home State: New York
Vice President: Richard M. Johnson

9 WILLIAM HENRY HARRISON
Born: 1773 **Died:** 1841
Years in Office: 1841
Political Party: Whig
Home State: Ohio
Vice President: John Tyler

10 JOHN TYLER
Born: 1790 **Died:** 1862
Years in Office: 1841–45
Political Party: Whig
Home State: Virginia
Vice President: None

11 JAMES K. POLK
Born: 1795 **Died:** 1849
Years in Office: 1845–49
Political Party: Democratic
Home State: Tennessee
Vice President: George M. Dallas

12 ZACHARY TAYLOR
Born: 1784 **Died:** 1850
Years in Office: 1849–50
Political Party: Whig
Home State: Louisiana
Vice President: Millard Fillmore

13 MILLARD FILLMORE
Born: 1800 **Died:** 1874
Years in Office: 1850–53
Political Party: Whig
Home State: New York
Vice President: None

14 FRANKLIN PIERCE
Born: 1804 **Died:** 1869
Years in Office: 1853–57
Political Party: Democratic
Home State: New Hampshire
Vice President: William R. King

15 JAMES BUCHANAN
Born: 1791 **Died:** 1868
Years in Office: 1857–61
Political Party: Democratic
Home State: Pennsylvania
Vice President: John C. Breckinridge

16 ABRAHAM LINCOLN
Born: 1809 **Died:** 1865
Years in Office: 1861–65
Political Party: Republican
Home State: Illinois
Vice Presidents: Hannibal Hamlin,
Andrew Johnson

17 ANDREW JOHNSON
Born: 1808   Died: 1875
Years in Office: 1865–69
Political Party: Republican
Home State: Tennessee
Vice President: None

18 ULYSSES S. GRANT
Born: 1822   Died: 1885
Years in Office: 1869–77
Political Party: Republican
Home State: Illinois
Vice Presidents: Schuyler Colfax, Henry Wilson

19 RUTHERFORD B. HAYES
Born: 1822   Died: 1893
Years in Office: 1877–81
Political Party: Republican
Home State: Ohio
Vice President: William A. Wheeler

20 JAMES A. GARFIELD
Born: 1831   Died: 1881
Years in Office: 1881
Political Party: Republican
Home State: Ohio
Vice President: Chester A. Arthur

21 CHESTER A. ARTHUR
Born: 1829   Died: 1886
Years in Office: 1881–85
Political Party: Republican
Home State: New York
Vice President: None

22 GROVER CLEVELAND
Born: 1837   Died: 1908
Years in Office: 1885–89
Political Party: Democratic
Home State: New York
Vice President: Thomas A. Hendricks

23 BENJAMIN HARRISON
Born: 1833   Died: 1901
Years in Office: 1889–93
Political Party: Republican
Home State: Indiana
Vice President: Levi P. Morton

24 GROVER CLEVELAND
Born: 1837   Died: 1908
Years in Office: 1893–97
Political Party: Democratic
Home State: New York
Vice President: Adlai E. Stevenson

25 WILLIAM MCKINLEY
Born: 1843   Died: 1901
Years in Office: 1897–1901
Political Party: Republican
Home State: Ohio
Vice Presidents: Garret A. Hobart, Theodore Roosevelt

26 THEODORE ROOSEVELT
Born: 1858   **Died:** 1919
Years in Office: 1901–09
Political Party: Republican
Home State: New York
Vice President: Charles W. Fairbanks

27 WILLIAM HOWARD TAFT
Born: 1857   **Died:** 1930
Years in Office: 1909–13
Political Party: Republican
Home State: Ohio
Vice President: James S. Sherman

28 WOODROW WILSON
Born: 1856   **Died:** 1924
Years in Office: 1913–21
Political Party: Democratic
Home State: New Jersey
Vice President: Thomas R. Marshall

29 WARREN G. HARDING
Born: 1865   **Died:** 1923
Years in Office: 1921–23
Political Party: Republican
Home State: Ohio
Vice President: Calvin Coolidge

30 CALVIN COOLIDGE
Born: 1872   **Died:** 1933
Years in Office: 1923–29
Political Party: Republican
Home State: Massachusetts
Vice President: Charles G. Dawes

31 HERBERT HOOVER
Born: 1874   **Died:** 1964
Years in Office: 1929–33
Political Party: Republican
Home State: California
Vice President: Charles Curtis

32 FRANKLIN D. ROOSEVELT
Born: 1882   **Died:** 1945
Years in Office: 1933–45
Political Party: Democratic
Home State: New York
Vice Presidents: John Nance Garner,
  Henry Wallace, Harry S Truman

33 HARRY S TRUMAN
Born: 1884   **Died:** 1972
Years in Office: 1945–53
Political Party: Democratic
Home State: Missouri
Vice President: Alben W. Barkley

34 DWIGHT D. EISENHOWER
Born: 1890   **Died:** 1969
Years in Office: 1953–61
Political Party: Republican
Home State: Kansas
Vice President: Richard M. Nixon

35 JOHN F. KENNEDY
Born: 1917   **Died:** 1963
Years in Office: 1961–63
Political Party: Democratic
Home State: Massachusetts
Vice President: Lyndon B. Johnson

36 LYNDON B. JOHNSON
Born: 1908   **Died:** 1973
Years in Office: 1963–69
Political Party: Democratic
Home State: Texas
Vice President: Hubert H. Humphrey

37 RICHARD M. NIXON
Born: 1913   **Died:** 1994
Years in Office: 1969–74
Political Party: Republican
Home State: California
Vice Presidents: Spiro T. Agnew,
     Gerald R. Ford

38 GERALD R. FORD
Born: 1913
Years in Office: 1974–77
Political Party: Republican
Home State: Michigan
Vice President: Nelson A. Rockefeller

39 JIMMY CARTER
Born: 1924
Years in Office: 1977–81
Political Party: Democratic
Home State: Georgia
Vice President: Walter F. Mondale

40 RONALD REAGAN
Born: 1911
Years in Office: 1981–89
Political Party: Republican
Home State: California
Vice President: George Bush

41 GEORGE BUSH
Born: 1924
Years in Office: 1989–93
Political Party: Republican
Home State: Texas
Vice President: J. Danforth Quayle

42 BILL CLINTON
Born: 1946
Years in Office: 1993
Political Party: Democratic
Home State: Arkansas
Vice President: Albert Gore Jr.

Facts About the States

STATE	YEAR OF STATEHOOD	1997 POPULATION	REPS. IN CONGRESS	AREA (SQ. MI.)	POPULATION DENSITY (SQ. MI.)	CAPITAL
Alabama	1819	4,319,154	7	51,705	83.5	Montgomery
Alaska	1959	609,311	1	591,004	1.0	Juneau
Arizona	1912	4,554,966	6	114,000	40.0	Phoenix
Arkansas	1836	2,522,819	4	53,187	47.4	Little Rock
California	1850	32,268,301	52	158,706	203.3	Sacramento
Colorado	1876	3,892,644	6	104,091	37.4	Denver
Connecticut	1788	3,269,858	6	5,018	651.6	Hartford
Delaware	1787	731,581	1	2,045	357.7	Dover
District of Columbia	—	528,964	—	69	7,666.1	—
Florida	1845	14,653,945	23	58,664	249.8	Tallahassee
Georgia	1788	7,486,242	11	58,910	127.1	Atlanta
Hawaii	1959	1,186,602	2	6,471	183.4	Honolulu
Idaho	1890	1,210,232	2	83,564	14.5	Boise
Illinois	1818	11,895,849	20	56,345	211.1	Springfield
Indiana	1816	5,864,108	10	36,185	162.1	Indianapolis
Iowa	1846	2,852,423	5	56,275	50.7	Des Moines
Kansas	1861	2,594,840	4	82,277	31.5	Topeka
Kentucky	1792	3,908,124	6	40,410	96.7	Frankfort
Louisiana	1812	4,351,769	7	42,752	101.8	Baton Rouge
Maine	1820	1,242,051	2	33,265	37.3	Augusta
Maryland	1788	5,094,289	8	10,460	487.0	Annapolis
Massachusetts	1788	6,117,520	10	8,284	738.5	Boston
Michigan	1837	9,773,892	16	58,527	167.0	Lansing
Minnesota	1858	4,685,549	8	84,402	55.5	St. Paul
Mississippi	1817	2,730,501	5	47,689	57.3	Jackson
Missouri	1821	5,402,058	9	69,697	77.5	Jefferson City
Montana	1889	878,810	1	147,046	6.0	Helena
Nebraska	1867	1,656,870	3	77,355	21.4	Lincoln
Nevada	1864	1,676,809	2	110,561	15.2	Carson City
New Hampshire	1788	1,172,709	2	9,279	126.4	Concord
New Jersey	1787	8,052,849	13	7,787	1,034.1	Trenton
New Mexico	1912	1,729,751	3	121,593	14.2	Santa Fe
New York	1788	18,137,226	31	49,108	369.3	Albany
North Carolina	1789	7,425,183	12	52,669	141.0	Raleigh
North Dakota	1889	640,883	1	70,702	9.1	Bismarck
Ohio	1803	11,186,331	19	41,330	270.7	Columbus
Oklahoma	1907	3,317,091	6	69,956	47.4	Oklahoma City
Oregon	1859	3,243,487	5	97,073	33.4	Salem
Pennsylvania	1787	12,019,661	21	45,038	266.9	Harrisburg
Rhode Island	1790	987,429	2	1,212	814.7	Providence
South Carolina	1788	3,760,181	6	31,113	120.9	Columbia
South Dakota	1889	737,973	1	77,116	9.6	Pierre
Tennessee	1796	5,368,198	9	42,144	127.4	Nashville
Texas	1845	19,439,337	30	266,807	72.9	Austin
Utah	1896	2,059,148	3	84,899	24.3	Salt Lake City
Vermont	1791	588,978	1	9,614	61.3	Montpelier
Virginia	1788	6,733,996	11	40,767	165.2	Richmond
Washington	1889	5,610,362	9	68,139	82.3	Olympia
West Virginia	1863	1,815,787	3	24,232	74.9	Charleston
Wisconsin	1848	5,169,677	9	56,153	92.1	Madison
Wyoming	1890	479,743	1	97,809	4.9	Cheyenne

Important Supreme Court Cases

MARBURY v. MADISON, 1 CRANCH (5 U.S.) 137 (1803)

Significance: This ruling established the Supreme Court's power of judicial review, giving the Court the power to decide whether laws passed by Congress are constitutional. This decision greatly increased the prestige of the Court and gave the judiciary branch a powerful check against the legislative and executive branches.

Background: William Marbury and several others were commissioned as judges by Federalist president John Adams during his last days in office. This act angered the new Democratic-Republican president, Thomas Jefferson. Jefferson ordered his secretary of state, James Madison, not to deliver the commissions. Marbury took advantage of a section in the Judiciary Act of 1789 that allowed him to take his case directly to the Supreme Court. He sued Madison, demanding the commission and the judgeship.

Decision: This case was decided on February 24, 1803, by a vote of 5 to 0. Chief Justice John Marshall spoke for the Court, which decided against Marbury. The court ruled that although Marbury's commission had been unfairly withheld, he could not lawfully take his case to the Court without first trying it in a lesser court. Marshall said that the section of the Judiciary Act that Marbury had used was actually unconstitutional, and that the Constitution must take priority over laws passed by Congress.

MCCULLOCH v. MARYLAND, 4 WHEAT. (17 U.S.) 316 (1819)

Significance: This ruling established that Congress had the constitutional right to charter a national bank. The case also established the principle of national supremacy, which stated that the Constitution and other laws of the federal government take priority over state laws. In addition, the ruling reinforced the loose construction interpretation of the Constitution favored by many Federalists.

Background: In 1816 the federal government set up the Second Bank of the United States to stabilize the economy following the War of 1812. Many states were opposed to the competition provided by the new national bank. Some of these states passed heavy taxes on the Bank. The national bank refused to pay the taxes. This led the state of Maryland to sue James McCulloch, the cashier of the Baltimore, Maryland, branch of the national bank.

Decision: This case was decided on March 6, 1819, by a vote of 7 to 0. Chief Justice John Marshall spoke for the unanimous Court, which ruled that the national bank was constitutional because it helped the federal government carry out the other powers granted to it by the Constitution. The Court declared that any attempt by the states to interfere with the duties of the federal government could not be permitted.

GIBBONS v. OGDEN, 9 WHEAT. (22 U.S.) 1 (1824)

Significance: This ruling was the first case to deal with the clause of the Constitution that allows Congress to regulate interstate and foreign commerce. This case was important because it reinforced both the authority of the federal government over the states and the division of powers between the federal government and the state governments.

Background: Steamboat operators who wanted to travel on New York waters had to obtain a state license. Thomas Gibbons had a federal license to travel along the coast, but not a state license for New York. He wanted the freedom to compete with state-licensed Aaron Ogden for steam travel between New Jersey and the New York island of Manhattan.

Decision: This case was decided on March 2, 1824, by a vote of 6 to 0. Chief Justice John Marshall spoke for the Court, which ruled in favor of Gibbons. The Court stated that the congressional statute (Gibbons's federal license) took priority over the state statute (Ogden's state-monopoly license). The ruling also defined commerce as more than simply the exchange of goods, broadening it to include the transportation of people and the use of new inventions (such as the steamboat).

WORCESTER v. GEORGIA, 6 PET. (31 U.S.) 515 (1832)

Significance: This ruling made Georgia's removal of the Cherokee illegal. However, Georgia, with President Andrew Jackson's support, defied the Court's decision. By not enforcing the Court's ruling, Jackson violated his constitutional oath as president. As a result, the Cherokee and other American Indian tribes continued to be forced off of lands protected by treaties.

Background: The state of Georgia wanted to remove Cherokee Indians from lands they held by treaty. Samuel Worcester, a missionary who worked with the Cherokee Nation, was arrested for failing to take an oath of allegiance to the state and to obey a Georgia militia order to leave the Cherokee's lands. Worcester sued, charging that Georgia had no legal authority on Cherokee lands.

Decision: This case was decided on March 3, 1832, by a vote of 5 to 1 in favor of Worcester. Chief Justice John Marshall spoke for the Supreme Court, which ruled that the Cherokee were an independent political community. The Court decided that only the federal government, not the state of Georgia, had authority over legal matters involving the Cherokee people.

SCOTT v. SANDFORD, 19 HOW. (60 U.S.) 393 (1857)

Significance: This ruling denied enslaved African Americans U.S. citizenship and the right to sue in federal court. The decision also contradicted the Missouri Compromise, which had prevented slavery in territories north of the 36° 30' line of latitude. The ruling increased the controversy over the expansion of slavery in new states and territories.

Background: John Emerson, an army doctor, took his slave Dred Scott with him to live in Illinois and then Wisconsin Territory, both of which had banned slavery. In 1842 the two moved to Missouri, a slave state. Four years later, Scott sued for his freedom according to a Missouri legal principle of "once free, always free." The principle meant that a slave was entitled to freedom if he or she had once lived in a free state or territory.

Decision: This case was decided March 6–7, 1857, by a vote of 7 to 2. Chief Justice Roger B. Taney spoke for the Court, which ruled that slaves did not have the right to sue in federal courts because they were considered property, not citizens. In addition, the Court ruled that Congress did not have the power to abolish slavery in territories because that power was not strictly defined in the Constitution. Furthermore, the Court overturned the once-free, always-free principle.

PLESSY v. FERGUSON, 163 U.S. 537 (1896)

Significance: This case upheld the constitutionality of racial segregation by ruling that separate facilities for different races were legal as long as those facilities were equal to one another. This case provided a legal justification for racial segregation for more than 50 years until it was overturned by *Brown v. Board of Education* in 1954.

Background: An 1890 Louisiana law required that all railway companies in the state use "separate-but-equal" railcars for white and

African American passengers. A group of citizens in New Orleans banded together to challenge the law and chose Homer Plessy to test the law in 1892. Plessy took a seat in a whites-only coach, and when he refused to move, he was arrested. Plessy eventually sought review by the U.S. Supreme Court, claiming that the Louisiana law violated his Fourteenth Amendment right to equal protection.

Decision: This case was decided on May 18, 1896, by a vote of 7 to 1. Justice Henry Billings Brown spoke for the Court, which upheld the constitutionality of the Louisiana law that segregated railcars. Justice John M. Harlan dissented, arguing that the Constitution should not be interpreted in ways that recognize class or racial distinctions.

LOCHNER v. NEW YORK, 198 U.S. 45 (1905)

Significance: This decision established the Supreme Court's role in overseeing state regulations. For more than 30 years *Lochner* was often used as a precedent in striking down state laws, minimum-wage laws, child labor laws, and regulations placed on the banking and transportation industries.

Background: In 1895 the state of New York passed a labor law limiting bakers to working no more than 10 hours per day or 60 hours per week. The purpose of the law was to protect the health of bakers, who worked in hot and damp conditions and breathed in large quantities of flour dust. In 1902 Joseph Lochner, the owner of a small bakery in New York, claimed that this law violated his Fourteenth Amendment rights by unfairly depriving him of the liberty to make contracts with employees. This case went to the U.S. Supreme Court.

Decision: This case was decided on April 17, 1905, by a vote of 5 to 4 in favor of Lochner. The Supreme Court judged that the Fourteenth Amendment protected the right to sell and buy labor, and that any state law restricting that right was unconstitutional. The Court rejected the argument that the limited workday and workweek were necessary to protect the health of bakery workers.

MULLER v. OREGON, 208 U.S. 412 (1908)

Significance: A landmark for cases involving social reform, this decision established the Court's recognition of social and economic conditions (in this case, women's health) as a factor in making laws.

Background: In 1903 Oregon passed a law limiting workdays to 10 hours for female workers in laundries and factories. In 1905 Curt Muller's Grand Laundry was found guilty of breaking this law. Muller appealed, claiming that the state law violated his freedom of contract (the Supreme Court had upheld a similar claim that year in *Lochner* v. *New York*). When this case came to the Court, the National Consumers' League hired lawyer Louis D. Brandeis to present Oregon's argument. Brandeis argued that the Court had already defended the state's police power to protect its citizens' health, safety, and welfare.

Decision: This case was decided on February 24, 1908, by a vote of 9 to 0 upholding the Oregon law. The Court agreed that women's well-being was in the state's public interest and that the 10-hour law was a valid way to protect their well-being.

BROWN v. BOARD OF EDUCATION, 347 U.S. 483 (1954)

Significance: This ruling reversed the Supreme Court's earlier position on segregation set by *Plessy* v. *Ferguson* (1896). The decision also inspired Congress and the federal courts to help carry out further civil rights reforms for African Americans.

Background: When the Browns, an African American family, moved into an all-white neighborhood in Topeka, Kansas, they were told that their daughter would have to attend a distant all-black school that was supposedly "separate but equal." Oliver Brown sued the school board, saying that school segregation violated the equal protection clause of the Fourteenth Amendment.

Decision: This case was decided on May 17, 1954, by a vote of 9 to 0. Chief Justice Earl Warren spoke for the unanimous Court, which ruled that segregation in public education created inequality. The Court held that racial segregation in public schools was by nature unequal, even if the school facilities were equal. The Court noted that such segregation created feelings of inferiority that could not be undone. Therefore, enforced separation of the races in public education is unconstitutional.

GIDEON v. WAINWRIGHT, 372 U.S. 335 (1963)

Significance: **This ruling was one of several key Supreme Court decisions establishing free legal help for those who cannot otherwise afford representation in court.**

Background: Clarence Earl Gideon was accused of robbery in Florida. Gideon could not afford a lawyer for the trial, and the judge refused to supply him with one for free. Gideon tried to defend himself and was found guilty. He eventually appealed to the U.S. Supreme Court, claiming that the lower court's denial of a court-appointed lawyer violated his Sixth and Fourteenth Amendment rights.

Decision: This case was decided on March 18, 1963, by a vote of 9 to 0 in favor of Gideon. The Court agreed that the Sixth Amendment (which protects a citizen's right to have a lawyer for his or her defense) applied to the states because it fell under the due process clause of the Fourteenth Amendment. Thus, the states are required to provide legal aid to those defendants in criminal cases who cannot afford to pay for legal aid.

MIRANDA v. ARIZONA, 384 U.S. 436 (1966)

Significance: **This decision ruled that an accused person's Fifth Amendment rights begin at the time of arrest. The ruling caused controversy because it made questioning suspects and collecting evidence more difficult for law enforcement officers.**

Background: In 1963 Ernesto Miranda was arrested in Arizona for a kidnapping. Miranda signed a confession and was later found guilty of the crime. The arresting police officers, however, admitted that they had not told Miranda of his right to talk with an attorney before his confession. Miranda appealed his conviction on the grounds that by not informing him of his legal rights the police had violated his Fifth Amendment right against self-incrimination.

Decision: This case was decided on June 13, 1966, by a vote of 5 to 4. Chief Justice Earl Warren spoke for the Court, which ruled in Miranda's favor. The Court decided that an accused person must be given four warnings after being taken into police custody: (1) the suspect has the right to remain silent, (2) anything the suspect says can and will be used against him or her, (3) the suspect has the right to consult with an attorney and to have an attorney present during questioning, and (4) if the suspect cannot afford a lawyer, one will be provided before questioning begins.

REED v. REED, 404 U.S. 71 (1971)

Significance: **This ruling was the first in a century of Fourteenth Amendment decisions to say that gender discrimination violated the equal protection clause. This case was later used to strike down several other statutes that violated women's rights.**

Background: Cecil and Sally Reed were separated. When their son died without a will, the law gave preference to Cecil to be appointed the administrator of the son's estate. Sally sued Cecil for the right to administer the estate, challenging the gender preference in the law.

Decision: This case was decided on November 22, 1971, by a vote of 7 to 0. Chief Justice Warren Burger spoke for the unanimous Supreme Court. Although the Court had upheld laws based on gender preference in the past, in this case it reversed its position. The Court declared that gender discrimination violated the equal protection clause of the Constitution and therefore could not be the basis for a law.

Gazetteer

Abilene Cattle town in east-central Kansas. (39°N 97°W) **660**

Acadia Region founded by the French in 1604. Includes present-day Nova Scotia. **161**

Afghanistan Country in southwest-central Asia. Invaded by the Soviet Union in 1979. Capital: Kabul. (33°N 63°E) **xxiv**

Africa Second-largest continent. Lies in both the Northern and the Southern Hemispheres. **xxiv**

Alabama (AL) State in the southern United States. Admitted as a state in 1819. Capital: Montgomery. (33°N 87°W) **xx**

Alaska (AK) U.S. state in northwestern North America. Purchased from Russia in 1867. Became a territory in 1912. Admitted as a state in 1959. Capital: Juneau. (64°N 150°W) **xx**

Albany Capital city of New York State. Site where the Albany Plan of Union was written in 1754. (42°N 78°W) **206**

Algiers Present-day Algeria. Former kingdom in northern Africa that was one of the Barbary States, along with Morocco, Tripoli, and Tunis. **347**

Andes Mountains Mountain range that extends along almost the entire western coast of South America. Former home of the Inca Empire. **69**

Annapolis Maryland seaport that was the location of the Annapolis Convention in 1786. (38°N 77°W) **xx**

Antarctica Continent that surrounds the South Pole. **xxiv**

Antietam Creek Creek in northern Maryland. Site of an important Union army victory during the Civil War. **581**

Appalachian Mountains Mountain system in eastern North America that extends from Canada to central Alabama. **161**

Appomattox Courthouse Town in central Virginia where Robert E. Lee surrendered to Ulysses S. Grant, ending the Civil War. **599**

Arabian Peninsula Large peninsula in southwest Asia. **26**

Arctic Ocean Ocean north of the Arctic Circle. **xxiv**

Arizona (AZ) State in the southwestern United States. Organized into a territory in 1863. Admitted as a state in 1912. Capital: Phoenix. (34°N 113°W). **xx**

Arkansas (AR) State in the south-central United States. Admitted as a state in 1836. Capital: Little Rock. (35°N 93°W) **xx**

Asia Largest continent. Occupies the same land mass as Europe. **xxiv**

Astoria City and former fur-trading post located at the mouth of the Columbia River in northwestern Oregon. (46°N 124°W) **504**

Atlanta Capital of Georgia. Captured and burned by the Union army during the Civil War in 1864. (33°N 84°W) **598**

Atlantic Ocean Vast body of water separating North and South America from Europe and Africa. **xxiv**

Austin Capital of Texas located in the central part of the state. Capital of the Republic of Texas from 1839 to 1842. (30°N 98°W) **498**

Australia Island, continent, and country located between the Indian and the Pacific Oceans. Capital: Canberra. (35°S 150°E) **xxiv**

Austria Republic in central Europe. Capital: Vienna. (16°E 48°N) **xxiv**

Austria-Hungary Monarchy in central Europe from 1867 to 1918. Consisted of Austria, Hungary, Bohemia, and parts of Poland, Romania, Yugoslavia, and Italy. **768**

Bahamas Country in the Atlantic Ocean consisting of hundreds of islands, one of which was the site of Christopher Columbus's first landing in the Americas in 1492. **xxiv**

Balkans Countries that occupy the Balkan Peninsula, including Albania, Bulgaria, Greece, Romania, Yugoslavia, and northwestern Turkey. **768**

Baltimore Maryland city northeast of Washington, D.C., on the Chesapeake Bay. (39°N 76°W) **354**

Barbary States North African states of Algiers, Morocco, Tripoli, and Tunis. Some of them warred with the United States in the early 1800s. **347**

Bay of Pigs Bay on the southwestern coast of Cuba. Site of a failed 1961 invasion by U.S.-backed Cuban nationals. **786**

Beringia Land bridge that connected present-day Alaska with Siberia. Enabled the first Americans to cross into North America between 50,000 and 10,000 B.C. **4**

Berlin Capital of Germany. Divided into East Berlin and West Berlin in 1945. Reunited in 1989. (52°N 13°E) **776**

Black Hills Mountains in western South Dakota and northeastern Wyoming where gold was discovered in 1864. Site of a battle between the United States Army and the Sioux in 1876. **646**

Bolivia Republic in west-central South America. Capital: La Paz. (16°S 68°W) **xxiv**

Bosnia and Herzegovina Country annexed by Austria-Hungary in 1908 and Yugoslavia in 1918. Capital: Sarajevo. (44°N 17°E) **xxiv**

Bosque Redondo Location of a Navajo reservation in New Mexico. **647**

Boston Capital of Massachusetts. Leading center of anti-British sentiment in the 1700s and abolitionist activity in the 1800s. (42°N 71°W) **189**

Boston Harbor Massachusetts port that was the scene of the Boston Tea Party in 1773. **189**

Brandywine Creek Creek in Pennsylvania and Delaware that was the site of the Revolutionary War's Battle of Brandywine Creek in 1777. **205**

Brazil Republic in eastern South America. Largest country on the continent. Ruled by Portugal from 1500 to 1822. Capital: Brasília. (9°S 53°W) **xxiv**

Breed's Hill Major site of the Revolutionary War's Battle of Bunker Hill, which cost the lives of more than 1,000 British soldiers. **189**

Brook Farm Site in eastern Massachusetts of a utopian community in the mid-nineteenth-century. **455**

Buena Vista City in northeastern Mexico. Site of the U.S. victory that ended the northern campaign of the Mexican War. **520**

Bull Run Creek in northeastern Virginia where the Confederates won two major battles during the Civil War. **581**

Bunker Hill One site of the Revolutionary War's Battle of Bunker Hill, which cost the lives of more than 1,000 British soldiers. **189**

Cahokia Settlement founded by the Mississippi culture near present-day St. Louis, Missouri. British trading village along the Mississippi River that Patriot soldiers captured during the American Revolution. **11**

Calicut Port in southwestern India into which Vasco da Gama first sailed in 1498. (11°N 76°E) **35**

California (CA) State in the western United States. Admitted as a state in 1850. Capital: Sacramento. (38°N 121°W) **xx**

Camden City in north-central South Carolina where the Continental Army suffered a serious loss to the British in 1780 during the American Revolution. (40°N 75°W) **206**

Canada Country in northern North America. Capital: Ottawa. (50°N 100°W) **xxiv**

Canary Islands Islands off the west coast of Africa where Christopher Columbus first stopped on his journey to the Americas. **xxiv**

Cape of Good Hope Southern tip of Africa named by Bartolomeu Dias, who became the first European to round it in the late 1480s. **35**

Caribbean Sea Arm of the Atlantic Ocean between North America and South America. **xxiv**

Catskill Mountains Range in the Appalachian Mountains in southeastern New York. **390**

Central America Region of land connecting North and South America. **368**

Chaco Canyon Canyon in northwestern New Mexico where the Anasazi built multistory pueblos. **8**

Chancellorsville Town in northeastern Virginia where Union forces won a major victory during the Civil War. **595**

Chapultepec Fort in Mexico City, Mexico. Site of a U.S. victory during the Mexican War. (19°N 99°W) **520**

Charleston Port city in southeastern South Carolina where the Continental Army surrendered to the British in 1780 during the American Revolution. Location of Fort Sumter, upon which Confederates launched an attack that started the Civil War. Originally called Charles Town. (33°N 80°W) **206**

Charlestown Site in present-day Boston that was almost destroyed during the Battle of Bunker Hill during the American Revolution. **189**

Chesapeake Bay Inlet of the Atlantic Ocean in Virginia and Maryland. **95**

Chicago City in northeastern Illinois on Lake Michigan. Major port and large U.S. city. (41°N 87°W) **xx**

Chile Country in southwestern South America. Capital: Santiago. (35°S 72°W) **xxiv**

China (Official name: People's Republic of China) Vast country in Asia. Most populous country in the world. Capital: Beijing. (36°N 93°E) **xxiv**

Cíbola Zuni town in present-day New Mexico that Spanish conquistador Francisco Vásquez de Coronado captured in hopes of finding gold. **71**

Coahuila State in northeastern Mexico that Texas was part of until the Texas Revolution. **490**

Colombia Country in the northwestern South America. Capital: Bogotá. (3°N 72°W) **xxiv**

Colorado (CO) State in the southwestern United States. Admitted as a state in 1876. Capital: Denver. (39°N 107°W) **xx**

Columbia River River that flows from southeastern British Columbia, in Canada, through Washington and Oregon, where it empties into the Pacific Ocean. **342**

Concord One of two northeastern Massachusetts towns (along with Lexington) where the first fighting of the American Revolution took place in 1775. (42°N 71°W) **189**

Connecticut (CT) State in the northeastern United States. One of the original thirteen colonies. Admitted as a state in 1788. Capital: Hartford. (41°N 73°W) **xx**

Constantinople Original name of Istanbul, Turkey. Large city that was an economic and cultural center of the Byzantine Empire in the Middle Ages. (42°N 28°E) **35**

Cuba Island-country in the Caribbean about 90 miles south of Florida. Capital: Havana. (22°N 79°W) **xxiv**

Czechoslovakia Former country in central Europe made up of present-day Czech Republic (Capital: Prague) and Slovakia (Capital: Bratislava). **xxiv**

Dakota Territory U.S. territory made up of North Dakota and South Dakota (1861-89). Divided into two states in 1889. **646**

Delaware (DE) State in the eastern United States. One of the original thirteen colonies. Capital: Dover. (38°N 75°W) **xx**

Delaware River River that forms the boundaries of Pennsylvania and New York, Pennsylvania and New Jersey, and Delaware and New Jersey. **114**

District of Columbia Federal district between Maryland and Virginia where the United States capital is located. (39°N 84°W) **xx**

Dodge City Town in Kansas that was the end of the Western Trail. **660**

Dominican Republic Island-country in the Caribbean. Makes up the eastern part of the island of Hispaniola. Capital: Santo Domingo. (19°N 70°W) **xxiv**

Dorchester Heights Hill south of Boston from which a Patriot attack during the American Revolution forced a British retreat from Boston. **189**

Dust Bowl Drought-ridden region in the 1930s that included parts of Colorado, Kansas, New Mexico, Oklahoma, and Texas. **774**

Egypt Country in northeastern Africa on the Mediterranean Sea. Capital: Cairo. (27°N 27°E) **xxiv**

El Paso City in western Texas. Site of the first Spanish mission in present-day Texas, founded in 1659. (32°N 106°W) **xx**

England Region of the United Kingdom that makes up most of the southern part of the island of Great Britain. Capital: London. (51°N 1°W) **xxiv**

Europe Continent occupying the same land mass as Asia. **xxiv**

Everglades Vast tract of marshland in southern Florida. **383**

Florence Important Renaissance city in central Italy. (44°N 11°E) **32**

Florida (FL) State in the southeastern United States. Organized as a territory in 1822. Admitted as a state in 1845. Capital: Tallahassee. (30°N 84°W) **xx**

Fort Christina First settlement of New Sweden, built in 1638. **88**

Fort Detroit Political and trading center of the Great Lakes region located along the Detroit River. Site of present-day Detroit. **206**

Fort Donelson Fort in northwestern Tennessee captured by Union troops during the Civil War. **587**

Fort Duquesne Site of a French defeat by the British in 1758. Eventually became Pittsburgh. **161**

Fort Henry Fort in northwestern Tennessee captured by Union troops during the Civil War. **587**

Fort McHenry U.S. fort that guarded Baltimore, Maryland. Site of an unsuccessful British attack during the War of 1812. **354**

Fort Mims Alabama site of a massacre of settlers by Creek Indians in 1813. **354**

Fort Necessity Site where the French defeated British colonists in 1754, in what was the first battle of the French and Indian War. **161**

Fort Sumter Fort on Charlestown Harbor, South Carolina. Attack by Confederate forces here began the Civil War. **578**

Fort Ticonderoga Strategic fort in northern New York that Patriots secured from the British in 1775 during the American Revolution. **206**

Fort Wagner Fort on Morris Island in Charleston Harbor, South Carolina, that was captured by Union forces during the Civil War. **592**

Four Corners Point in the southwestern United States where Arizona, Colorado, New Mexico, and Utah meet. **8**

France Country in Western Europe. Capital: Paris. (46°N 0°) **xxiv**

Georgia (GA) State in the southeastern United States. Admitted as a state in 1788. One of the original thirteen colonies. Capital: Atlanta. (32°N 84°W) **xx**

Germany Country in Western Europe. Capital: Berlin. (51°N 8°E) **xxiv**

Gettysburg Town in southern Pennsylvania where a major Union victory took place during the Civil War. Abraham Lincoln delivered the Gettysburg Address there in 1863. (40°N 77°W) **595**

814 Gazetteer

Goliad   Town in south-central Texas. Site of an important Texan loss during the Texas Revolution. (28°N 97°W) **493**

Gonzales   Town in south-central Texas where the first battle of the Texas Revolution took place in 1835. (30°N 97°W) **493**

Granada   Kingdom in present-day Spain held by the Moors from the eighth century until 1492. **39**

Grand Canyon   Enormous gorge in the Colorado River located along the Arizona-Nevada border. **72**

Great Basin   Elevated U.S. region made up of parts of California, Idaho, Nevada, Oregon, Utah, and Wyoming that was home to many American Indian groups. **11**

Great Lakes   Chain of lakes located in central North America and extending across the U.S.-Canada border. Includes Lake Superior, Lake Michigan, Lake Huron, Lake Erie, and Lake Ontario. **88**

Great Plains   Region of North America that lies between the Mississippi River and the Rocky Mountains and stretches north into Canada and south into Texas. **645**

Great Salt Lake   Salty lake in northern Utah. **504**

Guam   Pacific island that became a U.S. territory after the Spanish-American War. Capital: Agana. (14°N 143°E) **xxiv**

Gulf of Mexico   Gulf on the southeastern coast of North America, bordered by the United States, Mexico, and Cuba. **xxiv**

Gulf of Tonkin   Part of the South China Sea east of northern Vietnam. (20°N 108°E) **789**

Haiti   Island-country in the Caribbean located on the western part of the island of Hispaniola. Former U.S. protectorate. Capital: Port-au-Prince. (19°N 72°W) **xxiv**

Hampton Roads   Channel through which the Elizabeth, James, and Nansemond Rivers flow into Chesapeake Bay. Site of the naval battle between the *Virginia* and the *Monitor* during the Civil War. **584**

Harpers Ferry   Town in present-day northeastern West Virginia where John Brown attempted to begin a slave revolt. **566**

Havana Harbor   Harbor in the seaport of Havana on the northwestern coast of Cuba. Site of the explosion of a U.S. battleship, which led to the Spanish-American War. **745**

Hawaii (HI)   U.S. state in the central Pacific Ocean that is made up of the Hawaiian Islands. Organized as a territory in 1900. Admitted as a state in 1959. Capital: Honolulu. (20°N 157°W) **xx**

Haymarket Square   Site in Chicago where the Haymarket Riot of 1886 took place. **687**

Hiroshima   Japanese city bombed by a U.S. atomic weapon in August 1945. (34°N 132°E) **778**

Hispaniola   Island that includes the countries of Haiti and the Dominican Republic. Explored and settled by Christopher Columbus in 1492. **41**

Houston   Capital of the Republic of Texas from 1837 to 1839 and again from 1842 to 1845. Located in southeastern Texas. (30°N 95°W) **498**

Hudson Bay   Inland sea in east-central Canada. Explored by Henry Hudson in 1610. **88**

Hudson River   River flowing from northeastern to southern New York. **88**

Iberian Peninsula   Peninsula of southwestern Europe made up of Spain and Portugal. **23**

Idaho (ID)   State in the northwestern United States. Admitted as a state in 1890. Capital: Boise. (44°N 15°W) **xx**

Illinois (IL)   State in the north-central United States. Admitted as a state in 1890. Capital: Springfield. (40°N 90°W) **xx**

Independence   City in western Missouri that was the starting point of the Santa Fe Trail. (40°N 95°W) **504**

India   Large republic in southern Asia. Capital: New Delhi. (28°N 77°E) **xxiv**

Indiana (IN)   State in the north-central United States. Admitted as a state in 1816. Capital: Indianapolis. (40°N 86°W) **xx**

Indiana Territory   Region formed from the division of the Northwest Territory in 1800 that included Illinois, Indiana, Wisconsin, much of Michigan, and part of Minnesota. Capital moved from Vincennes to Corydon in 1813. **354**

Indian Ocean   Vast body of water east of Africa, south of Asia, west of Australia, and north of Antarctica. **xxiv**

Indian Territory   Former territory in the south-central United States established in the 1830s as a home for forcibly displaced American Indians. Western section, which became Oklahoma Territory, was opened to white settlement in 1889. In 1907 Indian Territory was merged with Oklahoma Territory to form the state of Oklahoma. **383**

Indies   Name given by Europeans to various lands in Asia. **39**

Iowa (IA)   State in the north-central United States. Admitted as a state in 1846. Capital: Des Moines. (42°N 94°W) **xx**

Iran   Country in southwestern Asia where 53 Americans were held hostage during the 1970s. Capital: Tehran. (31°N 53°E) **xxiv**

Iraq   Country in southwestern Asia. Invaded Kuwait in 1990, leading to war with UN forces led by the

United States in 1991. Capital: Baghdad. (32°N 43°E) **xxiv**

Ireland   Island in the British Isles. Divided into Northern Ireland (Capital: Belfast), which is part of Great Britain, and the independent Republic of Ireland (Capital: Dublin). (54°N 8°W) **xxiv**

Israel   Country in southwestern Asia on the eastern Mediterranean coast. Established by Jews after the UN division of Palestine in 1948. Capital: Jerusalem. (32°N 34°E) **xxiv**

Isthmus of Panama   Thin land mass that links North America to South America and separates the Atlantic and the Pacific Oceans. Forms the Republic of Panama. **752**

Italy   Country in southern Europe. Capital: Rome. (44°N 11°E) **xxiv**

Jamaica   Island-country in the Caribbean. Capital: Kingston. (18°N 78°W) **xxiv**

James River   River in Virginia that flows into Chesapeake Bay. **95**

Jamestown   First successful English colony in America, established in eastern Virginia in 1607. **95**

Japan   Country made up of a chain of islands in the western Pacific Ocean. Capital: Tokyo. (37°N 134°E) **xxiv**

Jerusalem   Capital of Israel, located in the east-central part of the country in the West Bank. Considered a holy city by Christians, Jews, and Muslims. (31°N 35°E) **xxiv**

Kansas (KS)   State in the central United States. Organized as a territory in 1854. Admitted as a state in 1861. Capital: Topeka. (38°N 99°W) **xx**

Kaskaskia   Former British trading village in southwestern Illinois along the Mississippi River. Site of Patriot victory in 1778 during the American Revolution. **206**

Kentucky (KY)   State in the east-central United States. Admitted as a state in 1792. Capital: Frankfort. (37°N 87°W) **xx**

Kilwa   Town on the coast of present-day Tanzania. Formerly an important city-state and market center for Arab-Bantu trading. (9°S 39°E) **26**

Kitty Hawk   Village in eastern North Carolina where the Wright brothers flew the first piloted flight in 1903. (36°N 76°N) **679**

Korea   Peninsula and former country of eastern Asia between the Yellow Sea and the Sea of Japan. Officially divided into two independent nations, North Korea and South Korea, in 1945. **xxiv**

Kuwait   Oil-rich country on the northeastern Arabian Peninsula at the northern end of the Persian Gulf. Invaded by Iraq and liberated by UN forces in the Persian Gulf War (1991). Capital: Al Kuwait. (29°N 48°E) **xxiv**

Labrador   Mainland section of the Newfoundland province in eastern Canada. Site of Viking sailor Leif Eriksson's landing in North America around A.D. 1000. **18**

Lake Erie   One of the Great Lakes, located in the United States and Canada. Site of the Battle of Lake Erie, an important U.S. victory during the War of 1812. **354**

La Navidad   First Spanish colony established by Christopher Columbus in 1492. Named after the Spanish term for Christmas Day—the day it was founded. **41**

Latin America   Spanish-speaking countries of North and South America that once belonged to the Spanish empire. **368**

Lawrence   Town in eastern Kansas. Center for free-soilers before the Civil War. (39°N 95°W) **559**

Lexington   One of two northeastern Massachusetts towns (along with Concord) where the first fighting of the American Revolution took place in 1775. (42°N 71°W) **189**

Liberia   Country on the west coast of Africa established in 1822 by the American Colonization Society for the resettlement of freed African Americans. Capital: Monrovia. (6°N 10°W) **xxiv**

Little Bighorn River   River in southern Montana. Site of the Battle of the Little Bighorn between the U.S. Army and the Sioux in 1876. **645**

Little Rock   Capital of Arkansas, located in the central part of the state. Federal troops were sent there in 1957 to enforce a 1954 U.S. Supreme Court ruling against segregation in public schools. (34°N 92°W) **xx**

Los Angeles   Large city in southern California originally founded by Spanish settlers. (34°N 118°W) **xx**

Louisiana (LA)   State in the southeastern United States carved out of the Louisiana Territory. Admitted as a state in 1812. Capital: Baton Rouge. (31°N 71°W) **xx**

Louisiana Territory   Huge region of land stretching west from the Mississippi River to the Rocky Mountains. Acquired by the United States government from France through the Louisiana Purchase of 1803. **342**

Lowell   Massachusetts city located on the Merrimack River northwest of Boston. Site where business-person Francis Cabot Lowell built textile mills. (42°N 71°W) **447**

Maine (ME)   State in the northeastern United States. Admitted as a state in 1820. Capital: Augusta. (45°N 70°W) **xx**

Manhattan Island   The island at north end of New York Bay, and one of the five boroughs that make up New York City. Purchased by Dutch settlers from an American Indian tribe in 1626. **87**

Manila Bay   Large inlet of the South China Sea, located on southwestern Luzon, an island in the Philippines. Scene of an important naval battle in the Spanish-American War in 1898. **745**

Maryland (MD)   State in the east-central United States. One of the original thirteen colonies. Admitted as a state in 1788. Capital: Annapolis. (39°N 76°W) **xx**

Massachusetts (MA)   State in the northeastern United States, first settled as the Plymouth Colony in 1620. One of the original thirteen colonies. Admitted as a state in 1788. Capital: Boston. (42°N 72°W) **xx**

Mediterranean Sea   Large sea bordered by southern Europe, southwest Asia, and northern Africa. **xxiv**

Menlo Park   Community in central New Jersey that was the site of Thomas Edison's research laboratory. **679**

Mesoamerica   Extremely fertile region made up of present-day Mexico and parts of Central America that was the home to the first Native American cultures. Also known as "middle" America. **4**

Mexico   Country in southern North America. Capital: Mexico City. (23°N 104°W) **xxiv**

Michigan (MI)   State in the north-central United States. Admitted as a state in 1837. Capital: Lansing. (46°N 87°W) **xx**

Middle East   Vast region made up of countries in southwestern Asia and northeastern Africa. **782**

Midway Islands   Two islands northwest of Hawaii that have been occupied by the U.S. Navy since 1867. Site of an important U.S. naval victory in World War II. **xxiv**

Minnesota (MN)   State in the north-central United States. Admitted as a state in 1858. Capital: St. Paul. (46°N 90°W) **xx**

Mississippi (MS)   State in the southeastern United States. Admitted as a state in 1817. Capital: Jackson. (32°N 89°W) **xx**

Mississippi River   River that flows from Minnesota down to the Gulf of Mexico. **xx**

Mississippi River valley   Vast area of land drained by the Mississippi River. **9**

Missouri (MO)   State in the central United States. Admitted as a state in 1821. Capital: Jefferson City. (38°N 93°W) **xx**

Missouri River   River that flows from southern Montana to join the Mississippi River north of St. Louis, Missouri. **xx**

Missouri River valley   Vast area of land drained by the Missouri River. **9**

Mogadishu   Capital of Somalia, located on the Indian Ocean. Formerly an important market center for Arab-Bantu trading. (3°N 44°E) **26**

Mombasa   Town in present-day Kenya located on the island of Mombasa off the coast of Kenya. Formerly an important city-state and market center for Arab-Bantu trading. (4°S 39°E) **26**

Monongahela River   River in northern West Virginia and southwestern Pennsylvania that merges with the Allegheny River to form the Ohio River at Pittsburgh. **161**

Montana (MT)   State in the northwestern United States. Admitted as a state in 1889. Capital: Helena. (47°N 112°W) **xx**

Monterrey   City in northeastern Mexico that was captured by U.S. forces in the Mexican War. (25°N 100°W) **520**

Montgomery   Capital of Alabama. Capital of the Confederate States of America from February to May 1861. (32°N 86°W) **xx**

Montreal   City in southeastern Canada founded by the French in 1642. Became a center for the fur trade in the 1600s and 1700s. (46°N 74°W) **161**

Morocco   Kingdom in northwestern Africa that was once one of the Barbary States, which also included Algiers, Tripoli, and Tunis. **347**

Nagasaki   Second Japanese city bombed by a U.S. atomic weapon in August 1945, ending World War II. (32°N 130°E) **778**

Nassau   Capital of the Bahamas. Site of an attack by the U.S. Navy during the American Revolution. (25°N 77°W) **209**

Nauvoo   City in western Illinois where the Mormons established a settlement in the late 1830s. (41°N 91°W) **504**

Nebraska (NE)   State in the central United States. Admitted as a state in 1867. Capital: Lincoln. (41°N 101°W) **xx**

Netherlands   Kingdom in northwestern Europe. Capital: Amsterdam. (52°N 5°E) **xxiv**

Nevada (NV)   State in the western United States. Organized as a territory in 1861. Admitted as a state in 1864. Capital: Carson City. (39°N 117°W) **xx**

New Amsterdam   Dutch settlement on Manhattan Island founded in 1626. **87**

New England   Northeastern section of the United States, made up of Connecticut, Maine,

Massachusetts, New Hampshire, Rhode Island, and Vermont. **109**

New France   French territory in North America that included eastern Canada and the Mississippi Valley. France lost all of its North American territory to Britain in 1763. **88**

Newfoundland   Island off the eastern coast of Canada. Site of Leif Eriksson's landing in North America around A.D. 1000. **88**

New Hampshire (NH)   State in the northeastern United States. One of the original thirteen colonies. Admitted as a state in 1788. Capital: Concord. (44°N 71°W) **xx**

New Jersey (NJ)   State in the northeastern United States. One of the original thirteen colonies. Admitted as a state in 1787. Capital: Trenton. (40°N 71°W) **xx**

New Mexico (NM)   State in the southwestern United States. Organized as a territory that included Arizona and part of Colorado in 1850. Admitted as a state in 1912. Capital: Santa Fe. (34°N 107°W) **xx**

New Mexico Territory   Territory consisting of New Mexico and parts of Arizona and Colorado (1850). **645**

New Netherland   Dutch colony in North America, existing from 1613 to 1664, that included parts of present-day Connecticut, Delaware, New Jersey, and New York. **87**

New Orleans   Port city in southeastern Louisiana between the Mississippi River and Lake Pontchartrain. Founded in 1718. Operated under both Spanish and French rule until it passed to the United States as part of the Louisiana Purchase of 1803. (30°N 90°W) **xx**

Newport   Port city in southeastern Rhode Island. (41°N 71°W) **128**

New Spain   Vast area of Spanish America that extended from Mexico to California and Florida in North America, and included some Caribbean islands and the Philippines. **75**

New Sweden   Swedish colony in North America that was located along the Delaware River. Founded in 1638. **88**

New York (NY)   State in the northeastern United States. One of the original thirteen colonies. Admitted as a state in 1788. Capital: Albany. (42°N 78°W) **xx**

New York City   Largest city in the United States. First capital of the United States, 1785–90. (41°N 74°W) **xx**

Niagara Falls   City in Canada where the Niagara Movement was founded in 1905. (43°N 80°W) **722**

Nicaragua   Country of Central America on the Caribbean Sea and the Pacific Ocean. Capital: Managua. (12°N 86°W) **xxiv**

Nicodemus   Town in Kansas settled by African Americans in the late 1800s. (39°N 100°W) **663**

Nile River valley   A vast area in northeastern Africa that was home to the ancient kingdoms of Kush and the Aksum. **26**

Normandy   Northern French province that was the site of the D-Day invasion during World War II. **776**

North America   Continent in the northern Western Hemisphere. **xxiv**

North Carolina (NC)   State in the southeastern United States. Admitted as a state in 1789. Capital: Raleigh. (35°N 81°W) **xx**

North Dakota (ND)   State in the north-central United States. Organized as the northern part of the Dakota Territory in 1861. Admitted as a state in 1889. Capital: Bismarck. (47°N 102°W) **xx**

Northwest Territory   Region of the north-central United States, extending from the Ohio and Missouri Rivers to the Great Lakes. Awarded to the United States by the Treaty of Paris of 1783 and organized as a territory in 1787. Later split up into the present-day states of Illinois, Indiana, Michigan, Ohio, Wisconsin, and part of Minnesota. **228**

Nova Scotia   Province of eastern Canada. Location of French settlements, but was won by Britain in Queen Anne's War. **161**

Nueces River   Texas river that Mexico claimed was the boundary between Mexico and Texas. **520**

Ohio (OH)   State in the north-central United States. Originally part of the Northwest Territory. Admitted as a state in 1803. Capital: Columbus. (40°N 83°W) **xx**

Ohio River   River that flows through Pennsylvania, Ohio, Indiana, and Illinois. **xx**

Ohio River valley   Region of land drained by the Ohio River. Location of a series of wars from the late 1600s through the mid-1700s involving the British, the French, and several American Indian tribes. Location of conflict between British settlers and Indians. **161**

Oklahoma (OK)   State in the south-central United States. Organized as a territory in 1890. Admitted as a state in 1907. Capital: Oklahoma City. (36°N 98°W) **xx**

Oklahoma City   Capital of Oklahoma and site of a terrorist bombing in 1995. (36°N 98°W) **xx**

Omaha   City in Nebraska that was the eastern starting point of the first U.S. transcontinental railroad. (41°N 96°W) **660**

Oregon (OR)   State in the northeastern United States. Admitted as a state in 1859. Capital: Salem. (43°N 122°W) **xx**

Oregon Country   Region in western North America that extended from the Pacific coast to the Rocky Mountains and from the northern border of

California to Alaska. So called from 1818 until it became Oregon Territory in 1846. **539**

Pacific Ocean   Body of water extending from the Arctic Circle to Antarctica and from western North America and South America to Australia, the Malay Archipelago, and East Asia. **xxiv**

Palo Alto   Site in south Texas of the first battle of the Mexican War. **520**

Panama   Country in southern Central America occupying the Isthmus of Panama. Location of the Panama Canal. Capital: Panama City. (8°N 81°W) **xxiv**

Pawtucket   City in Rhode Island. Location of Samuel Slater's first mill, built in 1793. (42°N 71°W) **447**

Pea Ridge   City in northwestern Arkansas. Site of a Union victory during the Civil War. (36°N 94°W) **588**

Pearl Harbor   Port in the Hawaiian Islands where the Japanese launched a surprise attack against the U.S. Pacific fleet in 1941. **778**

Pennsylvania (PA)   State in the eastern United States. One of the original thirteen colonies. Admitted as a state in 1787. Capital: Harrisburg. (41°N 78°W) **xx**

Persian Gulf   Arm of the Arabian Sea between the Arabian Peninsula and southwestern Iran in southwestern Asia. **xxiv**

Peru   Republic in western South America. The former location of the Inca Empire and a vast area of Spanish America. Capital: Lima. (10°S 75°W) **xxiv**

Philadelphia   City in southeastern Pennsylvania. Important political and educational center in the 1700s and early 1800s. Capital of the United States from 1790 to 1800. (40°N 75°W) **xx**

Philippines   Archipelago of about 7,100 islands, lying approximately 500 miles off the southeast coast of Asia. Gained full independence from the United States in 1946. Capital: Manila. (14°N 125°E) **xxiv**

Pikes Peak   Mountain in east-central Colorado that was part of an important mining region in the mid- to late 1800s. **342**

Pittsburgh   City in southwestern Pennsylvania. Built on the site of Fort Duquesne, which was constructed by the French around 1750 and fell to the British in 1758, when it was renamed Fort Pitt. (40°N 80°W) **xx**

Plains of Abraham   Plateau west of Quebec. Scene of battle in 1759 during which British troops defeated the French. **164**

Plymouth   Site in Massachusetts where the Pilgrims first landed in North America in 1620. (42°N 70°W) **109**

Port Royal   French colony founded on the coast of Nova Scotia in 1605. **86**

Portugal   Country of southwestern Europe on the western Iberian Peninsula. Includes the island groups of Madeira and the Azores in the Atlantic Ocean. Capital: Lisbon. (38°N 9°W) **xxiv**

Potomac River   River that flows through West Virginia, Virginia, and Maryland and empties into the Chesapeake Bay. **307**

Potosí   Large South American Spanish silver-mining center in the 1600s. Located in present-day Bolivia. **74**

Princeton   Town in west-central New Jersey that was the site of the Revolutionary War's Battle of Princeton in 1777. (40°N 75°W) **206**

Promontory   Point in northwestern Utah at which the Central and the Union Pacific Railroads were joined in 1869. **660**

Providence   Settlement established by Roger Williams in 1636, that later became Rhode Island. (42°N 71°W) **109**

Puerto Rico   Island east of Cuba and southeast of Florida. First explored by Europeans in 1508. Ceded to the United States after the Spanish-American War. Later became a self-governing commonwealth. Capital: San Juan. (18°N 67°W) **xx**

Pullman   Town established near Chicago, Illinois, in 1880 by the Pullman Palace Car Company for its workers. **688**

Quebec   City in eastern Canada on the St. Lawrence River. Early French settlement in North America. (47°N 71°W) **xxiv**

Redbank   Site of a nineteenth-century utopian community in east-central New Jersey. **455**

Red River   River that flows from eastern New Mexico through Texas, Arkansas, and Louisiana, where it empties into the Mississippi River. **342**

Red Sea   Inland sea between the Arabian Peninsula and northeastern Africa. **xxiv**

Resaca de la Palma   Mexican War site in south Texas where U.S. soldiers defeated the Mexican army. **520**

Rhode Island (RI)   State in the northeastern United States. One of the original thirteen colonies. Admitted as a state in 1790. Capital: Providence. (41°N 71°W) **xx**

Richmond   Capital of Virginia. Capital of the Confederate States of America during the Civil War and a major military target of the Union army; fell in 1865. (37°N 77°W) **581**

Río de la Plata Large river between Argentina and Uruguay. Explored by Ferdinand Magellan in 1520 as he searched for a sea passage through South America. **48**

Rio Grande "Great River" that forms the border between Texas and Mexico. **342**

Rio Grande valley Area in southern Texas surrounding the Rio Grande. **498**

Roanoke Island Island off the coast of present-day North Carolina. Site of Britain's first settlement in North America, founded in 1585 but disappeared by 1590. **88**

Rocky Mountains Mountain range in western North America that extends from Alaska down to New Mexico. **11**

Russia Country in Eastern Europe and northwestern Asia. Formerly part of the Soviet Union. Capital: Moscow. (61°N 60°E) **xxiv**

Sacramento Capital of California and western starting point of the first U.S. transcontinental railroad. (38°N 121°W) **660**

Sagres Town in southwestern Portugal where Prince Henry gathered mapmakers, sailors, and shipbuilders in the early 1400s. **35**

Sahara Vast desert of northern Africa. **26**

Saint Domingue French colony that was renamed Haiti after a slave revolt overthrew the government in the 1790s. **340**

Salt Lake City Capital of Utah. First settled by the Mormons in the late 1840s. (41°N 112°W) **504**

Samoa Group of volcanic islands in the southwest-central Pacific Ocean. Divided into American Samoa and Western Samoa. **xxiv**

San Antonio City in southern Texas where Mexican forces defeated Texans at the Alamo during the Texas Revolution. Beginning of the Chisholm Trail. (29°N 99°W) **493**

San Carlos Location of an Apache reservation in Arizona. **648**

Sand Creek Site in southeastern Colorado of the Sand Creek Massacre, in which the U.S. Army killed around 200 Cheyenne in 1864. **645**

San Diego City in southern California on San Diego Bay, an inlet of the Pacific Ocean near the Mexican border. (33°N 117°W) **xx**

San Francisco City in western California on a peninsula between the Pacific Ocean and San Francisco Bay. Discovery of gold nearby in 1848 turned the city into a thriving boomtown. (37°N 122°W) **xx**

San Jacinto River in southeastern Texas that flows into Galveston Bay. Site of the Mexican surrender to the Texans in 1836, ending the Texas Revolution. **493**

San Salvador An island in the Bahamas. Site of Christopher Columbus's first landing in the Americas in 1492. **xxiv**

Santa Fe Capital of New Mexico, located in the north-central part of the state. Important city in Spanish America that was founded around 1609-10. Ending point of the Santa Fe Trail. (35°N 106°W) **77**

Santiago de Cuba Seaport located on the southern part of Cuba. Captured by U.S. forces during the Spanish-American War. (20°N 76°W) **745**

Sarajevo Center of Serbian nationalist sentiment in the early 1900s. Site of Archduke Ferdinand's assassination in 1914. Current capital of Bosnia and Herzegovina. (44°N 17°E) **768**

Saratoga Site in eastern New York of the Revolutionary War's Battle of Saratoga in 1777. **206**

Savannah Port city in southeastern Georgia founded by James Oglethorpe in 1733. (32°N 81°W) **116**

Scandinavia Region of northern Europe including Denmark, Norway, and Sweden. Home of the Viking explorers. **xxiv**

Seneca Falls Village in west-central New York State where the first women's rights convention in the United States was held in 1848. (43°N 77°W) **477**

Serbia Part of Yugoslavia, located in southeastern Europe. Formerly an annexed territory of Austria-Hungary. Capital: Belgrade. (45°N 20°E) **768**

Sierra Nevada Large mountain range in eastern California. **504**

Snake River River in the northwestern United States that flows from northwestern Wyoming, across Idaho, and empties into the Columbia River in southeastern Washington. **504**

Somalia Country in eastern Africa. Capital: Mogadishu. (3°N 44°E) **xxiv**

South America Continent in the southern Western Hemisphere. **xxiv**

South Carolina (SC) State in the southeastern United States. One of the original thirteen colonies. Admitted as a state in 1788. Capital: Columbia. (34°N 81°W) **xx**

South Dakota (SD) State in the north-central United States. Organized as part of the Dakota Territory in 1861. Admitted as a state in 1889. Capital: Pierre. (44°N 102°W) **xx**

Soviet Union Former communist country in Eastern Europe and Asia. **780**

Spain Country in southwestern Europe, occupying the greater part of the Iberian Peninsula and including the Balearic and Canary Islands. Capital: Madrid. (40°N 4°W) **xxiv**

Springfield City in southwestern Massachusetts that was the scene of Shays's Rebellion. (42°N 73°W) **xx**

St. Augustine City in northeastern Florida on the Atlantic Ocean. The oldest permanent European settlement in the United States, founded by the Spanish in 1565. **75**

St. Lawrence River Long river in southeastern Canada. **88**

Strait of Magellan Strait at the southern tip of South America that connects the southern Atlantic Ocean with the southern Pacific Ocean. Named after Ferdinand Magellan, who sailed through the strait in 1520. **48**

Sutter's Fort Colony established in 1839 in northern California. **504**

Switzerland Federal republic in central Europe. Capital: Bern. (47°N 7°E) **xxiv**

Tallapoosa River River that flows from northwestern Georgia into eastern Alabama, where it joins the Alabama River. Site of a U.S. victory at the Battle of Horseshoe Bend in 1814, which ended the Creek War. **354**

Tampico Seaport in eastern Mexico. Arrest of U.S. soldiers there in 1914 led to the sending of troops to Mexico. (22°N 98°W) **757**

Tennessee (TN) State in the south-central United States. Admitted as a state in 1796. Capital: Nashville. (36°N 88°W) **xx**

Tennessee River River flowing through Tennessee, northern Alabama, and western Kentucky. **587**

Tenochtitlán Island-city located on the site of present-day Mexico City. Served as the center of the Aztec civilization and had a population of about 300,000. **69**

Texas (TX) State in the south-central United States. Was an independent republic from 1836 to 1845. Admitted as a state in 1845. Capital: Austin. (31°N 101°W) **xx**

Thames River River that flows from southeastern Ontario, Canada, and empties into Lake St. Clair. Site of an important U.S. victory during the War of 1812. **354**

Timbuktu Town in Mali, in western Africa. Center of Islamic culture and learning in the late 1200s. Reached height of prosperity as a commercial and cultural center under Songhai rule, c. 1500. (16°N 3°W) **26**

Tippecanoe River River that flows from northern Indiana to join the Wabash River in west-central Indiana. **349**

Topeka Capital of Kansas, located in the northeastern part of the state. (39°N 95°W) **xx**

Trenton Capital of New Jersey, located in the west-central part of the state. Site of an important Patriot victory during the Revolutionary War. (40°N 75°W) **206**

Troy Small city in eastern New York where Emma Willard started the first college-level educational institution for women in the United States. (43°N 74°W) **466**

Tula Toltec city in present-day central Mexico that had many grand buildings. **7**

Tunis Present-day Tunisia. Region in northern Africa that was one of the Barbary States, along with Algiers, Morocco, and Tripoli. **347**

United States of America Federal republic in central North America. Capital: Washington, D.C. (39°N 77°W) **xxiv**

Utah (UT) State in the western United States. Admitted as a state in 1896. Capital: Salt Lake City. (39°N 112°W) **xx**

Valley Forge Site in southeastern Pennsylvania where General George Washington and his troops spent the harsh winter of 1777-78. **206**

Venezuela Country in northern South America on the Caribbean Sea. Capital: Caracas. (8°N 65°W) **xxiv**

Venice Important Renaissance city and trading center in northeastern Italy. (45°N 12°E) **35**

Veracruz Seaport in eastern Mexico seized by U.S. forces in 1914. (19°N 96°W) **758**

Vermont (VT) State in the northeastern United States. One of the original thirteen colonies. Admitted as a state in 1791. Capital: Montpelier. (44°N 73°W) **xx**

Vicksburg City in western Mississippi on the bluffs above the Mississippi River. Besieged during the Civil War and finally captured by Union troops in 1863. (42°N 85°W) **587**

Vietnam Southeast Asian country (divided into North Vietnam and South Vietnam between 1954 and 1975) where U.S. and South Vietnamese forces fought a war against the communist North Vietnamese and their South Vietnamese allies. Capital: Hanoi. (18°N 107°E) **xxiv**

Vincennes Town in southwestern Indiana along the Wabash River. British soldiers surrendered to Patriot forces there in 1779 during the Revolutionary War's Battle of Vincennes. (39°N 88°W) **206**

Vinland Portion of the North American coast explored by the Vikings around A.D. 1000. **18**

Virginia (VA) State in the eastern United States. One of the original thirteen colonies. Admitted as a state in 1788. Capital: Richmond. (37°N 80°W) **xx**

Virginia City Town in western Nevada that was established in the 1860s when people came to

Virginia City   Town in western Nevada that was established in the 1860s when people came to mine the Comstock Lode. (39°N 119°W) **531**

Wabash River   River that flows from western Ohio to empty into the Ohio River in southwestern Indiana. **349**

Walden Pond   Pond in northeastern Massachusetts near Concord, where Henry David Thoreau lived from 1845 to 1847. **445**

Waltham   Massachusetts city west of Boston that was the location of Francis Cabot Lowell's first textile mill. (43°N 71°W) **447**

Washington (WA)   State in the northwestern United States, bounded by British Columbia, Canada, to the north and by the Pacific Ocean to the west. Admitted as a state in 1889. Capital: Olympia. (47°N 121°W) **xx**

Washington, D.C.   Capital of the United States, located on the Potomac River between Virginia and Maryland. (39°N 77°W) **xx**

West Indies   Islands between North and South America on the eastern boundary of the Caribbean Sea. **209**

West Virginia (WV)   State in the east-central United States. Part of Virginia until the area refused to endorse the Ordinance of Secession in 1861. Admitted as a state in 1863. Capital: Charleston. (39°N 81°W) **xx**

Willamette Valley   Fertile agricultural region of present-day Oregon. First settled in the 1830s by pioneers traveling west along the Oregon Trail. **503**

Wisconsin (WI)   State in the north-central United States. Became part of the Northwest Territory in 1787. Admitted as a state in 1848. Capital: Madison. (44°N 91°W) **xx**

Withlacoochee River   River in western Florida that was the site of a Seminole victory over U.S. troops in 1835. **386**

Wittenberg   City in eastern Germany where the Protestant Reformation began. **80**

Wounded Knee Creek   Site in southwestern South Dakota of the Massacre at Wounded Knee, in which the U.S. Army killed at least 150 Sioux in 1890. **645**

Wyoming (WY)   State in the northwestern United States. Admitted as a state in 1890. Capital: Cheyenne. (43°N 108°W) **xx**

Yorktown   Town in southeastern Virginia. Site of the last battle of the American Revolution. (41°N 74°W) **206**

Yucatán Peninsula   Region of land in Central America made up of southeastern Mexico, Belize, and northern Guatemala. Separates the Gulf of Mexico from the Caribbean Sea. **11**

Yukon Territory   Territory of northwestern Canada east of Alaska. Region first explored by fur traders in the 1840s and acquired by Canada from the Hudson Bay Company in 1870. Capital: Whitehorse. (63°N 135°W) **531**

Index

Acknowledgments

For permission to reprint copyrighted material, grateful acknowledgment is made to the following sources:

Harvard University Press: "World, in Hounding Me" by Sor Juana Inés de la Cruz from *A Sor Juana Anthology,* translated by A. S. Trueblood. Copyright © 1988 by the President and Fellows of Harvard College.

Harvard University Press and the Trustees of Amherst College: From "This is my Letter to the World" from *The Poems of Emily Dickinson,* edited by Thomas H. Johnson. Copyright © 1951, 1955, 1979, 1983 by the President and Fellows of Harvard College. Published by the Belknap Press of Harvard University Press, Cambridge, Mass.

JG Press, Inc. From "Southwest Indian Song" from *The Native Americans: An Illustrated History,* edited by Betty Ballantine and Ian Ballantine. Copyright © 1993 by JG Press, Inc.

The Heirs to the Estate of Martin Luther King, Jr., c/o Writers House, Inc. as agent for the proprietor: From "I Have a Dream" by Martin Luther King, Jr. Copyright © 1963 by Martin Luther King, Jr.; copyright renewed © 1991 by Coretta Scott King.

Alfred A. Knopf, Inc.: "I Too Sing America" from *Selected Poems* by Langston Hughes. Copyright © 1926 by Alfred A. Knopf, Inc.; copyright renewed © 1954 by Langston Hughes.

Random House, Inc.: From "On the Pulse of Morning" from *On the Pulse of Morning* by Maya Angelou. Copyright © 1993 by Maya Angelou.

Van Nostrand Reinhold: From "Creation Story of the Northwest Coast" from *Spirits of the Sacred Mountains: Creation Stories of the American Indian* by William E. Coffer. Copyright © 1978 by Van Nostrand Reinhold.

SOURCES CITED:

Quote by 'Abd al-Latif from *The Rise of Colleges: Institutions of Learning in Islam and the West,* translated by G. Makdisi. Published by Edinburgh University Press, 1981.

From interview with Madge Alford from *Indian-Pioneer Papers,* University of Oklahoma, Norman.

Quote by an Aztec messenger from *The Broken Spears: The Aztec Account of the Conquest of Mexico,* Expanded and Updated Edition, edited by Miguel León-Portilla. Published by Beacon Press, Boston, 1992.

From an Aztec poem from *Aztec Thought and Culture: A Study of the Ancient Nahuatl Mind* by Miguel León-Portilla, translated by Jack Emory Davis. Published by the University of Oklahoma Press, Norman, 1963.

From an Aztec poem from *The Broken Spears: The Aztec Account of the Conquest of Mexico,* Expanded and Updated Edition, edited by Miguel León-Portilla. Published by Beacon Press, Boston, 1992.

From "Whoopee Ti Yi Yo, Git Along Little Dogies" from *Cowboy Songs,* edited by J. A. Lomax. Published by Sturgis and Walton.

Quote by a Creek Indian woman from *A History of the Indians of the United States* by Angie Debo. Published by the University of Oklahoma Press, Norman, 1970.

Quotes by an Indian leader, a rifleman, Little Turtle, and Joseph Brant from *The Ohio Frontier: Crucible of the Old Northwest, 1720–1830* by R. Douglas Hurt. Published by Indiana University Press, Bloomington, 1996.

Quote by a Victorio follower from *In the Days of Victorio: Recollections of a Warm Springs Apache* by Eve Ball. Published by University of Arizona Press, Tucson, 1970.

From "Recantation of the women of Andover, 1692" from *The History of the Colony and Province of Massachusetts Bay* by Thomas Hutchinson, edited by Lawrence Shaw Mayo. Cambridge, Mass., 1936.

Quote by Ibn Battuta from *A Short History of Africa* by Roland Oliver and J. D. Fage. Published by Penguin Books Ltd., 1962, 1966.

From *Lucy Breckinridge of Grove Hill: The Journal of a Virginia Girl,* 1862–1864, edited by Mary D. Robertson. Published by Kent State University Press, Ohio, 1979.

Quote by Johannes Brenz from Protestants: *The Birth of a Revolution* by Steven Ozment. Published by Doubleday, New York, 1992.

From *Castaways: The Narrative of Alvar Núñez Cabeza de Vaca,* edited by Enrique Pupo-Walker, translated by Frances M. López-Morillas. Published by the University of California Press, Berkeley, 1993.

Quotes by Alvise da Cadamosto and Bartholomeu Dias from *The Discoverers* by Daniel J. Boorstin. Published by Random House, Inc., New York, 1983.

Quote by John Cash from "Howard University Becomes 'Hot Pick'" by Jonathan P. Decker from *Christian Science Monitor,* June 2, 1997, Philadelphia.

Quote by Tausha Carmack from "Grads Average Five-Figure Debt" by John Lang Scripps from *Ventura County Star,* October 12, 1997. Published by Howard News Service.

From *The Book of the Courtier* by Baldassare Castiglione, translated by George Bull. Published by Penguin Classics, London, 1967.

Quotes by Esther Clark, Mary Lyon, and Mary Roberts from *Pioneer Women: Voices from the Kansas Frontier* by Joanna L. Stratton. Published by Simon & Schuster, Inc., New York, 1981.

From *Fifty Years on the Old Frontier* by James H. Cook. Published by Yale University Press, 1994.

Quote by Chester Copeland and from interview with Paul and Pauline Griffith from *Like a Family: The Making of a Southern Cotton Mill World* by Jacquelyn Dowd Hall et al. Published by the University of North Carolina Press, 1987.

Quote by Hernán Cortés from *Hernán Cortés: Letters from Mexico,* translated and edited by Anthony Pagden. Published by Yale University Press, New Haven, 1986.

Quote by Count Henri de Marenches from *Friendly Spies: How America's Allies Are Using Economic Espionage to Steal Our Secrets* by Peter Schweizer. Published by The Atlantic Monthly Press, New York, 1993.

Quote by Bernal Díaz from *Cortés and the Downfall of the Aztec Empire* by Jon Manchip White. Published by Carroll & Graff Publishers, Inc., New York, 1971.

From "Life and Activities in Houston" from *Gustav Dresel's Houston Journal: Adventures in North America and Texas 1837–1841,* translated and edited by Max Freund. Published by the University of Texas Press, Austin, 1954.

Quote by the Gentleman of Elvas from *The De Soto Chronicles: The Expedition of Hernando de Soto to North America 1539–1543, Vol. 1,* translated by James Alexander Robertson, edited by Lawrence A. Clayton et al. Published by the University of Alabama Press, Tuscaloosa, 1993.

From "The Narrative of the Expedition of Hernando de Soto" by the Gentleman of Elvas, edited by Theodore H. Lewis from *Spanish Explorers: In the Southern United States 1528–1543.* Published by the Texas State Historical Association, Austin, 1990.

From *Ancient North America: The Archaeology of a Continent* by Brian M. Fagan. Published by Thames and Hudson Inc., New York, 1991, 1995.

From *Livre des oeuvres divines* by Hildegard of Bingen, translated by B. Gorceix. Published by Albin Michel, Paris, 1982.

From "Godfrey Barnsley, 1805–1873: British Cotton Factor in the South" by Nelson M. Hoffman, Jr. Ph.D. dissertation, University of Kansas, 1964.

Quote by Karlsevni from *Voyages to Vinland: The First American Saga,* translated and interpreted by Einar Haugen. Published by Alfred A. Knopf, Inc., New York, 1942.

Quote by Kolokotrones from "Antecedents to Balkan Revolutions" by L. S. Stavrianos from *Journal of Modern History,* XXXIX, 1957.

Quote by Bartolomé Las Casas from *The Conquest of America: The Question of the Other* by Tzvetan Todorov, translated by Richard Howard. Published by HarperCollins Publishers, Inc., New York, 1984.

Quote by Alonso de León from *The Spanish Frontier in North America* by David J. Weber. Published by Yale University Press, New Haven, 1992.

From "You can make a difference" by Cindy Lightner from *Time,* January 7, 1985. Published by Time, Inc., New York, 1985.

From "Fighting to Survive, A History of Survival" by Alison Ligon from the *Herald Sun.* Available on the World Wide Web at http://www.herald-sun.com/hbcu/docs/history.html, February 10, 1998.

Quote by Josia Reams from *Class and Tennessee's Confederate Generation* by Fred Arthur Bailey. Published by University of North Carolina Press, Chapel Hill, 1987.

From "Newsletters Find Haven Online" by Screenath Screenivasan from *The New York Times,* July 7, 1997. Published by The New York Times Company, New York, 1997.

From *My People the Sioux* by Luther Standing Bear. Published by Houghton Mifflin Company, 1928.

From "A Comparison Between Ancient and Modern Ingenuity" by Alessandro Tassoni from *Philosophy, Technology and the Arts in the Early Modern Era* by Paolo Rossi, translated by Salvator Attanasio. Published by HarperCollins Publishers, New York, 1970.

Quote by Shawnee chief Tecumseh from *Indian Wars* by Robert M. Utley and Wilcomb E. Washburn. Published by Houghton Mifflin Company, Boston, 1977.

Quote by Ten Bears of the Vamparika Comanche from *Bury My Heart at Wounded Knee: An Indian History of the American West* by Dee Brown. Published by Henry Holt and Company, New York, 1971.

Quote by Agnolo di Tura from *The Black Death, A Turning Point in History?* edited by William Bowsky. Published by Holt, Rinehart and Winston.

Quote by Caroline Louise Sacks von Roeder from "Life of Emilie von Roeder" by Benno von Roeder. Louis Lenz Collection, University of Texas.

From *Texas, 1844–1845* by Carl von Solms-Braunfels. Published by Anson Jones, Houston, 1936.

From *A Kid on the Comstock: Reminiscences of a Virginia City Childhood* by John Taylor Waldorf. Published by American West Publishing Company, Palo Alto, 1970.

From *The Long Winter* by Laura Ingalls Wilder. Published by HarperCollins Publishers, New York, 1940.

From *Yesterday: A Memoir of a Russian Jewish Family* by Miriam Shomer Zunser, edited by Emily Wortis Leider. Published by HarperCollins Publishers, New York, 1978.

Photography

Abbreviations used: (t) top, (c) center, (l) left, (r) right, (bckgd) background, (bdr) border.

Front Matter: Page iv, AKG Photo; v, (b), Rare Books and Manuscripts Division, The New York Public Library, Astor, Lenox and Tilden Foundations; vi, Art Resource, NY; ix (b), Corbis-Bettmann; x (b), Union drum with Federal Eagle, from Time-Life Books, Inc. Photo by Al Freni. Courtesy Don Troiani; xi, Peter Newark's Western Americana; xiv(t), Christie's Images; (b) Image Copyright ©1996 PhotoDisc, Inc.; xv (tl), Texas State Library & Archives Commission, (cl) Christie's Images; (c) HRW Photo Research Library; (cr), Image Copyright ©1996 PhotoDisc, Inc.; (bl), National Maritime Museum London; (br), Image Copyright ©1996 PhotoDisc, Inc.; xvi-xix (bdr), National Archives; xvi & xviii-border (t) Boltin Picture Library; (tc), Image Copyright ©1996 PhotoDisc, Inc.; (l) Figurehead, c. 1937, watercolor and graphite on paper, National Gallery of Art, Washington, Index of American Design; (bc-map), Map courtesy Oregon Historical Society, OrHi 79989; (bc-telescope), National Maritime Museum London; (br), From *The National Museum of American History* by Shirley Abbott, published by Harry N. Abrams Inc., New York; xvi(cl), Jerry Jacka/Courtesy Dennis Lyon Collection; (b), Stock Montage, Inc.; xvii, The Granger Collection, New York; xviii(cl), The Museum of the Confederacy Richmond, Virginia;(cr), Archive Photos;(tr & tcl), Image Copyright © 1997 PhotoDisc, Inc.; (tc), Image Copyright © 1996 PhotoDisc, Inc.; xviii(l), Figurehead, c. 1937, watercolor and graphite on paper, National Gallery of Art, Washington, Index of American Design; (bl), National Maritime Museum London; (br), From *The National Museum of American* History by Shirley Abbott, published by Harry N. Abrams Inc., New York; xvii & xix(t), Image Copyright © 1997 PhotoDisc, Inc.; (tr), HRW photo by Sam Dudgeon, courtesy Fred Hay; (c), Corbis-Bettmann; (cr), HRW Photo by Sam Dudgeon; (br), Image Copyright © 1996 PhotoDisc, Inc.; (bc), From *The National Museum of American History* by Shirley Abbott, published by Harry N. Abrams Inc., New York; (bl), Courtesy Jane Dixon.

Unit One: Page 1(c), Tate Gallery, London/Art Resource, NY. **Chapter One:** Page 2, "Gambling Patoli and the god, Xochipilli," from Codex Maghabecciano, Aztec manuscript, Private Collection/Bridgeman Art Library, London/New York; 3, George Lepp/Tony Stone Images; 5(t), Finley-Holiday Films/Page Museum; 5(b), HRW Photo by Sam Dudgeon; 6(c), Dean Conger/ Corbis; (bdr), see below; 7, Bodleian Library, Oxford, MS Arch. Selden A.1, Fol. 37R; 8(t), Michael Holford; (b), Rich Buzzelli/Tom Stack & Associates; 9, Superstock; 10, Jerry Jacka/Courtesy Dennis Lyon Collection; 12, Lawrence Migdale/Photo Researchers, Inc.; 13 (border), see below; (c), F. Stuart Westmorland/ AllStock/PNI; 14, Negatives/ Transparencies #K14285, Courtesy Department of Library Services, American Museum of Natural History; 15, Library of Congress; 16, The Granger Collection, New York; 17, Viking ship, the Gokstad model, Science Museum, London/ Bridgeman Art Library, London/ New York; 18(t), "Vikings Attacking a Greenland Eskimo Camp," Nationalmuseet, Copenhagen/Bridgeman Art Library, London/New York; (b), Greenwich suit of armor, C. 1550, Christie's Images/Bridgeman Art Library, London/New York; 19(l), Musee Conde, Chantilly/Giraudon; (r), Mansell Collection; 20(l), Michael Holford; (r), The British Library MS Royal 14e3f89; 21, Michael Teller/AKG Photo; 22, Public Record Office, Kew, Richmond, Surrey; 23, Erich Lessing/Art Resource, NY; 24, China Stock; 25(bdr), see below;(c) E.T. Archive; 27, Giraudon/Art Resource, NY; 29, Nick Saunders/Barbara Heller Photo Library, London/Art Resource, NY. **Chapter Two:** Page 30, AKG Photo; 31, British Library/E.T. Archive; 32(l), Ancient Art & Architecture Collection; (r), Ancient Art & Architecture Collection; 33(t), The Granger Collection, New York; (b), Scala/Art Resource, NY; 34, The Granger Collection, New York; 36(t), Paul Dupuy Museum, Toulouse, France/Lauros-Giraudon, Paris/SuperStock; 36(c), Image Copyright © 1996 PhotoDisc, Inc.; 36(b), Image Copyright © 1996 PhotoDisc, Inc.; 37, Boltin Picture Library; 38, The Metropolitan Museum of Art, Gift of J.Pierpont Morgan, 1900. (00.18.2) Photograph copyright 1979 The Metropolitan Museum of Art.; 39, Bettmann; 40(b), AKG Photo; 40(t), Superstock; 42(t), AKG Photo; 42(b), Corbis-Bettmann; 43, The Granger Collection, New York; 44, Michael Holford; 45, Corbis-Bettmann; 46, Ancient Art & Architecture Collection ; 47, AKG Photo; 48, The Granger Collection, New York; 49, Michael Holford; 50, AKG Photo; 51(t), Ancient Art & Architecture Collection; (b), Boltin Picture Library; 52, C. Chesek/ J.Becket/ Negatives/Transparencies #4051, Courtesy Department of Library Services, American Museum of Natural History; 53, Henry E. Huntington Library & Art Gallery; 55, Rare Books and Manuscripts Division, The New York Public Library, Astor, Lenox and Tilden Foundations; 56(l), National Maritime Museum/E.T. Archive; (r), Image Copyright © 1996 PhotoDisc, Inc.; (b), Image Copyright © 1997 PhotoDisc, Inc.; 57, Runk/ Schoensenger/Grant Heilman Photography, Inc.; 58, Image Copyright © 1996 PhotoDisc, Inc.; 59, Richard Weiss/Peter Arnold, Inc.; 60, Image Copyright © 1996 PhotoDisc, Inc.; 61(l), ©Scott Camazine/Photo Researchers, Inc.; (r), Image Copyright © 1997 PhotoDisc, Inc.; 63, Chuck Pefley/ Stock, Boston; 64, The Granger Collection, New York.

Unit Two: Page 65(c), "Sioux Ball Player Ah-No-Je-Nange, 'He Who Stands on Both Sides,' George Catlin, Private Collection/ Bridgeman Art Library, London/New York. **Chapter Three:** Page 66, "The Taking of Tenochtitlan by Cortes, 1521," British Embassy, Mexico City/Bridgeman Art Library, London/New York; 67, Corbis-Bettmann; 68(l), Piti Palace, Florence/E.T. Archive; (r), E.T. Archive; 70, Corbis-Bettmann; 71, The Granger Collection, New York; 72, The Granger Collection, New York; 73, Mark Nohl/New Mexico Magazine; 74(t), Bob Daemmrich Photo, Inc.; (b), Michael Holford; 76(t), "Cocoa Plantation in Grenada," O'Shea Gallery, London/Bridgeman Art Library, London/New York; (b), AKG Photo, London; 77, North Wind Picture Archives; 78, Art Resource, NY; 79, Culver Pictures; 80, Scala/Art Resource, NY; 82, Corbis-Bettmann; 83, Chart of Carthagena showing the fleet of Sir Francis Drake by Baptista Boazio, National Maritime Museum, London/Bridgeman Art Library, London/New York; 85, Corbis-Bettmann; 86, Corbis-Bettmann; 89, The Granger Collection, New York. **Chapter Four:** Page 92, The Granger Collection, New York; 93, Rare Books and Manuscripts Division, The New York Public Library, Astor, Lenox and Tilden Foundations; 94, Library of Congress; 95, Archive Photos; 96(l), The Granger Collection, New York; (r), Detail from the National Portrait Gallery, Smithsonian Institution, Washington, DC/Art Resource, NY; 97(t), The Granger Collection, New York; (b), Archive Photos; 99, King James I and VI of Scotland, Bridgeman Art Library, London/New York; 100(b), Archive Photos; 101(t, b), HRW Photo by Sam Dudgeon; 101(c), HRW Photo Research Library; 102(t), The Granger Collection, New York; 102(c), Culver Pictures; 102(b), Courtesy, Peabody Essex Museum, Salem, Massachusetts; 104, The Granger Collection, New York; 105(t), Stock Montage, Inc.; 106, The Granger Collection, New York; 107, Culver Pictures; 108(t), HRW Photo by Sam Dudgeon; 108(c), HRW Photo Research Library; 109, The Granger Collection, New York; 110, Courtesy, Peabody Essex Museum, Salem, Massachusetts; 111, Courtesy St. Ignatius Church; 112, The Granger Collection, New York; 113, "The Wrath of Peter Stuyvesant," painting by Asher B. Durand, from the Collection of the New-York Historical Society; 114, The Granger Collection, New York; 115(t), "Penn's Treaty with the Indians" (1771-72) by Benjamin West, oil on canvas, Courtesy of the Museum of American Art of the Pennsylvania Academy of the Fine Arts Philadelphia. Gift of Mrs. Sarah Harrison (The Joseph Harrison, Jr. Collection).; 117, The Granger Collection, New York. **Chapter Five:** Page 120, The Granger Collection, New York; 121, Archive Photos; 122, The Granger Collection, New York; 123(c), ©Daniel MacDonald/Stock Boston; 124(t), Courtesy of Winterthur Museum; 124, The Granger Collection, New York; 125, The Granger Collection, New York; 126, Detail from the National Portrait Gallery, Smithsonian Institution, Washington DC/Art Resource, NY; 127(t), Hulton Deutsch Collection Ltd./ Tony Stone Images; (b), The Granger Collection, New York; 129, Hulton Deutsch Collection Ltd./Tony Stone Images; 130, Maryland Historical Society, Baltimore; 131(b), The Granger Collection, New York; 131(t), Corbis-Bettmann; 132(c), Culver Pictures; 133(both), 134, The Granger Collection, New York; 135, Courtesy of the Free Library Of Philadelphia; 136, Art Resource; 137(b), Art Resource, NY; 137(t), The Granger Collection, New York; 138, Culver Pictures; 139, Corbis-Bettmann; 140, Scala/Art Resource, NY; 141 (l) Michael Holford; (r) Culver Pictures; 142(b), The Granger Collection, New York; 142(t), Image Copyright © 1996 PhotoDisc, Inc.; 142(bl), Image Copyright © 1997 PhotoDisc, Inc.; 142(c), Image Copyright © 1996 PhotoDisc, Inc.; 143(c), Historical Society of Pennsylvania title page, "Works of the Late Dr. Benjamin Franklin." AM 1793 FRA.; 144(b), HRW Photo Library; 144(r), Detail from The Pierpont Morgan Library/Art Resource, NY; 144(l), The Granger Collection, New York; 144(t), Detail from the Pierpont Morgan Library/Art Resource, NY; 145, Bowdoin College Museum of Art, Brunswick, Maine. Bequest of Mrs. Sarah Bowdoin Dearborn; 146(b), Victoria & Albert Museum/Bridgeman Art Library, London/New York; 146(t), Image Copyright © 1996 PhotoDisc, Inc.; 147, The New York Public Library; 147, Corbis-Bettmann; 148(t), The Granger Collection, New York; 148-149(b) "British Ships of War Landing Their Troops at Boston Harbor, 1768," Private Collection/Bridgeman Art Library, London/New York; 152, "The Slave Market" by Amadeo Preziosi (1816-1882), Victoria & Albert Museum/Bridgeman Art Library, London/New York; 153(r), Image Copyright © 1997 PhotoDisc, Inc.; 155, HRW Photo by Michelle Bridwell.

Unit Three: Page 156, "Patrick Henry Before the Virginia House of Burgesses" (1851) by Peter F. Rothermel. Red Hill, The Patrick Henry National Memorial, Brookneal, Virginia.; 157(c), Corbis-Bettmann; **Chapter Six:** Page 158, The Granger Collection, New York; 159, Corbis; 160, The Granger Collection, New York; 162, Washington/Curtis/Lee Collection, Washington and Lee University, Lexington, Virginia; 163, Archive Photos; 163(bc), (Detail), Courtesy of The Mariners' Museum, Newport News, VA ; 164, Medal commemorating the British capture of Quebec, 1759 (bronze), Private Collection/Bridgeman Art Library, London/New York; 165, The Granger Collection, New York; 166, Courtesy of the Hunt Institute for Botanical Documentation, Carnegie Mellon University, Pittsburgh, PA; 167(t), The Filson Club Historical Society; (b), Corbis-Bettmann; 168, The Granger Collection, New York; 169, Archive Photos; 170(t), Corbis; (b), Rare Books and Manuscripts Division, The New York Public Library, Astor, Lenox and Tilden Foundations; 172, Courtesy of the John Carter Brown Library at Brown University; 173, Colonial Williamsburg Foundation; (t), Corbis; 174(b), The Granger Collection, New York; 175(c), Peter Newark's American Pictures; 177, Archive Photos; 180(t), New-York State Historical Society; (c), HRW Photo Research Library; (b), Image Copyright © 1997 PhotoDisc, Inc.; 181, Archive Photos; 182, HRW Photo by Ken Karp; 183, Chuck Place/Chuck Place Photography; 184, Image Copyright © 1996 PhotoDisc, Inc.; 185, Corbis-Bettmann; 185(b), Image Copyright © 1997 PhotoDisc, Inc. **Chapter Seven:** Page 186, The Granger Collection, New York; 187, The Granger Collection, New York; 188, Superstock; 189, Christie's Images; 190, The Granger Collection, New York; 191, The Granger Collection, New York; 192(l), Historical Society of Pennsylvania; 192(r), The Granger Collection, New York; 193(t), Archive Photos; (bl), The Granger Collection, New York; (br), Stock Editions/ HRW Photo Research Library; 194(t), Culver Pictures; 194(b), Peter Newark's American Pictures; 195, Courtesy of the Massachusetts Historical Society; 196, Image Copyright © 1997 PhotoDisc, Inc.; 200, Mount Vernon Ladies' Association; 201(tl), Collection of The New-York Historical Society; (tr), The Granger Collection, New York; (b), Collection of The New-York Historical Society; 202(c), Benninghoff Collection of the American Revolution; 202 border: (tl), HRW photo by Sam Dudgeon, courtesy Fred Hay; (bl), Image Copyright © 1996 PhotoDisc, Inc.; (bcl), From *The National Museum of American History* by Shirley Abbott, published by Harry N. Abrams Inc., New York; (bcr), Courtesy, The Mariners' Museum, Newport News, VA; (br), Courtesy Jane Dixon; (br), From *The National Museum of American History* by Shirley Abbott, published by Harry N. Abrams Inc., New York; (tr), Science & Society Picture Library; (bkgd), U.S. Patent and Trade Office; (cr), HRW photo by Sam Dudgeon; 203, National Archives (NARA) ; 204, Anne S.K. Brown Military Collection, Brown University Library; 205, Art Resource, NY; 207(l), The Granger Collection, New York; (r), Erich Lessing/Art

Resource, NY; 208, The Historic New Orleans Collection, Museum/Research Center; 209, The Granger Collection, New York; 211, Peter Newark's American Pictures; 212(t), HRW Photo Research Library; (b), The Granger Collection, New York; 213 (c), The Granger Collection, New York; 217, Library of Congress; 219, Steve McBrady/PhotoEdit; 220, Library of Congress.

Unit Four: Page 221(c), The Granger Collection, New York; **Chapter Eight:** Page 222, Detail of "Washington Addressing the Constitutional Convention." Virginia Museum of Fine Arts, Richmond, VA. Gift of Edgar William and Bernice Chrysler Garbisch. Photo: Ron Jennings, © 2000 Virginia Museum of Fine Arts; 223, Independence National Historical Park Collection; 224, Stock Montage; 225(t), National Archives (NARA); (b), H. Armstrong Roberts; 226(t), The Granger Collection, New York; (b), Rare Books and Manuscripts Division, The New York Public Library, Astor, Lenox and Tilden Foundations; 227, Corbis-Bettmann; 229(r), North Wind Picture Archives; 230(t, b), HRW Photo by Sam Dudgeon; 230(border), HRW Photo Research Library; 231(border), HRW Photo by Sam Dudgeon; 232, Corbis-Bettmann; 233(b), Stock Montage, Inc.; 233(t), National Portrait Gallery, Smithsonian Institution/Art Resource, NY; 234(l), Baldwin H. Ward/Corbis-Bettmann; 234(r), Johns Hopkins University, Larry Stevens /Nawrocki Stock Photo Inc.; 234(c), Johns Hopkins University, Larry Stevens/Nawrocki Stock Photo Inc.; 235, North Wind Picture Archives; 236, The Granger Collection, New York; 237, National Portrait Gallery, Smithsonian Institution, Washington, DC, Gift of Henry Cabot Lodge/Art Resource, NY; 238, The Granger Collection, New York; 239(t), Courtesy Winterthur Museum; (b), North Wind Picture Archives; 240, Independence National Historic Park Collection; 241, Library Company of Philadelphia; 243, National Archives (NARA); 244, Library of Congress; 245(l), Archive Photos; (r), The Granger Collection, New York; 246, Smithsonian Institution; 247, The Granger Collection, New York; 248, UNIPHOTO; 249, Courtesy of the John Carter Brown Library at Brown University; 252(t,c), Image Copyright © 1996 PhotoDisc, Inc.; 252(b), Image Copyright © 1997 PhotoDisc, Inc.; 253, H. Abernathy/H. Armstrong Roberts; 254(t), Image Copyright © 1996 PhotoDisc, Inc.; (b), Tim Clary/Agence France Presse/Corbis-Bettmann; 255, SuperStock; 256(t), HRW Photo by Lance Schriner; 256(t), Image Copyright © 1996 PhotoDisc, Inc.; 256(t), Image Copyright © 1996 PhotoDisc, Inc.; 256(c), HRW Photo by Lance Schriner; 256(b), HRW Photo by Lance Schriner; 257(t), HRW Photo by Lance Schriner; 257(b), HRW Photo by Lance Schriner; 257(br), Image Copyright © 1997 PhotoDisc, Inc. **Chapter Nine:** Page 258, Paul S. Conklin; 259, The Granger Collection, New York; 260(l), Paul S. Conklin; (r), Jay Mallin Photos; 262, from THE HERBLOCK GALLERY (Simon & Schuster, 1968); 264, Collection, the Supreme Court of the United States, courtesy The Supreme Court Historical Society; 265, Paul Conklin; 266-285(bdr), HRW Photo by Sam Dudgeon; 266, Independence National Historical Park Collection; 286, Independence National Historical Park Collection; 287, The Granger Collection, New York; 288(t), AP/Wide World Photos; 288(b), Jeffrey Brown/Gamma Liaison; 289, Bob Daemmrich Photo, Inc.; 289(tl), NASA; 289(bl), John Taylor/FPG International; 291, Louie Psihoyos/ Woodfin Camp & Associates, Inc.; 292, Sandra Baker/Gamma Liaison; 293, Paul Sakuma/AP Photo/Wide World Photos; 294(l), David Young-Wolff/Photo Edit; 294(r), Spencer Grant/Photo Edit; 295, Jeff Greenberg / PhotoEdit; 296(b), Bob Daemmrich/ Stock, Boston; 296(t), Joe Marquette/AP/Wide World Photos; 297, Chris Gardner/AP/Wide World Photos. **Chapter Ten:** Page 300, (detail), L.M. Cooke, "Salute to General Washington in New York Harbor," Gift of Edgar William and Bernice Chrysler Garbisch, © 1997 Board of Trustees, National Gallery of Art, Washington; 301, The Free Library of Philadelphia ; 302, The Granger Collection, New York; 303, Daniel Huntington 1816-1906, "The Republican Court" 1861, Oil on Canvas, 167.6 x 277.0 (66 x 109), The Brooklyn Museum 39.536.1, Gift of the Crescent-Hamilton Athletic Club ; 304, Corbis-Bettmann; 305, The Granger Collection, New York; 306, Museum of American Financial History; 307, North Wind Picture Archives; 308(c), The Granger Collection, New York; 309(t), Corbis-Bettmann; (b), Larry Stevens/Nawrocki Stock Photo; 310, The Granger Collection, New York; 311, The Mansell Collection; 312(c), Giraudon/Art Resource, NY; 313(l), Giraudon/Art Resource, NY; (r), Culver Pictures; 314, Corbis-Bettmann; 315, The Historic New Orleans Collection; 316, New York State Historical Association, Cooperstown; 318(b), The Granger Collection, New York; 318(t), ©Laurie Platt Winfrey Inc./Woodfin Camp & Associates; 319, HRW Photo Research Library; 320, ©Laurie Platt Winfrey Inc./Woodfin Camp & Associates; 321, Sally Anderson-Bruce/The Museum of American Political Life, University of Hartford, West Hartford,CT; 322, McAlphin Collection, Miriam and Ira D. Wallach Division of Art, Prints and Photographs, The New York Public Library, Astor, Lenox and Tilden Foundations; 172(t), Archive Photos; 323, The Granger Collection, New York; 324(t), The Granger Collection, New York; (b), The Granger Collection, New York; 326, 327, The Granger Collection, New York; 329, The Metropolitan Museum of Art, Gift of Edgar William and Bernice Chrysler Garbisch, 1963. (63.201.2).

Unit Five: Page 332, Christie's Images; 333(c), Courtesy Oregon State Archives, Mural located in Oregon State Capitol by Frank H. Schwartz c. 1938. **Chapter Eleven:** Page 334, The Granger Collection, New York; 335(both), Collection of the American Numismatic Society; 336, The Granger Collection, New York; 337, The Granger Collection, New York; 338(b), Stock Montage, Inc.; 338(t), National Archives; 339, Nawrocki Stock Photo, Inc.; 340, North Wind Picture Library; 341, The Granger Collection, New York; 342(b), Fred J. Maroon; 343, The Granger Collection, New York; 344(t), North Wind Picture Archives; 344(b), The Granger Collection, New York; 345, North Wind Picture Archives; 346, Courtesy of The Mariners' Museum, Newport News, VA; 348, E.R.L./Sipa Press; 349(t), Image Copyright © 1996 PhotoDisc, Inc.; (b), Archive Photos; 350, The Granger Collection, New York; 351, Corbis-Bettmann; 352, Courtesy of The Mariners' Museum, Newport News, VA; 353(t), North Wind Picture Archives; 353(b), The Granger Collection, New York; 355(l), ©Laurie Platt Winfrey Inc./Woodfin Camp & Associates, Inc.; 355(r), 356, The Granger Collection, New York; 357, Peter Newark's American Pictures; 360(tl), New York Public Library; 360(c), Abby Aldrich Rockefeller Folk Art Center; 360(tr), Image Copyright © 1996 PhotoDisc, Inc.; 360(b), Image Copyright © 1997 PhotoDisc, Inc.; 362, The Granger Collection, New York; 363, HRW Photo Research Library; 364, Maryland Historical Society; 365(t), HRW Photo Research Library; 365(bl), Christie's Images; 365(br), Image Copyright © 1997 PhotoDisc, Inc. **Chapter Twelve:** Page 366, Culver Pictures/PNI; 367, The Granger Collection, New York; 368, National Portrait Gallery, Smithsonian Institution, Washington, DC/Art Resource, NY; 370, ©Laurie Platt Winfrey Inc./Woodfin Camp & Associates, Inc.; 371, The Shelburne Museum, Shelburne, Vermont, detail of the painting "Conestoga Wagon" by Thomas Birch, photograph by Ken Burris; 372, 373, The Granger Collection, New York; 375, Laurie Pratt Winfrey/Woodfin, Camp & Associates, Inc.; 376(l), Museum of Political Life, University of Hartford, West Hartford, CT; (r), Museum of Political Life, University of Hartford, West Hartford, CT; 377, National Portrait Gallery, Smithsonian Institution, Gift of the Swedish Colonial Society through Mrs. William Hacker/Art Resource, NY; 378(c), Rick Bowmer/AP/Wide World Photos; 378(border), see below; 379(bl), Library of Congress, Manuscript Division/HRW Photo Research Library; 379(tr), Bob Prestwood after a Phillip Dorf Illustration; 380, The Granger Collection, New York; 381, The Granger Collection, New York; 382, Corbis-Bettmann; 384(br), Robert D. Rubic/Rare Books and Manuscripts Division, the New York Public Library, Astor, Lenox and Tilden Foundations; 384(tc), The Granger Collection, New York; 385, Woolaroc Museum, Bartlesville, Oklahoma; 386, North Wind Picture Archives; 387, Patrick Henry pictured on a decorative pendant, Carnegie Institute, Pittsburgh, Pennsylvania/Bridgeman Art Library, London/New York; 388, North Wind Picture Archives; 389, The Granger Collection, New York; 390(tc), Corbis-Bettmann; 390(bl), The Granger Collection, New York; 391, Corbis-Bettmann; 396, The Granger Collection, New York.

Unit Six: Page 397, 398, The Granger Collection, New York. **Chapter Thirteen:** Page 399, The Granger Collection, New York; 400(t), Bridgeman Art Library, London/New York/Art Resource, NY; 4(b), The Granger Collection, New York; 401, Corbis-Bettmann; 402, VCG FPG International; 403(both), 404, Corbis-Bettmann; 405, 406, American Textile History Museum; 407, 408, The Granger Collection, New York; 409(l), "The Bay and Harbor of New York," C. 1855, Watercolor on Canvas, Museum of the City of New York, Gift of Mrs. Robert M. Littlejohn; (r), Corbis-Bettmann; 410, Culver Pictures, Inc.; 411, Archive Photos; 412, Corbis-Bettmann; 415(t), Peter Newark's American Pictures; 416, Stock Montage, Inc.; 417(l), Corbis-Bettmann; (r), The Granger Collection, New York; 418(b), Culver Pictures; 418(t), Archive Photos; 419, Corbis-Bettmann. **Chapter Fourteen:** Page 422, Detail of John Antrobus' "Plantation Burial," (1860), oil on canvas, The Historic New Orleans Collection; 424, Corbis-Bettmann; 425(both), Culver Pictures; 427, The Granger Collection, New York; 428, Corbis-Bettmann; 429(t), The Granger Collection, New York; (b), SuperStock; 430(c), Culver Pictures; 431, North Wind Picture Archives; 432, New York Public Library; 433, The Granger Collection, New York; 434(t), The Granger Collection, New York; (b), Stock Montage, Inc.; 435, Culver Pictures; 436(c), Corbis; 437(t), Courtesy of the Charleston Museum, South Carolina; (b), Stock Montage, Inc.; 438, The Granger Collection, New York; 439, Stock Montage, Inc.; 440(t), Kennedy Galleries; (b), From the Collection of the Louisiana State Museum; 441(t), Maryland Historical Society; (b), Smithsonian Institution neg. #75-2984; 442, The Granger Collection, New York; 443(l), The Granger Collection, New York; 443(r), The Library Company of Philadelphia; 445,The Granger Collection, New York; 446(t), Image Copyright © 1996 PhotoDisc, Inc.; (c), Image Copyright © 1996 PhotoDisc, Inc.; (b), Image Copyright © 1997 PhotoDisc, Inc.; 448, Courtesy Chicago Historical Society; 449(t), Culver Pictures; 449(b), Catherine Wetzel/The Museum of the Confederacy, Richmond, Virginia; 450(r), Superstock; (l), Image Copyright © 1997 PhotoDisc, Inc.; 451(l), Christie's Images/ SuperStock; 451(r), Image Copyright © 1997 PhotoDisc, Inc. **Chapter Fifteen:** Page 452, The Granger Collection, New York; 453, Corbis-Bettmann; 454(l), Photographs and Prints Division, Schomburg Center for Research in Black Culture, The New York Public Library, Astor, Lenox and Tilden Foundations; (r), George Goodwin/United Methodist Church; 455(t), Courtesy of Massachusetts Historical Society; (b), Paul Rocheleau/Metropolitan Museum of Art; 456(c), Brown Brothers; 457, The Granger Collection, New York; 458, Courtesy of the Bostonian Society Old State House; 460(both), The Granger Collection, New York; 462, North Wind Picture Archives; 463, The Granger Collection, New York; 464(t), Culver Pictures; (b), Corbis; 465(t), Archive Photos; (b), Stock Montage, Inc.; 466, The Granger Collection, New York; 467, I.N. Phelps Stokes Collection, Miriam & Ira D. Wallach Division of Art, Prints and Photographs, The New York Public Library, Astor, Lenox and Tilden Foundations; 468, Photographs and Prints Division,Schomberg Center for Research in Black Culture, The New York Public Library, Astor, Lenox and Tilden Foundations; 469, Photographs and Prints Division, Schomburg Center for Research in Black Culture, The New York Public Library, Astor, Lenox and Tilden Foundations; 470(t), The Granger Collection, New York; 471(l), Courtesy of Massachusetts Historical Society; (c), Courtesy of Massachusetts Historical Society; (r), Courtesy of Massachusetts Historical Society; 471(l), UPI/Corbis-Bettmann ; 472, Corbis-Bettmann; 474, The Granger Collection, New York; 475, Photographs and Prints Division, Schomburg Center for Research in Black Culture, The New York Public Library, Astor, Lenox and Tilden Foundations; 476(both), 477, Archive Photos; 478(t,b), HRW Photo by Sam Dudgeon; 478(c), HRW Photo Research Library; 479, Archive Photos; 482, The Granger Collection, New York.

Unit Seven: Page 484, Emanuel Gottlieb Leutze, "Westward the Course of Empire Takes Its Way," ca. 1861, oil on canvas, 0126.1615, From the Collection of Gilcrease Museum, Tulsa; 485(c), Corbis-Bettmann. **Chapter Sixteen:** Page 486, The National Cowboy Hall of Fame and Western Heritage Center, Oklahoma City, Oklahoma; 487, Corbis-Bettmann; 488, The Granger Collection, New York; 489, Corbis-Bettmann; 490, The Granger Collection, New York; 491, Daughters of the Republic of Texas Library Alamo Collection, #CT 97.23; 492, ©Laurie Platt Winfrey Inc./Woodfin Camp & Associates, Inc.; 493(t), The Granger Collection, New York; 494(b), "Fall of the Alamo" by Robert Jenkins Onderdonk, Courtesy of Friends of the Governor's Mansion, Austin, Texas; 494(t), ©Laurie Platt Winfrey Inc./Woodfin Camp & Associates, Inc.; 495, Archives Division - Texas State Library, Photographer, Eric Beggs; 496, The Granger Collection, New York; 497(b), Panhandle-Plains Historical Museum, Research Center, Canyon, Texas; 497(t), Archives Division - Texas State Library; 498(b), HRW Photo by Sam Dudgeon. From the Collection of the Yoakum Heritage Museum; 499(c), Bob Daemmrich Photography; 500, Stock Montage, Inc.; 501, Harcourt Brace Photo; 502(t), Joseph Drayton, "Indians and Trappers at Fort Walla Walla, Oregon Territory, 1841," Oregon Historical Society, Negative number OrHi 56364; 502(b), The Granger Collection, New York; 503, Culver Pictures; 505, Corbis-Bettmann; 506(both), Collection of the American Numismatic Society; 507(b), The Granger Collection, New York; 508(c), Stock Montage, Inc.; 509, National Museum of American Art, Washington, DC/Art Resource, NY. **Chapter Seventeen:** Page 512, Archives Division - Texas State Library; 513, Courtesy Cornell University Library, Ithaca, New York; 514, Christie's Images; 515(b) Stock Montage; 516, North Wind Picture Archives; 517, Culver Pictures, Inc.; 518(t), The Granger Collection, New York; (b), Stock Montage, Inc.; 519(c), National Portrait Gallery, Smithsonian Institution, Washington, DC/Art Resource, NY; 521(t), Sipa Press/Woodfin Camp & Associates, Inc.; 521(b), The Granger Collection, New York; 522, National Archives; 524, North Wind Picture Archives; 525(l), Corbis-Bettmann; 525(r), Corbis-Bettmann; 526(t), Sipa Press/Woodfin Camp & Associates, Inc.; (b), North Wind Picture Archives; 527(c), North Wind Picture Archives; 528, Culver Pictures, Inc.; 529, Courtesy of The Bostonian Society, Old State House; 530(t), Wells Fargo Bank; (b), The Granger Collection, New York; 531(l), Colorado Historical Society; 532, The Granger Collection, New York; 534, San Francisco History Center, San Francisco Public Library; 535, North Wind Picture Archives; 538(bc), North Wind Picture Archives; 538(tc), Courtesy "Texas Highways" Magazine; 538(t), Image Club Graphics ©1997 Adobe Systems; 538(b), Image Copyright © 1997 PhotoDisc, Inc.; 540, Image Copyright © 1997 PhotoDisc, Inc.; 541(t), The Granger Collection, New York; 541(b), North Wind Picture Archives; 542, Image Copyright © 1997 PhotoDisc, Inc.; 543(c), Vickie Silbert/PhotoEdit; 543(b), Image Copyright © 1997 PhotoDisc, Inc.; 544, © Llewellyn/Uniphoto; 545, Christopher Morris/Black Star/PNI.

Unit Eight: Page 547(c), Library of Congress; 548, The Granger Collection, New York. **Chapter Eighteen:** 549, Corbis-Bettmann; 551(t), Museum of American Political Life, University of Hartford, West Hartford, CT, photo by Steven Laschever; 551(b), The Granger Collection, New York; 552(l), Library of Congress; 552(r), The Granger Collection, New York; 553, National Archives (NARA); 554, The Granger Collection, New York; 554(tl), From *The National Museum of American History* by Shirley Abbott. Published by Harry N. Abrams, Inc., New York; 554(bl, stack), Image Copyright © 1996 PhotoDisc, Inc.; 554(bl, open book), Image Copyright © 1996 PhotoDisc, Inc.; 554(bl paper), Image Copyright © 1996 PhotoDisc, Inc.; 554(br, ink and pen), Image Copyright © 1996 PhotoDisc, Inc.; 554(br, book), HRW Photo by Sam Dudgeon; 555, 556, 557, The Granger Collection, New York; 558, Kansas State Historical Society; 559, The Granger Collection, New York; 560, The Granger Collection, New York; 561, The Granger Collection, New York; 562(t), Corbis-Bettmann; 562(br), Steven Laschever/Museum of American Political Life, University of Hartford, West Hartford, CT; 563(b), The Granger Collection, New York; 563(tl), Library of Congress; 563(tr), National Archives (NARA); 564, Illinois Secretary of State; 565, National Portrait Gallery, Smithsonian Institution, Art Resource, NY; 566, Library of Congress; 568, The Metropolitan Museum of Art, Gift of Mr. and Mrs. Carl Stoeckel, 1897. (97.5) @1982 by The Metropolitan Museum of Art; 569, Library of Congress; 570, 571, The Granger Collection, New York. **Chapter Nineteen:** Page 574, Museum of the City of New York/Scala/Art Resource, NY; 575, Library of Congress; 576(b), North Wind Picture Archives; 576(t), The Granger Collection, New York; 577(l), Corbis-Bettmann; 577(tr, br), HRW Photo by Sam Dudgeon; 577(cr), HRW Photo Research Library; 578, the Museum of the Confederacy, Richmond, Virginia, Photography by Katherine Wetzel; 579, Archive Photos; 580, from THE CIVIL WAR: FORWARD TO RICHMOND,Photograph by Al Freni, ©1983 Time-Life Books, Inc. Courtesy, Troiani Collection; 582(t), Virginia Historic Society; 583, Corbis-Bettmann; 584, Corbis-Bettmann; 585, U.S. War Dept. General Staff photo/National Archives (NARA); 586(l), Corbis-Bettmann; 586(r), Laurie Platt Winfrey/Woodfin Camp & Associates, Inc.; 588, 589, Library of Congress; 590, The Historical Society of Pennsylvania; 591(c), AKG Photo; 592, The Granger Collection, New York; 593, Corbis-Bettmann; 594, Lloyd Ostendorf Collection; 594(t), Corbis-Bettmann; 595, The Virginia Military Institute Archives, Lexington, VA; 597, State Museum of Pennsylvania; 598(t), Lloyd Ostendorf Collection; 598(b), National Archives (NARA); 599, National Geographic Image Collection; 600, 601(border), HRW Photo by Sam Dudgeon; 604(t), National Archives (NARA); (tr), National Archives (NARA); (c), The Granger Collection, New York; (b), Image Copyright © 1997 PhotoDisc, Inc.; 605, Stock Montage, Inc.; 606, Library of Congress, Manuscripts Division; 607(t), Image Copyright © 1997 PhotoDisc, Inc., (b), National Archives (NARA); 608, The Granger Collection, New York; 609(bl), Superstock; (br), Image Copyright © 1997 PhotoDisc, Inc. **Chapter Twenty:** Page 610, North Wind Picture Archives; 611, The Museum of the Confederacy Richmond, Virginia, Katherine Wetzel Photographer; 612, The Valentine Museum; 613, Library of Congress; 615(c), The Stock Market/© William Taufic; 616, Super Stock; 617, Corbis-Bettmann; 618, Stock Montage, Inc.; 619(t), The Granger Collection, New York; 619(b), Corbis-Bettmann; 620, The Granger Collection, New York; 621(t), Louisiana Collection, Howard Tilton Memorial Library, New Orleans, LA 70118; (b), The Granger Collection, New York; 622(b), The Granger Collection, New York; 623, Library of Congress; 624, Courtesy of South Caroliniana Library, University of South Carolina, Columbia.; 625(both), The Granger Collection, New York; 627, North Wind Picture Archives; 628(t), Architect of the Capitol, United States Capitol Art Collection; (b), The Granger Collection, New York; 629, H. Armstrong Roberts; 630, Corbis-Bettmann; 631(b), The Granger Collection, New York; 632(b), The Granger Collection, New York; 633(t), Archive Photos; 633(b), North Wind Picture Archives; 634(c), The Granger Collection, New York; 635, Jubilee Singers, Courtesy of Fisk University Library Special Collections; 638, © 1995 Jeffery Titcomb/Liaison International; 639, Ruth Fremson/AP/Wide World Photos.

Unit Nine: Page 640, Denver Public Library Western Collection; 641(c), Buffalo Bill Historical Center, Cody, Wyoming. **Chapter Twenty-One:** Page 642, Peter Newark's Western Americana; 643, The Granger Collection, New York; 644(t), Werner Forman Archive, Pohrt Collection, Plains Indian Museum, BBHC, Cody Wyoming, USA/Art Resource, NY; 644(b), Corbis-Bettmann; 646(b), The Granger Collection, New York; 647, Corbis-Bettmann; 648, Corbis-Bettmann; 649, The Granger Collection, New York; 650, E.R. Degginger/Color-Pic, Inc.; 651, National Archives (NARA); 652(l), Colorado Historical Society; 652(r), Peter Newark's Western Americana; 653, Hulton Deutsch Collection/Tony Stone Images; 653(tl), ©1997 Kathy Mansfield; 653(bl, telescope), National Maritime Museum London; 653(bl, map), Map courtesy Oregon Historical Society, OrHi 79989; 653(bc, coins), Boltin Picture Library; 653(br, cotton), Image Copyright © 1997 PhotoDisc, Inc.; 653(br, mat), The Ancient Art & Architecture Collection, Ltd.; 653(br, globe), Image Copyright © 1997 PhotoDisc, Inc.; 653(cr, medallion), From The National Archives of the United States by Herman J. Viola. Published by Harry N. Abrams, Inc., New York; 653(bkgd), Courtesy of the White House Website; 653(bl, Chinese), Courtesy of Jie Sun; 653(bl, vase), Christie's Images; 654(t), Peter Newark's Western Americana; 654(b), Peter Newark's American Pictures; 655(l), Peter Newark's Western Americana; 655(r), Union Pacific Museum Collection; 656, Boltin Picture Library; 657(t), Peter Newark's Western Americana; 657(b), Montana Historical Society, Helena; 658(t), Peter Newark's Western Americana; 658(b), Solomon D. Butcher Collection,Library of Congress; 659(r), Peter Newark's Western Americana; 659(l), Buffalo Bill Historic Center, Cody, Wyoming; 661, The Granger Collection, New York; 662, Peter Newark's Western Americana; 663(t), AKG London; 663(b), S.D. Butcher/ Denver Public Library, Western Historical Society; 665, Courtesy of the California History Room, California State Library, Sacramento, California; 666(t), HRW Photo Research Library; 666(b), Peter Newark's Western Americana; 667, Library of Congress; 670(t), Image Copyright © 1997 PhotoDisc, Inc.; 670(r), Colorado Historical Society; 670(r), Image Copyright © 1996 PhotoDisc, Inc.; 670(b), Image Copyright © 1997 PhotoDisc, Inc.; 672, National Archives (NARA); 673, 674, Image Copyright ©1997 PhotoDisc, Inc.; 675(l), North Wind Picture Archives; 675(r), Image Copyright © 1997 PhotoDisc, Inc. **Chapter Twenty-Two:** Page 676, The Granger Collection, New York; 677, Archive Photos; 679(l), The Granger Collection, New York; 679(r), Culver Pictures; 680(r), The Granger Collection, New York; 680(l), The Granger Collection, New York; 681, The Granger Collection, New York; 682, Carnegie Library of Pittsburg; 683, Culver Pictures; 684, Corbis-Bettmann; 685(both), The Granger Collection, New York; 686(both), Corbis-Bettmann; 688, The Granger Collection, New York; 689, The Granger Collection, New York; 691(t), Brown Brothers; 691(b), The Granger Collection, New York; 693(b), Detroit Publishing Co. Photo Collection/ Library of Congress; 693(t), Museum of the City of New York/Archive Photos; 694, The Granger Collection, New York; 695, 696, Corbis-Bettmann; 697, The Granger Collection, New York; 698, J.R. Holland/Stock, Boston; 699(t), The Granger Collection, New York; 699(b), Library of Congress; 700(br), The Granger Collection, New York; 701, Corbis-Bettmann; 703, The Granger Collection, New York. **Chapter Twenty-Three:** Page 704, The Granger Collection, New York; 705, Stock Montage, Inc.; 706, 707(both), 708, The Granger Collection, New York; 709, Brown Brothers; 710(l), Corbis-Bettmann; 710(r), Corbis-Bettmann, (tr) Culver Pictures; 711, UPI/Corbis-Bettmann; 712(t), National Archives (NARA); 712(b), Library of Congress; 713(l), Corbis-Bettmann; 713(r), Brown Brothers; 714, The Granger Collection, New York; 715(l), Corbis-Bettmann; 716(r), UPI/Corbis-Bettmann; 716(l), The Granger Collection, New York; 716(r), Wide World Photos; 717, Brown Brothers; 718, 719, Library of Congress; 720, Corbis-Bettmann; 721(t), The National Portrait Gallery/Art Resource, NY; (bdr), HRW Photo by Sam Dudgeon; (c), HRW Photo Research Library; 723(l), Corbis-Bettmann; 723(r), Rio Grande Press; 724, Keystone-Mast Collection, UCR/CALIFORNIA MUSEUM OF PHOTOGRAPHY, University of California, RIverside; 725, The Granger Collection, New York; 726, Corbis-Bettmann; 727(c), ©Laurie Platt Winfrey Inc./Woodfin Camp & Associates, Inc.; 728(b), Corbis-Bettmann; 728(t), Theodore Roosevelt Collection,Harvard College Library; 730(b), Corbis-Bettmann; 730(t), Theodore Roosevelt Collection,Harvard College Library; 731, Stock Montage, Inc. **Chapter Twenty-Four:** Page 734, Library of Congress; 735, Stock Montage, Inc.; 737(t), The Anchorage Museum of History and Art, Gift of Mr. and Mrs. John M. Sorenson; 737(b), Library of Congress; 738, UPI/Corbis-Bettmann; 739(t), Corbis-Bettmann; 739(bc), Bishop Museum, The State Museum of Natural and Cultural History; 740, Peabody Essex Museum, Salem Mass.; 741, Snark International/Art Resource, NY; 742, Brown Brothers; 744(b), ©Laurie Platt Winfrey Inc./Woodfin Camp & Associates, Inc.; 744(t), The Granger Collection, New York; 746(c), The Granger Collection, New York; 747, Library of Congress; 748, Keystone-Mast Collection #V33954, UCR/California Museum of Photography, University of California, Riverside; 749, U.S. Naval Institute; 750, The Granger Collection, New York; 751(t), The Granger Collection, New York; 751(b), Brown Brothers; 752(b), The Granger Collection, New York; 754, UPI/Corbis-Bettmann; 755, Culver Pictures; 756(t), The Granger Collection, New York; 756(t), Library of Congress; 758, The Granger Collection, New York; 759, The Granger Collection, New York; 761, The Granger Collection, New York; 762, David Young-Wolff/PhotoEdit; 763, Michelle Bridwell/Frontera Fotos. **Epilogue:** Page 764, Archive Photos; 765, Hirz/Archive Photos; 766, The Granger Collection, New York; 767(l), ©Hulton Getty/Woodfin Camp & Associates, Inc.; 767, Narwocki Stock Photo; 769, UPI/Bettmann Newsphotos; 770, The Granger Collection, New York; 771(r), ©Hulton Getty/Woodfin Camp & Associates, Inc.; 771(l), Archive Photos; 772, The Granger Collection, New York; 773, Dorthea Lange/Hulton Getty/Woodfin Camp & Associates, Inc.; 774(b), The Granger Collection, New York; 774(t), Corbis-Bettmann; 775, The Granger Collection, New York; 777(t), Library of Congress; 777(b), Woodfin Camp & Associates, Inc.; 778, The Granger Collection, New York; 779, Corbis-Bettmann; 780, UPI/Bettmann Newsphotos; 781(t), Corbis-Bettmann; 781(b), Pfc. James Cox/National Archive (NARA); 782, Federal Civil Defense Administration, courtesy of Harry S. Truman Library; 783, Archive Photos; 785, Brown Brothers; 786, AP/Wide World Photos; 787(l), Les Immel/Peoria Journal Star; 787(b), AP/Wide World Photos; 788(t), Corbis-Bettmann; 788(b), AP/Wide World Photos; 790, Sara Matthews/ Swarthmore College Peace Collection; 791, Photri; 792, AP/Wide World Photos; 793(t), Michael J. Okoniewski/Gamma Liason; 793(b), B. Bartholomew/Black Star; 794(b), Reuters/Corbis-Bettmann; 794(t), HRW Photo by Sam Dudgeon; 795, AP/Wide World Photos; 797, ©Frederico Mendes/Sipa Press/Woodfin Camp & Associates, Inc.

Back Matter: Page(tl), Image copyright ©1997 PhotoDisc, Inc.; (tr), HRW photo by Sam Dudgeon, courtesy Fred Hay; (r), The Granger Collection, New York; (b),

Independence National Historical Park; (l), F. Stuart Westmorland/Allstock/PNI; 801(t), Image Copyright © 1996 PhotoDisc, Inc.; 801(r), Sandra Baker/Gamma Liaison; 801(cl), ; (cr), Collection of the American Numismatic Society; (cl), Collection of the American Numismatic Society; (b), Peter Newark's Western Americana; Research Library; 800-801(bkgd), Maps Division, The New York Public Library; 802-806 (all) White House Collection, copyright White House Historical Association; 808-811(bdr), Jay Mallin Photos.

Feature Borders (full page):

American Arts, pages 13, 227, 308, 356, 408, 508, 694. Clockwise (1), Figurehead, c. 1937, watercolor and graphite on paper, National Gallery of Art, Washington, Index of American Design; (2), HRW Photo by Richard Haynes; (3), HRW Photo by Sam Dudgeon; (4), From *The Treasures of the Library of Congress* by Charles A. Goodrum, published by Harry N. Abrams, Inc., New York; (5), HRW Photo by Sam Dudgeon; (6), HRW Photo by Richard Haynes; (7), From *The Treasures of the Library of Congress* by Charles A. Goodrum, published by Harry N. Abrams, Inc., New York; (8), Christie's Images; (9), Christie's Images; (10), HRW photo by Sam Dudgeon, Courtesy of Candace Moore.

Global Connections, page 653, see above.

Science and Technology, Pages 6, 138, 325, 374, 413, 533, 596, 681. (clockwise, position 1), HRW photo by Sam Dudgeon, courtesy Fred Hay; (2), Science & Society Picture Library; (3), Science & Society Picture Library; (4), HRW photo by Sam Dudgeon; (5), From *The National Museum of American History* by Shirley Abbott, published by Harry N. Abrams Inc., New York; (6), Courtesy Jane Dixon, (7), Courtesy, The Mariners' Museum, Newport News, VA; (8), From *The National Museum of American History* by Shirley Abbott, published by Harry N. Abrams Inc., New York; (9), Image Copyright © 1996 Photodisc, Inc.; (bkgd), U.S. Patent and Trade Office.

Linking Past and Present, pages 378, 402, 499, 527: (tl), NASA; (bl), John Taylor/FPG International; (r-lamp, br-car), HRW photo by Sam Dudgeon; (r-kite)HRW photo by Russell Dian; (br-disc) Image Copyright © 1996 Photodisc, Inc.

American Literature, pages 389, 436, 519, 554, 727, 746. (tl), From *The National Museum of American* History by Shirley Abbott. Published by Harry N. Abrams, Inc., New York; (bl stack), Image Copyright © 1996 PhotoDisc, Inc.; (bl open book), Image Copyright © 1996 PhotoDisc, Inc.; (bl paper), Image Copyright © 1996 PhotoDisc, Inc.; (br ink and pen), Image Copyright © 1996 PhotoDisc, Inc.; (br book), HRW Photo by Sam Dudgeon

Feature Borders (3/4 page):

American Arts, pages 46, 149. Clockwise, (1), Figurehead, c. 1937, watercolor and graphite on paper, National Gallery of Art, Washington, Index of American Design; ; (2), HRW Photo by Richard Haynes; (3), HRW Photo by Sam Dudgeon, courtesy Candace Moore; (4), From *The Treasures of the Library of Congress* by Charles A. Goodrum, published by Harry N. Abrams, Inc., New York; (5), HRW Photo by Sam Dudgeon; (7), From *The Treasures of the Library of Congress* by Charles A. Goodrum, published by Harry N. Abrams, Inc., New York; (8,9), Christie's Images; (10), HRW photo by Sam Dudgeon, Courtesy of Candace Moore;

Linking Past and Present, page 34, 129, 615: (tl), NASA; (tr), HRW photo by Russell Dian; (bl), John Taylor/FPG International; (cr), HRW photo by Sam Dudgeon; (br-all), HRW photo by Sam Dudgeon.

Global Connections, pages 25, 312, 430, 717: (tl), ©1997 Kathy Mansfield; (bl telescope), National Maritime Museum London; (cr medallion), From *The National Archives of the United States* by Herman J. Viola. Published by Harry N. Abrams, Inc., New York; (bl map), Map courtesy Oregon Historical Society, OrHi 79989; (bl Chinese), Courtesy of Jie Sun; (bl vase), Christie's Images; (bc coins), Boltin Picture Library; (br cotton), Image Copyright © 1997 PhotoDisc, Inc.; (br mat), The Ancient Art & Architecture Collection, Ltd.; (br globe), Image Copyright © 1997 PhotoDisc, Inc. 25(bkgd), Courtesy of the White House Website.

American Literature, pages 78, 213, 261, 634. (tl), From *The National Museum of American History* by Shirley Abbott. Published by Harry N. Abrams, Inc., New York; 213(bl stack), Image Copyright © 1996 PhotoDisc, Inc.; 213(bl open book), Image Copyright © 1996 PhotoDisc, Inc.; 213(bl paper), Image Copyright © 1996 PhotoDisc, Inc.; 213(br ink and pen), Image Copyright © 1996 PhotoDisc, Inc.; 213(br book), HRW Photo by Sam Dudgeon.

Science and Technology, page 202, see above.

Young People In History, pages 1, 65, 157, 221, 333, 397, 485, 547, 641. (tl-parasol, cameo, books), HRW Photo by Sam Dudgeon; (tr-coonskin cap), HRW Photo by Sam Dudgeon; (tr-sled), Christie's Images; (l-Huck Finn), Christie's Images;(r-harmonica), Bygone Designs; (r-canteen), Image Copyright © 1996 PhotoDisc, Inc.; (r-canoe) HRW Photo by Sam Dudgeon;

(bl-bobbins), Image Copyright ©1997 PhotoDisc, Inc.; (bl-quilt), HRW Photo by Sam Dudgeon; (bl-buttons), HRW Photo by Sam Dudgeon; (br-marbles), Image Copyright © 1996 PhotoDisc, Inc.; (br-soldier), Image Copyright © 1996 PhotoDisc, Inc.

Feature Borders (half page):

American Arts, pages 175, 582. (tl), Figurehead, c. 1937, watercolor and graphite on paper, National Gallery of Art, Washington, Index of American Design; (c), HRW Photo by Sam Dudgeon, courtesy Candace Moore; (br), From *The Treasures of the Library of Congress* by Charles A. Goodrum, published by Harry N. Abrams, Inc., New York; (br), From *The Treasures of the Library of Congress* by Charles A. Goodrum, published by Harry N. Abrams, Inc., New York; (bkgd), HRW Photo by Richard Haynes.

American Literature, pages 107, 456, 647. (tl). From *The National Museum of American History* by Shirley Abbott. Published by Harry N. Abrams, Inc., New York; (br book), HRW Photo by Sam Dudgeon; (br- ink and pen), Image Copyright © 1996 PhotoDisc, Inc.

Linking Past and Present, pages 115, 247, 289, 699. 289(tl), NASA; (bl), John Taylor/FPG International; (br), HRW photo by Sam Dudgeon.

Global Connections, pages 81, 163, 208, 348, 470, 567, 591, 739. (tl), ©1997 Kathy Mansfield; (bl), Courtesy of Jie Sun; (br vase), Christie's Images; (br telescope), National Maritime Museum London; (br map), Map courtesy Oregon Historical Society, OrHi 79989; (bkgd), Courtesy of the White House Website.

Art

Abbreviated as follows: (t) top, (b) bottom, (l) left, (r) right, (c) center. All art, unless otherwise noted, created by Holt, Rinehart and Winston. Text maps, feature maps, Atlas, created by GeoSystems Global Corp. Bunting illustrations created by David Merrell/Suzanne Craig Represents Inc.

Chapter 2 Page: 36(t), Leslie Kell; 57(tl), Steven Stankiewicz.

Chapter 3 Page: 84(tl), Dave Merrill/Steven Edsey & Sons.

Chapter 4 Page: 116(bl), Leslie Kell.

Chapter 5 Page: 134(bl), Greathead Studios Inc.; 149(tl), Dave Merrill/Steven Edsey & Sons; 150(tl), Karen Minot; 153(tr), Charles Apple; 154(cr), Dave Merrill/Steven Edsey & Sons.

Chapter 6 Page: 171(br), Dave Merrill/Steven Edsey & Sons; 176(t), Leslie Kell; 179(br), Charles Apple; 180(b), Steven Stankiewicz; 182(tl), Charles Apple; 182(tr), Charles Apple; 183(tl), Dave Merrill/Steven Edsey & Sons.

Chapter 7 Page: 214(tl), Karen Minot.

Chapter 8 Page: 242(t), Leslie Kell; 248(t), Leslie Kell; 254(t), Karen Minot; 255(t), Dave Merrill/Steven Edsey & Sons; 256(t), Charles Apple; 257(t), Steven Stankiewicz.

Chapter 9 Page: 263(t), Leslie Kell; 285(b), Karen Minot; 290(tl), Karen Minot.

Chapter 10 Page: 306(tr), Saul Rosenbaum/Deborah Wolfe Ltd.; 325(b), Nenad Jakesevic.

Chapter 11 Page: 349(tl), Saul Rosenbaum/Deborah Wolfe Ltd.; 362(tl), Charles Apple; 364(bl), Charles Apple; 365(tr), Dave Merrill/Steven Edsey & Sons.

Chapter 12 Page: 374(b), Nenad Jakesevic; 380(tl), Saul Rosenbaum/Deborah Wolfe Ltd.; 393(br), The John Edwards Group.

Chapter 13 Page: 406(br), Charles Apple; 413(b), Nenad Jakesevic; 415(tr), Leslie Kell.

Chapter 14 Page: 435(tl), Charles Apple; 448(cl), Charles Apple; 448(tl), Charles Apple; 450(tl), Dave Merrill/Steven Edsey & Sons; 450(bl), Dave Merrill/Steven Edsey & Sons; 451(t), Karen Minot.

Chapter 15 Page: 459(br), Leslie Kell; 481(br), Dave Merrill/Steven Edsey & Sons.

Chapter 17 Page: 533(b), Nenad Jakesevic; 534(tl), Dave Merrill/Steven Edsey & Sons; 541(t), Saul Rosenbaum/Deborah Wolfe Ltd.; 543(tl), Charles Apple; 543(bl), Charles Apple.

Chapter 18 Page: 568(tl), Saul Rosenbaum/Deborah Wolfe Ltd.; 570(tr), Leslie Kell.

Chapter 19 Page: 596(b), Nenad Jakesevic; 603(br), Charles Apple; 605(t), Dave Merrill/Steven Edsey & Sons; 609(tl), Karen Minot.

Chapter 20 Page: 631(tr), The John Edwards Group; 632(t), Karen Minot.

Chapter 21 Page: 655(tr), Charles Apple; 666(t), Leslie Kell; 669(br), Saul Rosenbaum/Deborah Wolfe Ltd.; 671(all), Charles Apple; 674(all), Dave Merrill/Steven Edsey & Sons; 675(t), Charles Apple.

Chapter 22 Page: 678(bl), Charles Apple; 690(bl), Dave Merrill/Steven Edsey & Sons.

Chapter 23 Page: 715(br), Saul Rosenbaum/Deborah Wolfe Ltd.; 718(tr), Charles Apple.

Chapter 24 Page: 743(b), Charles Apple; 757(br), Charles Apple.

Epilogue Page: 790(t), Dave Merrill/Steven Edsey & Sons; 794(tl), Saul Rosenbaum/Deborah Wolfe Ltd.

Back Matter Page: 807, (all), Leslie Kell.